2012/13

3 0132 02108994 6

D1634762

THE GUIDE TO

MAJOR TRUSTS
VOLUME 2

TENTH EDITION

Denise Lillya, Catriona Chronnell
& Sarah Johnston

Additional research by:
Lucy Lernelius-Tonks, Jude Doherty,
Jenny McIntyre & Susanne Hollywell

DIRECTORY OF SOCIAL CHANGE

Published by
Directory of Social Change
24 Stephenson Way
London NW1 2DP
Tel: 08450 77 77 07; Fax: 020 7391 4804
Email: publications@dsc.org.uk
www.dsc.org.uk
from whom further copies and a full publications catalogue are
available.

Directory of Social Change Northern Office
Federation House, Hope Street, Liverpool L1 9BW
Policy & Research 0151 708 0136; email: research@dsc.org.uk

Directory of Social Change is a Registered Charity no. 800517

First published 1993
Second edition 1995
Third edition 1997
Fourth edition 1999
Fifth edition 2001
Sixth edition 2003
Seventh edition 2005
Eighth edition 2007
Ninth edition 2010
Tenth edition 2012

ISBN 978 1 906294 55 7

British Library Cataloguing in Publication Data
A catalogue record for this book is available from the British
Library

Cover design by Kate Bass
Text designed by Kate Bass
Typeset by Marlinzo Services, Frome
Printed and bound by Page Bros, Norwich

Contents

Introduction

Welcome to *The Guide to the Major Trusts Volume 2*. This edition contains more than 1,170 UK trusts, following on from the 400 largest detailed in Volume 1. The trusts in this book give almost £196 million a year collectively (trusts in Volume 1 gave a total of almost £2.14 billion).

The guide's main aim is to help people raise money from trusts. We aim to provide as much information as we can to enable fundraisers to locate relevant grantmakers and produce suitable applications. There is also a secondary aim: to be a survey of the work of grant-making trusts and to show where trust money is going and for what purposes.

For the 1,173 trusts included in the guide, grants totalled almost £196 million with income standing at £424 million. Assets amounted to around £4.27 billion in total (note that most of the financial information in this book was taken from 2009/10 accounts).

Comparing these figures to the previous edition shows that the value of trusts' assets has risen by £0.5 billion and income increased by £5 million to £424 million. Despite this, total grants decreased from £212 million to £196 million.

The continuing effects of the recession on charities

At the beginning of 2010, the UK and the rest of the world were only just starting to show signs of moving out of the worst recession in living memory (BBC 2010). Despite the increase in both total assets and income during the period on which the research for this book is based, grantmakers would appear to be exercising caution in their giving, resulting in a fall in the total amount awarded in grants.

In August 2011, research based on 265 Freedom of Information responses from local councils across England showed that, one year on from the launch of the Big Society, many charities and voluntary groups were facing deep funding cuts (Jayanetti 2011). An article following the study published by the TUC stated:

> More than 2,000 charities (2,215) are facing budget cuts as local authorities reduce their funding – or in some cases completely withdraw it – according to new research published today [2 August 2011] by the union backed anti-cuts campaign website False Economy.

> The False Economy research shows that charities face net funding reductions of more than £110 million this year, though the final figure is likely to be far higher given that some large authorities have not yet finalised where the cuts will hit.

> All charities or voluntary groups receiving a funding cut of at least five per cent are listed in the research, although most of the cuts are far deeper than this and many groups have had their funding cancelled completely. *TUC 2011*

Some organisations within the voluntary sector considered this estimate of £110 million for the year to be significantly underestimating the true scale of government funding cuts (Jones 2011).

Research carried out by NCVO found that the cuts to public spending as a whole would result in the sector losing eight times that amount during 2015 to 2016:

> With recent research showing that from 2011 the UK voluntary and community sector will lose around £911 million a year in public funding by 2015–16, two-thirds of respondents expect their organisation's financial situation to worsen over the next 12 months – up from 53% last quarter and approaching the level of concern (63%) felt during the height of the cuts in the last quarter of 2010. *Catenazzi 2011*

An example of local authority cuts is in Liverpool where the city council's community grants programme is being cut by 17.5%, which will be spread evenly across all organisations receiving the grant. This also means that the programme will not be open to new applicants, and all organisations currently receiving a grant will continue to do so, with a reduction of 17.5%.

These worrying forecasts and decisions will have a knock-on effect on grant-making trusts which will receive many more applications than they can hope to meet, and means that charities will be forced to look to other sources of funding to maintain their services. Many trusts have managed to keep up with their levels of grantmaking during 2009/10 but they still face huge challenges in maintaining their grant levels in the future and being sustainable themselves as organisations.

A comparison of the top 25 trusts in 2010/11 with the top 25 in 2012/13 (see the table opposite) shows that in this edition only six of the grant-making trusts that were in the top 25 in the last edition of this guide remain. Of the 19 that do not appear in the 2012/13 top 25, three have increased their grantmaking and now appear in Volume 1 of *The Guide to Major Trusts*; they are: Sir Siegmund Warburg's Voluntary Settlement, The Davidson Family Charitable Trust and The Geoff and Fiona Squire Foundation.

Top 25 trusts

Guide to the Major Trusts Volume 2 – 2012/13		Total grants
1	The Fuserna Foundation	£3.5 million
2	The David and Elaine Potter Foundation	£3.2 million
3	The Exilarch's Foundation	£2.8 million
4	The M A Hawe Settlement	£1.8 million
5	The Marjorie and Arnold Ziff Charitable Foundation	£1.5 million
6	The R D Crusaders Foundation	£1.4 million
7	Bourneheights Limited	£1.2 million
8	The Dinwoodie Settlement	£1.2 million
9	The Ian Karten Charitable Trust	£1.1 million
10	Country Houses Foundation	£1.1 million
11	Extonglen Limited	£1.1 million
12	The Lind Trust	£1 million
13	The Scotshill Trust	£1 million
14	Vyoel Moshe Charitable Trust	£1 million
15	The Langley Charitable Trust	£1 million
16	The English Schools' Football Association	£984,000
17	Truedene Co. Ltd	£960,000
18	The Charles Shorto Charitable Trust	£936,000
19	Ambika Paul Foundation	£930,000
20	The Barbour Foundation	£925,000
21	The Talbot Village Trust	£884,000
22	Coutts Charitable Trust	£864,000
23	The Ireland Fund of Great Britain	£863,000
24	The Queen Anne's Gate Foundation	£809,000
25	Lancashire Environmental Fund	£796,000
	Total	**£32.9 million**

Guide to the Major Trusts Volume 2 – 2010/11			Total grants
1	(-) *	The R D Crusaders Foundation	£3.8 million
2	(-)	Dr Mortimer and Theresa Sackler Foundation	£1.7 million
3	(11)	Bourneheights Limited	£1.5 million
4	(-)	Kollel and Co. Limited	£1.5 million
5	(-)	The Francis Winham Foundation	£1.5 million
6	(1)	John Laing Charitable Trust	£1.4 million
7	(3)	Lewis Family Charitable Trust	£1.4 million
8	(-)	The Alan Sugar Foundation	£1.3 million
9	(-)	The Edith Winifred Hall Charitable Trust	£1.3 million
10	(-)	J P Moulton Charitable Foundation	£1.2 million
11	(-)	The Exilarch's Foundation	£1.1 million
12	(-)	The Martin Smith Foundation	£1.1 million
13	(-)	The Muriel Edith Rickman Trust	£1.1 million
14	(18)	TJH Foundation	£1.1 million
15	(-)	Truedene Co. Ltd	£1.1 million
16	(-)	Sir Siegmund Warburg's Voluntary Settlement	£1 million
17	(15)	The Geoff and Fiona Squire Foundation	£1 million
18	(-)	Vyoel Moshe Charitable Trust	£1 million
19	(-)	Help the Hospices	£996,000
20	(-)	The Park Charitable Trust	£991,000
21	(-)	Davidson Charitable Trust	£927,000
22	(24)	Royal Artillery Charitable Fund	£904,000
23	(-)	Keren Mitzvah Trust	£881,000
24	(-)	Coutts Charitable Trust	£870,000
25	(-)	Melow Charitable Trust	£870,000
		Total	**£31.5 million**

* Figures in brackets show position in the previous edition

The remaining 16 trusts' grantmaking has reduced, precluding them from the top 25 for this edition, and there are various reasons for these reductions. Six trusts had received a large injection of funds during the financial year 2008/09 and had used this to increase their giving substantially. In the succeeding years, grants had fallen to their previous levels. Two trusts had experienced drops in income which affected their giving. One trust was undergoing a restructuring programme and this had affected the total amount it gave, another had given a large grant which was later withdrawn and one trustee body had made the decision to maintain reserves by limiting expenditure. For the five remaining grantmakers there appeared to be no specific reason for the reduction in their giving.

What's new?

There are a number of trusts which are new to the series. There have also been trusts added that were in the previous edition of Volume 1 as they no longer give enough money to qualify for the top 400. Some trusts that were in the last edition of this guide have grown and now warrant entries in Volume 1. Others are newly established or newly discovered and include Chrysalis Trust, Liberum Foundation, the Liebreich Foundation and TVML Foundation.

DSC survey 2011

In our survey of 2011 we asked trusts whether they had received fewer, about the same or more applications than in 2009/10. Out of 255 responses to this question, 162 trusts had received about the same number as the previous year, 79 had received more applications and 14 had received fewer.

Of those trusts that had received more applications, the majority stated that they had dealt with the increase by narrowing the eligibility criteria, reducing the average amount given or making fewer awards. A recurring comment was that it had been necessary for trustees to be more selective and spend more time when considering applications.

The following comments from trusts, when asked 'What was your reaction to the increased demand?', show how they have endeavoured to deal (or not deal) with the increase:

Slight panic! More admin and longer meetings.

Slower response rate from the foundation.

We have a set amount available for donations – the increase in applications makes the task of allocating funds much harder.

By being very selective.

We have narrowed the eligibility criteria.

More rationing.

Having to say no to some excellent applications.

They are listed and a copy sent to all trustees but they are effectively ignored.

Having to reduce the average amount of grants given.

By ignoring them.

And on a positive note:

Working harder!

Investing more time as more applications to evaluate. No difference in service to beneficiaries.

Attempting to increase the number of grants.

Every application is given careful consideration.

Considering an online application process.

Sending own application form to applicants to prevent pointless extra information [being submitted].

Update our website.

We now reply to applicants online to save time and money. Ideally we would like to receive applications online too. We have increased the amount that we donate each year to allow us to donate to more applicants.

Another recurring comment was the amount of time it was felt was wasted by applicants in applying to trusts that have stated clearly in both their own literature, and through publications such as this guide, that they do not consider unsolicited applications. Not only is this a waste of time for the applicant charity, it involves the grant-making trusts in unnecessary work. Our advice is that if trustees have stated that they will not consider applications they have not requested, then don't apply. If you consider that your project is so fitting to the grantmaker's criteria that they would welcome hearing about it, contact the trust and discuss the project briefly over the phone.

Asked what common mistakes applicants made, the overwhelming response was that applications fell outside publicised guidelines or criteria and that applicants had not read these carefully (or at all). Many complained of cold-calling, a scattergun approach, mail merged pro-forma appeal letters and generic applications.

Here is a selection of comments taken from the survey about common mistakes:

They don't read guidelines on the website.

Not reading the guidance and criteria; not providing all relevant supporting documents; not supplying the requested additional information.

Around 15 to 20% of applicants do not pay attention to criteria. However, this number is declining.

No application form; no accounts; have not read our website.

Applications outside the trust's grant-making categories.

Approximately 75% are ineligible. They are clearly outside our funding remit.

We receive a lot of 'round-robin' letters obviously sent to many charities with the exact same wording. Some such letters are not signed (!) therefore binned.

Cold correspondents wasting their resources by sending too much bumph.

Grant-making trusts are like all other charities: their resources are finite and often stretched. For this reason very few will spend time considering applications for projects which don't immediately appear to fall within their criteria, or where it is clear that the applicant has not read the trust's guidelines.

A large number of respondents also stated that applications often did not detail the need that would be met by the potential grant and how that need had been assessed, or failed to provide a properly considered budget with validated costs, or details of how the work to be carried out would be planned, executed and monitored. In some cases trustees said they received too much information but none of it was tailored or relevant.

Here are few relevant comments regarding these issues:

They don't justify the need for the work they are doing and/or fully explain how the work will be planned and implemented, i.e. they do not make a convincing case.

Poor applications lacking focus and statistical or sufficient evidence of need according to criteria; contact with other agencies in their field of work; referees.

They do not give enough detail about the benefit of the research nor the timeplan and project plan to support the application and validate the costs.

Fundraisers need to dedicate time when applying for funding: time spent on initial research of the funder and its criteria is well spent and saves resources in the long run for both the applicant and the grant-making trust.

Many of the larger trusts now have very detailed websites and application guidelines, which is an absolute lifeline to charities which are desperate for funding. It has been particularly interesting to see over the course of the research for this guide a great number of trusts which welcome and actively encourage dialogue with charities in order to ensure as many successful applications as possible, and also to help them to understand better the groups they set out to support.

However, whilst there are many open and accessible trusts, there are still those that neglect their obligations. Some fail to be transparent or do not have application procedures that are clear to applicants, some still do not comply with the Charity Commission's guidelines on submitting accounts or include grants lists. Unfortunately, in some cases contact is actively discouraged. It is hoped that DSC's continuing Great Giving campaign will encourage more transparency in the future.

What trusts do we include?

Our criteria are as follows: trusts must have the potential to give at least £30,000 a year in grants, and these grants should go to organisations in the UK. Many give far more than this: over 635 trusts have the potential to give £100,000 or more. There are actually 231 trusts that have the potential to give £300,000 or more. These would appear to be large enough to be included in Volume 1. However, in a number of cases the income of the trust was lower than the total given in grants for the latest financial year – perhaps due to a substantial one-off donation from its capital – and therefore it is expected that the level of giving by such trusts will decrease in future. Other reasons for a trust to be included in Volume 2 are that the majority of the trust's grants were distributed overseas or in a particular part of the UK, or its areas of work were too specific for Volume 1. For a full list of the trusts in size order see page xviii. Some trusts were included regardless of the fact that they gave less than £30,000 as they have the potential to increase this grant total in the future.

What is excluded?

Trusts which appear large enough to warrant inclusion in this guide may be excluded for the following reasons.

▶ Some or all of their money is given to individuals, meaning that £30,000 a year is not available for organisations. The following two guides provide information on trusts which support individuals: *The Guide to Grants for Individuals in Need* and *The Educational Grants Directory*, both published by DSC. Alternatively our subscription website, www.grantforindividuals.org.uk, contains the same information as these publications.

▶ They give exclusively to local causes in a restricted geographical area of England. There are many very large trusts which restrict their grantmaking in this way. So if a trust restricts its giving to a single county or city (or smaller geographical area) it is generally excluded. In this way we hope that Volume 2 remains a national directory and therefore relevant to more people.

▶ They only, or predominantly, support international charities. Such trusts were previously included in this guide, but information on these trusts can now be found in *The Directory of Grant Making Trusts*.

▶ They are company trusts, established as a vehicle for a company's charitable giving. These are detailed in *The Guide to UK Company Giving* or at www.companygiving.org.uk.

DSC's subscription-based website www.trustfunding.org.uk contains details of over 4,500 trusts including those that give locally, UK-wide and internationally.

The layout of this book

The layout of the entries is similar to that established in the previous editions of Volumes 1 and 2, illustrated on page xii. Please also see page xi for other information on how to use this guide. We have used the word Chair in preference to Chairman. We have also rounded off the financial figures to allow for easier reading of the guide, which explains why in some places the totals do not add up exactly.

Indexes

The trusts are listed alphabetically in this guide. To help you locate the most relevant trusts there are two indexes. They are a useful starting point.

▶ Subject index – page 448. This can be useful for identifying trusts that have a particular preference for your cause. There are many trusts which have general charitable purposes (either exclusively or as well as other specific criteria). However, we do not have a general category in the indexes. This is because it would

include so many trusts as to be useless. The subject index therefore should not be used as the definitive guide to finding the right trusts to apply to.

▶ Geographical index – page 471. Although trusts limiting their support to one particular area have been excluded, there are many which have some preference for one or more areas. These are listed in this index. Again, in a similar way to the subject index, care is needed. Many trusts state their beneficial area as the UK, so are not included in this index.

It is important to note that the trusts which appear under a particular index may have other criteria which exclude your organisation. Always read the entry carefully so that you can be sure you fit in with all the trust's criteria. Do not just use the index as a mailing list.

How the guide was compiled

The following practical guidelines were followed to produce this guide.

▶ Concentrate on what the trust does in practice rather than the wider objectives permitted by its formal governing document.

▶ Provide extensive information which will be of most use to readers; i.e. publish the trust's criteria and guidelines for applicants in full, where available.

▶ Include, where possible, details of a good sample of the organisations which have received grants to give the reader an idea of what the trust supports and the amounts it usually gives.

▶ Provide the most up-to-date information available at the time of the research.

▶ Include all trusts which meet our criteria for inclusion.

Availability of information

DSC believes that charities should be publicly accountable and it supports the implementation of the Charity Commission regulations and the 2005 SORP (Statement of Recommended Practice). DSC's Chief Executive, Debra Allcock Tyler, is a SORP Committee Member.

Many trusts recognise the importance of providing good, clear information about the work they do. However, there are some that wish to believe they are private bodies and ignore their statutory obligation to provide information to the public. The information that is held for these trusts at the Charity Commission is sometimes many years out of date.

Failing to supply accounts on request

Charities are required to send their annual report and accounts to the Charity Commission and also to any member of the public who requests them in writing. They are obliged to send the information, although they can make a 'reasonable charge' for this (i.e. the costs of photocopying and postage). Since the launch of the new format of the online Central Register of Charities on 1 October 2008, accounts that are overdue now have a red outline at the top of the page to show this, making it immediately apparent to the reader. When the overdue accounts are received the colour will revert to green. However, a record that a charity's accounts were late for a particular year will remain on the page for five years.

Failure to disclose grants

In SORP 2005, there is a clear emphasis on transparency. The report section is designed to help interested parties understand the work of charities and provide clarity and structure. It includes sections on charities':

- aims and objectives and the strategies and activities undertaken to achieve them
- achievements and performance
- plans for the future.

SORP 2005 also provides guidance on how grants payable during the year should be analysed. This should be sufficient to give an understanding of how its grant-making activity fits in with its particular charitable objectives.

As in SORP 2000, the 2005 update requires trusts to detail at least 50 grants (if these are of £1,000 or more). Of the trusts listed in this guide, *over 100 trusts* did not provide any details of the grants they made during the year. Where this is the case we have noted this in the 'information available' field.

Failing to provide a narrative report

All trusts should provide a narrative report describing its work. It is here that trusts should give an account of their work during the year with an explanation and analysis of the grants they have made. Many trust reports are extremely brief and give very little away about their activities. However, following the introduction of the Charities Act 2006, a charity must now be able to demonstrate that, for each of its aims, there is a clear benefit for the public as a whole or a sufficient section of it. Charity trustees have a new duty to report on their charity's public benefit in their trustee annual reports and this will necessitate those trustees who have been less than open in the past to give a more detailed account of the trust's activities.

Good trust reports

On a positive note, there are some trusts which provide excellent reports that go beyond the basic 'The objective of this charity is to make grants to charitable institutions.' When they have been particularly interesting or informative for applicants we have reproduced them in the entries.

Applying to trusts

There is a lot of competition for grants. Many trusts in this guide receive more applications than they can support. It is important to do the research: read the trust's criteria carefully and target the right trusts. This can lead to a higher success rate and save you writing applications which are destined only for the bin. Applying to inappropriate trusts is bad practice and, as well as annoying trustees, can potentially cause problems for future applicants. Trustees tell us that around half the applications they receive are from organisations that work outside their stated areas of support.

Unsolicited applications

A number of trusts do not want to receive applications (and for this reason usually do not want to appear in the guide). There can be good reasons for this. For example, the trust may do its own research or support the same list of charities each year. There are some trusts, however, which believe that they are 'private' trusts. No registered charity is a private body. We believe that trusts should not resent applications but should be committed to finding those charities most eligible for assistance.

We include these trusts for two reasons. First, some trusts state 'no unsolicited applications' simply as a deterrent in an effort to reduce the number of applications they receive, but will still consider the applications they receive. The second reason relates to the secondary purpose of the guide: to act as a survey of grant-making trusts.

If you choose to write to one of these trusts, do so with caution. Only write to those where your organisation very clearly fits a trust's criteria. We would advise you to include a stamped, addressed envelope and to state that you do not expect a response unless you are eligible. If they do not reply, do not chase them.

DSC policy and campaigning

Over the years DSC has campaigned on a number of fronts for better grantmaking. We believe that funders have a responsibility that extends far beyond providing funding. The way funders operate and develop their programmes has a huge impact on the organisations, causes and beneficiaries which their funding supports, as well as on the wider voluntary sector. Transparency is a key principle for us: by providing information about funders in this book and other DSC publications we have sought to open up their practices to greater scrutiny. Clearer and more accessible information enables fundraisers to focus their efforts effectively, and encourages open review and discussions of good practice. Our Great Giving campaign has grown out of these long-established beliefs.

We have identified some specific campaigning areas that we wish to focus on as part of an overall campaign for better grantmaking.

1) A clear picture of the funding environment

We think that to enable better planning and decision-making from funders and policymakers, more comprehensive information is needed about where money is going and what it supports. Many of the funders in this book are leading the way, although some fall short in terms of the level of detail they provide about their activities and effectiveness.

2) Accessible funding for campaigning

Financial support for campaigning is vital to the role organisations play in achieving social change. Greater clarity from grant-making trusts is needed so that campaigning organisations can find the support they need more easily.

3) An end to hidden small print

DSC is asking all funders to provide the terms and conditions which govern the use of the funds at the outset when people apply and to be open to negotiating terms when applicants request it.

4) No ineligible applications

We know that most funders receive applications that do not fall within the funder's guidelines. Clearer guidelines can help, but applicants also need to take more heed of funder guidelines and target their applications appropriately.

DSC has always believed that clear and open application and monitoring processes are essential for both funders and fundraisers to produce more effective applications and better eventual outcomes. The availability of such information has come a long way since the first edition of this guide. However, an important element of the funding process often remains hidden from wider scrutiny.

The detailed terms and conditions which set out what the applicant is required to do to obtain and retain the grant are too often unavailable until the point at which a formal offer of a grant is made. For an applicant, seeing these terms and conditions for the first time only when there is an offer of money on the table is not helpful. Even if negotiating the conditions is an option, the balance of power is still squarely with the funder. If the funder is not willing to negotiate, the applicant is faced with a difficult decision: should any conditions conflict with their organisation's values or the wider needs of their beneficiaries, they then face a dubious choice between accepting conditions which may threaten their independence, and turning down much needed funding.

We surveyed the largest charitable, corporate and government funders to find out more about the availability and accessibility of their terms and conditions, which culminated in a research report, *Critical Conditions* (DSC 2009). This research found that many trusts and foundations were demonstrating what we consider good practice – 72% of those that responded said they made their terms and conditions publicly available, and there were a number of good examples. However, nearly half of trusts that responded stated that their terms were non-negotiable, a stance we consider not in the best interests of funders or applicants. Overall these findings compared favourably to the central government funders that responded. By comparison these funders appeared to be less transparent and more averse to negotiating. They also tended to have more complicated and lengthy terms.

However, in late 2009 DSC asked similar questions of a much larger sample of trusts and foundations, and the results paint a different picture. In this research only half of respondents said their terms and conditions were publicly available, and a solid majority said they were non-negotiable. The rate of those which said their terms were not publicly available at all was three times greater than in the *Critical Conditions* survey. Some of the variation is accounted for by the fact that the larger sample contained a far greater number of smaller trusts and foundations that do not have any terms and conditions at all (49% of respondents to this survey said they had terms and conditions, compared with 86% in the *Critical Conditions* report). Nevertheless, this further research broadly suggests that there is room for improvement from trusts as regards the transparency of their funding terms and conditions.

Some may argue that providing more information at the beginning of the application process could make things more time consuming and costly, but DSC believes the benefits of greater transparency should take precedence. It is crucial that fundraisers have access to all the information they need to make an informed decision about whether to apply. It is also vital that such information is publicly available so that funders and others can make comparisons and share good practice. Further, in this age of digital communication, there is an ever-increasing expectation that all the relevant information, guidance and application forms will be available online. A link to a web page or a short document outlining the detailed terms and explaining their place in the application process is easy to provide and need not cost anything. Clear instructions should be provided for the fundraiser about the importance of the terms and conditions, why they are necessary and what they mean, along with exhortations to read them thoroughly.

Again the onus is not entirely on the funder – fundraisers have a responsibility to inform themselves as fully as possible and to ask for relevant information if it isn't available or is not clearly presented by the funder. Reading and evaluating the criteria, guidance and detailed terms and conditions is part of making a well-targeted application which is more likely to be successful. More crucially it is about protecting the organisation's independence and building funding relationships that will work well for both parties. The fundraiser, therefore, has an important role to play in scrutinising the conditions of the funding arrangement at the outset, and communicating their views to other decision-makers in the organisation (see www.dsc.org.uk for more advice on terms and conditions for fundraisers).

DSC's Big Lottery Refund campaign

The National Lottery occupies a unique place in the grant-making world. Whilst the various distributors are statutory bodies which distribute what is, technically speaking, public money, their activities, aims and beneficiaries have much in common with charitable grant-making trusts.

DSC's campaign will therefore be of interest to fundraisers, fundraising charities, and anyone interested in the Big Lottery Fund in particular. The aim of the campaign is for the government to refund to the Big Lottery Fund £425 million of Lottery revenue which was diverted to help pay for the London 2012 Olympics. We argue that this decision, taken in 2007, was wrong in principle, as it should have been given out in grants to voluntary and community groups across the country, not to make up the budgetary shortfall for a one-off sporting event.

Both the previous and current government have committed to refund the Lottery using proceeds from selling Olympics assets after the Games, and there have been a series of agreements between the various agencies involved. However, it is unfortunately not straightforward – asset sales are expected to take decades, which is not acceptable in our view. Learn more and stay updated with developments at www.biglotteryrefund.org.uk.

Finally . . .

The research for this book has been conducted as carefully as possible. Many thanks to those who have made this easier, especially the trusts themselves through their websites, their trust officers for providing additional information and the trustees and others who have helped us.

The availability of so much accessible, high-quality information from the Charity Commission website has been invaluable in the preparation of this guide. The staff at the Commission have been helpful in the support they have been able to offer when necessary.

We are aware that some of this information may be incomplete or will become out of date. We are equally sure we will have missed some relevant charities. We apologise for these imperfections. If you come across any omissions or mistakes, or if you have any suggestions for future editions of this book, do let us know. We can be contacted at the Liverpool Office Research Department at the Directory of Social Change either by phone on 0151 708 0136 or by email: research@dsc.org.uk

We hope this latest edition is as useful in its application as it has been interesting and inspiring in its preparation.

References

BBC (2010), 'UK economic growth revised up to 0.3%', BBC NEWS, news.bbc.co.uk, 26 February

Catenazzi, Nicole and Nick Wilson Young (2011), *Charity Forecast: a Quarterly Survey of Sector Leaders; Quarter 3*, London, NCVO

DSC (2009), *Critical Conditions*, London, Directory of Social Change

Jayanetti, Chaminda (2011), 'More than 2,000 charities and community groups face cuts', False Economy, falseeconomy.org.uk, 2 August

Jones, Gareth (2011), '£110m cuts estimate 'far too low', says NCVO', *Charity Finance*, London, Civil Society Media, 2 August

TUC (2011), 'Over 2,000 charities and community groups facing cuts or cull', Trades Union Congress, www.tuc.org.uk, 2 August

How to use this guide

The contents

The entries are in alphabetical order and describe the work of over 1,100 trusts. The entries are preceded by a listing of the trusts in order of size and are followed by a subject index and geographical index. There is also an alphabetical index at the back of this guide.

Finding the trusts you need

There are three basic ways of using this guide.

(a) You can simply read the entries through from A to Z (a rather time-consuming activity).

(b) You can look through the trust ranking table which starts on page xviii and use the boxes provided to tick the trusts which might be relevant to you (starting with the biggest).

(c) You can use the subject or geographical indexes starting on pages 448 and 471 respectively. Each has an introduction that explains how to use them.

If you use approaches (b) or (c), once you have chosen enough trusts to be getting on with, read each trust entry carefully before deciding to apply. Very often a trust's interest in your field will be limited and precise, and may demand an application specifically tailored to its requirements or often no application at all as they may not be currently accepting applications.

Sending off applications which show that the available information has not been read antagonises trusts and brings charities into disrepute within the grant-making sector. Carefully targeted applications, on the other hand, are usually welcomed by most trusts.

A typical trust entry

The Fictitious Trust

Welfare

£180,000 (2009)

Beneficial area

UK.

The Old Barn, Main Street, New Town ZC48 2QQ

Correspondent: Ann Freeman, Appeals Secretary

Trustees: Eva Appiah; Rita Khan; Lorraine Murphy.

CC Number: 123456

Information available

Accounts were on file at the Charity Commission.

The trust supports welfare charities in general, with an emphasis on homelessness. The trustees will support both capital and revenue projects. 'Specific projects are preferred to general running costs.'

In 2011 the trust had assets of £2.3 million and an income of £187,000. Over 200 grants were given totalling £180,000. Grants ranged from £100 to £20,000, with about half given in New Town. The largest grants were to: Homelessness UK (£18,000); and Shelter (£15,000). There were 10 grants of £2,000 to £10,000 including those to the Seafarers' Benevolent Society, Children without Families and Refugee Support Group.

Smaller grants were given to a variety of local charities, local branches of national charities and a few UK welfare charities.

Exclusions

No grants to non-registered charities, individuals or religious organisations.

Applications

In writing to the correspondent. Trustees meet in March and September each year. Applications should be received by the end of January and the end of July respectively.

Applications should include a brief description of the project and audited accounts. Unsuccessful applicants will not be informed unless a stamped, addressed envelope is provided.

Name of the charity

Summary of main activities – what the trust will do in practice rather than what its trust deed allows it to do.

Grant total – total grants given (not income) for the most recent year available.

Geographical area of grantgiving – including where the trust can legally give and where it gives in practice.

Contact address – telephone and fax numbers; and email and website addresses, if available.

Contact person

Trustees

Sources of information – what we used and what is available to the applicant.

Background/summary of activities – a quick indicator of the trust's policies to show whether it is worth reading the rest of the entry.

Financial information – noting the assets, ordinary income and grant total, and comment on unusual figures.

Typical grants range – indicates what a successful applicant can expect to receive.

Large grants – indicates where the main money is going, often the clearest indication of trust priorities.

Other examples of grants – a list of typical beneficiaries and, where possible, the purpose of the grant. We also indicate whether the trust gives one-off or recurrent grants.

Exclusions – a list of any area, subjects or types of grant the trust will not consider.

Applications – this includes how to apply and when to submit an application.

Dates for your diary

X = the usual month of trustees' or grant allocation meetings, or the last month for the receipt of applications.

Please note that these dates are provisional, and that the fact of an application being received does not necessarily mean that it will be considered at the next meeting.

	Jan	Feb	Mar	Apr	May	Jun	Jul	Aug	Sep	Oct	Nov	Dec
The A B Charitable Trust	X		X				X			X		
The Adamson Trust		X			X			X			X	
The Sylvia Aitken Charitable Trust			X						X			
The Ajahma Charitable Trust											X	
The Alabaster Trust			X			X			X			X
All Saints Educational Trust				X								
The Anchor Foundation	X						X					
The Appletree Trust				X								
The Ove Arup Foundation			X			X			X			X
The Astor Foundation				X						X		
The Baker Charitable Trust	X			X			X			X		
William P Bancroft (No. 2) Charitable Trust and Jenepher Gillett Trust					X							
Lord Barnby's Foundation		X				X					X	
The Misses Barrie Charitable Trust			X					X				X
The Bestway Foundation			X									
The Bisgood Charitable Trust (registered as Miss Jeanne Bisgood's Charitable Trust)		X							X			
Sir Alec Black's Charity			X						X			
The Charlotte Bonham-Carter Charitable Trust					X						X	
The Oliver Borthwick Memorial Trust					X							
The Bothwell Charitable Trust		X										
The Bransford Trust								X				X
Burdens Charitable Foundation			X			X			X			X
The Clara E Burgess Charity	X						X					

	Jan	Feb	Mar	Apr	May	Jun	Jul	Aug	Sep	Oct	Nov	Dec
The C Charitable Trust	X	X	X	X	X	X	X	X	X	X	X	X
Henry T and Lucy B Cadbury Charitable Trust			X									
The Richard Carne Trust						X						
The Joseph and Annie Cattle Trust	X	X	X	X	X	X	X	X	X	X	X	X
The Wilfrid and Constance Cave Foundation					X					X		
The Chapman Charitable Trust			X						X			
The Malcolm Chick Charity											X	
Chrysalis Trust						X						X
The Marjorie Coote Animal Charity Trust										X		
The Cotton Trust	X						X					
The Ronald Cruickshank Foundation										X		
The Cumber Family Charitable Trust			X							X		
The Daily Prayer Union Charitable Trust Ltd			X			X				X		
The Dickon Trust					X					X		
The DLM Charitable Trust		X					X				X	
The Dumbreck Charity				X	X							
The Edinburgh Trust, No. 2 Account				X								
Educational Foundation of Alderman John Norman		X			X	X				X		
The George Elias Charitable Trust	X	X	X	X	X	X	X	X	X	X	X	X
The Edith Maud Ellis 1985 Charitable Trust		X				X				X		
The Elmgrant Trust			X			X				X		
The Englefield Charitable Trust			X						X			
The Eventhall Family Charitable Trust	X	X	X	X	X	X	X	X	X	X	X	X
Elizabeth Ferguson Charitable Trust Fund	X						X					
Marc Fitch Fund				X						X		
The Fitton Trust				X				X				X
The Joyce Fletcher Charitable Trust										X	X	
The Forbes Charitable Foundation						X					X	
Ford Britain Trust						X					X	
The Oliver Ford Charitable Trust					X					X		
The Gordon Fraser Charitable Trust	X			X			X			X		
The Joseph Strong Frazer Trust			X						X			
The Frognal Trust		X			X			X			X	
The Gale Family Charitable Trust							X					
The Golsoncott Foundation		X			X			X			X	
The Good Neighbours Trust			X			X			X			X
Grand Charitable Trust of the Order of Women Freemasons							X					
The Grand Order of Water Rats' Charities Fund	X	X	X	X	X	X	X	X	X	X	X	X
The GRP Charitable Trust			X									

	Jan	Feb	Mar	Apr	May	Jun	Jul	Aug	Sep	Oct	Nov	Dec
The Harbour Foundation		X										
Hasluck Charitable Trust	X						X					
The Hawthorne Charitable Trust											X	
The Haymills Charitable Trust			X							X		
Help the Homeless	X			X			X			X		
The Christina Mary Hendrie Trust for Scottish and Canadian Charities			X	X						X	X	
The Holly Hill Charitable Trust						X				X		
The Charles Littlewood Hill Trust			X				X			X		
Hockerill Educational Foundation						X						
The Dorothy Holmes Charitable Trust	X		X									
The Mary Homfray Charitable Trust		X	X									
The Hope Trust						X						X
The Cuthbert Horn Trust												X
The Humanitarian Trust			X							X		
The Irish Youth Foundation (UK) Ltd (incorporating The Lawlor Foundation)		X										
The Ironmongers' Foundation	X		X					X		X		
The Ruth and Lionel Jacobson Trust (Second Fund) No. 2	X	X	X	X	X	X	X	X	X	X	X	X
The John Jarrold Trust	X					X						
Rees Jeffreys Road Fund	X			X			X		X		X	
The Jenour Foundation			X									
The Jephcott Charitable Trust				X						X		
The Johnson Foundation	X	X	X	X	X	X	X	X	X	X	X	X
The Anton Jurgens Charitable Trust						X				X		
The Kelly Family Charitable Trust			X						X			
The Nancy Kenyon Charitable Trust												X
The Peter Kershaw Trust					X						X	
The Kessler Foundation						X						X
The David Laing Foundation			X			X				X		X
The Lambert Charitable Trust								X				
Lancashire Environmental Fund	X			X			X			X		
LandAid Charitable Trust			X									
The Langdale Trust							X					
The R J Larg Family Charitable Trust		X					X					
Mrs F B Laurence Charitable Trust				X							X	
The Kathleen Laurence Trust	X					X						
The Law Society Charity				X			X		X			X
The Edgar E Lawley Foundation	X											
The Leche Trust		X				X				X		
The Linmardon Trust		X			X			X			X	
The Loseley and Guildway Charitable Trust		X			X				X			
The Michael Marks Charitable Trust	X						X					

	Jan	Feb	Mar	Apr	May	Jun	Jul	Aug	Sep	Oct	Nov	Dec
The Marsh Christian Trust	X	X	X	X	X	X	X	X	X	X	X	X
The Charlotte Marshall Charitable Trust			X									
John Martin's Charity				X			X			X		X
The Millfield House Foundation			X						X			
The Peter Minet Trust		X				X				X		
Monmouthshire County Council Welsh Church Act Fund			X			X			X			X
The Morgan Charitable Foundation				X						X		
S C and M E Morland's Charitable Trust			X									X
The Morris Charitable Trust	X	X	X	X	X	X	X	X	X	X	X	X
The Edwina Mountbatten & Leonora Children's Foundation									X	X		
Mountbatten Festival of Music	X						X					
Murphy-Neumann Charity Company Limited											X	X
The Music Sales Charitable Trust			X			X			X			X
The National Manuscripts Conservation Trust						X						X
The Norton Foundation							X					
The Oakdale Trust				X						X		
The Ogle Christian Trust					X						X	
The Oikonomia Trust		X										
The Ouseley Trust			X							X		
The Frank Parkinson Agricultural Trust				X								
Arthur James Paterson Charitable Trust			X						X			
The Constance Paterson Charitable Trust						X						X
Miss M E Swinton Paterson's Charitable Trust							X					
The David Pickford Charitable Foundation	X	X	X	X	X	X	X	X	X	X	X	X
The Bernard Piggott Trust					X						X	
The Austin and Hope Pilkington Trust						X					X	
The J S F Pollitzer Charitable Settlement				X							X	
The Porter Foundation			X				X				X	
The J E Posnansky Charitable Trust					X							
The Puebla Charitable Trust							X					
The R V W Trust				X				X				X
The Radcliffe Trust						X						X
The Rainford Trust			X				X				X	
The Fanny Rapaport Charitable Settlement			X						X			
The John Rayner Charitable Trust	X											
The Albert Reckitt Charitable Trust			X			X	X					
REMEDI						X						X
The Clive Richards Charity	X	X	X	X	X	X	X	X	X	X	X	X
Rix-Thompson-Rothenberg Foundation						X						X

	Jan	Feb	Mar	Apr	May	Jun	Jul	Aug	Sep	Oct	Nov	Dec
The Jean Sainsbury Animal Welfare Trust			X				X				X	
The Saintbury Trust				X							X	
The Sammermar Trust	X	X	X	X	X	X	X	X	X	X	X	X
Sir Samuel Scott of Yews Trust				X						X		
SFIA Educational Trust Limited			X	X								
The Linley Shaw Foundation		X	X									
The Shipwrights' Company Charitable Fund		X				X				X		
The John Slater Foundation					X					X		
The SMB Charitable Trust			X			X			X			X
The N Smith Charitable Settlement					X							X
The South Square Trust			X			X				X		
The W F Southall Trust		X	X							X		
The Worshipful Company of Spectacle Makers' Charity				X								
The Jessie Spencer Trust			X			X			X			X
Spring Harvest											X	
St Gabriel's Trust	X			X					X			
The Late St Patrick White Charitable Trust		X			X		X			X		
St Teilo's Trust		X			X				X			
The Stoller Charitable Trust			X			X			X			X
The W O Street Charitable Foundation	X			X			X			X		
Swan Mountain Trust		X				X			X			
The Tabeel Trust					X						X	
C B and H H Taylor 1984 Trust					X						X	
The Thomas Wall Trust									X			
The Ulverscroft Foundation			X			X			X			X
The Van Neste Foundation	X					X				X		
Mrs Maud Van Norden's Charitable Foundation					X							
The Scurrah Wainwright Charity		X				X				X		
The F J Wallis Charitable Settlement			X						X			
Blyth Watson Charitable Trust						X						X
The Weavers' Company Benevolent Fund		X				X				X		
The James Weir Foundation					X					X		
The Barbara Welby Trust			X							X		
The Wessex Youth Trust					X						X	
Dame Violet Wills Charitable Trust			X							X		
Anona Winn Charitable Trust		X					X					
Women's World Day of Prayer											X	
The Woodward Charitable Trust	X						X					
Zephyr Charitable Trust							X					

The major trusts ranked by grant total

Trust	Grants	Main grant areas
☐ The Fuserna Foundation	£3.5 million	Relief in need, children, older people, mental and physical illness
☐ The David and Elaine Potter Foundation	£3.2 million	Human rights, education, research and the arts
☐ The Exilarch's Foundation	£2.8 million	General, Jewish, education
☐ The M A Hawe Settlement	£1.8 million	General
☐ The Marjorie and Arnold Ziff Charitable Foundation	£1.5 million	General, education, Jewish, arts, youth, older people, medicine
☐ The R D Crusaders Foundation	£1.4 million	General
☐ Bourneheights Limited	£1.2 million	Orthodox Jewish
☐ The Dinwoodie Settlement	£1.2 million	Postgraduate medical education and research
☐ The Ian Karten Charitable Trust	£1.1 million	Technology centres for people with disabilities
☐ Country Houses Foundation	£1.1 million	Preservation of buildings of historic or architectural significance
☐ Extonglen Limited	£1.1 million	Orthodox Jewish
☐ The Lind Trust	£1 million	Social action, community and Christian service
☐ The Scotshill Trust	£1 million	General, particularly health, arts, conservation, education, social needs, animal welfare and conservation
☐ Vyoel Moshe Charitable Trust	£1 million	Education, relief of poverty
☐ The Langley Charitable Trust	£1 million	Christian, general
☐ The English Schools' Football Association	£984,000	Association football
☐ Truedene Co. Ltd	£960,000	Jewish
☐ The Charles Shorto Charitable Trust	£936,000	General
☐ Ambika Paul Foundation	£930,000	Education, young people
☐ The Barbour Foundation	£925,000	Health, welfare, conservation and restoration
☐ The Talbot Village Trust	£884,000	General
☐ Coutts Charitable Trust	£864,000	General, social welfare
☐ The Ireland Fund of Great Britain	£863,000	Welfare, community, education, peace and reconciliation, the arts
☐ The Queen Anne's Gate Foundation	£809,000	Education, medical and rehabilitative, disadvantage
☐ Lancashire Environmental Fund	£796,000	Environment and community

☐ The Kennel Club Charitable Trust	£780,000	Dogs
☐ Matliwala Family Charitable Trust	£753,000	Islam, general
☐ The Persula Foundation	£748,000	Homeless, people with disabilities, human rights, animal welfare
☐ E and E Kernkraut Charities Limited	£744,000	General, education, Jewish
☐ The Priory Foundation	£741,000	Health and social welfare, especially children
☐ The C Charitable Trust	£729,000	General
☐ East Kent Provincial Charities	£728,000	General, education, younger, older people
☐ The Stella and Alexander Margulies Charitable Trust	£725,000	Jewish, the arts, general
☐ Friends of Wiznitz Limited	£721,000	Jewish education, relief of poverty
☐ Achiezer Association Ltd	£691,000	Relief in need, elderly people, education, religion, general
☐ J P Moulton Charitable Foundation	£684,000	Medical, education, training and counselling
☐ The Ingram Trust	£672,000	General
☐ The Richard Wilcox Welfare Charity	£669,000	Health, medical research, welfare of patients, hospitals, animal welfare
☐ Elshore Ltd	£656,000	Jewish
☐ The Kohn Foundation	£650,000	Scientific and medical projects, the arts – particularly music, education, Jewish charities
☐ The Edith Winifred Hall Charitable Trust	£612,000	General
☐ Wychville Ltd	£600,000	Jewish, education, general
☐ The J Isaacs Charitable Trust	£595,000	General
☐ Newpier Charity Ltd	£579,000	Jewish, general
☐ Kirschel Foundation	£564,000	Jewish, medical
☐ Premierquote Ltd	£560,000	Jewish, general
☐ The Platinum Trust	£559,000	Disability
☐ Marchig Animal Welfare Trust	£554,000	Animal welfare
☐ The Schapira Charitable Trust	£552,000	Jewish, health, education
☐ Lewis Family Charitable Trust	£551,000	General, Jewish
☐ The Porter Foundation	£551,000	Jewish charities, environment, arts, general
☐ The Thames Wharf Charity	£531,000	General
☐ Kollel and Co. Limited	£517,000	Jewish, relief of poverty
☐ Ranworth Trust	£515,000	General
☐ D D McPhail Charitable Settlement	£511,000	Medical research, disability, older people
☐ The Barbara Ward Children's Foundation	£507,000	Children
☐ The Bestway Foundation	£500,000	Education, welfare, medical
☐ The Locker Foundation	£500,000	Mainly Jewish charities
☐ The Horne Trust	£492,000	Hospices
☐ The Law Society Charity	£491,000	Law and justice, worldwide
☐ The Swire Charitable Trust	£490,000	General
☐ The Bransford Trust	£485,000	General
☐ The Harbour Foundation	£482,000	Jewish, general
☐ The Rowlands Trust	£482,000	General, mainly medical research, social welfare, music, the arts, the environment
☐ The Catherine Cookson Charitable Trust	£481,000	General
☐ The John Swire (1989) Charitable Trust	£477,000	General
☐ Alvor Charitable Trust	£470,000	Christian, humanitarian, social change
☐ Bay Charitable Trust	£470,000	Jewish
☐ The William Allen Young Charitable Trust	£470,000	General, health, social welfare
☐ The Ruth Berkowitz Charitable Trust	£464,000	Jewish, medical research, youth, general
☐ The Matt 6.3 Charitable Trust	£462,500	Christian
☐ The Union of Orthodox Hebrew Congregation	£453,000	Jewish
☐ The Connie and Albert Taylor Charitable Trust	£450,000	Medical research, hospices, education and recreation, conservation
☐ The Robert McAlpine Foundation	£448,000	Children with disabilities, older people, medical research, welfare

☐ The Martin Laing Foundation	£445,000	General, environment and conservation, disadvantaged young people, older people, illness
☐ The Steinberg Family Charitable Trust	£441,000	Jewish, health
☐ Solev Co. Ltd	£435,000	Jewish charities
☐ Lloyd's Charities Trust	£431,000	General
☐ Wychdale Ltd	£430,000	Jewish
☐ The Fulmer Charitable Trust	£423,000	Developing world, general
☐ J A Clark Charitable Trust	£422,000	Health, education, peace, the environment, the arts
☐ The A B Charitable Trust	£406,000	Human rights
☐ The Normanby Charitable Trust	£405,000	Social welfare, disability, general
☐ The Tanner Trust	£396,000	General
☐ The John and Freda Coleman Charitable Trust	£395,000	Disadvantaged young people
☐ The Vandervell Foundation	£391,000	General
☐ The Evan Cornish Foundation	£387,000	Education, older people, health, human rights, poverty alleviation, penal reform
☐ The Avenue Charitable Trust	£384,000	General
☐ Trumros Limited	£384,000	Jewish
☐ The Ashley Family Foundation	£383,000	Art and design, higher education, local projects in mid-rural Wales
☐ The Harris Family Charitable Trust	£382,000	Health, illness
☐ The Norman Family Charitable Trust	£382,000	General
☐ The Norwich Town Close Estate Charity	£380,000	Education in and near Norwich
☐ Keren Mitzvah Trust	£379,000	General, Jewish
☐ The Rowland Family Foundation	£379,000	Relief in need, education, religion, community
☐ G R Waters Charitable Trust 2000	£375,000	General
☐ The Daniel Howard Trust	£375,000	Jewish causes
☐ The Laduma Dhamecha Charitable Trust	£375,000	General
☐ The Puebla Charitable Trust	£371,000	Community development work, relief of poverty
☐ Generations Charitable Trust	£367,000	Children, overseas projects
☐ The Whitley Animal Protection Trust	£367,000	Protection and conservation of animals and their environments
☐ The Tufton Charitable Trust	£363,000	Christian
☐ Help the Hospices	£362,000	Hospices
☐ The John Coates Charitable Trust	£362,000	General, arts, children, environment, medical
☐ Seamen's Hospital Society	£361,000	Seafarers
☐ Brian Mercer Charitable Trust	£360,000	Welfare, medical, visual arts
☐ The Dyers' Company Charitable Trust	£359,000	General
☐ The George Cadbury Trust	£355,000	General
☐ The Simon Heller Charitable Settlement	£355,000	Medical research, science and educational research
☐ Kupath Gemach Chaim Bechesed Viznitz Trust	£351,000	Jewish
☐ The Essex Youth Trust	£351,000	Youth, education of people under 25
☐ The Peter Stebbings Memorial Charity	£351,000	General
☐ The Hospital Saturday Fund	£350,000	Medical, health
☐ The Bowerman Charitable Trust	£349,000	Church, the arts, medical, youth
☐ The Cobalt Trust	£348,000	General
☐ The Breast Cancer Research Trust	£345,000	Breast cancer research
☐ The Holden Charitable Trust	£345,000	Jewish
☐ Millennium Stadium Charitable Trust	£344,000	Sport, the arts, community, environment
☐ Salo Bordon Charitable Trust	£344,000	Jewish
☐ The Mutual Trust Group	£340,000	Jewish, education, poverty
☐ The Panacea Society	£337,000	Christian religion, relief of sickness
☐ Sino-British Fellowship Trust	£334,000	Education
☐ Dromintee Trust	£334,000	General
☐ The John Beckwith Charitable Trust	£334,000	Youth, education, social welfare, medical research, arts
☐ The Radcliffe Trust	£334,000	Music, crafts, conservation
☐ The R V W Trust	£330,000	Music education and appreciation
☐ Mariapolis Limited	£327,000	Christian ecumenism

☐ Minton Charitable Trust	£325,000	General, education
☐ The De Laszlo Foundation	£321,000	The arts, general
☐ The Doris Field Charitable Trust	£321,000	General
☐ The Bishop Radford Trust	£319,000	Church of England
☐ The Batchworth Trust	£316,000	Medical, humanitarian aid, social welfare, general
☐ The D G Charitable Settlement	£316,000	General
☐ The Jean Sainsbury Animal Welfare Trust	£315,000	Animal welfare
☐ The W O Street Charitable Foundation	£314,000	Education, people with disabilities, young people, health, social welfare
☐ The David Lean Foundation	£311,000	Film production, education and visual arts
☐ The Mactaggart Third Fund	£311,000	General
☐ Viscount Amory's Charitable Trust	£309,000	Welfare, older people, older people, education, Christian churches
☐ The Anson Charitable Trust	£308,000	General
☐ The Norwood and Newton Settlement	£308,000	Christian
☐ John Laing Charitable Trust	£307,000	Education, community regeneration, youth, homelessness, environment
☐ Menuchar Ltd	£307,000	Jewish
☐ The Jean Shanks Foundation	£307,000	Medical research and education
☐ William Harding's Charity	£305,000	Education, welfare
☐ The Persson Charitable Trust	£302,000	Christian mission societies and agencies
☐ The Costa Family Charitable Trust	£300,000	Christian
☐ Michael Davies Charitable Settlement	£299,000	General
☐ The Leche Trust	£298,000	Preservation and restoration of Georgian art, music and architecture
☐ T and J Meyer Family Foundation Limited	£298,000	Education, healthcare, environment
☐ The Anton Jurgens Charitable Trust	£297,000	Welfare, general
☐ The Park Charitable Trust	£295,000	Jewish, patient care – cancer and heart conditions, hospitals
☐ The Yapp Charitable Trust	£293,000	Social welfare
☐ The Houghton Dunn Charitable Trust	£292,000	Medical, health, welfare, environment, wildlife, churches, heritage
☐ The M K Charitable Trust	£289,000	Jewish orthodox charities
☐ The Truemark Trust	£289,000	General
☐ The Christina Mary Hendrie Trust for Scottish and Canadian Charities	£288,000	Youth, people who are elderly, general
☐ The Huntingdon Foundation	£288,000	Jewish education
☐ The Stewards' Charitable Trust	£288,000	Rowing
☐ The Sidney and Elizabeth Corob Charitable Trust	£287,000	General, Jewish
☐ The Ajahma Charitable Trust	£286,000	Development, poverty, human rights, health, disability, social welfare
☐ The W F Southall Trust	£286,000	Quaker, general
☐ Friends of Boyan Trust	£283,000	Orthodox Jewish
☐ The Alan Sugar Foundation	£283,000	Jewish charities, general
☐ The Inman Charity	£283,000	General, medical, social welfare, disability, older people, hospices
☐ SFIA Educational Trust Limited	£280,000	Education
☐ The Alchemy Foundation	£280,000	Health and welfare, famine relief overseas
☐ The Philips and Rubens Charitable Trust	£280,000	General, Jewish
☐ R S Charitable Trust	£280,000	Jewish, welfare
☐ The Derek Butler Trust	£279,000	Medical research, health, music and music education
☐ The William Brake Charitable Trust	£279,000	General
☐ The Adint Charitable Trust	£276,000	Health, social welfare
☐ The Reta Lila Howard Foundation	£275,000	Children, arts, environment
☐ Mazars Charitable Trust	£272,000	General
☐ The Millichope Foundation	£272,000	General

☐ The Violet and Milo Cripps Charitable Trust	£272,000	Prison and human rights
☐ The Indigo Trust	£270,000	Prisons and criminal justice
☐ The Sir John Ritblat Family Foundation	£270,000	Jewish, general
☐ The Stanley Foundation Ltd	£269,000	Older people, medical care and research, education, social welfare
☐ Newby Trust Limited	£268,000	Welfare
☐ Tudor Rose Ltd	£268,000	Jewish
☐ Stervon Ltd	£267,000	Jewish
☐ Mountbatten Festival of Music	£266,000	Royal Marines and Royal Navy charities
☐ The Cayo Foundation	£266,000	Medical research, crime, children and young people, performing arts, general
☐ The Toy Trust	£266,000	Children
☐ The Robert Gavron Charitable Trust	£262,000	The arts, policy research, general
☐ Basil Samuel Charitable Trust	£261,000	General
☐ The Kennedy Charitable Foundation	£261,000	Roman Catholic ministries, general, especially in the west of Ireland
☐ The Clara E Burgess Charity	£260,500	Children and young people
☐ Songdale Ltd	£260,000	Jewish, education
☐ The Clover Trust	£260,000	Older people, young people, Catholic, health, disability
☐ The Loftus Charitable Trust	£260,000	Jewish
☐ The Ruzin Sadagora Trust	£260,000	Jewish
☐ The David Laing Foundation	£258,000	Youth, disability, the arts, general
☐ The Weavers' Company Benevolent Fund	£258,000	Disadvantaged young people, offenders and ex-offenders
☐ Sue Hammerson's Charitable Trust	£256,000	Health care, education, religion
☐ Burdens Charitable Foundation	£255,000	General
☐ C B and H H Taylor 1984 Trust	£255,000	Quaker, general
☐ The Weinstock Fund	£255,000	General
☐ Prairie Trust	£254,000	International development, climate change, conflict prevention
☐ The Association of Colleges Charitable Trust	£253,000	Further education colleges
☐ The Patrick Frost Foundation	£252,000	General
☐ The Russell Trust	£252,000	General
☐ The Stoller Charitable Trust	£252,000	Medical, children, general
☐ The Charlotte Heber-Percy Charitable Trust	£251,000	General
☐ The Second Joseph Aaron Littman Foundation	£251,000	General
☐ The Coltstaple Trust	£250,000	Medical, relief in need, education
☐ The Sir Jack Lyons Charitable Trust	£250,000	Jewish, arts, education
☐ The Lynn Foundation	£249,000	General
☐ Tomchei Torah Charitable Trust	£247,500	Jewish
☐ The Park House Charitable Trust	£247,000	Education, social welfare, ecclesiastical
☐ Sir Samuel Scott of Yews Trust	£245,000	Medical research
☐ Talteg Ltd	£245,000	Jewish, welfare
☐ The Noon Foundation	£245,000	General, education, relief of poverty, community relations, alleviation of racial discrimination
☐ The Petplan Charitable Trust	£245,000	Welfare of dogs, cats, horses and rabbits
☐ Roger Vere Foundation	£244,000	General
☐ The Melanie White Foundation Limited	£242,000	General
☐ Lord Barnby's Foundation	£241,000	General
☐ The Woodward Charitable Trust	£240,000	General
☐ The Forest Hill Charitable Trust	£239,000	Christian causes and relief work
☐ The Homelands Charitable Trust	£239,000	The New Church, health, social welfare
☐ The Millfield House Foundation	£238,000	Social disadvantage, social policy
☐ The Joseph and Annie Cattle Trust	£237,000	General
☐ The Elizabeth Frankland Moore and Star Foundation	£236,000	General
☐ The Annandale Charitable Trust	£235,000	Major UK charities

☐ The Esfandi Charitable Foundation	£235,000	Jewish
☐ Peter Barker-Mill Memorial Charity	£234,000	General
☐ The Chapman Charitable Trust	£234,000	Welfare, general
☐ Grimmitt Trust	£233,000	General
☐ The Sammermar Trust	£232,000	General
☐ Beauland Ltd	£231,000	Jewish causes
☐ Tegham Limited	£231,000	Orthodox Jewish, welfare
☐ The Grahame Charitable Foundation Limited	£231,000	Jewish
☐ The Ellinson Foundation Ltd	£230,000	Jewish
☐ The Haymills Charitable Trust	£230,000	Education, medicine, welfare, youth
☐ The Odin Charitable Trust	£230,000	General
☐ The Shanley Charitable Trust	£230,000	Relief of poverty
☐ Woodlands Green Ltd	£230,000	Jewish
☐ Marr-Munning Trust	£229,000	Overseas aid
☐ The George Elias Charitable Trust	£229,000	Jewish, general
☐ The King/Cullimore Charitable Trust	£228,500	General
☐ Women's World Day of Prayer	£228,000	Promotion of the Christian faith through education, literature and audio-visual material
☐ Child Growth Foundation	£227,000	Child/adult growth disorder treatment and research
☐ Monmouthshire County Council Welsh Church Act Fund	£227,000	General
☐ The Edgar E Lawley Foundation	£227,000	Older people, disability, children, community, hospices and medical
☐ The Andrew Anderson Trust	£226,000	Christian, social welfare
☐ R H Southern Trust	£225,000	Education, disability, relief of poverty, environment, conservation
☐ Macdonald-Buchanan Charitable Trust	£225,000	General
☐ The Henry C Hoare Charitable Trust	£225,000	General
☐ The Joanna Herbert-Stepney Charitable Settlement	£225,000	General
☐ The Cooks Charity	£224,000	Catering, welfare
☐ The Lolev Charitable Trust	£224,000	Orthodox Jewish
☐ The Mole Charitable Trust	£224,000	Jewish, general
☐ The Booth Charities	£223,000	Welfare, health, education
☐ The Bedfordshire and Hertfordshire Historic Churches Trust	£222,000	Churches
☐ The Michael Bishop Foundation	£220,000	General
☐ Royal Masonic Trust for Girls and Boys	£219,000	Children, young people
☐ The Iliffe Family Charitable Trust	£219,000	Medical, disability, heritage, education
☐ R J M Charitable Trust	£218,000	Jewish
☐ The Cecil Rosen Foundation	£218,000	Welfare, especially older people, illness, people who are mentally or physically disabled
☐ The Joseph Strong Frazer Trust	£218,000	General, particularly social welfare, education, religion and wildlife
☐ Marbeh Torah Trust	£217,000	Jewish education and religion, relief of poverty
☐ Old Possum's Practical Trust	£217,000	General, arts
☐ The Michael and Morven Heller Charitable Foundation	£217,000	University and medical research projects, the arts
☐ The Tisbury Telegraph Trust	£217,000	Christian, overseas aid, general
☐ Woodroffe Benton Foundation	£217,000	General
☐ The Eleanor Rathbone Charitable Trust	£216,000	Merseyside, women, 'unpopular causes'
☐ The Englefield Charitable Trust	£216,000	General, particularly local charities in Berkshire
☐ The Francis Winham Foundation	£216,000	Welfare of older people
☐ Ian Mactaggart Trust	£215,000	Education and training, culture, welfare and disability
☐ The South Square Trust	£215,000	General
☐ The Van Neste Foundation	£215,000	Welfare, Christian, developing world
☐ Toras Chesed (London) Trust	£215,000	Jewish, education

THE MAJOR TRUSTS RANKED BY GRANT TOTAL

☐	Calleva Foundation	£213,000	General
☐	The Lauffer Family Charitable Foundation	£213,000	Jewish, general
☐	The SMB Charitable Trust	£212,000	Christian, general
☐	Alan Edward Higgs Charity	£210,000	Child welfare
☐	Bill Brown's Charitable Settlement	£210,000	General, health, social welfare
☐	The Austin and Hope Pilkington Trust	£210,000	Music, the arts, community, medical, children and youth, older people
☐	The Sir John Eastwood Foundation	£209,500	Social welfare, education, health
☐	The Jephcott Charitable Trust	£209,000	Development worldwide, specifically health, education, population control and environment
☐	The M D and S Charitable Trust	£209,000	Jewish
☐	The Roger Raymond Charitable Trust	£209,000	Older people, education, medical
☐	The Bisgood Charitable Trust	£208,000	Roman Catholic purposes, older people
☐	The Clive Richards Charity	£208,000	Churches, schools, arts, disability and poverty
☐	The Leslie Silver Charitable Trust	£208,000	Jewish, general
☐	The Rothermere Foundation	£206,000	Education, general
☐	Finnart House School Trust	£205,000	Welfare and education of Jewish children and young people
☐	Saint Sarkis Charity Trust	£204,000	Armenian churches and welfare, offenders
☐	The Eventhall Family Charitable Trust	£204,000	General
☐	The Scouloudi Foundation	£204,000	General
☐	Fordeve Ltd	£203,000	Jewish, general
☐	Mercury Phoenix Trust	£203,000	AIDS, HIV
☐	The Armourers' and Brasiers' Gauntlet Trust	£203,000	Materials science, general
☐	The James Weir Foundation	£203,000	Welfare, education, general
☐	The Sackler Trust	£203,000	Arts and culture, science, medical
☐	Webb Memorial Trust	£202,500	Education, politics, social policy
☐	Royal Artillery Charitable Fund	£202,000	Service charities
☐	The Anchor Foundation	£201,000	Christian
☐	The Lotus Foundation	£201,000	Children and families, women, community, animal protection, addiction recovery, education
☐	Buckingham Trust	£200,000	Christian purposes, relief of poverty and sickness and support for older people
☐	Elizabeth Ferguson Charitable Trust Fund	£200,000	Children, medical research, health, hospices
☐	Gordon Cook Foundation	£200,000	Education and training
☐	The D W T Cargill Fund	£200,000	General
☐	The Linda and Gordon Bonnyman Charitable Trust	£200,000	General
☐	The Ripple Effect Foundation	£200,000	General, particularly disadvantaged young people, the environment and overseas development
☐	The Sigmund Sternberg Charitable Foundation	£200,000	Jewish, inter-faith causes, general
☐	Spring Harvest	£199,000	The promotion of Christianity
☐	John Coldman Charitable Trust	£198,000	General, Christian
☐	The Chevras Ezras Nitzrochim Trust	£198,000	Jewish
☐	The Friarsgate Trust	£197,000	Health and welfare of young and older people
☐	The Irish Youth Foundation (UK) Ltd	£197,000	Irish young people
☐	The Peter Minet Trust	£196,000	General, children/youth, health and people with disabilities, social welfare, culture and community
☐	The Sir Victor Blank Charitable Settlement	£196,000	Jewish organisations and general
☐	The William and Katherine Longman Trust	£195,000	General
☐	Farthing Trust	£194,000	Christian, general
☐	The Cotton Trust	£193,000	Relief of suffering, elimination and control of disease, people who are disabled or disadvantaged
☐	The Paul Bassham Charitable Trust	£192,000	General
☐	The Peggy Ramsay Foundation	£191,000	Writers and writing for the stage
☐	The David Webster Charitable Trust	£190,000	Ecological and broadly environmental projects
☐	John Martin's Charity	£189,000	Religious activity, relief in need, education
☐	Scott (Eredine) Charitable Trust	£189,000	Service and ex-service charities, medical, welfare

☐ The Amalur Foundation Limited	£189,000	General
☐ The Three Oaks Trust	£189,000	Welfare
☐ Stuart Hine Trust	£188,000	Evangelical Christianity
☐ The British Council for Prevention of Blindness	£187,000	Prevention and treatment of blindness
☐ The Misses Barrie Charitable Trust	£187,000	Medical, general
☐ The Sir Harry Pilkington Trust	£187,000	General
☐ Peltz Trust	£186,000	Arts, education, health, Jewish, general
☐ The M and C Trust	£186,000	Jewish, social welfare
☐ Rokach Family Charitable Trust	£185,000	Jewish, general
☐ The O'Sullivan Family Charitable Trust	£185,000	Children and young people, care homes, genetic research
☐ The Pharsalia Charitable Trust	£185,000	General, relief of sickness
☐ The Whitaker Charitable Trust	£185,000	Music, environment, countryside conservation
☐ The Bulldog Trust Limited	£184,000	General
☐ The Jewish Youth Fund	£184,000	Jewish youth work
☐ The Ove Arup Foundation	£184,000	Construction education and research
☐ Stevenson Family's Charitable Trust	£183,000	Culture and arts, conservation and heritage, health, education, overseas aid
☐ The Barbers' Company General Charities	£183,000	Medical and nursing education
☐ The Holly Hill Charitable Trust	£183,000	Environmental education, conservation and wildlife
☐ The Lillie Johnson Charitable Trust	£183,000	Children, young people who are blind or deaf, medical
☐ The John Oldacre Foundation	£182,500	Research and education in agricultural sciences
☐ The Florence Turner Trust	£182,000	General
☐ The Vivienne and Samuel Cohen Charitable Trust	£182,000	Jewish, education, health, medical, culture, general
☐ The Leslie Smith Foundation	£181,000	Children with illnesses, orphans and schools
☐ The Charles Littlewood Hill Trust	£180,000	Health, disability, service, children (including schools)
☐ The Christopher Laing Foundation	£180,000	Social welfare, environment, culture, health, children and youth
☐ The Sir Edward Lewis Foundation	£180,000	General
☐ The Tay Charitable Trust	£180,000	General
☐ C and F Charitable Trust	£179,000	Orthodox Jewish charities
☐ Philip and Judith Green Trust	£179,000	Christian and missions
☐ The C A Redfern Charitable Foundation	£179,000	General
☐ The Ellerdale Trust	£179,000	Children
☐ Cardy Beaver Foundation	£178,000	General
☐ G M Morrison Charitable Trust	£178,000	General
☐ The Craps Charitable Trust	£178,000	Jewish, general
☐ The Rock Foundation	£176,000	Christian ministries and charities
☐ The Doris Pacey Charitable Foundation	£175,000	Jewish, medical, educational and social
☐ The Sir Peter O'Sullevan Charitable Trust	£175,000	Animal welfare
☐ The Holst Foundation	£174,000	Arts
☐ Localtrent Ltd	£173,000	Jewish, education, religion
☐ Sueberry Ltd	£172,000	Jewish, welfare
☐ The Hilda and Samuel Marks Foundation	£171,000	Jewish, general
☐ The Lister Charitable Trust	£171,000	Outdoor activities for disadvantaged young people
☐ The Albion Trust	£170,000	General
☐ The Ratcliff Foundation	£170,000	General
☐ The John Slater Foundation	£169,000	Medical, animal welfare, general
☐ Double 'O' Charity Ltd	£168,000	General
☐ Jusaca Charitable Trust	£168,000	Jewish, arts, research, religion, housing
☐ Rees Jeffreys Road Fund	£167,000	Road and transport research and education
☐ Schroder Charity Trust	£165,000	General
☐ The Kobler Trust	£165,000	Arts, Jewish, general
☐ The Laurence Misener Charitable Trust	£165,000	Jewish, general

☐ Ford Britain Trust	£164,000	Community service, education, environment, disability, schools, special needs education, youth
☐ The CH (1980) Charitable Trust	£164,000	Jewish
☐ The Hyde Charitable Trust – Youth Plus	£164,000	Disadvantaged children and young people
☐ Michael Marks Charitable Trust	£163,000	Culture, environment
☐ Thackray Medical Research Trust	£163,000	Research of medical procedures/products, medical supply trade
☐ The Marchday Charitable Fund	£163,000	Education, health, social welfare, support groups, overseas aid
☐ The R D Turner Charitable Trust	£162,500	General
☐ Hockerill Educational Foundation	£162,000	Education, especially Christian education
☐ The Elise Pilkington Charitable Trust	£161,000	Equine animals, older people, illness, relief of poverty
☐ The Ironmongers' Foundation	£160,000	General
☐ The Jessie Spencer Trust	£160,000	General
☐ The John Jarrold Trust	£159,000	Social welfare, arts, education, environment/ conservation, medical research, churches
☐ The Gershon Coren Charitable Foundation	£158,000	Jewish, welfare, general
☐ The GRP Charitable Trust	£158,000	Jewish, general
☐ The Ward Blenkinsop Trust	£157,000	Medicine, social welfare, arts, education, general
☐ The Archie Sherman Cardiff Foundation	£156,000	Health, education, training, overseas aid, community and Jewish
☐ The Marsh Christian Trust	£156,000	General
☐ The Peter Kershaw Trust	£156,000	Medical research, education, social welfare
☐ The Susanna Peake Charitable Trust	£156,000	General
☐ The Schreiber Charitable Trust	£155,000	Jewish with a preference for education, social welfare and medical
☐ Largsmount Ltd	£154,400	Jewish
☐ The Catholic Trust for England and Wales	£154,000	Catholic
☐ The Martin Smith Foundation	£154,000	Art, music, sports and education
☐ The Thornton Foundation	£154,000	General
☐ The Thornton Trust	£152,000	Evangelical Christianity, education, relief of sickness and poverty
☐ The Follett Trust	£151,000	Welfare, education, arts
☐ The Wilfrid and Constance Cave Foundation	£151,000	Conservation, animal welfare, health, social welfare, general
☐ The CBD Charitable Trust	£150,000	General, children and young people
☐ The Cyril Shack Trust	£150,000	Jewish, general
☐ The Hope Trust	£150,000	Temperance, Reformed Protestant churches
☐ The Miller Foundation	£150,000	General
☐ The Saintbury Trust	£150,000	General
☐ Brian and Jill Moss Charitable Trust	£149,000	Jewish, healthcare
☐ George A Moore Foundation	£149,000	General
☐ The Delves Charitable Trust	£149,000	Environment, conservation, medical, general
☐ Riverside Charitable Trust Limited	£148,000	Health, welfare, older people, education, general
☐ The G W Cadbury Charitable Trust	£148,000	Family planning, conservation, general
☐ The Wessex Youth Trust	£147,000	Youth, general
☐ The Sir James Roll Charitable Trust	£145,000	General
☐ Melodor Ltd	£144,000	Jewish, general
☐ Mickleham Charitable Trust	£144,000	Relief in need
☐ The Gordon Fraser Charitable Trust	£144,000	Children, young people, environment, arts
☐ The Leigh Trust	£144,000	Addiction, children and youth, criminal justice, asylum seekers, racial equality and education
☐ The Morris Charitable Trust	£144,000	Relief in need, education, community support and development
☐ The GNC Trust	£143,000	General
☐ The Goodman Foundation	£143,000	General, social welfare, older people, health and disability

☐ The Stephen R and Philippa H Southall Charitable Trust	£143,000	General
☐ The London Law Trust	£142,500	Health and personal development of children and young people
☐ The Friends of Kent Churches	£142,000	Churches
☐ The Nani Huyu Charitable Trust	£142,000	Welfare
☐ The Ronald Cruickshank's Foundation	£142,000	Welfare, education, general
☐ The Scott Bader Commonwealth Ltd	£142,000	General, international
☐ Adenfirst Ltd	£141,000	Jewish
☐ The Rainford Trust	£141,000	Social welfare, general
☐ Golubovich Foundation	£140,000	Arts
☐ St Monica Trust Community Fund	£139,000	Older people, disability
☐ The J E Posnansky Charitable Trust	£139,000	Jewish charities, health, social welfare and humanitarian
☐ The Simon Whitbread Charitable Trust	£139,000	Education, family welfare, medicine, preservation
☐ St Gabriel's Trust	£138,000	Higher and further religious education
☐ The Felicity Wilde Charitable Trust	£138,000	Children, medical research
☐ The Suva Foundation Limited	£138,000	General
☐ Saint Luke's College Foundation	£137,000	Research or studies in theology
☐ The Arnold Burton 1998 Charitable Trust	£137,000	Jewish, medical research, education, social welfare, heritage
☐ The Beryl Evetts and Robert Luff Animal Welfare Trust	£137,000	Animal welfare
☐ The Cecil Pilkington Charitable Trust	£137,000	Conservation, medical research, general
☐ The Charlotte Bonham-Carter Charitable Trust	£137,000	General
☐ The Lord Faringdon Charitable Trust	£137,000	Medical, education, heritage, social welfare, the arts and sciences, recreation and general
☐ The Constance Green Foundation	£136,000	Social welfare, medicine, health, general
☐ The Doughty Charity Trust	£136,000	Orthodox Jewish, religious education, relief of poverty
☐ The Hugh and Ruby Sykes Charitable Trust	£136,000	General, medical, education, employment
☐ The Gale Family Charitable Trust	£135,000	General
☐ The Mayfield Valley Arts Trust	£135,000	Arts, especially chamber music
☐ The Pyne Charitable Trust	£135,000	Christian, health
☐ The Walter Guinness Charitable Trust	£135,000	General
☐ Christian Response to Eastern Europe	£134,000	Christian, emergency relief
☐ The David Tannen Charitable Trust	£134,000	Jewish
☐ Grand Charitable Trust of the Order of Women Freemasons	£133,000	General and overseas
☐ The Altajir Trust	£133,000	Islam, education, science and research
☐ The Hudson Foundation	£133,000	Older people, general
☐ The Hutton Foundation	£133,000	Christian
☐ The Lawson Beckman Charitable Trust	£133,000	Jewish, welfare, education, arts
☐ The Cotton Industry War Memorial Trust	£132,500	Education in textiles
☐ Lifeline 4 Kids	£132,000	Equipment for children with disabilities
☐ Quercus Trust	£131,000	Arts, general
☐ The J R S S T Charitable Trust	£131,000	Democracy and social justice
☐ The Magen Charitable Trust	£131,000	Education, Jewish
☐ The Oakdale Trust	£131,000	Social work, medical, general
☐ The Langdale Trust	£130,000	Social welfare, Christian, medical, general
☐ The Lanvern Foundation	£130,000	Education and health, particularly for children
☐ The Ouseley Trust	£130,000	Choral services of the Church of England, Church in Wales and Church of Ireland, choir schools
☐ The Raymond and Blanche Lawson Charitable Trust	£130,000	General
☐ Famos Foundation Trust	£129,000	Jewish
☐ The A M Fenton Trust	£129,000	General

☐ The Boshier-Hinton Foundation	£129,000	Children and adults with special educational or other needs
☐ The Hargrave Foundation	£129,000	General, medical, welfare
☐ The Idlewild Trust	£129,000	Performing arts, culture, restoration and conservation, arts education
☐ The J E Joseph Charitable Fund	£129,000	Jewish
☐ The Woodcock Charitable Trust	£129,000	General, children
☐ The Ogle Christian Trust	£128,000	Evangelical Christianity
☐ Gerald Micklem Charitable Trust	£127,000	General, health
☐ Richard Rogers Charitable Settlement	£127,000	General
☐ Salters' Charitable Foundation	£126,000	General, specifically the environment, citizenship, community development and health
☐ The Old Broad Street Charity Trust	£126,000	General
☐ Wallace and Gromit's Children's Foundation	£125,500	Improving the quality of life for sick children
☐ Criffel Charitable Trust	£125,000	Christianity, welfare, health
☐ The Worshipful Company of Chartered Accountants General Charitable Trust	£125,000	General, education
☐ Garrick Charitable Trust	£124,000	Theatre, music, literature, dance
☐ The Cyril Taylor Charitable Trust	£124,000	Education
☐ The Hammonds Charitable Trust	£124,000	General
☐ The Hawthorne Charitable Trust	£124,000	General
☐ The Kyte Charitable Trust	£123,000	Medical, disadvantaged and socially isolated people
☐ The Sandy Dewhirst Charitable Trust	£123,000	General
☐ The Spear Charitable Trust	£123,000	General, with some preference for animal welfare, the environment and health
☐ EAGA Partnership Charitable Trust	£122,000	Fuel poverty
☐ The Helen Roll Charitable Trust	£122,000	General
☐ The Kelly Family Charitable Trust	£122,000	Support for families
☐ The Harding Trust	£121,000	Arts, general
☐ The Sir Jeremiah Colman Gift Trust	£121,000	General
☐ The Stanley Smith UK Horticultural Trust	£121,000	Horticulture
☐ Miss A M Pilkington's Charitable Trust	£120,000	General
☐ Rosalyn and Nicholas Springer Charitable Trust	£120,000	Welfare, Jewish, education, general
☐ SEM Charitable Trust	£120,000	General, particularly educational special needs and Jewish organisations
☐ The Benham Charitable Settlement	£120,000	General
☐ The Billmeir Charitable Trust	£120,000	General, health and medical
☐ The Forte Charitable Trust	£120,000	Roman Catholic, Alzheimer's disease, senile dementia
☐ The Sylvia Aitken Charitable Trust	£120,000	Medical research and welfare, general
☐ The Tinsley Foundation	£120,000	Human rights, poverty, homelessness and health education in underdeveloped countries
☐ Yankov Charitable Trust	£120,000	Jewish
☐ Henry Lumley Charitable Trust	£119,000	General, medical, educational, relief of poverty/hardship
☐ Premishlaner Charitable Trust	£119,000	Jewish
☐ Rix-Thompson-Rothenberg Foundation	£118,000	Learning disabilities
☐ The Amelia Chadwick Trust	£118,000	General
☐ The Estelle Trust	£118,000	Overseas aid
☐ Dischma Charitable Trust	£117,000	General, education, arts and culture, conservation and human and animal welfare
☐ The Burden Trust	£117,000	Christian, welfare, medical research, education, general
☐ The Casey Trust	£117,000	Children and young people
☐ The David Brooke Charity	£117,000	Youth, older people, medical
☐ The Flow Foundation	£117,000	Welfare, education, environment, medical
☐ The Kiawah Charitable Trust	£117,000	Young people with health or education issues

☐ The N Smith Charitable Settlement	£117,000	General, social work, medical research, education, environment/animals, arts and overseas aid
☐ The Bassil Shippam and Alsford Trust	£116,000	Young and older people, health, education, learning disabilities, Christian
☐ The Duke of Cornwall's Benevolent Fund	£116,000	General
☐ The Mitchell Charitable Trust	£116,000	Jewish, general
☐ The Sheldon Trust	£116,000	General
☐ Vision Charity	£116,000	Children who are blind, partially sighted or dyslexic
☐ The Heathcoat Trust	£115,000	Welfare, local causes to Tiverton, Devon
☐ Diana and Allan Morgenthau Charitable Trust	£115,000	Jewish, general
☐ Spar Charitable Fund	£115,000	General, with a preference for children and young people
☐ The Sydney Black Charitable Trust	£115,000	Evangelical Christianity, social welfare, young people
☐ The Treeside Trust	£115,000	General
☐ The Bernard Kahn Charitable Trust	£114,000	Jewish
☐ Ulting Overseas Trust	£114,000	Theological training
☐ The Company of Actuaries' Charitable Trust Fund	£113,000	Actuaries, medical research, young and older people, disability
☐ The Kathleen Laurence Trust	£113,000	Heart disease, arthritis, mental disabilities, medical research, older people, children's charities
☐ The Strawberry Charitable Trust	£113,000	Jewish, youth
☐ Prison Service Charity Fund	£111,000	General
☐ The Ashworth Charitable Trust	£110,000	Welfare
☐ Hinchley Charitable Trust	£110,000	Mainly evangelical Christian
☐ Kinsurdy Charitable Trust	£110,000	General
☐ T and S Trust Fund	£110,000	Orthodox Jewish
☐ The Bay Tree Charitable Trust	£110,000	Development work, general
☐ The Charlotte Marshall Charitable Trust	£110,000	Roman Catholic, general
☐ The Richard Carne Trust	£109,000	Young people in the performing arts
☐ Balmain Charitable Trust	£109,000	General
☐ Jacqueline and Michael Gee Charitable Trust	£109,000	Health, arts, education, Jewish
☐ The Andy Stewart Charitable Foundation	£109,000	General
☐ The Argentarius Foundation	£109,000	General
☐ The Helene Sebba Charitable Trust	£109,000	Medical, disability and Jewish
☐ Vivdale Ltd	£109,000	Jewish
☐ Ryklow Charitable Trust 1992	£108,000	Education, health, environment and welfare
☐ The Bernhard Heuberger Charitable Trust	£108,000	Jewish
☐ The Kreitman Foundation	£108,000	Education, health, welfare and animal conservation
☐ The Marjorie Coote Animal Charity Trust	£108,000	Wildlife and animal welfare
☐ The Sue Thomson Foundation	£108,000	Christ's Hospital School, education
☐ The Willie and Mabel Morris Charitable Trust	£108,000	Medical, general
☐ Highcroft Charitable Trust	£107,000	Jewish, poverty
☐ Princess Anne's Charities	£107,000	Children, medical, welfare, general
☐ REMEDI	£107,000	Medical research
☐ The Cuby Charitable Trust	£107,000	Jewish
☐ The Maurice and Vivien Thompson Charitable Trust	£107,000	General
☐ Marc Fitch Fund	£106,000	Humanities
☐ Oizer Dalim Trust	£106,000	Jewish
☐ The Chownes Foundation	£106,000	Religion, relief-in-need, social problems
☐ The Leach Fourteenth Trust	£106,000	Medical, disability, environment, conservation, general
☐ The River Trust	£106,000	Christian
☐ Anona Winn Charitable Trust	£105,000	Health, welfare, general
☐ The Hon. M J Samuel Charitable Trust	£105,000	General, Jewish
☐ The Jenour Foundation	£105,000	General
☐ The Mason Porter Charitable Trust	£105,000	Christian

☐ The Nigel Vinson Charitable Trust	£105,000	Economic/community development and employment, general
☐ The Noel Buxton Trust	£105,000	Child and family welfare, penal matters, Africa
☐ The Leslie Mary Carter Charitable Trust	£104,500	Conservation/environment, welfare
☐ MYA Charitable Trust	£104,000	Jewish
☐ Alexandra Rose Charities	£103,000	People in need
☐ Sellata Ltd	£103,000	Jewish, welfare
☐ The Harbour Charitable Trust	£103,000	General
☐ The Colonel W H Whitbread Charitable Trust	£102,500	Education, preservation of places of historic interest and natural beauty
☐ The Rayne Trust	£102,000	Jewish organisations, older and young people and people disadvantaged by poverty or social isolation
☐ Coral Samuel Charitable Trust	£101,000	General, with a preference for educational, cultural and socially supportive charities
☐ Foundation for Management Education	£101,000	Management studies
☐ The Annie Schiff Charitable Trust	£101,000	Orthodox Jewish education
☐ The Arnold Lee Charitable Trust	£101,000	Jewish, educational, health
☐ The Edward and Dorothy Cadbury Trust	£101,000	Health, education, arts
☐ The Kreditor Charitable Trust	£101,000	Jewish, welfare, education
☐ Florence's Charitable Trust	£100,000	Education, welfare, illness, general
☐ St James' Trust Settlement	£100,000	General
☐ St Michael's and All Saints' Charities	£100,000	Health, welfare
☐ The Craignish Trust	£100,000	Arts, education, environment, general
☐ The Dellal Foundation	£100,000	General, Jewish
☐ The Galanthus Trust	£100,000	Medical, developing countries, environment, conservation
☐ The Gilbert and Eileen Edgar Foundation	£100,000	General
☐ The Humanitarian Trust	£100,000	Education, health, social welfare, Jewish
☐ The Inlight Trust	£100,000	Religion
☐ The J G Hogg Charitable Trust	£100,000	Welfare, animal welfare, general
☐ The Louis and Valerie Freedman Charitable Settlement	£100,000	General
☐ The R J Larg Family Charitable Trust	£100,000	Education, health, medical research, arts particularly music
☐ The Samuel and Freda Parkinson Charitable Trust	£100,000	General
☐ The Sutasoma Trust	£100,000	Education, general
☐ The Witzenfeld Foundation	£100,000	General
☐ Marmot Charitable Trust	£99,000	Environmentally friendly organisations, conflict resolution
☐ The DLM Charitable Trust	£99,000	General
☐ The Earl Fitzwilliam Charitable Trust	£99,000	General
☐ The Neville and Elaine Blond Charitable Trust	£99,000	Jewish, general
☐ Ner Foundation	£98,000	Orthodox Jewish
☐ The Norda Trust	£98,000	Prisoners, asylum seekers, disadvantaged communities
☐ The Wyseliot Charitable Trust	£98,000	Medical, welfare, arts
☐ The Almond Trust	£97,000	Christian
☐ Harbo Charities Limited	£97,000	Jewish causes, general and education
☐ Nesswall Ltd	£97,000	Jewish
☐ Philip Smith's Charitable Trust	£97,000	Welfare, older people, children, environment, armed forces
☐ R G Hills Charitable Trust	£97,000	Health, poverty, education, general
☐ The Edinburgh Trust, No. 2 Account	£97,000	Education, armed services
☐ The Edwina Mountbatten Trust	£97,000	Medical
☐ The James Trust	£97,000	Christianity

☐ The Jeremy and John Sacher Charitable Trust	£97,000	General, arts, culture and heritage, medical and disability, community and welfare, education, science and technology, children and youth, religion
☐ The Kasner Charitable Trust	£97,000	Jewish
☐ The Merchant Taylors' Company Charities Fund	£97,000	Education, training, church, medicine, general
☐ The Oliver Morland Charitable Trust	£97,000	Quakers, general
☐ The P and D Shepherd Charitable Trust	£97,000	General, particularly young people
☐ The Scurrah Wainwright Charity	£97,000	Social reform
☐ AM Charitable Trust	£96,000	Jewish, general
☐ Blyth Watson Charitable Trust	£96,000	UK-based humanitarian organisations, hospices
☐ Cullum Family Trust	£96,000	Social welfare, education and general
☐ Rosa – the UK fund for women and girls	£96,000	Women's organisations and projects supporting women
☐ The Emilienne Charitable Trust	£96,000	Medical, education
☐ The Joseph and Lena Randall Charitable Trust	£96,000	General
☐ The Forbes Charitable Foundation	£95,000	Adults with learning disabilities
☐ The Linley Shaw Foundation	£95,000	Conservation
☐ The Modiano Charitable Trust	£95,000	Arts, Jewish, general
☐ The Paragon Trust	£95,000	General
☐ The Saints and Sinners Trust	£95,000	General, mainly welfare and medical
☐ Hasluck Charitable Trust	£94,000	Health, welfare, disability, youth, overseas aid
☐ The Dugdale Charitable Trust	£94,000	Christian education, the advancement of Methodist education and the Catholic religion
☐ The Jill Franklin Trust	£94,000	Overseas, welfare, prisons, church restoration
☐ The Johnson Foundation	£94,000	Education, health, relief of poverty
☐ The Michael and Ilse Katz Foundation	£94,000	Jewish, music, medical, general
☐ The Nadezhda Charitable Trust	£94,000	Christian
☐ The W G Edwards Charitable Foundation	£94,000	Care of older people
☐ Peter Stormonth Darling Charitable Trust	£93,500	Heritage, medical research, sport
☐ The Gibbs Charitable Trust	£93,000	Methodism, international, arts
☐ The Samuel Storey Family Charitable Trust	£93,000	General
☐ The Westcroft Trust	£92,500	International understanding, overseas aid, Quaker, Shropshire
☐ Malbin Trust	£92,000	Jewish, general
☐ NJD Charitable Trust	£92,000	Jewish
☐ The Charles Skey Charitable Trust	£92,000	General
☐ The Demigryphon Trust	£92,000	Medical, education, children, general
☐ The Smith Charitable Trust	£92,000	General
☐ Truemart Limited	£92,000	General, Judaism, welfare
☐ Andor Charitable Trust	£91,000	Health, arts, Jewish, general
☐ John Bristow and Thomas Mason Trust	£91,000	Education, relief in need, people with disabilities, community amenities
☐ The Sants Charitable Trust	£91,000	General
☐ Spears-Stutz Charitable Trust	£90,000	Relief of poverty, general
☐ The Albert Van Den Bergh Charitable Trust	£90,000	Medical research, disability, community, general
☐ The Football Association National Sports Centre Trust	£90,000	Play areas, community sports facilities
☐ The John M Archer Charitable Trust	£90,000	General
☐ The M J C Stone Charitable Trust	£90,000	General
☐ The Peter Samuel Charitable Trust	£90,000	Health, welfare, conservation, Jewish care
☐ Annie Tranmer Charitable Trust	£89,000	General, young people
☐ Ashburnham Thanksgiving Trust	£89,000	Christian
☐ The David Uri Memorial Trust	£89,000	Jewish, general
☐ The Music Sales Charitable Trust	£89,000	Children and youth, musical education
☐ The Limbourne Trust	£88,000	Environment, welfare, arts
☐ The Mishcon Family Charitable Trust	£88,000	Jewish, social welfare, medical, disability, children

☐	The P Leigh-Bramwell Trust 'E'	£88,000	Methodist, general
☐	The Searle Charitable Trust	£88,000	Youth development with a nautical focus
☐	Audrey Earle Charitable Trust	£87,000	General, with some preference for animal welfare and conservation charities
☐	Dixie Rose Findlay Charitable Trust	£87,000	Children, seafarers, blindness and multiple sclerosis
☐	The Benjamin Winegarten Charitable Trust	£87,000	Jewish
☐	The Hesed Trust	£87,000	Christian
☐	The Shipwrights' Company Charitable Fund	£87,000	Maritime or waterborne connected charities
☐	Minge's Gift and the Pooled Trusts	£86,000	Medical, education, disadvantage, disability
☐	James Madison Trust	£86,000	The study of federal government
☐	Leslie Sell Charitable Trust	£86,000	Scout and guide groups
☐	Limoges Charitable Trust	£86,000	General, including health, heritage and community
☐	Peter Storrs Trust	£86,000	Education
☐	The Daily Prayer Union Charitable Trust Ltd	£86,000	Evangelical Christian
☐	The Rose Flatau Charitable Trust	£85,500	Jewish, general
☐	Briggs Animal Welfare Trust	£85,000	Animal welfare
☐	Coats Foundation Trust	£85,000	Textile and thread-related training courses and research
☐	Help the Homeless	£85,000	Homelessness
☐	The Frank Parkinson Agricultural Trust	£85,000	British agriculture
☐	The Hamamelis Trust	£85,000	Ecological conservation, medical research
☐	The Inland Waterways Association	£85,000	Inland waterways
☐	The John Spedan Lewis Foundation	£85,000	Natural sciences, particularly horticulture, environmental education, ornithology and conservation
☐	The Norman Whiteley Trust	£85,000	Evangelical Christianity, welfare, education
☐	The Weinberg Foundation	£85,000	General
☐	Mrs F B Laurence Charitable Trust	£84,000	Social welfare, medical, disability, environment
☐	The Barnsbury Charitable Trust	£84,000	General
☐	The Harold and Alice Bridges Charity	£84,000	General
☐	The Harry Bottom Charitable Trust	£84,000	Religion, education, medical
☐	The International Bankers Charitable Trust	£84,000	Recruitment and development of employees in the financial services
☐	The Millward Charitable Trust	£84,000	Social welfare, performing arts, medical research and animal welfare
☐	The Tory Family Foundation	£84,000	Education, Christian, medical
☐	The Gunter Charitable Trust	£83,000	General
☐	The John Feeney Charitable Trust	£83,000	Arts, heritage and open spaces
☐	British Humane Association	£82,000	Welfare
☐	The Chipping Sodbury Town Lands Charity	£82,000	Welfare, education, leisure
☐	The Denise Cohen Charitable Trust	£82,000	Health, welfare, arts, humanities, education, culture, Jewish
☐	The Moss Charitable Trust	£82,000	Christian, education, poverty, health
☐	Moshal Charitable Trust	£81,000	Jewish
☐	The Astor Foundation	£81,000	Medical research, general
☐	Sir John and Lady Amory's Charitable Trust	£80,000	General
☐	Sir Clive Bourne Family Trust	£80,000	Jewish
☐	The Bernard Morris Charitable Trust	£80,000	General
☐	The Carpenter Charitable Trust	£80,000	Humanitarian and Christian outreach
☐	The H and M Charitable Trust	£80,000	Seafaring
☐	The Mizpah Trust	£80,000	General
☐	The Philip Green Memorial Trust	£80,000	Young and older people, people with disabilities, people in need
☐	The Phillips Family Charitable Trust	£80,000	Jewish charities, welfare, general
☐	The Seedfield Trust	£80,000	Christian, relief of poverty
☐	The Spurrell Charitable Trust	£80,000	General
☐	The George and Esme Pollitzer Charitable Settlement	£79,500	Jewish, general

☐ P H Holt Foundation	£79,000	General
☐ The Adnams Charity	£79,000	General
☐ The Animal Defence Trust	£79,000	Animal welfare and protection
☐ The C S Kaufman Charitable Trust	£79,000	Jewish
☐ The Thriplow Charitable Trust	£79,000	Higher and further education and research
☐ EMI Music Sound Foundation	£78,000	Music education
☐ A J H Ashby Will Trust	£78,000	Wildlife, heritage, education and children
☐ David Solomons Charitable Trust	£78,000	Learning difficulties
☐ The Balney Charitable Trust	£78,000	Preservation, conservation, welfare, service charities
☐ The Charles Lloyd Foundation	£78,000	Construction, repair and maintenance of Roman Catholic buildings, advancement of the Roman Catholic religion, and music
☐ The Elaine and Angus Lloyd Charitable Trust	£78,000	General
☐ The Fred and Della Worms Charitable Trust	£78,000	Jewish, social welfare, health, education, arts, youth
☐ The Judith Trust	£78,000	Mental health and learning disabilities, particularly for women and Jewish people
☐ Lindale Educational Foundation	£77,000	Roman Catholic, education
☐ The Alan Evans Memorial Trust	£77,000	Preservation, conservation
☐ The C L Loyd Charitable Trust	£77,000	General
☐ The Good Neighbours Trust	£77,000	People with mental or physical disabilities
☐ The Lili Tapper Charitable Foundation	£77,000	Jewish
☐ The Lord Cozens-Hardy Trust	£77,000	Medical/health, welfare, general
☐ The Sandhu Charitable Foundation	£77,000	General
☐ The Taurus Foundation	£77,000	General
☐ TVML Foundation	£77,000	General
☐ Lord and Lady Lurgan Trust	£76,000	Medical charities, older people, children and the arts
☐ The E L Rathbone Charitable Trust	£76,000	Social work charities
☐ The Michael Harry Sacher Trust	£76,000	General, with a preference for arts, education, animal welfare, Jewish, health and social welfare
☐ The Olga Charitable Trust	£76,000	Health, welfare, youth organisations, children's welfare, carers' organisations
☐ The Shanti Charitable Trust	£76,000	General, Christian, international development
☐ The York Children's Trust	£76,000	Young people under the age of 25
☐ The Adamson Trust	£75,000	Children under 18 with a physical or mental disability
☐ The B G S Cayzer Charitable Trust	£75,000	General
☐ The David and Ruth Behrend Fund	£75,000	General
☐ The National Manuscripts Conservation Trust	£75,000	Conservation of manuscripts
☐ The Primrose Trust	£75,000	General
☐ Weatherley Charitable Trust	£75,000	General
☐ The Wilfrid Bruce Davis Charitable Trust	£74,500	Health
☐ Disability Aid Fund	£74,000	Disability
☐ The Aurelius Charitable Trust	£74,000	Conservation of culture and the humanities
☐ The G D Charitable Trust	£74,000	Animal welfare, the environment, disability, homelessness
☐ The Vernon N Ely Charitable Trust	£74,000	Christian, welfare, disability, sports, children and youth, overseas
☐ Children's Liver Disease Foundation	£73,000	Diseases of the liver and biliary system in children
☐ The Dumbreck Charity	£73,000	General
☐ The Ian Askew Charitable Trust	£73,000	General
☐ The Migraine Trust	£73,000	Study of migraine
☐ The Owen Family Trust	£73,000	Christian, general
☐ The Salamander Charitable Trust	£73,000	Christian, general
☐ Birthday House Trust	£72,000	General
☐ The David Pearlman Charitable Foundation	£72,000	Jewish, general
☐ The Epigoni Trust	£72,000	Health and welfare, disability, homelessness, addiction, children who are disadvantaged, environment

☐ The Matthews Wrightson Charity Trust	£72,000	General, smaller charities
☐ Panahpur	£71,000	Christian missionaries, general
☐ The Joyce Fletcher Charitable Trust	£71,000	Music, children's welfare
☐ The Searchlight Electric Charitable Trust	£71,000	General
☐ Bear Mordechai Ltd	£70,000	Jewish
☐ Houblon-Norman/George Fund	£70,000	Finance
☐ Murphy-Neumann Charity Company Limited	£70,000	Health, social welfare, medical research
☐ Nicholas and Judith Goodison's Charitable Settlement	£70,000	Arts, arts education
☐ The Ampelos Trust	£70,000	General
☐ The Andrew Salvesen Charitable Trust	£70,000	General
☐ The Blair Foundation	£70,000	Wildlife, access to countryside, general
☐ The Sir William Coxen Trust Fund	£70,000	Orthopaedic hospitals or other hospitals or charities doing orthopaedic work
☐ The Edith Lilian Harrison 2000 Foundation	£69,500	General
☐ The Portrack Charitable Trust	£69,500	General
☐ The Anna Rosa Forster Charitable Trust	£69,000	Medical research, animal welfare, famine relief
☐ The Dennis Curry Charitable Trust	£69,000	Conservation, general
☐ The Dorus Trust	£69,000	Health and welfare, disability, homelessness, addiction, children who are disadvantaged, environment
☐ The Fitton Trust	£69,000	Social welfare, medical
☐ The Leopold De Rothschild Charitable Trust	£69,000	Arts, Jewish, general
☐ The Stanley Kalms Foundation	£69,000	Jewish charities, general including arts, education and health
☐ Garvan Limited	£68,000	Jewish
☐ J A R Charitable Trust	£68,000	Roman Catholic, education, welfare
☐ Rita and David Slowe Charitable Trust	£68,000	General
☐ The Bernard Piggott Trust	£68,000	General
☐ The Bertie Black Foundation	£68,000	Jewish, general
☐ The Fidelio Charitable Trust	£68,000	The arts, in particular the dramatic and operatic arts, music, speech and dance
☐ The Horizon Foundation	£68,000	General, education, women and children
☐ The Millfield Trust	£68,000	Christian
☐ The Schmidt-Bodner Charitable Trust	£68,000	Jewish, general
☐ The Weinstein Foundation	£68,000	Jewish, medical, welfare
☐ Consolidated Charity of Burton upon Trent	£67,000	General
☐ The Huxham Charitable Trust	£67,000	Christianity, churches and organisations, development work
☐ Jack Livingstone Charitable Trust	£67,000	Jewish, general
☐ P G and N J Boulton Trust	£66,000	Christian
☐ The Oikonomia Trust	£66,000	Christian
☐ Meningitis Trust	£65,000	Meningitis
☐ Friends of Biala Ltd	£65,000	Jewish
☐ The B and P Glasser Charitable Trust	£65,000	Health, disability, Jewish, welfare
☐ The Harebell Centenary Fund	£65,000	General, education, medical research, animal welfare
☐ The McKenna Charitable Trust	£65,000	Health, disability, education, children, general
☐ The Michael and Anna Wix Charitable Trust	£65,000	Older people, disability, education, medicine and health, poverty, welfare, Jewish
☐ The Morel Charitable Trust	£65,000	Arts/culture, race relations, inner-city projects UK and the developing world
☐ The TUUT Charitable Trust	£65,000	General, particularly trade-union-favoured causes
☐ The Grand Order of Water Rats' Charities Fund	£64,000	Theatrical, medical equipment
☐ The Michael and Shirley Hunt Charitable Trust	£64,000	Prisoners' families, animal welfare
☐ The Worshipful Company of Spectacle Makers' Charity	£64,000	Visual impairment, City of London, general
☐ The Linden Charitable Trust	£63,500	Medical, healthcare, the arts
☐ Harold and Daphne Cooper Charitable Trust	£63,000	Medical, health, Jewish

☐ The Acacia Charitable Trust	£63,000	Jewish, education, general
☐ The Mahavir Trust	£63,000	General, medical, animal welfare, relief of poverty, overseas aid, religion
☐ The Michael and Clara Freeman Charitable Trust	£63,000	General
☐ The Pat Allsop Charitable Trust	£63,000	Education, medical research, children, relief of poverty
☐ The Tabeel Trust	£63,000	Evangelical Christian
☐ Chrysalis Trust	£62,500	General, education, social welfare
☐ The Sir Julian Hodge Charitable Trust	£62,500	General
☐ Dame Violet Wills Charitable Trust	£62,000	Evangelical Christianity
☐ Maranatha Christian Trust	£62,000	Christian, relief of poverty and education of young people
☐ R S Brownless Charitable Trust	£62,000	Disability, relief in need, ill health, accommodation and housing, education, job creation, voluntary work
☐ The Augustine Courtauld Trust	£62,000	General
☐ The Greys Charitable Trust	£62,000	General
☐ The Kathleen Trust	£62,000	Music
☐ The Ormsby Charitable Trust	£62,000	General
☐ The Janet Nash Charitable Settlement	£61,000	Medical, hardship, general
☐ GMC Trust	£61,000	Medical research, healthcare, general
☐ The Artemis Charitable Trust	£61,000	Psychotherapy, parent education, and related activities
☐ The David Pickford Charitable Foundation	£61,000	Christian, general
☐ The Naggar Charitable Trust	£61,000	Jewish, the arts, general
☐ The Norton Foundation	£61,000	Young people under 25 years of age in Birmingham, Coventry and the County of Warwick
☐ Wakeham Trust	£61,000	Community development, education, community service by young people
☐ The A H and E Boulton Trust	£60,000	Evangelical Christian
☐ AF Trust Company	£60,000	Higher education
☐ Altamont Ltd	£60,000	Jewish causes
☐ Sir John Evelyn's Charity	£60,000	Relief in need
☐ The Dorothy Holmes Charitable Trust	£60,000	General
☐ The Dunn Family Charitable Trust	£60,000	Medical, general, conservation
☐ The Eleni Nakou Foundation	£60,000	Education, international understanding
☐ The Fawcett Charitable Trust	£60,000	Disability
☐ The Gamma Trust	£60,000	General
☐ The Merchants' House of Glasgow	£60,000	General
☐ The Williams Charitable Trust	£60,000	Education, medicine, theatre, general
☐ Elizabeth Cayzer Charitable Trust	£59,000	Arts
☐ The Chetwode Foundation	£59,000	Education, churches, general
☐ The Christopher Cadbury Charitable Trust	£59,000	Nature conservation, general
☐ The G D Herbert Charitable Trust	£59,000	Medicine, health, welfare, environmental resources
☐ The Morgan Charitable Foundation	£59,000	Welfare, hospices, medical, Jewish, general
☐ The Moshulu Charitable Trust	£59,000	Humanitarian, evangelical
☐ The P and C Hickinbotham Charitable Trust	£59,000	Social welfare
☐ The Tresillian Trust	£59,000	Overseas aid, welfare
☐ The W L Pratt Charitable Trust	£59,000	General
☐ B E Perl Charitable Trust	£58,000	Jewish, general
☐ The Ulverscroft Foundation	£58,000	People who are blind or partially sighted, ophthalmic research
☐ Edith and Ferdinand Porjes Charitable Trust	£57,000	Jewish, general
☐ Evelyn May Trust	£57,000	Currently children, older people, medical, natural disaster relief
☐ Samuel William Farmer Trust	£57,000	Education, health, social welfare

☐ The Adrienne and Leslie Sussman Charitable Trust	£57,000	Jewish, general
☐ The Alborada Trust	£57,000	Veterinary causes, social welfare
☐ The Emerton-Christie Charity	£57,000	Health, welfare, disability, arts
☐ The Gretna Charitable Trust	£57,000	General
☐ The John Apthorp Charitable Trust	£57,000	General
☐ The Lambert Charitable Trust	£57,000	Health, welfare, education, disability, Jewish
☐ The Rofeh Trust	£57,000	General, religious activities
☐ CLA Charitable Trust	£56,000	People with disabilities or who are disadvantaged
☐ Panton Trust	£56,000	Animal wildlife – worldwide, environment – UK
☐ The Andrew Balint Charitable Trust	£56,000	General charitable causes, Jewish charities
☐ The Boris Karloff Charitable Foundation	£56,000	General
☐ The Goldmark Trust	£56,000	General
☐ Mrs H R Greene Charitable Settlement	£55,000	General, particularly at risk groups, poverty, social isolation
☐ The André Christian Trust	£55,000	Christian
☐ The Caron Keating Foundation	£55,000	Supports small but significant cancer charities
☐ The Forces Trust	£55,000	Military charities
☐ The Yardley Great Trust	£55,000	General
☐ The Bartlett Taylor Charitable Trust	£54,000	General
☐ The British Dietetic Association General and Education Trust Fund	£54,000	Dietary and nutritional issues
☐ The Diana Edgson Wright Charitable Trust	£54,000	Animal conservation, social welfare, general
☐ The Elephant Trust	£54,000	Visual arts
☐ The Equity Trust Fund	£54,000	Theatre
☐ The Francis Coales Charitable Foundation	£54,000	Historical
☐ The Lionel Wigram Memorial Trust	£54,000	General
☐ The Peter Morrison Charitable Foundation	£54,000	Jewish, general
☐ The Violet M Richards Charity	£54,000	Older people, ill health, medical research and education
☐ The Gamlen Charitable Trust	£53,500	Legal education, general
☐ Harry Bacon Foundation	£53,000	Medical, animal welfare
☐ The Alfred And Peggy Harvey Charitable Trust	£53,000	Medical, research, older people, children and young people with disabilities or disadvantages, visually and hearing impaired people
☐ The Brendish Family Foundation	£53,000	General, children, education, health care and access to food and water
☐ The Montague Thompson Coon Charitable Trust	£53,000	Children with muscular diseases, medical research, environment
☐ The Torah Temimah Trust	£53,000	Orthodox Jewish
☐ William Dean Countryside and Educational Trust	£53,000	Education in natural history, ecology and conservation
☐ Cowley Charitable Foundation	£52,000	General
☐ The Carr-Gregory Trust	£52,000	Arts, social welfare, health, education
☐ The Catholic Charitable Trust	£52,000	Catholic
☐ The Emmandjay Charitable Trust	£52,000	Social welfare, medicine, youth
☐ The Monica Rabagliati Charitable Trust	£52,000	Children, humanitarian, medical, general
☐ The Oakmoor Charitable Trust	£52,000	General
☐ The Oliver Ford Charitable Trust	£51,000	Mental disability, housing
☐ Nazareth Trust Fund	£51,000	Christian, and developing countries
☐ The Ardwick Trust	£51,000	Jewish, welfare, general
☐ The E C Sosnow Charitable Trust	£51,000	Mainly education and arts
☐ The MSE Charity	£51,000	Financial education, improving financial literacy
☐ The Pennycress Trust	£51,000	General
☐ William Arthur Rudd Memorial Trust	£50,500	General , and selected Spanish charities
☐ Blatchington Court Trust	£50,000	people under 30 with visual impairments
☐ Ellador Ltd	£50,000	Jewish
☐ Mary Homfray Charitable Trust	£50,000	General

☐ Mildred Duveen Charitable Trust	£50,000	General
☐ The Carvill Trust	£50,000	General
☐ The Cuthbert Horn Trust	£50,000	General
☐ The DLA Piper Charitable Trust	£50,000	General
☐ The Ericson Trust	£50,000	Older people, community including the arts, offender rehabilitation and research, refugees, the environment, the developing world
☐ The Eva Reckitt Trust Fund	£50,000	Welfare, relief in need, extension and development of education, victims of war
☐ The Golsoncott Foundation	£50,000	Arts
☐ The Gould Charitable Trust	£50,000	General
☐ The Rhododendron Trust	£50,000	Overseas aid and development, social welfare and culture
☐ The Whitecourt Charitable Trust	£50,000	Christian, general
☐ The Marina Kleinwort Charitable Trust	£49,500	Arts
☐ Daisie Rich Trust	£49,000	General
☐ MYR Charitable Trust	£49,000	Jewish
☐ The Barbara Whatmore Charitable Trust	£49,000	Arts and music, relief of poverty
☐ The Corona Charitable Trust	£49,000	Jewish
☐ The Hare of Steep Charitable Trust	£49,000	General
☐ The P Y N and B Hyams Trust	£49,000	Jewish, general
☐ The Ruth and Jack Lunzer Charitable Trust	£49,000	Jewish, children, young adults, education and the arts
☐ The Violet Mauray Charitable Trust	£49,000	General, medical, Jewish
☐ The Cleopatra Trust	£48,000	Mental health, cancer welfare/education, diabetes, physical disability, homelessness, addiction, children
☐ The Dickon Trust	£48,000	General
☐ The George Balint Charitable Trust	£48,000	General, education, poverty relief, Jewish
☐ The Mirianog Trust	£48,000	General
☐ The Paul Balint Charitable Trust	£48,000	General
☐ Zephyr Charitable Trust	£48,000	Community, environment, social welfare
☐ William P Bancroft (No. 2) Charitable Trust and Jenepher Gillett Trust	£47,500	Quaker
☐ The Geoffrey John Kaye Charitable Foundation	£47,000	Jewish, general
☐ G S Plaut Charitable Trust Limited	£47,000	Sickness, disability, Jewish, older people, general
☐ Onaway Trust	£47,000	General
☐ Percy Hedley 1990 Charitable Trust	£47,000	General
☐ The Alexis Trust	£47,000	Christian
☐ The Cumber Family Charitable Trust	£47,000	General
☐ The Isaac and Freda Frankel Memorial Charitable Trust	£47,000	Jewish, general
☐ The John Young Charitable Settlement	£47,000	General
☐ The Late St Patrick White Charitable Trust	£47,000	General
☐ The Thomas Sivewright Catto Charitable Settlement	£47,000	General
☐ Sumner Wilson Charitable Trust	£46,000	General
☐ The Burry Charitable Trust	£46,000	Medicine, health
☐ The Col W W Pilkington Will Trusts The General Charity Fund	£46,000	Medical, arts, social welfare, international charities, drugs misuse, environment
☐ The Ebenezer Trust	£46,000	Evangelical Christianity, welfare
☐ The Katzauer Charitable Settlement	£46,000	Jewish
☐ The Richard Kirkman Charitable Trust	£46,000	General
☐ Golden Charitable Trust	£45,000	Preservation, conservation, medical research
☐ Miss V L Clore's 1967 Charitable Trust	£45,000	General, arts, social welfare, health, Jewish
☐ The A B Strom and R Strom Charitable Trust	£45,000	Jewish, general
☐ The Crescent Trust	£45,000	Museums and the arts, ecology, health
☐ The Gerald Fogel Charitable Trust	£45,000	Jewish, general

☐ The Mountbatten Memorial Trust	£45,000	Technological research in aid of disabilities
☐ The Rayden Charitable Trust	£45,000	Jewish
☐ The Rest Harrow Trust	£45,000	Jewish, general
☐ Thomas Roberts Trust	£45,000	Medical, disability, relief in need
☐ The Monatrea Charitable Trust	£44,500	General
☐ All Saints Educational Trust	£44,000	Religious education, home economics
☐ Alan and Sheila Diamond Charitable Trust	£44,000	Jewish, general
☐ Lord Forte Foundation	£44,000	Hospitality
☐ The Baker Charitable Trust	£44,000	Mainly Jewish, older people, sickness and disability, medical research
☐ The J S F Pollitzer Charitable Settlement	£44,000	General
☐ The Roger Brooke Charitable Trust	£44,000	General
☐ The Scarfe Charitable Trust	£44,000	Churches, arts, music, environment
☐ LandAid Charitable Trust	£43,000	Homelessness, relief in need, young people
☐ The BACTA Charitable Trust	£43,000	General
☐ The Bintaub Charitable Trust	£43,000	Jewish, medical and youth
☐ The RRAF Charitable Trust	£43,000	General, medical research, children who are disadvantaged, older people, religious organisations, aid for the developing world
☐ The Simpson Education and Conservation Trust	£43,000	Environmental conservation
☐ The Charter 600 Charity	£42,000	General
☐ The Gur Trust	£42,000	Jewish causes
☐ The Huntly and Margery Sinclair Charitable Trust	£42,000	General
☐ The Leonard Trust	£42,000	Christian, overseas aid
☐ The Mushroom Fund	£42,000	General
☐ The Victor Adda Foundation	£42,000	Fan Museum, welfare
☐ The Lyndhurst Trust	£41,000	Christian
☐ Archbishop of Wales' Fund for Children	£41,000	Children
☐ St Teilo's Trust	£41,000	Evangelistic work in the Church in Wales
☐ The Barnett and Sylvia Shine No. 2 Charitable Trust	£41,000	General
☐ The Children's Research Fund	£41,000	Child health research
☐ The Eagle Charity Trust	£41,000	General, international, welfare
☐ The Edith Maud Ellis 1985 Charitable Trust	£41,000	Quaker work and witness, peace and conflict resolution, interfaith and ecumenical understanding, community development work and overseas, work with asylum seekers, refugees and internally displaced people
☐ The Nancy Kenyon Charitable Trust	£41,000	General
☐ The Peter Beckwith Charitable Trust	£41,000	Medical, welfare, general
☐ Bud Flanagan Leukaemia Fund	£40,000	Leukaemia research and treatment
☐ Michael and Leslie Bennett Charitable Trust	£40,000	Jewish
☐ Miss M E Swinton Paterson's Charitable Trust	£40,000	Church of Scotland, young people, general
☐ Mrs Maud Van Norden's Charitable Foundation	£40,000	General
☐ Rosanna Taylor's 1987 Charity Trust	£40,000	General
☐ The Birmingham Hospital Saturday Fund Medical Charity and Welfare Trust	£40,000	Medical
☐ The Colin Montgomerie Charitable Foundation	£40,000	General
☐ The Dorothy Hay-Bolton Charitable Trust	£40,000	Deaf, blind
☐ The E Alec Colman Charitable Fund Ltd	£40,000	Religion, especially Jewish, children, social welfare
☐ The E H Smith Charitable Trust	£40,000	General
☐ The Gay and Keith Talbot Trust	£40,000	Overseas aid, health, famine relief
☐ The Loseley and Guildway Charitable Trust	£40,000	General
☐ Philip Henman Trust	£39,000	Overseas development
☐ Barleycorn Trust	£39,000	Christian
☐ Gilbert Edgar Trust	£39,000	General, UK and overseas

☐ Llysdinam Charitable Trust	£39,000	Natural sciences, horticulture, Christian, relief of poverty
☐ Mageni Trust	£39,000	Arts
☐ The Bagri Foundation	£39,000	General
☐ The Cemlyn-Jones Trust	£39,000	Welsh heritage, medical research, animal welfare, music and religion
☐ The Marjorie and Geoffrey Jones Charitable Trust	£39,000	General
☐ The R M Douglas Charitable Trust	£39,000	General
☐ The Robert Clutterbuck Charitable Trust	£39,000	Service, sport and recreation, natural history, animal welfare and protection
☐ Col-Reno Ltd	£38,000	Jewish
☐ The Alabaster Trust	£38,000	Christian Church and related activities
☐ The Bothwell Charitable Trust	£38,000	Disability, health, older people, conservation
☐ The E M MacAndrew Trust	£38,000	Medical, children, general
☐ The Elmgrant Trust	£38,000	General , education, arts, social sciences
☐ The Joy and Malcolm Lyons Foundation	£38,000	Jewish
☐ The Wilkinson Charitable Foundation	£38,000	Scientific research
☐ The Oliver Borthwick Memorial Trust	£37,000	Homelessness
☐ Mejer and Gertrude Miriam Frydman Foundation	£37,000	Jewish, Jewish education
☐ Paul Lunn-Rockliffe Charitable Trust	£37,000	Christianity, poverty, illness, youth
☐ S C and M E Morland's Charitable Trust	£37,000	Quaker, sickness, welfare, peace and development overseas
☐ The F J Wallis Charitable Settlement	£37,000	General
☐ The JMK Charitable Trust	£37,000	Art and Music, religions and their relations with other faiths – Worldwide
☐ The Ruth and Stuart Lipton Charitable Trust	£37,000	Jewish charities and general
☐ The Stone-Mallabar Charitable Foundation	£37,000	Medical, arts, religion, overseas appeals, welfare and education
☐ The Carron Charitable Settlement	£36,000	Environment, education, medicine
☐ The Lady Eileen Joseph Foundation	£36,000	People who are disadvantaged by poverty or social isolation, at-risk groups, welfare, medical, general
☐ Beatrice Hankey Foundation Ltd	£35,000	Christian
☐ Edwin George Robinson Charitable Trust	£35,000	Medical research
☐ Jimmy Savile Charitable Trust	£35,000	General
☐ Nathan Charitable Trust	£35,000	Evangelical Christian work and mission
☐ The Becker Family Charitable Trust	£35,000	General, orthodox Jewish
☐ The Everard and Mina Goodman Charitable Foundation	£35,000	Jewish, general
☐ The Helen and Geoffrey De Freitas Charitable Trust	£35,000	Preservation of wildlife and rural England, conservation and environment, cultural heritage
☐ The Manny Cussins Foundation	£35,000	Older people, children, health, Jewish, general
☐ The Metropolitan Drinking Fountain and Cattle Trough Association	£35,000	Provision of pure drinking water
☐ Arthur James Paterson Charitable Trust	£34,000	Medical research, welfare of older people and children
☐ Laufer Charitable Trust	£34,000	Jewish
☐ The R H Scholes Charitable Trust	£34,000	General, children and young people who have disabilities or are disadvantaged, hospices, preservation and churches
☐ The Solo Charitable Settlement	£34,000	Jewish, general
☐ The Tony Bramall Charitable Trust	£34,000	Medical research, ill health, social welfare
☐ The Williams Family Charitable Trust	£33,500	Jewish
☐ D G Albright Charitable Trust	£33,000	General
☐ T B H Brunner's Charitable Settlement	£33,000	Church of England, heritage, arts, general
☐ The D C Moncrieff Charitable Trust	£33,000	Social welfare, environment
☐ The Drayson Foundation	£33,000	Relief of sickness, education

☐ The John Rayner Charitable Trust	£33,000	General
☐ The Lady Tangye Charitable Trust	£33,000	Catholic, overseas aid, general
☐ Vale of Glamorgan – Welsh Church Fund	£33,000	General
☐ The Angela Gallagher Memorial Fund	£32,500	Children and youth, Christian, humanitarian, education
☐ Alba Charitable Trust	£32,000	Jewish
☐ Maurice Fry Charitable Trust	£32,000	Medicine, health, welfare, humanities, environmental resources, international
☐ The Ann and David Marks Foundation	£32,000	Jewish charities, general
☐ The Beaufort House Trust Limited	£32,000	Christian, education
☐ The Homestead Charitable Trust	£32,000	Medicine, health, welfare, animal welfare, Christianity and the arts
☐ The Max Reinhardt Charitable Trust	£32,000	Deafness, fine arts promotion
☐ The Misselbrook Trust	£32,000	General
☐ Thomas Betton's Charity for Pensions and Relief-in-Need	£32,000	General, education for children and young people
☐ The Ian Fleming Charitable Trust	£31,000	Disability, medical
☐ The AS Charitable Trust	£31,000	Christian, development, social concern
☐ The Dwek Family Charitable Trust	£31,000	General
☐ The Thistle Trust	£31,000	Arts
☐ A H and B C Whiteley Charitable Trust	£30,000	Art, environment, general
☐ Buckland Charitable Trust	£30,000	General, health, international development and welfare
☐ Haskel Family Foundation	£30,000	Jewish, social policy research, the arts, education
☐ Leonard Gordon Charitable Trust	£30,000	Jewish
☐ Robyn Charitable Trust	£30,000	General, particularly young people
☐ Swan Mountain Trust	£30,000	Mental health, penal affairs
☐ Sydney E Franklin Deceased's New Second Charity	£30,000	Relief of poverty, children, communities
☐ The Barbara A Shuttleworth Memorial Trust	£30,000	People with disabilities
☐ The Carlton House Charitable Trust	£30,000	Jewish, education including bursaries, general
☐ The Carole and Geoffrey Lawson Foundation	£30,000	Child welfare, poverty, arts, education, research and Jewish organisations
☐ The Clifford Howarth Charity Trust	£30,000	General
☐ The Edgar Milward Charity	£30,000	Christian, humanitarian
☐ The Fairway Trust	£30,000	General
☐ The Frognal Trust	£30,000	Older people, children, disability, blindness and ophthalmological research, environmental heritage
☐ The Hanley Trust	£30,000	Social welfare and people who are disadvantaged
☐ The Harold Joels Charitable Trust	£30,000	Jewish
☐ The Huggard Charitable Trust	£30,000	General
☐ The ISA Charity	£30,000	The arts, health and education
☐ West London Synagogue Charitable Fund	£30,000	Jewish, general
☐ Gableholt Limited	£29,000	Jewish
☐ May Hearnshaw's Charity	£29,000	General
☐ The Culra Charitable Trust	£29,000	General
☐ The John and Celia Bonham Christie Charitable Trust	£29,000	General
☐ The Simpson Foundation	£29,000	Roman Catholic purposes
☐ The Soli and Leah Kelaty Trust Fund	£29,000	General, education, overseas aid, religion
☐ Eric Abrams Charitable Trust	£28,000	Jewish
☐ Henry T and Lucy B Cadbury Charitable Trust	£28,000	Quaker causes and institutions, health, homelessness, support groups, developing world
☐ The A and R Woolf Charitable Trust	£28,000	General
☐ The A M McGreevy No. 5 Charitable Settlement	£28,000	General
☐ The Barbara Welby Trust	£28,000	General
☐ The Calpe Trust	£28,000	Relief work
☐ The Dennis Alan Yardy Charitable Trust	£28,000	General

☐ The Derek Hill Foundation	£28,000	Arts, culture
☐ The Helen Isabella McMorran Charitable Foundation	£28,000	General, Christian
☐ The Jim Marshall Charitable Trust	£28,000	General
☐ The Oak Trust	£28,000	General
☐ The Rowing Foundation	£28,000	Water sports
☐ Brian Abrams Charitable Trust	£27,000	Jewish
☐ The Astor of Hever Trust	£27,000	Youth, medical research, education
☐ The Sylvanus Charitable Trust	£27,000	Animal welfare, Roman Catholic
☐ The Thomas Wall Trust	£27,000	Education, welfare
☐ The Kass Charitable Trust	£26,000	Welfare, education, Jewish
☐ John Huntingdon's Charity	£26,000	Welfare
☐ Mr and Mrs F E F Newman Charitable Trust	£26,000	Christian, overseas aid and development
☐ The Dorcas Trust	£26,000	Christian, relief of poverty and advancement of education
☐ The Duncan Norman Trust Fund	£26,000	General
☐ The Late Sir Pierce Lacy Charity Trust	£26,000	Roman Catholic, general
☐ The Pallant Charitable Trust	£26,000	Church music
☐ R E Chadwick Charitable Trust	£25,000	General
☐ The Cazenove Charitable Trust	£25,000	General
☐ The Jack Goldhill Charitable Trust	£25,000	Jewish, general
☐ The Minos Trust	£25,000	Christian, general
☐ The Moette Charitable Trust	£25,000	Jewish education and social welfare
☐ The Pamela Champion Foundation	£25,000	General, disability
☐ The Macfarlane Walker Trust	£24,000	Education, the arts, social welfare, general
☐ The Norman Joels Charitable Trust	£24,000	Jewish causes, general
☐ Lady Gibson's Charitable Trust	£23,500	General, arts, culture
☐ The Malcolm Chick Charity	£23,500	Youth character building, armed forces welfare, medical research and care
☐ Annette Duvollet Charitable Trust	£23,000	General
☐ P H G Cadbury Charitable Trust	£23,000	General, arts, conservation, cancer
☐ The Dorema Charitable Trust	£23,000	Medicine, health, welfare, education, religion
☐ The Hellenic Foundation	£23,000	Greek education
☐ The Star Charitable Trust	£23,000	General
☐ TJH Foundation	£22,000	Social welfare, medical, racing welfare
☐ Bellasis Trust	£22,000	General
☐ The Baltic Charitable Fund	£22,000	Seafarers, fishermen, ex-service and service people
☐ The Red Rose Charitable Trust	£22,000	General, particularly educational expenses for students and ill health
☐ The Seven Fifty Trust	£22,000	Christian causes
☐ C J Cadbury Charitable Trust	£21,000	Environment, conservation, music
☐ The Anthony and Elizabeth Mellows Charitable Settlement	£21,000	National heritage, Church of England churches
☐ The Green and Lilian F M Ainsworth and Family Benevolent Fund	£21,000	Youth, disability, health, medical research, disadvantage, older people, general
☐ The Beacon Trust	£20,000	Christian
☐ The Fanny Rapaport Charitable Settlement	£20,000	Jewish, general
☐ Sir Alec Black's Charity	£20,000	Relief in need
☐ The Geoffrey Burton Charitable Trust	£20,000	General
☐ The Gough Charitable Trust	£20,000	Youth, Episcopal and Church of England, preservation of the countryside, social welfare
☐ The Nicholas Joels Charitable Trust	£20,000	Jewish, medical welfare, general
☐ C B Richard Ellis Charitable Trust	£18,000	General
☐ The Blueberry Charitable Trust	£18,000	Jewish, relief in need
☐ The Millhouses Charitable Trust	£18,000	Christian, overseas aid, general
☐ The Nigel Moores Family Charitable Trust	£18,000	Arts
☐ The Rock Solid Trust	£18,000	Christian causes

☐ The Cheruby Trust	£17,000	Welfare, education, general
☐ T F C Frost Charitable Trust	£16,000	Medical
☐ The Earl of Northampton's Charity	£16,000	Welfare
☐ The Beaverbrook Foundation	£15,000	General
☐ The Constance Paterson Charitable Trust	£15,000	Medical research, health, welfare of children, older people, service people
☐ The Emmanuel Kaye Foundation	£15,000	Medical research, welfare and Jewish organisations
☐ The Geoffrey C Hughes Charitable Trust	£15,000	Nature conservation, environment, performing arts
☐ The Loke Wan Tho Memorial Foundation	£15,000	Environment and conservation, medical causes, overseas aid
☐ The Linmardon Trust	£14,000	General
☐ The Moss Spiro Will Charitable Foundation	£14,000	Jewish welfare
☐ Armenian General Benevolent Union London Trust	£13,000	Armenian education, culture and welfare
☐ The Henry Angest Foundation	£13,000	General
☐ The Ruth and Lionel Jacobson Trust No. 2	£13,000	Jewish, medical, children, disability
☐ The Kitty and Daniel Nabarro Charitable Trust	£12,000	Welfare, education, medicine, homeless, general
☐ Educational Foundation of Alderman John Norman	£11,000	Education
☐ Mandeville Trust	£11,000	Cancer, young people and children
☐ H and L Cantor Trust	£10,000	Jewish, general
☐ The Kessler Foundation	£10,000	General, Jewish
☐ The River Farm Foundation	£10,000	General, older people, young people, animal welfare and the environment
☐ The Richard and Christine Purchas Charitable Trust	£9,000	Medical research, medical education and patient care
☐ The Roger and Sarah Bancroft Clark Charitable Trust	£9,000	Quaker, general
☐ The Daniel Rivlin Charitable Trust	£8,000	Jewish, general
☐ Barchester Healthcare Foundation	£7,500	Health and social care
☐ The H P Charitable Trust	£5,600	Orthodox Jewish
☐ The Camilla Samuel Fund	£4,500	Medical research
☐ The Amanda Smith Charitable Trust	£1,400	General
☐ Dezna Robins Jones Charitable Foundation	£1,000	Medical, general
☐ The Bluff Field Charitable Trust	£1,000	General

The A B Charitable Trust

Human rights

£406,000 (2009/10)

Beneficial area
Mainly UK.

Monmouth House,
87–93 Westbourne Grove, London
W2 4UL
Tel: 020 7313 8070
Fax: 020 7313 9607
Email: mail@abcharitabletrust.org.uk
Website: www.abcharitabletrust.org.
uk
Correspondent: Sara Harrity,
Director
Trustees: Claire Bonavero; Olivier
Bonavero; Philippe Bonavero; Anne
Bonavero; Yves Bonavero; Athol
Harley; Alison Swan Parente; Peter
Day.
CC Number: 1000147

Information available
Accounts were available from the
Charity Commission.

The following information has been
taken from the trust's website:

A B Charitable Trust supports charities
working where human dignity is
imperilled and where there are
opportunities for human dignity to be
affirmed.

Applications are particularly welcomed
from charities working to support:
▷ refugees and victims of torture
▷ prisoners
▷ older people
▷ people with mental health problems.
In relation to the above, the following
cross-cutting themes are of interest to
the trustees:
▷ women
▷ homelessness
▷ therapeutic art.

Grants are awarded to charities
registered in the UK; usually to those
working in the UK, though a few are
awarded to charities working
internationally. It tends to support
charities with annual income between
£150,000 and £1.5 million which do
not have substantial investments or
surpluses.

The trust has a small-grants
programme (up to £5,000) which
responds to appeals on a one-off

basis. It seeks to identify charities
working on its priorities for larger
grants, which could be awarded on a
regular basis subject to annual reports
and an agreed exit strategy. It is
happy to provide funding for core
costs.

In 2009/10 the trust had assets of
£133,000 and an income of £184,000,
mostly from Gift Aid and other
contributions. From 146 applications
received, grants to 63 organisations
were made totalling £406,000. They
were distributed as follows:

Abuse, addiction and mental health	8	£88,000
Community and development	5	£25,000
Disabilities	4	£16,000
Homeless	3	£15,000
Human rights	9	£43,000
Older people and carers	8	£40,000
Prisoners	11	£95,000
Refugees and asylum seekers	15	£85,000

Beneficiaries included: Demos and
UK Drugs Policy Commission
(£50,000 each); Prison Reform Trust
(£30,000); Inquest and FPWP
Hibiscus (£10,000 each); Women's
Therapy Centre and Asylum Support
Appeals Project (£7,500 each); Yarl's
Wood Befrienders, Action on Elder
Abuse, Harrogate Homeless Project,
Living Options – Devon, Caxton
House and Lakelands Hospice (£5,000
each); Interact Reading Service
(£3,500); and Fahamu (£2,500).

Exclusions
No grants are made to organisations
principally concerned with:
▷ animals
▷ children
▷ environment
▷ formal education
▷ medicine
▷ religion
▷ research.

Capital appeals are not normally
supported, nor are charities with
large national or international links,
or areas which should reasonably be
funded by government.

Applications
Applications can be completed online
at the trust's website.

As well as administrative and
financial details, the online
application form will ask for a two
page summary of the organisation's
work, including:

▷ background
▷ aims and objectives
▷ activities
▷ achievements.

After filling in the online application
form you will be sent a reference
number. Please send the director the
following documents in hard copy
quoting the reference number:
▷ the two page overview of the
organisation's work
▷ a signed copy of the latest certified
accounts/statements, with a
reporting date that is no more than
12 months prior to the application
deadline chosen (the trustees meet
four times a year, in January,
April, July and October – please
see the trust's website for exact
deadline dates)
▷ up to two items of publicity
material that illustrate the work of
the organisation, such as annual
reviews or leaflets.

Eric Abrams Charitable Trust

Jewish

£28,000 (2009/10)

Beneficial area
UK.

c/o Lyon Griffiths Limited, Unit 17,
Alvaston Business Park, Middlewich
Road, Nantwich, Cheshire CW5 6PF
Tel: 01270 624 445
Correspondent: The Trustees
Trustees: Brian Abrams; Eric Abrams;
Marcia Anne Jacobs; Susan Melanie
Abrams.
CC Number: 275939

Information available
Accounts were available from the
Charity Commission, but without a
list of grants.

The charity makes grants to registered
charities established in the UK for the
advancement of education, welfare
and relief of poverty, particularly
amongst those persons of the Jewish
faith.

In 2009/10 the trust had assets of
£654,000 and an income of £37,000.
Grants to 32 organisations totalled
£28,000.

Previous beneficiaries have included: Friends of Ohr Akiva Institution, Centre for Torah Education Trust, Halacha Lemoshe Trust, Hale Adult Hebrew Education Trust, the Heathlands Village, Manchester Jewish Federation, Rabbi Nachman of Breslov Charitable Foundation, UK Friends of Magen David Adom and United Jewish Israel Appeal.

Exclusions
No grants to individuals.

Applications
'The trustees do not invite appeals, as the trust is fully committed until further notice.'

Brian Abrams Charitable Trust

Jewish

£27,000 (2009/10)

Beneficial area
UK.

c/o Lyon Griffiths Limited, Unit 17, Alvaston Business Park, Middlewich Road, Nantwich, Cheshire CW5 6PF
Correspondent: The Trustees
Trustees: Betty Abrams; Brian Abrams; Eric Abrams; Gail Gabbie.
CC Number: 275941

Information available
Accounts were available from the Charity Commission, but without a list of grants.

In 2009/10 this trust had an income of £36,000 and made 31 grants totalling £27,000.

Previous beneficiaries have included: Centre for Torah Education Trust, Friends of Ohr Akiva Institution, Halacha Lemoshe Trust, Hale Adult Hebrew Education Trust, the Heathlands Village, Manchester Jewish Federation, Rabbi Nachman of Breslov Charitable Foundation, Rainsough Charitable Trust, UK Friends of Magen David Adom and United Jewish Israel Appeal.

Exclusions
No grants to individuals.

Applications
The trust has stated that its funds are fully committed and applications are not invited.

The Acacia Charitable Trust

Jewish, education, general

£63,000 (2009/10)

Beneficial area
UK and Israel.

C/o H W Fisher & Co, Acre House, 11–15 William Road, London NW1 3ER
Tel: 020 7486 1884
Email: acacia@dircon.co.uk
Correspondent: The Secretary
Trustees: K D Rubens; Angela Gillian Rubens; S A Rubens; P H Rubens.
CC Number: 274275

Information available
Full accounts available from the Charity Commission website.

In 2009/10 the trust had assets of £1.7 million and an income of £67,000. 36 grants to 25 organisations totalled £63,000. Governance costs were high in relation to income and expenditure at £32,000.

Grants were given in the following categories:

Arts and culture	10	£42,000
Community care and welfare	13	£9,500
Education	3	£6,000
Overseas aid	3	£3,000
Medical and disability	6	£600
General	1	£100

Beneficiaries included: The Jewish Museum (£41,000); Community Security Trust (£5,000); Norwood and Yad Vashem (£1,000 each); Royal National Theatre (£500); Nightingale House (£250); and Shelter, Jewish Council for Racial Equality and Riding for the Disabled (£100 each).

Exclusions
No grants to individuals.

Applications
In writing to the correspondent.

Achiezer Association Ltd

The relief of elderly people and people in need, advancement of education, advancement of religion, and general charitable purposes

£691,000 (2008/09)

Beneficial area
Worldwide.

130–134 Granville Road, London NW2 2LD
Tel: 020 8209 3880
Email: genoffice@dasim.co.uk
Correspondent: David Chontow, Trustee
Trustees: David Chontow; Sydney S Chontow; Michael M Chontow.
CC Number: 255031

Information available
2008/09 accounts were most recent available from the Charity Commission. At the time of writing (November 2011) the 2009/10 accounts were 276 days overdue.

The trust's objects are to:
- offer relief to the 'aged, impotent and poor'
- advance education, religion and purposes beneficial to the community.

In 2008/09 the trust had assets of £1.2 million and a consolidated income of £965,000. Grants were made totalling £691,000. The accounts for the year do not include the individual beneficiaries of the grants made. According to the trust, a list of grant beneficiaries is 'detailed in a separate publication which is available from the Registered Office'. A copy has been requested but is yet to be received.

In the past, the trust has mainly supported Jewish charities with a few small grants being given to medical and welfare charities. No further information was available.

Exclusions

No grants to individuals.

Applications

In writing to the correspondent.

The Company of Actuaries' Charitable Trust Fund

Actuaries, medical research, young and older people, disability

£113,000 (2009/10)

Beneficial area

UK, with a preference for the City of London.

55 Station Road, Beaconsfield, Bucks HP9 1QL

Email: charity@companyofactuaries.co.uk

Website: www.actuariescompany.co.uk

Correspondent: Lyndon Jones, Honorary Almoner

Trustees: John A Jolliffe; Nick Dumbreck; Jeff Medlock; Fiona J Morrison; Michael Turner; David Barford.

CC Number: 280702

Information available

Accounts were available from the Charity Commission. The following is taken from the trust's accounts:

Objectives of the charity:

1 the relief of poverty of members of the profession of actuary
2 grants for the advancement of education of actuaries
3 grants for charitable research in the field of actuarial science and the award of bursaries
4 awards of educational exhibitions to persons intending to practice the profession of actuary
5 awards of prizes in connection with the examinations for actuaries
6 assisting the general education of persons in need who are preparing to be actuaries
7 assisting and benefiting persons who are endeavouring to qualify as actuaries
8 making donations to any registered charity.

We are a small charity with limited funds. We therefore only donate to those charities where our donation will 'make a difference' and be used efficiently and effectively.

We normally only donate to the following types of registered charities:

1 those involved with supporting the elderly or disabled
2 charities helping children and young people
3 those involved in treating medical conditions or funding medical research
4 other worthy charities, such as those working with the needy or disadvantaged.

In 2009/10 the trust had assets of £245,000 and an income of £121,000. Grants were made to 49 organisations totalling £113,000. Awards were given ranging from £500 to £4,000, with larger amounts where liverymen had a significant connection. Grant funding was distributed as follows:

Donations made to charities	£51,000
Donations made to Coram Life Education	£30,000
Awards made for educational purposes	£20,000
Master's donations	£9,000
Donations made from Master's events	£4,000

Beneficiaries included: City University (£7,000); Herriot Watt University (£4,000); Cure Parkinson's Trust (£3,500); Duke of Edinburgh's Award Scheme (£2,500); Lord Mayor's Appeal (£2,000); the Soldier's Charity (£1,000); and Mansion House Scholarship Appeal (£500).

Exclusions

No grants for the propagation of religious or political beliefs, the maintenance of historic buildings or for conservation. The trustees do not usually support an organisation which has received a grant from the fund in the previous 24 months.

Applications

On a form which can be downloaded from the fund's website. Further information about the trust can be obtained from the correspondent.

The Adamson Trust

Children under 18 with a physical or mental disability

Around £75,000 to organisations and individuals.

Beneficial area

UK, but preference will be given to requests on behalf of Scottish children.

PO Box 26334, Crieff, Perthshire PH7 9AB

Email: edward@elworthy.net

Correspondent: Edward Elworthy, Administrator

Trustees: R Alastair Mc Strickland, Chair; Mary Campbell; Dr Helen Kirkwood; Maureen Nicholson; Stuart Shields.

SC Number: SC016517

Information available

Information provided by the trust.

Formerly known as Miss Agnes Gilchrist Adamson's Trust, grants are made to individuals and organisations providing holidays for children under 18 with a physical or mental disability. Donations are usually one-off.

About £75,000 is given in grants each year, mostly to individuals.

Previous beneficiaries have included Barnardo's – Dundee Family Support Team, Children's Hospice Association Scotland, Lady Hoare Trust for Physically Disabled Children, Hopscotch Holidays, Over the Wall Gang Group, Peak Holidays, React, Scotland Yard Adventure Centre, Sense Scotland, Special Needs Adventure Play Ground and Scottish Spina Bifida Association.

Applications

In writing to the correspondent. A copy of the latest audited accounts should be included together with details of the organisation, the number of children who would benefit and the proposed holiday.

Common applicant mistakes

'Not enough back up information provided with applications.'

The Victor Adda Foundation

Fan Museum, welfare

£42,000 (2009/10)

Beneficial area

UK, but in practice Greenwich.

c/o Kleinwort Benson Trustees, PO Box 57005, 30 Gresham Street, London EC2V 7PG
Tel: 020 3207 7091
Correspondent: The Trustees
Trustees: Helene Alexander; Roy Gluckstein; Ann Mosseri.
CC Number: 291456

Information available

Accounts were available from the Charity Commission.

Virtually since it was set up in 1984, the foundation has been a stalwart supporter of the Fan Museum in Greenwich. Both the foundation and the museum share a majority of the same trustees; the foundation also owns the property in which the museum is sited and has granted it a 999-year lease.

In 2009/10 the trust had assets of £1.3 million and an income of £46,000. Grants were made totalling £42,000, all of which went to the Fan Museum.

Previous beneficiaries have included the Child Trust, Jewish Museum and St Christopher Hospice.

Applications

In writing to the correspondent. Only successful applications are notified of a decision.

Adenfirst Ltd

Jewish

£133,000 (2010)

Beneficial area

Worldwide.

34 Princes Park Avenue, London NW11 0JT
Correspondent: Leonard Bondi, Governor
Trustees: Mrs H F Bondi; Mr Leonard Bondi; Mrs R Cymerman; Mrs Sylvia Cymerman; Mr Ian Heitner; Mr Michael Cymerman; Mrs Sarah Heitner.
CC Number: 291647

Information available

Accounts were available from the Charity Commission.

The trust supports mostly Jewish organisations, with a preference for education and social welfare.

In 2010 the trust had assets of £1.5 million and made grants to 14 organisations totalling £133,000 which were broken down as follows:

Advancement of education	£78,000
Relief of poverty	£55,000

Beneficiaries included: Beis Aaron Trust (£30,000); Ezer Vehatzolo and Kahal Chassidim Wiznitz (£20,000 each); and Beis Rochel D'Satmar, Lolev Charitable Trust and Mercaz Hatorah Belz Machnovke (£10,000 each).

Grants of less than £5,000 totalled £2,500.

Applications

In writing to the correspondent.

The Adint Charitable Trust

Health, social welfare

£276,000 (2009/10)

Beneficial area

Worldwide, in practice UK.

Suite 42, 571 Finchley Road, London NW3 7BN
Email: adintct@gmail.com
Correspondent: Douglas R Oram, Trustee
Trustees: Anthony J Edwards; Mrs Margaret Edwards; Douglas R Oram; Brian Pate.
CC Number: 265290

Information available

Accounts were available from the Charity Commission.

This trust was established in 1972 by the settlor, Henry John Edwards. Most of the grants made are for £5,000 or £10,000 to a range of health and welfare charities, many concerned with children.

In 2009/10 the trust had assets of £6.1 million and an income of £324,500. Grants were made to 46 organisations totalling £276,000.

Beneficiaries included: CLIC Sargeant, Fight for Sight Eye Research, Mental Health Foundation and Shelter (£10,000 each); Army Benevolent Fund, British Lung Foundation and the Westminster Pastoral Foundation (£5,000 each); and the Anne Frank Trust UK and Headway London (£1,000 each).

Exclusions

Individuals are not supported.

Applications

In writing to the correspondent. Each applicant should make its own case in the way it considers best, but the application should include full details of the applicant charity. The trust notes that it cannot enter into correspondence and unsuccessful applicants will not be notified.

The Adnams Charity

General

£79,000 (2009/10)

Beneficial area

Within a 25-mile radius of St Edmund's Church, Southwold.

Sole Bay Brewery, Southwold, Suffolk IP18 6JW
Tel: 01502 727200
Email: rebecca.abrahall@adnams.co.uk
Website: www.adnams.co.uk/charity
Correspondent: Rebecca Abrahall, Charity Administrator
Trustees: Jonathan Adnams, Chair; Rob Chase; Lizzy Cantwell; Guy Heald; Emma Hibbert; Melvyn Horn;

Sadie Lofthouse; Simon Loftus; Andy Wood.

CC Number: 1000203

Information available

Accounts were available from the Charity Commission website.

The Adnams Charity was founded in 1990 to mark the centenary of the Adnams company and is funded by the annual donation of at least 1% of the profits of Adnams Plc and by the generosity of others – including a major legacy from a former shareholder. It supports a wide variety of organisations including those involved with health and social welfare, education, recreation, the arts, environment and conservation and historic buildings.

The charity prefers to make one-off grants for specific items. Though, in very exceptional circumstances, it may give a grant to cover ongoing running costs. Applications from national charities which operate within the 25-mile catchment area may be considered if assurances can be given that the money will be used for a specific purpose within the area. Grants normally range from £100 to £2,500 and the charity expects to see the result of its donations within twelve months.

In 2009/10 the charity held assets of £23,000 and had an income of £63,000. During the year grants made totalled £79,000.

Beneficiaries included: Westleton Village Hall and Deben Rowing Club (£2,500 each); St Edmund's Primary School – Hoxne (£2,400); Waveney Crossroads (£2,200); Blofield Primary School PTA (£2,000); North Suffolk and Great Yarmouth Cruse Bereavement Care (£1,800); Credit Action (£1,300); 1st Halesworth Scout Group (£1,000); Harleston Allotments Association (£920); Victim Support (£820); Open Space Theatre Company (£660); IDC Diamonds (£450); St James Village Orchard Project (£350); and Laxfield Village Hall (£200).

Exclusions

The charity does not normally make grants to religious organisations or private clubs unless they can demonstrate that the purpose of the grant is for something of clear public benefit, accessible to all. It does not provide raffle prizes or sponsorship of any kind. No grants are made to individuals. However, public bodies and charities may apply on behalf of individuals. Grants are not made in successive years.

Applications

Application forms are available on request to the Charity Administrator. Grants are considered at quarterly meetings, in January, April, July and October. Application deadlines usually fall in the previous month and are listed on the charity's website.

Common applicant mistakes

'Many applicants are not within catchment area.'

AF Trust Company

Higher education

£60,000 (2009/10)

Beneficial area

England.

34 Chapel Street, Thatcham, Reading, Berkshire RG18 4QL
Tel: 01635 867222
Correspondent: Paul Welch, Secretary
Trustees: Martin Wynne-Jones; David Charles Savage; Jeremy Lindley; Andrew Murphy; David Leah.
CC Number: 1060319

Information available

Accounts were available from the Charity Commission.

Support is given for charitable purposes connected with the provision of higher education in England. The company currently provides property services and leasing facilities to educational establishments on an arm's length basis.

In 2009/10 the trust had assets of £353,000. The total income and expenditure for the year was around £3 million. However, it is worth noting that this relates to the funds used to lease buildings from educational establishments and then enter into lease-back arrangements rather than describing the size of funds available. Grants were made totalling £60,000.

Beneficiaries were: University of Nottingham (£17,500); University of Reading (£14,250); Imperial College (£13,250); University of Canterbury Christ Church (£7,750); Royal Holloway (£3,000); University of Exeter (£2,250); and Royal Academy of Music and University of Central Lancashire (£1,000 each).

Exclusions

No grants to individuals.

Applications

In writing to the correspondent. However, unsolicited applications are only accepted from higher education institutions within England.

The Green and Lilian F M Ainsworth and Family Benevolent Fund

Youth, disability, health, medical research, disadvantage, older people, general

£21,000 (2009/10)

Beneficial area

UK, with some preference for northwest England.

RBS Trust Services, Eden, Lakeside, Chester Business Park, Wrexham Road, Chester CH4 9QT
Correspondent: The Trust Section Manager
Trustee: The Royal Bank of Scotland plc.
CC Number: 267577

Information available

Full accounts were available at the Charity Commission.

The trust states that each year it supports UK charities covering a wide range of interests mainly involving people of all ages who are disadvantaged by either health or other circumstances.

In 2009/10 the trust had an income of £29,000 and grants totalled £21,000.

Grants were either for £500 or £350 each. Beneficiaries included: Avon Riding Centre, Lost Chord, Young People Taking Action, Wirral Inroads and InterAct Reading Service (£500 each); and Frishta Children's Village, the Migraine Trust, Dogs for the Disabled, Red Squirrel Survival Trust and River and Sea Sence (£350 each).

Exclusions

No grants to individuals or non-registered charities.

Applications

In writing to the trustees, there is no application form.

The Sylvia Aitken Charitable Trust

Medical research and welfare, general

About £120,000 (2009/10)

Beneficial area

UK, with a preference for Scotland.

Fergusons Chartered Accountants, 24 Woodside, Houston, Renfrewshire PA6 7DD
Tel: 01505 610412
Correspondent: The Administrator
Trustees: Mrs S M Aitken; Mrs M Harkis; J Ferguson.
SC Number: SC010556

Information available

The following entry is based on information filed with the Office of the Scottish Charity Regulator.

Whilst this trust has a preference for medical projects, it has general charitable purposes, making small grants to a wide range of small local organisations throughout the UK, particularly those in Scotland. In 2009/10 the trust had an income of £119,000.

Previous grant beneficiaries have included: Association for International Cancer Research, Barn

Owl Trust, British Lung Foundation, British Stammering Association, the Roy Castle Lung Cancer Foundation, Disabled Living Foundation, Epilepsy Research Trust, Friends of the Lake District, Motor Neurone Disease Association, Network for Surviving Stalking, Royal Scots Dragoon Guards Museum Trust, Sense Scotland, Scottish Child Psychotherapy Trust, Tall Ships Youth Trust, Tenovus Scotland, Wood Green Animal Shelters and Young Minds.

Exclusions

No grants to individuals: the trust can only support UK registered charities.

Applications

In writing to the correspondent. Applicants should outline the charity's objectives and current projects for which funding may be required. The trustees meet at least twice a year, usually in March/April and September/October.

The Ajahma Charitable Trust

Development, poverty, human rights, health, disability, social welfare

£286,000 (2009/10)

Beneficial area

Unrestricted.

275 Dover House Road, London SW15 5BP
Tel: 020 8788 5388
Correspondent: Suzanne Hunt, Administrator
Trustees: Jennifer Sheridan; Elizabeth Simpson; James Sinclair Taylor; Carole Pound; Roger Paffard.
CC Number: 273823

Information available

Accounts were available from the Charity Commission.

This trust was established in 1977 for general charitable purposes. It aims to balance its donations between international and UK charities and focuses on the following areas of work:

- development
- health
- disability
- poverty
- women's issues
- family planning
- human rights
- social need.

Generally, established charities receive grants but new groups and those which may have difficulty finding funds from traditional sources are encouraged.

The 2009/10 trustees' report states that:

> The Trustees have adopted a policy of seeking and considering applications for charitable funding generally from established charities. They seek to maintain a reasonable balance between charitable activities overseas and in the United Kingdom. This is the third year of a new policy of making larger grants (currently of £50,000 p.a.) over a 3-year period from 2008 to 2010 to 4 specific charities working overseas.

In 2009/10 the trust had assets of £2.9 million and an income of £95,000. During the year the Charity made total grant payments of £286,000 (2009 – £269,000) with an approximate balance of 72% (2009 – 74%) benefiting overseas work and 28% (2009 – 26%) benefiting work in the UK. A continuing substantial commitment to local Headway groups has been maintained, with Headway groups awards totalling £50,000 (9 grants).

Other beneficiaries included: CAMFED, Global Witness and Womankind Worldwide (£50,000 each); and Blue Sky, Straight Talking and Switchback (£4,500 each).

Exclusions

Large organisations with a turnover above £4 million will not normally be considered, nor will applications with any sort of religious bias or those which support animal rights/welfare, arts, medical research, buildings, equipment, local groups or overseas projects where the charity income is less than £500,000 a year. Applications for grants or sponsorship for individuals will not be supported.

Applications

The trust has reviewed their grant-making criteria and will now proactively seek and select organisations to which they wish to award grants. They will no longer consider unsolicited applications.

The Alabaster Trust

Christian Church and related activities

£38,000 (2009/10)

Beneficial area

UK and overseas.

1 The Avenue, Eastbourne, East Sussex BN21 3YA
Tel: 01323 644579
Email: john@caladine.co.uk
Correspondent: John Caladine, Trust Administrator
Trustees: Jill Kendrick; Graham Kendrick; Abigail Sheldrake; Amy Waterman.
CC Number: 1050568

Information available

Accounts were available from the Charity Commission, but without a list of grants.

This trust was set up to make grants to evangelical Christian organisations in the UK and abroad. In 2009/10 it had assets of £54,000 and an income of £50,000, mostly derived from Gift Aid donations. Grants totalled £38,000. Further information was not available.

Exclusions

No grants to individuals.

Applications

In writing to the correspondent. The trustees meet to consider grants quarterly, usually in March, June, September and December.

Alba Charitable Trust

Jewish

£32,000 (2007/8)

Beneficial area

UK and overseas.

3 Goodyers Gardens, Hendon, London NW4 2HD
Tel: 020 7434 3494
Correspondent: Leslie Glatt, Trustee
Trustees: Leslie Glatt, Chair; Mrs R Glatt; Mrs D Kestel.
CC Number: 276391

Information available

The latest accounts available at the Charity Commission were for 2007/8.

This trust has stated that it mainly supports educational institutions in the UK and internationally, but also makes grants towards other causes.

The latest accounts available were for 2007/8 when the trust had assets of £286,000, an income of £66,000 and made grants totalling £32,000.

Beneficiaries included: Lolev Charitable Trust (£20,000); Chasdei Cohen (£5,500); Jewish Care (£4,000); and HAYE (£1,500). A further £600 was granted in donations of less than £500.

Applications

In writing to the correspondent.

The Albion Trust

General

£170,000 (2009/10)

Beneficial area

UK.

Coutts & Co, 440 The Strand, London WC2R 0QS
Tel: 020 7663 6838
Correspondent: Helen Porter, Administrator
Trustees: Peter Savage; Diane Savage; Philip Savage; Philip Clancey; Helen Stringer; Coutts & Co.
CC Number: 1117812

Information available

Basic accounts were available from the Charity Commission.

The trust was established in 2007 for general charitable purposes.

In 2009/10 it had assets of £300,500 and an income of £22,000. Grants were made to 14 organisations during the year totalling £170,500, although

the individual amounts awarded were not disclosed in the trust's accounts.

The beneficiaries were: Nordoff-Robbins Music Therapy; Enterprise Education Trust; Downside Fisher Youth Club; ECHO; Lawrence's Roundabout Well Appeal; Stonebridge City Farm; CLIC Sargent; Skill Force Development; Rainbow Trust; Groundwork Black Country; Second Chance; The Honeypot Charity; YMCA Winchester; and Ellen McArthur Trust.

Applications

In writing to the correspondent.

The Alborada Trust

Veterinary causes, social welfare

£57,000 (2009)

Beneficial area

Worldwide.

Fladgate Fielder, 16 Great Queen Street, London WC2 5DG
Tel: 020 3036 7308
Website: www.alboradatrust. com/alboradatrust_home/
Correspondent: Jamie Matheson
Trustees: Miss E K E Rausing; D J Way; R Lerner; Capt. J Nicholson.
CC Number: 1091660

Information available

Latest accounts available at the Charity Commission were for 2009.

This trust was established in October 2001 with an initial donation of £5 million being settled in April 2002. The trust is named after the racehorse Alborada.

Unsolicited applications are not requested as the trustees prefer to restrict the area of benefit to:

▶ Veterinary causes in the United Kingdom and Ireland with activities primarily devoted to the welfare of animals and/or in their associated research.

▶ Projects throughout the world associated with the relief of poverty, human suffering, sickness or ill health.

At the time of writing (December 2011) the latest accounts available were for the period April–December 2009. The trust had assets of £8.8 million and an income of £188,000. Grants to 2 organisations totalled £57,000, these were: Animal Health Trust (£35,000) and Wildlife Vets International (£22,000).

Applications

Funds are fully committed. The trust does not accept unsolicited applications.

Common applicant mistakes

We receive a lot of 'round-robin' letters obviously sent to many charities with the exact same wording. Some such letters are not signed and are therefore disregarded.

Some applicants obviously have no idea about our stated criteria for donations.

D G Albright Charitable Trust

General

£33,000 (2009/10)

Beneficial area

UK, with a preference for Gloucestershire.

Old Church School, Hollow Street, Great Somerford, Chippenham, Wiltshire SN15 5JD
Tel: 01249 720 760
Correspondent: Richard Wood, Trustee
Trustees: Hon. Dr Gilbert Greenall; Richard Wood.
CC Number: 277367

Information available

Accounts were on file at the Charity Commission.

In 2009/10 the trust had assets of £1.1 million and an income of £42,000. Grants were made to 26 organisations totalling £33,000.

Grants included those to: Bromesberrow Parochial Church Council (£4,000); Gloucestershire Macmillan Cancer Relief, National Star College, the Countryside Foundation for Education and the Family Haven – Gloucester (£2,000

each); Hands Around the World, Butterfly Conservation, Fields in Trust and the Calvert Trust (£1,000 each); Dulverton Patient Group and HOPE Family Centre (£500 each); and Bibles for Children (£300).

Exclusions

No grants to individuals.

Applications

In writing to the correspondent.

The Alchemy Foundation

Health and welfare, famine relief overseas

£280,000 (2009/10)

Beneficial area

UK and overseas.

Trevereux Manor, Limpsfield Chart, Oxted, Surrey RH8 0TL
Tel: 01883 730 600
Correspondent: Richard Stilgoe, Trustee
Trustees: Dr Jemima Stilgoe; Holly Stilgoe; Jack Stilgoe; Rufus Stilgoe; Richard Stilgoe; Alex Armitage; Andrew Murison; Annabel Stilgoe; Esther Rantzen; Joseph Stilgoe; Tony Elias.
CC Number: 292500

Information available

Accounts were available from the Charity Commission, but without a list of grants.

The charity was established, as The Starlight Foundation, by a charitable trust deed on 14 August 1985. The name was changed to The Alchemy Foundation on 2 June 1987.

The foundation's 2009/10 accounts state:

The charity's objects are particularly focused on The Orpheus Centre, water projects in the developing world, disability (particularly mobility, access, helplines and communications), social welfare (inner city community projects, disaffected youth, family mediation, homelessness), personal reform, penal reform (work with prisoners, especially young prisoners, and their families), medical research and aid (especially in areas of blindness and disfigurement), individual enterprise (by helping Raleigh

International and similar organisations to give opportunities to young people according to need) and respite for carers.

In 2009/10 it had a total income of £298,000, of which £258,000 came from donations received and £39,000 was generated from assets, which totalled £2.3 million. There were 371 grants made totalling £280,000. Donations were broken down as follows:

Disability – mobility, helplines, access	£75,000
Third world water projects	£54,000
Social welfare – inner city community projects	£51,000
Respite for carers	£25,000
Medical research and aid – blindness and disfigurement	£24,000
Individuals on behalf of registered charities	£8,800
Orpheus Centre	£8,300
Penal reform and work with prisoners and their families	£4,800
Other	£29,000

Exclusions

The foundation does not fund organisations exclusive to one faith or political belief.

Applications

In writing to the correspondent.

The Alexis Trust

Christian

£47,000 (2009/10)

Beneficial area

UK and overseas.

14 Broadfield Way, Buckhurst Hill, Essex IG9 5AG
Correspondent: Prof. Duncan Vere, Trustee
Trustees: Prof. Duncan Vere; Chris Harwood; Elisabeth Harwood; Vera Vere.
CC Number: 262861

Information available

Accounts were available from the Charity Commission.

Support is given to a variety of causes, principally Christian. In 2009/10 the trust had assets of £434,000 and an income of £50,000. Grants were made totalling £47,000.

The sum of £41,000 was distributed to various missionary societies with seven organisations receiving £1,000 or more, including: Nationwide Christian Trust (£10,000); Counties Workers Essex and Tearfund (£2,000 each); UCCF and Barnabas Fund (£1,200 each); and Epping Forest Youth for Christ and SGM Lifewords (£1,000 each). A further 95 unlisted beneficiaries received a total of £23,000.

A further £7,300 was distributed to 79 short term missionary projects.

Exclusions

No grants for building appeals, or to individuals for education.

Applications

In writing to the correspondent, although the trust states that most of the funds are regularly committed.

All Saints Educational Trust

Religious education, home economics

£44,000 to organisations (2009/10)

Beneficial area

UK and overseas.

Suite 8C, First Floor, VSC Charity Centre, Royal London House, 22–25 Finsbury Square, London EC2A 1DX
Tel: 020 7920 6465
Email: aset@aset.org.uk
Website: www.aset.org.uk
Correspondent: The Clerk
Trustees: Diane McCrea; Rev Canon Peter Hartley; Revd Dr Keith Riglin; David J Trillo; Clive Wright; Barbara E Harvey; Dr Augur Pearce; Prof Anthony R Leeds; Ven. Stephan J Welch; Stephanie Valentine; Joanna Moriarty; Dr Robert L Gwynne; Frances M Smith; Anna E Cumbers; Michael C Jacob; Stephen Brooker.
CC Number: 312934

Information available

Accounts were available from the Charity Commission.

The All Saints Educational Trust makes awards annually to students and organisations.

Its main purpose is to:

- help increase the number of new teachers with Qualified Teacher Status
- improve the skills and qualifications of experienced teachers
- encourage research that can assist teachers in their work
- support specifically the teaching of Religious Studies and Home Economics and related areas – such as the promotion of public health and nutrition, both at home and overseas.

The trust offers both *Personal* and *Corporate* awards.

Corporate awards

The following description of the *Corporate Award* scheme has been taken from the trust's helpful website.

> The trust wishes to stimulate and support imaginative new projects that will enhance the Church's contribution to education, in accordance with our charitable scheme.
>
> The trustees are keen to identify and support pro-active projects that promote the development of education, particularly in the areas of Religious Education, Home Economics and related areas or subjects, and Multi-cultural/Inter-faith Education.
>
> Priority is given to projects in our core disciplines – especially pump-priming projects – whereby teachers are helped directly or indirectly.
>
> Projects most favoured are those that have the potential to result in lasting benefit, either through the intrinsic quality of the new ideas being put forward, or through the quantity of teachers and/or pupils who will share in the benefit.
>
> Larger corporate applications will be scrutinised carefully to ensure that they are sustainable and give value for money.
>
> Grants will not normally be made for a period in excess of five years.
>
> Our most distinctive and long-term Corporate Award is the All Saints Saxton Fellowship. The fourth Saxton Fellowship is due to start in the academic year 2012–2013.

In 2009/10 the trust had assets totalling £9 million which generated an income of £380,000. Grants totalled £202,000 and were distributed as follows:

Corporate awards (organisations)	£39,000
Scholarships and bursaries (individuals)	£159,000
All Saints Saxton Fellowship	£4,900

Previous beneficiaries of corporate awards include: National Association of Teachers in Home Economics, Southwark Cathedral Education Centre, British Nutrition Foundation, Design and Technology Association, Sheffield Hallam University, Wulugu – Ghana, Scripture Union, Christian Education Movement and the Soil Association.

Exclusions

Please note that the trust will not support:

- general or core funds of any organisation
- public appeals
- school buildings, equipment or supplies (except library resources)
- the establishment of new departments in universities and colleges
- general bursary funds of other organisations.

Applications

For applications from organisations (not individuals): applicants are invited to discuss their ideas informally with the clerk before making an application. In some cases, a 'link trustee' is appointed to assist the organisation in preparing the application and who will act in a liaison role with the trust. Completed applications are put before the awards committee in April/May, with final decisions made in June.

Application forms are available on the trust's website, either in interactive or printable form.

Common applicant mistakes

'Failure to read carefully the trust's terms and conditions.'

The Pat Allsop Charitable Trust

Education, medical research, children, relief of poverty

£63,000 (2009/10)

Beneficial area

UK.

1 The Sanctuary, London SW1P 3JT
Tel: 020 7222 5381
Email: jrandel@lbmw.com
Correspondent: J P G Randel, Trustee
Trustees: J P G Randel; P W E Kerr; W J K Taylor; N W M MacKilligin.
CC Number: 1030950

Information available

Accounts were received at the Charity Commission but not available to view online.

A number of educational grants are made each year, e.g. towards research and organising educational events. The founder of the trust was a partner in Allsop and Co. Chartered Surveyors, Auctioneers and Property Managers, therefore the trust favours supporting those educational projects and charities which have connections with surveying and property management professions. The trustees have a policy of making a small number of major donations (over £2,500) and a larger number of smaller donations.

In 2009/10 it had an income of £25,000 and a total expenditure of £63,000.

Previous beneficiaries have included: Duke of Edinburgh's Award, Jewish Care – Minerva Business Lunch (£5,000 each); the Story of Christmas (£3,800); Cambridge International Land Institute, Geoff Marsh Scholarship Fund and Reading Real Estate Foundation (£2,500 each); Crisis, the Honeypot Charity and the Willow Foundation (£1,000 each); Cambridge Mencap, King Alfred School Trust, the Jumbalance Charity, MACS Charity, Maggie's Cancer Caring Centre and Scottish Community Charity (£500 each); Philip Green Memorial Trust (£400); Get Kids Going (£350); Barnardo's, Get Kids Going, Muscular Dystrophy and Race for Life (£250 each); Cancer Research UK (£200); Children in Need (£150); and Variety Club Children's Charity (£100).

Exclusions

No grants to individuals.

Applications

The trust does not accept unsolicited applications.

The Almond Trust

Christian

£97,000 to organisations (2009/10)

Beneficial area

UK and worldwide.

19 West Square, London SE11 4SN
Correspondent: Sir Jeremy Cooke, Trustee
Trustees: Sir Jeremy Cooke; Jonathan Cooke; Lady Cooke.
CC Number: 328583

Information available

Full accounts were available from the Charity Commission website.

The trust's aims are the support of evangelistic Christian projects, Christian evangelism and the translation, reading, study and teaching of the Bible. Donations are largely recurrent.

In 2009/10 the trust had assets of £94,000 and an income of £63,000, including £58,000 from donations. Grants totalled £105,000. The accounts listed 18 organisations receiving of £1,000 or more. All but two had received grants in the previous year.

Beneficiaries included: Lawyers' Christian Fellowship (£12,000 in two grants); St Mary's Warbleton PCC (£10,000); Agape, Haggai Institute, Jews for Jesus and Titus Trust (£5,000 each); Friends International (£3,000); and CVM (£1,500).

Five payments totalling £8,800 were made to individuals.

Applications

In writing to the correspondent, but please note that the trust states it rarely responds to uninvited applications.

The Altajir Trust

Islam, education, science and research

£133,000 (2010)

Beneficial area

UK and Arab or Islamic states.

11 Elvaston Place, London SW7 5QG
Tel: 020 7581 3522
Fax: 020 7584 1977
Email: awitrust@tiscali.co.uk
Website: www.altajirtrust.org.uk
Correspondent: The Trustees
Trustees: Prof. Alan Jones, Chair; Prof. Roger Williams; Dr Charles Tripp; Dr Noel Brehony.
CC Number: 284116

Information available

Full accounts were available online at the Charity Commission; the trust has a useful website.

The Altajir Trust is a UK based charity supporting exhibitions, publications, educational activities and other programmes related to Islamic culture and Muslim – Christian relations. The trust provides scholarships for undergraduates and graduates, mainly from the Arab world, to undertake further studies at approved colleges of higher education within the United Kingdom. Funding may also be given towards the cost of conservation of Islamic artefacts and manuscripts in the United Kingdom, assisting conservation in Muslim countries, and to charitable and academic institutions assisting in rebuilding societies in the Islamic world after conflict.

In 2010 the trust had an income of £719,000 mostly from donations. Direct charitable expenditure totalled £390,000 of which £133,000 was paid out in grants; £247,000 on student support and £9,100 on events and publications.

Grant beneficiaries included: University of York – Lectureship (£46,000); British Council – Chevening Scholarships (£38,000); British Museum – Curatorial Summer School (£20,000); St John of Jerusalem Eye Hospital (£12,000); Offscreen Education Programme

(£7,500); Council for British Research in the Levant (£5,100); University of Sterling – Scholarships (£2,500); and SOAS (£1,500).

Applications
On a form available from the trust's website. The trustees meet about four times a year. Applications can be submitted at any time but may have to await the next trustees' meeting for a decision. However, they will all be acknowledged when received and an indication of the time frame for a decision will be given.

Please note: applications should be printed and signed before being sent to the trust.

Altamont Ltd

Jewish causes
£60,000 (2009/10)

Beneficial area
Worldwide.

18 Green Walk, London NW4 2AJ
Correspondent: David Last, Trustee
Trustees: D Last; H Last; Mrs H Kon; Mrs S Adler; Mrs G Wiesenfeld.
CC Number: 273971

Information available
Accounts were not required at the Charity Commission due to the charity's low income.

In 2009/10 the trust made had an income of £1,800 and a total expenditure of £62,000. (2008/09 – £850,000 given in grants). We have no further information regarding this charity.

Applications
In writing to the correspondent.

Alvor Charitable Trust

Christian, humanitarian, 'social change'
Around £470,000 (2009/10)

Beneficial area
UK, with a preference for Sussex, Norfolk and north east Scotland.

Monks Wood, Tompsets Bank, Forest Row, East Sussex RH18 5LW
Correspondent: I Wilkins, Chair
Trustees: C Wills; Shaena Wills; M Atherton; Fiona Atherton; I Wilkins; Julie Wilkins.
CC Number: 1093890

Information available
Basic information was available from the Charity Commission website.

Established in August 2002, this Christian and humanitarian charity predominately supports Christian social change projects in the UK and overseas. A proportion of its target funding goes to local projects around Sussex, Norfolk and north east Scotland where the trust has personal interests. The trust tends to support smaller projects where the grant will meet a specific need. It typically makes a few larger donations each year and a number of smaller grants.

In 2009/10 it had an unusually low income of £14,700. Total expenditure was £477,000.

Accounts were not available from the Charity Commission due to the low income but previous beneficiaries included: Kenward Trust (£50,000 in two grants); Salt Sussex Trading Ltd (£40,000 in four grants); Anne Marie School, Ghana (£35,000); Urban Saints (£33,000); Hymns Ancient and Modern (£30,000 in two grants); Care for the Family and Romance Academy (£25,000 each); Care, Hope UK, the Lighthouse Group, Message Trust, Mid Sussex Citizen Advice Bureau, Saltmine Trust and World In Need (£20,000 each); Carey Films Ltd, Christians in Sport, Positive Parenting, Scripture Union, Trussell Trust and Youth For Christ (£15,000 each); Church Army, First Base Agency, Proclaim Trust and Release International (£10,000 each); Opera Brava (£8,000); Brighton Fareshare, Furniture Now and N:Vision (£5,000 each); Caring 4 Life and Chestnut Tree House (£2,000 each); and Impact Initiatives (£500).

Exclusions
The trust does not look to support animal charities or medical charities outside of the geographic areas mentioned above.

Applications
In writing to the correspondent.

AM Charitable Trust

Jewish, general
£96,000 (2009/10)

Beneficial area
UK and overseas.

Kleinwort Benson Trustees Ltd, 30 Gresham Street, London EC2V 7PG
Tel: 020 3207 7091
Correspondent: The Administrator
Trustee: Kleinwort Benson Trustees Ltd.
CC Number: 256283

Information available
Accounts were available from the Charity Commission.

This trust supports a range of causes, particularly Jewish organisations but also medical, welfare, arts and conservation charities. Certain charities are supported for more than one year, although no commitment is usually given to the recipient. Grants range between £100 and £15,000 each, but are mostly of £200 to £500.

In 2009/10 the trust had assets of £1.8 million and an income of £72,000. Grants were made to 43 organisations totalling £96,000 and were divided between 'Jewish' and 'general' donations.

Jewish	11	£82,000
General	32	£14,000

Beneficiaries included: World Jewish Relief and Youth Aliyah – Child Rescue (£15,000 each); British Technion Society (£12,000); Jerusalem Foundation (£10,000); Friends of Boys Town Jerusalem (£5,000); Cancer Research Campaign (£3,000); British Heart Foundation (£2,000); Blond McIndoe Research Foundation (£1,500); New Marlowe Theatre Development Trust (£1,000);

NSPCC (£500); Kent Air Ambulance and Oxford and St George's Jewish Youth (£200 each); and Centrepoint (£100).

Exclusions
No grants to individuals.

Applications
The trust's annual report states:

> Donations are decided periodically by the Trustee having regard to the wishes of the Settlor, and unsolicited appeals are considered as well as causes which have already been supported. Only successful applicants are notified of the trustee's decision.

The Amalur Foundation Limited

General

£189,000 (2009/10)

Beneficial area
Worldwide.

Fladgate LLP, 16 Great Queen Street, London WC2B 5DG
Correspondent: David Way, Trustee
Trustees: Claudia Garuti; David Way; Michael Giedroyc; Helen Mellor.
CC Number: 1090476

Information available
Accounts were available from the Charity Commission.

Registered in February 2002, in 2009/10 this charity had no income and a total expenditure of £189,000. Please refer to the Applications section of this entry.

Previous beneficiaries include: Absolute Return for Kids (£110,000); St Patrick's Catholic Church (£50,000); Prostate Research Campaign UK (£10,000); Brain Tumour Research Campaign (£5,500); Breakthrough Breast Cancer (£3,000); and the Extra Care Charitable Trust (£2,000).

Applications
We are informed (September 2011) by the correspondent that the charity's income is diminishing and that it does not have a long-term future. While the trustees have funds available, they are pleased to consider applications, though this will not be for a great deal longer. Applications should be made to the correspondent in writing.

Sir John and Lady Amory's Charitable Trust

General

£80,000 to organisations (2009/10)

Beneficial area
UK, with a preference for Devon and the South West.

The Island, Lowman Green, Tiverton, Devon EX16 4LA
Tel: 01884 254899
Correspondent: Lady Heathcoat Amory, Trustee
Trustees: Sir Ian Heathcoat Amory; Lady Heathcoat Amory; William Heathcoat Amory.
CC Number: 203970

Information available
Accounts were available from the Charity Commission.

The trust was set up in 1961 with a bequest from Sir John and Lady Amory. It supports general charitable purposes and has a preference for funding smaller organisations in the south west of England that 'do not have access to sophisticated fundraising campaigns and on which a relatively small donation may have a significant effect'.

In 2009/10 the trust had assets of £1.9 million and an income of £395,000. The sale and purchase of investments during the year showed an increase in income (£323,000) and expenditure (£312,000). Grants to charitable and other institutions totalled £80,000.

Donations of £5,000 or more went to: National Trust (£8,500); and Exeter Cathedral Third Millennium Campaign (£5,000).

A further £3,400 was given to individuals.

Applications
In writing to the correspondent.

Viscount Amory's Charitable Trust

Welfare, older people, education, Christian churches

£309,000 (2009/10)

Beneficial area
UK, primarily in Devon.

The Island, Lowman Green, Tiverton, Devon EX16 4LA
Tel: 01884 254899
Correspondent: The Trust Secretary
Trustees: Sir Ian Heathcoat Amory; Catherine Cavender.
CC Number: 204958

Information available
Accounts were on file at the Charity Commission.

The trust's annual report 2010/11 states:

> The trustees believe objectives of the trust are to donate the annual investment income to charitable institutions or other organisations primarily to benefit the inhabitants of the County of Devon; to assist young people, the poor and aged; and to advance education.

In 2009/10 the trust had assets of £11.9 million and an income of £424,000. Grants were made to 200 organisations totalling £309,000, broken down into the following categories:

Education
Beneficiaries included: Exeter Cathedral School: (£15,000)

Religious
Beneficiaries included: Devon Historic Churches Trust: (£5,000)

General
Beneficiaries included: Rona Sailing Trust (£74,000); and The National Trust (£8,000).

Exclusions
No grants to individuals from outside South West England.

Applications
In writing to the correspondent, giving general background information, total costs involved,

amount raised so far and details of applications to other organisations.

The Ampelos Trust

General

Around £70,000 (2009/10)

Beneficial area

UK.

Menzies LLP, 3rd Floor, Kings House, 12–42 Wood Street, Kingston upon Thames, Surrey KT1 1TG
Tel: 020 8974 7500
Email: kingston@menzies.co.uk
Correspondent: Ms R A Lomer, Secretary
Trustees: Baroness of Babergh Ruth Rendell; Ann Marie Witt; MMH Trustees Limited.
CC Number: 1048778

Information available

Accounts received at the Charity Commission but unavailable to view.

In 2009/10 the trust had an unusually low income of £3,800 (£192,000 in 2008/09) and a total expenditure of £76,000. No further information was available.

Previous beneficiaries have included: Kids for Kids, Handel House Trust, Chester Zoo, Medical Foundation for the Care of Victims of Torture, Shelter, Stroke Association, Princess Royal Trust for Carers and the Seeing Ear.

Applications

In writing to the correspondent.

The Anchor Foundation

Christian

£201,000 (2009/10)

Beneficial area

UK and occasionally overseas.

PO Box 21107, Alloa FK12 5WA
Email: secretary@theanchorfoundation.org.uk

Website: www.theanchorfoundation.org.uk
Correspondent: The Secretary
Trustees: Prudence Thimbleby; Revd Michael Mitton; Revd Robin Anker-Petersen; Nina Anker-Petersen.
CC Number: 1082485

Information available

Accounts were available online at the Charity Commission; good trust website.

The foundation was registered with the Charity Commission in September 2000, it supports Christian charities concerned with social inclusion, particularly through ministries of healing and the arts.

The grant range for a project is between £500 and £10,000. It is not the normal practice of the charity to support the same project for more than three years (projects which have had three years funding may apply again two years from the payment of the last grant). Applications for capital and revenue funding are considered. Only in very exceptional circumstances will grants be given for building work. Organisations with a number of projects operating are advised to choose a single project for their application.

In 2009/10 the trust had assets of £5.4 million generating an income of £143,000. Grants totalled £201,000.

Beneficiaries included: Breakout (£8,000); Greenbank Christian Centre (£7,500); NGM Trust (£7,000); the Bethseda Project – Burundi (£6,400); Good News Family Care (£6,000); Heart to Heart and Malt Cross Trust (£5,000 each); Perth YMCA (£4,500); Unlock – Sheffield, Scripture Union and Scottish Love in Action (£4,000 each); and Disha Asha – India (£2,500).

Exclusions

No grants to individuals.

Applications

An initial application form can be completed online at the Anchor Foundation website. Full guidelines for applicants are also available online.

Applications are considered at twice yearly trustee meetings in April and

November and need to be received by 31 January and 31 July each year. The foundation regrets that applications cannot be acknowledged.

Successful applicants will be notified as soon as possible after trustees' meetings – usually before the end of May or the end of November. Unsuccessful applicants may reapply after twelve months.

The Andrew Anderson Trust

Christian, social welfare

£226,000 to organisations (2009/10)

Beneficial area

UK and overseas.

1 Cote House Lane, Bristol BS9 3UW
Tel: 011 7962 1588
Correspondent: Revd Andrew Robertson Anderson, Trustee
Trustees: Revd Andrew Robertson Anderson, Chair; Anne Alexander Anderson; Margaret Lillian Anderson.
CC Number: 212170

Information available

Accounts were available from the Charity Commission, but without a list of grants.

The trust states in its trustees' report that it provides support to a wide range of charitable causes. Most of its money appears to go to evangelical organisations and churches, but it also makes a large number of small grants to health, disability and social welfare charities.

In 2009/10 it had assets of £9.9 million and an income of £278,000. Grants totalled £284,000, of which £226,000 was given to organisations and the remaining £58,000 to individuals. No further information was available.

Previous beneficiaries have included: Aycliffe Evangelical Church, Christian Medical Fellowship, Concern Worldwide, Emmanuel Baptist Church – Sidmouth, Fellowship of Independent Evangelical Churches, Good Shepherd Mission, Kenward Trust, Latin Link, Proclamation Trust, Rehoboth Christian Centre –

Blackpool, Scientific Exploration Society, St Ebbe's PCC – Oxford, St Helen's Church – Bishopsgate, TNT Ministries, Trinity Baptist Church – Gloucester, Whitefield Christian Trust, Weald Trust and Worldshare.

Exclusions

Individuals should not apply for travel or education.

Applications

The trust has previously stated that 'we prefer to honour existing commitments and initiate new ones through our own contacts rather than respond to applications'.

Common applicant mistakes

'Though we are not open to unsolicited applications, we are inundated with applications for grants, most of which we cannot help.'

Andor Charitable Trust

Health, arts, Jewish, general

£91,000 (2009/10)

Beneficial area

UK and overseas.

c/o Blick Rothenberg, 12 York Gate, Regent's Park, London NW1 4QS
Tel: 020 7486 0111
Correspondent: David Rothenberg, Trustee
Trustees: David Rothenberg; Nicholas Lederer; Dr Donald Dean; Jeanne Szego.
CC Number: 1083572

Information available

Accounts were available from the Charity Commission.

Registered with the Charity Commission in 2000, in 2009/10 the trust had assets of £3.2 million and an income of £88,000. Grants to 26 organisations totalled £91,000.

Beneficiaries included: National Hospital for Neurology and Neurosurgery (£10,000); the Chicken Shed Theatre Trust (£7,500 in two

grants); Macmillan Cancer Support and Médecins Sans Frontières – UK (£5,000 each); Rix Thompson Rothenberg Foundation (£4,000); Cystic Fibrosis Trust and Live Music Now Limited (£3,000 each); and Young Music Makers, Shape London, Riders for Health and Council for Music in Hospitals (£2,000 each).

Applications

In writing to the correspondent.

The André Christian Trust

Christian

£55,000 (2010)

Beneficial area

UK.

2 Clevedon Close, Exeter EX4 6HQ
Tel: 01392 258681
Correspondent: Andrew K Mowll, Trustee
Trustees: Andrew K Mowll; Stephen Daykin.
CC Number: 248466

Information available

Accounts were available from the Charity Commission.

The trust makes grants towards the advancement of Christianity, either through printing and distributing Bible scriptures or through evangelistic work. A number of charities are listed in the trust deed, and they are its principle beneficiaries. Grants appear to mainly be ongoing.

In 2010 the trust had assets of £1.16 million and an income of £49,000. Grants were made totalling £54,600.

Beneficiaries in 2010 included: Open Air Campaigners (West Country) (£11,000); Exeter Community Family Trust (£8,000); Care for the Family and SIFT (£5,000 each); and Bible Society, Karis Kids, Life Words and Open Doors Exmouth (£1,000 each).

Applications

In writing to the correspondent. However, the trust states: 'Applications are discouraged since

grants are principally made to those organisations which are listed in the trust deed.' Funds are therefore fully committed and unsolicited requests cannot be supported.

The Henry Angest Foundation

General

£13,000 (2010)

Beneficial area

UK and overseas.

Arbuthnot House, 20 Ropemaker Street, London EC2Y 9AR
Tel: 020 7012 2400
Correspondent: The Trustees
Trustees: H Angest; D Angest.
CC Number: 1114761

Information available

Basic information taken from the Charity Commission website.

Set up in 2006 for general charitable purposes, in 2010 its total expenditure was £13,000. The charity had no income in the accounting year 2010, however, so far it remains on the Central Register of Charities and its income may increase in the future.

Previous beneficiaries included: Perth College Development Trust (£80,000); World Pheasant Association (£6,000); Bowel and Cancer Research, British Olympic Association, the R D Crusaders Foundation and East Midlands Zoological Society (£5,000 each); Cancer Research UK (£2,000); the Salvation Army (£1,000); and Botanic Foundation, PACT, Scottish Ballet and Wycombe Abbey School Foundation (£500).

Applications

In writing to the correspondent.

The Animal Defence Trust

Animal welfare/ protection

£79,000 (2009/10)

Beneficial area

UK.

Horsey Lightly Fynn, Devon House, 12–15 Dartmouth Street, Queen Anne's Gate, London SW1H 9BL
Tel: 020 7222 8844
Email: ameyer@horseylightly.com
Website: www.animaldefencetrust. org/
Correspondent: Alan A Meyer, Secretary
Trustees: Marion Saunders; Carole Bowles; Richard J Vines; Jenny Wheadon.
CC Number: 263095

Information available

Accounts were available from the Charity Commission.

The trust makes grants for capital projects purely to animal welfare charities. In 2009/10 it had assets totalling £1.4 million and an income of £44,000. Grants were made to 47 organisations, including 30 that had been supported in the previous year, totalling £79,000.

Beneficiaries included: Brooke Hospital, Care4Cats, Ferne Animal Sanctuary and Worldwide Veterinary Service (£3,000 each); Animals in Distress, Barn Owl Trust, Bedfordshire Wildlife Rescue, Berwick Animal Rescue, The Cat and Rabbit Centre, Cat Register and Rescue, Compassion in World Farming, Haworth Cat Rescue, International Otter Survival Fund, Plantation Dog Rescue, Tia Greyhound and Lurcher Rescue and Yorkshire Swan and Wildlife Rescue (£1,500 each); and Lagos Animal Protection (£1,000).

Exclusions

No grants to individuals.

Applications

On a form which can be downloaded from the trust's website. Application must be returned by post to: PO Box 44, Plymouth, PL7 5YW.

Common applicant mistakes

'Applicants holding too much in assets or cash in the bank.'

The Annandale Charitable Trust

Major UK charities

£235,000 (2009/10)

Beneficial area

UK.

HSBC Trust Services, 10th Floor, Norwich House, Nelson Gate, Commercial Road, Southampton SO15 1GX
Tel: 02380 722 248
Correspondent: The Trust Manager
Trustees: Carole Duggan; HSBC Trust Company (UK) Ltd.
CC Number: 1049193

Information available

Accounts were available from the Charity Commission.

The trust supports a range of major UK charities. In 2009/10 it had assets of £11 million, an income of £254,000. Grants were made to 53 organisations totalling £235,000.

Beneficiaries included: Mayhaw Animal Home, Seeability, Rushmoor Healthy Living, Chestnut Tree House Children's Hospice, and Brain and Spine Foundation (£5,000 each); British Red Cross, Headway, NSPCC, Redwings Horse Sanctuary and Victim Support (£4,300 each); and Unicef Gaza Children's Appeal, Unicef Sri Lanka Children's Appeal and Unicef Sudan Children's Appeal (£3,000 each).

Applications

In writing to the correspondent. The trust has previously stated that it has an ongoing programme of funding for specific charities and all its funds are fully committed.

The Anson Charitable Trust

General

£308,000 (2009/10)

Beneficial area

UK.

The Lilies, High Street, Weedon, Aylesbury, Buckinghamshire HP22 4NS
Email: lilies@btinternet.com
Correspondent: George Anson, Trustee
Trustees: George Anson; Kirsty Anson; Peter Nichols.
CC Number: 1111010

Information available

Accounts were on file at the Charity Commission.

The trust was set up in 2005 and in 2009/10 it held assets of £27,000. During the year the trust had an income of £335,000 entirely from donations and made 243 grants totalling £308,000. Some organisations received more than one grant.

Beneficiaries included: Prostrate Cancer (£16,000); Norfolk Hospice (£10,000); Royal Opera House (£9,500); Southbank (£8,000); ABF The Soldiers' Charity (£6,000); Buckinghamshire Agricultural Association, British Red Cross and Children in Need (£5,000 each); Living Paintings (£3,600); Oundle School Foundation (£3,500); Alzheimer's Trust, Mission to Seafarers and Anthony Nolan Trust (£3,000 each); Prince's Trust (£2,500); Starlight Children and Braille Chess Association (£2,000 each); Build Africa and Watts Gallery (£1,000 each); Water Aid (£600); and Capellania Anglica (£200).

Grants can also be made to individuals.

Applications

In writing to the correspondent.

The Appletree Trust

Disability, sickness, poverty

Beneficial area
UK and overseas, with a preference for Scotland and the north east Fife district.

The Royal Bank of Scotland plc, Trust and Estate Services, Eden Lakeside, Chester Business Park, Wrexham Road, Chester, CH4 9QT
Correspondent: The Royal Bank of Scotland plc, Administrator
Trustees: The Royal Bank of Scotland plc; Revd W McKane; Revd Dr J D Martin; Revd L R Brown.
SC Number: SC004851

Information available
The following entry is based on information filed with the Office of the Scottish Charity Regulator.

This trust was established in the will of the late William Brown Moncour in 1982 to relieve disability, sickness and poverty. The settlor recommended that Action Research for the Crippled Child, British Heart Foundation and National Society for Cancer Relief should receive funding from his trust, particularly for their work in the north east Fife district.

In 2009/10 the trust had an income of £27,000. No further information was available.

Previous grant beneficiaries have included: 1st St Andrews Boys Brigade, Alzheimer Scotland, Arthritis Care In Scotland, the Broomhouse Centre, Children's Hospice Association, Discovery Camps Trust, Home Start East Fife, Marie Curie Cancer Care, PDSA, Prince and Princess of Wales Hospice, RNID, the Salvation Army, Scottish Motor Neurone Disease Association and Scottish Spina Bifida Association.

Exclusions
No grants to individuals.

Applications
In writing to the correspondent. Trustees meet to consider grants in April.

The John Apthorp Charitable Trust

General
£57,000 (2009/10)

Beneficial area
UK, with a preference for Radlett.

c/o Myers Clark, Iveco House, Station Road, Watford WD17 1DL
Correspondent: Paul Shaw, Correspondent
Trustees: John Apthorp; Justin Apthorp.
CC Number: 289713

Information available
Accounts were received at the Charity Commission but not available to view online.

The trust was established, and is funded by, its eponymous settlor in 1983 with general charitable purposes.

In 2009/10 it had an income of £64 and a total expenditure of over £57,000. No list of beneficiaries was available to view.

Previous beneficiaries have included: Tay Ghillies Association (£55,000); Radlett Choral Society (£7,000); RAFT (£6,000); Radlett Arts Society Exhibition (£5,300); Radlett Cricket Club, St Mary's Church Trefriw Organ Fund and Battersby Junction Residents (£5,000 each) and The Radlett Society and Green Belt Association (£1,000).

Applications
Unsolicited appeals are not welcome and will not be answered. The trustees carry out their own research into prospective grant areas.

Archbishop of Wales' Fund for Children

Children
£41,000 (2009)

Beneficial area
Wales.

Church in Wales, 39 Cathedral Road, Cardiff CF11 9WH
Tel: 029 2034 8234
Email: awfc@churchinwales.org.uk
Correspondent: Karen Phillips, Administrator
Trustees: Revd J Michael Williams, Chair; Cheryl Beach; Ruth Forrester; Caroline Owen; James Tovey.
CC Number: 1102236

Information available
Accounts were available from the Charity Commission, but without a list of grants.

This fund was established in 2004. Its purpose is to support children in need and their families and local communities, through the work of organisations in this order of priority:
- those in the Dioceses of the Church in Wales
- those associated with other Christian bodies which are members of Cytun (Churches Together in Wales)
- other organisations working with children in Wales.

The fund has received substantial donations from Church in Wales congregations, particularly from collections at the annual Christingle services. In 2009 the trust had assets of £99,000 and an income of £54,000. Grants totalled £41,000.

Previous beneficiaries have included: the Bridge Mentoring Plus Scheme; Cardiff People First; Family Awareness Drug and Support; MENFA; Pontllanfraith, Brecon, Aberdare and Merthyr Tydfil Contact Centres; and Valley Kids. A number of church-based projects were also supported.

Applications
Application forms are available from the correspondent.

The John M Archer Charitable Trust

General

About £90,000 (2009/10)

Beneficial area

UK and overseas.

10 Broughton Place, Edinburgh
EH1 3RS
Correspondent: Mrs W Grant,
Secretary
Trustees: Gilbert B Archer; Mrs
A Morgan; Mrs W Grant; Mrs
C Fraser; Mrs I C Smith.
SC Number: SC010583

Information available

The entry is based on information
filed with the Office of the Scottish
Charity Regulator.

The trust supports local, national and
international organisations, in
particular those concerned with:

▶ prevention or relief of individuals
   in need
▶ welfare of people who are sick,
   distressed or afflicted
▶ alleviation of need
▶ advancement of education
▶ advancement of religious or
   missionary work
▶ advancement of medical or
   scientific research and discovery
▶ preservation of Scottish heritage
   and the advancement of associated
   cultural activities.

In 2009/10 the trust had an income of
£49,000. The trust generally gives
around £90,000 a year.

Previous beneficiaries have included
Cambodian Hospital Siem Reap for
Children, the Canonmills Baptist
Church, Castlebrae School Tutoring
Programme, Erskine Stewarts Melville
College – Arts Centre, Mercy Corps
Scotland, the Bobby Moore Fund,
Red Cross – Aberdeen Guest House
and Royal Liverpool University
Hospital – Macular Degeneration
Research.

Applications

In writing to the correspondent.

The Ardwick Trust

Jewish, welfare, general

£51,000 (2009/10)

Beneficial area

UK, Israel and the developing world.

c/o Knox Cropper, 24 Petworth Road,
Haslemere, Surrey GU27 2HR
Tel: 01428 652788
Correspondent: Janet Bloch, Trustee
Trustees: Janet Bloch; Dominic
Flynn; Miss Judith Portrait.
CC Number: 266981

Information available

Accounts were available from the
Charity Commission.

The trust supports Jewish welfare,
along with a wide band of non-Jewish
causes to include social welfare,
health, education (especially special
schools), older people, conservation
and the environment, child welfare,
disability and medical research.
Although the largest grants made by
the trust are to Jewish organisations,
the majority of recipients are non-
Jewish.

In 2009/10 it had assets of £2 million
and an income of over £565,000.
Grants were made to 250
organisations totalling £51,000. The
main beneficiary, as in previous years,
was Nightingale House which
received £5,000.

A further five organisations received
grants of £1,000 or over each: British
Friends of the Hebrew University –
Jerusalem and Weizmann UK
(£2,500); World Jewish Relief
(£2,000); and Jewish Care and
Norwood (£1,000 each).

Remaining beneficiaries were all for
£500, £200 or £100 each. Beneficiaries
included: Book Aid International,
Bowel Disease Research Foundation,
Combat Stress, Council for Christians
and Jews, Dystonia Society,
Elimination of Leukaemia Fund, Help
the Aged, Jubilee Sailing Trust,
Meningitis Trust, National Trust,
North London Hospice, Princess
Royal Trust for Carers, RNIB, Shaare
Zedek UK, Talking Newspaper
Association of the UK, Tree Aid,
YWCA and Whizz-Kids.

Exclusions

No grants to individuals.

Applications

In writing to the correspondent.

Common applicant mistakes

'Not reading the guidelines set out in
DSC publications or other references,
i.e. the Ardwick Trust does not
donate to individuals, only to
registered charities.'

The Argentarius Foundation

General

Around £109,000 (2009/10)

Beneficial area

UK.

Goodman & Co, 14 Basing Hill,
London NW11 8TH
Tel: 0208 458 0955
Email: philip@goodmanandco.com
Correspondent: Philip Goodman
Trustees: Emma Marbach; Judy
Jackson; Anna Josse.
CC Number: 1079980

Information available

Basic information taken from the
Charity Commission website.

Set up in 2000 with general charitable
purposes, in 2009/10 the trust had an
income of £20,000 and a total
expenditure of £109,000. We have no
information regarding the
beneficiaries of the charity.

Applications

In writing to the correspondent.

Armenian General Benevolent Union London Trust

Armenian education, culture and welfare

Around £13,000 to organisations (2009)

Beneficial area

UK and overseas.

51c Parkside, Wimbledon Common, London SW19 5NE
Correspondent: The Chair
Trustees: Dr Berge Azadian; Berge Setrakian; Hampar Chakardjian; Aris Atamian; Mrs Annie Kouyoumdjian; Mrs Noushig Yakoubian Setrakian; Assadour Guzelian; Mrs Anahid Manoukian; Mrs Arline Medazoumian; Ms Armine Afrikian.
CC Number: 282070

Information available

Accounts were on file at the Charity Commission.

The purpose of the trust is to advance education among Armenians, particularly those in the UK, and to promote the study of Armenian history, literature, language, culture and religion.

In 2009 it had assets of almost £3.5 million and an income of £219,000. Grants were made totalling £61,000 including £46,000 in 21 student loans and grants.

Grants categorised as 'Aid to Armenia, charitable and other grants' included those to the Royal Geographical Society of Armenia (£2,300) and the Armenian Community and Church Council of Great Britain (£500). A further £10,000 was given under the grant category 'London community organisations' to the Armenian General Benevolent Union – London Branch.

Exclusions

No support for projects of a commercial nature.

Applications

In writing to the correspondent. Applications are considered all year round.

The Armourers' and Brasiers' Gauntlet Trust

Materials science, general

£203,000 (2009/10)

Beneficial area

UK, with some preference for London.

Armourers' Hall, 81 Coleman Street, London EC2R 5BJ
Tel: 020 7374 4000
Fax: 020 7606 7481
Email: info@armourersandbrasiers.co.uk
Website: www.armourersandbrasiers.co.uk
Correspondent: The Secretary
Trustees: S G B Martin, Chair; Prof. William Bonfield; Sir Timothy Edwards Rugglesbrise; Prof. Sir C J Humphreys; Ven. C J H Wagstaff; Lord Lifford.
CC Number: 279204

Information available

Accounts were available from the Charity Commission.

The trust, which provides the charitable outlet for the Worshipful Company of Armourers and Brasiers, was set up in 1979. The objectives of the trust are:

- support for education and research in materials science and technology and for basic science in schools
- encouragement of the understanding and preservation of historic armour
- encouragement of the armourers' trade in the armed services
- encouragement of professional excellence in the training of young officers in the Royal Armoured Corps
- to consider appeals in the following overall categories: (i) community, social care and armed forces; (ii) children, youth and general education; medical and health; (iii) art, arms and armour; and (iv) Christian mission.

The trust funds are relatively modest; therefore applications for large sums should be avoided. Regular annual grants are not a policy of the trust at present, but charities can still apply for grants on an annual basis.

In 2009/10 the trust had assets of £5.8 million, an income of £340,000 and made grants totalling £248,000. Grants of £46,000 were made to 63 individuals and grants of over £202,500 were made to organisations.

Beneficiaries included: Dream Connection, Greenwich Toy & Leisure Library Association, Let's Face It, Morning Star Trust, Students Exploring Marriage Trust and Welch Ally UK Limited (£1,000 each); ALD Life, Baby Lifeline Limited, Batten Disease Family Association, Bowel & Cancer Research, Childhood Eye Cancer Trust, Kids N' Action, Global Bengali Mohila Sharnity, Globetown Community Association, Holiday Endeavour for Lone Parents, Root Development Agency, The F N Charrington Tower Hamlets Mission, The Pavement, The Sequal Trust, The Seventy4 Foundation, The Thomas Morley Trust, Tower Hamlets Friends & Neighbours, Parents for the Early Intervention of Autism in Children, React, Special Toys Educational Postal Service, St Francis' Children's Society, Straight Talking Peer Education, The Child Accident Prevention Trust, The Child Care Action Trust, The Seeing Ear Limited, The Special Yoga Centre and The Trinity Sailing Trust (£500 each).

Exclusions

In general grants are not made to:

- organisations or groups which are not registered charities
- individuals (including sponsorship)
- organisations or groups whose main object is to fund or support other charitable bodies
- organisations or groups which are in direct relief of any reduction of financial support from public funds
- charities with a turnover of over £1 million

- charities which spend over 10% of their income on fundraising activities
- charities whose accounts disclose substantial financial reserves
- political or commercial appeals.

Nor towards general maintenance, repair or restoration of buildings, including ecclesiastical buildings, unless there is a long standing connection with the Armourers' and Brasiers' Company or unless of outstanding importance to the national heritage.

Applications
In writing to the correspondent, with a copy of the latest annual report and audited accounts. Applications are considered quarterly.

Common applicant mistakes
'They do not read the trust's website to confirm eligibility.'

The Artemis Charitable Trust

Psychotherapy, parent education, and related activities

£61,000 (2010)

Beneficial area
UK.

Brook House, Quay Meadow, Bosham, West Sussex PO18 8LY
Tel: 01243 573475
Correspondent: Richard Evans, Trustee
Trustees: R W Evans; D S Bergin; W A Evans; D J Evans; M W Evans.
CC Number: 291328

Information available
Accounts were available from the Charity Commission.

The trust was set up in 1985, its 2005 trustees' report states: 'The policy of the trust has continued to be the making of grants to aid the provision of counselling, psychotherapy, parenting, human relationship training and related activities.'

In 2010 it had assets of £1.5 million and an income of over £47,000.

Grants totalled £61,000. Beneficiaries were: Voluntary Sector Mental Health Providers Forum (£49,000); Relate (£7,000); Royal African Society (£4,000); and Core System Trust (£560).

Exclusions
Individuals or organisations which are not registered charities.

Applications
Applicants should be aware that most of the trust's funds are committed to a number of major ongoing projects and that spare funds available to meet new applications are very limited.

The Ove Arup Foundation

Construction – education and research

£184,000 (2009/10)

Beneficial area
Unrestricted.

c/o 13 Fitzroy Street, London W1T 4BQ
Tel: 020 7755 3184
Website: www.theovearupfoundation. com
Correspondent: Peter Klyhn, Ove Arup & Partners
Trustees: R B Haryott, Chair; A Chan; F Cousins; M Glover; J Kennedy; M Shears; D Michael; R T M Hill; C Cole; R Hough; P Dilley.
CC Number: 328138

Information available
Accounts were available from the Charity Commission.

The trust was established in 1989 with the principal objective of supporting education in matters associated with the built environment, including construction-related academic research. The trustees are appointed by the board of the Ove Arup Partnership. It gives grants for research and projects, including start-up and feasibility costs.

In 2009/10 the foundation had assets of £2.7 million and an income of

£239,000. Grants were made to 13 organisations totalling £184,000.

Beneficiaries included: London School of Economics (£45,000); Royal Academy of Engineering and the University of Edinburgh (£40,000 each); Royal College of Art (£12,000); Institute of Civil Engineers (£10,500); University of South Wales (£10,000); Constructionarium (£8,000); Midlands Architecture and the Design Environment (£7,000); College of Estate Management (£5,000); and University of Warwick Student Union (£500).

Exclusions
No grants to individuals, including students.

Applications
In writing to the correspondent, with brief supporting financial information. Trustees meet quarterly to consider applications (March, June, September and December).

The AS Charitable Trust

Christian, development, social concern

£31,000 (2008/09)

Beneficial area
UK and developing countries.

Bix Bottom Farm, Henley-on-Thames, Oxfordshire RG9 6BH
Correspondent: Roy Calvocoressi
Trustees: Roy Calvocoressi; Mrs Caroline Eady; George Calvocoressi; Simon Sampson.
CC Number: 242190

Information available
The most recent accounts available from the Charity Commission were for 2008/09.

This trust makes grants in particular to projects which combine the advancement of the Christian religion, with Christian lay leadership, with third world development, with peacemaking and reconciliation or with other areas of social concern. In the accounts for 2008/09 the trustees made donations to charities known to them and whose aims they support.

In 2008/09 the trust had assets of £6 million, an income of £266,000 and made grants totalling £31,000.

Beneficiaries receiving grants of £1,000 or more included: GRACE (£16,000 in 11 gifts); Christian International Peace Service (£12,000 in 13 gifts); Epic Arts and Eton College (£1,000 each).

Exclusions

Grants to individuals or large charities are very rare. Such applications are discouraged.

Applications

In writing to the correspondent.

Ashburnham Thanksgiving Trust

Christian

£89,000 to organisations (2009/10)

Beneficial area

UK and worldwide.

Agmerhurst House, Ashburnham, Battle, East Sussex TN33 9NB
Correspondent: The Charity Secretary
Trustees: Mrs M Bickersteth; E R Bickersteth; R D Bickersteth; Mrs R F Dowdy.
CC Number: 249109

Information available

Full accounts were on file at the Charity Commission.

The trust supports a wide range of Christian mission organisations and other Christian organisations which are known to the trustees, in the UK and worldwide. Individuals are also supported.

In 2009/10 the trust had assets of £5.6 million and an income of £174,000. Grants totalled £121,000, of which £89,000 was distributed in grants to 129 organisations. Further monies were distributed in restricted grants and grants to individuals.

There were 28 grants made of £1,000 or more. Beneficiaries included: New

Destiny Trust (£5,100); Genesis Arts Trust (£4,000); Open Doors (£3,000); Prison Fellowship (£2,800); Ashburnham Christian Trust (£2,600); Interserve (£2,000); Calvary Chapel – Hastings (£1,900); Micah Trust (£1,300); and Two Tim Two Trust and RZIM Zacharias Trust (£1,000 each).

Other beneficiaries included: St Luke's Hospital for Clergy (£800); Advantage Africa (£725); London City Mission (£600); SGM Lifewords (£500); Grace Publishing (£324); Cutting Edge Ministries (£200); Arts Centre Group (£180); and Crusade for World Revival (£104).

Exclusions

No grants for buildings.

Applications

The trust has stated that its funds are fully committed to current beneficiaries. Unfortunately, it receives far more applications than it is able to deal with.

A J H Ashby Will Trust

Wildlife, heritage, education and children

£78,000 (2009/10)

Beneficial area

UK, especially Lea Valley area of Hertfordshire.

HSBC Trust Company (UK) Ltd, Trust Services, Norwich House, Nelson Gate, Commercial Road, Southampton SO15 1GX
Tel: 023 8072 2243
Correspondent: Sandra Hill, Trust Manager
Trustee: HSBC Trust Company (UK) Ltd.
CC Number: 803291

Information available

Accounts were available from the Charity Commission.

The trust was established in 1990 to support wildlife throughout the UK, particularly birds, as well as heritage, education projects and young people

specifically in the Lea Valley area of Hertfordshire.

In 2009/10 the trust had an income of £854,000. There were eight grants made totalling £78,000.

Beneficiaries included: RSPB (£70,000 in five grants); Wormley Cricket Club (£3,000); West Lea School (£2,500); and Barking Boxing Club (£2,800).

Exclusions

No grants to individuals or students.

Applications

In writing to the correspondent.

The Ashley Family Foundation

Art and design, higher education, local projects in mid-rural Wales

£383,000 (2009/10)

Beneficial area

Mostly Wales, other areas considered.

Ladywell House, Park Street, Newtown SY16 1JB
Tel: 01686 610648
Email: lafwales@tiscali.co.uk
Website: www. ashleyfamilyfoundation.org.uk/
Correspondent: Jane Ashley, Trustee
Trustees: Jane Ashley; Prof. Susan Golombok; Martyn C Gowar; Emma Shuckburgh; Prof. Oriana Baddeley; Prof. Sue Timney; Mike Hodgson.
CC Number: 288099

Information available

Accounts were available from the Charity Commission.

The foundation was set up in 1986 in memory of Laura Ashley by her family. It has a strong commitment to fine and applied arts and design and also to Wales, particularly Powys, where the Ashley business was first established. The trustees plan to widen the geographical area within Wales and this is not to the exclusion of English projects which fall within the foundation's criteria for grant-making.

Awards are mainly one-off and for a period of up to three years.

In 2009/10 the foundation had assets of £10.7 million, an income of £302,000 and made grants totalling £383,000.

Beneficiaries included: Dylan Thomas Prize (£23,000); National Benevolent Fund for the Aged (£14,700); Garden Organic (£13,000): New Pathways and Age Concern Ceredigion (£10,000 each); Textprint (£7,000); Powys Mental Health Alliance (£5,000); Harvest Trust (£3,000); and Screen at Hay (£1,000).

Exclusions

The foundation does not fund individuals, business ventures, overseas projects, projects falling within the field of religion or retrospective work.

Applications

The Ashley Family Foundation will consider requests from charities, unincorporated organisations and community groups with a constitution or terms of reference and a charitable purpose. It will consider requests for: core funding, including salaries and overheads. Requests that are below £10,000 are favoured. The trust states that 'decisions are based upon benefit and value and each project is considered on its own merit. Final decisions are at the discretion of the trustees.' Potential applicants are encouraged to check the foundation's website before submitting an application. The website states:

> Due to the economic downturn we are receiving an unprecedented increase in requests. We are therefore changing our long held policy of replying to all requests. If you have submitted a stage one proposal and have not heard within eight weeks please assume you have been unsuccessful.

The Ashworth Charitable Trust

Welfare

£110,000 to organisations
(2010/11)

Beneficial area

UK and worldwide, with some preference for certain specific needs in Honiton, Ottery St Mary, Sidmouth and Wonford Green surgery, Exeter.

Foot Anstey, Senate Court, Southernhay Gardens, Exeter EX1 1NT
Tel: 01392 411221
Fax: 01392 685220
Email: ashworthtrust@btinternet.com
Website: www.ashworthtrust.org
Correspondent: Mrs G Towner
Trustees: Mr C F Bennett, Chair; Mrs K A Gray; Mrs H Rouhipour; Mrs S Rouhipour.
CC Number: 1045492

Information available

Accounts were available from the Charity Commission; the trust also has a useful website.

The trust was founded by Mrs C E Crabtree in 1995. The trust currently considers applications for and makes grants as appropriate to:

- Ironbridge Gorge Museum Trust
- people living in the areas covered by the medical practices and social services in Honiton, Ottery St Mary, Sidmouth and Wonford Green surgery, Exeter. Such grants are to be paid for particularly acute needs
- humanitarian projects either to other charities or to individuals.

The trust's website states that: 'for the most part, the trust looks to fund projects, not core funding'.

In 2010/11 the trust had assets of £3.7 million and an income of £127,000. Grants were made to 46 organisations totalling £110,000.

The largest grants were for £10,000 each and went to Hospiscare and Ironbridge Gorge Museum Trust.

Other grants included: Age UK, World in Need and West Suffolk Voluntary Association for the Blind (£3,000 each); Freedom Social Projects, Esther Benjamins Trust and Sunseed Tanzania Trust (£2,500 each); Acid Survivors Trust International and Home Start Exeter (£2,000 each); Community, Equality, Disability Action (£1,500); Widows' Rights International and Aberdare

Children's Contact Centre (£1,000 each); and Living Water Satisfies (£750).

A further £3,000 was given to 17 individuals from the Doctors' and Social Services Fund.

Please note: these grant examples are not necessarily indicative of future giving.

Exclusions

No grants for:

- research-based charities
- individuals
- non-UK registered charities
- charities with a turnover of more than £1 million
- charities with disproportionately large reserves, unless there is an exceptional reason. In such a case, we will require an explanation
- animal charities
- UK hospices – the trustees already contribute to one hospice of their choice
- heritage charities such as National Trust or other organisations whose aim is the preservation of a building, museum, library and so on (with the exception of the Ironbridge Gorge Museum)
- the promotion of religious or political activities.

Applications

In writing to the correspondent. There is no application form but applications should include:

- registered charity number
- an email address
- a recent set of accounts
- a brief (not more than two pages) analysis of the main objectives of your organisation and any particular project for which funding is required.

Please do not send brochures, DVDs, books, annual reviews or any other bulky promotional material. If we need more information we will contact you.

The trustees meet twice a year in May and November. Applications should be submitted by the middle of March or the middle of September respectively. Please note that we are unable to enter into any discussions regarding funding, successful or otherwise, as we have no funds designated for this purpose.

The Ian Askew Charitable Trust

General

£73,000 (2009/10)

Beneficial area

UK, with a preference for Sussex.

c/o Baker Tilly, 18 Mount Ephraim Road, Tunbridge Wells, Kent TN1 1ED
Correspondent: The Trustees
Trustees: J R Hecks, Chair; Mrs C Pengelley; R A R Askew; J B Rank; R P G Lewis.
CC Number: 264515

Information available

Accounts were available from the Charity Commission.

Grants are given to a wide variety of charitable bodies throughout the country with a preference for those connected with the county of Sussex.

In 2009/10 the trust had assets of £14 million and an income of £342,000. Grants to 159 charitable organisations totalled £92,000.

The majority of grants to organisations were for £500 or less, with 4 for £1,000 or more. Beneficiaries included: Save and Prosper (£1,000); Sussex Historic Churches Association (£750); Action for Kids Street Bruie, Brook Hospital for Animals, Church Urban Fund, Harambee Schools Kenya, National Kidney Federation and Ringmer District Youth Association (£500 each); and National Trust Scotland and the Royal Academy Trust (£25).

In addition to the above mentioned donations the trust maintains the woodlands at Plashett Estate, East Sussex, the main part of which is designated as a site of special and scientific interest. The woodlands are used principally for educational purposes.

Applications

In writing to the correspondent. Applications are considered every other month.

The Association of Colleges Charitable Trust

Further education colleges

£253,000 (2009/10)

Beneficial area

UK.

2–6 Stedham Place, London WC1A 1HU
Website: www.aoc.co.uk
Correspondent: The Trust Manager
Trustees: Alice Thiagaraj; Peter Brophy; David Forrester; John Bingham; Martin Doel; Richard Eve.
CC Number: 1040631

Information available

Accounts were on file at the Charity Commission.

The Association of Colleges was created in 1996 as the single voice to promote the interests of further education colleges in England and Wales. It is responsible for administering two programmes, the largest of these is the Beacon Awards, which provide monetary grants to specific initiatives within further education colleges. The other programme that operates within the trust is the AoC Gold Awards.

Established in 1994, the Beacon Awards recognise and promote the interdependence of further education colleges and business, and professional and voluntary sector organisations to their mutual advantage. The aim of the programme is to highlight the breadth and quality of education in colleges throughout the UK and increase understanding of colleges' contribution to UK educational skills policy and economic and social development.

The awards:
- recognise imaginative and exemplary teaching and learning practice in colleges
- draw attention to provision which encourages and supports learners to approach challenges positively and creatively
- support learning and continuous improvement through the dissemination of award-bearing practice.

Applications may be for a programme, course, or project or for some other aspect of college provision – teaching, learning, guidance or support. To be eligible, initiatives should show evidence of imaginative yet sustainable teaching and learning practice or other relevant provision. It must also fulfil the following criteria:
- it must meet the specific requirements set out by the sponsors of the particular award (see relevant page in the Awards section of the Prospectus)
- it must be subject to evaluation/ quality assurance to influence the continuing development of the initiative
- it must have been running for at least one academic session before the deadline for applications
- it must have features which actively promote exemplary teaching and learning
- it must be of benefit to one or more groups of students or trainees who will be identified and described in the application
- it must have wider relevance and applicability making it of value to other colleges as an example of good practice and innovation.

Each award has separate criteria in the interests of the area of work of the sponsor. They range from broad educational development to the promotion of particular courses or subjects, covering most aspects of further education.

The other scheme operated by the trust is the AoC Gold Awards for Further Education Alumni, which reward former members of further education colleges who have since excelled in their chosen field or profession.

In 2009/10 the trust's assets stood at £150,000, with an income of £318,000. Charitable activities for the year amounted to £253,000, of which the majority was given in Beacon Awards, with around £5,000 given through Gold Awards.

Exclusions

Grants are not made to individuals.

Applications

See the trust's website for further information.

Common applicant mistakes

'Individual students are applying – funding is for leadership teams in further education colleges. College applicants have not addressed all the Beacon Award or sponsor's criteria.'

The Astor Foundation

Medical research, general

£81,000 (2009/10)

Beneficial area

UK.

PO Box 3096, Marlborough, Wiltshire SN8 3WP
Email: astor.foundation@virgin.net
Correspondent: Lisa Rothwell-Orr, Secretary
Trustees: R H Astor, Chair; the Hon. Tania Astor; Lord Latymer; C Astor; Dr H Swanton; Prof J Cunningham.
CC Number: 225708

Information available

Accounts were on file at the Charity Commission. The following extract is taken from the trust's 2009/10 accounts:

> The primary object of the foundation is medical research in its widest sense, favouring research on a broad front rather than in specialised fields. For guidance, this might include general medical equipment or equipment for use in research, or grants to cover travelling and subsistence expenses for doctors and students studying abroad.
>
> In general, the foundation gives preference to giving assistance with the launching and initial stages of new projects and filling in gaps or shortfalls.
>
> In addition to its medical connection, historically the foundation has also supported initiatives for children and youth groups, the disabled, the countryside, the arts, sport, carers groups and animal welfare.

In 2009/10 the foundation had assets of £3.3 million and an income of £104,000. Grants were made to 68 organisations totalling just over £81,000.

Beneficiaries included: Friends of UCLH (£5,000); Independence at Home (£4,500); Help the Hospices (£4,000); RNLI (£3,000);UCL Medical School (£2,000); Samantha Dickson Brain Tumour Trust (£1,500); the Ulysses Trust (£1,000); Working Families (£500); and Red Squirrel Survival Trust (£250).

Exclusions

No grants to individuals or towards salaries. Grants are given to registered charities only.

Applications

There are no deadline dates or application forms. Applications should be in writing to the correspondent and must include accounts and an annual report if available.

The trustees meet twice yearly, usually in October and April. If the appeal arrives too late for one meeting it will automatically be carried over for consideration at the following meeting. An acknowledgement will be sent on receipt of an appeal. No further communication will be entered into unless the trustees raise any queries regarding the appeal, or unless the appeal is subsequently successful.

Common applicant mistakes

'Not putting sufficient postage on their applications.'

The Astor of Hever Trust

Youth, medical research, education

£27,000 (2009/10)

Beneficial area

UK and worldwide, with a preference for Kent and the Grampian region of Scotland.

Frenchstreet House, Westerham, Kent TN16 1PW
Tel: 01959 565070
Correspondent: Gill Willis, Administrator
Trustees: John Jacob, Third Baron Astor of Hever; Hon. Philip D P Astor; Hon. Camilla Astor.
CC Number: 264134

Information available

Accounts were on file at the Charity Commission.

The trust gives grants UK-wide and internationally. It states that there is a preference for Kent and the Grampian region of Scotland, although the preference for Kent is much stronger.

When Gavin Astor, second Baron Astor of Hever, founded the trust in 1955, its main areas of support were arts, medicine, religion, education, conservation, youth and sport. Reflecting the settlor's wishes, the trust makes grants to local youth organisations, medical research and educational programmes. Most beneficiaries are UK-wide charities or a local branch.

In 2009/10 the trust had assets of £1 million and an income of £37,000. Grants were made to 78 organisations totalling £27,000.

The largest grants went to: SBS Association (£2,000); and Rochester Cathedral Trust and Migvie Church (£1,000 each).

Grants of less than £1,000 went to: Home in Zimbabwe, Game and Wildlife Conservation Trust and Countryside Foundation for Education (CFE) (£500 each); Belmont Abbey Organ Trust (£300); Dogs for the Disabled and Luke Ree-Pulley Charitable Trust (£250 each); Battle of Britain Memorial Trust and Kids Company (£200 each); British Youth Opera (£150); and Breakthrough Breast Cancer (Too Many Women) (£50).

Exclusions

No grants to individuals.

Applications

In writing to the correspondent. Trustees meet twice each year. Unsuccessful applications are not acknowledged.

The Aurelius Charitable Trust

Conservation of culture and the humanities

£74,000 (2009/10)

Beneficial area

UK.

Briarsmead, Old Road, Buckland, Betchworth, Surrey RH3 7DU
Tel: 01737 842186
Email: philip.haynes@tiscali.co.uk
Correspondent: P E Haynes, Trustee
Trustees: W J Wallis; P E Haynes.
CC Number: 271333

Information available

Accounts were on file at the Charity Commission.

During the settlor's lifetime, the income of the trust was distributed broadly to reflect his interests in the conservation of culture inherited from the past, and the dissemination of knowledge, particularly in the humanities field. Since the settlor's death in April 1994, the trustees have continued with this policy.

Donations are preferred to be for seed-corn or completion funding not otherwise available. They are usually one-off and range from £500 to £3,000.

In 2009/10 the trust had assets of £2.1 million, which generated an income of £70,000. Donations were made to 26 organisations totalling £74,000.

Beneficiaries included: Old Royal Naval College, Royal Botanic Gardens – Kew and the British Academy (£5,000 each); the Carpet Museum Trust and English National Opera (£3,000 each); Friends of the Moot Hall, Maldon (£2,000); Friends of Herefordshire Museums and Arts (£1,500); the Quaker Tapestry at Kendal Ltd (£1,000); and St Margaret of Antioch (£600).

Exclusions

No grants to individuals.

Applications

In writing to the correspondent. Donations are generally made on the recommendation of the trust's board of advisors. Unsolicited applications will only be responded to if an sae is included. Trustees meet twice a year.

Common applicant mistakes

'They have not identified we are a conservation charity. Too many seem to fail to research the charities they approach.'

The Avenue Charitable Trust

General

£384,000 (2009/10)

Beneficial area

Worldwide.

Sayers Butterworth, 18 Bentinck Street, London W1M 5RL
Tel: 020 7935 8504
Correspondent: Susan Simmons
Trustees: R D L Astor; Hon. Mrs B A Astor; G W B Todd.
CC Number: 264804

Information available

Accounts were available from the Charity Commission.

In 2009/10 the trust assets declined to £45,500 (£297,000 in 2008/09). Although income from investments fell correspondingly a substantial donation of £150,000 brought total income for the year to £153,000. There were 10 grants made to organisations amounting to £384,000.

Beneficiaries included: Delta Trust (£225,000); Neuro-Psychoanalysis Fund (£65,000); David Astor Journalism Award Trust (£50,000); Adonis Mosat Project (£25,000); Living Landscape Project (£10,000); Adam von Trott Memorial Appeal (£5,000); Amnesty International, Cheek By Jowl and Koestler Trust (£1,000 each); and Prisoners Abroad (£500).

Applications

The trust has previously stated that all available income is now committed to existing beneficiaries.

Harry Bacon Foundation

Medical, animal welfare

£53,000 (2009/10)

Beneficial area

UK.

Natwest Bank Plc, Trustee Department, 5th Floor, Trinity Quay 2, Avon Street, Bristol BS2 0PT
Tel: 0117 940 3283
Correspondent: The Trust Manager
Trustee: NatWest Bank Plc.
CC Number: 1056500

Information available

Accounts were available from the Charity Commission.

In 2009/10 the trust had assets of £192,000, an income of £44,000 and made grants totalling £53,000.

Grants of £6,600 were given to the following eight charities: RNLI, Imperial Cancer Research, British Heart Foundation, PDSA, Parkinson's Disease Society, the Arthritis and Rheumatism Council for Research, Donkey Sanctuary and World Horse Welfare.

Applications

In writing to the correspondent. The trustees meet regularly to consider applications.

The BACTA Charitable Trust

General

£43,000 (2009/10)

Beneficial area

UK.

Alders House, 133 Aldersgate Street, London EC1A 4JA
Tel: 020 7726 9826
Email: info@bacta.org.uk
Website: www.bacta.org.uk
Correspondent: The Clerk to the Trustees
Trustees: J Stergides; M Horwood; J Thomas; S Hawkins; J Oversby-

Powell; A Boulton; P Weir; J Godden; D Petrie; G Stergides.

CC Number: 328668

Information available

Accounts were on file at the Charity Commission.

The trust only supports charities recommended by the British Amusement Catering Trade Association (BACTA) members.

In 2009/10 the trust had assets of £81,000 and an income of £49,000. Grants were made to five organisations totalling £43,000. The main beneficiary was Macmillan (£38,000).

Other grants went to: Rainbow Children's Hospice and Motor Neurone Disease Association (£2,000 each); Birmingham Sands and Child Bereavement Charity (£1,000 each).

Exclusions

No grants for overseas charities or religious purposes.

Applications

In writing to the correspondent via a BACTA member.

The Scott Bader Commonwealth Ltd

General, international

£142,000 (2010)

Beneficial area

UK, Eire, France, South Africa, Croatia, Dubai, USA, Czech Republic, Sweden, Spain.

The Scott Bader Commonwealth Limited, Wollaston Hall, Wellingborough, Northamptonshire NN29 7RL

Tel: 01933 666755

Fax: 01933 666608

Email: commonwealth_office@ scottbader.com

Website: www.scottbader.com/

Correspondent: Sue Carter, Secretary

Trustees: The Board of Management: Heather Puddephatt; Richard Stillwell; Richard Stillwell; Jacquie Findlay; Syed Omar Hayat; Anne

Atkinson-Clark; Mary Hilary Pinder; Julie Rodgers; John Wojakowsk and Charles Scott.

CC Number: 206391

Information available

Accounts were on file at the Charity Commission.

The charity fulfils its objects by making grants to charitable organisations around the world whose purposes are to help young/ disadvantaged people who suffer deprivation and discrimination or are poor, homeless, vulnerable children, women and minority communities and people affected by poverty, hunger and disease.

In 2010 the charity has assets of £45 million, an income of £175,000 and made grants totalling £142,000. The Global Charity Fund is divided into two categories:

Local Funds

The money in this category is shared between the Companies in the Scott Bader Group, for them to support Charities where they are located (UK, Eire, France, South Africa, Dubai, Croatia, USA, Czech Republic, Sweden, Spain). Some of the grants made in 2010 were:

- UK: donations ranging from £1,000–£6,000 were made in support of the following six charities – Kids Out, Plunket Foundation, The Kings Arms Project, June & Brian Cox Educational Trust, Volunteer Reading Help and Ro Ro Sailing Project
- France: donations ranging from £900–£2,500 were made to St Joseph De Cluny (in Haiti, Kuborroto, Zinder and Momambique) and Ecole FG de Hem
- Croatia: donations ranging from £1,200–£1,500 were made to SOS Children's Village Croatia, Croatian Association for the Blind, PUZ, SNAGA and Firefly
- Sweden: Handikappidrott Falkenberg who provide sport programmes for the disabled
- Czech Republic: School of Hearing for Handicapped Children in Liberec

- Spain: the decision was made in 2010 to use their allocation in support of the Haiti disaster
- South Africa: donations ranging from £1,500–£1,800 SOS Children's Village, Embocraft, Fulton School for the Deaf, Feed the Babies Fund and 100 Hills Community Helpers
- USA: donations of £200 each were made to support the work of Urban Community School, Providence House, GWRC Boy Scouts of America, The Flying House Farms and KIVA.
- Dubai: donations ranging from £2,000–£4,500 were made to support the work of four charities – Empacs, St Gregorios Balagram, Yusuf Meherally Centre and Rashi Paediatric Therapy Centre.

Central Fund

Currently this fund is to support two large community based environmental/educational projects to the value of £25,000 each. In 2010, LHC Foundation Trust I Care- South Africa and Concern Worldwide- Pakistan received the grants from this fund. The process and deadline for applications is posted on the website at the beginning of each year.

Exclusions

No support for charities concerned with the well-being of animals, individuals in need or organisations sending volunteers abroad. It does not respond to general appeals or support the larger well-established national charities. It does not provide grants for medical research. It does not make up deficits already incurred, or support the arts, museums, travel/ adventure, sports clubs or the construction, renovation or maintenance of buildings.

Applications

In writing or by email to the correspondent. Trustees meet in February, May, September and November.

The Bagri Foundation

General

£39,000 to organisations and individuals (2009/10)

Beneficial area

Worldwide.

80 Cannon Street, London EC4N 6EJ
Tel: 020 7280 0089
Correspondent: M C Thompson, Secretary
Trustees: Lord Bagri; Hon. A Bagri; Lady Bagri.
CC Number: 1000219

Information available

Accounts were available from the Charity Commission, but without a list of grants.

This foundation was set up in 1990 with general charitable purposes. In 2009/10 it had assets of £2.1 million and an income of £61,000. During the year grants were made to organisations and individuals totalling £39,000.

In previous years the majority of the foundation's charitable expenditure was given to organisations. No other information is given in its report and accounts.

Applications

In writing to the correspondent.

The Baker Charitable Trust

Mainly Jewish, older people, sickness and disability, medical research

£44,000 (2009/10)

Beneficial area

UK and overseas.

16 Sheldon Avenue, Highgate, London N6 4JT
Tel: 020 8340 5970
Correspondent: Dr Harvey Baker, Trustee

Trustees: Dr Harvey Baker; Dr Adrienne Baker.
CC Number: 273629

Information available

Accounts were available from the Charity Commission, but without a grants list.

The trust makes grants to organisations that support people who are elderly, have a chronic sickness or disability and people who have had limited educational opportunity. The trust also supports medical research related to the above groups. There is a preference for Jewish organisations.

In 2009/10 it had assets of £1.1 million and an income of £44,000. Grants to 27 organisations totalled £44,000. A full list of grants was not included in the accounts received at the Charity Commission although they do detail two grants of over £10,000 which were: Jewish Care (£12,500); and Norwood (£10,000).

Previous beneficiaries have included: British Council Shaare Zedek Medical Centre, Chai Cancer Care, Community Security Trust, Disabled Living Foundation, Friends of Magen David Adom in Great Britain, Hillel Foundation, Institute of Jewish Policy Research, Jewish Women's Aid, Marie Curie Cancer Care, National Society for Epilepsy, United Jewish Israel Appeal, St John's Hospice, United Synagogue, Winged Fellowship and World Jewish Relief.

Exclusions

No grants to individuals or non-registered charities.

Applications

In writing to the correspondent. The trustees meet to consider applications in January, April, July and October.

Common applicant mistakes

'Very few mistakes [are made by applicants].'

The Andrew Balint Charitable Trust

General charitable causes, Jewish charities

£56,000 (2010/11)

Beneficial area

UK; Israel; Hungary.

Carter Backer Winter, Enterprise House, 21 Buckle Street, London E1 8NN
Tel: 020 7309 3800
Trustees: Dr Gabriel Balint-Kurti; Mrs Angela Balint; Mr Roy Balint-Kurti; Mr Daniel Balint-Kurti.
CC Number: 273691

Information available

Accounts were available from the Charity Commission.

This trust gives to charitable organisations to assist with general causes in the UK and abroad. The 2010/11 accounts state:

> The Andrew Balint Charitable Trust, The George Balint Charitable Trust, The Paul Charitable Trust and the Trust for Former Employees of Balint Companies are jointly administered. They have some trustees in common and are independent in other matters.

In 2010/11 the trust held assets of £1.7 million and had an income of £52,000. Grants totalled £56,000.

Beneficiaries included: Nightingale House (£20,000); Hungarian Senior Citizens (£7,700); Former Employee Trust (£6,500); Toth – Gabor (£5,400); American Jewish Joint Distribution Committee (£5,000); United Jewish Israel Appeal (£2,600); and Goldschein Joseph (£1,000).

A further 36 grants of less than £1,000 were also made.

Applications

In writing to the correspondent.

The George Balint Charitable Trust

General, education, poverty relief and Jewish

Around £48,000 (2010–11)

Beneficial area

UK, Israel, Hungary.

Carter Backer Winter, Enterprise House, 21 Buckle Street, London E1 8NN
Tel: 0207 309 3800
Correspondent: Mr David Kramer
Trustees: Dr Andrew Balint; Mr George Rothschild; Mrs Marion Balint-Farkas.
CC Number: 267482

Information available

Basic information was available from the Charity Commission website.

In the 2010–11 year the trust had an income of £19,000 derived from investments. Total expenditure was £56,000. No further information was available.

In the past this trust has donated to general charitable organisations, this has included medical, educational and Jewish causes.

Previous beneficiaries include: United Jewish Israel Appeal (£15,000); Hungarian Senior Citizens (£10,200); Former Employees Trust (£8,500); Neviot Olam Institution and British Friends of Bar Ilan University (£2,000 each); Imperial College London (£1,000); Norwood: Children and Families First (£750); and Marie Curie Cancer Care (£200).

The 2008–9 accounts note:

> The George Balint Charitable Trust, the Paul Balint Charitable Trust and The Charitable Trust for Former Employees of Balint Companies operate from the same premises and are jointly administered. They have some trustees in common and are independent in all other matters.

Applications

In writing to the correspondent.

The Paul Balint Charitable Trust

General charitable purposes

£48,000

Beneficial area

UK; Hungary; Israel.

15 Portland Court, 101 Hendon Lane, London N3 3SH
Tel: 020 8346 1266
Correspondent: Dr Andrew Balint, Administrator
Trustees: Dr Andrew Balint; Dr Gabriel Balint-Kurti; Dr Marc Balint; Mr Paul Balint.
CC Number: 273690

Information available

Basic information was available from the Charity Commission website.

The trust was founded in 1977 and benefits organisations of general charitable purposes. It has helped a wide variety of organisations including those engaged in medical research, education, assisting the elderly and relieving poverty.

The trust makes grants to organisations operating in the UK, Israel and Hungary. In the year ending April 2011 the trust had an income of £3,500 and a total expenditure of £52,000. No further information was available.

Applications

In writing to the correspondent.

Balmain Charitable Trust

General

£109,000 (2009/10)

Beneficial area

UK.

c/o Rutter and Alhusen, 2 Longmead, Shaftesbury, Dorset SP7 8PL
Correspondent: Trust Administrator
Trustees: Paul G Eaton; Andrew B Tappin; Donald S Balmain; Iain D Balmain; Leonora D Balmain; Charles A G Wells.
CC Number: 1079972

Information available

Accounts were on file at the Charity Commission.

Registered with the Charity Commission in March 2000, in 2009/10 the trust had assets of £2.4 million, an income of £104,000 and made 48 grants totalling £109,000.

Beneficiaries included: British Red Cross and Oxfam (£8,000 each); Great Bustard Group (£6,000); Second Chance (£5,200); Royal Opera House Foundation (£5,000); Great Ormond Street Hospital (£4,000); Wiltshire Wildlife Trust and the National Art Collections Fund (£3,000 each); Crisis, Help for Heroes and the National Trust (£2,000 each); Age Concern, Cerebra, Foxglove Covert and Soil Association (£1,000 each); and the Royal Academy (£190).

Many of the beneficiaries are supported year after year.

Applications

In writing to the correspondent.

The Balney Charitable Trust

Preservation, conservation, welfare, service charities

£78,000 (2009/10)

Beneficial area

UK, with a preference for north Buckinghamshire and north Bedfordshire.

The Chicheley Estate, Bartlemas Office, Paveham, Bedford MK43 7PF
Tel: 01234 823663
Correspondent: Miss Helen Chapman, Correspondent
Trustees: Maj. J G B Chester; R Ruck-Keene; Ms J Heaton.
CC Number: 288575

Information available

Accounts were on file at the Charity Commission.

The objectives of the trust as stated in its accounts as follows:

- the furtherance of any religious and charitable purposes in connection with the parishes of Chicheley, North Crawley and the SCAN Group i.e. Sherington, Astwood, Hardmead and churches with a Chester family connection
- the provision of housing for persons in need
- agriculture, forestry and armed service charities
- care of older people and the sick and disabled from the Chicheley area
- other charitable purposes.

In 2009/10 the trust had assets of £800,000 and an income of £91,000. Direct charitable expenditure totalled £78,000.

The trust makes regular donations each year by standing order ranging from £25 to £1,000. A list of beneficiaries was not included in this year's accounts. However, previous beneficiaries included: Gurkha Welfare Trust (£1,000); St Lawrence Church – Chicheley (£500); Royal Agricultural Benevolent Institution (£350); Buckinghamshire Historic Churches Trust (£300); SSAFA (£250); Guards Museum Trust (£200); Country Landowners Association Charitable Trust (£100); and Friends of John Bunyan Museum – Bedford (£25).

Exclusions
Local community organisations and individuals outside north Buckinghamshire and north Bedfordshire.

Applications
In writing to the correspondent. Applications are acknowledged if an sae is enclosed, otherwise if the charity has not received a reply within six weeks the application has not been successful.

The Baltic Charitable Fund

Seafarers, fishermen, ex-service and service people
£22,000 (2009/10)

Beneficial area
UK, with a preference for the City of London.

The Baltic Exchange, 38 St Mary Axe, London EC3A 8BH
Correspondent: The Company Secretary
Trustee: The Directors of the Baltic Exchange Limited.
CC Number: 279194

Information available
Accounts were on file at the Charity Commission.

The fund aims to support causes relating to the sea, including training for professionals and children, the City of London, Forces charities and for sponsorship for Baltic Exchange members. Support is given to registered charities only.

In 2009/10 the fund had assets of £1.8 million and an income of £40,000. Grants were made to 16 organisations totalling just over £22,000, including £6,000 given from the Bonno Krull Fund. (Grants in 2007/08 totalled £90,000).

No single grant totalled over £10,000 this year. Beneficiaries included: Lord Mayor's Appeal (£7,000); City and Sea Exchange (£5,000); BLESMA (£500); Sailors Society (£300); and CORDA (£100).

Exclusions
No support for advertising or charity dinners, and so on.

Applications
Unsolicited applications are not considered.

William P Bancroft (No 2) Charitable Trust and Jenepher Gillett Trust

Quaker
£47,500 (2010)

Beneficial area
UK and overseas.

13 Woodbury Park Road, Tunbridge Wells, Kent TN4 9NQ
Tel: 01892 528 150
Correspondent: Dr D S Gillett, Trustee
Trustees: Dr Godfrey Gillett; Martin B Gillett; Dr D S Gillett; Mrs Jenepher Moseley; Dr C Bancroft Wolff; Mrs M McNaughton.
CC Number: 288968

Information available
Accounts were available from the Charity Commission.

This trust is unusual as it consists of two separate trusts which are operated as one. For historical reasons there is a William P Bancroft trust giving in the UK and a Jenepher Gillet trust giving in Delaware, USA which shared a common settlor/joint-settlor; the two trusts are now being run jointly with the same trustees and joint finances.

It makes grants towards charitable purposes connected with the Religious Society of Friends, supporting Quaker conferences, colleges and Friends' homes for older people.

In 2010 the trust held assets of £787,000 and had an income of £43,000. Between the two trusts a total of £47,500 was given in grants with the William P Bancroft trust responsible for £29,500 of that total and the Jenepher Gillet Trust donating £18,000.

Beneficiaries included: Charney Manor Quake Course (£14,000); BYM (£5,000); Woodbrooke College (£4,000); Quaker Social Action (£2,500); Quaker Peace Centre – Capetown, Fellowship of

Reconciliation and Street Talk (£1,000 each); West Midland Quaker Peace Education, Scholarships for Street Kids and Oxford Homeless Medical Fund (£500 each).

Exclusions

No appeals unconnected with Quakers. No support for individual or student grant applications.

Applications

In writing to the correspondent. Trustees meet in May, applications must be received no later than April.

The Barbers' Company General Charities

Medical and nursing education

£183,000 (2009/10)

Beneficial area

UK.

Barber-Surgeons' Hall, Monkwell Square, Wood Street, London EC2Y 5BL
Correspondent: The Clerk
Trustee: The Barbers' Company.
CC Number: 265579

Information available

Accounts were on file with the charity commission.

The charities were registered in May 1973; grants are made to organisations and individuals. It no longer has direct contact with the hairdressing fraternity. However, a small amount is given each year to satisfy its historical links. Causes supported include those related to medical education and nursing.

In 2009/10 the charity had assets of £1.3 million and an income of £209,000. Grants totalled £183,000.

There were 19 grants of £1,000 or more listed in the accounts. Beneficiaries included: Kings College London (£50,000); Royal College of Surgeons (£40,000); Phyliss Tuckwell Hospice (£22,000); The Guildhall School Trust (£6,400); Reeds School (£5,000); City of London Freeman's

School (£2,600) and ABF- The Big Curry, Treloars and The Lord Mayor's Appeal (£1,000 each).

Applications

The charities do not welcome unsolicited applications.

The Barbour Foundation

Health, welfare, conservation/ restoration

£925,000 (2009/10)

Beneficial area

Mainly Tyne and Wear, Northumberland and South Tyneside.

J Barbour & Sons Ltd, PO BOX 37, Jarrow, Tyne & Wear NE32 3YT
Tel: 0191 455 555
Website: www.barbour.com
Correspondent: Harold Tavroges
Trustees: Dame Margaret Barbour, Chair; Henry Jacob Tavroges; Helen Barbour.
CC Number: 328081

Information available

Basic information taken from the Charity Commission website.

The objects of the charity are to support any charitable institution (grants are not made directly to individuals) whose objects include:

- the relief of patients suffering from any form of illness or disease, the promotion of research into the causes and treatment of such illnesses or disease and the provision of medical equipment for such patients
- the furtherance of education of children and young people by award of scholarship, exhibitions, bursaries or maintenance allowances tenable at any school, university or other educational establishment in England
- the protection and preservation for the benefit of the public in England, such features of cities, towns, villages and the countryside as are of special environmental, historical or architectural interest

- the relief of persons, whether resident in England or otherwise who are in conditions of need, hardship or distress as a result of local, national or international disaster, or by reason of their social and economic circumstances.

In 2009/10 the trust had an unusually very low income of £12,000 and a total expenditure of £925,000.

Previous beneficiaries included: Northumbria Youth Action Limited (£30,000); Alzheimer's Trust (£13,000); Action Medical Research and Northern Institute for Cancer Treatment (£10,000 each); Derwentside Domestic Abuse Centre, Genesis Appeal, Marie Curie Cancer Care, Newcastle Healthcare Charity, North of England Children's Cancer Research Fund and Shelter (£5,000 each); Fairbridge Tyne and Wear (£3,000); Project Northumberland and Wellbeing of Women (£2,000 each); Listening Books and Rainbow Trust (£1,500 each); and Butterwick Hospice Care, Combat Stress, National Farmers Network, Refuge, Ruskin Museum, Save the Children, Someone Cares, STOP, Sunderland North Family Zone, Textile Benevolent Association, Walk the Walk Worldwide and Whizz-Kids (£1,000 each).

Exclusions

No support for:

- requests from outside the geographical area
- requests from educational establishments
- individual applications, unless backed by a particular charitable organisation
- capital grants for building projects.

Applications

On an application form available from PO Box 21, Guisborough, Cleveland, TS14 8YH. The applications should include full back-up information, a statement of accounts and the official charity number of the applicant.

A main grants meeting is held every three to four months to consider grants of £500 plus. Applications are processed and researched by the administrator and secretary and further information may be requested.

A small grants meeting is held monthly to consider grants up to £500.

The trust always receives more applications than it can support. Even if a project fits its policy priority areas, it may not be possible to make a grant.

Common applicant mistakes

'Lack of financial information; insufficient information on history of charity; lack of clarity or too much irrelevant information.'

The Barcapel Foundation

Health, heritage, youth

Beneficial area

Scotland and other parts of the UK.

The Mews, Skelmorlie Castle, Skelmorlie, Ayrshire PA17 5EY
Tel: 01475 521616
Email: admin@barcapelfoundation.org
Website: www.barcapelfoundation.org
Correspondent: Moira Givens
Trustees: Robert Wilson, Chair; James Wilson; Andrew Wilson; Jed Wilson; Clement Wilson; Niall Scott.
SC Number: SC009211

Information available

Information was available from the trust's website.

The foundation was established in 1964 after the sale of the family business, Scottish Animal Products.

The three priority areas of interest for funding are health, heritage and youth.

The foundation's website gives the following information on these areas of interest:

Health
The foundation supports all aspects of health, a wide ranging remit acknowledging that 'health is a state of complete physical, mental and social well-being and not merely the absence of disease or infirmity'.

Heritage
The original financiers of the foundation had a keen interest in our heritage, specifying that one of the foundations aims was *the preservation and beautification of historic properties*. The foundation continues to support the built environment and will support our literary and artistic heritage as well as architectural.

Youth
The *development of people* is one of the principal objectives of the Foundation. Whilst charitable giving can be used to alleviate problems it can also be used to empower people and this is particularly true of the young.

In 2010 the foundation had an income of £220,000.

Grant beneficiaries for 2010 include: The Royal Museum Project, Riverside Museum Appeal, Fairbridge and National Galleries of Scotland (£50,000 each); University of Westminster, The Cancer Thermal Ablation Fund and Castlemilk Youth Project (£25,000 each).

Exclusions

No support for:
- individual applications for travel or similar
- organisations or individuals engaged in promoting religious or political beliefs
- applications for funding costs of feasibility studies or similar.

Support is unlikely to be given for local charities whose work takes place outside the British Isles.

Applications

A preliminary application form can be downloaded from the foundation's website. Please ensure that interests, aims and objectives are compatible with those of the foundation.

Applications are not accepted by email.

Barchester Healthcare Foundation

Health and social care

£7,500 to organisations (2010)

Beneficial area

England, Scotland and Wales.

Suite 201, The Chambers, Chelsea Harbour, London SW10 0XF
Tel: 0800 328 3328
Email: info@bhcfoundation.org.uk
Website: www.bhcfoundation.org.uk
Correspondent: The Administrator
Trustees: Prof Malcolm Johnson; Elizabeth Mills; Lesley Flory; Christopher Vellenoweth; Michael D Parsons; Janice Robinson; Nick Oulton.
CC Number: 1083272

Information available

Accounts were on file at the Charity Commission. Information is available on the foundation's website.

The Barchester Healthcare Foundation was established in 2003 by Barchester Healthcare to reinvest into the communities it serves. It is a registered charity with independent trustees. The trust's website states:

We make grants available across England, Scotland and Wales to older people and other adults (18 plus) with a physical or mental disability whose health and/or social care needs cannot be met by the statutory public sector or by the individual. Our mission is to make a difference to the lives of older people and other adults with a physical or mental disability, supporting practical solutions that lead to increased personal independence, self-sufficiency and dignity.

The trustees are currently encouraging applications from individuals. The foundation can provide grants of any amount, up to a maximum of £5,000.

In 2010 the foundation had an income of £311,000 and made grants totalling £109,000 of which £7,500 went to small charities/community groups and the remaining funds to individuals.

Beneficiary organisations were: The Care Management Group (£2,000); NMBVA (£1,500); Cookley Playing Field and Village Hall Association, Integrated Neurological Services, Manordeillo & District Senior Citizens Association and the Sunnybank Trust (£1,000 each).

Exclusions

Funds will not normally be given to:
- Provide services for which the health and social care authorities have a statutory responsibility.

- Services normally offered in a care home operated by Barchester Healthcare or by any other company.
- Indirect services such as help lines, newsletters, leaflets or research.
- Core/ running costs or salaries or give financial support to general projects.
- Major building projects.
- Provide continuing year on year support for a project following an initial grant. Any further applications in respect of the same beneficiary will be considered after a period of three years from the initial grant.

The trustees reserve the right to put a cap on grants to a single charity (including all its branches) in any one year.

Applications

Application can be made via the foundation's website. A decision usually takes approximately ten weeks from the date of application.

All applications supported by Barchester Healthcare staff will be given priority.

Common applicant mistakes

'Applicants don't read or check our criteria before applying'

Peter Barker-Mill Memorial Charity

General

£234,000 (2009/10)

Beneficial area

UK, with a preference for Hampshire, including Southampton.

c/o Longdown Management Ltd, The Estate Office, Longdown, Marchwood, Southampton SO40 4UH
Tel: 02380 292107
Fax: 02380 293376
Correspondent: Christopher Gwyn-Evans, Administrator
Trustees: C Gwyn-Evans; T Jobling; R M Moyse.
CC Number: 1045479

Information available

Accounts were available from the Charity Commission.

In 2009/10 the trust had assets of £3.9 million and an income of £67,000. Grants were made to 61 organisations totalling £234,000.

Beneficiaries included: Solent Centre for Architecture and Design (£28,000); Hampshire and Isle of Wight Wildlife Trust (£15,000); Students Exploring Marriage Trust (£12,000); Sussex House School (£10,000); The Rose Road Association (£7,000); Christ Church Colbury and Wessex Medical Research (£5,000 each); Computer Aid International and Music of Life (£3,000 each); Dream Holidays, Headway and The Soldiers, Sailors, Airmen and Families Association (£2,000 each); Music Alive and Berkshire Multiple Sclerosis Therapy Centre (£1,000 each); and The Smile Train UK (£500).

Exclusions

No grants to individuals.

Applications

In writing to the correspondent.

Barleycorn Trust

Christian

£39,000 (2010)

Beneficial area

Worldwide.

32 Arundel Road, Sutton, Surrey SM2 6EU
Correspondent: The Trustees
Trustees: Mrs H M Hazelwood; Mrs S A Beckwith.
CC Number: 296386

Information available

Accounts were available from the Charity Commission.

The object of the charity is the advancement of the Christian faith, furtherance of religious or secular education, the encouragement of missionary activity, relief of the poor and needy and help and comfort of the sick and aged.

In 2010 its assets totalled £1.1 million, it had an income of over

£128,000 and made grants totalling nearly £39,000.

Beneficiaries included: Deaf Church Hove (£5,000); Romanian Aid Fund and Scripture Union International (£3,000); Kids for Kids, Kidz Klub Leeds, Langley House Trust, Magdalene Trust and Stepping Stones (£1,000); and Village Water (£500).

Applications

In writing to the correspondent.

Lord Barnby's Foundation

General

£241,000 (2009/10)

Beneficial area

UK.

PO Box 71, Plymstock, Plymouth PL8 2YP
Correspondent: Jane Lethbridge, Secretary
Trustees: Hon. George Lopes; Countess Peel; Sir Michael Farquhar; Algy Smith-Maxwell; Laura Greenall.
CC Number: 251016

Information available

Accounts were available from the Charity Commission.

The foundation has established a permanent list of charities that it supports each year, with the remaining funds then distributed to other charities.

Its priority areas include the following:

- heritage; the preservation of the environment; and the countryside and ancient buildings, particularly the 'great Anglican cathedrals'
- charities benefiting people who are ex-service and service, Polish, disabled or refugees
- welfare of horses and people who look after them
- youth and other local organisations in Ashtead – Surrey, Blyth – Nottinghamshire and Bradford – Yorkshire.

In 2009/10 the foundation had assets of £4.1 million and an income of £216,000. Grants totalled £228,000 and were divided between 'permanent' and 'discretionary' donations.

Examples of the 82 organisation receiving 'discretionary' donations included: Help for Heroes, Marie Curie Cancer Care and Countryside Foundation for Education (£10,000 each); European Squirrel Initiative (£7,500); Merlin (£6,000); Zane, Queen Alexandra Hospital Home and Independent Age (£5,000 each); Bradford Amateur Rowing Club (£3,000); Alzheimer's Research Trust (£2,000); Exeter Cathedral, Kids Company and Talking Space (£1,000 each); Scott Polar Research Institute (£500); and Yorkshire Air Ambulance (£250).

The foundation also has an 'appointed fund' under which certain investments have been set aside specifically for the benefit of the textile industry. During the year £13,000 was given through this fund.

Exclusions
No grants to individuals.

Applications
Applications will only be considered if received in writing accompanied by a set of the latest accounts. Applicants do not need to send an sae. Appeals are considered three times a year, in February, June and November.

The Barnsbury Charitable Trust

General

£84,000 (2009/10)

Beneficial area
UK, but no local charities outside Oxfordshire.

26 Norham Road, Oxford OX2 6SF
Correspondent: H L J Brunner, Trustee
Trustees: H L J Brunner; M R Brunner; T E Yates.
CC Number: 241383

Information available
Accounts were available from the Charity Commission.

In 2009/10 the trust had assets of £2.8 million and an income of

£82,000. Grants were made to 47 organisations totalling £84,000.

Beneficiaries included: Oxfordshire Chamber Music Festival (£10,000); Archway Foundation (£6,000); Blackfriars Priory and Pegasus Theatre (£5,000 each); Oxfordshire Family Mediation and the George Mackay Brown Fellowship (£2,500 each); PCC of Letcombe Bassett (£2,000); Charities Aid Foundation (£1,000); Oxfordshire Rural Community Council and Oxford District Mencap (£500 each); St Adhelm's RC Church (£300); Friends of Wychwood and Oxfordshire Museum (£100 each); PCC of St Giles (£50); and the Royal Society of St George (£25).

Exclusions
No grants to individuals.

Applications
In writing to the correspondent.

The Misses Barrie Charitable Trust

Medical, general

£187,000 (2009/10)

Beneficial area
UK.

Raymond Carter and Co, 1b Haling Road, South Croydon CR2 6HS
Tel: 020 8686 1686
Correspondent: The Trustees
Trustees: J A Carter; R S Ogg; Mrs R Fraser.
CC Number: 279459

Information available
Accounts were available from the Charity Commission.

In 2009/10 the trust had assets of £5.3 million and an income of £209,000. Grants to 95 organisations totalled £187,000.

Beneficiaries included: Scottish Chamber Orchestra and University of Oxford (£10,000 each); Canine Partners and East Neuk Festival (£5,000 each); All England Netball Association, ARC Addington, Downs

Syndrome, Hearts and Minds, Listening Books, Scooniehill Group Riding for the Disabled and Surrey Cricket Board (£3,000 each); Headstart 4 Babies, Helen Ley Respite Care Centre, Holidays for Heroes Jersey, Institute of Cancer Research, Integrated Neurological Services, Jumbulance Trust, Life Care (Edinburgh), Lifelites, Lord Cobham, Worcestershire Youth Cricket Trust, Maggie's Cancer Caring Centres, Marie Curie Cancer Care and Youth Link Dundee (£2,000 each); Answer, Braille Chess Association, British Forces Foundation, Broadway Youth Activities, Cued Speech, Dream Connections, East Surrey Carers Support Association, Four Wheels Travel Fellowship, Gatton Trust, Girlguiding 1st Broadway Guides, Gurkha Welfare Trust, Highlanders Museum, Spadework, The Albrighton Trust, Tree Club, Virtually Impaired Association Bristol, WRVS Archive and Young Virtuosi Festival (£1,000 each).

Exclusions
No grants to individuals.

Applications
In writing to the correspondent accompanied, where appropriate, by up to date accounts or financial information. Trustees meet three times a year, in April, August and December.

The trust states that: 'The trustees regret that due to the large number of unsolicited applications for grants received each week they are not able to notify those which are unsuccessful.'

The Bartlett Taylor Charitable Trust

General

£54,000 to organisations (2009/10)

Beneficial area
Preference for Oxfordshire.

24 Church Green, Witney, Oxfordshire OX28 4AT
Tel: 01993 703941

Email: krobertson@ johnwelchandstammers.co.uk
Correspondent: Katherine Robertson
Trustees: Richard Bartlett; Gareth Alty; Katherine Bradley; Brenda Cook; James W Dingle; Rosemary Warner; Mrs S Boyd.
CC Number: 285249

Information available

Accounts were available from the Charity Commission, but without a list of grants.

In 2009/10 the trust had assets of £1.7 million and an income of £71,000. Grants were made totalling £64,000. There were 101 grants totalling £54,000 awarded to organisations during the year which were covered in the following categories:

Local		
Community	25	£13,000
Medical	17	£11,000
Educational	8	£2,000
Other	16	£2,000
National		
Medical	18	£14,000
Educational	2	£2,500
Other	8	£5,000
International	7	£4,500
Individuals		
Relief	26	£9,000
Medical	13	£2,000
Educational	19	£500

There was no list of beneficiaries available.

Applications

In writing to the correspondent. Trustees meet bi-monthly.

The Paul Bassham Charitable Trust

General

£192,000 (2009/10)

Beneficial area

UK, mainly Norfolk.

c/o Howes Percival, The Guildyard, 51 Colegate, Norwich NR3 1DD
Tel: 01603 762103
Correspondent: R Lovett, Trustee
Trustees: A G Munro; R Lovett.
CC Number: 266842

Information available

Accounts were available from the Charity Commission.

This trust was established in the early 1970s and has general charitable purposes. The trust states: 'The trustees will seek to identify those projects where the greatest and widest benefit can be attained.'

In 2009/10 the trust had assets of £10.6 million and an income of £351,000. During the year 84 donations were made totalling £192,000.

Beneficiaries of the four largest grants were: East Anglia Children's Hospice Quidenham and Norfolk Heart Trust (£25,000 each); and Norfolk Wildlife Trust and YMCA Norwich (£20,000 each).

Other beneficiaries included: RNLI Norfolk and St Catherine's PCC (£5,000 each); Great Yarmouth Samaritans, Norfolk Brass, Norwich Theatre Royal and Norwich Preservation Trust (£2,000 each); and Brainwave, British Lung Foundation, Dream Holidays, Jubilee Family Centre, Skill Force and Buckingham Emergency Flood Appeal (£1,000 each).

Richard Lovett is also a trustee of Brigadier D V and Mrs H R Phelps Charitable Settlement (Charity Commission no. 249047).

Exclusions

Grants are not be made directly to individuals, nor to unregistered organisations.

Applications

Only in writing to the correspondent – no formal application forms issued. Telephone enquiries are not invited because of administrative costs. The trustees meet quarterly to consider general applications.

The Batchworth Trust

Medical, humanitarian aid, social welfare, general

£316,000 (2009/10)

Beneficial area

Worldwide.

CLB Gatwick LLP, Imperial Buildings, 68 Victoria Road, Horley, Surrey RH6 7PZ
Tel: 01293 776411
Email: mrn@clbgatwick.co.uk
Correspondent: M R Neve, Administrative Executive
Trustee: Lockwell Trustees Ltd.
CC Number: 245061

Information available

Accounts were available from the Charity Commission.

The trust mainly supports nationally-recognised charities in a wide range of areas. In 2009/10 it had assets of £9 million, which generated an income of £280,000. Grants were made to 41 organisations totalling £316,000. The trust has previously informed us that:

> The trustees have a policy of mainly distributing to nationally recognised charities but consider other charities where it felt a grant would be of significant benefit when matched with other funds to launch a new enterprise or initiative.

Beneficiaries included: University of Bristol – research post (£50,000); Cecily's Fund, Cure Parkinson's, the Halo Trust and the Sandpiper Trust (£10,000 each); African Medical Mission, Living Paintings, Mary's Meals and Smile (£5,000 each); Stewartry Trust (£3,000); Fet Lor Youth Club (£2,000); and Dumfries and Galloway Arts Festival (£1,000).

Exclusions

No applications from individuals can be considered.

Applications

In writing to the correspondent. An sae should be included if a reply is required.

Bay Charitable Trust

Jewish

£470,000 (2010)

Beneficial area

UK and overseas.

Hermolis House, Abbeydale Road, Wembley, Middlesex HA0 1AY
Correspondent: I M Kreditor, Trustee
Trustees: I M Kreditor; M Lisser.
CC Number: 1060537

Information available

Accounts were available from the Charity Commission, but without a grants list.

Registered with the charity Commission in February 2007, the objectives of the charity are to give charity for the relief of poverty and the advancement of traditions of the Orthodox Jewish Religion and the study of Torah.

In 2010 it had an income of £360,000, mainly from donations. Grants totalled £470,000. The sum of £122,000 was carried forward at year end.

Applications

In writing to the correspondent.

The Bay Tree Charitable Trust

Development work, general

£110,000 (2010)

Beneficial area

UK and overseas.

PO Box 53983, London SW15 1VT
Correspondent: The Trustees
Trustees: I M P Benton; Miss E L Benton; P H Benton.
CC Number: 1044091

Information available

Accounts were available from the Charity Commission.

In 2010 the trust had assets of £3.4 million, an income of £136,000 and made 11 grants totalling £110,000.

Beneficiaries were: DEC Haiti Earthquake Appeal (£25,000); DEC Pakistan Floods Appeal (£20,000); Age Concern East Cheshire, British Red Cross – Chilean Earthquake Appeal, Combat Stress and Fareshare (£10,000 each); and Children of the Andes, Friends of the Earth, Hop Skip & Jump (Swindon), Integrated Neurological Services and Samaritans (£5,000 each).

Exclusions

No grants to individuals.

Applications

The 2010 accounts advise:

All appeals should be by letter containing the following:
- aims and objectives of the charity
- nature of appeal
- total target if for a specific project
- contributions received against target
- registered charity number
- any other relevant factors.

Letters should be accompanied by a set of the charitable organisation's latest report and full accounts.

The Beacon Trust

Christian

£20,000 to organisations (2010/11)

Beneficial area

Mainly UK, but also some overseas (usually in the British Commonwealth) and Spain and Portugal.

Unit 3, Newhouse Farm, Old Crawley Road, Horsham, West Sussex RH12 4RU
Tel: 01293 851715
Correspondent: Grahame Scofield
Trustees: Miss J Benson; Miss J M Spink; M Spink.
CC Number: 230087

Information available

Accounts were available from the Charity Commission.

The trust's objects are to advance the Christian faith, relieve poverty and advance education.

In 2010/11 the trust had assets of £2.4 million, an income of £45,000 and made grants totalling £29,000 which includes £8,000 to individuals.

The emphasis of the trust's support is on Christian work overseas, particularly amongst students, although the trust does not support individuals. The trust has previously stated that it has a list of charities that it supports in most years. This leaves very little funds available for unsolicited applications.

Beneficiaries included: Latin Link (£9,500); L'Abri (£5,000); and Missionary Aviation, CARE, and Torch Trust for the Blind (£2,000 each).

Exclusions

Applications from individuals are not considered.

Applications

The trust does not respond to unsolicited applications.

Bear Mordechai Ltd

Jewish

£70,000 (2009/10)

Beneficial area

Worldwide.

40 Fountayne Road, London N16 7DT
Correspondent: The Secretary
Trustees: Chaim Benedikt; Eliezer Benedikt; Yechiel Benedikt.
CC Number: 286806

Information available

Accounts were available from the Charity Commission, but without a list of grants.

Grants are made to Jewish organisations. The trust states that religious, educational and other charitable institutions are supported.

In 2009/10 this trust had assets of £1.8 million, an income of £197,000 and made grants totalling £70,000.

Previous beneficiaries have included: Agudat Yad Yemin Jerusalem, Almat, Chevras Mo'oz Ladol, Craven Walk Charities Trust, Havenpoint, Keren Tzedaka Vachesed, Lolev, UTA and Yetev Lev Yerusholaim.

Applications

In writing to the correspondent.

The Jack and Ada Beattie Foundation

Social welfare, injustice and inequality

Beneficial area

The Midlands and London.

203 Larna House, 116 Commercial Street, London E1 6NF
Tel: 020 3287 8427
Email: info@beattiefoundation.com
Website: www.beattiefoundation.com
Correspondent: Alexandra Taliadoros, Director
Trustees: Trevor Beattie; Peter Beattie; Paul Beattie.
CC Number: 1142892

Information available

Information was available from the foundation's website.

The foundation was established in July 2011 by Trevor Beattie, the marketing executive whose advertising company, Beattie McGuinness Bungay, was responsible for high-profile campaigns for French Connection and Playtex amongst others.

The following information is taken from the foundation's website:

I set up The Jack and Ada Beattie Foundation in honour and memory of my parents. It will adhere to their life-long held principles of fair play, care for the vulnerable and getting the job done. It will fight against inequality in all its forms (when you come from a family of ten, you soon learn the importance of equality . . .) and it will probably bear the Beattie family trait of defiance in the face of adversity.

It is likely that the foundation will have around £175,000 in total available each year for grants.

Eligibility

- the Jack and Ada Beattie Foundation seeks to support those facing social injustice and inequality in the Midlands and London.
- our funding priorities are: Dignity; Freedom; and Sanctuary
- the foundation accepts applications from charitable organisations under these headings – please tailor your applications accordingly.
- we are interested in funding credible projects with measured objectives and deliverable tangible outcomes.

Guidelines for organisations

Applications can only be made to the Jack and Ada Foundation following a successful proposal submission.

Before completing your application form, please make sure you have read these guidelines. It will help you fill in the form.

The following guidelines will assist you in any application you make to the Foundation, regarding financial and/or non-financial support.

If you need advice or support to complete your application form, please contact the Foundation Director who will be happy to discuss your project or idea.

Please be aware that organisations that have an outstanding End of Grant Report relating to previous funding from us, will be unable to submit any new application for funding until you have returned the information requested.

The application form can be downloaded from the Jack and Ada Beattie Foundation website.

Our priorities

The foundation gives priority to initiatives against social injustice. Preference will be given to the support of projects undertaken by charitable organisations.

Priority funding will change from time to time. Please contact Alexandra Taliadoros, Foundation Director for further information.

Who can apply?

The foundation can only donate to registered charities and individuals in the UK whose work tackles areas of social injustice.

How much can you apply for?

Financial support is administered through our 'Grants Scheme'. Grants available are between £500 and £2,000. The foundation will be looking to the applicant to demonstrate that they can manage the amount they have applied for and the tangible results projected from the funding.

The foundation does not intend to engage in continual repeat funding of organisations.

The foundation also makes grants directly to individuals.

Applications

Initial proposals should be emailed to the foundation. Eligible applicants will then be notified if the foundation is interested in receiving a full application, which is made using a form available on the foundation's website. The foundation's website gives the following guidance on completing the application form:

Please complete all sections of the application form and mark 'not appropriate' if that applies.

Contact details

Please give all contact details as requested. This will enable the Jack and Ada Beattie Foundation to keep accurate records of your organisation and help speed up the application process should we need to contact you by telephone or email.

The contact details requested are of a member of the management committee and/or trustee. This again will help make the application process more efficient should we need to contact you.

Organisation details

In this section you will help us understand the structure and purpose of your organisation. You can tell us what you do and who is involved.

Project details

Please describe the project you are requiring support for, with time-scales attached. Please describe how this project furthers the aims and objectives of your organisation if applicable and the tangible results to be achieved.

Statement of need

Please describe how you have identified a need for the project requiring support. Who will be involved in the delivery of this project and who are to be the beneficiaries?

Coherence of values and objectives

Please outline how the values and objectives of your organisation and project align to those of the foundation.

Organisation finance

This information will provide us with an idea as to how your organisation is run; what funders are attached and how effectively you operate.

Cost of your project

If you are applying for a Grant, please outline the amount of money you need for your project and where the funds are coming from (if you have applied to multiple funders). Please give a thorough breakdown of costs with timescales if appropriate. The foundation offers grants in the region of

£500–£2,000. We reserve the right to partially fund a project if we feel this is appropriate.

Project outcomes and outputs
Please outline what you hope to tangibly achieve from this project and how support from the foundation can assist you in doing so.

If your application is successful you will be required to monitor and evaluate the project and report back to the foundation. Details will be sent with the grant.

Application forms will only be accepted by email unless there are exceptional circumstances. Contact the Foundation Director if you have any queries.

The foundation endeavours to acknowledge each stage of the application process. Decisions will be reached within two months of each stage.

The Beaufort House Trust Limited

Christian, education

£32,000 (2010)

Beneficial area
UK.

Beaufort House, Brunswick Road, Gloucester GL1 1JZ
Correspondent: Mrs R J Hall, Secretary
Trustees: M Chamberlain; W Yates; Revd Nigel Stock; F Hart; Sir P Mawer; C Smith; N Sealy; The Ven. A Cooper; S Meredith; D P Wilson.
CC Number: 286606

Information available
Accounts were on file at the Charity Commission. The trust's 2010 annual report states:

The object of the company is to promote all charitable objects and purposes including the advancement, promotion and furtherance of education and the Christian religion.

Primarily the trust awards grants in response to appeals received from schools, colleges, universities and other charitable bodies. Normally grants are made in the form of single payments but occasionally the trustees may support a special project over a longer period.

In 2010 the trust had assets of £99,000 and an income of £91,000, including £84,000 in school fee annuities from Ecclesiastical Life Limited. Ecclesiastical Life Limited is a subsidiary of Allchurches Trust Limited. Beaufort House Trust Limited and Allchurches Trust Limited are companies that are controlled by a common board of trustees. The sum of £32,000 was given in grants which were distributed accordingly: schools (82%); colleges (11%); other educational establishments (7%).

Beneficiaries included: Catholic Blind Institute – Liverpool, towards furnishing of the residential unit at the school; Brampton Abbotts Church of England Primary School – Herefordshire, towards building and security costs; Mater Dei School – Dublin, towards staff, equipment, training and transport costs; and Weston All Saints Church of England Primary School – Somerset, towards the installation of a bio-pool and natural pool to help pupils learn to swim.

Exclusions
No grants are made to organisations with political associations, UK wide charities or individuals.

Applications
On an application form. The following details will be required: the objectives of the charity; the appeal target; how the funds are to be utilised; funds raised to date; and previous support received from the trust.

Beauland Ltd

Jewish causes

£231,000 (2009/10)

Beneficial area
Worldwide, with some preference for the Manchester area.

32 Stanley Road, Salford M7 4ES
Correspondent: M Neumann, Trustee
Trustees: F Neumann; H Neumann; M Friedlander; H Rosemann; J Bleier; R Delange; M Neumann; P Neumann; E Neumann; E Henry.
CC Number: 511374

Information available
Accounts were on file at the Charity Commission, without a list of grants.

The trust's objects are the advancement of the Jewish religion in accordance with the Orthodox Jewish faith and the relief of poverty. Most grants are made to educational institutions (including adult education) and institutions for the relief of poverty; though depending on the circumstances the trust may award a large donation to 'any particular cause that may arise in any year'.

In 2009/10 the trust had assets of £2.8 million and an income of £184,000. Grants totalled £231,000.

A list of beneficiaries was not available for 2009/10 but in previous years grants have included those to Asos Chesed, Cosmon Belz, Famos Charity Trust, Radford Education Trust, Sunderland Yeshiva and Yetev Lev.

Applications
In writing to the correspondent.

The Beaverbrook Foundation

General

£15,000 (2010)

Beneficial area
UK and Canada.

Ms Ford, Third Floor, 11/12 Dover Street, London W1S 4LJ
Tel: 020 7042 9435
Email: jane@beaverbrookfoundation.org
Website: www.beaverbrookfoundation.org
Correspondent: The Secretary
Trustees: Lord Beaverbrook, Chair; Lady Beaverbrook; Lady Aitken; Hon. Laura Levi; J E A Kidd; Hon. M F Aitken.
CC Number: 310003

Information available
Accounts were available from the Charity Commission website.

The objects of this foundation include:

- the erection or improvement of the fabric of any church building
- the purchase of books, papers, manuscripts or works of art
- care of the aged or infirm in the UK.

The major project of the last decade has been the renovation of Beaverbrook's country house and gardens at Cherkley Court, near Leatherhead, Surrey. Since the completion of this project and sale of the Cherkley Estate, the trustee's plan is to fully focus on charitable giving and grant making.

In 2010 the foundation had assets of £13 million and an income of £197,000. Out of a total expenditure of £4.6 million, grants to organisations totalled £15,000.

The following extract was taken from the foundation's website:

One of the areas that the foundation has concentrated on over the past twenty years has been supporting small charitable projects. We recognise that it is often more difficult to raise a few thousand to refurbish a church hall than it is to raise millions for a major public building. In the past twenty years, the foundation has donated to more than 400 charities.

Grant beneficiaries include: Battle of Britain Memorial Trust (£5,000); Aids Ark and Calvert Trust (£2,000 each) and a number of other grants for under £2,000 each totalling £6,250.

Exclusions
Only registered charities are supported.

Applications
There is an online application form at the foundation's website.

The Becker Family Charitable Trust

General, orthodox Jewish
£35,000 (2010/11)

Beneficial area
UK and overseas.

33 Sinclair Grove, London, NW11 9JH

Correspondent: A Becker, Trustee
Trustees: A Becker; Ms R Becker; Ms D Fried.
CC Number: 1047968

Information available
Accounts were available from the Charity Commission, but without a list of grants.

The trust makes grants for general charitable purposes, particularly to orthodox Jewish organisations.

In 2010/11 the trust had assets of £339,000 and an income of £157,000, mainly from donations. Grants were made to organisations totalling £35,000 (£67,000 in 2009/10).

Unfortunately a list of beneficiaries was not included with the accounts but previous beneficiaries have included: Keren Shabbas, Lolev CT, Menora Grammar School, Torah Temima and WST.

Applications
In writing to the correspondent. However, please note that the trust has previously stated that its funds were fully committed.

The Peter Beckwith Charitable Trust

Medical, welfare, general
£41,000 (2009/10)

Beneficial area
UK.

Hill Place House, 55a High Street, Wimbledon Village, London SW19 5BA
Tel: 020 8944 1288
Correspondent: The Trustees
Trustees: P M Beckwith; Mrs P G Beckwith; Mrs C T Van Dam; Tamara Veroni.
CC Number: 802113

Information available
Accounts were available from the Charity Commission.

This trust was established in 1989. In 2009/10 it had an income from donations of £42,000 and made 52 grants totalling £41,000. Assets at the year end totalled £11,500.

Beneficiaries included: Wimbledon and Putney Common Conservators (£10,000); Richmond Theatre (£5,000); Imperial War Museum (£2,000); and BAAF, ORCHID and Starlight Children's Foundation (£1,000 each).

One grant was paid to an individual.

Applications
In writing to the correspondent.

The John Beckwith Charitable Trust

Youth, education, social welfare, medical research, arts
£334,000 (2009/10)

Beneficial area
UK and overseas.

124 Sloane Street, London SW1X 9BW
Correspondent: Ms Sally Holder, Administrator
Trustees: J L Beckwith; H M Beckwith; C M Meech.
CC Number: 800276

Information available
Accounts were on file at the Charity Commission.

In 2009/10 the trust had assets of £3.1 million and an income of £657,000. There were 66 grants made totalling £334,000, broken down as follows:

Education	7	£119,000
Arts	4	£100,000
Social welfare	37	£83,000
Medical Research	17	£32,000
Sport	1	£800

The accounts listed 22 donations. Beneficiaries included: Royal Opera House Trust (£100,000); Harrow Development Trust (£90,000); Wycome Abbey School (£21,000); Families of the Fallen (£17,000); Breast Cancer Care (£15,000); RNIB (£9,700); Special Boat Service Association, UNICEF and Sightsavers

(£5,000 each); Alzheimer's Society and Ghana Youth Sport Development Programme (£2,000 each); KIDS and Whizz Kids (£1,000 each); and The Mayor's Fund for London (£800).

Unlisted grants totalled £33,000.

Applications
In writing to the correspondent.

The Bedfordshire and Hertfordshire Historic Churches Trust

Churches

£222,000 (2009/10)

Beneficial area
Bedfordshire, Hertfordshire and that part of Barnet within the Diocese of St Albans.

Wychbrook, 31 Ivel Gardens, Biggleswade, Bedfordshire SG18 0AN
Tel: 01767 312966
Email: wychbrook@yahoo.co.uk
Website: www.bedshertshct.org.uk
Correspondent: Archie Russell, Grants Secretary
Trustees: R C H Genochio, Chair; C P Green; A A I Jenkins; P F D Lepper; P A Lomax; S A Russell; T Warburton; W Marsterson; P N Griffiths.
CC Number: 1005697

Information available
Accounts were on file at the Charity Commission; the trust has a helpful website.

The trust gives grants for the restoration, preservation, repair and maintenance of churches in Bedfordshire, Hertfordshire and that part of Barnet within the Diocese of St Albans. Annual income comes from member subscription and from the annual Bike 'n' Hike event. The trust also acts as a distributive agent for church grants made by the Wixamtree Trust and Waste Recycling Environmental Ltd (WREN).

In 2009/10 the trust had assets of £223,000 and an income of £222,000, including £40,000 from WREN. There

were 36 grants made totalling £222,000, which were in the range of £1,000 and £15,000.

Beneficiary Churches included: St Mary – Baldock, for tower repairs; All Saints, Odell – towards kitchen and toilets; Methodist Church – Clapham, for fabric repairs; St Andrew – Watford, towards stonework and repairs; All Saints – Houghton Conquest, wall repair; and Baptist – Marykate, roof repairs.

Exclusions
No grants to individuals.

Applications
Initial enquiries should be made to the Grants Secretary. Applications can only be made by members of the trust.

The David and Ruth Behrend Fund

General

£75,000 (2009/10)

Beneficial area
UK, with a preference for Merseyside.

151 Dale Street, Liverpool L2 2AH
Correspondent: The Secretary
Trustee: Liverpool Charity and Voluntary Services.
CC Number: 261567

Information available
Accounts were available from the Charity Commission.

The trust's annual reports state: 'The fund has been established to make grants for charitable purposes. Grants are only made to charities known to the settlors and unsolicited applications are therefore not considered.' Set up in 1969, it appears to give exclusively in Merseyside.

In 2009/10 the fund had assets of £1.4 million and an income of £73,000. Grants totalled £75,000. There were 27 listed beneficiaries in receipt of grants of £1,000 or more.

Beneficiaries included: Merseyside Development Foundation (£8,000); Birkenhead Youth Club (£6,000);

Amelia Chadwick Trust (£5,000); Liverpool Central Citizens Advice (£2,500); Liverpool Roots Trust and Liverpool International Nordic Community (£2,000 each); European Play – Work Association and KIND (£1,500 each); and Support for Asylum Seekers and Merseyside Holiday Service (£1,000 each).

Exclusions
Anyone not known to the settlors.

Applications
This fund states that it does not respond to unsolicited applications. 'The charity only makes grants to charities already known to the settlors as this is a personal charitable trust.'

Bellasis Trust

General

£22,000 (2009/10)

Beneficial area
UK.

4th Floor, 65 Kingsway, London WC2B 6TD
Correspondent: Paul Wates, Trustee
Trustees: Paul Wates; Annette Wates; Annabelle Elliott; Joseph Lulham.
CC Number: 1085972

Information available
Accounts were on file at the Charity Commission.

Established in March 2001, the trust states that it is the 'intention of the trustees to support local charities including those for the disadvantaged persons'. In 2009/10 the trust had assets of £821,000 and an income of £33,000. Grants totalled £22,000.

There were six beneficiaries of £500 or more listed in the accounts. They were: Royal Horticultural Society (£10,000); Mickleham PCC (£2,000); Surrey Community Development, MJC Stone Charitable Trust and Pancreatic Cancer UK (£1,000 each); and Facing Africa – Noma (£750).

Applications
The trustees research and consider applicants for grants.

The Benham Charitable Settlement

General

£120,000 (2010/11)

Beneficial area

UK, with very strong emphasis on Northamptonshire.

Hurstbourne, Portnall Drive, Virginia Water, Surrey GU25 4NR
Correspondent: The Secretary
Trustees: Mrs M M Tittle; Lady Hutton; E N Langley; D A H Tittle; Revd. J A Nickols.
CC Number: 239371

Information available

Accounts were available from the Charity Commission.

The charity was founded in 1964 by the late Cedric Benham and his wife Hilda, then resident in Northamptonshire, 'to benefit charities and other good causes and considerations'.

The object of the charity is the support of registered charities working in many different fields – including charities involved in medical research, disability, elderly people, children and young people, disadvantaged people, overseas aid, missions to seamen, the welfare of ex-servicemen, wildlife, the environment, and the arts. The trust also supports the Church of England, and the work of Christian mission throughout the world. Special emphasis is placed upon those churches and charitable organisations within the county of Northamptonshire [especially as far as new applicants are concerned].

In 2010/11 the charity had assets of £5.3 million and an income of £163,000. It made donations totalling £120,000 with the majority of grants ranging from £200 to £700.

Grants can be analysed as follows:

One-off cause (Northamptonshire Association of Youth Clubs)	1	£26,000
Medical	33	£19,500
General	22	£18,000
Persons with disabilities	25	£12,000
Overseas aid & mission	13	£12,000
Children, youth & schools	13	£6,400
Elderly	17	£8,600
Christian mission	11	£7,700
Church maintenance	13	£6,200
Wildlife & conservation	4	£2,000
Art & sport	2	£1,000
Animal welfare	2	£900

Beneficiaries included: Northamptonshire Association of Youth Clubs (£26,000); William Wilberforce Trust (£8,000); Christ Church – Peckham (£3,000); ZANE (Zimbabwe A National Emergency) (£2,000); Camphill Village Trust (£600); Deafblind UK and Friends of the Elderly (£500 each); and Myasthenia Gravis Association (£400).

Exclusions

No grants to individuals.

Applications

In recent years the trust has not been considering new applications.

Michael and Leslie Bennett Charitable Trust

Jewish

£40,000 (2009/10)

Beneficial area

UK.

Bedegars Lea, Kenwood Close, London NW3 7JL
Correspondent: Michael Bennett, Trustee
Trustees: Michael Bennett; Lesley V Bennett.
CC Number: 1047611

Information available

Accounts were available from the Charity Commission.

The trust supports a range of causes, but the largest donations are usually to Jewish organisations. In 2009/10 the trust had assets of £297,000 and an income of £36,000 including £20,000 from donations. There were 37 grants made totalling £40,000.

Grants of £750 or more were made to seven organisations: World Jewish Relief (£18,000); Norwood Ravenswood (£5,100); Chai Cancer Care (£3,800); United Jewish Israel Appeal and Nightingale (£3,000 each); LJCC (£1,000); and Macmillan Cancer Care (£750).

Applications

In writing to the correspondent.

The Ruth Berkowitz Charitable Trust

Jewish, medical research, youth, general charitable purposes

£464,000 (2009/10)

Beneficial area

UK and overseas.

39 Farm Avenue, London NW2 2BJ
Tel: 020 7388 3577
Correspondent: The Trustees
Trustees: Philip Beckman; Brian Beckman.
CC Number: 1111673

Information available

Accounts were available from the Charity Commission.

Established for general charitable purposes, the Trustees' current grant making policy is to make modest grants to numerous qualifying charities and some larger grants for specific projects. There is some preference for Jewish organisations.

In 2009/10 the trust had assets of £4 million and an income of £91,000. Grants totalled £464,000 and were broken down as follows:

Children/youth/education	15	£248,000
Community	9	£157,000
Medical	3	£38,000
Small Grants Fund	1	£22,000

Beneficiaries included: National Jewish Chaplaincy Board (£47,500); World Jewish Relief (£42,500); Community Security Trust (£40,000); Magen David Adom UK and North West London Jewish Day School (£25,000 each); Lord Ashdown Charitable Settlement (£21,500); Norwood Ravenswood (£20,000); Cancer Research UK and Marie Curie Cancer Care (£15,000 each); London Philharmonic Orchestra Limited

(£10,000); British Friends Ohel Sarah and The Z.S.V. Trust (£7,500 each); and Camp Simcha (£4,000).

Applications

In writing to the correspondent.

The Bestway Foundation

Education, welfare, medical

£500,000 (2009/10)

Beneficial area

UK and overseas.

Bestway Cash and Carry Ltd, Abbey Road, Park Royal, London
NW10 7BW
Tel: 0208 453 1234
Email: zulfikaur.wajid-hasan@ bestway.co.uk
Website: www.bestwaygroup.co.uk/
Correspondent: M Y Sheikh, Trustee
Trustees: A K Bhatti; A K Chaudhary; M Y Sheikh; Z M Choudrey; M A Pervez.
CC Number: 297178

Information available

Accounts were available from the Charity Commission.

The objects of this foundation are the advancement of education by grants to schoolchildren and students who are of Indian, Pakistani, Bangladeshi or Sri Lankan origin; relief of sickness, and preservation and protection of health in the UK and overseas, especially in India, Pakistan, Bangladesh and Sri Lanka. Grants are made to individuals, UK registered charities, non-registered charities and overseas charities. All trustees are directors and shareholders of Bestway (Holdings) Limited, the parent company of Bestway Cash and Carry Limited.

In 2009/10 this trust had assets of £5.4 million, an income of £885,000 and made grants totalling £500,000. During the year, 17 grants were awarded to institutions and 81 grants and donations to individuals accounting for 99.9% of the resources expended.

Grant beneficiaries included: Bestway Foundation Pakistan (£200,000); Crimestoppers (£34,000); Duke of Edinburgh Awards (£15,000); The Cayo Foundation (£5,000); Commonwealth Countries League and Al-Hijrah Trust (£2,000 each) and John Kelly Technology Girls' College (£1,000).

Exclusions

No grants for trips/travel abroad.

Applications

In writing to the correspondent, enclosing an sae. Applications are considered in March/April. Telephone calls are not welcome.

Thomas Betton's Charity for Pensions and Relief-in-Need

Education for children and young people, housing, disability, performing arts, family

£32,000 (2009/10)

Beneficial area

UK.

Ironmongers' Hall, Barbican, London EC2Y 8AA
Tel: 020 7776 2311
Email: helen@ironhall.co.uk
Website: www.ironhall.co.uk
Correspondent: The Charities Administrator
Trustee: The Worshipful Company of Ironmongers.
CC Number: 280143

Information available

Accounts were on file at the Charity Commission.

This charity makes grants for educational activities for children and young people up to the age of 25 from disadvantaged backgrounds. It also gives to specific charitable organisations with which the trustee has an ongoing relationship (a block grant is made to Housing the

Homeless which allocates grants to individuals).

In 2009/10 the trust had assets of £950,000 and an income of £42,500. Grants totalled £32,000.

Beneficiaries were: Housing the Homeless Central Fund (£10,000); Royal Academy for Dramatic Arts (£6,500); Autism initiatives UK (£6,000); Pascal Theatre Company (£5,000); Sheriff's and Recorder's Fund (£2,000); Chad Varah Appeal for Samaritans (£500); and the City of London Police Widows and Orphans Fund (£200).

Exclusions

Applications for grants to individuals are accepted only from registered social workers or other agencies, not directly from individuals.

Applications

In writing to the correspondent.

The Billmeir Charitable Trust

General, health and medical

£120,000 (2009/10)

Beneficial area

UK, with a preference for the Surrey area, specifically Elstead, Tilford, Farnham and Frensham.

Moore Stephens, 150 Aldersgate Street, London EC1A 4AB
Tel: 020 7334 9191
Correspondent: Keith Lawrence, Secretary
Trustees: B C Whitaker; M Whitaker; S Marriott; J Whitaker.
CC Number: 208561

Information available

Accounts were on file at the Charity Commission.

The trust states it supports a wide variety of causes. About a quarter of the grants are given to health and medical charities and about a third of the grants are given to local organisations in Surrey, especially the Farnham, Frensham, Elstead and Tilford areas.

In 2009/10 the trust had assets of £3.8 million, which generated an income of £162,000. Donations were made to 27 charities totalling £120,000, the majority of beneficiaries had received grants in the previous year.

Beneficiaries included: Reed's School – Cobham (£10,000); Marlborough College (£8,000); Arundel Castle Cricket Club and Old Kiln Museum Trust (£7,000 each); RNIB and the New Ashgate Gallery (£5,000 each); Helen Arkell Dyslexia Centre (£3,000); and Cancer Vaccine and Broomwood Hall School (£2,000 each);

Applications

The trust states that it does not request applications and that its funds are fully committed.

The Bintaub Charitable Trust

Jewish, medical and youth

£43,000 (2009/10)

Beneficial area

Greater London, worldwide.

125 Wolmer Gardens, Edgware HA8 8QF
Correspondent: Mrs Dahlia Rosenberg, Trustee
Trustees: James Frohwein; Tania Frohwein; Mrs Dahlia Rosenberg; Rabbi E Stefansky.
CC Number: 1003915

Information available

Accounts were on file at the Charity Commission.

This trust was set up in 1991 and provides grants to mainly London organisations, towards 'the advancement of education in and the religion of the Orthodox Jewish faith'. Grants are also given for other charitable causes, mainly towards medical and children's work.

In 2009/10 it had an income from donations of £52,000 and made grants to ten organisations totalling just over £43,000.

Grants went to: Gateshead Jewish Academy (£6,400); Yeshiva Be'er Hatorah (£6,000); Gateshead Jewish Primary School (£3,000); JTTC (£2,900); Menorah Foundation School (£2,600); Kupat Ha'ir (£2,500); Friends of Yeshivat Lomdei Torah, Friends of Mir and Va'ad Harabbanim L'inyanei Tzedaka (£2,000 each); and Sunderland Kollel (£700).

Applications

The trust has previously stated that new applications are not being accepted.

The Birmingham Hospital Saturday Fund Medical Charity and Welfare Trust

Medical

Around £40,000 (2009)

Beneficial area

UK, but mostly centred around the West Midlands and Birmingham area.

Gamgee House, 2 Darnley Road, Birmingham B16 8TE
Tel: 0121 454 3601
Email: charitabletrust@bhsf.co.uk
Correspondent: The Secretary
Trustees: Dr R P Kanas; S G Hall; E S Hickman; M Malone; D J Read; J Salmons.
CC Number: 502428

Information available

Accounts were overdue at the Charity Commission.

This trust supports the relief of sickness, with the trustees also holding an interest in medical research. The trustees continue to give priority to charities that benefit those living in the West Midlands area with some interest in the south west for historical reasons. The trust no longer receives an income from the parent company and so the trustees are now working purely with reserves and the interest from them.

This has resulted in a more critical look at projects at each meeting and donations are now generally less than £2,000. Projects that are appropriate and reflect well thought through projects with realistic cost breakdowns are given greater consideration.

In 2009 the trust had an income of £4,000 and a total expenditure of £50,000. Full accounts were not required at the Charity Commission due to the moderate income this year; therefore, further details on grants and beneficiaries was not available.

Previous beneficiaries included: Friends of Victoria School – Northfield (£3,800); NHS West Midlands (£3,400); Birmingham Centre for Arts Therapies and Starlight Children's Foundation (£2,500 each); Vascular Department, Selly Oak Hospital (£2,000); Dream Holidays, Isle of Wight (£1,900); the Mary Stevens Hospice, Stourbridge, West Midlands (£1,600); Institute of Ageing and Health, Birmingham (£1,500); Contact the Elderly, Birmingham (£1,200); Christian Lewis Trust – Cardiff (£1,100); Action Medical Research – Horsham, Children's Heart Foundation and REACT Surrey (£1,000); Katherine House – Stafford (£900); St Martin's Centre for Health and Healing (£750); Deep Impact Theatre Company and Birmingham Heart Care – Walsall (£500 each); and Acorns Children's Hospice – Birmingham (£315).

Exclusions

The trust will not generally fund: direct appeals from individuals or students; administration expenditure including salaries; bank loans/deficits/mortgages; items or services which should normally be publicly funded; large general appeals; vehicle operating costs; or motor vehicles for infrequent use and where subsidised vehicle share schemes are available to charitable organisations.

Applications

On a form available from the correspondent. The form requires basic information and should be submitted with financial details. Evidence should be provided that the project has been adequately considered through the provision of quotes or supporting documents, although the trust dislikes applications which provide too much general information or have long-winded descriptions of projects. Applicants should take great care to read the guidance notes on the application form. The trustees meet four times a year and deadlines are given when application forms are sent out.

Birthday House Trust

General

£72,000 to organisations (2009/10)

Beneficial area

England and Wales.

Dickinson Trust Ltd, Pollen House, 10–12 Cork Street, London W1S 3LW
Tel: 020 7439 9061
Email: charity@mfs.co.uk
Correspondent: Laura Gosling, Trust Administrator
Trustee: The Dickinson Trust Limited and Rathbone Trust Company Limited.
CC Number: 248028

Information available

Accounts were on file at the Charity Commission.

Established in 1966, the main work of this trust is engaged with the running of a residential home for people who are elderly in Midhurst, West Sussex. In 2009/10 it had assets of £6.1 million and an income of £239,000. Grants to 11 organisations totalled £72,000. A further £66,000 was distributed to pensioners.

Beneficiaries were: Druk White Loftus School (£50,000); Countryside Alliance (£10,000); Merton Road Scouts (£3,000); Sussex Community Foundation and Ecology Trust (£2,500 each); Chichester Cathedral Trust (£2,000); Fire Services National Benevolent Fund and Eastbourne Scout and Guide Hut Committee (£500 each); Fernhurst Recreation Ground Trust and Organic Research Trust (£250 each); and Murray Downland Trust (£50).

Exclusions

No applications will be considered from individuals or non-charitable organisations.

Applications

In writing to the correspondent, including an sae. No application forms are issued and there is no deadline. Only successful applicants are acknowledged.

The Bisgood Charitable Trust (registered as Miss Jeanne Bisgood's Charitable Trust)

Roman Catholic purposes, older people

£208,000 (2009/10)

Beneficial area

UK, overseas and locally in Bournemouth and Dorset, especially Poole.

12 Waters Edge, Brudenell Road, Poole BH13 7NN
Correspondent: J M Bisgood, Trustee
Trustees: J M Bisgood, Chair; P Schulte; P J K Bisgood.
CC Number: 208714

Information available

Accounts were available from the Charity Commission, but without a list of grants.

This trust has emerged following an amalgamation of the Bisgood Trust with Miss Jeanne Bisgood's Charitable Trust. Both trusts had the same objectives.

The General Fund has the following priorities:
1   Roman Catholic charities
2   Charities benefiting people in Poole, Bournemouth and the county of Dorset
3   National charities for the benefit of older people.

No grants are made to local charities which do not fall under categories 1 or 2. Many health and welfare charities are supported as well as charities working in relief and development overseas.

In 2009/10 the trust had assets of £5.2 million, which generated an income of £171,000. Donations to charities amounted £208,000. Previous beneficiaries from the general fund have included Apex Trust, ITDG, Horder Centre for Arthritis, Impact, St Barnabas' Society, St Francis Leprosy Guild, Sight Savers International and YMCA.

In considering appeals the trustees will give preference to charities whose fund-raising and administrative costs are proportionately low.

The trust was given 12 paintings to be held as part of the trust funds. Most of the paintings were sold and the proceeds were placed in a sub-fund, the Bertram Fund, established in 1998, the income of which is purely for Roman Catholic causes. It is intended that it will primarily support major capital projects. Most grants are made anonymously from this fund.

Exclusions

Grants are not given to local charities which do not fit categories 1 or 2 above. Individuals and non-registered charities are not supported.

Applications

In writing to the correspondent, quoting the UK registration number and registered title of the charity. A copy of the most recent accounts should also be enclosed. Applications should *not* be made directly to the Bertram Fund. Applications for capital projects should provide brief details of the main purposes, the total target and the current state of the appeal. The trustees regret that they are unable to acknowledge appeals. The trustees normally meet in late February/early March and September.

Common applicant mistakes

'We receive quite a number of applications from local charities operating outside Dorset (which is one of our priorities) and not under Roman Catholic auspices (which is our first priority).'

The Michael Bishop Foundation

General

£220,000 (2009/10)

Beneficial area

Worldwide with a preference for Birmingham and the Midlands.

26 Harrop Road, Hale, Altrincham
WA15 9DQ
Tel: 0161 904 8300
Correspondent: Grahame Elliott, Trustee
Trustees: Sir Michael Bishop, Chair; Grahame N Elliott; John T Wolfe; John S Coulson.
CC Number: 297627

Information available

Full accounts were available from the Charity Commission website.

Sir Michael Bishop of British Midland set up the foundation in 1987 by giving almost £1 million of shares in Airlines of Britain (Holdings) plc, the parent company of British Midland. A further sum was given in 1992.

In 2009/10 the trust had assets of nearly £2.4 million, and an income of £200,000. Grants to 22 organisations totalled £220,000.

Beneficiaries included: the Actors Benevolent Fund, The Human Trafficking Foundation, The Imperial War Museum, the Royal Flying Doctor Service of Australia and Terrance Higgins Trust (£25,000 each); Peter Tatchell Human Rights Fund (£15,000); Nightingale Trust (£10,000); Greyfriars Opera (£10,000); Hospices of Hope and Leicestershire Victoria County History Trust (£5,000 each); Barry & Martin's Trust and Birmingham Early Music Festival (£2,500 each); and Army Benevolent Fund (£500).

Applications

In writing to the correspondent.

The Sydney Black Charitable Trust

Evangelical Christianity, social welfare, young people

£115,000 (2009/10)

Beneficial area

UK.

30 Welford Place, London SW19 5AJ
Correspondent: The Secretary
Trustees: Mrs J D Crabtree; Mrs H J Dickenson; S J Crabtree; P M Crabtree.
CC Number: 219855

Information available

Accounts were received by the Charity Commission but not available to view online.

In 2001 The Edna Black Charitable Trust and The Cyril Black Charitable Trust were incorporated into this trust.

In 2009/10 the trust had an income of £18,000 and a total expenditure of £115,000. Previous beneficiaries included Endeavour (£20,000). Grants are generally in the region of £125 and £250 each with around 700 organisations benefiting.

Applications

Applications, made in writing to the correspondent, will be considered by the appropriate trust.

The Bertie Black Foundation

Jewish, general

£68,000 (2009/10)

Beneficial area

UK, Israel.

Abbots House, 198 Lower High Street, Watford WD17 2FG
Correspondent: Harry Black, Trustee
Trustees: I B Black; D Black; H S Black; Mrs I R Seddon.
CC Number: 245207

Information available

Accounts were available at the Charity Commission website, but without a list of beneficiaries.

The trust tends to support organisations which are known to the trustees or where long-term commitments have been entered into. Grants can be given over a three-year period towards major projects.

In 2009/10 the foundation had assets of £2.9 million and an income of £101,000. Grants were made to 31 organisations in the year totalling £68,000, of which 8 received funds in excess of £5,000 each. (This was compared with a much larger grant list of 116 grants amounting to £329,000 in 2007/08.)

A list of beneficiaries was not available in 2009/10. However, previous beneficiaries included: I Rescue (£50,000); Magen David Adom (£47,000 in three grants); Alyn Hospital (£49,000 in two grants); Emunah (£38,000); Laniardo Hospital and Shaare Zedek (£25,000 each); Friends of Israel Sports Centre for Disabled (£20,000); Child Resettlement Trust (£10,000 in four grants); Norwood (£7,600 in four grants); and Hope (£5,200 in four grants).

Applications

The trust states it 'supports causes known to the trustees' and that they 'do not respond to unsolicited requests'.

Sir Alec Black's Charity

Relief in need

£20,000 to organisations (2009/10)

Beneficial area

UK, with a preference for Grimsby.

Wilson Sharpe and Co., 27 Osborne Street, Grimsby, North East Lincolnshire DN31 1NU
Email: sabc@wilsonsharpe.co.uk
Correspondent: Stewart Wilson, Trustee
Trustees: Stewart Wilson; Dr Diana F Wilson; Michael Parker; Philip A Mounfield; John N Harrison.
CC Number: 220295

Information available

Accounts were available from the Charity Commission.

The primary purposes of the trust are:

▎ the purchase and distribution of bed linen and down pillows to charitable organisations caring for people who are sick or infirm

▎ the provision of pensions and grants to people employed by Sir Alec Black during his lifetime

▎ the benefit of sick, poor fishermen and dockworkers from the borough of Grimsby.

In 2009/10 it had assets of £1.5 million and an income of £88,000. Grants totalled £41,000 and were distributed as follows:

Bed linen/pillows for charitable organisations	£20,000
Former employees	£16,000
Fishermen	£4,700

Applications

In writing to the correspondent. Trustees meet in May and November; applications need to be received in March or September.

The Blair Foundation

Wildlife, access to countryside, general

£70,000 (2010/11)

Beneficial area

UK, particularly southern England and Scotland; overseas.

Smith and Williamson, 1 Bishops Wharf, Walnut Tree Close, Guildford, Surrey GU1 4RA
Tel: 01483 407100
Correspondent: The Trustees
Trustees: Robert Thornton; Jennifer Thornton; Graham Healy; Alan Thornton.
CC Number: 801755

Information available

Accounts were received at the Charity Commission but were unable to view.

This foundation was originally established to create environmental conditions in which wildlife can prosper, as well as improving

disability access to such areas. This work is focused on Scotland and southern England.

In 2010/11 the foundation had an income of £18,000 and a total expenditure of £76,000. Based upon expenditure in previous years grant expenditure probably totalled around £70,000.

Previous beneficiaries included: Ayrshire Wildlife Services (£12,000); King's School – Canterbury and Ayreshire Fiddler Orchestra (£10,000 each); Scottish National Trust (£7,000); Home Farm Trust (£5,000); CHAS (£2,000); Handicapped Children's Action Group and Penny Brohn Cancer Care (£1,500); Ro Ro Sailing Project and Sustrans (£1,000 each).

Exclusions

Charities that have objectives which the trustees consider harmful to the environment are not supported.

Applications

In writing to the correspondent, for consideration at trustees' meetings held at least once a year. A receipt for donations is requested from all donees.

The Sir Victor Blank Charitable Settlement

Jewish organisations and general charitable purposes

£196,000 (2009/10)

Beneficial area

Worldwide.

c/o Wilkins Kennedy, Bridge House, London Bridge, London SE1 9QR
Tel: 0207 403 1877
Correspondent: R Gulliver, Trustee
Trustees: Sir M V Blank; Lady S H Blank; R Gulliver.
CC Number: 1084187

Information available

Accounts were available from the Charity Commission.

Registered with the Charity Commission in December 2000, in 2009/10 this charity had assets of £1.6 million and an income of £251,000. Grants totalled £196,000.

There were 24 donations of £1,000 or more listed in the accounts. Beneficiaries included: Jewish Care (£30,000); United Jewish Israel Appeal (£27,000); Norwood Ravenswood (£22,000); Hillel Foundation and Jewish Community Secondary School (£10,000 each); Alexander Devine Children's Cancer Care Trust and Jewish Deaf Association (£5,000 each); Nightingale Patron Scheme (£3,000); University of Nottingham (£2,500); Wow Give Big Charity Event (£2,000); and Campaign to Protect Rural England and Spanish and Portuguese Jews' Home (£1,000 each).

Other grants of less than £1,000 each totalled £14,000.

Applications

In writing to the correspondent.

Blatchington Court Trust

Supporting vision-impaired people under the age of 30

£50,000 to organisations (2009/10)

Beneficial area

UK, preference for Sussex.

Ridgeland House, 165 Dyke Road, Hove, East Sussex BN3 1TL
Tel: 01273 727 222
Fax: 01273 722 244
Email: info@blatchingtoncourt.org.uk
Website: www.blatchingtoncourt.org. uk
Correspondent: The Executive Manager
Trustees: Richard Martin, Chair; Alison Acason; Daniel Ellman-Brown; Georgina James; Roger Jones; Stephen Pavey; Anna Hunter; Jonathan Wilson.
CC Number: 306350

Information available

Accounts were on file at the Charity Commission.

This trust's initial income arose from the sale of the former Blatchington Court School for people who are partially sighted at Seaford. Its aim is the promotion of education and employment (including social and physical training) of blind and partially sighted persons under the age of 30 years. There is a preference for Sussex.

The Charity has two grant making programmes; financial assistance and capital grants:

(a) Financial Assistance

The primary and largest is the Sussex Programme, which provides services to individual clients including advocacy, counselling, education, training and assistance in finding employment and family support.

(b) Capital Grants

The second programme is for capital grants which covers all of the UK and through which the charity, usually in partnership with sister charities, will:

(i) Award grants for the provision of recreational and leisure facilities (or contributions towards such facilities), which enable vision impaired people to develop their physical, mental and moral capacities.

(ii) Make grants to any voluntary or charitable organisation approved by the trustees, the objects of which include the promotion of education, training and/or employment of vision impaired young people and their general well-being in pursuance of all the foregoing.

In 2009/10 the trust had assets of £10 million and an income mainly from investments of £479,000. Grants paid totalled £130,000, of which £50,000 went to organisations. The remaining £80,000 was given to individuals.

Applications

On a form available from the correspondent. Applications can be considered at any time. An application on behalf of a registered charity should include audited accounts and up-to-date information on the charity and its commitments.

The Neville and Elaine Blond Charitable Trust

Jewish, general

£99,000 (2009/10)

Beneficial area

Worldwide.

c/o H W Fisher and Co, Chartered Accountants, Acre House, 11–15 William Road, London NW1 3ER
Tel: 020 7388 7000
Correspondent: The Trustees
Trustees: Dame Simone Prendergast; P Blond; Mrs A E Susman; S N Susman; Mrs J Skidmore.
CC Number: 206319

Information available

Full accounts were available from the Charity Commission website.

In 2009/10 the trust had assets of almost £1.2 million and an income of £60,000. Grants totalling £99,000 were made to 15 organisations, of which 12 had been supported in the previous year.

The main beneficiaries were: Beth Shalom Holocaust Memorial Centre (£30,000); United Jewish Israel Appeal (£30,000); and British WIZO and Community Security Trust (£10,000 each).

Smaller grants included: Holocaust Educational Trust (£5,000); Halle Orchestra (£4,000); Nordoff Robbins Music Therapy Centre (£2,000); Chicken Shed Theatre (£1,000); and Walk the Walk (£200).

Exclusions

Only registered charities are supported.

Applications

In writing to the correspondent. Applications should arrive by 31 January for consideration in late spring.

The Blueberry Charitable Trust

Jewish, relief-in-need

£18,000 (2009/10)

Beneficial area

UK.

Number 14, The Embankment, Vale Road, Heaton Mersey, Stockport, Cheshire
Correspondent: I Aspinall, Trustee
Trustees: J H Lyons; I Aspinall; K Pinnell.
CC Number: 1080950

Information available

Accounts were on file at Charity Commission

Registered with the Charity Commission in May 2000, the 2010 annual report states: 'the principal object of the charity is to use income for the relief of poverty and hardship amongst Jewish persons or the advancement of the Jewish religion, or for other charitable purposes'.

In 2009/10 the trust had assets of £694,000 and an income of £43,000 mostly coming from donations. It made grants to organisations totalling £18,000 (significantly less than in previous years, £53,000 in 2007/08). Assets stood at £694,000.

There were four grants made over £1,000 each. Beneficiaries were: Community Security Trust (£5,000); Manchester Jewish Federation and Manchester Jewish Youth Trust (£4,000 each); and Lubavitch South Manchester Trust (£2,500). A further amount of £2,500 was given out in grants of less than £1,000.

Applications

In writing to the correspondent.

The Boltons Trust

Social welfare, medicine, education

£0 (2009/10)

Beneficial area

Unrestricted.

12 York Gare, Regent's Park, London NW1 4QS
Correspondent: The Trustees
Trustees: C Albuquerque; R M Baldock; S D Albuquerque.
CC Number: 257951

Information available

Accounts were on file at the Charity Commission.

The main aims of the trust are:

- the pursuit of understanding and the reduction of innocent suffering
- support for education, research and welfare projects.

In 2009/10 the trust had assets of £1.2 million, an income of £46,000. No grants were made during the year, as the trustees stated that they were reserving their income to fund future donations.

Previously beneficiaries have included: Council for Christians and Jews; Dartington International Summer School; Jewish Association of Business Ethics; London Philharmonic Orchestra; Norwood; Trinity College of Music; and World ORT.

Applications

In writing to the correspondent. The trustees meet on a regular basis to consider applications.

The John and Celia Bonham Christie Charitable Trust

General

£29,000 (2009/10)

Beneficial area

UK, with some preference for the former county of Avon.

PO Box 9081, Taynton, Gloucester GL19 3WX
Correspondent: The Trustees
Trustees: Richard Bonham Christie; Robert Bonham Christie; Rosemary Ker.
CC Number: 326296

Information available

Accounts were available from the Charity Commission, but without a list of grants.

In 2009/10 the trust had assets of £1.3 million and a total income of £42,000. Grants were made to 27 organisations totalling £29,000.

Previous beneficiaries have included BIBIC, Butterwick Hospice, Cancer Research Campaign, Derby TOC, Digestive Disorder Foundation, Dorothy House, Elizabeth Finn Trust, Foundation for the Study of Infant Cot Deaths, Frome Festival, Home Start South Wiltshire, Inspire Foundation, Kings Medical Trust, Royal Society for the Blind Winsley, Sea Cadet Association, St John's Ambulance and Ten of Us.

Exclusions

No grants to individuals.

Applications

In writing to the correspondent. Only a small number of new applications are supported each year.

The Charlotte Bonham-Carter Charitable Trust

General

£137,000 (2009/10)

Beneficial area

UK, with some preference for Hampshire.

Chelwood, Rectory Road, East Carleton, Norwich NR14 8HT
Correspondent: Mrs Jenny Cannon, Administrator
Trustees: Sir Matthew Farrer; David Bonham-Carter; Eliza Bonham-Carter; Georgina Nayler.
CC Number: 292839

Information available

Accounts were available from the Charity Commission.

The trust is principally concerned with supporting charitable bodies and purposes which were of particular concern to Lady Bonham-Carter during her lifetime or are within the county of Hampshire. The trust's annual reports state:

> The trustees continue to support a core number of charities to whom they have made grants in the past as well as reviewing all applications received and making grants to new charities within their grant-giving criteria.

In 2009/10 the trust had assets of £3.9 million, which generated an income of £127,000. It gave £137,000 in 73 grants, ranging from £500 to £10,000.

Beneficiaries included: National Trust (£10,000); Florence Nightingale Museum (£5,000); City and London Guilds Bursary Fund (£4,000); British Museum – Friends of the Ancient Near East (£3,500); British Institute for the Study of Iraq (£3,000); Chelsea Physic Garden (£2,000); British Schools Exploring Society, Enterprise Education Trust and Firefly International (£1,000 each); Fields in Trust, National Council for the Conservation of Plants and Gardens and Sir Joseph Banks Archive Project (£500 each).

Exclusions

No grants to individuals or non-registered charities.

Applications

In writing to the correspondent. The application should include details of the funds required, funds raised so far and the timescale involved. The trust states that: 'unsolicited general applications are unlikely to be successful and only increase the cost of administration.' There are no application forms. Trustees meet in January and July; applications need to be received by May or November.

The Linda and Gordon Bonnyman Charitable Trust

General

Around £200,000 (2009/10)

Beneficial area
Unrestricted.

Ely Grange, Bells Yew Green Road, Frant, Tunbridge Wells, East Sussex TN3 9DY
Correspondent: Linda Bonnyman, Trustee
Trustees: James Gordon Bonnyman; Linda Bonnyman; James Wallace Taylor Bonnyman.
CC Number: 1123441

Information available
Limited information was available from the Charity Commission.

This trust was established in 2008 for general charitable purposes.

In 2009/10 the charity had an income of £14,360 and a total charitable expenditure of £205,000. No further information was available.

Applications
In writing to the correspondent.

The Booth Charities

Welfare, health, education

£223,000 to organisations (2009/10)

Beneficial area
Salford.

The William Jones Building, 1 Eccles Old Road, Salford M6 7DE
Tel: 0161 736 2989
Fax: 01270 764795
Email: enquiries@butcher-barlow.co.uk
Correspondent: Jonathan Shelmerdine, Clerk to the Trustees

Trustees: William Whittle, Chair; David Tully; Philip Webb; Richard Kershaw; Edward Tudor Evans; Edward Wilson Hunt; Richard Christmas; Roger Weston; Michael Prior; John Willis; Alan Dewhurst.
CC Number: 221800

Information available
Accounts were available from the Charity Commission.

The Booth Charities are two charities supporting disadvantaged people in Salford. Together they provide a wide range of support including pension payments to individuals and grants to local charities and facilities. A large number of grants go to organisations which have a direct connection with the charities and a substantial number of these institutions bear the Booth name.

Humphrey Booth the Elder's Charity is for the benefit of the inhabitants of Salford and is established 'for the relief of the aged, impotent or poor' with a preference for people over sixty years of age; the relief of distress and sickness; the provision and support of facilities for recreation and other leisure time occupation; the provision and support of educational facilities; and any other charitable purpose.

Humphrey Booth the Grandson's Charity is established for the income to be applied in or towards the repair and maintenance of the Church of Sacred Trinity, Salford, and in augmenting the stipend of the rector of the Church. The remaining income is then applied in furtherance of the same objects as apply to the Humphrey Booth the Elder Charity.

In 2009/10 the trust had assets of £29 million. Income stood at £918,000, down from £1.1 million in 2008/09, largely due to a 14% drop in investment income. Grants were made to 55 organisations during the year totalling £223,000. Support costs were relatively high at £214,000. Grants were categorised as follows:

Recreation and leisure	11	£69,000
Education	5	£61,000
Relief of distress and sickness	5	£25,000
Relief of aged, impotent and poor	22	£20,000
Sacred Trinity Church	1	£18,000
Other charitable purposes	11	£28,000

Beneficiaries included: the Heritage Learning Centre and Museum (£30,000); William Jones Bursary (£20,000); the Lowry Centre Trust (£10,000); Broughton House (£9,000); the Working Class Movement Library (£6,700); Music in Hospitals (£5,000); the Salfordian Trust Co Ltd (£4,000); Boundary Road Methodist Church (£2,000); PDSA (£1,000); and Rainsough Community Centre (£220).

Grants were also made to 31 individuals totalling £3,200.

Applications
In writing to the correspondent.

Salo Bordon Charitable Trust

Jewish

£344,000 (2009/10)

Beneficial area
UK and worldwide.

39 Gresham Gardens, London NW11 8PA
Correspondent: Marcel Bordon, Trustee
Trustees: Marcel Bordon; Salo Bordon; Lilly Bordon.
CC Number: 266439

Information available
Accounts were available from the Charity Commission, but without a list of grants.

This trust makes grants mainly to Jewish organisations, for social welfare and religious education. In 2009/10 it had assets amounting to £7.8 million and an income of £563,000 compared to £321,000 in 2008/09. The trust attributes this 75 per cent increase to the increase in investment income dividends receivable, which totalled £400,000 for the year (£134,000 in 2008/09). Grants totalled £344,000. A list of grant beneficiaries was not included in the accounts.

Previous beneficiaries include: Agudas Israel Housing Association Ltd, Baer Hatorah, Beth Jacob Grammar School, Brisk Yeshivas, Golders Green Beth Hamedrash Congregation Jaffa

Institute, Jewish Learning Exchange, London Academy of Jewish Studies, Society of Friends of Torah and WST Charity.

Applications
In writing to the correspondent.

The Oliver Borthwick Memorial Trust

Homelessness
£37,000 (2008/09)

Beneficial area
UK.

c/o Donor Grants Department, Charities Aid Foundation, Kings Hill, West Malling, Kent ME19 4TA
Tel: 01732 520 107
Email: jknight@cfaonline.org
Correspondent: Mr James Knight
Trustees: M H R Brethedon; R A Graham; J Macdonald; J R Marriott; Mrs V Wrigley; D Scott.
CC Number: 256206

Information available
Last accounts available at the Charity Commission website were for 2008/09.

The intention of the trust is to provide shelter and help the homeless. The trustees welcome applications from small but viable charities where they are able to make a significant contribution to the practical work of the charity, especially in disadvantaged inner-city areas.

In 2008/09 it had assets of £1 million which generated an income of £45,000. Grants totalling £37,000 were made to 8 organisations.

Beneficiaries included: Queens Cottages, Single Homeless Accommodation Project Ltd, Rape & Sexual Abuse Support Centre, St George's House Charity and Basement Night Drop-In Centre (£5,000 each).

Exclusions
No grants to individuals, including people working temporarily overseas

for a charity where the request is for living expenses, together with applications relating to health, disability and those from non-registered charitable organisations.

Applications
Letters should be set out on a maximum of two sides of A4, giving full details of the project with costs, who the project will serve and the anticipated outcome of the project. Meetings take place once a year in May. Applications should be received no later than April.

The Boshier-Hinton Foundation

Children and adults with special educational or other needs
£129,000 (2009/10)

Beneficial area
England and Wales.

Yeomans, Aythorpe Roding, Great Dunmow, Essex CM6 1PD
Tel: 01245 231032
Email: boshierhinton@yahoo.co.uk
Correspondent: Dr Peter Boshier, Trustee
Trustees: Thea Boshier, Chair; Dr Peter Boshier; James Tye; Janet Beale.
CC Number: 1108886

Information available
Accounts were available from the Charity Commission.

Set up in 2005, the foundation's main area of interest is children and adults with special educational or other needs and their families.

In 2009/10 the foundation had assets of £885,000 and an income of £123,000. Grants were made to 77 organisations totalling just over £129,000. During the year the foundation considered 253 applications.

Grants ranged from £250 to £6,000, although the majority of grants were for £2,000 or less.

Beneficiaries included: Accuro (£6,000); British Paralympic Association (£5,000); Meningitis Trust and Happy Days Children's Charity (£3,000 each); Arthritis Care, All Ability Sports and Leisure, Birmingham Royal Ballet, Cerebral Palsy Sport, Clothing Solutions, Friends of Penn Hall School, Lakelands Hospice and Sign Health (£2,000 each); Calibre Audio Library, Lunch on the Run, Green Light Trust and UK Voice (£1,500 each); BASIC, Deafness Support Network, Disability North, National Autistic Society and the National Blind Tenpin Bowling Association (£1,000 each); Sheffield Theatres Trust (£750); Camden Arts Centre, Dance Umbrella and Step By Step (£500 each); and Worcester Concert Club (£250).

Applications
A copy of the latest grant application form is available on request.

Common applicant mistakes
'They do not enquire regarding our system; they are often too imprecise regarding the reasons for seeking funds.'

The Bothwell Charitable Trust

Disability, health, older people, conservation
£38,000 (2009/10)

Beneficial area
England, particularly the South East.

25 Ellenbridge Way, South Croydon CR2 0EW
Tel: 020 8657 6884
Correspondent: Mr Paul Leonard James, Chair of Trustees
Trustees: Paul L James, Chair; Crispian M P Howard; Theresa McGregor.
CC Number: 299056

Information available
Information was available from the Charity Commission website.

The trust makes grants towards health, disability, conservation and older people's causes. In 2009/10 the trust had assets of £9,000, with an income of £42,000. Grants were made to 24 organisations totalling £38,000.

Grants were for either £2,000 or £1,000; beneficiaries included: Arthritis Research UK, Blackthorn Trust, British Heart Foundation, ECHO International Health Services Ltd, Friends of the Elderly, Invalid Children's Aid Nationwide, Leukaemia Research Fund (£2,000 each); and Brain Research Trust, British Trust for Conservation Volunteers, Childlink Adoption Society, Multiple Sclerosis Society and Riding for the Disabled Association (£1,000 each).

Exclusions

No grants for animal charities, overseas causes, individuals, or charities not registered with the Charity Commission.

Applications

In writing to the correspondent. Distributions are usually made in February or March each year.

The Harry Bottom Charitable Trust

Religion, education, medical

£84,000 (2009/10)

Beneficial area

UK, with a preference for Yorkshire and Derbyshire.

c/o Westons, Chartered Accountants, Queen's Buildings, 55 Queen Street, Sheffield S1 2DX
Correspondent: J S Hinsley
Trustees: Revd J M Kilner; Prof. T H Lilley; Prof. I G Rennie; Prof. A Rawlinson; T Moore.
CC Number: 204675

Information available

Accounts were available from the Charity Commission.

The trust states that support is divided roughly equally between religion, education and medical causes. Within these categories grants are given to:

- religion – small local appeals and cathedral appeals
- education – universities and schools
- medical – equipment for hospitals and charities concerned with disability.

In 2009/10 the trust had assets of £4.3 million, which generated an income of £212,000. Grants were made totalling £84,000 and were broken down as follows:

Educational and other activities	£36,000
Religious activities	£30,000
Medical activities	£18,000

Beneficiaries included: Yorkshire Baptist Association (£25,000); St Luke's Hospice (£5,000); Sheffield Association for Cerebral Palsy (£3,500); Sheffield Mencap (£3,000); and Girl Guiding (£2,500).

Exclusions

No grants to individuals.

Applications

In writing to the correspondent at any time.

Common applicant mistakes

'The trustees aim to support causes in South Yorkshire in North East Derbyshire. Many claims are from outside areas or abroad. The trustees also tend to support small charities etc. rather than large national ones.'

The A H and E Boulton Trust

Evangelical Christian

£60,000 to organisations (2009/10)

Beneficial area

Worldwide, with some preference for Merseyside.

c/o Moore Stephens LLP, 110–114 Duke Street, Liverpool L1 5AG
Tel: 0151 703 1080
Correspondent: The Trustees
Trustees: Dr Frank Gopsill; Jennifer Gopsill; Michael Gopsill; Peter Gopsill.
CC Number: 225328

Information available

Accounts were available from the Charity Commission.

The trust mainly supports the erection and maintenance of buildings to be used for preaching the Christian gospel and for relieving the sick or needy. The trustees can also support other Christian institutions, especially missions in the UK and developing world.

In 2009/10 the trust had assets of £2.8 million and an income of £52,000. Grants totalled £63,000.

Beneficiaries were: Liverpool City Mission (£30,000); and the Slavic Gospel Association and Pioneer People Wirral (£15,000 each). An additional grant of £500 was made to a parishioner and a further £2,200 was given in small grants to ministers.

Applications

In writing to the correspondent. The trust tends to support a set list of charities and applications are very unlikely to be successful.

P G and N J Boulton Trust

Christian

£66,000 (2009/10)

Beneficial area

Worldwide.

PO Box 72, Wirral, Merseyside CH46 6AA
Website: www.boultontrust.org.uk
Correspondent: Andrew L Perry, Trustee
Trustees: Andrew L Perry; Shirley Perry; Peter H Stafford; Margaret Jardine-Smith.
CC Number: 272525

Information available

Accounts were available from the Charity Commission.

The trust describes its general funding policy on its website as follows:

1 **Main Commitment** – Our giving is largely restricted to organisations and activities that are of special interest to the trustees and this is largely concentrated in the area of Christian missionary work.

2 **Other Areas** – The trust has from time to time made donations in the following areas:
  - disaster and poverty relief
  - medical research and healthcare
  - disability relief and care of elderly.

In 2009/10 it had assets of £3.6 million, an income of £125,000 and made grants totalling £66,000.

Grants of £1,000 or more were made to twelve organisations and were listed in the accounts. Beneficiaries were: Vision for China (£11,000); New Life Centre (£10,000); Children Alone (£8,500); Intercessors for Britain (£8,000); Shalom Christian Fellowship (£6,000); Longcroft Christian Trust (£4,500); Just Care (£4,000); Christian Institute and International Mission Project (£2,500 each); Barnabas Fund and Shepherd's Purse Trust (£1,500 each); and Cedars School (£1,000).

Other donations of £1,000 or less totalled £5,000.

Exclusions

No grants for:
- individuals
- environment and conservation
- culture and heritage
- sport and leisure
- animal welfare
- church building repairs.

Applications

Please note the following statement from the trust's website:

> We are currently undergoing a long term review of our policies and this means that in practice, we are currently only making donations to organisations to whom we have an existing commitment. This unfortunately means that any new requests for funding at the present time will almost certainly be unsuccessful.

Sir Clive Bourne Family Trust

Jewish

£80,000 (2009/10)

Beneficial area

UK.

134–136 High Street, Epping, Essex CM16 4AG
Correspondent: Janet Bater

Trustees: Lady Joy Bourne; Katie Cohen; Lucy Furman; Claire Lefton; Merryl Flitterman.
CC Number: 290620

Information available

Full accounts were available from the Charity Commission website.

The trustees favour Jewish causes. A number of health and medical charities (particularly relating to cancer) have also benefited.

In 2009/10 the trust's assets totalled £4.3 million and it had an income of £181,000. Grants were made totalling £80,000, which was around 20 per cent more than in 2008/09 due to the trustees increasing their support to the Prostate Cancer Research Fund (£39,000).

Other beneficiaries included: Sydney Gold Trust (£13,000); Norwood Ravenswood (£4,700); WIZO UK (£3,700); World Jewish Relief (£3,000); Drugsline (£2,500); Community Security Trust and Hazon Yeshaya (£2,000 each); Jewish Care (£1,500); Langdon Foundation (£1,000); International Spinal Research Trust (£500); Anne Frank Trust (£260); One to One (£200); Jewish Women's Aid (£150); and Institute of Cancer Research (£100).

Applications

In writing to the correspondent.

Bourneheights Limited

Orthodox Jewish

£1.2 million (2009/10)

Beneficial area

UK.

Flat 10, Palm Court, Queen Elizabeth's Walk, London N16 5XA
Correspondent: Schloime Rand, Trustee
Trustees: Chaskel Rand; Esther Rand; Erno Berger; Yechiel Chersky; Schloime Rand.
CC Number: 298359

Information available

Accounts were available from the Charity Commission, but without a list of grants.

Registered with the Charity Commission in February 1998, in 2009/10 this charity had assets of £6.5 million and an income of £2.1 million including £1.1 million from donations. Grants were made totalling £1.2 million.

Previous beneficiaries include: Moreshet Hatorah, Mercaz Torah Vahesed Ltd, BFOT, Belz Synagogue, Telz Academy Trust, Gevurath Ari Academy, UTA, Toreth Emeth, Olam Chesed Yiboneh, Before Trust, Heaven Point, Yeshivas Avas Torah and Lubavitch Mechina.

Applications

In writing to the correspondent.

The Bowerman Charitable Trust

Church, the arts, medical, youth

£349,000 (2009/10)

Beneficial area

UK, with a preference for West Sussex.

Champs Hill, Coldwatham, Pulborough, West Sussex RH20 1LY
Correspondent: D W Bowerman, Trustee
Trustees: D W Bowerman; C M Bowerman; J M Taylor; K E Bowerman; A M Downham; J M Capper; M Follis.
CC Number: 289446

Information available

Accounts were on file at the Charity Commission.

In 2009/10 the trust had assets of £11.4 million and an income of £284,000. Grants were made to organisations totalling £349,000 (£509,000 in the previous year) and were given in the following categories:

Church activities	£243,000
The arts	£79,000
Youth work	£13,000
Medical charities	£8,000
Other	£6,000

The largest grant went to St Margaret's Church, Angmering (£216,000). Other grants included those made to: English Chamber Orchestra (£13,000); British Youth Opera and Wigmore Hall Trust (£11,000 each); and the Titus Trust (£10,000).

Applications

In writing to the correspondent. The trustees have previously stated that they are bombarded with applications and unsolicited applications will not be considered.

The William Brake Charitable Trust

General

£279,000 (2009/10)

Beneficial area

UK, with a preference for Kent.

c/o Gill Turner and Tucker, Colman House, King Street, Maidstone, Kent ME14 1JE
Correspondent: The Trustees
Trustees: Philip R Wilson; Deborah J Isaac; Penelope A Lang; Michael Trigg.
CC Number: 1023244

Information available

Accounts were on file at the Charity Commission, without a list of recent grants.

The charity invites applications from the William Brake family for funding of worthy charitable causes each year, with a particular emphasis on local charities where the family know the charity's representative.

In 2009/10 the trust had assets of £9.5 million and an income of £114,000. The trust made 73 grants totalling £279,000.

Previous beneficiaries included: Whitely Fund for Nature; the Royal Masonic Benevolent Institution; NSPCC; the Duke of Edinburgh's

Award; the Ecology Trust; Wooden Spoon Society; Aurora Tsunami Orphanage; Mike Collingwood Memorial Fund; League of Remembrance; Friends of St Peter's Hospital Chertsey; Canterbury Cathedral Development; Cancer Research UK; Elimination of Leukaemia Fund; Maidstone Mencap Charitable Trust; RNLI; Alzheimer's Society; Breast Cancer Care; Courtyard – Petersfield; Dorothy Grinstead Memorial Fund; Macmillan Cancer Support; and Portland College.

Applications

In writing to the correspondent.

The Tony Bramall Charitable Trust

Medical research, ill health, social welfare

£34,000 (2009/10)

Beneficial area

UK, with some preference for Yorkshire.

12 Cardale Court, Beckwith Head Road, Harrogate, North Yorkshire HG3 1RY
Tel: 01423 535300
Email: johnholroyd64@hotmail.com
Correspondent: The Trustees
Trustees: D C A Bramall; Mrs K S Bramall Odgen; Mrs M J Foody; G M Tate; Miss A Bramall.
CC Number: 1001522

Information available

Accounts were available from the Charity Commission.

The charity was established in 1988 by Mr D C A Bramall with an initial sum of £600,000. The charity is focused on assisting persons less able to finance their medical/health needs, particularly children and particularly those causes based in the northern part of the country.

In 2009/10 the trust had assets of £3.9 million, an income of £98,000 and made 9 grants totalling £34,000.

Beneficiaries included: St Michael's Hospice (£20,000); Children Heart Surgery Fund (£3,000); Henshaw's

Society for Blind People (£2,500); Royal Horticultural Society (£2,000); Brain Tumor UK (£500); and Christie Charity (£200).

Applications

In writing to the correspondent.

The Bransford Trust

General

£485,000 (2009/10)

Beneficial area

Preference for the West Midlands.

5 Deansway, Worcester, Worcestershire WR1 2JG
Tel: 01905 612001
Email: doliver@harrison-clark.co.uk
Correspondent: Dawn Emma Oliver
Trustees: C A Kinnear; B Kinnear; L E S Freeman; A J C Kinnear; A J Neil.
CC Number: 1106554

Information available

Accounts were available from the Charity Commission.

Established in 2004, in 2009/10 the trust had assets of £8 million and an income of £1 million. Grants were made to over 25 organisations totalling almost £485,000.

Beneficiaries included: the Leys School (£190,000); St Richard Hospice (£100,000); Acorns Children's Trust (£30,000); Noah's Ark Trust and Young Enterprise West Midlands (£15,000 each); Vitalise Trust (£10,000); English Symphony Orchestra (£6,000); Bromsgrove Festival (£5,000); and Choice Radio (£1,000).

Applications

In writing to the correspondent.

The Breast Cancer Research Trust

Breast cancer research

£345,000 (2009/10)

Beneficial area

UK.

48 Wayneflete Tower Avenue, Esher, Surrey KT10 8QG
Tel: 01372 463235
Email: bcrtoffice@aol.com
Website: www.breastcancerresearchtrust.org.uk
Correspondent: The Honorary Administrator
Trustees: Dame Vera Lynn; Prof. Charles Coombes; Jean-Claude Gazet; Virginia Lewis-Jones; Bob Potter; Prof. Trevor J Powles; R M Rainsbury; Dr Margaret Spittle.
CC Number: 272214

Information available

Accounts were available from the Charity Commission.

The Breast Cancer Research Trust is a charity dedicated to funding clinical and laboratory project research, undertaken in recognised cancer centres or research institutions in the UK, directly aimed at improving the prevention, early diagnosis and treatment of breast cancer. Limited grants available up to a term of three years. Grants reviewed annually.

In 2009/10 the trust had assets of £244,000 and an income of £265,000. Grants were made to 11 institutions totalling £345,000. The University of Birmingham received the largest grant amounting to £72,000.

Other beneficiaries were: Mount Vernon Hospital (£60,000); University of Leeds (53,000); Imperial College (£42,000); University College London (£35,000); University of Nottingham (£30,000); Royal Marsden Hospital (£20,000); CBC Research (£10,000); Southampton General Hospital and Cardiff University (£9,000 each); and University of Dundee (£7,000).

Exclusions

No grants to students.

Applications

Application forms available only from the trust's website.

The Brendish Family Foundation

General, children, education, health care and access to food and water

£53,000 (2009/10)

Beneficial area

UK and overseas, with a preference for India.

Dixon Wilson Chartered Accountants, 22 Chancery Lane, London WC2A 1LS
Tel: 020 7680 8100
Correspondent: Graham Chambers, Trustee
Trustees: Graham Chambers; Susan Brendish; Clayton Brendish; Nathan Brendish; Natalie Brendish.
CC Number: 1079065

Information available

Accounts were available from the Charity Commission.

The trust was established in 2000 for general charitable purposes. The trust's recent accounts state that in the future the trustees would like to support projects including those that involved children, education, health care and access to food and water.

In 2009/10 the foundation had assets of £851,000 and an income of £264,000. Grants were made to seven organisations totalling £53,000.

The main beneficiary during the year was the Brendish Foundation, a connected foundation which is overseeing the building of a children's hospital in India, which received just over £30,000.

The other beneficiaries during the year were: Child in Need Institute – India (£10,000); the Children with Special Needs Foundation (£5,000); the Busoga Trust (£3,000); Marie Curie Cancer Care (£2,500); Digital Himalayan Project – Cambridge University (£1,500); and Haiti Earthquake Appeal (£1,000).

Applications

In writing to the correspondent.

The Harold and Alice Bridges Charity

General

£84,000 (2009/10)

Beneficial area

South Cumbria and North Lancashire (as far south as Preston).

Senior Calveley and Hardy Solicitors, 8 Hastings Place, Lytham FY8 5NA
Tel: 01253 733333
Email: rnh@seniorslaw.co.uk
Correspondent: Richard N Hardy, Trustee
Trustee: Richard N Hardy.
CC Number: 236654

Information available

Accounts were obtained from the Charity Commission website. The 2009/10 trustees' report provides the following information:

> The trustees normally make grants to local causes in the Lancashire and South Cumbria area with special preference to the River Ribble area and northwards, the Blackburn area, and the South Lakes area. Generally, grants are made to benefit the young and the elderly, are mainly towards capital projects in connection with rural and village life especially where there is associated voluntary effort.

In 2009/10 the charity had assets of £2.4 million and an income of £90,000. Grants to 46 organisations totalled £84,000. Donations ranged between £500 and £5,000.

Beneficiaries included: Stainton Institute and Rosemere Cancer Foundation – Preston (£5,000 each); St John's Churchyard – Tunstall (£4,000); Emmanuel Parish Church – Southport (£2,500); British Wireless for the Blind Fund (£2,000); Rainbow Trust Children's Charity (£1,000); and Dolly Mops and Springfield

Bowling Club – High Bentham (£500 each).

Exclusions

No grants to individuals.

Applications

In writing to the correspondent, followed by completion of a standard application form. The trustees meet three times a year to discuss and approve grant applications and review finances. Cheques are sent out to those successful applicants within days of each meeting.

Briggs Animal Welfare Trust

Animal welfare

£85,000 (2009/10)

Beneficial area

UK and overseas.

Little Champions Farm, Maplehurst Road, West Grinstead, Horsham, West Sussex RH13 6RN
Correspondent: The Trustees
Trustees: Louise Hartnett; Adrian Schouten.
CC Number: 276459

Information available

Accounts were received by the Charity Commission but were not available to view.

This trust derives most of its income from shares in the company Eurotherm International plc. Although the original objects of the trust were general, but with particular support for animal welfare, the trust's policy is to support only animal welfare causes. There are five named beneficiaries in the trust deed: RSPCA, Reystede Animal Sanctuary Ringmer, Brooke Hospital for Animals Cairo, Care of British Columbia House and the Society for the Protection of Animals in North Africa.

In 2009/10 the trust had an income of £2,100 and a total expenditure of £93,000. Grants were made totalling around £85,000. No further information was available.

Applications

In writing to the correspondent.

John Bristow and Thomas Mason Trust

Education, relief in need, people with disabilities, community amenities

£91,000 (2010)

Beneficial area

Parish of Charlwood (as the boundaries stood in 1926).

3 Grayrigg Road, Maidenbower, Crawley RH10 7AB
Tel: 01293 883950
Email: trust.secretary@jbtmt.org.uk
Website: www.jbtmt.org.uk
Correspondent: Miss M Singleton, Secretary
Trustees: Martin James, Chair; Revd Bill Campen; Feargal Hogan; Alison Martin; Howard Pearson; Deborah Shortland; Pat Wilson.
CC Number: 1075971

Information available

Accounts were available from the Charity Commission.

The trust's objectives are:

- the promotion of education in the area of benefit
- the relief of inhabitants who are in need, hardship or distress, or who are sick, convalescent, disabled, handicapped or infirm
- the provision and support of facilities for recreation and other leisure time occupation for the inhabitants or any sufficient sector of them
- the provision and support of other charitable purposes for the benefit of the inhabitants.

In 2010 the trust had assets of £2.2 million and an income of £78,000. Grants amounted to £91,000.

Grant beneficiaries included: Charlwood Parish Hall (£29,000); 9th Horley (Charlwood) Scouts (£4,000); St Catherine's Hospice (£3,300); Charlwood Village Infant School-

PTA (£3,100); Charlwood and Hookwood Community Steering Commitee (£2,300); 1st Horley Guides (£1,100); and the Charlwood Mothers Union (£200).

Exclusions

Any application that will not benefit the residents of the Parish of Charlwood (as the boundaries stood in 1926) will not be considered.

Applications

Applications should be made on a form available from the correspondent upon written request, and should include an estimate of the total cost of the project, with three quotations where applicable.

The British Council for Prevention of Blindness

Prevention and treatment of blindness

£187,000 (2009/10)

Beneficial area

Worldwide.

4 Bloomsbury Square, London WC1A 2RP
Tel: 020 7404 7114
Email: info@bcpb.org
Website: www.bcpb.org
Correspondent: The Trustees
Trustees: Dr J Jay: Chair; S M Brooker; Ms J Boulter; Dr C Harper; Prof. J Morgan; Ms C Walker.
CC Number: 270941

Information available

Accounts were available from the Charity Commission.

The BCPB's mission statement is to help prevent blindness and restore sight in the UK and developing world by:

- funding research (including fellowships) in UK hospitals and universities into the causes and treatments of the major eye diseases

- supporting practical treatment programmes and research in the developing world
- promoting vital skills, leadership, awareness and demand for the expansion of community eye health in the developing world through the education of doctors and nurses within communities.

The trust's policy is to divide its support equally between projects in the UK and abroad. Grants are given to hospitals, universities and health centres both in the UK and in developing countries. Grants are also given to individuals through the Boulter Fellowship Awards. Grants are usually for a maximum of £40,000 and given for a maximum of three years.

In 2009/10 the organisation had assets of £735,000 and an income of £665,000, mainly from legacy income. Grants totalled £187,000.

Exclusions

This trust does not deal with the individual welfare of blind people in the UK.

Applications

Applications can be made throughout the year.

The British Dietetic Association General and Education Trust Fund

Dietary and nutritional issues

£54,000 (2009/10)

Beneficial area

UK.

5th Floor, Charles House, 148–149 Great Charles Street, Queensway, Birmingham B3 3HT
Tel: 0121 200 8080
Email: info@bda.uk.com
Website: www.bda.uk.com
Correspondent: The Secretary to the Trustees

Trustees: P Brindley; E Elliot; W T Seddon; M Mackintosh; H Davidson.
CC Number: 282553

Information available

Accounts were on file at the Charity Commission.

The British Dietetic Association General and Education Trust exists to advance education and other purposes related to the science of dietetics. The trust has an annual grant giving budget of around £50,000 and can make grants to individuals and to recognised associations or groups of people engaged in dietetic research and associated activities.

In 2009/10 it had assets of £1.4 million and an income of £50,000. Grants were made totalling £54,000.

Exclusions

No direct support of dietetic students in training or postgraduate qualifications for individuals, i.e. the trust will not pay postgraduate fees/ expenses, or elective/MSc study for doctors.

Applications

Application forms can be downloaded from the trust's website.

British Humane Association

Welfare

£82,000 (2010)

Beneficial area

UK.

The Cottage, New Road, Cutnall Green, Droitwich WR9 0PQ
Tel: 01299 851588
Correspondent: H R J Grant, Company Secretary
Trustees: Dr J T Breen; B Campbell-Johnson; C Campbell-Johnston; C J Newbold; J M Huntington; P Gee; D J Eldridge; D A Cantlay; A H Chignell.
CC Number: 207120

Information available

Accounts were available from the Charity Commission.

The charity's 2010 trustees' report states:

> The primary aim of the company, which is a registered charity, is the promotion of benevolence for the good of humanity and the community, through grant making. The directors of the Association have decided, that in order to increase the amount available for grant distribution to beneficiaries, they will transfer funds to other charitable organisations, which have in place systems for identifying and assisting deserving cases in need. By so doing, they will not duplicate selection processes and the resultant costs. It is the intention that any one or more of the directors will examine requests for assistance received and submit a proposal to the board to award a one-off, set period or continuing grant to any body, which has applied for assistance.

Three classes of charities have been designated to receive support in accordance with its articles of association; these are:

- charities directly involved in the relief of inhumane activities
- charities distributing grants to individuals
- charities providing relief of poverty, sickness or benefit to the community.

In 2010 the charity had assets of £3.8 million and an income of £112,000. Grants were made to 11 organisations totalling £82,000.

Beneficiaries included: Send a Cow (£33,000); St John of Jerusalem Eye Hospital (£12,000); Argyll and Bute Care and Repair Children with Cancer and Leukaemia (£10,000); Phoenix Futures (£5,000); and Sir David Evans Bursary and Penarth Sea Scouts (£2,000 each).

Applications

Applications not considered – see 'General' section.

The Roger Brooke Charitable Trust

General

£44,000 (2009/10)

Beneficial area

UK, with a preference for Hampshire.

Withers, 16 Old Bailey, London EC4M 7EG
Tel: 020 7597 6123
Correspondent: J P Arnold, Trustee
Trustees: J P Arnold; C R E Brooke; Mrs N B Brooke; Ms J R Rousso; S H R Brooke.
CC Number: 1071250

Information available

Basic information taken from the Charity Commission website.

Established in 1998, this trust has general charitable purposes, including medical research, support for carers and social action.

In 2009/10 the trust had an income of £23,000 and a total expenditure of £44,000. No other financial information was available.

Previous beneficiary: The Southampton University Development Fund (£100,000).

Exclusions

In general, individuals are not supported.

Applications

The trustees advised us as follows:

We are suspending grants for the foreseeable future due to the decreased value of the underlying assets of the trust.

The David Brooke Charity

Youth, older people, medical

£117,000 (2009/10)

Beneficial area

UK.

Cook Sutton, Tay Court, Blounts Court Road, Sonning Common, Oxfordshire RG4 9RS
Correspondent: D J Rusman, Trustee
Trustees: D J Rusman; P M Hutt; N A Brooke.
CC Number: 283658

Information available

Accounts were available from the Charity Commission.

The charity supports youth causes, favouring disadvantaged young people, particularly through causes providing self-help programmes and outdoor-activity training. Grants are also given to medical organisations and organisations supporting older people.

In 2009/10 the charity had assets of £2 million and an income of £114,000. Grants were given to 38 organisations totalling £117,000, which were broken down into the following two categories:

Children and young people	11	£40,000
Other institutions	27	£77,000

Beneficiaries included: Thwaites Theatre (£6,000); Great Ormond Street Hospital (£5,000); ASTO and the British Stammering Association (£4,000 each); the Mission to Seafarers and the Samaritans (£3,500 each); Age Concern (£3,000); SSAFA Forces Help (£2,500); the Living Paintings Trust and the Sobriety Project (£2,000 each); and the Ramblers Association (£1,000).

Applications

The correspondent stated that the trust's annual income is not for general distribution as it is committed to a limited number of charities on a long-term basis.

Bill Brown's Charitable Settlement

General, health, social welfare

£210,000 (2009/10)

Beneficial area

UK.

BM BOX 4567, London WC1N 3XX
Correspondent: The Trustees
Trustees: G S Brown; A J Barnett.
CC Number: 801756

Information available

Accounts were on file at the Charity Commission.

This settlement supports general charitable purposes, particularly health and welfare causes.

In 2009/10 the trust had assets of £10 million and an income of £356,000. Grants to 19 organisations totalled £210,000. Grants are often recurrent.

Beneficiaries included: Charities Aid Foundation Trust (£60,000 in two grants); Bristol Grammar School (£43,000); Macmillan Cancer Support and Salvation Army (£13,000 each); DebRA, Leonard Cheshire Foundation, Princess Alice Hospice and the Scout Council – Greater London and Middlesex West Country (£6,500 each); and NCH Action for Children and Richmond Borough Association for Mental Health (£3,300 each).

Future commitments were made to Bristol Grammar School totalling £75,000.

Exclusions

No grants to individuals.

Applications

In writing containing the following:
- aims and objectives of the charity
- nature of appeal
- total target if for a specific project
- contributions received against target
- registered charity number
- any other relevant factors.

Appeals should be accompanied by a set of the organisation's latest report and full accounts.

R S Brownless Charitable Trust

Disability, relief-in-need, ill health, accommodation and housing, education, job creation, voluntary work

£62,000 (2009/10)

Beneficial area

Mainly UK and occasionally overseas.

Hennerton Holt, Hennerton, Wargrave, Reading RG10 8PD
Tel: 0118 940 4029
Correspondent: Philippa Nicolai, Trustee
Trustees: Frances Plummer; Philippa Nicolai.
CC Number: 1000320

Information available

Accounts were on file at the Charity Commission, without a list of grants.

The trust makes grants to causes that benefit people who are disabled, disadvantaged or seriously ill. Charities working in the fields of accommodation and housing, education, job creation and voluntary work are also supported. Grants are usually one-off, ranging between £100 and £2,000.

In 2009/10 the trust had assets of £1.2 million and an income of £53,000. Grants were made totalling £62,000.

Previous beneficiaries have included: Alzheimer's Society, Camp Mohawk, Casa Allianza UK, Crisis, Foundation for Study of Infant Deaths, Prader-Willi Foundation, St Andrew's Hall, UNICEF, Wargrave PCC and Witham on the Hill PCC.

Exclusions

Grants are rarely given to individuals for educational projects or to education or conservation causes or overseas aid.

Applications

In writing to the correspondent. The trustees meet twice a year, but in special circumstances will meet at other times. The trust is unable to acknowledge all requests.

The T B H Brunner Charitable Settlement

Church of England, heritage, arts, general

£33,000 to organisations and individuals (2009/10)

Beneficial area

UK with some preference for Oxfordshire.

Flat 4, 2 Inverness Gardens, London W8 4RN
Tel: 020 7727 6277
Correspondent: Timothy Brunner, Trustee
Trustees: Timothy Brunner; Helen Brunner; Dr Imogen Brunner.
CC Number: 260604

Information available

Accounts were available from the Charity Commission.

The trust offered the following guidance on its grantmaking policy in the latest accounts:

> The trustees seek to make donations to other charities and voluntary bodies for the benefit of Church of England preservation projects and other charities dealing with historical preservation, both local to Oxfordshire and nationally. The trustees may also seek to make donations to other charities, voluntary bodies and individuals relating to the arts, music and also for general charitable purposes.

In 2009/10 this trust had assets of £1.7 million and an income of £48,000. There were 56 grants made during the year totalling £33,000.

Beneficiaries included: Rotherfield Greys PCC (£4,100 in four grants); Institute of Economic Affairs (£2,500); York Minster Fund (£1,300); King Edward Hospital, National Centre for Early Music, Rugby Portobello Trust, Minority Rights Group, Royal Theatrical Fund and the National Federation of Women's Institutes (£1,000 each); British Suzuki Institute (£750); Lincoln Cathedral (£550 in two grants); London School of Economics and Trinity College – Oxford (£500 each); TZABA (£250); Royal British Legion (£200); Garrick Christmas Fund (£150); and the Society for the Protection of Ancient Buildings (£100).

Applications

In writing to the correspondent.

Buckingham Trust

Christian purposes, relief of poverty and sickness and support for older people

£200,000 to organisations (2009/10)

Beneficial area

UK and worldwide.

Foot Davson, 17 Church Road, Tunbridge Wells, Kent TN1 1LG
Tel: 01892 774774
Fax: 01892 774775
Correspondent: The Trustees
Trustees: Richard Foot; Tina Clay.
CC Number: 237350

Information available

Accounts were on file at the Charity Commission.

The trust's objects are the advancement of religion and other charitable purposes.

In 2009/10 the trust held assets of £892,000 and had an income of £182,000, mostly from voluntary donations. Grants were made totalling £202,000, broken down as follows:

Charities	£65,000
Churches	£135,000
Individuals	£2,100

Beneficiaries included: Cure International (£18,000); Grace Church (£10,000); St Andrew's Church – Oxford and Tear Fund (£8,200 each); Sewardstone Church (£6,600); St Mark's – Gillingham (£4,000); Titus Trust (£3,400); OMF

International (£2,500); Barnabas Fund (£2,200); Sheiling Trust (£2,000); Tonbridge Baptist Church (£1,900); World in Need (£1,500); Association of Evangelists (£1,300); and Langham Partnership and All Saints – Lindfield (£1,000 each).

Applications

Unsolicited applicants are not considered. As an agency charity, the trustees allow the donors to choose which registered charities or churches their funds are given to.

Buckland Charitable Trust

General, health, international development and welfare

£30,000 (2009/10)

Beneficial area

UK and overseas.

c/o Smith and Wlliamson Limited, 1 Bishops Wharf, Walnut Tree Close, Guildford, Surrey GU1 4RA
Tel: 01483 407 100
Correspondent: The Trustees
Trustees: Paul Bannister; Ali Afsari; Anna Bannister.
CC Number: 273679

Information available

Accounts were on file at the Charity Commission.

In 2009/10 the trust had an income of £346,000 and made grants to 36 organisations totalling £30,000. During the year the majority of support was given to health related activities.

Beneficiaries included: Médecins Sans Frontières (£4,000); Cumbria Community Foundation and Muslim Aid (£3,000 each); Macmillan Cancer Relief and Cancer Research UK (£2,000 each); Camphill Village Trust, Great North Air Ambulance Service, Bishop Simeon Trust, Children with Leukaemia and Eden Valley Hospice (£1,000 each); Alzheimer's Disease Society, Inspire Foundation, Scope and MIND (£500 each); Moredum

Foundation and Water Aid (£200 each); and British Lung Foundation (£100).

Applications

In writing to the correspondent.

The Bulldog Trust Limited

General

£184,000 (2009/10)

Beneficial area

Worldwide, with a preference for the South of England.

2 Temple Place, London WC2R 3BD
Website: www.bulldogtrust.org
Correspondent: The Trustees
Trustees: Patrick Burgess; Martin Riley; Brian Smouha; Mary Fagan; Charles Hoare; Richard Hoare.
CC Number: 1123081

Information available

Accounts were available from the Charity Commission.

Operating since 1983, the Bulldog Trust has donated more than £3 million to a range of charities and in recent years has made grants totalling around £200,000 annually. The trust aims to support charity in ways which ensure that smaller donations provide maximum benefit. In the past we have pledged to start match funding campaigns; offered interest-free loans to tide charities through cash-flow crises; funded innovative pilot projects that could not access funding elsewhere and facilitated scholarships and bursaries in fields that we believed were being overlooked. The trustees have supported charities as diverse as Humanitarian Aid Relief Trust, the Prince's Trust and the University of Winchester. The trust's website states:

> Bulldog also runs two separately administered, smaller educational grants funds. The Bulldog Arts Fund offers grants to innovative and interesting arts projects. The Bulldog Educational Grants Fund makes small grants towards special educational needs.

In 2009/10 the trust had assets of £9 million and an income of £609,000. Grants totalled £184,000.

Beneficiaries included: University of Winchester (£23,000); Dance United (£13,000); Public Catalogue Foundation, Covenant House-Homeless Kids Toronto and Holidays 4 Heroes (£10,000 each).

Exclusions

No grants are given to individuals or to unsolicited applications.

Applications

The trust regrets that unsolicited applications cannot be accepted.

The Burden Trust

Christian, welfare, medical research, education, general

£117,000 (2009/10)

Beneficial area

UK and overseas.

51 Downs Park West, Westbury Park, Bristol BS6 7QL
Tel: 0117 962 8611
Email: p.oconor@netgates.co.uk
Correspondent: Patrick O'Conor, Secretary
Trustees: A C Miles, Chair; Dr Joanna Bacon; R E J Bernays; Dr M G Barker; Prof. A Halestrap.
CC Number: 235859

Information available

Accounts were available from the Charity Commission.

The trust operates in accordance with various trust deeds dating back to 1913. These deeds provide for grants for medical research, hospitals, retirement homes, schools and training institutions, homes and care for the young and people in need. The trust operates with an adherence to the tenets and principles of the Church of England.

In 2009/10 the trust had assets of £3.7 million and an income of £145,000. Grants were made to 15 organisations totalling £117,000, which were made under the following categories:

Schools and Training Institutions	7	£70,000
Organisations for Care and Training of Young People	3	£25,000
Support of the Marginalised	4	£17,000
Neurological Research	1	£5,000

Grants included those made to: Trinity College, Bristol (£20,000); Langham Research Scholarships (£15,000); Easton Families Project; Easton Families Project (£12,000); St Mark's Baptist Church (£10,000); Changing Tunes (£6,000); Alzheimer's Research (£5,000) and the Seed Project (£2,500).

Exclusions

No grants to individuals.

Applications

In writing to the correspondent. Financial information is required in support of the project for which help is requested. No application is responded to without an sae. Recipients of recurring grants are notified each year that grants are not automatic and must be applied for annually. Applications are considered at the annual trustees meeting.

Burdens Charitable Foundation

General

£255,000 (2009/10)

Beneficial area

UK, but mostly overseas, with special interest in Sub-Saharan Africa.

St George's House, 215–219 Chester Road, Manchester M15 4JE
Correspondent: Arthur James Burden, Trustee
Trustees: Arthur James Burden; Godfrey Wilfred Burden; Hilary Margaret Perkins; Sally Anne Schofield; Anthony David Burden.
CC Number: 273535

Information available

Accounts were available from the Charity Commission.

The trustees' report gives the following information:

There are no formal restrictions on the charitable activities that can be supported, but the trustees' main activities currently embrace the prevention and relief of acute poverty, substantially through the medium of education and healthcare and most especially in countries such as those of sub-Saharan Africa.

In 2009/10 the foundation had assets of £20 million, an income of £596,000 and made 46 grants totalling £255,000 a significant number of which went overseas.

Beneficiaries of grants of £5,000 or more included: The Message Trust (£20,000); Kings World Trust India (£15,000); Build-it and Self Help Africa (£10,000 each); The Charity Service (£7,000); and Tenovus (£5,000).

Exclusions

Causes which rarely or never benefit include animal welfare (except in less developed countries), the arts and museums, political activities, most medical research, preservation etc. of historic buildings and monuments, individual educational grants and sport, except sport for people with disabilities. No grants are made to individuals.

Applications

In writing to the correspondent, accompanied by recent, audited accounts and statutory reports, coupled with at least an outline business plan where relevant. Trustees usually meet in March, June, September and December.

The Clara E Burgess Charity

Children and young people

£260,500 (2009/10)

Beneficial area

UK and worldwide.

RBS Trust Services, Eden, Lakeside, Chester Business Park, Wrexham Road, Chester CH4 9QT
Correspondent: The Trust Section Manager
Trustee: The Royal Bank of Scotland plc.
CC Number: 1072546

Information available

Accounts were available from the Charity Commission.

Registered in 1998, this trust makes grants to registered charities where children are the principal beneficiaries of the work. Grants are towards 'the provision of facilities and assistance to enhance the education, health and physical well-being of children particularly (but not exclusively) those under the age of 10 years who have lost one or both parents'. Within these boundaries grants can be made to the following causes: education/training, overseas projects, disability, social welfare, hospitals/hospices, medical/health and medical research.

In 2009/10 the trust had assets of £10.6 million and an income of £263,500. Grants were made to 81 organisations totalling £260,500. Most grants were for £5,000 or less.

Larger grants were made to: Save the Children Haiti Appeal and St Mary's Hospice (£15,000 each); Children & Families in Grief (£14,000); and This Way Up and Grief Encounter Project (£10,000 each).

Other beneficiaries included: Forget Me Not (£7,500); Nelson's Journey (£6,500); Richard House (£5,000); Norwood Children & Families First (£4,000); Trees for Cities (£3,000); Seesaw, Council for British Archaeology, Church Housing Trust and the International Refugee Trust (£2,000 each); and Human Relief and Donagh Wee Folk Playgroup (£1,000 each).

Exclusions

No grants to non-registered charities.

Applications

In writing to the correspondent. Applications are considered in January and July.

The Burry Charitable Trust

Medicine, health

£46,000 (2009/10)

Beneficial area

UK, with a preference for Highcliffe and the surrounding and further areas.

261 Lymington Road, Highcliffe, Christchurch, Dorset BH23 5EE
Correspondent: R J Burry, Trustee
Trustees: R J Burry; Mrs J A Knight; A J Osman: N J Lapage.
CC Number: 281045

Information available

Accounts were on file at the Charity Commission.

In 2009/10 the trust had assets of £924,000 and an income of £67,000. Grants were made to 22 mainly local organisations totalling £46,000.

Beneficiaries included: Oakhaven Hospital Trust (£10,000); Not Forgotten Association and Wessex Cardiac Trust (£5,000 each); Help for Heroes (£2,500); Julia's House Hospice and Wessex Autistic Society (£1,500 each); Meningitis UK (£1,000); and First Opportunities (£250).

Exclusions

No grants to individuals or students.

Applications

This trust states that it does not respond to unsolicited applications.

The Arnold Burton 1998 Charitable Trust

Jewish, medical research, education, social welfare, heritage

£137,000 (2009/10)

Beneficial area

Worldwide.

c/o Trustee Management Ltd, 19 Cookridge Street, Leeds LS2 3AG
Tel: 0113 243 6466
Correspondent: The Trust Managers
Trustees: A J Burton; J J Burton; N A Burton; M T Burton.
CC Number: 1074633

Information available

Accounts were available from the Charity Commission.

Established in 1998, this trust gives special consideration to appeals from Jewish charities and projects related to medical research, education, social welfare and heritage. No grants are made to individuals. In 2009/10 it had assets of £5 million, an income of £142,000 and made grants totalling £137,000. Donations were broken down as follows:

Social welfare	91	£43,000
Health	54	£36,000
Education	20	£30,000
Third world/overseas	23	£13,000
Jewish/Israel	32	£8,000
Arts and amenities	9	£7,000

Beneficiaries included: Lubavitch Foundation (£10,000); Fight for Sight and Leeds Art Collection Fund (£5,000 each); RNIB and William Meritt Disabled Living Centre (£1,000 each); Leeds Jewish Welfare Board and Hope and Homes for Children (£500 each); War Memorials Trust (£250); and Pony Sanctuary and RNLI (£100 each).

Applications

In writing to the trust managers. Unsuccessful appeals will not necessarily be acknowledged.

The Geoffrey Burton Charitable Trust

General

£20,000 (2009/10)

Beneficial area

UK, especially Suffolk and the Needham Market area.

Salix House, Falkenham, Ipswich IP10 0QY
Tel: 01394 448339
Email: ericmaule@hotmail.com

Correspondent: Eric Maule, Trustee
Trustees: Roger Nash; Ted Nash; Eric Maule.
CC Number: 290854

Information available

Accounts were available from the Charity Commission.

In 2009/10 the trust had assets of £551,000, which generated an income of £25,000. Grants were made totalling £20,000.

The trust continued to support the Mid-Suffolk Citizens Advice Bureau with a contribution of £2,900 for its Benefit Uptake and Income Maximisation Project.

Other grant beneficiaries included: Bacton United Football Club – contribution towards cost of new facilities, Needham Market Entertainment Company – contribution towards sound facilities, Marie Curie Cancer care -funding for work in Suffolk (£1,000 each); Red Rose Chain -general funding (£750); Optua -Share Fun Arts Day, Suffolk Wildlife Trust – Snape Marshes and Waveney Stardust – contribution towards boat (£500 each); Jubilee Sailing Trust – general funding and British Dyslexics – information pack project (£300 each); and Autism Suffolk – general funding (£250).

Exclusions

No grants to individuals.

Applications

In writing to the correspondent.

Consolidated Charity of Burton upon Trent

General

£67,000 to organisations (2010)

Beneficial area

The former county borough of Burton upon Trent and the parishes of Branston, Stretton and Outwoods.

Talbot and Co, 148 High Street, Burton upon Trent, Staffordshire DE14 1JY
Tel: 01283 564716

Email: clerk@
consolidatedcharityburton.org.uk
Website: www.
consolidatedcharityburton.org.uk/
Correspondent: T J Bramall, Clerk to
the Trustees
Trustees: Mrs V Burton, Chair; Mrs
G M Foster; Mrs P P Hill; T Dawn;
Mrs B Toon; Mrs A M Parker; Mr
D E Salter; Mr J Mariott Peach; Mrs
L Nash; Mr P R Davies; Mrs
M A Heather; Cllr Mr D F Fletcher;
P Ackroyd; Mr G M Hamilton; Cllr
Mrs E J Staples; Mr D Clegg Leese;
Rev R Styles; Cllr Mr L G Milner.
CC Number: 239072

Information available

Full accounts were on file at the
Charity Commission.

This large local trust supports
individuals and organisations within
the area of benefit. In 2010 the trust
had assets of £11.1 million and an
income of £426,000. Grants to
organisations totalled £67,000 and a
further £94,000 was given to
individuals for relief-in-need
purposes and educational purposes.
This included 39 bursaries of £400
per annum for three years.

Numerous organisations receive
funding from the charity including
churches, other registered charities,
and voluntary groups within the area
of benefit.

Beneficiaries included: SARAC
(£11,000); Burton upon Trent &
District YMCA (£5,000); Burton
Venture Trust (£9,000 between two
grants); Queen's Hospital, Mellow
Dramatics (£3,000 each); Carers
Association Southern Staffordshire,
Newlife Foundation for Disabled
Children (£2,000 each); Holy Rosary
Catholic Primary School and Winshill
Cricket Club (£1,000 each).

Applications

On a form which can be downloaded
from the trust's website. Applications
for grants from organisations are
considered by the main committee
which meets three times a year.

The Derek Butler Trust

Medical research, health, music and music education

£279,000 (2009/10)

Beneficial area

Worldwide, in practice UK.

c/o Underwood Solicitors LLP,
40 Welbeck Street, London W1G 8LN
Tel: 020 7526 6000
Email: info@thederekbutlertrust.org.
uk
Website: www.thederekbutlertrust.
org.uk
Correspondent: Bernard W Dawson,
Trustee
Trustees: Bernard W Dawson;
Donald F Freeman; Revd Michael
Fuller; Hilary A E Guest.
CC Number: 1081995

Information available

Accounts were available from the
Charity Commission.

The trust was established in 2000 for
general charitable purposes, with an
interest in medical research, health,
music and music education. The
charity is particularly interested in
supporting research into the study of
oesophageal and related cancers of
the digestive tract, projects for public
education in respect of HIV/AIDS
and relief of sufferers from HIV/
AIDS.

In 2009/10 it had assets of
£12 million and an income of
£347,000. Grants were made during
the year totalling £279,000, which
included £44,000 in awards through
the Derek Butler London Prize.

There were 32 grants made to
organisations, with beneficiaries
including: Imperial College (£63,000);
Food Chain UK (£20,000); Crusaid
(£15,000); Naz Project (£13,000);
Westminster Cathedral Choir School
Choristers Fund (£12,000); GMFA
Charity and National Opera Studio
(£10,000 each); British Youth Opera –
2010 (£7,800); Jesuit Refugee Service
(£6,000); Royal Brompton and
Harefield Charitable Fund (£4,500);

Purcell School (£2,000); London Song
Festival (£1,500); and Prisoner's
Education Trust (£1,000).

Applications

In writing to the correspondent. 'The
trustees continue to seek new
charities to which they can make
suitable donations.'

The Noel Buxton Trust

Child and family welfare, penal matters, Africa

£105,000 (2010)

Beneficial area

UK, eastern and southern Africa.

PO Box 393, Farnham, Surrey
GU9 8WZ
Website: www.noelbuxtontrust.org.
uk/index.htm
Trustees: Richenda Wallace; Joyce
Morton; Simon Buxton; Jon Snow; Jo
Tunnard; John Littlewood; Brendan
Gormley; Miss Emma Ponsonby; Miss
Katie Aston; Katie Buxton.
CC Number: 220881

Information available

Accounts were available from the
Charity Commission.

Grants are made for the following:
- the welfare of children in
  disadvantaged families and of
  children in care. This will normally
  cover families with children of
  primary school age and younger,
  although work with children in
  care will be considered up to the
  age at which they leave care.
  (Grants are NOT given for
  anything connected with physical
  or mental disability or any medical
  condition.)
- the prevention of crime, especially
  work with young people at risk of
  offending; the welfare of prisoners'
  families and the rehabilitation of
  prisoners (housing of any kind is
  excluded).
- education and development in
  eastern and southern Africa.

The trust is a small one and seldom
makes grants of more than £4,000,

often considerably less. The average grant in 2008 was around £1,650. The trust will fund core costs and will consider making a series of annual grants for up to three years. Due to the size of grant, appeals whose major component is salary costs will not be considered.

The trustees very much welcome appeals from small local groups in England, Scotland and Wales. The emphasis of their giving is on areas outside London, south-east England and Northern Ireland. The trust does not respond to appeals from large and well-supported charities or to general appeals.

In 2010 the trust had assets of £2.3 million and an income of £109,000. Donations were made totalling £105,000. They were broken down as follows and are shown here with examples of beneficiaries:

Africa – 14 grants totalling £36,000
Dig Deep (£4,000); Tirrim Development Program (£3,600); International Refugee Trust (£3,300); Vision Africa, TWAM – Tools with a Mission and Education Uganda (£3,000 each); African Initiatives, Jubilee Debt Campaign and Zimbabwe Benefit Foundation (£2,500 each); Zanzibar Action Project and Retrak (£2,000 each); Edinburgh Global Partnerships (£1,000); and Burley-Téréli Friendship Trust (£500).

Family – 22 grants totalling £36,000
Family Rights Group (£5,000); YKids (£2,500); Voice of the Child and Corby Furniture Turnaround Project (£2,000 each); Rushmoor Healthy Living, Befrienders and Bristol Children's Playhouse (£1,500 each); Havering Women's Aid and Wood Street Mission (£1,000 each).

Penal – 20 grants totalling £33,000
Cleveland Housing Advice Centre, HACRO and Howard League for Penal Reform and String of Pearls Project (£2,000 each); Consequences, Families/Friends of Prisoners (£1,500 each); Church Housing Trust and Nene & Ouse Community Transport (£1,000 each).

Exclusions
The trust does not give to: academic research; advice centres; animals; the arts of any kind; buildings; conferences; counselling; development education; drug and alcohol work; the elderly; the environment; expeditions, exchanges, study tours, visits, and so on, or anything else involving fares; housing and homelessness; human rights; anything medical or connected with illness or mental or physical disability; anywhere overseas except eastern and southern Africa; peace and disarmament; race relations; youth (except for the prevention of offending); and unemployment. Grants are not made to individuals for any purpose.

Applications
By letter, setting out the reasons why a grant is being requested. Applications should include the applicant's charity registration number and the name of the organisation to which cheques should be made payable if different from that at the head of the appeal letter. Applications should include: budget for current and following year; details of funding already received, promised or applied for from other sources; latest annual report/accounts in the shortest available form.

Applications may be made at any time and are not acknowledged. Successful applicants will normally hear from the trust within six months. The trust will not discuss applications on the telephone or correspond about rejected appeals.

C and F Charitable Trust

Orthodox Jewish charities
£179,000 (2009/10)

Beneficial area
UK and overseas.

c/o Cohen Arnold, New Burlington House, 1075 Finchley House Road, London NW11 0PU
Correspondent: The Trustees

Trustees: Fradel Kaufman; Simon Kaufman.
CC Number: 274529

Information available
Accounts on file at the Charity Commission, without a list of grants.

The trust income derives mainly from investment properties and other investments. Grants are made to Orthodox Jewish charities.

In 2009/10 the trust had assets of £1.2 million, an income of £138,000 and made grants totalling £179,000.

Previous beneficiaries have included Community Council of Gateshead, Ezras Nitrochim, Gur Trust, Kollel Shaarei Shlomo, SOFT and Yetev Lev Jerusalem Trust.

Exclusions
Registered charities only.

Applications
In writing to the correspondent.

The C Charitable Trust

General
£729,000 (2009/10)

Beneficial area
UK.

Farrer & Co, 66 Lincoln's Inn Fields, London WC2A 3LH
Email: admin@ccharitabletrust.org
Website: www.ccharitabletrust.org/
Correspondent: Richard Pierce-Saunderson, Administrator
Trustees: Mark Langhorn Coombs; Laura O'Grady; James Hurbert Carleton.
CC Number: 1118899

Information available
Accounts were available from the Charity Commission. The trust also has a clear and simple website.

The trust was established in 2007 for general charitable purposes. The trustees will consider awarding grants to charities that:
 ▪ are for the benefit of persons who are making an effort to improve their lives

61

- are for the benefit of persons who are no longer physically or mentally able to help themselves
- have a long term beneficial impact on the future of individuals, groups of individuals or organisations
- preserve buildings or works of heritage value
- are for the benefit of endangered or mistreated animals
- protect the environment
- are small or minority charities where a small grant will have a significant impact.

In 2009/10 the trust had assets of £2.4 million and an income of £548,000. Grants made to institutions amounted £729,000 which was significantly more than in the previous year(£159,000 in 2008/09).

The largest grants went to: Scott Polar Research Institute (£225,000); St John's College, Cambridge University (£155,000); and East Anglia's Children's Hospices and Fairshare (£50,000 each). Other beneficiaries included: Pace Centre (£12,000); Cancer Counselling Trust, DEMAND, Jessie May Trust and Multiple Sclerosis Society (£10,000 each); James Hopkins Trust (£6,000); Edinburgh Young Carers Project, Normandy Community Therapy and Primrose Hospice (£5,000 each); Viva Chamber Orchestra (£4,000); Independent Age (£3,000); Vitalise (£2,500); and Marches Family Network (£1,500).

Other grants of less than £1,000 amounted to £800.

Exclusions

The trust will not consider grants for:
- Citizens Advice
- community centres
- environmental projects not directly involving land purchase
- heritage and building projects
- higher education
- housing associations
- individuals
- medical research
- minibuses
- non-departmental government bodies
- overseas projects
- previously unsuccessful applicants
- Scouts, Cubs, Guides, Brownies and similar organisations
- secondary education
- single-faith organisations
- sports clubs, unless for the mentally and physically disabled

- village halls
- youth centres.

Applications

The trust gives the following guidance on its website on making an application:

How to apply
Electronic applications are preferred, and should be sent to **admin@ccharitabletrust.org**.

Please send details and budget of the proposed project, how many people would benefit, how those benefits might be measured (not just financially), what the estimated cost of raising funds for the project is. It is important to include in your email application full accounts for your most recent completed financial year.

If sending a hardcopy application to our correspondence address, please note that hardcopy applications take longer to process. **Please do not send DVDs, CDs, glossy brochures or other additional information.**

It normally takes 12 weeks from application to applicants being informed of the trustees' decision. There are no application deadlines as trustees make grant decisions on a monthly basis. Please note that less than 10% of all applications are successful.

The G W Cadbury Charitable Trust

Family planning, conservation, general

£148,000 (2009/10)

Beneficial area
Worldwide.

PKF (UK) LLP, New Guild House, 45 Great Charles Street, Queensway, Birmingham B3 2LX
Tel: 0121 212 2222
Correspondent: The Trust Administrator
Trustees: Miss J C Boal; Mrs L E Boal; P Cadbury Boal; Miss J Lyndall Woodroffe; Mrs C A Woodroffe; N B Woodroffe.
CC Number: 231861

Information available
Accounts were available from the Charity Commission.

In 2009/10 the trust had assets of £5.6 million, generating an income of £229,000. There were 62 grants made totalling £248,000, given in the following geographical areas:

UK	£76,000
USA	£50,000
Africa	£16,000
Canada	£6,000
South America	£350

There were 13 grants of £5,000 each or more listed in the accounts. Beneficiaries included: Pacific NorthWest Ballet (£20,000); Cancer Counselling Trust (£15,000); AFRODAD – African Forum and Network on Debt and Development and Brook Northern Ireland (£10,000 each); School of American Ballet (£8,000); Help the Rural Child (£6,000); and Compassion in Dying (£5,000).

A further 20 donations of between £1,000 and £5,000 each were made. Beneficiaries included: Family Planning Association and Asylum Seekers in Islington Relief Trust (£3,000); Fred Hutchinson Cancer Research Centre and Planned Parenthood of Western Washington (£2,700); Brook London (£2,000); Doctors without Borders, Momenta Foundation and Schools First (£1,000 each).

Other smaller grants of less than £999 were made to 29 organisations and totalled £6,700.

Exclusions
No grants to individuals or non-registered charities, or for scholarships.

Applications
In writing to the correspondent.

P H G Cadbury Charitable Trust

General, arts, conservation, cancer

£23,000 (2010/11)

Beneficial area
UK and overseas.

KS Carmichael Accountants, PO Box 4UD, London W1A 4UD
Tel: 020 7258 1577

Email: dlarder@kscarmichael.com
Correspondent: Derek Larder, Trustee
Trustees: Derek Larder; Peter Cadbury; Sally Cadbury.
CC Number: 327174

Information available

Accounts were available from the Charity Commission.

The trust makes grants to registered charities for general charitable purposes, with a preference for the arts, conservation and cancer-related causes. Grants range from between £25 and £3,500.

In 2010/11 the trust had assets of £553,000 and an income of £26,000. There were 47 grants made totalling £23,000, of which 19 were for £1,000 or more.

Beneficiaries included: Garsington Opera, Helen and Douglas House and the Royal Academy (£1,500 each); The National Trust (£1,200); English National Ballet, Natural History Museum and The Wallace Collection (£1,000 each).

Applications

The trust does not usually respond to unsolicited applications.

The Christopher Cadbury Charitable Trust

Nature conservation, general

£59,000 (2009/10)

Beneficial area

UK, with a preference for the Midlands.

PKF (UK) LLP, New Guild House, 45 Great Charles Street, Queensway, Birmingham B3 2LX
Tel: 0121 212 2222
Correspondent: The Trust Administrator
Trustees: R V J Cadbury; Dr C James Cadbury; Mrs V B Reekie; Dr T N D Peet; P H G Cadbury; Mrs C V E Benfield.
CC Number: 231859

Information available

Accounts were available from the Charity Commission.

In 2009/10 the trust had assets of £1.8 million, which generated an income of £70,000. Grants totalled £59,000. The trustees have drawn up a schedule of commitments covering charities which they have chosen to support.

The majority of beneficiaries were supported in the previous year; grants included those made to: Fircroft College and Island Conservation Society UK (£11,000 each); Playthings Past Museum Trust (£7,500); Devon Wildlife Trust (£6,000); Norfolk Wildlife Trust (£5,000); Bower Trust, R V J Cadbury Charitable Trust, R A and V B Reekie Charitable Trust and Sarnia Charitable Trust (£2,000 each); Survival International (£1,000); and Avoncroft Arts Society and Selly Oak Nursery School (£500 each).

Exclusions

No support for individuals.

Applications

Unsolicited applications are unlikely to be successful.

C J Cadbury Charitable Trust

Environment, conservation, music

£21,000 (2009/10)

Beneficial area

UK.

Martineau, No. 1 Colmore Square, Birmingham B4 6AA
Tel: 0870 763 2000
Fax: 0870 763 2001
Correspondent: The Clerk
Trustees: Hugh Carslake; Joy Cadbury; Thomas Cadbury; Lucy Cadbury.
CC Number: 270609

Information available

Accounts were on file at the Charity Commission.

In 2009/10 the trust had assets of £669,000 and an income of £35,000. Grants totalled £21,000.

Only those beneficiaries in receipt of £1,000 or more in grants were listed in the accounts. They were: Island Conservation Society UK (£14,000 in three grants) and Hertfordshire Nature Trust (£3,000).

Applications

The trust does not generally support unsolicited applications.

Henry T and Lucy B Cadbury Charitable Trust

Quaker causes and institutions, health, homelessness, support groups, developing world

Around £28,000 (2010)

Beneficial area

Mainly UK, but also the Third World.

c/o B C M, Box 2024, London WC1N 3XX
Correspondent: The Secretary
Trustees: Candia Carolan; C Ruth Charity; Suzannah Gibson; M Bevis Gillett; Tristram Hambly; Elizabeth Rawlins; Tamsin Yates; Dr Emma Hambly.
CC Number: 280314

Information available

Basic information available from the Charity Commission website.

In 2010 the trust had an income of £21,000 and a total expenditure of almost £29,000

Grant recipients are usually those that are personally chosen by one of the trustees. Previously beneficiaries were: Quaker United Nations Office (£5,000); Battle Against Tranquillizers, British Pugwash Trust, the People's Kitchen and Slower Speeds Trust (£2,000 each); Action for ME, Money for Madagascar and Tools for Self Reliance (£1,500 each); and Calcutta Rescue Fund, Quaker Opportunity Playgroup and Youth

Education Service Midnapore (£1,000 each).

Exclusions

No grants to non-registered charities.

Applications

The trust's income is committed each year and so unsolicited applications are not normally accepted. The trustees meet in March to consider applications.

The George Cadbury Trust

General

£355,000 (2009/10)

Beneficial area

Preference for the West Midlands, Hampshire and Gloucestershire.

PKF (UK) LLP, New Guild House, 45 Great Charles Street, Queensway, Birmingham B3 2LX
Tel: 0121 212 2222
Correspondent: Sarah Moss
Trustees: Anne L K Cadbury; Sir Adrian Cadbury; Mark Cadbury; Roger V J Cadbury; A Janie Cadbury.
CC Number: 1040999

Information available

Accounts were available from the Charity Commission.

The trust was set up in 1924 and maintains a strong financial interest in the Cadbury company. In 2009/10 the trust had assets of £9.9 million, which generated an income of £336,000. There were donations made totalling £355,000.

The largest beneficiaries of grants over £5,000 or more included: St John's of Jerusalem Eye Hospital (£52,000); Performance Birmingham Limited (£25,000); Dean and Chapters Gloucester Cathedral (£20,000); Elmhurst Ballet School Trust and Rift Valley Tree Trust (£10,000 each); Age Concern and Birmingham Opera Company (£5,000 each).

Grants for less than £1,000 went to beneficiaries including: West Bromwich and District YMCA (£4,000); Save the Elephants (£3,600);

Tourism Concern (£2,500); Combat Stress (£2,000); and Gosford Forest Guide House – Co Armagh, Kings College Cambridge and Dunluce Guide House (£1,000 each).

Exclusions

No support for individuals for projects, courses of study, expeditions or sporting tours. No support for overseas appeals.

Applications

In writing to the correspondent to be considered quarterly. Please note that very few new applications are supported due to ongoing and alternative commitments.

The Edward and Dorothy Cadbury Trust

Health, education, arts

£101,000 (2009/10)

Beneficial area

Preference for the West Midlands area.

Rokesley, University of Birmingham Selly Oak, Bristol Road, Selly Oak, Birmingham B29 6QF
Tel: 0121 472 1838
Correspondent: Miss S Anderson, Company Secretary/Trust Manager
Trustees: Mrs P A Gillett, Chair; Dr C M Elliott; Mrs P S Ward; Mrs S E Anfilogoff; Mrs J E Gillett; Mrs J A Cadbury.
CC Number: 1107327

Information available

Accounts were available from the Charity Commission.

This trust was registered in December 2004, and is the recipient of funds transferred from the now defunct Edward and Dorothy Cadbury Trust (1928), registered charity number 221441. The objects of the new trust remain the same, i.e. general charitable purposes in the West Midlands, with areas of work funded including music and the arts, children's charities, disadvantaged groups and support for the voluntary sector. The normal range of grants is

between £500 and £2,500, with occasional larger grants made.

In 2009/10 it had assets of £5.3 million, which generated an income of £131,000. Grants were made to 111 organisations totalling £101,000, which were distributed under the following categories:

Compassionate support	45	£44,000
Community projects and integration	27	£26,000
Education and training	18	£18,000
Arts and culture	12	£8,000
Conservation and the environment	6	£4,000
Research	3	£1,500

Beneficiaries included: Worcester Breast Unit Campaign (£15,000); Age Concern – Bromsgrove and District Elmhurst School for Dance – Birmingham (£5,000 each); Bromsgrove Festival (£4,000); Bromsgrove Bereavement Counselling (£1,500); National Playbus Association, St Francis Church – Bournville and the Willow Trust (£1,000 each); Cued Speech Association and SENSE (£750 each); Big Brum Theatre in Education, Design and Manufacture for Disability -DEMAND, Ellen MacArthur Trust, Brain Tumour UK and Fight for Sight (£500 each).

Exclusions

No grants to individuals.

Applications

In writing to the correspondent, giving clear, relevant information concerning the project's aims and its benefits, an outline budget and how the project is to be funded initially and in the future. Up-to-date accounts and annual reports, where available, should be included. Applications can be submitted at any time but three months should be allowed for a response. Applications that do not come within the policy as stated above may not be considered or acknowledged.

Calleva Foundation

General

£213,000 (2009)

Beneficial area
UK and worldwide.

4 Cottesmore Gardens, London W8 5PR
Correspondent: The Trustees
Trustees: S C Butt; C Butt.
CC Number: 1078808

Information available
Accounts were on file at the Charity Commission, without a list of grants.

Registered with the Charity Commission in January 2000, this trust can give in the UK and worldwide for general charitable purposes.

The latest accounts available were for 2009 when donations were split between education, children's holidays, social services, medical research, medical equipment, overseas/international relief, environment, arts, culture and animal welfare.

In 2009 the trust had assets of £85,000, an income of £256,000, and paid out £213,000 in grants. Grants can be categorised as follows:

Social services	£64,000
Children's holidays	£25,000
Overseas/international relief	£16,000
Education	£25,000
Arts and culture	£8,000
Medical research	£25,000
Animal welfare	£10,000

No further information on beneficiaries was available.

Applications
In writing to the correspondent.

Common applicant mistakes
'Too much wasteful paper. A letter and a website reference is all that is needed.'

The Calpe Trust

Relief work

£28,000 (2009/10)

Beneficial area
Worldwide.

The Hideaway, Sandy Lane, Hatford Down, Faringdon, Oxfordshire SN7 8JH
Tel: 01367 870665
Email: reggienorton@talktalk.net
Correspondent: R Norton, Trustee
Trustees: R H L R Norton, Chair; B E M Norton; E R H Perks.
CC Number: 1004193

Information available
Accounts were available from the Charity Commission.

The trust makes grants towards registered charities benefiting people in need including refugees, homeless people, people who are socially disadvantaged, victims of war, victims of disasters and so on.

In 2009/10 the trust had assets of £1 million and an income of £32,000. It made 10 grants totalling £28,000.

Beneficiaries included: Ecumenical Project for International Cooperation Inc (£9,000); New Israel Fund, OXFAM and Salt of the Earth (£5,000 each); Samaritans (£4,000); The World Children's Fund (£1,000); and TRAX – Oxfordshire Motor Project (£400).

Exclusions
No grants towards animal welfare or to individuals.

Applications
In writing to the correspondent. Applicants must contact the trust before making an application.

Common applicant mistakes
'Applicants should phone first.'

H and L Cantor Trust

Jewish, general

Around £10,000 (2009/10)

Beneficial area
UK, with some preference for Sheffield.

3 Ivy Park Court, 35 Ivy Park Road, Sheffield S10 3LA
Correspondent: Lilly Cantor, Trustee
Trustees: Lily Cantor; Nicholas Jeffrey.
CC Number: 220300

Information available
Due to the trust's low income in 2009/10, only basic financial information was available from the Charity Commission.

The principal objective of the trust is to provide benefit for charities, particularly Jewish charities.

In 2009/10 the trust had an unusually low income of £12,000 (£272,000 in 2008/09) and expenditure of £15,000 (£30,000 in 2008/09). No further information was available.

Previous beneficiaries include: Delamere Forest School Ltd, Sheffield Jewish Congregation & Centre, Sheffield Jewish Welfare Organisation, I Rescue, Jewish Childs Day, Sense, Share Zadek UK, Brain Research Trust, PDSA – Sheffield and World Cancer Research.

Applications
Unsolicited applications are not considered.

Cardy Beaver Foundation

General

£178,000 (2009/10)

Beneficial area
UK with preference for Berkshire.

Clifton House, 17 Reading Road, Pangbourne, Berkshire RG8 7LU
Tel: 0118 984 4713
Correspondent: Sandra Rice, Trustee
Trustees: John James; Mary Cardy; Sandra Rice.
CC Number: 265763

Information available
Accounts were available from the Charity Commission.

Registered with the Charity Commission in May 1973, in 2009/10 the foundation had assets of £2.3 million and an income of £93,000. Grants totalled £178,000. During the year 38 grants were made,

23 of which were given to organisations that were also supported in the previous year. All but four were for £5,000 each.

Beneficiaries included: Cancer Research UK, Watermill Theatre Appeal, Wallingford Museum, NSPCC, Berkshire Blind Society, Adventure Dolphin, St Peter's PCC, Church House Trust, RNLI and Asthma Relief (£5,000 each); Julia's House and Elizabeth Foundation (£2,500 each); Com Exchange – Newbury (£2,000); and Pangbourne Fete 2010 (£500).

Exclusions

Registered charities only.

Applications

In writing to the correspondent.

The D W T Cargill Fund

General

Around £200,000 (2008/09)

Beneficial area

UK, with a preference for the West of Scotland.

Miller Beckett and Jackson Solicitors, 190 St Vincent Street, Glasgow G2 5SP
Correspondent: Norman A Fyfe, Trustee
Trustees: A C Fyfe; W G Peacock; N A Fyfe; Mirren Elizabeth Graham.
SC Number: SC012703

Information available

Despite making a written request for the accounts of this charity (including an sae) these were not provided. The following entry is based on information filed with the Office of the Scottish Charity Regulator.

This fund has the same address and trustees as two other trusts, W A Cargill Charitable Trust and W A Cargill Fund, although they all operate independently.

It supports any hospitals, institutions, societies or others whose work in the opinion of the trustees is likely to be beneficial to the community.

In 2008/09 the fund had an income of £244,000. Grants have previously totalled around £200,000 a year.

Previous beneficiaries have included: City of Glasgow Society of Social Service, Colquhoun Bequest Fund for Incurables, Crathie Opportunity Holidays, Glasgow and West of Scotland Society for the Blind, Glasgow City Mission, Greenock Medical Aid Society, North Glasgow Community Forum, Scottish Maritime Museum – Irvine, Scottish Episcopal Church, Scottish Motor Neurone Disease Association, Lead Scotland and Three Towns Blind Bowling/Social Club.

Exclusions

No grants are made to individuals.

Applications

In writing to the correspondent, supported by up-to-date accounts. Trustees meet quarterly.

The Carlton House Charitable Trust

Jewish, education/ bursaries, general

£30,000 (2009/10)

Beneficial area

UK and overseas.

Craven House, 121 Kingsway, London WC2B 6PA
Tel: 0207 242 5283
Correspondent: Stewart S Cohen, Trustee
Trustees: S Cohen; P G Cohen; F A Stein.
CC Number: 296791

Information available

Accounts were on file at the Charity Commission.

The charity's main aim is to provide support to other charities in the UK and overseas. The charity supports a limited number of graduate and post graduate students – in particular those in engineering, the physical sciences, drama and stage management.

In 2009/10 the trust had assets of £1 million and an income of £57,000. Grants were made to 179 organisations totalling £31,000. Grants ranged from £100–£4,500.

Beneficiaries of the 26 largest grants of £100 or more included: Western Marble Arch Synagogue (£4,500); Community Security Trust (£2,500); Bnai Brith Hillel Foundation, National Trust and Westminster Advocacy Service (£2,000 each); Royal Academy of Music and Imperial College (£1,000 each); British Technion Society and London Philharmonic Orchestra (£500); Nightingale House (£250) and Magon David Adorn (£150).

A further 153 donations were made for £100 or less totalling £5,800.

Applications

In writing to the correspondent.

The Richard Carne Trust

Young people in the performing arts

Around £109,000 to organisations and individuals (2010)

Beneficial area

UK.

Kleinwort Benson Trustees Ltd, 14 St George Street, London W1S 1FE
Tel: 020 3207 7356
Correspondent: Christopher Gilbert, Administrator
Trustees: Kleinwort Benson Trustees Limited; Philip Edward Carne; Mrs Marjorie Christine Carne.
CC Number: 1115903

Information available

Accounts were on file at the charity Commission.

Set up in 2006, the trust states that:

> The objects of the charity are to assist young people in the performing arts, and will be largely focused towards individuals in institutions dedicated to music and theatre. In addition, the trust may also wish to help fringe theatrical groups or musical groups in the early stages of their careers.

In 2010 the trust had an income of £20,000 and a total expenditure of £121,000. No further information was available.

Previous beneficiaries included: Royal College of Music (£50,000); Royal Academy of Dramatic Art (£30,000); London Academy of Music and Drama (£25,000); Royal Welsh College of Music and Drama (£20,000); Classical Opera Company and Trinity College of Music (£10,000 each); South Bank Sinfonia (£7,000); Rakhi Sing/Barbiroili Quartet (£4,000); and ENO Young Singers Programme (£2,500).

The trustees' current policy is to annually distribute the trust's income to certain selected charities, although no commitment is given to the recipients.

Applications

The trust's latest available accounts state:

> The trustees' current policy is to consider all written appeals received, but only successful applications are notified of the trustees' decision. [. . .] The trustees review the selected charities, and consider new appeals received at their annual trustee meeting, normally held in June. Only successful applicants are notified of the trustees' decision.

The Carpenter Charitable Trust

Humanitarian and Christian outreach

Around £80,000 (2009/10)

Beneficial area

UK and overseas.

The Old Vicarage, Hitchin Road, Kimpton, Hitchin, Hertfordshire SG4 8EF
Correspondent: M S E Carpenter, Trustee
Trustees: M S E Carpenter; G M L Carpenter.
CC Number: 280692

Information available

Accounts were received at the Charity Commission but unavailable to view.

The trust's latest available report and accounts (2008) provides the following information:

> The charity is established on wide grant giving terms. The trustees continue to pursue their 'preferred' list approach – a list of charities with which the trustees have developed a good relationship over the years.

In 2009/10 the trust had an income of £19,000 and a total expenditure of £85,000. A full list of beneficiaries for the year was unavailable.

Previous grants have included: Mission Aviation Fellowship Europe (£7,500); ORBIS Charitable Trust (£6,000); Andrew Christian Trust, Barnabas Fund, Help in Suffering UK, and Relationships Foundation (£5,000 each); DEC Bangladesh (£2,500); Brooke Hospital for Animals, Crisis UK, Merlin and Salvation Army (£1,000 each); Blue Cross, Fight for Sight, Mercy Ships, Prison Fellowship, RSPB, Send a Cow and Tibet Relief (£500 each); and Cats Protection League (£250).

Exclusions

The trust's report and accounts go on to state:

> The trustees do not consider applications for church repairs (other than in respect of Kimpton Church) nor applications from individuals nor any applications received from abroad unless clearly 'sponsored' by an established charity based in England and Wales.

Applications

In writing to the correspondent including sufficient details to enable a decision to be made. However, as about half the donations made are repeat grants, the amount available for unsolicited applications remains small.

The Carr-Gregory Trust

Arts, social welfare, health, education

£52,000 (2010)

Beneficial area

UK.

56 Pembroke Road, Clifton, Bristol BS8 3DT
Correspondent: Russ Carr, Trustee
Trustees: Russ Carr; Heather Wheelhouse; Linda Carr; H J Nicholls.
CC Number: 1085580

Information available

Accounts were on file at the charity Commission.

Grants are mainly made to charities operating in London or the Bristol area. Priority is given to the performing arts and health and social needs.

In 2010 the trust had assets of £460,000 and an income of £54,000. Grants totalled £52,000.

Donations were broken down as follows:

Arts/culture	£28,750
Social needs	£14,300
Health	£8,600

Grant beneficiaries included: the Royal National Theatre (£11,000); The Royal Academy of Music (£7,000); University of Bristol (£3,000); Alzheimer's Society (£2,000); Calibre Audio Library, Help the Hospices and Prisoner's Education Trust (£1,000 each); The Salvation Army, St Mungo's and The Stroke Foundation (£500 each).

Applications

Applications should be made in writing to the correspondent and should not exceed two A4 pages.

The Carron Charitable Settlement

Environment, education, medicine

Around £36,000 (2009/10)

Beneficial area

UK and overseas.

c/o Rothman Panthall and Co., 10 Romsey Road, Eastleigh, Hampshire SO50 9AL
Tel: 023 8061 4555
Correspondent: Ms Carolyn Cox

Trustees: P G Fowler; W M Allen; D L Morgan.
CC Number: 289164

Information available

Basic information taken from the Charity Commission website.

The trust was created for charitable purposes in connection with wildlife, education, medicine, the countryside and the printing and publishing trade. Ongoing support is given to the St Bride's Church – Fleet Street.

In 2009/10 the settlement's income was £6,000 which was substantially lower than in previous years (£77,000 in 2007/08). There was a total expenditure of £36,000.

Previous beneficiaries included: St Bride's Church Appeal (£20,000); INTBAU (£10,000); Academy of Aviation and Space Medicine (£3,000); and Curwen Print Study Centre (£1,500).

Exclusions

No grants to individuals.

Applications

The trust does not invite applications from the general public.

The Leslie Mary Carter Charitable Trust

Conservation/ environment, welfare

£104,500 (2010)

Beneficial area

UK, with a preference for Norfolk, Suffolk and North Essex.

c/o Birketts, 24–26 Museum Street, Ipswich IP1 1HZ
Tel: 01473 232300
Correspondent: Sam Wilson, Trustee
Trustees: Miss L M Carter; S R M Wilson; Martyn Carr.
CC Number: 284782

Information available

Accounts were available from the Charity Commission.

The trust has a preference for welfare organisations and conservation/ environment causes, with an emphasis on local projects including those in Suffolk, Norfolk and North Essex. Grants generally range from £500 to £5,000 but larger grants are sometimes considered.

In 2010 the trust had assets of £3 million, an income of £123,000 and made grants totalling £104,500.

Beneficiaries included: Norfolk Wildlife Trust and St Elizabeth Hospice (£10,000 each); Campaign to Protect Rural England, Colchester Archaeological Trust and Combat Stress (£5,000 each); Barn Owl Trust and Waveney Stardust (£3,000 each); Bat Conservation Trust and Witham Boys Brigade (£2,000 each); and RSPB and Suffolk Preservation Society (£1,000 each).

Trustees prefer well thought-out applications for larger gifts, than many applications for smaller grants.

Exclusions

No grants to individuals.

Applications

In writing to the correspondent. Telephone calls are not welcome. There is no need to enclose an sae unless applicants wish to have materials returned.

Applications made outside the preferred areas for grant giving will be considered, but acknowledgements may not always be sent.

The Carvill Trust

General

£50,000 (2009/10)

Beneficial area

UK.

5th Floor, Minories House, 2–5 Minories, London EC3N 1BJ
Tel: 020 7780 6900
Correspondent: K D Tuson, Trustee
Trustees: R K Carvill; R E Pooley; K D Tuson.
CC Number: 1036420

Information available

Accounts received at the Charity Commission but unavailable to view.

The trust was established for general charitable purposes in 1994. In 2009/10 the trust had an income of £13,000 and a total expenditure of £109,000.

Previous beneficiaries included: Irish Youth Foundation (£14,000); and Academy Ocean Reef and War Child (£10,000 each).

Applications

In writing to the correspondent, although the trust states that it only supports beneficiaries known to or connected with the trustees. Unsolicited applications from individuals will not be supported.

The Casey Trust

Children and young people

£117,000 (2009/10)

Beneficial area

UK and developing countries.

27 Arkwright Road, London NW3 6BJ
Website: www.caseytrust.org
Correspondent: Kenneth Howard, Trustee
Trustees: Kenneth Howard; Edwin Green; Hon. Judge Leonard Krikler.
CC Number: 1055726

Information available

Full accounts were available at the Charity Commission.

This trust was established to help children and young people in the UK and developing countries by supporting new projects, in a variety of countries.

In 2009/10 it had assets of £2.7 million, which generated an income of £114,000. Grants were made to 90 organisations totalling £117,000.

Beneficiaries included: Norwood (£10,000); World Medical Fund (£8,000); World Jewish Relief (£5,000); Kisharon (£4,000); Voces Cantabiles Music (£3,500); FRODO

(£3,000); the Movement Centre (£2,500); Anit-Slavery, Action for Kids and Headstart for Babies (£2,000 each); TSYJ Transplant Active, the Children's Adventure Farm Trust, the Cruse Bereavement Centre and Theodora Trust (£1,500 each); Computer Aid International, Hospices of Hope, Philharmonia Orchestra, Books Abroad and Lennox Children's Cancer Fund (£1,000 each).

Exclusions

Grants are not given to 'individual applicants requesting funds to continue studies or travel'.

Applications

The trust's accounts note that:

> Not being a reactive trust, it is regretted that the trustees will be unable to respond to the majority of requests for assistance. In order to both reduce costs and administration the trustees will respond mainly to those charitable institutions known to them.

There is no application form.

Common applicant mistakes

'They don't read the guidelines on our website, or are individuals; or don't have charitable status; or are not exclusively for children.'

The Catholic Charitable Trust

Catholic

£52,000 (2009)

Beneficial area

America and Europe.

Vernor, Miles and Noble, 5 Raymond Buildings, Gray's Inn, London WC1R 5DD
Correspondent: J C Vernor Miles, Trustee
Trustees: J C Vernor Miles; W E Vernor Miles; D P Orr.
CC Number: 215553

Information available

Accounts were on file at the Charity Commission.

The trust supports traditional Catholic organisations in America and Europe.

In 2009 it had assets of £1.7 million, which generated an income of £55,000. Grants were made to 18 organisations totalling £52,000.

Beneficiaries included: Society of Saint Pius X – England (£12,000); Latin Mass Society, Fraternity of St Pius X Switzerland and Little Sisters of the Poor (£4,000 each); Cardinal Hume Centre and St Benets Hall Oxford (£2,000 each); and Holy Cross Parish Fulham (£1,000).

Three grants were made to American organisations: the Carmelite Monastery Carmel California and California Friends of the Society of St Pius X, (US$2,000 each); and Oratory of Monterey California ($1,000).

Exclusions

The trust does not normally support a charity unless it is known to the trustees. Grants are not made to individuals.

Applications

Applications can only be accepted from registered charities and should be in writing to the correspondent. In order to save administration costs replies are not sent to unsuccessful applicants. For the most part funds are fully committed.

The Catholic Trust for England and Wales

Catholic

£154,000 (2010)

Beneficial area

England and Wales.

39 Eccleston Square, London SW1V 1BX
Tel: 020 7901 4810
Email: secretariat@cbcew.org.uk
Website: www.catholicchurch.org.uk
Correspondent: Revd Marcus Stock, Secretary
Trustees: Rt Revd Malcolm McMahon, Chair; Mgr Michael McKenna; Ben Andradi; Alison Cowdall; John Gibbs; Peter Lomas; Canon Nicholas Rothon; Robin Smith; Dr James Whiston; Richard King; Mjr John Nelson; Michael Prior; Elizabeth Walmsley.
CC Number: 1097482

Information available

Accounts were available from the Charity Commission.

The fund was established in 1968 and is concerned with 'the advancement of the Roman Catholic religion in England and Wales'. In order to fulfil its charitable aims and objectives, the activities of CatEW are determined by the requirements of the Bishops' Conference of England and Wales.

The 2010 accounts give this background detail:

> The Catholic Bishops' Conference of England and Wales is a permanent body within the organisation of the Catholic Church that brings together the Bishops of England and Wales. As a Conference the Bishops 'jointly exercise certain pastoral functions for the Christian faithful... in order to promote the greater good which the Church offers to humanity, especially through forms and programs of the apostolate fittingly adapted to the circumstances of time and place' (cf.Code of Canon Law can 447).

> The departments of CatEW identify the present broad areas of activity for the Bishops in supporting the Dioceses of England and Wales and witnessing to the Gospel in the contemporary world: Catholic Education and Formation, Christian Life and Worship, Christian Responsibility and Citizenship, Dialogue and Unity, Evangelisation and Catechesis and International Affairs.

> Each committee is concerned with a different area of work of the Church. Grants are only given to organisations which benefit England and Wales as a whole, rather than local projects.

The accounts include those of the trust's subsidiary companies: Colloquium Limited, The Papal Visit Limited and The Papal Visit 2010 Limited and this is why the income and assets do not reflect the amounts paid or payable in grants. In 2010 the trust had assets of £11 million and an income of £15 million. Grants totalled £154,000.

Beneficiaries included: CARITAS Social Action Network (£56,000); Churches Legislation Advisory Service (£18,000); National Board of Catholic Women (£13,000); Churches Media Council (£6,000); Churches Committee Hospital Chaplaincy (£4,000); and SIGNIS (£2,000).

Exclusions

No grants to individuals, local projects or projects not immediately advancing the Roman Catholic religion in England and Wales.

Applications

In writing to the correspondent. The trust has stated previously that it does not respond to unsolicited applications.

The Joseph and Annie Cattle Trust

General

£237,000 to organisations (2009/10)

Beneficial area

Worldwide, with a preference for Hull and East Yorkshire.

389–395 Anlaby Road, Hull HU3 6AB
Tel: 01482 211198
Correspondent: Roger Waudby, Administrator
Trustees: J A Collier; M T Gyte; S C Jowers.
CC Number: 262011

Information available

Detailed accounts available from the Charity Commission website.

The object of the charity is to provide for general charitable purposes by making grants, principally to applicants in the Hull area. Older people and people who have disabilities or who are underprivileged are assisted wherever possible, and there is a particular emphasis on giving aid to children with dyslexia.

In 2009/10 the trust had assets of £7.2 million and an income of £353,000. Grants totalled £257,000 of which £20,500 was given to 39 individuals. The 161 grants to organisations were broken down into four main categories as follows:

	No. of grants over £1,000
Local societies and activities	48
National societies	20
Churches and missions	12
Charities for disabled people	11

Beneficiaries included: Hull City Council Social Services (£80,000); Sobriety Project (£15,000); Dyslexia Action (£13,000); Holderness Road Methodist Church and Market Weighton Scout & Guide Head Quarters Project (£5,000 each); Cherry Burton Tennis Club (£3,000); Sutton Methodist Church and Yorkshire Eye Research (£2,000 each); and Andrew Marvell Youth Centre, Beeford Cricket Club, House of Light, Hull Boys Club, Leven Playing Fields Association, Walkington Pre-School and Wilf Ward Family Trust (£1,000 each).

Exclusions

Grants are very rarely given to individuals and are only supported through social services or relevant charitable or welfare organisations.

Applications

In writing to the correspondent. Meetings are usually held on the third Monday of each month.

The Thomas Sivewright Catto Charitable Settlement

General

£47,000 (2009/10)

Beneficial area

Unrestricted (for UK-based registered charities).

PO Box 47408, London N21 1YW
Correspondent: The Secretary to the Trustees
Trustees: Lord Catto; Olivia Marchant; Zoe Richmond-Watson.
CC Number: 279549

Information available

Accounts were received at the Charity Commission but unable to view.

This trust has general charitable purposes, making a large number of smaller grants to a wide range of organisations and a few larger grants of up to £20,000. Despite the large number of grants made, there appears to be no strong preference for any causes or geographical areas.

In 2009/10 the trust had an income of £1,000 and a total expenditure of £47,000. No information was available as to why the income and expenditure had dropped so significantly over the past year and we are unable to say if this is a permanent reduction.

Previous beneficiaries included: Royal College of Music (£14,000); Royal Scottish Academy of Music and Drama (£12,000); Bowel Cancer Research and King VII's Hospital for Officers (£10,000 each); Haddo House Choral and Operatic Society and World YWCA (£5,000 each); Aviation for Paraplegics and Tetraplegics Trust (£2,000); NACRO (£1,500); Alzheimer's Research Trust, Elizabeth Finn Care, Concern Worldwide, the Fostering Network, Outward Bound Trust, Refugee Council, St Mungo's, Shelter and Charlie Waller Memorial Trust (£1,000 each); Crisis, Disabled Living Foundation, Matthew Trust, REACT and Royal London Society for the Blind (£750 each); and Clubs for Young People, Motability, Nepal Leprosy Trust, Prisoners' Advice Service, Queen Elizabeth's Foundation, Sportability and VSO (£500 each).

Exclusions

The trust does not support non-registered charities, expeditions, travel bursaries and so on, or unsolicited applications from churches of any denomination. Grants are unlikely to be considered in the areas of community care, playschemes and drug abuse, or for local branches of national organisations.

Applications

In writing to the correspondent, including an sae.

The Wilfrid and Constance Cave Foundation

Conservation, animal welfare, health, social welfare, general

£151,000 (2009/10)

Beneficial area

UK, with preference for Berkshire, Cornwall, Devon, Dorset, Hampshire, Oxfordshire, Somerset, Warwickshire and Wiltshire.

New Lodge Farm, Drift Road, Winkfield, Windsor SL4 4QQ
Email: tcf@eamo.co.uk
Correspondent: The Secretary
Trustees: Mrs T Jones; P Simpson; F H C Jones; Mrs J Archer; Mrs J Pickin; M Pickin; Mrs M Waterworth; Mrs N Thompson; R Walker; G Howells; W Howells; M Beckett.
CC Number: 241900

Information available

Accounts were on file at the Charity Commission.

The trust supports local and UK-wide organisations and has general charitable purposes.

In 2009/10 it had assets of £4.1 million which generated an income of £155,000. Grants were made to 47 organisations totalling £151,000, with Oxford Museum of Children's Literature receiving the largest grant of £50,000.

Other beneficiaries included: Farmers' Club Pinnacle Award (£7,000); East Berkshire Women's Aid (£6,000); West Country River Trust (£6,000); Fairground Heritage Trust (£5,000); Two Moors Festival (£3,000); and Shooting Star Children's Hospice (£1,000).

Exclusions

No grants to individuals.

Applications

In writing to the correspondent a month before the trustees' meetings held twice each year, in May and October.

The Cayo Foundation

Medical research, crime, children and young people, performing arts, general

£266,000 (2009/10)

Beneficial area

UK.

7 Cowley Street, London SW1P 3NB
Tel: 0207 248 6700
Correspondent: Angela E McCarville
Trustees: Angela E McCarville; Stewart A Harris.
CC Number: 1080607

Information available

Accounts were available from the Charity Commission.

The foundation supports the fight against crime, medical research and training, performing arts and children's charities.

In 2009/10 it had assets of £371,000 and an income of £339,000. Grants were made to 8 organisations totalling £266,000.

Previous beneficiaries included: NSPCC (£125,000); the Disability Foundation, PACT, the Royal Opera House (£25,000 each); the Princes Foundation (£20,000); Wessex Youth Trust (£10,000); Christian Blind Mission (£6,000); Wellbeing of Women (£3,000); Institute for Policy Research and Royal Humane Society (£2,500 each); and Sue Ryder Care – St John's Hospice (£1,000).

Applications

In writing to the correspondent.

The B G S Cayzer Charitable Trust

General

£75,000 (2009/10)

Beneficial area

UK.

The Cayzer Trust Company Limited, Cayzer House, 30 Buckingham Gate, London SW1E 6NN
Correspondent: The Administrator
Trustees: P R Davies; Mrs M Buckley; Mrs A M Hunter; Mrs R N Leslie.
CC Number: 286063

Information available

Accounts were on file at the Charity Commission, without a list of beneficiaries.

In 2009/10 the trust had assets of over £2.8 million, an income of £151,000 and made grants totalling £75,000, broken down as follows:

Heritage and conservation	£27,000
Education and training	£13,500
Medical	£11,000
Art and culture	£10,000
General	£6,000
Relief of poverty	£5,000
Religion	£2,500

Previous beneficiaries have included: Friends of the National Maritime Museum, Hike for Hope, Marie Curie Cancer Care, RAFT, St Paul's Cathedral Foundation, Scottish Countryside Alliance Education Trust and Worshipful Company of Shipwrights Charitable Fund.

Exclusions

No grants to organisations outside the UK.

Applications

The trust tends to support only people/projects known to the Cayzer family or the trustees. Unsolicited appeals will not be supported.

Elizabeth Cayzer Charitable Trust

Arts

£59,000 (2009/10)

Beneficial area

UK.

The Cayzer Trust Company Limited, Cayzer House, 30 Buckingham Gate, London SW1E 6NN
Tel: 020 7802 8080
Correspondent: The Hon. Elizabeth Gilmour, Trustee

Trustees: The Hon. Elizabeth Gilmour; Diana Lloyd; Dominic Gibbs.
CC Number: 1059265

Information available

Accounts were on file at the Charity Commission, without a list of grants.

This charity was established by The Honourable Elizabeth Gilmour, who has made significant donations to the charity since 1996. In formulating policy the trustees have taken into account the wishes of the settlor, which are that the assets of the charity should be used in supporting and promoting the work of museums, galleries and the architectural heritage of the British Isles.

In 2009/10 the trust had assets of £2.4 million, an income of £62,000 and made grants totalling £59,000, broken down as follows: education (£13,000); and conferences and exhibitions (£46,000).

Previous beneficiaries have included Elias Ashmole Trust; Dulwich Picture Gallery; the National Gallery and Sir John Soane's Museum.

Applications

Note the following statement taken from the charity's 2009/10 accounts:

> The trustees identify the projects and organisations they wish to support and so do not consider grants to people or organisations who apply speculatively. The trust also has a policy of not responding to any correspondence unless it relates to grants it has agreed to make or to the general management of the trust.

The Cazenove Charitable Trust

General

£25,000 (2008)

Beneficial area

UK.

Cazenove, 20 Moorgate, London EC2R 6DA
Tel: 020 7155 6147
Correspondent: Sophia Pryor
Trustees: Sophia Pryor, Chair; Edward M Harley; Michael Wentworth-Stanley; Michael Power.

CC Number: 1086899

Information available

The latest accounts available at the Charity Commission website were for 2008.

Established in 1969, this trust primarily supports the charitable activities sponsored by current and ex Cazenove employees.

In 2008 the trust had assets of £1 million and an income of £44,000. Grants totalled £25,000.

Beneficiaries included: Wheelpower (£3,000); Cancer Research, Macmillan Cancer Relief (£2,000 each); Army Benevolent Fund (£1,300); Global Vision International, National Autistic Society and Wooden Spoon (£1,000 each).

£12,500 worth of grants were made in sums of less than £1,000.

Applications

This trust does not respond to unsolicited applications.

The CBD Charitable Trust

General, children and young people

Around £150,000 (2010/11)

Beneficial area

Worldwide.

Trustee Dept, Coutts & Co, 440 Strand, London WC2R 0QS
Tel: 020 7663 6825
Correspondent: Coutts & Co
Trustees: Coutts & Co; Ingrid Scott.
CC Number: 1136702

Information available

Basic information was available from the Charity Commission.

The trust was established in 2010 for general charitable purposes and is connected to CBD Interfaith Ministries. The trust has a preference for organisations working with children and young people.

In 2010/11 the trust had both an income and a total expenditure of £171,000. Unfortunately, no further information was available.

Applications

In writing to the correspondent.

The Cemlyn-Jones Trust

Welsh heritage, medical research, animal welfare, music and religion

£39,000 (2009/10)

Beneficial area

North Wales and Anglesey.

59 Madoc Street, Llandudno LL30 2TW
Tel: 01492 874391
Email: philip.brown@brewin.co.uk
Correspondent: P G Brown, Trustee
Trustees: P G Brown; Mrs J E Lea; Mrs E G Jones.
CC Number: 1039164

Information available

Accounts were available from the Charity Commission.

This trust was registered in 1994, and has a welcome preference for making grants to small local projects in North Wales and Anglesey. Its objects, listed in the annual report, are:
1 conservation and protection of general public amenities, historic or public interests in Wales
2 medical research
3 protection and welfare of animals and birds
4 study and promotion of music
5 activities and requirements of religious and educational bodies.

In 2009/10 the trust had assets of £1 million, which generated an income of £36,000. Grants were made totalling £39,000.

Four grants went to Bangor University towards the following funds, schools and departments: Stewardship (£12,000); C J Fellowship fund (£8,000); Outreach (£6,000); School of Ocean Sciences (£4,000); and Royal Society (£3,000).

Other beneficiaries included: Music in Hospitals Wales (£2,000); Beaumaris Festival, All Saints Church – Deganwy and Snowdonia Society (£1,000 each);

and Llandudno Youth Music Theatre (£500).

Exclusions

No grants to individuals or non-charitable organisations.

Applications

In writing to the correspondent.

The CH (1980) Charitable Trust

Jewish

£164,000 (2009/10)

Beneficial area

UK and Israel.

30 Gresham Street, London EC2V 7PG
Correspondent: The Administrator
Trustee: Kleinwort Benson Trustees Limited.
CC Number: 279481

Information available

Accounts were available from the Charity Commission.

Established in 1980, in 2009/10 the trust had assets of £1.6 million and an income of £36,000. Grants made to 8 organisations totalled £164,000.

Grants went to: Oxford Centre for Hebrew and Jewish Studies (£100,000); Traditional Alternatives Foundation (£25,000); Jerusalem Foundation (£18,000); Israel Diaspora Trust and Anglo Israel Foundation (£8,000 each); West London Synagogue Charitable Fund (£3,000); B'nal B'rith Hillel Foundation (£1,000); and British Friends of the Israel Guide Dog Centre for the Blind (£500).

Applications

In writing to the correspondent.

R E Chadwick Charitable Trust

General

Around £25,000 (2009/10)

Beneficial area

UK.

Newlaithes Manor, Newlaithes Road, Horsforth, Leeds LS18 4LG
Tel: 01132 446 100
Correspondent: Peter Chadwick, Trustee
Trustees: Peter Chadwick; Esme Knowles; Paul Knowles; Ann Chadwick.
CC Number: 1104805

Information available

Basic information was available from the Charity Commission website.

Set up in 2004, in 2009/10 the trust had an income of £25,000 and a total expenditure of £30,000. No further information was available.

Previous beneficiaries include: Grammar School at Leeds, British Red Cross, Crisis, Leeds Festival Chorus, Myasthenia Gravis Association, RNIB, UNICEF, Arthritis Research, CAFOD, the Country Trust, Friends of St Winifred's , Gloucester Choral Society, Leeds Parish Church Choral Foundation Appeal, Meanwood Valley Urban Farm, Muslim Hands, NSPCC, the Simon Community, Yorkshire Dales Millennium Trust, Landmark Trust, Mission to Deep Sea Fishermen, Nightstop and Royal Horticultural Society – Harlow Carr.

Applications

In writing to the correspondent.

The Amelia Chadwick Trust

General

£118,000 (2009/10)

Beneficial area

UK, especially Merseyside.

Guy Williams Layton, Pacific Chambers, 11–13 Victoria Street, Liverpool L2 5QQ
Tel: 0151 236 7171
Correspondent: John McGibbon, Trustee
Trustees: John McGibbon; Christopher Bibby.
CC Number: 213795

Information available

Accounts were available from the Charity Commission.

The trust supports a wide range of charities, especially welfare causes. Although grants are given throughout the UK, there is a strong preference for Merseyside.

In 2009/10 the trust had assets of £3.3 million, an income of £112,000 and made 39 grants totalling £118,000.

Beneficiaries included: Merseyside Development Foundation (£25,000); St Helen's and District Women's Aid (£18,000); Liverpool PSS (£12,000); European Play-Work Association (£7,000); Birkenhead Youth Club (£5,000); Merseyside Holiday Service (£3,000); Centrepoint, Kid's Cookery School and Sue Ryder Home (£2,000 each); Sheila Kay Fund (£1,500); Age Concern – Liverpool and Shrewsbury House (£1,000 each); British Red Cross (£750); Fortune Centre (£500); and Wirral Independent Support Forum (£100).

Exclusions

No grants to individuals.

Applications

All donations are made through Liverpool Charity and Voluntary Services. Grants are only made to charities known to the trustees, and unsolicited applications are not considered.

The Pamela Champion Foundation

General, disability

£25,000 (2010)

Beneficial area

UK, with a preference for Kent.

Wiltons, Newnham Lane, Eastling, Faversham, Kent ME13 0AS
Tel: 01795 890233
Correspondent: Elizabeth Bell, Trustee
Trustees: Miss M Stanlake; Mrs C Winser; Mrs E Bell; P M Williams.
CC Number: 268819

Information available

Accounts were available from the Charity Commission.

In 2010 the trust had assets of over £718,000 and an income of over £31,000. There were 28 grants made totalling £25,000 and administration costs including expenses and accountancy fees were almost £3,000.

Beneficiaries included: Fairbridge in Kent and Salvation Army (£2,000 each); Kent MS Society, Farms for City Children, Kingfisher Medway, Lord Whisky and Combat Stress (£1,000 each); London Centre for Children with Cerebral Palsy (£750 each); Canterbury Oast Trust, Deafblind, Livability and Willow Foundation (£500 each); and Hope Appeal (£250).

Exclusions

No grants to non-registered charities.

Applications

In writing to the correspondent.

The Chapman Charitable Trust

Welfare, general

£234,000 (2009/10)

Beneficial area

Eastern and South East England, including London, and Wales.

Crouch Chapman, 62 Wilson Street, London EC2A 2BU
Tel: 020 7782 0007
Email: cct@crouchchapman.co.uk
Correspondent: Roger S Chapman, Trustee
Trustees: Roger Chapman; Richard Chapman; Bruce Chapman; Guy Chapman; Bryony Chapman.
CC Number: 232791

Information available

Accounts were available from the Charity Commission.

Established in 1963 with general charitable purposes, the trust mainly supports culture and recreation, education and research, health, social services, environment and heritage causes. In 2009/10 the trust has assets of £6 million and an income of £221,000. Overall, 114 grants were made totalling £234,000. See the table below for more information on the trust's grant giving.

Beneficiaries included: Hampstead & Westminster Hockey Club (£25,000); Pesticide Action Network UK (£15,000 in two grants); Fragile X Society and Queen Alexandra Hospital Home (£12,000 in two grants each); Cherry Trees – respite care for children (£6,000), Phoenix Cinema Trust (£2,500); and CoolTan Arts (£1,500).

In addition, there were 69 grants of £1,000 each and 8 Grants of £500 each made to organisations.

Exclusions

No grants to or for the benefit of individuals, local branches of UK charities, animal welfare, sports tours or sponsored adventure holidays.

Applications

In writing at any time. The trustees currently meet to consider grants twice a year at the end of September and in March. They receive a large number of applications and regret that they cannot acknowledge receipt of them. The absence of any communication for six months would mean that an application must have been unsuccessful.

Common applicant mistakes

'Falling outside our stated area of operation. Applications come from individuals, which are not considered.'

The Charter 600 Charity

General

£42,000 (2009/10)

Beneficial area

UK.

Mercers' Hall, Ironmongers Lane, London EC2V 8HE
Website: www.mercers.co.uk/
Correspondent: The Clerk
Trustee: The Mercers Company.
CC Number: 1051146

Information available

Accounts were available from the Charity Commission.

The Charter 600 charity was established to commemorate the 600th anniversaries of the Grant of the Mercers' Company's first Charter in 1394 and of the first Mastership of Sir Richard Whittington in 1395. Established in 1994, it operates under a trust deed dated October 1995.

The 2010/11 trustees' report states:

> The trustee's aims are to support a range of organisations with the common theme of delivering charitable services and facilities to those in need and to local communities. The Charity has achieved these aims during the period by supporting community-based, grass-roots organisations with particular emphasis on education, social and medical welfare support for young people and communities.
>
> It is the intention of the trustees in 2012 and beyond to maintain the current grant-making programme with a particular focus on smaller charities personally endorsed by members of the Mercers Company with grants of up to £2,000.

In 2009/10 the charity has assets of £803,000 and an income of £70,000. Grants made during the year totalled £42,000 and were distributed for the following purposes:

Welfare: social and medical	£19,250
Welfare: youth and community	£8,500
Education	£6,800
Performing arts	£2,350
Church	£1,750
Welfare: the elderly	£1,500
Heritage: material conservation	£750
Heritage: wildlife	£750

Beneficiaries included: Russian Orphan Opportunity Fund (£2,000); Cornwall Multiple Sclerosis Therapy

THE CHAPMAN CHARITABLE TRUST

	Local	National	Total
Culture and heritage	£22,000 (8)	£8,000 (6)	£30,000
Education and research	– (0)	£7,000 (6)	£7,000
Activity, health and wellbeing	£26,000 (2)	£2,000 (2)	£28,000
Social Care	£35,000 (7)	£110,000 (51)	£145,000
Environment	£1,000 (1)	£24,000 (11)	£25,000

Centre' Faversham Amateur Boxing Club and Touch of Light (£1,500 each); Bray Senior Citizens Club, Croydon Community Against Trafficking and Shirts for Soldiers (£1,000 each); Cherished Memories Support Group, Fewen Educational Trust, St Barnabas Parish Church and Trustees of King George's Field Whitwell (£750 each); Friends in St Helier, Hereford String Orchestra and Willow Foundation (£500 each); and Federation of Youth Clubs and Westminster House Youth Club (£250 each).

Exclusions
Applications for charitable grants will only be accepted when put forward by a member of the Mercers' Company.

Applications
The charity does not consider unsolicited applications.

Common applicant mistakes
'Applicants not reading and following criteria and, therefore, submitting ineligible applications.'

The Worshipful Company of Chartered Accountants General Charitable Trust (also known as CALC)

General, education
£125,000

Beneficial area
UK.

Hampton City Services, Hampton House, High Street, East Grinstead, West Sussex RH19 3AW
Tel: 01342 319038
Email: peterlusty@btconnect.com
Correspondent: Peter Lusty, Clerk
Trustees: Henry Gold; Rachel Adams; Colin Brown; John Cardnell; James Macnamara; David Allvey.

CC Number: 327681

Information available
Accounts were on file at the Charity Commission.

In general, the trust supports causes advancing education and/or benefiting disadvantaged people. It has a tendency to focus on a particular theme each year, as well as making grants to other causes and organisations of particular relevance to members of the company.

In 2009/10 the trust had assets of £1.2 million, an income of £146,000 and made grants totalling £125,000.

£24,000 was distributed between 29 Primary Schools to promote numeracy and literacy.

Major beneficiaries included: The Master's project (£56,000); Institute of Chartered Accountants bursary (£10,000); MANGO (£5,000); and The Lord Mayor's Appeal 2010 (£2,500).

Applications
Applications must be sponsored by a liveryman of the company.

The Cheruby Trust

Welfare, education, general
£17,000 (2009/10)

Beneficial area
UK and worldwide.

62 Grosvenor Street, London W1K 3JF
Tel: 020 7499 4301
Correspondent: Mrs S Wechsler, Trustee
Trustees: A L Corob; L E Corob; T A Corob; C J Cook: S A Wechsler.
CC Number: 327069

Information available
Full accounts were available from the Charity Commission.

The trust's charitable objectives are the relief of poverty, the advancement of education and such other charitable purposes as the trustees see fit. Its policy is to: 'hold a level of reserves sufficient for the Charity to meet any long term commitments and obligations.' In 2009/10 the trust had assets of £31,000 and an income of £32,000, mostly from donations. There were 7 grants made totalling £17,000 (£105,000 in 2007/08).

Grants went to: Water Aid (£5,000); Breadline Africa and British Humanitarian Aid (£3,000 each); WJR – Indonesia Appeal (£2,500); Indian Rural Health Trust (£2,000); DEC – Haiti Earthquake Appeal (£1,000); and Rainforest Concern (£500).

Applications
In writing to the correspondent.

The Chetwode Foundation

Education, churches, general
£59,000 (2009/10)

Beneficial area
UK, with a preference for Nottinghamshire, Leicestershire and Derby.

Samworth Brothers (Holdings) Ltd, Chetwode House, 1 Samworth Way, Leicester Road, Melton Mowbray, Leicestershire
Tel: 01664 414500
Correspondent: J G Ellis, Trustee
Trustees: J G Ellis; R N J S Price; A C Price.
CC Number: 265950

Information available
Full accounts were on file at the Charity Commission.

This foundation has general charitable purposes, giving without exclusion across the UK. Whilst it has preferences for education, churches and work in Nottinghamshire, Leicestershire and Derby, this is not at the expense of other causes.

In 2009/10 the foundation had assets of £1.5 million and an income of £75,000. Grants totalling £59,000 were made to 13 organisations.

Grants went to: North Notts Independent Domestic Abuse Services

– NNIDAS (£26,000); Canaan Trust (£10,000); Hope for the Homeless (£8,000); Belvoir Castle Cricket Trust (£4,000); Tythby and Cropwell Butler PCC (£3,000); Newark and Nottinghamshire Agricultural Society (£2,000); Help for Heroes, NSPCC, Brough Methodist Chapel and Hand in Hand Trust (£1,000 each); Bingham and District Choral Society (£750); British Limbless Ex-Service Men's Association (£500); and Chance to Shine (£250).

Applications

'The foundation's grant making policy is to support a limited number of causes known to the trustees, particularly those supported by the settlor. Unsolicited applications are not normally considered.'

The Malcolm Chick Charity

Youth character building, armed forces welfare, medical research and care

£23,500 (2009/10)

Beneficial area

UK.

Pothecary Witham Weld, 70 St George's Square, London SW1V 3RD
Tel: 020 7821 8211
Email: charities@pwwsolicitors.co.uk
Website: www.pwwsolicitors.co.uk
Correspondent: Jayne Day, Administrator
Trustees: D J L Mobsby; R S Fowler; N D Waldman.
CC Number: 327732

Information available

Information taken from the Charity Commission website.

This trust has been in existence for some time with the trustees making small grants to organisations they were familiar with. On the death of one of the trustees, Malcolm Chick, the trust received part of his estate and has grown in size.

Grants are given in the following categories:
- youth character building
- armed service charities
- Medical research and care.

In 2009/10 the charity had an income of £23,000 and an expenditure of £23,500.

Previous beneficiaries included: AHOY Centre and St Dunstan's (£9,000 each); Children's Heart Foundation (£4,000); Barts and the London Charity, the Daneforth Trust, Hove and the Adur Sea Cadet Unity and Tall Ships Youth Trust (£3,000 each); and Soft Power Education, Ocean Youth Trust South and Project Trust (£500 each).

Applications

Applicants should first write to ask for a copy of the criteria and application forms. Telephone calls are not welcomed. The trustees meet to consider applications in November and completed forms must be returned by the middle of October. There is a separate application form and guidance notes for individual applicants.

Common applicant mistakes

'Not supplying required supporting documentation. After initial request many do not go on to return the standard application form.'

Child Growth Foundation

Institutions researching child/adult growth disorders, and people with such diseases

£227,000 (2009/10)

Beneficial area

UK.

2 Mayfield Avenue, Chiswick W4 1PY
Tel: 020 8995 0257
Email: info@childgrowthfoundation.org
Website: www.childgrowthfoundation.org
Correspondent: Tam Fry, Hon. Chair

Trustees: Tam Fry, Chair; Nick Child; Russell Chaplin; Rachel Pidcock; Linda Washington; Mark Coyle; Sue Davies; Nick Fullagar.
CC Number: 274325

Information available

Accounts were available from the Charity Commission.

Among the objects of this foundation are to promote and fund research into the causes and cure of growth disorders in children within the area of benefit and to publish the results of such research.

The conditions covered by the foundation are:
- Turner syndrome
- Russell-Silver syndrome/intrauterine growth retardation
- bone dysplasia
- Sotos syndrome
- premature sexual maturity
- growth/multiple pituitary hormone deficiency.

In 2009/10 the trust had assets of £654,000 and an income of £303,000. Out of a total expenditure of £351,000, grants were made totalling £227,000.

Beneficiaries were: Institute of Child Health (£96,000); University of Edinburgh (£46,000); Central Manchester University Hospitals (£35,000); Queen Mary's College (£34,000); King's College (£11,000); and Imperial College (£4,400).

Applications

In writing to the correspondent.

Children's Liver Disease Foundation

Diseases of the liver and biliary system in children

£73,000 (2009/10)

Beneficial area

UK.

36 Great Charles Street, Queensway, Birmingham B3 3JY
Tel: 0121 212 3839

Fax: 0121 212 4300
Email: info@childliverdisease.org
Website: www.childliverdisease.org
Correspondent: Catherine Arkley, Chief Executive
Trustees: Tom Ross, Chair; Bob Benton; Nick Budd; Jayne Carroll; Kellie Charge; Mairi Everard; Michele Hunter; Ann Mowat; David Tildesley.
CC Number: 1067331

Information available

Accounts were on file at the Charity Commission.

The Children's Liver Disease Foundation (CLDF) is a national registered charity founded in 1980. Its mission is to advance knowledge of childhood liver disease through:

- funding pioneering medical research
- providing effective education
- giving a professional and caring support service to families and young people with liver disease.

CLDF supports a wide range of projects, including clinical and laboratory-based research, and social research which looks at topics such as how to improve quality of life. Further details on the research priorities for 2011–14 are available to download from the website.

The foundation has a major grants programme which awards project grants for a maximum three years. The small grants programme distributes £20,000 per annum in grants of up to £5,000. PhD fellowship funding is also offered on an ad hoc basis.

In 2009/10 the foundation had assets of £728,000, an income of £670,000 and a total expenditure of £638,000. Expenditure on research and grants totalled £73,000.

Previous beneficiaries include: Birmingham Children's Hospital, King's College Hospital – London, Institute of Reproductive and Developmental Biology – Imperial College London, St James's University Hospital – Leeds, Liver Research Group – Southampton University, National Heart and Lung Institute – London and Queens Medical Centre – University of Nottingham.

Exclusions

The charity does not accept applications from organisations whose work is not associated with paediatric liver disease. No grants to individuals, whether medical professionals or patients. No grants for travel or personal education. No grants for general appeals.

Applications

Applicants are strongly advised to look at the relevant pages on the Children's Liver Disease Foundation website where further information and application forms are available.

The Children's Research Fund

Child health research

£41,000 (2009/10)

Beneficial area

UK.

Head Office, 6 Scarthill Property, New Lane, Aughton, Ormskirk, Lancashire L39 4UD
Tel: 01695 420928
Website: www.childrensresearchfund.org.uk
Correspondent: The Trustees
Trustees: Hugh Greenwood, Chair; Gerald Inkin; Hugo Greenwood; Rt Hon. Lord Morris of Manchester; Elizabeth Theobald; David Lloyd.
CC Number: 226128

Information available

Full accounts were available from the Charity Commission.

The fund supports research into children's diseases, child health and prevention of illness in children, carried out at institutes and university departments of child health. The policy is to award grants, usually over several years, to centres of research. It will also support any charitable project associated with the well being of children.

In 2009/10 it had assets of £1.4 million, an income of £42,000 and made research grants totalling £41,000 (£120,000 in 2008/09).

Grants went to: the British Association of Paediatric Surgeons

(£25,000); Liverpool School of Tropical Medicine (£7,000); Dr Saula – Africa (£6,000); War Children of Kuwait (£3,000); and KIND (£1,000).

Exclusions

No grants for capital projects.

Applications

Applicants from child health research units and university departments are invited to send in an initial outline of their proposal; if it is eligible they will then be sent an application form. Applications are considered in March and November.

The Chipping Sodbury Town Lands Charity

Welfare, education, leisure

£82,000 (2010)

Beneficial area

The parishes of Chipping Sodbury and Old Sodbury.

Town Hall, 57–59 Broad Street, Chipping Sodbury, Bristol, South Gloucestershire BS37 6AD
Tel: 01454 852223
Email: nicola.gideon@chippingsodburytownhall.co.uk
Correspondent: Nicola Gideon, Clerk
Trustees: P J Elsworth, Chair; B Ainsley; C A R Hatfield; B Seymour; D Shipp; R Smith; M Cook; Paul L; P S Robins; W Whittle.
CC Number: 236364

Information available

Accounts were on file at the Charity Commission.

The trust gives grants for relief-in-need and educational purposes, and also other purposes within Sodbury, including the provision of leisure facilities.

In 2010 the trust had assets of £8.2 million, an income of £324,000 and made grants totalling £82,000. £57,500 of this total was made in grants to organisations and the remainder was given in grants to individuals.

Beneficiaries included: Chipping Sodbury Endowed School (£20,000); Chipping Sodbury Scouts (£6,500); St John Baptist Church, Chipping Sodbury Cricket Club (£6,000 each); Chipping Sodbury Festival (£3,000); Chipping Sodbury Golf Club and Woodmans Close Residents Club (£1,000 each).

Applications

In writing to the correspondent. The trustees meet on the third week of each month except August. Retrospective applications are not considered.

The Chownes Foundation

Religion, relief-in-need, social problems

£106,000 (2009/10)

Beneficial area

UK, priority is given to charities based in Sussex, particularly in mid Sussex.

The Courtyard, Beeding Court, Shoreham Road, Steyning, West Sussex BN44 3TN
Tel: 01903 816699
Email: chownes@russellnew.com
Correspondent: Sylvia Spencer, Secretary
Trustees: Mrs U Hazeel; The Rt Revd S Ortiger; M Woolley.
CC Number: 327451

Information available

Accounts were available from the Charity Commission.

According to the foundation's 2009/10 annual report, its objects are: 'the advancement of religion, the advancement of education among the young, the amelioration of social problems, the relief of poverty amongst the elderly and the former employees of Sound Diffusion PLC who lost their pensions when the company went into receivership and the furtherance of any other lawful charitable purpose.' Priority is given to charities based in Sussex,

particularly in mid Sussex, being the former home of the Founder. Preference will be given to projects where a donation by the Chownes Foundation may have some meaningful impact on an identified need rather than simply being absorbed into a larger funding requirement.

In 2009/10 the foundation had assets of £1.6 million, which generated an income of £100,000. Grants were made totalling £106,000 which included £48,000 in grants to individuals and £58,000 in grants to organisations, which was distributed as follows:

Social problems	£42,000
Religion	£6,000
General	£11,000

Applications

In writing to the correspondent.

Christian Response to Eastern Europe

Christian, emergency relief

£134,000 to organisations (2010)

Beneficial area

Eastern Europe (in practice Romania and Moldova).

Cherith, 130 Honiton Road, Exeter EX1 3EW
Website: www.cr2ee.org.uk/
Correspondent: David Northcote-Passmore, Chair
Trustees: David Northcote Passmore, Chair; Timothy Mason; Hugh Scudder.
CC Number: 1062623

Information available

Accounts were available from the Charity Commission.

The 2009/10 trustees' annual report outlines the trust's objects as follows:

The objects of the charity are to provide relief to disadvantaged and vulnerable people living in Eastern Europe. Help is given by supporting families, churches and medical organisations through financial gifts, taking humanitarian aid and medical supplies, and setting up projects to

provide long term benefits and independence.

In 2010 the trust had assets of £70,000 and an income of £204,000. Grants were made totalling £249,000 mainly to assist people in Romania and Moldova.

Grants to individuals and families totalled £115,000. 'Institutional grants' totalled £134,000.

Beneficiaries included: Gura Biculu Centre building project (£85,000); Gura Biculu farm project (£20,000); Orhei Church and Soup Kitchen (£6,000); Repairs to road in Gambut Village (£3,000); Street Children's home, Beltsey and Well at Gribova (£2,000 each); and God's Vineyard Foundation (£1,000).

Applications

In writing to the correspondent.

Chrysalis Trust

General, education, social welfare

£62,500 (2010/11)

Beneficial area

North East of England, UK national organisations providing benefit across the UK, overseas.

Dickinson Dees, One Trinity Gardens, Broad Chare, Newcastle upon Tyne NE1 2HF
Tel: 08449 841500
Fax: 08449 841501
Email: info@chrysalis-trust.co.uk
Website: www.chrysalis-trust.co.uk
Correspondent: Sarah Evans, Trustee
Trustees: Mark Price Evans; Sarah Evans; Andrew Playle; Alba Lewis.
CC Number: 1133525

Information available

Brief accounts were available from the Charity Commission. The trust also has a simple and informative website.

The trust was registered in 2010 for general charitable purposes, with a particular interest in education, social welfare and disability. The trust considers funding unpopular causes and projects that may find it difficult to attract funding elsewhere. Funding is divided between North East

England, the rest of the UK and overseas. The following further information is taken from the trust's website:

All grants are made at the discretion of the trustees without discrimination on any grounds. Amongst other things, the trustees will consider the following criteria:

▶ the ability of the applicant to demonstrate that they already provide or will provide public benefit
▶ the impact the grant will make with regard to relieving hardship, distress or sickness and/or promoting social welfare
▶ the number of people the grant will benefit and for how long
▶ how any shortfall in funding for the project will be raised
▶ the time scale for the project.

In 2010/11 the trust had an income of £1.4 million and made grants totalling £62,500.

Beneficiaries included: Cry in the Dark (£20,000), towards medical and vehicle running costs for Casa Lumina and Hospice Casa Albert – Romania; Excellent Development (£10,000), capital cost of one sand dam – Kenya; Greggs Foundation (£5,000), towards a hardship fund for making small grants to individuals in extreme financial hardship in the North East of England; Deafway (£4,000), towards bedding for a school for deaf children – Nepal; Circle of Life Rediscovery (£2,000), towards outdoor education for young carers; and British Wireless for the Blind Fund (£1,000), towards audio equipment for seven blind people in Newcastle.

Exclusions

Grants are not made for:
▶ research – academic or medical
▶ holidays or outings
▶ arts or entertainment activities
▶ animal welfare
▶ general appeals.

Applications

The trust provides the following helpful information on its website:

Application Checklist

There is no application form. Please outline your project on no more than 4 A4 sides using the following checklist:

1   What is the name of your organisation and what is your charitable registration number if you have one?
2   What does your organisation do?
3   Who are you helping, how many and how?
4   How many staff and volunteers do you have?
5   Which statutory and voluntary organisations do you have links with, if any?
6   How much money do you need? [e.g., a contribution of £X towards a total budget of £Y]. Where will the balance of the funds required come from?
7   What do you need the money for?
8   When do you need the money?
9   Have you applied to other sources? If so, give details and outcomes.
10 Who is your key contact regarding this application and what are their contact details (including telephone, email and mailing address)?

Please attach:
▶ A 250 word summary of your proposal.
▶ The contact details of 2 organisations or individuals able to provide a reference on your behalf.
▶ A copy of your latest audited annual report and accounts or a copy of your most recent bank statement if you do not have accounts.
▶ A budget for the project for which the application is made.
▶ Please do not attach any unnecessary documentation.

Applications should then be submitted preferably by email; if necessary, applications may be sent by post.

What will happen next?

▶ You will receive an acknowledgement that your application has been received.
▶ Applications are considered by the Trustees twice a year – usually in June and December, however, applications for amounts less than £1,001 may be considered sooner.
▶ We may contact you by telephone or email to discuss your application or to arrange a visit.
▶ We aim to let applicants know whether or not their application has been successful within 2 weeks of the trustees meeting at which the application is being considered.

What are the terms and conditions of a grant?

▶ Successful applicants will be asked to sign a simple grant agreement setting out their obligations in relation to the grant.
▶ Grants must be used for the purposes outlined in the application. If the project is unable to go ahead as planned we are happy to consider variations as to how the money is to be spent, however, the money must not be used for any other purposes without our agreement. It must be returned if the project does not go ahead.

▶ Recipients of a grant will be required to provide a report on the funded project to the trustees within 6 months of receiving the grant.

Common applicant mistakes

'General appeals; many are ineligible, particularly as they are outside North East England.'

CLA Charitable Trust

People with disabilities or who are disadvantaged

£56,000 (2009/10)

Beneficial area

England and Wales only.

Hopbine Farm, Main Street, Ossington, Newark NG23 6LJ
Tel: 01636 823 835
Website: www.cla.org.uk
Correspondent: Peter Geldart, Director
Trustees: Sir Henry Aubrey-Fletcher; Gordon Lee Steere; Anthony Duckworth-Chad; Hugh Duberly; Neil Mainwaring.
CC Number: 280264

Information available

Accounts were available from the Charity Commission.

The trust was founded in 1980 by CLA members. Its objects are threefold:

▶ to encourage education about the countryside for those who are disabled or disadvantaged, particularly youngsters from urban areas
▶ to provide facilities for those with disabilities to have access to recreation in the countryside
▶ to promote education in agriculture, forestry, horticulture and conservation for those who are disabled or disadvantaged.

It prefers to support smaller projects where a grant from the trust can make a 'real contribution' to the success of the project'. It gives grants for specific projects or items rather than for ongoing running costs.

In 2009/10 it had assets of £316,000 and an income of £67,000. Grants totalled £56,000.

There were 20 grants of £1,000 or more listed in the accounts. Beneficiaries included: Harper Adams College (£6,000); Avon Riding Centre for the Disabled (£3,200); Woolverstone Project (£3,000); Elizabeth Fitzroy Support (£2,800); Noah's Ark and Watershed RDA (£2,000 each); Queen Alexandra Hospital Home (£1,700); Clapton Common Boys Club (£1,500); Menro Lluest (£1,300); and Nancy Oldfield Trust (£1,100).

Other grants of less than £1,000 each totalled £11,000.

Exclusions
No grants to individuals.

Applications
In writing to the correspondent. Trustees meet four times a year.

Common applicant mistakes
'Not checking eligibility criteria.'

J A Clark Charitable Trust

Health, education, peace, preservation of the earth, the arts

£422,000 to organisations (2009)

Beneficial area
UK, with a preference for South West England.

PO Box 1704, Glastonbury, Somerset BA16 0YB
Correspondent: Mrs P Grant, Secretary
Trustees: Tom Clark, Chair; Lance Clark; William Pym; Aidan Pelly.
CC Number: 1010520

Information available
Last accounts available at the Charity Commission website were for 2009.

In 2009 the trust had assets of £13.7 million and an income of £444,000. Grants totalled £433,000, of this total £422,000 was made to

organisations and £11,000 was given to individuals.

Beneficiaries included: Eucalyptus Charitable Foundation (£73,000); Khwendo Kor-Pakistan (£36,000); SHIN (£22,000); Hope Flowers School, Society for Empowering Human Resource, Rwanda Women's Network, CDA Sudan Women and Conflicts Forum (£20,000 each); Odanadi UK and Arab Women's Solidarity Association (£15,000 each); SKADA (£13,000); Oxford Research Group (£10,000); ABC Trust (£6,000); and Hai Ninh Project (£900).

Applications
This trust does not respond to unsolicited applications.

Common applicant mistakes
'Unsolicited enquiries are never processed.'

The Roger and Sarah Bancroft Clark Charitable Trust

Quaker, general

£9,000 (2009)

Beneficial area
UK and overseas, with preference for Somerset and Scotland.

c/o KPMG LLP, 100 Temple Street, Bristol BS1 6AG
Correspondent: The Trustees
Trustees: Mary P Lovell; Sarah C Gould; Roger S Goldby; Alice Clark; Robert B Robertson; Martin Lovell.
CC Number: 211513

Information available
Recent accounts were overdue at the Charity Commission, the latest accounts available were for 2009.

The objects of the trust are general charitable purposes with particular reference to:
- Religious Society of Friends and associated bodies
- charities connected with Somerset
- education (for individuals).

Accounts were overdue at the Charity Commission therefore the last available accounts were for 2009. In this year the trust had an income of £36,000 and assets of £1.3 million. Grants were made totalling £9,000 consisting of £2,500 to the University of Edinburgh and £6,500 to the Architectural Heritage Society of Scotland.

Previous beneficiaries have included Alfred Gillett Trust, Artlink Edinburgh, Bury St Edmunds Meeting House Appeal, Greenbank Swimming Pool, Holburne Museum of Art, Médecins Sans Frontières, Quaker Peace and Social Witness, Oxfam, Retreat York Ltd, Session's Book Trust, Society for the Protection of Ancient Buildings, Ulster Quaker Service Committee, Wilmington Friends School and Woodbrooke Quaker Study Centre.

Applications
In writing to the correspondent. There is no application form and telephone calls are not accepted. Trustees meet about three times a year. Applications will be acknowledged if an sae is enclosed or an email address given.

The Cleopatra Trust

Mental health, cancer welfare/education, diabetes, physical disability, homelessness, addiction, children

£48,000 (2010)

Beneficial area
Mainly UK.

c/o Charities Aid Foundation, 25 Kings Hill Avenue, King's Hill, West Malling, Kent ME19 4TA
Tel: 01732 520028
Correspondent: C H Peacock, Trustee
Trustees: Dr C Peacock; B Bond; C H Peacock.
CC Number: 1004551

Information available

Accounts were on file at the Charity Commission.

The trust has common trustees with two other trusts, the Dorus Trust and the Epigoni Trust (see separate entries), with which it also shares the same aims and polices. All three trusts are administered by Charities Aid Foundation. Generally the trusts support different organisations each year.

The trust makes grants in the following areas:

- mental health
- cancer welfare/education – not research
- diabetes
- physical disability – not research
- homelessness
- addiction
- children who are disadvantaged.

There is also some preference for environmental causes. It only gives grants for specific projects and does not give grants for running costs or general appeals. Support is only given to national organisations, not for local areas or initiatives.

In 2010 it had assets of almost £3.3 million, which generated an income of £113,000. Grants were made totalling £48,000.

Beneficiaries included: Fairbridge, Cystic Fibrosis Trust, Maggie Keswick Jencks Cancer Caring Centres Trust and Shooting Star Hospice (£10,000 each); Wellington College (£5,000); and West Wittering Flood Defence (£2,000).

Exclusions

No grants for individuals, expeditions, research, scholarships, charities with a local focus, local branches of UK-wide charities or towards running costs.

Applications

This trust no longer accepts applications.

Miss V L Clore's 1967 Charitable Trust

General, arts, social welfare, health, Jewish

Around £45,000 (2009/10)

Beneficial area

UK.

Unit 3, Chelsea Manor Studios, Flood Street, London SW3 5SR
Tel: 020 7351 6061
Email: info@cloreduffield.org.uk
Website: www.cloreduffield.org.uk
Correspondent: Sally Bacon
Trustees: Dame V L Duffield; David Harrel; Caroline Deletra.
CC Number: 253660

Information available

Accounts were available from the Charity Commission.

The trust has general charitable purposes, but broadly speaking is concerned with the performing arts, education, social welfare, health and disability. Grants usually range from £500 to £5,000. It is administered alongside the much larger Clore Duffield Foundation.

In 2009/10 the trust had assets of £1.2 million, an income of £43,000 and a total expenditure of £45,000. No list of grant beneficiaries was available.

Previous beneficiaries included: Chelsea Physic Gardens, Family Friends and Maccabi GB (£5,000 each); North London Hospice (£4,000); West London Synagogue (£2,500); Friends of Castle of Mey, NSPCC, the Pearl Foundation and UF Elias Ashmole Trust (£1,000 each); and Institute for Polish-Jewish Studies and JTMM Mission (£500 each).

Exclusions

No grants are given to individuals.

Applications

In writing to the correspondent on one to two sides of A4, enclosing an sae.

Common applicant mistakes

'Most common mistake is not specifying how much money is being requested.'

The Clover Trust

Older people, young people, Catholic, health disability

£260,000 (2009)

Beneficial area

UK, and occasionally overseas, with a slight preference for West Dorset.

DTE Business Advisory Services Limited, Park House, 26 North End Road, London NW11 7PT
Correspondent: G F D Wright, Trustee
Trustees: N C Haydon; Mrs S Woodhouse.
CC Number: 213578

Information available

Accounts were available from the Charity Commission.

This trust supports organisations concerned with health, disability, young people, older people and Catholic activities. However, most grants are given to a 'core list' of beneficiaries and the trust states: 'the chances of a successful application from a new applicant are very slight, since the bulk of the income is earmarked for the regular beneficiaries, with the object of increasing the grants over time rather than adding to the number of beneficiaries.'

Grants are given towards general running costs. Unsolicited applications which impress the trustees are given one-off grants, although only a tiny percentage of the many applications are successful.

In 2009 the trust had assets of £4.2 million and an income of £223,000. Grants were made to 45 organisations totalling £260,000. Grants ranged from £1,000 to £50,000, but were mainly for amounts of £5,000 or less.

Grants included those made to: Friends of Children in Romania

(£50,000); Downside Fisher Youth Club and Childhood First (£10,000 each); 999 Club (£7,500); Bridport Stroke Club and Orchard Vale Club (£5,000 each); Wireless for the Bedridden (£3,000); National Eczema Society (£2,000); and English Catholic History Association (£1,000).

Exclusions

The arts, monuments and non-registered charities are not supported. No grants are given towards building work.

Applications

In writing to the correspondent. Replies are not given to unsuccessful applications.

The Robert Clutterbuck Charitable Trust

Service, sport and recreation, natural history, animal welfare and protection

£39,000 (2009/10)

Beneficial area

UK, with preference for Cheshire and Hertfordshire.

28 Brookfields, Calver, Hope Valley, Derbyshire S32 3XB
Tel: 01433 631308
Email: secretary@clutterbucktrust.org.uk
Website: www.clutterbucktrust.org.uk
Correspondent: G A Wolfe, Secretary
Trustees: Maj. R G Clutterbuck; I A Pearson; R J Pincham.
CC Number: 1010559

Information available

Accounts were available from the Charity Commission.

The trust normally only makes grants to registered charities in the following areas:

- personnel within the armed forces and ex-servicemen and women
- sport and recreational facilities for young people benefiting Cheshire and Hertfordshire

- the welfare, protection and preservation of domestic animal life benefiting Cheshire and Hertfordshire
- natural history and wildlife
- other charities associated with the counties of Cheshire and Hertfordshire
- charities which have particular appeal to the founder, Major Robert Clutterbuck.

The trust prefers to make grants towards buying specific items rather than running costs. No grants are made below £500.

In 2009/10 the trust had assets of almost £1.2 million, an income of £35,000 and made 53 grants totalling £39,000.

Beneficiaries included: Sue Ryder Care (£1,800); Boys' Brigade, Henshaw's Society for the Blind and Mercyships (£1,500); Dogs Trust, David Lewis Centre, Grasslands Trust and Vincent Wildlife Trust (£1,000 each); and Leonard Cheshire Disability and Red Squirrel Survival Trust (£500 each).

Exclusions

No grants to individuals.

Applications

In writing to the correspondent. There are no application forms. Applications are acknowledged and considered by the trustees twice a year. The trustees will not normally consider appeals from charities within two years of a previous grant being approved.

Common applicant mistakes

'Not looking at published material.'

The Francis Coales Charitable Foundation

Historical

£54,000 (2010)

Beneficial area

UK, with a preference for Bedfordshire, Buckinghamshire, Hertfordshire and Northamptonshire.

The Bays, Hillcote, Bleadon Hill, Weston-super-Mare, Somerset BS24 9JS
Tel: 01934 814009
Email: enquiries@franciscoales.co.uk
Website: franciscoales.co.uk/
Correspondent: Trevor Parker, Administrator
Trustees: H M Stuchfield, Chair; A G Harding; Revd B H Wilcox; I G Barnett.
CC Number: 270718

Information available

Accounts were on file at the Charity Commission.

In 1885 Francis Coales and his son, Walter John Coales, acquired a corn merchant's business in Newport Pagnell, Buckinghamshire. Over the years similar businesses were acquired, but after a major fire it was decided to close down the business. From the winding-up was established The Francis Coales Charitable Trust in 1975. The following information is taken from the foundation's website:

> The objectives of the foundation are: 'to provide grants for the structural repair of buildings (built before 1875) which are open to the public. Preference is given to churches in the counties of Bedfordshire, Buckinghamshire, Hertfordshire and Northamptonshire.
>
> There is no territorial restriction in respect of the conservation of monuments and monumental brasses.
>
> Grants are occasionally made towards publication of architectural and archaeological books and papers; towards the purchase of documents and items for record offices and museums; for archaeological research and related causes.

In 2010 the foundation had assets of £3.4 million and an income of £661,000 including £649,000 from legacies. Grants were made totalling £54,000.

Exclusions

In respect of buildings, assistance is only given towards fabric repairs, but not to 'domestic' items such as heating, lighting, wiring, installation of facilities etc.

Applications

On a form which can be downloaded from the foundation's website. Trustees normally meet three times a year to consider grants. The foundation's website offers the following guidance:

> In respect of a building or contents, include a copy of the relevant portion only of the architect's (or conservator's) specification showing the actual work proposed. Photographs illustrating this are a necessity, and only in exceptional circumstances will an application be considered without supporting photographs here.
>
> It is of help if six copies of any supporting documentation are submitted in order that each trustee may have a copy in advance of the meeting.

Common applicant mistakes

'They do not meet the objectives, i.e. structural repairs only or outside the geographic area.'

The John Coates Charitable Trust

General, arts, children, environment, medical

£362,000 (2009/10)

Beneficial area

UK, mainly southern England.

PO Box 529, Cambridge CB1 0BT
Correspondent: Mrs R J Lawes, Trustee
Trustees: Mrs G F McGregor; Mrs C A Kesley; Mrs R J Lawes; Mrs P L Youngman; Mrs C P Cartledge.
CC Number: 262057

Information available

Accounts were obtained from the Charity Commission website.

This trust has general charitable purposes. Grants are made to large UK-wide charities, or small charities of personal or local interest to the trustees.

In 2009/10 the trust had assets of £10.2 million, an income of £376,000 and made 82 grants totalling £362,000. About a third of organisations supported also received support in the previous year.

Beneficiaries of larger grants included: Changing Faces, Great Ormond Street Hospital, Lymington Museum Trust, National Trust, Painshill Park Trust

Limited, Royal Hospital for Neuro-Disability, The Royal Marsden Hospital Charity and Tommy's The Baby Charity (£10,000 each).

Other beneficiaries included: Natural History Museum (£6,000); Action on Addiction, Age UK, Canine Partners, Chase Hospice Care for Children, Chichester Cathedral Restoration and Development Trust, Cleft Lip and Palate Association, Combat Stress, Farms for City Children, Fields in Trust, Help for Heroes, NSPCC, Pimlico Opera, Royal Albert Hall Trust, St Mungo's, Salvation Army, The Samaritans, Scope and Shakespeare's Globe (£5,000 each); Petersfield Swimming Pool, Rainbow Trust, The Solent Protection Society and Two Moors Festival Limited (£2,000 each); and Best Beginnings and The Nowhere Trust (£1,000 each).

Exclusions

Grants are given to individuals only in exceptional circumstances.

Applications

In writing to the correspondent. Small local charities are visited by the trust.

Coats Foundation Trust

Textile and thread-related training courses and research

£85,000 (2009/10)

Beneficial area

UK.

Coats plc, Coats Pensions Office, Pacific House, 70 Wellington Street, Glasgow G2 6UB
Tel: 014 1207 6820
Email: gwen.mckerrell@coats.com
Correspondent: Sheila Macnicol
Trustee: The Coats Trustee Company Limited.
CC Number: 268735

Information available

Basic information was available from the Charity Commission website.

Preference is given, but not specifically restricted, to applicants from textile and thread-related training courses.

In 2009/10 the foundation had an income of £22,000. Total expenditure was over £89,000.

Previous beneficiaries include: Copthall School, Leeds University and Nottingham Trent University.

Applications

Please write, enclosing a CV and an sae, giving details of circumstances and the nature and amount of funding required. There is no formal application form. Only applicants enclosing an sae will receive a reply. Applications are considered four times a year.

Common applicant mistakes

'We tend to only support applications which have a textile connection so those applying for an education grant for a different subject are often unsuccessful.'

The Cobalt Trust

General

£348,000 (2009/10)

Beneficial area

UK and overseas.

17 New Row, London WC2N 4LA
Correspondent: Stephen Dawson, Trustee
Trustees: Stephen Dawson; Brigitte Dawson; Jan Dawson.
CC Number: 1096342

Information available

Accounts were on file at the Charity Commission.

This trust was set up in 2002 with general charitable purposes. The trustees do not respond to unsolicited applications.

The trust's 2009/10 report states:

> Criteria for grants are reviewed on a regular basis. The latest review has led to focusing a substantial proportion of the amounts donated on a small number of larger and regular donations. These are generally to organisations well known to the trustees or where the trustees have undertaken a thorough review before deciding to donate. The

trustees have a preference in their strategic donations for smaller organisations where they feel their contribution will have a greater impact.

In 2009/10 the trust had assets of £1.9 million and an income of £127,000. Grants totalled £348,000.

Beneficiaries included: Impetus Trust (£169,000); EVPA (£26,000); Streets Limited (£14,000); Enable Ethiopia and Tree Aid (£12,000 each); Rose Trees Trust and Money for Madagascar (£10,000 each); Beat – Eating Disorders Association (£5,000); Wherever the Need (£1,000); Red Squirrel Survival Trust (£500); Wessex MS Therapy Centre (£100); and Bath RSPB (£50).

Many of the beneficiaries were supported in the previous year.

Applications
The trustees do not respond to unsolicited applications.

The Vivienne and Samuel Cohen Charitable Trust

Jewish, education, health, medical, culture, general

£182,000 (2009/10)

Beneficial area
UK and Israel.

Clayton Start & Co, 5th Floor, Charles House, 108–110 Finchley Road, London NW3 5JJ
Tel: 020 7431 4200
Correspondent: Dr Vivienne Cohen, Trustee
Trustees: Dr V L L Cohen; M Y Ben-Gershon; J S Lauffer; Dr G L Lauffer; D G Cohen.
CC Number: 255496

Information available
Accounts were available from the Charity Commission.

The majority of the trust's support is to Jewish organisations. In 2009/10 the trust had assets of £2.8 million and an income of £102,000. Grants totalled £182,000.

There were 306 grants made in the year which were broken down into the following categories:

Medical care and welfare	113	£68,000
Education	45	£59,000
Care and welfare	62	£34,500
Cultural and recreation	65	£16,000
Religious activities and communal	21	£4,000

Beneficiaries included: Ariel (£14,000); University College London (£10,000); Variety Club (£7,000); World Jewish Relief (£5,000); Hamesorah School (£4,000); the Spiro Ark (£3,000); Israel Free Loan Association and University Jewish Chaplaincy Board (£2,000 each); Chai Cancer Care, Machanaim and Royal Society of Medicine (£1,000 each).

Exclusions
No grants to individuals.

Applications
In writing only, to the correspondent.

The Denise Cohen Charitable Trust

Health, welfare, arts, humanities, education, culture, Jewish

£82,000 (2009/10)

Beneficial area
UK.

Berwin Leighton and Paisner, Adelaide House, London Bridge, London EC4R 9HA
Correspondent: Martin Paisner, Trustee
Trustees: Denise Cohen; Martin Paisner; Sara Cohen.
CC Number: 276439

Information available
Full accounts were available at the Charity Commission.

Registered with the Charity Commission in 1978, the trust has general charitable purposes, with a preference for work in the following areas: health, welfare, arts, humanities, education, culture, and Jewish organisations. In 2009/10 the trust had assets of £2.1 million and

an income of £93,000. Grants were made to 96 charities totalling £82,000.

Grants included those made to: Chai Cancer Charity (£9,000); Nightingale (£6,000); Jewish Woman's Aid (£4,500); Community Security Trust (£3,000); Lifeline for the Old Jerusalem (£2,500); Combat Stress (£2,000); Caring 4 Carers and British Friends of the Edith Wolfs (£1,000 each); British Friends of Rambam Medical Centre (£750); Sadler's Wells Theatre (£600); Wellbeing of Women and Royal Star and Garter Home (£500 each); Youth Aliyah-Child Rescue (£250); and British WIZO and Zionist Federation (£100 each).

Applications
In writing to the correspondent.

John Coldman Charitable Trust

General, Christian

£198,000 (2009/10)

Beneficial area
UK, with a preference for Edenbridge in Kent.

Bank House, Bank Street, Tonbridge, Kent TN9 1BL
Tel: 01732 770 660
Fax: 01732 362 452
Email: charles.warner@ warners-solicitors.co.uk
Correspondent: Charles Warner, Trustee
Trustees: John Coldman; Graham Coldman; Charles Warner.
CC Number: 1050110

Information available
Accounts were available from the Charity Commission.

The trust gives grants to community and Christian groups in Edenbridge, Kent and UK organisations whose work benefits that community such as children's and medical charities and schools.

In 2009/10 the trust had assets of £1.8 million and an unusually low income of £35,000. Grants to 25 organisations totalled £198,000.

Beneficiaries included: Great Ormond Street Hospital Children's Charity (£32,000); NSPCC Special Investigation Unit and Prince's Trust (£20,000 each); National Gardens Scheme (£18,000); Oasis International (£15,000); Citizen's Advice – Edenbridge and Westerham Branch (£12,000); Edenbridge Community Warden (£10,000); Eden Christian Trust (£7,500); Stangrove Area Community Action Group (£5,000); African Foundation (£3,000); Compaid Trust (£1,000); and Help the Hospices (£500).

During the year an additional £31,000 went towards the running of the Holcot Residential Centre, which operates as a hostel, holiday centre and community centre for the use of young people and others.

Applications

In writing to the correspondent.

The John and Freda Coleman Charitable Trust

Disadvantaged young people

£39,5000 (2010/11)

Beneficial area

Hampshire and Surrey and surrounding areas.

Alderney House, 58 Normandy Street, Alton, Hampshire GU34 1DE
Tel: 01420 86888
Email: paul.coleman@btinternet.com
Correspondent: Sue Poulter
Trustees: I Williamson; Mrs J L Bird; P H Coleman; B R Coleman.
CC Number: 278223

Information available

Accounts were available from the Charity Commission.

The trust aims to provide:

An alternative to an essentially academic education, to encourage and further the aspirations of young people with talents to develop manual skills and relevant technical knowledge to fit them for satisfying careers and useful employment. The aim is to develop the self-confidence of individuals to

succeed within established organisations or on their own account and to impress upon them the importance of service to the community, honesty, good manners and self discipline.

In 2010/11 the trust had assets of £870,000, an income of £31,000 and made 8 grants totalling £39,500. The following statement is taken from the trustees 2010/11 report:

The charitable donations this year have again been targeted at the core aims of the trust in helping young people to obtain the skills they need for both work and life. Principal donations are currently directed towards a number of organisations, in Surrey and Hampshire, focussed on providing practical training, skills and support where the normal education system has failed and young people are not reaching their full potential.

Beneficiaries were: Surrey SATRO (£10,500); Surrey Care Trust (£10,000); Surrey Community Development Trust (£5,000); Reigate and Redhill YMCA and Second Chance (£3,000 each); The Yvonne Arnaud Theatre Youth Drama Training (£2,000); and Step by Step (£1,000).

Exclusions

No grants are made to students.

Applications

In writing to the correspondent. Telephone calls are not welcome.

Common applicant mistakes

'We get a lot of applicants outside the geographical area of support.'

The E Alec Colman Charitable Fund Ltd

Religion, especially Jewish, children, social welfare

Around £40,000

Beneficial area

UK and worldwide.

Colman House, 6–10 South Street, Harborne, Birmingham B17 0DB

Tel: 0121 427 7700
Correspondent: A N Carless, Secretary
Trustees: S H Colman; Cecilia R Colman; M Harris; Susan R Stone.
CC Number: 243817

Information available

Accounts had been received at the Charity Commission, but were not available to view.

In 2009/10 the trust had an income of £11,000 and a total expenditure of £42,000. Further information was not available.

Previous beneficiaries included: World Jewish Relief (£5,000); Send a Cow (£2,500); Army Cadet Force Association, the Royal British Legion and RNIB (£2,000 each); Practical Action and St Dunstan's (£1,500 each); the Smile Train UK (£1,200); British Friends of Ohel Sarah, Institute for the Special Child, the Queen Alexandra Hospital Home, Rochdale Special Needs Cycling Club, the Salvation Army and Yad Vashem UK Foundation (£1,000 each); Brighton and Hove Parents and Children Group (£850); Operation New World and the Universal Beneficent Society (£750 each); 3H Fund, Amherst Heritage Centre, Deptford Action Group for the Elderly, Food Lifeline and the Tree Club (£500 each); At Risk Teenagers (£250); and 95th Birmingham Scout Group (£150).

Exclusions

No grants to individuals.

Applications

In writing to the correspondent; however, the trust has stated that new beneficiaries are only considered in exceptional circumstances. The trust aims to pinpoint areas of interest and take the initiative in funding organisations working in these fields.

The Sir Jeremiah Colman Gift Trust

General

£121,000 (2009/10)

Beneficial area

UK, with a preference for Hampshire, especially Basingstoke.

Malshanger, Basingstoke, Hampshire RG23 7EY
Tel: 01256 780252
Correspondent: Mrs V R Persson, Secretary to the Trustees
Trustees: Sir Michael Colman; Lady Colman; Oliver Colman; Hon. Cynthia Colman; Jeremiah Colman; Sue Colman.
CC Number: 229553

Information available

Accounts were available from the Charity Commission.

The trust makes grants for general charitable purposes with special regard to:

- advancement of education and literary scientific knowledge
- moral and social improvement of people
- maintenance of churches of the Church of England and gifts and offerings to the churches
- financial assistance to past and present employees/members of Sir Jeremiah Colman at Gatton Park, J and J Colman Ltd or other clubs and institutions associated with Sir Jeremiah Colman.

In 2009/10 the trust had assets of £4.7 million and an income of £131,000. Grants totalled £121,000 and were broken down as follows: 'special' donations (£65,000); 'annual' donations (£55,000); and 'extra' donations (£550).

Beneficiaries included: Warham (£7,500); National Art Collections and The Centre for Social Justice (£2,000 each); Cruse, Seeability, Wessex Counselling Service and Youth for Christ (£1,000 each).

Exclusions

Grants are not made to individuals requiring support for personal education, or to individual families for welfare purposes.

Applications

No unsolicited applications.

Common applicant mistakes

'The fact that we're not inviting them to apply.'

Col-Reno Ltd

Jewish

£38,000 (2009/10)

Beneficial area

UK, USA and Israel.

15 Shirehall Gardens, Hendon, London NW4 2QT
Correspondent: The Trustees
Trustees: Martin Stern; Alan Stern; Keith Davis; Rhona Davis; Chaim Stern; Libbie Goldstein.
CC Number: 274896

Information available

Accounts were on file at the Charity Commission.

The trust appears to support only Jewish organisations, with a preference for medical aid organisations and education.

In 2009/10 it had assets of £1.1 million and an income of £96,000. Grants to 18 organisations totalled £38,000.

Beneficiaries included: Society of Friends of the Torah (£16,000); Tiffert Gimzo (£7,500); Friends of Ascent (£2,400); Jerusalem Park Authority (£2,000); Friends of Yeshivat Chedvat Hatalmud (£1,600); Israel Museum – New Items Fund (£1,500); Chabad House of Hendon (£1,000); Chabad of Oxford (£720); Shaare Zedeck (£600); Yad Eliezer Trust (£200); and British Friends of Reut (£100).

Applications

In writing to the correspondent.

The Coltstaple Trust

Medical, relief in need, education

£250,000 (2010/11)

Beneficial area

Worldwide.

c/o Pollen House, 10–12 Cork Street, London W1S 3NP
Tel: 020 7439 4400
Correspondent: Lord Oakshott of Seagrove Bay, Trustee
Trustees: Lord Oakshott of Seagrove Bay; Dr P Oakshott; B R M Stoneham; E G Colville.
CC Number: 1085500

Information available

Accounts were available from the Charity Commission.

The trust was set up in 2001 with the following objects: 'the relief of persons in need, poverty or distress in third world countries and the relief of persons who are homeless or in housing need in the UK or any other part of the world'.

In 2010/11 it had assets of £4.6 million, an income of £207,000 and made grants totalling £250,000.

Four grants were made and these were awarded to: Oxfam (£130,000); St Mungo's and Opportunity International (£50,000 each); and Sport for Life (£20,000).

Applications

Unfortunately the trust's funds are fully committed: 'We give to a very small number of charities on a long term basis and have recently been receiving many requests which must have taken the applicants a lot of time [...] which we cannot deal with.'

Gordon Cook Foundation

Education and training

Around £200,000

Beneficial area

UK.

3 Chattan Place, Aberdeen AB10 6RB
Tel: 01224 571010
Email: gordoncook@btconnect.com
Website: www.gordoncook.org
Correspondent: Sharon Hauxwell, Foundation Secretary
Trustees: Miss A Harper, Chair; G Ross; Dr I Sutherland; D A Adams; J Anderson.
SC Number: SC017455

Information available

Limited information was filed with the Office of the Scottish Charity Regulator; the trust has a useful website.

This foundation was set up in 1974 and is dedicated to the advancement and promotion of all aspects of education and training which are likely to promote 'character development' and 'citizenship'. The following information is taken from the foundation's website.

> In recent years, the foundation has adopted the term 'Values Education' to denote the wide range of activity it seeks to support. This includes:
>
> ▶ the promotion of good citizenship in its widest terms, including aspects of moral, ethical and aesthetic education, youth work, cooperation between home and school, and coordinating work in school with leisure time pursuits
> ▶ the promotion of health education as it relates to values education
> ▶ supporting relevant aspects of moral and religious education
> ▶ helping parents, teachers and others to enhance the personal development of pupils and young people
> ▶ supporting developments in the school curriculum subjects which relate to values education
> ▶ helping pupils and young people to develop commitment to the value of work, industry and enterprise generally
> ▶ disseminating the significant results of relevant research and development.

In 2009/10 the foundation had an income of £303,000. Grants usually range from around £3,000 to £30,000.

The foundation collaborates with a wide range of other institutions involved in values education including: Comino Foundation, Institute for Global Ethics (UK) Trust, Learning and Teaching Scotland, Royal Highland Education Trust, Association of Directors of Education in Scotland and various universities. Many projects support and facilitate discussions of relevant issues among a wide variety of participants. In particular the foundation sponsors the Five Nations Network, a unique forum in England, Ireland, Northern Ireland, Scotland and Wales for sharing practice in formal education for citizenship and values. The network holds an annual conference bringing together teachers, policy makers, curriculum planners, inspectors, NGO representatives and others. Participants share practice, take part in interactive workshops, develop collaborative projects and plan for improving the effectiveness of citizenship and values education across the five distinct education systems of the UK and Ireland.

Exclusions

Individuals are unlikely to be funded.

Applications

The trustees are proactive in looking for projects to support and do not normally invite or respond to unsolicited applications for grant aid.

Common applicant mistakes

'We do not invite or respond to unsolicited applications for grant aid. All of the grants we provide are through areas of work that are identified by the trustees themselves.'

The Cooks Charity

Catering, welfare

Around £224,000

Beneficial area

UK, especially City of London.

Coombe Ridge, Thursley Road, Churt, Farnham, Surrey GU10 2LQ
Email: clerk@cookslivery.org.uk
Correspondent: Michael C Thatcher, Clerk and Solicitor
Trustees: H F Thornton; G A V Rees; B E G Puxley.
CC Number: 297913

Information available

Information was available, but accounts had yet to be received at the Charity Commission.

The charity was established in 1989 to support educational and welfare projects concerned with people involved in catering, and then any charitable purposes (with some sort of catering connection) in the City of London.

In 2009/10 it had an income of £451,000 and a total expenditure of £231,000. At the time of writing accounts had yet to be received at the Charity Commission, therefore further information was not available. Previously grants were made to 14 organisations totalling £224,000, which were broken down as follows:

Advancement of education	9	£189,000
The City of London	3	£25,000
General welfare	2	£10,000

Past beneficiaries have included: Academy of Culinary Arts (£55,000); Food Education At Schools Today (£42,000); Hackney Community College (£30,000); Springboard (£25,000); Ironbridge Museum (£15,000); Crisis Skylight Cafe (£12,000); Bournemouth University (£10,000); and Treloar Trust, Broadway and Pembroke House (£5,000 each).

Applications

In writing to the correspondent. Applications are considered in spring and autumn.

The Catherine Cookson Charitable Trust

General

£481,000 (2009/10)

Beneficial area

UK, with some preference for the North East of England.

Thomas Magnay and Co, 13 Regent Terrace, Gateshead, Tyne and Wear NE8 1LU
Tel: 0191 488 7459
Correspondent: Peter Magnay, Trustee
Trustees: David S S Hawkins; Peter Magnay; Hugo F Marshall; Daniel E Sallows; Jack E Ravenscroft.
CC Number: 272895

Information available

Accounts were available from the Charity Commission.

This trust was registered with the Charity Commission in February 1977. In 2009/10 the trust had assets of £22 million and an income of just over £733,000 derived from investments and royalties from many of the literary works of Dame Catherine Cookson. Grants were made during the year totalling £481,000 and were broken down as follows:

Medical, health and sickness	24	£249,000
Religious activities	23	£88,000
Education and training	8	£44,000
Children and young people	17	£11,000
Disability	23	£8,000
Arts and culture	15	£6,000
Animal welfare	2	£500
Other	28	£76,000

Beneficiaries of the largest grants included: Cancer Research UK (£100,000); Newcastle Diocese Education Board, the Puffin Appeal and the Stroke Association (£50,000 each); Newcastle upon Tyne Royal Grammar School (£35,000); and Great Ormond Street Hospital Children's Charity (£25,000).

Other beneficiaries included: East Sussex Hospitals NHS Trust (£8,000); HMS Trincomalee Trust (£5,000); Royalty Theatre Sunderland (£2,000); Blind Voice UK, St Cuthberts Centre Crook and Finchale Training College

(£1,000 each); Coping with Cancer Northeast, Peach Berkshire and Gangshow Newcastle and the Old Vicarage (£500 each); Brampton Primary School, Martlett's Hospice, and Rainbow Trust Durham (£250 each); and British Dyslexics North East, Elim Church Newcastle, and Jack and Jill Pre School Nursery (£100 each).

Applications

In writing to the correspondent.

Harold and Daphne Cooper Charitable Trust

Medical, health, Jewish

£63,000 (2009/10)

Beneficial area

UK.

c/o Portrait Solicitors, 1 Chancery Lane, London WC2A 1LF
Tel: 020 7092 6984
Correspondent: Alison Burton, Trust Administrator
Trustees: Sally Roter; Judith Portrait; Timothy Roter; Abigail Roter; Dominic Roter.
CC Number: 206772

Information available

Accounts were on file at the Charity Commission.

The trust was established in 1962 with general charitable purposes, though in practice support is focused on medical research, health and Jewish charities. Most grants are small and one-off but on-going support may be considered.

In 2009/10 the trust had assets of £2.6 million and an income of £93,000. Grants to 12 organisations were made totalling £63,000.

Beneficiaries were: Jewish Care (£46,000); Norwood Ravenswood (£5,000); Dogs for the Disabled and Variety Club of Great Britain (£2,000 each); and Live Music Now, Marie Curie Cancer Care, Arthritis Research UK, Jewish Blind and Disabled, Moorfields Eye Hospital, Spadework,

Thrive and Wheelpower (£1,000 each).

Exclusions

No grants to individuals.

Applications

In writing to the correspondent; applications are not acknowledged.

The Marjorie Coote Animal Charity Trust

Wildlife and animal welfare

£108,000 (2009/10)

Beneficial area

Worldwide.

Dykelands Farm, Whenby, York YO61 4SF
Email: info@mcacharity.org.uk
Correspondent: Mrs J P Holah, Trustees
Trustees: Sir Hugh Neill; Mrs. J P Holah; Lady Neill; Mrs. S E Browne.
CC Number: 208493

Information available

Accounts were available from the Charity Commission.

The trust was established in 1954 for the benefit of five named charities and any other charitable organisation which has as its main purpose the care and protection of horses, dogs or other animals or birds.

The trustees concentrate on research into animal health problems and on the protection of the species, whilst applying a small proportion of the income to general animal welfare, including sanctuaries.

In 2009/10 it had assets of £3.2 million and an income of £111,000. Grants paid totalled £108,000.

Ongoing support (£77,000 in 28 grants)

Grants were in the range of £500 and £10,000 and included those to: Animal Health Trust, RSPCA Sheffield and The Langford Trust for Animal Health & Welfare (£10,000 each); PDSA (£8,000); WWF-UK (£6,000); the Whiteley Wildlife Conservation Trust and Devon Wildlife Trust (£4,000 each); Brooke Hospital for Animals and Friends of Conservation (£3,000 each); The Gorilla Organization and Tusk Trust (£2,500 each); Devon Horse and Pony Sanctuary (£1,500); and Sheffield Wildlife Trust and SPANA (£1,000 each).

One-off grants (£31,000 in 13 grants)

The largest grant went to RSPCA Sheffield's Rebuild Project (£20,000). Other beneficiaries were: Royal Veterinary College Animal Health Trust (£10,000); Save the Rhino International (£1,000); and Alberts Horse Sanctuary and Dogs for the Disabled (£500 each).

Exclusions

No grants to individuals.

Applications

In writing to the correspondent. Applications should reach the correspondent during September for consideration in October/November.

The Gershon Coren Charitable Foundation

Jewish, welfare, general

£158,000 (2009/10)

Beneficial area

UK and the developing world.

5 Golders Park Close, London NW11 7QR
Correspondent: Muriel Coren, Trustee
Trustees: Muriel Coren; Anthony Coren; Walter Stanton.
CC Number: 257615

Information available

Accounts were available from the Charity Commission.

The trust supports registered charities, particularly Jewish organisations. In 2009/10 its assets totalled £2.5 million and it had an

income of £175,000. Grants were made to 41 organisations totalling £158,000.

Beneficiaries included: Gategi Village Self Help Group (£65,000); Spiro Ark (£8,000); Aish UK (£7,000); Magen David Adom UK (£5,000); Jewish Medical Association UK (£3,000); British ORT (£2,500); Kisharon (£2,000); One Voice and Smile Train (£1,000 each); and National Trust and Strongbone Children's Charitable Trust (£500).

Applications

In writing to the correspondent.

The Evan Cornish Foundation

Education, older people, health, human rights, poverty alleviation, penal reform

£387,000 (2009/10)

Beneficial area

UK and developing countries.

c/o Provincial House, Solly Street, Sheffield S1 4BA
Email: contactus@ evancornishfoundation.org.uk
Website: www. evancornishfoundation.org.uk
Correspondent: The Trustees
Trustees: Barbara Ward; Sally Cornish; Rachel Cornish.
CC Number: 1112703

Information available

Accounts were available from the Charity Commission.

The foundation was created by the widow and four daughters of businessman Evan Cornish who died in 2002. Support is given for 'charitable good causes'.

In 2009/10 the foundation had assets of £7 million, which generated an income of £156,000. A total of 86 donations were made ranging from £500 to £10,000 totalling £387,000.

Beneficiaries included: Inquest, Photovoice and Twin Charity

(£10,000 each); Practical Action (£9,500); AMREF and Civil Liberties Trust (£7,500); Brighton and Hove Fare Share, Extra Care and the Jenifer Trust (£5,000 each); Arts for Recovery and Rural Solar Light (£2,500 each); Village Water and Tools for Self Reliance (£1,000 each); and Power International (£700).

Exclusions

No grants for animal welfare charities or religious or political activities.

Applications

The trustees will consider applications as well as seeking out causes to support. They normally meet at least four times a year. They have a three step application process which can be found on the trust's website.

The Duke of Cornwall's Benevolent Fund

General

£116,000 (2009/10)

Beneficial area

UK, with a number of grants made in the Cornwall area.

10 Buckingham Gate, London SW1E 6LA
Tel: 020 7834 7346
Correspondent: Robert Mitchell
Trustees: Hon. James Leigh-Pemberton; W R A Ross.
CC Number: 269183

Information available

Accounts were available from the Charity Commission.

The fund receives donations from the Duke of Cornwall (Prince Charles) based on amounts received by the Duke as Bona Vacantia (the casual profits of estates of deceased intestates dying domiciled in Cornwall without kin) after allowing for costs and ex-gratia payments made by the Duke in relation to claims on any estate.

The fund's objectives are the relief of people in need, provision of almshouses, homes of rest, hospitals and convalescent homes, advancement of education, advancement of religion, advancement of the arts and preservation for the benefit of the public of lands and buildings. Grants are made to registered charities only.

In 2009/10 the fund had assets of £2.8 million and an income of £121,000. Grants were made totalling £116,000.

Of the 149 grants made during the year, there were 21 grants of £1,000 or more listed in the accounts. Beneficiaries included: the Prince's Foundation (£15,000); Business in the Community (£9,000); the Cleveland Pools Trust and Dartmoor Farmers Association (£5,000 each); Soil Association (£2,500); Wells Cathedral (£2,000); Isle of Scilly Veterinary Support Group, Shekinah Mission, Coombe Community Association and Woodland Heritage (£1,000 each).

Applications

In writing to the correspondent. Applicants should give as much detail as possible, especially information on how much money has been raised to date, what the target is and how it will be achieved. Applications can be made at any time. Trustees meet quarterly.

The Sidney and Elizabeth Corob Charitable Trust

General, Jewish

£287,000 (2009/10)

Beneficial area

UK.

62 Grosvenor Street, London W1K 3JF
Correspondent: The Trustees
Trustees: A L Corob; E Corob; C J Cook; J V Hajnal; S A Wechsler; S Wiseman.
CC Number: 266606

Information available

Basic information was available from the Charity Commission website.

The trust has general charitable purposes, supporting a range of causes including education, arts, welfare and Jewish charities.

In 2009/10 the trust had an income of just £4,000 (£48,000 in the previous year). Total expenditure was £287,000

Previous beneficiaries of larger grants included: Oxford Centre for Hebrew and Jewish Studies (£47,000); Autism Speaks (£20,000); United Synagogue (£10,000); and British Technion Society, the HOPE Charity, Jewish Care and Magen David Adom UK (£10,000 each).

Exclusions

No grants to individuals or non-registered charities.

Applications

In writing to the correspondent. The trustees meet at regular intervals.

The Corona Charitable Trust

Jewish

£49,000 (2009/10)

Beneficial area

UK and overseas.

16 Mayfield Gardens, Hendon, London NW4 2QA
Correspondent: A Levy, Chief Executive Officer
Trustees: A Levy; A Levy; B Levy.
CC Number: 1064320

Information available

Accounts were available from the Charity Commission.

In 2009/10 the trust had an income, mainly from donations, of £44,000 and made grants totalling £49,000. Assets stood at £76,000 at the year end.

Beneficiaries included: Menorah Foundation School (£8,000); Hasmonean high School (£7,000); the ZSV Trust (£6,000); Ahavas Shalom Charity Fund (£5,000); WST Charity Limited (£2,500); and Edgware Jewish Primary School (£1,500).

In addition, £3,000 was given out in grants of less than £1,000.

Applications

In writing to the correspondent.

The Costa Family Charitable Trust (formerly the Morgan Williams Charitable Trust)

Christian

£300,000 (2009/10)

Beneficial area

UK.

50 Stratton Street, London W1J 8LL
Tel: 020 7352 6592
Correspondent: K J Costa, Trustee
Trustees: K J Costa; Mrs A F Costa.
CC Number: 221604

Information available

Full accounts were available from the Charity Commission.

In 2009/10 the trust had assets of £64,000 and an income of £277,000 derived mostly from donations. Grants were made totalling £300,000.

The largest grant went to Alpha International (£250,000). Other beneficiaries included: VSO (£12,000); Pentecost Festival (£10,000); the Chasah Trust and the Philo Trust (£5,000 each); British Museum (£2,000); and the Wallace Collection (£1,000).

Applications

The trust states that only charities personally connected with the trustees are supported and absolutely no applications are either solicited or acknowledged.

The Cotton Industry War Memorial Trust

Education in textiles

£132,500 (2010)

Beneficial area

UK.

c/o 42 Boot Lane, Heaton, Bolton BL1 5SS
Tel: 01204 491810

Information available

Accounts were available from the
Charity Commission.

This trust makes grants to
educational bodies to assist eligible
students in furtherance of their textile
studies, to other bodies which
encourage recruitment into or
efficiency in the industry or
organisations otherwise researching
or benefiting the cotton industry.
Major support has also been given to
other causes, including those related
to young people and people with
disabilities.

In 2010 it had assets of £5.7 million
and an income of £296,000. Grants
totalled £132,500.

Beneficiaries were: Manchester
University (£45,000); Adventure Farm
Trust (£32,000); Texprint –
Contribution to Operating Costs of
Exhibition (£20,000); Primary
Engineers (£15,000); the Society of
Dyers and Colourists (£10,000); Shri
Krishna Temple (£5,000); and The
Jack Brown Scholarship Award
(£4,500).

Two grants of £500 each were made
to individuals.

Applications

In writing to the correspondent.

Common applicant mistakes

'Only support textile – applicants
have to have connection with
Lancashire textiles.'

The Cotton Trust

Relief of suffering, elimination and control of disease, people who have disabilities and disadvantaged people

£193,000 (2009/10)

Beneficial area

UK and overseas.

PO Box 6895, Earl Shilton, Leicester
LE9 8ZE
Tel: 01455 440917
Correspondent: Joanne Burgess
Congdon, Trustee
Trustees: Joanne Burgess Congdon;
Tenney Ellen Cotton; Erica Suzanne
Cotton.
CC Number: 1094776

Information available

Accounts were on file at the Charity
Commission.

The trust's policy is: the relief of
suffering; the elimination and control
of diseases; and helping people of any
age who have a disability or who are
disadvantaged. Grants are primarily
awarded for capital expenditure for
specific projects or items of specialist
equipment. A limited number of
grants are awarded for running costs
where the grant will provide direct
support for a clearly identifiable
charitable project.

The trust receives upwards of 600
applications each year. It awards
about 80 to 100 grants to UK
registered charities working both at
home and overseas each year, ranging
between £250 and £5,000. In
exceptional cases the trust may award
grants of between £10,000 and
£15,000.

In 2009/10 the trust had assets of
£5.7 million, an income of £151,000
and made grants totalling £193,000. A
total of 51 organisations were
supported. Of these awards, 33 grants
totalling a sum of around £126,000,
and representing 65% of the total
amount distributed were awarded to
projects operating overseas, primarily
in Africa, Asia and South America.
The remaining £67,000 was awarded
to charities operating within the UK.
Of this amount £41,000 was granted
to Leicester Charity Link,
representing just over 21% of all
grants in the year.

Donations were broken down as
follows:

Emergency disaster appeals and relief efforts	7	£62,000
Miscellaneous support costs for equipment and services	13	£40,000
Health and welfare	22	£38,000
Medical and specialist therapeutic equipment	20	£29,000
Access to education	7	£23,500

Previous beneficiaries have included:
Leicester Charity Link towards
support/equipment for families
(£41,000); CamFed (£15,000); Merlin
(£10,000); Africa Now (£5,000);
Angels International (£4,000); John
Fawcett Foundation, International
Medical Corps and Leukaemia
Research (£2,500 each); Harvest Help
(£2,250); Edinburgh Young Carers
Project and International Childcare
Trust (£1,500 each); Shelter, St Giles
Trust and Village Service Trust
(£1,000 each); People for Animal
Care Trust (£750); and Youth Action
Wiltshire – young carers educational
project (£580).

Exclusions

Grants are only given to UK-
registered charities that have been
registered for at least one year. No
grants to animal charities,
individuals, students, further
education, travel, expeditions,
conservation, environment, arts, new
building construction, the purchase
of new buildings or 'circular' appeals.
The trustees will only support the
purchase of computer systems and
equipment if it is to be directly used
by people who are disadvantaged or
have disabilities, but not general IT
equipment for the running of
organisations.

Applications

In writing to the correspondent with
latest accounts, evidence of charitable
status, detailed budget, timetable and
details of funds raised.

Guidelines are available with an sae.
Deadlines for applications are the end
of July and the end of January, with
successful applicants being notified
within three months of these dates. It
is regretted that only successful
applications can be answered. The
trustees only accept one application
in a 12-month period.

Country Houses Foundation

Preservation of buildings of historic or architectural significance

£1.1 million (2009/10)

Beneficial area

England.

The Manor, Sheephouse Farm, Uley Road, Dursley, Gloucestershire GL11 5AD

Tel: 0845 402 4102

Fax: 0845 402 4103

Email: david@ countryhousesfoundation.org.uk

Website: www. countryhousesfoundation.org.uk/

Correspondent: David Price, Company Secretary

Trustees: Christopher Taylor, Chair; Oliver Pearcey; Nicholas Barber; Michael Clifton; Norman Hudson; Sir John Parsons; Mary King.

CC Number: 1111049

Information available

Accounts were available at the Charity Commission website. Full guidelines are available on the foundation's website.

The CHF was born out of the Country Houses Association, an industrial and provident society which was formed in 1955 by Admiral Greathed for the purposes of preserving for the benefit of the nation historic buildings. During its lifetime, the Association acquired nine large country houses, and restored and preserved these until their sale in 2003 and 2004. During their ownership by the Association, all the houses were converted into retirement apartments, with the rental income helping to pay for extensive renovations and repairs. The houses were open to members of the Association and also members of the public.

Following a restructuring of the Association in 2004, all the properties were sold which resulted in a substantial surplus. The majority of

these funds have been donated to the Country Houses Foundation to ensure that the work of preserving historic buildings continues. It is the intention of the CHF Trustees that these funds will be used to award substantial grants to the most deserving of qualifying projects.

The main aims of the foundation are to support the preservation of buildings of historic or architectural significance together with their gardens and grounds, and/or to protect and augment the amenities and furnishings of such buildings, for the public benefit. Beneficiaries can include registered charities, building preservation trusts and private owners. The following extract is taken from the foundation's 2009/10 accounts:

> Since the launch of the grants scheme in February 2006, the number of applications for funding has increased significantly. At the end of the financial year [2009/10] the foundation had supported 46 projects with grant offers totalling over £3 million.

The following guidelines are taken from the foundation's website:

Guidelines

We aim to give grants for repairs and restoration work required to prevent loss or damage to historic buildings located in England, their gardens, grounds and any outbuildings. We would normally expect your building to be listed, scheduled, or in the case of a garden included in the English Heritage Register of Parks and Gardens. However, we may also make grants to projects which involve an unlisted building of sufficient historic or architectural significance or importance if it is within a conservation area.

In addition, to qualify for any grant you must be able to show the following:

- there is a compelling need for the work you want to undertake to be done within the next 2 to 3 years
- the project will enhance our historic environment
- there will be appropriate public access
- the project will have a sustainable future
- there is a financial need for the grant
- the project can proceed within a reasonable time frame (i.e. 1–2 years)
- we aim to make grants for projects which are ready to proceed (i.e. can be started within 1–2 years) but which either do not qualify for funding from any of the mainstream sources or have been awarded only partial funding and require significant

further funds to complete the resource package.

We will also consider making grants to effectively 'kickstart' a project but will expect your other funding to be completed within 1–2 years.

In 2009/10 the foundation had assets of £12.3 million and an income of £394,000. Grants totalled £1.1 million. Projects supported during the year include those at: Stanford Hall – Leicestershire; Homme House near Ledbury; Red House within the Painswick Roccoco Gardens; Temple of Vaccinea in the garden of the Jenner Museum in the Vale of Berkeley; Faringdon Folly Tower; Sulgrave Manor; Tyringham Hall – Buckinghamshire; Howsham Mill; Stoneleigh Park; Launde Abbey; Woodchester Mansion and Wothorpe Towers Preservation Trust.

Exclusions

As a general rule we do not offer grants for the following:

- Projects which do not have a heritage focus.
- Alterations and improvements.
- Routine maintenance and minor repairs.
- General running costs.
- Demolitions.
- Rent, loan or mortgage payments.
- Buying furniture, fittings and equipment except where they have an historic relationship with the site and are relevant to the project.
- Work carried out before a grant offer has been made in writing and accepted.

Applications

Pre-application forms can be completed online, or in a hard copy and returned by post. The foundation tries to respond within 28 days of receipt. If a project fits the criteria then a unique reference number will be issued which must be quoted on the full application form.

Applications can be made at anytime.

Common applicant mistakes

'They do not read criteria for support, complete all sections of form or check the form for mistakes.'

The Augustine Courtauld Trust

General

£62,000 (2009/10)

Beneficial area

UK, with a preference for Essex.

Birkett Ballard, No.1 Legg Street, Chelmsford, Essex CM1 1JS
Website: www. augustinecourtauldtrust.org
Correspondent: Bruce Ballard, Clerk
Trustees: Revd. A C C Courtauld, Chair; The Lord Lieutenant of Essex; The Bishop of Chelmsford; Julien Courtauld; D E Fordham; Lt General Sir Anthony Denison-Smith; T J R Courtauld; W M Courtauld.
CC Number: 226217

Information available

Accounts were on file at the Charity Commission.

This trust was founded in 1956 by Augustine Courtauld, an Arctic explorer who was proud of his Essex roots. His charitable purpose was simple: 'My idea is to make available something that will do some good.' Among the main areas of work supported before his death in 1959 were young people, people with disabilities, the countryside, certain churches, Arctic exploration and the RNLI. The current guidelines are to support organisations that are:

▶ working within the historical boundaries of the county of Essex
▶ involved in expeditions to the Arctic and Antarctic regions
▶ known to one of the trustees.

Within Essex, the preference is to support disadvantaged young people, conservation projects and certain charities that the founder specifically wanted to help. Grants for projects and core costs and can be for multiple years, but only if the charity applies for a grant in consecutive years.

In 2009/10 the trust had assets of £1.1 million and an income of £126,000. There were 40 grants made to organisations totalling £62,000.

The largest grants went to: Friends of Essex Churches Trust and Gino

Watkins Memorial Trust (£9,000 each); Cirdan Sailing Trust (£5,000); and Essex Association of Boys' Clubs (£4,500). Other beneficiaries included: Rural Community Council of Essex (£2,400); British Schools Exploring Society, Hope UK and Stanley Hall Opera (£1,000 each); and Association of Wheelchair Children, Braintree and Bocking Public Gardens Trust and Happy Days Children's Charity (£500 each).

Exclusions

No grants to individuals. No grants to individual churches for fabric repairs or maintenance.

Applications

Applications must be submitted via the trust's website. Written applications will not be accepted.

Common applicant mistakes

'Not applying using the online application form.'

Coutts Charitable Trust

General, social need

£864,000 (2009/10)

Beneficial area

UK, preference is given to areas where Coutts & Co. has a physical presence, specifically London.

Coutts & Co, 440 Strand, London WC2R 0QS
Tel: 020 7957 2822
Email: kay.boland@coutts.com
Correspondent: Kay Boland, Trust Administrator
Trustees: The Earl of Home; Mark Bevan; Sally Doyle; Gerald Bailey; Nicholas Gornall.
CC Number: 1000135

Information available

Detailed accounts were on file at the Charity Commission.

The trust was set up by the company Coutts & Co. which provides banking and allied services. It is funded by the bank under a deed of covenant equivalent to one half of 1% of the

bank's pre-tax profit with a minimum of £100,000.

Grants are given to UK registered charities only and the trust prefers to support social need organisations in areas where the bank has a presence, mainly London. Charities supported include those involved with helping the homeless, rehabilitation and teaching self-help (drug; alcohol; young offenders), disadvantaged adults and children, youth organisations, the elderly, medical research, heritage, education and the relief of poverty. Most donations are in the range of £500 to £1,000 'where a comparatively small amount can still make a great difference'. Many donations are between £1,000 and £2,000 with a portion of the charitable budget being used for larger donations.

In 2009/10 the trust had an income of £1.3 million and made 1,199 grants totalling £864,000.

Beneficiaries included: Charles Dickens Museum (£24,000); Samaritans (£7,000); Prostate Scotland (£6,500); DebRA (£5,000); Help for Heroes (£4,500); Little Treasures Children's Trust (£4,000); 2Simple Trust (£3,000); Amber Foundation (£2,500); 4 Sight (£1,700); Africa Challenges, Camp Horizon, PHAB, Christies Hospital, Go North Devon and Bromley Road PTA (£1,000 each).

Exclusions

No response to circular appeals. No support for appeals from individuals or overseas projects.

Applications

In writing to the trust administrator, at any time. Applications should include clear details of the purpose for which the grant is required. Grants are made regularly where amounts between £500 and £1,000 are deemed to be appropriate. The trustees meet quarterly to consider larger donations.

Cowley Charitable Foundation

General

£52,000 (2009/10)

Beneficial area

Worldwide, with some preference for south Buckinghamshire and the Aylesbury area.

140 Trustee Co. Ltd, 36 Broadway, London SW1H 0BH
Tel: 020 7973 8044
Correspondent: The Secretary
Trustees: 140 Trustee Co. Ltd; Harriet M M Cullen.
CC Number: 270682

Information available

Accounts were on file at the Charity Commission.

The charity was established in 1973 with general charitable purposes.

In 2009/10 the trust had assets of £922,000 and an income of £44,000. Grants to 32 organisations totalled £52,000.

Beneficiaries included: Thinking Foundation (£20,000); Global Warming Policy (£6,000); Alzheimer's Society (£2,000); Tate Britain (£1,800); Pere Jean Zambe (£1,600); International Dark Sky Association – USA, Médecins Sans Frontières and Wordsworth Trust (£1,500 each); John Soames Museum and Hemihelp (£1,000 each); Royal Court, Save the Children and London Shakespeare Workout (£500 each); and Voluntary Services Overseas (£50).

Exclusions

No grants to non-registered charities. No grants to individuals or for causes supposed to be serviced by public funds or with a scope considered to be too narrow.

Applications

The trust states that unsolicited applications are not invited, and that the trustees carry out their own research into charities.

The Sir William Coxen Trust Fund

Orthopaedic hospitals or other hospitals or charities doing orthopaedic work

£70,000 (2009/10)

Beneficial area

England.

The Town Clerk's Office, City of London, PO Box 270, Guildhall, London EC2P 2EJ
Tel: 020 7332 1408
Correspondent: Rakesh Hira, Correspondent
Trustees: Ian Luder; David Hugh Wootton; John Stuttard; Neil Redcliffe; Sir David Lewis; Sir Michael Savory.
CC Number: 206936

Information available

Accounts were available from the Charity Commission.

This trust was established following a bequest from the late Sir William Coxen in 1940. Expenditure is mainly applied for the support of orthopaedic hospitals or other hospitals or charities doing orthopaedic work.

In 2009/10 the trust had assets of over £1.8 million and an income of £76,000. Grants of £2,500 were made to 28 organisations totalling £70,000.

Beneficiaries included: Action for Kids, Brainwave, Child Care Action Trust, Fire Fighters' Charity, Motability, Neuromuscular Centre, Spinal Injuries Association, Stick and Step, The New Children's Hospital Appeal and The Orthopaedic Research Fund.

Exclusions

No grants to individuals or non-charitable institutions.

Applications

In writing to the correspondent.

The Lord Cozens-Hardy Trust

Medical/health, welfare, general

£77,000 (2009/10)

Beneficial area

UK with preference for Merseyside and Norfolk.

PO Box 28, Holt, Norfolk NR25 7WH
Correspondent: The Trustees
Trustees: Hon. Beryl Cozens-Hardy; J E V Phelps; Mrs L F Phelps; J J P Ripman.
CC Number: 264237

Information available

Accounts were available from the Charity Commission.

The trustees' policy is to assist as many UK registered charities as possible but with particular interest in supporting medicine, health, education and welfare causes in Norfolk and Merseyside.

In 2009/10 the trust had assets of £2.6 million and an income of £92,000. Grants totalled £77,000 (of which 15 totalling £45,000 were listed in the accounts) and were broken down as follows:

Medical	£28,000
Community	£23,000
Children, youth and education	£22,000
Other	£4,000

Beneficiaries included: Norfolk and Norwich Association for the Blind and Grooms-Shaftesbury (£10,000 each); Help for Heroes and Norfolk and Norwich Families House (£5,000 each); Raleigh International Trust (£1,250); Breast Cancer Campaign, Liverpool School of Tropical Medicine, Norfolk and Norwich Association for the Blind, Princes Trust, Salvation Army and World Association of Girl Guides and Girl Scouts (£1,000 each).

Exclusions

No grants to individuals.

Applications

In writing to the correspondent. Applications are reviewed quarterly.

The Craignish Trust

Arts, education, environment, general

Around £100,000 each year

Beneficial area

UK, with a preference for Scotland.

c/o Geoghegan and Co, 6 St Colme Street, Edinburgh EH3 6AD
Correspondent: The Trustees
Trustees: Ms M Matheson; J Roberts; Ms C Younger.
SC Number: SC016882

Information available

Despite making a written request for the accounts of this trust (including an sae) these were not provided. The following entry is based on information filed with the Office of the Scottish Charity Regulator.

This trust was established in 1961 by the late Sir William McEwan Younger; its funding criteria are summarised as follows:

- no grants to large national charities
- there is a Scottish bias, but not exclusively
- arts, particularly where innovative and/or involved in the community
- education
- environment
- organisations/projects of particular interest to a trustee.

In 2007/08 the trust had an income of £151,000.

Previous beneficiaries have included Art in Healthcare, Boilerhouse Theatre Company Ltd, Butterfly Conservation – Scotland, Cairndow Arts Promotions, Centre for Alternative Technology, Edinburgh International Book Festival, Edinburgh Royal Choral Union, Friends of the Earth Scotland, Human Rights Watch Charitable Trust and Soil Association Scotland.

Exclusions

Running costs are not normally supported.

Applications

There is no formal application form; applicants should write to the correspondent. Details of the project should be included together with a copy of the most recent audited accounts.

The Craps Charitable Trust

Jewish, general

£178,000 (2009/10)

Beneficial area

UK, Israel.

Grant Thornton, Chartered Accountants, 202 Silbury Boulevard, Milton Keynes MK9 1LW
Correspondent: The Trustees
Trustees: J P M Dent; Miss C S Dent; Miss L R Dent.
CC Number: 271492

Information available

Accounts were available from the Charity Commission.

This trust mostly supports Jewish charities, although medical and other organisations are also supported. There is a list of eight charities mentioned in the trust deed, although not all of these are supported every year and other groups in the UK and overseas can be supported.

In 2009/10 it had assets of £3.8 million, which generated an income of £323,000. Grants were made to 32 organisations totalling £178,000.

Beneficiaries included: British Technion Society (£25,000); Jewish Care (£20,000); Nightingale House, Home for Aged Jews (£16,000); the New Israel Fund (£12,000); CBF World Jewish Relief (£5,000); Save the Children (£2,000); Anglo Israel Association (£1,000); and London Jewish Cultural Centre (£500).

Applications

The trust states that funds of the trust are fully committed and the trust does not invite applications for its funds.

The Crescent Trust

Museums and the arts, ecology, health

£45,000 (2009/10)

Beneficial area

UK.

9 Queripel House, 1 Duke of York Square, London SW3 4LY
Correspondent: Ms C Akehurst
Trustees: J C S Tham; R A F Lascelles.
CC Number: 327644

Information available

Accounts were available from the Charity Commission.

The trust concentrates on arts (especially larger museums), heritage and ecology. Smaller grants are mainly given in the medical field. Only specific charities of which the trustees have personal knowledge are supported.

In 2009/10 the trust had assets of £386,000 and an income of £70,000, the majority of which came from donations. Grants were made to 15 organisations totalling £45,000 (£109,000 in the previous year).

Beneficiaries included: Service Funds RAF and the Attingham Trust (£10,000 each); Public Catalogue Foundation (£5,000); National Youth (£2,500); Swan Rescue Sanctuary (£2,000); Fund for Refugees (£1,000); and Shooting Star Children's Hospice (£250).

Applications

This trust states that it does not respond to unsolicited applications.

Criffel Charitable Trust

Christianity, welfare, health

£125,000 (2009/10)

Beneficial area

UK and overseas.

Ravenswood Lodge, 1a Wentworth Road, Sutton Coldfield, West Midlands B74 2SG
Tel: 0121 308 1575
Correspondent: Mr and Mrs Lees, Trustees
Trustees: Jim Lees; Juliet Lees; Joy Harvey.
CC Number: 1040680

Information available

Accounts were available from the Charity Commission.

The objectives of the trust are the advancement of Christianity and the relief of poverty, sickness and other needs. In 2009/10 it had assets of £847,000 and an income of £65,000. Grants totalled £125,000 and were broken down as follows:

Advancement of Christianity	£87,000
Relief-in-need	£23,000
Relief of sickness	£14,000
Miscellaneous	£2,000

Beneficiaries of the largest grants over £2,000 each were: Lichfield Inspires (£50,000); Tear Fund (£10,000); Links International (£5,000); and Four Oaks Methodist Church (£2,600).

Applications

All funds are fully committed. The trust states that no applications are considered or acknowledged. Please do not apply.

Common applicant mistakes

'Making application for funding when we have stated that no unsolicited applications considered; applications for funding for individuals.'

The Violet and Milo Cripps Charitable Trust

Prison and human rights

£272,000 (2007/08)

Beneficial area

UK.

52 Bedford Row, London WC1R 4LR
Correspondent: The Trustees
Trustees: Anthony J R Newhouse; Richard J Lithenthal; Jennifer Beattie.

CC Number: 289404

Information available

Accounts were available from the Charity Commission.

The trust supports large prison and human rights organisations. In 2009/10 it had assets of £734,000 and an unusually large income of over £2 million due to receiving £2 million from the estate of the late Lord Parmoor. Grants to six organisations totalled £2.2 million and included £2 million to the Howard League for Penal Reform.

Other beneficiaries were: Lancaster University (£100,000); The Prison Advice and Care Trust (£50,000); Dorothy House Hospice Care, Frank Langford Charitable Trust and Trinity Hospice (£25,000 each).

Applications

The trust states that unsolicited applications will not receive a response.

The Ronald Cruickshanks' Foundation

Welfare, education, general

£142,000 (2009/10)

Beneficial area

UK, with some preference for Folkestone, Faversham and the surrounding area.

34 Cheriton Gardens, Folkestone, Kent CT20 2AX
Tel: 01303 251742
Correspondent: I F Cloke, Trustee
Trustees: I F Cloke, Chair; J S Schilder; Mrs S E Cloke.
CC Number: 296075

Information available

Accounts were obtained from the Charity Commission.

The settlor of this charity died in 1995 leaving his shareholding in Howe Properties Ltd to the foundation, under the terms of his will. The foundation's objects are to provide general charitable and

educational assistance as the trustees deem suitable with the knowledge of the wishes given to them by the settlor in his lifetime. The assistance is to include those in poverty and need in Folkestone and Faversham and their surrounding areas.

In 2009/10 the foundation had assets of £1.7 million and an income of £134,000. There were 134 grants were made totalling £142,000. Donations ranged from £250 to £8,000.

Beneficiaries of larger grants included: Demelza House Children's Hospice, Pilgrims Hospice on the Hill and the Pilgrims Hospice – Canterbury (£8,000 each); Parish Church of St Mary & St Eanswythe – Fabric Fund (£6,000); Kent Air Ambulance (£4,500); and Barnardo's, Cats Protection and Canterbury Horse Rescue (£1,000 each).

Other beneficiaries included: PDSA and Hearing Dogs for Deaf People (£750 each); The Genesis Appeal and Volunteer Reading Help (£500 each); and Kent Kids, Miles of Smiles, The Caldecott Foundation and Samaritans (£250 each).

Applications

In writing to the correspondent. Applications should be received by the end of September for consideration on a date coinciding closely with the anniversary of the death of the founder, which was 7 December.

The R D Crusaders Foundation

General

£1.4 million (2010).

Beneficial area

Worldwide.

The Northern and Shell Building, No. 10 Lower Thames Street, London EC3R 6EN
Tel: 0208 612 7760
Email: allison.racher@express.co.uk
Correspondent: The Trustees
Trustees: R C Desmond; Northern and Shell Services Ltd and Northern and Shell Media Group Ltd.

CC Number: 1014352

Information available

Accounts were available from the Charity Commission.

The trust gives one-off and recurrent grants for core, capital and project funding for general charitable purposes, especially for the relief of poverty and sickness amongst children.

In 2010 the trust had assets of £550,000 and an income of £1.3 million. The trust made 60 grants totalling £1.4 million.

Grant beneficiaries include: Jewish Care (£125,000); United Jewish Israel Appeal (£100,000); Fight for Sight (£50,000); CST- Community Service Trust (£10,000); The Stroke Association (£5,000); Kindred (£2,000); Little Heroes, Pathway Project and Sainsbury's Sport Relief (£1,000 each).

Applications

In writing to the correspondent.

The Cuby Charitable Trust

Jewish

£107,000 (2009/10)

Beneficial area

UK, overseas.

16 Mowbray Road, Edgware, Middlesex HA8 8JQ
Tel: 020 7563 6868
Correspondent: S Cuby, Secretary
Trustees: S Cuby, Chair; Mrs C Cuby; J Cuby; Mrs R Talmor.
CC Number: 328585

Information available

Accounts were available from the Charity Commission, but without a list of grants.

The main objectives of this charitable trust are 'providing charitable assistance in any part of the world and in particular for the advancement of Orthodox Jewish religious education'.

In 2009/10 the trust had assets of £323,000 and an income of £102,000,

mainly from donations. Grants totalled £107,000. No list of grants was provided with the accounts to indicate the size or number of beneficiaries during the year.

Applications

In writing to the correspondent.

Cullum Family Trust

Social welfare, education and general charitable purposes

£96,000 (2009/10)

Beneficial area

UK.

Wealden Hall, Parkfield, Sevenoaks, Kent TN15 0HX
Correspondent: Peter Geoffrey Cullum, Trustee
Trustees: Peter Geoffrey Cullum; Ann Cullum; Claire Louise Cullum; Simon Timothy Cullum.
CC Number: 1117056

Information available

Accounts were available from the Charity Commission.

Established in 2006, this trust is the vehicle for the philanthropy of Peter Cullum, executive chairman of the Towergate insurance group. Mr Cullum was voted Entrepreneur of the Year by Ernst & Young in 2006.

The trust's accounts state its objects as:

▪ to relieve poverty and the advancement of education and religion; and
▪ any other charitable purposes for the benefit of the public

In 2009/10 the foundation had assets of £24 million and an income of £625,000. Grants were made totalling £96,000.

The main grant beneficiaries were: Kids Company and Sussex Community Foundation (£40,000 each). Other grants to institutions totalled £16,000.

Applications

In writing to the correspondent.

The Culra Charitable Trust

General

£29,000 (2009/10)

Beneficial area

UK.

1 College Hill, London EC4R 2RA
Correspondent: Mrs Mary Kitto
Trustees: C Byam-Cook; H Byam-Cook; G Needham; G Francis.
CC Number: 274612

Information available

Accounts were available from the Charity Commission.

This trust has general charitable purposes, giving grants to a wide variety of active charitable organisations throughout the UK. In 2009/10 the trust had an income of £74,000 and made grants totalling £29,000. Assets stood at £556,000.

> During the year there were 43 grants awarded between £250 – £500 to local and national UK charities, in addition, a grant of £6,000 was made to the Royal Air Force Benevolent Fund.

Exclusions

Grants are not given to non-registered charities or individuals.

Applications

The trust tends to support organisations known to the trustees, rather than responding to unsolicited applications. The trustees meet twice a year.

The Cumber Family Charitable Trust

General

£47,000 (2009/10)

Beneficial area

Worldwide, with a preference for the developing world and Berkshire and Oxfordshire.

Manor Farm, Marcham, Abingdon, Oxfordshire OX13 6NZ
Tel: 01865 391327

Email: mary.tearney@hotmail.co.uk
Website: www.
cumberfamilycharitabletrust.org.uk
Correspondent: Mrs M E Tearney,
Secretary
Trustees: A R Davey; W Cumber;
Mrs M J Cumber; Mrs M J Freeman;
Mrs M E Tearney; Mrs J E Mearns.
CC Number: 291009

Information available

Accounts were available from the
Charity Commission.

This trust has a preference for UK-
wide needs, developing countries and
local organisations in Oxfordshire
and Berkshire. It favours the
following causes: health,
homelessness, disability, welfare, rural
development, housing, overseas aid,
Christian aid, agricultural
development, youth and children's
welfare and education. About 50% of
the funding given is for work
overseas.

In 2009/10 the trust had assets of
£781,000 and an income of £44,000.
Grants ranging from £250 to £2,000
were made to 61 organisations
totalling £47,000.

Beneficiaries included: Bradfield
Primary Project and Vale and
Ridgeway Trust (£2,000 each); Amity,
International Refugee Trust, Kaloko
Trust, Operation New World,
Practical Action, and the Unicorn
School (£1,000 each); Abingdon
Alzheimer's, Leys Youth Programme,
Reading Deaf Centre, RoRo Sailing
Project and the Friends of Hope
(£500 each); and Balsam Family
Project, Mareham Society and the
Sunshine Club (£250 each).

Exclusions

No grants for animal welfare. Only
very few to individuals with local
connections and who are personally
known to the trustees are supported.
Local appeals outside Berkshire and
Oxfordshire are not usually
supported.

Applications

In writing to the correspondent. The
trustees usually meet twice a year.

Common applicant mistakes

'We support national charities but
not local charities that work outside

Oxfordshire and Berkshire. We
receive many applications for work
outside the area and for individuals
not know to us that are ineligible.'

The Dennis Curry Charitable Trust

Conservation, general

£69,000 (2009/10)

Beneficial area

UK.

Alliotts, 5th Floor, 9 Kingsway,
London WC2B 6XF
Correspondent: N J Armstrong,
Secretary to the Trust
Trustees: M Curry; Mrs A S Curry;
Mrs M Curry-Jones; Mrs P Edmond.
CC Number: 263952

Information available

Accounts were available from the
Charity Commission.

The trust has general charitable
objects with a special interest in the
environment and education;
occasional support is given to
churches and cathedrals. In 2009/10 it
had an income of £69,000, nearly all
of which it distributed in grants
(98%) to nine organisations. Assets
stood at £3 million.

Grants went to: Durrell Wildlife
Conservation Trust (£20,000);
University of Oxford – Dept. of
Zoology, Wildlife Conservation
Research Unit (£15,000); the Art
Fund and Galapagos Conservation
Trust (£10,000 each); Botanic
Gardens Conservation International
(£8,000); Project Trust (£3,000);
University of Glasgow Trinidad
Expedition (£1,500); Friends of Little
Chalfont Library (£1,000); and the
Open Spaces Society (£500).

Applications

In writing to the correspondent.

The Manny Cussins Foundation

Older people, children, health, Jewish, general

£35,000 (2009/10)

Beneficial area

Mainly UK, with some emphasis on
Yorkshire.

c/o Ford Campbell Freedman,
34 Park Cross Street, Leeds, LS 1
2QH
Correspondent: Derek Corby,
Correspondent
Trustees: A Reuben; A Cussins;
A J Cussins; J R Cussins; Mrs.
A Reuben.
CC Number: 219661

Information available

Accounts were available at the
Charity Commission website, without
a list of grants

The foundation's objects are as
follows:
- to support the welfare and care of
  the elderly
- welfare and care of children at risk
- health care in the Yorkshire region
  and abroad
- charities in Yorkshire and the
  former county of Humberside
- charitable need amongst Jewish
  communities in the UK and
  abroad
- general charitable purposes.

In 2009/10 the foundation had assets
of £765,000, an income of £159,000
and made grants totalling £35,000.
The accounts did not include a list of
beneficiaries.

Previous beneficiaries have included:
Angels International, Christie
Hospital – Children Against Cancer,
Forgiveness Project, Hadassah Lodge,
Leeds International Piano
Competition, Leeds Jewish Education
Authority, Leeds Jewish Welfare
Board, Lifeline for the Old Jerusalem,
Martin House Hospice, United Jewish
Israel Appeal, Wheatfields Hospice
and Women's International Zionist
Organisation.

Exclusions

No grants to individuals.

Applications

The correspondent states that applications are not sought as the trustees carry out their own research.

The D G Charitable Settlement

General

£316,000 (2009/10)

Beneficial area

UK.

PO Box 62, Heathfield, East Sussex
TN21 8ZE
Tel: 01435 867604
Email: joanna.nelson@btconnect.com
Correspondent: Ms P A Samson, Trustee
Trustees: D J Gilmour; P Grafton-Green; Ms P A Samson.
CC Number: 1040778

Information available

Accounts were available from the Charity Commission.

This trust makes regular donations to a fixed list of charities and does not consider unsolicited applications. In 2009/10 the trust had assets of £1.7 million and an income of £2 million. Grants were made totalling £316,000.

Poverty overseas	£120,000
Other medical	£66,000
Homeless	£65,000
Human rights	£22,500
Environment	£20,000
Elderly	£10,000
Other	£2,000

Beneficiaries included: Age Concern, Amnesty International, Battersea Home for Dogs, Crisis, Cancer Research UK, Environmental Investigation Agency Charitable Trust, Great Ormond Street Hospital, Greenpeace, Terrence Higgins Trust, Hoping Foundation, Medical Foundation for Victims of Torture, Otto Wolff Child Health Research, Oxfam, Prisoners Abroad, Prisoners of Conscience Appeal Fund,

St Richard's Hospital Charitable Trust and Shelter.

Applications

This trust does not consider unsolicited applications.

Common applicant mistakes

'They should NOT apply.'

The Daily Prayer Union Charitable Trust Ltd

Evangelical Christian

£86,000 (2009/10)

Beneficial area

UK.

12 Weymouth Street, London
W1W 5BY
Correspondent: Mrs C Palmer, Secretary
Trustees: Revd G C Grinham; Mrs F M Ashton; Mrs E D Bridger; Revd D J Jackman; Revd T J Sterry; Dr J Sudell; Mrs A V Tompson.
CC Number: 284857

Information available

Accounts were available from the Charity Commission.

The trust supports evangelical Christian causes. Grants range from £1,000 to £7,000. In 2009/10 the trust had assets of £132,000 and an income of £66,000. Grants totalled £86,000, of which £24,000 went to organisations and £62,000 to 51 individuals.

Beneficiaries included: Monkton Combe School (£7,000); SUMT Isle of Man (£6,000); St Andrew's Ministry Trust (£2,000); CPAS (£1,800); Jesus Lane Trust (£1,600); and UCCF (£1,000).

Exclusions

No grants for bricks and mortar.

Applications

The trust supports causes already known to the trustees. Unsolicited applications are unlikely to be successful. Trustees meet at different times throughout the year, usually around March, June and October.

Oizer Dalim Trust

Jewish

£106,000 (2009/10)

Beneficial area

UK and overseas.

68 Osbaldeston Road, London
N16 7DR
Correspondent: Mordechai Cik, Trustee
Trustee: Mordechai Cik.
CC Number: 1045296

Information available

Accounts were on file at the Charity Commission, but without a list of grants.

The trust was established to help alleviate poverty amongst members of the Orthodox Jewish faith in the UK and overseas. It also assists in the furtherance of Orthodox Jewish education throughout the world.

In 2009/10 the trust had an income of £161,000, entirely from donations. Assets stood at £59,000. Grants were made for 'poverty alleviation' totalling £106,000. A list of grant beneficiaries was not available.

Applications

In writing to the correspondent.

Michael Davies Charitable Settlement

General

£299,000 to organisations (2008/9)

Beneficial area

UK.

Lee Associates, 5 Southampton Place, London WC1A 2DA
Tel: 0207 025 4600
Correspondent: K Hawkins, Administrator
Trustees: M J P Davies; K A Hawkins.
CC Number: 1000574

Information available

Full accounts were available from the Charity Commission.

In 2008/09 the settlement had assets of £576,000 and an income of £323,000. Grants were made totalling £299,000. A full list of beneficiaries was not included in the trust's accounts.

Previous beneficiaries included: BTYC Sailsports Club (£15,000); Camden Arts Centre, Camp and Trek, Marie Curie Cancer Care, North London Hospice, School Aid India and Tools for Training Overseas (£10,000 each); Médecins du Monde and The Study Gallery (£5,000 each); Architects For Aid (£3,500); Thames Wharf Charity (£2,000); The Langford Trust for Animal Health and Welfare (£1,000); and the Architectural Association Inc. (£750).

Applications

In writing to the correspondent.

The Wilfrid Bruce Davis Charitable Trust

Health

£74,500 (2009/10)

Beneficial area

UK, but mainly Cornwall; India.

La Feock Grange, Feock, Truro, Cornwall TR3 6RG
Tel: 01872 862795
Correspondent: W B Davis, Trustee
Trustees: W B Davis; Mrs D F Davis; Mrs D S Dickens; Mrs C A S Pierce.
CC Number: 265421

Information available

Accounts were on file at the Charity Commission.

The trust was set up in 1967, the objects being 'such charities as the settlor in his lifetime and the trustees after his death shall determine'. The trust presently concentrates on 'improving the quality of life for those who are physically disadvantaged and their carers'. The geographical area covered is almost exclusively Cornwall, however the main thrust of the trust's activities is now focused on India.

The trust is fully committed to its current beneficiaries.

In 2009/10 the trust had assets of £184,000 and an income of £33,000. Grants totalled £74,500.

Beneficiaries included: Pallium India (£50,000); Cornwall Community Foundation (£6,000); Pain and Palliative Care Society Calicut (£5,000); and Médecins Sans Frontières (£1,000).

Exclusions

No applications from individuals are considered.

Applications

No replies are made to unsolicited applications. The correspondent has stated that the budget for many years to come is fully committed and that the trust receives hundreds of applications, none of which can be supported.

The Helen and Geoffrey De Freitas Charitable Trust

Preservation of wildlife and rural England, conservation and environment, cultural heritage

Around £35,000 (2009/10)

Beneficial area

UK.

Speechly Bircham LLP, 6 New Street Square, London EC4A 3LX
Correspondent: Richard Kirby, Trustee
Trustees: R C Kirby; Frances de Freitas; Roger de Freitas.
CC Number: 258597

Information available

Accounts were received at the Charity Commission but unavailable to view.

The latest accounts available (2007/08) state:

The main object of the trust is to benefit UK charitable organisations and voluntary umbrella bodies which seek to:
- conserve countryside and environment in rural Britain
- preserve Britain's cultural heritage
- assist the underprivileged through community facilities and services, advice centres and community arts and recreation.

Once a year the trustees may respond to a national or international humanitarian crisis which may be outside the terms of reference of the trust.

Grants are usually one-off for feasibility studies, project and occasionally for start-up costs and range from £500 to £5,000 each.

In 2009/10 the trust an income of £19,000 and a total expenditure of £47,000. Grants usually total around £35,000.

Previous beneficiaries included: Staffordshire Wildlife Trust and GINA (£5,000 each); Tarka Country Trust (£3,000); Dartington Hall Trust (£2,800); the Grasslands Trust, Marine Conservation Society, Nailsea Tithe Barn Trust and Suffolk Building Preservation Trust (£2,500 each); Devon Wildlife Trust (£1,500); St Michael and All Angels – London Fields (£1,500); and Community Can Cycle (£500).

Exclusions

No grants to non-registered charities, individuals, or to charities on behalf of individuals. Definitely no support for charities concerned with medical or health matters, or with physical, mental or sensory impairments.

Applications

In writing to the correspondent at the following address:
PO Box 18667
London
NW3 5WB

Trustees meet quarterly.

The De Laszlo Foundation

The arts, general

£321,000 (2009/10)

Beneficial area

UK and worldwide.

5 Albany Courtyard, London
W1J 0HF
Correspondent: Christabel Wood
Trustees: Damon de Laszlo, Chair;
Lucy Birkbeck; Robert de Laszlo;
William de Laszlo.
CC Number: 327383

Information available

Accounts were available from the
Charity Commission.

Registered with the Charity
Commission in March 1987, the
foundation has the following objects:
1   The advancement and promotion
    of education and interest in the
    visual arts with special reference
    to encouraging knowledge of the
    works of contemporary painters,
    in particular those of the late
    Philip de Laszlo.
2   To encourage research into the
    restoration of works of art and
    their preservation and the location
    of suitable venues for them.
3   To acquire and maintain a
    collection of the works of art of
    the late Philip de Laszlo and of
    appropriate works of art of the
    same or any other period.
4   To advance education and research
    generally in the areas of arts,
    science, economics and medicine.
5   To encourage the study,
    reproduction and cataloguing of
    works of art and the publication
    of books and literature in
    connection therewith.
6   To promote the founding of
    scholarships and prizes related to
    the above.

It has increasingly been the policy of
the trustees to make a small number
of targeted large grants. In 2009/10 it
had assets of £2.8 million and an
income of £343,000, including
£212,000 from donations. Grants
totalled £321,000.

Grants were broken down into the
following categories:

Archive Trust	£140,000
Science	£43,000
Arts	£42,000
Education	£33,000
Medicine	£15,000
Scholarship and grants	£7,000
Other charities	£42,000

Previous beneficiaries included: the
De Laszlo Archive Trust (£188,000);
Gordonstoun School Arts Centre
(£20,000); Durham University and
Royal Marsden (£10,000 each);
Foundation for Liver Research
(£8,000); Southampton University
(£5,000); Federation of British Artists
(£3,000); AGORA (£2,500); National
Youth Orchestra (£1,500); Tate
Foundation (£1,000); Cardboard
Citizens (£500); and Chelsea Open
Air Nursery School (£250).

Applications

No grants to unsolicited applications.

The Leopold De Rothschild Charitable Trust

Arts, Jewish, general

£52,000 (2005/06)

Rothschild Trust Corporation Ltd,
New Court, St Swithin's Lane,
London EC4P 4DU
Tel: 020 7280 5000
Correspondent: The Clerk
Trustee: Rothschild Trust
Corporation Ltd.
CC Number: 212611

Information available

Accounts were available from the
Charity Commission.

The trust gives most of its support to
the arts and has some preference for
Jewish organisations, with limited
support to other causes covering
heritage, welfare, medical and
children.

In 2009/10 the trust had assets of
almost £1.5 million and an income of
£54,000. Grants totalled £69,000,
including £26,000 made from capital.

Beneficiaries included: Glynde Bourne
and Jewish Music Institute (£10,000
each); INTOUniversity (£3,000);
Liberal Jewish Synagogue (£2,700);

Aldeburgh Foundation, David
Shepherd Wildlife Foundation,
Jerusalem Foundation, Lord Mayor's
Appeal, National Museum of Science
& Industry, National Railway
Museum, Newbury Spring Festival
and Sir John Soane Museum (£1,000
each); and Contemporary Applied
Arts, Friends of Holland Park, The
Big Issue and Wiener Library (£100
each).

Applications

In writing to the correspondent.

William Dean Countryside and Educational Trust

Education in natural history, ecology and conservation

£53,000 (2010)

Beneficial area

Principally Cheshire; also Derbyshire,
Lancashire, Staffordshire and the
Wirral.

St Mary's Cottage, School Lane,
Astbury, Congleton, Cheshire
CW12 4RG
Tel: 01260 290194
Email: bellstmarys@hotmail.com
Correspondent: Mrs Brenda Bell
Trustees: David Daniel, Chair;
William Crawford; John Ward; David
Crawford; Margaret Williamson.
CC Number: 1044567

Information available

Accounts were available from the
Charity Commission.

This trust gives grants towards
enterprises in its immediate locality
which promote education in natural
history, ecology and the conservation
of the natural environment.

In 2010 it had assets of £1.3 million,
an income of £56,000 and made
grants totalling almost £53,000.

There were 46 organisations in receipt
of grants, including: Cheshire Wildlife
Trust (£16,000); Congleton
Sustainability Group Apple Project
and Lower Moss Wood Animal
Hospital (£2,000 each); Bromley

Farm Development Trust, Game and Wildlife Conservation Trust and Lymm Angling Club (£1,000 each); and NSPCC Show Garden RHS Tatton and Victoria School & Specialist Arts College (£500 each).

Exclusions

The trust stated that education is not funded, unless directly associated with one of the eligible categories.

Applications

In writing to the correspondent.

Common applicant mistakes

'Because the word 'educational' appears on the Charity Commission website, the trust gets applications for purposes other than for 'education in natural history, ecology or conservation of the natural environment'.'

The Dellal Foundation

General, Jewish

Around £100,000

Beneficial area

UK.

25 Harley Street, London W1G 9BR
Correspondent: The Administrator
Trustees: J Dellal; E Azouz; J Azouz; G Dellal.
CC Number: 265506

Information available

Accounts had been received by the Charity Commission, but were unavailable to view.

The foundation states that it continues to give 'a significant proportion of the grants towards charities whose aim is the welfare and benefit of Jewish people'.

In 2009/10 it had an income of £1,000 and a total expenditure of £106,000. Previously grants totalled £119,000; unfortunately further information was not available.

Exclusions

No grants to individuals.

Applications

In writing to the correspondent.

The Delves Charitable Trust

Environment, conservation, medical, general

£178,000 (2005/06)

Beneficial area

UK.

Luminary Finance LLP, PO Box 135, Longfield, Kent DA3 8WF
Correspondent: The Trust Administrator
Trustees: Elizabeth Breeze; John Breeze; George Breeze; Charles Breeze; William Breeze; Mark Breeze; Catharine Mackey.
CC Number: 231860

Information available

Accounts were available from the Charity Commission.

This trust has a list of organisations that receive an annual subscription from the trust, and also provides a small number of grants to other organisations.

In 2009/10 the trust had assets of £6.4 million, which generated an income of £206,000. Grants to 35 organisations totalled £149,000. These were broken down into 26 'subscriptions' (£136,000) and 'donations' (£12,000).

The largest grants went to: British Heart Foundation (£25,000); Action Medical Research, MacMillan Cancer Support and Médecins Sans Frontières (£10,000 each); SEQUAL Trust (£8,000); and Medical Foundation for the Care of Victims of Torture (£6,000).

Other beneficiaries of subscriptions and donations included: CRISIS (£5,000); Parkinson's Disease Society (£4,000); Ghana Education Project (£3,000); Big Issue Foundation (£2,500); Sussex Wildlife Trust (£1,500); Samaritans (£1,000); and Combat Stress (£500).

Exclusions

The trust does not give sponsorships or personal educational grants.

Applications

The trust's 2011 annual report states:

> Requests for funding should be made to the Trust Administrator in writing, concisely explaining the objective, activities, intended public benefit and anticipated achievements. Applications are accepted on a rolling basis and reviewed by the Trustees quarterly, whose decision is final. No response is made to unsuccessful unsolicited applications.

The Demigryphon Trust

Medical, education, children, general

£92,000 (2009/10)

Beneficial area

UK, with a preference for Scotland.

Pollen House, 10–12 Cork Street, London W1S 3LW
Correspondent: The Secretary
Trustee: The Cowdray Trust Ltd.
CC Number: 275821

Information available

Accounts were available from the Charity Commission.

The trust supports a wide range of organisations and appears to have a preference for education, medical, children and Scottish organisations.

In 2009/10 the trust had assets of £2.6 million, which generated an income of £60,000. Grants were made totalling £92,000 including £53,000 in grants to pensioners and 17 grants to organisations totalling just over £39,000. There was one major beneficiary during the year, the Duke of Edinburgh Award Scheme, which received £25,000 (£25,000 in the previous year).

Other beneficiaries included: Game and Wildlife Conservation Trust (£5,000); Houston Tampico Sister City Association (£2,000); Welsh guards Afghanistan Appeal (£1,000); Facing Africa and Chichester

Cathedral Trust (£500 each); Cancer Vaccine Institute (£250); and Macmillan Cancer Support (£50).

Exclusions

No grants to individuals; only registered charities are supported.

Applications

No grants to unsolicited applications.

The Sandy Dewhirst Charitable Trust

General

£123,000 (2009)

Beneficial area

UK, with a strong preference for East and North Yorkshire.

Addleshaw Goddard LLP, Sovereign House, Sovereign Street, Leeds LS1 1HG
Correspondent: The Secretary
Trustees: Timothy Dewhirst; Paul Howell.
CC Number: 279161

Information available

Accounts were on file at the Charity Commission for 2009.

The trust was established in 1979, firstly for the welfare of people connected through employment with I J Dewhirst Holdings Ltd or the settlor of the trust and secondly for general charitable purposes, with a strong preference for East and North Yorkshire.

The latest accounts available were for 2009. In this year the trust held assets of £1.5 million and had an income of £55,000. They made grants totalling £123,000 and of this £3,000 was given to an individual, £86,000 to local organisations and £34,000 to national organisations.

21 grants to organisations included: Bramcote School (£50,000); Stroke Association (£20,000); All Saints Church, Driffield (£16,000); Royal British Legion (Driffield Branch); Help for Heroes; Driffield Boxing and Fitness Club (£1,000 each); and All Saints Church Kilham, Filey Sea

Cadets TS Unseen and St Catherine's Hospice (£500 each).

Applications

The trust does not accept unsolicited applications.

The Laduma Dhamecha Charitable Trust

General

£375,000 (2009/10)

Beneficial area

UK and overseas.

2 Hathaway Close, Stanmore, Middlesex HA7 3NR
Correspondent: Pradip Dhamecha, Trustee
Trustees: K R Dhamecha; S R Dhamecha; P K Dhamecha.
CC Number: 328678

Information available

Accounts were on file at the Charity Commission, without a list of grants.

The trust supports a wide range of organisations in the UK and overseas. The aims of the trust are listed in the annual report as being:

- to provide relief of sickness by the provision of medical equipment and the establishing or improvement of facilities at hospitals
- to provide for the advancement of education and/or an educational establishment in rural areas to make children self-sufficient in the long term
- other general charitable purposes.

In 2009/10 the trust had assets of almost £1.7 million and an income of £293,000 including £262,000 from Dhamecha Foods Limited. Grants totalled £375,000. No information was available on the size or number of beneficiaries during this year.

Applications

In writing to the correspondent.

Alan and Sheila Diamond Charitable Trust

Jewish, general

£60,000 (2006/07)

Beneficial area

UK.

Mazars LLP, 8 New Fields, 2 Stinsford Road, Nuffield, Poole, Dorset BH17 0NF
Tel: 01202 680777
Correspondent: The Trustees
Trustees: Alan Diamond, Chair; Sheila Diamond; Jonathan Kropman; Kate Goldberg.
CC Number: 274312

Information available

Accounts were available from the Charity Commission.

About two-thirds of the trust's grant-making is to Jewish organisations. The trust supports the same organisations each year which are listed in its trust deed, and cannot consider other applications.

In 2009/10 the trust had assets of £1.5 million and an income of £53,000. There were 59 grants made totalling £44,000.

Beneficiaries included: British School of Osteopathy (£10,000); Norwood (£7,000); Anglo Israel Association (£4,900); Community Security Trust (£4,500); British WIZO (£3,400); Jewish Museum and Sidney Sussex College (£2,500 each); and Central Synagogue (£2,200).

Exclusions

No grants to individuals.

Applications

The trust states that it will not consider unsolicited applications. No preliminary telephone calls. There are no regular trustees' meetings. The trustees frequently decide how the funds should be allocated. The trustees have their own guidelines, which are not published.

The Dickon Trust

General

£48,000 (2009/10)

Beneficial area

North East England and Scotland.

Dickinson Dees, St Anne's Wharf, 112 Quayside, Newcastle NE99 1SB
Tel: 0191 279 9698
Website: www.dickontrust.org.uk
Correspondent: Helen Tavroges
Trustees: Mrs D L Barrett; Major-General R V Brims; R Y Barrett; M L Robson; A Copeman.
CC Number: 327202

Information available

Accounts were available from the Charity Commission.

The trust has general charitable purposes giving grants to local groups in north east England (from the Tees in the south to Cumbria in the west) and Scotland. The trustees in particular favour charities that are beneficial to young people.

In 2009/10 the trust had assets of £1.3 million and an income of £54,000. Grants to organisations totalled £48,000.

All grants but four were for £1,000 each. Beneficiaries included: Holy Island Village Hall and Hopscotch Children's Charity (£2,000 each); Age Concern Gateshead, Blyth Young People's Centre LTD, Disability North, React, Skill Force, the Arkwright Scholarship Trust, St Oswald's Hospice and the Shirlie Project (£1,000 each).

Exclusions

No support for individuals, unregistered charities or churches.

Applications

Applications can be made online at the trust's website. The trustees meet twice a year in summer and winter to consider appeals. Any applications received by the end of October will be considered at the winter meeting and any applications made after that time, up to the end of May, will be considered at the summer meeting.

The Dinwoodie Settlement

Postgraduate medical education and research

£1.2 million (2009/10)

Beneficial area

UK.

c/o Thomas Eggar, The Corn Exchange, Baffins Lane, Chichester, West Sussex PO19 1GK
Correspondent: The Clerk to the Trustees
Trustees: William A Fairbairn; Dr John M Fowler; Miss Christian Webster; Rodney B N Fisher; John A Gibson.
CC Number: 255495

Information available

Accounts were available from the Charity Commission.

The trust outlined its grant policy in its 2009/10 accounts:

> The trustees endeavour to be pro-active in pursuing the objectives of the charity by supporting eligible projects in the field of postgraduate medical education and research in England.

The maximum grant towards a Postgraduate Medical Centres (PMCs) project in any one area is normally £1 million. Medical research is for no more than the salary of two research workers in any one year. The trust's funds can be committed for three years when supporting major projects.

In 2009/10 the trust had assets of £3.5 million and an income of £323,000. Grants were made to four organisations totalling £1.2 million. Beneficiaries were: Kings College London (£750,000); Portsmouth Hospital (£259,000); Southport and Ormskirk Hospital (£150,000); and Imperial College London (£43,000).

Exclusions

Anything falling outside the main areas of work referred to above. The trustees do not expect to fund consumable or equipment costs or relieve the NHS of its financial responsibilities.

Applications

The trustees state they are proactive rather than reactive in their grant-giving. Negotiating for new PMCs and monitoring their construction invariably takes a number of years.

Disability Aid Fund (The Roger and Jean Jefcoate Trust)

Disability

£74,000 to organisations (2009/10)

Beneficial area

UK.

2 Swanbourne Road, Mursley, Milton Keynes MK17 0JA
Correspondent: Roger Jefcoate, Trustee
Trustees: Vivien Dinning, Chair; Roger Jefcoate; Valerie Henchoz; Rosemary McCloskey; Carol Wemyss.
CC Number: 1096211

Information available

Accounts were on file at the Charity Commission.

The following statement was taken from the trust's 2009/10 accounts and explains its grantmaking strategy:

> We support a few carefully selected local, regional and small national healthcare and disability charities for older people in Buckinghamshire and Milton Keynes and adjacent counties, especially charities which promote health and wellbeing through information, advice and practical help like developing or providing special needs technology. We look for charities showing strong support from service users and volunteers and only modest expenditure on fundraising and administration.
>
> We also provide a nationwide funding advice service for severely disabled individuals who seek special needs technology like an adapted computer for their writing or communication needs or their voluntary work. Occasionally we might also fund such equipment, but we prefer to do so through specialist charities like AbllityNet (0800 269545) which provides good independent advice on the most suitable equipment and how to get it.

In 2009/10 the trust had assets of £3.1 million, an income of £161,000 and made grants totalling £86,000 of which £74,000 went to 16 organisations and the remaining £12,000 went to 11 individuals.

Beneficiaries included: Demand – Watford – for the launch of the Yorkshire premises appeal (£20,000); L'Arche Community – Bognor – to refurbish the Fieldway supported home (£6,000); Bath Institute of Medical Engineering – for general needs and St John Ambulance – improvement for wheelchair visitors (£5,000 each); MS Therapy Centre – Bristol – for electrically adjustable beds and Macular Disease Society – Andover – for a training course at Chilton (£3,000 each); Advocacy Project – London – for general needs and Help the Hospices – London – for the Drapers' company appeal (£2,000 each); and Exeter Gateway Centre – for allotment tools for people with mental disabilities (£1,000).

Applications

In writing to the correspondent.

Common applicant mistakes

'Failure to read carefully their entry in DSC publications!'

Dischma Charitable Trust

General, with a preference for Education, Arts and Culture, Conservation and Human and Animal Welfare

£138,000 (2006)

Beneficial area

Worldwide, with a strong preference for London and the south east of England.

Rathbone Trust Company Ltd, c/o 159 New Bond Street, London W15 2UD
Tel: 020 7399 0820
Email: linda.cousins@rathbones.com

Correspondent: Linda Cousins, The Secretary
Trustees: Simon Robertson; Edward Robertson; Lorna Robertson Timmis; Virginia Robertson; Selina Robertson; Arabella Brooke.
CC Number: 1077501

Information available

Accounts were available from the Charity Commission.

Registered with the Charity Commission in September 1999, this trust has recently reviewed their grant-giving policy and have decided to support principally, but not exclusively, projects concerned with education, arts and culture, conservation and human and animal welfare.

In 2010 the trust had assets of £4.8 million and income of £62,000. Grants were made to 53 organisations totalling £117,000 and were broken down as follows:

General medical, mental health and disabilities	£24,000
Wildlife and conservation	£23,500
Education	£23,000
General	£18,000
Children and youth welfare	£17,000
Relief of poverty	£9,000
Elderly welfare	£3,000

Grants included those made to: Alton College and Treloar Trust (£5,000 each); Epic Arts and International Animal Rescue (£4,000 each); Compassion in World Farming (£3,500); Listening Books, Sign Health and Wild Things (£3,000 each); Bear Baiting in Pakistan (£2,500); Action Against Hunger, Almshouse Association, ASBAH, Chernobyl Children's Project, Fields in Trust, Grasslands Trust and Marine Stewardship Council (£2,000 each); Albert Kennedy Trust, Child to Child Trust, Get Connected, Gorilla Organisation and WWF (£1,500 each); and The 999 Club (£500).

Exclusions

The trust does not support charities that carry out medical research.

Applications

The trustees meet half-yearly to review applications for funding. Only successful applicants are notified of the trustees' decision. Certain charities are supported annually, although no commitment is given.

The DLM Charitable Trust

General charitable purposes

£99,000 (2009/10)

Beneficial area

UK, especially the Oxford area.

c/o Cloke and Co., Warnford Court, Throgmorton Street, London EC2N 2AT
Tel: 020 7638 8992
Correspondent: J A Cloke, Trustee
Trustees: Dr E A de la Mare; Mrs P Sawyer; J A Cloke; Miss J E Sawyer.
CC Number: 328520

Information available

Accounts were available from the Charity Commission.

The trust was established in 1990, after R D A de la Mare left 25% of the residue of his estate for charitable purposes. It supports charities that were supported by the settlor and local Oxford organisations 'where normal fundraising methods may not be successful.' In 2009/10 the trust had assets of £5 million and an income of £150,000. Grants were given to 22 organisations totalling £99,000.

Beneficiaries included: the Ley Community (£25,000); See Saw (£15,000); Wildlife Conservation Research Unit (£10,000); National Society for Epilepsy (£5,000); Brainwave, Christians Against Poverty, Prison Phoenix Trust and Reading Quest (£2,000 each); and Dogs for the Disabled (£1,000).

Exclusions

No grants to individuals.

Applications

In writing to the correspondent. Trustees meet in February, July and November to consider applications.

The Dorcas Trust

Christian, relief of poverty and advancement of education

£26,000 (2009/10)

Beneficial area
UK.

Port of Liverpool Building, Pier Head, Liverpool L3 1NW
Tel: 0151 236 6666
Correspondent: I Taylor
Trustees: J C L Broad; J D Broad; P L Butler.
CC Number: 275494

Information available
Accounts were available from the Charity Commission, but without a grants list.

The trust has a preference for Christian causes, although other charities have also been supported. The trustees will also consider making loans to organisations and individuals. In 2009/10 the trust had assets of £1.5 million and an income of £40,000. Grants were made totalling £26,000.

Previous beneficiaries included: Dorcas Developments Limited (£103,000); Navigators (£15,000); Newmarket Day Centre (£14,000); World Vision (£5,000); Mildmay Mission (£3,000); Integra (£2,000); Shaftesbury Society and Moorlands Bible College (£1,000 each); Send a Cow (£500); Chernobyl Children's Lifeline (£100); and RNIB (£50).

Applications
In writing to the correspondent, although the trust stated that applications cannot be considered as funds are already committed.

The Dorema Charitable Trust

Medicine, health, welfare, education, religion

£23,000 (2009/10)

Beneficial area
UK.

4 Church Grove, Amersham, Buckinghamshire HP6 6SH
Correspondent: D S M Nussbaum, Trustee
Trustees: D S M Nussbaum; Mrs K M Nussbaum; S Murray-Williams.
CC Number: 287001

Information available
Accounts were received at the Charity Commission, but were unavailable to view.

This trust supports medicine, health, welfare, education and religion. In 2009/10 the trust had an income of £2,000 and a total expenditure of £23,000. Further information was not available.

Applications
The trust strongly stated that unsolicited applications are not considered, describing such appeals as a waste of charitable resources.

Common applicant mistakes
'Applying is a mistake. Unsolicited applications are not considered.'

The Dorus Trust

Health and welfare, disability, homelessness, addiction, children who are disadvantaged, environment

£69,000 (2009)

Beneficial area
Mainly UK.

c/o Charities Aid Foundation, Kings Hill, West Malling, Kent ME19 4TA

Tel: 01732 520028
Correspondent: C H Peacock, Trustee
Trustees: C H Peacock; Mrs B Bond; A M Bond.
CC Number: 328724

Information available
Full accounts were provided by the trust.

The trust has common trustees with two other trusts, the Cleopatra Trust and the Epigoni Trust (see separate entries) with which it also shares the same aims and polices. All three trusts are administered by Charities Aid Foundation. Generally the trusts support different organisations each year.

The trust makes grants in the following areas:
▷ mental health
▷ cancer welfare/education – not research
▷ diabetes
▷ physical disability – not research
▷ homelessness
▷ addiction
▷ children who are disadvantaged.

There is also some preference for environmental causes. It only gives grants for specific projects and does not give grants for running costs or general appeals. Support is only given to national organisations, not local areas or initiatives. In 2009 the trust had assets of £3.1 million, which generated an income of £85,000. Grants were made to 11 organisations totalling £69,000.

Grants went to: Wildfowl & Wetlands Trust (£9,000); DebRA; Just a Drop and St Raphael's Hospice (£8,000 each); Practical Action and Home Start Merton (£7,000 each); Crisis UK (£6,000); Fairbridge and Switchback (£5,000 each); Landmark Trust (£4,000); and Royal Choral Society (£3,000).

Exclusions
No grants to individuals, expeditions, research, scholarships, charities with a local focus, local branches of UK charities or towards running costs.

Applications
This trust no longer accepts applications.

Double 'O' Charity Ltd

General

£104,000 (2005/06)

Beneficial area

UK and overseas.

c/o 4 Friars Lane, Richmond, Surrey TW9 1NL
Tel: 020 8940 8171
Correspondent: The Trustees
Trustees: Peter Townshend; Karen Townshend.
CC Number: 271681

Information available

Accounts were available from the Charity Commission.

The primary objective of the trust is to make grants towards the relief of poverty, preservation of health and the advancement of education. The trust considers all requests for aid.

In 2009/10 the trust held assets of £121,000 and an income of £108,000. Grants to organisations totalled £168,000, with a further £32,000 given to individuals.

Beneficiaries included: Spirit of Recovery (£48,000); Avatar Meher Baba (£33,000); Refuge (£30,000); NAPAC (£28,000); Richmond Bridge Friendship Club (£13,000); Arvon Foundation and One World Action (£5,000 each); Wroxham Trust (£3,000); Art and Soul (£2,000); and SRLV 2009 Adventure (£500).

Exclusions

No grants to individuals towards education or for their involvement in overseas charity work.

Applications

In writing to the correspondent.

The Doughty Charity Trust

Orthodox Jewish, religious education, relief of poverty

£136,000 (2009)

Beneficial area

England, Israel.

22 Ravenscroft Avenue, Golders Green, London NW11 0RY
Tel: 020 8209 0500
Correspondent: Gerald B Halibard, Trustee
Trustees: G Halibard, Chair; Mrs M Halibard.
CC Number: 274977

Information available

Full accounts were available from the Charity Commission.

This trust appears to confine its giving to Orthodox Jewish causes. In 2009 the trust had an income of £213,000 and made grants totalling £136,000. Its assets stood at £56,000.

Beneficiaries included: Zichron Menachem (£25,000); Tomchei Sharei Zion (£20,000); Beif Hayeld (£17,000); Sylvella Charity (£12,000); FKHKS (£10,000); JET and Achiezer (£5,000 each); and NW London Sephardi Synagogue (£1,300).

Various donations of £1,000 and under amounted to £16,000.

Exclusions

No grants to individuals.

Applications

In writing to the correspondent.

The R M Douglas Charitable Trust

General

£39,000 to organisations (2009/10)

Beneficial area

UK with a preference for Staffordshire.

c/o 68 Liverpool Road, Stoke-on-Trent ST4 1BG
Correspondent: Juliet Rees, Trustee
Trustees: J M Douglas; Juliet E Lees; F W Carder; M J D Lees.
CC Number: 248775

Information available

Accounts were available from the Charity Commission, but without a list of grants.

The trust was set up for the relief of poverty (including provision of pensions) especially for present and past employees (and their families) of Robert M Douglas (Contractors) Ltd, and for general charitable purposes especially in the parish of St Mary, Dunstall. In practice grants are only given to organisations previously supported by the trust. Grants range from £200 to £5,000, although only a few are for over £500.

In 2009/10 the trust had assets of £883,000 and an income of £189,000. Grants were made to organisations totalling £39,000. A further £2,000 was distributed to individuals connected with the company.

Previous beneficiaries have included: Bible Explorer for Christian outreach, British Red Cross for general purposes, Burton Graduate Medical College to equip a new lecture theatre, Four Oaks Methodist Church for its centenary appeal, Lichfield Diocesan Urban Fund for Christian mission, St Giles Hospice – Lichfield for development, SAT-7 Trust for Christian outreach and John Taylor High School – Barton in Needwood for a performing arts block.

Applications

The trust has previously stated that its funds were fully committed.

The Drayson Foundation

Relief of sickness, education

£33,000 (2009/10)

Beneficial area

UK.

1 Threadneedle Street, London EC2R 8AY
Correspondent: Clare Maurice, Trustee
Trustees: Lord Drayson; Lady Drayson; Clare Maurice.
CC Number: 1076700

Information available

Accounts were available from the Charity Commission.

Set up in 2009, the main objects of the foundation are the relief of sickness, with particular emphasis on children and the advancement of education.

In 2009/10 it had assets of £3.6 million, mostly from investment income of £90,000. There was one grant made to National Centre for Young People with Epilepsy (£33,000).

Applications

In writing to the correspondent.

Dromintee Trust

General

£118,000 (2006/07)

Beneficial area

UK and developing countries.

The Manor House, Main Street, Thurnby, Leicester LE7 9PN
Tel: 0116 241 5100
Correspondent: Hugh Murphy, Trustee
Trustees: Hugh Murphy; Margaret Murphy; Mary Murphy; Patrick Hugh Murphy; Robert Smith; Paul Tiernan.
CC Number: 1053956

Information available

Accounts were available from the Charity Commission.

Established in March 1996, this trust gives for people in need by reason of age, illness, disability or socio-economic circumstances; for charitable purposes connected with children's welfare; the advancement of health and education; research into rare diseases and disorders, in particular metabolic disorders; and for general charitable purposes. Grants are made locally, nationally and in developing countries.

In 2009/10 the trust had assets of £1.3 million and an income of £323,000. Grants were made to 16 organisations totalling £334,000.

The three largest grants went to: Great Ormond Street Hospital Charity (£151,000); Consolata Fathers (£35,000 in two grants); and CAFOD – St Francis Community West Kenya (£34,000).

Other beneficiaries were: Let the Children Live and the National Hospital for Neurology and Neurosurgery – Brain Tumour Unit (£25,000 each); InterCare – Medical Aid for Africa and the Parish of Dromintee and Jonesboro' (£20,000 each); Holy Cross Priory (£8,400); Atiamah Trust and International Reconstructive Plastic Surgery (Ghana) Project (£3,000 each); International Refugee Trust – Uganda (£2,600); Hospices of Hope and Home-Start International – Uganda (£2,500 each); and Feed the Children and Broom Street Children Project (£1,000 each).

Applications

In writing to the correspondent.

The Dugdale Charitable Trust

Christian education, the advancement of Methodist education and the Catholic religion

£94,000 (2008/9)

Beneficial area

UK, with a preference for Hampshire and West Sussex, and overseas.

Yewtrees, Curbridge, Botley, Southampton SO30 2HB
Tel: 1489788343
Correspondent: Robert Dugdale, Trustee
Trustees: Robert Dugdale; Bebe Dugdale; Jeremy Dugdale; Simon Dugdale.
CC Number: 1052941

Information available

Full accounts were on file at the Charity Commission.

The trust has general charitable purposes and supports the advancement of the Methodist religion and Christian education in the UK. Increasingly, the trust supports overseas mission, relief and development work particularly in Africa and the Indian subcontinent.

In 2008/9 the trust had an income of £60,000, held assets of £441,000 and made grants totalling £94,000 of which £31,000 was allocated for specific development projects in Uganda.

Beneficiaries included: Winchester Family Church (£12,000); New Life Church (£9,000); OMS International (£6,000); and Waltham Chase Methodist Church, Christians Against Poverty, Mission Aviation Fellowship, WPCC and Open Doors (£5,000 each).

Applications

This trust only supports causes known personally to the trustees. Unsolicited applications are not considered.

The Dumbreck Charity

General

£73,000 (2009/10)

Beneficial area

Worldwide, especially the west Midlands.

c/o PS Accounting, 41 Sycamore Drive, Hollywood, Birmingham B47 5QX
Correspondent: Mrs P M Spragg
Trustees: A C S Hordern; H B Carslake; Mrs J E Melling.
CC Number: 273070

Information available

Accounts were available from the Charity Commission.

In 2009/10 the charity had assets of £3.4 million and an income of £241,000. Grants to organisations totalled £73,000. A small number of new grants are awarded each year to charities in Worcestershire, Warwickshire and West Midlands. Grants included regular donations and one-off payments which were given in the following categories:

Miscellaneous	18	£23,000
Medical	12	£14,000
Care of the elderly and physically/mentally disabled	18	£12,000
Animal welfare/conservation	6	£7,000
Children's Welfare	9	£6,000

Beneficiaries included: DEC Haiti Earthquake Appeal (£10,000); Worcester Cathedral for Music and Light, Macular Disease Support Group Leamington and Spear (£2,000 each); Home from Hospital Care, British Blind Sport, St Matthews Holiday Play Scheme and Birmingham Royal Ballet (£1,000 each); Momentum Midlands and the Singalong Group (£750 each); and Elgar School of Music, Trinity Christian Group, War Memorials Trust and Bowel and Cancer Research (£500 each).

Exclusions

No grants to individuals.

Applications

In writing to the correspondent. The trustees meet annually in April/May. Unsuccessful applications will not be acknowledged. In general, priority is given to applications from the Midlands counties.

The Houghton Dunn Charitable Trust

Medical, health, welfare, environment, wildlife, churches, heritage

£292,000 (2009/10)

Beneficial area

UK, with an interest in Lancashire.

Carlton Place, 22 Greenwood Street, Altrincham WA14 1RZ
Correspondent: A M H Dunn, Trustee
Trustees: A M H Dunn; R C H Dunn.
CC Number: 261685

Information available

Accounts were on file at the Charity Commission, without a list of grants.

Support is given to organisations working in the Lancashire area or UK-wide. It mostly makes small recurrent grants towards core costs of small organisations to enable them to maintain and improve their services.

Larger grants can also be made towards capital projects.

In 2009/10 the trust had assets of £6 million and an income of £303,000. Grants were made to 26 organisations totalling £292,000. Grants were broken down as follows:

Medical and health – general	5	£80,000
Medical and health – research	2	£25,000
Medical and health – children	2	£25,000
Welfare in the community – children and youth	10	£101,000
Welfare in the community – general	4	£26,000
Environment and wildlife	2	£25,000
Church and heritage	1	£10,000

Previous beneficiaries have included: AMEND, Arthritis Research Campaign, Cancer BACUP, Cancer Research UK, Christie Hospital NHS Trust, East Lancashire Hospice Fund, Lancashire Wildlife Trust, Marie Curie Cancer Care, Macmillan Cancer Relief , National Eczema Society, National Trust Lake District Appeal and National Youth Orchestra.

Exclusions

No grants to individuals.

Applications

In writing to the correspondent. There is no set time for the consideration of applications, but donations are normally made in March each year.

The Dunn Family Charitable Trust

Medical, general, conservation

£60,000 (2009/10)

Beneficial area

UK, with a strong preference for Nottinghamshire.

Rushcliffe Developments, Tudor House, 13–15 Rectory Road, West Bridgford, Nottingham NG2 6BE
Tel: 0115 945 5300
Email: nad@rushcliffe.co.uk
Correspondent: The Trustees
Trustees: Graham R Dunn; Mrs Jacky R Dunn; Mrs Lisa J Dunn; Nigel A Dunn; Peter M Dunn; Richard M Dunn.

CC Number: 297389

Information available

Full accounts were available at the Charity Commission.

This trust supports health, multiple sclerosis research, conservation, ecology and general community and voluntary organisations.

In 2009/10 the trust had assets of £1.7 million, which generated an income of £63,000. Grants were made to 25 organisations totalling £60,000.

Beneficiaries included: the Oakes Trust – Sheffield (£4,500); Nottingham Multiple Sclerosis Therapy Centre Ltd (£4,000); St Luke's Hospice (£3,000); Macmillan Cancer Support (£2,500); CP Sport and Friary Drop-in Ltd (£2,000 each); Rainbow Children's Hospice (£1,500); RSPB and RNLI – Wells-next the-Sea (£1,000 each).

Exclusions

No grants to individuals or unsolicited applications.

Applications

In writing to the correspondent.

Mildred Duveen Charitable Trust

General

£50,000 (2009/10)

Beneficial area

Worldwide.

Devonshire House, 60 Goswell Road, London EC1M 7AD
Tel: 020 7566 4000
Correspondent: Peter Holgate, Trustee
Trustees: Peter Holgate; Adrian Houstoun; Peter Loose; John Shelford.
CC Number: 1059355

Information available

Accounts were available from the Charity Commission.

Registered with the Charity Commission in November 1996, in 1999/2000 this trust received a substantial income of £1.3 million. In 2009/10 the trust had assets of

£1.1 million, which generated an income of £29,000. Grants to 26 organisations totalled £50,000.

Beneficiaries included: Almeida Theatre (£7,000); CPRE – Wiltshire, Theatre Royal Haymarket Masterclass and Hoopers Africa Trust (£5,000 each); Monica Cantwell Trust (£3,000); Charlie Waller Memorial Trust (£2,500); the Passage (£2,000); Provincial Grand Masters Benevolent Fund – Cumberland (£1,500); PDSA, Deafblind UK, South East Cancer Help Centre, Martlets Hospice and Midlands Air Ambulance (£1,000 each); and Walk the Walk Worldwide, Cat and Rabbit Rescue Centre and Whittington Babies (£500 each).

Applications

In writing to the correspondent.

The Annette Duvollet Charitable Trust

General

£23,000 (2009/10)

Beneficial area

UK.

18 Nassau Road, London SW13 9QE
Tel: 020 8748 5401
Correspondent: Peter Clarke, Trustee
Trustees: Peter Clarke; Caroline Dawes; Richard Shuttleworth.
CC Number: 326505

Information available

Accounts were available from the Charity Commission.

Registered with the Charity Commission in 1984, this trust gives grants to charities whose work supports young people aged 14 to 25. In 2009/10 the trust had assets of £679,000 and an income of £32,000. Grants were given to nine organisations totalling £23,000.

Beneficiaries were: Norfolk and Norwich Scope Association – NANSA (£5,700); Depaul Trust (£5,000); Journey of a Lifetime (£4,500); Changing Faces and Notting Hill Housing Trust (£2,000 each); Cued

Speech Association, Mencap – Keynsham and Children's Trust – Tadworth (£1,000 each); and Sayers Croft Environmental Educational Trust (£500).

Applications

In writing to the correspondent.

The Dwek Family Charitable Trust

General

£31,000 (2009/10)

Beneficial area

UK, with a preference for the Greater Manchester area.

Suite One, Courthill House, 66 Water Lane, Wilmslow, Cheshire SK9 5AP
Correspondent: J C Dwek, Trustee
Trustees: J C Dwek; J V Dwek; A J Leon.
CC Number: 1001456

Information available

Accounts were received at the Charity Commission.

In 2009/10 the trust had assets of £308,000 and an income of £41,000. Charitable donations amounted to £31,000, but there were no details of the number of grants or who they were made to.

Applications

In writing to the correspondent.

The Dyers' Company Charitable Trust

General

£359,000 (2009/10)

Beneficial area

UK.

Dyers Hall, Dowgate Hill, London EC4R 2ST
Tel: 020 7236 7197
Correspondent: The Clerk
Trustee: The Court of The Dyers' Company.
CC Number: 289547

Information available

Accounts were on file at the Charity Commission website.

In 2009/10 the trust had assets of £8.2 million and an income of £1 million, mostly from voluntary donations. Grants to organisations totalled £359,000, which were in the following categories:

Education and young people	34	£107,000
The Craft	9	£51,000
Norwich School	1	£51,000
Health and welfare	27	£29,000
The Arts	14	£18,000
The Services	7	£15,000
Local community/city/inner London	9	£7,000
The Church	8	£6,000
Other Appeals	6	£10,000

Beneficiaries included: the Chesil Trust (£20,000); St Saviour's and St Olave's School (£18,000); Heriot-Watt University (£14,000); University of Manchester (£10,000); Society of Dyers and Colourists (£7,000); Royal College of Art (£6,000); Help for Heroes (£5,000); HANDS (£3,000); St Peter's Hospice – Bristol and Orchid Cancer Appeal (£2,000 each); City and Guilds of London Arts School and River Thames Boat Project (£1,000 each); and the Scargill Movement and PACE (£500 each).

Exclusions

No grants to individuals.

Applications

The trust does not welcome unsolicited applications.

Common applicant mistakes

'Making unsolicited applications, international charities applying and also individuals.'

EAGA Partnership Charitable Trust

Fuel poverty

£122,000 (2009/10)

Beneficial area

UK and European Union.

PO Box 225, Kendal LA9 9DR
Tel: 01539 736 477
Email: eagact@aol.com

Website: www.eagacharitabletrust.org
Correspondent: Dr Naomi Brown, Trust Manager
Trustees: William Baker; Zoe Dick; Prof Dave Gordon; Elizabeth Gore; Virginia Graham; Pedro Guertler; Jack Harrison; Annette Rowe.
CC Number: 1088361

Information available

Accounts were on file at the Charity Commission; the trust has a very useful website.

The trust currently provides grants to fund research and other projects within two grant programmes.

- The first programme aims to clarify the nature, extent and consequences of fuel poverty and offer insights into the energy efficient and cost-effective relief of fuel poverty.
- The second programme aims to explore issues related to vulnerable consumers and their multiple needs and preferences. It explores the overlap between fuel poverty and wider deprivation, in order to develop a better understanding of different groups of vulnerable and/ or deprived consumers.

The trust gives priority to funding proposals that have the potential to inform or influence national perceptions and policies and have a wide geographic focus. A project that operates at a local level will only be considered for a grant if it: clearly demonstrates innovation; identifies the policy relevance of the project; has wide applicability; and has well developed and accurately costed evaluation and dissemination plans.

The work funded by the trust can be divided into three categories:

- policy-related research
- action projects (such as practical, community based initiatives which have wider applicability)
- the promotion of good practice (such as tool kits and workshops).

The trust does not have minimum or maximum grant levels but it does encourage the co-funding of projects where appropriate. Grants usually run from one to three years. The trust will accept the inclusion of reasonable overhead costs within a project budget (in addition to the project's direct costs) providing the applicant can explain what the overhead costs include, how the full costs have been analysed and how the allocation was calculated.

In 2009/10 the trust had assets of £790,000, an income of £180,000 and approved two new grants totalling £122,000. Beneficiaries were: Blooming Green – for a community energy makeover (£43,000); and the University of Ulster – for research into the health impacts of fuel poverty on infants towards an action plan for intervention (£78,000).

Exclusions

No grants for: general fund-raising appeals; projects that comprise solely of capital works; retrospective funding; energy advice provision materials; maintenance of websites; or local energy efficiency/warm homes initiatives. No grants to individuals.

Applications

Application forms and detailed guidance on the application process are available on the trust's website. Meetings are held three times a year to consider submissions.

The Eagle Charity Trust

General, international, welfare

£41,000 (2009)

Beneficial area

UK, in particular Manchester, and overseas.

Nairne Son and Green, 477 Chester Road, Cornbrook, Manchester M16 9HF
Tel: 0161 872 1701
Correspondent: The Trustees
Trustees: Mrs L A Gifford; Miss D Gifford; Mrs E Y Williams; Mrs S A Nowakowski; R M E Gifford.
CC Number: 802134

Information available

Accounts were available from the Charity Commission, but without a grants list.

The trust stated it supports a wide variety of charities, including UK and international charities and local charities in Manchester. There is a preference for those concerned with medicine and welfare. Grants are made on a one off basis, with no commitment to providing ongoing funding. In 2009 the trust had assets of £892,000, which generated an income of £40,000. There were 31 grants made totalling £41,000.

Previous beneficiaries included: Oxfam – Darfur and Chad (£2,500); Médecins Sans Frontières, UNICEF and Shelter (£2,000 each); British Red Cross – Bangladesh and MacMillan Cancer Support (£1,500 each); Amnesty International, Sight Savers International and Samaritans (£1,000 each); and Turning Point, Claire House and WaterAid (£500 each).

Applications

Unsolicited applications are not invited.

Common applicant mistakes

'We don't really consider unsolicited applications; we will look at them but then they are thrown out.'

Audrey Earle Charitable Trust

General, with some preference for animal welfare and conservation charities

£87,000 (2009/10)

Beneficial area

UK.

c/o Moon Beever, 24 Bloomsbury Square, London WC1A 2PL
Tel: 020 7637 0661
Fax: 020 7436 4663
Email: psheils@mail.com
Correspondent: Paul Sheils, Trustee
Trustees: Paul Andrew Shiels; Roger James Weetch.
CC Number: 290028

Information available

Accounts were on file at the Charity Commission.

In 2009/10 this trust had assets of £3.8 million and an income of

£181,000. Grants were made to 23 organisations totalling £87,000. Most of the beneficiaries are supported year after year.

Beneficiaries included: Wells Hospital and Hospice Trust (£7,000); Animal Health Trust, British Red Cross Society, Royal British Legion, People's Dispensary for Sick Animals – PDSA, Age Concern England, Redwings Horse Sanctuary, Salvation Army and Oxfam (£4,000 each); Burnham Market and Norton Village Hall (£3,000); Burnham Overy PCC (£1,000); and Farming and Wildlife Advisory Group (£500).

Applications

In writing to the correspondent.

East Kent Provincial Charities

General, education, younger, older people

£728,000 (2009/10)

Beneficial area

UK, with a preference for Kent.

11 Boorman Way, Estuary View Business Park, Whitstable, Kent CT5 3SE
Tel: 01227 272944
Email: office@ekpca.org.uk
Website: www.ekpca.org.uk
Correspondent: Lyndon Jones
Trustees: Stewart Cale; Nicholas Waller; Peter Daniels; Peter Rodd; Brian Powell; Thomas Denne.
CC Number: 1023859

Information available

Accounts were available from the Charity Commission.

The following statement concerning the future of this charity is taken from the trustees 2009/10 report:

The upheaval in the financial markets continues. With the continuing need to have funds readily available to meet anticipated outward payments the association has been unable to obtain an adequate rate of return on investments. Thus by the time last years report was issued the rate of interest on offer to members was

already down to 0.1%, and by the end of April 2010 it had to be reduced to zero. In order to ensure that the association had sufficient liquid funds to cover the projected level of outflows; the two remaining term money market investments were withdrawn: 2151k in September and the remaining 2154k in late November. All the association's funds are now held in cash deposits with UK banks.

At a special general meeting held in March 2010, the provincial grand master proposed that a review of charitable activity, undertaken by the provincial executive, had concluded that the combined impact of turmoil in the financial markets, and the arrangements for the Freemasons' Grand Charity 2014 Festival, meant that the association was becoming less viable as a vehicle for charitable giving. A vote of members present at the SGN agreed, by a substantial majority, that the management committee should commence the dissolution of the EKPCA in accordance with its rules. Following this meeting, the Chairman wrote to all members explaining the position, and recommending that they look to moving their donations to other charities as soon as possible.

In 2009/10 the trust had assets of £20,000 and an income of £92,000. Grants totalled £728,000 and were broken down as follows:

General charitable purposes	£643,000
Education	£52,000
Care of people who are sick and older people	£31,000
Relief of poverty	£700

Beneficiaries included:

Masonic registered charities – £37,000

Freemasons Grand Charity – Festival 2014 (£250,000); Kent Masonic Library and Museum (£50,000); Masonic Centre Benevolent Funds – Castle Lodge and Ramsgate (£20,000 each); and Kent Mark Benevolent Fund (£2,500).

Non-Masonic registered charities – £43,000

Leonard Cheshire Disability (£7,000); Hospices (£4,000); Scout groups (£2,750); and Pie Factory Music, Greenhill Gymnastics Club and Veterans' Aid (£1,000 each).

Applications

See 'General' section.

The Sir John Eastwood Foundation

Social welfare, education, health

£209,500 (2009/10)

Beneficial area

UK, but mainly Nottinghamshire in practice.

PO Box 9803, Mansfield, Nothinghamshire NG18 9FT
Fax: 01623 847955
Correspondent: David Marriott, Secretary
Trustees: Gordon G Raymond, Chair; Diana M Cottingham; Valerie A Hardingham; Constance B Mudford; David Marriott.
CC Number: 235389

Information available

Accounts were obtained from the Charity Commission.

The trust makes grants to registered charities benefiting Nottinghamshire, although other applications are considered. Priority is given towards people with disabilities, older people and children with special needs. The settlor of the foundation, the late Sir John Eastwood, was a successful farmer and businessman.

In 2009/10 the trust had assets of £7.3 million and an income of £338,500. The foundation's income has reduced significantly following the cessation of trading of Adam Eastwood & Sons Limited, a company which is wholly owned by the foundation and from where income was derived. Grants were made during the year totalling £209,500. Most grants were for less than £4,000, with some organisations receiving more than one grant during the year.

The larger beneficiaries, listed in the accounts, were: Nottingham Hospice (£24,000); Newark and Nottinghamshire Agricultural Society (£10,000); NSPCC (£6,000); and Age Concern – Sybil Levin Centre, Macmillan Cancer Support and the Disability Living Centre (£5,000 each).

Exclusions

No grants to individuals.

Applications

In writing to the correspondent.

The Ebenezer Trust

Evangelical Christianity, welfare

£46,000 (2009/10)

Beneficial area

UK and overseas.

Longwood Lodge, Whites Hill, Stock, Ingatestone, Essex CM4 9QB
Tel: 01277 829893
Correspondent: Nigel Davey, Trustee
Trustees: Nigel Davey; Ruth Davey.
CC Number: 272574

Information available

Accounts were available from the Charity Commission.

The trust gives grants to Evangelical Christian charities for education, medical, religion and welfare purposes. In 2009/10 the trust had assets of £672,000 and an income of £31,000. Grants were made to 35 organisations totalling £46,000.

Beneficiaries included: Spacious Places and TEAR Fund (£4,000 each); Avant Ministries (£3,500); Baptist Missionary Society, Christian Concern for our Nation and Leeds Faith in Schools (£2,000 each); St Francis Hospice, Livability and Baptist Union Home Mission (£1,000 each); Bible in Literacy (£500); Treasures in Heaven Trust (£300); and the Brainwave Centre (£50).

Exclusions

No grants to individuals.

Applications

The trust states that they 'are most unlikely to consider unsolicited requests for grants.'

Common applicant mistakes

'Cold correspondents wasting their resources by sending too much information such as accounts etc.

Despite saying that we do not normally consider unsolicited requests, organisations still send, and some say 'I know you don't normally consider unsolicited requests but our cause is particularly special'.'

The Gilbert and Eileen Edgar Foundation

General – see below

£100,000

Beneficial area

UK (and a few international appeals).

James Cowper LLP, North Lea House, 66 Northfield End, Henley on Thames, Oxfordshire, RG92BE
Tel: 01491 848500
Email: info@jamescowper.co.uk
Correspondent: The Trustees
Trustees: Adam Gentilli; Simon Gentilli.
CC Number: 241736

Information available

Accounts for 2009 were received at the Charity Commission but unavailable to view.

Registered with the Charity Commission in 1965, the settlor of this trust expressed the desire that preference be given to the following objects:

- Medical research – the promotion of medical and surgical science in all forms.
- Care and support – helping people who are young, old and in need.
- Fine arts – raising the artistic taste of the public in music, drama, opera, painting, sculpture and the fine arts.
- Education in the fine arts – the promotion of education in the fine arts.
- Religion – the promotion of religion.
- Recreation – the provision of facilities for recreation or other leisure time activities.

There is a preference for smaller organisations 'where even a limited grant may be of real value'. The majority of grants are around £500 to £1,000 each. Many of the organisations supported are regular beneficiaries.

In 2009 the trust had an income of £69,000 and a total charitable expenditure of £108,000. No further information was available for this year however based on previous years grants made probably totalled around £100,000.

Previous beneficiaries included: Cystic Fibrosis Trust and Prostate Cancer Research Charity, Multiple Sclerosis and Prostate Cancer Charity (£1,000 each); Royal College of Surgeons of England (£500); NSPCC and Weston Spirit (£1,000); Books Abroad (£500); Ghurkha Welfare Trust and Nightingale House (£500 each); Brains Trust (£2,000); Not Forgotten Association (£1,000); English National Ballet (£2,000); Royal Academy of Arts – Scholarship (£6,000); and Survival for Tribal Peoples and Marine Conservation Society (£500 each).

Exclusions

Grants for education in the fine arts are made by way of scholarships awarded by academies and no grants are made directly to individuals in this regard.

Applications

In writing to the correspondent. There are no application forms.

Gilbert Edgar Trust

General, UK and overseas

£36,000 (2005/06)

Beneficial area

Predominantly UK, limited overseas.

c/o James Cowper LLP, North Lee House, 66 Northfield End, Henley-on-Thames, Oxfordshire RG9 2BE
Tel: 01491 848500
Correspondent: The Trustees
Trustees: Simon Gentilli; Adam Gentilli; Dr Richard Solomons.
CC Number: 213630

Information available

Accounts were available from the Charity Commission.

Registered with the Charity Commission in 1955, this trust supports organisations whose work is concerned with the welfare of people in the UK and overseas.

In 2009/10 the trust had assets of £941,000 and an income of £38,000. Charitable expenditure came to £39,000 given in 57 grants, which were broken down as follows:

Children	8	£5,500
Deaf/blind	3	£1,500
Disabled	11	£5,500
Drug abuse	4	£2,000
Homeless	5	£7,000
Hospice	3	£1,500
Medical	3	£2,000
Overseas	5	£5,000
Research	5	£3,000
Social	6	£4,000
Youth	3	£1,500
Other	1	£100

Beneficiaries included: Samaritans, NSPCC, Simon Community and British Red Cross (£1,500 each); Prostate Cancer Charity, Macmillan Cancer Relief and National Institute of Conductive Education (£1,000 each); YMCA, Hambleden Church Council, Hospice of St Francis, Prisoners Abroad, Barts Research Trust, Woodcraft Folk, Release, Sense and Orchard Vale Trust (£500 each); and Worshipful Company of Clockmakers (£100).

Exclusions

No grants to individuals or non-registered charities.

Applications

In writing to the correspondent, with a copy of a brochure describing your work.

The Edinburgh Trust, No 2 Account

Education, armed services

£97,000 (2009/10)

Beneficial area

UK and worldwide.

Buckingham Palace, London
SW1A 1AA
Tel: 020 7930 4832
Correspondent: The Secretary
Trustees: Sir Brian McGrath; C Woodhouse; Sir Miles Hunt-Davis.
CC Number: 227897

Information available

Full accounts were available at the Charity Commission.

In 2009/10 the trust had assets of £2.3 million and an income of £99,000. Grants were made to 88 organisations totalling £97,000 and were distributed into the following categories:

General	£66,000
Armed Services	£26,000
Education	£5,000

Beneficiaries included: International Sacred Literature Trust (£7,000); Edwina Mountbatten Trust (£3,000); the Federation of London Youth Clubs, Royal Commonwealth Ex Serviceman's League and King George Fund for Sailors (£2,500 each); King Edward VII Hospital for Officers, St George's House and the Game & Wildlife Conservancy Trust (£2,000 each); Burma Star Association, the Cutty Sark Trust, SSAFA and British Trust for Conservation Volunteers (£1,500 each); Interact Worldwide, the Sail Training Association and the Zoological Society of London (£1,000 each).

Exclusions

No grants to individuals; only scientific expeditions are considered with the backing of a major society. No grants to non-registered charities.

Applications

In writing to the correspondent. The trustees meet to consider grants in April each year. Applications must be submitted by January.

Educational Foundation of Alderman John Norman

Education

£11,000 to organisations (2009/10)

Beneficial area

Norwich and Old Catton.

Brown and Co, The Atrium, St George's Street, Norwich NR3 1AB
Tel: 01603 629 871
Correspondent: N F Saffell, Clerk
Trustees: Revd Jonathan Boston, Chair; Roger Sandall; Dr Julia Leach; Revd Canon Martin Smith; Derek Armes; Christopher Brown; Tracey Hughes; Stephen Slack; James Hawkins; Roy Hughes; Francis Whymark.
CC Number: 313105

Information available

Accounts were on file at the Charity Commission.

The foundation was originally founded by the terms of the will of Alderman Norman dated February 1720. It is currently regulated by schemes from 1972 and 1973. Grants made by the foundation are to assist the education of:

- young persons descended from Alderman John Norman
- young persons resident in the parish of Old Catton
- young persons resident in the city of Norwich and for the benefit of schools established for charitable purposes only or for the benefit of local authority schools for benefits not provided by local authority.

In 2009/10 the foundation held assets of £6 million and had an income of £253,000. Grants to 531 descendents and 5 Old Catton residents totalled £210,000. A further £11,000 was given to 10 organisations.

Beneficiaries were: Norfolk County Council Children's Services (£3,000); Norwich Cathedral Choir Endowment Fund (£2,500); Claimants Unity Trust (£2,000); Community Action Norwich, the Whitlingham Project, Handicapped Children Action Group, the Matthew Project, the Hamlet Centre and Norwich and District Carers Forum (£500 each); and Norfolk and Norwich Chamber Music (£300).

Exclusions

No grants to non-registered charities. No applications from outside Norwich and Old Catton will be considered.

Applications

In writing to the correspondent. Grants to organisations are considered at the trustees meeting in May/June, however, the trustees usually meet three times each year, in February, May and October.

The W G Edwards Charitable Foundation

Care of older people

£94,000 (2009/10)

Beneficial area

UK.

c/o 123a Station Road, Oxted, Surrey RH8 0QE
Tel: 01883 714412
Fax: 01883 714433
Email: janetbrown@ wgedwardscharitablefoundation.org. uk
Website: www. wgedwardscharitablefoundation.org. uk
Correspondent: Janet Brown, Clerk to the Trustees
Trustees: Margaret E Offley Edwards; Prof. Wendy D Savage; Gillian Shepherd Coates; Ms Yewande Savage.
CC Number: 293312

Information available

Accounts were available from the Charity Commission.

The W G Edwards Charitable Foundation is constituted under a trust deed of 1985 following the death of William George Edwards. Although the trust deed does not specify any particular beneficiaries, the trustees have agreed to adopt the following grant making policy statement in order to reflect more closely the wishes of the late Mr W G Edwards, and have signed a statement of wishes to this effect:

> To assist with the provision of care for older people through existing charities, principally with capital projects but also other innovative schemes for ongoing care.

In addition, the aims of the foundation are:-

i) to support as many projects as possible, even if this means smaller individual grants

ii) to donate to refurbishment/building projects nearing completion rather than those in the planning stage

iii) to support all kinds of groups of older people such as blind, homeless etc. but not necessarily groups that might include older people, for example disabled organisations

iv) to sponsor individual named items of expenditure rather than donate into a pool/unrestricted fund

v) to ensure that any funding is properly spent on those specific items sponsored.

In 2009/10 the foundation had assets of £2.8 million and an income of £90,000. A total of 143 applications were received, of which 36 were successful. Grants totalled £94,000. Types of donations as listed in the accounts were broken down as follows:

Refurbishment	£32,000
Furniture/Equipment	£18,000
Recreational Activity	£12,000
Outreach/care projects	£5,000
Homeless	£2,000
I.T. for older people	£2,000
Research	£16,000

Beneficiaries included: RICE (£10,000); Alzheimer's Support, Bromley Council on Ageing, Help the Aged, Rushmore Healthy Living and Sevenoaks Almshouse Charity (£3,000 each); Age Concern Hackney, Parwich Memorial Hall, Reading YMCA, Rio Cinema and STARS (£2,000 each); and Abbeyfield Bognor Regis (£1,000 each).

Exclusions

No grants to individuals.

Applications

In writing to the correspondent, including: confirmation of charitable status (charity number on letterhead will suffice); brief details of the project; budget statement for the project; current fundraising achievements and proposals for future fundraising; items of expenditure within project costing approx £1,000 to £5,000 – trustees currently prefer to give towards a named item rather than into a pool building fund; copy of latest accounts if available.

There are no forms or deadlines for applications. If your project fulfils the foundation's policy criteria, your details will be passed on to the trustees for consideration at their next meeting.

Common applicant mistakes

'Requesting revenue funding.'

The Elephant Trust

Visual arts

£54,000 (2009/10)

Beneficial area

UK.

512 Bankside Lofts, 65 Hopton Street, London SE1 9GZ
Email: ruth@elephanttrust.org.uk
Website: www.elephanttrust.org.uk
Correspondent: Ruth Rattenbury
Trustees: Dawn Ades; Elizabeth Carey -Thomas; Benjamin Cook; Jeremy Deller; Antony Fonvood; Melissa Gronlund; Antony Penrose; Elizabeth Price; Rob Tufnell; Richard Wentworth; Sarah Whitfield.
CC Number: 269615

Information available

Accounts were available from the Charity Commission.

The trust makes grants to individual artists, arts organisations and publications concerned with the visual arts. It aims to extend the frontiers of creative endeavour, to promote the unconventional and the imaginative and, to make it possible for artists and arts organisations to realise and complete specific projects.

In 2009/10 the trust assets totalled £1.6 million, which generated an income of £57,000. Grants were given totalling £54,000 with £33,000 distributed to individuals and £21,000 distributed to 11 organisations.

Grants went to: Auto Italia, Bookworks, Cubitt Artists Limited, Pump House Gallery, Sheffield Contemporary Art Forum, Site Gallery, Stour Valley Arts, Studio Voltaire, Wandsworth Council (£2,000 each); and the Drawing

Room and Durham Art Gallery (£1,500 each).

The trust also administers the George Melhuish Bequest, which has similar objectives.

Exclusions

No education or other study grants.

Applications

In writing to the correspondent. Guidelines are available. The trustees meet four times a year.

Common applicant mistakes

'Ignoring guidelines regarding the types of projects and categories supported as listed on our website.'

The George Elias Charitable Trust

Jewish, general

£229,000 (2009/10)

Beneficial area

Some preference for Manchester.

Elitex House, 1 Ashley Road, Altrincham, Cheshire WA14 2DT
Tel: 0161 928 7171
Email: textiles@kshaw.com
Correspondent: S E Elias, Trustee
Trustees: E C Elias; S E Elias.
CC Number: 273993

Information available

Accounts were available from the Charity Commission.

The trust states that it gives grants to charities supporting educational needs and the fight against poverty as well as organisations promoting the Jewish faith.

In 2009/10 the trust had assets of £132,000 and an income of £293,000. Grants were made to organisations totalling £229,000.

Beneficiaries included: UK Friends of Nadar Deiah (£50,000); Ahavat Shalom (£45,000); UJIA (£30,000); Hale and District Hebrew Congregation (£24,000); JEM (£5,000); South Manchester Mikva Trust (£4,000); British Friends of Rinat Aharon (£2,500); Moracha LTD (£1,000); Chai Lifeline Cancer Trust

(£300); and Friends of the Sick (£100).

Applications

In writing to the correspondent. Trustees meet monthly.

Ellador Ltd

Jewish

£50,000 (2009/10)

Beneficial area

UK.

20 Ashtead Road, London E5 9BH
Tel: 020 7242 3580
Correspondent: Helen Schreiber, Trustee
Trustees: Joel Schreiber; Simon Schreiber; Helen Schreiber; Rivka Schreiber.
CC Number: 283202

Information available

Accounts were on file at the Charity Commission, but without a grants list.

The trust supports organisations benefiting Jewish people and also Jewish individuals, mainly for educational and religious purposes. In 2009/10 it had assets of £505,000 and an income of £79,000. Grants totalled £50,000, however, a list of beneficiaries was not included in the accounts.

Applications

In writing to the correspondent.

The Ellerdale Trust

Children

£179,000 (2009/10)

Beneficial area

Mainly Norfolk.

The Parlour, The High Street, Ketteringham, Wymondham, Norfolk NR18 9RU
Tel: 01603 813 340
Email: mary.adlard@btconnect.com
Correspondent: Mary Adlard, Director of Grant-making

Trustees: A T R Macfarlane; P C Kurthausen; S P Moores.
CC Number: 1073376

Information available

Accounts were available from the Charity Commission.

This trust was established to relieve poverty, distress or suffering in any part of the world particularly children who are disadvantaged or in need. In practice, the majority of funding is given to local and national organisations for projects based in Norfolk.

In 2009/10 the trust had assets of £6.6 million, which generated an income of £393,000. Grants were made to organisations totalling £179,000.

Beneficiaries included: Action for Kids and Rainbow Centre (£30,000 each); Break and East Anglian Children's Hospice (10,000 each); Fairbridge Merseyside (£7,000); Over The Wall (£5,000); Avon Wildlife Trust (£2,000); Brainwave and Whirlow Hall Farm Trust (£3,000 each); Scottish Spina Bifida (£2,000); CCHF (£1,000); and National Association of Toys and Leisure (£500).

Applications

In writing to the correspondent.

Common applicant mistakes

'Applications from outside of our area.'

The Ellinson Foundation Ltd

Jewish

£230,000 (2009/10)

Beneficial area

Worldwide.

Messrs Robson Laidler and Co, Fernwood House, Fernwood Road, Jesmond, Newcastle upon Tyne NE2 1TJ
Tel: 0191 281 8191
Correspondent: The Trustees
Trustees: A Ellinson; A Z Ellinson; U Ellinson.
CC Number: 252018

Information available

Full accounts were available from the Charity Commission.

The foundation supports hospitals, education and homelessness in the UK and overseas, usually with a Jewish-teaching aspect. The trust regularly supports organisations such as boarding schools for boys and girls teaching the Torah. In 2009/10 it had assets of £3.3 million and an income of £284,000. Grants totalled £230,000.

Beneficiaries included: Kesser Yeshua Refua – Israel (£120,000); British Friends of Rinat Aharon (£30,000); Three Pillars (£20,000); Kollel Ruach Chaim – Jerusalem (£12,000); Friends of Yeshivas Brisk and Baer Hatora Ltd (£5,000 each); Institute of Torah and Charity – A Light for Israel (£2,000); and BLBH Building Fund (£1,000).

Donations to institutions of less than £1,000 each amounted to £6,000.

Exclusions

No grants to individuals.

Applications

In writing to the correspondent. However, the trust generally supports the same organisations each year and unsolicited applications are not welcome.

The Edith Maud Ellis 1985 Charitable Trust

Quaker work and witness, international peace and conflict resolution, interfaith and ecumenical understanding, community development work in the UK and overseas, work with asylum seekers and refugees including internally displaced people

£41,000 (2009/10)

Beneficial area

UK, Ireland and overseas.

Virtuosity Executive Support, Prospect House, 6 Westgate, Thirsk, North Yorkshire YO7 1QS
Website: www. theedithmellischaritabletrust.org
Correspondent: Jackie Baily
Trustees: Jane Dawson; Michael Phipps; Nicholas Sims; Elizabeth Cave.
CC Number: 292835

Information available

Accounts were available at the Charity Commission and further information was supplied by the trust.

Edith M Ellis was a passionate Quaker and worked tirelessly for international peace and reconciliation. The Edith Ellis Charitable Trust was established by her for general charitable purposes. The Trust aims to give small grants to a broad range of Quaker and other UK registered charities, on governmental organisations or social enterprises with a turnover of less than £250,000.

Grants tend to be either: one-off; time limited in support; or are given in the form of seed money for startup projects. Usually small grants of up to £3,000 (in exceptional circumstances larger grants may be given) or interest free loans of up to £5,000 repayable over 5 years. Grants are usually made in the following categories:

- Quaker work and witness
- International peace and conflict resolution
- Interfaith and ecumenical understanding
- Community development work in the UK and overseas
- Work with asylum seekers and refugees including internally displaced people

In 2009/10 the trust had assets of £391,000 and an income of £139,000. Grants were made to 38 organisations totalling £41,000.

Beneficiaries included: Chilterns Area Quaker meeting (£10,000); Disaster E Committee (£3,000); Wyton Meeting House (£2,000); Afghanistan & Central Asian Association, Irish School of Ecumenics and SFAC

(£1,000 each); Off the Fence, Music Alive and International Rescue Committee (£500 each); and South Belfast Friends Meeting (£300).

Exclusions

In general the trust *does not* support the following:

- Core funding for organisations
- Individuals
- Infrastructure organisations
- Conferences or seminars
- Ongoing work
- General appeals
- Educational bursaries
- Humanitarian relief appeals
- Medical research and services
- Organisations with a turnover exceeding £250,000

Applications

Applications should be received by the end of January, May and September in order to be considered at one of the Trustee Meetings. It is sensible to get applications in well ahead of these dates. Late applicants will be considered in the next funding round. Successful applicants will be informed as soon as possible of the Trustees decision. If you have not heard within one calendar month of the relevant closing date you should assume you have been unsuccessful. Successful applicants will be encouraged to contribute to our website in a variety of ways and may be approached to showcase the work of the Trust. Applications should be made in writing to the correspondence address.

The Elmgrant Trust

General charitable purposes, education, arts, social sciences

£38,000 (2009/10)

Beneficial area

UK, with a preference for the South West of England.

The Elmhirst Centre, Dartington Hall, Totnes, Devon TQ9 6EL
Tel: 01803 863160

Correspondent: Angela Taylor, Secretary

Trustees: Marian Ash, Chair; Sophie Young; Paul Elmhirst; David Young; Mark Sharman.

CC Number: 313398

Information available

Accounts were on file at the Charity Commission.

This trust has general charitable purposes, but in particular aims to encourage local life through education, the arts and social sciences. Although there is a preference for South West England, grants to organisations are awarded throughout the UK.

In 2009/10 the trust had assets of £1.9 million and an income of £84,000. Grants totalling £38,000 were distributed including £2,000 in grants to individuals and the remainder paid to 60 organisations, distributed under the following categories:

Social sciences and scientific grants	30	£18,000
Arts and arts research grants	17	£10,000
Education and educational research grants	13	£4,000
Pension, donations and compassionate grant	7	£3,000

Beneficiaries included: Dartington International Summer School (£2,000); Kinergy and the Prison Phoenix Trust (£1,000 each); Centre for the Spoken Word (£750); Dawlish Gardens Trust, the Towersey Foundation and the Daisy Garland (£500 each); and Guild of St Lawrence (£250).

A further £2,000 was given in grants to five individuals.

Exclusions

The following are not supported:
▶ large scale UK organisations
▶ postgraduate study, overseas student grants, expeditions and travel and study projects overseas
▶ counselling courses
▶ renewed requests from the same (successful) applicant within a two-year period.

Applications

In writing to the correspondent, giving full financial details and, where possible, a letter of support. Initial telephone calls are welcome if advice is needed. There are no application forms. Guidelines are issued. An sae would be very helpful, although this is not obligatory. Currently, meetings are held three times a year in March, June and October. Applications need to be received one clear month prior to meeting.

Elshore Ltd

Jewish

£656,000 (2009/10)

Beneficial area

Worldwide.

c/o Michael Pasha & Co., 220 The Vale, Golders Green, London NW11 8SR

Tel: 020 8209 9880

Correspondent: Hersz M Lerner, Trustee

Trustees: Hersz M Lerner; Susan Yanofsky; Goldie Grahame.

CC Number: 287469

Information available

Accounts were on file at the Charity Commission, but without a list of grants.

This trust appears to make grants solely to Jewish organisations. In 2009/10 the trust held assets of £214,000 and it had an income of £442,000, mainly from donations. Grants were made totalling £656,000. A grants list was not included with the accounts for this year.

Further information has been unavailable since 1994/95, when grants to 40 beneficiaries totalled £178,000. The larger grants were £26,000 to Eminor Educational Centre and £20,000 to Cosmon Belz. Grants of £10,000 were given to 10 organisations, including Gur Trust and Marbe Torah Trust. Most other grants were less than £1,000, although some were for up to £8,000.

Applications

In writing to the correspondent.

The Vernon N Ely Charitable Trust

Christian, welfare, disability, sports, children and youth, overseas

£74,000 (2009/10)

Beneficial area

Worldwide, with a preference for London borough of Merton.

Grosvenor Gardens House, 35–37 Grosvenor Gardens, London SW1W 0BY

Tel: 020 7828 3156

Email: dph@helmores.co.uk

Correspondent: Derek Howorth, Trustee

Trustees: J S Moyle; D P Howorth; R S Main.

CC Number: 230033

Information available

Accounts were available from the Charity Commission, but without a list of grants.

The trust makes grants to Christian, welfare, disability, sports, children, youth and overseas charities. In 2009/10 the trust had assets of £1.5 million and an income of £44,000. Grants were made to organisations mainly in the London Borough of Merton, totalling £74,000. There was no list of beneficiaries with the accounts.

Previous beneficiaries included: Age Concern, Cardiac Risk in the Young, Samaritans, London Sports Forum for Disabled People, Christchurch URC, Polka Children's Theatre and Community Housing Therapy (£4,000 each); British Tennis Foundation (£1,750); and West Barnes Singers and Sobell Hospice (£500 each).

Exclusions

No grants to individuals.

Applications

In writing to the correspondent.

The Emerton-Christie Charity

Health, welfare, disability, arts

£57,000 (2009/10)

Beneficial area

UK.

c/o Cartmell Shepherd, Viaduct House, Carlisle CA3 8EZ
Tel: 01228 516666
Email: jmj@cartmells.co.uk
Correspondent: The Trustees
Trustees: Dr N A Walker; Dr C Mera-Nelson; Lt Col W D Niekirk; Dr S E Walker.
CC Number: 262837

Information available

Accounts were available from the Charity Commission.

The Emerton Charitable Settlement was established in 1971 by Maud Emerton, with additional funds subsequently added by Vera Bishop Emerton. In April 1996, it became the Emerton-Christie Charity following a merger with another trust, The Mrs C M S Christie Will Trust.

In 2009/10 it had assets totalling £2.3 million and an income of £65,000. Grants were made to organisations totalling £57,000.

Beneficiaries included: Raising the Roof – The Greenwich Toy Library (£5,000); Awards for Young Musicians – Pathways Appeal, Canine Partners, Friends of the Elderly, Hospice at Home, Music in Hospitals, Queen Alexandra Hospital Home, RoRo Project, the Life Centre and the Treehouse Trust (£3,000 each); and Women's Health Concern (£2,000).

Exclusions

Generally no grants to: individuals; religious organisations; restoration or extension of buildings; start-up costs; animal welfare and research; cultural heritage; or environmental projects.

Applications

In writing to the correspondent. A demonstration of need based on budgetary principles is required and applications will not be acknowledged unless accompanied by an sae. Trustees normally meet once a year in the autumn to select charities to benefit.

EMI Music Sound Foundation

Music education

£78,000 to organisations (2009/10)

Beneficial area

UK and Ireland.

EMI Music Sound Foundation, 27 Wrights Lane, London W8 5SW
Tel: 020 7795 7000
Fax: 020 7795 7296
Email: enquiries@ musicsoundfoundation.com
Website: www. musicsoundfoundation.com
Correspondent: Janie Orr, Chief Executive
Trustees: Eric Nicoli, Chair; Jim Beach; John Deacon; Paul Gambaccini; Leslie Hill; David Hughes; Rupert Perry; Tony Wadsworth; Christine Walter; Charles Ashcroft.
CC Number: 1104027

Information available

Accounts were on file at the Charity Commission.

The foundation's website states:

> EMI Music Sound Foundation is an independent music education charity, established in 1997 to celebrate the centenary of EMI Records and to improve young peoples' access to music education in the UK & Ireland.
>
> We are now the single largest sponsor of Specialist Performing Arts Colleges and have created vital bursaries at seven music colleges to assist music students in need of financial support. We have also helped hundreds of schools and individual students improve their access to music through the purchase or upgrade of instruments and music making equipment.

EMI Music Sound Foundation is the largest sponsor for Specialist Performing Arts Colleges in the UK. Together with the Specialist Schools and Academies Trust it has sponsored 36 schools to become Performing Arts Colleges. The foundation is the major sponsor in every case and still remains the largest single schools sponsor in this sector. Sponsorship has now been extended to Music Colleges as part of the foundation's ongoing support for specialist schools. All enquiries for EMI Music Sound Foundation sponsorship must be made through the Specialist Schools and Academies Trust (Bidding Support Department 0207 802 2300) in the first instance, as initial recommendations are taken from them.

Funds are distributed in the following ways:

Bursaries for music students in eight chosen colleges

Individual grants not exceeding £2,000

General Awards

EMI Music Sound Foundation is dedicated to the improvement of music education with a focus on youth. Preference is given to full-time students under the age of 25.

Support is given to:
- non-specialist schools to fund music education
- music students in full time education to fund instrument purchase
- music teachers to fund courses and training.

In 2007/8 the foundation offered each of its sponsored schools funding to support Key Stage 1 Music- 25 of which accepted the offer. After reviewing the sponsorship the trustees decided to continue their Key Stage 1 Music funding to schools which have been independently evaluated as having made a difference in this area.

Bursary Awards

Every year EMI MSF awards bursaries to students at seven music colleges in the UK and Ireland. These bursaries are distributed at each college's discretion, based on criteria provided by EMI MSF. For more information, please contact the colleges directly (Birmingham Conservatoire, Drumtech/Vocaltech/GuitarX – London, Institute of Popular Music – Liverpool, Irish World Music Centre – Limerick, Royal Scottish Academy of Music and Drama – Glasgow, Royal Academy – London and Royal

Welsh College of Music and Drama – Cardiff).

In 2009/10 the foundation had assets totalling £7.3 million and an income of £355,000. Grants totalled £203,000 of which £125,000 was awarded to individuals and £78,000 to organisations.

Grant beneficiaries include: University of Limerick (£7,300); Royal Welsh College of Music and Drama, Birmingham City University, National Children's Orchestra and Brighton Institute (£5,000 each).

Exclusions

No support for:

- applications from outside the United Kingdom and Ireland
- non-school based community groups, music therapy centres, etc.
- applications over £2,500.

Applications

On a form which can be downloaded from the foundation's website.

The Emilienne Charitable Trust

Medical, education

£96,000 (2009/10)

Beneficial area

Not defined.

Ashton House, 12 The Precinct, Winchester Road, Chandlers Ford, Eastleigh, Hampshire
Correspondent: M Howson-Green, Trustee
Trustees: M Howson-Green; B M Baxendale; Mrs M A Howson-Green.
CC Number: 327849

Information available

Accounts were available from the Charity Commission.

Set up in 1988, the trustees are particularly interested in support for charities involved in the treatment of addiction and in promoting education.

In 2009/10 it had assets of £620,000 and an income of £32,000. Grants to organisations totalled £96,000.

Beneficiaries of grants over £1,000 each were: Streetscene (£16,000); Wulfris Educational Foundation (£10,000); SCRATCH (£7,000); Wessex Cancer Trust (£4,000); Myositis Support Group (£2,000); and Great Oaks School (£1,500).

A further 57 grants of less than £1,000 were made to organisations totalling £38,000.

Applications

In writing to the correspondent.

The Emmandjay Charitable Trust

Social welfare, medicine, youth

£52,000 (2009/10)

Beneficial area

UK, with a special interest in West Yorkshire.

PO Box 60, Otley, West Yorkshire BD23 9DP
Correspondent: Mrs A E Bancroft, Administrator
Trustees: Mrs Sylvia Clegg; John A Clegg; Mrs S L Worthington; Mrs E A Riddell.
CC Number: 212279

Information available

Accounts were available from the Charity Commission, but without a list of grants.

The trust's annual report states:

> The trust gives most particularly to help disadvantaged people, but many different projects are supported – caring for the disabled and terminally ill, work with young people and medical research. The trust likes projects which reach a lot of people. The trustees are keen that grants are actually spent.

In 2009/10 the trust had assets of £1.8 million, which generated an income of £30,000. Grants totalled £52,000. A grants list was not included in the accounts, although it contained a breakdown of the areas in which it gives grants as follows:

Hospices, terminally ill, care	£16,000
Children's charities and care	£7,000
Special schemes, workshops, disabled	£7,000
Local community groups	£6,000
National charities	£6,000
Special overseas appeals	£3,000
Youth activities, schools	£2,000
Medical research	£2,000
Hospital appeals	£1,800
Homeless	£1,100
Social services, probation services	£700
Counselling services	£250

Previous beneficiaries have included: Abbeyfield Bradford Society, Bradford's War on Cancer, British Heart Foundation, British Red Cross, Cancer Support Centre, Caring for Life – Leeds, Marie Curie Cancer Centre, Research into Ageing and West Yorkshire Youth Association.

A substantial capital donation of £3 million to the MHA Care Group was approved during the year, which accounts for the reduced level of grant expenditure (£389,000 in 2007/08).

Exclusions

The trust does not pay debts, does not make grants to individual students, and does not respond to circulars. Grants are only given, via social services, to individuals if they live in Bradford.

Applications

In writing to the correspondent.

The Englefield Charitable Trust

General charitable purposes with a preference for local charities in Berkshire

£216,000 (2009/10)

Beneficial area

Worldwide. In practice, UK with a special interest in Berkshire.

The Quantocks, North Street, Theale, Reading RG7 5EX
Tel: 01189 323 582
Fax: 01189 323 748
Email: sandyreid@englefield.co.uk
Correspondent: Alexander S Reid, Secretary to the Trustees
Trustees: Sir William Benyon; James Shelley; Lady Elizabeth Benyon; Richard H R Benyon; Mrs Catherine Haig; Zoe Benyon.
CC Number: 258123

Information available

Accounts were available from the Charity Commission.

The trust was established in 1968 for general charitable purposes by the settlor Sir William Benyon. The trustees consider each application on its own merit and give preference to local causes in Berkshire.

In 2009/10 the trust had assets of £10.5 million and an income of £269,500. During the year the trustees approved donations of almost £216,000. 118 donations were made, varying in size from £200 to £5,000. Approximately 700 applications were received during the year and the trustees continued their policy of examining each one on its merits.

Beneficiaries included: Watermill Theatre (£10,000); Mary Hare Foundation and Museum of English Rural Life (£5,000 each); British Red Cross Berkshire Branch (£4,000); Bucklebury Memorial Hall and Lambeth Fund (£3,000 each); Kennet Opera, Kensworth Church, Morrell Room, Mortimer St John's C of E Infant School, Polish Catholic Mission Reading Parish, Thames Valley & Chiltern Air Ambulance and Volunteer Centre West Berkshire (£2,000 each); Heart Research UK, Heritage of London Trust Ltd, Highland Hospice, Swaziland Charitable Trust and West Berkshire District Council (£1,000 each); and Healing Hands India (£500).

Exclusions

Individual applications for study or travel are not considered.

Applications

In writing to the correspondent enclosing the latest accounts, stating the charity's registered number and the purpose for which the money is to be used. Applications are considered in March and September. Only applications going before the trustees will be acknowledged.

Common applicant mistakes

'Asking for too much funding.'

The English Schools' Football Association

Association football

£984,000 (2009)

Beneficial area

England.

4 Parker Court, Staffordshire Technology Park, Stafford, Staffordshire ST18 0WP
Tel: 01785 785970
Fax: 01785 256246
Email: dawn.howard@schoolsfa.com
Website: www.esfa.co.uk
Correspondent: Dawn Howard, Finance Officer
Trustees: Philip J Harding, Chair; Gerry Smith; Nigel Brown.
CC Number: 306003

Information available

Accounts and annual report were provided by the association.

Support is given for the mental, moral and physical development and improvement of schoolchildren and students through the medium of association football. Assistance is also given to teachers' charities and 'other such charitable purposes'.

In 2009 the association had an income of £977,000. Charitable expenditure for the year totalled £984,000, and was broken down as follows:

National Competitions	£143,000
Council and AGM	£42,000
Coaching Courses	£33,000

Exclusions

Grants are restricted to membership and teacher charities.

Applications

In writing to the correspondent. Check the association's website for up-to-date information on future deadlines.

The Epigoni Trust

Health and welfare, disability, homelessness, addiction, children who are disadvantaged, environment

£72,000 (2010)

Beneficial area

UK.

c/o Charities Aid Foundation, King's Hill, West Malling, Kent ME19 4TA
Tel: 01732 520028
Correspondent: Charles Peacock, Trustee
Trustees: C H Peacock; Mrs B Bond; A M Bond.
CC Number: 328700

Information available

Full accounts were on file at the Charity Commission.

The trust has common trustees with two other trusts, the Cleopatra Trust and the Dorus Trust (see separate entries) with which it also shares the same aims and policies. All three trusts are administered by Charities Aid Foundation. Generally the trusts support different organisations.

The trust makes grants in the following areas:

- mental health
- cancer welfare/education – not research
- diabetes
- physical disability – not research
- homelessness
- addiction
- children who are disadvantaged.

There is also some preference for environmental causes. It only gives grants for specific projects and does not give grants for running costs or general appeals. Support is only given to national projects, not local areas or initiatives.

In 2010 the trust had an income of £113,000 and assets of £3.3 million. It made 7 grants totalling £72,000.

Beneficiaries were: Mondo Challenge Foundation (£17,000); Pallant House Gallery (£15,000); Breakthrough

(£13,800); Fairbridge (£7,000); Wheelyboat Trust (£6,000); Chichester Festival Theatre- Create and Children on the Edge (£5,000 each); and Snowdrop Trust (£3,000).

Exclusions

No grants to individuals, expeditions, research, scholarships, charities with a local focus, local branches of UK charities or towards running costs.

Applications

This trust no longer accepts applications.

The Equity Trust Fund

Theatre

£54,000 (2009/10)

Beneficial area

UK.

222 Africa House, 64 Kingsway, London WC2B 6AH
Tel: 020 7404 6041
Correspondent: Keith Carter, Secretary
Trustees: Colin Baker; Glen Barnham; James Bolam; Annie Bright; Jo Cameron Brown; Robin Browne; Oliver Ford Davies; Graham Hamilton; Frank Hitchman; Barbara Hyslop; Milton Johns; Harry Landis; Ian McGarry; Frederick Pyne; Gillian Raine; Jean Rogers; John Rubinstein; Rosalind Shanks; Ian Talbot; Josephine Tewson; Jeffry Wickham; Frank Williams; Johnny Worthy; Glen Barnham; Jo Cameron Brown; Caroline Smith.
CC Number: 328103

Information available

Accounts were available from the Charity Commission.

The charity is a benevolent fund for professional performers and stage managers and their dependants. It offers help with welfare rights, gives free debt counselling and information and can offer financial assistance to those in genuine need. It also has an education fund to help members of the profession with further training provided they have at least 10 years' professional adult experience. It also

makes grants and loans to professional theatres or theatre companies.

In 2009/10 the trust had assets of £8.1 million and an income of £350,000, mostly from investment income. Grants were made to six organisations totalling £54,000.

Beneficiaries were: Dancers' Career Development (£40,000); Lyric Theatre Hammersmith and Northern Actors Centre (£4,000 each); Attic Theatre (£2,000); High Tide Festival (£3,000); and Stone Crabs (£1,000).

Exclusions

No grants to non-professional performers, drama students, non-professional theatre companies, multi-arts venues, community projects or projects with no connection to the professional theatre.

Applications

In the first instance please call the office to ascertain if the application is relevant. Failing that, submit a brief letter outlining the application. A trustee meeting takes place about every six to eight weeks, please ring for precise dates. Applications are required at least two weeks beforehand.

The Ericson Trust

Older people, community including the arts, offender rehabilitation and research, refugees, the environment, the developing world

Around £50,000

Beneficial area

UK, developing countries, Eastern and Central Europe.

Flat 2, 53 Carleton Road, London N7 0ET
Email: claudia.cotton@googlemail.com
Correspondent: The Trustees
Trustees: R C Cotton; V J Barrow; A M C Cotton.

CC Number: 219762

Information available

Accounts had been received at the Charity Commission but were unavailable to view.

The trust provides grants to previously supported organisations in the following fields: (a) older people; (b) community projects/local interest groups, including arts; (c) prisons, prison reform, mentoring projects, as well as research in this area; (d) refugees; (e) mental health; (f) environmental projects and research; and (g) aid to developing countries provided by a UK-registered charity.

In 2009/10 the trust had an income of £25,000 and a total expenditure of £55,000. Further information was not available.

Previous beneficiaries have included: Action on Elder Abuse, Anti-Slavery International, Ashram International, Bhopal Medical Appeal, Headway East London, Howard League for Penal Reform, the Koestler Trust, Minority Rights Group, Psychiatric Rehabilitation Association, Quaker Social Action, the Rainforest Foundation, the Relatives and Residents Association, Tools for Self Reliance and the Umalini Mary Brahma Charitable Trust.

Exclusions

No grants to individuals or to non-registered charities. Applications from the following areas are generally not considered unless closely connected with one of the above: children's and young people's clubs, centres and so on; schools; charities dealing with illness or disability (except psychiatric); or religious institutions, except in their social projects.

Applications

Unsolicited applications cannot be considered as the trust has no funds available. The correspondent stated:

> We are increasing worried by the waste of applicants' resources when they send expensive brochures at a time when we are unable to consider any new appeals and have, indeed, reduced some of our long standing grants due to the bad economic situation. It is particularly sad when we receive requests from small charities in Africa and Asia.

The Esfandi Charitable Foundation

Jewish

£235,000 (2009/10)

Beneficial area

UK and overseas.

36 Park Street, London W1K 2JE
Correspondent: J Esfandi, Trustee
Trustees: J Esfandi; Mrs D Esfandi.
CC Number: 1103095

Information available

Accounts were available from the Charity Commission.

Set up in 2004, in 2009/10 the foundation had an income of £257,000 and made grants totalling £235,000. The largest donation was made to Norwood totalling £55,000 (£110,000 in 2007/08).

Other beneficiaries included: Jewish Care (£25,000); Community Security Trust (£25,000); WST Charity LTD (£17,000); Chief Rabbinate Trust (£15,000); Jewish Community Secondary School Trust (£13,000); Ahavat Shaloh Charity Fund (£11,000); Royal National Theatre (£10,000); UK Friends of Association for Wellbeing of Israel's Soldiers (£5,000); European Council of Jewish Communities (£2,500); Achisomoch (£2,000); and the Chicken Soup Shelter, the Variety Club Children's Charity and JABE (£1,000 each).

Donations of £1,000 or less totalled £5,000.

Applications

In writing to the correspondent.

The Essex Youth Trust

Youth, education of people under 25

£351,000 (2009/10)

Beneficial area

Essex.

Gepp and Sons, 58 New London Road, Chelmsford, Essex CM2 0PA
Tel: 01245 493939
Fax: 01245 493940
Email: douglas-hughesj@gepp.co.uk
Correspondent: J P Douglas-Hughes, Clerk
Trustees: Richard Wenley; Julien Courtauld; Michael Dyer; Revd Duncan Green; William David Robson; Lady Julia Denison-Smith; Claire Coltwell; Michael Biegel; Mrs Julie Rogers.
CC Number: 225768

Information available

Accounts were available from the Charity Commission.

The Essex Youth Trust comprises four charities administered under a scheme dated 24 February 1993. The four charities are Essex Home School for Boys, The Charity of George Stacey Gibson, The Charity of George Cleveley and The Charity of Adelia Joyce Snelgrove.

The trust's objectives are the advancement of education for people under the age of 25 who are in need of assistance. Preference is given to those who are in need owing to 'being temporarily or permanently deprived of normal parental care or who are otherwise disadvantaged'.

This information and the following quote are taken from the trustees' 2011 report and financial statements:

> The trustees award grants which favour organisations which develop young people's physical, mental and spiritual capacities through active participation in sports and indoor and outdoor activities. As a result they are particularly supportive of youth clubs and other organisations which provide facilities for young people to take active part in an assortment of activities as well as single activity organisations.

In 2009/10 the trust had assets of £7 million and an income of £421,000. Grants paid to 45 organisations in the year totalled £351,000.

Beneficiaries included: Cirdan Sailing Trust (£57,000 in three grants); Stubbers Adventure Centre (£45,000); Essex Boys' and Girls' Clubs (£28,000 in two grants); North Avenue Youth Centre (£19,000 in three grants); Solid (£15,000); St Mark's College (£10,000); the Ark Family Resource

Centre (£8,000); Frenford Clubs and Maldon Essex Mind (£5,000 each); Roots in the River (£4,000); Beyond Youth (£3,000); Motorvations Project (£2,000); Hope UK (£1,000); and Colchester Institute (£750).

Exclusions

No grants to individuals.

Applications

On a form available from the correspondent. The trustees meet on a quarterly basis.

Common applicant mistakes

'Wrong location; applications made by individuals.'

The Estelle Trust

Overseas aid

£118,000 (2009/10)

Beneficial area

Not defined, but in practice Zambia.

Fisher Phillips, 170 Finchley Road, London NW3 6BP
Tel: 0207 483 6100
Correspondent: Ged Ornstein, Trustee
Trustees: N AN E Farrow; G R Ornstein; K-M Britain; S Farrow; D Wise.
CC Number: 1101299

Information available

Accounts were available from the Charity Commission.

Registered in December 2003, in 2009/10 the trust had assets of £1.4 million and an income of £132,000, the majority of which came from voluntary income (£103,000). Grants totalled £118,000.

Beneficiaries included: Wind pump programme in Africa (£62,000); Chipembele Wildlife Education Trust (£18,000); Arulussa School Development (£11,000); Lorry (£9,000); Queen's College Cambridge (£7,000); International Rescue Committee (£5,000); Action Age (£1,000); Kids Company (£1,000); Prostate Research Campaign UK (£250); and the Sabre Charitable Trust (£100).

Applications

In writing to the correspondent.

The Alan Evans Memorial Trust

Preservation, conservation

£77,000 (2009/10)

Beneficial area

UK.

Coutts & Co., Trustee Department, 440 Strand, London WC2R 0QS
Tel: 020 7753 1000
Correspondent: The Trust Manager
Trustees: Coutts & Co.; David Halfhead; Deirdre Moss.
CC Number: 326263

Information available

Accounts were available from the Charity Commission, but without a list of grants.

The objects of the trust are 'to promote the permanent preservation, for the benefit of the nation, of lands and tenements (including buildings) of beauty or historic interest and as regards land, the preservation (so far as practicable) of the natural aspect, features and animal and plant life'.

In 2009/10 the trust had assets of £1.6 million and an income of £96,000. Grants ranged from £250 to £1,000 and were given to 94 organisations totalling £77,000. A list of beneficiaries was not available.

Previous beneficiaries include: English Hedgerow Trust, Landmark Trust, Zoological Society of London, St Wilfrid's Church – Leeds, Thatcham Charity, Cathedral Church of the Holy Spirit – Guildford, Peterborough Cathedral Development and Preservation Trust, Wells Cathedral – Somerset, Lincoln Cathedral and the Church of Our Lord, St Mary and St Germaine – Selby Abbey.

Exclusions

No grants to individuals or for management or running expenses, although favourable consideration is given in respect of the purchase of land and restoration of buildings. Grants are given to registered charities only. General appeals will not be acknowledged.

Applications

There is no formal application form, but appeals should be made in writing to the correspondent, stating why the funds are required, what funds have been promised from other sources (for example, English Heritage) and the amount outstanding. The trust has also stated previously that it would be helpful when making applications to provide a photograph of the project. The trustees normally meet four times a year, although in urgent cases decisions can be made between meetings.

Sir John Evelyn's Charity

Relief of the poor

£60,000 to organisations (2010)

Beneficial area

Ancient parishes of St Nicholas Deptford and St Luke Deptford.

Clerk's Office, Armada Court Hall, 21 McMillan Street, Deptford, London SE8 3EZ
Tel: 020 8694 8953
Correspondent: Mrs Colette A Saunders
Trustees: Bridget Perry, Chair; Revd J K Lucas; Jasmine Barnett; Kay Ingledew; Mrs J Miller; Cllr M O'Mara; Cllr Margaret Mythen.
CC Number: 225707

Information available

Accounts were available from the Charity Commission.

Originally registered in 1876, the charity received a small boost to its endowment with the amalgamation of 19 small charities under a Charity Commission scheme of 1992. It operates within the ancient parishes of St Nicholas and St Luke in Deptford.

The 2010 trustees report states:

> The Charity has continued to support two vital community projects in the area namely, the Armada Community Project and the 190 Centre. This has enabled the Armada Community Project to employ an administrator who is able to provide additional support to the Charity's beneficiaries. By supporting this project, the Charity gives residents in the area of benefit access to projects which contribute to individual lifelong learning skills. The 190 Centre also provides support to residents in the area, delivering welfare projects, advice and guidance as well as a wide range of social activities.

In 2010 the trust had assets of £2.7 million and an income of over £56,000. Grants were made to individuals (£365) and four organisations and totalled over £60,000. Beneficiary organisations included: Armada Community project (£42,000); Henrietta and Hughes Field Young People's Project (£13,000); Evelyn 190 Centre (£5,000); and St Nicholas and St Luke's (£400).

Applications

In writing to the correspondent.

The Eventhall Family Charitable Trust

General

£204,000 (2009/10)

Beneficial area

Preference for North West England.

PO Box 490, Altrincham WA14 22T
Correspondent: The Trustees
Trustees: Julia Eventhall; David Eventhall.
CC Number: 803178

Information available

Accounts were available from the Charity Commission, but without a list of grants.

In 2009/10 the trust had assets of £2.9 million, which generated an income of £124,000. Grants were made to 60 organisations totalling £204,000. A list of the beneficiaries was not provided with the accounts.

Previous beneficiaries have included: Aish Hatorah, ChildLine, Clitheroe Wolves Football Club, Community Security Trust, Greibach Memorial, Guide Dogs for the Blind, Heathlands Village, International Wildlife Coalition, JJCT, MB Foundation Charity, Only Foals and Horses Sanctuary, Red Nose Day, RNLI, Sale Ladies Society, Shelter and South Manchester Synagogue.

Exclusions
No grants to students.

Applications
In writing to the correspondent. Please note, however, previous research highlighted that the trust stated it only has a very limited amount of funds available. Telephone calls are not accepted by the trust. Trustees meet monthly to consider grants. A pre-addressed envelope is appreciated (stamp not necessary). Unsuccessful applicants will not receive a reply.

The Beryl Evetts and Robert Luff Animal Welfare Trust

Animal welfare
£137,000 (2009/10)

Beneficial area
UK.

294 Earls Court Road, London SW5 9BB
Correspondent: The Administrator
Trustees: Sir R Johnson; Revd M Tomlinson; J Tomlinson; R P J Price; B Nicholson; Lady Johnson; G Favot; M Condon.
CC Number: 283944

Information available
Full accounts were available from the Charity Commission website.

The principal objective of the trust is the funding of veterinary research and the care and welfare of animals. It appears to make substantial commitments to a few organisations over several years, whether to build up capital funds or to establish

fellowships. The trust gives priority to research projects and bursaries. In practice, the trust supports the same beneficiaries each year.

In 2009/10 the trust had assets of £1 million, which generated an income of £45,000. Grants were made to 12 organisations totalling £137,000.

Grants went to: Animal Welfare Trust (£65,000); Royal Veterinary College (£60,000); Blue Cross (£2,500); and Greek Animal Welfare Trust, Battersea Dogs Home, St Tiggy Winkles, Brooke Hospitals for Animals, Mayhew Animal Home, Songbird Survival, Kent Wildlife Trust, Animal Samaritan and the Cats (£1,000 each).

Applications
The trust states: 'No applications, thank you.' The trust gives grants to the same beneficiaries each year and funds are often allocated two years in advance.

The Exilarch's Foundation

General, Jewish, education
£2.8 million (2010)

Beneficial area
Mainly UK.

4 Carlos Place, Mayfair, London W1K 3AW
Tel: 020 7399 0850
Correspondent: Naim Dangoor, Trustee
Trustees: Naim Dangoor; David Dangoor; Elie Dangoor; Robert Dangoor; Michael Dangoor.
CC Number: 275919

Information available
Information was available at the Charity Commission.

The trust has the following charitable aims for the next three years:

1   **Iraq:** To build up and hold a designated reserve of £10 million for the specific purpose of assisting the setting up of educational and religious institutions in a future re-established Jewish community in

Iraq. Once the position and security of that country has been stabilised it is anticipated that some Jews may choose to live in Iraq when they will be free to pursue their religious faith without fear of persecution and discrimination. These funds will be used to help rebuild synagogues and communal buildings, and to assist in providing Jewish schools in Iraq as and when the community's need arises, and when it becomes possible for Jews to again live there.

2   **Monotheism:** In 2010 a report was published jointly with Birkbeck college that contained five key recommendations on the feasibility of creating an institute for ethical monotheism. The trust intends to continue this work.

3   **Grants for educational institutions:** Funding has been sustained through 2010 with academic results continuing to improve at Westminster Academy, which the foundation continues to support.

4   **Other major grants and applications:** grants of £1.1 million to Cancer Research UK and £1.05 million to Age UK were made.

Alongside continuing to support other applications the charity wishes to continue to focus its charitable activities on the above areas over the next three years.

In 2010 the foundation had assets of £57 million, £10 million of which is specifically designated towards the plans for Iraq. Income totalled £6.3 million and grants were made to the value of £2.8 million, broken down as follows:

Social welfare	£2.3 million
Education	£401,000
The arts	£100,000

Other beneficiaries included: Westminster Academy (£306,000); Jewish Museum (£100,000); Weizmann UK (£25,000); and Jewish Association for Business Ethics (£11,000).

Applications
The trust stated that it does not respond to unsolicited applications for grants.

Extonglen Limited

Orthodox Jewish

£1.1 million (2009)

Beneficial area

UK.

New Burlington House, 1075 Finchley Road, London NW11 0PU
Tel: 020 8731 0777
Email: ml@rowdeal.com
Correspondent: C Levine
Trustees: M Levine; Mrs C Levine; I Katzenberg.
CC Number: 286230

Information available

Latest accounts available at the Charity Commission were for 2009.

Registered with the Charity Commission in January 1983, this trust accepts applications from representatives of Orthodox Jewish charities. The trust has a particular focus on education and the relief of poverty.

The latest accounts available were for 2009. The trust had assets of £13 million and an income of £511,000. Grants totalled over £1 million.

No further information concerning grants was available but previous beneficiaries have included: Kol Halashon Education Programme (£470,000); Ahavas Chesed (£95,000); Pikuach Nefesh (£50,000); Kupath Gemach Chaim Bechesed Viznitz Trust (£40,000); British Friends of Nishmat Yisrael (£12,000); and Children's Town Charity (£3,600).

Applications

In writing to the correspondent.

The Fairway Trust

General

£30,000 (2009/10)

Beneficial area

UK and worldwide.

The Gate House, Coombe Wood Road, Kingston-upon-Thames, Surrey KT2 7JY
Correspondent: Mrs J Grimstone, Trustee
Trustees: Janet Grimstone; Ms K V M Suenson-Taylor.
CC Number: 272227

Information available

Accounts were available from the Charity Commission.

The trust's accounts state it will continue support for charities engaged in the fields of education, religion and social welfare.

In 2009/10 the trust an income almost entirely from donations of £36,000, most of which was given in grants. The largest grant was given to Family Education Trust (£20,000).

Other beneficiaries were: Clubs for Young People Northern Ireland and the Welsh National Opera (£2,000 each); Prayer Book Society (£1,250); and Sight Savers, Kids Out, Thames Philharmonic Choir and the Bishop of Wakefield (£1,000 each).

Exclusions

No grants to medical charities.

Applications

The trustees have an established list of charities which they support on a regular basis. Unsolicited applications are not therefore considered.

Famos Foundation Trust

Jewish

£129,000 (2009/10)

Beneficial area

UK and overseas.

4 Hanover Gardens, Salford, Greater Manchester M7 4FQ
Tel: 0161 740 5735
Correspondent: Rabbi S M Kupetz, Trustee
Trustees: Rabbi S M Kupetz; Mrs F Kupetz; I D Kupetz; J S Kupetz.
CC Number: 271211

Information available

Accounts were on file at the Charity Commission.

The trust supports a wide range of Jewish organisations, including those concerned with education and the relief of poverty. Many grants are recurrent and are of up to £5,000 each.

In 2009/10 the trust had assets of £1.7 million and an income of £212,000. Grants totalled £129,000, broken down into the following categories:

Medical	£10,000
Education	£55,000
Relief of Poverty	£49,000
Places of Worship	£15,000

Exclusions

No grants to individuals.

Applications

In writing to the correspondent, at any time. The trust does not accept telephone enquiries.

The Lord Faringdon Charitable Trust

Medical, educational, heritage, social welfare, the arts and sciences, recreation and general

£137,000 (2009/10)

Beneficial area

UK.

The Estate Office, Buscot Park, Oxfordshire SN7 8BU
Tel: 01367 240786
Email: estbuscot@aol.com
Correspondent: Mrs S L Lander, Secretary to the Trustees
Trustees: A D A W Forbes; Hon. J H Henderson; Mrs S J Maitland Robinson; B Cazenove.
CC Number: 1084690

Information available

Accounts were available from the Charity Commission.

This trust was formed in 2000 by the amalgamation of the Lord Faringdon First and Second trusts. It supports:

- educational objectives
- hospitals and the provision of medical treatment for the sick
- purchase of antiques and artistic objects for museums and collections that have public access
- care and assistance of people who are elderly or infirm
- development and assistance of arts and sciences, physical recreation and drama
- research into matters of public interest
- relief of poverty
- support of matters of public interest
- maintaining and improving the Faringdon Collection.

In 2009/10 it had assets of £6.3 million and an income of £178,500. Grants to 41 organisations totalled £137,000.

Beneficiaries included: Institute of Cancer Research (£20,000); Autism Speaks and National Trust Buscot C & M Fund (£10,000 each); Royal Horticultural Society, Oxford Playhouse, Oxford Philomusica, Royal Choral Society, Young Musicians Symphony Orchestra, Ashmolean Museum and The Hunt Servants Fund (£5,000 each); Lifelites and Campaign for Cirencester Parish Church (£2,500 each); and Furniture Recycling Project, Living Memory Historical Museum, Cirencester Cyber Cafe, Noah's Ark Children's Venture, Swindon Counselling Service and Asthma Relief (£1,000 each).

Exclusions

No grants to individuals, just to registered charities.

Applications

In writing to the correspondent.

Samuel William Farmer's Trust

Education, health, social welfare

£57,000 (2010)

Beneficial area

Mainly Wiltshire.

71 High Street, Market Lavington, Devizes, Wiltshire SN10 4AG
Tel: 01380 813299
Correspondent: Mrs M Linden-Fermor, Secretary
Trustees: P G Fox-Andrews, Chair; Mrs J A Liddiard; W J Rendell; B J Waight; C K Brockis.
CC Number: 258459

Information available

Accounts were available from the Charity Commission.

The trust was established in 1928 for: the benefit of poor people who through ill health or old age are unable to earn their own livelihood; for educational purposes; and for the benefit of hospitals, nursing and convalescent homes or other similar objects. The trustees apply a modern interpretation of these aims when assessing applications, supporting both individuals and organisations.

In 2010 the trust had assets of £2.2 million and an income of £75,000. 'Special' grants for this year totalled £51,000. An additional £6,000 was distributed in 'annual' grants to Royal Agricultural Benevolent Institution and Independent Age (£3,000 each). The sum of £240 went to individuals.

Special grants went to 29 organisations. Beneficiaries included: Wiltshire Air ambulance Appeal (£8,000); Great Bedwyn CE Primary School (£5,600); Farming & Countryside Education and Prospect Hospice (£2,500 each); Drews Pond Wood project, Greatwood and The Guide Dogs for the Blind Association (£2,000 each); and South Wiltshire Intervention for Trauma, Strongbones Children's Charitable Trust and SWAN Advocacy Network (£1,000 each).

Exclusions

No grants to students, or for schools and colleges, endowments, inner-city welfare or housing.

Applications

In writing to the correspondent. Trustees meet half-yearly.

Farthing Trust

Christian, general

£194,000 to organisations and individuals (2009/10)

Beneficial area

UK and overseas.

PO Box 277, Cambridge CB7 9DE
Correspondent: The Trustees
Trustees: C H Martin; Mrs E Martin; Mrs J Martin; Mrs A White.
CC Number: 268066

Information available

Accounts were on file at the Charity Commission.

This trust was established to meet charitable causes in any area of the world. It has wide charitable objectives but the main focus is on the advancement of religion, education, health and human rights and the reconciliation and promotion of religious and racial harmony, equality and diversity.

In 2009/10 the trust had assets of £3.1 million and an income of £85,000. Grants were made totalling £194,000, and were broken down as follows:

Education – UK and overseas	£37,000
UK churches	£35,000
UK Christian causes	£32,000
UK general charities	£2,500
Local grants	£3,700
Christ's servants	£25,000
Individuals in need – UK and overseas	£16,000
Overseas Christian causes	£38,000
Overseas general charities	£4,000

Applications

Applications and enquiries should be made in writing to the correspondent. Applicants, and any others requesting information, will only receive a response if an sae is enclosed. Most beneficiaries are known to the trustees personally or through their acquaintances, though applications from other organisations are considered.

The Fawcett Charitable Trust

Disability

£60,000 (2008/9)

Beneficial area

UK with a preference for Hampshire and West Sussex.

10 Helena Close, Portslade, Brighton
Correspondent: Julie Fawcett
Trustees: Johanna Fawcett; Roger Fawcett.
CC Number: 1013167

Information available

Latest accounts received at the Charity Commission were for 2008/9.

The trust was set up in 1991 by Derek and Frances Fawcett with an endowment of shares in their company with an initial value of £1.6 million.

According to the trust, it supports work aimed at increasing the quality of life of people with disabilities by facilitating and providing recreation opportunities. Preference is normally given to organisations and projects located in Hampshire and West Sussex.

The latest accounts available for this trust were for 2008/9. During this year the trust had an income of £24,000 and a total expenditure of £64,000. A breakdown of expenditure was not available but based upon previous years the grants total was likely to be approximately £60,000.

Previous beneficiaries have included: Chichester Harbour Trust (£75,000); RYA Sailability (£65,000); Naomi House (£50,000); Wessex Children's Hospice (£30,000); St Wilfred's Hospice (£25,000); NSPCC (£20,000); Portsmouth Cathedral (£15,000); Sailing Academy and Jubilee Sailing Trust (£5,000 each); and Bikeability (£1,000)

Exclusions

Large national charities are excluded as a rule.

Applications

In writing to the correspondent.

The John Feeney Charitable Bequest

Arts, heritage and open spaces

£83,000 (2009)

Beneficial area

Birmingham.

55 Wychall Lane, Kings Norton, Birmingham B38 8TB
Tel: 0121 624 3865
Email: secretary@feeneytrust.org.uk
Correspondent: Ms P J Byatt, Secretary
Trustees: C R King-Farlow; D M P Lea; S J Lloyd; Mrs M F Lloyd; H B Carslake; J R L Smith; M S Darby; Mrs S R Wright; William J E Southall; Ms Anouk Perinpanayagam.
CC Number: 214486

Information available

Accounts were available from the Charity Commission.

The trust was set up in 1907 when John Feeney directed that one tenth of his residue estate be invested and the income used for the benefit of public charities in the city of Birmingham, for the promotion and cultivation of art in the city and for the acquisition and maintenance of parks, recreation grounds or open spaces in or near the city.

In 2009 the charity had assets of £1.5 million and an income of £65,000. There were 21 grants made to organisations totalling £83,000, which are broken down as follows:

Special projects	3	£32,000
Arts	6	£23,000
Music	7	£15,000
Heritage and open spaces	4	£9,500
General	4	£3,500

Beneficiaries of grants included: City of Birmingham Symphony Orchestra (£15,000); Elmhurst Ballet School – Scholarship fund (£10,000); Midlands Arts Centre (£7,500); Ackers Adventure (£3,500); Royal Birmingham Society of Artists and Ironbridge Gorge Museum Trust (£2,000 each); Birmingham Botanical Gardens, Theodora Children's Trust and Ikon Gallery (£1,000 each); and Cruse Bereavement (£500).

Exclusions

Applications will not be accepted: from, or on behalf of, individuals; which do not directly benefit the Birmingham area or Birmingham charitable organisations; which could be considered as political or denominational.

Additionally, applications from large national charities, even with a Birmingham base, are unlikely to succeed.

Applications

Application forms are now available from the trust's website. When the form is completed please **post** or **email** it with a supporting letter and other documents to the correspondent.

Common applicant mistakes

'Not keeping to the terms set out on our website. Providing too much irrelevant material (or, less often, not enough!).'

The A M Fenton Trust

General

£129,000 (2010)

Beneficial area

UK, preference for North Yorkshire, and overseas.

14 Beech Grove, Harrogate, North Yorkshire HG2 0EX
Tel: 01423 504442
Correspondent: James Fenton, Trustee
Trustees: J L Fenton; C M Fenton.
CC Number: 270353

Information available

Accounts were obtained from the Charity Commission website.

The trust was created by Alexander Miller Fenton in 1975. After his death in 1977, the residue of his estate was transferred to the trust which is established for general charitable purposes.

In 2010 the trust had assets of £3.9 million, an income of £117,000, and made grants totalling £129,000.

Beneficiaries included: Yorkshire County Cricket Club Charitable Youth Trust (£20,000); Hipperholme Grammar School (£10,000); Dewsbury League of Friendship (£8,000); Cleckheaton Central Methodist Church (£7,500); Tweed Foundation (£4,000); Kenmore Leonard Cheshire Disability and St John of Jerusalem Eye Hospital (£2,500 each); Ghurka Welfare Trust and Disability Action Yorkshire (£2,000 each); Age Concern Knaresborough and Crime Stoppers Trust (£1,000).

Exclusions
The trust is unlikely to support local appeals, unless they are close to where the trust is based.

Applications
In writing to the correspondent.

Elizabeth Ferguson Charitable Trust Fund

Children, medical research, health, hospices
Around £200,000 to organisations and individuals

Beneficial area
UK, with some interest in Scotland.

c/o 27 Peregrine Crescent, Droylsden, Manchester M43 7TA
Correspondent: The Trustees
Trustees: Sir Alex Ferguson; Cathy Ferguson; Huw Roberts; Ted Way; Les Dalgarno; Paul Hardman; Jason Ferguson.
SC Number: SC026240

Information available
Limited information was available from the Office of the Scottish Charity Regulator.

This trust was created by Sir Alex Ferguson in 1998 in memory of his

mother. It supports a range of children's and medical charities. Grants range from £250 to £10,000 and can be recurrent. Various high-profile events have contributed to the trust's income in recent years. Grants are distributed in the areas where the income is raised.

In 2009/10 the trust had an income of £260,000. Grants totalled around £200,000.

Charities supported by the founder in his home town of Govan will continue to be supported through the trust. Recent beneficiaries have included the Govan Initiative and Harmony Row Boys' Club.

Exclusions
Non-registered charities and individuals are not supported. The trust does not make grants overseas.

Applications
An application form and guidelines should be requested in writing from the correspondent. The committee meets to consider grants at the end of January and July. Applications should be received by December and June respectively.

The Fidelio Charitable Trust

The arts, in particular the dramatic and operatic arts, music, speech and dance
£68,000 to institutions (2009/10)

Beneficial area
UK.

2nd Floor, 20–22 Stukeley Street, London WC2B 5LR
Email: fidelio@act.eu.com
Correspondent: Tony Wingate, Trustee
Trustees: J R S Boas; A J Wingate; J M Wingate.
CC Number: 1112508

Information available
Accounts were available from the Charity Commission.

In 2009/10 the trust had assets of £1.3 million and an income of £21,000. Grants were made to institutions totalling £68,000.

Beneficiaries included: Royal Academy of Music, Shakespeare's Globe and Wigmore Hall Productions (£5,000 each); National Centre Early Music (£4,000); Presteigne Festival (£3,000); Ark Schools (£2,500); Barbican Centre Trust, Birmingham Opera Co, Hills Road 6th Form College, Joined Up Thinking and Oxford Lieder Limited (£2,000 each); SWAYED (£1,500); Actors' Centre (£800); and IV Folk Dance Festival (£400).

Exclusions
Applications from **individuals or groups** seeking support for themselves will **not** be accepted.

Applications
Applications forms are available from the trust's website, with full details on how to apply.

The Doris Field Charitable Trust

General
£321,000 (2009/10)

Beneficial area
UK, with a preference for Oxfordshire.

c/o Morgan Cole, Buxton Court, 3 West Way, Oxford OX2 0SZ
Tel: 01865 262183
Correspondent: The Trustees
Trustees: N A Harper; J Cole; Mrs W Church.
CC Number: 328687

Information available
Accounts were available from the Charity Commission.

One-off and recurrent grants are given to large UK organisations and small local projects for a wide variety of causes. The trust states that it favours playgroups and local causes in Oxfordshire. In 2009/10 the trust had assets of £7.8 million and an income of £294, 000. Grants were made totalling £321,000 to 188 organisations.

Grants included those made to: OCCTOPUS (£50,000); Cancer Research UK and the Thames Valley Air Ambulance Trust (£30,000 each); Maggie's Centres and Oxford Radcliffe Hospitals Charitable Trust (£5,000 each); the Mulberry Bush Organisation and Oxfordshire Netball (£2,500 each); Oxford Welsh Male Voice Choir and United Response (£2,000 each); Appleton with Eaton Parish Council and Footsteps Foundation (£1,000 each); and Charlbury Corner House, Didcot Cricket Club and Opera Anywhere (£500 each).

Exclusions

It is unlikely that grants would be made for overseas projects or to individuals for higher education.

Applications

On a form available from the correspondent. Applications are considered three times a year or as and when necessary.

Common applicant mistakes

'Asking for salaries, training and higher education costs.'

The Bluff Field Charitable Trust

General

Around £1,000 (2010)

Beneficial area

UK.

8 The Little Boltons, London SW10 9LP
Tel: 020 7373 1863
Email: bfct@btinternet.com
Correspondent: Peter Field, Trustee
Trustees: Peter Field; Sonia Field; Stanley Salter.
CC Number: 1057992

Information available

Accounts were on file at the Charity Commission.

Established in 1996, in 2010 this trust had an income of just £44 and an expenditure of £1,000. This was

similar to last year which indicates that the trust may be inactive or winding down. In previous years it has received substantial income from donations and Gift Aid.

Previous beneficiaries have included Emmanuel Church Billericay, Leukaemia Research Fund, Risk Waters' World Trade Centre UK Appeal, St George's Hospital Medical School and Wigmore Hall Trust.

Applications

In writing to the correspondent.

Dixie Rose Findlay Charitable Trust

Children, seafarers, blindness and multiple sclerosis

£151,000 (2005/06)

Beneficial area

UK.

HSBC Trust Co. (UK) Ltd, 10th Floor, Norwich House, Nelson Gate, Commercial Road, Southampton SO15 1GX
Tel: 023 8072 2226
Correspondent: A Fryers, Trust Manager
Trustee: HSBC Trust Co. (UK) Ltd.
CC Number: 251661

Information available

Accounts were available from the Charity Commission.

The trust is concerned with children, seafarers, blindness, multiple sclerosis and similar conditions. In 2009/10 it had assets of £4.1 million, an income of £86,000 and made grants to 33 organisations totalling £87,000.

Grants included those made to: Leukaemia Research and Royal National Lifeboat Institution (£6,000 each); Cassell Hospital, Keech Hospice Care, Dorset Blind Association, St John's Wood Adventure Playground and Barnado's (£3,000 each); Family Support – Clacton and the Cleft Lip and Palate Association (£2,000 each); and Deewentside Domestic Abuse Service

and Disabled Travel Service (£1,000 each).

Applications

In writing to the correspondent.

Finnart House School Trust

Jewish children and young people in need of care and/or education

£142,000 (2006/07)

Beneficial area

Worldwide.

PO Box 603, Edgware, Middlesex HA8 4EQ
Tel: 020 3209 6006
Email: info@finnart.org
Website: www.finnart.org
Correspondent: Peter Shaw, Clerk
Trustees: Dame Hilary Blume; Mark Sebba; Robert Cohen; Linda Paterson; Sue Leiffer; Gideon Lyons.
CC Number: 220917

Information available

Accounts were available from the Charity Commission.

The trust supports the relief of children and young people (aged under 21) of the Jewish faith. Bursaries and scholarships are given to Jewish secondary school pupils and university entrants who are capable of achieving, but would probably not do so because of family and economic pressures. The trust may also support work concerned with people who are disaffected, disadvantaged socially and economically through illness or neglect or in need of care and education.

In 2009/10 the trust had assets of £4.3 million, which generated an income of £161,000. Grants totalled £205,000.

The largest grant was made to Finnart Scholarship (£180,000), this included awards made during the period to 65 students for amounts of between £500 and £2,000 per annum for courses of between three and seven years.

Other grants went to: Jewish Free School (£12,000); King Solomon High School (£12,000); and King David High School (£1,000).

Applications

Please note the following statement taken from the trust's website:

> If you are a charity (working for Jewish children in need) seeking support, please understand that the major part of Finnart's income goes to fund the Finnart Scholars. If you wish to apply, though realising the chances of success are slim, please check by telephone, email or letter before doing so. If you are a school seeking a hardship fund, please remember that our trust deed restricts our grant giving to Jewish children in need. We may also require evidence of the eligibility of any pupil. We will require a report on how any funds have been dispersed.

Common applicant mistakes

'Not reading the criteria which are clearly stated on our website and in the application pack.'

Marc Fitch Fund

Humanities

£106,000 to organisations and individuals (2009/10)

Beneficial area

UK.

19 The Avenue, Cirencester, Gloucestershire GL7 1EJ
Tel: 01608 811944
Email: admin@marcfitchfund.org.uk
Website: www.marcfitchfund.org.uk
Correspondent: Christopher Catling, Director
Trustees: David White; Lindsay Allason-Jones; Alan Scott Bell; Andrew Howard Murison; Dr Helen Forde; Dr John Blair; Professor David Hey; Michael Hall.
CC Number: 313303

Information available

Accounts were on file at the Charity Commission.

The trust makes grants to organisations and individuals for publication and research in archaeology, historical geography, history of art and architecture, heraldry, genealogy, use and preservation of archives, conservation of artefacts and other antiquarian, archaeological and historical studies. The primary focus of the fund is the local and regional history of the British Isles.

Grants range from relatively minor amounts to more substantial special project grants which may be paid over more than one year. In many cases, the awards enable work to be undertaken, or the results published either in print or online form, which would not otherwise be achieved.

In 2009/10 the trust had assets of £5 million and an income of £184,000. Grants to 28 organisations totalled £83,000, whilst £23,000 was given in research grants to individuals.

Beneficiaries included: Manorial Documents Register (£10,000); Tate Gallery (£8,500); Institute of Historical Research – Centre for Metropolitan History (£8,500); Lambeth Palace Gallery (£7,000); Wordsworth Trust (£6,000); North West Wales Dendrochronology Project (£5,000); Victoria County History (£4,500); National Archives (£4,000); British School at Rome (£3,000); North Yorkshire County Record Office (£2,500); Corpus Vitrearum Medii Aevi (£2,000); Northmoor Trust for Countryside Conservation (£1,500); Tayside and Fife Archaeological Committee (£1,300); South Ainsty Archaeological Society (£1,000); and Centre for English Local History – Leicester (£500).

Exclusions

No grants are given towards foreign travel or for research outside the British Isles (unless the circumstances are exceptional); building works; mounting exhibitions; or general appeals. No awards are made in connection with vocational or higher education courses or to people reading for higher degrees.

Applications

In writing to the correspondent, providing a brief outline of the project. The Council of Management meets twice a year, in spring and autumn, to consider applications. The deadlines for receipt of completed applications and references are 1 March and 1 August. The fund requests that any application enquiries be made well in advance of these deadlines as the application process is likely to take at least a few weeks to complete.

The Fitton Trust

Social welfare, medical

£69,000 (2009/10)

Beneficial area

UK.

PO Box 649, London SW3 4LA
Correspondent: Mrs Rosalind Gordon-Cumming, The Secretary
Trustees: Dr R P A Rivers; D V Brand; R Brand; K J Lumsden; E M Lumsden; L P L Rivers.
CC Number: 208758

Information available

Accounts were available from the Charity Commission.

In 2009/10 the trust had assets of £1.6 million and an income of £85,000. There were approx 271 grants made to organisations totalling £69,000. The majority of beneficiaries received £150 to £350. Only one organisation received over £1,000, which was the King's Medical Research Trust (£2,100).

Exclusions

No grants to individuals.

Applications

In writing to correspondent. The trustees meet three times each year, usually in April, August and December. The trust states:

> No application considered unless accompanied by fully audited accounts. No replies will be sent to unsolicited applications whether from individuals, charities or other bodies.

The Earl Fitzwilliam Charitable Trust

General

£99,000 (2009/10)

Beneficial area

UK, with a preference for areas with historical family connections, chiefly in Cambridgeshire, Northamptonshire and Yorkshire.

Estate Office, Milton Park, Peterborough PE6 7AH
Tel: 01733 267740
Email: agent@miltonestate.co.uk
Correspondent: R W Dalgleish, Secretary to the Trustees
Trustees: Sir Philip Naylor-Leyland; Lady Isabella Naylor-Leyland.
CC Number: 269388

Information available

Accounts were available from the Charity Commission.

The trust tends to favour charities that benefit rural communities, especially those with a connection to Cambridgeshire, Peterborough, South Yorkshire and Malton in North Yorkshire where the Fitzwilliam family have held their landed estates for many centuries. It was established in 1975 by the Rt Hon. Earl Fitzwilliam and has since had various capital sums and property gifted to it.

In 2009/10 it had assets of £10.6 million and an income of £135,000. Grant were made to 68 organisations totalling £100,000. Grants tend to be given as one-off payments and range between £100 and £10,000. In this year, no grants exceeded £6,000.

Beneficiaries included: Ryedale Voluntary Action re Milton Rooms (£7,500); Hunt Servants' Fund (£6,000); Game and Wildlife Conservation Trust (£5,000); Cambridgeshire High Sheriff's Award Scheme (£2,500); Breast Cancer Campaign (£2,000); Countryside Restoration Trust, Anna's Hope and Bag Books (£1,000 each); Tashi Lhunpo Monastery UK Trust, Rutland Sailability and Peterborough Cathedral Trust (£500 each).

Exclusions

No grants to individuals.

Applications

In writing to the correspondent. Trustees meet about every three months.

Bud Flanagan Leukaemia Fund

Leukaemia research and treatment

£40,000 (2010)

Beneficial area

UK.

10 Royal Sovereign View, Eastbourne, East Sussex BN23 6EQ
Tel: 01323 642843
Email: budflanagan-fund@hotmail.co.uk
Website: www.bflf.org.uk
Correspondent: Julie Rudland-Wood
Trustees: Joseph Goodman; K Kaye; Martin King; Tony Robinson.
CC Number: 1092540

Information available

Accounts were on file at the Charity Commission.

Established in 1969 from the estate of the late Bud Flanagan, according to the fund its principle objects are 'the promotion of clinical research into the treatment and possible cure of leukaemia and allied diseases and the publication of the results of all such research'. The fund makes grants to hospitals and research institutions for research into the causes, diagnosis and treatment of leukaemia.

In 2010 it had assets totalling £633,000 and an income of £104,000. Grants to three organisations were made during the year totalling £40,300.

The three beneficiaries receiving grants were: The Royal Marsden Hospital (£40,000); Help for Heroes (£200) and St Catharine's Hospice (£100).

Exclusions

The fund does not normally make grants to welfare charities or to individuals.

Applications

In writing to the correspondent.

The Rose Flatau Charitable Trust

Jewish, general charitable purposes

About £52,000 (2006/07)

Beneficial area

UK.

Friend-James, Chartered Accountants, 169 Preston Road, Brighton BN1 6AG
Tel: 01273 562563
Correspondent: The Trustees
Trustees: Naomi Woolf; A E Woolf; N L Woolf.
CC Number: 210492

Information available

Accounts were available from the Charity Commission.

The trust supports Jewish and other organisations which relieve those in need by reason of youth, age, disability, ill health and social circumstances.

In 2009/10 the trust had assets of £1.6 million and an income of £71,000. Grants were made to 26 organisations totalling £85,500.

Beneficiaries included: Brantwood Trust (£10,000); British Red Cross, Cherry Trees and Children's Trust Tadworth (£5,000 each); Institute of Cancer Research, New Horizons Research and Nightingales (£2,500 each); London Catalyst and Royal Hospital Disability (£2,000 each); and MacMillan Cancer Support and St Mary's Wrestwood Trust (£1,000 each).

Exclusions

No grants to individuals.

Applications

The trust stated: 'Our funds are fully committed to the foreseeable future'.

Speculative applications will therefore be fruitless.

The Ian Fleming Charitable Trust

Disability, medical

£31,000 to organisations (2009/10)

Beneficial area

UK.

Haysmacintyre, Fairfax House, 15 Fulwood Place, London WC1V 6AY
Tel: 020 7969 5500
Email: mjones@haysmacintyre.com
Correspondent: A A I Fleming, Trustee
Trustees: A A I Fleming; N A M McDonald; A W W Baldwin; A H Isaacs.
CC Number: 263327

Information available

Accounts were on file at the Charity Commission.

This trust's income is allocated equally between: (a) UK charities actively operating for the support, relief and welfare of men, women and children who are disabled or otherwise in need of help, care and attention, and charities actively engaged in research on human diseases; and (b) Music Education Awards under a scheme administered by the Musicians Benevolent Fund and advised by a committee of experts in the field of music.

In 2009/10 it had assets of £2.5 million, which generated an income of £96,000. Grants were made totalling £77,000, of which £31,000 was given in 18 grants to organisations and £46,000 was awarded to the Musicians Benevolent Fund Awards.

Beneficiaries included: Apex Trust, Diabetes UK and Stroke Association (£2,000 each); Camphill Family and Salvation Army (£1,500 each); Centrepoint and Variety Club Children's Charity (£1,000 each).

Exclusions

No grants to individuals except under the music education award scheme. No grants to purely local charities.

Applications

In writing to the correspondent.

The Joyce Fletcher Charitable Trust

Music, children's welfare

£71,000 (2009/10)

Beneficial area

England, almost entirely South West.

68 Circus Mews, Bath BA1 2PW
Tel: 01225 314355
Correspondent: R A Fletcher, Trustee and Correspondent
Trustees: R A Fletcher; W D R Fletcher; Susan C Sharp; S P Fletcher.
CC Number: 297901

Information available

Accounts were available from the Charity Commission.

The policy of the trust is to support institutions and organisations that are registered charities, specialising in music in a social or therapeutic context, music and special needs, and children and young people's welfare. Other organisations which are supported outside these areas are usually known to the trustees and/or are in the South West. Grants usually range between £450 and £5,000, occasionally more is given. A good proportion are repeat grants although there are always some new ones.

In 2009/10 the trust had assets of £2.1 million, an income of £59,000 and made grants totalling £71,000. Of the 41 organisations receiving support, 29 were based in the south west, six were national charities, five were based in other UK regions and one was based overseas. Grants were broken down as follows:

Music education and performance	£27,000
Music in a social/therapeutic context	£21,000
Children and young people	£5,000
Disability and deprivation	£9,000
Organisations outside the immediate objectives	£9,000

Beneficiaries included: Welsh National Opera (£5,000); Wiltshire Music Centre (£4,000); Buxton Festival, Drake Music Project and Ilford Arts (£3,000 each); Bath Area Play Project, Bath Fringe Festival, Bath Mozartfest and Jessie's Fund (£2,000 each); Project Trust and Hope and Homes for Children (£1,000 each); and National Trust (£600).

Exclusions

Grants to individuals and students are exceptionally rare; applications are not sought. No support for areas which are the responsibility of the local authority. No support is given to purely professional music/arts promotions. No support for purely medical research charities.

Applications

In writing to the correspondent before 1 November each year. Applications are considered in the months of October and November. There are no application forms. Letters should include the purpose for the grant, an indication of the history and viability of the organisation and a summary of accounts. Preliminary telephone calls are accepted. Acknowledgements are only given if the application is being considered or if an sae is sent.

Common applicant mistakes

'Applications have improved over the year but there are signs of more desperate/remote applications, i.e. outside our area of interest and region.'

Florence's Charitable Trust

Education, welfare, sick and infirm, general

£100,000 to organisations (2009/10)

Beneficial area

UK, with a preference for Rossendale in Lancashire.

E Suttons and Sons, PO Box 2, Riverside, Bacup, Lancashire OL13 0DT
Correspondent: B Terry, Secretary to the Trustees
Trustees: C C Harrison; A Connearn; G D Low; R D Uttley; S Holding; M Kelly; A Jepson.
CC Number: 265754

Information available

Accounts were on file at the Charity Commission, without a list of grants.

The trust was formed, amongst other things, to:

- establish, maintain and support places of education and to give scholarships and other awards to encourage proficiency in education
- establish, maintain and support places providing relief for sickness and infirmity, and for the aged
- relieve poverty of any person employed or formerly employed in the shoe trade
- provide general charitable public benefits.

In 2009/10 the trust had assets of £999,000 and an income of £58,000. Grants totalled £100,000 and were broken down as follows:

Educational support	34	£40,000
General charitable purposes	32	£40,000
Relief for sickness and infirmity	9	£19,000

A list of grant beneficiaries was not included in the latest accounts.

Previous beneficiaries have included: Pioneer Community Club; Bacup Family Centre; Whitworth Water Ski; Rossendale Search and Rescue; Rossendale United Junior Football Club; North West Air Ambulance; British Heart Foundation; Rochdale Special Needs; Macmillan Cancer Support; Children with AIDS; SENSE; Tenovus; All Black Netball Fund; Sport Relief and Heart of Lancashire appeal. A number of local primary schools and playgroups also benefited.

Exclusions

No grants to individuals for educational fees, exchange visits or gap year activities.

Applications

In writing only to the correspondent (no telephone calls please). To save on administration costs, unsuccessful applications will not be acknowledged even if an sae is provided.

Common applicant mistakes

'Making applications for salaries.'

The Flow Foundation

Welfare, education, environment, medical

£117,000 (2009/10)

Beneficial area

UK.

22 Old Bond Street, London W1S 4PY
Tel: 0207 499 9099
Correspondent: Mrs Nita Sowerbutts, Trustee
Trustees: Mrs N Shashou; Mrs Nina Sowerbutts; H Woolf; Mrs J Woolf.
CC Number: 328274

Information available

Accounts had been submitted to the Charity Commission, but were not available to view.

In 2009/10 it had an income of £11,000 and a total expenditure of £117,000.

Previous beneficiaries have included After Adoption, Brain Research Trust, British Friends of Haifa University, British ORT, Chicken Shed Theatre Company, Honey Pot Charity, International Centre for Child Studies, Jewish Care, Norwood, Royal Pharmaceutical Society, Tate Gallery Foundation, Toynbee Hall Foundation, Unite for the Future, Variety Club Children's Charity, Weizmann Institute Foundation and West London Synagogue.

Applications

In writing to the correspondent on one sheet of paper only.

The Gerald Fogel Charitable Trust

Jewish, general

£45,000 (2009/10)

Beneficial area

UK.

Morley and Scott, Lynton House, 7–12 Tavistock Square, London WC1H 9LT
Correspondent: J Clay, Accountant
Trustees: J G Fogel; B Fogel; S Fogel; D Fogel.
CC Number: 1004451

Information available

Accounts were available from the Charity Commission.

The trust stated in its annual report that its policy is 'to make a wide spread of grants', however mainly Jewish charities are supported in practice.

In 2009/10 the trust had assets of £873,000 and an income of £68,000. Grants totalled £45,000.

During the year organisations received support of £1,000 or more, including: Chai Cancer Care – nine grants (£9,000); World Jewish Relief (£6,000); Jewish Care (£5,000); Community Security Trust (£2,500); London Jewish Cultural Centre (£1,000).

Small grants below £1,000 each totalled £5,000.

Exclusions

No grants to individuals or non-registered charities.

Applications

In writing to the correspondent.

The Follett Trust

Welfare, education, arts

£151,000 (2009/10)

Beneficial area

UK and overseas.

Po Box 4, Knebworth, Herts SG3 6UT
Correspondent: Brian Mitchell, Trustee/Administrator

Trustees: Brian Mitchell; Ken Follett; Barbara Follett.
CC Number: 328638

Information available

Accounts were available from the Charity Commission.

The trust's policy is to: give financial assistance to organisations in the field of education and individual students in higher education including theatre; support organisations concerned with disability and health; support trusts involved with writers and publishing; and respond to world crisis appeals for help.

In 2009/10 the trust had an income of £162,000. Grants totalled £151,000.

Grants of £1,000 or more included those to: Donald Woods Foundation (£30,000); Canon Collins Education Trust (£20,000); Canterbury Cathedral (£10,000); Human Rights Watch (£5,000); and IPSEA, Melanoma, Real Victorian Trust, Tricycle Theatre and World Cinema Collective (£1,000 each).

Grants of less than £1,000 totalled £28,000.

Applications

The trust states:

> A high proportion of donees come to the attention of the trustees through personal knowledge and contact rather than by written application. Where the trustees find it impossible to make a donation they rarely respond to the applicant unless a stamped addressed envelope is provided.

The Football Association National Sports Centre Trust

Play areas, community sports facilities

£90,000 (2010)

Beneficial area

UK.

The Football Association, Wembley Stadium, London HA9 0WS
Tel: 084 4980 8200
Email: mike.appleby@thefa.com

Correspondent: Mike Appleby, Secretary to the Trustees
Trustees: William T Annable; Raymond G Berridge; Barry W Bright; Geoff Thompson; Jack Perks.
CC Number: 265132

Information available

Accounts were received at the Charity Commission but not available to view.

The trust supports the provision, maintenance and improvement of facilities for use in recreational and leisure activities. Grants are made to county football associations, football clubs and other sports associations.

In 2010 the trust had an income of £24,504 and a total expenditure of £93,000 of which £90,000 was probably given in grants. No further information for this year was available.

A small grant aid scheme was introduced in 2008 to assist clubs at the lower end of the FA's National League System. The maximum grant available was £10,000, which was designed to assist clubs seeking funding from other funding agencies such as the Football Foundation. The trustees allowed £500,000 for this project, which has now been fully allocated.

The trustees will however continue to consider applications from organisations for assistance towards the cost of community based projects.

Applications

In writing to the correspondent.

The Forbes Charitable Foundation

Adults with learning disabilities

£95,000 (2009/10).

Beneficial area

UK.

14 Nursery Court, Kibworth Harcourt, Leicester LE8 0EX

Correspondent: The Secretary to the Trustees
Trustees: C G Packham, Chair; I Johnson; R Bunting; ; N J Townsend; J M Waite; J. W. Williamson; R Warburton.
CC Number: 326476

Information available

Accounts were available from the Charity Commission.

The trust supports charities involved with the care of adults with learning difficulties. It prefers to support capital rather than revenue projects.

In 2009/10 it had assets of £3 million and an income of £937,000, which mostly came from a substantial legacy donation. Grants to organisations totalled £95,000.

Beneficiaries included: Leicester City Council-Special Olympics (£50,000); Cottage and Rural Enterprises Ltd (£8,000); See Ability (£5,000); Mires Beck Nursery (£3,000); Wirral Autistic Society (£2,600); and Merseyside Tuesday Club (£1,000).

Applications

In writing to the correspondent. Applications are considered in June and November.

The Forces Trust

Military charities

Around £55,000 (2009/10)

Beneficial area

UK.

Viaduct House, Victoria Viaduct, Carlisle CA3 8EZ
Tel: 01228 516666
Email: joanna.jeeves@cartmells.co.uk
Correspondent: Joanna Jeeves
Trustees: Capt. A P C Niekirk; Lieu. Col. W D Niekirk; Brig. R E Nugee; B E V Bowater.
CC Number: 211529

Information available

Information taken from the Charity Commission website.

The trust can only support military charities or institutions. The trustees prefer to support service charities that assist people rather than support buildings or property.

In 2009/10 the trust had an income of £43,000 and a total expenditure of £55,000. Further information was not available regarding beneficial organisations.

Previous beneficiaries included: British Limbless Ex-Service Men's Association, Erskine Hospital, Gordon Highlanders London Association Benevolent Fund, League of Remembrance, Scottish National Institution for the War Blinded, Sir Oswald Stoll Foundation, SSAFA Forces Help Cumbria and St David's Nursing Home.

Exclusions

No grants to any non-naval or military charities, individuals, scholarships or education generally.

Applications

In writing to the correspondent at any time, preferably on one side of A4.

Ford Britain Trust

Community service, education, environment, disability, schools, special needs education, youth

£164,000 (2009/10)

Beneficial area

Local to the areas in close proximity to Ford Motor Company Limited's locations in the UK. These are Essex (including East London), Bridgend, Southampton and Daventry.

Room 1/445, c/o Ford Motor Company Limited, Eagle Way, Brentwood, Essex CM13 3BW
Tel: 01277 252551
Email: fbtrust@ford.com
Website: www.ford.co.uk/fbtrust
Correspondent: Andy Taylor
Trustees: Michael Callaghan; David Russell; Michael Brophy; Jennifer Ball; Dr June-Alison Sealy; Mitra Janes.
CC Number: 269410

Information available

Accounts were available from the Charity Commission.

Registered with the Commission in 1975, the trust supports organisations in the areas where the Ford Motor Company is based, with special attention paid to projects that concern the trusts main objectives: education, the environment, children, disabilities, youth education and projects that benefit the local communities that Ford operates in. When this is a town it will support the surrounding area, i.e. where the employees are likely to be living. There is also a preference for charities where a member of staff is involved. Grants are typically one-off, provided for specific capital projects or parts of a project, and fall into two categories:

- small grants – for amounts up to £250, available four times a year
- large grants – for amounts over £250 and usually up to £3,000, available twice a year

Applications for new Ford vehicles are considered when two-thirds of the purchase price is available from other sources. These grants are not usually more than £2,000, but registered charities may be able to arrange a reduction from the recommended retail price. Grants are not available for second-hand vehicles. Applications relating to core funding, operating costs, salaries, revenue expenditure and other general funding will be considered for small grants only.

In 2009/10 the trust had assets of £221,000 and an income of £192,000, of which £114,000 came from a donation from the Ford Employee Benefit Trust. Grants totalled £164,000, broken down as follows:

Community service	99	£36,000
Youth	51	£48,000
Schools/education	36	£34,000
Disability	12	£13,000
Special needs education	2	£3,900

The five largest grants went to: Thames Gateway Youth Football Programme (£10,000); and Harold Hill Youth Football Club, 1st Miskin Mill Scout Group, St Mary's Primary School and Woodbridge High School (£3,000 each).

Grants of £3,000 each or less totalled £113,000.

Exclusions

Grant applications are not considered if they support the following purposes or activities: major building works; sponsorship or advertising; research; overseas projects; travel; religious projects; political projects; purchase of second hand vehicles; third party fundraising initiatives (exceptions may be made for fundraising initiatives by Ford Motor Company Limited employees and retirees).

National charities are assisted rarely and then only when the purpose of their application has specific benefit to communities located in close proximity to Ford locations.

Applications

On a form available from the correspondent or to download from the trust's website. Applications for large grants should include a copy of the organisation's most recent report and accounts.

Small grant applications are considered in March, June, September and November and should be submitted by the 1st of each month. Applications for large grants are considered in May and September and again should be submitted by the 1st of each month.

The Oliver Ford Charitable Trust

Mental disability, housing

£105,000 (2006/07)

Beneficial area

UK.

20 Cursitor Street, London EC4A 1LT
Tel: 020 7831 9222
Correspondent: Matthew Pintus
Trustees: Lady Wakeham; Martin Levy.
CC Number: 1026551

Information available

Accounts were available from the Charity Commission.

The objects of the trust are to educate the public and advance knowledge of the history and techniques of interior decoration, the designs of fabric and other decorative materials and landscape gardening including Oliver Ford's own work. Income and capital not used for these purposes is used for the Anthroposophical Society of Great Britain, Camphill Village Trust, Norwood or any other charity providing housing, educational or training facilities for children, young persons or adults who have learning disabilities or learning difficulties.

In 2009/10 the trust had assets of £2.4 million and an income of £96,000. Grants to 21 organisations totalled £51,000. Grants were also given to students at the Furniture & History Society (£3,000); the Royal Horticultural Society (£5,000); and the Victoria & Albert Museum (£18,000).

Beneficiaries included: Norwood Ravenswood (£20,000); L'Arche (£5,000); Hansel Foundation (£2,500); Norman Laud Association (£1,500); and Independent Options (£700).

Applications

In writing to the correspondent. Trustees meet in March and October.

Fordeve Ltd

Jewish, general

£203,000 (2009/10)

Beneficial area
UK.

c/o Gerald Kreditor & Co, Hallswelle House, 1 Hallswelle Road, London NW11 0DH
Tel: 020 8209 1535
Correspondent: Jeremy Kon, Trustee
Trustees: Jeremy Kon; Helen Kon.
CC Number: 1011612

Information available

Accounts were available from the Charity Commission.

The trust makes grants to Jewish causes and for the relief of need.

In 2009/10 it had assets of £686,000, an income of £123,000 and gave grants totalling £203,000. No further information about the beneficiaries or

the grants they received was available from this year's accounts.

Previous beneficiaries include: the Gertner Charitable Trust; Lubavitch Foundation; the Yom Tov Assistance Fund; the Society of Friends of the Torah; Lolev Charitable Trust; Beth Jacob Grammar School for Girls.

Applications
In writing to the correspondent.

The Forest Hill Charitable Trust

Mainly Christian causes and relief work

£239,000 (2009/10)

Beneficial area
UK and overseas.

104 Summercourt Way, Brixham, Devon TQ5 0RB
Tel: 01803 852857
Email: horacepile@tiscali.co.uk
Correspondent: Mrs P J Pile, Secretary to the Trustees
Trustees: H F Pile, Chair; Mrs P J Pile; R S Pile; Mrs M S Tapper; M Thomas.
CC Number: 1050862

Information available

Accounts were available from the Charity Commission.

This trust gives grants mainly to Christian causes and for relief work (80%), although support is given to agencies helping people who are disabled, in need or sick.

In 2009/10 the trust had assets of £3.2 million, which generated an income of £943,000. Grants were made totalling £239,000. There were two grants of more than £5,000 which were made to: LiNX (£22,000) and Great Parks Chapel (£12,000).

All other grants of £5,000 or less amounted to £205,000.

Applications
The trustees have previously stated that their aim was to maintain regular and consistent support to the charities they are currently supporting. New requests for funding

are therefore very unlikely to succeed and unsolicited applications are rarely considered.

The Anna Rosa Forster Charitable Trust

Medical research, animal welfare, famine relief

£69,000 (2009/10)

Beneficial area
Worldwide.

c/o R W Napier Solicitors, Floor E, Milburn House, Dean Street, Newcastle upon Tyne NE1 1LF
Tel: 0191 230 1819
Correspondent: R W Napier, Trustee
Trustees: R W Napier; A W Morgan.
CC Number: 1090028

Information available

Accounts were available from the Charity Commission, but without a list of grants.

Registered with the Charity Commission in January 2002, in 2009/10 the trust had assets of £2 million and an income of £68,000. Grants totalled £69,000 with a third of funds going in each of the following areas:

Medical research	£23,000
Animal welfare	£23,000
Famine relief	£23,000

A full list of grants was not included but previous beneficiaries included: Alzheimer's Research Trust, Cancer Research UK, British Red Cross, Farm Africa, Cats Protection League, CARE International UK, Motor Neurone Disease Association, the Donkey Sanctuary, PDSA, RSPCA, International Spinal Research Trust and the World Medical Fund.

Applications
In writing to the correspondent.

The Forte Charitable Trust

Roman Catholic, Alzheimer's disease, senile dementia

£120,000 (2009/10)

Beneficial area
UK and overseas.

Lowndes House, Lowndes Place, London SW1X 8DB
Tel: 020 7235 6244
Email: hmcconville@roccofortehotels. com
Correspondent: Mrs Heather McConville
Trustees: Hon. Sir Rocco Forte; Hon. Olga Polizzi di Sorrentino; G F L Proctor; Lowndes Trustees Ltd.
CC Number: 326038

Information available
Information was provided by the trust.

The trust has narrowed its areas of work down to those in relation to the Roman Catholic faith, Alzheimer's disease and senile dementia.

The trust stated that grants total about £120,000 a year.

Applications
In writing to the correspondent.

Lord Forte Foundation

Hospitality

£44,000 (2009/10)

Beneficial area
UK.

Lowndes House, Lowndes Place, Belgrave Square, London SW1X 8DB
Tel: 020 7235 6244
Email: hmcconville@ roccofortecollection.com
Correspondent: Heather McConville, Foundation Administrator
Trustees: Hon Sir Rocco Forte, Chair; Lord Janner; Hon Olga Polizzi di

Sorrentino; George Proctor; Nick Scade; Andrew McKenzie.
CC Number: 298100

Information available
Accounts were available from the Charity Commission.

This trust was set up in 1987, 'to encourage excellence in the fields of hospitality encompassing the hotel, catering, travel and tourism industries'. It does this by giving grants directly to educational establishments which provide training courses or carry out research projects in these fields.

In 2009/10 it had assets of £2.1 million, which generated an income of £56,000. Grants were made totalling £44,000 to ten educational institutions providing training courses in the hospitality industry.

Beneficiaries were: University of Bedfordshire (£7,000); Thames Valley University (£5,600); Leeds City College, Llandrillo College, the Bournemouth and Poole College Foundation, Fifteen Foundation and Westminster Kingsway College (£5,000 each); Crisis UK (£3,900); and Bournemouth University and the University of Strathclyde (£1,300 each).

Applications
In writing to the correspondent.

Foundation for Management Education

Management studies

£101,000 (2009/10)

Beneficial area
UK.

TBAC Business Centre, Avenue Four, Station Lane, Witney OX28 4BN
Tel: 01993 848722
Email: fme@lineone.net
Website: www.management-education.org.uk
Correspondent: The Director
Trustees: Geoffrey Armstrong; Valerie Boakes; Tim Boswell; Robert Lintott; G C Olcott; David Thomas;

Lord J E Tomlinson of Walsall; James Watson; John Wybrew; Miss P B Graham; J L James; J Colley; M Flanagan; Dr P Hahn; Dr J Hodges; Dr B Howieson; Dr O Mathias; S Pepper.
CC Number: 313388

Information available
Accounts were available from the Charity Commission.

This extract is taken from the charity's 2009/10 trustees' report:

> The Foundation exists to promote, fund and facilitate initiatives within the UK university business schools, with a particular emphasis on connecting business education with the world of work. It sets out to represent to policy makers and to management education providers an independent view on business education and fund activities that lead to the provision, development and dissemination of such, either independently or in partnership/ collaboration with others. As such the Foundation has a deserved reputation for its involvement in business and management education and its views are regularly sought in this connection.

Since its inception in 1960, funds have been used to support many initiatives, firstly to establish the Business School Sector within UK universities and latterly to fund a fellowship scheme which assists mid-career business practitioners to translate to a second career as business school academics.

In 2009/10 the charity had assets of £159,000 and an income of £42,000. Educational grant-making amounted to £101,000.

Previous beneficiaries include the universities of Surrey, Bath, Cambridge, Nottingham, and the London School of Economics.

Exclusions
Individual applications for further studies cannot be supported.

Applications
Unsolicited applications are not encouraged.

Common applicant mistakes
'Under-researched applications.'

The Isaac and Freda Frankel Memorial Charitable Trust

Jewish, general

£47,000 (2009/10).

Beneficial area

UK and overseas, particularly Israel.

33 Welbeck Street, London W1G 8LX
Tel: 020 7872 0023
Correspondent: M D Frankel, Secretary
Trustees: M D Frankel; G Frankel; J Steinhaus; J Silkin.
CC Number: 1003732

Information available

Accounts were available from the Charity Commission, but without a grants list.

The Isaac and Freda Frankel Memorial Charitable Trust was established in July 1991 by members of the Frankel family to support mainly Jewish causes.

In 2009/10 the trust had assets of £420,000 and an income of £27,000. Grants totalled £47,000. A list of beneficiaries was not included with the accounts filed at the Charity Commission.

Exclusions

No grants to individuals or students, for expeditions or scholarships.

Applications

In writing to the correspondent.

The Elizabeth Frankland Moore and Star Foundation

General in the UK

£236,000 (2009/10)

Beneficial area

UK.

c/o Neuhoff & Co, 11 Towcester Road, Whittlebury, Northamptonshire, NN 12 8XU
Tel: 01327 858171
Correspondent: Marianne Neuhoff
Trustees: Mrs J Cameron; R A Griffiths; Mrs A E Ely; Dr David Spalton.
CC Number: 257711

Information available

Information was available from the Charity Commission website.

Registered with the Charity Commission in February 1969, in 2009/10 the trust had an income of £186,000, assets of £8.7 million and made grants to 42 organisations totalling £236,000.

Beneficiaries included: Star Appeal – East Lothian (£25,000); Kids Company (£15,000); BLESMA, Eye Hope, The Hansel Foundation and Salvation Army Scotland (£10,000 each); Barnardo's Scotland, Special Forces Benevolent Fund and SANDS (£5,000 each); Royal Blind Society (£2,500); Accord Hospice and Glasgow Lodging House Mission (£1,000 each); Search and Rescue Dog Association, UK Youth and Wiltshire Air Ambulance Appeal (£500 each).

Applications

In writing to the correspondent. Trustees meet twice a year.

Sydney E Franklin Deceased's New Second Charity

Relief of poverty, children, communities

Around £30,000 (2009/10)

Beneficial area

Worldwide. Priority is given to developing world projects.

c/o 39 Westleigh Avenue, London SW15 6RQ
Correspondent: Dr Rodney Franklin, Trustee
Trustees: Dr Rodney Franklin; Natasha Franklin; Caroline Holliday.

CC Number: 272047

Information available

Limited information was available from the Charity Commission website.

The trust supports small charities with low income (under £300,000), which are involved in the relief of poverty and disability and the protection of endangered species. Priority is given to children in the developing world, education and communities working towards self sufficiency.

In 2009/10 the trust had an income of £20,000 and a total expenditure of £32,000. No further information was available.

Previous beneficiaries have included: Kerala Federation for the Blind, Water for Kids, Narwhal/Niaff, United Charities Fund, Ashram International, Books Abroad, Children of the Andes, Kaloko Trust, Microloan Foundation, Tools for Self Reliance, Tree Aid, Window for Peace UK, Forest Peoples Project, African Initiatives, Lake Malawi Projects, World Medical Fund and Gwalior Children's Hospital.

Applications

Donations may only be requested by letter, including a copy of latest accounts, and these are placed before the trustees at their meeting which is normally held at the end of each year. Applications are not acknowledged.

The Jill Franklin Trust

Overseas, welfare, prisons, church restoration

£94,000 (2009/10)

Beneficial area

Worldwide.

Flat 5, 17–19 Elsworthy Road, London NW3 3DS
Tel: 020 7722 4543
Email: info@jill-franklin-trust.org.uk
Website: www.jill-franklin-trust.org.uk

Correspondent: N Franklin, Trustee
Trustees: Andrew Franklin; Norman Franklin; Sally Franklin; Sam Franklin; Tom Franklin.
CC Number: 1000175

Information available

Accounts were available from the Charity Commission.

In June 2009 the assets of the Sally Franklin Charitable Trust were absorbed into The Jill Franklin Trust following a resolution of its trustees, all of whom are also trustees of this trust. Apart from special grants selected by the trustees, the six areas the trustees have concentrated their giving on are:

- Self-help groups etc for people with a mental illness or learning difficulties.
- Holidays for carers to provide respite from their caree. This is mainly as a block grant to the Princess Royal Trust for Carers.
- Organisations helping and supporting asylum seekers and refugees coming to the UK.
- Restoration of churches of architectural importance,
- Grants to prisoners for education and training. This is given as a block grant to the Prisoners Education Trust.
- Camden Bereavement Service, with which Jill Franklin was closely associated.

In 2009/10 the trust had assets of £1.5 million, an income of £170,000 and made grants totalling £94,000, broken down as follows.

Church restoration	25	£14,000	14.6%
Refugees	26	£13,000	13.8%
Bereavement	1	£12,000	12.8%
Prisoners	1	£10,000	10.6%
Mental health and learning difficulties	18	£10,000	10.5%
Respite/holidays	7	£12,000	12.8%

Grant beneficiaries included: Linden Lodge School (£20,000); Camden City Islington and Westminster Bereavement Services (£12,000); Princess Royal Trust for Carers (£7,000); Pevsner Book Trust (£2,250); Kiloran Trust, Hoffman Foundation for Autism and Respite Association (£1,000 each).

Exclusions

Grants are not given to:

- appeals for building work;
- endowment funds;
- branches of a national organisations, and to the centre itself (unless it is a specific grant, probably for training in the branches);
- replace the duties of government, local authorities or the NHS;
- encourage the 'contract culture', particularly where authorities are not funding the contract adequately;
- religious organisations set up for welfare, education etc. of whatever religion, unless the service is open to and used by people from all denominations;
- overseas projects;
- heritage schemes;
- animal charities;
- students, nor to any individuals nor for overseas travel;
- medical research.

Applications

In writing to the correspondent, enclosing a copy of the latest annual report and accounts and a budget for the project. Organisations based outside the UK should provide the name, address and telephone number of a correspondent or referee in the UK.

The trust states: 'The trustees tend to look more favourably on an appeal which is simply and economically prepared: glossy, 'prestige' and mail sorted brochures do not impress the trustees.'

Unsolicited enquiries are not usually acknowledged. The trust states: 'We have very little uncommitted cash, and so most applications are rejected, for the only reason that we have insufficient money.'

Common applicant mistakes

'They apply without having read our conditions, which are available on our website.'

The Gordon Fraser Charitable Trust

Children, young people, environment, arts

£144,000 (2009/10)

Beneficial area

UK, with a preference for Scotland.

Gaidrew Farmhouse, Drymen, Glasgow G63 0DN
Correspondent: Claire Armstrong, Administrator
Trustees: Mrs Margaret A Moss; William F T Anderson; Sarah Moss; Susannah Rae; Alexander Moss; Alison Priestly.
CC Number: 260869

Information available

Accounts were on file at the Charity Commission.

The trustees are particularly interested in supporting children/ young people in need, the environment (including the built environment) and visual arts (including performance arts). Most grants are given within these categories. Applications from or for Scotland will receive favourable consideration, but not to the exclusion of applications from England, Wales or Northern Ireland.

In 2009/10 the trust had assets of £2.7 million and an income of £179,000. Grants were made to 100 organisations totalling £144,000.

The trustees rarely make donations to the same charity more than once in the same year and a donation rarely exceeds £20,000 or is less than £100 although there are no minimum or maximum amounts for donations.

Beneficiaries included: National Galleries of Scotland (£9,500); The MacRoberts Centre (£7,000); Scottish International Piano Competition (£6,500); Artlink Central and the University of Cambridge (£5,000 each); Royal Scottish National Orchestra (£4,000); London Children's Flower Society (£3,500); British Red Cross and the Riverside

Museum Appeal Trust (£2,000 each); Borderline and Dance Umbrella (£1,000 each); and Factory Skatepark and the York Foundation for Conservation & Craftsmanship (£500 each).

Exclusions

No grants are made to organisations which are not recognised charities, or to individuals.

Applications

In writing to the correspondent. Applications are considered in January, April, July and October. Grants towards national or international emergencies can be considered at any time. All applicants are acknowledged; an sae would, therefore, be appreciated.

The Joseph Strong Frazer Trust

General, with broad interests in the fields of social welfare, education, religion and wildlife

£218,000 (2009/10)

Beneficial area

Unrestricted, in practice, England and Wales only.

Floor A, Milburn House, Dean Street, Newcastle upon Tyne NE1 1LE
Tel: 0191 232 8065
Fax: 0191 222 1554
Email: uf@joseph-miller.co.uk
Correspondent: The Trustees
Trustees: Sir William A Reardon Smith, Chair; David A Cook; R M H Read; William N H Reardon Smith; William I Waites.
CC Number: 235311

Information available

Accounts were available from the Charity Commission.

Established in 1939, the trust has general charitable purposes and gives to a wide range of causes, with broad interests in the fields of medical and other research, social welfare, people with disabilities, children, hospitals, education, maritime, youth, religion and wildlife. Recipients are based throughout England and Wales.

In 2009/10 the trust had assets of £11.9 million and an income of £400,000. There were 162 grants made totalling £218,000, categorised in the accounts as follows:

Medical and other research	35	£48,500
Hospitals and home	16	£21,500
Other trusts, funds and voluntary organisations	19	£21,500
Caring organisations	14	£18,500
Youth	13	£14,000
Deaf and blind	8	£14,000
Leisure activities, animals and wildlife	9	£14,000
Children	9	£13,500
Disabled	8	£12,500
Maritime	10	£10,500
Armed forces	4	£8,500
Older people	4	£6,500
Religious bodies	7	£6,500
Mental Health	4	£4,500
Schools and colleges	2	£3,500

Combat Stress received £3,000 while grants of £2,000 were paid to 46 organisations including: Addaction, Archway Project, British Retinitis Pigmentosa Society, Carers UK, Counsel & Care for the Elderly, Downside Fisher Youth Club, Iris Fund, Leonard Cheshire Wales & West, Prostate Cancer Charity, Royal School for the Blind Liverpool and Welsh National Opera. There were a further 115 grants to organisations of less than £2,000 which were not detailed in the accounts.

Exclusions

No grants to individuals.

Applications

In writing to the correspondent. Trustees meet twice a year, usually in March and September. Application forms are not necessary. It is helpful if applicants are concise in their appeal letters, which must include an sae if acknowledgement is required.

The Louis and Valerie Freedman Charitable Settlement

General

£100,000 (2009/10)

Beneficial area

UK, especially Burnham.

c/o Bridge House, 11 Creek Road, East Molesey, Surrey KT8 9BE
Tel: 020 8941 4455
Correspondent: F H Hughes, Trustee
Trustees: M A G Ferrier; F H Hughes.
CC Number: 271067

Information available

Accounts were available from the Charity Commission.

The trust supports health and welfare interests in which the Freedman family has a particular interest. Local education and youth charities in Burnham are also supported. The trustees report for 2009/10 states:

> Now that the Freedman family have no direct connection with the Burnham area, new focuses are being defined by the trustees, which will continue to be related to areas of interest of the Freedman family, and also in continuation of support of areas of interest of the late Louis & Valerie Freedman.

It is not clear currently, what the new focuses are.

In 2009/10 it had assets of £3.6 million, an income of £109,000 and made grants totalling £100,000.

Beneficiaries were: Burnham Health Promotion Trust (£50,000); Prostrate Research Campaign UK and The PSP Association (£10,000 each); and Care International, Children's Trust, Helena Kennedy Foundation, Every Child a Chance, Newlife Foundation for Disabled Children and Red Cross Haiti Earthquake Appeal (£5,000 each).

Burnham Health Promotion Trust is a related charity, also established by Louis Freedman.

Exclusions

No grants to individuals. Only registered charities are considered for support.

Applications

There is no application form. Applications should be in writing to the correspondent and they will not be acknowledged. Notification of a failed application will only be given if an sae is enclosed.

The Michael and Clara Freeman Charitable Trust

General

£63,000 (2009/10)

Beneficial area

UK and overseas.

9 Connaught Square, London
W2 2HG
Correspondent: Michael Freeman, Trustee
Trustees: Michael Freeman; Clara Freeman; Laura Freeman; Edward Freeman.
CC Number: 1125083

Information available

Accounts were available from the Charity Commission.

The trust was established in 2008 for general charitable purposes with an initial donation of almost £2 million from the settlors, Michael Freeman, co-founder of Argent Property Developers and his wife Clara, a former executive on the board of Marks & Spencer and currently on the University of the Arts London board of governors.

In 2009/10 the trust had assets of £2.1 million and an income of £275,000. 16 grants were made totalling £63,000.

Beneficiaries included: Help for Heroes (£23,000); Balliol College – University of Oxford (£7,500); Chipping Norton Theatre (£5,000); Combat Stress and the British Legion (£2,500); Kids Company and St Giles' Trust (£2,000 each); and Mary's Meals (£1,000).

The annual accounts for this financial year states:

> The trustees have pledged a gift of £450,000 to Balliol College, Oxford towards the permanent endowment of one of the Classical Literature Fellowships, conditional upon the College being able to raise the balance of the capital required.

Applications

In writing to the correspondent.

The Friarsgate Trust

Health and welfare of young and older people

£197,000 (2009/10)

Beneficial area

UK, with a strong preference for West Sussex, especially Chichester.

The Corn Exchange, Baffins Lane, Chichester, West Sussex Po19 1GE
Tel: 01243 786111
Fax: 01243 775640
Correspondent: Miss Amanda King-Jones
Trustees: A C Colenutt; T J Bastow; Mrs V Higgins.
CC Number: 220762

Information available

Accounts were available from the Charity Commission.

The objectives of the trust are:

- To provide funds for the academic and general education of orphans and children (whether infant or adult) whose parents are in poor or reduced circumstances.
- To promote the mental, moral, physical, technical and social education of children, young persons and adults.
- To provide, equip and maintain for the purposes referred to above camping grounds, holiday camps, playing fields, club rooms or other accommodation and facilities.
- To provide for the relief and care of impotent persons including in that expression all persons suffering either temporarily or permanently from disease or disability of any kind affecting their body or mind.
- To provide for the relief of persons over the age of sixty years by the provision of maintenance, food, clothing and housing.
- To promote and support or aid any charitable institutions, purposes or projects in any way connected with the objects aforesaid or calculated to further such objects or any of them.

In 2009/10 the trust had assets of £2.1 million and an income of £87,000. There were 50 grants made during the year totalling £197,000, split into two categories: education (£85,000) and care and welfare (£112,000).

Beneficiaries of the three largest grants were: Chichester Boys Club (£75,000 in three grants); Fordwater School (£50,000); and the Apuldram Centre (£30,000).

All other grants ranged between £500 and £2,000. Beneficiaries included: CYE Sailing Centre, the Honey Pot Charity and St Barnabus Hospice (£2,000 each); Enterprise Educational Trust, Sussex Autistic Trust and the Association of Wheelchair Children (£1,000 each); and Life Centre, Pallant House Gallery and Whizz Kidz (£500 each).

Exclusions

Local organisations outside Sussex are unlikely to be supported.

Applications

In writing to the correspondent. Applicants are welcome to telephone first to check they fit the trust's criteria.

Friends of Biala Ltd

Jewish

Around £65,000 (2009/10)

Beneficial area

UK and overseas.

Rosenthal and Co, 106 High West Street, Gateshead, Tyne and Wear NE8 1NA
Tel: 0191 477 2814
Correspondent: The Secretary
Trustees: B Z Rabinovitch; Mrs T Weinberg.
CC Number: 271377

Information available

Basic information was available from the Charity Commission website.

The trust supports religious education in accordance with the orthodox Jewish faith and registered welfare charities.

In 2009/10 the trust had an income of £11,000 and a total expenditure of

£68,000. No further information was available.

Previous beneficiaries include: Friends of Biala Israel, Aguda Hadadit, Yeshiva Beis Ephraim, Gemach Ezra Hadadit and Freebee Foundation Limited.

Applications

In writing to the correspondent.

Friends of Boyan Trust

Orthodox Jewish

£283,000 (2010)

Beneficial area

Worldwide.

23 Durley Road, London N16 5JW
Tel: 020 8809 6051
Correspondent: Jacob Getter, Trustee
Trustees: J Getter; M Freund; N Kuflik.
CC Number: 1114498

Information available

Accounts were available from the Charity Commission.

Set up in 2006, the charity was formed for the advancement of the orthodox Jewish faith, orthodox Jewish religious education, and the relief of poverty in the orthodox Jewish community.

In 2010 the trust had income of £297,000 from donations and made grants totalling £283,000. The sum of £18,000 was carried forward at year end.

A list of beneficiaries was not available with the accounts. Previous beneficiaries included: Gomlei Chesed of Chasidei Boyan (£84,000); Mosdot Tiferet Yisroel Boyan (£31,000); Kimcha De'Pischa Boyan (£21,000); Kimcha De'Pischa Beitar Ilit (£13,000); Chevras Mo'oz Ladol (£12,000); Kolel Avrechim Boyan, Betar Ilit (£6,000); Ezer Mikoidesh Foundation (£2,000); Beis Rizhin Trust (£1,500); and Yad Vochessed (£1,000).

Applications

In writing to the correspondent.

The Friends of Kent Churches

Churches

£142,000 (2010)

Beneficial area

County of Kent, particularly the dioceses of Canterbury and Rochester.

Parsonage Farm House, Hampstead Lane, Yalding, Maidstone ME18 6HG
Tel: 01622 815569
Website: www.friendsofkentchurches. co.uk
Correspondent: Jane Bird
Trustees: Charles Banks; Charles Oliver; Mary Gibbins; Paul Smallwood; Angela Parish; Leslie Smith; Jane Bird; Richard Latham; Jane Boucher.
CC Number: 207021

Information available

Accounts were available from the Charity Commission.

The objective of the trust is to promote the preservation of any Christian churches in use of architectural merit or historic interest in the dioceses of Canterbury and Rochester, and to help maintain in good order their fabric and fixtures of special importance.

A large amount of the trust's income is raised by an annual sponsored bike ride where half of the money raised is returned to the church of the riders' choice and the other half is allocated by the trust to the churches that have applied for a grant.

The following is taken from the trustees 2010 annual report:

> The Friends paid out £142,000 (2009 £147,000) in grants to churches in 2010 on completion of work carried out. During the year 26 successful applications were made for help and grants offered amounting to £122,500 (2009 £132,000), payable on completion of works.

In 2010 the trust had assets of £501,000 and an income of £183,000. Grants were paid out totalling £142,000.

Grants approved included: St Mildred – Canterbury, St Nicholas – St Nicholas at Wade (£10,000 each);

Newnham – St Peter and St Paul and Ruckinge – St Mary Magdalene (£7,500 each); Newington – St Nicholas (£5,000); Kilndown Christchurch (£3,000); and St Botolph – Lullington (£1,000).

Exclusions

No grants for reordering, new extensions, toilets and kitchens; heating, redecorating and rewiring; bells, clocks and organs.

Applications

In writing to the correspondent.

Friends of Wiznitz Limited

Jewish education, relief of poverty

£721,000 (2009/10).

Beneficial area

UK and overseas.

8 Jessam Avenue, London E5 9DU
Correspondent: E Gottesfeld
Trustees: H Feldman; E Kahan; R Bergmann; S Feldman.
CC Number: 255685

Information available

Accounts were available from the Charity Commission.

This trust is mainly concerned with supporting major educational projects being carried out by orthodox Jewish institutions.

In 2009/10 the trust had assets of £953,000 and an income of £714,000. Grants were made totalling £721,000 and distributed as follows:

Religious education	£480,000
Relief of poverty	£232,000
Advancement of religion	£7,500
Medical	£1,600

Beneficiaries listed in the accounts were: Igud Mosdos Wiznitz (£264,000); L'Hachzicom Ve'lehachyosom (£187,000); CMA Trust Ltd (£95,000); and Mosdos Wiznitz (£89,000).

Applications

In writing to the correspondent.

143

The Frognal Trust

Older people, children, disability, blindness/ophthalmological research, environmental heritage

£30,000 (2009/10)

Beneficial area

UK.

Steynings House, Summerlock Approach, Salisbury, Wiltshire SP2 7RJ
Correspondent: Donor Grants Officer
Trustees: Philippa Blake-Roberts; Jennifer Helen Fraser; P Fraser.
CC Number: 244444

Information available

Accounts were available from the Charity Commission.

The trust supports smaller charities rather than national organisations or local branches of large national charities. In 2009/10 it had assets of £2.1 million, which generated an income of £71,000. Grants were made to organisations totalling £30,000, which were broken down as follows:

Children and young people	£6,600
Disability and blindness	£6,400
Medical research	£6,300
Environmental heritage	£5,500
Old people	£5,500

Unfortunately a grants list was not available in this year's accounts.

Previous beneficiaries have included: Action Medical Research, Aireborough Voluntary Services to the Elderly, Canniesburn Research Trust, Elderly Accommodation Counsel and Leeds Society for Deaf and Blind People, Friends of the Elderly, Gloucestershire Disabled Afloat Riverboat Trust, National Rheumatoid Arthritis Society, Royal Liverpool and Broad Green University Hospitals, Samantha Dickson Research Trust, Stubbers Adventure Centre, Wireless for the Bedridden Society and Yorkshire Dales Millennium Project.

Exclusions

The trust does not support:
- any animal charities
- the advancement of religion
- charities for the benefit of people outside the UK
- educational or research trips
- branches of national charities
- general appeals
- individuals.

Applications

In writing to the correspondent. Applications should be received by February, May, August and November, for consideration at the trustees' meeting the following month.

T F C Frost Charitable Trust

Medical

£16,000 (2009/10).

Beneficial area

UK and overseas.

Holmes and Co Accountants, 10 Torrington Road, Claygate, Esher, Surrey KT10 0SA
Tel: 01372 465378
Email: holmes_and_co@hotmail.com
Correspondent: John Holmes
Trustees: Thomas Frost; Michael Miller; Prof John Marshall; Dr Elizabeth Graham.
CC Number: 256590

Information available

Limited accounts were available from the Charity Commission website.

The trust supports research associates of recognised centres of excellence in ophthalmology, individuals and organisations benefiting academics, medical professionals, research workers and people with sight loss.

In 2009/10 it had assets of £2.7 million and an income of £80,000. Grants totalled £16,000.

Previous beneficiaries have included: University of Southampton – Professor Andrew Lotery; University of Bristol – Chair in Experimental Ophthalmology; and the Rayne Institute St Thomas' Hospital – Professor John Marshall.

Exclusions

There are no available resources for the relief of blind people or people suffering from diseases of the eye.

Applications

In writing to the correspondent. Trustees meet twice a year.

The Patrick Frost Foundation

General

£252,000 (2009/10)

Beneficial area

Worldwide, but only through UK charities.

c/o Trowers and Hamlins LLP, Sceptre Court, 40 Tower Hill, London EC3N 4DX
Tel: 020 7423 8000
Fax: 020 7423 8001
Correspondent: Mrs Helena Frost, Trustee
Trustees: Mrs Helena Frost; Donald Jones; Luke Valner; Dominic Tayler.
CC Number: 1005505

Information available

Accounts were available from the Charity Commission.

The foundation makes general welfare grants to organisations and grants to help small charities that rely on a considerable amount of self-help and voluntary effort.

In 2009/10 the foundation had assets of £4.9 million and an income of £313,500. Grants were paid to 36 registered charities totalling £252,000.

Beneficiaries included: London Narrow Boat Project, Humberside Police Authority and The Smile Train UK (£20,000 each); Dogs for the Disabled, Opportunity International and Toynbee Hall (£10,000 each); Chance for Children, Deafblind UK and Family Holiday Association (£5,000 each); and Acorn Christian Foundation and Medical Foundation for the Care of Victims of Torture (£4,000 each).

Exclusions

No grants to individuals or non-UK charities.

Applications

In writing to the correspondent, accompanied by the last set of audited accounts. The trustees regret that due to the large number of applications they receive, they are unable to acknowledge unsuccessful applications.

Maurice Fry Charitable Trust

Medicine, health, welfare, humanities, environmental resources, international

£32,000 (2009/10)

Beneficial area

UK and overseas.

98 Savernake Road, London NW3 2JR
Correspondent: L E A Fry, Trustee
Trustees: L E A Fry; Mrs F Cooklin; Mrs L Weaks; Sam Cooklin-Smith.
CC Number: 327934

Information available

Accounts were available from the Charity Commission.

The trust's main areas of interest are welfare, humanities, environmental resources and international causes, but it is not restricted to these.

In 2009/10 the trust had assets of £1.1 million and an income of £37,000. Grants to 14 organisations totalled £32,000.

Beneficiaries were: Médecins Sans Frontières and British Red Cross (£8,000 each); The Maypole Project (£4,000); Royal Marsden Cancer Campaign, Friends of the Earth Trust, Amnesty International and Southbank Centre (£2,000 each); and Carers Bromley, Bromley Mencap, St Christopher's Hospice and FROK (£1,000 each).

Exclusions

No grants to individuals.

Applications

The trust states that it does not respond to unsolicited applications.

Mejer and Gertrude Miriam Frydman Foundation

Jewish, Jewish education

£37,000 (2009/10)

Beneficial area

UK and overseas.

Westbury Chartered Accountants, 145–157 St John Street, London EC1V 4PY
Tel: 020 7253 7272
Correspondent: David H Frydman, Trustee
Trustees: Keith Graham; David H Frydman; Gerald B Frydman; Louis J Frydman.
CC Number: 262806

Information available

Accounts were available from the Charity Commission, but without a list of grants.

The trust supports new and established charitable projects for study and research, including scholarships, fellowships, professorial chairs, lectureships, prizes, awards and the cost of purchasing or erecting any building or land required for such projects.

In 2009/10 the foundation had assets of £88,000 and an income of £41,000. Grants were made totalling £37,000.

Previous beneficiaries include: North West London Jewish Day School, Jewish Care, Norwood Ravenswood, Kisharon, Chai Cancer Care, Kesser Torah, Friends of Yeshiva O H R Elchanan, the Merephdi Foundation, Institute for Higher Rabbinicial Studies and Talia Trust for Children.

Exclusions

No grants to individuals for scholarships or any other purpose.

Applications

In writing to the correspondent.

The Fulmer Charitable Trust

Developing world, general

£423,000 (2009/10)

Beneficial area

Worldwide, especially the developing world and Wiltshire.

Estate Office, Street Farm, Compton Bassett, Calne, Wiltshire SN11 8SW
Tel: 01249 760410
Fax: 01249 760410
Correspondent: The Trustees
Trustees: J S Reis; Mrs S Reis; Mrs C Mytum; Miss E J Reis.
CC Number: 1070428

Information available

Accounts were available from the Charity Commission.

Most of the support is given in the developing world, although UK charities are also supported, especially those working in Wiltshire.

In 2009/10 the trust had assets of £5.6 million and an income of £435,000. Grants to 193 organisations totalled £423,000.

The largest donations included those to: Sight Savers and Sense (£11,000 each); Save the Children and Shelter (£10,000 each); NSPCC and the Sequal Trust (£9,000 each); Age Concern and Macmillan Cancer Relief (£8,000 each); the Brain Research Trust, Brainwave and Extracare (£7,000 each); I.M.P.S., the Leys Youth Programme and TRAX (£5,000 each); Coventry Cathedral Development Trust (£4,000); and Disasters Emergency Committee (£3,000).

Other beneficiaries included: Bath and District Samaritans, Bibles for Children, Book Aid International, Karen Hill Tribes Trust, Sailors Society and Topsy Foundation (£2,000 each); Traidcraft, Y Care International and Youth Action Wiltshire (£1,750 each); Zimbabwe A National Emergency – ZANE (£1,500); Able Child Africa, Acid Survivors Trust International, Food for the Hungry UK, Kenyan

Children's Project, Lamb Health Care Foundation, Transrural Trust (£1,000 each); King's Care (£500); and Salisbury & South Wiltshire Museum (£100).

Exclusions
No support for gap year requests.

Applications
In writing to the correspondent. Very few unsolicited applications are accepted.

The Fuserna Foundation

Relief-in-need, children, older people, mental and physical illness

£3.5 million (2009)

Beneficial area
UK and overseas.

Sixth Floor, 6 Chesterfield Gardens, Mayfair, London W1J 5BQ
Tel: 020 7409 3900
Email: info@fusernafoundation.org
Website: www.fusernafoundation.org
Correspondent: The Trustees
Trustees: Louise Creasly; Ariadne Getty; Patrick Maxwell.
CC Number: 1107895

Information available
Accounts were available from the Charity Commission.

The Fuserna Foundation was formed in February 2005 and it stated in the most recent annual report that its charitable objects are as follows:

- To revitalise existing charities and individual charitable projects that are failing in their objectives due to financial constraints and or lack of exposure and publicity. This will include vital projects that have difficulty in raising funds to continue in their operations or get off the ground and without any form of reserve, good contacts or patrons to assist them.
- To fund projects that intend to alleviate poverty and financial hardship, to relieve sickness and poor health. The emphasis will be on self help and community.

- To enable individuals to reach their potential despite their social, physiological or environmental limitations. This will include providing new opportunities and experiences for children and the elderly that they may not otherwise have access to.
- To assist, promote, encourage sustainable projects that create long term benefits for disadvantaged local communities that are trying to improve their area. This will include the making of grants to projects that assist individuals who by reason of their youth, age, infirmity or disablement, financial hardship or social and economic circumstances have need of such facilities, particularly projects which assist young people in the long term through education and training.
- To assist in the treatment and care of individuals suffering from mental or physical illness or those in need of rehabilitation as a result of such illness. This will include projects for mentally ill, drug, alcohol and other addictions.

The trustees of the Fuserna Foundation have an informal policy that they will not generally support charities that have annual incoming resources in excess of £3,000,000, or charities that have a high level of publicity through high profile patrons. The foundation focuses on supporting smaller charities and unpopular causes where any donation made can make a real and sustained impact.

The trustees have in the past made exceptions to this policy and have donated to charities with higher levels of incoming resources and publicity but this is not regarded by them as their core focus.

Grants are usually of between £5,000 and £15,000 each.

In 2009 the foundation had an income of £3.4 million mostly from voluntary income and made grants totalling £3.5 million.

The largest grant by far was made to the National Gallery for £3 million; the foundation commented upon this in its 2009 annual report:

We would not normally consider such a large donation to a high profile arts charity. However the trustees consider that the retention of these artworks in Great Britain is of the utmost importance and of the overall benefit to the general public and therefore contributed to the successful retention of Diana and Actaeon.

Other beneficiaries included: William J Clinton Foundation UK (£194,000); Fuserna Foundation – US (£136,000); Metropolitan Opera (£102,000);

Africa Foundation (£25,000); Reprieve (£15,000); Brainwave (£5,000); and Barton Training Trust (£2,000).

Exclusions
The foundation will not generally consider projects that include the following:
- animals
- religious activities/institutions
- general appeals.

Applications
The foundation asks for all initial applications to be in writing and to include the following:
- background information about the charity or charitable project in question
- details of the project that currently requires funding including the objective of the project and full operational details of how that objective will be achieved.
- a copy of your most recent financial statutory accounts
- details of the budget outlined in respect of the project
- details of existing sources of finance, including donations from other Charitable Trusts and details of other fundraising activities in place in respect of raising the funds needed for the project.

Upon receipt of the above information, a member of the foundation's day to day operational staff may wish to visit the charity prior to presenting its application to the trustees or alternatively to commence discussions with you. Further to this your application will be put forward to the trustees of the Fuserna Foundation for their consideration.

However, please note that due to a high volume of applications during 2009, the foundation is not currently accepting new applications. Please check the foundation's website for up-to-date information.

The G D Charitable Trust

Animal welfare, the environment, disability, homelessness

£74,000 (2009)

Beneficial area
Worldwide.

c/o Bircham Dyson Bell LLP,
50 Broadway, Westminster, London
SW1H 0BL
Tel: 020 7227 7000
Correspondent: The Trustees
Trustees: George Lincoln Duffield;
Natasha Velvet Duffield; Alexander
Seamus Fitzgibbons.
CC Number: 1096101

Information available
Accounts were available from the
Charity Commission.

Registered in February 2003, the trust
aims to support the following
charitable areas:
- the relief of animal suffering
- the preservation of the
  environment
- the promotion of equal
  opportunities for people who are
  disabled
- the relief of people who are
  homeless.

In 2009 the trust had assets of
£3.5 million, an income of £135,000
and made grants totalling £74,000.

Beneficiaries were: the Whitely Fund
for Nature (£50,000); the Aspinall
Foundation and the Eve Appeal
(£10,000 each); Naomi House
Children's Hospice (£2,000); and
Brook Hospital for Animals and
Royal Parks Foundation (£1,000
each).

Exclusions
No grants to individuals.

Applications
In writing to the correspondent.

Gableholt Limited

Jewish

£29,000 (2009/10)

Beneficial area
UK.

115 Craven Park Road, London
N15 6BL
Tel: 020 8802 4782
Correspondent: Mrs E Noe, Secretary
Trustees: S Noe; Mrs E Noe;
C Lerner; P Noe; A E Bude.
CC Number: 276250

Information available
Accounts were available from the
Charity Commission.

Set up as a limited company in 1978,
the trust gives practically all of its
funds to Jewish institutions,
particularly those working in
accordance with the Orthodox Jewish
faith.

In 2009/10 the trust held assets of
£21 million and an income of
£1 million. Grants to organisations
and individuals totalled £29,000.

Unfortunately no information on
grants was included with the trust's
accounts that were on file at the
Charity Commission. In previous
years beneficiaries have included:
Afula Society; Child Resettlement;
Friends of Harim Establishment;
Friends of the Sick; Gur Trust;
Mengrah Grammar School; Rachel
Charitable Trust and Torah
Venchased Le'Ezra Vasad.

Applications
In the past this trust has stated that 'in
the governors' view, true charitable
giving should always be coupled with
virtual anonymity' and for this reason
they are most reluctant to be a party to
any publicity. Along with suggesting
that the listed beneficiaries might also
want to remain unidentified, they also
state that the nature of the giving (to
orthodox Jewish organisations) means
the information is unlikely to be of
much interest to anyone else. Potential
applicants would be strongly advised
to take note of these comments.

The Galanthus Trust

Medical, developing countries, environment, conservation

Around £100,000 (2009/10)

Beneficial area
UK and overseas.

West Farm House, Newton Tony,
Salisbury SP4 OHF
Tel: 01980 629345
Email: galanthustrust@yahoo.co.uk
Correspondent: Mrs J M Rogers,
Trustee
Trustees: S F Rogers; Mrs
J M Rogers.
CC Number: 1103538

Information available
Accounts were on file at the Charity
Commission, without a list of grants.

This trust was registered with the
Charity Commission in April 2004.
The trust's latest available annual
report (2008/09) provides the
following information:

> Our aim is to help finance a variety of
> smaller local projects and good causes,
> in addition to supporting the work of
> existing organisations, both in the UK
> and abroad.

> There are several areas of particular
> interest to the trustees:
> - Medical and healthcare needs
>   including research, and patient
>   support (for example, stroke, MS,
>   heart disease and cancer). This
>   might also include help for disability
>   access, support groups or
>   individuals with special needs
>   resulting from illness or injury.
> - Projects in the third world: health,
>   education, water supplies and
>   sustainable development. Here the
>   intention is to fund on-going projects
>   being managed by charitable
>   organisations in the developing
>   world.
> - Environmental and wildlife concerns,
>   including the restoration and
>   maintenance of the UK's natural
>   habitats, such as local woodlands
>   and chalk downland. The trust will
>   also give grants for the creation of
>   new footpaths, particularly those
>   facilitating access for disabled
>   people.

▶ Conservation and preservation projects of historic and cultural value (for example, the National Trust's work at Tyntesfield).

In 2009/10 the trust had an income of £5,000 and a total expenditure of £114,000. Previously grants had been distributed between three categories: medical and healthcare, projects in the third world and environment and welfare.

Applications

In writing to the correspondent. The trust states: 'All requests for grants are considered carefully by the trustees. The trustees decide whether to donate and the amount to donate.'

Common applicant mistakes

'Most applications are vague, non-specific, unobjective and results are unmeasurable. Requests are also made for gap year travel costs, which are not considered.'

The Gale Family Charitable Trust

General

£135,000 (2009/10)

Beneficial area

UK, mainly Bedfordshire.

Garner Associates, Northwood House, 138 Bromham Road, Bedford MK40 2QW
Tel: 01234 354 508
Fax: 01234 349 588
Email: ggg@garnerassociates.co.uk
Correspondent: G Garner, Administrator
Trustees: G D Payne, Chair; J Tyley; J Williams; A J Ormerod; Mrs D Watson; R Beard; W Browning; D Stanton.
CC Number: 289212

Information available

Accounts were available from the Charity Commission.

The trust gives support in three areas:
▶ for churches and church ministries, with emphasis on Bunyan Meeting Free Church in Bedford and the ministries of the Baptist Union in England and Wales

▶ donations to charities and organisations active in the community life of Bedford and Bedfordshire
▶ donations to UK charities and organisations active in community life.

In 2009/10 the trust had assets of £5.4 million and an income of £213,000. Grants were made totalling £135,000.

There were 35 grants made to organisations, which included payments to: BECHAR – Prebend Street Day Centre (£10,000); Bedford Day Care Hospice (£6,000); Cecil Higgind Art Gallery (£5,000); Bedfordshire Festival of Music, Speech and Drama (£3,000); Lady Taverners (£2,000); MS Therapy Centre and the Corner Club (£1,000 each); Marlins – Special Needs Water Activity Club and Whitbread Wanderbus Limited (£500 each).

A further 13 grants made to churches, including those made to: Bunyan Meeting Free Church (£17,000); Baptist Union (£11,000); St Paul's Church – Bedford (£7,000); and. All Saints Church – Odell, St Leonard's Church – Stagsden and St Mary the Virgin Church – Woolton (£1,000 each).

Exclusions

Grants are rarely given to individuals.

Applications

In writing to the correspondent. Grants are distributed once a year and applications should be made by May for consideration in July.

The Angela Gallagher Memorial Fund

Children and youth, Christian, humanitarian, education

£32,500 (2010)

Beneficial area

UK and international organisations based in the UK.

Church Cott, The Green, Mirey Lane, Woodbury, Devon EX5 1DX
Tel: 01395 232097
Correspondent: Diana R Moss, Secretary
Trustees: N A Maxwell-Lawford; Diana R Moss; Wendy Manfield; H Rising.
CC Number: 800739

Information available

Accounts were available from the Charity Commission.

The aim of the fund is to help children within the UK. The fund will also consider Christian, humanitarian and educational projects worldwide, although international disasters are only aided through British Red Cross or CAFOD. Small charities which do not have access to large corporate donors are given priority.

In 2010 the trust had assets of £1.5 million and an income of £38,000. Grants to 57 organisations totalled £32,500.

Grants of £1,000 each were made to Anglo-Peruvian Child Care Mission, Cathedral Camps, Derby Toc H Children's Camp, North East Help Link, Over the Wall, The BTT John Fawcett Foundation, The Singalong Group and The Spiti Projects. Remaining donations were mostly for £500 each and included those to African Village Support, Bahia Street Trust, Bibles for Children, Children of Fiji, Cirencester Cyber Cafe, Clothing Solutions, Kindz Club – Leeds, Merthyr Tydfil Children Contact Centre, Mosaic, One in a Million, Rutland Sailability, Sail, Shelterbox for Haiti, Sunny smiles, Thumbs Up Club and Women in Need in Jinja.

Exclusions

Donations will not be made to the following: older people; scientific research; hospitals and hospices; artistic and cultural appeals; animal welfare; or building and equipment appeals. No grants to individuals.

Applications

In writing to the correspondent, for consideration at trustees' meetings twice a year. Applicants must include a set of accounts or the appeal will not be considered. Applications are not acknowledged without an sae.

Common applicant mistakes

'Failure to submit full recent accounts; appeals which have nothing to do with disadvantaged children. Applicants having management costs which are too high (above 60%!).'

The Gamlen Charitable Trust

Legal education, general

£53,500 (2009/10)

Beneficial area

UK.

c/o Thomas Eggar LLP, Newbury House, 20 Kings Road West, Newbury, Berkshire RG14 5XR
Tel: 01635 571000
Correspondent: J W M Chadwick, Trustee
Trustees: R G Stubblefield; P G Eaton; J W M Chadwick.
CC Number: 327977

Information available

Accounts were available from the Charity Commission.

Established in 1988, in 2009/10 this trust had assets of £28,000 and an income of £127,000. Grants to five organisations totalled £53,500.

Beneficiaries were: Christ Church (Law Fellowship) (£39,000); City Solicitors Educational Trust (£5,000); Newbury Spring Festival (£4,000); Grange Park Opera (£3,000); and Garsington Opera (£2,000).

Applications

The trust does not accept unsolicited applications.

The Gamma Trust

General

About £60,000 (2009/10)

Beneficial area

UK, with a possible preference for Scotland.

c/o Mazars CYB Services Limited, 90 St Vincent Street, Glasgow G2 5UB
Tel: 0141 225 4953
Email: glasgowtrustteam@mazars.co.uk
Correspondent: The Trust Secretary
SC Number: SC004330

Information available

Information was provided by the trust.

This trust has general charitable purposes. It appears that new grants are only given to UK-wide organisations although most grants are ongoing commitments to local organisations in Scotland. It has a grant total of about £60,000 a year.

Previous beneficiaries have included British Red Cross, British Heart Foundation, Cancer Research Campaign and Erskine Hospital.

Exclusions

No grants to individuals.

Applications

In writing to the correspondent for consideration quarterly.

Garrick Charitable Trust

Theatre, music, literature, dance

£142,000 (2005/06)

Beneficial area

UK.

Garrick Club, 15 Garrick Street, London WC2E 9AY
Tel: 020 7395 4111
Email: charitabletrust@garrickclub.co.uk

Correspondent: Fiona Murray, Trust Administrator
Trustees: John Nigel Newton; David Sigall; Stephen Waley-Cohen; Roger Braban; Stephen Peter Aris.
CC Number: 1071279

Information available

Accounts were available from the Charity Commission.

This trust supports institutions which are seeking to further the profession of theatre (including dance), literature or music. Grants are usually for amounts of £2,500, only in exceptional circumstances will they exceed £10,000.

In 2009/10 the trust had assets of £4.6 million, which generated an income of £141,000. Grants were made to 46 organisations totalling £124,000 and were broken down as follows:

Theatre	20	£48,000
Literature	5	£17,000
Music	17	£47,000
Dance	4	£13,000

Beneficiaries included: Orange Tree Theatre, Dance Umbrella, Two Moors Festival and National Academy of Writing (£5,000 each); Poetry School (£3,000); Opera UK Limited, National Youth Ballet, Royal Society of Literature, Sinfonietta Production, Tobacco Factory Theatre and Lyric Players Theatre Productions Limited (£2,500 each); Tete a Tete (£2,100); Appledore Book Festival (£1,300); Sticking Place (£1,000); and Sibmas (£300).

Applications

Initial applications are reviewed by the trustees who decide whether or not to send an application form. Trustees meet quarterly.

Garvan Limited

Jewish

£68,000 (2009/10)

Beneficial area

UK.

Flat 9, Windsor Court, Golders Green Road, London NW11 9PP
Correspondent: The Trustees
Trustees: A Ebert; L Ebert.

CC Number: 286110

Information available

Accounts were available from the Charity Commission.

The objectives of this charity are the advancement of religion in accordance with the Orthodox Jewish faith and the relief of poverty.

In 2010 the trust had assets of £1.2 million and an income of £239,000. It gave grants totalling £68,000. No further information was available.

Applications

In writing to the correspondent.

The Robert Gavron Charitable Trust

The arts, policy research, general

£262,000 (2009/10)

Beneficial area

Mainly UK.

44 Eagle Street, London WC1R 4FS
Tel: 020 7400 4300
Fax: 020 7400 4245
Correspondent: Ms Yvette Dear, Secretary
Trustees: Lord Robert Gavron; Charles Corman; Lady Katharine Gavron; Jessica Gavron; Sarah Gavron.
CC Number: 268535

Information available

Accounts were available from the Charity Commission.

This is a personal and family trust, with no full-time paid staff, whose grants go mainly, though not exclusively, to charities already known to the trustees.

The trust concentrates its funding on health and welfare (including charities for people with disabilities), prisons and prison reform, arts and arts education, social policy and research and education.

The trustees stated in their latest accounts that:

In many cases the trustees prefer to make grants to organisations whose work they personally know and admire. This does not, however, mean that charities unknown to the trustees personally do not receive grants. One freelance adviser visits and reports on new applicants to the trust and his reports are taken into account by the trustees when they make their decisions. This leads to a number of grants to new organisations during each financial year. These include small charities working in areas which cannot easily raise funds and which are without the resources themselves for professional fund raising. Small charities supported during the year include those working in prisons and with ex-offenders, and those working with adults and children with disabilities. The trust has also continued to help previously funded small charities which come into these categories.

In 2009/10 the trust had assets of £8.5 million and an income of £646,000. Grants were made totalling £262,000 and ranged from £25 to £100,000.

There was a sharp fall in donations made in the year as a large proportion of the outgoings had been provided for in previous years' accounts as committed donations. The fall in total donations charged to the accounts for this financial year reflected a drop in income due to lower investment returns in the last two years and also a reduction in the total value of investments.

Major beneficiaries during the year were: Menerbes Sports Centre (£179,000); King Alfred School (£100,000); Arab Israel Children's Tennis Charity (£76,500); and Barbados Cricket Association (£41,000).

Smaller grants included those to: Runnymede Trust (£25,000); Friends of Highgate Cemetery (£15,000); REFRESH (£10,000); Rainbow Drama Group (£5,000); Holocaust Educational Trust (£1,000); and Jewish Community Centre UK (£300).

Exclusions

The trust does not give donations to individuals or to large national charities.

Applications

Although the trust indicates that its funds are fully committed and that it would have difficulty in considering further appeals, particularly due to the current financial climate, new projects may be supported.

In writing only to the correspondent. Please enclose a stamped addressed envelope and latest accounts. There are no regular dates for trustees' meetings, but they take place about five times a year.

Jacqueline and Michael Gee Charitable Trust

Health, arts, education, Jewish

£109,000 (2009/10)

Beneficial area

UK.

27 Berkeley House, 15 Hay Hill, London W1J 8NS
Tel: 020 7493 1904
Correspondent: Michael Gee, Trustee
Trustees: Michael Gee; Jacqueline Gee.
CC Number: 1062566

Information available

Accounts were available from the Charity Commission.

This charity's policy is to benefit almost exclusively health, arts and educational charities. In practice this includes many Jewish organisations. It was created in 1997 by the settlement of £50 from the Archie Sherman Charitable Trust.

In 2009/10 the trust had assets of £68,000 and an income of £125,000 made up mostly from donations. Grants were made to 54 organisations totalling £109,000 and were distributed as follows:

General donations	18	£29,000
Arts and culture	16	£37,000
Education and training	9	£16,000
Medical, health and sickness	11	£26,000

Beneficiaries included: Royal Opera House (£17,000); Philip and Nicola Gee Charitable Trust, Purcell School, Chai-Lifeline Cancer Care and Dalaid

(£10,000 each); Royal National Theatre (£5,000); British Emunah (£3,300); Jewish Leadership Council (£2,500); St John's Hospice (£2,200); United Synagogue (£1,800); Heart Cells Foundation (£1,500); Camphill Village Trust (£1,400); WIZO UK (£1,100); SSAFA – Forces Help and Grange Park Opera (£1,000 each); Drugsline (£500); and Swiss Global Artistic Foundation (£100).

Applications

In writing to the correspondent.

Generations Charitable Trust

Children, overseas projects

Around £367,000 (2009/10)

Beneficial area

UK, Merton and overseas.

36 Marryat Road, Wimbledon, London SW19 5BD
Tel: 020 8946 7760
Email: rfinch@rfinch.plus.com
Website: www.generationsct.co.uk
Correspondent: Rohini Finch, Trustee
Trustees: Robert Finch; Stephen Finch; Rohini Finch.
CC Number: 1110565

Information available

Accounts were available from the Charity Commission.

The trust's website provides a useful overview of its activities:

Generations Charitable trust was set up in July 2005 by the Finch Family. The trust is funded by the family and aims to provide a better quality of life for children who need it the most; those who are disabled, disadvantaged, or struggle with ill health. The trust supports local causes in the Borough of Merton where the family is resident and also works abroad in developing countries. The trust also supports projects for environmental protection and conservation; the central aim being to leave a gift for future generations.

In 2009/10 the trust had assets of £38,000 and an income of £192,000. Grants totalled £367,000.

Awards ranging from £5,000 to £50,000 were made to 30 organisations, including: World Land Trust, Global Hospital and Research Centre and Save the Children – Haiti (£50,000 each); Right to Dream, Network 81 and In-Touch (£10,000 each); Sports Relief 2010 (£8,000); Shooting Stars Children's Hospice (£7,000); MARE Hostel (£6,300); and Scope, Variety Club of Jersey, the Sing-along Group and Tree Aid (£5,000 each).

A further 32 grants of less than £5,000 were made totalling £39,000.

Applications

In writing to the correspondent.

The Gibbs Charitable Trust

Methodism, international, arts

£93,000 (2009/10)

Beneficial area

UK with a preference for the south of England and worldwide.

8 Victoria Square, Clifton, Bristol BS8 4ET
Email: jamesgibbs@btinternet.com
Website: www.gibbstrust.org.uk
Correspondent: Dr James M Gibbs, Trustee
Trustees: John N Gibbs, Chair; James Gibbs; Andrew Gibbs; Celia Gibbs; Elizabeth Gibbs; Jessica Gibbs; John E Gibbs; Juliet Gibbs; Patience Gibbs; Rebecca Gibbs; William Gibbs; James D Gibbs.
CC Number: 207997

Information available

Accounts were available from the Charity Commission.

The trust supports Methodist churches and organisations, other Christian causes (especially those of an ecumenical nature), creative arts, education, and social and international causes. It has a slight preference for projects which can be easily visited by the trustees and it also occasionally supports overseas applications.

In 2009/10 the trust had assets of £2 million and an income of £105,000. Grants totalled £93,000, which were broken down as follows:

International	25	£49,000
Arts, drama and music	12	£15,000
Other Christian initiatives	6	£9,000
Other Methodist initiatives	5	£8,000
Social, educational and medical need	6	£7,000
Methodist churches, circuits and districts	11	£6,000

Beneficiaries included: Village Aid for Youth and Women's Empowerment (£6,000); Biblical Literacy – University of Durham (£5,000); Oxfam – West African peace project (£4,000); Africa Now (£3,000); Llangynidr Village Hall – for Tennis Courts (£2,000); Shakespeare at the Tobacco Factory – Bristol (£1,000); Sudden Productions (£750); Daventry Project (£500).

Exclusions

A large number of requests are received by the trust from churches undertaking improvement, refurbishment and development projects, but only a few of these can be helped. In general, Methodist churches are selected, sometimes those the trustees have particular knowledge of.

No unsolicited applications from individuals and no animal charities.

Applications

The trust has no application forms, although an application cover sheet is available on the trust's website along with a policy and guidelines page. Requests should be made in writing to the correspondent. The trustees meet three times a year, after Christmas, near Easter and late summer. Unsuccessful applicants are not normally notified. The trustees do not encourage telephone enquiries or speculative applications. They also state that they are not impressed by applicants that send a huge amount of paperwork.

Common applicant mistakes

'There has been much increased activity in the applications industry. Only some applicants used the trust's website. Very few look at previous accounts to see who else was funded. We want to be flexible and be able to respond to the enthusiasm of trustees

– this leaves us open to applicants from left field.'

Lady Gibson's Charitable Trust

General, arts, culture

£23,500 (2010/11)

Beneficial area

Overseas and the UK, with a preference for East Sussex, Kent, Surrey and West Sussex.

Pollen House, 10–12 Cork Street, London W1S 3LW
Tel: 020 7439 9061
Email: charity@mfs.co.uk
Correspondent: Laura Gosling
Trustee: The Cowdray Trust Limited.
CC Number: 261442

Information available

Accounts were received at the Charity Commission but not available to view.

The trust makes grants to a range of organisations including a number that are arts and culture related. Priority is given to grants for one year or less; grants for up to two years are considered. Grants range from £20 up to around £10,000, but the majority tend to be below £1,000.

In 2010/11 the trust had an income of £17,000 and an expenditure of £23,500.

Previous beneficiaries included: Withyham Parochial Church Council (£11,000); Royal National Theatre (£1,500); Royal Academy Trust (£1,300); Blond McIndoe Centre (£1,000); Bowles (£500); Chichester Cathedral Restoration and Development Trust (£350); Combat Stress (£250); London Philharmonic Orchestra (£120); Southbank Centre (£45); and Friends of Friendless Churches (£20).

Exclusions

No grants to individuals or non-registered charities.

Applications

In writing to the correspondent. Acknowledgements will only be sent if a grant is being made.

The B and P Glasser Charitable Trust

Health, disability, Jewish, welfare

£65,000 (2009/10)

Beneficial area

UK and worldwide.

Stafford Young Jones, The Old Rectory, 29 Martin Lane, London EC4R 0AU
Correspondent: B S Christer
Trustees: J D H Cullingham; M J Glasser; J A Glasser.
CC Number: 326571

Information available

Accounts were on file at the Charity Commission.

This trust makes grants mainly to health and disability-related charities and Jewish charities, but also for general social welfare purposes.

In 2009/10 the trust had assets of £2 million and an income of £76,000. Grants to 25 organisations totalled £65,000.

Grant beneficiaries include: Practical Action (£8,000); Nightingale House (£7,500); Jewish Care (£5,500); Royal National Institute for the Blind and Sight Savers International (£5,000 each); Ian Rennie Hospice at Home (£2,500); Camphill Village Trust (£2,000); Help the Aged (£1,500); Gurkha Welfare Trust and The Samaritans – Chiltern branch (£500 each).

Exclusions

No grants to individuals or students.

Applications

In writing to the correspondent. To keep administrative costs to a minimum the trust is unable to reply to unsuccessful applicants.

GMC Trust

Medical research, healthcare, general

£61,000 (2009/10)

Beneficial area

UK, predominantly West Midlands.

Flat 4, Fairways, 1240 Warwick Road, Knowle, Solihull, West Midlands B93 9LL
Tel: 01564 779971
Fax: 01564 770499
Correspondent: Rodney Pitts, Secretary
Trustees: Sir A Cadbury; B E S Cadbury; M J Cadbury; Mrs C E Fowler-Wright.
CC Number: 288418

Information available

Accounts were available from the Charity Commission.

The trust supports medical research, healthcare and causes related to inner city disadvantage. Income is substantially committed to a range of existing beneficiaries.

In 2009/10 the trust had assets of £2.4 million and an income of £155,000. Grants to 53 organisations totalled £61,000 (£170,000 in 2008/09).

Beneficiaries included: Birmingham Settlement (£6,000); Sense (£5,100); Runnymede Trust (£5,000); King's College Cambridge and Birmingham Women's NHS Foundation Trust Charities (£2,500 each); Mind and King's Lynn Arts Centre (£2,000 each); Depaul Trust, Dodford Children's Holiday Farm, Practical Action, Save the Children and Princess Royal Trust for Carers (£1,000 each); Derek Johnson Leukaemia Fund, No Panic, Royal Birmingham Society of Artists, Shelter and Abbeyfield Society (£500 each); Schools Outreach (£250); and Christian Aid (£100).

Exclusions

No grants to individuals, or to local or regional appeals outside the West Midlands. The trust does not respond to national appeals, except where there are established links.

Applications

In writing to the correspondent. The trust largely supports projects which come to the attention of its trustees through their special interests and knowledge. General applications for grants are not encouraged.

The GNC Trust

General

£143,000 (2010)

Beneficial area

UK, with preferences for Birmingham and Cornwall.

41 Sycamore Drive, Hollywood, Birmingham B47 5QX
Tel: 0121 265 5000
Correspondent: Mrs P M Spragg
Trustees: G T E Cadbury; R J Cadbury; Mrs P J Richmond-Watson; Mrs I J Williamson.
CC Number: 211533

Information available

Accounts were obtained from the Charity Commission's website.

Support is given to registered charities that the trustees have special interest in, knowledge of or association with.

In 2009/10 the trust had assets of 1.5 million, an income of £43,000 and made grants totalling £145,000.

Beneficiaries included: Lymington Museum Trust (£60,000); National Youth Ballet (£25,000); St John of Jerusalem Eye Hospital (£15,000); Downing College (£5,000); Friends of Bournville Cantlor (£3,000); Local Solutions (£2,500); Milton Abbey School (£2,000); and Alzheimer's Society and Treloar Trust- 5 donations totalling £1,750.

Grants for under £1,750 totalled £24,000.

Exclusions

No grants are made to national appeals, London-based charities or to individuals.

Applications

In writing to the correspondent at any time. There are no application forms and applications are not acknowledged.

The Sydney and Phyllis Goldberg Memorial Charitable Trust

Medical research, welfare, disability

£0 (2009/10)

Beneficial area

UK.

Coulthards Mackenzie, 17 Park Street, Camberley, Surrey GU15 3PQ
Tel: 01276 65470
Correspondent: M J Church, Trustee
Trustees: H G Vowles; M J Church; C J Pexton.
CC Number: 291835

Information available

Accounts were available from the Charity Commission.

The income for the trust comes from its investments which are mainly held in Syona Investments Limited. Phyllis Goldberg initially bequeathed her shareholding in Syona Investments Limited to the trust and since then the trust has bought the balance of the shares.

In 2009/10 the trust had assets of £3.1 million with an income of £61,000 and total expenditure of over £10,000 (spent almost entirely on management and administration). The 2009/10 trustee report states: 'However, no distributions were made during the current year.' It is not made clear why the remaining £51,000 was not distributed. The report goes on to say: 'The trustees feel that they have achieved the objects throughout the year and future plans are to carry on in the same manner.'

Previous beneficiaries include: £13,500 each to Children of St Mary's Intensive Care Department of Child Health, the British Stammering Association, the Dystonia Society, Children with Special Needs Foundation, Life Centre and the Prostate Cancer Charity; and £7,500 to the Isaac Goldberg Charity Trust.

Applications

In writing to the correspondent. Telephone requests are not appreciated. Applicants are advised to apply towards the end of the calendar year.

Golden Charitable Trust

Preservation, conservation, medical research

Around £45,000 (2009/10)

Beneficial area

UK with a preference for West Sussex.

Little Leith Gate, Angel Street, Petworth, West Sussex GU28 0BG
Tel: 01798 342434
Correspondent: Lewis Golden, Secretary to the Trustees
Trustees: Sara Solnick; Jeremy Solnick.
CC Number: 263916

Information available

Due to the trust's low income in 2009–10, only basic financial information was available from the Charity Commission.

The trust appears to have a preference in its grantmaking for organisations in West Sussex in the field of the preservation and conservation of historic articles and materials; church restoration and medical research charities.

In 2009/10 the trust had an income of £20,000 and a total expenditure of £46,000. No further information was available.

Previous beneficiaries include: Westminster Synagogue; Petworth Cottage Nursing Home; Music Mind Spirit Trust; Wordsworth Trust; Langdon Foundation; Chichester Cathedral Trust; Royal School of Needlework; Inter-Cultural Youth Exchange; Reform Foundation Trust; Macmillan Cancer Trust; Dermatitis and Allied Diseases Research Trust;

Helen and Douglas House; and Cancer Research UK.

Exclusions

No grants to individuals.

Applications

In writing to the correspondent.

The Jack Goldhill Charitable Trust

Jewish, general

£25,000 (2010)

Beneficial area

UK.

85 Kensington Heights, Campden Hill Road, London W8 7BD
Tel: 020 7727 4326
Correspondent: Jack Goldhill, Trustee
Trustees: G Goldhill; J A Goldhill; M L Goldhill.
CC Number: 267018

Information available

Accounts were available from the Charity Commission.

In 2010 the trust had assets of £582,000 and an income of £84,000. Grants were made totalling £25,000, however no details of beneficiaries were provided in the trust's accounts.

Previous beneficiaries have included CST; City and Guilds of London School of Art; Jack Goldhill Award Fund; JNF Charitable Trust; Jewish Care; Joint Jewish Charitable Trust; Nightingale House; Royal Academy of Arts; Royal London Hospital; Tate Gallery; Tricycle Theatre Co.; West London Synagogue; and Atlantic College.

Exclusions

No support for individuals or new applications.

Applications

The trustees have a restricted list of charities to whom they are committed and no unsolicited applications can be considered.

The Goldmark Trust

General

£56,000 (2009/10)

Beneficial area

UK.

30 St Giles, Oxford OX1 3LE
Correspondent: Graham Cole
Trustees: A O M Goldsmith; P L Luckett; M J Snell.
CC Number: 1072901

Information available

Accounts were available from the Charity Commission.

Registered with the Charity Commission on 10 December 1998, in 2009/10 the trust had assets of £2.5 million, an income of £110,000 and made grants to organisations totalling £56,000. The trustees' report stated that this level of giving would continue in the future.

Beneficiaries included: Children's Hospices UK and NCYPE (£2,500 each); Foundation for Conductive Education (£2,000); Autism West Midlands (£1,500); and Birmingham Royal Ballet, Discover Children's Centre and Tourettes Action (£1,000 each).

Applications

In writing to the correspondent. The trustees meet at least twice a year.

The Golsoncott Foundation

The arts

£50,000 (2009/10)

Beneficial area

UK.

53 St Leonard's Rd, Exeter EX2 4LS
Tel: 01392 252855
Email: golsoncott@btinternet.com
Website: www.golsoncott.org.uk/
Correspondent: Hal Bishop, Administrator

Trustees: Josephine Lively, Chair; Penelope Lively; Stephen Wick; Dr Harriet Harvey Wood.
CC Number: 1070885

Information available

Accounts were available from the Charity Commission.

The trust states its objects as follows:

> To promote, maintain, improve and advance the education of the public in the arts generally and in particular the fine arts and music. The fostering of the practice and appreciation of the arts, especially amongst young people and new audiences, is a further specific objective.

> Grants vary according to context and are not subject to an inflexible limit, but they are unlikely to exceed £5,000 and are normally given on a non-recurrent basis.

In 2009/10 the foundation had assets of £1.6 million and an income of £64,000. Grants to organisations totalled £50,000 and ranged between £100 and £4,000.

Beneficiaries included: Marian Consort (£4,000); Lake Land Arts (£2,500); New London's Children's Choir and Little Angel Theatre (£2,000 each); Gainsborough House and Shakespeare at the Tobacco Factory (£1,000 each); Hexham Abbey (£750); Magdalen Farm Strings (£500); Wildfire Folk (£200); and Purbeck Strings (£100).

Exclusions

No grants to individuals.

Applications

The trustees meet quarterly to consider applications, in February, May, August and November. Applications should be sent to the correspondent by the end of the month preceding the month of the trustees meeting. The full guidelines are stated on the foundation's website and include the following:
- A clear and concise statement of the project, whether the award sought will be for the whole project or a component part. Is the applicant organisation of charitable status?
- Evidence that there is a clear benefit to the public, i.e. does the project conform with the declared object of the trust.
- The amount requested should be specified, or a band indicated. Is this the only source of funding being sought? All other sources of funding

should be indicated, including those that have refused funding.

- If the grant requested is part of the match-funding required by the Heritage Lottery Foundation (HLF) following an award, state the amount of that award and the percentage of match-funding required by the HLF and the completion date.
- Wherever possible an annual report and accounts should accompany the application, as may other supporting information deemed relevant.

Second or further applications will not be considered until a minimum of 12 months has elapsed since determination of the previous application, whether successful or not.

Common applicant mistakes

'Generic applications that indicate they have neither read the guidelines nor the trustees' preferences, which are published on our website. Conversely, detailed applications which lie outside the foundation's legal objective.'

Golubovich Foundation

Arts

£140,000 (2009/10)

Beneficial area

UK.

c/o MVL Business Services, 15a High Street, Battle, East Sussex TN33 0AE
Tel: 01424 830 723
Email: tim.lewin@btinternet.com
Correspondent: Tim Lewin
Trustees: Alexei Golubovich; Olga Mirimskaya; Andrey Lisyanski; Arkadiy Golubovich.
CC Number: 1113965

Information available

Accounts were available from the Charity Commission.

Set up in 2006, the foundation seeks to foster relationships between Russia and the UK in the area of performing arts. This is done mainly through encouraging established UK arts centres to identify and develop the talents of young Russian nationals.

In 2009/10 the foundation had assets of £7,800 and an income of £171,000. Grants were made to two beneficiaries, Trinity College of Music

London (£75,000) and University of the Arts London (£65,000).

A further £31,000 was spent on governance costs.

Applications

In writing to the correspondent.

The Good Neighbours Trust

People with mental or physical disabilities

£77,000 (2010)

Beneficial area

UK, with preference for Bristol, Somerset and Gloucestershire.

16 Westway, Nailsea, Bristol
BS48 2NA
Tel: 01275 851051
Email: gntbristol@aol.com
Correspondent: P S Broderick, Secretary
Trustees: G V Arter, Chair; J C Gurney; P S Broderick; J L Hudd.
CC Number: 201794

Information available

Accounts were available from the Charity Commission.

The present policy of the trust is to principally support registered charities whose activities benefit people who are physically or mentally disabled. It mainly gives one-off grants for low-cost specific projects such as purchase of equipment or UK holidays for people with disabilities.

In 2010 the trust had assets of £2.7 million and an income of £83,000. Grants totalling £77,000 were made to 122 organisations, ranging from £250 to £10,000. Donations were broken down as follows:

Beneficiaries included: Children's Hospice South West (£10,000); Avon Riding Centre For the Disabled and St Peter's Hospice (£1,000 each); Keynsham and District Mencap Society and Whizz-Kidz – London (£500 each); and Theodora Children's Trust and Listening Books (£250 each).

Exclusions

Support is not given: for overseas projects; general community projects*; individuals; general education projects*; religious and ethnic projects*; projects for unemployment and related training schemes*; projects on behalf of offenders and ex-offenders; projects concerned with the abuse of drugs and/or alcohol; wildlife and conservation schemes*; and general restoration and preservation of buildings, purely for historical and/or architectural reasons. (* If these projects are mainly or wholly for the benefit of people who have disabilities then they may be considered.)

Ongoing support is not given, and grants are not usually given for running costs, salaries, research or items requiring major funding. Loans are not given.

Applications

The trust does not have an official application form. Appeals should be made in writing to the secretary. Telephone calls are not welcome. The trust asks that the following is carefully considered before submitting an application:

Appeals must:
- be from registered charities
- include a copy of the latest audited accounts available (for newly registered charities a copy of provisional accounts showing estimated income and expenditure for the current financial year)
- show that the project is 'both feasible and viable' and, if relevant, give the starting date of the project and the anticipated date of completion
- include the estimated cost of the project, together with the appeal's target-figure and details of what funds have already been raised and any fundraising schemes for the project.

The trustees state that 'where applicable, due consideration will be given to evidence of voluntary and self-help (both in practical and fundraising terms) and to the number of people expected to benefit from the project'. They also comment that their decision is final and 'no reason for a decision, whether favourable or otherwise, need be given' and that 'the award and acceptance of a grant will not involve the trustees in any other commitment'.

Appeals are dealt with on an ongoing basis, but the trustees meet formally four times per year usually in March, June, September and December.

Common applicant mistakes

'Applying for funds outside criteria, e.g. for core funds which we do not consider. Providing insufficient back up information i.e. financial.'

Nicholas and Judith Goodison's Charitable Settlement

Arts, arts education

£70,000 (2009/10)

Beneficial area

UK.

PO Box 2512, London W1A 5ZP
Correspondent: Nicholas Goodison, Trustee
Trustees: Nicholas Goodison; Judith Goodison; Katharine Goodison.
CC Number: 1004124

Information available

Accounts were available from the Charity Commission.

The trust supports registered charities in the field of the arts and arts education. Grants are often given to institutions in instalments over several years towards capital projects.

In 2009/10 the trust had assets of £1.3 million and an income of £48,000. Grants were made to 19 organisations totalling £70,000. Management and administration expenses for the year were very low at just £666.

The two largest grants of £20,000 were given to Victoria and Albert Museum – Ceramic Galleries and Courtauld Institute of Art.

Other beneficiaries included: Fitzwilliam (£7,100); Academy of Ancient Music (£5,000); Handel House (£4,000); Tate Gallery

(£3,500); English National Opera (£2,500); British Museum (£2,000); Burlington Magazine Travel Scholarship (£1,200); MEMO and Attingham Trust (£1,000 each); Wigmore Hall (£500); World Monuments Fund (£350); and Venice in Peril (£200).

Exclusions

No grants to individuals.

Applications

The trust states that it cannot respond to unsolicited applications.

The Everard and Mina Goodman Charitable Foundation

Jewish, general

Around £35,000

Beneficial area

UK and Israel.

Flat 5, 5 Bryanston Court, London W1H 7HA
Tel: 020 7355 3333
Correspondent: Dr Everard Goodman, Trustee
Trustees: Dr Everard Goodman; Mina Goodman; Michael Goodman; Suzanne Goodman; David Goodman.
CC Number: 220474

Information available

Accounts had been submitted at the Charity Commission, but were unavailable to view.

As well as supporting causes related to the Jewish faith, this trust also makes grants for: the relief of poverty; the advancement of education; children and youth; medicine and health; and rehabilitation and training. Grants are predominantly small, totalling less than £500. Although, larger grants of around £15,000 are also made.

In 2006 the foundation's income increased significantly due to a substantial donation from the settlor Everard Goodman, former chief executive of property company Tops Estates. Although, a substantial part

of this went to the Faculty of Life Sciences at Bar-Ilan University in Israel (£2 million), which is now named after the settlor and his wife, the foundation's increase in income has allowed the level of general grantmaking to rise significantly, although income and expenditure have been reduced somewhat in recent years.

In 2009/10 the foundation had an income of £15,000 and a total expenditure of £39,000. Further information was not available.

Previous beneficiaries include: British Friends of Bar-Ilan University – Life Sciences Faculty, Variety Club – Sunshine Coach Appeal, British Friends of Laniado Hospital, Child Resettlement Fund, Institute for Jewish Policy Research, Western Marble Arch Synagogue, Smile Train UK, Jewish Women's Aid, National Autistic Society and High Blood Pressure Foundation.

Exclusions

No grants to individuals or organisations which are not registered charities.

Applications

In writing to the correspondent.

The Goodman Foundation

General, social welfare, older people, health and disability

£143,000 (2009/10)

Beneficial area

England, Wales and the Republic of Ireland.

c/o APB, Unit 6290, Bishops Court, Solihull Parkway, Birmingham Business Park, Birmingham B37 7YB
Correspondent: The Trustees
Trustees: L J Goodman; C Goodman; R M Cracknell; L Tidd.
CC Number: 1097231

Information available

Accounts were available from the Charity Commission, but without a grants list.

Registered in April 2003, in 2009/10 the foundation had assets of £12.3 million and an income of £377,000, largely from investment income. Grants to organisations totalled £143,000 and were broken in the accounts as follows:

Third world and disasters	6	£60,000
'Poor, elderly, sick and disabled'	14	£53,000
Other	5	£18,000
Children's charities	5	£12,000

Applications

In writing to the correspondent.

Leonard Gordon Charitable Trust

Jewish

Around £30,000 (2009/10)

Beneficial area

England and Wales.

17 Park Street, Salford M7 4NJ
Tel: 0161 792 3421
Correspondent: Leonard Gordon, Chair
Trustees: Leonard Gordon, Chair; Michael Gordon; Jan Fidler.
CC Number: 1075185

Information available

Basic financial information was available from the Charity Commission.

Established in 1999, this trust supports Jewish religious, educational and welfare organisations.

In 2009/10 it had an income of £11,000 and a total expenditure of £33,000. Grants were made totalling around £30,000. No further information was available.

Applications

In writing to the correspondent.

The Gough Charitable Trust

Youth, Episcopal and Church of England, preservation of the countryside, social welfare

Around £20,000 (2009/10)

Beneficial area

UK, with a possible preference for Scotland.

Lloyds TSB Private Banking Ltd, UK Trust Centre, 22–26 Ock Street, Abingdon OX14 5SW
Tel: 01235 232712
Correspondent: The Trust Manager
Trustee: Lloyds Bank plc.
CC Number: 262355

Information available

Accounts were received at the Charity Commission, but were not available to view.

The trust has previously shown a preference for Scotland. In 2009/10 the trust had an income of £25,000. Grants generally total around £20,000.

Previous beneficiaries included: Irish Guards Lieutenant Colonels Fund, Prince of Wales Lodge No 259 Benevolent Fund, The Lifeboat Service Memorial Book Trust, National Army Development Trust, Household Brigade Benevolent Fund, Lloyds Charities Fund, Lloyds Benevolent Fund, Crown and Manor Boys Club and Trinity Hospice.

Exclusions

No support for non-registered charities and individuals including students.

Applications

In writing to the correspondent at any time. No acknowledgements are sent. Applications are considered quarterly.

The Gould Charitable Trust

General

£64,000 (2006/07)

Beneficial area

UK, Israel, Philippines.

Cervantes, Pinner Hill, Pinner, Middlesex HA5 3XU
Correspondent: S Gould, Trustee
Trustees: Mrs J B Gould; L J Gould; M S Gould; S Gould; S H Gould.
CC Number: 1035453

Information available

Accounts were received at the Charity Commission but not available to view.

In 2009/10 the trust had an income of £23,000 and a total expenditure of £52,000. No further information was available.

Previous beneficiaries included: Alzheimer's Research Trust, Child Hope, FCED Foundation Philippines, Friends of Hebrew University, Hackney Quest, Jewish World Relief, Médecins Sans Frontières, New Israel Fund, NSPCC, One to One, Project Trust and SOS Children.

Exclusions

No support for non-registered charities. No grants to individuals.

Applications

In writing to the correspondent, although the trust states: 'We never give donations to unsolicited requests on principle.'

The Grahame Charitable Foundation Limited

Jewish

£231,000 (2009)

Beneficial area

UK and worldwide.

5 Spencer Walk, Hampstead High Street, London NW3 1QZ
Tel: 020 7794 5281
Correspondent: Mrs G Grahame, Secretary
Trustees: A Grahame; J M Greenwood.
CC Number: 1102332

Information available

Accounts were available from the Charity Commission.

'The charity's objects and its principal activities are that of the advancement of education, religion and the relief of poverty anywhere in the world and to act as a charitable fund.'

In 2009 the trust's assets totalled £1.2 million. It had an income of £83,000. Grants totalled £231,000, with the following beneficiaries listed in the accounts: Beit Haknesset Caesarea (£33,000); Jerusalem College of Technology (£25,000); Child Resettlement Fund (£20,000); Beis Ruzhim Trust (£11,000); and British Friends of the Shaare Zedek Medical Centre, Colel Torah Mi Yerushalayim, Jerusalem Foundation, United Jewish Israel Appeal, United Jewish Students Hillel and Yesodey Hatorah School (£10,000 each).

Exclusions

No grants to individuals.

Applications

The trustees allocate funds on a long-term basis and therefore have none available for other applicants.

Grand Charitable Trust of the Order of Women Freemasons

General in the UK and overseas

£68,000 to non-masonic organisations (2005/06)

Beneficial area

UK and overseas.

27 Pembridge Gardens, London W2 4EF
Tel: 020 7229 2368

Website: www.owf.org.uk/
Correspondent: Mrs Joan Sylvia Brown, Trustee
Trustees: B I Fleming-Taylor; M J P Masters; H I Naldrett; J S Brown; Z D Penn.
CC Number: 1059151

Information available

Accounts were available at the Charity Commission, but without a list of all beneficiaries.

The charity's objectives are the general charitable purposes which the trustees shall in their absolute discretion think fit to support or establish throughout England and Wales. These include:

- medical – assistance in getting operations or treatment carried out privately to relieve pain or suffering where there is a long wait for NHS treatment
- relief of poverty – assistance with costly utility bills where hardship has occurred
- accommodation – help given especially where floods or serious fires have occurred
- children, elderly and disabled – donations mainly to hospitals, hospital appeals and help with mobility appliances
- grants to individuals/organisations – sponsorship always considered and special appeals
- other charities and voluntary bodies – donations given when applications are made. The amount is at the trustees discretion.

In 2009/10 the trust had assets of £756,000, an income of £175,000 and made grants totalling £133,000. During the year the trust has gifted £75,000 (2009 -£73,000) to outside charities. Specific gifts from members have also enabled the trust to make donations to the Adelaide Litten Charitable Trust totalling £57,000 (2009 – £57,000).

Applications

In writing to the correspondent. Applications should be submitted by the end of July each year for consideration by the trustees.

The Grand Order of Water Rats' Charities Fund

Theatrical, medical equipment

£64,000 (2009)

Beneficial area

UK.

328 Gray's Inn Road, London WC1X 8BZ
Tel: 020 7407 8007
Email: charities@gowr.net
Website: www.gowr.net
Correspondent: John Adrian, Secretary
Trustees: Chas McDevitt, Chair; Wyn Calvin; Roy Hudd; Kaplan Kaye; Keith Simmons; Ken Joy.
CC Number: 292201

Information available

Accounts were available from the Charity Commission, but without a grants list.

The trust was established to assist members of the variety and light entertainment profession and their dependants who, due to illness or age, are in need. The fund also buys medical equipment for certain institutions and also for individuals who have worked with or who have been closely connected with the same profession.

In 2009 the trust had an income of £140,000 and assets of £1.5 million, with income coming mainly from the profit gained from functions organised by the members of the Grand Order of Water Rats. Charitable activities amounted to £64,000, which included £58,000 in monthly allowances, £2,000 for fruit and flowers, £850 listed as donations, grants and gifts and £800 in museum expenses.

Previous grants included those made to Actors Church Union, British Legion Wales, Bud Flanagan Leukaemia Fund, Cause for Hope, Northwick Park Hospital and Queen Elizabeth Hospital for Children.

Exclusions

No grants to students.

Applications

In writing to the correspondent. The trustees meet once a month.

The Constance Green Foundation

Social welfare, medicine, health, general

£136,000 (2009/10)

Beneficial area

Mainly England, with some preference for West Yorkshire, overseas.

FCM Limited, Centenary House, La Grande Route de St Pierre, St Peter, Jersey JE3 7AY
Tel: 01534 487757
Fax: 01534 485261
Email: management@fcmtrust.com
Correspondent: S Hall
Trustees: M Collinson; Col. H R Hall; Mrs M L Hall; Mrs S Collinson.
CC Number: 270775

Information available

Accounts were available from the Charity Commission.

The foundation makes grants mainly in the fields of social welfare and medicine. There is a special emphasis on the needs of young people and people who are mentally or physically disabled. Preference is given to making grants to assist in funding special projects being undertaken by charities rather than grants to supplement funds used for general purposes.

In 2009/10 the foundation had assets of £8 million and an income of £339,000. Grants were made to 40 organisations totalling £136,000, of which 69% was given within the UK, 31% was given to charities undertaking work outside of the UK, and 18% was given to charities either operating in, or with projects focused on, various parts of Yorkshire. A

further breakdown of grants by category and expenditure can be seen as follows:

Category	%	£
Medical and social care	62	£86,000
Children and young persons	11	£22,000
'Disabled and aged'	16	£15,000
Homeless	10	£13,000
Church and community projects	1	£1,000

Beneficiaries included: British Red Cross Haiti Appeal (£10,000); Brainwave, Martin House Hospice – Wetherby and the Libra Foundation (£5,000 each); Family Holiday Association (£3,000); Friends of Michael Sobell House (£2,000); KIDS (£1,500); Transplant Active and Women in Prison (£1,000 each).

Exclusions

Sponsorship of individuals is not supported.

Applications

At any time in writing to the correspondent (no special form of application required). Applications should include clear details of the need the intended project is designed to meet, plus an outline budget.

The Philip Green Memorial Trust

Young and older people, people with disabilities, people in need

£81,000 (2009/10)

Beneficial area

UK and overseas, particularly Israel and Nepal.

105 Trafalgar House, Grenville Place, Mill Hill, London NW7 3SA
Tel: 020 8906 8732
Email: info@pgmt.org.uk
Website: www.pgmt.org.uk
Correspondent: The Committee
Trustees: D Kosky; M Campbell; S Paskin.
CC Number: 293156

Information available

Accounts were available from the Charity Commission.

During the year the trust had assets of £101,000 and an income of £311,000. Grants were made to 12 organisations totalling £81,000.

Beneficiaries included: Colnbrook School (£20,000); Jewish Community Secondary School (£15,000); Community Security Trust (£12,000); Norwood (£31,000); Namaste Children's Home and London Ex-Boxers Association (£1,000).

D Kosky is also a trustee of Friends of the Museum of the History of Polish Jews (Charity Commission no. 1087537) and Kosky Seal Charitable Trust (Charity Commission no. 1014309).

The accounts state that Mr C Paskin and Mrs N Paskin are both employed as administrators of the trust.

Applications

In writing to the correspondent.

Philip and Judith Green Trust

Christian and missions

£179,000 to organisations and individuals (2009/10)

Beneficial area

UK and Africa.

Marchfield, Flowers Hill, Pangbourne, Berkshire RG8 7BD
Correspondent: Philip Green, Trustee
Trustees: Philip Green; Judith Green.
CC Number: 1109933

Information available

Accounts were available from the Charity Commission.

Registered with the Charity Commission in 2005, the 2009/10 accounts state that the charity's objects are:

> To advance the education and support the development of pupils in underprivileged communities both overseas and in the UK and to advance the Christian faith for the benefit of the public by supporting missionaries and to include the upkeep and provision of places of worship both overseas and in the UK.

In 2009/10 the trust had an income of £85,000 and made grants totalling £179,000, up from £119,000 in

2008/09. However, assets dropped to £70,000 (£165,000 in 2008/09) largely due to this increase in grantmaking.

Grant beneficiaries included: Hope Through Action (£105,000); Bible Society (£30,000); African Enterprises (£15,000); Greyfriars Church (£8,300); Stewardship Services (£6,600); Rinell Carey Holmquist (£2,200); and Mission Aviation (£2,000). One further grant of £1,700 was made to an individual.

Other grants of smaller amounts were made totalling £8,400, however these were not listed in the charity's accounts.

Applications

In writing to the correspondent.

Mrs H R Greene Charitable Settlement

General, particularly at risk-groups, poverty, social isolation

£55,000 (2009/10)

Beneficial area

UK, with a preference for Norfolk and Wistanstow in Shropshire.

Birketts LLP, Kingfisher House, 1 Gilders Way, Norwich, Norfolk NR3 1UB
Tel: 01603 232300
Correspondent: N G Sparrow, Trust Administrator
Trustees: A C Briggs; Revd J B Boston; D A Moore.
CC Number: 1050812

Information available

Basic accounts were available from the Charity Commission website.

The founder of this trust lived in Wistanstow in Shropshire and the principal trustee was for many years based in Norwich. Both these factors influence the grant-making of the trust, with several grants given in both the parish of Wistanstow and in the Norfolk area. The trust has an additional preference for supporting organisations helping at-risk groups

and people who are disadvantaged by poverty or socially isolated.

In 2009/10 the trust had assets of £2.1 million, an income of £71,000 and made grants totalling £55,000 which included £3,500 in Christmas gifts. This is the only information available for this year. The most recent grants list available comes from 1997/98, when the trust had an income of £61,000, a total expenditure of £72,000 and gave £60,000 in grants.

Beneficiaries included: St Michael's Hospital Bartestree, Norfolk and Norwich Clergymen's Widows' and Children's Charity, Brittle Bone Society, Children's Food Fund, Macmillan Cancer Relief, Muscular Dystrophy Group, Orbis, Beeston Church Organ, Friends of Norwich Cathedral, Horsford and St Faith's Scout Group and Litcham Parochial Church Council.

Applications

The trust states that it does not respond to unsolicited applications.

The Gretna Charitable Trust

General

£57,000 (2009/10)

Beneficial area

UK, with a preference for Hertfordshire and London.

Imperial London Hotels Limited, Russell Square, London WC1B 5BB
Correspondent: The Trustees
Trustees: H R Walduck; Mrs S M C Walduck; A H E P Walduck; C B Bowles.
CC Number: 1020533

Information available

Accounts were available from the Charity Commission.

This trust gives grants to a wide range of voluntary organisations in the UK, with a preference for Hertfordshire and London.

In 2009/10 the trust had assets of £1.4 million, an income of £43,000 and made grants totalling £57,000 which ranged from £250–£6000.

Beneficiaries included: Lord Major's Appeal (£6,000); Basketmakers Company – Charitable trust (£1,750); St Albans Cathedral (£4,000); Royal British Legion (£500); University of Hertfordshire Scholarship (£2,000); St Mary's Essendon (£4,250); Potters Bar Cricket (£1,000); Nicholas Biddle Choir (£1,000) and Potters Bar Museum (£500).

Exclusions

The trust will not provide support to fund salaries or administration costs.

Applications

This trust does not encourage applications.

Common applicant mistakes

'Sending too much expensive printed material and using a first class stamp.'

The Greys Charitable Trust

General

£62,000 (2009/10)

Beneficial area

UK and locally in Oxfordshire.

c/o Lawrence Graham LLP, 4 More London, Riverside, London SE1 2AU
Correspondent: The Trustees
Trustees: J S Brunner; T B H Brunner.
CC Number: 1103717

Information available

Accounts were available from the Charity Commission.

Registered in May 2004, this charity's trust fund consists solely of shares in the Brunner Investment Trust plc and cash. The trust's 2010/11 accounts state:

'The trustees seek to make donations to other charities and voluntary bodies for the benefit of Church of England preservation projects, other charities dealing with historical preservation, both local to Oxfordshire and nationally, and may seek to make donations to the arts.'

In 2009/10 it had assets of £994,000 and income of £28,000. Grants were made totalling £62,000.

Beneficiaries included: Rotherfield Greys PCC (£11,000 in three grants); the National Trust (£9,000 in two grants); Institute of Economic Affairs (£5,000); the Royal Opera House (£4,000 in two grants); Vincents Club – Oxford University (£3,000 in two grants); Save Canterbury Cathedral (£2,000); the Art Fund (£1,500); and the Landmark Trust (£1,000).

Applications

In writing to the correspondent, the trustees usually meet twice a year.

Grimmitt Trust

General

£233,000 (2009/10)

Beneficial area

Birmingham and district and areas where trustees have a personal connection.

Orchard House, 4a St Catherines Road, Blackwell, Worcestershire B60 1BN
Tel: 0121 445 2197
Email: admin@grimmitt-trust.org.uk
Correspondent: Kate Chase, Secretary
Trustees: Patrick Welch; Sue Day; Leon Murray; David Owen; Tim Welch; Jenny Dickins; Sarah Wilkey.
CC Number: 801975

Information available

Accounts were obtained from the Charity Commission website.

The trust is focused on encouraging and strengthening local communities. Grants are given to organisations in the Birmingham area. Local branches of UK organisations are supported, but larger UK appeals are not.

In 2009/10 the trust had assets of £6.4 million and an income of £269,000. There were 197 grants made in the year totalling £233,000, broken down as follows:

Community	61	£65,000
Cultural and educational	40	£59,000
Children and youth	38	£34,000
Overseas	21	£39,000
Medical and health	31	£32,000
Elderly	6	£3,300

Beneficiaries included: Methodist Relief and Development Fund (£15,000); City of Birmingham Symphony Orchestra (£14,000);

WaterAid (£10,000); Walk Through the Bible Ministries (£7,500); Go Africa (£7,000); Birmingham Law Centre and Midlands Art Centre (£5,000 each); Wellbeing of Women (£4,000); Barton Training Trust (£3,000); and Edwards Trust, Walsall Hospice, St John the Evangelist – Sparkhill and Acacia (£2,000 each).

Smaller grants of less than £2,000 were made to 172 organisations, totalling £98,000, and four grants were made to individuals during the year.

Applications

Potential applicants should contact the secretary who will advise on the best way to design a grant request and to ensure that all the necessary information is included. The trustees meet three times a year to consider applications.

The GRP Charitable Trust

Jewish, general

£158,000 (2009/10)

Beneficial area

UK.

Kleinwort Benson Trustees Ltd, PO Box 57005, 30 Gresham Street, London EC2V 7PG
Tel: 020 3207 7356
Correspondent: The Secretary
Trustee: Kleinwort Benson Trustees Ltd.
CC Number: 255733

Information available

Full accounts were on file at the Charity Commission.

The GRP of the title stands for the settlor, George Richard Pinto, a London banker who set up the trust in 1968. Most of the grants are given to Jewish organisations.

In 2009/10 the trust had assets of £4.8 million and an income of £176,000. A total of £158,000 was given in grants, there were 16 made to Jewish causes and 14 made to general causes.

Beneficiaries included: Oxford Centre for Hebrew and Jewish Studies

(£50,000); Jewish Care (£20,000); British ORT (£17,000); United Jewish Israel Appeal (£10,000); Barts and the London Charity and the Politics and Economics Research Trust (£5,000 each); the Fare Share Foundation (£2,500); Jerusalem Foundation (£1,000); Oxford Playhouse Trust (£500); Spotlight Appeal (£200); and St Peter's Trust for Kidney, Bladder and Prostrate Research (£100).

Exclusions

No grants to individuals.

Applications

In writing to the correspondent. However, the trustees prefer to provide medium-term support for a number of charities already known to them, and unsolicited applications are not acknowledged. Trustees meet annually in March.

The Walter Guinness Charitable Trust

General

£135,000 (2009/10)

Beneficial area

UK with a preference for Wiltshire and overseas.

Biddesden House, Andover, Hampshire SP11 9DN
Correspondent: The Secretary
Trustees: Hon. F B Guinness; Hon. Mrs R Mulji; Hon. Catriona Guinness.
CC Number: 205375

Information available

Accounts were available from the Charity Commission.

The trust was established in 1961 by Bryan Walter, the second Lord Moyne, in memory of his father, the first Lord Moyne. Most grants are given to a number of charities which the trust has been consistently supporting for many years. In 2009/10 the trust had assets of £6.3 million and an income of £165,000. There were 127 grants made totalling £135,000.

Beneficiaries included: NSPCC (£10,000); Andover Mind, Hunt Servants Fund and National Society for Epilepsy (£4,000 each); Oxford Medical Students Elective Trust (£3,000); Friends of the Elderly, Prisoners Advice Service, RNIB and Sailors Society (£2,000 each); and Asylum Aid, Brainwave, Charity Search, Children's Safety Education Foundation and Diabetes UK South West (£1,000 each).

Exclusions

No grants to individuals.

Applications

In writing to the correspondent. Replies are only sent when there is a positive decision. Initial telephone calls are not possible. There are no application forms, guidelines or deadlines. No sae is required.

The Gunter Charitable Trust

General

£83,000 (2009/10)

Beneficial area

UK.

c/o Forsters, 31 Hill Street, London W1J 5LS
Tel: 020 7863 8333
Correspondent: The Trustees
Trustees: J de C Findlay; R G Worrall.
CC Number: 268346

Information available

Full accounts were available from the Charity Commission.

The trust gives grants to a wide range of local and UK organisations, including countryside, medical and wildlife causes. In 2009/10 the trust had assets of £2.1 million and an income of £111,000. There were 29 grants made totalling £83,000.

Beneficiaries included: Marie Stopes International (£8,000); Woodland Trust (£4,500); Médecins Sans Frontières (£4,000); the Great Bustard Group (£3,000); the Ne w Bridge Foundation and Womankind Worldwide (£2,000 each); the Smile

Train UK and Sandleheath Sea Scouts (£1,000 each); Oxfam (£650); Plantlife International (£350); Royal National Mission for Deep Sea Fishermen (£250).

Exclusions

No support for unsolicited applications.

Applications

Applications are considered by the trustees twice a year. No unsolicited applications are accepted, and all such applications are immediately returned to the applicant.

The Gur Trust

Jewish causes

£42,000 (2009/10)

Beneficial area

Worldwide.

206 High Road, London N15 4NP
Tel: 020 8801 6038
Correspondent: The Trustees
Trustees: David Cymerman; M Mandel; S Morgenstern.
CC Number: 283423

Information available

Accounts were available from the Charity Commission, but without a list of grants.

In 2009/10 the trust had assets of £1.3 million and an income of £54,000. Grants were made totalling £42,000, however a list of beneficiaries was not available in this year's accounts.

Previous beneficiaries have included Beis Yaacov Casidic Seminary, Beth Yaacov Town, Bnei Emes Institutions, Central Charity Fund, Gur Talmudical College, Kollel Arad, Yeshiva Lezeirim, Pri Gidulim, Maala and Mifal Gevura Shecehessed.

Applications

In writing to the correspondent. The trust has previously stated that: 'Funds are raised by the trustees. All calls for help are carefully considered and help is given according to circumstances and funds then available.'

The H and M Charitable Trust

Seafaring

£80,000 (2009/10)

Beneficial area

UK, with some preference for Kent.

Abbey House, 342 Regents Park Road, London N3 2LJ
Tel: 020 8445 9104
Correspondent: David Harris, Trustee
Trustees: Pamela M Lister; D Harris; J Lister
CC Number: 272391

Information available

Accounts were available from the Charity Commission.

The trust supports charities concerned with seamanship, divided between educational and welfare causes. In 2009/10 the trust had assets of £2.7 million and an income of £69,000. Grants totalled £80,000.

Previous beneficiaries included: Arethusa Venture Centre, Fairbridge – Kent, Guide Dogs for the Blind, Hand in Gillingham, Jubilee Sailing Trust, Kent Air Ambulance, North London Hospice, RSPCA, Royal Engineers Association, Royal National Lifeboat Association and Royal Star and Garter Home.

The trust has previously stated that 'resources are committed on a regular annual basis to organisations that have come to rely upon us for their funding'.

Applications

The trustees said they do not wish their trust to be included in this guide since it leads to disappointment for applicants. Unsolicited applications will not be successful.

The H P Charitable Trust

Orthodox Jewish

£5,600 (2009/10)

Beneficial area

UK.

26 Lingwood Road, London E5 9BN
Tel: 020 8806 2432
Correspondent: Aron Piller, Trustee
Trustees: A Piller; Mrs H Piller;
A Zonszajn.
CC Number: 278006

Information available

Accounts were available from the Charity Commission, but without a grants list.

The H P Charitable Trust was created by Hannah Piller in 1979 and makes grants to orthodox Jewish charities. In 2009/10 its assets stood at £1.5 million and it had an income of £181,000.

Grants totalled £5,600, a substantial drop from the previous year's figure (£353,000). There was no explanation for this in the trust accounts, except the following quote:

> During the year, the charity's incoming resources exceeded the outgoing resources. The trustees are satisfied with the results for the year. The trustees do not seek to maintain reserves, other than to ensure that they can continue the activities of the charity.

Previous beneficiaries included: Craven Walk Charities, Emuno Educational Centre Ltd, Gur Trust, Ponivez, Yad Eliezer, Yeshuas Caim Synagogue and Yetev Lev.

Applications

In writing to the correspondent.

The Edith Winifred Hall Charitable Trust

General

£612,000 (2009/10)

Beneficial area

UK, with a preference for Northamptonshire.

Spratt Endicott, 52–54 South Bar Street, Banbury, Oxfordshire OX16 9AB
Tel: 01295 204000
Correspondent: D Endicott, Trustee
Trustees: David Reynolds; David Endicott; P P Reynolds; L C Burgess-Lumsden.
CC Number: 1057032

Information available

Full accounts were available from the Charity Commission.

This trust has stated that it wants its funds to make a difference. It prefers to make a small number of large grants. Two of the trust's trustees, David Reynolds and David Endicott, are also trustees of the following organisations: East of England Agricultural Society, St Peter's Independent School – Northampton, the Countryside Alliance Foundation, Cabi Trust and the Twinkle Trust, which may indicate a preference for agricultural and bioscience based organisations.

In 2009/10 the trust had assets of £2.3 million and an income of £111,000. Grants were made to 20 organisations totalling £612,000.

Beneficiaries included: Balscote Village Hall (£80,000); Luton Churches Education Trust (£75,000); Friends of St Paul's Church – Bedford (£60,000); the Country Trust and Reach Out Projects (£50,000 each); All Saints Church with St Katherine and St Peter (£20,000); Keystone Escape Youth Centre (£14,000); St Peter's Church – Lowick (£10,000); and St Leonard Fabric Fund and Leicester and Rutland Crime Beat Limited (£5,000 each).

Applications

In writing to the correspondent.

The Hamamelis Trust

Ecological conservation, medical research

£85,000 (2009/10)

Beneficial area

UK, but with a special interest in the Godalming and Surrey areas.

c/o Penningtons Solicitors LLP, Highfield, Brighton Road, Godalming, Surrey GU7 1NS
Tel: 01483 791800
Correspondent: Mrs L Dadswell, Trustee
Trustees: Mrs L Dadswell; Dr A F M Stone; Ms L J Stone.
CC Number: 280938

Information available

Accounts were available from the Charity Commission.

The trust was set up in 1980 by John Ashley Slocock and enhanced on his death in 1986. The main areas of work are medical research and ecological conservation. Grants are occasionally made to other projects. Preference is given to projects in the Godalming and Surrey areas.

In 2009/10 the trust had assets of £2.9 million and an income of £79,000. Grants totalled £85,000 and were awarded to 37 beneficiaries, which included: the Chiddingfold Conservation Trust (£15,000); SOIL Association and Friends of the Earth (£4,000 each); Blond McIndoe Research Foundation, Bowel Cancer Research and Wildfowl and Wetlands Trust (£2,000 each); Busbridge Infants School (£1,500); Rural Life Centre and the Bluebell Railway Trust (£1,000 each); and Plantlife (£500).

Exclusions

Projects outside the UK are not considered. No grants to individuals.

Applications

In writing to the correspondent. All applicants are asked to include a short summary of the application along with any published material and references. Unsuccessful appeals will not be acknowledged. Dr Adam Stone, one of the trustees, who is medically qualified, assesses medical applications.

Sue Hammerson's Charitable Trust

Health care, education, religion

£256,000 (2009/10)

Beneficial area

UK, with a preference for London.

c/o H W Fisher and Co, Acre House, 11–15 William Road, London NW1 3ER
Tel: 020 7388 7000
Correspondent: The Trustees
Trustees: Sir Gavin Lightman; David Hammerson; Patricia Beecham; Peter Hammerson; Anthony Bernstein; Anthony Thompson; Rory Hammerson.
CC Number: 235196

Information available

Accounts were available from the Charity Commission.

The objects of this trust are to advance medical learning and research and the relief of sickness and poverty; it also supports a range of other charities including a number of Jewish and arts organisations.

In 2009/10 it had assets of £7.3 million and an income of £242,000. Grants were made to 192 organisations totalling £256,000, and were broken down as follows:

Arts and culture	£26,000
Education, international and religious causes	£27,000
Healthcare and relief of poverty	£203,000

The largest beneficiary by far was Lewis W Hammerson Memorial Home, which received a grant of £151,000.

Other beneficiaries included: NA and GA Lightman Charitable Trust (£8,000); West London Synagogue (£6,900); National Theatre (£6,500); English National Opera (£6,000); Royal Academy of Arts (£3,500); Bobby Moore Fund for Cancer Research (£2,500); Diabetes UK (£2,000); St John's Hospice (£1,300); Shalom Foundation (£1,000); Alzheimer's Society (£750); Youth Aliyah Child Rescue and Motability (£500 each); CHASE (£250); Independent Age (£200); and Breadline Africa (£100).

Exclusions

No grants to individuals.

Applications

In writing to the correspondent.

The Hammonds Charitable Trust

General

£124,000 (2009/10)

Beneficial area

Mainly Birmingham, London, Leeds, Bradford and Manchester.

Hammonds Solicitors, Rutland House, 148 Edmund Street, Birmingham B3 2JR
Email: linda.sylvester@hammonds.com
Website: www.hammonds.com
Correspondent: Linda Sylvester
Trustees: S M Gordon; J S Forrest; S R Miller; S Kelly
CC Number: 1064028

Information available

Accounts were available from the Charity Commission.

This trust (formerly known as The Hammond Suddards Edge Charitable Trust) usually makes donations to charitable organisations based locally to the trust.

In 2009/10 the trust 'supported a number of national charities in a wide variety of areas, but in particular the trustees were pleased to support smaller charities working within the areas in which its firm's offices are based – situated in Birmingham, London, Leeds and Manchester'.

During the year, the trust had assets of £105,000, an income of £67,000 and made grants to 185 organisations totalling £124,000.

Medical/health/sickness	77	£43,000
Education/training	42	£28,000
General purposes	34	£18,000
Disability	7	£9,000
Economic/ community development/employment	1	£9,000
Relief of poverty	5	£6,000
Overseas aid/famine relief	3	£4,250
Sport and recreation	4	£4,000
Children	4	£1,200
Arts/Culture	1	£1,000
Animal welfare	2	£300
Religious activity	3	£275
Other purposes	1	£270
Environment/conservation/ heritage	1	£100

Beneficiaries included: Business in the Community (£9,250); the Royal National Institute for Deaf People (£7,000); the Nordoff-Robbins Music Therapy Centre (£5,000); Orchid (£4,000); NSPCC (£3,400); the Prince's Trust (£2,500); Crohns and Colitis in Childhood (£2,000); Shaare Zedek UK and the Healing Foundation (£1,000 each); Elim Church (£500); Brathay Trust (£300); Birmingham Centre for Arts Therapies (£200); Guy's Gift (£100); and Dodford Children's Holiday Farm (£70).

Applications

This trust does not accept unsolicited applications.

Beatrice Hankey Foundation Ltd

Christian

£35,000 (2010)

Beneficial area

UK and overseas.

11 Staverton Road, Werrington, Peterborough, Cambridgeshire PE4 6LY
Tel: 01733 571794
Correspondent: Melanie Churchill, Secretary
Trustees: Rev David Faulks; H W Bright; Rev David Savill; T Halliday; A Y Stewart; H Walker; Canon David Haokip; Christine Legg; Pamela Macey; Wendy Hill; Selina Ormond; Daphne Sampson; Margaret Faulks; Crispin Wedell.
CC Number: 211093

Information available

Accounts were available from the Charity Commission.

Grants are made to individuals and groups known personally to the foundation members that carry out activities that will promote the values of Christian teaching. It gives mostly small grants of up to £5,000 each.

In 2010 the foundation had assets of £1 million and an income of £46,000. Grants were made to organisations totalling £35,000.

Beneficiaries included: Lagan College (£14,000); Corrymeela Community (£3,500); St Alfege's School Project (£3,000); The Dalitsu Trust – Malawi (£2,000); Friends of Burma (£1,500); and Mathieson Music Trust (£1,000).

Exclusions

No grants for buildings or equipment.

Applications

Unsolicited applications cannot be considered.

The Hanley Trust

Social welfare and people who are disadvantaged

£30,000 (2009/10)

Beneficial area

UK, with a preference for Corby and Rutland.

21 Buckingham Gate, London SW1E 6LS
Correspondent: Hon. Mrs Sarah Price, Trustee
Trustees: Hon. Sarah Price, Chair; Hon. Samuel James Butler; William Swan.
CC Number: 299209

Information available

Full accounts were available from the Charity Commission website.

This trust states that it has various funding priorities, for social welfare and people who are disadvantaged. It makes grants to registered charities only, usually small, up to a maximum of £4,000.

In 2009/10 the trust had assets of £1 million and an income of £33,000. Grants were made to 72 organisations totalling £30,000 and ranged between £100 and £2,500.

Beneficiaries included: Butler Trust and Irene Taylor Trust (£2,500 each); Uppingham PCC (£2,000); Helen Arkell Dyslexia Centre and Shelter (£1,000 each); Young Minds, the Royal National Mission to Deep Sea Fishermen and Deafness Research UK (£500 each); Conservation Foundation, Ladywood Furniture Project and Suffolk Punch Trust (£250 each); and Corby Furniture Turnabout Foundation (£100).

Exclusions

Grants are not made to individuals or to non-registered charities.

Applications

In writing to the correspondent.

Harbo Charities Limited

Jewish causes, general and education

£97,000 (2009/10)

Beneficial area

UK.

c/o Cohen Arnold and Co., New Burlington House, 1075 Finchley Road, London NW11 0PU
Correspondent: The Trustees
Trustees: Harry Stern; Barbara Stern; Harold Gluck.
CC Number: 282262

Information available

Accounts were available from the Charity Commission, but without a grants list.

The trust supports orthodox Jewish charities, particularly those which provide financial support and basic necessities to 'the poor', support Jewish education and places of worship for the Jewish community and provide relief of sickness and disability.

In 2009/10 the trust had assets of £760,000, an income of £104,000 and made grants totalling £97,000.

Previous beneficiaries have included: Beis Chinuch Lebonos Girls' School, Beth Rochel d'Satmar, Bobov Trust, Chevras Maoz Ladol, Craven Walk Charitable Trust, Edgware Yeshiva Trust, Keren Yesomim, Kollel Shomrei HaChomoth, Tevini Limited, Tomchei Shabbos, Yad Eliezer, Yesode Ha Torah School and Yeshiva Chachmay Tsorpha.

Applications

In writing to the correspondent.

The Harbour Charitable Trust

General

£103,000 (2009/10)

Beneficial area

UK.

Barbican House, 26–34 Old Street, London EC1V 9QQ
Correspondent: The Trustees
Trustees: Mrs B B Green; Mrs Z S Blackman; Mrs T Elsenstat; Mrs E Knobil.
CC Number: 234268

Information available

Accounts were available at the Charity Commission, but without a list of grants.

The trust makes grants for the benefit of childcare, education and healthcare and to various other charitable organisations. In 2009/10 it had assets of £3.5 million and an income of £291,000. Grants were made totalling £103,000 and were categorised as follows:

Joint Jewish Charitable Trust	£38,000
Healthcare	£40,000
Education	£6,000
Aged care	£4,000
Childcare	£2,000
Other donations	£13,000

No further information was available on the charities supported.

Exclusions

Grants are given to registered charities only.

Applications

In writing to the correspondent.

The Harbour Foundation

Jewish, general

£482,000 (2009/10)

Beneficial area

Worldwide, with a preference for London.

1 Red Place, London W1K 6PL
Tel: 020 7456 8180
Correspondent: The Trustees
Trustees: D Harbour; Rex Harbour; Anthony C Humphries; Susan Harbour.
CC Number: 264927

Information available

Accounts were available from the Charity Commission.

The principal activities of the trust are providing relief among refugees and people who are homeless, the advancement of education, learning and research, and to make donations to any institution established for charitable purposes throughout the world. It focuses on grants for educational and research advancement, for medical research and for the advancement of arts and culture. The trustees stated the following in their annual report:

> The foundation's current and future charitable programme is directed towards general support for charities and individuals involved in work to aid those in need and to helping with programmes of education both generally and in technology and music. Support will be given to help musical organisations and musically talented individuals with their training. Donations are also made to wider community charities engaged on both social and educational work as well as to organisations of the Jewish community and other bodies.

In 2009/10 the trust had an income of £1.5 million, assets of £56 million and made 96 grants totalling £480,000 of which 75 were to charities in the UK.

Area		
Area	96	£482,000
Education	14	£250,000
Relief	55	£122,000
Music	19	£67,000
Religious	8	£43,000

Beneficiaries included: Royal College of Music, London and the Tel Aviv Foundation, Israel (£15,000 each)

Applications

In writing to the correspondent. Applications need to be received by February, as trustees meet in March.

The Harding Trust

Arts, general charitable purposes

£121,000 (2009/10)

Beneficial area

Mainly, but not exclusively, north Staffordshire and surrounding areas.

Brabners Chaffe Street, Horton House, Exchange Flags, Liverpool L2 3YL
Tel: 0151 600 3000
Email: peter.orourke@brabnerscs.com
Correspondent: Peter O'Rourke
Trustees: G G Wall; J P C Fowell; M N Lloyd; G B Snow.
CC Number: 328182

Information available

Accounts were available from the Charity Commission, but without a grants list.

The aim of this trust is to promote, improve, develop and maintain public education in, and appreciation of, the art and science of music, by sponsoring or by otherwise supporting public concerts, recitals and performances by amateur and professional organisations.

In 2009/10 the trust had assets of £3.6 million and an income of £116,000. Grants were made totalling £121,000.

Previous grants beneficiaries included: Donna Louise Trust, Douglas Macmillan Hospice, Harding Trust Piano Recitals, Katharine House Hospice, Patrons Victoria Hall Organ, St John's Ambulance, Stoke on Trent Festival, Stoke on Trent Music School – Education Scheme, Wolverhampton Civic Hall Orchestra and Wolverhampton Recital Series.

Applications

In writing to the correspondent. The trustees meet annually in spring/early summer. Accounts are needed for recurrent applications.

William Harding's Charity

Education, welfare

£305,000 (2010)

Beneficial area

Aylesbury.

Parrott and Coales LLP, 14 Bourbon Street, Aylesbury, Buckinghamshire HP20 2RS
Tel: 01296 318501
Website: www.bucksinfo.net/william-harding-s-charity
Correspondent: J Leggett
Trustees: Bernard Griffin, Chair; William Chapple; Mrs Freda Roberts; Leslie Sheldon; Mrs Betty Foster; John Vooght; Mrs Kathleen Brooker; Mrs Pennie Thorne; Roger Evans.
CC Number: 310619

Information available

Accounts were on file at the Charity Commission.

Under a scheme of 1978, Harding's Eleemosynary Charity and Harding's Educational Charity (both set up in the eighteenth century) merged to become William Harding's Charity. Its objects, limited to the town of Aylesbury, include the provision of almshouses and special benefits of any kind not normally provided by the local authority for any maintained school or any college of education or other institution of further education in or substantially serving the town of Aylesbury; awarding maintenance allowances tenable at any school, university or college of further education; relief in need and provision of general benefit in Aylesbury.

The trustees are made up of two nominative members from Buckinghamshire County Council and from Aylesbury Charter Trustees, and seven co-optive trustees who, the trust states: 'shall be persons who through residence, occupation or employment or otherwise shall have special knowledge of the Town of Aylesbury'.

The trust owns 35 properties in Aylesbury itself, land in or adjacent to Aylesbury and is a member of the National Association of Almshouses.

In 2010 the charity had assets of £23.3 million, an income of £692,000 and made grants totalling £305,000.

Grants to organisations totalled £220,000 and were broken down into the following categories:

Travel for clubs/societies/schools	£52,000
Schools and other educational establishments	£47,000
Equipment and tools for young people	£7,000
General benefits/relief in need	£84,000
Youth groups	£30,000

A further £85,000 was awarded to 143 individuals.

Grant beneficiaries include: Skill Centre UK (£15,000); Aylesbury Grammar School and Aylesbury Citizens Advice Bureau (£10,000 each); and Gerald Simmonds Healthcare (£6,000); Aylesbury Homestarts (£5,000); Grange Youth Centre (£3,500); Girl Guide Bucks (£2,250); Yours Social Club (£1,500); Cansel's 60 Club (£1,250) and Thursday Morning Club (£1,100).

Exclusions

All persons and organisations not based in Aylesbury Town.

Applications

In writing to the correspondent. Trustees meet on a monthly basis to consider and determine applications for charitable assistance.

Common applicant mistakes

Applications from outside our of remit area, which is Aylesbury.'

The Hare of Steep Charitable Trust

General

£49,000 (2009/10)

Beneficial area

UK, with preference for the south of England, especially Petersfield and East Hampshire.

6 Heath Road, Petersfield, Hampshire GU31 4EJ

Tel: 01730 267953
Correspondent: Mrs S M Fowler, Hon. Secretary
Trustees: P L F Baillon; J S Grenfell; J R F Fowler; S M Fowler; S E R Johnson-Hill.
CC Number: 297308

Information available

Accounts were available from the Charity Commission.

In 2009/10 the trust had assets of £145,000 and an income of £41,000. Grants were made to 41 organisations totalling £49,000. The Trust made only one donation greater than 5% of the total distributed, a grant of £2,500 paid to the King's Arms, a charity which supports local youth clubs. There's a preference for local charities and other community projects in the south of England particularly in East Hampshire.

Unfortunately an exact breakdown of the grant beneficiaries was not provided by the trust. Previous grants have been made to Alzheimer's Disease Society, Arthritis and Rheumatism Council – Petersfield, British Heart Foundation, Rainbow House Trust and SSAFA.

Exclusions

No funding for overseas charities, students, visits abroad or political causes.

Applications

The trust has previously stated that the trustees already support as many charities as they could wish and would certainly not welcome any appeals from others. Unsolicited requests are not acknowledged.

The Harebell Centenary Fund

General, education, medical research, animal welfare

£65,000 (2009)

Beneficial area

UK.

50 Broadway, London SW1H 0BL

Tel: 020 7227 7000
Email: pennychapman@bdb-law.co.uk
Correspondent: Ms P J Chapman
Trustees: J M Denker; M I Goodbody.
CC Number: 1003552

Information available

Accounts were available from the Charity Commission.

Established in 1991, this trust provides funding towards the promotion of neurological and neurosurgical research and the relief of sickness and suffering amongst animals, as well as holding an interest in the education of young people.

The current policy of the trustees is to concentrate on making donations to charities that do not receive widespread public support and to keep administrative expenses to a minimum. For this reason the trustees have decided to make donations only to registered charities and not to individuals.

In 2009 it had assets of £1.9 million, which generated an income of £69,000. Grants totalling £65,000 were made to 28 organisations, many of which were hospices. Governance costs were high at £11,000.

All grants ranged between £2,000 and £3,500 each. Beneficiaries included: Crathie School (£3,500); Daws Hall Trust, DEMAND, Ferriers Barn and Hebridean Trust – the Treshnish Isles (£2,500 each); and Little Haven Children's Hospice, St Christopher's Hospice, the Rachael Hospice and the Trinity Hospice (£2,000 each).

Exclusions

No grants are made towards infrastructure or to individuals.

Applications

In writing to the correspondent. Unsolicited applications are not requested, as the trustees prefer to make donations to charities whose work they have come across through their own research.

Common applicant mistakes

'Applications from individuals are stated not to be considered but many individuals still apply.'

The Hargrave Foundation

General, medical, welfare

£129,000 (2009/10)

Beneficial area
Worldwide.

47 Lamb's Conduit Street, London WC1N 3NG
Correspondent: Stephen Hargrave, Trustee
Trustees: Stephen Hargrave; Dominic Moseley; Mark Parkin.
CC Number: 1106524

Information available
Accounts were on available from the Charity Commission.

Registered with the Charity Commission in November 2004, in its first year of operation this trust received income of £2.8 million.

In 2009/10 it had assets of £2.9 million, an income of £151,000 and made grants to organisations totalling £129,000.

Beneficiaries included: Institute of Healing of Memories (£38,000); Reform Research Trust (£20,000); British Liver Trust, Prostate Cancer Charity, Writers & Scholars Educational Trust and English Pen (£10,000 each). Grants were made to other charities amounting to £32,000, with an additional £5,000 given in grants to individuals.

Applications
In writing to the correspondent.

The Harris Family Charitable Trust

Health, sickness

£382,000 (2009/10)

Beneficial area
UK.

65 New Cavendish Street, London W1G 7LS
Tel: 020 7467 6300
Correspondent: R M Harris, Trustee

Trustees: R M Harris; Loretta Harris; Charlotte Emma Harris.
CC Number: 1064394

Information available
Basic information taken from the Charity Commission website.

Set up in 1997, the trust makes grants to organisations dealing with health issues and the alleviation of sickness.

In 2009/10 it had, for the second year running, an unusually low income of £10,500 and total expenditure of £382,000.

Applications
The trustees' 2010/11 report and accounts states:

> The charity invites applications for funding of projects through various sources. The applications are reviewed by the trustees who ensure that they are in accordance with the charity's objectives.

The Edith Lilian Harrison 2000 Foundation

General

£69,500 (2009/10)

Beneficial area
UK.

TWM Solicitors, 40 West Street, Reigate, Surrey RH2 9BT
Tel: 01737 221212
Fax: 01737 240120
Email: reigate.reception@twmsolicitors.com
Correspondent: Geoffrey Peyer, Trustee
Trustees: Geoffrey Peyer; Clive Andrews; Paul Bradley.
CC Number: 1085651

Information available
Accounts were available from the Charity Commission.

The foundation was established in 2000 for general charitable purposes, although grantmaking activities only commenced in 2008/09 after receiving £3.5 million from the estate of the late Edith Lilian Harrison.

The foundation's accounts give this insight into its funding strategy:

> In terms of identifying grant recipients, the trustees have followed the general directions set out in a Letter of Wishes signed by Mrs Harrison on 5th September 2000. The level of grants payable during the year largely matches the level of incoming resources. Although the trustees have unfettered discretion in identifying future grant recipients, it is likely that they will attempt to support projects which reflect their understanding of the charitable aims of Mrs Harrison.

In 2009/10 the foundation had assets of £2.6 million and an income of £72,000. Grants were made to three organisations totalling £69,500.

The beneficiaries that received a grant in this year are likely to represent the charitable wishes and interests of the settlor. They were: Alzheimer's Society (£29,500); and Cardiac Risk in the Young – CRY and Salisbury Hospice (£20,000 each).

Applications
In writing to the correspondent. The trustees meet quarterly. At each regular meeting, applications for grants are considered and duly dealt with.

The Alfred And Peggy Harvey Charitable Trust

Medical, research, older people, children and young people with disabilities or disadvantages, visually and hearing impaired people

£53,000 (2009/10)

Beneficial area
UK, with a strong preference for Kent, Surrey and South East London.

c/o Manches LLP, Aldwych House, 81 Aldwych, London WC2B 4RP
Tel: 020 7404 4433
Correspondent: The Trustees
Trustees: Colin John Russell; John Duncan; Kevin James Custis.

CC Number: 1095855

Information available

Accounts were available from the Charity Commission.

The trust has four main objects:

- the advancement and funding of medical and surgical studies and research
- the care of the elderly and the provision of accommodation for the elderly
- the care of and provision of financial support for disabled children and young people and for children and young people suffering from the lack of stable family upbringing or other social or educational disadvantages
- the care of blind and deaf people.

The trust will only consider applications from charities in Kent, Surrey and South East London.

In 2009/10 the trust had assets of £330,000 and an income of £84,000. Grants to 15 organisations totalled £53,000.

Beneficiaries included: Macular Disease Society (£10,000); Country Holidays For Inner City Kids (£6,400); Lighthouse Educational Scheme (£4,700); E-Learning Foundation (£4,000); Hope UK (£3,800); Children's Country Holiday Fund (£3,500); Kidscape (£3,000); Happy Days (£2,500); Action for Kids (£2,000); and Child Victims of Crime (£1,000).

Applications

In writing to the correspondent.

The Haskel Family Foundation

Jewish, social-policy research, arts, education

£30,000 (2009)

Beneficial area

UK.

12 Rosemont Road, Richmond-upon-Thames, Surrey TW10 6QL
Tel: 0208 948 7711

Correspondent: Lord Simon Haskel
Trustees: A M Davis; S Haskel; M Nutman; Lord Haskel.
CC Number: 1039969

Information available

Accounts were on file at the Charity Commission.

The charity funds projects concerned with social-policy research, Jewish communal life, arts and education.

In 2009 it had assets of £536,000 and an income of £29,000. Grants totalled £30,000 and were: Aldeburgh Music (£15,000); Liberal Judaism and the Rosetree Trust (£5,000 each); Children Leukaemia (£3,500); Jewish Research (£1,100) and The Rainbow Trust (£500).

Applications

This trust states that it does not respond to unsolicited applications.

Hasluck Charitable Trust

Health, welfare, disability, youth, overseas aid

£94,000 (2009/10)

Beneficial area

UK.

Rathbone Trust Company Limited, 159 New Bond Street, London W1S 2UD
Tel: 020 7399 0447
Email: john.billing@rathbones.com
Correspondent: John Billing, Trustee
Trustees: Matthew James Wakefield; John Billing.
CC Number: 1115323

Information available

Accounts were on file at the Charity Commission.

This trust was registered with the Charity Commission on 14 July 2008. Half of the income received is allocated to eight charities (Barnardo's, Mrs R H Hotblacks Michelham Priory Endowment Fund, International Fund for Animal Welfare, Macmillan Cancer Relief, the Riding for the Disabled Association,

RNLI, RSPB and Scope), which are of particular interest to the settlor. The remaining monies are distributed to such charitable bodies as the trustees decide.

In 2009/10 the trust had assets of £1.2 million and an income of £126,000. Grants totalled £94,000.

The sum of £48,000 was given to the trust's eight primary beneficiaries. There were a further 33 grants made in the range of £1,000 to £4,000. Beneficiaries included: World Vision, Kent Air Ambulance, London Narrow Boat Project, Children's Liver Disease Foundation, Coram, Adoption Support, Wildfowl and Wetlands Trust, Signpost Stockport for Carers, Credit Action, Beat Bullying and Friends of the Elderly.

Applications

In writing to the correspondent. Grants are generally distributed in January and July, although consideration is given to appeals received at other times of the year.

Common applicant mistakes

'We ask applicants not to send copies of their accounts as these can be viewed online. We only reply to successful applicants and do not wish to receive stamped addressed envelopes from any seeking acknowledgement of their application.'

The M A Hawe Settlement

General

£1.8 million to organisations and individuals (2009/10)

Beneficial area

UK, with a preference for the north west of England, particularly the Fylde coast area.

94 Park View Road, Lytham St Annes, Lancashire FY8 4JF
Tel: 01253 796888
Correspondent: M A Hawe, Trustee
Trustees: M A Hawe; Mrs. G Hawe; M G Hawe.
CC Number: 327827

Information available

Accounts were available from the Charity Commission.

In 2009/10 the trust had assets of £3.4 million and an income of £77,000. Grants to organisations totalled over £1.8 million with over £1.7 million donated to Kensington House Trust Limited and £4,000 being distributed to individuals. Future donations to Kensington House Trust will be at a reduced rate.

In April 1993 the trustees purchased a property with the intention that it should be converted in order to provide suitable accommodation on a short stay basis for young homeless people. A company, The Kensington House Trust Limited, operating under the name The Kensington Foundation (Charity commission no. 1044235) was established for the purpose of operating the accommodation. The hostel was closed in 2008/09.

This company now provides a Crisis Grant Line, furniture and equipment to people in need, Adventure Time, a project designed to give children from the Blackpool area a five day holiday to experience challenging outdoor activities and the Daisy Chain Project which provides holidays in Blackpool for families with special needs children.

The foundation will now focus on the Daisy Chain Project at Normoss Farm as its main activity. In order to help fund this, the trustees have decided to put Kensington House on the market and the proceeds will be invested or used to fund the further development required.

The remaining grants ranged between £200 and £5,500. Beneficiaries were The Cross and Passion Sisters (£5,500); Haiti Earthquake and Holy Cross Church and Soup Kitchen (£1,000 each); Kenyan Orphan Project (£500); Home Start Fund Day and Claremont School (£250 each); and Rev Ballard – Sri Lanka (£200).

Applications

In writing to the correspondent.

The Hawthorne Charitable Trust

General

£124,000 (2009/10)

Beneficial area

UK, especially Hereford and Worcester.

c/o Baker Tilly, 25 Farringdon Street, London EC4A 4AB
Tel: 020 3201 8298
Correspondent: Mrs Evaline Sarbout
Trustees: Mrs A S C Berington; R J Clark.
CC Number: 233921

Information available

Full accounts were available from the Charity Commission.

The trust supports a wide range of organisations, particularly health and welfare causes but also charities concerned with animal welfare, disability, heritage and young people.

In 2009/10 it had assets of £6.7 million, which generated an income of £161,000. Grants were made to 66 organisations totalling £124,000. Donations were broken down into the following categories:

Environment, conservation and heritage	9	£30,000
Medical, health and sickness	13	£29,000
Disability	7	£11,000
Caring for animals	4	£6,000
Relief of poverty	3	£7,000
Other	30	£47,000

Grants ranged between £100 and £6,000; beneficiaries included: National Trust (£6,000); Friends of the Elderly – Davenham & Perrans House (£5,000); St Andrew's Club (£3,000); Ability Net and Compassion in World Farming Trust (£2,500 each); County Air Ambulance Trust (£2,000); Acquired Aphasia Trust (£1,000); Vale Wildlife Hospital and Rehabilitation Centre (£500); MacMillan Cancer (£200); and Primrose Hospice (£100).

A number of the above beneficiaries have been supported in previous years.

Exclusions

Grants are given to registered charities only. No grants to individuals.

Applications

In writing to the correspondent, including up-to-date accounts. Applications should be received by October for consideration in November.

The Dorothy Hay-Bolton Charitable Trust

Deaf, blind

Around £40,000 (2009/10)

Beneficial area

UK, with a preference for the South East of England and overseas.

c/o F W Stephens, 3rd Floor, 24 Chiswell Street, London EC1Y 4YX
Tel: 0207 382 1820
Email: brian.carter@fwstephens.co.uk
Correspondent: Brian E Carter, Trustee
Trustees: Brian E Carter; Stephen J Gallico.
CC Number: 1010438

Information available

Accounts had been received at the Charity Commission, but were unavailable to view.

The trust makes grants towards charities working with people who are deaf or blind, particularly children, young people and elderly people. In 2009/10 the trust had an income of £24,000 and a total expenditure of £65,000. Further information was not available.

Previous beneficiaries included: Hearing Dogs for the Deaf (£3,500); Action for Blind People, Sussex Lantern and Telephones for the Blind (£2,500); Eyeless Trust (£1,500); British Blind Sport and Esther Benjamin's Trust (£1,250); East Sussex Association for the Blind (£1,000); The Seeing Ear (£750); and East Kent Cycling Club (£250).

Exclusions

The trust states that it does not generally give to individuals.

Applications

In writing to the correspondent.

Common applicant mistakes

'Many applications are outside of our grant criteria.'

The Haymills Charitable Trust

Education, medicine, welfare, youth

£230,000 to organisations and individuals (2009/10)

Beneficial area

UK, but particularly the west of London and Suffolk, where the Haymills group is sited.

7 Wildwood, Northwood HA6 2DB
Tel: 01923 825989
Email: ian.w.ferres@btinternet.com
Correspondent: I W Ferres, Secretary
Trustees: W G Underwood, Chair; E F C Drake; I W Ferres; J A Sharpe; J L Wosner; I R Brown.
CC Number: 277761

Information available

Accounts were available from the Charity Commission. The trustees' 2010/11 report states:

> The trustees endeavour to make the best use of the monies available from the funds of the trust. In particular donations are made to projects they believe to be inadequately supported.

In the past grants have fallen into four main categories:

- Education: grants to schools, colleges and universities
- Medicine: grants to hospitals and associated institutions and to medical research
- Welfare: primarily to include former Haymills' staff, and to those who are considered to be 'in necessitous circumstances' or who are otherwise distressed or disadvantaged

- Youth: support for training schemes to assist in the education, welfare and training of young people

In 2009/10 it had assets of £6.8 million and an income of £170,000. Grants totalled £230,000 and were broken down as follows:

Youth and welfare	£157,000
Medical	£41,000
Educational	£32,000

Beneficiaries included: Merchant Taylors' School for the Geoffrey Cox Scholarships (£30,000); and the Royal College of Physicians and the British Red Cross (£5,000 each).

In addition, research societies supported included Cancer, Plastic Surgery and Ischaemia. League of Friends at Ealing, Central Middlesex and Bournemouth Eye Hospitals have continued to be supported as well as the London and St John's Ambulances.

Payments in the past have also been made to support retired employees of Haymills Contractors Ltd.

Exclusions

No personal applications will be considered unless endorsed by a university, college or other appropriate authority.

Applications

In writing to the correspondent, but note the comments in the general section. Trustees meet at least twice a year, usually in March and October. Applications are not acknowledged.

May Hearnshaw's Charity

General

£29,000 (2009/10)

Beneficial area

UK, particularly South Yorkshire, North Nottinghamshire, Derbyshire, East Lancashire and Cheshire areas.

Barber Harrison and Platt, 2 Rutland Park, Sheffield S10 2PD
Correspondent: Michael Ferreday, Trustee

Trustees: Marjorie West; Michael Ferreday; Richard Law; William Munro; D C Law.
CC Number: 1008638

Information available

Accounts were available from the Charity Commission.

This trust was established by the will of the late May Hearnshaw who died in 1988. It was her wish that the trust be used for the promotion of education, advancement of religion and relief of poverty and sickness. Support is mostly given to children's organisations within these themes. Grants are made to UK-wide charities or local charities working in the South Yorkshire, North Nottinghamshire, Derbyshire, East Lancashire and Cheshire areas.

In 2009/10 the trust had assets of £1.8 million and an income of £71,000. Grants were made to 14 organisations totalling £29,000.

Beneficiaries were: Holmesfield Scouts (£5,000); Neurocare – Sheffield Hallamshire Hospital (£4,100 in two grants); Action for Kids (£3,500); National Kidney Foundation (£3,000); Yorkshire Air Ambulance (£2,500); Meadowhead Community Learning Trust, Stroke Association and Barnardo's (£2,000 each); Tansley Methodist Church, Independent Age, Shelter Housing Difficulties, Christians Against Poverty and Ecclesall Live at Home Scheme (£1,000 each); and NORSACA (£750).

Applications

The trustees' 2010/11 report states:

> The trustees usually meet three times a year when they decide on and make major grants to charitable organisations but may decide to make grants at any time. They do not include in their consideration appeals received direct from individuals.

The Heathcoat Trust

Welfare, local causes to Tiverton, Devon

£115,000 to organisations
(2009/10)

Beneficial area

Mainly Tiverton, Devon.

The Factory, Tiverton, Devon
EX16 5LL
Tel: 01884 254949
Website: www.heathcoat.co.uk
Correspondent: Mr E W Summers, Secretary
Trustees: Sir Ian Heathcoat Amory; M J Gratton; J Smith; Mr C Dunster; Mr S Butt.
CC Number: 203367

Information available

Accounts were available from the Charity Commission.

The trust was established in 1945. Its objectives as stated in the 2010/11 accounts are:

> For the relief of financial hardship, for education and training, for building or making grants to health institutions, and in certain circumstances for making contributions to any charity but mostly in Tiverton in Devon and its neighbourhood, or in places where the firms John Heathcoat and Company Limited and Lowman Manufacturing Company Limited and their subsidiaries carry on business. In so far as the income cannot be applied towards the objects specified in the trust deed, it may be applied for any charitable purpose.

Over 100 grants a year, mostly under £1,000 each, are made to organisations and nearly all to local causes around the Tiverton area. Other grants are made to individuals, employees and pensioners of the Heathcoat group of companies. Educational grants are given to children of those employees or pensioners and also to local students attending schools and colleges in Tiverton, or beyond if courses are not available locally.

In 2009/10 the trust had assets of £19.3 million and an income of £684,000. Grants totalled £586,000 of which £115,000 went to organisations and £454,000 to individuals.

Applications

In writing to the correspondent. There are application forms for certain education grants.

The Charlotte Heber-Percy Charitable Trust

General

£251,000 (2009/10)

Beneficial area

Worldwide, with a preference for Gloucestershire.

Rathbones, 159 New Bond Street, London W1S 2UD
Tel: 020 7399 0820
Correspondent: The Administrator
Trustees: C S Heber Percy; J A Prest.
CC Number: 284387

Information available

Full accounts were on file at the Charity Commission.

Set up by a deed created in 1981, the trust has a stated preference for Gloucestershire. In addition to local appeals, non-local applications are accumulated and considered annually by the trustees.

In 2009/10 the trust had assets of £5.6 million, which generated an income of £212,000. Grants were made to organisations totalling £251,000, which were distributed in the following categories:

Medical, cancer and hospices	£62,000
Animal welfare and the local environment	£57,000
Education and children	£53,000
Local organisation	£32,000
International charities	£13,000
The arts and museums	£8,000
General charitable purposes	£28,000

Exclusions

No grants to individuals.

Applications

The correspondent stated that unsolicited applications are not required.

Percy Hedley 1990 Charitable Trust

General charitable purposes

£47,000 (2009/10)

Beneficial area

UK with a preference for Northumberland and Tyne and Wear.

10 Castleton Close, Newcastle upon Tyne NE2 2HF
Tel: 0191 281 5953
Correspondent: John Armstrong, Trustee
Trustees: John Armstrong; Bill Meikle; Fiona Ruffman.
CC Number: 1000033

Information available

Accounts were available from the Charity Commission.

In 2009/10 the trust had assets of £1.3 million and an income of £47,000. Grants were made to 69 organisations totalling £47,000.

Beneficiaries included: Percy Headley Foundation (£5,000); Newcastle Royal Grammar School Bursary Fund and Central Newcastle High School GDST Bursary Fund (£3,000 each); St Oswald's Hospice, Anaphylaxis Campaign and Samaritans – Newcastle (£1,000 each); Employment Opportunities, Combat Stress, Girl Guiding – North Tyneside, Koestler Trust, Natural History Society of Northumberland, Newcastle Dog and Cat Shelter, Age UK, British Blind Sport, Embleton Cygnets Nursery, National Youth Orchestra, Perthes Association and Woodland Trust (£500 each); and Bamburgh Church – St Aidan's (£250).

Applications

In writing to the correspondent. Trustees meet twice a year.

Common applicant mistakes

'No application form; no accounts; they have not read the website.'

The Hellenic Foundation

Greek education in the UK

Around £23,000 (2010)

Beneficial area
UK.

150 Aldersgate Street, London
EC1A 4AB
Tel: 020 7251 5100
Correspondent: The Secretary
Trustees: Stamos J Fafalios; Nicos H Sideris; Constantinos I Caroussis; Mary Bromley; George J D Lemos; Louisa Williamson; Joanna Caroussis; Nikki Chandris; Pantelis Michelakis.
CC Number: 326301

Information available
Basic information taken from the Charity Commission website.

The foundation was set up in 1982 to advance and propagate education and learning in Great Britain in the cultural tradition and heritage of Greece and particularly in the subjects involving education, research, music and dance, books and library facilities and university symposia.

In 2010 the trust had an income of £21,000 and a total expenditure of £23,000. We have no information regarding beneficiaries.

Previously beneficiaries included: Royal Academy Byzantine exhibition (£15,000); Theatro Technis (£1,000); and Aghia Shophia School (£200).

Exclusions
The foundation is unable to offer scholarships or grants to cover tuition fees and living expenses.

Applications
In writing to the correspondent.

The Michael and Morven Heller Charitable Foundation

University and medical research projects, the arts

£217,000 (2009/10)

Beneficial area
Worldwide.

Carlton House, 22a St James's Square, London SW1Y 4JH
Tel: 020 7415 5000
Fax: 020 7415 0611
Correspondent: M A Heller, Trustee
Trustees: Michael Heller; Morven Heller; W S Trustee Company Limited.
CC Number: 327832

Information available
Accounts were available from the Charity Commission.

This trust was established in 1972, and funds specific projects relating to medical research, science and educational research. This usually involves making large grants to universities for research purposes, particularly medical research. In practice, there appears to be some preference for Jewish organisations.

In 2009/10 the trust had assets of £3.9 million and an income of £302,000. Grants totalled £217,000, broken down as follows:

Education	£166,000
Humanitarian	£31,000
Research	£20,000

Exclusions
No support for individuals.

Applications
In writing to the correspondent.

The Simon Heller Charitable Settlement

Medical research, science and educational research

£355,000 (2009/10)

Beneficial area
Worldwide.

Carlton House, 22a St James' Square, London SW1Y 4JH
Tel: 020 7415 5000
Correspondent: The Trustees
Trustees: M A Heller; Morven Heller; W S Trustee Company Limited.
CC Number: 265405

Information available
Accounts, without a list of beneficiaries, were available from the Charity Commission website.

This trust was established in 1972, and funds specific projects relating to medical research, science and educational research. This usually involves making large grants to universities for research purposes, particularly medical research. In practice, there appears to be some preference for Jewish organisations.

In 2009/10 the trust had assets of £7.2 million and an income of £384,000. Grants were made totalling £355,000. Broken down as follows: education (£262,000); humanitarian (£73,000); and research (£20,000). No list of grants was included with the accounts filed at the Charity Commission.

Previous beneficiaries include: Institute for Jewish Policy Research (£35,000); Jewish Care (£30,000), Aish Hatora (£15,000 in two grants), Spiro Institute (£13,000), Scopus (£12,000 in two grants) and Chief Rabbinate Charitable Trust (£10,000).

Exclusions
No grants to individuals.

Applications
In writing to the correspondent.

Help the Homeless

Homelessness

£85,000 (2009/10)

Beneficial area

UK.

6th Floor, 248 Tottenham Court Road, London W1T 7QZ
Fax: 020 7636 1428
Email: hth@help-the-homeless.org.uk
Website: www.help-the-homeless.org.uk
Correspondent: Terry Kenny, Secretary
Trustees: F J Bergin; T S Cookson; L A Bains; T Rogers; P Fullerton; J Rose.
CC Number: 271988

Information available

Accounts were available from the Charity Commission and the trust has a useful website.

The trust makes grants to smaller or new voluntary organisations (with a turnover of less than £1 million a year), who are registered charities, for capital costs directly relating to projects that assist individuals in their return to mainstream society, rather than simply offer shelter or other forms of sustenance. Grants to larger charities are considered if the project is suitably innovative and it is only possible for a large organisation to develop it. Grants do not normally exceed £3,000.

In 2009/10 the trust had assets of £1.2 million and an income of £60,000. Grants were made totalling £85,000.

The largest grant made during the year was given to the Wellspring – Stockport (£30,000). Other beneficiaries included: Pilsdon Community (£5,000); Bridge Trust Corporation (£4,300); Streetwork UK and the Amber Foundation (£3,000 each); One25 Limited (£2,800); Hornsey YMCA (£2,600); Pavement (£2,000); Clock Tower Sanctuary – Brighton (£1,800); Causeway Irish Housing Association (£1,400); and Burntwood Pathway Project (£1,000).

Exclusions

Charities with substantial funds are not supported. No grants to individuals.

Applications

Application forms can be downloaded from the trust's website. The quarterly deadlines for applications each year are: 31 March, 30 June, 30 September and 31 December.

Help the Hospices

Hospices

£362,000 to organisations and individuals (2009/10)

Beneficial area

UK and overseas.

34–44 Britannia Street, London WC1X 9JG
Tel: 020 7520 8277
Fax: 020 7278 1021
Email: info@helpthehospices.org.uk
Website: www.helpthehospices.org.uk
Correspondent: Grants Team
Trustees: Rt Hon. Lord Howard of Lympne; Peter Holliday; Sally Taylor; Bay Green; Paul Dyer; Dr Ros Taylor; Beverley Brooks; Gary Hawkes; Marina Phillips; Sheila Tonge; Isabelle Whaite; Peter Ellis; Shaun O'Leary; Sue Newman.
CC Number: 1014851

Information available

Accounts were available from the Charity Commission; the charity has a useful website.

The objects of the charity are:
- to facilitate and promote the relief, care and treatment of the sick, especially of the dying, and the support and care of their families and carers and of the bereaved
- to facilitate and promote the charitable activities of independent hospices
- to provide or facilitate education and training for professionals and volunteers engaged in palliative care

- to increase awareness among the general public of the values, principles and practice of hospice and palliative care.

These objectives are met by providing education and training as well as funding hospices and palliative care units through a number of grant schemes. See the charity's website for up-to-date details of open and forthcoming programmes.

In 2009/10 the trust had assets of £7.2 million and an income of £6.1 million, mostly from voluntary income.

Out of a total charitable expenditure of £5.9 million, grants were made totalling £362,000, of which £314,000 was given in the UK and £48,000 overseas. Grants were given to 177 hospices and 386 individuals.

Applications

The trust's website provides guidelines for each programme and clear information on application procedures and deadlines. Depending on the programme, application forms can be downloaded or completed through the online application system.

Common applicant mistakes

'Not reading our eligibility criteria.'

The Christina Mary Hendrie Trust for Scottish and Canadian Charities

Youth, people who are elderly, general

£288,000 (2008/09)

Beneficial area

Scotland and Canada.

Anderson Strathern Solicitors, 1 Rutland Court, Edinburgh EH3 8EY
Tel: 0131 270 7700
Fax: 0131 270 7788
Website: www.christinamaryhendrietrust.com
Correspondent: Alan Sharp, Secretary

SC Number: SC014514

Information available

Accounts were available from the trust's website in the 'legal' section.

The trust was established in 1975 following the death in Scotland of Christina Mary Hendrie. The funds constituting the trust originated in Canada and grants are distributed to charities throughout Scotland and Canada. Its main preference is to support charities that are connected with young or older people, although it will consider charities with general charitable purposes.

In 2009/10 the trust's assets stood at £6.3 million with an income of £223,000. Grants totalled £288,000.

Grant beneficiaries included: William Simpson's Home (£40,000); Barnardo's Scotland (£22,500); Black Watch (£25,000); Elgin Youth Development Group, Place 2 Be and Queen Victoria School (£15,000 each); Canine Partners and Rock Trust (£10,000 each); Aberlour, Alzheimer's Research Trust and Edinburgh Young Carers Project (£5,000 each); Alcohol Focus Scotland(£2,000); and Junction and Royston Youth Project (£1,000 each).

Exclusions

Grants are not given to individuals.

Applications

In writing to the correspondent.

Philip Henman Trust

Overseas development

£39,000 to organisations (2009/10)

Beneficial area

Worldwide.

16 Pembury Road, Tonbridge TN9 2HX
Tel: 01732 362227
Email: info@pht.org.uk
Website: www.pht.org.uk

Correspondent: Joseph Charles Clark, Trustee
CC Number: 1054707

Information available

Accounts were available from the Charity Commission, but without a list of grants.

The Philip Henman Trust offers grants to major UK development organisations based overseas requiring partnership funding for projects lasting between three and five years. These grants are split into annual payments (normally between £3,000 and £5,000 per annum) with a maximum total of £25,000. Once the grant has been approved the organisation will be guaranteed an annual grant for the duration of the project, as long as receipts and reports are sent back to the trust. Once a grant has been given, the organisation cannot apply for a grant in respect of a project for which they have already received funding.

The trust only has resources to guarantee an average of two new long term grants a year, and therefore it is important to be sure any project fits the criteria before applying. Successful applications are normally those that prove the following:

- the project is being run professionally by an established major UK registered charity (normally defined as having an income of over £100,000 per annum)
- the project is concerned with long term overseas development
- the project will start and finish within five years – no funding is given for ongoing concerns
- the funding from the trust is important to the project (normally the grant should account for between 20% and 80% of the total project budget)
- the project will provide a lasting beneficial impact to the people or environment it seeks to help
- the project is being partly funded by other sources – voluntary work and central office administration costs can be counted as other source funding.

In 2009/10 the trust had assets of £1.8 million and an income of £59,000. Grants totalled £40,000, and were broken down as follows:

Overseas aid	£34,000
Medical and community work	£5,000
Individuals	£1,100
Other	£145

Unfortunately, a list of beneficiaries was not included in the accounts.

Applications

Applications are only considered once a year – the deadline is always 10 September. Applications are no longer accepted by post. Please use the online form (available on the 'Applications' page on the trust's website) to submit a request for funding.

The G D Herbert Charitable Trust

Medicine, health, welfare, environmental resources

£59,000 (2009)

Beneficial area

UK.

Barnards Inn, 86 Fetter Lane, London EC4A 1EN
Tel: 0207 405 1234
Correspondent: J J H Burden, Trustee
CC Number: 295998

Information available

Accounts were available from the Charity Commission, but without a grants list.

The trust makes grants in the areas of medicine, health, welfare and environmental resources. It mainly gives regular grants to a set list of charities, with a few one-off grants given each year.

In 2009/10 this trust had assets of £1.8 million, which generated an income of £46,000. There were 25 'regular donations' made totalling £59,000.

Previous beneficiaries of 'special donations' included: Ashford and Tenterden Samaritans, Children's Fire and Burn Trust, The Queen Alexandra Hospital Home, National ME Centre for Fatigue Syndromes, The Rainbow Centre, St Raphael's Hospice and Deafness Research UK (£2,000 each).

Previous beneficiaries of 'regular donations' included: The National Trust, Friends of the Elderly, Marie Curie Cancer Care, PDSA, Royal College of Surgeons of England, Royal Hospital for Neuro-Disability and The Woodland Trust (£2,500 each); Ogbourne St Georges PCC and Wiltshire Wildlife Trust (£500 each).

Applications

In writing to the correspondent. No applications are invited other than from those charities currently supported by the trust.

The Joanna Herbert-Stepney Charitable Settlement (also known as The Paget Charitable Trust)

General – see below

£225,000 (2009/10)

Beneficial area

Worldwide, with an interest in Loughborough.

Old Village Stores, Dippenhall Street, Crondall, Farnham, Surrey GU10 5NZ
Tel: 01252 850253
Correspondent: Joanna Herbert-Stepney, Trustee
Trustees: Joanna Herbert-Stepney; Lesley Mary Blood; Meg Williams.
CC Number: 327402

Information available

Accounts were available from the Charity Commission.

The trust supports UK and local charities for general charitable purposes. Priorities include international aid and development, children who are disadvantaged, older people, animal welfare and environmental projects. The trust states that there is a preference for the 'unglamorous' and 'projects where a little money goes a long way'. In many cases ongoing support is given to organisations.

In 2009/10 the trust had assets of £6.8 million and an income of £154,000. During the year 201 grants were made to organisations totalling £225,000.

Grant beneficiaries include: Manacare Foundation (£7,600); Oxfam (£7,000); Tibet Relief Fund of UK (£3,325); International Development Partnerships and Soil Association (£3,000 each); Children's Family Trust, Vitalise, Mali Medics and Medical Foundation for Care of Victims (£2,000 each); Contact the Elderly, FARM Africa, Friends of Student Educational Trust and Mexico Child Link (£1,000 each) and Marie Stopes International, Mother's Union and St Cuthbert's Hospice (£500 each).

Exclusions

The trust states that 'sheer need is paramount, in practice, nothing else is considered'. Grants are only given to registered UK charities. Overseas projects can only be funded via UK charities; no money can be sent directly overseas. The trust does not support individuals (including students), projects for people with mental disabilities, medical research or AIDS/HIV projects.

Applications

In writing to the correspondent; there is no application form. The trustees meet in spring and autumn. The trust regrets that it cannot respond to all applications.

Common applicant mistakes

'Applications from individuals, usually students for gap years.'

The Hesed Trust

Christian

£87,000 (2009/10)

Beneficial area

UK and overseas.

14 Chiltern Avenue, Cosby, Leicestershire LE9 1UF
Tel: 0116 286 2990
Email: glynrawlings@btopenworld.com
Correspondent: G Rawlings, Secretary
Trustees: P Briggs; R Eagle; G Rawlings; J C Smith.
CC Number: 1000489

Information available

Accounts were available from the Charity Commission.

The trust's objectives are:
- the advancement of the Christian faith
- the relief of persons who are in conditions of need, hardship or distress or who are aged or sick
- the provision of instruction the Christian faith at any educational establishment
- the provision of facilities for recreation for persons in need and for the benefit of the public at large with the object of improving the conditions of life for such persons.

In 2009/10 the trust had assets of £81,000 and an income of £180,000. Grants were made to five charitable organisations totalling £87,000.

Beneficiaries were: Ministries without Borders (£42,000); All Nations Church (£24,000); Blackpool Church and City Church Coventry (£10,000 each); and Covenant Life Church Leicester (£750).

Exclusions

No support for expeditions and individual requests.

Applications

The trust states that no applications are now being considered.

The Bernhard Heuberger Charitable Trust

Jewish

£108,000 (2008/09)

Beneficial area

Worldwide.

12 Sherwood Road, London
NW4 1AD
Correspondent: The Trustees
Trustees: D H Heuberger;
S N Heuberger.
CC Number: 294378

Information available

Accounts were available from the
Charity Commission.

This trust was established in 1986. In
2008/09 the trust had assets of
£2.3 million and an income of
£111,000. During the year 24 grants
totalling £108,000 were approved,
compared with 17 grants totalling
£161,000 in the previous year.

General Purposes	5	£97,000
Education/training	4	£11,000
Medical/health/sickness	1	£1,000

Grants went to: C.M.M (£80,000);
Beis Harnadrash (£7,500); Gateshead
Jewish High School (£6,000); Kemble
Charitable Trust (£4,000); Hendon
United Synagogue (£2,400); Binoh
(£2,000); JFS School (£1,700);
Congregation Ateres ZVI Trust, the
Hebrew University and Norwood
(£1,000 each).

Other small charitable donations
amounted to £1,800.

Applications

In writing to the correspondent.

The P and C Hickinbotham Charitable Trust

Social welfare

£59,000 (2009/10)

Beneficial area

UK, with a preference for
Leicestershire and Rutland.

9 Windmill Way, Lyddington,
Oakham, Leicestershire LE15 9LY
Tel: 01572 821236
Email: rogerhick@gmail.com
Correspondent: Roger
Hickinbotham, Trustee
Trustees: Catherine Hickinbotham;
Roger Hickinbotham; Rachel
Hickinbotham; Anna Steiger.
CC Number: 216432

Information available

Accounts were available from the
Charity Commission.

Grants are generally not recurrent
and are largely to social welfare
organisations, with some churches
and Quaker meetings also receiving
support. Grants are mainly between
£1000 – £2,000, with some smaller
grants made to a variety of registered
charities. The trust gives occasional,
one-off larger grants usually between
£5,000 and £20,000.

In 2009/10 the trust had assets of
almost £3.3 million and an income of
£65,000. Grants were made to 26
organisations totalling £59,000.

Beneficiaries included: Rainbows
Children's Hospice (£5,000); De
Montfort University (£2,600); The
Mummers Foundation and The
Woodland Trust (£2,000); Society of
Friends – Leicester PM (£1,600); and
Belgrave Playhouse Cruise
Bereavement Care and NSPCC
(£1,000 each).

Exclusions

No grants to individuals applying for
bursary-type assistance or to large UK
charities.

Applications

In writing to the correspondent,
giving a brief outline of the purpose
of the grant. Replies will not be sent
to unsuccessful applicants.

Common applicant mistakes

'The trust states that it supports
applications for very specific
geographical areas – many
applications are from way outside
these areas.'

Alan Edward Higgs Charity

Child welfare

£210,000 (2009/10).

Beneficial area

Within 25 miles of the centre of
Coventry only.

Ricoh Arena Ltd, Phoenix Way,
Coventry CV6 6GE
Tel: 024 7622 1311
Email: clerk@higgscharity.org.uk
Correspondent: Peter Knatchbull-
Hugessen, Clerk
Trustees: Peter J Davis; Marilyn
F Knatchbull-Hugessen; Andrew
Young.
CC Number: 509367

Information available

Accounts were available from the
Charity Commission, but without a
grants list.

Grants are made to benefit 'wholly or
mainly the inhabitants of the area
within 25 miles of the centre of
Coventry'. The main activity
supported is 'the promotion of child
welfare, and particularly the welfare
of underprivileged children'. It is the
aim of the trustees to reach as wide a
selection of the community as
possible within the geographical
limitations. They are happy to receive
applications for grants from local
bodies or associations and from
national organisations that can show
that any grant from the charity would
be used to benefit people resident
within the geographical area [...] the
increasing range and diversity of
donations continue to be welcomed.

In the past, the majority of grants
awarded were for relatively small
amounts to a broad range of local
causes, however, during 2009/10 the
trustees decided to devote grant
making to a small number of larger
projects directly benefiting those in
the local area.

In 2009/10 the trust had assets of
£18 million and an income of
£520,000. Grants totalled £210,000
with the average grant amount being
£5,000. The trust continues to
support the Alan Higgs Centre Trust,

a multi-sports facility in a deprived area of South East Coventry.

Previous grant beneficiaries included: Coventry Institute of Creative Enterprise (£40,000); The Living Environment Trust (£28,000); Belgrade Theatre (£20,000); Family Holiday Association (£10,000); Shakespeare Hospice Appeal (£5,000); Guideposts Trust (£3,000); and the RSPB (£1,000).

Exclusions

No grants for individuals or the funding of services usually provided by statutory services, medical research, travel outside the UK or evangelical or worship activities.

Applications

In writing to the clerk to the trustees, along with:

- a copy of the latest audited accounts
- charity number (if registered)
- a detailed description of the local activities for the benefit of which the grant would be applied
- the specific purpose for which the grant is sought
- a copy of the organisation's policy that ensures the protection of young or vulnerable people and a clear description of how it is implemented and monitored.

Common applicant mistakes

'Applications from outside the eligible area; non-registered charities and individuals applying. Applications received which are addressed to the wrong charity, i.e. a mail merge failure.'

Highcroft Charitable Trust

Jewish, poverty

£107,000 (2009/10)

Beneficial area

UK and overseas.

15 Highcroft Gardens, London NW11 0LY
Correspondent: Rabbi R Fischer, Trustee
Trustees: Rabbi R Fischer; Mrs S L Fischer.

CC Number: 272684

Information available

Accounts were available from the Charity Commission.

The trust supports the advancement and study of the Jewish faith and the Torah, and also the relief of poverty and advancement of education among people of the Jewish faith. Grants have previously ranged between £150 and £5,000.

In 2009/10 the trust had assets of £406,000 and an income of £112,000. Grants totalled £107,000.

Unfortunately, a list of beneficiaries was not available in this year's accounts, however previous beneficiaries have included: Friends of Beer Miriam, Institute For Higher Rabbinic Studies and Kollel Ohr Yechiel (£5,000 each); Kollel Chibas Yerushalayim (£4,200); Craven Walk Charity Trust (£2,500); London Friends of Kamenitzer (£2,000); Hachzakas Torah Vachesed Charity (£1,900); Amutat Shaarei Harama, Beis Yaacov High School and Tashbar Manchester (£1,000 each); Belt Haknesset Kehilat Yaacov (£700) and British Friends of College Technology and Delamere Forest School (£100 each).

Applications

In writing to the correspondent.

The Holly Hill Charitable Trust

Environmental education, conservation and wildlife

£183,000 (2009/10)

Beneficial area

UK.

Unit No. 525, Citibox Kensington Ltd, 2 Old Brompton Road, London SW7 3DQ
Correspondent: The Trustees
Trustees: M D Stanley; A Lewis.
CC Number: 1044510

Information available

Accounts were available from the Charity Commission.

This trust was established in 1995 to support environmental education, conservation and wildlife organisations.

In 2009/10 it had assets of £734,000 and an income of £29,000, made from investments. Grants were made totalling £183,000.

Beneficiaries included: Landshare (£38,000); Wildcru (£27,000); Client Earth (£25,000); Rainforest Concern (£23,000); West Country Rivers Trust (£10,000); St Columbans (£5,000); EIRIS Foundation (£2,000); Fair Pensions (£1,000).

Exclusions

No grants to individuals.

Applications

In writing to the correspondent. Applications need to be received in April and September, and trustees meet in June and November.

The Derek Hill Foundation

Arts/culture

£28,000 (2009/10)

Beneficial area

UK.

c/o Rathbone Trust Company Limited, 159 New Bond Street, London W1S 2UD
Correspondent: The Trustees
Trustees: Rathbone Trust Company Limited; Earl of Gowrie; Lord Armstrong of Ilminster; Mrs Josephine Batterham; Ian Patterson.
CC Number: 801590

Information available

Accounts were available from the Charity Commission.

This foundation was set up in 1989, by the writer and artist Derek Hill. Following his death in 1990, a specific legacy was left to the foundation including properties, furniture and pieces of art. In 2009/10 it had assets of £1.4 million and an income of

£27,000. Grants totalled £62,000, of which £28,000 went to organisations.

Beneficiaries included: the British School at Rome (£9,000); Welsh National Opera (£5,000); Memorial Arts Charity (£2,500); Llanfyllin Festival Association (£2,000); Royal College of Music (£1,500); National Arts Collection (£1,000); and Lyme Regis Organ Appeal (£300).

In addition, grants were made to five individuals amounting to £34,000.

Applications
In writing to the correspondent.

The Charles Littlewood Hill Trust

Health, disability, service, children (including schools)

£180,000 (2010)

Beneficial area
UK, with a preference for Nottinghamshire and Norfolk.

Berryman Shacklock LLP, Park House, Friar Lane, Nottingham NG1 6DN
Tel: 0115 945 3700
Fax: 0115 948 0234
Correspondent: W F Whysall, Trustee
Trustees: C W L Barratt; W F Whysall; T H Farr; N R Savory.
CC Number: 286350

Information available
Accounts were on file at the Charity Commission.

The trust supports schools, disability, health, service and children's organisations. It gives UK-wide, although particular preference is given to applications from Norfolk and Nottinghamshire.

In 2010 the trust had assets of £4.1 million, which generated an income of £190,000. Grants were made totalling £180,000 and were broken down as follows, shown here with examples of beneficiaries in each category:

Norfolk – 19 grants totalling £72,500
YMCA Norfolk (£7,500); NORCAS (£5,000); Norfolk Eating Disorders Association (£3,000) and Purfleet Trust and St Edmunds Society (£1,000).

Nottinghamshire – 25 grants totalling £70,500
Maggie's Nottingham (£10,000); St John Waterwing (£6,000); Nottinghamshire Hospice (£5,000); The Army Benevolent Fund – Nottinghamshire (£3,000); Family Care (£2,000) and St Peter's Church – Toton (£1,000).

Elsewhere – 14 grants totalling £19,100
The Arkwright Scholarships (£3,600); Leonard Cheshire Disability (£2,000); Marie Curie Cancer Care and The Heather Trust (£1,000 each).

Other grants totalled £20,000.

Exclusions
Applications from individuals are not considered. Grants are seldom made for repairs of parish churches outside Nottinghamshire.

Applications
In writing to the correspondent, including the latest set of audited accounts, at least one month before trustees' meetings in March, July and November. Unsuccessful applications will not be notified.

R G Hills Charitable Trust

Health, poverty, education, general

£97,000 (2009/10)

Beneficial area
UK and overseas.

Furley Page, 39 St Margaret's Street, Canterbury, Kent CT1 2TX
Tel: 01227 763939
Correspondent: Harvey Barret, Trustee
Trustees: David Pentin; Harvey Barrett.
CC Number: 1008914

Information available
Accounts were available from the Charity Commission.

This trust was dormant until Mrs E M Hill's death in March 1996, when she left three-quarters of the residue of her estate to the trust. The balance was received in June 1999. The trust supports local and national registered charities mainly, but not exclusively, in the fields of health, poverty and education.

In 2009/10 it held assets of almost £2.9 million and had an income of £102,000. The trust made grants to 51 organisations totalling £97,000.

Beneficiaries included: Fauna and Flora International (£3,800); Motor Neurone Disease Association (£3,500); Blonde McIndoe Research Foundation and Fynvola (£3,000 each); Spurgeons, Mission to Seafarers and Salvation Army – Canterbury Corps (£2,500 each); International Animal Rescue, Crime Diversion Scheme and Farm Africa (£2,000 each); Combat Stress (£1,900); Best Beginnings (£1,500); Cardboard Citizens (£1,200); and Toynbee Hall, Welcome Day Centre, Mental Health Foundation and L'Arche Overseas Development Fund (£1,000 each).

Applications
In writing to the correspondent.

Hinchley Charitable Trust

Mainly evangelical Christian

£110,000 (2009/10)

Beneficial area
UK and overseas.

10 Coplow Terrace, Coplow Street, Birmingham B16 0DQ
Tel: 0121 455 6632
Email: bs217@cam.ac.uk
Correspondent: Prof Brian Stanley, Chair
Trustees: Prof Brian Stanley, Chair; John Levick; Mark Hobbs; Roger Northcott.
CC Number: 1108412

Information available

Accounts were available from the Charity Commission.

The trust gives grants in the following categories:

- training of Christian leaders
- holistic mission and evangelism
- Christian youth organisations
- Christian organisations in local communities
- Christian influence in the public sphere.

It is particularly keen to support smaller charities where a grant can make a significant difference to their work.

In 2009/10 the trust had assets of £2.4 million and an income of £150,000. Grants to 19 organisations totalled £110,000. This is a partial recovery from 2008/09 when the trust could only make grants of £84,000 but grantmaking has yet to return to 2007/08 levels when £140,000 was distributed. As part of the trust's strategy to maintain the effectiveness of its grantmaking during this period, it has reduced the number of grants made while increasing the value of those grants. In 2009/10, for example, 56 per cent of grants were over £5,000, compared with only 27 per cent in 2008/09.

During the year beneficiaries included: Urban Saints – formerly Crusaders Union (£23,000); Langham Partnership (£13,000); Cleenish Renewal (£10,000); LICC (£8,000); Emmanual International (£7,500); and St Edmunds College and Willowfield Community Project (£5,000 each).

Applications

The trustees adopt a proactive approach to grant making meaning unsolicited applications are rarely supported.

Stuart Hine Trust

Evangelical Christianity

£188,000 (2009/10)

Beneficial area

UK and overseas.

'Cherith', 23 Derwent Close, Hailsham, East Sussex BN27 3DA

Tel: 01323 843948
Correspondent: Raymond Bodkin, Trustee
Trustees: Raymond Bodkin; Amelia Gardner; Philip Johnson; Jonathan Birdwood Juby; Leonard Chipping.
CC Number: 326941

Information available

Accounts were available from the Charity Commission.

The trust gives grants to evangelical Christian organisations that have been supported by the trustees or by the settlor during his lifetime and that are known to the trustees.

In 2009/10 the trust held assets of £206,000. The trust had an income of £137,000, mainly from royalties received from the song 'How Great Thou Art' written by Stuart Hine. Grants were made totalling £188,000. Governance costs rose significantly to £29,000 (£14,000 in 2008/09), due to an increase in legal fees and copyright consultancy costs.

The only grant beneficiary listed in the accounts was Wycliff Bible Translators, which received a donation of £150,000. Grants to other organisations totalled £38,000.

Applications

The trust states that 'unsolicited requests for funds will not be considered'. Funds are basically distributed in accordance with the wishes of the settlor.

The Hinrichsen Foundation

Music

£0 (2009) Previously around £40,000.

Beneficial area

UK.

PO Box 309, Leatherhead, Surrey KT22 2AT
Email: hinrichsen.foundation@ editionpeters.com
Website: www.hinrichsenfoundation. org.uk/
Correspondent: The Secretary
Trustees: P Standford, Chair; T Berg; Dr J Cross; Dr Linda Hirst; Sue

Lubbock; K Potter; P Strang; Prof S Walsh; Mrs T Estell.
CC Number: 272389

Information available

Accounts were on file at the Charity Commission from 2009. The trust also has a useful website. It gives the following information:

> The Hinrichsen Foundation is a charity devoted to the promotion of music. Although the objects of the trust are widely drawn, the trustees have decided for the time being to concentrate on assisting in the 'written' areas of music, that is, assisting contemporary composition and its performance and musical research.

Support is given to the public performance of living composers; grants include those to performing ensembles for concerts and festivals. Organisations supported include both UK organisations and local groups throughout the UK. The trust also supports the publication of musicological research.

This trust announced in 2009 that it was suspending its grants giving programme 'for the time being, largely as a result of the present uncertainty in world markets and the weakness of its investment currency'. As of late 2011 the trustees believed that they were resolving the issues surrounding income generation and would be able to renew support in 2012. For further information please check for updates on the trust's website.

The last accounts available were for 2009 when there were no grants made, however in 2008 29 grants were made totalling £38,000. The trustees believe that grantmaking will resume in the not too distant future.

Previous beneficiaries included: Huddersfield Contemporary Music Festival (£5,000); Dartington International Summer School and Spitalfields Festival (£2,000 each); Birmingham Contemporary Music Group and Kettle's Yard (£1,500 each); Swaledale Festival and York Late Music Festival (£1,000 each); The Red Violin (£750); Dmitri Ensemble (£500); and Pro Nobis Singers (£450).

Exclusions

The foundation does not:

- fund the commissioning of new works
- make donations towards the costs of making recordings, either by private or commercial companies
- as a general rule, finance degree courses. The aim is to encourage composition and research, but not to finance the acquisition of basic skills in these subjects.
- consider applications for assistance in purchasing musical instruments or equipment including the electronic or computer variety
- make grants retrospectively.

Applications

On a form which can be downloaded from the foundation's website.

The trustees have noted that in a number of applications they have been invited to make a grant equal to the total cost of the project where a commercial organisation has a specific interest whether as a publisher or as an impresario. While the trustees are prepared to consider making grants in such circumstances towards the cost of a project which is essentially non-commercial, they will always have greater sympathy for those projects where the organisation involved is making some contribution towards the risk.

The trustees will be pleased to receive applications for assistance with projects that fall within these terms, and such applications may come from individuals, organisations, or other charities. The Trustees do not wish to consider applications for which there are existing official schemes of help, but rather to devote their efforts to areas at present neglected.

Trustees meet quarterly.

The Henry C Hoare Charitable Trust

General

£225,000 (2009/10)

Beneficial area

UK.

C Hoare and Co, 37 Fleet Street, London EC4P 4DQ
Tel: 020 7353 4522

Trustees: Henry C Hoare; Messrs Hoare Trustees.
CC Number: 1088669

Information available

Accounts were available from the Charity Commission.

This trust was established in 2001 with general charitable purposes. One-off and annual donations are made.

In 2009/10 the trust had an income of £164,000 and made grants totalling £225,000. Assets stood at £3.5 million.

Donations were broken down as follows:

Youth, age, ill health, disability and financial hardship	£70,000
Environment protection and improvement	£46,000
Health	£44,000
Religion	£37,500
Education	£10,500
Arts	£8,500
Animal Welfare	£7,000
Citizenship & Community Development	£2,300

A list of beneficiaries was not included with the accounts but previous beneficiaries of grants of £5,000 or more have included: Trinity College Cambridge (£25,000); Transform Drug Policy Foundation and Foundation for People with Learning Disabilities (£20,000 each); For Dementia (£15,000); and The Abby CEVA Primary School (£7,000).

Applications

In writing to the correspondent.

Hockerill Educational Foundation

Education, especially Christian education

£162,000 to organisations
(2009/10)

Beneficial area

UK, with a preference for the dioceses of Chelmsford and St Albans.

3 The Swallows, Harlow, Essex CM17 0AR
Email: info@hockerillfoundation.org.uk

Website: www.hockerillfoundation.org.uk
Correspondent: Derek J Humphrey, Secretary
Trustees: Ven. Trevor Jones, Chair; Rt Revd Stephen Cottrell; Rt Revd Dr Alan Smith; Lesley Barlow; Rt Revd Paul Bayes; Colin Bird; Ven. Elwin Cockett; Rob Fox; Jonathan Longstaff; Revd Coralie McCluskey; Canon Harry Marsh; Rt Revd Christopher Morgan; Hannah Potter; Canon Jonathan O Reynolds; Janet Scott.
CC Number: 311018

Information available

Accounts were available from the Charity Commission.

The foundation was set up in 1978 following the closure of Hockerill College, which was established in 1852 to train women teachers who 'would go to schools in the service of humanity'. When the Secretary of State for Education and Science decided in 1976 to wind down Hockerill College, the proceeds of the sale of its assets were given to this foundation to use for the purposes for which the college was created.

The foundation makes grants in the field of education in three main areas:

- individual grants to support the education and training of teachers
- grants to organisations to support teachers and research and development in religious education
- grants to develop the church's educational work in the dioceses of Chelmsford and St Albans.

The trustees will normally consider applications from corporate bodies or institutions associated with education on Christian principles. There is a religious dimension to all education, but the trustees expect any activity, course, project or research supported to be of real benefit to religious education and/or the church's educational work. They will give priority to imaginative new projects which will enhance the Church of England's contribution to higher and further education and/or promote aspects of religious education in schools.

Grants are renewable for up to three years, or occasionally a maximum of five years, subject to the trustees being satisfied on an annual basis that the grant has been used satisfactorily. Grants for the funding of research or the appointment of staff may be paid by instalments and are subject to funds being available. The foundation monitors research or the progress of a project as appropriate, and expects regular progress reports. It may also ask for a line of credit in the final report of a research project.

In 2009/10 the foundation had assets of £4.9 million and an income of £263,000. Grants totalling £214,000 were paid during the year and were distributed as follows:

Diocese of St Albans	£70,000
Diocese of Chelmsford	£70,000
Corporate grants for research and development in education	£22,000
Individuals	£52,000

Exclusions

Grants are not given for general appeals for funds, 'bricks and mortar' building projects or purposes that are the clear responsibility of another body.

Applications

On a form available to download from the foundation's website. Applications should include some official documentation, such as the most recent annual report and accounts, which clearly show the status, objects and ideals of the organisation and its financial position, and an sae. They should be submitted by 31 March each year. Grants are usually awarded between July and September.

The Sir Julian Hodge Charitable Trust

General

£62,500 (2009/10)

Beneficial area

UK.

Ty Gwyn, Lisvane Road, Lisvane, Cardiff CF14 0SG
Correspondent: Joyce Harrison, Trustee

Trustees: Julian J Hodge; Joyce Harrison; Derrek L Jones; Margaret Cason; Eric M Hammonds.
CC Number: 234848

Information available

Accounts were available from the Charity Commission.

The trust was established by a gift from Sir Julian Hodge and in 2006 received a further substantial bequest under the terms of his will.

The principal objective of the trust is to allocate trust income for charitable purposes, with special regard to the following areas:

- the encouragement of medical and surgical studies and research and in particular the study and research in connection with the causes, diagnosis, treatment and cure of cancer, poliomyelitis, tuberculosis and diseases affecting children;
- the general advancement of medical and surgical science;
- the advancement of education;
- the advancement of religion;
- the relief of aged and disabled persons in needy circumstances.

In 2009/10 the trust had assets of £1.3 million and an income of £50,000. Grants were made totalling £62,500 and were broken down as follows:

Medical	£35,000
Other	£17,500
Education	£8,000
Religion	£2,000

Beneficiaries included: Hope House Children's Hospices (£5,000); The St John of Jerusalem Eye Hospital (£3,000); Compton Hospice, Headway and National Autistic Society (£2,000 each); Albrighton Trust, Derby Kids Camp, Good Companions Bolton, Guide Dogs, Walsall Disability Centre and Youth for Christ (£1,000 each).

Exclusions

No grants to individuals or companies.

Applications

In writing to the correspondent. The trust invites applications for grants from charitable institutions. Institutions submit a summary of their proposals to the trustees in a

specific format. Applications for grants are considered by the trustees against its objectives.

Common applicant mistakes

'Applicants which are not registered charities.'

The J G Hogg Charitable Trust

Welfare, animal welfare, general

Around £100,000 (2009/10)

Beneficial area

UK.

Chantrey Vellacott DFK, Russell Square House, 10 -12 Russell Square, London WC1B 5LF
Tel: 020 75099000
Email: cjones@cvdfk.com
Correspondent: C M Jones, Trustees' Accountant
Trustees: Sarah Jane Houldsworth; Joanna Wynfreda Turvey.
CC Number: 299042

Information available

Basic information was available from the Charity Commission website.

The trust states that it has no set policy on the type of charity supported, but would give favourable consideration to those based primarily in the UK that support the relief of human and animal suffering.

In 2009/10 the trust had an income of £19,000 and total expenditure of £109,000. We have no information regarding beneficiary organisations but previously the trust made awards to: Kids Company and Oxfam (£15,000 each); Medicinema and Teddy Bear Air Care (£10,000 each); and Addiction Recovery Foundation (£7,000).

Exclusions

No grants to individuals. Registered charities only are supported.

Applications

In writing to the correspondent. To keep administration costs to a minimum, the trust is unable to reply to unsuccessful applicants.

The Holden Charitable Trust

Jewish

£345,000 (2009/10)

Beneficial area

UK, with a preference for the Manchester area.

c/o Lopian Gross Barnett and Co., Cardinal House, 20 St Mary Parsonage, Manchester M3 2IG
Tel: 0161 832 8721
Correspondent: The Clerk
Trustees: David Lopian; Marion Lopian; Michael Lopian.
CC Number: 264185

Information available

Accounts were available from the Charity Commission.

The charity states that: 'The Holden Charitable Trust exists to receive and distribute charitable donations to worthy causes primarily within the Jewish community.' In 2009/10 the trust had assets of £835,000 and an income of £248,000. Grants amounted to £345,000.

There were grants of £1,000 or more listed in the accounts. Beneficiaries included: Broom Foundation (£59,000); Ohel Bnei Yaakob (£50,000); Ohr Yerushalayim Synagogue (£33,000); Friends of Beis Eliyahu Trust (£24,000); the FED (£7,500); and King David's School (£5,000).

Donations of less than £5,000 each totalled £67,000.

Applications

In writing to the correspondent.

The Dorothy Holmes Charitable Trust

General

Around £60,000 (2010/11)

Beneficial area

UK, with a preference for Dorset.

Smallfield Cody and Co, 5 Harley Place, Harley Street, London W1G 8QD
Tel: 0207 636 6100
Correspondent: Michael Kennedy
Trustees: Miss M Cody; Dr S Roberts; J Roberts.
CC Number: 237213

Information available

Accounts had been received at the Charity Commission, but were unavailable to view.

The trust's policy is to make a substantial number of relatively small donations to groups working in many charitable fields – including those involved in medical research, disability, older people, children and young people, churches, the disadvantaged, the environment and the arts. The trust can give throughout the UK but has a preference for Dorset, especially Poole. In practice nearly all grants are given to either national charities or those based in Dorset. In 2010/11 the trust had an income of £22,000 and an expenditure of £60,000. Further information was not available.

Previous beneficiaries included: Wallingford School (£6,000); Children in Touch, Crisis and Christmas and RNLI (£5,000 each); Hyman Cen Foundation (£4,000); Army Benevolent Fund (£3,000); Action on Elder Abuse and Clic Sargent Cancer Fund (£2,000 each); National Autistic Society and Raleigh International (£1,000 each); and Royal Free Hospital Retirement Fellowship (£300).

Exclusions

Only applications from registered charities will be considered.

Applications

In writing to the correspondent, preferably in January to March each year.

The Holst Foundation

Arts

£174,000 (2009/10)

Beneficial area

UK.

179 Great Portland Street, London W1W 5LS
Tel: 020 8673 4215 (answerphone only)
Email: holst@dpmail.co.uk
Correspondent: The Grants Administrator
Trustees: Rosamund Strode, Chair; Noel Periton; Prof. Arnold Whittall; Peter Carter; Andrew Clements; Julian Anderson.
CC Number: 283668

Information available

Accounts were available from the Charity Commission.

The trust has two objects: firstly, to promote public appreciation of the musical works of Gustav and Imogen Holst; and secondly, to encourage the study and practice of the arts.

In practice the trust tends to be proactive. Funds are available almost exclusively for the performance of music by living composers. The trust has historical links with Aldeburgh in Suffolk and is a major funder of new music at the annual Aldeburgh Festival. It also promotes the recording of new music by means of substantial funding to the recording label NMC, which the foundation also provided the funds to set up.

In 2009/10 it had assets of £1.3 million and an income of £74,000. Grants totalled £174,000.

By far the largest donation of £123,000 went to NMC Recordings. Other beneficiaries included: University of York music Press (£7,500); Aldeburgh Music (£5,000); Birmingham Contemporary Music Group (£4,000); Cheltenham Music Society and Huddersfield Festival (£1,000 each).

A further 32 unlisted grants totalled £14,000.

Exclusions

No support for the recordings or works of Holst that are already well supported, nor for capital projects. No grants to individuals for educational purposes.

Applications

In writing to the correspondent. Trustees meet four times a year. There is no application form. Seven copies of the application should be sent. Applications should contain full financial details and be as concise as possible. Funding is not given retrospectively.

Common applicant mistakes

'We are a musical charity, but our funding only goes towards the work of living composers. Many applicants apply for educational support.'

P H Holt Foundation

General

£79,000 (2009/10)

Beneficial area

UK, with a preference for Merseyside.

Room 607, India Buildings, Liverpool L2 0RA
Tel: 0151 473 4693
Fax: 0151 473 4693
Correspondent: Roger Morris, Secretary
Trustees: Neil Kemsley, Chair; Tilly Boyce; Martin Cooke; Paige Earlam; Nikki Eastwood; Anthony Hannay; Derek Morris; Ken Ravenscroft.
CC Number: 1113708

Information available

Detailed accounts were available from the Charity Commission website.

The foundation makes a large number of mostly small grants, about three quarters of them in Merseyside. It is a welcome and exceptional example of Liverpool shipping money staying in and around the city. The foundation organises its giving in two established grant programmes concerned with Merseyside and the 'Holt tradition'.

In 2009/10 it had assets of £12.8 million and an investment income of £200,000. Grants committed during the year totalled £79,000, categorised in the table below.

Merseyside

Major grants included those made to: Speke Baptist Church (£10,000); Lodestar Theatre Company (£6,000); Collective Encounters and Liverpool Arts Interface Ltd (£5,000 each); Plaza Community Cinema (£4,400); Garston and District Community Council (£3,000); Hurricane Film Foundation (£2,500); Creative Ideas in Action and Merseyside Refugee and Asylum Seekers Pre and Post Natal Support Group (£2,000 each); Steps to Freedom (£1,500); Kensington Remembers (£1,000); and China Pearl, Rotunda Community College and Elim Christian Centre (£500 each).

There were also 17 routine grants to organisations with which the foundation has regular contact.

The 'Holt Tradition'

No grants were made under this category in response to appeals but there were 12 routine grants to organisations with which the foundation has regular contact.

Beneficiaries were: Outward Bound Trust and Runnymede Trust (£1,000 each); Inter-Faith Network for UK, Anti-Slavery International and Contemporary Art Society (£500 each); and Ancient Monuments Society, Society for Protection of Ancient Buildings, Victorian Society, Campaign to Protect Rural England, Campaign for the Protection of Rural Wales, Friends of the Lake District and John Muir Trust (£250 each).

Exclusions

No grants for:
- individuals
- sectarian causes
- appeals for help with minibuses, holidays and animal welfare work
- organisations based outside of Merseyside (in some circumstances help may be given to organisations in parts of Cheshire, Halton and West Lancashire which have strong links with Merseyside).

Wherever possible, grants are paid to or through registered charities.

Applications

In writing to the correspondent including, as appropriate, a budget, annual report and accounts and indications of who else is supporting the work or willing to recommend it. Full and detailed guidance notes are available from the foundation.

The Homelands Charitable Trust

The New Church, health, social welfare

£239,000 (2009/10)

Beneficial area

UK.

c/o Alliotts, 4th Floor, Imperial House, 15 Kingsway, London WC2B 6UN
Tel: 020 7240 9971

P H HOLT FOUNDATION

Activity 2009/10

	Merseyside	'Holt tradition'
No. of applications received	213	25
No. of grants made	44	12
of which		
recipients previously supported	30	12
recipients supported for the first time	14	0
Total value of commitments made	£73,000	£5,300
Average size of grant	£1,700	£440
Median size of grant	£1,000	£250

Grants by category 2009/10

	Merseyside	'Holt tradition'
Community development and participation	£43,000	£1,500
Social welfare	£4,300	£500
Education	£8,400	£1,000
Visual and performing arts	£16,000	£500
Heritage and built environment	£1,100	£750
Natural environment	£750	£1,000
Total committed in year	**£73,000**	**£5,300**

Correspondent: N J Armstrong, Trustee

Trustees: D G W Ballard; N J Armstrong; Revd C Curry; R J Curry.

CC Number: 214322

Information available

Accounts were available from the Charity Commission.

This trust was established in 1962, the settlors were four members of the Curry family and the original endowment was in the form of shares in the Curry company.

In 2009/10 it had assets of £6.5 million and a total income of £517,000. Grants were made totalling £239,000 in five main categories (which the trustees usually have a funding bias for each year) as follows:

New Church	£115,000
Other charities	£58,000
Hospices	£29,000
Care and protection of children	£21,000
Medical	£17,000

Beneficiaries included: General Conference of the New Church (£68,000); Broadfield Memorial Fund (£15,000); New Church College (£11,000); Bournemouth Society (£10,000); Jubilee Sailing Trust, Manic Depression Fellowship and National Children's Homes (£2,400 each); and the Attic Charity – Youth Project, Bikeability, Eyeless Trust and Pestalozzi (£1,600 each).

The trust's annual report stated:

The trustees have set up a designated fund of £250,000 in respect of an interest-free loan to the New Church towards the extension and refurbishment of the New Church's residential centre.

Exclusions

No grants to individuals.

Applications

In writing to the correspondent.

The Homestead Charitable Trust

Medicine, health, welfare, animal welfare, Christianity and the arts

£32,000 (2009/10)

Beneficial area

UK.

Flat 7, Clarence Gate Gardens, Glentworth Street, London NW1 6AY

Tel: 020 7258 1051

Correspondent: Lady Nina Bracewell-Smith, Trustee

Trustees: Sir C Bracewell-Smith; Lady N Bracewell-Smith.

CC Number: 293979

Information available

Accounts were on file at the Charity Commission.

This trust makes grants towards medical, health and welfare, animal welfare, Christianity and the arts.

In 2009/10 it had assets of £5.2 million, which generated an income of £210,000. The trust fund of the Sir Charles Bracewell-Smith Voluntary Settlement, worth £1.6 million, was transferred to the trust in October 2004. Grants given to individuals and institutions totalled £32,000.

Beneficiaries included: CVS (£10,000); Stroke Association and UN World Food Programme (£5,000 each); Sight Savers (£180); and WaterAid (£100).

Applications

In writing to the correspondent.

The Mary Homfray Charitable Trust

General

£50,000 (2009/10)

Beneficial area

UK, with a preference for Wales.

5 Callaghan Square, Cardiff CF10 5BT

Tel: 029 2026 0000

Correspondent: Angela Homfray, Trustee

Trustees: Angela Homfray; Simon Gibson; Josephine Homfray.

CC Number: 273564

Information available

Accounts were on file at the Charity Commission.

The trust supports a wide range of organisations, including many in Wales.

In 2009/10 the trust had assets of £1.4 million and an income of £33,000. Grants were made to 23 organisations totalling £50,000 and were mostly recurrent.

Beneficiaries included: Thomas Mansel Franklen Trust (£5,000); Age Concern, Salvation Army, Shelter – Cymru, Amelia Trust Farm and Wallich Clifford Community (£3,000 each); Coram Family, National Botanic Garden of Wales and Kiloran Trust (£2,000 each); Maes-y-Dyfan and Army Benevolent Fund (£1,000 each); and Y Bont (£500).

Applications

In writing to the correspondent. Applications should be made towards the end of the year, for consideration at the trustees' meeting in February or March each year.

Common applicant mistakes

'Applications from charities outside Wales'

The Hope Trust

Temperance, Reformed Protestant churches

About £150,000 (2009)

Beneficial area

Worldwide, with a preference for Scotland.

Drummond Miller, 31–32 Moray Place, Edinburgh EH3 6BZ

Tel: 0131 226 5151

Email: rmiller@drummond-miller.co.uk

Correspondent: The Secretary

Trustees: Prof. G M Newlands; Prof. D A S Ferguson; Revd G R Barr; Revd Dr Lyall; Carole Hope; Revd Gillean McLean.

SC Number: SC000987

Information available

Despite making a written request for the accounts of this trust/foundation/charity (and including an sae), these were not provided. The following entry is based, therefore, on information filed with the Office of the Scottish Charity Regulator

The trust was established to promote the ideals of temperance in the areas of drink and drugs, and Protestant church reform through education and the distribution of literature. PhD students of theology studying at Scottish universities are also supported.

In 2009 its income was £171,000. Grants totalled around £150,000.

Previous beneficiaries have included Church of Scotland Priority Areas Fund, World Alliance of Reformed Churches, National Bible Society for Scotland, Feed the Minds and Waldensian Mission Aid.

Exclusions

No grants to gap year students, scholarship schemes or to any individuals, with the sole exception of PhD students of theology studying at Scottish universities. No grants for the refurbishment of property.

Applications

In writing to the correspondent. The trustees meet to consider applications in June and December each year. Applications should be submitted by mid-May or mid-November each year.

The Horizon Foundation

General, education, women and children

£68,000 (2009/10)

Beneficial area

Unrestricted.

Coutts & Co, 440 The Strand, London WC2R 0QS
Tel: 020 7663 6814
Trustees: Kirkland Caroline Smulders; Patrick Lance Smulders; Coutts & Co.
CC Number: 1118455

Information available

Limited information was available from the Charity Commission.

Established in 2009/10, the objects of the foundation are:

▶ to promote and advance the education of women and children
▶ the relief of financial hardship, either generally or individually, of women and children by making grants of money for providing or paying for items services or facilities
▶ general charitable purposes.

In 2009/10 the foundation had an income of £68,000 and made six grants to three organisation totalling £68,000. These were made to:
▶ Eton College
▶ University of Essex
▶ Pembroke College

The amount received by each recipient was not disclosed in the brief report filed with the Charity Commission. Other past beneficiaries have included: Atlantic College, Lessons with Love, Mongolian Children's Aid Foundation, and The Hotchkiss School.

Applications

In writing to the correspondent.

The Cuthbert Horn Trust

General charitable purposes

£50,000 (2009)

Beneficial area

Worldwide.

Capita Trust Company Limited, Phoenix House, 18 King William Street, London EC4N 7HE
Tel: 020 7800 4126
Email: trusts@capitatrust.co.uk
Correspondent: Laurie Wilson, Trust Manager
Trustees: AA Flint; H Flint; P H Marr-Johnson; Capita Trust Co Ltd
CC Number: 291465

Information available

Accounts were available from the Charity Commission.

Registered with the Charity Commission in 1985, this trust makes

grants for general charitable purposes. In 2009 the trust had assets of £1.3 million and a total income of £356,000. Grants were made to 16 organisations totalling £50,000.

Beneficiaries included: Farms for City Children, International Bee Research Association, Progressive Farming Trust (£4,000 each); the Fishermans Mission, Sevenoaks Symphony Orchestra and Ovingdean Hall School (£3,000 each); and the Charleston Trust and Norwegian Locomotive Trust (£2,000).

Exclusions

No grants are made to individuals.

Applications

Unsolicited applications are discouraged. For the time being the trustees have decided to rely on their own research, usually giving to organisations who have an income of less than £100,000.

The Horne Trust

Hospices

£492,000 (2009/10)

Beneficial area

UK and the developing world.

Kingsdown, Warmlake Road, Chart Sutton, Maidstone, Kent ME17 3RP
Tel: 01622 842638
Email: mail.jh@horne-trust.org.uk
Correspondent: J T Horne, Trustee
Trustees: J T Horne; J L Horne; N J Camamile.
CC Number: 1010625

Information available

Accounts were available from the Charity Commission.

The trust supports homelessness charities and hospices, particularly children's hospices. Grants can also be given to medical support charities and organisations helping to develop self-reliant technology in Africa and the developing world.

In 2009/10 it had assets of £6.2 million and an income of £343,000. Grants to 88 organisations and totalled £492,000.

Beneficiaries included: Demelza House Children's Hospice, Humberstone Hydrotherapy Pool and World Medical Fund (£10,000 each); AbilityNet, Share Community and Woodlands Hospice – Liverpool (£7,500); Laura Campbell-Preston Trust (£6,700); Deafblind UK, FACT, and Fisherman's Mission (£5,000 each); Winfield Trust, Disability Aid Fund, and Whitby Dog Rescue (£1,000 each).

Applications

Normally in writing to the correspondent, although the trust has stated that currently unsolicited applications cannot be supported.

The Hospital Saturday Fund

Medical, health

£350,000 to organisations (2010)

Beneficial area

UK, the Republic of Ireland, the Channel Islands and the Isle of Man.

24 Upper Ground, London SE1 9PD
Tel: 020 7928 6662
Email: charity@hsf.eu.com
Correspondent: Keith R Bradley, Chief Executive
Trustees: John Greenwood; Jane Laidlaw Dalton; Michael Boyle; John Randel; David Thomas.
CC Number: 1123381

Information available

Accounts were available from the Charity Commission.

The Hospital Saturday Fund is a healthcare cash plan organisation, which was founded in 1873. In 1987 it established a charitable trust to support a wide range of hospitals, hospices and medical charities for care and research, as well as welfare organisations providing similar services. The trustees continue to provide support to smaller, lesser-known charities connected with diseases and disabilities about which there is little public awareness. Individuals can also be supported by the trust, usually for special equipment to relieve their condition or in cases where their health has

contributed to their financial hardship, and sponsorship can be given to people studying for a medically-related career.

In 2010 it had an income of £27 million, a huge increase from the last entry (£166,000 in 2008). This was mostly from trading turnover from the charity's subsidiary company HSF health plan Limited. Grants were made to organisations totalling £350,000 and to individual medical students totalling £5,000. Grants to organisations were broken down as follows:

- Medical charities – £243,000
- Hospices – £107,000

Unfortunately a grants list was not available with this year's accounts, however previous beneficiaries have included: Alzheimer's Society (£3,000); Teenage Cancer Trust and International Glaucoma Association (£1,500); BasicNeeds UK Trust, LEPRA, Motivation Quality of Life (£750 each); and Age Concern England, Brain Tumour UK, ChildLine, DebRA, the Ear Foundation, Friends of the Elderly, the National Autistic Society, OCD Action, Rethink, the Shaftesbury Society, the Sunflower Trust, Terrence Higgins Trust and Wellbeing of Women (£500 each).

Exclusions

Unless there are exceptional circumstances, organisations are not supported in successive years.

Applications

Hospitals, hospices and medically-related charities are invited to write detailed letters or to send a brochure with an accompanying letter. There is a form for individuals to complete available from the personal assistant to the trust administrator.

Houblon-Norman/George Fund

Finance

£70,000 (2009/10)

Beneficial area

UK.

Bank of England, Threadneedle Street, London EC2R 8AH
Tel: 020 7601 3778
Fax: 020 7601 4423
Email: ma-hngfund@bankofengland. co.uk
Website: www.bankofengland.co. uk/research/houblonnorman/index. htm
Correspondent: The Secretary
Trustees: C R Bean; Brendan Barber; Andrew Haldane.
CC Number: 213168

Information available

Accounts were available from the Charity Commission.

The trust supports research into the interaction and function of financial and business institutions, the economic conditions affecting them, and the dissemination of knowledge thereof. Fellowships are tenable at the Bank of England. The research work to be undertaken is intended to be full-time work, and teaching or other paid work must not be undertaken during the tenure of the fellowship, without the specific consent of the trustees. In considering applications the trustees will pay particular regard to the relevance of the research to current problems in economics and finance.

In 2009/10 the trust had assets of £1.8 million, an income of £58,000 and made grants totalling £70,000 in the form of four fellowships.

Applications

On an application form available from the website.

The Reta Lila Howard Foundation

Children, arts, environment

£275,000 (2009/10)

Beneficial area

UK and Republic of Ireland.

Jamestown Investments Ltd, 4 Felstead Gardens, Ferry Street, London E14 3BS

Tel: 020 7537 1118
Email: jamestown@btinternet.com
Correspondent: The Company Secretary
Trustees: Emma Adamo; Christian Bauta; Charles Burnett; Garfield Mitchell; Alannah Weston; Graham Weston; Claudia Hepburn; Melissa Murdoch.
CC Number: 1041634

Information available

Accounts were available from the Charity Commission, but without a list of grants.

The founder of this trust had an interest in children's charities and the trust's grantmaking focus is 'to support a few innovative projects that benefit children up to the age of 16 within the British Isles'. Funds are directed to selected projects, 'to support the education of young people or to ameliorate their physical and emotional environment'. In practice the trust also supports arts and environmental organisations. Donations are given over a finite period, with the aim that the project can be self-supporting when funding has ended.

In 2009/10 the trust had assets of £13.6 million and an income of £217,000. The trustees' report states that grants were made to 14 organisations totalling £275,000.

Previous beneficiaries included: Countryside Education Trust (£70,000); Barnardo's (£68,500); Civitas (£60,000); The Tree Council (£53,000); Farms for City Children (£40,000); Children's Hospice Association Scotland (£35,000); Teach First (£30,000); New Forest Museum & Library (£20,000); The Bridge End Community Centre (£15,000); and Bibles for Children (£10,000).

Exclusions

Grants are not given to individuals, organisations which are not registered charities, or towards operating expenses, budget deficits, (sole) capital projects, annual charitable appeals, general endowment funds, fundraising drives or events, conferences, or student aid.

Applications

The trust states that it does not accept unsolicited applications, since the trustees seek out and support projects they are interested in.

The Daniel Howard Trust

Jewish causes

£375,000 (2008/9)

Beneficial area

UK and Israel.

St James's House, 23 King Street, London SW1Y 6QY
Tel: 020 78395169
Correspondent: Sarah Hunt
Trustees: Dame Shirley Porter; Linda Streit; Steven Porter; Brian Padgett; Andrew Peggie.
CC Number: 267173

Information available

Accounts were on file at the Charity Commission up to 2008/9.

The trust mostly supports Jewish or Israeli organisations, in particular those promoting education, culture, the environment and welfare. There is ongoing support for the Daniel Amichai Education centre and the Israel Philharmonic Orchestra.

The latest accounts available for the trust were for 2008/9. In this year the trust had an income from investments of £130,000 and assets of 7.5 million. Grants were made totalling £375,000

Grants were broken down as follows:

Education	£131,000
Culture	£93,000
Environment	£0
Welfare	£151,000

Beneficiaries included: Association of Friends Tel Aviv Sourasky Medical Centre (£52,000); Friends of Daniel for Rowing Association (£45,000); National Theatre; Israel Family Therapy Advancement Fund (£30,000 each); Mousetrap Theatre Projects (£25,000); University of Pennsylvania (USA) Foundation Limited (£13,000); Ra'anana Symphonette Orchestra; British Friends of the Israel Opera (£4,000 each); Weizmann Institute

(£1,000) and Eliya (Israel Association for the Blind) (£570).

Exclusions

Grants are only made to registered charities. No grants to individuals.

Applications

In writing to the correspondent.

The Clifford Howarth Charity Trust

General

£30,000 (2009/10)

Beneficial area

UK, with a preference for Lancashire (Burnley/Rossendale).

14A Hall Garth, Kelbeck, Barrow in Furness, Cumbria LA13 0QT
Correspondent: James Howarth, Trustee
Trustees: James Howarth; Judith Howarth; Cara Tinning.
CC Number: 264890

Information available

Accounts received at the Charity Commission but unavailable to view.

The charity has general charitable purposes assisting local and UK charities supported by the founder. This is generally for work within Burnley and Rossendale.

In 2009/10 the charity had an income of £17,000 and a total expenditure of £30,000. Grants usually total around £30,000 each year.

Previous beneficiaries have included: Cumbria Cerebral Palsy (£15,000); St Marys Hospice (£5,000); St Nicholas Church – Newchurch (£3,000); Hospice in Rossendale (£2,500); and Ulverstone Inshore Rescue, Beaver Scouts, Spurgeons and Burnley Garrick Club (£2,000 each).

Exclusions

Only registered charities will be supported. No grants to individuals, for scholarships or for non-local special projects.

Applications

The charity states that grants are only made to organisations known to the trustees, and that applications are unlikely to be successful.

The Hudson Foundation

Older people, general

£133,000 (2009/10)

Beneficial area

UK, with a preference for the Wisbech area.

1–3 York Row, Wisbech, Cambridgeshire PE13 1EA
Correspondent: David W Ball, Trustee
Trustees: Hayward A Godfrey; David W Ball; Stephen G Layton.
CC Number: 280332

Information available

Accounts were obtained from the Charity Commission website.

The object of the foundation is the relief of infirm and/or older people, in particular the establishment and maintenance of residential accommodation for relief of infirm and/or older people and to make donations to other charitable purposes with a preference for the Wisbech area. The accounts state that 'whilst the trustees do make contributions to revenue expenditure of charitable organisations, they prefer to assist in the funding of capital projects for the advancement of the community of Wisbech and district'.

In 2009/10 the foundation had assets of £1.8 million and an income of £947,000. Grants to 11 organisations totalled £133,000.

Beneficiaries were: Wisbech Parish Church of St Peter and St Paul (£80,000); Ely Diocesan Board of Finance (£64,000); Wisbech St Mary Sports and Community Centre (£30,000); Wisbech Grammar School (£29,000); Wisbech Swimming Club (£8,400); Methodist Homes for the Aged (£6,200); Alzheimer's Society (£1,200); Wisbech and Fenland

Museum (£250); and Wisbech Music Society (£150).

Applications

In writing to the correspondent. Trustees meet quarterly.

The Huggard Charitable Trust

General

Around £30,000 (2009/10)

Beneficial area

UK, with a preference for South Wales.

Blacklands Farm, Five Mile Lane, Bonvilston, Cardiff CF5 6TQ
Correspondent: S J Thomas, Trustee
Trustees: Mrs A Helme; S J Thomas; A Chiplin.
CC Number: 327501

Information available

Accounts were on file at the Charity Commission.

In 2009/10 the trust had an income of £7,000 and a total expenditure of £35,000.

Previous beneficiaries included: Amelia Methodist Trust, Vale of Glamorgan, Bro Morgannwg NHS Trust, CURE Fund – Cardiff, Laparoscopy Laser Fund – UHW, SWS Cymru and Whitton Rosser Trust – Vale of Glamorgan.

Applications

The trustees are not inviting applications for funds.

Common applicant mistakes

'As is stated on Charity Commission website and elsewhere, we are a family run charity who do not solicit donations or incur costs but who are not looking to fund any new applications, therefore most times any application is in vain.'

The Geoffrey C Hughes Charitable Trust

Nature conservation, environment, performing arts

£15,000 (2009/10)

Beneficial area

UK.

c/o Mills & Reeve, Francis House, 112 Hills Road, Cambridge CB2 1PH
Tel: 01223 222290
Correspondent: P C M Solon, Trustee
Trustees: J R Young; P C M Solon; W A Bailey.
CC Number: 1010079

Information available

Basic information taken from the Charity Commission website.

This trust is essentially interested in two areas: nature conservation/ environment and performing arts, particularly ballet or opera with a bias towards modern work.

In 2009/10 the trust had an income of £6,000 and total expenditure of £15,000. In the previous year expenditure was £119,000.

Exclusions

No grants to individuals.

Applications

In writing to the correspondent.

The Humanitarian Trust

Education, health, social welfare, Jewish

Around £100,000

Beneficial area

Worldwide, mainly Israel.

27 St James's Place, London SW1A 1NR
Tel: 0207 409 1376

Correspondent: Mrs M Myers, Secretary

Trustees: Jacques Gunsbourg; Pierre Halban; Anthony Lerman.

CC Number: 208575

Information available

Accounts were available from the Charity Commission.

The trust was founded in 1946. In the early years donations were made overwhelmingly to educational causes in Israel. Nowadays the trust is giving to a wider range of causes, still mainly Jewish, but some smaller grants are given to non-Jewish organisations.

The trust's grant-making policy is outlined in its annual report:

> The trustees consider grant applications from organisations and individuals in the UK and abroad, especially in the fields of education, health, social welfare, civil society, Jewish communal life and general charitable purposes.

In 2009/10 it had an income of £132,000 and a total expenditure of £136,000.

Previously grants included those made to: Friends of the Hebrew University of Jerusalem towards: the Humanitarian Trust Fellowship and the M Gunsbourg Memorial Scholarships (£10,000 each). Other beneficiaries included: New Israel Fund (£6,000); Institute for Jewish Policy Research (£5,000); University of Oxford (£4,500); Jerusalem Foundation Bilingual School, Association for Civil Rights in Israel and The Samaritans (£2,000 each); King's College London, University of Dundee and University of Birmingham (£500 each).

Applications

In writing to the correspondent, including annual report and accounts, projected budgets and future plans. Applications are considered at trustees' meetings in March and October.

The Michael and Shirley Hunt Charitable Trust

Prisoners' families, animal welfare

£64,000 to organisations and individuals (2009/10)

Beneficial area

UK and overseas.

Ansty House, Henfield Road, Small Dole, West Sussex BN5 9XH

Tel: 01903 817116

Fax: 01903 879995

Correspondent: Mrs D S Jenkins, Trustee

Trustees: W J Baker; C J Hunt; S E Hunt; D S Jenkins; K D Mayberry.

CC Number: 1063418

Information available

Accounts were available from the Charity Commission.

The trust makes grants for the benefit of prisoners' families, animals which are unwanted, sick or ill-treated and general charitable purposes. The trustees prefer to award grants for emergency operational funding rather than capital projects or overhead expenses.

In 2009/10 it had assets of almost £5.6 million and an income of £223,000. Grants were made totalling £64,000, broken down as follows:

Prisoners and their families	6	£7,000
Animal welfare	22	£22,600
Miscellaneous	7	£26,000

Grants to 70 individuals totalled £8,800.

Beneficiaries included: DEC Haiti Earthquake Appeal (£10,000); St Barnabus Hospice (£5,000); Macmillan Cancer Support and Prisoners Families and Friends Service (£2,500 each); East Sussex WRAS, Eden Animal Rescue, S.H.A.R.P., and Wood Green Animal Shelters, (£2,000 each); and Action for Prisoners Families, Capricorn Animal Rescue, Lincolnshire Trust for Cats, National Probation Service, Sussex and Willows Animal Sanctuary (£1,000 each).

Exclusions

No grants for capital projects, support costs, fines, bail, legal costs, rent deposits and so on.

Applications

In writing to the correspondent. The trustees meet to consider applications 'as and when necessary, and at least annually'.

The Huntingdon Foundation

Jewish education

£288,000 (2009/10)

Beneficial area

Mainly Jewish communities in the UK. There is some grant giving in the US.

8 Goodyers Gardens, London NW4 2HD

Tel: 020 8202 2282

Correspondent: Benjamin Perl

Trustees: Benjamin Perl, Chair; Dr Shoshana Perl; R Jeidel (USA); Jonathan Perl; Naomi Sorotzkin; Joseph Perl.

CC Number: 286504

Information available

Accounts were available from the Charity Commission.

The foundation was established in 1960 for general charitable purposes. It defines its principal activity as 'the establishment and continued support of Jewish schools'. The foundation also supports other educational organisations, charities and orthodox Jewish higher education establishments in the U.S.

In 2009/10 the trust had assets of £10.6 million and an income of almost £1.1 million. Grants were made totalling £288,000.

Beneficiaries included: Yavneh College; Yesodey Hatorah Schools; Sylvella Charity Limited; Edgware Jewish Primary School; Morasha Jewish Primary School; Aish; Noam Primary School; and Bais Yaccov Primary School.

The accounts do not list the amounts given to individual recipient organisations.

Exclusions

No grants to individuals.

Applications

In writing to the correspondent. The trustees meet several times a year.

John Huntingdon's Charity

Welfare

£26,000 (2010)

Beneficial area

The parish of Sawston.

John Huntingdon House, Tannery Road, Sawston, Cambridge CB22 3UW
Tel: 01223 830599
Email: office@johnhuntingdon.org.uk
Website: www.johnhuntingdon.org.uk/
Correspondent: Revd Mary Irish, Charity Manager
Trustees: Thomas Butler; Sally Hatton; Susan Reynolds; Reg Cullum; Christine Ingham; Eugene Murray; Eleanor Clapp; Catherine Gilmore; Alan Partridge; Josephine Shickell; David Basilington.
CC Number: 203795

Information available

Accounts were available from the Charity Commission.

The charity states that it 'serves the people of Sawston and gives new opportunities to individuals, families and groups in the community. Its aims are to alleviate disadvantage in whatever form it presents and to monitor and respond to changing need'. This includes the relief of sickness, the provision of almshouses, assistance to the elderly, educational needs for the under 25's and assisting the under 25's in their development through leisure activities.

They work closely with a wide range of statutory organisations and have a team of support workers who help with advice on housing, debt, benefits, and form filling.

The charity has grants available for individuals and families who are on low incomes. They are given for a variety of essential items including cookers, washing machines or beds. They also give grants for school trips, school uniforms and sometimes assistance is given with nursery or playgroup fees. Grants of up to £1,000 are given to groups and organisations that operate in the village of Sawston.

In 2010 the charity held assets of £7.7 million and had an income of £372,000. Grants totalled £26,000. 107 small grants were given to residents of Sawston who were in need, amounting to £14,000. Grants totalling £625 were given from the Spicer Fund. Twelve young people received bursaries to help them study for a first degree.

£6,100 was given in grants to the following organisations: Cogwheel Adult Counselling (£1,000); Centre 33 (young people's drop in and counselling (£2,100); Alzheimer's Society Singing for the Brain project (£2,000); STARS 9children's bereavement counselling (£500); Camsight visual impairment (£500).

Applications

In writing to the correspondent.

The Hutton Foundation

Christian

£133,000 (2010)

Beneficial area

Worldwide.

Spring Cottage, Cranes Road, Sherborne St John, Hampshire RG24 9HY
Correspondent: Graham Hutton, Trustee
Trustees: Graham Hutton; Amanda Hutton; Richard Hutton; James Hutton.
CC Number: 1106521

Information available

Accounts were available from the Charity Commission.

Set up in 2004, in 2010 the foundation had an income of £28,000. Grants totalled £133,000. Assets stood at £1.9 million at year end.

Previously: the Catholic Trust for England and Wales and Hampshire (£100,000 each); NSPCC (£34,000); Catholic Bishops Conference (£25,000); Aid to the Church in Need (£25,000); and International Theologies Institute (£21,000).

Applications

In writing to the correspondent.

The Huxham Charitable Trust

Christianity, churches and organisations, development work

£67,000 to organisations (2009/10)

Beneficial area

Now mainly Albania and Kosova.

Thatcher Brake, 37 Whidborne Avenue, Torquay TQ1 2PG
Tel: 01803 380399
Correspondent: Adrian W Huxham
Trustees: Rev Deacon; Revd Percy; Mr Corney; Mr Hawkins.
CC Number: 1000179

Information available

Accounts were available from the Charity Commission.

In 2009/10 the trust had assets of £135,000 and an income of £55,000. Grants to organisations and individuals totalled £80,000, with £67,000 being made to organisations. No further information was available.

Applications

Grants cannot be made to unsolicited applicants. The trust states that it now concentrates solely on its own projects.

The Nani Huyu Charitable Trust

Welfare

£142,000 (2009/10)

Beneficial area

UK, particularly but not exclusively within 50 miles of Bristol.

Rusling House, Butcombe, Bristol BS40 7XQ
Tel: 01275 474433
Email: maureensimonwhitmore@btinternet.com
Correspondent: The Trustees
Trustees: Simon Whitmore; Ben Whitmore; Charles Thatcher; Maureen Whitmore.
CC Number: 1082868

Information available

Accounts were on file at the Charity Commission, without a list of grants.

The trust was registered with the Charity commission in October 2000. Its aims are to assist people who are underprivileged, disadvantaged or ill, young people in matters of health, accommodation and training and those requiring assistance or medical care at the end of their lives, principally within Bristol and its surroundings.

In 2009/10 the trust had assets of £3.7 million and an income of £142,000. Grants were made to 25 organisations totalling £141,500.

Grant beneficiaries include: Rainbow, Womankind and Southside Family Project (£11,000 each); Young Bristol and Jessie May Trust (£10,000 each); Family Centre for Deaf (£8,000); Crossroads (£7,000); Wellspring Counselling (£4,000); Bristol Meditation and Grounds for Change (£3,000 each) and Preanes Green Junior Activity Club (£1,500).

Applications

In writing to the correspondent.

The P Y N and B Hyams Trust

Jewish, general

£49,000 (2009/10)

Beneficial area

Worldwide.

Lubbock Fine, Russell Bedford House, City Forum, 250 City Road, London EC1V 2QQ
Tel: 020 7490 7766
Correspondent: N Shah, Trustee
Trustees: Mrs M Hyams; D Levy; N Shah.
CC Number: 268129

Information available

Accounts were available from the Charity Commission, but without a list of grants.

In 2009/10 the trust had assets of almost £1.1 million and an income of £83,000. Grants to organisations totalled £49,000. No list of grants was included with the accounts.

In previous years, grants have been mostly given to Jewish organisations, although other causes are also funded.

Applications

In writing to the correspondent, but please note, the trust states that funds are fully committed and unsolicited applications are not welcomed.

The Hyde Charitable Trust – Youth Plus

Disadvantaged children and young people

£164,000 (2009/10)

Beneficial area

The areas in which the Hyde Group operates (currently London, Kent, Surrey, Sussex and Hampshire).

Youth Plus, Hyde Charitable Trust, Hollingsworth House, 181 Lewisham High Street, London SE13 6AA
Tel: 020 8297 7575

Email: youthplus@hyde-housing.co.uk
Website: www.hyde-housing.co.uk
Correspondent: The Trustees
Trustees: Peter Matthew; Stephen Hill; Patrick Elliott; Geron Walker; Martin Wheatley; Derek Biggs; Baroness Kishwer Falkner.
CC Number: 289888

Information available

Accounts were available from the Charity Commission.

Hyde Charitable Trust is a charitable company established in 1984. The trust states that it 'works to help improve the condition and quality of life of people from the poorest communities'.

Youth Plus works throughout the areas where the Hyde Group, one of the biggest housing association groups in the country, currently operates (London, Kent, Surrey, Sussex and Hampshire).

The following information is available on the trust's website:

> Youth Plus aims to support disadvantaged children and young people in communities suffering high social deprivation in London and the South East of England. Each year, approximately £70,000 is available for distribution to projects that meet the Youth Plus objectives.

> Youth Plus is supported by Hyde Plus, Hyde's economic and community regeneration arm. Hyde Plus administers the grants and supports groups in the development of projects seeking Youth Plus funding.

> *What have we funded previously and why?*
> We are mainly interested in innovative projects seeking to address problems faced by children and young people in areas typified by social deprivation. These areas will often have high levels of unemployment and disenchantment within the community and offer very few prospects for young people.

> We are keen to hear about projects that demonstrate a partnership approach and which are committed to involving children and young people in both the planning and delivery of their services.

Grants of up to £200 each can also be made to young Hyde residents (16 years or under) for education or development training and equipment under the Hyde Young Pride Award.

In 2009/10 the trust had assets of £2.6 million and an income of

£167,000. Grants were made totalling £164,000 to various youth-related charitable projects, which were made to the following projects and areas:

Family support/parenting	£65,000
Young Pride Awards	£46,000
Holiday play fund	£39,000
Jobs plus	£10,000
New business	£5,000
Sustainability and environmental	£2,000
Other	£6,000

Exclusions

No funding for:

▶ Projects outside of the area where Hyde is working. No areas outside the South East of England.
▶ Sporting, social or fund-raising events.
▶ Medical research, hospices, residential homes for the elderly.
▶ Any other projects which the trustees deem to fall outside our main criteria.

Applications

The trust has recently informed us that it can no longer accept unsolicited applications.

The Idlewild Trust

Performing arts, culture, restoration and conservation, occasional arts education

£129,000 (2010)

Beneficial area

UK.

1a Taylors Yard, 67 Alderbrook Street, London SW12 8AD
Tel: 020 8772 3155
Email: info@idlewildtrust.org.uk
Website: www.idlewildtrust.org.uk
Correspondent: Mrs Angela Hurst, Administrator
Trustees: Lady Judith Goodison, Chair; J A Ford; M Wilson; J Ouvry; Dr T Murdoch.
CC Number: 268124

Information available

Accounts were available from the Charity Commission.

The trust was founded in 1974 by Peter Brissault Minet, who had previously set up the Peter Minet Trust. Its policy is to support charities concerned with the encouragement of performing and fine arts and preservation for the benefit of the public of lands, buildings and other objects of beauty or historic interest. Occasionally support is given to bodies for educational bursaries in these fields or for conservation of the natural environment. The trust prefers to support UK-charities and it is unlikely to support a project of local interest only.

In 2010 the trust had assets of £4.4 million, an income of £150,000 and made grants totalling £128,000.

Grants were categorised in the trust's annual report as follows:

Preservation and Restoration	31	£60,000
Performing Arts	13	£25,000
Education	11	£22,000
Museums and Galleries	6	£14,000
Fine Art	4	£8,000

Beneficiaries included: All Hallows Church – Allerton and National Galleries of Scotland (£3,000 each); Buxton Festival, Candocc Dance Festival, the Rosslyn Chapel Trust and Ulster Youth Orchestra (£2,000 each); Sound and Music and St Thomas' Church – Rhyl Organ Fund (£1,500 each); Shobana Jeyasingh Dance Company (£1,000); Dulwich Picture Gallery (£800).

Exclusions

Grants to registered charities only. No grants are made to individuals. The trust will not give to:

▶ repetitive UK-wide appeals by large charities
▶ appeals where all, or most, of the beneficiaries live outside the UK
▶ local appeals unless the artistic significance of the project is of more than local importance
▶ appeals whose sole or main purpose is to make grants from the funds collected
▶ endowment or deficit funding.

Applications

On a form available from the correspondent, or as a download from the trust's website. This can be sent via post or emailed as a Microsoft Word file. Applications

should include the following information:

▶ budget breakdown (one page)
▶ most recent audited accounts
▶ a list of other sponsors, including those applied to
▶ other relevant information.

Potential applicants are welcome to telephone the trust on Tuesdays or Wednesdays between 10am and 4pm to discuss their application and check eligibility. Trustees meet twice a year usually in March and November.

All eligible applications, which are put forward to the trustees, are acknowledged; other applications will not be acknowledged unless an sae is enclosed. Applications from organisations within 18 months of a previous grant will not be considered.

The Iliffe Family Charitable Trust

Medical, disability, heritage, education

£219,000 (2009/10)

Beneficial area

UK and Worldwide.

Barn Close, Yattendon, Berkshire RG18 0UX
Tel: 01635 203929
Correspondent: The Secretary to the Trustees
Trustees: N G E Petter; G A Bremner; Lord Iliffe; Hon. Edward Iliffe.
CC Number: 273437

Information available

Full accounts were on file at the Charity Commission.

The trust gives grants towards groups concerned with medical causes, disability, heritage and education. The bulk of the grants made are to charities already known to the trustees, to which funds are committed from year to year. Other donations are made for a wide range of charitable purposes in which the trust has a special interest.

In 2009/10 the trust had assets of £1.2 million and an income of £204,000. Grants totalled £219,000 and were broken down as follows:

Welfare	£69,000
Heritage	£53,000
Medical	£41,000
Education	£34,000
Conservation	£15,000
Religious	£8,000

Beneficiaries included: Marine Society & Sea Cadets (£30,000); Royal Shakespeare Company and Bradfield Foundation (£20,000); Game & Wildlife Conservation Trust (£15,000); Arthur Rank Centre (£12,000); Jubilee Sailing Trust (£10,000); Priors Court Foundation (£5,000); Ufton Court Education Centre (£1,000); FAAOA (£900); and Elizabeth Finn Care (£500).

Exclusions
No grants to individuals and rarely to non-registered charities

Applications
In writing to the correspondent. Only successful applications will be acknowledged. Grants are considered at ad hoc meetings of the trustees, held throughout the year.

The Indigo Trust

Prisons and criminal justice
£270,000 (2009/10)

Beneficial area
UK and overseas.

Allington House, 1st Floor, 150 Victoria Street, London SW1E 5AE
Tel: 020 7410 0330
Fax: 020 7410 0332
Website: www.sfct.org.uk
Correspondent: Alan Bookbinder, Director
Trustees: Dominic Flynn; Bernard Chi-Chung Fung; Francesca Perrin; William Perrin.
CC Number: 1075920

Information available
Accounts were available from the Charity Commission.

Summary
This is one of the Sainsbury Family Charitable Trusts, which share a joint administration. They have a common approach to grantmaking which is generally discouraging to organisations not already in contact with the trust concerned, but some appear increasingly open to unsolicited approaches.

General
The trust's 2009/10 accounts offer the following analysis of its grantmaking policy:

Last year the trustees decided to focus their grant-making entirely in the field of criminal justice. During the course of this year the trustees have concentrated on researching parts of the sector where support from the Indigo Trust could have significant impact and create sustained change. As a result of this work, the trustees are likely to wish to fund programmes in the areas of:

- improved use of resources in the sector, particularly in resettlement and education
- the development of innovation and best practice in the sector, particularly in terms of the use of the web and new technologies
- research and dissemination to support the areas above.

Over the next year the trustees will make a small number of grants to organisations or programmes that have the potential to bring about systematic change both in prisons and within the criminal justice system more widely.

Proposals are generally invited by the trustees or initiated at their request. Unsolicited applications are not encouraged and are unlikely to be successful. Grants are not normally made to individuals.

Grants in 2009/10
In 2009/10 the trust had assets of £7.4 million and a significantly lower income (than in previous years) of £117,000 (£5.8 million in 2006/07). However, the high income in 2006/07 was mainly due to a large gift of £5.5 million from the settlor. This has since been invested by the trust and the higher returns generated should allow for increased grantmaking in future years.

Grants payable during the current year totalled £270,000.

Beneficiaries were: Impetus Trust (£72,000); New Philanthropy Capital (£63,000); Open Book (£45,000); My Society (£40,000); Butler Trust (£36,000); University of Cambridge – Robinson College (£10,000); and the Sainsbury Archive (£3,000).

A grant of £1,300 was also made but not listed.

Exclusions
Grants are not usually made to individuals.

Applications
In writing to the correspondent, no more than two pages long describing the organisation (including most recent income and expenditure), the project and the funding needed. At this stage applicants should not send full accounts.

The Ingram Trust

General
£672,000 (2009/10)

Beneficial area
UK and overseas, with a local preference for Surrey.

c/o 8th Floor, 101 Wigmore Street, London W1U 1QU
Email: theingramtrust@sandaire.com
Correspondent: Joan Major, Administrator
Trustees: C J Ingram; Mrs J E Ingram; Ms C M Maurice.
CC Number: 1040194

Information available
Accounts were on file at the Charity Commission.

The trust's policies are as follows:
- it selects a limited number of charities which it commits itself to support for three to five years
- it prefers to support specific projects which can include identifiable costs for special services provided by the charity or equipment that is required
- beneficiaries will generally be major UK-wide or international charities together with some local ones in the county of Surrey
- the majority of grants will be made for periods of three to four years at a time in order to better assess grant applications and monitor progress

- the only overseas aid charities which are considered are those dedicated to encouraging self-help and providing more permanent solutions to problems
- no animal charities are considered except those concerned with wildlife conservation.

In 2009/10 the trust had assets of £12.2 million, an income of £206,000 and made grants to 27 organisations totalling £672,000.

Beneficiaries included: WWF – UK (£75,000); ACTIONAid (£50,000); the National Theatre (£30,000); St Mungo's (£20,000); St Giles Trust (£15,000); and Disability Challengers and Pimlico Opera (£10,000 each).

Exclusions

No grants to non-registered charities or to individuals. No charities specialising in overseas aid are considered except those dedicated to encouraging self help or providing more permanent solutions. No animal charities except those concerned with wildlife conservation.

Applications

In writing to the correspondent, although the trust states that it receives far more worthy applications than it is able to support.

The Inland Waterways Association

Inland waterways

£85,000 (2010)

Beneficial area

UK and Ireland.

Island House, Moor Road, Chesham, Buckinghamshire HP5 1WA
Tel: 01923 711114
Fax: 01923 897000
Email: iwa@waterways.org.uk
Website: www.waterways.org.uk
Correspondent: The Chair of the IWA Restoration Committee
Trustees: The Council of the Association; Doug Beard; Ray Carter; Leslie Etheridge; John Fletcher; Anthony Harrison; Michael Palmer;

John Pomfret; Paul Strudwick; Vaughan Welch; Ian West.
CC Number: 212342

Information available

Accounts were available from the Charity Commission, but without a list of grants.

The trust supports organisations promoting the restoration of inland waterways (i.e. canal and river navigations).

It makes grants for:
1 construction, especially works relating to the restoration of navigation such as locks, bridges, aqueducts, culverts, weirs, pumps, excavation, dredging, lining and so on
2 administration – support for a particular purpose, such as a project officer, a funding appeal or for promotional literature or events
3 professional services, such as funding of feasibility studies or detailed work on engineering, economic or environmental issues
4 land purchase
5 research on matters affecting waterway restoration, including original research, reviews of research undertaken by others and literature reviews
6 education, such as providing information to local authorities or agencies to promote the nature and benefits of waterway restoration.

In 2010 the trust had assets of £276,000 and an income of £1.5 million, most of which was derived from membership subscriptions, legacies, donations and related funds such as Gift Aid. Charitable expenditure during the year totalled approximately £800,000 of which a large amount (£575,000) was designated to campaign and restoration costs which included donations and grants of £85,000.

Previous grant beneficiaries include: the Driffield Navigation Trust (£7,500); Lichfield & Hatherton Canals Restoration Trust and Caldon & Uttoxeter Canal Trust (£5,000 each); British Waterways (£2,500); Rolle Canal and North Devon Waterways Society, Wiltshire and Berkshire Canal Trust and Foxton

Locks Partnership (£2,000 each); and River Gipping Trust (£1,000).

Exclusions

No grants to individuals. No retrospective grants for projects where expenditure has already been incurred or committed.

Applications

In writing to the correspondent. Applications should comply with the 'Guidelines for Applicants', also available from the correspondent. Each applicant should provide a full description of its proposal, show that the organisation can maintain a satisfactory financial position and demonstrate that it is capable of undertaking the proposed project.

Applications for up to £2,000 are assessed under a simplified procedure – each application should demonstrate that the grant would be used to initiate or sustain a restoration scheme or significantly benefit a specific small project.

Applications for over £2,000 should demonstrate that the grant would be applied to one of the types of projects (1–6). Applicants should also demonstrate the extent to which the project satisfies one or more of the following conditions:
- the grant would unlock (lever) a grant several times larger from another body
- the grant would not replace grants available from other sources
- the project does not qualify for grants from major funding sources
- the grant would enable a key project to be undertaken which would have a significant effect on the prospect of advancing the restoration and gaining funds from other sources for further restoration projects
- the result of the project would have a major influence over the progress of a number of other restoration projects
- The Inland Waterways Association Restoration Committee would have a major influence in the management of the project, including monitoring of expenditure.

The Inlight Trust

Religion

£100,000 (2009/10)

Beneficial area

UK.

PO Box 2, Liss, Hampshire
GU33 6YP
Tel: 01730 894120
Correspondent: The Trustees
Trustees: Sir T Lucas; Mrs W Collett;
S Neil; R Wolfe; D Hawkins; Mrs
J Hayward.
CC Number: 236782

Information available

Accounts were available from the
Charity Commission.

The trust makes grants for the
advancement of religion only. It states
that its funding priorities are:

> To make donations on an
> undenominational basis to charities
> providing valuable contributions to
> spiritual development and charities
> concerned with spiritual healing and
> spiritual growth through religious
> retreats.

Grants are usually one-off for a
specific project or part of a project.
Bursary schemes may also be
supported. Core funding and/or
salaries are rarely considered.

In 2009/10 it had assets of
£5.2 million, which generated an
income of £218,000, through which
15 grants were made totalling
£100,000.

The main beneficiaries included:
Drukpa UK (£10,000); St Albans
Cathedral Music Trust (£5,000):
Christians in Care (£3,000); and
Acorn Christian Healing Foundation
(£2,000).

Exclusions

Grants are made to registered
charities only. Applications from
individuals, including students, are
ineligible. No grants are made in
response to general appeals from
large national organisations. Grants
are seldom available for church
buildings.

Applications

In writing to the correspondent
including details of the need the
intended project is designed to meet
plus an outline budget and the most
recent available annual accounts of
the charity. Only applications from
eligible bodies are acknowledged.
Applications must be accompanied by
a copy of your trust deed or of your
entry in the Charity Commission
register. They are considered four
times a year. Only successful
applicants are informed.

The Inman Charity

General, medical, social welfare, disability, older people, hospices

£283,000 (2010)

Beneficial area

UK.

Payne Hicks Beech, 10 New Square,
Lincoln's Inn, London WC2A 3QG
Correspondent: The Trustees
Trustees: A L Walker; Miss
B M A Strother; M R Matthews; Prof.
J D Langdon.
CC Number: 261366

Information available

Full accounts were on file at the
Charity Commission. The charity's
2009/10 annual report states:

> The directors operate a grant giving
> policy, providing funds for such
> charitable object or institution as the
> directors think fit. In addition to
> supporting a wide range of charitable
> organisations, the charity makes a
> regular payment to the Victor Inman
> Bursary Fund at Uppingham School of
> which the settlor had been a lifelong
> supporter.
>
> The charity makes a payment of
> £20,000 per annum and is reviewed
> annually.

The directors aim to make grants
totalling approximately £250,000 per
year. Previously grants have been
given in the areas of social welfare,
disability, older people and hospices.

In 2010 it had assets of £4.9 million
generating an income of £156,000.
Grants to 64 organisations totalled
£283,000.

Beneficiaries included: The Roy Castle
Lung Cancer Foundation and Fight
for Sight (£5,000 each); World Cancer
Research Fund and Gurkha Welfare
Trust (£4,000 each); Redbridge
Concern Mental Health (£3,000); the
Dystonia Society and Right
Employment (£2,500 each); Missing
People (£1,500); and Optua (£500).

Exclusions

No grants to individuals.

Applications

In writing to the correspondent
accompanied by the charity's latest
report and full accounts. Applications
should contain the following: aims
and objectives of the charity; nature
of the appeal; total target if for a
specific project; contributions
received against target; registered
charity number; any other relevant
factors.

The International Bankers Charitable Trust (The Worshipful Company of International Bankers)

The recruitment and development of employees in the financial services

£84,000 (2009/10)

Beneficial area

UK with preference for inner London.

3rd Floor, 12 Austin Friars, London
EC2N 2HE
Tel: 020 7374 0214
Email: tim.woods@
internationalbankers.co.uk
Website: www.internationalbankers.
co.uk
Correspondent: Tim Woods, Clerk

Trustee: The Worshipful Company of International Bankers.

CC Number: 1087630

Information available

Accounts were on file at the Charity Commission. The Worshipful Company of International Bankers' website provides the following information:

As a representative of the major commercial activity in the city, banking and financial services, the company combines the traditions of the City Livery Companies with a modern outlook on the financial services sector. With more than 600 members, drawn from over 250 companies and institutions and with almost 50 nationalities represented, the company has a truly international character.

The 'Charity Applications' section of the website states:

The company will seek to promote recruitment and development of employees in the financial services industry with particular emphasis on those younger people in the immediate area of the city who would not normally be able to aspire to a city job.

Grants are made to registered charities only.

The company may support:

1 Specific projects where a donation from the company would cover either a significant proportion of the cost or an identified element of it.

2 Long-term funding of scholarships and/or bursaries.

In 2009/10 the trust had assets of £815,000 and an income of £123,000, mostly from members of the Worshipful Company of International Bankers. Grants were made totalling £84,000.

Beneficiaries included: the Brokerage Citylink (£30,000); Reed's School (£16,000 in two grants); Museum of London (£2,500); and the Social Mobility Foundation and Archway (£1,000 each).

Exclusions

The following areas are excluded from company grants:

- large projects towards which any contribution from the company would have limited impact
- general appeals or circulars
- replacement of statutory funds
- salaries

- counselling
- course fees for professionals
- medical research
- fundraising events and sponsorship.

Applications

On a form with can be downloaded from the trust's website. Previous grant recipients must allow two years from the date the original grant was awarded to reapply.

The Inverforth Charitable Trust

General

Nil (2010); £49,000 (2009).

Beneficial area

UK.

58A Flood Street, London SW3 5TE
Tel: 0870 770 2657
Correspondent: The Secretary
Trustees: Elizabeth Lady Inverforth; Dr Andrew Weir; Hon. Mrs J Kane.
CC Number: 274132

Information available

Accounts were available from the Charity Commission.

Established in 1977 the trust exists to support general charitable causes. It has given widely in the past by supporting organisations concerned with health, the arts, youth & education, churches and heritage. The trust supports UK and international charities.

In 2010 the trust had assets of £4.1 million, which generated an income of £39,000. No grants were made during 2010 (2009: £49,000). The trustees annual report for 2010 states:

The charity continues to take a long view and Trust assets are primarily invested in securities. The Trust has power to distribute capital and income. In the past, the Trustees have made full distributions of income together with part of the capital appreciation. For the future, the Trustees will distribute the estimated net annual income to the selected charities, after expenses.

Previous beneficiaries have included: Help for Heroes (£5,000); Helriot Hospice Homecare and CHASE

Hospice Care for Children (£2,000 each); the ART Fund, British Lung Foundation, Voluntary Services Overseas and National Youth Orchestra of Great Britain (£1,500 each); National Playbus Association, Kidscape, Contact the Elderly and Farms for City Children (£1,000 each); and Book Aid International, Bowel Cancer UK and the Gurkha Welfare Trust (£500 each).

Applications

In writing to the trustees.

Common applicant mistakes

'Applicants providing excessive information. Concise applications are preferred.'

The Ireland Fund of Great Britain

Welfare, community, education, peace and reconciliation, the arts

£863,000 (2010)

Beneficial area

Ireland and Great Britain.

2nd Floor, Wigglesworth House, 69 Southwark Bridge Road, London SE1 9HH
Tel: 0207 9409 850
Fax: 0207 378 8376
Email: info@irelandfund.org
Website: www.theirelandfunds.org
Correspondent: Sheila Bailey
Trustees: Sheila Bailey; Seamus McGarry; Basil Geoghegan; Peter Kiernan; John Rowan; Ruth McCarthy; Ivan Fallon; Michael Casey; Ruari Conneely; Conor Foley; Zach Webb; Eileen Kelliher.
CC Number: 327889

Information available

Accounts were on file at the Charity Commission; the trust has a useful website.

Founded in 1976 by Sir Anthony O'Reilly and a number of key American businessmen, The Ireland Funds is an international charitable organisation operating in 11 countries and has raised over

$300 million for worthy causes in Ireland.

The Ireland Fund of Great Britain (IFGB) states in its annual report that it: 'was established to distribute funding to community groups, voluntary organisations, charities and establishments who seek to promote Irish arts and culture and develop relationships between our communities; advancement of education; [and] promote Irish culture to the friends of Ireland.'

At present the trust is undertaking a strategic shift in its fundraising policy as it attempts to move away from event led fundraising towards a donation based income stream.

In 2010 the fund had assets of £613,000 an income of £1.2 million, mainly from donations and memberships. Grants totalled £863,000 and were broken down as follows:

Community development and relief of poverty	£367,000
Sharing and developing Irish arts and culture	£60,000
Education	£436,000

In 2010 beneficiaries included: Leeds Irish Health and Homes, Coventry Irish Society, Irish Community Care Merseyside, Aisling Return to Ireland Project, Cricklewood Homeless Concern, Solace Women's Aid (£10,000 each); The Hibernian Society, Milton Keynes Irish Welfare Support Group, Irish in Greenwich, Immigrant Counselling & Psychotherapy (£7,000 each); Irish Arts Foundation, Sandwell Irish Society Birmingham (£6,000 each); Tyneside Irish Centre (£5,000); Southwark Irish Pensioners Project (£4,500); St John Bosco Club (£2,000); and Tara Irish Pensioners (£1,500).

Some beneficiaries in 2011 included: Irish Women's Survivors Support Network, Irish Support and Advice Service Hammersmith, Irish Elderly Advice Network (£7,000 each); Coventry Irish Society (£4,000); and Birchfield Residents Action Group (£3,500).

Eligibility

IFGB supports projects in the following categories:

- arts and culture
- community development
- education
- peace and reconciliation.

Each category is accorded equal importance.

Arts and culture

IFGB wishes to support excellence and innovation in the arts and culture and especially projects that make the arts more accessible to the wider community. In particular, the IFGB will focus on the following:

- arts/cultural activities applied in settings of socio-economic disadvantage
- arts/cultural activities applied in educational or health settings
- arts/cultural activities promoting tolerance and reconciliation.

Community Development/Relief of Poverty

IFGB is seeking ways to promote an inclusive and integrated society and to ensure the regeneration of marginalised sections of the Irish community. IFGB sees the following areas as priorities:

- increasing the capacity of the social economy
- promotion of social inclusion
- promotion of tolerance and diversity.

Education

Investment in education is investment in the future. Economic and social development depends on a well-educated population. For this reason, IFGB will focus on programmes supporting:

- access and progression to further education
- pre-school education
- lifelong learning
- tolerance through education.

Peace and Reconciliation

IFGB seeks to support communities working together towards a shared future. The skills and culture of negotiation and compromise need to be honed politically and organisationally within and between communities. To this end, programmes supporting the following areas have been prioritised for assistance:

- citizenship and participation
- a greater understanding of cultural identity within and between communities
- social inclusion.

Exclusions

Grants are generally not given for: general administration costs; travel or accommodation costs; payments for buildings or land; general appeals; other grant making trusts; payments for vehicles; medical expenses i.e. applications must be made for clearly specified purposes. No multi-annual awards.

Applications

Application forms and full details of how to apply are available from the IFGB website.

The Irish Youth Foundation (UK) Ltd (incorporating The Lawlor Foundation)

Irish young people

£197,000 (2010)

Beneficial area

UK.

The Irish Cultural Centre, Blacks Road, Hammersmith, London W6 9DT
Tel: 020 8748 9640
Email: info@iyf.org.uk
Website: www.iyf.org.uk
Correspondent: Linda Tanner
Trustees: John O'Neill, Chair; John Dwyer; Fred Hucker; Virginia Lawlor; Mary Clancy; Mark Gilbert; David Murray; Jim O'Hara.
CC Number: 328265

Information available

Accounts were available at the Charity Commission, but without a list of grant beneficiaries.

Irish Youth Foundation (UK) Ltd merged with the Lawlor Foundation (effective from 30 June 2005). The work of the Lawlor Foundation, towards the advancement of education in Northern Ireland, continues with support for Irish students and educational organisations.

The foundation supports organisations anywhere in the UK working with young Irish people aged up to 25 who are socially, educationally or culturally disadvantaged.

A wide range of projects are supported which include: training/counselling; drug rehabilitation; advice/advocacy; youth work; family support; homelessness; educational, cultural & social activities; cross-community initiatives; travellers and disability.

Grants range from £500 to £25,000 and are awarded annually. Grants for organisations in England, Scotland and Wales fall into the following three categories:

- Small grants for up to £2,500
- Medium grants for over £2,500 and under £12,000
- Large grants for one year or more ranging from £12,000 to £25,000

The Irish Youth Foundation (UK) and the Irish Youth Foundation (Ireland) have established a joint fund to provide support for community and voluntary groups in Northern Ireland. Grants for organisations in Northern Ireland are up to £5,000.

In 2010 the foundation had assets of £2.2 million and an income of £190,000. Grants totalled £200,000.

Previous beneficiaries in the UK (excluding Northern Ireland) include: Brent Adolescent Centre – London (£15,000 in two grants for three years); Irish Community Care – Merseyside (£12,000); London Gypsy and Traveller Unit (£9,000); Irish Arts Foundation – Leeds (£4,000); Warwickshire Schools Gaelic Athletics Association (£2,000); and Liverpool Irish Festival Society (£1,000).

Previous beneficiaries in Northern Ireland included: The National Deaf Children's Society, Northern Ireland (£4,500); Artillery Youth Centre – Belfast (£4,000); Drake Music Project – Newry (£3,500); Down Community Arts – Downpatrick (£3,000); Headliners – Derry (£2,500); and Our

Lady Queen of Peace Youth Club – Belfast (£1,000).

Exclusions

The foundation generally does not support: projects for people over 25; general appeals; large/national charities; academic research; alleviating deficits already incurred; individuals; capital bids; or overseas travel.

Applications

Applications are assessed on an annual basis and application forms are only available during the annual round either on the website or by request. The application period is short as forms are only available during December and January, with grant awards being made the following April.

Applications are assessed on the following requirements: need; continuity; track record/evaluation; disadvantaged young people; innovativeness; funding sources; and budgetary control. Faxed or emailed applications are not considered. Unsolicited applications outside the annual round of grant applications will not be considered or acknowledged.

Common applicant mistakes

'Poor applications lacking focus and statistical or sufficient evidence of need according to criteria; contacts with other agencies in their field of work; not providing referees.'

The Ironmongers' Foundation

General, see below

£160,000 (2009/10)

Beneficial area

UK with some preference for inner London.

Ironmongers' Hall, Barbican, London EC2Y 8AA
Tel: 020 7776 2311
Fax: 020 7600 3519
Email: helen@ironhall.co.uk
Website: www.ironhall.co.uk
Correspondent: Helen Sant, Charities Administrator

Trustee: Worshipful Ironmongers' Company.
CC Number: 238256

Information available

Accounts were available from the Charity Commission.

The charity's 2009/10 annual report provides the following information:

> The primary purpose of the Foundation is to enable the Company to support charitable activities it keeping with its historic origins. Any surplus income is used to further the Trustee's objectives to promote relief in need. The Charity aims to encourage the continued development of use of iron and steel. This is achieved through supporting ferrous-related educational activities at selected schools, colleges and universities. Two award schemes funded by the charity promote excellence and innovation in the steel industry. In addition, appeals are accepted from charitable organisations engaged in the conservation or creation of fine iron and steel work.

Grants will be made for projects that meet all of the following criteria:

1 Children and young people up to the age of 25;
2 Educational activities;
3 Specific projects with clear aims and objectives to be met within a planned timescale.

Most grants are in the region of £1,000 to £5,000. The trustees will consider making grants over more than one year to longer term projects, subject to a satisfactory evaluation of progress at the end of each year. The company's support should make a recognisable difference; therefore preference will be given to requests which cover a significant element of the cost and to those from smaller organisations.

In 2009/10 the foundation had assets of £2.2 million, an income of £135,000 and made grants to organisations totalling £160,000.

The accounts listed beneficiaries in receipt of awards over £1,000 each, with examples of beneficiaries, divided as follows:

Foundation Bursary Scheme	£58,000
Universities and industry	£28,000
Ironwork	£21,000
Relief in need	£13,000
Iron education	£9,000
City organisations	£8,000

Beneficiaries included: St Katharine Cree (£6,000); the Industrial Trust

(£4,500); University of Birmingham (£3,500); the National Trust (£2,000); and Lincoln Cathedral (£1,250).

Exclusions

No grants towards:

- Large projects towards which any contribution from the Company would have limited impact.
- General appeals or circulars.
- Replacement of statutory funds.
- General running costs. (A reasonable proportion of overheads will be accepted as part of project costs.)
- Counselling.
- Course fees for professionals.
- Medical research.
- Fundraising events and sponsorship.
- Retrospective appeals and projects starting before the date of the relevant Committee meeting.

Applications

The Company's 'Grant Application Summary Sheet' must be completed and returned including a description of the project, of no more than three A4 pages. Summary sheets can be downloaded from the fund's website.

The Appeals Committee meets twice a year in March and October. The deadlines for receipt of applications are 31 January and 31 August respectively. Please note that applications are not accepted by email.

Grants must be spent within twelve months from the date of the award.

Common applicant mistakes

'They don't justify the need for the work they are doing and/or fully explain how the work will be planned and implemented, i.e. they do not make a convincing case.'

The ISA Charity

The arts, health and education

£30,000 (2009/10)

Beneficial area

UK.

2 The Mansion, Northwick Park, Blockley, Moreton-in-Marsh Gl56 9RJ

Website: www.isacharity.net
Correspondent: R Paice, Trustee
Trustees: R Paice; Mrs M Paice; Miss A Paice.
CC Number: 326882

Information available

Accounts were available at the Charity Commission, but without a list of grants. Detailed information is available on the charity's website.

Founded in 1985 by Richard Paice, the ISA Charity supports causes related to the arts, health and education in the broadest sense. This can include both UK and overseas initiatives. The charity selects various organisations which help to find the individual beneficiaries. Up to £50,000 is distributed each year.

In 2009/10 the charity had assets of £1.7 million and an income of £31,000. Grants totalled £30,000.

Unfortunately a list of the beneficiaries was not available.

Applications

The charity's website included the following statement:

The charity adopts a venture philanthropy approach and identifies its own projects. It does not accept funding requests from individuals, organisations or other charities. As a consequence it will not acknowledge any unsolicited funding requests.

The J Isaacs Charitable Trust

General

£595,000 (2009/10)

Beneficial area

England and Wales.

c/o Touch Group PLC, Saffron House, 6–10 Kirby Street, London EC1N 6TS
Email: peter.katz@touchgroupplc.com
Correspondent: Peter Katz
Trustees: Jeremy Isaacs: Joanne Isaacs; Helen Eastick.
CC Number: 1059865

Information available

Accounts were available from the Charity Commission.

Registered with the Charity Commission in 1996, the trust states that it:

Strives to support causes connected to the following:

- Children
- Respite for parents/children
- Cancer
- Sponsorship for causes supported by Lehman employees
- London-based organisations

In 2009/10 it had assets of £16.6 million and an income of £31,000. Grants were made totalling £595,000.

Beneficiaries included: Jewish Care (£200,000); the Jewish Museum London (£100,000); Community Security Trust (£75,000); Greenhouse Schools Project (£25,000); Policy Exchange Ltd (£15,000); UCLH Fund (£7,500); UK Jewish Film (£5,000); and Royal National Theatre (£1,000).

Applications

In writing to the correspondent.

J A R Charitable Trust

Roman Catholic, education, welfare

£68,000 (2010/11)

Beneficial area

Worldwide.

Hunters, 9 New Square, London WC2A 3QN
Tel: 020 7412 0050
Correspondent: Philip R Noble, Trustee
Trustees: Philip R Noble; Revd William Young; Revd Paschal Ryan.
CC Number: 248418

Information available

Accounts were on file at the Charity Commission.

The trust makes grants towards: Roman Catholic missionaries, churches and other causes; education for people under 30; and food and clothing for people over 55 who are in need. In practice, the trust gives regular grants to support mainly Roman Catholic organisations.

In 2010/11 the trust had assets of £2.4 million which generated an income of £72,000. Grants were made to 30 organisations totalling £68,000.

Beneficiaries included: Oxford Oratory and the Passage (£4,000 each); Liverpool Archdiocesan Youth Pilgrimage, the Venerable English College Rome and Catholic Children's Society (£3,000 each); Friends of Turnaini, Little Sisters of the Poor and Church of St James (£2,000 each); and Tongabezi Trust School, Court Meadow School and Marriage Care (£1,000 each).

Exclusions

The trust does not normally support a charity unless it is known to the trustees and it does not support individuals.

Applications

In writing to the correspondent. Please note that the trust's funds are fully committed to regular beneficiaries and it states that there is very little, if any, for unsolicited appeals. In order to save administration costs replies are not sent to unsuccessful applicants.

The JRSST Charitable Trust

Democracy and social justice

£131,000 (2010)

Beneficial area

UK.

The Garden House, Water End, York YO30 6WQ
Tel: 01904 625744
Fax: 01904 651502
Email: info@jrrt.org.uk
Website: www.jrrt.org.uk
Correspondent: Tina Walker
Trustees: Christine J Day; Christopher J Greenfield; Paedar Cremin; Mandy Cormack; Lord Archy Kirkwood; Andrew Neal.
CC Number: 247498

Information available

Accounts were available from the Charity Commission.

The trust was originally endowed by the non-charitable Joseph Rowntree Reform Trust Ltd. It will consider and sometimes instigate charitable projects which relate specifically to the work of The Joseph Rowntree Reform Trust Ltd in supporting the development of an increasingly democratic and socially-just society in Great Britain.

In 2010 the trust had assets of £2.7 million and an income of over £93,000. Grants paid to organisations totalled £131,000.

Beneficiaries of grants approved during the year included: Institute for Government (£50,000); Democratic Audit (£14,000); Northern Ireland Family Planning Association (£10,000); and Demos, Mysociety and Reuters Institute (£5,000 each).

Exclusions

No student grants are funded.

Applications

The trustees meet quarterly. They do not invite applications.

Common applicant mistakes

'Not contacting trust before applying; not reading guidelines.'

The Ruth and Lionel Jacobson Trust (Second Fund) No 2

Jewish, medical, children, disability

£13,000 (2009/10)

Beneficial area

UK, with a preference for North East England.

14 The Grainger Suite, Dobson House, The Regent Centre, Newcastle upon Tyne NE3 3PF
Correspondent: The Trustees
Trustees: Anne Jacobson; Malcolm Jacobson.
CC Number: 326665

Information available

Accounts were available from the Charity Commission.

The trust supports UK charities and organisations based in the north east of England. The trust states that it supports the advancement of Jewish religious education and healthcare charities. Charities outside the north east of England are supported whenever possible.

In 2009/10 the trust had assets of £1.1 million, an income of £46,000 and made grants totalling £13,000.

Although the trustees' report for this financial year states: 'The charity was pleased to assist the United Jewish Israel Appeal with its educational purposes and family support programme', an amount has not been listed in the accounts and so we assume this refers to previous years. There was only one beneficiary organisation in the year 2009/10 which was WIZO UK (£13,000).

Exclusions

No grants for individuals. Only registered charities will be supported.

Applications

In writing to the correspondent. Please enclose an sae. Applications are considered every other month.

The James Trust

Christianity

£97,000 (2009/10)

Beneficial area

UK and overseas.

27 Radway Road, Upper Shirley, Southampton, Hampshire SO15 7PL
Tel: 023 8078 8249
Correspondent: R J Todd, Trustee
Trustees: R J Todd; G Blue.
CC Number: 800774

Information available

Accounts were available from the Charity Commission.

Principally, the trust has a preference for supporting Christian organisations. It operates primarily as a channel for the giving of a small group of donors. Grants are primarily to churches and Christian organisations involved in overseas development and work with young people.

In 2009/10 it had an income of £40,000 and made grants to totalling £97,000. Donations were in the range of £30 and £10,000 and were broken down as follows:

Organisations working in the UK	£37,000
Organisations working overseas	£28,000
Churches and church organisations	£23,000
Development and relief work	£9,000
Individuals	£650

During the year donations were made to the local churches of the donors and to a wide range of Christian organisations. The main beneficiaries were Above Bar Church, Ambassadors in Sport, Food for the Hungry, UCCF and Wycliffe Translators.

Unfortunately a full grants list was not provided in this year's set of accounts, however previous beneficiaries have included: Archbishops Council (£10,000); Above Bar Church (£7,700); Food For the Hungry (£5,000); UCCF (£3,600); Crusaders (£4,100); TearFund (£1,900); Christian Aid (£1,300); Bible Society (£800); Church Missionary Society (£500); and Cancer Research (£200).

Exclusions
No grants to individuals not personally known to the trustees.

Applications
In writing to the correspondent. Unsolicited applications are not acknowledged.

Common applicant mistakes
'Not making a phone call, to discuss whether to apply, before sending costly brochures and material that goes into the bin.'

The John Jarrold Trust

Social welfare, arts, education, environment/ conservation, medical research, churches

£159,000 to organisations
(2009/10)

Beneficial area
Norfolk.

Jarrold and Sons Ltd, Whitefriars, Norwich NR3 1SH
Tel: 01603 677360
Email: caroline.jarrold@jarrold.com
Website: www.jarrold.com
Correspondent: Caroline Jarrold, Secretary
Trustees: A C Jarrold, Chair; R E Jarrold; P J Jarrold; Mrs D J Jarrold; Mrs J Jarrold; Mrs A G Jarrold; Caroline Jarrold; Mrs W A L Jarrold.
CC Number: 242029

Information available
Full accounts were available from the Charity Commission.

The trust supports a wide range of organisations including churches, medical, arts, environment/ conservation and welfare. It prefers to support specific projects, rather than contribute to general funding. In practice, most of the funds are given in Norfolk.

In 2009/10 the trust had assets of nearly £1.5 million and an income of £187,000. Grants made to 145 organisations totalled £159,000, and were broken down as follows:

Arts	£13,000
Social and Welfare	£83,000
Education	£27,000
Churches and historic buildings	£7,500
Developing countries	£9,000
Health and Medical	£16,000
Environment	£3,000

Beneficiaries included: Hamlet Centre and YMCA Norfolk (£25,000 each); Arkwright Scholarship and Norfolk & Norwich Festival (£5,000 each); Britten Sinfonia (£2,500); Age Concern, East Anglian Air Ambulance, Hebron Trust, Leeway Norwich Women's Aid, Norfolk Association for the Disabled, Norfolk Deaf Association, Poppy Centre Trust, Real Health Action, Against Breast Cancer, Asperger's East Anglia, Blood Pressure Association, Brain Research Trust, Fight For Sight, Scout Group, 1st Blofield & Brundall St Stephen's Church Norwich (£1,000 each); Sailors' Families' Society, Stalham Community Gym and Feed the Minds (£500 each); and Hellesdon High School, Sewell Park College, Sprowston Community High School and Wymondham College (£25 each).

Exclusions
Educational purposes that should be supported by the state will not be helped by the trust. Local groups outside Norfolk are very unlikely to be supported unless there is a personal connection to the trust. Individual educational programmes and gap year projects are not supported.

Applications
Trustees meet in January and June each year and applications should be made in writing by the end of November and April respectively. Grants of up to £250 can be made between meetings.

Common applicant mistakes
'Not reading criteria properly; applications which are too generalised.'

Rees Jeffreys Road Fund

Road and transport research and education

£167,000 to organisations and individuals (2010)

Beneficial area
UK.

Merriewood, Horsell Park, Woking, Surrey GU21 4LW
Tel: 01483 750758
Email: briansmith@reesjeffreys.org
Website: www.reesjeffreys.co.uk
Correspondent: Brian Smith, Fund Secretary
Trustees: David Bayliss, Chair; Mike Cottell; Tony Depledge; Ann Frye; Prof Mike McDonald; Prof Stephen Glaister; David Hutchinson; Martin Shaw.
CC Number: 217771

Information available
Accounts were available online at the Charity Commission; good trust website.

The late William Rees Jeffreys established the trust in 1950, shortly after he wrote 'The King's Highway'. He campaigned extensively for the improvement of better roads and transport and was described by Lloyd George as 'the greatest authority on roads in the United Kingdom and one of the greatest in the world', due to his unrivalled expertise in this field.

The trust's objectives are:

- to contribute to the cost of lectures, studies and scholarship calculated to foster the improvement of design and layout of public highways and adjoining lands
- to promote schemes for the provision of roadside parks and open spaces
- to encourage the improvement of existing and provision of additional public highways, bridges, tunnels, footpaths, verges, and cycleways to secure the maximum of safety and beauty
- to do any other matter or thing which may conduce to the carrying out of the foregoing object and thereby carry out the wishes and continue the life work of the founder.

The trust will support projects and pump priming for longer-term ventures for up to a maximum of five years. Operational or administrative staff costs are rarely supported. In almost all cases applicants are expected to provide or arrange match funding.

In 2010 the fund had assets of £6.8 million and an income of £32,000. Grants totalled £167,000 and were broken down as follows:

Educational bursaries and support	£83,000
Research and other projects	£68,000
Roadside rests and land adjoining	£15,000

The fund offers the following commentary on its grantmaking in the 2010 accounts:

The largest proportion of this sum related to bursary awards, which remained a key priority for trustees during 2010, providing vital support and encouragement to nine highly impressive candidates, who, it is anticipated, will make a significant impact upon the UK transport world in future years.

Grants for physical projects continued to rely upon the long-standing relationship which the fund has with Wildlife Trusts, and in 2010 the partnership resulted in financial support for four schemes in England and Wales.

The fund's chairman has continued to express a desire to extend the number of research grant recipients. The trustees see the support that they can give to projects which can influence UK transport policy as a core objective, and they would very much wish to encourage more applicants in this area. In 2010 £72,000 was awarded in grants under this heading, including major awards to the Road Safety Foundation and to the Sir Colin Buchanan Archive project.

Exclusions

Grants are not given to environmental projects not related to highways, individual works for cycle tracks or works of only local application. Also, operational and administrative staff costs are rarely considered.

Applications

Applications should be made in writing to the Fund Secretary and include the following details:

- the purpose for which funding is sought – outlining the objects, relevance and the proposed methodology of the project including the names of the principal participants
- the expected costs by category, along with the project timetable
- evidence of the willingness of other parties (where the project requires their contribution or participation) to get involved.

Applications should not be more than three A4 pages. All necessary supporting material and a digital version of the application should also be submitted.

The trustees meet five times a year, usually in January, April, July, September and November (please see the fund's website for specific dates). The deadline for submission of applications or other agenda items is normally a fortnight before the meeting.

The Jenour Foundation

General
£105,000 (2009/10)

Beneficial area

UK, with a special interest in Wales.

Deloitte and Touche, Blenhein House, Fitzalan Court, Newport Road, Cardiff CF24 0TS
Tel: 02920 264348
Correspondent: The Trustees
Trustees: Sir P J Phillips; G R Camfield; D M Jones; J L Zorab.
CC Number: 256637

Information available

Accounts were available from the Charity Commission.

This foundation has general charitable purposes, with a preference for Welsh causes.

In 2009/10 the foundation had assets of £3 million, an income of £111,000 and made 32 grants totalling £105,000.

Beneficiaries included: Atlantic College (£8,000); Welsh National Opera and British Heart Foundation (£7,000 each); Red Cross International (£5,000 each); George Thomas Society (£4,000); Llandovery College (£3,000); St Woolos Cathedral (£2,000);Society for Welfare of Horses and Ponies (£1,000); and Send a Cow Appeal (£500).

Exclusions

No support for individuals.

Applications

Applications should be in writing and reach the correspondent by February for the trustees' meeting in March.

The Jephcott Charitable Trust

Development worldwide specifically in the areas of health, education, population control and environment

£209,000 (2009/10)

Beneficial area

Worldwide.

The Threshing Barn, Ford, Kingsbridge, Devon TQ7 2LN
Website: www. jephcottcharitabletrust.org.uk
Correspondent: Dr Felicity Gibling
Trustees: Lady Jephcott, Chair; Judge A North; M Jephcott; K Morgan; Mrs D Ader; Mrs C Thomas.
CC Number: 240915

Information available

Accounts were on file at the Charity Commission.

The trust's funding priorities are:
- **Population control:** The trust is prepared to consider support for schemes, particularly educational ones, which help to control excessive growth in population.
- **The natural environment:** The trust has supported a number of projects involved in conserving the natural environment. It does not support projects involving animal welfare or heritage sites or buildings.
- **Education:** Projects will be considered benefiting people of all ages and backgrounds. They may be able to provide formal education, to teach vocational skills to enhance the possibility of employment, to enhance computer skills, health awareness, distance learning.
- **Health:** A wide range of healthcare projects are supported.

The trust prefers to support projects which are pump-priming – helping to get an organisation up and running, or make a significant step forward. The trust states:

> We like to make grants which will make a difference, preference will be given to charities or projects which are having difficulty getting started, or raising funds from other sources. This often means that the trust is funding capital projects, e.g. for equipment or materials, rather than running costs.

It is not usual for the trust to make more than one grant to any organisation, preferring to help many new projects get started.

Grants are made in the range of £2,000 to £10,000, and in exceptional cases only, up to £20,000. In 2009/10 the trust had assets of £4.5 million, an income of £205,000 and made grants totalling £209,000, which were distributed as follows:

Educational	£109,000
Health	£70,000
Population control	£17,000
Environmental relief	£12,000

Beneficiaries included: Toe in the Water and Kariandusi School Trust (£25,000 each); Starehe UK (£15,000) Building Blocks (£9,000); Berkeley Reforestation Trust (£9,000); Tree for Cities (£4,000); and Human Relief (£2,500).

Exclusions

The trust does not support:
- organisations whose administrative expenses form more than 15% of their annual income
- individuals
- animal welfare
- heritage.

Projects which require long-term funding are not normally considered. The trust prefers to make one-off donations to get many projects started, rather than support fewer projects charities over a long period.

Applications

Full and detailed guidelines and application forms can be downloaded from the trust's website. Trustees meet twice a year (in April and October) and must have detailed financial information about each project before they will make a decision. Only applications from eligible bodies are acknowledged, further information about the project may be requested. Monitoring of grant expenditure is a requirement of all successful grants and donations from the trust.

Common applicant mistakes

'Large organisations and charities just sending what is obviously a random mailshot request for money without completing the application form and providing specific information requested.'

The Jewish Youth Fund

Jewish youth work

£184,000 (2009/10)

Beneficial area

UK.

Third Floor, 24 Chiswell Street, London EC1Y 4YX
Tel: 020 7443 5169
Email: info@jyf.org.uk
Correspondent: Julia Samuel, Secretary
Trustees: Lady Morris of Kenwood; Adam D Rose; Phillipa Strauss; Lord Jonathan Morris; David Goldberg.
CC Number: 251902

Information available

Accounts were available from the Charity Commission.

The fund's objectives are to promote and protect religious, moral, educational, physical and social interests of young members of the Jewish community in the UK.

In 2009/10 the trust had assets of £3.5 million and an income of £375,000. Grants totalling £184,000 went to 11 organisations. The grants ranged in size from £1,000 to £6,500.

Beneficiaries included: Step by Step (£6,500); B'nai Akiva UK and JAT (£5,000 each); The BBYO Charitable Trust (£2,500); Bushey Youth (£1,800) and London Jewish Cultural Centre (£1,000).

Exclusions

Grants are not made in response to general appeals. Formal education is not supported.

Applications

On an application form available from the correspondent, enclosing a copy of the latest accounts and an annual report.

The JMK Charitable Trust

Art and Music, religions and their relations with other faiths – Worldwide

£37,000 (2009/10)

Beneficial area

Worldwide.

Chantrey Vellacott DFK, Prospect House, 58 Queen's Road, Reading, Berkshire RG1 4RP
Tel: 0118 952 4700
Correspondent: The Trustees
Trustees: Mrs J M Karaviotis; J Karaviotis.
CC Number: 274576

Information available

Accounts were on file at the Charity Commission.

This trust supports registered charities, with a current preference for those concerned with the appreciation of art and music. 'We also assist religious organisations to help relations with other faiths.'

In 2009/10 the trust had assets of almost £2 million and an income of £65,000. Grants to 18 organisations totalled £37,000.

Grant beneficiaries included: English Touring Opera (£10,000); Royal Academy of Music- Scholarship (£5,000); Royal Academy of Music- Pavarotti Prize (£3,000); Royal Opera House (£2,500); Royal Academy of Arts (£2,000); Diva Opera and Keeping Kids Company (£1,000 each); West London Synagogue (£500) and Friends Royal Academy (£100).

Applications

In writing to the correspondent. No acknowledgement of receipt is given.

The Nicholas Joels Charitable Trust

Jewish, medical welfare, general

Around £20,000 (2009/10)

Beneficial area

UK and overseas.

20 Copse Wood Way, Northwood HA6 2UF
Tel: 01923 841376
Correspondent: N Joels, Trustee
Trustees: N Joels; H Joels; Mrs A Joels.
CC Number: 278409

Information available

Accounts had been received at the Charity Commission but were not available to view.

The trust makes grants to registered charities only, and from the list of beneficiaries it appears to support Jewish causes and medical and welfare charities.

In 2009/10 it had an income of £14,000 and a total expenditure of £20,000. No information was available regarding beneficiary organisations.

Previous beneficiaries included: World Jewish Relief (£9,000); Norwood (£5,300); Emunah (£4,300); United Jewish Israel Appeal (£3,800); Jewish Care (£2,000); Zionist Federation (£1,000); United Synagogue (£900); I Rescue (£750); Chinese Disaster Fund (£500); Jewish Women's Aid (£200); and Friends of the Tate Gallery (£100).

Applications

In writing to the correspondent.

The Harold Joels Charitable Trust

Jewish

£30,000 (2009/10)

Beneficial area

UK and overseas.

11a Arkwright Road, London NW3 6AA
Email: hjoles7@aol.com
Correspondent: H Joels, Trustee
Trustees: H Joels; Dr N Joels; Mrs V Joels; N E Joels.
CC Number: 206326

Information available

Accounts were available from the Charity Commission.

The trust makes grants to Jewish organisations in the UK and US.

In 2009/10 the trust had an income of £24,000 and a total expenditure of £36,000.

Previous beneficiaries in the US included: The American Jewish Committee, Emunah of America, Family Law Connection, Florida

Holocaust Museum, Florida Studio Theatre, Gocio Elementary School, Jewish Family and Children's Service, Temple Beth Sholom, Women's Resource Centre of Sarasota County World, Jewish Congress and Young Judea.

Previous beneficiaries in the UK included: Bet Elazraki Home, British Friend of the Hebrew University, Chai Cancer Care, Hampstead Synagogue, I Rescue, Jewish Care, National Theatre, Royal Academy of Arts, the Tel Aviv Foundation, Tricycle Theatre Co Ltd, United Synagogue and World Jewish Relief.

Applications

In writing to the correspondent.

The Norman Joels Charitable Trust

Jewish causes, general

£24,000 (2009/10)

Beneficial area

UK, Israel and the Middle East.

Grunberg and Co Ltd, 10 - 14 Accommodation Road, London NW11 8EP
Tel: 020 8458 0083
Fax: 0208 458 0783
Correspondent: The Trustees
Trustees: Jessica L Joels; Norman Joels; Harold Joels; Myriam Joels.
CC Number: 206325

Information available

Accounts were received but not available to view online at the Charity Commission website.

In 2009/10, the trust had an income of £25,000 and total expenditure of £24,000. We have no details of beneficiaries for this financial year.

Previous beneficiaries have included: Friends of Magen David Action in Great Britain, Jewish Aid Committee, Jewish Care, Joint Jewish Charitable Trust, New London Synagogue, Norwood Ravenswood, The Spiro Institute and World Jewish Relief.

Applications

In writing to the correspondent.

The Lillie Johnson Charitable Trust

Children, young people who are blind or deaf, medical

£183,000 (2009/10)

Beneficial area

UK, with a preference for the West Midlands.

Heathcote House, 39 Rodbourne Road, Harborne, Birmingham B17 0PN
Correspondent: J W Desmond, Trustee
Trustees: V M C Lyttle; P W Adams; J W Desmond; Mrs V C Adams.
CC Number: 326761

Information available

Accounts were obtained from the Charity Commission website.

In 2009/10 the trust had assets of £5.2 million and an income of £194,000. Grants to 131 organisations were made totalling £183,000.

Donations under £1,000 were made to 91 organisations. Beneficiaries of grants of £1,000 or more included: LEC – Worcester (£60,000); Web Care (£13,000); West House School (£10,000); Cancer Care and St Mary's and St Margaret's (£5,000 each); Solihull Samaritans (£4,000); Barnardo's, Castle Bromwich hall Gardens, Focus Parkinson's Society and Primrose Hospital (£1,000 each).

Exclusions

No support for individuals.

Applications

Applications are only considered from charities which are traditionally supported by the trust. The trust stated that it is inundated with applications it cannot support and feels obliged to respond to all of these.

The Johnson Foundation

Education, health, relief of poverty

£94,000 (2009/10)

Beneficial area

Merseyside.

Westmount, Vyner Road South, Birkenhead, Wirrall CH43 7PN
Tel: 0151 653 1700
Correspondent: P R Johnson, Trustee
Trustees: P R Johnson; C W Johnson.
CC Number: 518660

Information available

Accounts were available from the Charity Commission.

The objects for which the Foundation is established are:

- to promote any charitable purposes for the benefit of the City of Liverpool or the immediate neighbourhood at the discretion of Liverpool City Council
- to promote any charitable purposes and in particular the advancement of education, the preservation and protection of health and relief of poverty and sickness.

In 2009/10 the foundation had assets of £1.8 million and an income of £140,000. Grants totalled £94,000.

Beneficiaries included: Birkenhead School Scholarship (£35,000); Cardiothoracic Centre (£15,000); Life Education Centres (£10,000); New Brighton Rugby Junior Development (£5,000); Lord Mayor's Charity Appeal (£4,000); Women's Enterprising Breakthrough (£2,500); Royal Navy and Marine Charity (£2,000); Empowering Youth Foundation and Harvest Trust for Deprived Children (£1,500 each); and Henshaw Society for the Blind and Local Solutions (£1,000 each).

Other grants and donations (25 less than £1,000) amounted to £6,000.

Exclusions

Grants are not normally given to individuals.

Applications

In writing to the correspondent. The trustees meet monthly.

Common applicant mistakes

'Applications which are out of our specific area; applicants applying too often.'

The Johnson Group Cleaners Charity

General charitable purposes

£0 (2009/10)

Beneficial area

Merseyside only.

Abbots Park, Monks Way, Preston Brook, Cheshire WA7 3GH
Tel: 1928704600
Correspondent: Yvonne Monaghan
Trustees: Yvonne Monaghan; Karen Castle; Christopher Sander; Margo Green.
CC Number: 802959

Information available

Accounts were not required at the Charity Commission however were able to be viewed with the accounts from the Johnson Charitable Trust. Some additional information was provided by the trust.

The trust was created in January 1990, evolving from a previous company-linked trust first created in 1914. Grants have been given to Merseyside charities, including CVS's, for care in the community and holidays and outings.

In 2009/10 the trust had assets of £136,000, an income of £1,700 and gave no grants.

This trust is connected to the Johnson Charitable Trust, they have the same trustees and the accounts for this trust were included in those for the Johnson Charitable Trust. The trust reported that they gave no grants in the previous year due to the low income.

Previous beneficiaries have included: Johnson Group Welfare Charity

(£80,000); Bootle YMCA, Stroke Association, Salvation Army and Claire House (£5,000 each); Royal School for the Blind, Slightline Vision and Merseyside Holiday Services (£3,000 each); Rainbow Charity Children's Hospice (£750); Halton Haven Hospice and Merseyside Gymnastic Club (£500 each); and Wellchild (£250).

Exclusions

No grants to national charities or individuals.

Applications

In writing only to the correspondent.

Dezna Robins Jones Charitable Foundation

Medical, general

£1,000 (2009/10)

Beneficial area

Preference for Wales.

Greenacres, Laleston, Bridgend, Mid Glamorgan CF32 OHN
Tel: 01656 768584
Correspondent: Bernard Jones, Trustee
Trustees: B W R Jones; Alexia Cooke; Louise Boobyer.
CC Number: 1104252

Information available

Basic information taken from the Charity Commission website.

Registered in June 2004, the main object of the foundation is to support local medical charities. It has an ongoing relationship with Cancer Care Cymru.

In 2009/10 this trust had an income of just £4 and a total expenditure of almost £1,000.

Previous beneficiaries include: Cancer Care Cymru (£462,000); University Hospital of Wales – Cardiff (£138,000); Cory band (£72,000); and Performance Arts Education (£48,000).

Applications

In writing to the correspondent. Trustees meet at least twice a year.

The Marjorie and Geoffrey Jones Charitable Trust

General

£39,000 (2009/10)

Beneficial area

UK, preference south west of England.

Carlton House, 30 The Terrace, Torquay, Devon TQ1 1BN
Tel: 01803 213251
Email: nigel.wollen@hooperwollen.co.uk
Correspondent: N J Wollen, Trustee
Trustees: N J Wollen; W F Coplestone Boughey; P M Kay; E M J Richards.
CC Number: 1051031

Information available

Accounts were received but not available online at the Charity Commission website.

The trust was set up under the terms of the will of Rose Marjorie Jones, who died in 1995, leaving the gross of her estate amounting to £2.2 million for grant making purposes. In her will she donated amounts of £15,000 and £10,000 to charities based in Devon, such as the Donkey Sanctuary – Sidmouth, Paignton Zoological and Botanical Gardens Limited, the Rowcroft Hospital – Torquay, the Torbay Hospital League of Friends and RNIB – Torquay. Other organisations named in the will were UK-wide, such as RNLI, RSPCA and NSPCC – although grants were probably given to local branches.

In 2009/10 the trust had an income of £24,000 and an expenditure of £39,000.

Previous beneficiaries included: Torbay Coast and Countryside Trust (£4,000); Pilgrim BM45 Trust Ltd, Living Paintings and Teign Heritage (£3,000 each); Children's Hospice South West and Fire Services Benevolent Fund (£2,500); DeafBlind UK and West Country Rivers (£2,000 each); and Rural Stress South West, The Two Moors Festival and Apollo Football Club (£1,000 each).

Applications

In writing to the correspondent. The trustees meet four times a year to consider applications.

Common applicant mistakes

'The trustees favour organisations based in, or with projects in the Devon area. The trustees do not favour individuals.'

The J E Joseph Charitable Fund

Jewish

£129,000 (2010/11)

Beneficial area

London, Manchester, Israel, India and Hong Kong.

Flat 10, Compass Close, Edgware, Middlesex HA8 8HU
Tel: 020 8958 0126
Correspondent: Roger J Leon, Secretary
Trustees: F D A Mocatta, Chair; P Sheldon; J H Corre; J S Horesh; Abe Simon; Robert Shemtob; Susan Kendal.
CC Number: 209058

Information available

Accounts were available from the Charity Commission.

The trust was established for the benefit of Jewish communities for any purposes, mainly in the fields of education, disability and the relief of poverty. In 2010/11 it had assets of £4 million, an income of £122,000 and made grants totalling £129,000.

Grants included those made to: The Future Generation Fund (£13,000); Od Yosef Hai Yeshiva (£7,000); Edinburgh House (Home for Elderly) (£6,000); Kisharon Day School, Spanish and Portuguese Synagogue Welfare Board and University Jewish Chaplaincy Board (£5,000 each); Ilford Synagogue (Eastern) (£3,000); and Hospital Kosher Meals (£2,000).

Exclusions

No grants to individuals. No support for capital projects.

Applications

In writing to the correspondent, including a copy of the latest accounts. The trustees respond to all applications which are first vetted by the secretary. The trust stated that many applications are unsuccessful as the number of appeals exceeds the amount available from limited income.

The Lady Eileen Joseph Foundation

People who are disadvantaged by poverty or socially isolated and 'at-risk' groups. Largely welfare, medical causes and general charitable purposes are supported

Around £36,000 (2009/10)

Beneficial area

UK.

Colbrans Farm, Cow Lane, Laughton, Lewes BN8 6BZ
Correspondent: Thurlstan W Simpson, Trustee
Trustees: Judith M Sawdy; Thurlstan W Simpson; Gael Lynn Simpson.
CC Number: 327549

Information available

Information available from the Charity Commission website.

The trust was registered in 1987. It supports people who are disadvantaged by poverty or who are socially isolated. Medical causes are also supported.

In 2009/10 the foundation had an income of £22,000 and a total expenditure of £36,000.

Previous beneficiaries included: Second Chance (£7,500); Coldstream

Guards Association (£6,500); Alzheimer's Research Trust and Friends of the Home Physiotherapy Service (£5,000 each); Havens Hospices (£4,500); Ellenor Foundation and Queen Alexandra Hospital (£3,000 each); Independent Age and Wellbeing of Women (£2,000 each); and Cystic Fibrosis Trust, Foundation for the Prevention of Blindness and Action for Kids (£1,000 each).

Applications

The trust states that unsolicited requests will not be considered.

The Judith Trust

Mental health and learning disabilities with some preference for women and Jewish people

£78,000 (2009/10)

Beneficial area

UK.

5 Carriage House, 88–90 Randolph Avenue, London W9 1BG
Tel: 020 7266 1073
Fax: 020 7289 5804
Email: judith.trust@lineone.net
Website: www.judithtrust.org.uk
Correspondent: Dr A R Lawson, Trustee
Trustees: Dr Annette Lawson; Peter Lawrence; Dr George Lawson; Charlotte Collins; Dr Geraldine Holt; Dr Colin Samson.
CC Number: 1063012

Information available

Information was available from the Charity Commission.

The Judith Trust aims to improve the quality of life of people who have both learning disabilities and mental health needs.

The trust's website gives an account of the trust's history.

> The Judith Trust was founded in 1997 by Judith's family and set up to ensure the concerns of the trustees would closely follow the nature of Judith's own problems, her background and personal characteristics.

It is because Judith has both learning and mental health problems that the trust explores how to improve the quality of life with and for people with both these issues. It is because Judith is a woman and our background is Jewish that we take a particular interest in the needs and concerns of women and Jewish people. ... we have learned how much is also still shared with people of all ages in varied backgrounds with these problems. And with their families, carers and friends.

The trust supports multi-disciplinary, preventative and innovative approaches and pays particular attention to the needs of women and Jewish people.

The Judith Trust:

- commissions and carries out research supports innovative projects;
- forms strategic alliances with government departments, voluntary organisations and academic institutions;
- brings together groups of professionals and others, including service users, for specific purposes;
- campaigns on behalf of and with people with learning disabilities and mental health needs;
- promotes examples of good practice and the sharing of knowledge in its publications, seminars and conferences;

In 2009/10 the trust had an income of £18,000 and an expenditure of £78,000. A list of grants was not available but previous beneficiaries have included: Living in the Community Project (£26,000) and 'Healthcare needs and experiences of care' (£11,000).

Exclusions

No grants to individuals.

Applications

In writing to the correspondent; however, please note that most grants are made through experts and advisors. The trust does not accept unsolicited applications for funding, but is pleased to hear from organisations who wish the trust to be aware of their work.

Common applicant mistakes

'Applications are not invited as there is no current plan for funding.'

The Anton Jurgens Charitable Trust

Welfare, general

£297,000 (2009/10)

Beneficial area
UK with a preference for the south east of England.

Saffrey Champness, Lion House, 72–75 Red Lion Street, London WC1R 4GB
Tel: 020 7841 4000
Fax: 020 7841 4100
Correspondent: Maria E Edge-Jurgens, Trustee
Trustees: Eric M C Deckers; R Jurgens; Frans A V Jurgens; F A W Jurgens; Maria E Edge-Jurgens; M A J Jurgens; I L M van Oosten Slingeland.
CC Number: 259885

Information available
Accounts were available from the Charity Commission.

This trust has general charitable purposes, although welfare and children's groups feature prominently in the grants, as do organisations based in the south east of England. The trust states its main aim is 'alleviating suffering by making grants to charitable organisations that try to help those who are vulnerable in our society'.

In 2009/10 the trust had assets of £6.3 million and an income of £256,000. Grants to over 80 organisations were made totalling £297,000.

Beneficiaries included: JDRF (Juvenile Diabetes Research Foundation) (£10,000); Downside Fisher Youth Club (£8,000); Cerebra, Cherry Trees, Combat Stress, Edinburgh Young Carers, Families for Children, Headway East London and National Blind Children's Society (£5,000 each); Reading Single Homeless Project and Fine Cell Work (£4,000 each); New Horizon Youth Centre, Radicle and Regain (£3,000 each); Leicester Charity Link and Rainbow Children's Hospice (£2,000 each); and

Rocking Horse and Willow Burn Hospice (£1,000 each).

Applications
In writing to the correspondent. The trustees meet twice a year in June and October. The trustees do not enter into correspondence concerning grant applications beyond notifying successful applicants.

Jusaca Charitable Trust

Jewish, arts, research, religion, housing

£168,000 (2009/10)

Beneficial area
UK, Israel and worldwide.

17 Ashburnham Grove, London SE10 8UH
Correspondent: The Trustees
Trustees: Ralph Neville Emanuel; Sara Jane Emanuel; Carolyn Leonora Emanuel; Maurice Seymour Emanuel; Diana Clare Franklin; Donald Franklin; Rachel Paul.
CC Number: 1012966

Information available
Accounts were available from the Charity Commission, but without a grants list.

The following statement from the trust's 2009/10 annual accounts outlines its grant policy:

> The trust aims to give grants to alleviate poverty, promote health and education, to support the arts, research, religious activities and the provision of decent housing. The objective is to distribute at least 50% of donations to Jewish charities (in the UK, overseas and Israel), of the remainder about 40% to be donated to charities operating in the UK and about 60% outside the UK.

The majority of grants are given to the same organisations each year in order to provide a long term stream of funding.

In 2009/10 the trust had assets of £1.3 million and an income of £92,000. Grants to 102 organisations totalled £168,000, and were broken down as follows:

Welfare	28	£88,000
Overseas	2	£1,500
Education	19	£21,000
Religious	4	£6,100
Housing	6	£13,000
Health	19	£21,000
Community relations	7	£13,000
General	5	£950
Arts	8	£1,900
Research	4	£1,900

Applications
Grants are made at the discretion of the trustees. Unsolicited applications are not encouraged.

The Bernard Kahn Charitable Trust

Jewish

£114,000 (2008/09)

Beneficial area
UK and Israel.

24 Elmcroft Avenue, London NW11 0RR
Correspondent: The Trustees
Trustees: Mrs C B Kahn; S Fuehrer; Y E Kahn.
CC Number: 249130

Information available
Accounts were available from the Charity Commission.

In 2008/09 the trust had assets of £1.7 million and an income of £84,000. Grants were made to 31 organisations totalling £114,000.

Beneficiaries of the largest grants were: Achisomoch Aid Company Ltd, Gevuras Ari Trust and Orthodox Council of Jerusalem Limited (£20,000); Tely (£15,000); and Friends of Be'er Miriam and Marbeh Torah Trust (£11,000 each).

Other beneficiaries included: Beth Hamedrash Elyon Golders Green Limited (£4,500); Margenita D'Avrohom (£1,500); British Friends of Yeshivath – Ofakim (£900); Lopian Sofer (£750); Yeshivas Shaarei Torah (£500); Tel Hai Fund (£300); the Friends of Neve Yerushalaym Seminary Trust (£200); and Yad Ezrah – Helping Hand (£100).

Applications
In writing to the correspondent.

The Stanley Kalms Foundation

Jewish charities, general including arts, education and health

Around £69,000 (2009/10)

Beneficial area
UK and overseas.

84 Brook Street, London W1K 5EH
Tel: 020 7499 3494
Correspondent: Mrs Jane Hunt-Cooke
Trustees: Lord Stanley Kalms; Lady Pamela Kalms; Stephen Kalms.
CC Number: 328368

Information available
Accounts were received at the Charity Commission but not available to view online.

Established in 1989 by Lord Stanley Kalms, the president of DSG International plc (formerly Dixons Stores Group plc), this charity states its objectives as the encouragement of Jewish education in the UK and Israel. Other activities include support for the arts and media and other programmes, both secular and religious.

In 2009/10 the foundation had an income of £70,000 and a total expenditure of £69,000. No further information was available.

Previous grants have been to mainly Jewish organisations (social and educational) with grants also going to the arts, education and health. Beneficiaries have included: Dixons City Academy (£25,000), Milliken Community High (£23,000), Royal Opera House Foundation (£17,000), Jewish Care (£14,000) and Jewish National Fund (£12,000); Norwood (£7,600), British Friends of Haifa University (£7,200), Keren Klita (£7,000), Civitas, Centre for Social Justice, Institute of Economic Affairs, Jewish Policy Research, Royal Academy Trust (£5,000 each), Stephen Wise Temple (£4,500), the Kabbalah Centre (£2,900), Anglo Israel Association (£2,000), British ORT (£1,500) and St James Conversation Trust (£1,000).

Applications
In writing to the correspondent, but note that most of the trust's funds are committed to projects supported for a number of years.

The Boris Karloff Charitable Foundation

General

£56,000 (2009/10)

Beneficial area
Worldwide.

Peachey and Co., 95 Aldwych, London WC2B 4JF
Tel: 0207 316 5200
Correspondent: The Trustees
Trustees: Ian D Wilson; P A Williamson; O M Lewis.
CC Number: 326898

Information available
Full accounts were available from the Charity Commission website.

This foundation was set up in 1985, by Evelyn Pratt (Karloff), wife of the famous horror actor, Boris Karloff (whose real name was William Henry Pratt). When Evelyn Pratt died in June 1993, she bequeathed over £1.4 million to the assets of the foundation.

In 2009/10 the foundation had assets of £2.2 million and an income of £52,000. Grants were made to institutions in the area of acting, theatre. television and cinema amounting to £56,000.

Beneficiaries included: Royal Theatrical Fund, RADA – Boris Karloff Scholarship Fund and Cinema and Television Benevolent Fund (£10,000 each); Shakespeare Global Trust (£6,500); LAMDA – the London Academy of Music and Dramatic Arts, Surrey County Cricket and the Royal Shakespeare Community (£5,000 each); and the Royal National Theatre (£4,000).

Exclusions
Charities with large resources are not supported.

Applications
In writing to the correspondent.

The Ian Karten Charitable Trust

Technology centres for people with disabilities

£1.1 million to organisations (2009/10)

Beneficial area
Great Britain and Israel, with some local interest in Surrey and London.

The Mill House, Newark Lane, Ripley, Surrey GU23 6DP
Tel: 01483 225020
Fax: 01483 222420
Email: iankarten@btinternet.com
Website: www.karten-network.org.uk
Correspondent: Timothy Simon, Administrator
Trustees: Ian H Karten, Chair; Mrs Mildred Karten; Tim Simon; Angela Hobbs.
CC Number: 281721

Information available
Accounts were available from the Charity Commission.

The trust states its objects in its 2009/10 accounts:

> The objects of the trust are to carry out legally charitable purposes for the relief of poverty, the advancement of education or religion or otherwise for the benefit of the community.

> The trust currently concentrates on
> ▷ Improving the quality of life and independence of people with severe physical, sensory, cognitive disability or mental health problems by providing Centres for Computer-aided Training, Education and Communication (CTEC Centres). These are typically established by and located in colleges of further education or (mainly residential) host charities concerned with rehabilitation and education, especially vocational, of people with one or more of the above mentioned disabilities.

the support of higher education by funding studentships for postgraduate studies and research at selected universities in the UK

The trust also has a separate modest budget from which it makes small donations to other selected registered charities, mostly local to the trust (London or Surrey).

In 2009/10 it had assets of £7 million and an income of £254,000. Grants paid to organisations totalled £1.1 million, broken down as follows and shown with examples of beneficiaries:

CTEC Centres – 19 grants totalling £1,126,000

New Bridge Learning Centre (£186,000); Lufton, Mencap (£142,000); Aspire (£108,000); David Lewis Centre (£90,000); East Sussex Disability Centre (£50,000); Portland College, Mansfield (£18,000); and Scope (£3,000).

Large grants – 12 grants totalling £18,000

Institute for the Advancement of Deaf Personal in Israel (£8,000); the Meeting Place (£2,500); Jewish Care (£1,500); Yad Vashem UK Foundation (£1,000); and Anne Frank Educational Trust (£250).

Further funding was given for scholarships to nine institutions, including Haifa University and University College London, totalling £84,000; an individual scholarship of £900; and, the sum of £5,300 was also given in small grants.

Exclusions

No grants to individuals.

Applications

The trust currently only considers grants to charities supported in the past. Individual scholarships are no longer available directly to students, instead the trust's chosen universities select the Karten Scholarships themselves. The trustees meet every six weeks to consider applications.

The Kasner Charitable Trust

Jewish

£97,000 (2009/10)

Beneficial area

UK and Israel.

1a Gresham Gardens, London NW11 8NX
Tel: 020 8455 7830
Correspondent: Josef Kasner, Trustee
Trustees: Baruch Erlich; Josef Kasner; Judith Erlich.
CC Number: 267510

Information available

Accounts were on file at the Charity Commission.

The objects of the trust are for general charitable purposes and in practice grants are given to Jewish organisations. They are subject to the approval of Josef Kasner during his lifetime and thereafter at the discretion of the trustees.

In 2009/10 the trust had assets of £734,000, an income of £127,000 and made grants to over 150 organisations totalling £97,000.

Beneficiaries included: The Gevourah Ari Torah Academy Trust and The Sunderland Kolel (£20,000 each); United Jewish Appeal (£10,000); British Friends of Bnei Bracha Hospital (£5,000); S.O.F.T. (£4,000), Yesoda Hatorah School (£1,250); and British Friends of Nishmas Yisroel, British Friends of Shemaya Trust, British Friends of the Hebrew University, British Friends of Tiferet Shlomo, Friends of Lubavitch Scotland, Friends of Melachos Schomayim, Friends of Ohel Torah Trust, Talmud Torahs Torat Emet, and The JNF Charitable Trust (£100 each).

Applications

In writing to the correspondent. The trust gives grants to most of the organisations that apply. Certain organisations are investigated personally by the trustees and may receive larger grants.

The Kass Charitable Trust

Welfare, education, Jewish

£26,000 to organisations (2009/10).

Beneficial area

UK.

37 Sherwood Road, London NW4 1AE
Tel: 020 8371 3111
Email: dkass@vintange.co.uk
Correspondent: D E Kass, Trustee
Trustees: David Elliot Kass; Shulamith Malkah Sandler.
CC Number: 1006296

Information available

Accounts were available from the Charity Commission, but without a list of grants.

The trust now focuses on 'poverty and education for disadvantaged children'.

In 2009/10 it had assets of £13,000 and an income of £40,000 mostly from donations received. Grants totalled £40,000, of which £26,000 was given in grants to organisations. £6,000 was given to 'provide support for a needy family'.

Unfortunately a full list of grant beneficiaries was not included with the accounts, however the trust stated that approximately 500 donations were made to institutions during the year, mostly for small amounts and were provided for educational purposes or relief of poverty.

The largest beneficiary organisation was British Friends of Mercaz Hatorah (£5,000), for the promotion of charitable and educational work.

Applications

In writing to the correspondent.

Common applicant mistakes

'Wrong cause; incomplete verifiable information; the sheer audacity of the demand.'

The Kathleen Trust

Music

£62,000 (2009/10)

Beneficial area

UK, with a preference for London.

Currey and Co, 21 Buckingham Gate, London SW1E 6LS
Tel: 0207 828 4091
Correspondent: E R H Perks, Trustee
Trustees: E R H Perks; Sir O C A Scott; Lady P A Scott; Mrs C N Withington.
CC Number: 1064516

Information available

Accounts were received at the Charity Commission but not available to view online.

Established in 1997, it is the policy of the trustees to 'assist young and impecunious musicians'.

In 2009/10 the trust had an income of just under £25,000 and expenditure was nearly £62,000. In previous years grants were given mainly to individuals. Previous beneficiary organisations have included: Oxford Chamber Music Festival and the British Kidney Patient Association (Young Clarinetist).

Applications

In writing to the correspondent.

The Michael and Ilse Katz Foundation

Jewish, music, medical, general

About £94,000 (2009/10)

Beneficial area

Worldwide.

The Counting House, Trelill, Bodmin, Cornwall PL30 3HZ
Tel: 01208 851814
Correspondent: Osman Azis, Trustee
Trustees: Norris Gilbert; Osman Azis.
CC Number: 263726

Information available

Accounts were available from the Charity Commission.

Established in 1971, this foundation supports many Jewish organisations, although musical and medical charities also received funds.

In 2009/10 it had assets of £888,000 and an income of £206,000. Grants to organisations totalled £94,000, of which £8,000 was allocated in grants not exceeding £1,000 each.

Beneficiaries included: Jewish Care (£25,000); Community Security Trust (£14,000); Norwood Children and Families First (£10,000); Bournemouth Orchestral Society (£8,000); The Worshipful Company of Butchers (£4,000); Nightingale House for Aged Jews (£1,500); Hillel Foundation and Magen David Adom UK (£2,000 each); Bournemouth Reform Synagogue, Holocaust Education Trust, MacMillan Cancer Relief, and Tel Aviv Sourasky Medical Centre (£1,000 each).

Applications

In writing to the correspondent.

The Katzauer Charitable Settlement

Jewish

£46,000 (2009/10)

Beneficial area

UK, but mainly Israel.

c/o Devonshire House, 1 Devonshire Street, London W1W 5DR
Tel: 0207 304 2000
Email: walter.lian@citroenwells.co.uk
Correspondent: Gordon Smith, Trustee
Trustees: G C Smith; Mrs E Moller; M S Bailey; W Lian.
CC Number: 275110

Information available

The annual update was received at the Charity Commission for the year 2009/10, however, the charity was below the annual return threshold of £10,000.

In 2009/10 the trust had an income of £3,000 and an expenditure of £46,000.

Previous beneficiaries included: Chabad Ra'anana (£26,000); Moriah Community and Meir Hospital (£10,000); Nahalat Yehiel (£6,000); Mercaz Hatorah (£4,000); Rabbi K Gross (£3,800); KollelRalanana (£3,200); Friends of Lubavitch (£2,900); Beit Hatavshil (£1,000);

Applications

In writing to the correspondent.

The C S Kaufman Charitable Trust

Jewish

£79,000 (2009/10)

Beneficial area

UK.

162 Whitehall Road, Gateshead, Tyne and Wear NE8 1TP
Correspondent: C S Kaufman
Trustees: I I Kaufman; Mrs L L Kaufman; J J Kaufman; S Kaufman.
CC Number: 253194

Information available

Accounts were available from the Charity Commission.

In 2009/10 the trust had assets of £888,000 and an income of £92,000. There were 48 grants made totalling £79,000; many of the beneficiaries received more than one grant each during the year.

Grants included those made to: Tomchei Yotzei Anglia (£20,000); Ezer Mikoidesh Foundation (£15,000); Kollel Sha'rei Shlomo (£10,000 in two grants); Tomchei Torah Family Relief (£5,000); Jewish Teacher Training College (£3,000 in two grants); SOFT (£1,000 in four grants); Yeshiva Tiferes Yaakov (£750); and ZVT (£150).

Exclusions

No grants to individuals.

Applications

In writing to the correspondent.

The Geoffrey John Kaye Charitable Foundation

Jewish, general

£47,000 to organisations (2009/10)

Beneficial area

UK and overseas.

7 St John's Road, Harrow, Middlesex HA1 2EY
Tel: 0208 863 1234
Email: charity@mmrca.co.uk
Correspondent: Robert Shaw, Chartered Account
Trustees: G J Kaye; Mrs S Rose; J Pears.
CC Number: 262547

Information available

Accounts were available from the Charity Commission.

In 2009/10 the foundation had assets of £996,000 and an income of £56,000.

There were three grants made totalling £47,000; these went to: UJIA (£26,000); Animal shelter A. C (£20,000); and JNF 1,000.

A further £11,000 went to one individual.

Applications

In writing to the correspondent, but please note that the foundation has previously stated that funds were fully committed.

The Emmanuel Kaye Foundation

Medical research, welfare and Jewish organisations

£15,000 (2009/10)

Beneficial area

UK and overseas.

Oakleigh House, High Street, Hartley Wintney, Hampshire RG27 8PE
Tel: 01252 843773

Correspondent: The Secretary to the Trustees
Trustees: David Kaye; Lady Kaye; John Forster; Michael Cutler.
CC Number: 280281

Information available

Accounts were received at the Charity Commission but were unavailable to view.

The foundation supports organisations benefiting medical professionals, research workers, scientists, Jewish people, at risk groups, people who are disadvantaged by poverty and socially isolated people.

In 2009/10 it had an income of £19,000 and total expenditure of £15,000.

Previous beneficiaries included: St James Conservation Trust (£6,000); Imperial College London and Nightingale (£5,000 each); Royal Academy of Arts and St Michaels Hospice – North Hampshire (£2,500 each); Jewish Care, the Holocaust Education Trust, Shaare Zedek UK, Community Links Trust, Laniado UK and UK Friends of Magen David Adom (£2,000 each); and Caius (£1,500).

Exclusions

Only registered charities are supported.

Applications

In writing to the correspondent.

The Caron Keating Foundation

Supports small but significant cancer charities

£55,000 (2009/10)

Beneficial area

UK.

PO Box 122, Sevenoaks, Kent TN13 1UM
Email: info@caronkeating.org
Website: www.caronkeating.org

Correspondent: The Secretary
Trustees: M Keating; G Hunniford.
CC Number: 1106160

Information available

Information was obtained from the foundation's website.

Registered with the Charity Commission in October 2004, this foundation is a fundraising charity that aims to target and financially assist 'small but significant cancer charities and support groups'.

The foundation's overall aim is to help small cancer charities in their work with professional carers, complimentary healing practitioners as well as groups that provide support and advice to cancer patients and the people closest to them who are affected by the disease. The website stated that:

> It will also financially help a number of cancer charities with their ongoing quest for prevention, early detection and hopefully ultimate cure.

In 2009/10 the foundation had assets of £800,000 and an income of £217,000. Grants totalled £55,000, which included £30,000 made in small grants of less than £20,000.

One main grant was made this year to Action Cancer Belfast (£25,000).

Previous beneficiaries included: The Lavendar Touch; The Rosemary Foundation; Sarah Lee Trust; Variety Club; and the Rainbow Centre (for children affected by cancer and bereavement).

Exclusions

No grants to individuals.

Applications

In writing to the correspondent.

The Soli and Leah Kelaty Trust Fund

General, education, overseas aid, religion

£29,000 (2009/10)

Beneficial area

Not defined.

Block O, OCC Building, London
N4 1TJ
Tel: 0208 800 2000
Email: freddy.kelaty@asiatic.co.uk
Correspondent: F S Kelaty, Secretary
Trustees: David Lerer; Fredrick
Kelaty; Sharon Mozel Kelaty.
CC Number: 1077620

Information available

Accounts were available from the
Charity Commission.

Registered with the Charity
Commission in September 1999,
grants can be made to organisations
and individuals.

In 2009/10 the trust had assets of
£34,000 and an income of £36,000.
Grants were made totalling £29,000; a
list of beneficiaries was not provided
with the accounts.

Applications

In writing to the correspondent.

The Kelly Family Charitable Trust

Support for families

£122,000 (2009/10)

Beneficial area

UK.

8 Mansfield Place, Edinburgh
EH3 6NB
Tel: 0131 3154879
Email: s.armstrong@kfct.org
Website: www.kfct.org.uk
Correspondent: Stuart Armstrong,
Administrator
Trustees: Annie Kelly; Brian
Mattingley; Jenny Kelly; Sheldon
Cordell; Michael Field; Emma Maier.
CC Number: 1102440

Information available

Accounts were available from the
Charity Commission. The trust also
has a clear and helpful website.

Established in 2004, the trust
supports organisations that encourage
family welfare and cohesion. The
following information is taken from
the trust's website:

> The trust has decided to prioritise its
> funding in favour of charities whose

activities involve all or most family
members in initiatives that support and
encourage the family to work as a
cohesive unit in tackling problems that
face one or more of its members. The
overall objective is to reinforce the
potential benefit and support that
family members as a unit can give to
each other.

> Applications are also welcomed from
> sports and health-related charities
> whose activities comply with the above
> criteria.

> The trust will consider both capital and
> revenue grants. The trust is happy to
> support requests for core funding as
> well as project-based grants, and
> actively encourages applications from
> relatively new organisations to help
> them become established.

In 2009/10 the trust had assets of
£2.7 million and an income of
£126,500. Grants were made to 16
organisations during the year
totalling £122,000.

The following information is noted in
the latest annual report:

> The Grants Administrator has been
> pleased to report the growing number
> of applications received which fall
> within the desired criteria for awards,
> which indicates the increasing success
> of the trust's publicity. It is felt that the
> [trust's] website has played a
> significant part in this. The trust
> continues to receive very encouraging
> responses on the effect of the grants
> awarded from successful applicants,
> and these were reviewed at each
> meeting and taken into consideration
> when repeat applications for funding
> are received. The trust now has
> awarded several second and third time
> grants to certain of the approved
> charities.

> The Grants Administrator continues to
> contact the majority of short-listed
> applicants either by personal visit or
> telephone, which has been appreciated
> by both the trustees and applicants.
> This has facilitated one of the trust's
> objectives to disseminate information
> amongst the charities it supports where
> appropriate and to put similar charities
> in touch with each other.

The beneficiaries during the year
were: 3D Drumchapel; Addaction;
Cambridge Mediation; Circle;
Families First; Guys Gift; HomeStart
Havant; Made of Money Project;
MOSAC; Multi-Cultural Family Base;
Norfolk Playvan; Parent to Parent;
Positive Help; Richmond's Hope; The
Zone; and Westminster Befriend a
Family. Individual grant amounts are
not stated, however are likely to be
between £1,000 and £5,000.

Exclusions

The following will not be considered:
- non-registered charities
- grants directly to individuals
- national charities (only regional
  projects will be considered)
- general appeals
- organisations with specific
  religious or political agendas.

Applications

Applications should be made using
the application form, which can be
downloaded from the trust's website.
Applications should be sent by email,
and should be supported by annual
accounts where available.

Grants are awarded twice a year to
charities and are usually between
£1,000 and £5,000, but the trustees
will consider requests for higher
amounts.

Applications must be submitted by
1 March and 1 September to be
considered at the subsequent meeting.
The trustees will ask for more detail
for those applications that pass the
initial screening and may visit the
projects they wish to support.

Common applicant mistakes

'Although we have a website many
charities get their information from
other sources who have not kept their
information up to date.'

The Kennedy Charitable Foundation

Roman Catholic ministries, general, especially in the west of Ireland

£261,000 (2009/10)

Beneficial area

Unrestricted, but mainly Ireland with
a preference for County Mayo and
County Sligo.

12th Floor, Bank House, Charlotte
Street, Manchester M1 4ET
Tel: 0161 236 8191
Fax: 0161 236 4814
Email: kcf@pye158.freeserve.co.uk

Correspondent: The Trustees
Trustees: Patrick James Kennedy; Kathleen Kennedy; John Gerard Kennedy; Patrick Joseph Francis Kennedy; Anna Maria Kelly.
CC Number: 1052001

Information available

Accounts were available from the Charity Commission.

Established in 1995, the foundation is funded by donations. Grants are predominantly made to organisations connected with the Roman Catholic faith, mainly in Ireland.

In 2009/10 the foundation had an income of £123,000 and made 65 grants totalling £261,000.

Beneficiaries included: Newman Institute (£87,000); Ballintubber Abbey Trust (£23,000); Lower Shankhill Community Association (£18,000); Elizabeth Hardie Ferguson Trust (£10,000); St Ann's Hospice (£6,000); Archdiocese of Cardiff and Diocese of Hexham and Newcastle (£5,000 each); Destination Florida, Lancaster Roman Catholic Diocese Trustees and St Vincent de Paul Society – Wythenshawe (£2,000 each); East Belfast Mission and Society of African Missions (£1,000 each); Leukaemia Research (£500); and NSPCC (£100).

Applications

The foundation says that 'unsolicited applications are not accepted'.

The Kennel Club Charitable Trust

Dogs

£780,000 (2010).

Beneficial area

UK.

1–5 Clarges Street, Piccadilly, London W1J 8AB
Tel: 0207 518 1037
Email: dholford@the-kennel-club.org.uk
Website: www.mad4dogs.org.uk
Correspondent: Mrs Cas Oakes
Trustees: M Townsend, Chair; M Herrtage; W H King; J Spurling; Mrs J Ziman.

CC Number: 327802

Information available

Accounts were available from the Charity Commission.

The trust describes its objects as science, welfare and support. It supports the furthering of research into canine diseases and hereditary disorders of dogs and also organisations concerned with the welfare of dogs in need and those which aim to improve the quality of life of humans by promoting dogs as practical or therapeutic aids.

The trust gives both ongoing and one-off grants, generally up to £35,000 each a year for research and of up to £10,000 each for support of dogs and those who care for them or benefit from them.

Kennel Club Charitable Trust worked in conjunction with Pedigree on the Pedigree Adoption Drive, which in 2008 raised over £496,000 for distribution by the trust. The trust was selected for its expertise and experience in allocating funds and the money has been distributed through its welfare initiative to organisations in the United Kingdom and Republic of Ireland. The drive was re-run in 2009 and raised a further £565,000.

In 2010 the trust had assets of £2.7 million and an income of £850,000. Grants were made under the trust's charitable objectives, totalling £780,000. These were divided into 'scientific and research project support' which amounted to £410,000, and 'Educational and other grants' totalling £295,000.

Beneficiaries of the trust's annual grant-making included: University of Cambridge (£53,000); Support Dogs (£24,000); Oldies Club (£6,000); Royston Animal Welfare (£3,000) and Dun-Roamin Rehoming and Staffordshire Bull Terrier Rescue (£2,000 each).

Exclusions

The trust does not give grants directly to individuals; veterinary nurses can apply to the British Veterinary Nursing Association where bursaries are available. The trustees tend not to favour funding the costs of building work.

Applications

In writing to the administrator, including latest accounts. Please state clearly details of the costs for which you are requesting funding, and for what purpose and over what period the funding is required. The trustees meet three or four times a year.

The Nancy Kenyon Charitable Trust

General

£41,000 to organisations (2009/10)

Beneficial area

UK.

Brook Financial Management Ltd, Meads Barn, Ashwell Business Park, Ilminster, Somerset TA19 9DX
Tel: 01460 259852
Correspondent: Alison Smith
Trustees: Lucy Phipps; Maureen Kenyon; Christopher Kenyon; Sally Kenyon; Peter Kenyon.
CC Number: 265359

Information available

Accounts were available from the Charity Commission.

The trust makes grants primarily for people and causes known to the trustees.

In 2009/10 the trust's assets totalled around £1.4 million. It had an income totalling £37,000 and distributed grants totalling £41,000 to organisations and £6,000 to individuals.

Beneficiaries in the year included: Nancy Oldfield Trust (£10,500); the Rainbow Farm Trust (£8,500); Nehemiah Project (£3,000); The Good Shepherd Project, Cheltenham Youth for Christ and The Starfish Cafe, Cambodia (£2,000 each); Cheltenham Youth for Christ and the Starfish Cafe – Cambodia (£2,000 each); Emthonjeni Trust, Epic Arts and Cheltenham Open Door (£1,000 each); and Uganda Shoe Box Appeal (£400).

Applications

In writing to the correspondent at any time. Applications for causes not known to the trustees are considered annually in December.

E and E Kernkraut Charities Limited

General, education, Jewish

£744,000 (2009/10)

Beneficial area

UK.

c/o Cohen Arnold, New Burlington House, 1075 Finchley Road, London NW11 0PU
Tel: 020 8731 0777
Correspondent: The Trustees
Trustees: Eli Kernkraut, Chair; Esther Kernkraut; Joseph Kernkraut; Jacob Kernkraut.
CC Number: 275636

Information available

Accounts were on file at the Charity Commission, but without a list of grants.

The trust states that it makes grants for educational, Jewish and other charitable purposes. Unfortunately the trust did not include a list of beneficiaries with their annual accounts.

In 2009/10 the trust had assets of £5.8 million and an income of £930,000. Grants were made totalling £744,000.

Applications

In writing to the correspondent.

The Peter Kershaw Trust

Medical research, education, social welfare

£156,000 (2009/10)

Beneficial area

Manchester and the surrounding district only.

22 Ashworth Park, Knutsford, Cheshire WA16 9DE
Tel: 01565 651086
Email: pkershawtrust@btinternet.com
Correspondent: Bryan Peak, Secretary and Trustee
Trustees: R P Kershaw, Chair; Mrs H F Kershaw; Mrs M L Rushbrooke; D Tully; Mrs R Adams; T Page.
CC Number: 268934

Information available

Accounts were on file at the Charity Commission website.

The principal activities of the trust are to provide grants for social welfare and to provide school bursaries in the Greater Manchester and North Cheshire area; to provide grants for medical research; and to make an annual award in memory of Peter Kershaw, of £50,000 spread over three years and specifically targeted at innovative youth work.

In 2009/10 the trust had assets of £6.3 million and an income of £195,000. Grants were made totalling £156,000 and were broken down as follows:

Social welfare	22	£83,900
School bursaries	8	£38,000
Memorial bursary	2	£25,000
Medical research	0	£nil

Beneficiaries included: H-Pan and Stonehouse Gang (£15,000 each); Fairbridge, Sycamore Project and United Estates of Wythenshawe (£10,000 each); Mustard Tree (£8,000); Bolton School and Manchester High School for Girls (£6,000 each); Barnabus, Jigsaw and m13 Youth Project (£5,000 each); St Bede's (£3,500); Cornerstone Day Centre (£2,000); Booth's Centre and Salford Child Contract Centre (£1,000 each); and Christie Hospital (£250).

David Tully and Peter Kershaw are also trustees of Edward Holt Trust (Charity Commission no. 224741) and The Booth Charities (Charity Commission no. 221800); David Tully is also a trustee of CHR Charitable Trust (Charity Commission no. 213579); and Tim Page is also a trustee of Cheadle

Royal Industries Charitable Trust (Charity Commission no. 509813).

Exclusions

No grants to individuals or for building projects.

Applications

In writing to the correspondent, however the trust is always oversubscribed. The trustees normally meet twice a year in May and November to consider recommendations for grant aid which will be disbursed in June and December respectively.

Common applicant mistakes

'Applicants who do not read the basic advertised conditions, i.e. we do not fund capital costs. Applicants must be registered charity and in Greater Manchester.'

The Kessler Foundation

General, Jewish

Around £10,000 (2008/09)

Beneficial area

UK.

Jewish Chronicle Newspaper Ltd, 25 Furnival Street, London EC4A 1JT
Correspondent: Gwen Horwitz
Trustees: G Horwitz, Chair; Mrs J Jacobs; Prof. M Geller; Mr N P J Saphir; Mrs J F Mayers; P Morgenstern.
CC Number: 290759

Information available

Accounts were received at the Charity Commission but were unavailable for view.

The foundation makes grants for general charitable causes, with particular emphasis on supporting Jewish organisations. Generally the trust will support relatively small institutions (with an income of less than £100,000 a year) which do not attract funds from the larger charities. In exceptional circumstances grants to individuals will be considered. The foundation's funds depend upon dividends from its shareholdings in the Jewish Chronicle and grants made by the newspaper. Grants generally range from £250 to £2,000 each, mostly at the lower end of this scale. The foundation will assist organisations which may be devoted to:

- the advancement of Jewish religion, learning, education and culture
- the improvement of inter-faith, community and race relations, and the combating of prejudice
- the alleviation of the problems of minority and disadvantaged groups
- the protection, maintenance and monitoring of human rights
- the promotion of health and welfare
- the protection and preservation of records and objects with special significance to the Jewish and general community
- the encouragement of arts, literature and science including archaeology, natural history and protection of the environment with special reference to the Jewish community

In 2008/09 the foundation had an income of £17,000 and a total expenditure of £11,000. No further information was available.

Previous beneficiaries have included: Jewish Council for Racial Equality, Asylum Aid and Bedouin Women for Themselves (£2,000 each); International Council of Jewish Women (£1,500); Project Harar Ethiopia (£1,200); Peace Child Israel, Makor Charitable Trust, Jewish Bereavement Counselling Service and Theatre Objektiv (£1,000 each); Friends of Israel Educational Foundation and Quest New London Synagogue (£750 each); Ipswich Community Playbus and Aid for Romanian Orphanages (£500 each); and Arts to Share (£250).

Exclusions
In general the foundation will not support the larger well-known charities with an income in excess of £100,000, and will not provide grants for social, medical and welfare projects which are the responsibility of local or national government.

Applications
On a form available from the correspondent. The trustees meet at

least twice a year in June and December. Applicants will be notified of decisions as soon as possible after then.

The Kiawah Charitable Trust

Young people whose lives are vulnerable due to health and/or education issues

£117,000 (2009/10)

Beneficial area
Primarily sub Saharan Africa and southern India.

c/o Farrer and Co, 65–66 Lincoln's Inn Fields, London WC2A 3LH
Tel: 020 7242 2022
Correspondent: Anne Marie Piper, Correspondent
Trustees: Peter Smitham; Lynne Smitham; Vic Miles.
CC Number: 1107730

Information available
Accounts were on file at the Charity Commission.

Registered in January 2005, in 2009/10 the trust had assets of £838,000 and an income of £492,000. Three grants totalled £117,000.

Beneficiary organisations were: Sight Savers International (£47,000); Hope and Homes for Children (£40,000); and Railway Children (£30,000).

Applications
The trustees consider any applications received for grants and adopt a proactive approach in seeking worthy causes requiring support.

The King/ Cullimore Charitable Trust

General

£228,500 (2009/10)

Beneficial area
UK.

52 Ledborough Lane, Beaconsfield, Buckinghamshire HP9 2DF
Tel: 01494 678811
Correspondent: P A Cullimore, Trustee
Trustees: P A Cullimore; C Gardner; C J King; A G McKechnie.
CC Number: 1074928

Information available
Accounts were on file at the Charity Commission.

This trust has general charitable purposes and was registered with the Charity Commission on 30 March 1999.

In 2009/10 it had assets amounting to £5.4 million and an income of £310,000. Grants were paid to 13 organisations totalling £228,500.

Organisations to benefit in the year were: Prostate Cancer (£100,000); Jubilee Sailing Trust (£25,000); Study Group Sea Turtles and Woodrow High House (£20,000 each); Crisis, Leonard Cheshire Foundation and Woodland Trust (£10,000 each); and Countryside Foundation for Education and Music in Hospitals (£5,000 each).

Applications
In writing to the correspondent.

Kinsurdy Charitable Trust

General

£110,000 (2009/10)

Beneficial area
UK.

c/o Cheviot Asset Management Limited, 90 Long Acre, London WC2E 9RA
Tel: 020 7438 5600
Correspondent: The Trustees
Trustees: R P Tullett; A H Bartlett.
CC Number: 1076085

Information available
Accounts were on file at the Charity Commission.

Registered in June 1999, in 2009/10 this trust had assets of £1.6 million and an income of £167,000. Grants to 18 organisations totalled £110,000

Beneficiaries included: RABI, RNLI and Alzheimer's Society (£7,500 each); Save the Children, Age Concern, Guide Dogs, WWF – UK, Macmillan Cancer Support, British Red Cross and the Samaritans (£6,000 each); and League of Friends – West Berkshire Hospice (£3,500).

Applications

The trustees do not respond to unsolicited requests.

The Richard Kirkman Charitable Trust

General charitable purposes

£46,000 (2009/10)

Beneficial area

UK, with a preference for Hampshire.

Ashton House, 12 The Precinct, Wincester Road, Chandlers Ford, Eastleigh, Hampshire
Tel: 023 8027 4555
Fax: 023 8027 5766
Correspondent: M Howson-Green, Trustee
Trustees: M Howson-Green; Mrs F O Kirkman; B M Baxendale; D A Hoare; Mrs M Howson-Green.
CC Number: 327972

Information available

Accounts were available from the Charity Commission.

This trust supports a range of causes with a preference for Hampshire, especially Southampton.

In 2009/10 the trust had assets of £1.5 million and an income of £50,000. Grants were made to 40 organisations totalling £46,000.

There were 11 grants of £1,500 or more listed in the accounts. Beneficiaries included: British Limbless Ex-Servicemen Association (£4,000); Enham Trust (£3,000); British Diabetic Association and Stroke Association (£2,000 each); and Haemophilia Society and Police Dependants Trust (£1,500 each).

The total grants figure includes 29 grants of £1,000 or less, given to organisations and totalling £21,000.

Applications

The trust carries out its own research for beneficiaries and does not respond to applications by post or telephone.

Kirschel Foundation

Jewish, medical

£564,000 (2009/10)

Beneficial area

UK.

26 Soho Square, London W1D 4NU
Tel: 020 7437 4372
Correspondent: Stephen Pinshaw, Trustee
Trustees: Laurence Grant Kirschel; Ian Lipman; Stephen Pinshaw.
CC Number: 1067672

Information available

Accounts were available from the Charity Commission.

This trust states its aims and objectives are 'to provide benefits to underprivileged persons, who may be either disabled or lacking resources'. In practice this includes many Jewish organisations.

In 2009/10 the foundation had assets of £107,000 and an income of £251,000. Grants were made totalling £564,000.

There were 54 grants of £1,000 or more listed in the accounts. Beneficiaries included: Ahavat Shalom Charity Fund (£95,000); Jewish Learning Exchange (£55,000); Friends of Shamir and Tikkun (£40,000 each); Anshei Shalom Friends of Lubavitch Scotland (£18,000 each); Achisomoch (£12,000); Norwood Children's and Families Trust (£10,000); Lolev Charitable Trust (£7,000); Kabbalah Centre, Kisharon and Variety Club (£5,000 each); BSD and Camp Simcha (£3,000 each); Children with Leukaemia, Make a Wish and Seed (£2,500 each); Bas Melech, Evelina Children's Hospital Appeal and Keren Moisdos Eretz Yisroel (£2,000 each);

and Keen London, Palace for All and Shooting Star (£1,000 each).

The total of all other donations, individually less than £1,000 each was £7,000.

Applications

In writing to the correspondent.

The Marina Kleinwort Charitable Trust

Arts

£49,500 (2009/10)

Beneficial area

UK.

Kleinwort Benson, 30 Gresham Street, London EC2V 7PG
Tel: 020 3207 7109
Email: emily.verdeyen@ kleinwortbenson.com
Correspondent: Miss Emily Verdeyen, Correspondent
Trustees: Miss Marina Rose Kleinwort, Chair; David James Roper Robinson; Miss Zenaida Yanowsky; Mrs Tessa Elizabeth Bremmer.
CC Number: 1081825

Information available

Accounts were available from the Charity Commission.

In 2009/10 this trust had assets of £1.2 million and an income of £48,000. Grants totalling £49,500 were made to 17 organisations.

Beneficiaries included: RADA (£6,500); Almeida Theatre Co Ltd and The Old Vic (£5,000 each); The Clonter Farm Music Trust and Endymion Ensemble (£3,000 each); Natural History Museum and the Royal Court (£2,500 each); and Live Music Now (£1,000).

Exclusions

No grants to individuals.

Applications

The trustees' current policy is to consider written appeals from charities working in the field of the arts, but only successful applications are notified of the trustees' decision.

The trustees do not normally respond favourably to appeals from individuals, nor to those unconnected with the arts. The charity requests a copy of the most recent report and financial statements from applicants.

The Kobler Trust

Arts, Jewish, general

£165,000 (2009/10)

Beneficial area

UK.

c/o Lewis Silkin LLP, 5 Chancery Lane, Clifford's Inn, London EC4A 1BL
Correspondent: Ms J L Evans, Trustee
Trustees: A Xuereb; A H Stone; Ms J L Evans; J W Israelsohn.
CC Number: 275237

Information available

Accounts were available from the Charity Commission.

The Kobler Charitable Trust was established in 1963 by the settlor, Fred Kobler, for charitable purposes in the UK. In 2009/10 the trust had assets of £2.9 million and an income of £81,500 from investments. Grants totalling £165,000 were given to 65 organisations.

Beneficiaries included: Jewish Aids Trust, Brighton Dome & Festival Limited and Sadler's Wells (£15,000 each); Pavilion Opera Educational Trust (£12,000); UK Jewish Film Festival and West London Synagogue Interfaith Project (£10,000 each); Royal Academy of Music (£5,000); Rich Mix and St Giles Trust (£2,000 each); Soho Theatre Company, Spadework and Touchstones 12 (£1,000 each); and Thomas Hospice Care (£500).

Exclusions

Grants are only given to individuals in exceptional circumstances.

Applications

Applications should be in writing and incorporate full details of the charity for which funding is requested. Acknowledgements are not generally sent out to unsuccessful applicants.

The Kohn Foundation

Scientific and medical projects, the arts – particularly music, education, Jewish charities

£650,000 (2010)

Beneficial area

UK and overseas.

Wilkins Kennedy & Co, Bridge House, 4 Borough High Street, London SE1 9QR
Correspondent: Dr R Kohn, Trustee
Trustees: Dr Ralph Kohn, Chair; Zahava Kohn; Anthony A Forwood.
CC Number: 1003951

Information available

Accounts were available from the Charity Commission.

The foundation supports advancement of scientific and medical research, promotion of the arts – particularly music, general educational projects and Jewish charities.

In 2010 the foundation had assets of £1.2 million, an income of £847,000 and made grants totalling £650,000. Donations were broken down as follows, shown here with examples of beneficiaries in each category:

Medical and scientific	£390,000
Performing Arts	£181,000
Advancement of the Jewish religion, education and charitable institutions	£81,000

The Royal Society (£300,000); Manchester University (£25,000); Emunah (£18,000); Imperial College (£15,000); Jesus College Oxford (£12,000); National Osteoporosis Society (£5,000); Nash Concert Society (£2,500); Rudolph Kemp Society (£1,500).

Applications

In writing to the correspondent.

Kollel and Co. Limited

Jewish, relief of poverty

£517,000 (2009/10)

Beneficial area

Worldwide.

Lieberman and Co, 2L Cara House, 339 Seven Sisters Road, London N15 6RD
Correspondent: A Low, Secretary
Trustees: S Low; J Lipschitz; Z Rothschild.
CC Number: 1077180

Information available

Accounts were available from the Charity Commission.

Set up in 1999, the objects of the charity are the:
1 advancement of education and religion in accordance with the doctrines of the Jewish religion
2 relief of poverty.

In 2009/10 it had assets of £2 million and an income of £476,000. Grants totalled £517,000 and were given under the following headings:

Education	£50,000
General	£150,000
Integrated nursery	£250
Needy	£12,000
Orphanage	£2,500
Publication of religious books	£45,000
Relief of poverty	£76,000
Religious institutions	£113,000
Synagogues	£57,000
Talmudical colleges	£2,500
Training	£8,000

Only the largest grants were listed in the accounts. They were: Ezer V'hatzolah (£128,000); Tchaba Kollel (£60,000); Hadras Kodesh Trust and Shaarei Chesed – London (£45,000 each); and Satmar Kollel (Antwerp) Ltd (£44,000).

Applications

Grants are made upon application by the charity concerned. Grants are made in amounts thought appropriate by the directors/trustees.

The Kreditor Charitable Trust

Jewish, welfare, education

£101,000 (2009/10)

Beneficial area

UK, with preferences for London and North East England.

Gerald Kreditor and Co., Chartered Accountants, Hallswelle House, 1 Hallswelle Road, London NW11 0DH
Tel: 020 8209 1535
Fax: 020 8209 1923
Email: admin@gerald-kreditor.co.uk
Correspondent: Paul M Kreditor
Trustees: Paul M Kreditor; Merle P Kreditor; Sharon Kreditor.
CC Number: 292649

Information available

Accounts were available at the Charity Commission, without a list of grants.

This trust was established in 1985 for general charitable purposes, including the relief of poverty and the advancement of the Jewish religion.

In 2009/10 the trust had assets of £55,000 and an income of £70,000. Grants totalled £101,000.

In previous years, grants have been mostly for less than £100 and have been given mainly to Jewish organisations working in education and social and medical welfare. Beneficiaries have been scattered across London and the north-east of England. The vast majority of grants were for less than £100. Recipients have included Academy for Rabbinical Research, British Friends of Israel War Disabled, Fordeve Ltd, Jerusalem Ladies' Society, Jewish Care, Jewish Marriage Council, Kosher Meals on Wheels, London Academy of Jewish Studies, NW London Talmudical College and Ravenswood. Non-Jewish organisations supported included British Diabetic Association, RNID and UNICEF UK.

Applications

In writing to the correspondent.

220

The Kreitman Foundation

Education, health, welfare and animal conservation

£108,000 (2009/10)

Beneficial area

UK.

Citroen Wells, Devonshire House, 1 Devonshire Street, London W1W 5DR
Trustees: Mrs Jill Luck-Hille; P M Luck-Hille.
CC Number: 269046

Information available

Accounts were on file at the Charity Commission.

This trust was established in 1975 as the Jill Kreitman Charitable Trust which changed its name to the Luck-Hille Foundation and in 2009 changed its name again to The Kreitman Foundation. Grants are made to registered and exempt charities in the UK concerned with education, health and welfare and animal conservation.

In 2009/10 the trust held assets of £4.9 million and had a total income of £157,000. Two grants totalling £108,000 were made. Middlesex University received £105,000 and Hile Pandana received £2,500.

Exclusions

No grants to individuals.

Applications

To the correspondent in writing. The trustees seem to have a list of regular beneficiaries and it may be unlikely that any new applications will be successful.

Kupath Gemach Chaim Bechesed Viznitz Trust

Jewish

£351,000 to organisations (2009/10)

Beneficial area

UK and Israel.

171 Kyverdale Road, London N16 6PS
Tel: 020 8442 9604
Correspondent: Saul Weiss, Trustee
Trustees: Israel Kahan; Saul Weiss; Alexander Pifko.
CC Number: 1110323

Information available

Accounts were available from the Charity Commission.

The charity was established by Deed of Trust dated 18 May 2005.

The objects of the charity are:

- the relief of the poor, sick, feeble and frail throughout the world and in particular but not exclusively amongst members of the Jewish faith
- the advancement of the Orthodox Jewish faith
- the advancement of the Orthodox Jewish religious education.

In 2009/10 the trust had an income of £297,000 from donations and made grants to organisations totalling £351,000, which were broken down as follows:

Education	£55,000
Advancement of religion	£290,000
Relief of poverty	£5,500

Organisations to benefit included: BHW Ltd – for the advancement of religion (£256,000); and Tchabe Kollel Ltd – for education (£37,000).

During the year, a further £113,000 was granted to individuals.

Applications

In writing to the correspondent.

The Kyte Charitable Trust

Medical, disadvantaged and socially isolated people

£123,000 (2009/10)

Beneficial area

UK.

Business Design Centre, 52 Upper Street, London N1 0QH

Tel: 020 7704 7791
Correspondent: The Trustees
Trustees: D M Kyte; T M Kyte; J L Kyte; I J Kyte.
CC Number: 1035886

Information available

Accounts were available from the Charity Commission.

The trust supports organisations benefiting medical professionals and research workers. Support may go to organisations working with at- risk groups, and people who are disadvantaged by poverty or socially isolated.

In 2009/10 the trust had assets of £18,000 and an income of £131,000 from covenants and Gift Aid received. Grants were made totalling £123,000, and were broken down into the following categories:

Community support	£88,000
Healthcare	£11,000
Sports	£10,000
Arts, culture and heritage	£6,500
International Aid	£3,000
Children	£1,500
Educational support	£500
Miscellaneous	£2,500

Organisations receiving grants during the year included: United Jewish Israel Appeal (£27,000); Jewish Care (£21,000); Community Security Trust and Norwood Ravenswood (£15,000 each) and Myeloma UK (£1,000).

Applications

In writing to the correspondent.

The Late Sir Pierce Lacy Charity Trust

Roman Catholics, general

About £26,000 (2009/10)

Beneficial area

UK and overseas.

Aviva, Trustee Department, Pitheavlis, Perth PH2 0NH
Tel: 01738 895590
Fax: 01738 895903
Correspondent: Aviva, Trustee Department
Trustee: Aviva Insurance Ltd

CC Number: 1013505

Information available

Information was obtained from the Charity Commission website.

In 2009/10 the trust had an income of £22,000 and an expenditure totalling £26,000. Grants are only made to Roman Catholic and associated institutions. Newly established and UK organisations are supported, benefiting children, young adults, older people, Roman Catholics, at-risk groups, carers, people who have disabilities and people disadvantaged by poverty.

Grants are made in the areas of medicine and health, welfare, education, religion and for general charitable purposes. The trust particularly supports charities working in the field of infrastructure development, residential facilities and services, Christian education, Christian outreach, Catholic bodies, charity or voluntary umbrella bodies, hospices, rehabilitation centres, advocacy, education and training, community services and community issues.

Recurrent small grants of £1,000 or less are made, and grants can be for buildings, capital, core costs, project, research and start-up costs. Funding for more than three years may be considered.

Previous grants have included the following: £1,400 to Crusade of Rescue, £920 to St Francis' Children's Society, £810 to Poor Mission Fund, £800 to St Cuthbert's Mayne RC School – special donation, £720 to Society of St Vincent De Paul, £610 to Poor Mission Fund, £550 to Catholic Children's Society and £530 to St Francis' Leprosy Guild.

Exclusions

The trust only supports the Roman Catholic Church or associated institutions.

Applications

In writing to the correspondent, at any time.

John Laing Charitable Trust

Education, community regeneration, youth, homelessness, environment

£307,000 to organisations (2010)

Beneficial area

UK.

33 Bunns Lane, Mill Hill, London NW7 2DX
Tel: 020 8959 7321
Email: michael.a.hamilton@laing.com
Website: www.laing.com/lct.htm
Correspondent: Michael Hamilton, Secretary
Trustees: C M Laing; Sir Martin Laing; D C Madden; R I Sumner; P Jones; D Whipp; L Krige.
CC Number: 236852

Information available

Accounts were available from the Charity Commission. The following information is taken from the 'Charitable Donations' section within 'Corporate Responsibility' on the John Laing website:

> The John Laing Charitable Trust has always tried to match its areas of donations to sectors allied to the Company's business.
>
> More recently, the trust has concentrated its support on charities which support the following main themes:
> 1 education
> 2 community regeneration
> 3 disadvantaged young people
> 4 homelessness with a particular emphasis on day centres
> 5 environment.
>
> The John Laing Charitable Trust takes a pro-active role in seeking charities that fit the criteria.
>
> Donations range from £250 to £25,000 with up to 12 charities receiving more than £10,000. Usually, charities receive one-off donations, but a small number are supported for an agreed period, often up to three years.

In addition, the trust will match the fundraising efforts of the staff of John Laing plc with predetermined limits.

In 2010 the trust had assets of £50 million, an income of £1.7 million and 'distributed and accrued' grants totalling £938,000 of which £307,000 went to organisations. The trustees' report for 2010 states:

> The total of approved and accrued donations made to charitable organisations in 2010 amounted to £307,000 (£625,000: 2009). During the year the offer made to Atlantic College in 2008 of a donation of £400,000 was withdrawn whilst the College reconsiders its development plans. Without this withdrawal of the offer the total of approved and accrued donations would have been £400,000 higher.

Beneficiaries included: National Communities Resource Centre (£50,000); ContinYou (£35,000); Young Enterprise London (£30,000); Prince's Trust (£29,000); Victim Support, Croydon Commitment, Hertfordshire Groundwork and Learning Thro' Landscapes (£25,000 each); National Literacy Trust and The Reading Agency (£20,000 each); Kidscape and Springboard for Children (15,000 each); Church Action on Poverty, Fairshare, and Groundswell (£10,000 each); Depaul Trust (£7,500); CRASH (£6,000); Bentilee Dad's Group, Child Victims of Crime, Clouds of Hope, Discover, Maryland Primary School Quaker Social Action and Self Help Housing (£5,000 each); Upper Room and Wood Street Mission (£2,500 each).

Exclusions

No grants to individuals (other than to Laing employees and/or their dependants).

Applications

In writing to the correspondent. The trust does not have an application form and applicants are asked to keep the initial request as brief as possible. There is no deadline for receipt of applications. All applications are dealt with on a rolling basis. The trust says that all applications are acknowledged.

The Martin Laing Foundation

General, environment and conservation, disadvantaged young people and the elderly and infirm

£445,000 (2009/10)

Beneficial area

UK and worldwide, particularly Malta.

33 Bunns Lane, London NW7 2DX
Tel: 020 8238 8890
Correspondent: Ms Elizabeth Ann Harley, Correspondent
Trustees: Sir John Martin Laing; Colin Fletcher; Edward Charles Laing; Nicholas Gregory; Lady Stephanie Stearn Laing.
CC Number: 278461

Information available

Accounts were available from the Charity Commission.

This foundation is established for general charitable purposes and operates through its grantmaking programme. Through this programme, the trustees support charitable projects in areas identified as being of particular interest to them. These areas include environmental and conservation work, projects benefiting disadvantaged young people or the elderly/infirm, and Norfolk-based activities. A small number of grants are made to overseas projects, particularly in Malta; in such cases the trustees will have a thorough working knowledge of the organisations involved.

A small number of larger grants are made, including one to the Charities Aid Foundation (CAF) which is then disbursed in smaller grants to a large number of organisations 'at the Settlor's discretion'. The foundation is administered alongside the Beatrice Laing Trust, Kirby Laing Foundation and Maurice & Hilda Laing Charitable Trust. Administrative staff, who are employed by the Kirby Laing Foundation, office space, which is

owned by the Reculver Trust, and costs are shared with the other three trusts.

In 2009/10 the foundation had assets of £5.6 million and an income of £189,000. Governance and support costs totalled £20,000, while the investment manager's charges totalled £18,000. Grants were made totalling £445,000 of which £45,000 was distributed through CAF. The significant increase in the total amount given in grants is almost entirely attributable to an exceptional grant of £250,000 to the Home Farm Trust for the purchase of a property in Bishop's Stortford to provide shared living accommodation for people with learning disabilities.

Grants made directly by the foundation were broken down as follows:

Health and medicine	5	£270,000
Overseas aid	6	£42,000
Cultural and environmental	5	£35,000
Social welfare	5	£27,500
Child and youth	3	£15,000
Religion	1	£10,000
Charities Aid Foundation		£45,000

Beneficiaries included: Home Farm Trust Limited (£250,000); Students' Education Trust (£20,000); Malta Aviation Museum Foundation and WWF-UK (£10,000 each); Action for M E, Bird College, CPRE Norfolk, Cowes Community Partnership, The Poppy Centre Trust and The Pushkin Prizes (£5,000 each); Flimkien ghal Ambient Ahjar (£3,000); and The Malta Hospice Movement (£1,000).

Applications

The trust has previously informed us that:

> The trustees receive an enormous and increasing number of requests for help. Unfortunately the trustees are only able to help a small proportion of the requests and consequently they limit their support to those charities where they have an interest in their activities.

The trustees meet twice a year.

The Christopher Laing Foundation

Social welfare, environment, culture, health and, children and youth

£180,000 (2009/10)

Beneficial area

UK, with an interest in Hertfordshire.

c/o TMF Management UK Ltd, 400 Capability Green, Luton LU1 3AE
Tel: 01582 439200
Email: paula.doraisamy@tmf-group. com
Correspondent: Paula Doraisamy, Trust Consultant
Trustees: Christopher M Laing; John Keeble; Peter S Jackson; Diana C Laing.
CC Number: 278460

Information available

Accounts were available from the Charity Commission.

In 2009/10 the trust had assets of £5.9 million, which generated an income of £193,000. Grants totalled £180,000, which were distributed under the following categories:

Cultural and environmental	£50,000
Child and youth	£39,000
Health and medicine	£26,000
Social welfare	£15,000
Charities Aid Foundation	£50,000

Beneficiaries included: the Lord's Taverners (£30,000 in two grants); Fields in Trust (£25,000); Hertfordshire Groundwork (£15,000 in two grants); Alastair Hignall Multiple Sclerosis Fund (£10,000); Sport Aid and Worshipful Company of Paviors (£5,000 each).

Exclusions

Donations are only made to registered charities.

Applications

In writing to the correspondent.

The David Laing Foundation

Youth, disability, the arts, general

£258,000 (2009/10)

Beneficial area

Worldwide, with an apparent preference for the South of England.

Fermyn Woods Hall, Brigstock, Northamptonshire, NN 14 3JA
Tel: 01536 373886
Correspondent: David E Laing, Trustee
Trustees: David Eric Laing; John Stuart Lewis; Richard Francis Dudley Barlow; Frances Mary Laing.
CC Number: 278462

Information available

Accounts were available from the Charity Commission.

The foundation has general charitable purposes with an emphasis on youth, disability and the arts. Previous information has shown the foundation to make large grants to a wide and varied number of organisations as well as donating smaller grants through Charities Aid Foundation.

In 2009/10 the foundation had assets of £4.4 million and an income of £101,000. Grants totalled £258,000, which were broken down into the following categories:

General charitable purposes	£197,000
Disability/disadvantage/health/ sickness/medical	£32,000
Arts & culture	£13,000
Social welfare/sports/recreation	£11,000
Child & youth (including education)	£4,000
Religion	£600

Previous beneficiaries included: Northamptonshire Community Foundation (£120,000 in three grants); Grove House Hospice (£21,000); International Organ Festival (£15,000); Lord's Taverners (£6,500 in four grants); St John Ambulance (£6,000); Peterborough Cathedral (£5,000); British Olympic Foundation (£4,700 in three grants); Firfield Primary School PTA, Game Conservancy Trust, Hertfordshire Agricultural Society and Interact Reading Service (£2,000 each).

Exclusions

No grants to individuals.

Applications

In writing to the correspondent. Trustees meet in March, June, October and December, although applications are reviewed weekly. Due to the large number of applications received, and the relatively small number of grants made, the trust is not able to respond to all requests.

The Lambert Charitable Trust

Health, welfare, education, disability, Jewish

£57,000 (2009/10)

Beneficial area

UK and Israel.

Mercer & Hole, 72 London Road, St Albans, Hertfordshire AL1 1NS
Tel: 01727 869141
Correspondent: George Georghiou, Correspondent
Trustees: M Lambert; Prof. H P Lambert; Jane Lambert; O E Lambert; D J R Wells.
CC Number: 257803

Information available

Accounts were available from the Charity Commission.

The trust supports Jewish and Israeli causes, and organisations for people with disabilities, the elderly, medical, welfare, education and the arts.

In 2009/10 the trust had assets of £3 million and an income of £85,000. Grants totalled £57,000 and investment management and governance costs totalled £30,000.

Beneficiaries included: Jewish Care (£15,000); Action Medical Research, Medical Foundation for the Care of Victims of Torture, Meningitis Research Foundation, and Quaker Social Action (£2,000 each); Crossroads Caring for Carers Headway and Jewish Association for the Mentally Ill (£1,000); and Ponevez Yeshivah Israel (£250).

Applications

In writing to the correspondent before July for payment by 1 September.

Lancashire Environmental Fund

Environment and community

£796,000 (2010)

Beneficial area

Lancashire.

The Barn, Berkeley Drive, Bamber Bridge, Preston, Lancashire PR5 6BY
Tel: 01772 317 247
Fax: 01772 628 849
Email: andyrowett@lancsenvfund.org.uk
Website: www.lancsenvfund.org.uk
Correspondent: Andy Rowett, Administration Officer
Trustees: Gary Mayson; P Greijenberg; D Tattersall; Albert Atkinson; Roger Hardman.
CC Number: 1074983

Information available

Accounts were available from the Charity Commission.

This fund was established in June 1998 from a partnership of four organisations: SITA (Lancashire) Ltd, Lancashire County Council, the Wildlife Trust for Lancashire, Manchester and North Merseyside and Community Futures. The fund enables community groups and organisations throughout the country to take advantage of the funding opportunities offered by landfill tax credits. It achieves this by supporting organisations and projects based within Lancashire, or nationwide research or development with a relevance to Lancashire, which are managed by an Enrolled Environmental Body, as recognised by Entrust.

The Fund operates three funding schemes:

Small Grants (formerly Community Chest)

The Small Grants programme is available for small schemes usually to support groups who are seeking one off funding for a project. Applications are accepted for grants between £3,000 and £15,000. The overall cost of the project should not exceed £30,000. The Fund may act as Environmental Body for the project and administer the paperwork required by the regulator.

Main Grants (formerly Strategic Fund)

The Main Grants programme Fund is available to organisations who are registered as Environmental Bodies with Entrust, the scheme regulator. Applications are accepted for grants up to £40,000 but the overall cost should not exceed £300,000.

Dirtworks

The Dirtworks programme is funding to encourage young people to volunteer and get involved with practical environmental schemes. Applications are invited from organisations with the capacity to supervise and deliver a high quality project with young people. Schemes should cost up to £25,000 with the Fund contributing £20,000. The capital works element of the project should be at least 40% of the cost.

Note: The fund does not normally consider applications for 100% funding therefore, support from other grant sources is welcome.

In 2010 the fund had assets of £2.5 million and an income of £916,000. Grants awarded for the year totalled £796,000.

Grants awarded in the year included: Thornton Methodist Church and The Woodlands – Clayton le Moors (£30,000 each); Longholme Methodist Church – Rawtenstall (£25,000); Martin Mere, The Secret Garden – Penwortham and Yarrow Valley – Chorley (£15,000 each); Willow Lane – Lancaster (£9,000); and Briercliffe Memorial Bowling Green – Burnley (£5,000).

Exclusions

Funding is not given for the following:
- core cost of an organisation
- retrospective funding
- projects in school grounds
- allotment or food growing projects
- car parks and public conveniences
- recycling projects
- projects within the unitary authority districts of Blackpool and Blackburn.

All projects must satisfy at least one objective of the Landfill Communities Fund. For more information about the scheme contact Entrust, the regulatory body, by visiting its website or telephoning 0161 972 0074.

Applications

Detailed and helpful guidance notes and application forms for each funding strand is available from the correspondent or may be downloaded from the fund's website. Completed forms should contain all possible relevant material including maps, photographs, plans, and so on.

The board meets quarterly in January, April, July and October.

Staff are willing to have informal discussions before an application is made. Potential applicants are strongly advised to visit the website and view the guidelines before contacting the trust.

Common applicant mistakes

'Not reading the guidance and criteria; not providing all relevant supporting documents; not supplying the requested additional information.'

LandAid Charitable Trust

Homelessness, relief of need, young people

£43,000 (2009/10)

Beneficial area

UK.

St Albans House, 5th Floor, 57–59 Haymarket, London SW1Y 4QX
Tel: 020 3102 7190
Email: enquiries@landaid.org
Website: www.landaid.org
Correspondent: Lucy-Jayne Cummings, Administrator

Information available

Accounts were on file at the Charity Commission; good website.

LandAid is a charity established by the property industry to bring the resources, expertise and influence of the industry together in promoting effective charitable work.

The trust's grantmaking reflects its commitment to giving those who are less advantaged, particularly the young and homeless, an opportunity to transform their lives and achieve their full potential.

The trust's annual grants programme supports disadvantaged or homeless people, particularly the young, by funding projects which:

- provide accommodation or assist in meeting accommodation needs
- refurbish or renew facilities
- deliver training, life skills or other educational programmes.

Applications for grant support of between £5,000 and £25,000 are invited. The trust will not normally consider funding staff costs, unless the project is of limited duration or the applicant has shown how such costs will be met on an ongoing basis.

In 2009/10 the trust had assets of £281,000 and an income of £873,000, mainly from donations. Grants under the annual grants programme totalled £43,000.

Beneficiaries included: New Horizons Youth Centre (£8,800); Robert Blair Primary School (£7,500); Astell Foundation (£6,500); Chartered Surveyors Training Trust (£5,300); and Booth Centre, Space Trust and Canterbury Housing Advice Centre (£5,000 each).

In addition to the above, the trust has made large donations in support of Foundations for Life. This is an innovative partnership between LandAid and Centrepoint which aims to deliver real help to homeless young people in order to turn their lives around and progress to independent adulthood, with their own career and home.

Exclusions

No grants to individuals.

Applications

Organisations should apply online through the trust's website. Supporting documentation, including a copy of the latest annual report and financial statements, is required.

The Langdale Trust

Social welfare, Christian, medical, general

£130,000 (2009/10)

Beneficial area

Worldwide, but with a special interest in Birmingham.

c/o Cobbetts Solicitors, One Colmore Square, Birmingham B4 6AJ
Tel: 0845 404 2404
Correspondent: Mrs C G O'Brien, Secretary
Trustees: Jethro Elvin; Timothy R Wilson; Teresa Whiting;
CC Number: 215317

Information available

Accounts were available from the Charity Commission.

The trust was established in 1960 by the late Antony Langdale Wilson. There is a preference for local charities in the Birmingham area and those in the fields of social welfare and health, especially with a Christian context.

In 2009/10 the trust had assets of £3.4 million, which generated an income of £117,000. Grants were made to 44 organisations totalling £130,000. Grants ranged from £1,000 to £9,000.

Grant beneficiaries include: Yorkshire Swan and Wildlife Rescue Hospital (£9,000); Rainforest Concern (£6,000); The One Foundation (£5,000); Oxfam (£4,000); Prisoners Abroad (£3,000); Survival International (£2,000) and Tall Ships Youth Trust, Galapagos Conservation Trust and Apprentices are MAD (£1,000 each).

Applications

In writing to the correspondent. The trustees meet in July.

The Langley Charitable Trust

Christian, general

£1,040,000 (2009)

Beneficial area

UK and worldwide, with a preference for the West Midlands.

Wheatmoor Farm, 301 Tamworth Road, Sutton Coldfield, West Midlands B75 6JP
Tel: 0121 308 0165
Correspondent: The Trustees
Trustees: J P Gilmour; Mrs S S Gilmour.
CC Number: 280104

Information available

Latest accounts available from the Charity Commission were for 2009.

The trust makes grants to evangelical Christian organisations and to other charities in the fields of welfare, medicine and health. It makes grants in the UK and worldwide, but appears to have a slight preference for the West Midlands.

The last accounts available were for 2009. The trust had an income of £183,000 and assets of £5 million. They made grants totalling over £1 million most of which was given to the local youth clubs association.

Significant beneficiaries were: Northamptonshire Association of Youth Clubs (£1 million); Wide horizons (£15,000); Friends of Ludhiana (£25,000).

Beneficiaries of less than £1,000 were: United Christian Broadcaster (£500); Trauma Heading Workshop; Bible Society (£100 each); Manna House (£150); St Andrews Hospice Airdrie; St Giles Hospice (£25 each); Soul Survivor (£400); British Red Cross (£250).

One Individual received a grant of £1,000 for the Coton Green Church.

Exclusions

No grants to animal or bird charities.

Applications

In writing to the correspondent. The trust states: 'The trustees only reply where they require further information and so on. Neither telephone calls nor correspondence will be entered into concerning any proposed or declined applications.'

The Lanvern Foundation

Education and health, especially relating to children

£130,000 (2009)

Beneficial area

UK.

P O Box 34475, London W6 9YB
Tel: 020 8741 2930
Correspondent: J C G Stancliffe, Trustee
Trustees: J C G Stancliffe; A H Isaacs.
CC Number: 295846

Information available

Accounts were on file at the Charity Commission up to 2009

The foundation was established in 1986. The trustees state that it supports registered charities working primarily in the fields of education and health, with particular emphasis on children. There are never any grants to individuals.

The latest accounts available were for 2009 when the trust had an income of £108,000 and assets of £2.7 million. The trust made grants totalling £130,000. £125,000 was given to The Moorfields Eye Hospital and £5,000 to The Marchant-Holliday School.

Exclusions

Absolutely no grants to individuals.

Applications

In writing to the correspondent.

The R J Larg Family Charitable Trust

Education, health, medical research, arts – particularly music

About £100,000

Beneficial area

UK but generally Scotland, particularly Tayside.

Whitehall House, Yeaman Shore, Dundee DD1 4BJ
Correspondent: The Trustees
Trustees: R W Gibson; D A Brand; Mrs S A Stewart.
SC Number: SC004946

Information available

Information provided by the trust and basic information taken from the website of the Office of the Scottish Charity Register.

The trust has an annual income of approximately £140,000. Grants, which total about £100,000 each year, range between £250 and £6,000 and are given to a variety of organisations.

These include organisations concerned with cancer research and other medical charities, youth organisations, university students' associations and amateur musical groups. No further recent information was available.

Previous beneficiaries include High School – Dundee, Whitehall Theatre Trust, Macmillan Cancer Relief – Dundee and Sense Scotland Children's Hospice.

Exclusions

Grants are not available for individuals.

Applications

In writing to the correspondent. Trustees meet to consider grants in February and August.

Largsmount Ltd

Jewish

£154,400 (2009)

Beneficial area

UK and Israel.

50 Keswick Street, Gateshead NE8 1TQ
Tel: 0191 490 0140
Correspondent: Simon Kaufman, Trustee
Trustees: Z M Kaufman; Naomi Kaufman; Simon Kaufman.
CC Number: 280509

Information available

Accounts were overdue at the Charity Commission. Accounts for previous years were available without a list of grants.

Registered in 1980, this trust states its aims as:

- the advancement of religion in accordance with the Orthodox Jewish Faith
- the relief of poverty
- general charitable purposes.

Recent accounts were overdue at the Charity Commission so information was obtained from accounts for 2009. During the year the trust had an income of £526,000 and assets of £3.5 million. The charitable activities total was given in the accounts as £154,400 without a grants breakdown.

Details of beneficiaries during the year were not available, although previously the M Y A Charitable Trust, a connected charity, has been the largest beneficiary every year.

Applications

In writing to the correspondent.

Laufer Charitable Trust

Jewish

£34,000 (2009/10)

Beneficial area

UK.

342 Regents Park Road, London N3 2LJ

Tel: 020 8343 1660
Correspondent: R Aarons, Trustee
Trustees: S W Laufer; Mrs
D D Laufer; S C Goulden; R Aarons;
M Hoffman.
CC Number: 275375

Information available

Accounts were on file at the Charity Commission, without a list of grants.

The trust makes grants mainly to Jewish organisations and has a list of charities which it has a long-term commitment to and supports annually or twice a year. It rarely adds new charities to the list.

In 2009/10 the trust had assets of £836,000 and an income of £89,000. Grants were made totalling £34,000.

Unfortunately, we have no information regarding the beneficiaries.

Exclusions

No grants to individuals, as grants are only made to registered charities.

Applications

New beneficiaries are only considered by the trust in exceptional circumstances, as the trustees seek to maintain support for an existing group of charities. In view of this it is suggested that no applications be made.

The Lauffer Family Charitable Foundation

Jewish, general

£213,000 (2009/10)

Beneficial area

Commonwealth countries, Israel and USA.

Clayton Stark & Co, 5th Floor, Charles House, 108–110 Finchley Road, London NW3 5JJ
Tel: 020 7431 4200
Email: bethlauffer@lineone.net
Correspondent: J S Lauffer, Trustee
Trustees: Mrs R R Lauffer;
J S Lauffer; G L Lauffer; R M Lauffer.
CC Number: 251115

Information available

Accounts were available from the Charity Commission.

The trust has general charitable purposes, supporting Jewish causes in the UK, Commonwealth, Israel and USA.

In 2009/10 it had assets of £5.2 million, which generated an income of £138,000. Grants totalled over £213,000. Management and administration costs were £45,000.

Grants were broken down as follows:

Education	47	£102,000
Welfare and care of children and families	73	£39,000
Recreation and Culture	39	£30,000
Medical Healthcare	21	£23,000
Religious Activities	23	£19,000
Environment	9	£1,400

Beneficiaries included: Jewish Learning Exchange (£20,000); Hasmonean High School (£15,000); British Friends of Sarah Herzog Memorial Hospital (£10,000); United Joint Israel Appeal (£6,000); Spiro Ark (£5,000); and British Friends of Ezer Mizion (£1,200).

Exclusions

No support for individuals.

Applications

In writing to the correspondent; applications are considered once a year.

Mrs F B Laurence Charitable Trust

Social welfare, medical, disability, environment

£84,000 (2009/10)

Beneficial area

UK and overseas.

BM Box 2082, London WC1N 3XX
Correspondent: The Trustees
Trustees: Caroline Fry; Camilla Carr; Elizabeth Lyle.
CC Number: 296548

Information available

Accounts were on file at the Charity Commission.

The trust produces guidelines which state:

The stated object of the charity in its deed of trust is to provide for the benefit of the Royal National Lifeboat Institution, King George's Fund for Sailors (now known as Seafarers UK), Stock Exchange Benevolent Fund, Royal Air Force Benevolent Fund and such other charitable object or institution as the trustees in their absolute discretion think fit.

The trustees' preference is to make grants for the care and improvements of conditions experienced by disadvantaged members of society both within the United Kingdom and overseas for whom the United Kingdom owes a duty of care.

The trustees are willing to support small organisations and those that by the nature of their work, find it difficult to attract funding.

In 2009/10 the trust had assets of £2.3 million and a total income of £72,000. Grants were made totalling £84,000. Management and administration expenses were high at £20,000, including a payment of £17,000 to a firm in which one of the trustees is a partner. Whilst wholly legal, these editors always regret such payments unless, in the words of the Charity Commission, 'there is no realistic alternative'.

Grant recipients during the year included: Gurkha Welfare Trust and ZANE – Zimbabwe a National Emergency (£3,000 each); Seafarers UK and Barnado's (£2,500 each); Blue Cross, Stroke Association and Winston's Wish (£2,000 each); BHEST, Carers UK and Women for Women (£1,500 each); and Children with Leukaemia (£1,300). Other grants of £1,000 or less totalled £29,000.

Exclusions

No support for individuals. The following applications are unlikely to be considered:

- appeals for endowment or sponsorship
- overseas projects, unless overseen by the charity's own fieldworkers
- maintenance of buildings or landscape
- provision of work or materials that are the responsibility of the state
- where administration expenses, in all their guises, are considered by the trustees to be excessive
- where the fundraising costs in the preceding year have not resulted in

an increase in the succeeding years' donations in excess of these costs.

Applications

In writing to the correspondent, including the latest annual report and accounts, as filed with the Charity Commission. The guidelines state:

Write to us on not more than two sides of A4 paper with the following information:
- who you are
- what you do
- what distinguishes your work from others in your field
- where applicable describe the project that the money you are asking for is going towards and include a business plan/budget
- what funds have already been raised and how
- how much are you seeking from us
- how do you intend to measure the potential benefits of your project or work as a whole?

Only registered charities will be considered.

The Kathleen Laurence Trust

Heart disease, arthritis, mental disabilities, medical research, older people, children's charities

£113,000 (2009/10)

Beneficial area

UK.

Coutts and Co, Trustee Department, 440 Strand, London WC2R 0QS
Tel: 020 7753 1000
Fax: 020 7753 1090
Correspondent: Trust Manager
Trustee: Coutts and Co.
CC Number: 296461

Information available

Accounts were on file at the Charity Commission.

Donations are given to a wide range of organisations, particularly favouring smaller groups and those raising funds for specific requirements, such as for the caring and support of people with mental disabilities, arthritic and rheumatoid

research, cancer research, research into respiratory and cardiac illnesses, and children's charities.

In 2009/10 the trust had assets of £2.9 million and an income of £886,000. Grants were made to 82 organisations totalling £113,000.

Beneficiaries included: Action for Kids, Age Concern, Colchester Cat Rescue, Heart Research UK, Institute of Cancer Research, Just Different, Marfan Trust, Prostate Cancer Charity, Roy Castle Lung Cancer Foundation, Sunnybank Trust and West Norfolk Schools for Parents.

Exclusions

No donations are made for running costs, management expenses or to individuals.

Applications

In writing to the correspondent. Trustees meet in January and June.

The Law Society Charity

Law and justice, worldwide

£491,000 (2009/10)

Beneficial area

Worldwide.

113 Chancery Lane, London WC2A 1PL
Tel: 020 7316 5597
Email: lawsocietycharity@lawsociety.org.uk
Website: www.lawsociety.org.uk
Correspondent: Andrew Dobson, Company Secretary
Trustee: The Law Society Trustees Ltd.
CC Number: 268736

Information available

Information available from the Charity Commission website.

As the name suggests, this trust is concerned with causes connected to the legal profession, particularly in advancing legal education and access to legal knowledge. Organisations protecting people's legal rights and lawyers' welfare are also supported, as

are law-related projects from charities without an identifiable legal connection.

In 2009/10 the trust had an income of £16,500 and a total expenditure of £491,000.

Previous beneficiaries have included: The Citizenship Foundation (£90,000); LawCare Limited (£82,500); Howard League for Penal Reform (£17,500); Environmental Law Foundation and Solicitors' Benevolent Society (£15,000 each); Nottinghamshire Law Society and Working Families (£10,000 each); Asylum Support Appeals Project (£7,500); Book Aid International (£6,400); Peace Brigades International and Youthnet UK (£5,000 each).

Applications

In writing to the correspondent. Applications are considered at quarterly trustees' meetings, usually held in April, July, September and December.

Further details of the aims and objectives of the charity, together with an application form, can be downloaded from the trust's website.

The Edgar E Lawley Foundation

Older people, disability, children, community, hospices and medical

£227,000 (2010/11)

Beneficial area

UK, with a preference for the West Midlands.

P.O. Box 456, Esher KT10 1DP
Tel: 01372 805 760
Email: frankjackson1945@yahoo.com
Website: www.edgarelawleyfoundation.org.uk
Correspondent: F S Jackson, Trustee
Trustees: J H Cooke, Chair; Mrs G V H Hilton; P J Cooke; F S Jackson.
CC Number: 201589

Information available

Accounts were available from the Charity Commission.

The foundation currently funds six broad areas to ensure balance in its grant giving programme. These areas are: hospices; children and young people; older people; community; disabled; medical, research and other miscellaneous projects. There is a preference for the West Midlands.

In 2010/11 the foundation had assets of £4.1 million and an income of £197,000. Grants were made to 142 organisations and totalled £227,000.

Beneficiaries were listed in the accounts, but without any indication of the size of grant received. They included: Acorns Children's Hospice, Aston & Birchfield Community Association, Extra Care Charitable Trust, Gospel Oak Community Centre, Guide Dogs, Home from Hospital Care, Lifelites, Redditch Association for the Blind, Walsall Hospice, Who Cares Trust and Zoe's Place for Baby Hospice.

Exclusions

No grants to individuals.

Applications

Applications should be made in writing to the correspondent by 31 October. Applicants should outline the reasons for the grant request and the amount of grant being sought. Any supporting information that adds to the strength of the application should be included.

The trustees make grant decisions in January. The foundation regrets that it is not possible, unless a stamped addressed envelope has been provided, to communicate with unsuccessful applicants and the fact that a grant has not been received by mid August indicates that it has not been possible to fund it.

Common applicant mistakes

'Applying when they are not eligible.'

The Lawson Beckman Charitable Trust

Jewish, welfare, education, arts

£133,000 (2009/10)

Beneficial area

UK.

A Beckman plc, PO Box 1ED, London W1A 1ED
Tel: 020 7637 8412
Fax: 020 7436 8599
Correspondent: Melvin Lawson, Trustee
Trustees: M A Lawson; F C Katz; L R Stock.
CC Number: 261378

Information available

Accounts were on file at the Charity Commission.

The trust gives grants for the relief of poverty, support of the arts and general charitable purposes. Grants are allocated two years in advance.

In 2009/10 the trust had assets of £1.8 million and an income of £107,000. A total of £133,000 was distributed in 11 grants broken down as follows:

Medical/Health/Sickness	£115,300
General charitable purposes	£9,400
Education/Training	£4,500
Relief of poverty	£3,100
Religious activities	£1,100

Beneficiaries included: Jewish Care (£100,000), Norwood Ravenswood (£10,000), Nightingale House and United Jewish Israel Appeal (£5,000 each); Dalaid Limited and Project Seed (£2,500 each); and World Jewish Relief (£600).

Exclusions

No grants to individuals.

Applications

In writing to the correspondent, but please note that grants are allocated two years in advance.

The Raymond and Blanche Lawson Charitable Trust

General

£130,000 (2009/10)

Beneficial area

UK, with an interest in West Kent and East Sussex.

28 Barden Road, Tonbridge, Kent TN9 1TX
Tel: 01732 352 183
Fax: 01732 352 621
Trustee: Mrs S A Hill and Mr P Thomas.
CC Number: 281269

Information available

Accounts were on file at the Charity Commission.

The trust has a preference for local organisations and generally supports charities within the following categories:

- Local voluntary organisations
- Preservation of buildings
- Local hospices
- Care in the community
- Assistance for people who are disabled
- Armed forces and benevolent funds

In 2009/10 the trust had assets of £1.6 million, an income of £107,000 and made grants to 80 organisations totalling £130,000. Grants ranged from £250–£5,000.

The three largest grants during the year were for £5,000 and awarded to the following charities: Royal British Legion, Citizens Advice Bureau and Marden Memorial Village Hall.

Smaller grants included: Weald of Kent Hospice (£3,000); St Georges Community Children's Project and Royal London Society for the Blind (£2,000 each); Multiple Sclerosis Society, Independence at Home and League of Friends of Pembury Hospital (£1,000 each).

Exclusions

No support for churches or individuals.

Applications

In writing to the correspondent.

The Carole and Geoffrey Lawson Foundation

Child welfare, poverty, arts, education, research and Jewish organisations

Around £30,000 (2009/10)

Beneficial area

Worldwide, in practice UK.

Stilemans, Munstead, Godalming, Surrey GU8 4AB
Tel: 01483 420757
Correspondent: Geoffrey Lawson, Trustee
Trustees: Geoffrey C H Lawson; Carole Lawson; Harold I Connick; Edward C S Lawson; Jeremy S Lawson.
CC Number: 801751

Information available

Accounts were available from the Charity Commission.

This foundation was established in 1989 for general charitable purposes and focuses on child welfare, relief of poverty, the advancement of education, the arts, research and Jewish organisations.

In 2009/10 the foundation had an income of £6,000 and a total expenditure of £33,000. Accounts for this year were not required for the Charity Commission website, therefore further information concerning beneficiaries was not available. Expenditure was significantly reduced from the previous year when grants amounted to £273,000 (2007/08).

Previous beneficiaries included: World ORT Trust (£113,000); the Princes Trust (£33,000); Chase Children's Hospice Service (£29,000); St David's Care in the Community (£15,000); and Jewish Care (£13,000); Community Security Trust and World Jewish Relief (£10,000 each); Nightingale Home (£8,000); King

Silver Lining Appeal (£5,000); Young Enterprise (£3,500); Meath Epilepsy Trust (£2,000); and Royal Opera House, the Sanctuary and Coexistence Trust (£1,000 each).

Exclusions

In principal, no grants to individuals.

Applications

In writing to the correspondent.

The Leach Fourteenth Trust

Medical, disability, environment, conservation, general

£106,000 (2009/10)

Beneficial area

UK, with some preference for south west England and overseas only via a UK charity.

Barron & Barron, Chartered Accountants, Bathurst House, 86 Micklegate, York Y01 6LQ
Tel: 01904 628 551
Fax: 01904 623 533
Email: info@barronyork.co.uk
Correspondent: Guy Ward, Trustee
Trustees: W J Henderson; Mrs J M M Nash; G S Ward; Roger Murray-Leach.
CC Number: 204844

Information available

Accounts were available from the Charity Commission.

Although the trust's objectives are general, the trustees tend towards medical and disability organisations. The trust also has a preference for conservation (ecological) organisations. In practice there is a preference for south west England and the Home Counties.

A few charities receive regular donations. The trustees prefer to give single grants for specific projects rather than towards general funding and also favour small organisations or projects.

In 2009/10 the trust had assets of £2.8 million, an income of £92,000 and gave 66 grants totalling £106,000.

Beneficiaries for the year included: Merlin (£15,000); Plan International UK (£4,000); Army Benevolent Fund (£3,000); Salvation Army (£2,500); Mercy Ships and Youth Action Wiltshire (£2,000); and British Blind Sport, Countryside Restoration Trust, React and The Princess Royal Trust for Carers (£1,000 each).

Exclusions

Only registered charities based in the UK are supported (the trust only gives overseas via a UK-based charity). No grants to: individuals, including for gap years or trips abroad; private schools other than for people with disabilities or learning difficulties; no pet charities.

Applications

In writing to the correspondent. Applications for a specific item or purpose are favoured. Only successful appeals can expect a reply. A representative of the trust occasionally visits potential beneficiaries. There are bi-annual meetings of trustees in summer and late autumn. Grants tend to be distributed twice a year, but exceptions are made.

The David Lean Foundation

Film production, education and visual arts

£311,000 to organisations (2010)

Beneficial area

UK.

KJD Freeth LLP, Churchill House, Regent Road, Stoke-on-Trent ST1 3RQ
Tel: 01782 202 020
Fax: 01782 266060
Email: aareeves@kjd.co.uk
Website: www.davidleanfoundation. org
Correspondent: The Trustees
Trustees: A A Reeves; J G Moore.
CC Number: 1067074

Information available

Accounts were on file at the Charity Commission.

The foundation was registered on 23 December 1997 and was given rights to the royalties of four of the major films directed by the late Sir David Lean. This provides the foundation's principal, current and future source of income.

The foundation's objects are to promote public interest in the visual arts by stimulating original and creative work in the field of film production. The foundation's grant making policy is to achieve its objects by making awards:

- to other charitable institutions whose aims are similar to those of the foundation
- to the National Film and Television School for student scholarships on recommendations of the school
- to institutions/individuals for film literature and research with associations with the work of Sir David Lean associations.

In 2010 the foundation had assets of £391,000 and an income of £390,000. The income figure has been drawn from the trust's accounts and not the consolidated accounts of the foundation. The foundation's accounts for the year were very thorough; in 2010 the foundation paid grants totalling £311,000.

The beneficiaries were: National Film and Television School (£135,000 for lectures/scholarships); British Academy of Film and Television (£67,000); British Film Institute (£49,000); Royal Academy of Arts (£23,000 for schools/public lectures); University of Southampton (£20,000 for archives); Royal Holloway University of London (£16,500 for David Lean award/scholarships); and Leighton Park School (£500 for scholarships).

Applications

Scholarship grants for students attending the National Film and Television School, Royal Holloway or Leighton Park School, are normally only awarded on the recommendation of the course provider with the trustees.

Other applications for grants that would meet the aims of the foundation are invited in writing, enclosing full details of the project and including financial information and two references.

The Leche Trust

Preservation and restoration of Georgian art, music and architecture

£298,000 to organisations and a further £19,000 to individuals (2009/10).

Beneficial area

UK.

84 Cicada Road, London SW18 2NZ
Tel: 020 8870 6233
Fax: 020 8870 6233
Email: info@lechetrust.org
Website: www.lechetrust.org
Correspondent: Mrs Louisa Lawson, Secretary
Trustees: Dr Ian Bristow; The Hon. Mrs Felicity Guinness; Simon Jervis; Lady Greenstock; Martin Williams; Simon Wethered; Mrs Caroline Laing.
CC Number: 225659

Information available

Accounts were on file at the Charity Commission.

The trust was founded and endowed by the late Mr Angus Acworth in 1950. It supports the following categories (as stated on the trust's website):

1   the promotion of amity and good relations between Britain and third world countries by financing visits to such countries by teachers or other appropriate persons, or providing financial assistance to students from overseas especially those in financial hardship during the last six months of their postgraduate doctorate study in the UK or those engaged in activities consistent with the charitable objects of the trust;
2   assistance to academic, educational or other organisations concerned with music, drama, dance and the arts;
3   the preservation of buildings and their contents and the repair and conservation of church furniture

(including such items as monuments, but excluding structural repairs to the church fabric); preference is to be given to buildings and objects of the Georgian period;
4   assistance to conservation in all its aspects, including in particular museums and encouraging good practice in the art of conservation by supporting investigative and diagnostic reports;
5   the support of charitable bodies or organisations associated with the preservation of the nation's countryside, towns, villages and historic landscapes.

In 2009–10 the trust had assets of £5.7 million and an income of £283,000. Grants paid to individuals totalled £316,000 and were broken down as follows:

Historic buildings: 17 grants totalling £75,000. These included: Middlesex, Twickenham, Strawberry Hill; SAVE Europe's Heritage (£10,000 each); Painswick Rococo Garden Trust, North East Scotland Preservation Trust, The Nelson Monument – Edinburgh (£5,000 each); The National Trust – Erdigg (£4,000); The Hebridean Trust and Osterley Park (£2,500).

Churches: 23 grants totalling £74,000. These included: St Thomas's Church – Stourbridge, St George's Church – Southall, St Alkmund's Church, Shrewsbury (£5,000 each); St Michael & All Angels Church – Great Moulton, All Saints Church – Burton Dassett (£4,000 each); St Peter's Church – Knowstone (£3,500); and St Mary's Church – Stoke Newington (£2,000).

Institutions and museums: 17 grants totalling £66,000. These included: Sir John Soane's Museum – London (£30,000); City and Guilds London School of Art – London, The Watts Gallery, Compton (£5,000 each); College of Arms – London (£3,000); The Royal College of Surgeons of England – London, Frome Museum – Somerset, University of York (£2,500 each); British School at Rome (£2,000); and Wisbech & Fenland Museum – Cambridgeshire (£1,000).

Arts: 34 grants totalling £82,000. These included: Opera Circus – Dorset, Welsh National Opera (£5,000 each); Exaudi Vocal Ensemble – London, Brighton Early Music Festival (£3,000 each); Central School of Ballet – London, New London Children's Choir (£2,500 each); The Oxford Playhouse, Shobana Jeyasingh Dance Company, Shakespeare's Globe – London (£2,000 each); Lichfield Festival and London Song Festival (£1,000 each).;

Education (individuals): 1 grant of £1,500. Made in the form of bursaries to West Dean College.

Overseas students: 16 grants totalling £17,000. These were given to students who are in the final six months of their PhD courses. The average grant was just over £1,100.

Exclusions

No grants are made for: religious bodies; overseas missions; schools and school buildings; social welfare; animals; medicine; expeditions; or British students other than music students.

Applications

In writing to the secretary. Trustees meet three times a year, in February, June and October; applications need to be received the month before.

The Arnold Lee Charitable Trust

Jewish, educational, health

£101,000 (2010/11)

Beneficial area

UK.

Hazlems Fenton LLP, Palladium House, 1–4 Argyll Street, London W1F 7LD
Tel: 020 7437 7666
Correspondent: Hazlems Fenton LLP
Trustees: Edward Michael Lee; Alan Lee.
CC Number: 264437

Information available

Accounts were on file at the Charity Commission, but without an up-to-date grants list.

The policy of the trustees is to distribute income to 'established charities of high repute' for any charitable purpose or object. The

trust supports a large number of Jewish organisations.

In 2010/11 the trust had assets of £1.6 million and an income of £104,000. Grants were made totalling £101,000. The annual report states that grants were made to charities of high repute but there was no list of beneficiaries.

Previous beneficiaries have included Joint Jewish Charitable Trust, Project SEED, Jewish Care, Lubavich Foundations, The Home of Aged Jews, Yesodey Hatorah School and Friends of Akim.

Exclusions

Grants are rarely made to individuals.

Applications

In writing to the correspondent.

The Leigh Trust

Addiction, children and youth, criminal justice, asylum seekers, racial equality and education

£144,000 (2009/10)

Beneficial area

UK and overseas.

Begbies Chettle Agar, Epworth House, 25 City Road, London EC1Y 1AR
Tel: 020 7628 5801
Fax: 020 7628 0390
Correspondent: The Trustees
Trustees: Hon. David Bernstein; Dr R M E Stone; Caroline Moorehead.
CC Number: 275372

Information available

Accounts were available from the Charity Commission.

The Leigh Trust was registered in 1978. Its current policy is to distribute investment revenue and a proportion of capital gains. The trust makes grants to a variety of registered charities concerned with:

- drug and alcohol rehabilitation
- criminal justice
- asylum seekers/racial equality
- education.

The trust states: 'The policy of the trustees is to support those

organisations which they believe to be in greatest need. The trustees can respond favourably to very few applicants.'

In 2009/10 the trust had assets of £2.8 million and an income of nearly £80,000. 25 grants totalling £144,000 were categorised by the trust as follows:

Criminal justice	10	£40,000
Asylum seekers and racial equality	8	£25,000
Addiction	5	£18,000
Children and youth	2	£8,000
Other	1	£5,000

Beneficiaries included: Shelter (£10,000); Birmingham Law Centre (£6,000); Hebron Trust, ASAP, REALLITY, Remedi, Justice First and The Anna Freud Centre (£5,000 each); Tower Hamlets Mission, Church Action on Poverty, Article 1, Renecassin, Not Shut Up Limited and Leeway Women's Aid £3,000 each); Refugee Support Group Devon and New Bridge (£2,000 each); Open Hands Coventry, Barwaqa Relief Organisation, Glenthorne Quaker Centre and OSW (£1,500 each).

Exclusions

The trust does not make grants to individuals.

Applications

Organisations applying for grants must provide their most recent audited accounts, a registered charity number, a cash flow statement for the next 12 months, and a stamped addressed envelope.

Applicants should state clearly on one side of A4 what their charity does and what they are requesting funding for. They should provide a detailed budget and show other sources of funding for the project.

The P Leigh-Bramwell Trust 'E'

Methodist, general charitable purposes

£88,000 (2009/10)

Beneficial area

UK, with a preference for Bolton.

W and J Leigh and Co., Tower Works, Kestor Street, Bolton BL2 2AL
Tel: 01204 521771
Correspondent: Mrs L Cooper, Secretary
Trustees: Mrs H R Leigh-Bramwell; Mrs J Leigh Mitchell; B H Leigh-Bramwell.
CC Number: 267333

Information available

Accounts were available from the Charity Commission, but without a list of grants.

The objects of the charity are to 'advance Christian religion, education, the RNLI and any other legal charitable institution'.

In 2009/10 the trust had assets of over £1.8 million, an income of £89,000 and made grants totalling £88,000. Distributions were made to both regular beneficiaries together with ten additional charitable organisations. There was no list of beneficiary organisations.

Previous beneficiaries include: King's College School (£30,000). Other large beneficiaries included: Leigh-Bramwell Fund (£23,000); The Methodist Church – Bolton (£11,000); Rivington Parish Church (£7,500); The Unicorn School (£7,000); and The Methodist Church – Delph Hill and The Methodist Church – Breightmet (£3,400 each); Barnabus, Bolton Choral Union, Bolton Deaf Society, ChildLine North West, NCH Bypass, West London Mission and YWCA (£500 each).

Exclusions

No grants to individuals.

Applications

In writing to the correspondent; however, please note that previous research suggests that there is only a small amount of funds available for unsolicited applications and therefore success is unlikely.

The Leonard Trust

Christian, overseas aid

£42,000 (2010)

Beneficial area

Overseas and UK, with a preference for Winchester.

18 Edgar Road, Winchester, Hampshire SO23 9TW
Tel: 01962 854 800
Correspondent: Tessa E Feilden
Trustees: Dominic Gold; Christopher Smiley.
CC Number: 1031723

Information available

Accounts were available from the Charity Commission, but without a narrative report.

The trust informed us that it generally makes grants totalling about £30,000 each year, ranging between £1,000 and £5,000 each. It supports Christian and overseas aid organisations. In 2010 the trust had an income of £27,000 and made grants to 8 organisations totalling over £42,000.

Grant recipients were: Tower Hamlets Mission (£25,000); Christian Aid (£6,000); L'Arche Overseas Development Fund (£5,000); Chernobyl Children (£3,000); and Brendon Care and Credit Action (£2,000 each).

Exclusions

No grants to individuals. Medical research or building projects are no longer supported.

Applications

Unsolicited applications cannot be considered.

Lewis Family Charitable Trust

General, Jewish

£551,000 (2009/10)

Beneficial area

UK and Israel.

Chelsea House, West Gate, Ealing, London W5 1DR
Tel: 020 8991 4601
Correspondent: The Secretary
Trustees: David Lewis; Julian Lewis.
CC Number: 259892

Information available

Accounts were available from the Charity Commission.

The trust's annual report stated that:

> The Lewis Family Charitable Trust was established to give expression to the charitable intentions of members of the families of David, Bernard, Geoffrey and Godfrey Lewis and certain companies which they control. The legally permitted objectives are very wide and cover virtually every generally accepted charitable object.

However, in practice the causes to which the trustees have devoted the bulk of their resources in recent years have been medical research, particularly into possible treatments for cancer, Jewish community general charities, general medical support and educational funding.

In 2009/10 the trust had assets of £6.1 million and an income of £1.7 million. Grants were made totalling £551,000, broken down as follows:

Medical research	£139,000
General charitable funding	£126,000
Educational funding	£97,000
Medical – general support	£74,000
Support for the elderly	£56,000
Child care	£33,000
Jewish religious support	£27,000

Though, the vast majority of beneficiaries had a Jewish connection, support was also given to a number of non-Jewish organisations.

Beneficiaries included: Institute of Cancer Research (£80,000); Jewish Care (£56,000); United Jewish Israel Appeal (£50,000); Reform Judaism (£30,000); Weizmann Institute (£25,000); University of Nottingham (£14,000); Policy Exchange Limited, Child Resettlement Fund and Alzheimer's Research Trust (£10,000 each); Casa Shalom (£7,000); UJS Hillel (£5,000); Amutat Orr Shalom (£4,400); Dermatrust, Cancer Backup and Camp Simcha (£2,000 each); Ben Gurion University (£1,600); and Royal British Legion and Kisharon (£1,000 each).

Exclusions

No grants to individuals.

Applications

In writing to the correspondent.

The John Spedan Lewis Foundation

Natural sciences, particularly horticulture, environmental education, ornithology and conservation

£85,000 (2009/10)

Beneficial area
UK.

Partnership House, Carlisle Place, London SW1P 1BX
Tel: 020 7592 6121
Email: bridget_chamberlain@ johnlewis.co.uk
Correspondent: Ms Bridget Chamberlain, Secretary
Trustees: Charlie Mayfield, Chair; David Jones; Dr Vaughan Southgate; Simon Fowler; Miss Tessa Colman.
CC Number: 240473

Information available
Accounts were available from the Charity Commission.

The trust makes grants in the areas of horticulture, environmental education, ornithology and conservation, and to associated educational and research projects. Donations are mainly one-off.

In 2009/10 it had assets of £2.2 million, which generated an income of £94,000. Grants were made to 15 organisations and one individual totalling £85,000.

The beneficiaries included: Learning through Landscapes (£12,000); Cumbria Wildlife Trust (£7,500); Derbyshire Wildlife Trust (£6,000); National Museums Liverpool and University of Sussex (£5,000 each); Freshwater Biological Association, The British Trust for Ornithology and The Grasslands Trust (£4,000 each); and The Charleston Trust and People's Trust for Endangered Species (£1,000 each).

The individual donation was to fund the final year of a PhD student at the University of Reading.

Exclusions
Local branches of national organisations, or for salaries, medical research, welfare projects, building works or overseas expeditions.

Applications
In writing to the correspondent with latest report and accounts and a budget for the proposed project.

Common applicant mistakes
'Approximately 75% of applications are ineligible. They are clearly outside our funding remit.'

The Sir Edward Lewis Foundation

General charitable purposes

£180,000 (2009/10)

Beneficial area
UK and overseas, with a preference for Surrey.

Rawlinson and Hunter, The Lower Mill, Kingston Road, Ewell, Surrey KT17 2AE
Tel: 020 7842 2000
Correspondent: Darren Wing
Trustees: R A Lewis; K W Dent; Christine J A Lewis; Sarah J N Dorin.
CC Number: 264475

Information available
Accounts were available from the Charity Commission.

The trust was established in 1972 by Sir Edward Roberts Lewis. The trust has revised its policy and now plans to make one substantial donation every two or three years to an appropriate cause as well as smaller donations on an annual basis. Therefore it will not distribute all its income every year. The trustees prefer to support charities known personally to them and those favoured by the settlor.

In 2009/10 the foundation had assets of £7.5 million, an income of £477,000 and made grants to 95 organisations totalling £180,000.

Major beneficiaries included: Fareshare (£20,000); The Children's Trust Tadworth; Focus Kensington & Chelsea Foundation; and Ridgegate Home (£10,000 each); and Gurkha Welfare Trust, The David Shepherd Wildlife Foundation and St Anthony's Foundation (£5,000 each).

Other beneficiaries included; The Rugby Clubs (£4,000); Council for Music in Hospitals (£3,000); Ophthalmic Aid to Eastern Europe and Musicians Benevolent Fund (£2,500 each); UK Antarctic Heritage Trust and Trinity Hospice (£2,000 each); Cary Dickinson Breast Cancer and Shipwrecked Fisherman's Society (£1,500 each); RNLI and Soundaround (£1,000 each); and Barnardo's and The Uphill Ski Club (£500 each).

Exclusions
Grants are only given to charities, projects or people known to the trustees. No grants are given to individuals.

Applications
In writing to the correspondent. The trustees meet every six months.

Liberum Foundation

General charitable purposes with a focus on disadvantaged young people

Beneficial area
Not defined, in practice UK.

Ropemaker Place, Level 12, 25 Ropemaker Street, London EC2Y 9LY
Tel: 020 3100 2000
Email: info@liberumfoundation.com
Correspondent: Justine Rumens, Secretary to the Foundation
Trustees: Ms Carolyn Doherty; Simon Stilwell; Antony Scawthorn.
CC Number: 1137475

Information available
Basic information available from the Charity Commission website, further

information received from Carolyn Doherty, Trustee.

This charity was set up in March 2010 for general charitable purposes. The area of benefit is not defined but in practice will be national and the focus will be on disadvantaged young people. Grants will be given to individuals and organisations and will include those for education/training; the prevention or relief of poverty; sport/recreation and community development/employment.

In 2011 funds held were in the region of £60,000.

Exclusions

Adult health; hospitals; animals; older people; the armed services; housing; heritage; environment; and religion.

Applications

In writing to the Secretary.

The Liebreich Foundation

General charitable purposes

Beneficial area

Undefined, in practice the UK and overseas.

11 Pembridge Mews, London W11 3EQ
Email: info@liebreichfoundation.org
Website: www.liebreichfoundation. org/
Correspondent: M D J Liebreich, Correspondent and Trustee
Trustees: M D J Liebreich; Dr J B W Levy; N J Newman.
CC Number: 1136835

Information available

Basic information available from the Charity Commission. Accounts not due for this new charity.

This charity was established in March 2010 for general charitable purposes. It makes grants to other charities and voluntary organisations.

Michael Liebreich is also a trustee of St Mark's Hospital Foundation (Charity Commission No. 1088119).

Applications

In writing to the correspondent.

Lifeline 4 Kids

Equipment for children with disabilities

£132,000 (2010)

Beneficial area

Worldwide.

215 West End Lane, West Hampstead, London NW6 1XJ
Tel: 020 794 1661
Fax: 020 7794 1161
Email: rda@lifeline4kids.org
Website: www.lifeline4kids.org
Correspondent: Roger Adelman
Trustees: Roger Adelman, Chair; Paul Maurice; Beverley Emden; Mrs Roberta Harris; Irving Millman; Jeffrey Bonn.
CC Number: 200050

Information available

Accounts were on file at the Charity Commission, but without a list of grants. Information was available on the trust's website.

This charity supports children who are disabled up to 18 years old. The following description is taken from its website:

> We are a London based children's charity established in 1961. Originally known as 'The Handicapped Children's Aid Committee', our working name has now changed to Lifeline 4 Kids. Our members work on an entirely voluntary basis and we have no paid staff.
>
> We were formed for one purpose – to provide essential equipment to help improve the quality of life for children with disabilities and special needs irrespective of their race or creed.
>
> ▹ Schools, children's hospices, respite care homes and support centres throughout the UK receive our help with equipment including playground equipment, soft play and multi-sensory rooms and special beds.
> ▹ For the individual child we provide the full spectrum of specialised equipment such as electric wheelchairs, mobility aids and varying items including specialised computers. We are also one of the only UK charities prepared to help a special needs child from a low-income family with essential smaller items such as shoes, clothing, bedding and specialist toys.
> ▹ We are able to give emergency and welfare appeals immediate approval within the authorised limits of our welfare sub-committee.
> ▹ We also help equip hospital neonatal units with the latest incubators, infusion pumps and ultrasonic monitors amongst other life saving equipment.
> ▹ No appeal is too large or too small for us to consider.

In 2010 the charity had assets of £659,000, an income of £187,000 and gave £132,000 in response to appeals. Details of the successful applicants were not included with the accounts.

Please note that the trust does not give financial support, but purchases equipment directly for and on behalf of the beneficiary.

Assistance given in 2006 included that to: Central Middlesex Hospital, towards equipment for its outdoor play area (£5,000); the Living Paintings Trust, funding the production of 20 copies of a new Living Picture Book (£2,500); the New Jumbulance Travel Trust, providing two portable instant resuscitation packs (£2,400); Vision Aid, providing a specialised flat screen video magnifier (£2,000); and the Lothian Autistic Society, for equipment for its various play schemes (£1,500).

Exclusions

Building projects, research grants and salaries will not be funded.

Applications

Applications for help indicating specific requirements and brief factual information must initially be made in writing, addressed to the correspondent, or by email (appeals@lifeline4kids.org).

The charity states on its website that:

> Each request will be acknowledged and provided it meets our criteria, an application form will be sent by post or email. The form contains comprehensive questions relating to the child/children's medical condition and requires backup information from health professionals together with a financial statement of the applicant/ organisation.
>
> After we have received the completed application form, if appropriate, the appeal will be investigated personally by one of our members.

The majority of appeals are discussed and decided upon at our monthly meetings. If approved, a maximum sum is allocated and we take full responsibility for the purchase and safe delivery of the approved item.

Initial telephone calls from applicants are not welcome.

The Limbourne Trust

Environment, welfare, arts

£88,000 (2009/10)

Beneficial area

UK and overseas.

Downs Farm, Homersfield, Harleston, Norwich IP20 0NS
Correspondent: Elisabeth Anne Thistlethwayte, Trustee
Trustees: Elisabeth Thistlethwayte; Katharine Thistlethwayte; Jennifer Lindsay; Jane Chetwynd Atkinson; Jocelyn Magnus.
CC Number: 1113796

Information available

Accounts were available from the Charity Commission.

The trust's financial statements for 2011 state:

The charity has wide charitable objects, which encompass the benefit of communities throughout the world, and in particular the advancement of education, the protection of health, and the relief of poverty, distress and sickness.

The charity will also seek to challenge all forms of oppression and inequality, and will prioritise funding for groups who assist people who are unable to take a full role in society due to economic, political and social disadvantage.

The charity will seek to achieve these objectives by providing grant funding for other charities working in the following fields:

- research into renewable energy sources
- development of organic farming methods
- development of environmentally sustainable projects
- overcoming adverse effects of climate change
- community projects to assist those at disadvantage

- protection and conservation of the environment
- promote the public education in and appreciation of literature, music and drama
- other charitable purposes as the trustees from time to time may decide.

In 2009/10 the trust had assets of £2.2 million and an income of £86,000. Grants totalled £88,000.

Beneficiaries included: Chicks (£13,000); Norfolk and Norwich Families House and Journey of a Lifetime Trust (£12,000 each); EACH (£10,000); Vauxhall City Farm (£10,000); Whirlow Hall Farm Trust (£5,500); Aldeburgh Music (£5,000); Grasslands Trust (£4,000); Buckingham Emergency Fund Appeal (£1,000); and Metfield United Charities (£660).

Applications

The trust states: 'The trustees will seek to identify those projects where the greatest and widest benefit can be attained, and usually will only consider written applications and, where necessary, make further enquiries.' Trustees meet three times a year.

Limoges Charitable Trust

General, including health, heritage and community

£50,000 (2005/06)

Beneficial area

UK, with a preference for Birmingham.

c/o Tyndallwoods Solicitors, 29 Woodbourne Road, Edgbaston, Birmingham B17 8BY
Tel: 0121 693 2222
Fax: 0121 693 0844
Correspondent: Judy Ann Dyke, Trustee
Trustees: Mike Dyer; Albert Kenneth Dyer; Judy Ann Dyke; Andrew Milner.
CC Number: 1016178

Information available

Full accounts were available from the Charity Commission website.

The trust has general charitable purposes, although there are preferences for animal, health, heritage and community organisations. Many of the beneficiaries are based in Birmingham.

In 2009/10 the trust had assets of £862,000 and an income of £31,000. Grants totalled £86,000 and were distributed as follows:

Education	£3,300
Health and welfare	£39,000
Animals	£2,800
Youth	£4,000
Environment	£3,500
Nautical	£2,100
Heritage and community	£31,000

Beneficiaries included: Birmingham Museum and Art Gallery (£18,000 in two grants); Moseley Community Development Trust and Moseley Street Wardens (£10,000 each); Edward's Trust Limited (£6,000 in two grants); THSH, University of Birmingham, National Memorial Arboretum and Birmingham Early Music Festival (£2,000 each); and St Ildiernas Church (£1,600).

Applications

In writing to the correspondent.

The Lind Trust

Social action, community and Christian service

£1 million to organisations and individuals (2009/10)

Beneficial area

UK.

Tithe Barn, Attlebridge, Norwich, Norfolk NR9 5AA
Tel: 01603 262 626
Correspondent: Gavin Croft Wilcox, Trustee
Trustees: Leslie C Brown; Dr Graham M Dacre; Gavin C Wilcock; Mrs Julia M Dacre; Russell B Dacre; Samuel E Dacre
CC Number: 803174

Information available

Accounts were available from the Charity Commission.

This trust makes grants to individuals and organisations and also lets its properties to charities at a peppercorn rent.

In 2009/10 the trust had assets of £14.7 million and an income of £3 million. Grants were made to charities, organisations and individuals totalling £1 million. No breakdown of this was available, except for a donation of £190,000 to the Open Youth Trust.

In April 2010 the Trustees made commitments to donate £5,000 per year for two years to the Prince's Trust and £5,000 per year for two years to the Matthew Project.

Applications

In writing to the correspondent at any time. However, the trust commits most of its funds in advance, giving the remainder to eligible applicants as received.

Lindale Educational Foundation

Roman Catholic, education

£77,000 (2009/10)

Beneficial area

UK and overseas.

6 Orme Court, London W2 4RL
Tel: 020 7243 9417
Correspondent: J Valero
Trustees: Netherhall Educational Association; Dawliffe Hall Educational Foundation; Greygarth Association.
CC Number: 282758

Information available

Accounts were available from the Charity Commission.

The foundation supports the Roman Catholic religion and the advancement of education. Its aims are to:

- train priests
- establish, extend, improve and maintain churches, chapels, oratories and other places of worship
- establish, extend, improve and maintain university halls and halls of residence for students of all nationalities
- arrange and conduct courses, camps, study centres, meetings, conferences and seminars
- provide financial support for education or research by individuals or groups of students
- provide financial support for other individuals or institutions which meet the trust's criteria, including the corporate trustees.

In 2009/10 the foundation had assets of £30,000 and an income of £77,000. Grants were made totalling £77,000.

Beneficiaries were: Netherhall Educational Association Centre for Retreats and Study (eight grants totalling £56,500); Thornycroft Hall (four grants totalling £20,200).

Exclusions

No grants to individuals.

Applications

In writing to the correspondent, but note that most funds are already committed.

The Linden Charitable Trust

Medical, healthcare, the arts

£63,500 (2009/10)

Beneficial area

UK, with a preference for West Yorkshire.

c/o Baker Tilly, The Waterfront, Salts Mill Road, Shipley BD17 7EZ
Tel: 01274 536400
Correspondent: Miss M H Pearson, Trustee
Trustees: Miss M H Pearson; J F H Swales; G L Holbrook.
CC Number: 326788

Information available

Accounts were available from the Charity Commission.

Currently, the trust's policy is to benefit charities specialising in cancer relief and research, those particularly involved with hospices, those involved in arts and also a wider range of charities based in and around Leeds, West Yorkshire. The trustees have agreed (2009/10) to make a regular donation to Leeds International Pianoforte Competition of £10,000 per year.

In 2009/10 the trust had assets of £2.4 million and an income of £55,000. Grants were made totalling £63,500. Beneficiaries included: Leeds International Pianoforte Competition (£10,000); Macmillan Cancer Relief (£5,000); Marie Curie Cancer Care (£3,000); Leeds Lieder, Martin House Hospice and Mission for Seafarers (£2,000 each); Caring for Life, Combat Stress and Live Music Now (£1,000 each); and Listening Books (£500).

Exclusions

No grants to individuals.

Applications

In writing to the correspondent.

The Linmardon Trust

General

£14,000 (2009/10)

Beneficial area

UK, with a preference for the Nottingham area.

HSBC Trust Company (UK) Limited, Norwich House, Nelson Gate, Commercial Road, Southampton SO15 1GX
Tel: 023 8072 2240
Correspondent: Lee Topp, Trust Manager
Trustee: HSBC Trust Company (UK) Limited.
CC Number: 275307

Information available

Accounts were available from the Charity Commission.

The trust supports charities in the UK with a preference for those in the Nottingham area. The trustees prefer to support a greater number of small donations to various charities throughout the year.

In 2009/10, it had assets of nearly £1.2 million and an income of £787,000. Grants totalling £14,000 were made to nine organisations.

Beneficiaries were: Jubilee Sailing Trust (£3,000); Children with Leukaemia, Young Minds and Children's Liver Disease Foundation (£2,000 each); and 3H Fund, Princess Royal Trust for Carers, React, Martha Trust and Streatham Youth and Community Trust (£1,000 each).

Exclusions

Grants are made to registered charities only. No support to individuals.

Applications

In writing to the correspondent. The trustees meet quarterly, generally in February, May, August and November.

The Ruth and Stuart Lipton Charitable Trust

Jewish charities and general charitable purposes

£37,000 (2009/10)

Beneficial area

UK and overseas.

Lewis Golden and Co., 40 Queen Ann Street, London W1G 9EL
Tel: 020 7580 7313
Correspondent: N W Benson, Trustee
Trustees: Sir S Lipton; Lady Lipton; N W Benson.
CC Number: 266741

Information available

Accounts were available from the Charity Commission.

The trust was founded by property/art mogul Stuart Lipton and his wife in 1973.

In 2009/10 the trust had assets of £562,000 and an income of £30,000. Grants to 28 organisations totalled £37,000. There is no minimum limit for any grant and all grants must be approved unanimously by the trustees.

Grant beneficiaries included: Nightingale (£9,500); Royal Opera House (£7,000); Jewish Care (£5,500); United Synagogue (£4,000); British Technion Society (£500); Well Being of Women (£250); and Help for Heroes (£100).

Exclusions

No grants to individuals.

Applications

In writing to the correspondent.

The Lister Charitable Trust

Outdoor activities for disadvantaged young people

£171,000 (2009/10)

Beneficial area

UK.

43 High Street, Marlow, Buckinghamshire SL7 1BA
Tel: 01628 477879
Email: info@apperleylimited.co.uk
Correspondent: Nicholas Yellowlees, Accountant
Trustees: Noel A V Lister; David A Collingwood; Penny A Horne; Paul A Lister; Sylvia J Lister.
CC Number: 288730

Information available

Accounts were available from the Charity Commission.

The trust's annual report and accounts for 2008/09 included the following statement:

> The trust formerly had strong links to the UK Sailing Academy but this is now primarily supported by the Whirlwind Charitable Trust having been seeded with £4m capital sum by the trust in June 2007. This has enabled the Lister Charity to have greater impact in other areas of charitable support as demonstrated by the list of donations made during the year.

In 2009/10 the trust had assets of £7.5 million and an income of £173,000. Grants were made during the year to seven organisations totalling £171,000.

The beneficiaries during the year were: The European Nature Trust (£88,000); University of Miami (£64,000); Home Start Ashford (£10,000); Embercombe (£3,000); The Juvenile Diabetes Research Foundation (£2,500); Light Dragons (£2,000); and Sport Relief (£1,000).

Exclusions

Applications from individuals, including students, are ineligible. No grants are made in response to general appeals from large UK organisations or to smaller bodies working in areas outside its criteria.

Applications

In writing to the correspondent. Applications should include clear details of the need the intended project is designed to meet, plus an outline budget. Only applications from eligible bodies are acknowledged, when further information may be requested.

The Second Joseph Aaron Littman Foundation

General charitable purposes

£251,000 (2009/10)

Beneficial area

UK.

Berkeley Law (Ref: GCH/L2556/1), 19 Berkeley Street, London W1J 8ED
Correspondent: Glenn Hurstfield, Trustee
Trustees: Mrs C C Littman; R J Littman; Glenn Hurstfield.
CC Number: 201892

Information available

Accounts were available from the Charity Commission.

This trust has general charitable purposes with special preference for academic and medical research.

In 2009/10 it had assets of £5.4 million and an income of £300,000. Grants were made totalling £251,000.

The main beneficiary, as in previous years, was Littman Library of Jewish Civilisation which received £208,000. There were 10 further donations listed in the accounts. Beneficiaries included: The Spiro Ark (£10,000); Hadassah UK (£5,000); Westminster Synagogue (£3,500); The Misholin Children's Centre and JNF (£2,500 each); and Libra Foundation (£250).

Exclusions
Applications from individuals are not considered.

Applications
The trust's funds are fully committed and no new applications are considered.

Jack Livingstone Charitable Trust

Jewish, general
£67,000 (2009/10)

Beneficial area
UK and worldwide, with a preference for Manchester.

Westholme, The Springs, Bowdon, Altrincham, Cheshire WA14 3JH
Tel: 0161 928 3232
Correspondent: Janice Livingstone, Trustee
Trustees: Janice Livingstone; Terence Livingstone; Brian White.
CC Number: 263473

Information available
Accounts were on file at the Charity Commission.

In 2009/10 the trust had assets of £2 million, an income of £85,000 and made grants totalling £67,000.

Beneficiaries included: Manchester City Art Gallery (£10,000); R Chritake Trust (£6,000); King David School, SO Community Security and Morris F Homes (£5,000 each); London FDN Patrons and Manchester Jewish

Federation (£3,000 each); British Friends (£1,500); and Stockdales, Southport New Synagogue, Israel Children's Tennis Centers and Aish Hatorah (£1,000 each).

Other grants of less than £1,000 totalled £8,600.

Applications
The trust does not respond to unsolicited applications.

The Elaine and Angus Lloyd Charitable Trust

General
£78,000 (2009/10)

Beneficial area
UK, with a preference for Surrey, Kent and the South of England.

3rd Floor, North Side, Dukes Court, 32 Duke Street, St James's, London
Tel: 0207 930 7797
Correspondent: Ross Badger
Trustees: C R H Lloyd; A S Lloyd; J S Gordon; Sir Michael Craig-Cooper; Mrs V E Best; J S Lloyd; Mrs Philippa Satchwell Smith; Revd R J Lloyd.
CC Number: 237250

Information available
Accounts were available from the Charity Commission.

In 1992, the Elaine Lloyd Charitable Trust and the Mr Angus Lloyd Charitable Settlement were amalgamated and are now known as the Elaine and Angus Lloyd Charitable Trust. Many grants are recurrent, some may be paid quarterly. Grants are mainly to UK charities and local organisations in the Surrey and Kent area and elsewhere in the South of England. Grants are given in practice to those charities known to one or more of the trustees. Donations are made to:

- any charitable institution whether incorporated or not
- any individual recipients to assist them in meeting education expenses either for themselves or their children

- any individual recipients whose circumstances are such they come within the legal conception of poverty.

In 2009/10 the trust had assets of £2.3 million and an income of £86,000. Grants totalled £78,000 including £5,000 in grants to individuals and £73,000 in grants to organisations.

Beneficiaries included: EHAS (£4,000); Alive and Kicking and Positive Initiative Trust (£2,500 each); Brighton and Hove Parents and Children's Group, Monday to Wednesday Club, Rhema Partnership Mission Hospital and Rhema Religious and Charitable Trust (£2,000 each); the Grange Centre and the Willow Foundation (£1,000 each).

Exclusions
No support for overseas aid.

Applications
In writing to the correspondent. The trustees meet regularly to consider grants.

The Charles Lloyd Foundation

Construction, repair and maintenance of Roman Catholic buildings, the advancement of Roman Catholic religion, and music
£78,000 (2009/10)

Beneficial area
The Roman Catholic Dioceses of Menevia and Wrexham.

8–10 Grosvenor Road, Wrexham, Clwyd LL11 1BU
Tel: 01978 291 000
Fax: 01978 290493
Email: vincentryan@allingtonhughes. co.uk
Correspondent: Vincent Ryan, Trustee
Trustees: Revd C D S Lloyd; P Walters; T V Ryan; R C A Thorn.
CC Number: 235225

Information available

Accounts were available from the Charity Commission.

The foundation supports the construction, repair or maintenance of Roman Catholic churches, houses, convents and monasteries, the advancement of Roman Catholic charities in the beneficial area and the promotion and advancement of music, either religious or secular, for public appreciation in or towards national Catholic charities operating in the area of benefit. It prefers to give one-off donations for specific projects.

In 2009/10 it had assets of £1.2 million, which generated an income of £45,000. Grants were made to four organisations totalling £78,000; which went to: Welshpool Catholic Church (£42,000); the Carmelites – Dolgellau (£25,000); Abergele Catholic Church (£7,000); and Tywyn Catholic Church (£2,000).

Applications

In writing to the correspondent. The trust asks for 'evidence of hardship'. Unsuccessful applications are not acknowledged.

Lloyd's Charities Trust

General

£431,000 (2010)

Beneficial area

UK, with particular interest in East London.

One Lime Street, London EC3M 7HA
Tel: 020 7327 6075
Fax: 020 7327 6368
Email: communityaffairs@lloyds.com
Website: www.lloyds.com
Correspondent: Mrs Vicky Mirfin, Secretary
Trustees: Ms Holly Bellingham; Grahame Chilton; Graham White; David Gittings; Lawrence Holder; John Spencer; Iain Wilson; Ms Sue Langley; Rupert Atkin; Charles Harbord- Hamond.
CC Number: 207232

Information available

Accounts were available from the Charity Commission.

The charity was set up in 1953, and is the charitable arm of Lloyd's insurance market in London. In 2010 the trust had assets of £2.5 million and an income of £490,000. Grants were made in the form of donations and bursaries totalling £431,000. Grant making during the year is described in the 2010 report as follows:

General fund

Following the 2009 review of the Lloyd's Charities Trust's charitable giving strategy, new funding priorities were introduced in 2010 to maximise the impact of the Trust's charitable giving, by focusing on three key areas:

Making a great city greater: supporting London-based charities to help those that are disadvantaged and foster opportunity.

Responding to disasters and emergencies: responding to emergency appeals to help relieve suffering and rebuild lives.

Preparing for the future: providing support to equip individuals and communities with the resources and skills they need to meet the challenges of a rapidly changing world.

To meet the above funding priorities, Lloyd's Charities Trust continued with its policy of working closely with a small number of partner charities over a three-year period, made ad-hoc donations in response to international emergencies and City appeals and made donations through the Lloyd's Market Charity Awards scheme.

Cuthbert Heath Centenary Fund

In the 2009 review it was agreed that the income of the Cuthbert Heath Centenary Fund, which had previously been providing bursaries at nine public schools, should be used to benefit a greater number of young people with a particular focus on young people. The management board of Lloyd's Community Programme is now providing recommendations for the use of the fund.

Lloyd's Community Programme

Lloyds Community Programme (LCP) aims to meet its objective of improving the opportunities and the environment for communities in Tower Hamlets and neighbouring East London boroughs by mobilising the support and involvement of individuals and companies in the Lloyds market, primarily through volunteering. LCP also funds local organisations in the field of education, employability and enterprise.

Lloyd's Market Charity Awards

These provide employees within the Lloyd's markets to apply for donations of £1,000 on behalf of their chosen charities. During 2010 30 £1,000 donations were rewarded.

Exclusions

No grants for any appeal where it is likely that the grant would be used for sectarian purposes or to local or regional branches of charities where it is possible to support the UK organisation. Support is not given to individuals.

Applications

Lloyd's Charities Trust makes ad hoc donations, however the majority of funds are committed to supporting the partnership charities the trust works with. The trust has previously stated that as funds are committed over a three-year period 'we are unable to respond positively to the numerous appeals we receive'. Applications are not being invited for partner charity status.

Llysdinam Charitable Trust

Natural sciences, horticulture, Christian, relief of poverty

£39,000 (2009/10)

Beneficial area

Wales.

Rees Richards and Partners, Druslyn House, De La Beche Street, Swansea SA1 3HH
Tel: 01792 650 705

Fax: 01792 468 384
Email: post@reesrichards.co.uk
Correspondent: The Trustees
Trustees: Mary Elster; Norman Tyler; Emma Birkmyre.
CC Number: 255528

Information available

Accounts were on file at the Charity Commission.

The trust has four main areas of interest:

▶ the advancement of education in the natural sciences, particularly botany and biology
▶ the advancement (so far as legally charitable) of horticulture, agriculture and silviculture
▶ the advancement of the Christian religion in Wales and in particular by support of the Church of Wales
▶ the relief of poverty in Wales and particularly in the parishes of Llysdlnam, Llanfihangel-Bryn-Pabuan and Llanafan Fawr in the County of Brecon and the Parish of Llanyre in the county of Radnor.

In 2009/10 the trust had assets of £4.4 million and an income of £119,000. Grants were made totalling £39,000.

Beneficiaries included: University of Wales – Cardiff (£16,000); Llysdinam Field Centre (£11,000); Powys Arts Forum and Shakespeare Link (£2,000 each); National Gardens Scheme (£1,300); Llandokery College Arts Centre and Combat Stress (£1,000 each); Cyrnryd Rhan (£800); the Sequel Trust (£750); Wales Air Ambulance (£210); and NSPCC (£180).

Exclusions
No grants to individuals.

Applications
The trust has previously stated that it is overloaded with applications and does not welcome unsolicited applications.

Common applicant mistakes
'Applications for assistance outside designated area, i.e. Wales.'

Localtrent Ltd

Jewish, education, religion
£173,000 (2009/10)

Beneficial area
UK, with some preference for Manchester.

Lopian Gross Barnett and Co, 6th Floor, Cardinal House, 20 St Mary's Parsonage, Manchester M3 2LG
Tel: 0161 832 8721
Fax: 0161 835 3085
Correspondent: A Kahan, Administrator
Trustees: Hyman Weiss; Mina Weiss; Philip Weiss; Zisel Weiss; Bernardin Weiss; Yocheved Weiss.
CC Number: 326329

Information available
Full accounts were on file at the Charity Commission.

The trust was established in 1983 for the distribution of funds to religious, educational and similar charities for the advancement of the Jewish religion.

In 2009/10 the trust had assets of £246,000 and an income of £217,000. Grants totalling £173,000 were described in the trust's accounts as being made to:

> A number of institutions which carry out activities such as providing Orthodox Jewish education and other activities which advance Jewish religion in accordance with the Orthodox Jewish faith (e.g. the Chasdei Yoel Charitable Trust: grant £53,000; Kesser Torah School: grant £4,000).

Previous beneficiaries have also included: Modos Belz, Yeshivas Sharei Zion, Congregation Beth Medrash Chemed, 3 Pillars Charity, Asser Bishvil, BAT, Manchester Killel and Talmudical Torah Yetev Lev.

Applications
In writing to the correspondent.

The Locker Foundation

Mainly Jewish charities
£500,000 (2009/10)

Beneficial area
UK and overseas.

28 High Road, East Finchley, London N2 9PJ
Tel: 020 8455 9280
Correspondent: Irving Carter, Trustee
Trustees: I Carter; M Carter; Mrs S Segal.
CC Number: 264180

Information available
Accounts were available from the Charity Commission.

The trust mainly supports Jewish organisations. Its objects are for general charitable purposes with a preference for the welfare of the sick and those with disabilities and the teaching of the Jewish religion. In 2009/10 it had assets of £4.5 million and an income of £540,000. It made 33 grants totalling £500,000.

Beneficiaries included: Magen David Adom (£100,000); Kahal Chassidim Babov (£60,000); British Friends of Israel War Disabled (£35,000); Ezer Mizion (£25,000); Chai Cancer Care and WIZO (£20,000 each); Jewish Blind and Disabled and Jewish Care (£15,000 each); World Jewish Relief (£10,000); North London Hospice (£6,000); Wolfson Hillel Primary School (£5,000); Birmingham Jewish Community Care (£2,000); St John's Wood Synagogue and Zionist Federation (£1,000 each); Jewish Women's Week British WIZO (£200); and St Peter & St James Hospice (£100).

Applications
In writing to the correspondent.

The Loftus Charitable Trust

Jewish

£260,000 (2009/10)

Beneficial area

UK and overseas.

Asher House, Blackburn Road, London NW6 1AW
Tel: 020 7604 5900
Correspondent: Anthony Loftus, Trustee
Trustees: R I Loftus; A L Loftus; A D Loftus.
CC Number: 297664

Information available

Accounts were available from the Charity Commission.

The trust was established in 1987 by Richard Ian Loftus. Its objects are the:
▸ advancement of the Jewish religion
▸ advancement of Jewish education and the education of Jewish people
▸ relief of the Jewish poor.

In 2009/10 the trust had an income of £264,000 and made grants totalling £260,000. These were categorised as follows: relief of poverty and ill-health (£111,000); religious organisations (£94,000); and education (£56,000).

The largest grants were to: Chabad Lubavitch (£25,000); Norwood (£21,500); Kisharon and UK Friends of AWIS (£20,000 each); Community Security Trust (£15,000); and British Friends of Sulam (£12,500).

Smaller grants included those to: One Family (£7,800); Lubavitch Foundation (£7,500); Chief Rabbinate Trust Magen David Adom UK and Nightingale House (£5,000 each); British Friends of Affa Institute (£4,000); and JNF Charitable Trust and TZEDEK (£2,500 each).

Applications

The trustees' state that all funds are committed and unsolicited applications are not welcome.

The Lolev Charitable Trust

Orthodox Jewish

£224,000 to organisations (2009)

Beneficial area

Worldwide.

14a Gilda Crescent, London N16 6JP
Correspondent: Abraham Tager, Trustee
Trustees: Abraham Tager; Eve Tager; Michael Tager.
CC Number: 326249

Information available

The latest accounts available at the Charity Commission were for 2009.

The objects of the charity are the relief of the sick and needy and the support of Orthodox Jewish education.

The latest accounts available were for 2009. In this year the trust had an income of £3 million and assets of £37,000. The trust gave £3 million in grants of which £224,000 was given to organisations and £2.7 million was given to individuals.

Grants to organisations were broken down as follows:

Religious education	£125,000
Poor and needy	£56,000
Medical	£29,000
Schools	£12,000

Applications

In writing to the correspondent.

The London Law Trust

Health and personal development of children and young people

£142,500 (2009/10)

Beneficial area

UK.

Hunters, 9 New Square, Lincoln's Inn, London WC2A 3QN
Tel: 020 7412 0050

Email: londonlawtrust@ hunters-solicitors.co.uk
Website: www.thelondonlawtrust.org
Correspondent: G D Ogilvie, Secretary
Trustees: Prof. Anthony R Mellows; R A Pellant; Sir Michael Hobbs; Sir Ian Gainsford.
CC Number: 1115266

Information available

Accounts were available from the Charity Commission.

The trust's aims have been to support charities which:
▸ prevent or cure illness and disability in children and young people – via seed-corn grants and grants towards small research projects
▸ alleviate or reduce the causes or likelihood of illness and disability in children and young people – via grants for new ventures and to small support groups for children and young people suffering from more obscure conditions
▸ encourage and develop in young people the qualities of leadership and service to the community – via grants to national organisations for specific purposes.

During the year 2009/10, the trustees decided to discontinue for the future supporting charities in the first of these categories, and they made their final grants in this field. They continued to make grants in the other two categories. Instead of making further grants to charities in the first of the categories, the trustees have continued with the recently introduced The London Law Trust Medal, in association with King's College London. The Medal carries with it an eighteen-month Research Career Establishment Fellowship which is funded jointly by the trustees and the College.

The Fellowship is awarded for research in medicine or dentistry which is designed to impact on patient care. Candidates are selected on merit by a panel constituted by the College and including up to two trustees of The London Law Trust. Two Medals may be awarded in any year.

In 2009/10 the trust had assets of £3.5 million and an income of

£128,000. Grants were made to organisations totalling £67,500. The beneficiaries were not listed in the accounts. In addition the trustees resolved to make 2 of The London Law Trust Medal awards totalling £75,000 (2009: 1 award of £37,500).

Previous beneficiaries have included: BRIC, British Lung Foundation, Deans & Canons of Windsor, Great Ormond Street and St George's Hospital Medical School (£5,000 each); Envision (£3,000); Activenture and Swan Syndrome (£2,500 each); and Circomedia (£1,000).

Exclusions

Applications from individuals, including students, are ineligible.

Applications

Usually, in writing to the correspondent. However, the Secretary to the Trust has informed us (July 2011) that: 'The funds for the London Law Trust are fully committed for the present and for the foreseeable future. Therefore the trust regrets that it is unable to consider any new applications for grants at the moment.'

The trustees employ a grant advisor whose job is to evaluate applications. Grant applicants are requested to supply detailed information in support of their applications. The grant advisor makes on-site visits to all applicants and makes a written report

The directors of the trust meet twice a year to consider the grant advisor's individual visit reports together with the application form, latest accounts and other supporting information. Most grants are awarded in late Autumn.

The William and Katherine Longman Trust

General

£195,000 (2009/10)

Beneficial area

UK.

Charles Russell LLP, 8–10 New Fetter Lane, London EC4A 1RS
Tel: 020 7203 5196
Correspondent: Mrs G Feeney
Trustees: W P Harriman; A C O Bell.
CC Number: 800785

Information available

Accounts were on file at the Charity Commission.

The trust supports a wide range of organisations with grants ranging from £1,000 to £30,000 each, mostly at the lower end of the scale.

In 2009/10 it had assets of £3.5 million, which generated an income of £102,000. Grants were made totalling £195,000. Management and administration charges were relatively high at £30,000.

Past beneficiaries of grants of £10,000 or more included: Vanessa Grant Trust (£30,000); Chelsea Festival and World Child Cancer Fund (£20,000 each); Care (£12,000); and Hope Education Trust and RADA (£10,000 each).

Other beneficiaries included: Action for ME (£5,000); The Children's Society (£4,500); Age Concern – Kensington & Chelsea (£3,500); RSPCA – Harmsworth Hospital (£3,000); St Mungo's (£2,500); and Prisoners Abroad (£1,000).

Exclusions

Grants are only made to registered charities.

Applications

The trustees believe in taking a proactive approach in deciding which charities to support and it is their policy not to respond to unsolicited appeals.

The Loseley and Guildway Charitable Trust

General

£40,000 (2009/10)

Beneficial area

International and UK, with an interest in Guildford.

The Estate Offices, Loseley Park, Guildford, Surrey GU3 1HS
Tel: 01483 405 114
Fax: 01483 302 036
Email: charities@loseleypark.co.uk
Website: www.loseley-park.com/charities.asp
Correspondent: Mrs Julia Barnes, Secretary
Trustees: Maj. James More-Molyneux, Chair; Susan More-Molyneux; Michael More-Molyneux; Alexander More-Molyneux; Glye Hodson.
CC Number: 267178

Information available

Accounts were available from the Charity Commission.

The trust was founded in 1973, when the More-Molyneux family injected private capital and transferred five of their own properties to the trust. The rent of these properties provides about half the trust's present income. Two of these properties have now been sold in order to finance the purchase of land on which CHASE Children's Hospice has now been built.

The trust's accounts state that:

> The objects of the charity are widely drawn to include making grants to charitable associations, trusts, societies and corporations whether they are local, national or international. The major part of the available funds tend to be distributed locally to charitable institutions which the trustees consider to be particularly worthy of support.

In effect this means that major grants tend to be given to charities with which various members of the More-Molyneux family and trustees are associated.

In 2009/10 the trust had assets of £1.2 million, an income of £63,000 and made grants totalling £40,000 of which those over £1,000 (18) were listed in the accounts. Beneficiaries included: CHASE and Disability Challengers (£5,000 each); Brooke Hospital, Cherry Trees, Crisis, Gurkha Welfare Trust, National Society for Epilepsy, Phyllis Tuckwell Hospice, RNLI and Wells for India (£1,000 each).

Exclusions

No grants to individuals or non-registered charities.

Applications

In writing to the correspondent. The trustees meet in February, May and September to consider applications. However, due to commitments, new applications for any causes are unlikely to be successful.

The Lotus Foundation

Children and families, women, community, animal protection, addiction recovery, education

£201,000 (2010)

Beneficial area

UK, especially London and Surrey; occasionally overseas.

c/o Startling Music Ltd, 90 Jermyn Street, London SW1Y 6JD
Tel: 020 7930 5133
Website: www.lotusfoundation.com
Correspondent: Barbara Starkey, Trustee
Trustees: Mrs B Starkey; R Starkey; Mrs E Turner.
CC Number: 1070111

Information available

Accounts were on file at the Charity Commission.

The trust was established in 1998 and aims to make grants to other established and newly-formed charities. The primary objectives of the trust are: 'to support those charities that fall within our aims, [i.e.] children and youth, medical, substance abuse and domestic violence, education, animal welfare and community charities'.

In 2010 the trust had an income of £216,000 and holds assets of £72,000. They made grants totalling £201,000 which were broken down as follows:

Children/Youth	£60,000
Medical	£60,000
Substance abuse/ Domestic Violence	£37,000
Community	£33,000
Animals	£10,000
Education	£1,000

Beneficiaries included: Great Ormond Street Tick Tock Club (£25,000); Whizz Kids (£10,000); Marie Curie Cancer Care (£10,000); Médecins Sans Frontières (£20,000); Action on Addiction (£5,000); RAPT (£32,000); Gosden House School (£1,000); Battersea Dogs and Cats Home (£10,000); Cranleigh Lions Club (£2,000); Samaritans (£1,000).

Exclusions

No response to circular appeals. No grants to individuals, non-registered charities, charities working outside of the foundation's areas of interest, or for research purposes.

Applications

In writing to the correspondent giving a brief outline of the work, amount required and project/programme to benefit. The trustees prefer applications which are simple and economically prepared rather than glossy 'prestige' and mail sorted brochures.

Note: In order to reduce administration costs and concentrate its efforts on the charitable work at hand, unsolicited requests will no longer be acknowledged by the foundation.

Common applicant mistakes

'Applications which do not meet the stated criteria.'

The C L Loyd Charitable Trust

General

£77,000 (2009/10)

Beneficial area

UK, with a preference for Berkshire and Oxfordshire.

Betterton House, Lockinge, Wantage, Oxfordshire OX12 8QL
Tel: 01235 833 265
Correspondent: C L Loyd, Trustee

Trustees: A Loyd; T C Loyd; C L Lord.
CC Number: 265076

Information available

Accounts were available from the Charity Commission.

The trust supports UK charities and local charities (in Berkshire and Oxfordshire) involved in welfare, animals, churches, medical and disability, children, youth and education.

In 2009/10 the trust had assets of £2.2 million, which generated an income of £73,000. Grants were made to organisations totalling £77,000.

Grants of £1,000 or more went to ten organisations which were: County Buildings Protection Trust (£27,000); Ardington & Lockinge PCC (£20,000); King Alfred Educational Charity and Leighton House (£5,000 each); King Alfred's School (£3,500); Christian Aid (£2,000); Ardington & Lockinge Churches (£1,600); Injured Jockey's Fund (£1,100); and William Rowden Trust and National Hospital Development Fund (£1,000 each).

Other grants of less than £1,000 amounted to £9,000.

Exclusions

No support for individuals or medical research.

Applications

In writing to the correspondent. Grants are made several times each month.

Henry Lumley Charitable Trust

General, medical, educational, relief of poverty/hardship

£119,000 (2010)

Beneficial area

England and Wales.

c/o Lutine Leisure Ltd, Windlesham Golf Club, Bagshot, Surrey GU19 5HY
Tel: 01276 472273

Correspondent: Peter Lumley, Trustee
Trustees: Henry Lumley; Peter Lumley; Robert Lumley; James Porter.
CC Number: 1079480

Information available

Accounts were available from the Charity Commission.

Registered in February 2000, the income of the trust is derived from the dividends and interest received from shares in the private company Edward Lumley Holdings Ltd. Charities supported should be known to at least one trustee. Aside from the founder's initial list of beneficiaries, new charities have been added as funds permit and are usually of a one-off nature to assist medical or educational projects.

In 2010 the trust had assets of £3.4 million and an income of £75,000. Grants totalling £119,000 were made to 33 organisations, many of which were recurring in nature. Although established as a general charitable trust, grants usually cover three main areas, namely, medical, educational and relief of poverty and hardship (although in this financial year there were no educational grants made). Grants were broken down as follows:

Medical	28	£105,500
Relief of poverty and hardship	3	£7,500
Other	2	£6,000

Beneficiaries included: Royal College of Surgeons (£20,000); Cancer Research UK, Stroke Association and Broderers Charitable Appeal (£5,000 each); Asthma UK, British Liver Trust and Meningitis Research Fund (£4,000 each); Ghurka Welfare Trust, Friends of St Michael's Hospice, Royal British Legion and Royal Star, Garter Home for Disabled Ex-service Men and Women and Wellbeing of Women (£2,500 each); and Royal School of Needlework (£1,000).

Applications

In writing to the correspondent.

Paul Lunn-Rockliffe Charitable Trust

Christianity, poverty, infirm people, youth

£37,000 (2009/10)

Beneficial area

UK and developing world.

4a Barnes Close, Winchester, Hampshire SO23 9QX
Tel: 01962 852 949
Fax: 01962 852 949
Correspondent: Jacqueline Lunn-Rockliffe, Trustee
Trustees: Jacqueline Lunn-Rockliffe; James Lunn-Rockliffe; Bryan Boult.
CC Number: 264119

Information available

Accounts were available from the Charity Commission.

The 2009/10 annual report states that:

> The object of the charity is to make grants to any charity or for any charitable purpose, at the trustees discretion, but preferably to those recipients likely to further Christianity, support the relief of poverty and assist the aged and infirm.

Furthermore, that:

> The charity has supported 73 separate charities during the year ... [and] maintains a database of details and financial data for the charities supported. The latest financial information for recipient charities is reviewed and their achievements assessed, prior to donating further funds.

> The trustees have a policy of restricting the total number of recipient charities in order to ensure that each receives a more significant donation and has a preference for smaller and locally based charities, or those known to the trustees or members of their families.

> The trustees allocate a proportion of the funds for donation to be applied to charities not previously supported and for special one-off causes.

In 2009/10 the trust had assets of £760,000 and an income of £35,000. Grants totalled £37,000 and were distributed as follows:

Aged	£1,300
Children	£2,500
Disabled	£4,300
Education and students	£1,600
Family	£2,900
Mission	£4,500
Needy, drug addicts, homeless and unemployed	£4,500
Prisoners	£3,500
Radio/mission	£1,700
Third world	£4,700
Youth	£3,500
Others	£2,100

Beneficiaries included: Christians Against Poverty and British Red Cross (£1,000 each); Church Urban Fund, Langley House Trust and Community of Holy Fire – Zimbabwe Children (£600 each); Action for Elder Abuse, Children Country Holiday Fund, Shepherds Down School, Hope Pregnancy Crisis, Street Pastors, Society of St Dismas, Touchstones 12, Hour of Revival, Appropriate Technology Asia, Fairbridge Solent and Armed Forces Christian Union (£500 each); Way to Life, Consequences, Friends of the Family and People International (£400 each); and Gateway Club (£300).

Exclusions

The trustees will not fund individuals; for example, student's expenses and travel grants. Repair and maintenance of historic buildings are excluded.

Applications

The trust encourages preliminary phone calls to discuss applications. It will generally only reply to written correspondence if an sae has been included.

The Ruth and Jack Lunzer Charitable Trust

Jewish, children, young adults, education and the arts

£49,000 (2009/10)

Beneficial area

UK.

c/o Berwin Leighton Paisner, Adelaide House, London Bridge, London EC4R 9HA
Tel: 020 7760 1000
Correspondent: M D Paisner, Trustee
Trustees: J V Lunzer; M D Paisner.

CC Number: 276201

Information available

Accounts were available from the Charity Commission.

The trust says it makes grants to organisations benefiting children, young adults and students; primarily educational establishments. In practice many such beneficiaries are Jewish organisations.

In 2009/10 the trust had assets of £43,000 and an income of £51,000 with 37 grants totalling £49,000.

The largest grants went to Kahal Chassidim Bobov (£14,000) and Yesoday Hatorah Schools (£6,200).

Other beneficiaries included: Lubavich Foundation (£5,500); Adath Yikroet Synagogue and Moreshet Hatorah (£3,000 each); Beis Yehudis Moscow (£1,000); Closehelm Limited and Community Concern Limited (£500 each); Federation of Synagogues (£200); and Collel Chibath Yerushatayim (£100).

Applications

In writing to the correspondent. Unsuccessful applicants are not acknowledged.

Lord and Lady Lurgan Trust

Medical charities, older people, children and the arts

£76,000 (2010)

Beneficial area

UK and South Africa.

45 Cadogan Gardens, London SW3 2AQ
Tel: 0207 591 3333
Fax: 2075913300
Email: charitymanager@pglaw.co.uk
Website: www.lurgantrust.org/
Correspondent: Mrs Diana Burke
Trustees: Simon Ladd; Andrew Stebbings; Diana Graves; Brendan Beder.
CC Number: 297046

Information available

Accounts were on file at the Charity Commission. The trust also has a useful website.

The registered objects of this trust are:

- the relief and medical care of older people
- medical research, in particular cancer research and the publication of the useful results of such research
- the advancement of education including education in the arts for the public benefit by the establishment of educational and artistic bursaries
- other charitable purposes at the discretion of the trustees.

There is also special interest in: South Africa (due to the settlers spending the latter part of their lives there) with about one quarter of the funds available being distributed there) in music, and in Northern Ireland because of family origins.

In 2010 the trust had assets of £1 million, an income of £27,000 and made grants totalling £76,000.

Grant distribution is divided into two key areas:

Institutional grants in the UK (excluding Scotland): £56,000 in 21 grants, beneficiaries included: Central School of Ballet (£7,500); Royal College of Music (£10,000); Music in Hospitals (£1,800); Polka Children's Theatre (£1,500); Claremont Project (£1,000); Deafness Research UK (£2,000); and Age NI (£2,000).

South Africa: £20,000 in 16 grants, beneficiaries included: ACFS Community Nutritional Education and Feeding Scheme; BUSKAID; Johannesburg Children's Home; South African Federation for Mental Health; National creative Arts Youth Festival (£1,250 each).

Exclusions

No grants to individuals or for expeditions. No support for organisations in Scotland.

Applications

Complete the downloadable application form which is available on the trust's website. Please read the grant policy on the website before completing the form. Trustees meet three or four times a year.

The Lyndhurst Trust

Christian

£41,000 to organisations in the UK (2010)

Beneficial area

UK and overseas, with preferences for north east England and the developing world.

PO Box 615, North Shields, Tyne and Wear NE29 1AP
Correspondent: The Secretary
Trustees: Revd Dr R Ward; Jane Hinton; Ben Hinton; Sally Tan.
CC Number: 235252

Information available

Accounts were available from the Charity Commission.

The trust's accounts stated:

> The trustees have continued to support opportunities to promote and advance the spreading of the Christian religion in any part of the world.
>
> The policy has been continued of supporting regularly charities that are promoting the awareness of the Christian gospel, in those areas of the World where people are prevented from hearing it through normal channels of communication. Agencies operating in difficult circumstances are given special consideration.
>
> The trustees have continued their policy of making funds available to the disadvantaged in the United Kingdom. In addition, the trustees give special consideration to charities involved in supporting members of the persecuted church around the world. Churches in the North East of England have been given increased support due to the particular needs of the communities where they are operating.

In 2010 the trust had an income of £46,000 and grants totalled £69,000, of which £41,000 went to organisations within the UK. Assets stood at £1.4 million.

Grants in the UK and north east of England included: Sowing Seeds (£8,000); Message Trust (£7,000); Northumbria Community (£6,000); St Luke's Church (£5,000); Friends

International (£3,000); St Barnabus Church and Icthus Christian Fellowship (£2,000 each); and Guildford Town Centre Chaplaincy – Street Angels, Street Pastors and Youth for Church NE (prison work) (£1,000 each).

Exclusions

No support for individuals or buildings.

Applications

In writing to the correspondent, enclosing an sae if a reply is required. Requests are considered half-yearly.

The Lynn Foundation

General

£249,000 (2009/10)

Beneficial area

UK and overseas.

Blackfriars, 17 Lewes Road, Haywards Heath, West Sussex RH17 7SP
Tel: 01444 454773
Fax: 01444 456 192
Correspondent: Guy Parsons, Chair of the Trustees
Trustees: Guy Parsons, Chair; F Emmott; Dr P E Andry; P R Parsons; Ian Fair; John Sykes.
CC Number: 326944

Information available

Accounts were available from the Charity Commission website with a breakdown of categories but no beneficiary list.

The trust has previously stated that it supports a very wide range of organisations, including those in the areas of music, the arts, Masonic charities, people with disabilities, older people and children.

In 2009/10 the trust had assets of £4.7 million, an income of £300,000 and made grants totalling £249,000. Grants were made to 444 organisations and totalled £249,000. Details of individual beneficiary organisations were not available, although the total was broken down as follows:

Disabled adults	138	69,000
Disabled children	133	66,000
Youth sponsorship	52	31,000
Arts	8	25,000
Medical research	39	19,000
Music	35	18,000
Hospices	35	18,000
Sundry	4	2,000

Applications

In writing to the correspondent.

Common applicant mistakes

'Badly written letters; often 'computerised', impersonal letters.'

The Lyons Charitable Trust

Health, animals, medical research, children

£0 (2009/10) Usually around £70,000

Beneficial area

UK.

74 Broad Walk, London N21 3BX
Tel: 020 8882 1336
Correspondent: Michael Scott Gibbon, Trustee
Trustees: M Scott Gibbon; J Scott Gibbon; G Whitelock Read; Robin Worby.
CC Number: 1045650

Information available

Accounts were available from the Charity Commission.

The trust in particular makes grants in the fields of health, medical research, animals and children in need. Historically, the same 11 charities are supported each year.

In 2009/10 it had assets of £1.6 million and an income of £66,000. No grants were made in this financial year. As the trust usually gives to the same 11 charities on an annual basis, we have retained its details in the belief that grant making will resume.

The 11 beneficiaries each year are: The Royal Marsden Hospital and Macmillan Cancer Relief, Helen House, St Thomas Hospital and Streetsmart, CLIC, One25 Ltd., Cambridge Curwen Print Study Centre, Cats Protection League,

Children with Aids and Walthamstow Stadium Greyhound.

Applications

The trust has stated that it is closed to new applications.

The Sir Jack Lyons Charitable Trust

Jewish, arts, education

£250,000 (2009/10)

Beneficial area

UK and Israel.

Gresham House, 5–7 St Pauls Street, Leeds LS1 2JG
Tel: 0133 297 6789
Correspondent: Paul Mitchell
Trustees: Lady Roslyn Marion Lyons; M J Friedman; D S Lyons; Miss A R J Maude-Roxby; P D Mitchell; Belinda Lyons-Newman.
CC Number: 212148

Information available

Full accounts were available from the Charity Commission website.

This trust shows a particular interest in Jewish charities and also a consistent interest in the arts, particularly music. In 2009/10 it had assets of £3.2 million and an income of £189,000. Grants were made to eight organisations totalling over £250,000.

Beneficiaries were: UJIA – Tel Hal Academic College (£67,500); Youth Futures in Beer Sheva (£61,000), Beer Sheva Start Up and Sparks of Science (£30,000 each); UJIA (£25,000); Jerusalem Foundation (£24,000); Beit Halohem Geneva (£11,000); and University of York Celebration Prize (£1,500).

Exclusions

No grants to individuals.

Applications

In writing to the correspondent. In the past the trust has stated: 'In the light of increased pressure for funds, unsolicited appeals are less welcome and would waste much time and money for applicants who were looking for funds which were not available.'

The Joy and Malcolm Lyons Foundation

Jewish

Around £38,000 (2009/10)

Beneficial area

UK.

BDO, 55 Baker Street, London W1U 7EU
Tel: 020 7893 2602
Correspondent: Jeremy Newman, Trustee
Trustees: Malcolm Lyons; Joy Lyons; Jeremy Newman.
CC Number: 1050689

Information available

Accounts received at the Charity Commission but unavailable to view.

This trust supports Jewish and Israeli organisations. In 2009/10 it had an income of £12,000 and a total expenditure of £39,000. No further information was available.

Previous beneficiaries include: Sage, L'Ecole Juive du Cannes, Chai Cancer Care, Lubavitch Foundation, Child Resettlement Fund, Noam Primary School, British Friends of Ezer Mizion, Jewish Care, Camp Simcha and British Emunah.

Applications

The trust does not consider unsolicited applications.

The M and C Trust

Jewish, social welfare

£186,000 (2009/10)

Beneficial area

UK.

c/o Chantrey Vellacott DFK, Russell Square House, 10–12 Russell Square, London WC1B 5LF
Tel: 020 7509 9000
Fax: 020 7509 9219

Correspondent: Chris Jones, Secretary
Trustees: Kate Bernstein; Rachel J Lebus; Julia Marks
CC Number: 265391

Information available

Accounts were available from the Charity Commission.

The trust's primary charitable objects are Jewish causes and social welfare. The trust is connected with Quercus Trust, being under the same administration and having similar objectives.

In 2009/10 the trust had assets of £4.5 million and an income of £118,000. Grants totalled £186,000.

The three largest grants went to Jewish Care, Norwood and One Voice Europe (£20,000 each). Other beneficiaries included: World Jewish Relief, Connect and Jewish Children's Holiday Fund (£10,000 each); and Deaf Blind UK and Princess Royal Trust (£5,000 each).

Exclusions

No grants to individuals.

Applications

In writing to the correspondent, but the trust states that funds are currently earmarked for existing projects. In order to keep administration costs to a minimum, they are unable to reply to any unsuccessful applications.

The M D and S Charitable Trust

Jewish

£209,000 (2008/09)

Beneficial area

UK and Israel.

15 Riverside Drive, Golders Green Road, London NW11 9PU
Tel: 020 7272 2255
Correspondent: Martin D Cymerman, Trustee
Trustees: M D Cymerman; Mrs S Cymerman.
CC Number: 273992

Information available

Latest accounts available at the Charity Commission website were for 2008–09.

The trust supports Jewish organisations in the UK and has general charitable purposes in Israel.

In 2008–09 the trust had assets of £2.3 million and an income of £164,000. Grants were made to 72 organisations totalling £209,000.

Beneficiaries included: Yeshivat Kolel Breslaw (£28,000); Ichud Mosdos Gur (£23,000); Emunah Education Centre (£22,000); Yeshivat Magen Avrohom (£11,000); Centre for Torah Education Trust, Mercaz Lechinuch Torami (£10,000 each); Hechel Moishe Fund and Tomchey Torah Yeshivat Rasbi (£5,000 each).

A total of £53,000 was disbursed in grants of less than £4,000.

Applications

In writing to the correspondent.

The M K Charitable Trust

Jewish orthodox charities

£289,000 (2009/10)

Beneficial area

Unrestricted, in practice mainly UK.

c/o Cohen Arnold and Co., New Burlington House, 1075 Finchley Road, Regent Street, Temple Fortune, London
Tel: 020 8731 0777
Correspondent: Simon Kaufman, Trustee
Trustees: Z M Kaufman; S Kaufman; A Piller; D Katz.
CC Number: 260439

Information available

Accounts were available at the Charity Commission, but without a list of grants.

This trust was established in 1966 for general charitable purposes and applies its income for the provision and distribution of grants and donations to Orthodox Jewish Charities. The trust's income is derived from investments and from donations from the trustees and associates.

In 2009/10 it had assets of £6.7 million and an income of £1.2 million. Grants were made totalling £289,000.

Unfortunately, no further information was available regarding the trust's grant making activities.

Applications
In writing to the correspondent. The trust accepts applications for grants from representatives of Orthodox Jewish charities, which are reviewed by the trustees on a regular basis.

The E M MacAndrew Trust

Medical, children, general
£38,000 (2009/10)

Beneficial area
UK.

J P Thornton and Co., The Old Dairy, Adstockfields, Adstock, Buckingham MK18 2JE
Tel: 01296 714886
Fax: 01296 714711
Correspondent: J P Thornton, Administrator
Trustees: Amanda Nicholson; J K Nicholson; Sally Grant; Verity Webster.
CC Number: 290736

Information available
Accounts were on file at the Charity Commission.

The trust is mainly interested in medical and children's charities. In 2009/10 it had assets of £990,000 and an income of £49,000. Grants totalling £38,000 were made to 20 organisations.

Major beneficiaries included: Calibre (£4,000); Bucks Association for the Care of Offenders (£3,000); St Laurence Room Development Fund, Toe in the Water and Chilterns MS Centre (£2,000 each); and Anxiety UK, Cancer and Bio-detection Dogs and Puzzle Pre School Playgroup (£1,000 each).

Applications
The trustees state that they do not respond to any unsolicited applications under any circumstances, as they prefer to make their own decisions as to which charities to support.

The Macdonald-Buchanan Charitable Trust

General
£225,000 (2010)

Beneficial area
UK, with a slight preference for Northamptonshire.

Rathbone Trust Co. Ltd, 159 New Bond Street, London W1S 2UD
Tel: 020 7399 0820
Email: linda.cousins@rathbone.com
Correspondent: Miss Linda Cousins
Trustees: Capt. John Macdonald-Buchanan, Chair; A J Macdonald-Buchanan; A R Macdonald-Buchanan; H J Macdonald-Buchanan; Mrs M C A Philipson.
CC Number: 209994

Information available
Accounts were available from the Charity Commission.

The Hon. Catherine Macdonald-Buchanan set up this trust in 1952 for general charitable purposes and endowed it with 40,000 shares in the then Distillers Company.

In 2010 the trust had assets of £3.2 million and an income of £123,000. Grants were made to 123 organisations and totalled £225,000. The majority of these were for £400.

Overall, grants by category of the recipient charity were broken down as follows:

Medical and research	£89,000
General welfare	£87,000
Animal welfare	£25,000
Forces welfare	£8,000
Charities for people with disabilities	£6,000
Youth welfare	£4,000
Elderly welfare	£3,000
Hospices	£2,000
Religion	£600

Beneficiaries included: Langham Hospital Trust (£80,000); Carriejo Charity and Orrin Charitable Trust

(£30,000 each); British Racing School (£20,000); Oracle Cancer Trust (£10,000); Scotts Guards Colonel's Fund (£3,000); and Artists General Benevolent Institution, Hearing Dogs for the Deaf, Migraine Trust, Order of St John, Salvation Army and Sightsavers International (£400 each).

Exclusions
No grants to individuals.

Applications
In writing to the correspondent, for consideration once a year. Appeals will not be acknowledged.

The Macfarlane Walker Trust

Education, the arts, social welfare, general
£24,000 to organisations (2009/10)

Beneficial area
UK, with priority for Gloucestershire.

4 Shootershill Road, Blackheath, London SE3 7BD
Correspondent: Miss C Walker, Secretary
Trustees: D F Walker; N G Walker; Miss C Walker.
CC Number: 227890

Information available
Accounts were available from the Charity Commission.

This trust has a particular interest in the provision of facilities for recreation and social welfare in Gloucestershire, the relief of poverty and hardship among employees and former employees of Walker Crosweller and Co Ltd, the provision of educational facilities particularly in scientific research and the encouragement of music, drama and the fine arts. The trust also prefers to support small projects where it believes its 'contribution will be significant'.

In 2009/10 the trust had assets of £642,000, an income of £26,000 and made grants to organisations totalling £24,000. Beneficiaries included: Vicar's Relief Fund (£8,000); The Family Haven (£3,000); and Music Space (£2,700).

Exclusions

No grants for expeditions, medical expenses, nationwide appeals, animal charities or educational fees.

Applications

In writing to the correspondent giving the reason for applying, and an outline of the project with a financial forecast. An SAE must accompany the initial application.

The Mactaggart Third Fund

General

£311,000 (2009/10)

Beneficial area

UK and abroad.

One Red Place, London W1K 6PL
Website: www.mactaggartthirdfund.org
Correspondent: The Trustees
Trustees: Sandy Mactaggart; Robert Gore; Fiona Mactaggart; Andrew Mactaggart; Sir John Mactaggart.
SC Number: SC014285

Information available

Accounts were available to download from the charity's website from which the following information is taken:

> The Mactaggart Third Fund is a grant-making charity, established in 1968 by Deed of Trust granted by Western Heritable Investment Company Limited. The objectives of the Trust are to distribute funds by way of charitable donations to suitable charities in the United Kingdom and abroad. The trustees have decided to take a proactive approach to their grant-making. Their present policy is to make grants to those charities whose aims they support and who they believe have demonstrated excellence in their achievements. Please note the fund does not accept unsolicited applications.

> The trust aims to make grants of circa £250,000 each year and since its inauguration it has made grants of over £4 million to a range of charitable organisations.

In 2009/10 it had assets of £11 million and an income of £472,000. Grants totalled £311,000. Beneficiaries included: University of Miami (£50,000); Robin Hood Trust (£13,000); Bahamas National Trust (£11,000); Amazon Conservation Team (£8,000); Mactaggart Community Cybercafé (£7,000); Terence Higgins Trust (£5,000); Hearing Dogs for Deaf People (£4,000); Harris Manchester College (£2,000); Greatwood (£1,000); and Diabetes UK (£100).

Applications

The fund's website states:

> The trustees are solely responsible for the choice of charitable organisations to be supported. Trustees are proactive in seeking out charities to support and all projects are chosen on the initiative of the trustees. Unsolicited applications are not supported.

Ian Mactaggart Trust

Education and training, culture, welfare and disability

£215,000 (2009/10)

Beneficial area

UK, with a preference for Scotland.

2 Babmaes Street, London SW1Y 6HD
Website: www.ianmactaggarttrust.org/index.htm
Correspondent: The Trustees
Trustees: Sir John Mactaggart; Philip Mactaggart; Jane Mactaggart; Fiona Mactaggart; Lady Caroline Mactaggart; Leora Armstrong.
SC Number: SC012502

Information available

Accounts were available on the trust's website.

The Ian Mactaggart Trust is a grant-making charity, established in 1984. The objectives of the trust are to distribute funds by way of charitable donations to suitable charities in the United Kingdom and abroad. The trustees have decided to take a proactive approach to their grant-making. Their present policy is to make grants to those charities whose aims they support and who they believe have demonstrated excellence in their achievements.

In 2009/10 the trust had assets of £7.9 million and an income of £471,000. Grants were made to 74 organisations totalling £215,000.

Major beneficiaries were: University of Miami – Miami Project (£50,000); Robin Hood Foundation (£28,000); University of Glasgow Trust (£18,000); Oxfordshire Community Foundation and Alzheimer's Society (£15,000 each); and KIPP NY inc (£10,000).

Other beneficiaries included: Muirhead Outreach Project (£7,000); Institute for Public Policy Research (£6,000); Game and Wildfire Conservation Trust (£5,000); Checkerboard Foundation (£4,300); the Promise (£3,000); Women's Aid (£2,000); NSPCC (£1,800); Coisir Og Ghadhlig Ile (£1,000); Ashmolean Museum (£750); Scottish Ballet Ruby Slipper Fund (£500); Islay, Jura and Colonsay Agricultural Association (£300); Sheppard Trust (£200); and Boltons Association (£100).

Applications

The trustees are committed to seeking out charitable organisations that they wish to support and therefore they do not respond to unsolicited applications.

James Madison Trust

The study of federal government

Around £86,000 (2009/10)

Beneficial area

UK.

68 Furnham Road, Chard TA20 1AP
Tel: 01460 67368
Correspondent: D Grace, Secretary to the Trustees
Trustees: Robert Emerson; Ernest Wistrich; John Pinder; John Bishop; Richard Corbett.
CC Number: 1084835

Information available

Accounts were on file at the Charity Commission. The trust's latest available annual report (2008/09) gives the following information:

The objects of the charity are to support and promote studies of federal government whether within or among states and of related subjects, including the processes that may lead towards the establishment of such government, and to support or promote education and dissemination of knowledge of these subjects. These objects govern all decisions of trustees without the need for further specific annual objectives.

In 2009/10 the trust had an income of £19,000 and a total expenditure of £97,000. No further information was available.

Previous beneficiary organisations have included: University of Kent (£102,000); Federal Trust (£94,000); University of Edinburgh (£30,000); Unlock Democracy, University of Middlesex (£19,000); London Metropolitan University (£7,500); and University of Cardiff (£5,000).

The trust has also usefully broken down grant totals according to project, as well as by recipient organisations. Previous projects funded by grants have included: Comparative Devolution (£155,000); Centre for Federal Studies (£106,000); Federal Trust Projects (£105,000); Additional Constitutionalism (£24,000); Autonomy Website, Regions of England (£19,000); European Foreign & Security Policy (£7,500); Welsh Papers (£5,000); Climate Change Research and Book of Federal Studies 06 (£3,500).

The 2008/09 accounts note that: 'together the projects have produced seminars, conferences, studies and publications'.

Applications

In writing to the correspondent. The trustees meet approximately every six weeks to approve grants.

The Magen Charitable Trust

Education, Jewish

£131,000 (2009/10)

Beneficial area

UK.

New Riverside, 439 Lower Broughton, Salford M7 2FX

Tel: 0161 792 2626
Correspondent: The Trustees
Trustees: Jacob Halpern; Mrs Rose Halpern.
CC Number: 326535

Information available

Accounts were available at the Charity Commission website, but without a list of grants.

The trust's objects are for the relief of poverty; supporting educational establishments; and supporting religious education.

In 2009/10 the trust had assets of £1.5 million and an income of £234,000. Grants were made totalling £131,000. There was no list of grant recipients included in the accounts.

Previous beneficiaries have included Manchester Yeshiva Kollel, Talmud Educational Trust, Bnos Yisroel School and Mesifta Tiferes Yisroel.

Applications

In writing to the correspondent.

Mageni Trust

Arts

£39,000 to organisations (2009/10)

Beneficial area

UK.

5 Hyde Vale, Greenwich SE10 8QQ
Tel: 020 8469 2683
Email: garfcollins@gmail.com
Correspondent: Garfield Collins, Trustee
Trustees: Garfield Collins; Gillian Collins; Stephen Hoare.
CC Number: 1070732

Information available

Accounts were on file at the Charity Commission.

In 2009/10 the trust had assets of £1.1 million, an income of £41,000 and made grants to the total of £39,000.

Beneficiaries included: Charities Aid Foundation (£10,000); Farms for City Children and LPO Thomas Beecham Group (£5,000 each); BYMT (£4,500); National Theatre, Tools for Self Reliance and National Youth Orchestra (£2,500 each); DAGE and Foundation for Young Musicians (£2,000); LPO Annual Appeal (£1,000); Primavera (£600); Derby Toc H Camp and Greenwich and Bexley Hospice (£500 each); and LSO Benefactor (£350).

Applications

In writing to the correspondent.

The Mahavir Trust (also known as the K S Mehta Charitable Trust)

General, medical, animal welfare, relief of poverty, overseas aid, religion

£63,000 (2009/10)

Beneficial area

UK.

19 Hillersdon Avenue, Edgware, Middlesex HA8 7SG
Tel: 020 8958 4883
Email: mahavirtrust@googlemail.com
Correspondent: Jay Mehta, Trustee
Trustees: Jay Mehta; Nemish Mehta; Pravin Mehta; Pushpa Mehta; Kumud Mehta; Sudha Mehta; Sheena Mehta Sabharwal; Kumar Mehta.
CC Number: 298551

Information available

Accounts were available from the Charity Commission.

In 2009/10 the trust had assets of £361,000 and an income of £117,000, mainly from donations and gifts. Grants totalled £63,000 and were broken down as follows:

Jain religion	£6,300
Infrastructure to promote Jain philosophy	£30,000
Relief of poverty, sickness and distress	£13,000
Relief of financial need for victims of natural disaster	£1,300
Advancement of education in rural areas	£7,200
Promotion of humane behaviour towards animals and vegetarianism	£4,900

Applications

In writing to the correspondent. The trust states:

> Ours is a small family trust with limited resources. Trustees meet three or four times a year to consider applications. There are no fixed criteria for applicants to observe – our objectives must be met by their activities. Grants are usually of the order of £250.

Malbin Trust

Jewish, general

£92,000 (2008/9)

Beneficial area

Worldwide.

8 Cheltenham Crescent, Salford M7 4FP
Tel: 0161 792 7343
Correspondent: Benjamin Leitner, Trustee
Trustees: Benjamin Leitner; Margaret Leitner; Jehuda Waldman.
CC Number: 1045174

Information available

Latest accounts available at the Charity Commission were for 2008/9.

The latest accounts available for this trust were from 2008/9. In this year the trust held assets of £551,000 and had an income of £66,000. Grants totalled £92,000 and the trust also has investments to provide long term support for orphaned children.

A list of beneficiaries was not included with the accounts.

Applications

In writing to the correspondent.

The Mandeville Trust

Cancer, young people and children

Around £11,000 (2009/10)

Beneficial area

UK.

The Hockett, Hockett Lane, Cookham Dean, Berkshire SL6 9UF
Tel: 01628 484 272

Correspondent: R C Mandeville, Trustee
Trustees: Robert Cartwright Mandeville; Pauline Maude Mandeville; Peter William Murcott; Justin Craigie Mandeville.
CC Number: 1041880

Information available

Basic information taken from the Charity Commission website.

In 2009/10 the trust had an income of £14,000 and a total expenditure of £11,800. Due to the trust's low income no further information was available.

Previous beneficiaries have included: University College London (£26,000) and Imperial College (£20,000) for research purposes; and the Berkshire Community Foundation (£10,000). Other smaller grants totalled £2,500.

Applications

In writing to the correspondent.

Maranatha Christian Trust

Christian, relief of poverty and education of young people

£62,000 (2009/10)

Beneficial area

UK and overseas.

208 Cooden Drive, Bexhill-on-Sea, East Sussex TN39 3AH
Tel: 01424 844741
Correspondent: The Secretary
Trustees: Alan Bell; Revd Lyndon Bowring; Rt Hon. Viscount Brentford.
CC Number: 265323

Information available

Accounts were available from the Charity Commission, but without a list of grants.

The trust's objectives are the promotion of education among young persons and the relief of poverty, particularly among those professing the Christian religion or working to promote such religion.

In 2009/10 the trust had assets of £856,000 and an income of £28,000. Grants were made totalling £62,000. Unusually, a list of beneficiaries was not included in the accounts.

Previous beneficiaries include: Christian Action Research and Education, Vanessa Grant Memorial Trust, Cafe Africa Trust, Micah Trust, Friends of St Andrew's Church, Office for International Diplomacy, Concordis International, Cheer, Re Source, Forty-Three Trust and Christians in Entertainment.

Applications

In writing to the correspondent, but please note, the trust does not consider unsolicited applications.

Marbeh Torah Trust

Jewish education and religion, and the relief of poverty

£217,000 (2010)

Beneficial area

UK and Israel.

116 Castlewood Road, London N15 6BE
Correspondent: M C Elzas, Trustee
Trustees: Moishe Chaim Elzas; Jacob Naftoli Elzas; Simone Elzas.
CC Number: 292491

Information available

Accounts were on file at the Charity Commission.

The trust's objects are to further and support Jewish education and religion as well as the relief of poverty. The trust primarily supports Jewish educational establishments.

In 2010 the trust had an income of £217,000 and spent £217,000 on grants to Jewish educational organisations.

The beneficiaries included: Yeshiva Marbeh Torah (£81,000); Chazon Avraham Yitzchak (£38,000); Tashbar (£25,000);Kol Eitan (£11,600); Mishkenos Yaakov (£10,000); Shaarei Limund (£6,800); Torat Bezalel (£6,400); Yad Gershon and Margenita

De Avraham (£6,000 each); Kollel Oneg Shabbos (£4,000); and Kol Zvi (£3,500).

Applications

In writing to the correspondent.

Marchig Animal Welfare Trust

Animal welfare

£554,000 (2010)

Beneficial area

Worldwide.

10 Whitehorn Close, Ash, Aldershot GU12 6NZ

Tel: 0131 225 6039

Fax: 0131 220 6377

Email: info@marchigtrust.org

Website: www.marchigtrust.org

Correspondent: Colin Moor

Trustees: Mrs Jeanne Marchig; Dr Jerzy A Mlotkiewicz; Colin Moor; Les Ward.

CC Number: 802133

Information available

Accounts were on file at the Charity Commission. The trust also has a very useful website.

The objects of the trust are to protect animals and to promote and encourage practical work in preventing cruelty. There are no restrictions on the geographical area of work, types of grants or potential applicants, but all applications must be related to animal welfare and be of direct benefit to animals. Projects supported by the trust have included mobile spay/neuter clinics, alternatives to the use of animals in research, poster campaigns, anti-poaching programmes, establishment of veterinary hospitals, clinics and animal sanctuaries.

There are no restrictions on the geographical area of the work (with the exception of the USA and Canada), the type of grant, or the applicant. All applications meeting the following criteria will be considered by the trust:

▷ those encouraging initiatives designed to improve animal welfare

▷ those promoting alternative methods to animal experimentation and their practical implementation

▷ those promoting and encouraging practical work in alleviating suffering and preventing cruelty to animals.

As well as giving grants, the trust also makes Jeanne Marchig Awards. These awards, which take the form of a financial donation in support of the winner's animal welfare work, are given in either of the following two categories: (a) The development of an alternative method to the use of animals in experimental procedures and the practical implementation of such an alternative resulting in a significant reduction in the number of animals used in experimental procedures; (b) Practical work in the field of animal welfare resulting in significant improvements for animals either nationally or internationally.

In 2010 the trust had assets of £17.6 million, an income of £2.7 million and made grants totalling £554,000.

Grants in 2010

In the annual report of the trustees for 2010 some of the work carried out by the trust is noted:

> During the year in furtherance of these objectives, the Trust made a number of grants to organisations and individuals at home and abroad. Projects included: spay/neuter programmes and their promotion in the UK, Tanzania, Gibraltar, Greece, Spain, South Africa, Romania, Israel and India; provision of a vehicle for rescued animals in the Philippines; improving the welfare of dairy cows and their calves; exploring the use of 'human cells' to replace animals in pesticide toxicity trials; assisting with the construction, renovation, maintenance and ongoing operations of animal shelters in the UK, India, Gibraltar, Philippines, Thailand, Israel and Greece; support was provided for animal welfare and protection education programmes in Romania, Yugoslavia and Tanzania; in addition, support was given for the purchase of veterinary medicines, equipment and for the provision of care to relieve the suffering of animals in a number of countries. A major grant was awarded to the Royal (Dick) School of Veterinary Studies in Edinburgh to establish an International Centre for Animal Welfare Education.

The trust has continued this work into 2011 making grants to

organisations, in the UK: All Creatures Great & Small, Care4Cats, The Scratching Post and Mayhew Animal Home.

Grants made abroad: SAPT – Greece, Rudozem Street Dog Rescue – Bulgaria, Karuna Society for Animals and Nature – India and Soi Dog Foundation – Thailand.

Exclusions

The trust will reject any application failing to meet its criteria. Additionally, applications relating to educational studies or other courses, expeditions, payment of salaries, support of conferences and meetings, or activities that are not totally animal welfare related, will also be rejected.

Applications

On an application form available from the correspondent or via the website.

All applications must be completed in full and include:

▷ a detailed account of the purpose for which the grant is required

▷ a copy of your most recent financial accounts

▷ a copy of your latest annual report.

Any incomplete applications received or those which fail to meet our criteria (as outlined above) will be rejected.

The Stella and Alexander Margulies Charitable Trust

Jewish, the arts, general

£725,000 (2009/10)

Beneficial area

UK.

34 Dover Street, London W1S 4NG

Tel: 020 7343 7200

Fax: 020 7343 7201

Correspondent: Leslie Michaels, Trustee

Trustees: Marcus J Margulies; Martin D Paisner; Sir Stuart Lipton;

Alexander M Sorkin; Leslie
D Michaels.
CC Number: 220441

Information available

Accounts were available from the
Charity Commission.

Established in 1962, the trust has
general charitable purposes, with a
preference for Jewish organisations.
The trustees search out appropriate
projects to fulfil the objectives of the
trust and grants are made at their
discretion. A significant project with
The Jerusalem Foundation has now
commenced and is expected to be
completed in June 2011.

In 2009/10 it had assets of
£8.3 million and an income of
£231,000. Grants were made to 13
organisations totalling £725,000. The
largest grant for the year went to
Jerusalem Foundation (Mount Herzl)
(£645,000).

Other beneficiaries included: Alma
Hebrew College (£30,000); Royal
Opera House Foundation (£25,000);
Community Security Trust (£6,000);
Nightingale House (£5,000); YMER
(£2,000); and Royal Academy of Arts
and Tate Foundation (£1,000 each).

Applications

In writing to the correspondent.

Mariapolis Limited

Christian ecumenism

£327,000 (2009/10)

Beneficial area

UK and overseas.

38 Audley Road, London W5 3ET
Tel: 020 8991 2022
Email: rumold@btconnect.com
Correspondent: Rumold Van Geffen
Trustees: Timothy King; Manfred
Kochinky; Barry Redmond.
CC Number: 257912

Information available

Accounts were available from the
Charity Commission.

The trust promotes the international
Focolare Movement in the UK, and

grant making is only one area of its
work. It works towards a united
world and its activities focus on peace
and cooperation. It has a related
interest in ecumenism and also in
overseas development. Activities
include organising conferences and
courses, and publishing books and
magazines.

In 2009/10 assets stood at
£2.5 million and income, mostly from
various donations received and
earned income, at £521,000. Grants
totalling £327,000 were made to the
following: Pia Associazione Maschile
Opera di Maria (£323,000); family
welfare grants (£1,500); Anglican
Priests Training Fund (£1,000);
Focolare Trust (£408); and 'other'
(£1,600).

Applications

In writing to the correspondent.

The Michael Marks Charitable Trust

Culture, environment

£163,000 (2009/10)

Beneficial area

UK and overseas.

5 Elm Tree Road, London NW8 9JY
Tel: 020 7286 4633
Fax: 020 7289 2173
Correspondent: The Trustees
Trustees: Marina, Lady Marks; Prof.
Sir Christopher White; Noel
Annesley.
CC Number: 248136

Information available

Accounts were available from the
Charity Commission.

The trust supports the arts (including
galleries and museums), and
environmental groups, with grants
generally ranging from £1,000 to
£25,000, although larger grants have
been given.

In 2009/10 it had assets of
£5.8 million and an income of
£203,000. Grants totalling £163,000
were made to 20 organisations many
of which are supported annually.

Beneficiaries of the largest grants
included: British Museum (£25,000);
British Library (£19,000); Sainsbury
Institute (£12,000); Woodland Trust,
National Theatre, Burlington
Magazine and Academy of Ancient
Music (£10,000 each).

Other beneficiaries included:
St Pancras Community Trust
(£7,700); Spitalfields Music (£7,500);
Benaki Museum (£6,000); Royal
Horticultural Society (£4,500); Polish
Association of the Knights of Malta
(£3,000); and Scottish Poetry Library
and Greek Archdiocese of Thyateria
and Great Britain (£2,000 each).

Exclusions

Grants are given to registered
charities only. No grants to
individuals or profit organisations.

Applications

In writing to the correspondent.
Applications should include audited
accounts, information on other
bodies approached and details of
funding obtained. The trustees meet
twice a year, usually in January and
July, to consider applications.
Requests will not receive a response
unless they have been successful.

The Hilda and Samuel Marks Foundation

Jewish, general

£171,000 (2009/10)

Beneficial area

UK and Israel.

1 Ambassador Place, Stockport Road,
Altrincham, Cheshire WA15 8DB
Tel: 0161 941 3183
Fax: 0161 927 7437
Email: davidmarks@mutleyprperties.
co.uk
Correspondent: D L Marks, Trustee
Trustees: S Marks; Mrs H Marks;
D L Marks; Mrs R D Selby.
CC Number: 245208

Information available

Accounts were available from the
Charity Commission.

The foundation mainly gives support to UK charities and to charities based in Israel. The 2007/08 annual report states that:

> The object of the Foundation is to provide relief and assistance to poor and needy persons; for the advancement of education, religion or for other purposes beneficial to the community.

> As stated in previous years, the Foundation has supported a number of organisations on a long-term basis.

In 2009/10 the foundation had assets of £3.1 million and an income of £111,000. Grants totalling £171,000 were made during the year.

In line with the trustees' general rule to not comment on individual donations, grants were broken down as follows:

▶ Community/Education – £42,500 (24.92%)
▶ Health £56,900 – (33.36%)
▶ Welfare £71,175 – (41.73%)

However, notwithstanding this, the following observations were made by the trustees in their annual report:

> During the year under review the emphasis of the grants were to support Welfare based Charities (primarily in Israel), bearing in mind the current global economic conditions.

> A donation of $37,000 (approximately £25,000) was given to the ALYN Pediatric and Adolescent Rehabilitation Centre in Jerusalem which is an officially registered non-profit facility rehabilitating infants, children and adolescents who are afflicted with a broad range of physical disabilities including, children who have been injured in road accidents and terror attacks, children suffering from congenital conditions and children suffering from physical limitations due to various illnesses. Children from all over Israel and the world are treated at ALYN regardless of religion or ethnic origin. Due to the long term nature of the care it is necessary to provide classes for differing age groups. The Foundation has, over a number of years, sponsored one of the Classes.

> In additions, the Foundation made grants totalling £25,000 to Child Settlement Fund (Emunah). The Foundation has for many years supported a number of the Emunah projects in Israel .

Exclusions

No grants to individuals.

Applications

The trust primarily supports projects known to the trustees and its funds are fully committed. Therefore unsolicited applications are not being sought.

The Ann and David Marks Foundation

Jewish charities, general charitable purposes

£32,000 (2010)

Beneficial area

Worldwide with a preference for Manchester.

Mutley House, 1 Ambassador Place, Stockport Road, Altrincham, Cheshire WA15 8DB
Tel: 0161 941 3183
Email: davidmarks@mutleyproperties.co.uk
Correspondent: D L Marks, Trustee
Trustees: D L Marks; Mrs A M Marks; Dr G E Marks; A H Marks; M Purcell.
CC Number: 326303

Information available

Accounts were obtained from the Charity Commission website, but without a list of grants.

The trust mainly supports Jewish charities, especially in the Manchester area. It has a number of regular commitments and prefers to distribute to charities known to the trustees.

In 2010 the foundation had assets of £597,000 and an income of £71,000. Grants totalled £32,000. Unfortunately a list of grants was unavailable, although we do know from the trustees' report that the following organisations were beneficiaries: Finchley Jewish School (£4,000); UJIA £3,000); and Magen (£1,500).

Applications

Previous research suggested that the trust's funds are mostly committed and unsolicited applications are not welcome.

Common applicant mistakes

'Not reading or adhering to guidelines; not responding to or ignoring feedback, advice and questions asked previously. Basic errors like getting our name wrong or figures not adding up. Making unsubstantiated claims without evidence, or making claims which our local knowledge tells us are blatantly untrue. Failing to send supporting documents. Not reading our extensive guidance on outcomes and therefore not telling us about the changes they hope their project will make to beneficiaries.'

Marmot Charitable Trust

'Green' organisations, conflict resolution

£99,000 (2009/10)

Beneficial area

Worldwide.

c/o BM Marmot, London WC1N 3XX
Correspondent: The Secretary
Trustees: Jean Barlow; Martin Gillett; Jonathan Gillett.
CC Number: 1106619

Information available

Accounts were on file at the Charity Commission.

The trust was registered with the Charity Commission in November 2004. It has general charitable purposes.

> In practice, a policy reflecting the interests of the settlors has been implemented along with the interests of the late David Gillett, who left a major legacy to the trust. There is a concentration on funding 'green' organisations that support changes that will pave the way for a sustainable future. In addition, there is an interest in supporting peace organisations that are seeking new ways of dealing with conflict particularly at an international level and lessening the dependence on armaments including the eventual elimination of nuclear weapons.

In 2009/10 the trust had assets of £2.5 million and an income of

£367,000. Grants totalling £99,000 were made to 17 organisations. This included further grants to support the development of ways of investing in renewables and energy saving methods known as the Green New Deal (Earth Resources Research), and Friends of the Earth Trust in their Climate Change programme.

Beneficiaries included: British American Security Information Council (£15,000); Friends of the Earth Trust; and Unit for Research into Changing Institutions (£10,000 each); Martin Ryle Trust (Scientists for Global Responsibility) (£5,000); Poverty and Environment Trust (Sustainable Communities Act); Margaret Hayman Charitable Trust (Talkworks); and Tree Aid; (£2,000 each).

Applications

In writing to the correspondent.

The Marr-Munning Trust

Overseas aid

£229,000 (2009/10)

Beneficial area

Worldwide, mainly developing world.

9 Madeley Road, Ealing, London W5 2LA
Tel: 020 8998 7747
Fax: 020 8998 9593
Email: dongleeson@tiscali.co.uk
Correspondent: Donford Gleeson, Trust Administrator
Trustees: Glen Barnham; Marianne Elliott; Julian Kay; Guy Perfect; David Strachan; Pierre Thomas; Martin Sarbicki; Dr Geetha Oommen.
CC Number: 261786

Information available

Accounts were available from the Charity Commission.

The trust was founded in 1970 by the late Frank Harcourt-Munning. An extract from the trusts 2009/10 accounts encapsulate its purposes:

> To support charities giving overseas aid ... for the relief of poverty suffering and distress particularly among the inhabitants of territories which are economically underprivileged through want of development or of support of the necessities of life or of those commodities and facilities which enhance human existence enriched by education and free from the threat of poverty, disease, under nourishment or starvation.

Income is derived primarily from the letting of property. The trustees have been addressing the historically low proportion of charitable expenditure by modernising the management of its assets and the effects are already being seen in an increased level of grant.

In 2009/10 the trust had assets of £12 million and an income of £578,000. Grants totalling £229,000 were made to organisations working overseas and were broken down as follows:

Providing educational support	£67,000
Supporting self-sustaining projects	£60,000
Providing healthcare to poor people	£39,000
Providing shelter to destitute people	£37,000
Helping natural disaster victims	£26,000

Major beneficiaries were: Marr-Munning Asram – India (£14,000); Aysanew Kassa Trust (£11,000); and Médecins Sans Frontières (£10,000).

Recipients of smaller grants included: Africa Equipment for School (£5,400); CAFOD (£5,000); UNICEF (£4,500); World Orthopaedic Concern (£4,000); Homeless International and Joliba Trust (£3,000 each); Build It International (£2,500); Rural Solar Lighting, the Spiti Project and Mercy Ships (£2,000 each); Action for Children in Conflict and VETAID (£1,500 each); and Ss. Cyril and Methodious University (£1,000).

Exclusions

No grants to individuals or for work taking place within the UK.

Applications

The trustees meet quarterly and usually review applications twice yearly, in the spring and autumn. Sometimes a request may be carried forward to a later meeting. However, emergency appeals may be considered at any meeting.

Applications should be concise, ideally limited to no more than two sides of A4 plus a project description, budget and summary accounts or annual report. Clear financial information is essential, and applications from small or new organisations may benefit from reference to any better-known supporters or partners. Charitable or equivalent status of the applicant organisation should be made clear.

Please note: Any other supporting literature should be kept to a minimum. Do not waste stamps on an sae; the trust regrets that it does not have the administrative resources at present to return papers or respond to telephone or email enquiries (a website is under consideration). A trustee has agreed to look at the requests each month and where necessary seek further information. Otherwise, applicants will normally only hear if their bid has been successful which may be more than six months from receipt of application.

The Marsh Christian Trust

General

£156,000 (2009/10)

Beneficial area

UK.

2nd Floor, 36 Broadway, London SW1H 0BH
Tel: 020 7233 3112
Website: www.marshchristiantrust. org
Correspondent: Brian Peter Marsh, Trustee
Trustees: B P Marsh; R J C Marsh; Miss N C S Marsh; Mrs. L Ryan; Miss A Marsh.
CC Number: 284470

Information available

Full accounts were available from the Charity Commission website.

The trust was established in 1981 and has increased steadily in size with each passing year. In 2009/10 the trust had assets of £6 million and an income of £469,000. Grants and awards were made to 247 organisations and totalled £156,000. Support costs were £67,000 and governance costs £5,000.

A breakdown of the grants is presented in the table below.

Charitable donations

Grants generally range from £250 to £4,000, with responses to new applications being at the lower end of this scale. The trust engages in long-term core funding and prefers to build up the level of grant-making over time.

Grants of £1,000 or more included: Bible Reading Fellowship, Christians Against Poverty, English Speaking Union of the Commonwealth and Prisoners Abroad (£1,000 each).

Grants of under £1,000 each included: Cruse Bereavement Care (£900); Addaction and Historic Chapels Trust (£800 each); Impact Foundation (£700); Awareness Foundation (£600); London Early Years Foundation and London Philharmonic Orchestra (£500 each); Lloyd's Patriotic Fund (£450); Migraine Action and Mind (£400 each); The Charleston Trust (£275); and Little and David Construction and Small Woods Association (£100 each).

The trust offers this overview of its grantmaking on its website:

Marsh Awards

The trust runs a portfolio of awards with a number of internationally and nationally recognised organisations such as Barnardos, the National Trust and the Zoological Society of London. The awards seek to recognise unsung heroes who all aim to improve the world we live in. Recipients of Marsh Awards range from scientists working in conservation biology and ecology, to authors and sculptors from the arts world, and those who give their time unselfishly to work with the young, the elderly, people with mental health issues and for our heritage.

These partners recommend a short-list of worthy award winners, but the final decision lies with the award trustees, ensuring complete independence and giving real value to the winners in terms of the recognition earned.

The Marsh Awards now total 41 and continue to grow. The main areas of focus for the awards include conservation, science, the arts, heritage, literature and volunteering.

27 awards were made during the year and totalled £55,000.

Exclusions

No grants can be made to individuals, organisations not registered as charities, or for sponsorships. No start-up grants. No support for building funds, ordinary schools, colleges, universities or hospitals, or research.

Applications

In writing to the correspondent. All applications for grants must be accompanied by a copy of the most recent audited accounts. Decisions are made at monthly trustee meetings.

The trustees attempt to visit each long-term recipient at least once every three years to review the work done, to learn of future plans and renew acquaintance with those responsible for the charity.

The Jim Marshall Charitable Trust

General

Around £28,000 (2010)

Beneficial area

Milton Keynes.

Simpson Wreford and Co, Wellesley House, Duke of Wellington Avenue, London SE18 6SS

Tel: 020 8317 6460

Trustees: Dr James Marshall, Chair; Kenneth Saunders; Brian Charlton; Jonathon Ellery; Victoria Marshall.
CC Number: 328118

Information available

Accounts were available from the Charity Commission.

Established in 1989 by the founder of Marshall Amplification plc, this trust supports organisations concerned with children, young people, families and people who are sick or have disabilities and the local community generally. Grants are also made directly to individuals.

In 2010 the trust had an income of £1,000 and a total expenditure of £28,000. No further information was available.

A list of grant recipients was not available for the year but previous beneficiaries have included: MK Victors Boxing Club, Luton and Bedfordshire Youth Association and Action 4 Youth (£25,000); Foundation for Promoting the Art of Magic (£5,000); Comedians' Golfing Society (£2,500); Hazeley School Charitable Trust (£2,000); Nathan Edwards Mobility Bike Fund (£1,100); and Music Alive, Brainwave and Music for All (£1,000 each).

Applications

In writing to the correspondent at any time.

Common applicant mistakes

'Applying from the wrong geographic area.'

The Charlotte Marshall Charitable Trust

Roman Catholic, general

£110,000 (2009/10)

Beneficial area

UK.

Sidney Little Road, Churchfields Industrial Estate, St Leonards on Sea, East Sussex TN38 9PU
Tel: 01424 856655

THE MARSH CHRISTIAN TRUST			
Area	Awards £	Donations £	Total £
Social and welfare	10700	61000	71700
Literature, arts and heritage	22000	17000	39000
Environmental causes and animal welfare	22500	10000	32500
Education and training		5500	5500
Healthcare and medical research		4800	4800
Overseas appeals		2500	2500
Total in awards and grants			156000

Note: The above figures do not include supports costs.

Correspondent: The Trustees
Trustees: Mrs E M Cosgrove;
J Crosgrove; K B Page; J M Russell;
Rachel Cosgrove.
CC Number: 211941

Information available

Accounts were on file at the Charity Commission.

The trust has general charitable purposes in the UK, mainly supporting educational, religious and other charitable purposes for Roman Catholics.

In 2009/10 the trust had assets of £522,000 and an income of £119,000. During the year, grants were made to organisations and totalled £110,000. Of this, over £73,000 went towards Roman Catholic activities in the UK. Grants were further broken down as follows:

Education	11	£26,000
Disability and illness	29	£22,000
Homelessness	11	£21,000
Families and youth	14	£21,000
Needy and disadvantage	7	£6,000
Abuse addiction, refugee and torture	4	£5,000
Elderly	4	£2,000
Other	7	£12,000

Beneficiaries included: St Winifred's Centre – Sheffield (£8,000); St Gregory's Youth and Community Centre – Liverpool and St Mary's Star of the Sea (£6,000 each); Sacred Heart Primary School and St Mary Magdalen Catholic School (£5,000 each); Scottish Marriage Care (£4,000); St James Priory Project – Bristol and Westminster Children's Society (£3,000 each); Speak Out Hounslow (£1,500); Independent Age (£1,000): and Birmingham Settlement and Derby TOC H (£500 each).

Exclusions

No grants are given to individuals.

Applications

On a form available from the correspondent. Completed forms must be returned by 31st December for consideration in March.

John Martin's Charity

Religious activity, relief-in-need, education

£189,000 to schools and organisations (2009/10)

Beneficial area

Evesham and 'certain surrounding villages' only.

16 Queen's Road, Evesham, Worcestershire WR11 4JN
Tel: 01386 765 440
Fax: 01386 765 340
Email: enquiries@johnmartins.org.uk
Website: www.johnmartins.org.uk
Correspondent: John Daniels, Clerk
Trustees: Nigel Lamb; John Smith; Richard Emson; Revd Barry Collins; Cyril Scorse; Revd Andrew Spurr; Cllr Diana Raphael; Cllr Frances Smith; Joyce Turner; Julie Westlake; John Wilson; Revd Mark Binney; Catherine Evans; Gabrielle Falkiner.
CC Number: 527473

Information available

Accounts were available from the Charity Commission.

The charity was created following the death of John Martin of Hampton, Worcestershire in 1714. His property was left for the benefit of local residents, and over the years some of this property has been sold to generate income to enable the charity to carry out its objectives in accordance with his wishes. It was formally registered with the Charity Commission in 1981.

Aims and objectives

Under the terms of the original will and the amended Charity Commission Scheme, the overall aim of the charity is to benefit the residents of the town and neighbourhood of Evesham, Worcestershire.

It does this through the implementation of four specific aims:

- propagation of the Christian Gospel (religious support)
- relief in need
- promotion of education
- health.

Objectives

- religious support – to assist the Vicars and Parochial Church Councils within the town of Evesham
- relief in need – to assist individuals and organisations within the town of Evesham who are in conditions of need, hardship and distress
- promotion of education – to promote education to persons who are or have a parent residing within the town of Evesham and to provide benefits to schools within Evesham
- health – the trustees have wide ranging authority within the scheme to provide such charitable purposes as they see fit, for either assisting beneficiaries within the town of Evesham or within the immediate neighbourhood. The trustees currently utilise this authority to support people with chronic health problems and other related health issues.

Grants are available towards the cost of equipment (normally paid against an agreed invoice, either direct to the supplier or by direct credit to the organisation's bank account); project or on-going costs (normally paid in stages by direct credit); and general expenditure (normally paid by direct credit).

General

In 2009/10 the charity had assets of £18 million and an income of £716,000. Grants were made to 35 organisations (including schools) totalling £189,000, broken down as follows:

Religious support	3	£64,000
Relief in need	16	£52,000
Promotion of education	13	£54,000
Health	3	£19,000

Beneficiaries included: St Andrews PCC – Hampton (£29,000); Citizens Advice – Wychavon (£20,000); St Richard's Hospice and All Saints' PCC – Evesham (£18,000 each); Acquired Aphasia Trust (£14,000); Prince Henry's High School (£11,000); Hampton First School (£8,800); Evesham College (£6,100); Shop Mobility – Evesham (£3,000); Noah's Ark Trust (£2,500); St Mary's

Primary School (£1,300); and Breast Cancer Haven (£200).

Grants were also made to individuals across all four categories totalling £398,000.

Exclusions

No grants for the payment of rates or taxes, or otherwise to replace statutory benefits.

Applications

Grant applications are considered from organisations in, or supporting, the town of Evesham where the requested support is considered to fit within the governing schemes of the charity. Application periods close on 1 March, 1 June, 1 September and 20 November. Forms are available from the correspondent or via the charity's website. Applicants are asked to provide the following with their application: the latest set of annual accounts; latest bank statement showing the current balance and name of the organisation; any relevant literature about the organisation e.g. a leaflet or flyer.

Details of the application procedure for individuals are also contained on the trust's website.

The Mason Porter Charitable Trust

Christian

£105,000 (2009/10)

Beneficial area

UK.

Liverpool Charity and Voluntary Services, 151 Dale Street, Liverpool L2 2AH
Tel: 0151 227 5177
Correspondent: The Secretary
Trustees: Sue Newton, Chair; Mark Blundell; Dil Daly; Adeyinka Olushonde ; Charles Feeny; William Fulton; Prof. Phillip Love; Andrew Lovelady; Christine Reeves; Hilary Russell; Heather Akehurst; Perminder Bal.
CC Number: 255545

Information available

Accounts were available from the Charity Commission.

The trust supports mainly Christian causes in the UK, including those which provide relief or missionary work overseas.

In 2009/10 the trust had assets of £1.6 million and an income of £111,000. Grants to organisations totalled £105,000.

Grants of £1,000 and over were made to: Hoylake Cottage Hospital (£50,000); Abernethy Trust Ltd and Cliff College (£10,000 each); ECG Trust (£5,000); Just Care (£4,000); Proclaim Trust (£3,000); St Luke's Methodist Church Hoylake; (£2,000); and Share Jesus International and Wirral Christian Centre (£1,000 each). Other grants totalled £19,000.

Applications

The trust states that it only makes grants to charities known to the settlor and unsolicited applications are not considered.

Matliwala Family Charitable Trust

Islam, general

£753,000 (2009/10)

Beneficial area

UK and overseas, especially Bharuch – India.

9 Brookview, Fulwood, Preston PR2 8FG
Tel: 01772 706 501
Correspondent: Ayub Vali Bux, Trustee
Trustees: Ayub Vali Bux; Usman Salya; Abdul Aziz Vali Patel; Yousuf Bux; Ibrahim Vali Patel.
CC Number: 1012756

Information available

Accounts were available from the Charity Commission.

The trust's areas of giving are:
- the advancement of education for pupils at Matliwala School of Bharuch in Gujerat – India, including assisting with the provision of equipment and facilities
- the advancement of the Islamic religion
- the relief of sickness and poverty
- the advancement of education.

In 2009/10 the trust had assets of £4.4 million and an income of £310,000. Grants totalled £753,000, the vast majority of which was given to various projects in Bharuch, Gujarat – India. These included the building of a school, hospital care, purchase of educational books and materials, provision of clothing for the poor and the supply of free medicine.

In support of the trust's other objectives, £100,000 was given towards the advancement of religion in the UK and £3,400 towards the advancement of education overseas.

Applications

In writing to the correspondent.

The Matt 6.3 Charitable Trust

Christian

£462,500 (2009/10) to organisations and individuals

Beneficial area

UK.

Progress House, Progress Park, Cupola Way, Off Normanby Road, Scunthorpe, North Lincolnshire
Tel: 01724 863 666
Correspondent: I H Davey
Trustees: Christine Ruth Barnett; Doris Dibdin; T P Dibdin; R O Dauncey.
CC Number: 1069985

Information available

Accounts were available from the Charity Commission.

Established in 1998, this trust mainly supports Christian organisations. The trustees' report for 2009/10 states: 'The trust has established a number of long term relationships with organisations and individuals who share its vision to promote the Christian Faith.'

In 2009/10 the trust had assets of £7 million and an income of £262,000. Grants totalling £462,000 were made and the following beneficiaries were named in the accounts: Christian Centre (Humberside) Limited (£358,000); European Gospel Mission Limited (£65,000); and The Ice House Christian Centre (£2,000). Grants were awarded in the following amounts in the specified areas:

Promotion of the Christian faith	£369,000
Christian broadcasting	£65,000
Education	£7,500
Relief of poverty	Nil this year
Grants to individuals	£21,000

No further information regarding the beneficiaries was available.

Applications

The trust does not accept unsolicited applications and states that 'funds are committed to ongoing projects.'

The Violet Mauray Charitable Trust

General, medical, Jewish

£49,000 (2009/10)

Beneficial area

UK.

9 Bentinck Street, London W1U 2EL
Tel: 020 7935 0982
Correspondent: John Stephany, Trustee
Trustees: Alison Karlin; John Stephany; Robert Stephany.
CC Number: 1001716

Information available

Accounts were available from the Charity Commission.

The trust supports general charitable causes, with preference for medical charities and Jewish organisations.

In 2009/10 the trust had assets of £1.7 million and an income of £40,000. Grants totalled £49,000.

Beneficiaries included: Mango Tree and Tzedek (£5,000 each); Médecins Sans Frontières (£4,000); Employment Resource Centre and

Jewish Care (£3,000 each); Merlin and Shelterbox (£2,000 each); Kids Company and National Animal Welfare Trust (£1,000 each); and Concertina Charitable Trust (£500).

Exclusions

No grants to individuals.

Applications

In writing to the correspondent.

Evelyn May Trust

Currently children, older people, medical, natural disaster relief

Around £57,000 (2010)

Beneficial area

Worldwide.

Pothecary, Witham, Weld, White Horse Court, 70 St George's Square, London SW1V 3RD
Tel: 0207 821 8211
Correspondent: Ms Kim Gray
Trustees: Ms Lisa Webb; Ms K Gray; Ms J Tabersham.
CC Number: 261038

Information available

Accounts were on file at the Charity Commission.

Registered in 1970, this trust supports a variety of charities but appears to focus on specific areas every couple of years. One-off grants are given for specific projects but general funding is also considered.

In 2010 the trust had an income of £26,000 and a total expenditure of £78,000. No further information was available on the trust's activities in the year ending 31st December 2010.

In 2009 the trust had assets of £182,000, an income of £329,000 and made grants to 10 organisations totalling £20,000.

In 2009 beneficiaries included: Queen Alexandra Hospital (£3,000); Child Hope, Children's Heart Foundation, NSPCC Trust, Frishta Children's Village, Child Health Advocacy International, Children in Crisis, Richards House (£2,000 each) and Tabor centre (£1,000).

Exclusions

No grants to individuals, including students, or to general appeals or animal welfare charities.

Applications

In writing to the correspondent.

The Mayfield Valley Arts Trust

Arts, especially chamber music

£135,000 (2009/10)

Beneficial area

Unrestricted, but with a special interest in Sheffield and South Yorkshire.

Hawsons, Pegasus House, 463a Glossop Road, Sheffield S10 2QD
Tel: 0114 266 7141
Correspondent: P J Kennan, Administrator
Trustees: A H Thornton; J R Thornton; Mrs P M Thornton; D Whelton; D Brown; J R Rider.
CC Number: 327665

Information available

Accounts were on file at the Charity Commission.

Established in 1987, the objects of this trust are the advancement of education by the encouragement of art and artistic activities of a charitable nature, especially music; and the promotion and preservation of concerts and other musical events and activities.

In 2009/10 the trust had assets of nearly £2.2 million and an income of £115,000. Grants totalling £135,000 were made as follows: Wigmore Hall (£40,000); Live Music Now (£35,000); York Early Music Foundation (£30,000); Music in the Round (£20,000); and Prussia Cove (£10,000).

Exclusions

No grants to students.

Applications

The trust states that no unsolicited applications are considered.

Mazars Charitable Trust

General

£272,000 (2010)

Beneficial area

UK, overseas.

1 Cranleigh Gardens, South Croydon CR2 9LD
Tel: 020 8657 3053
Correspondent: Bryan K Rogers, Trust Administrator
Trustees: Alan T H Edwards; David J Evans; Peter R Hyatt; Robert H Neate.
CC Number: 287735

Information available

Accounts were available from the Charity Commission.

The trust is a conduit for most of the charitable giving of Mazars LLP, a national firm of Chartered Accountants (formerly known as Mazars Neville Russell), from which the major contribution is received each year.

The 2010 trustee report states:

The trustees operate through the management committee who meet annually to consider nominations for national (major) grants. Some funds are allocated to ten regional 'pots' whose appointed representatives approve smaller grant nominations from within their own region.

Nominations for national grants must be known to and be sponsored by team members of Mazars LLP and comply with stated criteria. Applicants known to team members of Mazars LLP can obtain a copy of the stated criteria upon request to the trust administrator. National and regional criteria are regularly reviewed but, in general, the trustees consider that the national grant-making policy should avoid core funding. Most national grants are therefore made towards one-off projects covering a defined period. Successful national nominations cannot normally be repeated within three years.

At 31 December 2010 the trust had assets of £74,000 and an income of £227,000. Grants were made to 183 organisations totalling £272,000.

Beneficiaries included: UK Youth (£25,000); Chickenshed and Parkinson's Disease Society of the United Kingdom (£15,000 each); The Johari Foundation (£12,000); Hope HIV and The Waterside Charitable Trust (£10,000 each); Emmanuel Global Network (UK) Limited, Hope for Konya and Redbridge Breast Funds (£5,000 each); and Sense and The National Deafblind & Rubella Association (£2,250 each).

Grants to 157 other charities of between £60 and £1,800 each totalled (£71,500).

Exclusions

Please refer to the General information section.

Applications

See General information for further details. Unsolicited appeals are usually rejected.

The Robert McAlpine Foundation

Children with disabilities, older people, medical research, welfare

£448,000 (2009/10)

Beneficial area

UK.

Eaton Court, Maylands Avenue, Hemel Hempstead, Hertfordshire HP2 7TR
Tel: 01442 233444
Correspondent: Brian Arter
Trustees: Hon. David McAlpine; Malcolm H D McAlpine; Kenneth McAlpine; Cullum McAlpine; Adrian N R McAlpine.
CC Number: 226646

Information available

Accounts were available from the Charity Commission.

This foundation generally supports causes concerned with children with disabilities, older people, medical research and social welfare. A small number of other charities are also supported, through a long-term connection with the foundation and therefore no new beneficiaries are considered from outside the usual areas.

In 2009/10 the trust had assets of almost £13 million and had an income of £463,000. Grants paid during the year totalled £448,000.

There were 35 grants paid during the year. Major beneficiaries included: The Ewing Foundation (£80,000); Age Concern (£40,000); Sevenoaks School Charity and From Boyhood to Manhood Foundation (£25,000 each); and Community Self Build Agency, Merchants Academy Withywood and The Towers School and Sixth Form Centre (£20,000 each).

Other beneficiaries included: The Respite Association (£15,000); Berkshire Community Foundation, Children's Aid Team and Dulwich Helpline (£10,000 each); The Pirate Club (£5,000); and Greenfingers Appeal (£2,500).

Exclusions

The trust does not like to fund overheads. No grants to individuals.

Applications

In writing to the correspondent at any time. Considered annually, normally in November.

Common applicant mistakes

'Being too large in income to meet our basic funding criteria.'

The A M McGreevy No 5 Charitable Settlement

General

£28,000 (2009/10)

Beneficial area

UK, with a preference for the Bristol and Bath area.

KPMG, 100 Temple Street, Bristol BS1 6AG
Tel: 0117 905 4000
Correspondent: Karen Ganson, Trust Administrator

Trustees: Avon Executor and Trustee Co. Ltd; Anthony McGreevy; Elise McGreevy-Harris; Katrina Paterson.
CC Number: 280666

Information available

Accounts were available from the Charity Commission.

The trust was established in 1979 by Anthony M McGreevy. In previous years there has been a preference for charities based in the former county of Avon.

In 2009/10 the trust had assets of £2.2 million, generating an income of £27,000. Grants were made to three organisations totalling £28,000.

The beneficiaries were: NSPCC (£25,000); Prostate Cancer Charity (£2,000); and the Stroke Association (£500).

Exclusions

No support for individuals.

Applications

In writing to the correspondent.

The McKenna Charitable Trust

Health, disability, education, children, general

£65,000 to organisations (2009/10)

Beneficial area

England and Wales.

Ingenious Asset Management, 15 Golden Square, London W1F 9JG
Tel: 020 7319 4000
Correspondent: J L Boyton, Trustee
Trustees: P A McKenna; Mrs. M E A McKenna; J L Boyton; H R Jones.
CC Number: 1050672

Information available

Accounts were available from the Charity Commission.

The trust's aims are to:
- assist with education, medical welfare and relief of need amongst people with disabilities
- provide funds for education as a means of relieving poverty

- make grants to children's charities
- Make grants for general charitable purposes.

In 2009/10 the trust had assets of £27,000 and an income of £87,500. Grants were made to six beneficiaries and totalled £65,000. The beneficiaries were: National Film and Television School (£50,000); Georgia's Teenage Cancer Appeal and The Royal Free Hampstead Charities (£5,000 each); CWMT (£2,600); Nordoff Robins Music Therapy (£1,500); and Animals Asia Foundation (Moon Bear) (£500).

Applications

The 2009/10 trustees report and accounts states:

> The trustees will consider applications for grants from individuals and charitable bodies on their merits but will place particular emphasis on the educational needs and the provision of support for disabled people.

The Helen Isabella McMorran Charitable Foundation

General, Christian

About £28,000 (2009/10)

Beneficial area

UK and overseas.

NatWest Trust Services, 5th Floor, Trinity Quay 2, Avon Street, Bristol BS2 0PT
Tel: 0117 940 3283
Correspondent: NatWest Trust Services
Trustee: NatWest Trust Services.
CC Number: 266338

Information available

Accounts were received at the Charity Commission but unavailable to view.

The trust makes one-off grants towards older people's welfare, Christian education, churches, the arts, residential facilities and services, social and moral welfare, special schools, cultural and religious teaching, special needs education,

health, medical and religious studies, conservation, animal welfare, bird sanctuaries and heritage.

In 2009/10 the foundation had an income of £22,000 and a total expenditure of £28,000.

Previous beneficiaries include: Christian Aid, Marine Conservation, Moon Bear Rescue, National Association for Crohn's Disease, National Children's Bureau, React, St Matthews PCC, St Nicholas Church, Sense International and Stoneham Housing Association.

Exclusions

No grants to individuals.

Applications

In writing to the correspondent. Brief guidelines are available. The closing date for applications is February each year.

D D McPhail Charitable Settlement

Medical research, disability, older people

£511,000 (2009/10)

Beneficial area

UK.

PO Box 285, Pinner, Middlesex HA5 3FB
Correspondent: Mrs Sheila Watson, Administrator
Trustees: Julia Noble; Patricia Cruddas; Catherine Charles-Jones; Christopher Yates; Tariq Kazi; Michael Craig; Mary Meeks.
CC Number: 267588

Information available

Accounts were on file at the Charity Commission.

In 2009/10 the trust had assets of £8.2 million and an unusually high income of £957,000 (£303,000 in 2008/09), due to a 'recoup of investment impairment' worth £721,000. Grants were made to 28 organisations totalling £511,000.

Two major grants were given to the Association of Wheelchair Children

(£170,000) and Combat Stress (£150,000).

Other beneficiaries included: Meningitis Research Foundation (£53,000); Demand (£25,000); Princess Royal Carers Trust (£20,000); Vocal Eyes (£10,000); Sir William Burrough School (£5,000); and Barbara Bus Fund, International League for the Protection of Horses, BLISS, National Society for Epilepsy, Hospice in the Weald and the Kidney Association Children's Holiday Fund (£2,000 each).

Applications

In writing to the correspondent.

The Anthony and Elizabeth Mellows Charitable Settlement

National heritage, Church of England churches

£21,000 (2010/11)

Beneficial area

UK.

22 Devereux Court, Temple Bar, London WC2R 3JR
Tel: 020 7583 8813
Correspondent: Prof. Anthony Mellows, Trustee
Trustees: Prof. Anthony R Mellows; Mrs Elizabeth Mellows.
CC Number: 281229

Information available

Accounts were available from the Charity Commission.

The trust gives support to charities in four main areas:

- the arts and national heritage
- churches of the Church of England
- hospitals and hospices
- the training and development of children and young people.

The trust states in its 2011 trustees report that it aims:

To further the charitable work of the operational charities supported by grants. The grants for the arts and

national heritage are made only to national institutions and, save in exceptional circumstances, grants for churches of the Church of England are made only to churches and other bodies of which the trustees have particular knowledge. [...] During the year under review [2010/11], the trustees decided that, in view of the reduced income available to them, they would in the future make no further grants for conservation purposes. Save for this, there have been no material changes to these policies since the last annual report.

In 2010/11 the trust had assets of £704,000 and an income of £32,000. Grants were made totalling £21,000 and were broken down as follows:

Arts and national heritage	6	£6,000
Churches – Council for the Care of Churches	6	£6,000
Hospitals, hospices and welfare	4	£5,000
Church of England	5	£3,500

Beneficiaries included: Royal Opera House Foundation (£2,900); Heath Chapel (£2,000); The Order of St John (£1,900); National Art Collection Fund (£1,125); and St Martin-in-the Fields (£500).

Exclusions

Applications from individuals, including students, are ineligible.

Applications

Applications are considered when received, but only from UK institutions. No application forms are used. Grants decisions are made three times a year when the trustees meet to consider applications.

Melodor Ltd

Jewish, general

£144,000 (2009/10)

Beneficial area

UK and overseas.

10 Cubley Road, Salford M7 4GN
Tel: 0161 720 6188
Correspondent: Bernardin Weiss, Secretary
Trustees: Hyman Weiss; Philip Weiss; Zisel Weiss; Pinchas Neumann; Yocheved Weiss; Eli Neumann; Esther Henry; Henry Neumann; Janet Bleier; Maurice Neumann; Miriam Friedlander; Rebecca Delange; Rivka

Ollech; Rivka Rabinowitz; Pesha Kohn; Yehoshua Weiss.
CC Number: 260972

Information available

Accounts were available from the Charity Commission, but without a list of grants.

The trust supports Orthodox Jewish institutions in the areas of education (including adult education), relief of poverty and the advancement of religion in accordance with the orthodox Jewish faith.

In 2009/10 it had assets of £751,000 and an income of £174,000. Grants to organisations totalled £144,000. A list of grants was not available.

Previously, beneficiaries of the largest grants were the Centre for Torah Education Trust, Beis Rochel and Chasdei Yoel.

Other beneficiaries include: Beth Hamedrash Hachodosh, Yeshivas Ohel Shimon, Beis Minchas Yitzhok, Talmud Torah Education Trust, Dushinsky Trust, Kollel Chelkas Yakov, Yetev Lev, Delman Charitable Trust, Ovois Ubonim and Friends of Viznitz.

Applications

In writing to the correspondent.

Meningitis Trust

Meningitis in the UK

£65,000 to organisations (2009/10)

Beneficial area

UK.

Fern House, Bath Road, Stroud, Gloucestershire GL5 3TJ
Tel: 01453 768000
Fax: 01453 768001
Email: helpline@meningitis-trust.org
Website: www.meningitis-trust.org
Correspondent: Financial Grants Officer
Trustees: Bernadette McGhie; Gill Noble; Mike Hall; Peter Johnson; Bob Johnson; Les Green; Richard Greenhalgh; James Kilmister; Alastair Irvine; Prof Keith Cartwright; Mitchell Wolfe; Eddie Wilson.
CC Number: 803016

Information available

Accounts were available from the Charity Commission; the trust has a useful website.

The trust is an international charity with a strong community focus, which aims to fight meningitis through the provision of support, education and awareness and research.

In 2009/10 the trust held assets of £1.5 million, an income of £3.1 million and a total charitable expenditure of £2.2 million. Grants to organisations for research purposes totalled £65,000. The sum of £193,000 was distributed to individuals in support grants.

Applications

Application forms are available from the correspondent. Requests for financial support are reviewed regularly by the Financial Grants Review Panel.

Common applicant mistakes

'Apply for areas we do not cover by the grant scheme, e.g. building adaptations in rented property.'

Menuchar Ltd

Jewish

£307,000 (2009/10)

Beneficial area

UK.

c/o Barry Flack & Co, Knight House, 27–31 East Barnet Road, Barnet EN4 8RN
Tel: 020 8275 5186
Correspondent: The Trustees
Trustees: Norman Bude; Gail Bude.
CC Number: 262782

Information available

Accounts were on file at the Charity Commission, but without a list of grants.

The main objects of the trust are the advancement of religion in accordance with the Orthodox Jewish faith and the relief of people in need.

In 2009/10 the trust had assets of £485,000 and an income of £635,000. Grants 'to religious organisations' totalled £307,000. A list of beneficiaries was not available.

Exclusions

No grants to non-registered charities or to individuals.

Applications

In writing to the correspondent.

Brian Mercer Charitable Trust

Welfare, medical, visual arts

£360,000 (2009/10)

Beneficial area

UK and overseas.

c/o Beever and Struthers, Central Buildings, Richmond Terrace, Blackburn BB1 7AP
Tel: 01254 686 600
Website: www.beeverstruthers.co.uk
Correspondent: Alan Rowntree, Trustee
Trustees: Christine Clancy; Kenneth Merrill; Alan Rowntree; Roger Duckworth; Mary Clitheroe.
CC Number: 1076925

Information available

Accounts were on file at the Charity Commission.

The trust's objectives are:
- the advancement of education and in particular, but not restricted to, the provision of grants for the promotion of medical and scientific research and the dissemination of the useful results thereof
- the furtherance and promotion of any other exclusively charitable objects and purposes in any part of the world as the trustees may in their absolute discretion think fit.

The trust's annual report 2009/10 states:

> Amongst other objects, the causes which they will most seek to benefit will be:
> - the prevention, treatment and cure of diseases effecting eyesight
> - the prevention, treatment and cure of cancer, particularly liver cancer
> - the promotion of the visual arts.

The trustees are seeking to develop close relationships with a number of charities with a view to working in partnership with those charities on specific projects and thus being in a position to influence the manner in which funds are expended in order to ensure that maximum benefit is derived from them.

In 2009/10 the trust had assets of £21 million and an income of £529,000. Grants, many of which are recurrent, were made to 33 organisations and totalled £360,000.

Beneficiaries included: Fight for Sight and British Council for the Prevention of Blindness (£50,000 each); SightSavers International (£25,000); Computer Aid International (£19,000); Macular Disease Society and Macmillan Cancer Relief (£15,000 each); DEC Haiti Earthquake Appeal and Vision Aid (£10,000 each); Micro Loan Foundation and North West Air Ambulance (£5,000 each); Burnley College and Cardinal Newman College (£2,500 each); and St Paul's PCC – Lindale (£1,000).

Applications

In writing to the correspondent. Trustees meet at least twice yearly to allocate grants.

The Merchant Taylors' Company Charities Fund

Education, training, church, medicine, general

£97,000 to organisations (2010)

Beneficial area

UK, especially inner London.

Merchant Taylor's Hall, 30 Threadneedle Street, London EC2R 8JB
Tel: 020 7450 4440
Email: charities@merchant-taylors.co.uk
Website: www.merchanttaylors.co.uk
Correspondent: Matthew Dear, Charities Officer

Trustees: Sir David Brewer; Mr. Richard Wingate Edward Charlton and Mr. Christopher Morley Keville.
CC Number: 1069124

Information available

Full accounts were available from the Charity Commission.

Grants are considered for the arts, social care and community development, disability, the elderly, poverty, medical studies and research, chemical dependency, homelessness, children, and education, with priority for special needs.

In 2010 the trust had assets of £600,000 and an income of £260,000 including a £52,000 corporate donation from The Merchant Taylors' Company. Grants were made totalling £72,000 and were broken down as follows:

Educational awards

Grants totalling £2,600 were made to six institutions. Beneficiaries include Wolverhampton Grammar School (£6,500); Foyle College, Londonderry (£4,200); Merchant Taylors School-Northwood (£3,700) and Wallingford School: Oxford (£900).

Training awards

Grants were made to three organisations totalling £7,000 and went to: Guildhall School of Music (£6,000) and St Paul's Cathedral Choir School and Royal School of Needlework (£500 each).

Church and clergy

Grants were made to five organisations totalling £5,000. Grant beneficiaries included: St Helen's Church – Bishopsgate (£2,000); St Paul's Cathedral of Friends and St Margaret's Church – Lee (£1,000 each) and St Michael's – Cornhill (£500).

Miscellaneous

One grant of £300 was made to the Brandram Road Community Centre Association.

Grants totalling £97,000 were made to eight organisations from the designated 'Livery and Freeman Fund'. Grant beneficiaries included: Sparks (£50,000); St Mungo's and East Potential (£10,000 each); Hope & Homes (£6,400); UNLOCK (£5,000) and Dean Close School (£2,000).

Applications

Awards are restricted at present to charities nominated by the Livery Committee.

The Merchants' House of Glasgow

General

About £60,000 to organisations a year.

Beneficial area

Glasgow and the west of Scotland.

7 West George Street, Glasgow
G2 1BA
Tel: 0141 221 8272
Fax: 0141 226 2275
Email: theoffice@merchantshouse.org.uk
Website: www.merchantshouse.org.uk
Correspondent: The Directors
Trustee: The Directors.
SC Number: SC008900

Information available

Information available from the OSCR website.

The charity's main activities included paying: 'pensions to pensioners, who may or may not have membership qualifications, and to provide assistance in the form of grants to charitable institutions within and around Glasgow'. It will normally consider applications from the following:

- organisations providing care and assistance to people with disabilities, older people, people who are terminally ill and people who have been socially deprived
- organisations providing for the care, advancement and rehabilitation of youth
- universities, colleges of further education and schools
- organisations connected with the arts, including music, theatre and the visual arts
- institutions that are connected with and represented by the Merchants' House.

The charity has an income of around £900,000 and makes grants to organisations of about £60,000 a year.

Previous grant recipients have included: Erskine Hospital, the National Youth Orchestra of Scotland, Scottish Motor Neurone Disease, the Castle Howard Trust, Delta, the National Burns Memorial Homes, Quarriers Village and Shelter.

Exclusions

The trust will not, unless in exceptional circumstances, make grants to:
- individuals
- churches other than Glasgow Cathedral
- organisations that have received support in the two years preceding an application

Applications

In writing to the correspondent at any time, supported by copy of accounts and information about the organisation's principal activities.

Mercury Phoenix Trust

AIDS, HIV

£203,000 (2009/10)

Beneficial area

Worldwide.

22 Cottage Offices, Latimer Park, Latimer, Chesham, Buckinghamshire HP5 1TU
Tel: 01494 766 799
Email: mercuryphoenixtrust@idrec.com
Website: www.mercuryphoenixtrust.com
Correspondent: Peter Chant, Administrator
Trustees: Brian May; Henry James Beach; Mary Austin; Roger Taylor.
CC Number: 1013768

Information available

Accounts were available from the Charity Commission; the trust has a useful website.

The trust was set up in memory of Freddie Mercury by the remaining members of the rock group, Queen, and their manager. The trust states that it makes grants to 'help relieve the poverty, sickness and distress of people with AIDS and HIV and to stimulate awareness and education in connection with the disease throughout the world'.

The trust's website states:

> Since 1992 the Mercury Phoenix Trust has been responsible for donating more than $15 million in the fight against AIDS making over 750 grants to charities worldwide. Applications for grants have come in from many countries around the world and collaboration has been realised with groups as far removed as the World Health Organisation to grass-root organisations run partly by voluntary workers in Uganda, Kenya, South Africa, Zambia, Nepal and India. The trust has adapted its policy to concentrate on HIV/AIDS education and awareness in the developing world.

In 2009/10 the trust had assets of £1.3 million and an income of £255,000. Grants totalled £203,000, of which 33 were listed in the accounts.

Beneficiaries included: Save The Children – UK (£15,000); Preana – Nepal (£12,000); Care International – UK and Gemini – UK (£10,000 each); British Red Cross – UK (£9,200); Mfesane – South Africa (£8,000); Christian Social Services – South Africa (£7,000); OGLM – US (£4,500); Sawed Trust – India and Rural Consciousness Unit – Bangladesh (£4,000 each); Social Welfare Environment and Conservation – Nepal (£3,500); and Dhiverse – India (£1,000).

Exclusions

No funding for individuals or travel costs.

Applications

Application forms are available on request from funding@mercuryphoenixtrust.com. In addition to a completed application form, the trust requires the following documents:

- a budget
- registration certificate
- audited accounts for the last financial year
- constitution or memorandum and articles of association
- annual report
- equal opportunities policy.

The Metropolitan Drinking Fountain and Cattle Trough Association

Provision of pure drinking water

£35,000 (2010)

Beneficial area

UK, mainly London, and overseas.

Oaklands, 5 Queenborough Gardens, Chislehurst, Kent BR7 6NP
Tel: 020 8467 1261
Email: ralph.baber@tesco.net
Website: www.drinkingfountains.org
Correspondent: R P Baber, Secretary
Trustees: J E Mills, Chair; R P Baber; Mrs S Fuller; Sir J Smith; M W Elliott; M Nation; A King; M Bear; Mrs L Erith.
CC Number: 207743

Information available

Accounts were available from the Charity Commission.

The objectives of the association are to promote the provision of drinking water for people and animals in the United Kingdom and overseas, and the preservation of the association's archive materials, artefacts, drinking fountains, cattle troughs and other installations.

Over the years the association has recognised a need for supplying fountains to schools throughout the United Kingdom. The association typically gifts a Novus drinking fountain to a school on the condition that the school pays £25 to join the association. Generally one fountain is donated per 100 children. The school is responsible for the installation and the maintenance of the fountain.

In 2010 the trust had assets of £590,000 and an income of £29,000. Grants totalling around £35,000 were made to organisations. Beneficiaries included: Appropriate Technology (£2,500); Dhaka Ahsania Mission, Resolve and The Spiti Project (£2,000 each); The Salvation Army (£1,500); and TescoSpana (£1,400).

Applications

In writing to the correspondent. In addition, in considering an application for a grant trustees also require the following information:

- a copy of the most recent audited accounts
- how has the cost of the project been ascertained, e.g. qualified surveyor?
- how many people/animals is it estimated would use the fountain/ trough in a day?
- will the charity supervise the project, if not who would?
- where is it anticipated the remainder of the funds to complete the project will come from?

T and J Meyer Family Foundation Limited

Education, healthcare, environment

£298,000 (2010)

Beneficial area

UK and overseas.

3 Kendrick Mews, London SW7 3HG
Email: info@tjmff.org
Correspondent: T H Meyer
Trustees: A C Meyer; J D Meyer; Q H Meyer; I T Meyer; M M Meyer.
CC Number: 1087507

Information available

Accounts were on file at the Charity Commission in dollars and were converted at a rate of 0.625 dollars to the pound.

Set up in 2001, this foundation focuses primarily on education, healthcare and the environment. The criteria for charities are:

- organisations which alleviate the suffering of humanity through health, education and environment
- organisations with extremely high correlation between what is gifted and what the beneficiary receives
- organisations who struggle to raise funds either because either they are new, their size or their access to funds is constrained

organisations who promote long-term effective sustainable solutions.

In 2010 the trust had assets of £16.3 million and an income of £298,000. It made grants to organisations totalling £534,000.

Beneficiaries included: Sisters of Sacred Heart of J & M (£63,000); Living Heart, Peru (£4,700); Room to Read (£50,000); Barefoot College (£6,300); Trees Water People (£12,500); Friends without Borders (£31,000); Partners in Health (£63,000); Village Health Workers (£16,000); Angels Choir (£7,700); Bowel Cancer UK (£7,300); Hope and Homes for Children (£39,000); Royal Marsden Cancer Trust (£68,000); and Samantha Dixon Brain Tumour (£15,000).

Applications

No grants to unsolicited applications. Trustees meet four times a year.

Mickleham Charitable Trust

Relief-in-need

£144,000 (2009/10)

Beneficial area

UK, with a preference for Norfolk.

c/o Hansells, 13–14 The Close, Norwich NR1 4DS
Tel: 01603 615 731
Email: philipnorton@hansells.co.uk
Correspondent: Philip Norton, Trustee
Trustees: Philip Norton; Rev Sheila Nunney; Anne Richardson.
CC Number: 1048337

Information available

Accounts were available from the Charity Commission.

Set up in 1995, the trusts main object is to provide relief for the abused and disadvantaged, particularly young people, and the blind.

In 2009/10 the trust had assets of £3.1 million and an income of £126,000. Grants totalling £144,000 were made to 62 organisations, many of which had been supported in the previous year. The grants were split across the objectives of the charity

with £91,000 made in support of charities providing assistance to the abused and disadvantaged and £53,000 in support of the blind or partially sighted.

Beneficiaries included: Orbis International (£12,000); Harvest Trust (£6,000); Deafness Research UK, Age Concern – Norwich and Motability – Norfolk (£5,000 each); NR5 Project (£2,000); Whizz Kids (£1,500); and St Dunstans, Rethink, Norwich Youth for Christ, Canine Partners, Norfolk Family Mediation Service, Elizabeth Fitzroy Support, Musical Keys and Parkinson's Disease Society (£1,000 each).

Applications

In writing to the correspondent.

Gerald Micklem Charitable Trust

General, health

£127,000 (2010)

Beneficial area

UK and East Hampshire.

Bolinge Hill Farm, Buriton, Petersfield, Hampshire GU31 4NN
Tel: 01730 264 207
Email: mail@geraldmicklemct.org.uk
Website: www.geraldmicklemct.org.uk/
Correspondent: Mrs S J Shone, Trustee
Trustees: Susan J Shone; Joanna L Scott-Dalgleish; Helen Ratcliffe.
CC Number: 802583

Information available

Information was available from the Charity Commission

The trust was established in November 1989 with a bequest left in the will of Gerald Micklem. The trust states that the charities it is most interested in are UK charities working on a national basis in the following areas: disability; deafness and blindness; medical conditions affecting both adults and children; medical research, but not in substitution of NHS spending; people with learning disabilities; children and young people, especially the

disadvantaged; environment and wildlife.

On occasion, the trust will make grants to charities working in East Hampshire outside the above fields. It does not make grants to local charities operating elsewhere in the UK. Donations are generally for between £2,000 and £3,000.

In 2010 the trust had assets of £977,000 and an income of £440,000. Grants totalled £127,000.

Major beneficiaries included: Self Unlimited (£6,000); Support for Living, Osteopathic Centre for Children, The Rosemary Foundation, Whizz-Kidz (£4,000 each); The Bendrigg Trust; St Wilfrid's Ribchester PCC, Hampshire Deaf Association, Refuge, and Diabetes UK (£3,000 each); Bhola's Children, The Royal Forestry Society and St Mary's Convent & Nursing Home – Chiswick (£2,000 each).

Exclusions

The trust does not make grants to individuals, does not enter into sponsorship arrangements with individuals and does not make grants to organisations that are not UK-registered charities.

The areas of charitable activity that fall outside the trust's current funding priorities are: drug/alcohol abuse and counselling; museums, galleries and heritage; performing arts and cultural organisations; churches; and, overseas aid.

Applications

Applications may be made to the correspondent by letter – not by email. Enquiries prior to any application may be made by email.

The trust offers this overview of the application process in its latest annual report:

There is no application form. Applications may be made at any time, but preferably not in December, and should be accompanied by the latest report & accounts of the applicant organisation.

Applicants should note that, at their main meeting early in the calendar year, the trustees consider applications received up to 31 December each year, but do not carry them forward. Having regard for the time of year when this meeting takes place, it makes sense for applications to be made as late as possible in the calendar year so that the information they contain is most up to date when the trustees meet.

Note: The trustees receive a very substantial number of appeals each year. It is not their practice to acknowledge appeals, and they prefer not to enter into correspondence with applicants other than those to whom grants are being made or from whom further information is required. Only successful applicants are notified of the outcome of their application.

Common applicant mistakes

'They don't read the guidelines on our website.'

The Migraine Trust

Study of migraine

£73,000 in research grants (2009/10)

Beneficial area

UK and overseas.

2nd Floor, 55–56 Russel Square, London WC1B 4HP
Tel: 0207 462 6604
Email: info@migrainetrust.org
Website: www.migrainetrust.org
Correspondent: Adam Speller
Trustees: Andrew Jordan; J P S Wolff-Ingham; Prof. P J Goadsby; Ms S Hammond; Dr H McGregor; Dr Anne McGregor; Mrs Jennifer Mills; Dr Mark Wetherall; Dr Brendan Davies; Ian Watmore; Mrs Suzanne Marriot.
CC Number: 1081300

Information available

Accounts were available from the Charity Commission.

Amongst other objects in relation to the study of migraine, the trust provides research grants, fellowships and studentships (studentships are applied for by host institution only). Funds provide for research into migraine at recognised institutions, such as hospitals and universities.

In 2009/10 the trust had assets of £388,000, an income of £583,000 and made grants for research purposes totalling £73,000.

Applications

By application form available from trust. Applications will be acknowledged.

Millennium Stadium Charitable Trust

Sport, the arts, community, environment

£344,000 (2009/10)

Beneficial area

Wales.

c/o Fusion, Loft 2, Ocean House, Clarence Road, Cardiff Bay CF10 5FR
Tel: 029 2049 4963
Fax: 029 2049 4964
Email: msct@fusionuk.org.uk
Website: www. millenniumstadiumtrust.co.uk
Correspondent: The Trust Officer
Trustees: Russell Goodway, Chair; Louise Casella; Ian Davies; Gerald Davies; Paul Glaze; Gerallt Hughes; Peredur Jenkins; Mike John; John Lloyd-Jones; Linda Pepper; Louise Prynne; Simon Wakefield; Wendy Williams.
CC Number: 1086596

Information available

Accounts were available from the Charity Commission, but without a list of grants.

The trust was established by an agreement between the Millennium Commission and the Millennium Stadium plc. Its income is generated through a levy on every ticket purchased for public events at the stadium.

The trust states the following aims on its website:

The trust's aims

Through its grant funding the trust aims to improve the quality of life of people who live and work in Wales. In particular the trust aims to promote education, history, language and culture, particularly for those who face disadvantage or discrimination.

Wales is a country rich in culture, history, language and sporting

successes. In today's era of globalisation people often forget what is in their locality. As a result the trust is keen to help young people learn more about their country via exchange programmes and has made provision to support youth exchange programmes which fall in to any of the funding categories of the trust.

In 2009/10 the trust held assets of £676,000 and had an income of £393,000, mainly from donations from the Millennium Stadium. Grants were made totalling £344,000.

Guidelines

The trust outlines its funding programmes on its website:

Sport

Sport embraces much more than traditional team games and competition. Sport can mean physical activity or the improvement of physical fitness and mental well-being, and can assist in the formation of social relationships and individual and team confidence.

The trust is particularly interested in supporting projects that improve the quality of life of people and communities facing disadvantage.

Funding Priorities

The trust strives to make a difference to sporting organisations throughout Wales and appreciates that sport relies heavily on volunteers.

The trust is keen to support volunteer-based projects, particularly from ethnic minorities and people with disabilities. In addition, the trust recognises the difference that coaching can make to the development of a sport and is keen to fund equipment and coaching costs if the need has been clearly identified.

The arts

The trust is keen to support arts projects that are creative, unique and work with the disadvantaged or deprived individuals and groups throughout Wales. In particular, the trust wishes to develop and improve the knowledge and practice of the arts and to increase opportunities for people to see and participate in the arts throughout Wales.

Funding Priorities

The trust aims to give more people the opportunity to enjoy the diversity of performing and visual arts in Wales. The trust particularly favours proposals which expand and improve arts provision in parts of the country less well served than others and will give priority to organisations which strive to work together to share experiences, practices and ideas.

The environment

The environment of Wales varies dramatically between north, south, east and west of the country. From the mountains of the north to the valleys of the south, the trust welcomes applications relating to environmental groups from both rural and urban areas in Wales.

Funding Priorities
The trust encourages applications relating to recycling, developing green spaces, the development and promotion of green practices and the promotion of public transport schemes. Projects that improve the quality of Wales' environment, protect and create a vibrant countryside, and develop and promote sustainable land-use planning will be a priority for support.

The trust aims to fund programmes that protect and enhance Wales' natural heritage and promote its sustainable use and enjoyment in a way which contributes to local economic prosperity and social inclusion.

The community
The trust is keen to target local communities suffering from greatest disadvantage in Wales.

Funding Priorities
The trust will give priority to organisations that are looking to tackle social, personal, economic or cultural barriers within their own communities. In particular projects that lead to greater independence and give people more control over their lives will be given priority. The trust welcomes applications that give people a voice to express their needs and hopes.

The trust is keen help disabled people to challenge barriers and to be active and visible in their local communities.

Youth Exchange Programmes
The trust will give priority to projects [in the above categories] that foster greater understanding and friendship among the young people of Wales through exchange programmes. Organisations may wish to consider applying for costs towards travel and accommodation to visit another similar group in Wales. Examples of projects such as this may include one football club in Wales travelling to visit another football club to undertake a sporting and social weekend. In particular the trust is keen to support youth programmes that bring together 11 to 25 year olds through sporting or cultural exchanges. Exchange projects should demonstrate long-term benefits for the groups and communities involved and must be between groups based within Wales. These benefits will be as a result of new experiences that are educative, participative, empowering and expressive. The trust recognises that such exchanges can lead to a better appreciation of the different cultural, linguistic and social characteristics that make up the communities of Wales.

The trust supports:
- not-for-profit organisations
- properly constituted voluntary organisations
- charitable organisations
- voluntary groups working with local authorities (applicant cannot be the local authority)
- applications from groups of any age (not just youth projects).

Priority is given to organisations serving groups and communities suffering from the greatest disadvantage.

The trust issues funding according to the size of geographical area that an organisation has a remit to cover:
- national organisations (covering the whole of Wales) – up to £12,500
- regional organisations (covering a region or local authority area) – up to £7,500
- local organisations (covering a local community or town) – up to £2,500.

Exclusions
The trust does not support:
- projects outside of Wales
- day-to-day running costs
- projects that seek to redistribute grant funds for the benefit of third party organisations
- payments of debts/overdrafts
- retrospective requests
- requests from individuals
- payment to profit making organisations
- applications made solely in the name of a local authority.

Note: In addition to the above, successful applicants may not-reapply to the trust until a three year period from the date of grant offer has elapsed. The grant offer letter will advise applicants of the date when they will be eligible to re-apply.

Applications
The trust holds three rounds a year one for each type of application – national, regional and local. Deadline dates can be found on the trust's website, along with full guidelines and application forms.

The Miller Foundation

General
About £150,000 (2009/10)

Beneficial area
UK, with a preference for Scotland, especially the west of Scotland.

Maclay Murray and Spens, 151 St Vincent Street, Glasgow G2 5NJ
Correspondent: The Secretary
Trustees: C Fleming-Brown; G R G Graham; J Simpson; G F R Fleming-Brown.
SC Number: SC008798

Information available
Basic information available from the website of the Office of the Scottish Charity Regulator.

The foundation supports a wide range of charitable activities, primarily in Scotland, but also in other parts of the UK. Grants generally range from £500 to £2,000, with the majority of them recurrent.

In 2009/10 the foundation had a gross income of £158,000. Grants are made totalling around £150,000 each year. No further information was available.

Exclusions
No grants to individuals.

Applications
In writing to the correspondent.

The Millfield House Foundation

Social disadvantage, social policy
£238,000 (2009/10)

Beneficial area
North east England particularly Tyne and Wear.

19 The Crescent, Benton Lodge, Newcastle upon Tyne NE7 7ST
Tel: 0191 266 9429

Email: finley@lineone.net
Website: www.mhfdn.org.uk
Correspondent: Terence Finley, Administrator
Trustees: Rosemary Chubb; Grigor McClelland; Jen McClelland; Stephen McClelland; Sheila Spencer; Robert Williamson; Toby Lowe; Jane Streather; Rhiannon Bearne.
CC Number: 271180

Information available

Accounts were available from the Charity Commission.

Millfield House Foundation (MHF) helps to tackle poverty, disadvantage and exclusion and to promote social change in the North East of England, particularly Tyne and Wear. The foundation states: 'The current priority is to promote social change by funding projects that inform discussion and influence public policy and attitudes, with the aim of diminishing social deprivation and empowering communities.'

The following information is taken from the foundation's website:

In November 2010 MHF's Trustees considered the changing political scenario and the impact of new policies in the NE region. They confirmed the current grants policy and wish to emphasize the following:

▷ MHF's funds continue to be available for policy-related work and campaigning.

▷ It is not MHF's role, nor does it have the resources, to protect those parts of the VCS which may be facing substantial cuts and MHF cannot provide a safety net for organisations at risk of failing or closing. But the Trustees are committed to continuing to support policy functions, and particularly the 'voices' of vulnerable groups in North East communities, especially if they are disproportionately affected by public expenditure cuts, reduction in services and the withdrawal or loss of grant aid to the VCS.

▷ The focus for policy-related work and campaigning may have shifted from regional to national structures but new opportunities should arise through regional bodies such as the LEPs. National organisations may be expected to find new ways of responding to needs within the region.

▷ The Trustees are aware that monitoring of the medium and longer term effects of new policies is necessary to provide evidence for policy action and campaigning. The implications of more public services being provided by the VCS and the private sector require careful consideration, as do new models of finance such as Social Impact Bonds and Payment by Results, and there may be opportunities for closer links with the private sector.

▷ Potential applicants are urged to refer to the grants list page [on the foundation's website] for examples of impact and influence and for possibilities of partnership working and alliances with current grant-holders.

Guidelines for applicants

MHF aims to provide, alone or in partnership with other funders, significant and medium-term support to a small number of carefully selected projects or organisations. It is unlikely to have more than about 6–12 grants in payment at the same time and can therefore approve only a small number of new grants in any one year. One-off grants may be between £5,000 and £50,000. Grants for more than one year could be between £20,000 and £30,000 p.a. for two or three years.

Applicants are asked to note the following:

▷ MHF will support national as well as local bodies, provided that projects are based in the North East of England (includes regional and sub-regional projects; projects which are locally based may be considered so long as they are of wider benefit).

▷ The financial resources of MHF are a tiny fraction of the total available for charitable activity in the North East. The Trustees therefore wish to concentrate their resources on projects which most other funding bodies cannot or will not support.

▷ As a charity, the Foundation must confine its grants to purposes accepted in law as charitable. However, official guidance makes it clear that charities may include a variety of political and campaigning activities to further their purposes.

▷ The Foundation wishes to promote equal opportunities and diversity through its grant-making. It will do its best to ensure that applications are dealt with fairly and that no one is denied access to information or funding on grounds of race, colour, ethnicity or national origin, religious affiliation, gender, sexual orientation, age or disability. If appropriate, the Foundation will offer help with the completion of an application.

▷ The Foundation welcomes applications from stand-alone projects, from organisations which sponsor or manage projects, from two or more projects applying jointly, and particularly from projects involving service users.

▷ In certain cases, and strictly subject to compliance with the Charity Commission's guidance CC9, the Foundation may be willing to support proposals which involve non-violent direct action.

▷ The Trustees may consider an additional element of grant to allow for support from a consultant to assist with campaigning, lobbying, media and public relations.

▷ The Trustees are willing to take some risks in funding projects which strongly reflect the above policy. The Administrator is available to discuss and give guidance on the submission of innovative proposals.

In 2009/10 the foundation had assets of £5.6 million and an income of £144,000. Grants were made to ten organisations totalling £238,000. Beneficiaries were: Institute for Public Policy Research (£40,000); Gateshead Carers Association (£34,000); Regional Refugee Forum North East (£32,000); Age Concern and Shelter (£30,000 each); Barnardo's (£24,000); Mental Health North East (£23,000); Living Streets (£15,000); Compass (£10,000); Voluntary Organisations Network North East (£500).

Exclusions

The foundation states that it 'will not fund straightforward service provision, or mainline university research, or the wide range of other projects that are eligible for support elsewhere'.

Applications

Initial outline proposals should be made in writing to the correspondent. If the application meets the stated guidelines the administrator may request further information or arrange a meeting. Applications unconnected with Tyne and Wear are not acknowledged.

The trustees meet twice a year, in May and November and the deadlines for the trustees' meetings are mid April and mid October. The administrator is willing to provide guidance for the preparation of final applications, but not without first receiving an outline proposal.

Applications should include:

▷ Full contact details, including email address if available. A covering letter containing a brief summary of the purpose of the project and the amount sought from MHF, and a substantive paper of no more than 4 pages. All other information should be provided as Appendices.

- A description of the project including its aims and intended outcomes, with specific reference to possible policy implications, an action programme and proposed timescale for delivery.
- A budget for the project giving a breakdown of total expenditure and of sources of anticipated income.
- A copy of the most recent annual report and audited accounts for the project and/or the sponsoring body.
- The constitution of the responsible body.
- Details of the organisation's policy and procedures for equal opportunities and diversity.
- If appropriate, plans for dissemination of the results of the project. (Research reports should be summarised in a format similar to that of the 'Findings' series produced by the Joseph Rowntree Foundation.
- Details of arrangements for monitoring and evaluation.
- If funding is sought towards the costs of a salaried post, a job description.
- The names of two independent referees (references may not be taken up in every case).

For further information potential applicants are strongly advised to visit the trust's website.

Common applicant mistakes

'They don't research the trust's policy and priorities, despite this information being available on our website; they don't take account of our specific requirements; 'round robin' appeals rather than targeted appeals – they just think they can have a go!'

The Millfield Trust

Christian

£68,000 to organisations (2009/10)

Beneficial area

UK and worldwide.

Millfield House, Bell Lane, Liddington, Swindon, Wiltshire SN4 0HE
Tel: 01793 790 181
Correspondent: D Bunce, Trustee
Trustees: D Bunce; P W Bunce; S D Bunce; A C Bunce; Mrs. Rita Bunce.
CC Number: 262406

Information available

Accounts were available from the Charity Commission.

The trust was setup to provide grants to Christian organisations, and has supported a number of missionary societies for the last 50 years. Grants are given solely to organisations known to the trustees and new applications are not considered.

In 2009/10 the trust had assets of £138,000 and an income of £71,000, including £52,000 in Gift Aid donations from two of its trustees. Grants to organisations totalled £68,000 of which 12 were listed in the accounts. A further £3,900 was given in grants to individual missionaries and evangelists, and £60 in gifts to older people.

Beneficiaries included: Gideon's International (£12,500); Gospel Mission to South America (£8,500); Mark Gillingham Charitable Trust (£4,200); Ashbury Evangelical Free Church (£3,500); Mission to Europe (£3,000); Bible lands (£2,500); and Send a Cow and TEAR Fund (£1,100 each).

Items of up to £1,000 were not individually listed in the accounts.

Applications

No replies to unsolicited applications. The trust has informed us that: 'Most of the organisations and individuals we support are ones in which we have a personal interest and have supported for many years.'

The Millhouses Charitable Trust

Christian, overseas aid, general

£18,000 (2009/10)

Beneficial area

UK and overseas.

c/o MacFarlane and Co., Cunard Building, Water Street, Liverpool L3 1DS
Tel: 0151 236 6161
Correspondent: Paul Charles Kurthausen, Correspondent
Trustees: Revd Jeanetta S Harcus; Dr A W Harcus; Dr J L S Alexander; Ms Penelope A Thornton; Mrs Fiona J van Nieuwkerk.
CC Number: 327773

Information available

Accounts were received at the Charity Commission but not available online.

In 2009/10 the trust had an income of £20,000 and a total expenditure of £18,000.

Previous beneficiaries included: NSPCC and Christian Solidarity (£5,000 each); Release International and Barnabus Fund (£2,500 each); Children's Society, Crisis and Oasis (£1,000 each); Rehab UK and Medical foundation (£500 each); and Mercy Ships, Operation Mobilisation and Smile (£250 each).

Exclusions

Grants are made to registered charities only; no grants to individuals.

Applications

In writing to the correspondent, but note that most of the grants given by this trust are recurrent. If new grants are made, they are usually to organisations known to the trustees.

The Millichope Foundation

General

£272,000 (2009/10)

Beneficial area

UK, especially the West Midlands and Shropshire.

Millichope Park, Munslow, Craven Arms, Shropshire SY7 9HA
Tel: 01584 841 234
Email: sarah@millichope.com

Correspondent: Mrs S A Bury, Trustee
Trustees: L C N Bury; Mrs S A Bury; Mrs B Marshall.
CC Number: 282357

Information available

Accounts were available from the Charity Commission.

The foundation makes donations to a wide range of different organisations including:

- UK charities
- local charities serving Birmingham and Shropshire
- arts and culture
- conservation/heritage
- Education.

In 2009/10 the foundation had assets of £6 million and an income of £398,000. Grants were made to organisations totalling £272,000.

Beneficiaries included: Brazilian Atlantic Rainforest Forest (£15,000); Hope and Homes for Children (£10,000); Community Council of Shropshire and Megan Baker House (£5,000 each); Cambridge Foundation (£4,000); Teme Valley Youth Project and Galapagos Conservation Trust (£2,000 each); Birmingham City Mission and Sandwell MultiCare (£2,000 each); Age Concern – Birmingham, Juvenile Diabetes Research Foundation and Riding for the Disabled (£1,000 each); and Marches Family Network (£500).

Exclusions

No grants to individuals or non-registered charities.

Applications

In writing to the correspondent.

Common applicant mistakes

'They don't meet our criteria.'

The Millward Charitable Trust

Social welfare, performing arts, medical research and animal welfare

£84,000 (2009/10)

Beneficial area

UK and overseas.

c/o Burgis & Bullock, 2 Chapel Court, Holly Walk, Leamington Spa, Warwickshire CV32 4YS
Tel: 01926 451 000
Correspondent: John Hulse, Trustee
Trustees: Maurice Millward; Sheila Millward; John Hulse.
CC Number: 328564

Information available

Accounts were available from the Charity Commission.

The trust has general charitable purposes and during the year supported a variety of causes including social welfare, performing arts, medical research and animal welfare.

In 2009/10 the trust had assets of nearly £2 million and an income of £68,000. Grants were made totalling £84,000 and were broken down as follows:

Performing arts	8	£61,500
Social welfare	19	£16,500
Animal welfare	5	£3,500
Medical research	6	£2,600

Institutional grants greater than £1,000 each included: Birds Eye View (£36,000 in three grants); Music in the Round (£6,400); City of Birmingham Symphony Orchestra (£10,000 in two grants); CORD Sudan Appeal and Leamington Music (£5,000 each); and Barnardo's, Christian Relief, Howard League for Penal Reform and RSPCA (1,000 each).

Applications

In writing to the correspondent.

The Edgar Milward Charity

Christian, humanitarian

£30,000 (2009/10)

Beneficial area

UK and overseas, with an interest in Reading.

53 Brook Drive, Corsham, Wiltshire SN13 9AX

Correspondent: A S Fogwill, Corresponding Secretary
Trustees: J S Milward, Chair; Mrs M V Roberts; G M Fogwill; S M W Fogwill; A S Fogwill; Mrs F Palethorpe; Mrs J C Austin.
CC Number: 281018

Information available

Accounts were available from the Charity Commission.

The object of the charity is to distribute all of its income as it arises in the following manner:

- one-half for the furtherance of the Christian religion within the UK and throughout the world
- two-fifths for general charitable purposes
- one-tenth for educational purposes within a 15-mile radius of the Civic Centre in Reading.

Within this, the trust's grant making policy is to support a limited number of causes known to the trustees, particularly those supported by the settlor.

In 2009/10 the charity had assets of £1.2 million, which generated an income of £49,000. Grants were made totalling £30,000, which were distributed under the following categories:

Furtherance of Christian religion		
£1,000 or more	7	£10,000
Under £1,000	11	£6,000
Total	18	£16,000
At trustees' discretion		
£1,000 or more	4	£8,000
Under £1,000	1	£500
Total	15	£13,000
Educational purposes		
£1,000 or more	–	–
Under £1,000	1	£500
Total	1	£500
Total		
£1,000 or more	11	£18,000
Under £1,000	23	£12,000
Total	34	£30,000

Beneficiaries included: the Bible Society and UCB (£2,000); Interserve (£1,500); Africa Inland Mission, Greyfriars Missionary Trust, OSCAR and Urban Saints (£1,000 each).

Exclusions

No new applications will be supported.

Applications

Unsolicited applications cannot be considered.

The Peter Minet Trust

General, children/ youth, health and people with disabilities, social welfare, culture and community

£196,000 (2009/10)

Beneficial area

Mainly south east London boroughs, particularly Lambeth and Southwark.

1a Taylors Yard, 67 Alderbrook Road, London SW12 8AD

Tel: 020 8772 3155

Email: info@peterminet.org.uk

Website: www.peterminet.org.uk

Correspondent: The Administrator

Trustees: J C B South, Chair; Ms P C Jones; R Luff; Revd Bruce Stokes; Mrs L Cleverly.

CC Number: 259963

Information available

Accounts were available from the Charity Commission.

In the mid-sixties, the Minet family sold much of their property to local councils. Part of the proceeds were used by Peter Brissault Minet to set up the trust in 1969.

The trust aims to improve the quality of life for people living in the inner city boroughs of South East London, especially Lambeth and Southwark. It does this by making grants to UK registered charities that run social welfare, health, cultural and community projects, working with people of all ages who are in need.

The Peter Minet Trust is interested in new ventures as well as established projects. It awards main grants of up to £5,000 and runs a small grants programme (£500 and under) for one-off events and smaller projects.

In 2009/10 the trust had assets of £4.2 million, an income of £168,000 and awarded grants to 57 organisations totalling £196,000 with 47 main grants and 10 small grants. Grants were distributed in the following categories:

Children and youth	19	£39,000
Health and people with disabilities	12	£27,000
Community projects	11	£23,000
General and cultural	5	£11,500
Small grants	10	£4,500

Beneficiary organisations included: Bermondsey Arts Group, Southwark Playhouse Theatre Company, Putney Samaritans and The Young Vic (£3,000 each); Action Space London Events, Children with AIDS Charity, Live Music Now! and UK Sailing Academy (£2,000 each) and Bells Gardens Tenants and Residents Association, Southwark Homeless Information Project and The Food Chain (£1,000 each).

Bruce Malcolm Stokes is also a trustee of First Fruit (Charity Commission no. 1066749); and Kick London (Charity Commission no. 1100072). Rodney Luff is also a trustee of The Simon Trust (Charity Commission no. 1029570); and The Will Charitable Trust (Charity Commission no. 801682).

Exclusions

The trust does not make grants for:

- Individuals
- National appeals by large charities
- Appeals outside the inner boroughs of South East London
- Appeals whose sole purpose is to make grants from collected funds
- Research

Applications

Application forms along with guidelines are available either, by post from the correspondent or, by downloading them from the trust's website. The following application guidelines were available from the trust's website:

How to Apply for Main Grants and Small Grants:

1. Please complete an Application Form that can be downloaded from www.peterminet.org.uk. We use the same form for Main Grants and Small Grants.
2. This application form should be completed in Microsoft Word and emailed as a Word attachment (not a pdf) to info@peterminet.org.uk.
3. Please do not email brochures, letters or annual reports with your application. We only need an attachment of your application form. We do not need a copy of your latest signed audited accounts as we look at these on your Charity Commission's record on www.charity-commission.gov.uk.
4. We prefer you to email us your application form, but if you cannot access the internet, please complete the form in black ink and send by post. Please do not use registered or recorded delivery as the office is not open full-time and this can delay your application.

If you have any questions about your application or how to send in your form, contact the office on 020 8772 3155 or info@peterminet.org.uk

Minge's Gift and the Pooled Trusts

Medical, education, disadvantage, disability

£86,000 to organisations (2009/10)

Beneficial area

UK, with some preference for the City of London.

The Worshipful Company of Cordwainers, Clothworkers Hall, Dunster Court, Mincing Lane, London EC3R 7AH

Tel: 020 7929 1121

Fax: 020 7929 1124

Email: office@cordwain.org

Website: www.cordwainers.org

Correspondent: John Miller, Company Clerk

Trustee: The Master and Wardens of the Worshipful Company of Cordwainers.

CC Number: 266073

Information available

Accounts were available from the Charity Commission.

Minge's Gift

The trust was established for general charitable purposes as directed by the Master and Wardens of the Worshipful Company of Cordwainers. The income of Minge's Gift is generally allocated for the support of educational and medical establishments with which the company has developed long term relationships, ex-Service organisations and towards assistance for disabled and/or disadvantaged youth.

In 2009/10 the trust had assets of £2.8 million and an income of £169,000. Grants were made to organisations totalling nearly £86,000, broken down as follows:

Standard grants – £82,000 in 27 grants, the largest of which went to: Royal Society for the Blind (£16,000); University of Northampton (£15,000); and University of the Arts – London (£10,000). Other beneficiaries included: De Montfort University (£5,000); Footwear Friends (£3,000); Lord Mayors Fund (£2,000); Guildhall School of Music and Dance (£1,500); Museum of London (£1,000); St Olave's Church (£625); Queen Alexandra Hospital Home – Worthing (£500); Action for the Blind (£300); British Red Cross – City of London (£200); United Guilds Service (£125); and Shawe and Fisher Service (£110).

Master's gifts – during the year £850 was given from this fund.

Pooled trusts

Also included in the accounts for Minge's Gift, were details of the giving of the Common Investment Fund (Pooled Trusts). This combines a number of small trusts which are administered by the Worshipful Company of Cordwainers for the benefit of scholars, the blind, deaf, clergy widows, spinsters of the Church of England, ex-servicemen and their widows and those who served in the merchant services. It also provides for the upkeep of the Company's almshouses in Shorne, Kent. A total of £18,000 was given to individuals (£15,000) and organisations (£3,000) in 2009/10.

Exclusions

Grants to individuals are only given through the Pooled Trusts.

Applications

In writing to the correspondent.

Common applicant mistakes

'They send what is clearly a general letter without focusing on our organisation.'

The Minos Trust

Christian, general

Around £25,000 (2009/10)

Beneficial area

UK and overseas.

Kleinwort Benson Trustees Ltd, 30 Gresham Street, London EC2V 7PG
Tel: 020 3207 7091
Correspondent: The Trustees
Trustees: Revd K W Habershon; Mrs E M Habershon; Mrs D M Irwin-Clark.
CC Number: 265012

Information available

Accounts were received at the Charity Commission but not available to view online.

Previously we were advised that the trust gives most of its support to Christian charities in grants ranging up to £15,000. Remaining funds are given to other causes, with a preference for animals and wildlife, although these grants tend to be less than £1,000. Many of the organisations receiving the larger grants are regularly supported by the trust.

In 2009/10 the trust had an income of £7,000 and a total expenditure of £25,000. This is in line with previous years when its expenditure has regularly exceeded its income. Further information was not available.

Previous beneficiaries include: Care Trust (£2,500), Tearfund (£2,000) and Ashburnham Christian Trust (£1,500), with £1,000 each to Bible Society, Friends of the Elderly and Youth with a Mission; Worldwide Fund for Nature (£450); Africa Christian Press (£400); Aid to Russian Christians (£300); Gideon's International (£100); Sussex Farming Wildlife Advisory Group and RSPB (£50 each).

Applications

In writing to the correspondent, for consideration on an ongoing basis.

Minton Charitable Trust

General, education

£325,000 (2009/10)

Beneficial area

UK.

26 Hamilton House, Vicarage Gate, London W8 4HL
Correspondent: Sir Anthony Armitage Greener, Trustee
Trustees: Sir Anthony Armitage Greener; Richard Edmunds; Lady Audrey Greener.
CC Number: 1112106

Information available

Accounts were available from the Charity Commission.

Set up in 2005, the trusts' objects, as taken from the Charity Commission website, are: 'the advancement and promotion of the education of the public through the provision of, or assisting with, the provision of facilities, support, education, advice and financial assistance to individuals and organisations'.

In 2009/10 the trust had assets of £388,000 and an income of £224,000, mostly from donations. Grants totalled £325,000.

The two beneficiaries were: Swindon Academy (£200,000); and St Giles Trust (£125,000).

Applications

In writing to the correspondent.

Common applicant mistakes

'They are ineligible or inappropriate.'

The Mirianog Trust

General

£48,000 (2009/10)

Beneficial area

UK.

Moorcote, Thornley, Tow Law, Bishop Auckland DL13 4NU
Tel: 01388 731350

Correspondent: Canon W E L Broad, Trustee

Trustees: Canon William Broad, Chair; Daphne Broad; Elizabeth Jeary.

CC Number: 1091397

Information available

Accounts were available from the Charity Commission.

Set up in 2002 with general charitable purposes, currently the trustees give preference to:

- relief of poverty
- overseas aid and famine relief
- accommodation and housing
- environment, conservation and heritage.

In 2009/10 the trust had assets of £623,000 and an income of £44,000. Grants totalled £48,000 and were made to 14 organisations.

Beneficiaries included: Justice First (£8,000); Bwindi Hospital, Uganda, Oxfam and Women in Need (£6,000 each); Medical Foundation for the Victims of Torture (£4,000); Butterwick Hospice and Listening Books (£2,000 each); and Intercare (£1,000).

Applications

In writing to the correspondent. The trustees meet twice each year.

The Laurence Misener Charitable Trust

Jewish, general

£165,000 (2009/10)

Beneficial area

UK.

c/o Leonard Jones & Co, 1 Printing Yard House, London E2 7PR

Tel: 020 7739 8790

Correspondent: David Lyons, Correspondent

Trustees: Mrs J Legane; Capt. G F Swaine.

CC Number: 283460

Information available

Accounts were available from the Charity Commission.

In 2009/10 the trust had assets of £2.4 million and an income of £93,000. Grants were made totalling £165,000.

The largest grants were to: Jewish Association for the Physically Handicapped, Jewish Care and Nightingale House (£15,000 each).

Other grants included: Jewish Temporary Shelter (£8,000); Blond McIndoe Centre, Cassel Hospital Families Centre Appeal, Elimination of Leukaemia Fund, Great Ormond Street Children's Hospital Fund, Seafarers UK, Sussex Stroke and Circulation Fund, Royal Marsden Hospital and World Jewish Relief (£7,000 each).

Applications

In writing to the correspondent.

The Mishcon Family Charitable Trust

Jewish, social welfare, medical, disability, children

£88,000 (2009/10)

Beneficial area

UK.

Summit House, 12 Red Lion Square, London WC1R 4QD

Correspondent: The Trustees

Trustees: P A Mishcon; R O Mishcon; Mrs J Landau.

CC Number: 213165

Information available

Full accounts available from the Charity Commission website.

The trust supports mainly Jewish charities, but also gives grants to general social welfare and medical/disability causes, especially children's charities.

In 2009/10 the trust had assets of £1.8 million, and an income of £57,000. Grants were made to almost 100 organisations totalling £88,000.

The largest grant went to the United Jewish Israel Appeal (£37,000). Smaller grants included: Sick

Children's Trust (£6,500); The Board of Deputies Charitable Trust (£6,000); Friends of Progressive Judaism (£5,000); Friends of Alyn (£2,000); The Lubavich Foundation and World Jewish Relief (£1,000 each); One World Action (£450); Jewish Book Council, Jewish Care, NSPCC and Rainbow Trust (£100 each); and The Stroke Association (£50).

Applications

In writing to the correspondent.

The Misselbrook Trust

General

£32,000 (2009/10).

Beneficial area

UK with a preference for the Wessex area.

Ashton House, 12 The Central Precinct, Winchester Road, Chandlers Ford, Eastleigh, Hampshire, SO53 2GB

Tel: 023 8027 4555

Correspondent: M Howson-Green, Trustee

Trustees: M Howson-Green; B M Baxendale; D A Hoare; Mrs M A Howson-Green.

CC Number: 327928

Information available

Accounts were available from the Charity Commission.

In 2009/10 the trust had assets of £1 million and an unusually high income of £337,000 after receiving a legacy of £303,000. Grants were made totalling £32,000 and those over £500 were listed in the accounts.

Grants of more than £500 went to 11 organisations including: Cantell Maths and Computing College (£10,000); Marwell Preservation Trust (£1,500); AIDS Trust, Royal Star & Garter Home and Southampton Women's Aid (£1,000 each); and St John's Church, Alresford (£600).

Other grants of £500 or less were made to 24institutions and totalled £11,600.

Applications

In writing to the correspondent.

The Mitchell Charitable Trust

Jewish, general

£116,000 (2009/10)

Beneficial area

UK, with a preference for London and overseas.

28 Heath Drive, London NW3 7SB
Tel: 020 7794 5668
Correspondent: Ashley Mitchell, Trustee
Trustees: Ashley Mitchell; Elizabeth Mitchell; Antonia Mitchell; Keren Mitchell.
CC Number: 290273

Information available

Accounts were available from the Charity Commission.

The trust was established in 1984. It has general charitable purposes but in practice appears to have a strong preference for welfare charities, Jewish organisations and health charities.

In 2009/10 the trust had assets of £1.1 million and an income of £43,000. There were 17 grants made during the year totalling £116,000, broken down as follows:

Medical and disability	£99,000
Community and welfare	£11,600
Education	£5,800
Arts and Culture	£Nil
Overseas Aid	£Nil

The main beneficiaries during the year were: Hammersmith Clinical Research (£37,000); Ovarian Cancer Care (£34,500) and Prostate Cancer Research Foundation (£25,000). Smaller grants included: London School of Economics and Political Science (£5,750); Community Security Trust and Norwood (£5,000 each); National Council for Epilepsy (£500); and Kidney for Kids (£30).

Exclusions

No grants to individuals or for non-Jewish religious appeals. Applicants from small charities outside London are unlikely to be considered.

Applications

In writing to the correspondent. Applications must include financial information. The trust does not reply to any applications unless they choose to support them. Trustees do not meet on a regular basis, thus applicants may not be advised of a grant for a considerable period.

Common applicant mistakes

'They don't do any research to find out the type of charities we support.'

Keren Mitzvah Trust

General, Jewish

£379,000 (2010)

Beneficial area

UK.

53 Sugden Road, Thames Ditton, Surrey KT7 0AD
Tel: 020 3219 2600
Correspondent: Naomi Crowther
Trustees: Manny Weiss; Alan McCormack; Neil Bradley.
CC Number: 1041948

Information available

Accounts were on file at the Charity Commission.

In 2010 the trust had an income of £374,000 mainly from donations. Grants totalled £379,000. The grants were broken down into the following categories:

Religious advancement	£147,000
Education	£142,000
Poverty relief	£42,000
Health	£40,000
Other	£10,000

Major beneficiaries included: Menorah High School for Girls (£32,000); Ezer Mizion (£22,000); Torah & Chessed, Kisharon (£20,000 each); Friends of Vishnas Mir (£16,000); Lezion Berina (£15,000); Achisomoch (£11,000); Side by Side (£10,000); CML (£8,000); The Shechita Defence Fund and UJIA (£5,000 each).

A total of £121,000 was also disbursed in grants of £5,000 or less.

Applications

The trust stated that the trustees support their own personal charities.

The Mizpah Trust

General

£80,000 to organisations and individuals (2009/10)

Beneficial area

UK and overseas.

Foresters House, Humbly Grove, South Warnborough, Hook, Hampshire RG29 1RY
Correspondent: A C O Bell, Trustee
Trustees: A C O Bell; Mrs J E Bell.
CC Number: 287231

Information available

Accounts were available from the Charity Commission.

The trust is proactive and makes grants to a wide range of organisations in the UK and, to a lesser extent, overseas.

In 2009/10 the trust had assets of £42,000 and an income of £36,000. Grants of £78,000 were made to 22 organisations. £1,500 was given to individuals.

The major beneficiary was The Vanessa Grant Trust (£30,000). Smaller grants included those to: The Warham Trust (£6,000); CURE International and Tearfund (£5,000 each); World Vision (£4,000); Friends of St Andrew's and The Christian Orphanage (£1,000 each); The Barnabus Trust (£150); and The Crosswinds Care Trust (£100).

Applications

The trust has stated that 'no applications will be considered'.

The Modiano Charitable Trust

Arts, Jewish, general

£95,000 (2009/10)

Beneficial area

UK and overseas.

Broad Street House, 55 Old Broad Street, London EC2M 1RX
Tel: 020 7012 0000
Correspondent: G Modiano, Trustee
Trustees: G Modiano; Mrs B Modiano; L S Modiano; M Modiano.
CC Number: 328372

Information available
Accounts were available from the Charity Commission.

In 2009/10 the trust had assets of £85,000, an income of £150,000 and made 88 grants totalling £95,000. The trust supports the arts, Jewish charities and those which relieve poverty, both in the UK and overseas.

The largest grants were to: Philharmonic Orchestra (£20,000); the Weiznam Institute Foundation (£10,000); and DEC Haiti Appeal, St Paul's School and UJIA (£5,000 each).

Smaller grants included: World Jewish Relief (£4,000); Life Action Trust (£3,500); CCJ and The Holocaust Educational Trust (£2,500 each); YMCA and the Reform Research Trust (1,000 each); and British Forces Association, Jewish Assoc. for the Mentally Ill (JAMI) and The St John of Jerusalem Eye Hospital (£100 each).

Applications
In writing to the correspondent.

The Moette Charitable Trust

Jewish education and social welfare
£25,000 (2009/10)

Beneficial area
UK and overseas.

1 Holden Road, Salford M7 4NL
Tel: 0161 832 8721
Correspondent: Simon Lopian, Trustee
Trustees: Simon Lopian; Pearl Lopian.
CC Number: 1068886

Information available
Accounts were available from the Charity Commission, but without a list of grants.

The principal activity of the trust is to make grants for the support of 'the poor and needy as well as other charitable institutions'.

In 2009/10 the trust had assets of £327,000 and an income of £60,000. Grants made in accordance with the trust's objectives totalled £25,000. A list of beneficiaries was unavailable.

Previous grants have included: £15,000 to Finchley Road Synagogue, £2,500 each to King David Schools (Manchester) and Manchester Charitable Trust, £2,000 to The Purim Fund, £1,000 each to Yad Voezer and Yeshivas Lev Aryeh and £500 each to Hakalo and London School of Jewish Studies, £400 to Manchester Jewish Federation and £50 to Manchester Seminary for Girls.

Applications
In writing to the correspondent.

The Mole Charitable Trust

Jewish, general
£224,000 (2009/10)

Beneficial area
UK, with a preference for Manchester.

2 Okeover Road, Salford M7 4JX
Tel: 0161 832 8721
Email: martin.gross@lopiangb.co.uk
Correspondent: Martin Gross, Trustee
Trustees: M Gross; Mrs L P Gross.
CC Number: 281452

Information available
Accounts were available from the Charity Commission, but without a grants list.

The objects of the charity are to make donations and loans to educational institutions and charitable organisations, and for the relief of poverty.

In 2009/10 the trust had assets of £2.3 million and an income of £151,000. Grants totalling £223,000 were broken down as follows:

- education (£116,000)
- Religious institutions and charitable organisations (£108,000).

A list of beneficiaries for the year was unavailable.

Grants have previously included those to: Three Pillars Charity (£60,000); Manchester Jewish Grammar School (£26,000); Chasdei Yoel Charitable Trust and United Talmudical Associates Limited (£20,000 each); Binoh of Manchester (£6,000); Beis Ruchel Girls' School (£3,000); Manchester Jewish Federation (£2,500); and Our Kids (£1,000).

Applications
The following is taken from the trustees' report 2009/10:

Grant-Making Policy
The trustees receive many applications for grants, mainly personal contact, but also verbally. Each application is considered against the criteria established by the Charity.

Although the Charity does not advertise, it is well known within its community and there are many requests received for grants. Feedback received is used to monitor the quality of grants.

The Monatrea Charitable Trust

General
£44,500 (2009/10)

Beneficial area
UK.

Coutts & Co, 440 Strand, London WC2R 0QS
Correspondent: Coutts & Co
Trustees: Patrick Stephen Vernon; Mary Vernon; Coutts & Co.
CC Number: 1131897

Information available
Basic accounts were available from the Charity Commission.

The trust was established in 2009 with an endowment of £503,500 for general charitable purposes. It is the charitable trust of Stephen Vernon, chairman of Green Property Limited.

In 2009/10, the trust's first year of operation it had an income of £50,000 and grants were made to five organisations totalling £44,500. Grants ranged from £2,000 to £21,000 and were made to: Capital Community Foundation; Prisoners' Advice Service; Roses Charitable Trust; Family Action; and South Central Youth.

Applications

In writing to the correspondent.

The D C Moncrieff Charitable Trust

Social welfare, environment

£33,000 (2009/10)

Beneficial area

UK and worldwide, with a preference for Norfolk and Suffolk.

8 Quinnell Way, Lowestoft, Suffolk NR32 4WL
Correspondent: R E James, Trustee
Trustees: M I Willis; R E James; M F Dunne.
CC Number: 203919

Information available

Accounts were available from the Charity Commission.

The trust was established in 1961. It supports a number of large UK organisations but tends to concentrate on charities local to the Norfolk and Suffolk areas.

In 2009/10 the trust had assets of £1.9 million and an income of £43,000, derived mostly from investment income. Grants were made to organisations totalling £33,000. A list of beneficiaries for the year was unavailable.

Previous grants have included those to: All Hallows Hospital, East Anglia's Children's Hospices, the Society for Lincolnshire History and Archaeology, Hemley Church PCC, Lowestoft Girl Guides Association and The Scouts Association, BREAK, Strongbones Children's Charitable

Trust and East Anglian Air Ambulance Association.

Exclusions

No grants for individuals.

Applications

In writing to the correspondent. The trust has previously stated that demand for funds exceeded available resources; therefore no further requests are currently invited.

Monmouthshire County Council Welsh Church Act Fund

General

£227,000 to organisations (2009/10)

Beneficial area

Blaenau Gwent, Caerphilly, Monmouthshire, Torfaen and Newport.

Treasurer's Department, Monmouthshire County Council, County Hall, Croesyceiliog, Cwmbran NP44 2XH
Tel: 01633 644644
Fax: 01633 644260
Correspondent: S K F Greenslade
Trustee: Monmouthshire County Council.
CC Number: 507094

Information available

Accounts were available from the Charity Commission.

An annual budget set by the Authority for grant payments is split between the administrative areas of Blaenau Gwent, Caerphilly, Monmouthshire, Torfaen and Newport on a population basis. A committee set up by the Authority approves grant applications on a quarterly basis. The trust supports individuals or organisations that are known to the trustees. It has supported a wide variety of causes including education, people who are blind, sick or in need, older people, medical and social research, recreation, culture and the arts,

historic buildings, churches and burial grounds, emergencies and disaster appeals.

In 2009/10 assets stood at £5 million. The trust had an unusually low income of £68,000 (£280,000 in 2008/09), which it attributed to underperforming financial markets. Grants to organisations during the year totalled £227,000.

Previous beneficiaries include: Parish Church Llandogo, Parish Church Llangybi, Bridges Community Centre, St David's Foundation Hospice Care and North Wales Society for the Blind.

Applications

On a form available from the correspondent, this must be signed by a county councillor. They are considered in March, June, September and December.

The Montague Thompson Coon Charitable Trust

Children with muscular diseases, medical research, environment

£53,000 (2009/10)

Beneficial area

UK.

Old Rectory, Church Lane, Colton, Norwich NR9 5DE
Tel: 07766 072592
Correspondent: Mrs Philippa Blake-Roberts, Trustee
Trustees: P A Clarke, Chair; J P Lister; Mrs P Blake-Roberts
CC Number: 294096

Information available

Accounts were available from the Charity Commission.

This trust was registered with the Charity Commission in 1986. The trust states that its objects are: 'to relieve sickness in children with muscular dystrophy and/or other muscular diseases, to carry out and provide for research into infant diseases and to advance the education of the public in the study of ecology and wildlife'.

In 2009/10 the trust had assets of almost £1.2 million and an income of £48,000. There were 11 grants made in the year totalling £53,000.

Beneficiaries included: Dogs for the Disabled (£11,500); SCOPE (£6,500); Muscular Dystrophy Campaign (£6,000); Action for Kids Charitable Trust (£5,000); The Jennifer Trust (£3,000); and Exmoor Calvert Trust (£2,000).

Exclusions
No grants to individuals.

Applications
In writing to the correspondent.

The Colin Montgomerie Charitable Foundation

General
Around £40,000 (2009)

Beneficial area
UK.

c/o Catella, Chiswick Gate, 3rd Floor, 598–608 Chiswick High Road, London W4 5RT
Correspondent: Miss Donna Cooksley, Trustee
Trustees: Colin Montgomerie; Guy Kinnings; Jonathan Dudman; Miss Donna Cooksley.
CC Number: 1072388

Information available
Limited information was obtained from the Charity Commission.

Set up in November 1998, the foundation aims to support the relief of poverty, the advancement of education and religion, and any other charitable purposes as decided by the trustees.

In 2009 the trust had an income of £1,600 and a total expenditure of £46,000. Grants usually total around £40,000. Details of beneficiaries were not available for the year. However, previous recipients have included: British Lung Foundation; Cancer

Vaccine Institute; NSPCC for the Full Stop Campaign; and University of Glasgow MRI Scanner Fund.

Applications
In writing to the correspondent.

George A Moore Foundation

General
£149,000 (2009/10)

Beneficial area
Principally Yorkshire and the Isle of Man.

The Stables, Bilton Hall, Bilton-in-Ainsty, York YO26 7NP
Tel: 01423 359446
Fax: 01423 359018
Email: info@gamf.org.uk
Website: www.gamf.org.uk
Correspondent: Angela James, Chief Administrator
Trustees: George Moore; Elizabeth Moore; Jonathan Moore; Paul Turner.
CC Number: 262107

Information available
Accounts were on file at the Charity Commission

The trustees of the foundation select causes and projects from applications received during the year, as well as using independent research to identify specific objectives where they wish to direct assistance.

In 2009/10 the trust had assets of £5.6 million and an income of £261,000. A total of £149,000 was distributed in grants, the majority of which were for £1,000 or less.

The largest grant of £35,000 went to Henshaws Yorkshire. Other major beneficiaries included: Boston Charitable Foundation (£28,000); Marie Curie Cancer Care (£19,000); Caring for Life – Crag House Farm (£14,000); and Saxton Village Pavilion (£10,000).

Other grants went to: Heart Research UK (£2,500); FEVA (£1,500); AbilityNet, Endeavour Training and Swaledale Festival (£1,000 each); Stroke Association (£600); Brain

Tumour UK (£500); Knaresborough Horticultural Society (£250); and Sulby and District Rifle Club (£100).

Exclusions
No assistance will be given to individuals, courses of study, expeditions, overseas travel, holidays, or for purposes outside the UK. Local appeals for UK charities will only be considered if in the area of interest. Because of present long-term commitments, the foundation is not prepared to consider appeals for religious property or institutions.

Applications
In writing to the correspondent. No guidelines or application forms are issued. The trustees meet approximately four times a year, on variable dates, and an appropriate response is sent out after the relevant meeting. For large grants of over £5,000, the trust will normally hold a meeting with the applicant to determine how the money will be spent.

Common applicant mistakes
'Applicants which have: not kept their databases/records up to date; not signed letters personally; not addressed letters properly (i.e. 'Dear Mrs A L James' or have been too informal or personal, i.e. 'Dear Angela'). Applicants have also sent mail merge letters but not checked that all the 'merged' data has been correctly incorporated.'

The Nigel Moores Family Charitable Trust

Arts
£18,000 (2007/08)

Beneficial area
UK, but mostly Liverpool and Wales.

c/o Macfarlane and Co., 2nd Floor, Cunard Building, Water Street, Liverpool L3 1DS
Tel: 0151 236 6161
Fax: 0151 236 1095
Email: all@macca.co.uk

Correspondent: P Kurthausen, Accountant and Trustee
Trustees: J C S Moores; Mrs P M Kennaway.
CC Number: 1002366

Information available

Accounts were received at the Charity Commission but not available to view online.

The trustees have determined that their principal objective should be the raising of the artistic taste of the public, whether in relation to music, drama, opera, painting, sculpture or otherwise in connection with the fine arts, the promotion of education in the fine arts and academic education, the promotion of the environment, the provision of facilities for recreation or other leisure time occupation and the advancement of religion.

Unusually, in 2009/10 there were very low levels of income and expenditure with the trust having an income of just £16 and total expenditure of £1,800. Accounts had been received at the Charity Commission but were not available online.

Previous beneficiaries have included: the A Foundation (£525,000); London Library (£20,000); Mostyn Gallery (£10,000); University of York (£6,750); Art School Palestine (£1,000); and Matts Gallery (£500).

Applications

In writing to the correspondent.

The Morel Charitable Trust

Arts/culture, race relations, inner-city projects. UK and the developing world

£65,000 (2009/10)

Beneficial area

UK and the developing world.

34 Durand Gardens, London SW9 0PP
Tel: 020 7582 6901
Correspondent: S E Gibbs, Trustee

Trustees: J M Gibbs, Chair; W M Gibbs; S E Gibbs; B M O Gibbs; Dr T Gibbs; Dr Emily Parry; Abigail Keane; Susanna Coan.
CC Number: 268943

Information available

Accounts were available from the Charity Commission.

The trust supports: the arts, particularly drama; organisations working for improved race relations; inner-city projects and developing-world projects. Also supported are: culture and recreation; health; conservation and environment; education and training; and social care and development. Projects supported are usually connected with places that the trustees have lived and worked, including the cities of Bristol, Leeds, Brecon and London and the countries of Ghana, Zambia, Malawi and the Solomon Islands.

In 2009/10 the trust had assets of £1.3 million and an income of £54,000. 38 grants were made totalling £65,000 and were broken down as follows:

Social and development	£41,000
Health	£13,000
Drama and the arts	£11,000

Beneficiaries included: Health Unlimited (£5,000); Medical Aid for Palestine (£3,000); African Initiatives, Congo Children's Trust, Excellent Development, Kaloko Trust, Zambia, Nigeria Health Care Project and The Capricorn African Trust (£2,000 each); Ace Arts Community Exchange, and The Young Vic (£1,500 each); and Age UK and Soho Trust (£1,000 each).

Exclusions

No grants to individuals.

Applications

In writing to the correspondent. The trustees normally meet three times a year to consider applications.

The Morgan Charitable Foundation

Welfare, hospices, medical, Jewish, general

£59,000 (2010)

Beneficial area

UK.

PO Box 57749, London Nw11 1FD
Tel: 079 6882 7709
Correspondent: The Trustees
Trustees: The Morgan Charitable Foundation Trustees Ltd. (A Morgan; L Morgan; Mrs C Morgan).
CC Number: 283128

Information available

Accounts were available from the Charity Commission.

The Morgan Charitable Foundation (previously known as The Erich Markus Charitable Foundation) was established in 1979 when, following Erich Markus's death, half of his residual estate was left to the trust.

In 2010 the foundation had assets at £3.8 million and an income of £52,000. Grants were made to 25 organisations and totalled £59,000.

Beneficiaries included: Magen David Adom and World Jewish Relief (£6,000 each); Chai Cancer Care (£4,000); In Kind Direct Charity (£3,000); Jewish Care and Jewish Blind and Disabled (£2,000 each); and Afrikids, Aleh Charitable Foundation, Institute for Philanthropy, London Pro Arte Choir, Marie Curie Cancer Care, Ohel Sarah, Pears Foundation, and Royal National Lifeboat Institution (£1,000 each).

Exclusions

No grants to individuals.

Applications

In writing to the correspondent. Applications will only be considered if accompanied by a copy of the charitable organisation's latest report and accounts. Trustees meet twice a

ear, usually in April and October.
Jo telephone enquiries please.

Diana and Allan Morgenthau Charitable Trust

Jewish, general

£115,000 to organisations
(2009/10)

Beneficial area
Worldwide.

Flat 27, Berkeley House, 15 Hay Hill, London W1J 8NS
Tel: 020 7493 1904
Correspondent: Allan Morgenthau, Trustee
Trustees: Allan Morgenthau; Diana Morgenthau.
CC Number: 1062180

Information available
Accounts were on file at the Charity Commission.

Registered with the Charity Commission in April 1997, grants are made to a range of Jewish, medical, education and arts organisations. In 2009/10 the trust had assets of £7,300 and an income of £95,000, virtually all of which came from the Archie Sherman Charitable Trust. Grants to 29 organisations totalled £115,000 and were broken down as follows:

General donations and overseas aid	£89,000
Medical, health and sickness	£12,000
Arts and culture	£7,200
Education and training	£7,000

The two largest grants were made under the general category to the British Friends of the Jaffa Institute (£35,000) and the Belsize Square Synagogue (£28,000).

Other beneficiaries included: Central British Fund for World Jewish Relief (£8,500); London Jewish Cultural Centre and Jewish Care (£7,000 each); Brent Adolescent Centre (£5,000); Nightingale House (£3,500); Ben Uri Gallery (£2,000); Tricycle Theatre (£1,700); Marie Curie (£1,000); and Camphill Village Trust (£200).

A further £14,000 was given in grants to individuals.

Applications
In writing to the correspondent.

The Oliver Morland Charitable Trust

Quakers, general

£97,000 (2009/10)

Beneficial area
UK.

Thomas's House, Stower Row, Shaftesbury, Dorset SP7 0QW
Tel: 01747 853524
Correspondent: J M Rutter, Trustee
Trustees: Priscilla Khan; Joseph Rutter; Jennifer Pittard; Kate Lovell; Charlotte Jones; Simon Pittard.
CC Number: 1076213

Information available
Accounts were available from the Charity Commission.

The trustees state that the majority of funds are given to Quaker projects or Quaker-related projects, which are usually chosen through the personal knowledge of the trustees. In 2009/10 the trust had assets of £1.5 million, an income of £82,000 and made 39 grants totalling £97,000.

Grants were broken down as follows:

Quaker and schools	18	£80,000
Health and social care	5	£4,400
Meeting House appeals	6	£4,100
International and environment	3	£3,800
Sundry	3	£2,500
Animals and nature	4	£2,300

Quaker and schools: 25 grants totalling £91,000
Beneficiaries included: Quaker Peace and Service (£32,500); Quaker Home Service – children and young people (£16,000); Refugee Council (£2,000); Leap Confronting Conflict, Living Again, Medical Aid for Palestine and Sightsavers International (£1,000 each); Come to God (£850); and Brooke Animal Hospital (£300).

Exclusions
No grants to individuals.

Applications
In our communication with the trust they have informed us that: 'Most of our grants are for continuing support of existing beneficiaries (approx 90%) so there is little left for responding to new appeals. We receive unsolicited applications at the rate of 6 or 7 each week, 99% are not even considered.'

Common applicant mistakes
'Most of our resources are devoted to Quaker charities and most of the applicants do not qualify. Personal knowledge by trustees is important.'

S C and M E Morland's Charitable Trust

Quaker, sickness, welfare, peace and development overseas

£37,000 (2009/10)

Beneficial area
UK.

Gable House, Parbrook, Glastonbury, Somerset BA6 8PB
Tel: 01458 850804
Correspondent: Victoria Morland, Trustee
Trustees: Esther Boyd; Joseph Morland; Janet Morland; Howard Boyd; David Boyd.
CC Number: 201645

Information available
Accounts were available from the Charity Commission.

The trust states in its annual report and accounts that it 'gives to Quaker, local and national charities which have a strong social bias, and also to some UK-based international charities'. Also, that it supports those charities concerned with the relief of poverty and ill health, and those promoting peace and development overseas.

The trust generally makes grants to charities it has supported on a long term basis, but each year this list is reviewed and new charities may be added.

In 2009/10 the trust had assets of £899,000 and an income of £35,000. Grants to 87 charities totalled £37,000. Only two grants of £1,000 or over were made and thus required listing in the accounts. These were to Britain Yearly Meeting (£7,500) and Oxfam (£1,000).

Exclusions

The trust does not usually give to animal welfare, individuals or medical research.

Applications

In writing to the correspondent. The trustees meet two times a year to make grants, in March and December. Applications should be submitted in the month before each meeting.

The Morris Charitable Trust

Relief of need, education, community support and development

£144,000 (2009/10)

Beneficial area

UK, with a preference for Islington; and overseas.

c/o Management Office, Business Design Centre, 52 Upper Street, London N1 0QH
Tel: 020 7359 3535
Fax: 020 7226 0590
Email: info@morrischaritabletrust. com
Website: www.morrischaritabletrust. com
Correspondent: Jack A Morris, Trustee
Trustees: Jack A Morris, Chair; Paul B Morris; Alan R Stenning; Gerald Morris; Dominic Jones.
CC Number: 802290

Information available

Accounts were available from the Charity Commission.

The Morris Charitable Trust was established in 1989 to provide support for charitable causes. It was

founded by the Morris Family, whose principal business – The Business Design Centre Group Ltd – is based in Islington, London. The group contributes a proportion of its annual profits to facilitate the trust's charitable activities.

The trust has general charitable purposes, placing particular emphasis on alleviating social hardship and deprivation, supporting national, international and local charities. There is a preference for supporting causes within the borough of Islington.

In 2009/10 the trust had assets of £152,000 and an income of £125,000 mainly from donations received from the above mentioned company. Grants totalling £144,000 were made to 182 beneficiaries, the majority of which (114) received a grant of less than £500 each. 42 organisations received a grant of between £501 and £1,000, while 26 received grants of between £1,001 and £5,000. No further information was available.

Exclusions

No grants for individuals. No repeat donations are made within 12 months.

Applications

By application form available from the trust or downloadable from its website. The completed form should be returned complete with any supporting documentation and a copy of your latest report and accounts.

The trustees generally meet monthly.

The Bernard Morris Charitable Trust

General

£40,000 (2005/06)

Beneficial area

UK.

5 Wolvercote Green, Oxford OX2 8BD
Tel: 01865 516593
Correspondent: Simon Ryde, Trustee

Trustees: Simon Ryde; Judith Silver; Simon Fineman; Jessica Ryde.
CC Number: 266532

Information available

Basic information was available from the Charity Commission website.

In 2010/11 the trust had an income of £23,000 and a total expenditure of £80,000. No details of the beneficiaries were available.

Previous grant recipients included: Oxford Synagogue (£16,000); Dragon School Trust (£12,000); One Voice (£2,500), OCJHS – Oxford Centre for Jewish and Hebrew Studies (£2,000), Soundabout (£1,000), the Story Museum (£500) and Centrepoint Homeless (£200).

Applications

In writing to the correspondent.

The Willie and Mabel Morris Charitable Trust

Medical, general

£108,000 (2009/10)

Beneficial area

UK.

41 Field Lane, Letchworth Garden City, Hertfordshire SG6 3LD
Tel: 01462 480 583
Correspondent: Angela Tether
Trustees: Michael Macfadyen; Alan Bryant; Peter Tether; Andrew Tether; Angela Tether; Suzanne Marriott.
CC Number: 280554

Information available

Full accounts were available from the Charity Commission website.

The trust was established in 1980 by Mr and Mrs Morris. It was constituted for general charitable purposes and specifically to relieve physical ill-health, particularly cancer, heart trouble, cerebral palsy, arthritis and rheumatism. Grants are usually only given to registered charities.

In 2009/10 the trust had assets of £3.5 million and an income of £108,000. 91 Grants were made totalling £70,000, 80% of which went o medical charities. Administration costs were £32,000

t Thomas Lupus; PBC Foundation or Life; Marie Curie Cancer Care £4,000 each); Strongbones Child Charitable Trust (£2,000); Stroke association (£2,000); Salvation Army £250) and English National Ballet £100).

Exclusions

No grants for individuals or non-registered charities.

Applications

The trustees 'formulate an independent grants policy at regular meetings so that funds are already committed'.

The Peter Morrison Charitable Foundation

Jewish, general

£54,000 (2009/10)

Beneficial area

UK.

Begbies Chettle Agar, Chartered Accountants, Epworth House, 25 City Road, London EC1Y 1AR
Tel: 020 7628 5801
Correspondent: J Payne
Trustees: M Morrison; I R Morrison.
CC Number: 277202

Information available

Full accounts were available from the Charity Commission website.

In the trust's annual report it states that 'the trustees are concerned to make donations to charitable institutions which in the opinion of the trustees are most in need and which provide a beneficial service to the needy'.

In 2009/10 the trust had assets of £901,000 and an income of over £28,000. Grants totalling over £54,000 were made during the year, mostly for £500 each or less.

The largest grants included those to: London Philharmonic Orchestra £7,600); Kingston Theatres Trust

St Giles Church (£5,000); Grange Park Opera (£3,750); RNLI (£3,100); World Jewish Relief (£3,000); Barnfield Riding for the Disabled, Community Security Trust and RNIB (£2,500); and Comic Relief and The Donkey Sanctuary (£1,000 each).

Smaller grants included those to: Alexander School PTA (£500); Life Line for the Old (£300); MIND (£200); The Woodland Trust (£100); and West London Synagogue Charitable Fund (£30).

Ian Morrison is also a trustee of Kemis's Lectureship Charity (Charity Commission no. 1013259); and The Andover Charities (Charity Commission no. 206587).

Applications

In writing to the correspondent.

G M Morrison Charitable Trust

General

£178,000 (2009/10)

Beneficial area

UK.

Currey and Co, 21 Buckingham Gate, London SW1E 6LS
Tel: 020 7802 2700
Correspondent: A E Cornick, Trustee
Trustees: N W Smith, Chair; Miss E Morrison; A E Cornick; Mrs J Hunt.
CC Number: 261380

Information available

Detailed accounts were available from the Charity Commission.

Grants are mostly given to a wide variety of activities in the social welfare, medical and education/training fields. The trust maintains a list of beneficiaries that it has regularly supported.

In 2009/10 the trust had assets of £7.5 million and a total income of £169,000. Grants were made to 220 organisations totalling £178,000 and ranged from £600 to £5,000 each. The average size of grant was £807.

There were 50 grants of £1,000 or more, including those to: British Red

Cross – Haiti Earthquake Appeal (£5,000); Oxfam – Emergency Response Horn of East Africa (£3,000); Royal College of Surgeons (£2,200); Royal Society of Arts Endowment Fund (£2,000); Help the Aged (£1,300); Enterprise Education Trust and University of Liverpool (£1,100 each); and Alternatives to Violence Project, Child in Need – India and Refugee Council Day Centre (£1,000 each).

Grants under £1,000 each included those to: Bath Institute of Medical Engineering (£900); Corporation for the Sons of the Clergy (£850); Family Holiday Association (£800); Fight for Sight and Castle Howard Arboretum Trust (£750 each); Gastroenterology and Nutrition Research Trust (£700); Prisoners Abroad (£650); and British Limbless Ex-servicemen's Association, Canine Partners for Independence, the Tree Register, Bible Society and Victim Support – Sussex (£600 each).

Exclusions

No support for individuals, charities not registered in the UK, schemes or activities which are generally regarded as the responsibility of statutory authorities, short-term projects or one-off capital grants (except for emergency appeals).

Applications

The trust's annual report states:

Beneficiaries of grants are normally selected on the basis of the personal knowledge and recommendation of a trustee. The trust's grant making policy is however to support the recipient of grants on a long term recurring basis. The scope of its giving is determined only by the extent of its resources, and is not otherwise restricted. The trustees have decided that for the present, new applications for grants will only be considered in the most exceptional circumstances, any spare income will be allocated to increasing the grants made to charities currently receiving support. In the future this policy will of course be subject to periodic review. Applicants understanding this policy who nevertheless wish to apply for a grant should write to the [correspondent].

Monitoring is undertaken by assessment of annual reports and accounts which are required from all beneficiaries, and by occasional trustee visits. During the year 38 existing beneficiaries failed to submit

283

their latest report and accounts and consequently lost their annual grant.

Common applicant mistakes

'Not having read our annual report and accounts, which clearly lay down our requirements, and what we fund.'

Moshal Charitable Trust

Jewish

£81,000 (2010/11)

Beneficial area

UK.

c/o Sefton Yodaiken & Co., 40a Bury New Road, Prestwich, Manchester M25 0LD
Correspondent: The Trustees
Trustees: D Halpern; L Halpern.
CC Number: 284448

Information available

Accounts were on file at the Charity Commission, without a list of grants.

In 2010/11, the trust had assets of £324,000 and an income of £61,000 mainly from donations. Grants during the year totalled £81,000 but a list of beneficiaries was not included in the accounts.

Applications

In writing to the correspondent.

Vyoel Moshe Charitable Trust

Education, relief of poverty

£1 million (2007/08)

Beneficial area

UK and overseas.

2–4 Chardmore Road, London N16 6HX
Correspondent: J Weinberger, Secretary
Trustees: Y Frankel; B Berger; S Seidenfeld.
CC Number: 327054

Information available

Latest accounts available at the Charity Commission website were for the 2007/08 financial year.

In 2007/08 the trust's assets totalled £56,000 and it had an income, mainly from donations, of £1.1 million. Grants were made totalling £1 million and were broken down as follows: Overseas (£984,000); Zorchei yom tov – UK (£43,000); and UK (£13,000).

Applications

In writing to the correspondent.

The Moshulu Charitable Trust

Humanitarian, evangelical

£59,000 to organisations (2009/10)

Beneficial area

UK.

Devonshire Road, Heathpark, Honiton, Devon EX14 1SD
Tel: 01404 540 770
Correspondent: H J Fulls, Trustee
Trustees: H J Fulls; D M Fulls; G N Fulls; S M Fulls; G F Symons.
CC Number: 1071479

Information available

Accounts were available from the Charity Commission.

Set up in September 1998, in 2009/10 the trust had assets of £167,000 and an income of £43,000. Grants were made totalling £62,000, of which 8 were listed in the accounts. £2,700 was paid to individuals.

Beneficiaries included: SWYM (£15,900); Christ Church (£11,700); Tear Fund (£5,400); Partnership UK (£3,000); Care for the Family (£2,400) and Seaway Trust (£1,600).

Applications

In writing to the correspondent.

The Moss Charitable Trust

Christian, education, poverty, health

£82,000 to organisations (2009/10)

Beneficial area

Worldwide, with an interest in Dorset, Hampshire and Sussex.

7 Church Road, Parkstone, Poole, Dorset BH14 8UF
Tel: 01202 730002
Correspondent: P D Malpas
Trustees: J H Simmons; A F Simmons; P L Simmons; D S Olby.
CC Number: 258031

Information available

Accounts were available from the Charity Commission.

The objects of the trust are to benefit the community in the county borough of Bournemouth and the counties of Hampshire, Dorset and Sussex, and also the advancement of religion in the UK and overseas, the advancement of education and the relief of poverty, disease and sickness.

The trust achieves this by providing facilities for contributors to give under Gift Aid or direct giving and redistributes them according to their recommendations. The trustees also make smaller grants from the general income of the trust.

In 2009/10 the trust had assets of £113,000, an income of £158,000 and made 120 grants totalling over £90,000, including £8,500 to individuals. These were categorised by the trust as follows:

- UK institutions (£80,400)
- overseas institutions (£1,600)
- UK individuals (£2,800)
- Overseas individuals (£5,800).

Beneficiaries receiving grants of £1,000 or more, included: Christ Church – Westbourne (£6,400); Great Wood Trust (£6,100); Slindon PCC (£5,800 each); Scripture Union (£4,600); Salvation Army (£2,000); and Worthing Churches Homeless Trust (£1,000).

Applications

No funds are available by direct application. Because of the way in which this trust operates it is not open to external applications for grants.

Brian and Jill Moss Charitable Trust

Jewish, healthcare

£149,000 (2009/10)

Beneficial area

Worldwide.

c/o Deloitte, 5 Callaghan Square, Cardiff CF10 5BT
Tel: 029 2046 0000
Correspondent: Miss K Griffin
Trustees: Brian Peter Moss; Jill Moss; David Paul Moss; Sarah Levy.
CC Number: 1084664

Information available

Basic information was available from the Charity Commission website.

Established in 2000, this trust makes grants for capital projects and towards 'ordinary charity expenditure'. In 2009/10 its income was £8,500. Total expenditure was £149,000.

Previous beneficiaries included: United Jewish Israel Appeal (£43,000); Magen David Adom UK (£31,000); Jewish Care (£16,000); World Jewish Relief (£15,000); Norwood (£13,000); Chai Cancer Care (£12,000); United Synagogue-Tribe (£11,000); Cancer Bacup (£6,300); WIZO UK (£6,000); National Jewish Chaplaincy Board (£5,500); Prostate Cancer Charitable Trust (£5,000); Jewish Association for the Mentally Ill (£3,500); Myeloma UK (£3,000); Holocaust Centre and Israel Folk Dance Institute (£500 each); and Jewish Museum and Operation Wheelchairs (£250 each).

Exclusions

Donations are made to registered charities only.

Applications

In writing to the correspondent. 'Appeals are considered as they are received and the trustees will make donations throughout the year.'

J P Moulton Charitable Foundation

Medical, education, training and counselling

£684,000 (2010)

Beneficial area

UK.

C/O Better Capital LLP,
39–41 Charing Cross Road, London WC2H 0AR
Tel: 020 7440 0860
Correspondent: J P Moulton, Trustee
Trustees: J P Moulton; Mrs P M Moulton; Sara Everett.
CC Number: 1109891

Information available

Accounts were on file at the Charity Commission.

The foundation's trustees report states that it provides: 'charitable donations for community service projects of any kind and to further the aims of the community by promoting education, training, counselling for disadvantaged persons of any age; to provide donations to hospitals, hospices, medical and care projects of any kind and to generally promote the relief of suffering'.

In 2010 the trust had assets of £6.1 million and an income of £1.3 million. Grants were made totalling £684,000, the majority of which went towards funding medical research projects. Major beneficiaries in this category included: University of Lancaster (£258,000); University College London (£65,000); University of Liverpool (£63,000); Meningitis Research Foundation (£57,000); University of Manchester (£49,000); University of Southampton (£48,000); and Imperial College (£33,000).

Other donations included: Les Bourgs Hospice (£40,000); CSV -'Summer of Service' initiative (£20,000);

St Martin-in-the-Fields Development Trust (£10,000); Papworth Hospital (£5,000); and Sevenoaks Citizens Advice (£2,500).

Applications

In writing to the correspondent.

The Edwina Mountbatten & Leonora Children's Foundation

Medical

£97,000 (2010)

Beneficial area

UK and overseas.

Estate Office, Broadlands, Romsey, Hampshire SO51 9ZE
Tel: 01794 529 750
Correspondent: John Moss, Secretary
Trustees: Countess Mountbatten of Burma, Chair; Hon. Alexandra Knatchbull; Lord Brabourne; Peter H T Mimpriss; Dame Mary Fagan; Lady Brabourne; Sir David Frost; Myrddin Rees; Sir Evelyn De Rothschild.
CC Number: 228166

Information available

Full accounts were available from the Charity Commission website.

The Edwina Mountbatten Trust was established in 1960 to honour the causes Edwina, Countess Mountbatten of Burma was involved with during her lifetime. Each year support is given to St John Ambulance (of which she was superintendent-in-chief) for work in the UK and its Commonwealth, and Save the Children (of which she was president) for the relief of children who are sick, distressed or otherwise in need. Nursing organisations are also supported, as she was the patron or vice-president of a number of nursing organisations. Grants, even to the core beneficiaries, are only given towards specific projects rather than core costs.

Charity Commission approval was received to merge the trust with The

Leonora Children's Cancer Fund and to adopt a working title of The Edwina Mountbatten & Leonora Children's Foundation. The merger took place on 1st January 2010, the assets of The Leonora Children's Cancer Fund being transferred to the Edwina Mountbatten Trust.

In 2010 the trust had assets of £4.9 million and an income of £121,000. Grants totalling £97,000 were made to 10 organisations.

The two major beneficiaries were: Save the Children and Rainbow Trust (£25,000 each).

Other grant recipients included: Cancer Research UK, St John Ambulance and St John Jerusalem Eye Hospital (£10,000 each); Help for Heroes (£5,000); Action Aid (£4,000); National Leprosy Fund (£3,000); The Fred Hollows Foundation (£3,400); and InterCare Medical Aid for Africa (£2,000).

Exclusions

No grants for research or to individual nurses working in the UK for further professional training.

Applications

In writing to the correspondent. The trustees meet once a year, generally in September/October.

Mountbatten Festival of Music

Royal Marines and Royal Navy charities

Around £266,000 (2009/10)

Beneficial area

UK.

The Corps Secretariat, Building 32, HMS Excellent, Whale Island, Portsmouth PO2 8ER
Tel: 02392 547 201
Email: royalmarines.charities@ charity.vfree.com
Website: www. royalmarinesregimental.co.uk
Correspondent: Lt Col I W Grant, Corps Secretary
Trustees: Commandant General Royal Marines; Director of Royal

Marines; Naval Personnel Team (RM) Team Leader.
CC Number: 1016088

Information available

Information was on file at the Charity Commission.

The trust was set up in 1993 and is administered by the Royal Marines. It raises funds from band concerts, festivals of music and beating retreat. Unsurprisingly, the main beneficiaries are service charities connected with the Royal Marines and Royal Navy. The only other beneficiaries are those hospitals or rehabilitation centres and so on, which have recently directly aided a Royal Marine in some way and Malcolm Sergeant Cancer Care. One-off and recurrent grants are made.

In 2009/10 the trust had an income of £512,000 and expenditure of £351,000. £266,000 of this total was dedicated to charitable activities. No further information was available. The Royal Marines website states that the proceeds of the festival go to the Royal Marines Charitable Trust Fund and CLIC Sargent.

Previous beneficiaries have included: Malcolm Sergeant Cancer Fund (£20,000); Metropolitan Police Benevolent Trust (14,000); RN Benevolent Fund; RNRMC and RM Museum (£10,000 each); Wrens Benevolent Trust, Seafarers UK, Royal British Legion, The 'Not Forgotten' Society, Queen Ann Hospital Home, and Scottish Veterans Residences (£1,000 each).

Exclusions

Charities or organisations unknown to the trustees.

Applications

Unsolicited applications are not considered as the trust's income is dependent upon the running and success of various musical events. Any money raised is then disbursed to a set of regular beneficiaries.

The Mountbatten Memorial Trust

Technological research in aid of disabilities

£45,000 (2010)

Beneficial area

Mainly UK, but some overseas.

The Estate Office, Broadlands, Romsey, Hampshire SO51 9ZE
Tel: 01794 529 750
Correspondent: John Moss, Secretary
Trustees: Countess Mountbatten of Burma; Lady Pamela Hicks; Ben Moorhead; Ashley Hicks; Hon. Michael John Knatchbull; Hon. Philip Knatchbull; William Fox and Kelly Knatchbull.
CC Number: 278691

Information available

Full accounts were on file at the Charity Commission.

The trust was set up in 1979 to honour the ideals of the Admiral of the Fleet, the Earl Mountbatten of Burma. The trust states that it supports charities and causes 'working to further the humanitarian purposes with which he was associated in his latter years'. The trust mainly focuses on making grants towards the development of technical aids for people with disabilities. Another focus has been to support the United World Colleges movement, which has the aim of providing a broad education to students from around the world and community projects are also an interest of the trust.

Following the merger with the Mountbatten Community Trust in January 2008, grants are now also made to aid the young and disadvantaged in various communities throughout Britain.

In 2010 the trust had assets of £520,000 and an income of £47,000. Grants totalling £50,000 were made to the following organisations: Atlantic College (£45,000); Inspire Foundation (£1,150); The Naval Review, Royal National Institute for the Deaf and The Sequal Trust (£1,000 each) and Motivation Charitable Trust (£600).

Exclusions

No grants are made towards the purchase of technology to assist people with disabilities.

Applications

In writing to the correspondent, at any time.

The MSE Charity

Financial education, improving financial literacy

£51,000 (2010/11)

Beneficial area

UK.

Tesciuba, Tesciuba Ltd, The Chambers, 13 Police Street, Manchester M2 7LQ
Tel: 0161 834 9221
Email: stuart@msecharity.com
Website: www.msecharity.com
Correspondent: Anthony Jeffrey, Administrator
Trustees: Tony Tesciuba; John Hewison, Chair; Katie Birkett; Vanessa Bissessur.
CC Number: 1121320

Information available

Accounts were available from the Charity Commission.

This trust was founded in 2007 by the popular television and radio personality and founder of the Money Saving Expert website, Martin Lewis.

According to the trust's website it aims to address:

> The UK's massive problem of financial illiteracy by funding relevant guidance and education for individuals and groups.
>
> The MSE Charity will support eligible individuals and groups who want to help eradicate this illiteracy through self-development or innovative projects.

The trust sets out a number of helpful criteria for groups or applicants seeking to establish innovative projects:

- projects must assist people to improve their quality of life through knowledge and understanding of how to manage and take control of their own financial situation
- groups will need to demonstrate that they have researched and assessed the need for the project
- groups must demonstrate that the project will make a significant difference to the beneficiaries so the OUTPUTS must be achievable, measurable, deliverable within budget and within a time frame and be sustainable
- groups will also need to show that the project will also provide outcomes that will benefit their wider communities
- groups should demonstrate that they have the skills, ability and experience to deliver the project
- the trust will consider full project cost recovery, but costs must only relate to the project itself and not the organisation's core funding
- projects must demonstrate value for money
- projects should seek to provide long term solutions rather than short one off events
- for existing projects with a proven success record, consideration will only be given to those that can demonstrate that funding will be used to extend the project beyond its existing boundaries in terms of the scope of project, number of beneficiaries and/or time frame.

In 2010/11 the trust held assets of £179,000 and had an income of £95,000, the majority of which was derived from donations. The trust gave £51,000 in grants, £43,000 of which was towards funding projects and £8,000 of which went towards funding training courses.

Although no list of beneficiaries for the period was included in the accounts the trust website lists some of the beneficiaries who have benefited from £263,000 in project grants since the trust was established (over £28,000 has been paid in individual grants to assist 78 people complete courses in money management in the same period).

Previous beneficiaries include: Bristol Debt Advice Centre; Tadley and District CAB; Cleanslate National CIC; Helping Hands for Refugees; Pen y Enfys; Nottingham Deaf Society; Bolton Lads' & Girls' Club; Stoke on Trent CAB; and The Holy Catholic School.

Exclusions

No funding for career development, vocational courses, undergraduate or postgraduate courses. No applications directly from persons under 18 years of age, such applicants will need a parent or guardian to apply on their behalf.

Applications

Applications must be made by a 'constituted group'. This roughly means an organisation with its own bank account and rules to make it accountable. Applicants can apply using the online application form on the trust's website.

For up-to-date programme information, including closing dates, please consult the trust's website. The trust welcomes queries from applicants who need help with the application process.

The website emphasises the following point:

> Please note only the first 40 applications that meet the criteria will be considered by the panel. Groups whether successful or not may only submit one application in any two year period.

If you have a project you consider to be special, and which does not appear to fit into the other criteria, then write directly to the Operations Manager (stuart@msecharity.com), who will bring it to the attention of the trustees.

Murphy-Neumann Charity Company Limited

Health, social welfare, medical research

£70,000 (2009/10)

Beneficial area

UK.

Hayling Cottage, Upper Street, Stratford-St-Mary, Colchester, Essex CO7 6JW
Tel: 01206 323685
Email: mncc@keme.co.uk
Correspondent: Mark J Lockett, Trustee
Trustees: Mark J Lockett; Colette Safhill; Marcus Richman.
CC Number: 229555

Information available

Full accounts were available from the Charity Commission website.

The trust has three main objects:
- to support projects aimed at helping those in society who suffer economic or social disadvantages or hardship arising from disability and/or social exclusion
- to assist those working to alleviate chronic illness and disabling disease
- to help fund research into medical conditions (particularly among the very young and the elderly) for which there is not yet a cure.

In 2009/10 the trust had assets of £1.4 million, an income of £69,000 and made grants totalling £70,000. The trust provided the following analysis of its grantmaking in the latest accounts:

Of the sixty seven charities to which donations were made around twenty fell into the core category with whom Murphy Neumann has had an on-going, long term relationship. In most cases these are relatively high profile organisations serving a large and well attested client base. Murphy Neumann made donations to around some fifteen charities primarily concerned with ameliorating the conditions of those who suffer specific economic or social disadvantage or hardship, approximately twenty charities most active in the investigation and alleviation of disabling and potentially terminal diseases and the remainder, charities mostly fairly small and community based, providing a mix of services to a clientele broadly drawn from among those who fall within the charity's overall catchment.

The trustees do not have a fixed policy with regard to the number of charities that can be supported. Each year a decision is taken on how much money is available for distribution without putting Murphy Neumann at risk. The trustees are mindful that donations should not be so small that they make little or no impact on the needs of the recipient. Not only could such donations hinder rather than help recipients but they would diminish the funds available to other charities with a perceived greater claim. With these considerations in mind the trustees have reached the conclusion that for the time being grants should be fixed at a maximum of £2,500 and a minimum of £500. The majority of grants fall within the range £750 -£2,000.

[...] It is difficult to measure the impact of (relatively) small grants on large organisations. In a number of cases grants are made to general funds rather than to support specific initiatives. In the case of smaller charities grants are invariably made towards named and known projects. This might include the purchase of specialist equipment, sponsoring programmes or activities or funding long term research into disabling diseases. In recent years charities have been obliged to comply with new legislation and in many cases this has entailed the provision of new facilities and the adaptation of old buildings to meet current needs. In several such cases the trustees have been able to support projects essential to the well-being or even survival of relatively large organisations. In one or two cases top-up grants have been made to small charities, particularly those with outreach programmes, where funding is essential to maintain their role in the community.

Beneficiaries during the year included: Contact the Elderly and Evening Argus Christmas Appeal (£2,500 each); Haemophilia Society, Hebron Trust and Beacon House (£1,800 each); Acorn Villages, SE Cancer Help Centre and Hospice in the Weald (£1,500 each); Prostate Cancer Charity, Dementia Care Trust and RUKBA (£1,300 each); RNIB Sunshine House Nursery School, Chicks Camping Holidays, Bowel Disease Research Foundation and Tourettes Action (£1,000 each); REACT, Jesse May Trust and Hamlet Centre Trust (£750 each); and Tuberous Sclerosis Association (£500).

Exclusions

No grants to individuals, or non-registered charities.

Applications

In writing to the correspondent, in a letter outlining the purpose of the required charitable donation. Telephone calls are not welcome. There are no application forms, guidelines or deadlines. No sae required. Grants are usually given in November and December.

Common applicant mistakes

'Around 15% to 20% of applicants do not pay attention to criteria. (However, this number is declining.)'

The Mushroom Fund

General charitable purposes

£42,000 (2009/10)

Beneficial area

UK and overseas, with a preference for St Helens.

Liverpool Charity and Voluntary Services, 151 Dale Street, Liverpool L2 2AH
Tel: 0151 227 5177
Email: enquiries@charitycheques.org.uk
Correspondent: The Trustees
Trustees: Mrs Rosalind Christian; Guy Pilkington; James Pilkington; Harriet Christian; Liverpool Charity and Voluntary Services.
CC Number: 259954

Information available

Accounts were available from the Charity Commission.

The trust has general charitable purposes, usually supporting causes known to the trustees.

In 2009/10 the trust had assets of £922,000 and an income of £31,000. Grants were made totalling £42,000 of which 17 were listed in the accounts.

Beneficiaries receiving grants of £1,000 or more each included: Pilkington Glass Collection Trust (£7,000); St Patrick's Church, Patterdale (£5,250); Samantha Dickson Brain Trust (£5,000); Pegasus Child Care Centre (£2,500); and National Wildflower Centre, St Helen's Women's Aid and Southport Offshore Rescue Team (£1,000 each).

Exclusions

No grants to individuals or to organisations that are not registered charities.

Applications

The trust does not consider or respond to unsolicited applications.

The Music Sales Charitable Trust

Children and youth, musical education, see below

£89,000 (2009)

Beneficial area
UK, but mostly Bury St Edmunds and London.

Music Sales Ltd, Dettingen Way, Bury St Edmunds, Suffolk IP33 3YB
Tel: 01284 702 600
Email: neville.wignall@musicsales.co.uk
Correspondent: Neville Wignall, Clerk
Trustees: Mr Robert Wise; Mr T Wise; Mr Ian Morgan; Mr Christopher Butler; Mr David Rockberger; Mrs Mildred Wise; Mr A E Latham.
CC Number: 1014942

Information available
Accounts were on file at the Charity Commission, but without a list of grants.

The trust was established in 1992 by the company Music Sales Ltd. It supports registered charities benefiting children and young adults, musicians, people who are disabled and people disadvantaged by poverty', particularly those resident in London and Bury St Edmunds. The trust is also interested in helping to promote music and musical education, again with a particular interest in children attending schools in London and Bury St Edmunds.

In 2009 the trust had assets of £4,000 and an income of £88,000. During the year grants were made totalling £89,000. The grants were categorised like so:

Education/training	13	£38,000
Arts and culture	18	£26,000
Medical, health, sickness	26	£17,000
Religion	2	£5,000
Disability	2	£1,500
General	1	£1000
Overseas aid/famine relief	1	£250

Major beneficiaries were: Purcell School (£30,000); Bury St Edmunds Bach Society (£10,000); The Worshipful Company of Musicians,

St Nicholas Hospice Care (£6,000 each); Westminster Synagogue (£5,000); Witold Lutoslawski Society (£2,500); Ipswich Community Play Bus, Citizens Advice Bureau, Maidstone Symphony Orchestra and Combat Stress (£1,000 each).

Exclusions
No grants to individuals.

Applications
In writing to the correspondent. The trustees meet quarterly, generally in March, June, September and December.

The Mutual Trust Group

Jewish, education, poverty

£340,000 (2010).

Beneficial area
UK.

12 Dunstan Road, London NW11 8AA
Tel: 020 8458 7549
Correspondent: B Weitz, Trustee
Trustees: B Weitz; M Weitz; A Weisz.
CC Number: 1039300

Information available
Brief accounts were available from the Charity Commission.

In 2010 the trust had assets of £157,000, an income of £316,000 and made grants totalling £340,000.

Beneficiaries included: Yeshivat Kesser Hatalmud (£175,000); Yeshivat Shar Hashamayim (£156,000); Congregation Beis Hamedrash (£6,500) and 'other' (£2,400).

Applications
In writing to the correspondent.

MYA Charitable Trust

Jewish

£104,000 to organisations (2009/10)

Beneficial area
Worldwide.

Medcar House, 149a Stamford Hill, London N16 5LL
Tel: 020 8800 3582
Correspondent: Myer Rothfeld, Trustee
Trustees: Myer Rothfeld; Eve Rothfeld; Hannah Schraiber; Joseph Pfeffer.
CC Number: 299642

Information available
Accounts were available from the Charity Commission, but without a list of grants.

In 2009/10 the trust had assets of £840,000 and an income of £104,000. Grants totalled £126,000 of which £104,000 was given to organisations and £22,000 to individuals. No further information was available.

In 2004/05 there were nine grants listed in the accounts of £1,000 each or more. Beneficiaries included: ZSV Trust (£3,500), KZF (£3,300), Beis Rochel and Keren Zedoko Vochesed (£2,500 each), London Friends of Kamenitzer Yeshiva and Maos Yesomim Charitable Trust (£2,000 each), Bikkur Cholim De Satmar (£1,100) and Keren Mitzva Trust and Wlodowa Charity Rehabilitation Trust (£1,000 each).

A further nine smaller grants to organisations of under £1,000 each totalled £1,200. The sum of £7,200 was distributed to nine 'poor and needy families'.

Applications
In writing to the correspondent.

MYR Charitable Trust

Jewish

£49,000 (2010)

Beneficial area
In practice, Israel, USA and England.

50 Keswick Street, Gateshead, Tyne and Wear NE8 1TQ
Correspondent: Z M Kaufman, Trustee

Trustees: Z M Kaufman; S Kaufman; A A Zonszajn; J Kaufman.
CC Number: 1104406

Information available

Accounts were available from the Charity Commission, but without a list of grants.

In 2010 the trust had assets of £1.1 million, an income of £78,000 and made grants totalling £49,000. No further information was available.

Previous beneficiaries have included: Cong Beth Joseph (£26,000); HP Charitable Trust (£2,300); UTA (£2,200); Gateshead Jewish Boarding School (£2,000); Keren Eretz Yisorel (£1,800); SCT Sunderland (£1,400) and GJLC (£1,000).

Applications

In writing to the correspondent.

The Kitty and Daniel Nabarro Charitable Trust

Welfare, education, medicine, homeless, general

£12,000 (2009/10)

Beneficial area

UK.

PO Box 7491, London N20 8LY
Email: admin.nabarro.charity@gmail.com
Correspondent: D J N Nabarro, Trustee
Trustees: D J N Nabarro; Katherine Nabarro; Allan Watson.
CC Number: 1002786

Information available

Accounts were on file at the Charity Commission.

The trust makes grants towards the relief of poverty, advancement of medicine and advancement of education, with some preference for work with homeless people. This trust will consider funding: information technology and computers; support and self-help groups; nature reserves; environmental issues; IT training;

literacy; training for work; vocational training; and crime prevention schemes.

In 2009/10 the trust had assets of £715,000 and an income of £27,000. Grants were made totalling £12,000 of which two were listed in the accounts: Cambridge Foundation Discovery Fund (£5,000); and OCD Action (£2,000). Other grants (£5,000).

Exclusions

No grants to individuals.

Applications

The trustees allocate grants on an annual basis to an existing list of charities. The trustees do not at this time envisage grants to charities which are not already on the list. This trust states that it does not respond to unsolicited applications.

Common applicant mistakes

'Failure to understand that we make very few grants.'

The Nadezhda Charitable Trust

Christian

£94,000 (2009/10)

Beneficial area

UK and worldwide, particularly Zimbabwe.

C/o Ballard Dale Syree Watson LLP, Oakmore Court, Kingswood Road, Hampton Lovett, Droitwich Spa WR9 0QH
Correspondent: Mrs Jill Kingston, Trustee
Trustees: William M Kingston; Mrs Jill M Kingston; Anthony R Collins; Ian Conolly.
CC Number: 1007295

Information available

Accounts were available from the Charity Commission.

The trust makes grants to projects for the advancement of Christianity in the UK and overseas, especially Zimbabwe.

In 2009/10 the trust had assets of £37,500, an income of £83,500 and made grants totalling £94,000 of

which nine were listed in the accounts. Of the grant total, £21,000 came from restricted funds which are designated for use in Zimbabwe.

Beneficiaries included: Mind the Gap Africa (£24,000); Friends of the Theological College of Zimbabwe in the USA (£23,000); Bulawayo Orphanage Zimbabwe (£16,000); Crosslinks (£11,000); George Whitefield College (£4,000); and Shaw Trust (£2,000).

Exclusions

No grants to individuals.

Applications

The majority of funds are presently directed to supporting the Christian Church in Zimbabwe. The trust does not, therefore, respond to unsolicited applications.

The Naggar Charitable Trust

Jewish, the arts, general

£61,000 (2009/10)

Beneficial area

UK and overseas.

61 Avenue Road, London NW8 6HR
Tel: 0207 034 1919
Correspondent: G Naggar, Trustee
Trustees: Guy Naggar; Hon. Marion Naggar; Marc Zilkha.
CC Number: 265409

Information available

Accounts were available from the Charity Commission.

The trust mainly supports Jewish organisations and a few medical charities. Arts organisations also receive some support.

In 2009/10 the trust had assets of £132,000, an income of £142,000 and made 24 grants totalling £61,000.

Beneficiaries included: British Friends of the Art Museums of Israel (£15,000); Western Marble Arch Synagogue (£11,000); CST (£8,500); The Contemporary Arts Society and The Royal Parks Foundation (£5,000 each) Jewish Care and One Family

UK (£2,500 each); Royal Academy of Arts (£1,000); and St John's Wood Society (£15).

Applications

In writing to the correspondent.

The Eleni Nakou Foundation

Education, international understanding

Around £60,000 (2009/10)

Beneficial area

Worldwide, mostly Continental Europe.

c/o Kleinwort Benson Trustees Ltd, 30 Gresham Street, London EC2V 7PG
Email: chris.gilbert@kbpb.co.uk
Correspondent: Chris Gilbert, Secretary
Trustee: Kleinwort Benson Trustees Ltd.
CC Number: 803753

Information available

Basic information was available from the Charity Commission.

The main aim of the trust is to advance the education of the people of Europe in each other's culture. Kleinwort Benson Trustees Ltd are also trustees of the following six trusts:

▶ C H (1980) Charitable Trust
▶ The A M Charitable Trust
▶ The G R P Charitable Trust
▶ The GP Charitable Trust
▶ The Richard Carne Trust
▶ The Sir Mark and Lady Turner Charitable Settlement

In 2009/10 the foundation had an income of £2,500 and an expenditure of £104,000. No further details were available.

Previous beneficiaries have included: Danish Institute at Athens (£45,000); Hellenic Foundation (£17,500); Eleni Nakou Scholarship Athens (£9,000); Scandinavian Society for Modern Greek Studies (£1,100).

Applications

In writing to the correspondent. Applications are considered

periodically. However, the trustees' state: 'It is unusual to respond favourably to unsolicited appeals'.

The Janet Nash Charitable Settlement

Medical, hardship, general

£61,000 to organisations (2009/10)

Beneficial area

UK.

Ron Gulliver and Co. Ltd, The Old Chapel, New Mill Lane, Eversley, Hampshire RG27 0RA
Tel: 01189 733 194
Correspondent: R Gulliver, Trustee
Trustees: Ronald Gulliver; M S Jacobs; Mrs C E Coyle.
CC Number: 326880

Information available

Accounts were available from the Charity Commission.

Registered with the Charity Commission in November 1985 this foundation supports medical research and education, particularly in the area of pathology. Grants are made to fund medical students who wish to have an extra research year at medical school and also to other research projects the trustees consider worthwhile.

In 2009/10 the charity had assets of £72,000 and an income of £375,000. Grants made to organisations totalled £61,000.

Beneficiaries included: the Royal Air Force Museum and the Get-a-Head Charitable Trust (£15,000); Acorns (£10,000); Shirley Medical Centre (£4,000); and Vision Charity (£3,000).

Applications

Absolutely no response to unsolicited applications. The trustees have stated: 'The charity does not, repeat not, ever consider any applications for benefit from the public.' Furthermore, that: 'Our existing charitable commitments more than use up our potential funds and were found personally by the

trustees themselves, never as a result of applications from third parties.'

Nathan Charitable Trust

Evangelical Christian work and mission

Around £35,000 (2009/10)

Beneficial area

UK and overseas.

The Copse, Sheviock, Torpoint, Cornwall PL11 3DZ
Tel: 01503 230 413
Correspondent: T R Worth, Trustee
Trustees: Thomas R Worth; Paula J Worth; Glyn A Jones.
CC Number: 251781

Information available

Full accounts were not required by the Charity Commission.

In recent years, the trust has had an unusually low income (£1 in 2010/11; £86 in 2009/10). The trust seemed to expend almost all of its capital in 2009/10 (£37,000); with a total expenditure of just £400 in 2010/11. As a result the trust has stated that no further donations will be made in the foreseeable future.

Previous beneficiaries have included: Operation Mobilisation, Carrot Tops, Leprosy Mission, Mission Aviation Fellowship, Open Doors, African Inland Mission, Bridges for Peace, Open Air Campaigners, Rhema Theatre Company and Christian Friends of Israel.

Applications

Funds are fully committed to current beneficiaries. No donations to be made in the foreseeable future.

The National Manuscripts Conservation Trust

Conservation of manuscripts

£75,000 (2010)

Beneficial area

UK.

c/o The National Archives, Ruskin Avenue, Kew, Surrey TW9 4DU
Tel: 020 8392 5218
Email: nmct@nationalarchives.gov.uk
Website: www.nmct.co.uk
Correspondent: Dr Anna Bulow, Secretary to the Trustees
Trustees: Lord Egremont; B Naylor; C Sebag-Montefiore.
CC Number: 802796

Information available

Full accounts were available from the Charity Commission website.

The object of the trust is to advance the education of the public by making grants towards the cost of conserving manuscripts which are of historic or educational value. The trust's 2010 annual report and accounts state:

> In a normal year, grants are awarded bi-annually, each June and December, for up to 90% of the cost of conservation of manuscripts held by any record office, library or by an owner of manuscript material that is exempt from capital taxation or owned by a charitable trust. In 2010, the Trustees met twice (in June and December) but only considered grant applications at the second of these meetings as a consequence of the change in the charity's administrative arrangements.

In 2010 the trust had assets of £1.8 million and an income of £80,000. During the year six grants were approved amounting to £75,000. The smallest grant was for £2,500 which went to the University of Edinburgh and the largest was for £40,000 which was awarded to the Fitzwilliam Museum, Cambridge.

Other beneficiaries include: Great Britain Trust towards the conservation of original ship's plans from the David McGregor collection (£10,000); University of Glasgow towards the conservation of MS Hunter 83 (£8,000) and Peterhouse, Cambridge towards the Peterhouse Partbooks Conservation Project (£5,000).

The trust is administered by the National Archives.

Exclusions

The following are not eligible: public records within the meaning of the Public Records Act; official archives of the institution or authority applying except in the case of some older records; loan collections unless exempt from capital taxation or owned by a charitable trust; and photographic, audio-visual or printed materials.

Applications

Applicants must submit six copies of the application form including six copies of a detailed description of the project. The applicant should also submit one copy of their most recent annual reports and accounts and details of its constitution.

Visit the trust's website for full details of how to apply. The trust's 2010 annual report and accounts give the following information on the trustees' decision-making process:

> In deciding whether an application should be awarded a grant, the trustees take into account the significance of the manuscript or archive, the suitability of the storage conditions, the applicant's commitment to continuing good preservation practice, and the requirement for the public to have reasonable access to it. Written reports on each application are given to the trustees by specialist staff from The National Archives working on a pro bono basis, but there is no other contribution by volunteers.

Nazareth Trust Fund

Christian, in the UK and developing countries

£51,000 to organisations (2009/10)

Beneficial area

UK and developing countries.

Barrowpoint, 18 Millennium Close, Salisbury, Wiltshire SP2 8TB
Tel: 01722 349 322
Correspondent: Dr Robert W G Hunt, Trustee
Trustees: Revd David R G Hunt; Eileen M Hunt; Dr Robert W G Hunt; Elma R L Hunt; Philip R W Hunt; Nicola M Hunt.
CC Number: 210503

Information available

Accounts were available from the Charity Commission.

The trust funds churches, Christian missionaries, Christian youth work and overseas aid. Grants are only made to people or causes known personally to the trustees.

In 2009/10 the trust held assets of £35,000 and had an income of £57,000. Grants were made totalling £54,000, of which £51,000 was given to organisations and £2,800 to individuals.

Beneficiaries included: Harnham FC Youth Club (£17,000 in two grants); Harnham Free Church (£8,400 in 12 grants); Durham Road Baptist Church (£5,600 in 15 grants); IREF (£3,300 in two grants); Urban Saints – previously 'Crusaders' (£4,000 in three grants); Northwood Hills Evangelical Church (£2,000); IREF – UK (£1,400 in three grants); London School of Theology (£800 in three grants); Scripture Union (£400 in two grants); Christian Viewpoint for Men (£250); and Faith Missions Trust (£30).

Exclusions

No support for individuals not known to the trustees.

Applications

In writing to the correspondent, although the trust tends to only support organisations it is directly involved with.

Ner Foundation

Orthodox Jewish

£98,000 (2009/10)

Beneficial area
UK and Israel.

409 Bury New Road, Salford,
Manchester M7 2YN
Correspondent: A Henry, Trustee
Trustees: A Henry; N Neumann; Mrs
E Henry.
CC Number: 1104866

Information available
Accounts were available from the
Charity Commission.

Set up in July 2004 as a company
limited by guarantee, the trustee's
2010 annual report states:

> The objects of the charity are the relief
> of poverty amongst the elderly or
> persons in need, hardship or distress in
> the Jewish Community; the
> advancement of the Orthodox Jewish
> Religion and the advancement of
> education according to the tenets of
> the Orthodox Jewish Faith.

In 2009/10 the foundation had assets
of £323,000 and an income of
£96,000. A list of beneficiaries was
not included in the accounts but
grants totalling £98,000 were broken
down as follows:

Relief of poverty	£47,000
Schools	£17,000
Yeshivos and seminaries	£17,000
Advancement of religion	£2,500
Grants under £1,000 each	£14,000

Applications
In writing to the correspondent.

Nesswall Ltd

Jewish

£97,000 (2009/10)

Beneficial area
UK.

28 Overlea Road, London E5 9BG
Tel: 020 8806 2965
Correspondent: Mrs R Teitelbaum,
Secretary
Trustees: I Teitelbaum, Chair; Mrs
R Teitelbaum; I Chersky; Mrs
H Wahrhaftig.

CC Number: 283600

Information available
Accounts were available from the
Charity Commission, but without a
grants list.

In 2009/10 the trust had assets of
£556,000 and an income of £99,000.
Grants and donations totalled
£97,000. A list of grants was not
available. Previous beneficiaries have
included: Friends of Horim
Establishments, Torah Vochesed
L'Ezra Vesaad and Emunah
Education Centre.

Applications
In writing to the correspondent, at
any time.

Newby Trust Limited

Welfare

£268,000 to organisations and
individuals (2009/10)

Beneficial area
UK.

Hill Farm, Froxfield, Petersfield,
Hampshire GU32 1BQ
Tel: 01730 827 557
Email: info@newby-trust.org.uk
Website: www.newby-trust.org.uk
Correspondent: Wendy Gillam,
Secretary
Trustees: Anna L Foxell; Anne
S Reed; Jean M Gooder; Ben Gooder;
Dr Richard D Gooder; Susan
A Charlton; Evelyn F Bentley; Nigel
Callaghan.
CC Number: 227151

Information available
Full accounts were available from the
Charity Commission website.

The following information regarding
the trust's work is taken from its
2009/10 annual report and accounts.

> The company works nationally, in
> particular to promote medical welfare,
> education, training and research, and
> the relief of poverty. The company does
> not generally provide funding for non
> UK activities or education, but takes
> steps to ensure the grants disbursed
> are spread as widely as possible to
> those in need within the United
> Kingdom.

Medical Welfare
To help alleviate physical and mental
suffering within the United Kingdom,
the company provides:
- small grants to individuals towards
  essential equipment, such as
  mobility aids, specialist chairs and
  beds
- larger grants on occasions, to
  registered charities for medical
  research, equipment, building
  improvements, etc. These are often
  related to the company's annual
  special category, as noted below.

Education, Training and Research
The company promotes education by
providing grants to:
- United Kingdom educational
  establishments in the form of
  bursaries and scholarships for
  postgraduate and post-doctoral
  research students, a condition of the
  grant being that its disbursement is
  based on merit and need
- registered charities and educational
  establishments for educational,
  cultural, sporting, or other projects.
  These are often associated with the
  annual special category.

Relief of Poverty
Recognising that there is widespread
poverty and deprivation within the
United Kingdom, some of which
manifests itself as crime, violence,
bullying, or domestic intimidation, the
company makes:
- small grants to individuals for home
  comforts, clothing, school uniforms,
  footwear, white goods, flooring etc
- larger grants to registered charities
  for community projects,
  refurbishment of community halls
  and buildings, the alleviation of
  homelessness, etc, again often
  related to the company's annual
  special category.

Annual Special Category
Under the general headings above, the
directors have a policy of selecting one
category for special support each year:
- in 2009/10 it was projects and/or
  training that encouraged artisanal
  skills e.g. sculpture, printing,
  thatching, weaving, art restoration
  etc
- in 2010/11 it was supporting families
  in poverty.

In 2009/10 the trust had assets of
£13 million and an income of
£313,000. Grants were made totalling
£268,000, of which £161,000 was
given to organisations and £107,000
to individuals. Of the total number of
applications made by organisations
and individuals, the success rate was
39 per cent. This was even lower for
registered charities, where out of 158

applications made, only 12 per cent were successful.

Grants were broken down as follows:

Medical welfare	£12,000
Education, training and research	£118,000
Medical welfare	£55,000
Special category and other special expenditure	£84,000

Major beneficiaries included: Down Syndrome Education International (£30,000 in three grants); Ditchling Museum (£20,000); Chichester College (£10,000); Bedales Grants Trust Fund (£7,500); Greenhouse Schools Project (£6,000); Weald and Downland Open Air Museum (£5,500); Medical Foundation for the Care of Victims of Torture and Academy of Ancient Music Trust (£5,000 each); and Hope in the Valley Riding Group (£1,000).

Applications

The application procedure differs between each category as follows:

Annual special category

Unsolicited applications will not be considered.

Education, training and research

Since 2008 the trust has supported education at the post-graduate or post-doctoral level only by allocating funds to selected universities or institutions in the United Kingdom. These are: City University, London, the London School of Economics and Political Science, the University of Edinburgh and the University of Manchester. Grants are awarded at the discretion of these universities subject to guidelines related to the purposes of the trust.

Medical welfare and Relief of poverty

Social Services or similar organisations may apply online only on behalf of individuals in need using the pre-application screening form on the trust's website.

Mr and Mrs F E F Newman Charitable Trust

Christian, overseas aid and development

£26,000 (2009/10)

Beneficial area

UK and overseas.

c/o David Quinn Associates, Southcroft, Caledon Road, Beaconsfield, Buckinghamshire HP9 2BX
Tel: 01494 674 396
Correspondent: David Quinn, Administrator
Trustees: Frederick Newman; Margaret Hayes; David Newman; Michael Newman; George Smith.
CC Number: 263831

Information available

Accounts were available from the Charity Commission.

In 2009/10 the trust had assets of £243,000 and an income of just over £26,000. Grants were made totalling £26,000 and were distributed from two funds as follows:

Donations: 'A' Fund (£6,200)

Grants were made to 24 organisations, ranging from £50 to £3,000. Beneficiaries included: Save Launde Abbey (£3,000); Christian Aid (£560 in three grants); Thal Village Project (£400); Guildford Samaritans (£200); Woking Hospice (£150 in two donations); Royal British Legion (£115); Amos Trust, Age Concern and Oxfam (£100 each); and St John Ambulance (£50).

Donations: 'B' Fund (£20,000)

Grants were made to 25 organisations, ranging from £50 to £2,000. Beneficiaries included: Tear Fund and Bible Society (£2,000 each); Acorn Christian Healing Foundation (£1,000); Riding Lights Trust, Traidcraft Exchange and Amnesty International (£600 each); TESS and SOMA (£500 each); and Community of the Holy Cross (£50).

Exclusions

No grants to individuals.

Applications

In writing to the correspondent. The trustees usually meet once a year to consider applications.

Newpier Charity Ltd

Jewish, general

£579,000 (2009/10)

Beneficial area

UK.

186 Lordship Road, London N16 5ES
Correspondent: Charles Margulies, Trustee
Trustees: Charles Margulies; Helen Knopfler; Rachel Margulies.
CC Number: 293686

Information available

Accounts were available from the Charity Commission, but without a list of grants.

The main objectives of the charity are the advancement of the orthodox Jewish faith and the relief of poverty.

In 2009/10 it had assets of £3.8 million and an income of £1 million. Grants totalling £579,000 were made during the year. Unfortunately, no list of grantees was included with the accounts at the Charity Commission.

Previous beneficiaries include: BML Benityashvut, Friends of Biala, Gateshead Yeshiva, KID, Mesdos Wiznitz and SOFT for redistribution to other charities.

Applications

In writing to the correspondent.

The Chevras Ezras Nitzrochim Trust

Jewish

£198,000 (2010)

Beneficial area

UK, with a preference for London.

53 Heathland Road, London N16 5PQ
Tel: 020 8800 5187
Correspondent: Hertz Kahan, Trustee
Trustees: Kurt Stern; Hertz Kahan; Moshe Rottenberg.

CC Number: 275352

Information available

Accounts were available from the Charity Commission, without a full list of grants.

The objects of the charity are the relief of the poor, needy and sick and the advancement of Jewish religious education. There is a preference for Greater London, but help is also given further afield. The majority of grants are made to individuals.

In 2010 the trust had assets of £3,000 and an income of £204,000. Grants totalled £198,000, of which £169,000 went to individuals and £29,000 went to organisations. Grants were awarded in the following categories and for the stated totals:

Poor and needy	£18,000
Education	£8,300
Religion	£2,800

There was no detailed list of beneficiary organisations but the trustees report states that the following organisations benefited: Notzar Chesed (£4,500); and Lemaan Hashabos (£1,500). Previous beneficiaries included Mesifta, Kupas Tzedoko Vochesed, Beis Chinuch Lenonos, Hachzokas Torah Vochesed Trust, Ezras Hakohol Trust, Woodstock Sinclair Trust, Side by Side, Yeshivas Panim Meiros, Yeahuas Chaim Synagogue, TYY Trust, Square Yeshiva and Stanislow.

Applications

In writing to the correspondent.

NJD Charitable Trust

Jewish

£92,000 to organisations and individuals (2009/10)

Beneficial area

UK and Israel.

Crowe Clark Whitehill, St Brides' House, 10 Salisbury Square, London EC4Y 8EH

Tel: 020 7842 7306
Email: info@igpinvest.com
Correspondent: Alan Dawson, Trust Administrator

Trustees: Nathalie Dwek; Jean Glaskie; Jacob Wolf; Alexander Dwek.
CC Number: 1109146

Information available

Accounts were available from the Charity Commission.

Set up in 2005, the objects of this trust are:

- the relief of poverty and hardship of members of the Jewish faith
- the advancement of Jewish religion through Jewish education.

In 2009/10 the trust had assets of £115,000, an income of £100,000 and made grants totalling £92,000.

Beneficiaries included: UJIA (£42,000); Jewish Care (£15,000); Hadassah Medical Relief Association UK (£10,000); Holocaust Educational Trust and Shaare Hayim Synagogue (£5,000 each). The remaining £16,000 represented a number of donations of £2,000 and under.

Applications

In writing to the correspondent.

The Noon Foundation

General, education, relief of poverty, community relations, alleviation of racial discrimination

£245,000 to organisations (2010)

Beneficial area

UK.

25 Queen Anne's Gate, St James' Park, London SW1H 9BU
Tel: 020 7654 1600
Email: grants@noongroup.co.uk
Correspondent: The Trustees
Trustees: Lord Noon; Akbar Shirazi; Mrs Zeenat Harnal; A M Jepson; A D Robinson; Mrs Zarmin N Sekhon.
CC Number: 1053654

Information available

Full accounts were available from the Charity Commission website.

The trust was set up in 1996 by Sir Gulam Noon, the founder of Noon Products. In 2010 the trust had assets of £1.9 million and an income of £47,000. Grants were made totalling £245,000 summarised as follows:

- **Education:** £55,000.
- **Sickness:** £166,000
- **Community relations:** £20,000.
- **Arts:** £3,300

Institutional beneficiaries included: Marie Curie Cancer Care (£56,000); Birkbeck University of London, Breast Cancer Care (£50,000 each); Macmillan Cancer Support (£48,000); Co-existence Trust (£15,000); Horizon Medical (£10,000); Garsington Opera (£2,500); London School of Economics, Oxfam (£2,000 each); Muslim Aid and Wellbeing (£1,000 each).

Other grants made to institutions of less than £1,000 totalled £4,000.

The trust's annual report and accounts commented on its current and future grant making as follows:

During the year the trust continued to support Birkbeck University of London with a further grant of £50,000. Birkbeck University of London, are working in conjunction with the University of East London and these grants will finance bursaries and top up grants for students in the East London area. The funding provided by the Noon Foundation will provide 35 full year bursaries and 60 top up grants for mainly evening work based courses to enhance employment prospects in some of the most deprived areas of London suffering from the lowest participation rate in higher education.

Plans for future periods
In addition to making grants out of income, the trustees are also considering the possibility of continuing to make substantial capital grants, where appropriate, to specific charities whose work and activities are considered would further and enhance the Foundation's purposes over the longer term.

Applications

All applications and queries should be made by email.

The Norda Trust

Prisoners, asylum seekers, disadvantaged communities

£98,000 (2010)

Beneficial area

UK.

The Shieling, St Agnes, Cornwall
TR5 0SS
Tel: 01871 553822
Email: enquiries@thenordatrust.org.uk
Website: www.thenordatrust.org.uk/
Correspondent: Martin Ward, Administrator
Trustees: J N Macpherson; P Gildener.
CC Number: 296418

Information available

Accounts were on file at the Charity Commission.

The trustees allocate funds principally in support of those working for the rehabilitation of prisoners both before and after release and support for the partners and families of prisoners. A special interest is taken in charities and organisations that support immigration detainees and the welfare of young offenders.

As funds permit, the trust can also support small local charities whose primary aim should be to improve the quality of life for the most severely disadvantaged communities or individuals.

The majority of awards are made on a one off basis, with very few commitments made over two or more years.

The trustees have a particular interest in helping to support new initiatives where there is a high level of volunteer involvement.

When funds allow applications will be considered from charities and organisations that, by the nature of the work they undertake, do not attract popular support.

In 2010 the trust's assets stood at nearly £2.9 million. It had an income of £101,000 and made grants totalling £98,000. Grants were made in four categories as follows:

Prisoners and their families	15	£53,000
Asylum seekers and refugees	12	£44,000
General	1	£1,000

Beneficiaries included: Dover Detainee Visitor Group (£6,400); NEPACS (£6,000); Asylum Welcome, Families/Friends of Prisoners and Maggies Day Centre (£5,000 each); Asylum Aid and Burnbake Trust (£3,000 each); A4e HMP Dorchester and Youth Empowerment Crime Diversion Scheme (£2,000 each) Solihull Churches (£1,000); and Samaritans South West (£600).

Exclusions

The following areas are not funded by the trust:

- medical causes
- animal causes
- individuals
- school fees
- Proselytising.

Applications

Via letter or email, outlining the appeal. All applicants should leave at least a year before re-applying. Up to date financial information is required from all applicants. The trust will then make contact to request any further information they need.

Common applicant mistakes

'Not reading our aims and objectives.'

The Norman Family Charitable Trust

General

£382,000 (2009/10)

Beneficial area

Primarily Cornwall, Devon and Somerset.

14 Fore Street, Budleigh Salterton, Devon EX9 6NG
Tel: 01395 446 699
Fax: 01395 446698
Email: enquiries@normanfct.plus.com
Website: www.nfct.org
Correspondent: R J Dawe, Chair of the Trustees
Trustees: R J Dawe, Chair; Mrs M H Evans; M B Saunders; Mrs M J Webb; Mrs C E Houghton.
CC Number: 277616

Information available

Accounts were available from the Charity Commission.

In November 2009 the trust acquired a commercial property investment leased to Kwik-Fit at 19a Tavistock Road, Plymouth for £751,000. The current rent is £39,500 per annum. The charity has also completed the purchase of 'Foreland', 12a Fore Street, Budleigh Salterton and the property is now being refurbished. This acquisition~ directly adjoins 14 Fore Street, which is already owned by the Trust and provides the potential opportunity to enhance the value of both properties. These investments have reduced the capital cash awaiting investment.

In 2009/10 the trust had assets of £8.6 million and an income of £387,000. Grants totalling £382,000 were made to 364 organisations and were mainly for less than £5,000 each. Grants were broken down by category as follows:

Community, sport and leisure	101	£92,000
Medical (inc. research)	62	£75,000
Environmental and conservation	12	£8,000
Youth	31	£35,000
Senior	14	£25,000
Blind, deaf, physically disabled	45	£26,000
Children	54	£51,500
Animals	18	£9,500
Homeless	11	£11,000
Drugs, alcohol and prison	6	£2,500
Mentally disabled	9	£5,000
Other	1	£250

Beneficiaries of larger grants were: Children's Hospice South West (£30,000); Peninsular Medical School (£20,000); Kenn Parish Hall and Resthaven (£15,000 each); and Budleigh Youth Project (£7,500).

Other beneficiaries included: Exeter Cathedral, Firefighters Charity and Help for Heroes (£5,000 each); Prince's Trust (£4,000); Alzheimer's Society and Motor Neurone Disease Association (£2,500 each); and Blue Cross, Cats Protection League and Shelter (£2,000 each).

Exclusions

No grants to individuals. No funding for religious buildings or to assist any organisations using animals for live experimental purposes or generally to fund overseas work.

Applications

In writing to the correspondent. A subcommittee of trustees meet regularly to make grants of up to £5,000. Grants in excess of £5,000 are dealt with at one of the quarterly meetings of all the trustees.

The Duncan Norman Trust Fund

General

£26,000 (2009/10)

Beneficial area

UK, with a preference for Merseyside.

Liverpool Charity and Voluntary Services, 151 Dale Street, Liverpool L2 2AH
Tel: 0151 227 5177
Email: enquiries@charitycheques.org.uk
Website: www.merseytrusts.org.uk
Correspondent: The Trustees
Trustees: R K Asser; Mrs C Chapman; Mrs V S Hilton; Mrs E Lazar; W Stothart; C L Venner.
CC Number: 250434

Information available

Accounts were obtained from the Charity Commission website.

The trust has general charitable purposes, but particularly supports organisations in the Merseyside area. In 2009/10 the trust had assets of £758,000 and an income of £29,000. Grants were made totalling £26,000.

Grants over £1,000 were made to: Catherine House Hospice (£1,300); The Campaign for Drawing (£1,200); and Moor Park Charitable Trust (£1,000). Grants of less than £1,000 each totalled £22,000.

Exclusions

No grants to individuals.

Applications

The trust states that it only makes grants to charities known to the settlor and unsolicited applications are not considered.

The Normanby Charitable Trust

Social welfare, disability, general

£405,000 (2009/10).

Beneficial area

UK, with a special interest in North Yorkshire and north east England.

52 Tite Street, London Sw3 4JA
Correspondent: The Trustees
Trustees: The Marquis of Normanby; The Dowager Marchioness of Normanby; Lady Lepel Kornicki; Lady Evelyn Buchan; Lady Peronel Phipps de Cruz; Lady Henrietta Burridge.
CC Number: 252102

Information available

Accounts were available from the Charity Commission. The trust's 2009/10 annual report states:

> The trustees have decided that only exceptionally will they help individuals in the future, and that they will confine their assistance for the moment, to mainly North Yorkshire and the North East of England.
>
> In accordance with the objectives under the trust deed the trustees do exceptionally make grants outside the preferred area and this has happened during the current year in respect of the grant paid to The Moyne Institute.

The trust concentrates its support on general charitable purposes, however previous research has suggested a preference for supporting social welfare, disability and the arts. The trust has occasionally considered giving grants for the preservation of religious and secular buildings of historical or architectural interest.

In 2009/10 the trust had assets of £8.8 million and an income of £292,000. Grants to 27 organisations were made totalling £405,000. The largest grants included those to: Moyne Institute (£228,000); Lythe Village Hall (£100,000); Mulgrave

Community Sports Association (£25,000); Keats/Shelley Memorial Association (£10,000).

Other grants included: Order of the Holy Paraclete (£5,000); Churches Regional Commission for Yorkshire and the Humber North York Moors Chamber Music Festival (£3,500 each); Hinderwell Methodist Church and Inter Active Whitby and District (£2,000 each); St Mungo's, The Salvation Army and Tom Carpenter Centre (£1,000 each); and St Catherine's Hospice (£500).

Exclusions

No grants to individuals, or to non-UK charities.

Applications

In writing to the correspondent. There are no regular dates for trustees' meetings. Please note, only successful applications will be acknowledged.

The Earl of Northampton's Charity

Welfare

£16,000 (2009/10)

Beneficial area

England, with a preference for London and the South East.

Mercers' Company, Mercers' Hall, Ironmonger Lane, London EC2V 8HE
Tel: 020 7726 4991
Fax: 020 7600 1158
Email: mail@mercers.co.uk
Website: www.mercers.co.uk
Correspondent: M McGregor, Clerk to the Mercers' Company
Trustee: The Mercers' Company.
CC Number: 210291

Information available

Full accounts were on file at the Charity Commission.

Shortly before his death in 1614, Henry Howard, Earl of Northampton, founded a hospital or almshouse for poor men at Greenwich, known as Trinity Hospital, and although he was not a member of the Mercers

Company he entrusted the management to the Company's care. The charity stated in their annual accounts that due to the refurbishment of the original almshouse at Trinity Hospital Greenwich, due to be complete in 2012, the charity's grant making programme will remain curtailed until the work is complete and the reserves fund reaches an appropriate level.

In 2009/10 the charity's assets stood at £22 million. It had an income of £769,000, of which most (£481,000) went towards maintaining its almshouses for the elderly.

Grants totalled £16,000 and were made to four organisations as follows: Trinity Hospital – Castle Rising (£10,000); Trinity Hospital – Clun (£4,000); Jubilee Trust Almshouses (£2,000); and St M Michael's Church Framlington (£250).

Applications

Please note: The trust is currently not accepting any applications. It is under the trusteeship of the Mercers' Company and one application to the Company is an application to all of its trusts including the Mercers' Charitable Foundation and the Charity of Sir Richard Whittington.

The Norton Foundation

Young people under 25 years of age (currently restricted to the areas of Birmingham, Coventry and the County of Warwick)

£61,000 to organisations (2009/10)

Beneficial area

UK, with a preference for Birmingham, Coventry and the County of Warwick.

Richard Perkins & Co, 50 Brookfield Close, Hunt End, Redditch B97 5LL
Tel: 01527 544 446
Email: correspondent@ nortonfoundation.org
Website: www.nortonfoundation.org

Correspondent: Richard C Perkins, Correspondent
Trustees: R H Graham Suggett, Chair; Alan Bailey; Michael R Bailey; Parminder Singh Birdi; Mrs Jane Gaynor; Mrs Sarah V Henderson; Richard G D Hurley; Brian W Lewis; Robert K Meacham; Richard C Perkins; Mrs Louise Sewell.
CC Number: 702638

Information available

Accounts were obtained from the Charity Commission website.

The trust was created in 1990. Its stated objects are to help children and young people under 25 who are in 'need of care or rehabilitation or aid of any kind, particularly as a result of delinquency, deprivation, maltreatment or neglect or who are in danger of lapsing or relapsing into delinquency'.

Once every five years the trust intends making a donation of £100,000 to a capital project and a designated fund has been created for this purpose. At 5 April 2010 the trustees set aside £100,000 towards the next major capital grant. In addition, the trustees received a donation of £100,000 from The Depot (South Warwickshire) on the winding up of that charity. This amount was given on condition it was used for the benefit of young persons in the Stratford on Avon District. The Trustees set up a small sub-committee to administer the promotion and award of the capital grants and, since the year end, two grants of £100,000 each have been awarded.

In 2009/10 the trust had assets of £4.1 million and an income of £233,000. Grants totalling £105,000 were made to individuals (£44,000) and organisations (£61,000). The latter amount included £32,000 in 'discretionary awards' to organisations which, at their discretion, can make grants to individuals. Grants were made to 54 organisations for the following purposes: social work (£31,000); education and training (£24,000); medical (£3,000); holidays (£2,000); and clothing (£1,000).

Beneficiaries of grants of £1,000 or more included: South Birmingham Young Homeless Project (£11,000);

Warwickshire County Council, Youth and Community Service (£9,000); React (£2,700); The Industrial Trust and Arthur Rank Centre (£2,500 each); Birmingham Battalion of the Boys' Brigade, Lifelites, The PCC of St Marks and Warwickshire Association of Youth Clubs (£2,000 each); and Birmingham Rathbone, Birmingham Royal Ballet, Coventry Boys' Club, Depaul Trust, Dyslexia Association of Birmingham, Guy's Gift, Happy Days Children's Charity, The National Deaf Children's Society, Warwick Corps of Drums and Whizz Kids (£1,000 each).

Exclusions

No grants for the payment of debts that have already been incurred. Grants are not made for further education (except in very exceptional circumstances).

Applications

By letter which should contain all the information required as detailed in the guidance notes for applicants. Guidance notes are available from the correspondent or from the foundation's website. Applications from organisations are normally processed by the trustees at their quarterly meetings. Application forms may be obtained from the correspondent or from the trust's website.

Common applicant mistakes

'Failure to understand the terms and conditions. Also, failure to be precise and specific about the uses the grant will be put to.'

The Norwich Town Close Estate Charity

Education in and near Norwich

£380,000 to organisations and individuals (2009/10)

Beneficial area

Within a 20-mile radius of the Guildhall of the city of Norwich.

Mr David Walker, 1 Woolgate Court,
St Benedict's Street, Norwich
NR2 4AP
Tel: 01603 621023
Email: david.walker@
norwichcharitabletrusts.org.uk
Correspondent: David Walker, Clerk
Trustees: David Fullman; John
Rushmer; Michael Quinton; Brenda
Ferris; Geoffrey Loades; Joyce
Hopwood; Philip Blanchflower; Sally
Barham; Anthony Hansell; Nigel
Black; Richard Gurney; Jeanette
Southgate; Robert Self.
CC Number: 235678

Information available

Accounts were available from the
Charity Commission.

The charity has the following objects:
  to provide 'relief in need' and
  pensions to Freemen or their
  widows or daughters where
  required
  the promotion of education of
  those in need of financial
  assistance who are Freemen or the
  sons or daughters of Freemen
  To make grants for educational
  purposes to bodies whose
  beneficiaries reside within the 20-
  mile radius of the Norwich
  Guildhall.

In 2009/10 the charity had assets of
£19.3 million and an income of
£720,000. Grants were made to
organisations and individuals
totalling £380,000, broken down as
follows:

Pensions	£106,000
Educational	£118,000
Relief in need	£3,000
Television licences	£3,000
Grant to 'other bodies'	£153,000

Beneficiaries of grants to 'other
bodies' include: Central Norwich
Hockey Consortium (£15,000); Eaton
Primary School and Norfolk
Homemakers Association (£10,000
each); Norfolk and Norwich Families
House (£9,000); St Peter's Church
Park Lane (£7,500); Hungate
Medieval Art (£5,500); East Anglia
Art Fund (£2,500); Wymondham Arts
Forum (£2,000) and Magdelen Gates
Pre-school (£300).

Exclusions

No grants to: individuals who are not
Freemen (or dependants of Freemen)

of the city of Norwich; charities more
than 20 miles from Norwich; or
charities which are not educational.
Revenue funding for educational
charities is not generally given.

Applications

After a preliminary enquiry, in
writing to the clerk.

When submitting an application the
following points should be borne in
mind:

- Brevity is a virtue. If too much
  written material is submitted there
  is a risk that it may not all be
  assimilated.
- The trustees like to have details of
  any other financial support
  secured.
- An indication should be given of
  the amount that is being sought
  and also how that figure is arrived
  at.
- The trustees will not reimburse
  expenditure already incurred.
- Nor, generally speaking will the
  trustees pay running costs, e.g.
  salaries.

Norwood and Newton Settlement

Christian

£308,000 (2009/10)

Beneficial area

England and Wales.

126 Beauly Way, Romford, Essex
RM1 4XL
Tel: 01708 723 670
Correspondent: David M Holland,
Trustee
Trustees: P Clarke; D M Holland;
Mrs Stella Holland; R Lynch; Mrs
Susan Newsom.
CC Number: 234964

Information available

Accounts were available from the
Charity Commission.

The trust supports Methodist and
other mainline Free Churches and
some other smaller UK charities in
which the founders had a particular
interest. As a general rule, grants are
for capital building projects which

aim to improve the worship, outreach
and mission of the church.

Where churches are concerned, the
trustees take particular note of the
contribution and promised
contributions towards the project by
members of the church in question.

In 2009/10 the settlement had assets
of £6.9 million and an income of
£324,000. Grants were made to 37,
mainly Methodist, organisations and
totalled £308,000.

The largest grants made included
those to: Colchester Baptist Church
and Fulwood Methodist Church
(£20,000 each); Whaddon Way
Baptist/CofE Church, Bletchley
(£15,000); and Vine Baptist Church,
Sevenoaks, The Mint Methodist
Church and Fathers House Elim
Church, Lancaster (£10,000 each).

Other grants made included those to:
Red Lodge Community Church, Ely
(£7,500); Ampthill Methodist Church,
Bedfordshire and High Bentham
Methodist Church, North Yorkshire
(£5,000 each); Cheriton Baptist
Church, Folkestone (£3,000); and
Brailsford Methodist Church, Derby
(£1,000).

Exclusions

Projects will not be considered where
an application for National Lottery
funding has been made or is
contemplated. No grants to
individuals, rarely to large UK
charities and not for staff/running
costs, equipment, repairs or general
maintenance.

Applications

In writing to the correspondent. In
normal circumstances, the trustees'
decision is communicated to the
applicant within seven days (if a
refusal), and if successful,
immediately after the trustees'
quarterly meetings.

Common applicant mistakes

'Not checking their eligibility; not
asking for advice if they do not
understand a question on the
application form.'

The Sir Peter O'Sullevan Charitable Trust

Animal welfare

£175,000 (2009/10)

Beneficial area

Worldwide.

The Old School, Bolventor,
Launceston PL15 7TS
Tel: 01566 880 292
Email: nigel@earthsummit.demon.co.uk
Website: www.thevoiceofracing.com
Correspondent: Nigel Payne, Trustee
Trustees: Christopher Spence; Lord
Oaksey; Sir Peter O'Sullevan; Nigel
Payne; Geoffrey Hughes; Bob
McCreery; Michael Dillon.
CC Number: 1078889

Information available

Accounts were available from the
Charity Commission.

Registered with the Charity
Commission in January 2000, in
2009/10 the trust had assets of
£75,000 and an income of £318,000
(mainly from fundraising events).
Grants were made totalling £175,000.

A total of six grants were made, as in
previous years, to Blue Cross, Brooke
Hospital for Animals, Compassion in
World Farming, World Horse
(formerly International League for the
Protection of Horses), the Racing
Welfare Charities and the
Thoroughbred Rehabilitation Centre
(£32,500 each).

Applications

In writing to the correspondent.

The Oak Trust

General

£28,000 (2009/10)

Beneficial area

UK.

Essex House, 42 Crouch Street,
Colchester CO3 3HH
Tel: 01206 217300

Email: bruce.ballard@birkettlong.co.uk
Website: www.oaktrust.org.uk
Correspondent: The Clerk to the
Trustees
Trustees: Revd A C C Courtauld;
J Courtauld; Dr Elizabeth Courtauld;
Miss C M Hart.
CC Number: 231456

Information available

Accounts were received at the Charity
Commission but not available to view
online.

The trust has a preference for
supporting those charities that it has
a special interest in, knowledge of or
association with and with a turnover
of below £1 million. In 2009/10 the
trust had an income of £24,000 and a
total expenditure of £28,000.

Previous grant recipients have
included: The Cirdan Sailing Trust
(£3,000); Christian Aid and Prader-
Willi Syndrome Association UK
(£2,000 each); Children's Overseas
Relief Fund and Voice (£1,000 each);
Cambridge Society for the Blind and
Partially-sighted, Detention Advice
Service, Practical Action – Darfor
Appeal, The Swiften Charitable Trust
and Westcott House (£500 each); and
Grace of God Church – Malawi and
Maranatho Orphanage Ministries –
Malawi (£250 each).

Exclusions

No support to individuals.

Applications

Written applications will no longer be
accepted. Applications must be
submitted via the online form
available from the trust's website.

Details of the next submission date
are included on the application form.
Applicants will receive an
acknowledgement of their application
and notification of the outcome
within 10 days of the Review Meeting
by email.

Common applicant mistakes

'Applying for grants in areas outside
the stated geographical area. Not
applying by using the online
application form available from the
trust's website.'

The Oakdale Trust

Social work, medical, general

£131,000 (2009/10)

Beneficial area

UK, especially Wales, and overseas.

Tansor House, Tansor, Oundle,
Peterborough PE8 5HS
Tel: 01832 226386
Email: oakdale@tanh.demon.co.uk
Correspondent: Rupert Cadbury,
Correspondent and Trustee
Trustees: Brandon Cadbury; Mrs
Flavia Cadbury; Rupert Cadbury;
Bruce Cadbury; Mrs Olivia Tatton-
Brown; Dr Rebecca Cadbury.
CC Number: 218827

Information available

Accounts were available from the
Charity Commission.

The trust's main areas of interest
were outlined in their most recent
accounts:

- Welsh-based social and community projects
- medical – support groups operating in Wales and UK-based research projects
- UK-based charities working in the third world
- environmental conservation in the UK and overseas
- Penal reform.

Some support is also given to the arts,
particularly where there is a Welsh
connection. The average grant is
approximately £650.

In 2009/10 the trust had assets of
£8.2 million and an income of
£165,000. Grants were made to 196
organisations totalling £131,000.

The main beneficiary organisations
were: The Brandon Centre (£14,000)
and Radnordshire Wildlife Trust
(£9,600).

Other grant recipients included:
Concern Universal (£7,000); F.P.W.P
Hibiscus (£6,000); Friends of
Swanirvar and Howard League for
Penal Reform (£1,500 each); Institute
of Orthopaedics, MDF The BiPolar
Organisation Cymru, Médecins Sans
Frontières, Mid Wales Chamber
Orchestra Ltd and Quaker Peace and

Social Witness (£1,000 each); Able Child Africa, Anti-Slavery International, Pain Relief Foundation and Peace Direct(£500 each); and Pond Conservation Trust and River and Sea Sense (£250 each).

Exclusions

No grants to individuals, holiday schemes, sport activities or expeditions.

Applications

An official application form is available on request. However applicants are free to submit requests in any format so long as applications are clear and concise, covering aims, achievements, plans and needs supported by a budget. Applicants applying for grants in excess of £750 are asked to submit a copy of a recent set of audited annual accounts (which can be returned on request). The latest accounts state that:

The trustees meet twice a year in April and October to consider applications and to award grants. No grants are awarded between meetings. The deadline for the April meeting is 1 March and for the October meeting 1 September.

The trust is administered by the trustees at no cost, and owing to a lack of secretarial help and in view of the numerous requests received, no applications are acknowledged even when accompanied by a stamped addressed envelope.

Common applicant mistakes

'Applications submitted for projects outside the geographical area (Wales) that the trust covers.'

The Oakmoor Charitable Trust

General

£52,000 (2009/10)

Beneficial area

UK.

Rathbone Trust Company Limited, 159 New Bond Street, London W1S 2UD
Tel: 020 7399 0807
Correspondent: The Administrator, Rathbone Trust Company Limited

Trustees: Rathbone Trust Company Ltd; P M H Andreae; Mrs R J Andreae.
CC Number: 258516

Information available

Accounts were received at the Charity Commission but not available to view online.

Established in 1969 the trust receives regular donations from the settlor, Peter Andreae.

In 2009/10 the trust had an income of £22,000 and total expenses of £52,000. We have no information regarding the 2009/10 beneficiary organisations.

The trust generally divides its grant giving into the following categories:

- the arts and museums
- youth and education
- other national and international charities
- local charities and hospices
- religious organisations

Previous beneficiaries have included: The London Library and Mary Rose Trust (£10,000 each); Save Britain's Heritage (£7,500); and CAFOD (£5,000); Institute of Economic Affairs (£3,000); Downe House Trust (£2,000); Armed Forces Memorial, Elias Ashmole Group and Hampshire Country Learning (£1,000 each); Bembridge Harbour Trust and Convent of St Lucy – Chichester (£500 each); Cancer Research (£250); and Friends of the Royal Opera House Foundation (£100).

Exclusions

No grants to individuals.

Applications

The trust states that it does not respond to unsolicited applications.

The Odin Charitable Trust

General

£230,000 (2009/10)

Beneficial area

UK.

PO Box 1898, Bradford-on-Avon, Wiltshire BA15 1YS

Email: kelly.donna@virgin.net
Correspondent: Mrs S G P Scotford, Trustee
Trustees: Mrs S G P Scotford; Mrs A H Palmer; Donna Kelly; Mrs P C Cherry.
CC Number: 1027521

Information available

Accounts were available from the Charity Commission.

In 2009/10 the trust had assets of £4.8 million and an income of £354,000. Grants paid during this financial year totalled £230,000.

Although the objects of the charity are wide, the trust has a preference for making grants towards: furthering the arts; providing care for people who are disabled and disadvantaged; supporting hospices, the homeless, prisoners' families, refugees, gypsies and 'tribal groups'; and furthering research into false memories and dyslexia.

The trustees are more likely to support small organisations and those that by the nature of their work, find it difficult to attract funding. Grants range from one-off donations to three year awards.

By far the largest grant was to: British False Memory Society (£44,000). Beneficiaries of smaller one year grants went to: Helen Arkell Dyslexia Centre and The Dorothy House Foundation (£5,000 each); Julian House PACT and Survival International (£3,000 each); Jessie's Fund, Dressability and St Pancras Thanet Street Trust (£2,000 each); and Kennet Furniture Recycling (£1,500).

Exclusions

Applications from individuals are not considered.

Applications

All appeals should be by letter containing the following:

- aims and objectives of the charity
- nature of appeal
- total target if for a specific project
- contributions received against target
- registered Charity Number
- any other relevant factors.

Letters should be accompanied by a set of the charitable organisation's latest report and full accounts and should be addressed to the correspondent.

Common applicant mistakes

'We receive applications from non-charities. Also commonly people address the letter to the wrong charitable trust when using mail merge etc.'

The Ogle Christian Trust

Evangelical Christianity

£128,000 (2009)

Beneficial area

Worldwide.

43 Woolstone Road, Forest Hill, London SE23 2TR
Tel: 020 8699 1036
Correspondent: Mrs F J Putley, Trustee
Trustees: Mrs F J Putley; R J Goodenough; S Proctor; Mrs L M Quanrud; Dr D Harley.
CC Number: 1061458

Information available

Accounts were on file at the Charity Commission.

The trust mainly directs funds to new initiatives in evangelism worldwide, support of missionary enterprises, publication of scriptures and Christian literature, pastor training and famine and other relief work.

In 2009 it had assets of £2.3 million and an income of £118,000. Grants totalled £128,000. 32 organisations received grants of £1,000 or more as listed in the accounts.

By far the largest grant, as in previous years, went to Operation Mobilisation (£21,000). Other beneficiaries included: Langham Partnership, Romans One Eleven Trust (£7,000 each); ELAM Ministries, OMF International, The Source (£5,000 each); ANCC, CCSM, Redcliffe College (£4,000 each); Lok Hospital, Oasis International, Starfish Asia (£3,000 each); France Mission Trust, Pakistan Fellowship of Evangelical

Students (£2,000 each); Caring for Life, Enlighten, Keswick Ministries and Saltworkz (£1,000 each).

Unlisted grants totalled £13,500.

Exclusions

Applications from individuals are discouraged; those granted require accreditation by a sponsoring organisation. Grants are rarely made for building projects. Funding will not be offered in response to general appeals from large national organisations.

Applications

In writing to the correspondent, accompanied by documentary support and an sae. Trustees meet in May and November, but applications can be made at any time.

The Oikonomia Trust

Christian

£66,000 (2009/10)

Beneficial area

UK and overseas.

98 White Lee Road, Batley, West Yorkshire WF17 8AF
Tel: 01924 502 616
Email: c.mountain@ntlworld.com
Correspondent: Colin Mountain, Trustee
Trustees: D H Metcalfe; R H Metcalfe; S D Metcalfe; C Mountain; Revd R O Owens.
CC Number: 273481

Information available

Accounts were received at the Charity Commission but not available to view online.

The trust supports evangelical work, famine and other relief through Christian agencies. The trust is not looking for new outlets as those it has knowledge of are sufficient to absorb its available funds.

In 2009/10 it had an income of £4,000 and a total expenditure of £66,000. We have no details of beneficiary organisations.

Previous beneficiaries included: Barnabus Trust (£5,500); Slavic

Gospel Association (£5,000); Bethel Church (£4,000); Asia Link, Association of Evangelists and Caring for Life (£3,000 each); Japan Mission (£2,500); Starbeck Mission (£2,000); People International (£1,000); and Carey Outreach Ministries (£500).

Exclusions

No grants made in response to general appeals from large national organisations.

Applications

In writing to the correspondent, although the trust has stated that most grants are made to the same organisations each year and as such new applications are unlikely to be successful. If an applicant desires an answer, an sae should be enclosed. Applications should arrive in January.

The Old Broad Street Charity Trust

General

£126,000 to organisations (2009/10)

Beneficial area

UK and overseas.

Rawlinson and Hunter, Eighth Floor, 6 New Street Square, London EC4A 3AQ
Tel: 020 7842 2000
Correspondent: Simon Jennings, Secretary to the Trustees
Trustees: Mrs Martine Cartier-Bresson; Adrian T J Stanford; Peter A Hetherington; Christopher J Sheridan; Clare Gough.
CC Number: 231382

Information available

Accounts were available from the Charity Commission.

The objects of the trust are general, although most of the funds are given towards the arts. It was the wish of Louis Franck, the founder, that part of the income should be used to fund scholarships, preferably for UK citizens to reach the highest levels of executive management in banking and financial institutions. The trust makes provision for this each year by setting aside an annual amount and funding scholarships for people serving in a bank or financial institution in the UK to spend time in any seat of learning (principally INSEAD) to attain the highest level of executive management. £35,000 was given for this purpose in the financial year 2009/10.

In 2009/10 the trust had assets of £1.7 million and an income of £71,000. Grants totalling £126,000 were made to 13 organisations; all but four were supported in the previous year.

Beneficiaries were: Foundation Henri Cartier-Bresson (£58,000); Societe Francaise le Lutte contre la Cecite et contre le Tranchome (£13,000), Bezirksfursorge – Saanen (£12,000), The Mulberry Bush Organisation and Changing Faces (£10,000 each); Royal Marsden NHS Foundation (£7,500); International Menuhin Music Academy (£6,000), Royal Academy of Arts and St Mungo's (£2,500 each), The National Gallery Trust (£2,000), Whitechapel Gallery (£1,000) and Artangel (£750); and Tate Gallery Foundation (£600).

Exclusions

The trustees only support organisations of which they personally have some knowledge.

Applications

In writing to the correspondent. Unsolicited applications are not considered.

Common applicant mistakes

'Applying for individual grants.'

Old Possum's Practical Trust

General, arts

£217,000 to organisations and individuals (2009/10)

Beneficial area

UK.

PO Box 5701, Milton Keynes MK9 2WZ
Email: generalenquiry@ old-possums-practical-trust.org.uk

Website: www.old-possums-practical-trust.org.uk
Correspondent: The Trustees
Trustees: Esme Eliot; Judith Hooper; Deidre Simpson; Clare Reihill.
CC Number: 328558

Information available

Accounts were available from the Charity Commission. The trust also has a useful website.

The following information on its aims and objectives is taken from the trust's website:

> The trust's mission is to manage the funds at its disposal to support literary, artistic, musical and theatrical projects and organisations.
>
> Priority is given to requests that display enterprise in artistic endeavour and demonstrate high sustainability and contextual impact. Particular interest is taken in those projects that will have an impact on future literary work.
>
> Special contributions made by the trust to other related types of organisation reflect both the personal history of Old Possum's Practical Trust and the wishes of the trustees. Support is more likely for those projects which best reflect the literary reputation and name of T. S. Eliot and the special interests of his wife.

In 2009/10 the trust had assets of £7.1 million and an income of £173,000. Grants were made totalling £217,000 and were broken down into the following categories:

Educational support	£20,000
Arts and historical conservation	£170,000
Support for the disabled and disadvantaged	£27,000

Beneficiaries included: High Tide (£80,000); First Story (£20,000); Poetry Book Society (£14,000); Arete, Victoria and Albert Museum and Book Trade Benevolent Society (£10,000 each); Dogs for the Disabled and the Times Stephen Spender Prize (£5,000 each); TS Eliot Festival (£4,000); Sue Coles School of Dance (£3,500); Garsington Opera, Animal Care Trust and London Children's Ballet (£3,000 each); Oxford CS Lewis Society (£2,000); and MK Snap (£1,000).

One grant of £7,500 was given to an individual.

Exclusions

The trust does not support the following:

- activities or projects already completed
- capital building projects
- personal training and education e.g. tuition or living costs for college or university
- projects outside the UK
- medical care or resources
- feasibility studies
- national charities having substantial amounts of potential funding likely from other sources.

Applications

Applications can only be made online through the trust's website. The trustees meet regularly to consider applications but state in the latest accounts that: 'the emphasis will be on continued support of those institutions and individuals who have received support in the past. Unfortunately we have to disappoint the great majority of applicants who nevertheless continue to send appeal letters.'

To keep administration costs to a minimum the trust does not give reasons for unsuccessful applications or allow applicants to appeal a decision.

The John Oldacre Foundation

Research and education in agricultural sciences

£182,500 (2009/10)

Beneficial area

UK.

Bohicket, 35 Broadwater Close, Burwood park, Walton on Thames, Surrey KT12 5DD
Correspondent: Stephen J Charnock, Trustee
Trustees: H B Shouler; S J Charnock; Ian Bonnett.
CC Number: 284960

Information available

Full accounts were on file at the Charity Commission.

Grants are made to universities and agricultural colleges towards the advancement and promotion, for public benefit, of research and education in agricultural sciences and the publication of useful results.

In 2009/10 the foundation had assets of £7.7 million and an income of £111,000. Grants were made to ten organisations and totalled £182,500.

Beneficiaries included: University of Bristol (£51,000); Royal Agricultural College (£20,000), University of Wolverhampton (£17,000); Harper Adams University College (£15,000); Game & Wildlife Conservation Trust (£12,000).

Exclusions

No grants towards tuition fees.

Applications

In writing to the correspondent.

The Olga Charitable Trust

Health, welfare, youth organisations, children's welfare, carers' organisations

£76,000 (2009/10)

Beneficial area

UK and overseas.

The Old Stables, Gracious Street, Selborne, Alton GU34 3JD
Tel: 020 7353 1597
Correspondent: Adam Broke, Accountant
Trustees: HRH Princess Alexandra; James Robert Bruce Ogilvy.
CC Number: 277925

Information available

Accounts were available from the Charity Commission.

The trust supports health, welfare and youth organisations, children's welfare and carers' organisations. All must be known to the trustees.

In 2009/10 the trust had assets of £936,000 and an income of £49,000. Grants totalling £76,000 were made to 43 organisations including: Columba

1400 (£10,000); Holy Trinity Church, Haiti Earthquake Appeal and Kew Botanical Gardens (£5,000 each); CFAB (£3,000); The Exhuma Foundation (£2,000); Comfort Rwanda, New Bridge, PDSA and Queen Alexandra's Hospice Home (£1,000 each); and Perth YMCA (£500).

Applications

In writing to the correspondent, although the trust states that its funds are fully committed and applications made cannot be acknowledged.

The Onaway Trust

General

£47,000 (2010)

Beneficial area

UK, USA and worldwide.

Donavourd Farmhouse, Donavourd, Pitlochry PH16 5JS
Tel: 0179 647 0047
Email: david@onaway.org
Website: www.onaway.org
Correspondent: David Watters, Trust Administrator
Trustees: A Breslin; C Howles; Ms Annie Smith; Ms V A Worwood; D Watters.
CC Number: 268448

Information available

Full accounts were available from the Charity Commission website.

This trust's objects are stated on its website as follows:

> To relieve poverty and suffering amongst indigenous peoples by providing seed grants for (small) self-help, self-sufficient and environmentally sustainable projects. This is expressed in many areas and includes the protection of the environment, the support of children and adults with learning difficulties, the assistance of smaller charities whose aim is to safeguard sick, injured, threatened or abandoned animals and emergency relief for victims of disaster.

The trust has a special emphasis on Native Americans.

The review of 2010 activity notes that: 'Onaway's trustees make the majority

of their grants through small charities operating at a grassroots level.'

Overall grantmaking was down in 2010, chiefly due to the trust moving to new premises. In 2010 the trust had assets of £4.4 million and an income of £133,000. Grants were made to organisations totalling £47,000 and were awarded in the following categories:

Indigenous – America (£17,000)
Three grants were made to Plenty USA (£12,000) and one was made to the Centre of Sacred Studies (£5,000).

Indigenous – Rest of the world (£25,000)
Beneficiaries included: Institute for Development Exchange (India) (£6,600); Academy for Development of Science (India), Literates Welfare Association (India) (£4,000 each); Adaho Youth Environmental (Africa) (£2,500); and Tanzania Marginalised Are (£1,000).

Other Onaway projects (£6,000)
Beneficiaries included: D.E.C Asia Quake Appeal (£5,000); and Khadeejey Ayyad (Middle East) (£600).

No money was given to charities in the environmental or animal welfare categories in 2010, although these are causes the charity considers.

Exclusions

No grants for administration costs, travel expenses or projects considered unethical or detrimental to the struggle of indigenous people.

Applications

In writing to the correspondent, enclosing an sae.

The Ormsby Charitable Trust

General

£62,000 (2009/10)

Beneficial area

UK, London and the South East.

The Red House, The Street, Aldermaston, Reading RG7 4LN
Tel: 0118 971 0343

Correspondent: Mrs K McCrossan, Trustee
Trustees: Rosemary Ormsby David; Angela Ormsby Chiswell; Katrina Ormsby McCrossan.
CC Number: 1000599

Information available

Accounts were available from the Charity Commission.

In 2009/10 the trust had assets of £1.6 million and an income of £42,000. Donations were made to 25 organisations totalling £62,000 and ranged from £500 to £5,000 each.

Beneficiaries included: In Kind (£5,000); Newbury Community Resource Centre (£4,500); Home Farm Trust and Breast Cancer Haven Trust (£3,800 each); Cornwall Air Ambulance (£3,000); NSPCC (£2,000) and Ramsdell Village Hall (£500).

Exclusions

No grants to individuals, animals or religious causes.

Applications

In writing to the correspondent.

The O'Sullivan Family Charitable Trust

Children and young people, care homes, genetic research

£185,000 (2009/10).

Beneficial area

Unrestricted, UK in practice.

36 Edge Street, London W8 7PN
Correspondent: Diana O'Sullivan, Trustee
Trustees: Diana O'Sullivan; Finian O'Sullivan; Emily O'Sullivan; Sophie O'Sullivan; Tessa O'Sullivan.
CC Number: 1123757

Information available

Information was available from the Charity Commission without a list of grants.

The trust was established in 2008 with a £5 million donation from Finian O'Sullivan, founder of Burren Energy, who reportedly made £67 million from the sale of the company in 2007.

The trust states in its 2010 financial statements that its objects and principal activities are to:

> Provide advancement of health or relief for those in need because of ill health, disability, financial hardship or other disadvantage; particularly by the provision of respite care for children and young adults affected by severe long-term disability and the promotion of genetic research into the causes of such disability and the dissemination of the useful results of such research.

The main focus of the trust in the long term is to support a large scale capital project which will provide respite care for severely disabled children, although applications from other organisations whose work fits in with the trustees' interests will also be considered.

In 2009/10 the trust had assets of £3.8 million and an income of £70,000. Grants during the year totalled £185,000. Previous grant beneficiaries include: The Honeypot Charity (£10,000); and Canine Partners (£5,000).

Applications

In writing to the correspondent.

The Ouseley Trust

Choral services of the Church of England, Church in Wales and Church of Ireland, choir schools

£130,000 (2010)

Beneficial area

England, Wales and Ireland.

PO Box 281, Stamford, Lincolnshire PE9 9BU
Tel: 01780 752 266
Email: ouseleytrust@btinternet.com
Website: www.ouseleytrust.org.uk
Correspondent: Martin Williams, Clerk
Trustees: Dr Christopher Robinson, Chair; Dr J A Birch; Rev Canon Mark Boyling; Dr S M Darlington; Mrs Gillian Perkins; Martin Pickering; Adam Ridley; Dr John Rutter; Revd A F Walters; Richard White; Timothy Byram-Wigfield.
CC Number: 527519

Information available

Accounts were available from the Charity Commission.

The trust administers funds made available from trusts of the former St Michael's College, Tenbury. The trust's 2009/10 annual report states that the trust's object is to:

> Promote and maintain to a high standard the choral services of the Church of England, the Church in Wales or the Church of Ireland (whether simple or elaborate) in such ways as the trustees think fit ... including the promotion of the religious, musical and secular education of pupils attending any school in which instruction in the doctrines of any of the said churches is given and performance of their choral liturgy is observed.

In 2010 the trust had assets of £3.8 million and an income of £146,000. Grants were made totalling £130,000.

Grants *authorised* in the year were broken down as follows:

Fees	26	74,000
Endowments	3	25,000
Other	3	12,000
Music	3	2,500

Grants will be awarded only where there is a clear indication that an already acceptable standard of choral service will be raised. Under certain circumstances grants may be awarded for organ tuition. Each application will be considered on its merits, keeping in mind the specific terms of the trust deed. Unique, imaginative ventures will receive careful consideration.

The trust does not normally award further grants to successful applicants within a two-year period. The trustees' policy is to continue making grants to cathedrals, choral foundations and parish churches throughout England, Wales and Ireland.

Exclusions

Grants will not be awarded to help with the cost of fees for ex-choristers, for chant books, hymnals or psalters. Grants will not be made for the purchase of new instruments or for the installation of an instrument from another place of worship where this involves extensive reconstruction. Under normal circumstances, grants will not be awarded for buildings, cassettes, commissions, compact discs, furniture, pianos, robes, tours or visits. No grants are made towards new organs or the installation of one which involves extensive reconstruction.

Applications

Applicants are strongly advised to refer to the trust's guidelines and FAQ section of its website before drafting an application. Applications must be submitted by an institution on a form available from the correspondent. Closing dates for applications are 31 January for the March meeting and 30 June for the October meeting.

Common applicant mistakes

'Failure to understand what categories of project are ineligible.'

The Owen Family Trust

Christian, general

£73,000 (2009/10)

Beneficial area

UK, with a preference for West Midlands.

C/o Rubery Owen Holdings Limited, PO Box 10, Wednesbury WS10 8JD
Tel: 0121 526 3131
Correspondent: A D Owen, Trustee
Trustees: Mrs H G Jenkins; A D Owen.
CC Number: 251975

Information available

Full accounts were available from the Charity Commission website.

Grants are given to independent and church schools, Christian youth centres, churches, community organisations, arts, conservation and medical charities. Support is given throughout the UK, with a preference for the West Midlands.

In 2009/10 the trust had assets of £1.1 million and an income of £37,000. During the year 41 grants were made totalling £73,000.

The largest grants were made to: Oundle School Foundation (£15,000); Black Country Museum Development Trust, Lichfield Cathedral, The Feast and Frontier Youth Trust (£5,000 each).

Other beneficiaries included: Acorns Children's Hospice and Lozells Project Trust (£3,000 each); The Friends of Whitchurch Heritage (£2,000); Cancer Support Centre, Sutton Coldfield, Lichfield Festival, St Chad's, Bagnall and The Extra Care Charitable Trust (£1,000 each); and Gloucester Cathedral (£255).

Exclusions

The trust states: 'No grants to individuals unless part of a charitable organisation.'

Applications

In writing to the correspondent including annual report, budget for project and general information regarding the application. Organisations need to be a registered charity; however an 'umbrella' body which would hold funds would be acceptable. Only a small number of grants can be given each year and unsuccessful applications are not acknowledged unless an sae is enclosed. The trustees meet quarterly.

Common applicant mistakes

'They do not check if they are eligible to receive a grant.'

The Doris Pacey Charitable Foundation

Jewish, medical, educational and social

£175,000 (2009/10)

Beneficial area

UK and Israel.

30 Old Burlington Street, London W1S 3NL
Tel: 020 7468 2600
Correspondent: J D Cohen, Trustee

Trustees: J D Cohen; R Locke; L Powell.
CC Number: 1101724

Information available

Accounts were available from the Charity Commission.

In 2009/10 the foundation had assets of £5.8 million, which generated an income of £104,000. Grants totalled £175,000.

Grants were made to: OR Movement (£50,000); Jewish Chaplaincy and UJIA – Jewish Curriculum (£40,000 each); Magen David Adom (£20,000); Courtauld Institute of Art (£13,000); Norwood (£8,000); Surrey Opera (£4,000); National Deaf Children's Society (£1,000); the Noam Primary School (£250).

Applications

Unsolicited applications are not considered.

The Pallant Charitable Trust

Church music

£26,000 to organisations and individuals (2009/10)

Beneficial area

UK, with a preference for areas within 50 miles of Chichester.

c/o Thomas Eggar, The Corn Exchange, Baffins Lane, Chichester, West Sussex PO19 1GE
Tel: 01243 786 111
Fax: 01243 532 001
Correspondent: Simon Macfarlane, Trustee
Trustees: Dr A J Thurlow; S A E Macfarlane; C Smyth; C J Henville.
CC Number: 265120

Information available

Accounts were available from the Charity Commission.

The trust's objective is to promote mainstream church music both in choral and instrumental form. Consideration will be given for schemes that provide training and opportunities for children or adults in the field of church music and with an emphasis on traditional services. Such schemes may include:

- vocal or instrumental (in particular organ) training
- choral work in the context of church services
- the training of choir leaders, organists or directors
- the provision and the purchase of equipment necessary for the above.

In 2009/10 the trust had assets of £1 million and an income of £41,000. Grants totalled £26,000 to organisations and individuals.

Beneficiary organisations were: The Dean and Chapter of Chichester (£3,600); and St Stephen's Organ Account (£5,000).

Grants were also made to: Chichester Cathedral Choristers Scholarships – Prebendal School Fees (£17,800 for two individuals).

Dr Alan Thurlow is also a trustee of the following charities: Church Music Society (Charity Commission no. 290309); The Friends of Pallant House Gallery (Charity Commission no. 278943); The ON Organ Fund (Charity Commission no. 289160); and West Sussex Organists' Association (Charity Commission no.279892).

Alistair Macfarlane is also a trustee of the following charities: Lavant House School Educational Trust Limited (Charity Commission no. 307372); Life Centre (Charity Commission no. 1127779); and The Bassil Shippam and Alsford Trust (Charity Commission no. 256996).

Exclusions

No grants to individuals, or for computer equipment or sponsorship of concerts.

Applications

In writing to the correspondent. Applications should be submitted by recognised organisations such as churches, schools, colleges or charities working in the field of church music.

PALLANT / PANACEA

The Panacea Society

Christian religion, relief of sickness

£337,000 (2010)

Beneficial area

UK, with a strong preference for Bedford and its immediate region.

14 Albany Road, Bedford MK40 3PH
Tel: 01234 359 737
Email: admin@panacea-society.org
Website: www.panacea-society.org
Correspondent: David McLynn, Business Administrator
Trustees: G Allan; L Aston; Revd Dr Jane Shaw; Prof. C Rowland; Dr J Meggitt.
CC Number: 227530

Information available

Full accounts were available from the Charity Commission website.

The charity is a Christian society. It was originally set up as a religious community, which thrived in Bedford between the First and Second World Wars. Over the years members of the Society have donated money and property to the charity to further the life of the community and its religious aims. A small donation flow continues to be received, however the charity's income today is derived primarily from its property and other investments.

The charity's 2010 report and financial statements provide the following information:

> The principal aim of the Society is to encourage the study of the Christian religion with particular emphasis on the teachings of Joanna Southcott and other prophets of the Visitation. It achieves this aim primarily by funding academic research and the sponsoring, publishing and distribution of publications. In addition to this work the Society also supports recognised local organisations dealing with the relief of sickness within the Bedford area.

> The Society also continues to offer its healing method by water and the spirit to all who apply, free of charge.

The work of this Christian charity, established in 1926, is informed by the teachings of Joanna Southcott. In meeting its charitable objects the society from time to time makes grants out of its income.

The report and financial statements go on to outline the charity's charitable activities:

> The charity has two main strands of charitable activity: (i). the restoration and bringing back into use of the functional buildings that have formed the historic and cultural core of the Panacea for over 80 years (the Bedford Project), ii. The grant making activities which commenced in 2001 and now form a significant element of the charity's work.

> The trustees' primary focus remains the Bedford Project, developing the Society's archive material including its unique collection of Joanna Southcott related manuscripts, books, and artefacts. A part of the Bedford project is the substantial refurbishment of Castleside in order to mount a permanent exhibition of the history of the Society and its antecedents (the Visitation).

> Closely linked with the Bedford Project is the charity's association with the University of Oxford under the auspices of the Prophecy Project. This entered its ninth year in 2010 and research is currently funded to late 2011. The Charity receives periodic reports and financial expenditure statements from the University on the progress of the work.

In addition to the above the charity makes grants and donations to deserving causes. The trustees expect to be able to continue applying a proportion of the Society's income towards the work of recognised local health and social care related organisations, insofar as available funding permits, provided applications fall within the designated criteria.

Funding criteria

The trustees have agreed the following policy criteria should apply in all cases for a funding application to be selected for further consideration. The purpose of the funding should be:

- work related to the advancement of the religious beliefs of the society as defined by its original charitable objects
- sponsoring the writing, publication, and distribution of religious works associated with the visitation

307

- undertaking the duties and responsibilities incumbent on being the custodian of Joanna Southcott's Box of Sealed Writings
- sponsoring research by recognised academic institutions into the history and theology of the society and its antecedents
- supporting the work of the Church of England in advancing the Christian religion especially in the Bedford area, or in aspects of theology or liturgy that relate to the society's specific interests
- Supporting recognised local organisations dealing with the relief of sickness within the Bedford area.

The charity states:

> At the end of 2010 and after much consideration, the Society decided that it would approach its Poverty and Sickness grant making in a different manner. Rather than invite organisations and groups to apply directly to the Society, for 2011 onwards funding would be provided to specialist funders working within the not for profit sector with the remit to then deal with all applications directly on behalf of the Society.

> The Bedfordshire and Luton Community Foundation working in partnership with Community and Voluntary Service Mid and North Beds manage the Society's non-educational grant making activities within the local community.

> Educational grants are still awarded and assessed directly by the Society.

The trust states that grants will be made for charitable purposes to UK-based organisations only. Priority will be given to funding requests that promote the religious aims of the society, benefit large numbers of people and are made on behalf of organisations rather than individuals.

In 2010 the society had assets of £24 million and an income of £489,000. Grants were made totalling £337,000 broken down as follows:

Universities research and conference	£198,000
Health/social	£71,000
Bedford Project	£60,000
Oxford University Prophecy Project	£4,000
Religious	£3,000
Miscellaneous scholarships/educational	£3,000

Beneficiaries in the health/social grants category and committed at 1st January 2010 included: Pasque Charity – Keech Children's Hospice (£10,000); Bedford Open Door (£6,000); Beds and Northants MS Centre and Bedford MENCAP (£5,000 each); BeCHAR, Deafblind and Friendship Link & Action Group (£2,000 each); and Cruse Bedfordshire (£1,000).

Exclusions

The society will not consider funding:

- political parties or political lobbying
- pressure groups
- which supports commercial ventures
- non-charitable activities
- which could be paid out of central or local government funds

Applications

The trust has previously stated that it receives many applications that they are unable or unwilling to support. Please read the grant criteria carefully before submitting an application. Unsolicited applications are not responded to.

Any organisation considering applying for funding support should make a formal application in writing to the correspondent. The application should set out the purpose for which the funding is required, and explain how it falls within the funding criteria and complies with their requirements. Full information on the work of the applicant body together with details of how the proposed funding will be applied should be given.

The correspondent will acknowledge receipt of an application, and indicate if the application falls within their parameters. At this point the society may call for additional information, or indicate that it is unable to consider the application further. Most applications fail because they fall outside the criteria, however the society does not provide additional reasons why it is unable to support a particular application.

When all relevant information has been received the application will be discussed at the next meeting of the society's trustees together with other valid applications. The trustees may at that meeting refuse or defer any application or request further information without giving reasons.

Applicants will be advised in writing of the trustees' decision.

For full details visit the society's website.

Panahpur

Christian missionaries, general

£71,000 (2009/10)

Beneficial area

UK, overseas.

84 High Street, Tonbridge, Kent TN9 1AP

Correspondent: Andrew Perry, Trustee

Trustees: Paul East; Andrew Perry; Dorothy Haile; Andrew Matheson.

CC Number: 1130367

Information available

Full accounts were available from the Charity Commission website under charity no. 214299.

The activities of the Panahpur Charitable Trust (charity no. 214299) have recently been transferred to a new incorporated body, Panahpur (charity no. 1130367). In November 2009 the charitable trust moved its unrestricted net assets to Panahpur, while its restricted net assets were given to the Penhurst Church Trust (charity no. 1134097).

The new trust will continue to support Christian missionary organisations operating both in the UK and overseas. It will also continue the trend of forming long term partnerships with a small number of suitable organisations and individuals.

In its last year of operation, 2009/10, the charitable trust made grants to seven organisations totalling £71,000.

Beneficiaries were: Oasis International (£38,000); Relationships Foundation (£10,000); Egypt Emerging Leadership – Xmedia (£9,000); CHGN – InterHealth Worldwide (£8,000); Ambassadors in Sport (£5,000); Redcliff College (£1,200); and Mena – Xmedia (£600).

Applications

The trustees do their own research and do not respond to unsolicited applications.

The Panton Trust

Animal wildlife worldwide, environment UK

£56,000 to organisations (2009/10).

Beneficial area

UK and overseas.

Ramsay House, 18 Vera Avenue, Grange Park, London N12 1RA
Tel: 020 8370 7700
Correspondent: Laurence Slavin, Trustee
Trustees: L M Slavin; R Craig.
CC Number: 292910

Information available

Full accounts were on file at the Charity Commission.

The trust states that it is 'concerned with any animal or animals or with wildlife in any part of the world, or with the environment of the UK or any part thereof. [...] The trustees consider applications from a wide variety of sources and favour smaller charities which do not have the same capacity for large-scale fundraising as major charities in this field.'

In 2009/10 the trust had assets of £182,000 and an income of £52,000. Grants were made totalling £56,000.

Beneficiaries included:
St Tiggywinkles Wildlife Hospital, Whale and Dolphin Conservation Society, PDSA (£5,000 each); Flora and Fauna International (£4,000); Murray Edwards College (£3,500); Royal Botanic Garden – Kew (£3,000); Galapagos Conservation Trust (£2,000); and National Wood Recycling Project (£1,000).

Other grants of less than £1,000 totalled £11,000.

Applications

In writing to the correspondent.

The Paragon Trust

General

£95,000 (2009/10)

Beneficial area

UK and overseas.

c/o Thomson Snell and Passmore Solicitors, 3 Lonsdale Gardens, Tunbridge Wells, Kent TN1 1NX
Tel: 01892 701 211
Correspondent: Mrs Kathy Larter, Ref: 1211
Trustees: The Lord Wrenbury; Revd Canon R Coppin; Miss L J Whistler; P Cunningham; Dr Fiona Cornish.
CC Number: 278348

Information available

Accounts were available from the Charity Commission.

In 2009/10 the trust had assets of £1.7 million and an income of £81,000. Grants totalled £95,000.

Grants of £1,000 or more included those to: British Red Cross (£3,000); Canterbury Cathedral and Demelza House (£2,000 each); Amnesty International, Home Farm Trust, Medical Foundation (Victims of Torture), Send A Cow and Sightsavers (£1,000 each).

Grants of less than £1,000 included those to: Changing Faces, Leonard Cheshire Homes and Open Arms Malawi (£500 each).

Dr Fiona Cornish is also a trustee of Medical Support in Romania (Charity Commission no. 1058339) and Miss L Whistler is also a trustee of St Bede's School Trust, Sussex (Charity Commission no.278950).

Applications

The trust states that it does not respond to unsolicited applications; all beneficiaries 'are known personally to the trustees and no attention is paid to appeal literature, which is discarded on receipt. Fundraisers are therefore urged to save resources by not sending literature.'

The Park Charitable Trust

Jewish, patient care – cancer and heart conditions, hospitals

£295,000 (2009/10)

Beneficial area

UK.

69 Singleton Road, Salford M7 4LX
Correspondent: E Pine, Trustee
Trustees: D Hammelburger; Mrs M Hammelburger; E Pine.
CC Number: 1095541

Information available

Accounts were available from the Charity Commission, but without a grants list.

The trust states:

> The objects of the charity are the advancement of the Jewish Faith; the advancement of Jewish education; the relief of poverty amongst the Jewish community; the relief of patients suffering from cancer and heart conditions; giving financial support to hospitals and furthering such other charitable purposes as the trustees may from time to time determine in support of their charitable activities.

Registered in January 2003, in 2009/10 the trust had assets of £3.7 million, an income of £1.3 million and made grants totalling £295,000.

Grants were broken down as follows:

Community projects	£46,000
Kollelim	£6,000
Relief of poverty	£151,000
Schools	£17,000
Yeshivot and seminaries	£49,000
Grants paid under £1,000	£25,000

Applications

In writing to the correspondent.

The Park House Charitable Trust

Education, social welfare, ecclesiastical

£247,000 (2010)

Beneficial area

UK and overseas, with a preference for the Midlands, particularly Coventry and Warwickshire.

Dafferns LLP, One Eastwood, Harry Weston Road, Binley Business Park, Coventry CV3 2UB
Tel: 024 7622 1046
Correspondent: Paul Varney
Trustees: N P Bailey; Mrs M Bailey; P Bailey; Dr M F Whelan.
CC Number: 1077677

Information available

Accounts were available from the Charity Commission.

The trust was established in September 1999. In 2010 it had assets of £1.4 million and an income of £181,000. Grants totalled £247,000 and were categorised as follows:

Social Welfare (£218,000) – Scottish International Relief – Mary's Meals (£100,000); St Joseph and the Helpers Charity (£20,000); Diocese of Bijnor, Friends of the Holy Land (£15,000 each); CAFOD, Good Rock Foundation (£10,000 each); Guys Gift (£5,000); Calcutta Rescue Fund (£3,000); and Coventry Medjugorge Centre (£2,000).

Education (£24,000) - Maryvale Institute (£15,000); Community of Holy First (£5,000); and Bateman Trust (£4,000).

Religious (£3,000) – St Paul's School for Girls (£3,000).

Medical (£2,000) – Tiny Tim's Children's Centre (£2,000).

Exclusions

No grants to individuals.

Applications

In writing to the correspondent. The trust has stated that it does not expect to have surplus funds available to meet the majority of applications.

The Frank Parkinson Agricultural Trust

British agriculture

£85,000 (2010)

Beneficial area

UK.

11 Alder Drive, Pudsey LS28 8RD
Tel: 0113 257 8613
Email: janetpudsey@live.co.uk
Correspondent: Miss Janet Smith, Secretary to the Trustees
Trustees: C Bourchier; J S Sclanders; Prof. Paul Webster; D Gardner.
CC Number: 209407

Information available

Accounts were available from the Charity Commission.

The trust's principal object is the improvement and welfare of British agriculture. Its aims are:

- the improvement and welfare of British agriculture;
- the undertaking of agricultural research or the provision of grants for such means;
- the establishment of scholarships, bursaries and exhibitions at any university, college or other technical institution in any branch of the agricultural industry;
- the granting of financial assistance to young people of ability who are in need of assistance and are working in the agricultural industry to improve their education and experience by working, training or otherwise;
- the encouragement and assistance of the social and cultural welfare of people working in the agricultural industry;
- the making of grants to any charity or organisation which is carrying on any work in connection with the provision of any such benefits as aforesaid.

In 2010 it had assets of £1.2 million and an income of £57,000. Grants were made to four organisations and totalled £85,000.

Grant beneficiaries included: Harper Adams University College (£75,000); Royal Agricultural Society of England and St George's House, Windsor Castle (£5,000 each) and AgriFood Charities Partnership (£500).

Exclusions

Grants are given to corporate bodies and the trust is not able to assist with financial help to any individuals undertaking postgraduate studies or degree courses.

Applications

In writing to the correspondent. The trustees meet annually in April and applicants are expected to make an oral presentation. Further details of the whole application process can be found in the useful 'Guidelines for Grant Applications' which is available from the trust. Note that the trust states: 'The chairman has the authority to approve small grants between annual meetings, but these are only for minor sums and minor projects.'

The Samuel and Freda Parkinson Charitable Trust

General

£100,000 (2009/10)

Beneficial area

UK.

Thomson Wilson Pattinson, Solicitors, Stonecliffe, Lake Road, Windermere, Cumbria
Tel: 01539 442 233
Fax: 01539 488 810
Correspondent: Trust Administrator
Trustees: D E G Roberts; J A Todd; M J Fletcher.
CC Number: 327749

Information available

Accounts were on file at the Charity Commission.

This trust was established in 1987 with £100. The fund stayed at this level until 1994/95 when £2.1 million worth of assets were placed in the trust on the death of the settlor. It supports the same eight beneficiaries each year, although for varying amounts.

In 2009/10 the trust had assets of £2.8 million, an income of £93,000 and made grants totalling £100,000.

Grant beneficiaries were: Salvation Army; Leonard Cheshire Foundation (£24,000 each); Church Army (£15,000); RNLI (£14,500); RSPCA (£7,500); and Animal Concern, Animal Rescue and Animal Welfare (£5,000 each).

Applications

The founder of this charity restricted the list of potential beneficiaries to named charities of his choice and accordingly the trustees do not have discretion to include further beneficiaries, although they do have complete discretion within the stated beneficiary list.

Arthur James Paterson Charitable Trust

Medical research, welfare of older people and children

£34,000 (2009/10)

Beneficial area
UK.

Royal Bank of Canada Trust Corporation Limited, 71 Queen Victoria Street, London EC4V 4DE
Tel: 020 7653 4756
Email: anita.carter@rbc.com
Correspondent: Anita Carter, Trust Administrator
Trustee: Royal Bank of Canada Trust Corporation Ltd.
CC Number: 278569

Information available
Accounts were on file at the Charity Commission.

In 2009/10 the trust had assets of £1.6 million and an income of £48,000. Grants to 14 organisations totalled £34,000.

Beneficiaries were: Glenalmond College and Worcester College (£4,400 each); Over the Wall, St Giles Centre, Birmingham Royal Ballet, Guild Care, Make a Wish and University College London Hospitals

(£3,300 each); Catch 22 and St Christopher Hospice (£900 each); and Friends of the Elderly, Home Start, National Society for Epilepsy and Prostate Cancer Charity (£875 each).

Applications
There are no application forms. Send your application with a covering letter and include the latest set of report and accounts. Deadlines are February and August.

The Constance Paterson Charitable Trust

Medical research, health, welfare of children, older people, service people

£15,000 (2009/10)

Beneficial area
UK.

Royal Bank of Canada Trust Corporation Limited, 71 Queen Victoria Street, London EC4V 4DE
Tel: 020 7653 4756
Email: anita.carter@rbc.com
Correspondent: Miss Anita Carter, Administrator
Trustee: Royal Bank of Canada Trust Corporation Ltd.
CC Number: 249556

Information available
Full accounts were available from the Charity Commission.

The trust makes grants in support of medical research, healthcare, welfare of elderly people and children (including accommodation and housing) and service people's welfare. In 2009/10 the trust had assets of £1.3 million and an income of £33,000. Grants were made to 11 organisations totalling £15,000.

Grants included those made to: NDCS, Caring for Life and STEPS (£2,300 each); Down Syndrome Education and Independence at Home (£600 each); and the Genesis Appeal (£400).

Exclusions
No grants to individuals.

Applications
In writing to the correspondent, including covering letter and the latest set of annual report and accounts. The trust does not have an application form. Deadlines for applications are June and December.

Miss M E Swinton Paterson's Charitable Trust

Church of Scotland, young people, general
Around £40,000

Beneficial area
Scotland.

Lindsays' Solicitors, Calendonian Exchange, 19a Canning Street, Edinburgh EH3 8HE
Correspondent: The Trustees
SC Number: SC004835

Information available
Limited information was filed with the Office of the Scottish Charity Regulator.

The trust was set up by the will of Miss M E Swinton Paterson who died in October 1989. The objectives of the trust are the support of charities in Scotland, specifically including schemes of the Church of Scotland.

In 2010/11 the trust had an income of £48,000. The trustees usually makes grants totalling £40,000 annually.

Previous beneficiaries include: L'Arche Edinburgh Community, Livingstone Baptist Church, Lloyd Morris Congregational Church, Haddington West Parish Church, Acorn Christian Centre, Stranraer YMCA, Care for the Family, Boys' and Girls' Clubs of Scotland, Fresh Start, Friends of the Elms, Iona Community, Edinburgh Young Carers' Project, Epilepsy Scotland, Stoneykirk Parish Church, Scotland Yard Adventure Centre, Atholl Centre, Scottish Crusaders,

Disablement Income Group Scotland and Artlink.

Exclusions

No grants to individuals or students.

Applications

In writing to the correspondent. Trustees meet once a year in July to consider grants.

Ambika Paul Foundation

Education, young people

£930,000 (2009/10)

Beneficial area

Mainly UK and India.

Caparo House, 103 Baker Street, London W1U 6LN
Tel: 020 7486 1417
Correspondent: Lord Paul of Marylebone, Trustee
Trustees: Lord Paul of Marylebone; Lady Aruna Paul; Hon. Angad Paul; Hon. Anjli Paul; Hon. Ambar Paul; Hon. Akash Paul.
CC Number: 276127

Information available

Accounts were available from the Charity Commission.

The foundation supports large organisations, registered charities, colleges and universities benefiting children, young adults and students mostly in the UK and India. Main areas of interest are to do with young people and education. Grants usually range from £100 to £3,000.

In 2009/10 the foundation had assets of £6.9 million and an income of £370,000. Grants were made totalling £930,000 and were broken down as follows:

Educational projects	£884,000
Social projects	£14,000
Medical trust funds	£32,000
Other grants	£100

The beneficiary of the largest grant was MIT Sloan School of Management (£657,000).

Other beneficiaries included: University of Wolverhampton (£200,000); Great Ormond Street

Hospital Children's Charity (£21,000); Magic Bus (£20,000); Zoological Society of London (£14,000); PiggyBankKids (£8,000); the Shela Dispensary (£3,000); Bhavan (£1,000); CST – Protecting Jewish Community (£500); and Anthony Nolan Trust and Mary Seacole Appeal (£100 each).

Exclusions

Applications from individuals, including students, are mainly ineligible. Funding for scholarships is made directly to colleges/universities, not to individuals. No expeditions.

Applications

In writing to the trustees at the correspondence address. Acknowledgements are sent if an sae is enclosed. However, the trust has no paid employees and the enormous number of requests it receives creates administrative difficulties.

Common applicant mistakes

'We do not fund individuals. The Ambika Paul Foundation is a small charity and people who apply for funding do not realise this. Also they expect all charities to be run with full time staff which the foundation does not have.'

The Susanna Peake Charitable Trust

General

£156,000 (2009/10)

Beneficial area

UK, with a preference for the South West of England, particularly Gloucestershire.

Rathbone Trust Company Limited, 159 New Bond Street, London W1S 2UD
Tel: 020 7399 0811
Correspondent: The Administrator
Trustees: Susanna Peake; David Peake.
CC Number: 283462

Information available

Accounts were available from the Charity Commission.

This is one of the Kleinwort family trusts. It was set up by Susanna Peake in 1981 for general charitable purposes and has a preference for charities based in the Gloucestershire area. In addition, non-local appeals when received are accumulated and considered by the trustees annually.

In 2009/10 the trust had assets of £5.2 million and an income of £153,000. Grants were made to 54 organisations totalling £156,000 and were broken down as follows:

Medical, cancer and hospices	£37,500
Local charities	£37,500
International and overseas	£24,000
Older people	£21,000
Education and children	£20,500
General and animal charities	£17,000

Beneficiaries included: Auditory Verbal UK (£10,000); ATP Enterprise, Chipping Norton Theatre Trust and Loughborough School PTA (£5,000 each); Cotswold Care Hospice and Crime Diversion Scheme (£4,000); Cheltenham Housing Aid Centre and Interact Wildlife (£3,000 each); Royal Blind Society and WaterAid (£2,000 each); Fine Cell Work (£1,000); and Christian Aid (£100).

Exclusions

No grants to individuals.

Applications

In writing to the correspondent. The trust states that: 'The trustees meet on an ad hoc basis to review applications for funding, and a full review is undertaken annually when the financial statements are available. Only successful applications are notified of the trustees' decision.'

The David Pearlman Charitable Foundation

Jewish, general

£72,000 (2009–10)

Beneficial area

UK.

New Burlington House, 1075 Finchley Road, London NW11 0PU
Tel: 020 8731 0777
Correspondent: Mr D Goldberger, Trustee
Trustees: D A Pearlman; M R Goldberger; S Appleman; Hager.
CC Number: 287009

Information available

Accounts were on file at the Charity Commission, but without a grants list.

Set up in 1983, in 2009–10 the foundation had assets of £1.7 million and an income of £196,000. Grants totalled £72,000. The accounts did not contain a list of beneficiaries.

Previous recipients of grants of £500 or more have included: British Friends of Igud Hakolelim B'Yerushalayim (£60,000); Lolev Charitable Trust (£30,000); Jewish Care (£16,000); Chevras Mo'oz Ladol (£15,000); Norwood (£12,000); the Duke of Edinburgh Trust (£7,000); Community Security Trust (£6,000); Life's 4 Living Trust Ltd (£6,400); Children Number One Foundation (£3,750); the Variety Club Children's Charity (£2,750); London Academy of Jewish Studies (£1,500); Jewish Music Institute and United Jewish Israel Appeal (£1,000).

Applications

In writing to the correspondent.

Peltz Trust

Arts, education, health, Jewish, general

£186,000 (2009/10)

Beneficial area

UK and Israel.

Berwin Leighton Paisner, Adelaide House, London Bridge, London EC4R 9HA
Tel: 020 7760 1000
Correspondent: Martin Paisner, Trustee
Trustees: Martin Paisner; Daniel Peltz; Hon. Elizabeth Wolfson Peltz.
CC Number: 1002302

Information available

Full accounts were available from the Charity Commission website.

In 2009/10 the trust had assets of £36,000 and an income of £171,000. Grants were made to 30 organisations totalling £186,000, broken down into the following categories:

Education and training	6	£90,000
Medical, health and sickness	4	£8,500
Arts and culture	7	£27,000
Relief of poverty	1	£500
Religious activities	1	£1,200
Economic and community development	5	£25,000
General charities	6	£34,000

Beneficiaries included: Oxford Centre for Hebrew and Jewish Studies (£33,000 in two grants); British Technion Society (£30,000); Facing History and Ourselves (£19,000 in two grants); Norwood Children and Families Trust (£11,000); Tate Gallery and ICSR Kings College (£10,000 each); Artichoke, One Family, St Stephen's Trust and UK Friends of Mogen David Adom (£5,000 each); Presidents Club Charitable Trust (£2,500); War Memorials Trust (£1,500); United Synagogue (£1,200); Royal Opera House Foundation, Jaffa Institute and Lifeline for the Old (£1,000 each); DALAID and Mousetrap Theatre Projects (£500 each); and the Rehabilitation Trust (£250).

Exclusions

No grants to individuals for research or educational awards.

Applications

In writing to the correspondent. The trustees meet at irregular intervals during the year to consider appeals from appropriate organisations.

The Pennycress Trust

General charitable purposes

£51,000 (2009/10)

Beneficial area

UK and worldwide, with a preference for Cheshire and Norfolk.

Flat D, 15 Millman Street, London WC1N 3EP
Tel: 020 7404 0145
Correspondent: Mrs Doreen Howells, Secretary to the Trustees
Trustees: Lady Aline Cholmondeley; Anthony J M Baker; C G Cholmondeley; Miss Sybil Sassoon.
CC Number: 261536

Information available

Accounts were available from the Charity Commission, but without a list of grants.

The trust's policy is to make donations to smaller charities and especially those based in Cheshire and Norfolk, with some donations to UK and international organisations.

In 2009/10 the trust had assets of £1.9 million and an income of £67,000. During the year 196 donations were made totalling £51,000. These were mostly between £100 and £500, with three of £1,000 each. A list of beneficiaries was not included with the latest accounts.

Previous beneficiaries have included All Saints' Church – Beeston Regis, Brain Research Trust, Brighton and Hove Parents' and Children's Group, British Red Cross, Crusaid, Depaul Trust, Elimination of Leukaemia Fund, Eyeless Trust, Genesis Appeal, Help the Aged, Matthew Project, RUKBA, St Peter's – Eaton Square Appeal, Salvation Army, Tibet Relief Fund, West Suffolk Headway, Women's Link and Youth Federation.

Lady Aline and Charles Cholmondeley are also trustees of Aaron David Sassoon (Charity Commission no. 210731; and Anthony Baker is also a trustee of Aaron David Sassoon and Beeston Regis Church Field (Charity Commission no. 241840).

Exclusions

No support for individuals.

Applications

In writing to the correspondent. 'No telephone applications please.' Trustees meet regularly. They do not have an application form as a simple letter will be sufficient.

B E Perl Charitable Trust

Jewish, general

£58,000 (2009/10)

Beneficial area

UK.

Foframe House, 35–37 Brent Street, Hendon, London NW4 2EF
Correspondent: Benjamin Perl, Chair
Trustees: Benjamin Perl, Chair; Dr Shoshanna Perl; Jonathan Perl; Joseph Perl; Naomi Sorotzkin; Rachel Jeidal.
CC Number: 282847

Information available

Accounts were on file at the Charity Commission.

The trusts main focus is the advancement of education in, and the religion of, the Orthodox Jewish faith. Grants are made to Jewish schools, other educational organisations and other charities.

In 2009/10 the trust had assets of £13 million and an income of £1.6 million. Grants totalled £58,000.

Major beneficiaries were: Torah (5759) Limited, Shaare Zedek, Society of Friends of the Torah, Torah Temimah Primary School, WJR and Hendon Adath Yisroel Congregation. No details of grant amounts were available.

Plans for future periods

Please note the following statement taken from the 2009/10 annual report and accounts:

> The trustees have considered and approved plans for the establishment of a major educational project in the UK. It is anticipated that the cost of this project will be in the order of £5 million and it is the intentions of the trustees to accumulate this amount over the next ten years. During the period an amount of £500,000 (2009–£500,000) was transferred to the Educational Reserve in order to fund this project. The Educational Reserve for this purpose stands at £2,000,000 as at the balance sheet date.

> The trustees are pleased to report that by the balance sheet date they had paid a total amount of £825,000 for the purchase of a freehold property to be utilised as an advanced study centre for teenagers.

Applications

In writing to the correspondent.

The Persson Charitable Trust (formerly Highmoore Hall Charitable Trust)

Christian mission societies and agencies

£302,000 (2009/10)

Beneficial area

UK and overseas.

Long Meadow, Dark Lane, Chearsley, Aylesbury, Buckinghamshire HP18 0DA
Tel: 01844 201955
Correspondent: P D Persson, Trustee
Trustees: P D Persson; Mrs A D Persson; J P G Persson; A S J Persson.
CC Number: 289027

Information available

Accounts were available from the Charity Commission.

The trust states that: 'The trustees have a policy of awarding grants to charitable, not-for-profit, organisations which are predominantly involved in humanitarian aid.'

In 2007/08 the trust had assets of £542,000 and an income of £322,000. Grants totalled £302,000, broken down as follows:

Home missions	£152,000
Overseas missions	£150,000
Other charities	£nil

Beneficiaries included: Tearfund – Christian relief (£80,000); All Nations Christian College and Bible Reading Fellowship (£50,000 each), Alpha International (£40,000); Church Renewal Trust (£25,000); and Relationships Foundation (£10,000). Smaller grants totalled £47,000.

Exclusions

No grants to non-registered charities.

Applications

The trust states that it does not respond to unsolicited applications. Telephone calls are not welcome.

The Persula Foundation

Homeless, people with disabilities, human rights, animal welfare

£748,000 (2009/10)

Beneficial area

Predominantly UK; overseas grants are given, but this is rare.

Richer House, Hankey Place, London SE1 4BB
Tel: 020 7357 9298
Fax: 020 7357 8685
Email: fiona@persula.org
Website: www.persula.org
Correspondent: Fiona Brown, Chief Executive
Trustees: J Richer; D Robinson; D Highton; Mrs R Richer; Mrs H Oppenheim.
CC Number: 1044174

Information available

Accounts were available from the Charity Commission.

The trust works in collaboration with organisations to support projects that are innovative and original in the UK and worldwide.

The foundation has core charity interests which they call Generic Research Projects (GRPs) and from this base, they decide on the charity and amount they donate.

- animal welfare
- disabilities (blind and visually impaired, deaf and hard of hearing, learning disabilities, mental health, physical disabilities)
- human welfare (bullying, children and young people, homeless, welfare)
- human rights.

During the 12 months ended 30 April 2010 the generic research groups of the foundation continued their work and support of various projects established within the previous year including the World Society of the

Protection of Animals – Humane Slaughter World programme; Animal Defenders International's Stop Circus Suffering campaign in South America; the National Autistic Society supporting their befriending scheme; and Action on Elder Abuse supporting their national helpline.

The foundation has also supported new projects such as Community Network, providing support groups for isolated elderly people; support to Changing Faces for their Face Equality poster campaign; and People for the Ethical Treatment of animals giving support to the anti-Foie Gras and anti-fur campaigns.

In 2009/10 the trust had an income of £898,000. The principal source of funding was donated by Richer Sounds plc of which Julian Richer is the founder. The following table gives a breakdown of the purposes for which the grants were made:

Human welfare	£394,000
Animal welfare	£210,000
Human rights	£56,000
People with disabilities	£42,000
Tapesense	£30,000
Storytelling	£15,000
Other	£20

One of the largest listed went to Tapesense (£30,000). This project was set up a few years ago by the foundation and offers subsidised equipment and accessories to blind and visually impaired people. Three other listed organisations were: Amnesty International UK (£20,000); and the Howard league for Penal Reform and League Against Cruel Sports (£20,000 each).

Previous beneficiaries have included Action for ME, African Children's Educational Trust, the Aids Trust, the Backup Trust, The Helen Bamber Foundation, Bullying Online, Disability Challengers, Dogs Trust, Emmaus, Humane Slaughter Association, Interact Worldwide, Kidscape, League Against Cruel Sports, The Mango Tree, the MicroLoan Foundation, National Deaf Children's Society, Practical Action, Prisoners Abroad, Prison Reform Trust, Respect for Animals, RNIB, RNID, St Mungo's, SOS Children, Stonewall, VIVA! And WSPA.

Exclusions

No grants to individuals, including sponsorship, for core costs, buildings/building work or to statutory bodies.

Applications

In writing to the correspondent. Trustees meet every two months. The foundation states:

> We consider applications which fit our broad criteria, but they must also fulfill the following:
> 1   They must come from a registered charity or other appropriate organisation.
> 2   The project should be an original idea, and not duplicating an existing service or suchlike.
> 3   The project should be or have the potential to be of national application, rather than local to one area.
> 4   We will not consider applications from charities that have substantial financial reserves (3 to 6 months running costs), and ask to see an annual report from any charity making an application.
> 5   Any charity with whom we work must be prepared to co-operate in a professional manner, for example, meet deadlines, return calls, perform mutually agreed work, in short, to behave 'commercially'.
> 6   The project, in most cases, must fall within the remit of one or more GRPs.
> 7   They must provide value for money.
>
> This list is by no means exhaustive, nor is it final. We will attempt to consider every application but, in general, the above should apply.

Full guidelines can be downloaded from the foundation's website.

Common applicant mistakes

'Not reading guidelines or our remit.'

The Petplan Charitable Trust

Welfare of dogs, cats, horses and rabbits

£245,000 (2009)

Beneficial area

UK.

Great West House GW2, Great West Road, Brentford, Middlesex TW8 9EG
Tel: 020 8580 8013
Fax: 020 8580 8186
Email: catherine.bourg@allianz.co.uk

Website: www.petplantrust.org
Correspondent: Catherine Bourg, Administrator
Trustees: David Simpson, Chair; Clarissa Baldwin; Patsy Bloom; John Bower; Ted Chandler; George Stratford; Neil Brettell.
CC Number: 1032907

Information available

Full accounts were available from the Charity Commission website.

The trust was established in 1994 by a pet insurance company by adding an optional £1.50 a year to the premiums paid by its members. The trust's annual reports state that:

> The trust provides grants towards the welfare of dogs, cats, horses and rabbits by funding clinical veterinary investigation, education and welfare projects. The trust does not and will not consider applications which involve experimental or invasive surgery.
>
> The principal activity of the trust is to make grants from donations received to fund clinical veterinary investigation, education and welfare projects. Two rounds of grants are awarded each year, welfare and scientific. Capital grants for major projects may also be awarded to veterinary schools when funds allow, from time to time.

In 2009 the trust had assets of £483,000 and an income of £531,000. There were 40 grants made (28 welfare and 12 scientific) totalling £245,000.

The largest grants for scientific purposes were awarded to the University of Edinburgh (£99,000) to investigate the effect of cyclosporine on glucose metabolism in dogs; and Royal Veterinary College (£30,000) for an immunological and genomic study of canine hypoadrenocorticism (Addison's disease).

Smaller scientific grants were made varying from £4,000 to £10,000 including those to: University College London, University of Liverpool (£10,000 each); Animal Health Trust (£8,000); Royal Veterinary College (£11,000 between two grants); and University of Edinburgh (£4,000).

Welfare grants were smaller but more numerous and included: Brooke Hospital for Animals (£7,000); Blue Cross, Margaret Green Foundation, Stokechurch Dog Rescue (£5,000 each); Animal Care, Three Counties Dog Rescue (£3,000 each); Jerry

Green Foundation Trust (£2,500); Veterinary Fees (£2,000) and Greek Animal Welfare Fund (£1,000).

Exclusions

No grants to individuals or non-registered charities. The trust does not support or condone invasive procedures, vivisection or experimentation of any kind.

Applications

Closing dates for scientific and welfare applications vary so please check the trust's website first. Grant guidelines and application forms can be downloaded from there.

The Pharsalia Charitable Trust

General, relief of sickness

£185,000 (2009/10).

Beneficial area

Unrestricted, with a particular interest in Oxford.

14 Hyde Place, Oxford OX2 7JB
Tel: 01367 870962
Correspondent: Trudy Sainsbury, Trustee
Trustees: Nigel Stirling Blackwell; Christina Blackwell; Trudy Sainsbury.
CC Number: 1120402

Information available

Accounts were available from the Charity Commission.

Established in 2007, the trust gives grants for general charitable purposes, with particular emphasis on the relief of sickness. It is the charitable trust of Nigel Stirling Blackwell of Blackwell's books and publishing – the name of the trust derives from a Roman epic poem by Lucan.

In 2009/10 the trust had assets of £2.1 million and an income of £330,000. Grants were made to 35 organisations, totalling £185,000.

The major beneficiary during the year was Oxford Radcliffe Hospital Charitable Funds, which received £65,000.

Other grant beneficiaries included: St Edmund Hall (£50,000); Macmillan Cancer Support (£20,000); Help for Heroes (£8,000); Vincent's Club, Oxford University (£6,000); Royal British Legion and Age Concern- Oxford (£4,000 each); Helen & Douglas House (£3,000); Cancer Research UK (£2,000); Motability (£1,000); Canine Partners (£750) and SWGC Captains Charity (£500).

Applications

In writing to the correspondent.

The Phillips and Rubens Charitable Trust

General, Jewish

£280,000 (2009/10)

Beneficial area

UK.

Fifth Floor, Berkeley Square House, Berkeley Square, London W1J 6BY
Tel: 020 7491 3763
Fax: 020 7491 0818
Correspondent: M L Phillips, Trustee
Trustees: Michael L Philips; Mrs Ruth Philips; Martin D Paisner; Paul Philips; Gary Philips; Carolyn Mishon.
CC Number: 260378

Information available

Full accounts were available from the Charity Commission website.

The trust supports a wide range of causes, including medical research, education, disability, old age, poverty, sheltered accommodation and the arts. In practice, almost all the grants are made to Jewish/Israeli organisations.

In 2009/10 the trust had assets of £9.4 million and an income of £256,000. Grants were made totalling £280,000 of which 16 were over £1,000.

The largest grant was the £80,000 donated to the connected Phillips Family Charitable Trust, followed by those to United Jewish Israel Appeal (£52,000), Community Security Trust (£25,000), and Jewish Community Secondary School (£21,000).

Other beneficiaries included: Royal Opera House Foundation (£12,000); British ORT (£8,000); Charities Aid Foundation (£5,000); World Jewish Relief (£3,000); and The Michael Palin Centre for Stammering Children (£2,500).

Grants to organisations of less than £1,000 each totalled £20,000.

Exclusions

No grants are made to individuals.

Applications

In writing to the correspondent at any time.

The Phillips Family Charitable Trust

Jewish charities, welfare, general

£80,000 (2009/10)

Beneficial area

UK.

Berkeley Square House, Berkeley Square, London W1J 6BY
Tel: 020 7491 3763
Correspondent: Paul S Phillips, Trustee
Trustees: Michael L Phillips; Mrs Ruth Phillips; Martin D Paisner; Paul S Phillips; Gary M Phillips.
CC Number: 279120

Information available

Full accounts were available from the Charity Commission website.

This trust stated that it makes grants to Jewish organisations and to a range of other organisations, including elderly, children and refugee charities and educational establishments.

In 2009/10 the trust had assets of £4,000 and an income of £60,000 which came from J B Rubens Charitable Trust (Charity Commission no. 218366). Grants were made to 81 organisations totalling £80,000.

Beneficiaries included: Community Security Trust (£5,500 in two grants); Chief Rabbinate Trust and Friends of Ohr Someach (£5,000 each); Jews' College (£3,000); Beth Shalom Ltd, Dalaid, My Israel and Sylvella Charity Ltd (£1,000 each).

Exclusions

No grants to individuals.

Applications

In writing to the correspondent. Please note, the trust informed us that there is not much scope for new beneficiaries.

The David Pickford Charitable Foundation

Christian, general

£61,000 (2009/10)

Beneficial area

UK (with a preference for Kent and London) and overseas.

Benover House, Rectory Lane, Saltwood, Hythe, Kent CT21 4QA
Tel: 01303 268 322
Fax: 01233 720 522
Correspondent: E J Pettersen, Trustee
Trustees: C J Pickford; E J Pettersen;
CC Number: 243437

Information available

Accounts were on file at the Charity Commission.

The general policy is to make gifts to Christian organisations especially those helping youth, and with special needs in the UK and overseas.

In 2009–10 the foundation had assets of £1.1 million and an income of £29,000. Grants were made totalling £61,000. A list of beneficiaries was not included.

Previous beneficiaries included: CARE (£5,000); Chaucer Trust (£4,000); Oasis Trust (£2,500); Brighter Future and Pastor Training international (£1,000 each); Toybox (£750); Alpha International, Flow Romania and Mersham Parish Church (£500 each);

Compassion (£300); Samaritans (£250); and Lionhart (£15).

Exclusions

No grants to individuals. No building projects.

Applications

In writing to the correspondent. Trustees meet every other month from January. Applications will not be acknowledged. The correspondent states: 'It is our general policy only to give to charities to whom we are personally known'. Those falling outside the criteria mentioned above will be ignored.

The Bernard Piggott Trust

General

£68,000 (2009/10)

Beneficial area

North Wales and Birmingham.

Jenny Whitworth, 4 Streetsbrook Road, Shirley, Solihull, West Midlands B90 3PL
Tel: 0121 744 1695
Fax: 0121 744 1695
Correspondent: J P Whitworth
Trustees: Mark Painter; D M P Lea; N J L Lea; R J Easton; Venerable Meurig Llwyd Williams.
CC Number: 260347

Information available

Full accounts were available from the Charity Commission website.

This trust provides one-off grants for Church of England, Church in Wales, educational, medical, drama and youth organisations in Birmingham and North Wales only. It is the trustees' policy to allocate approximately one-third of income to charitable organisations operating within North Wales and two-thirds to the Birmingham area.

In 2009/10 the trust's assets stood at £1.3 million. It had an income of £103,000 and made grants totalling £68,000. Grants ranged from £500 to £3,000.

Grant recipients included: Birmingham Clubs for Young People

and St Gwenfaen's, Rhoscolyn (£3,000 each); Castle Bromwich Hall Gardens and DebRA (£2,000 each); Birmingham Boys' & Girls' Union, Cornerstone, Marie Curie, Oesphagael Patients Association, Headway, Queen Alexandra College, The Ackers and The Dystonia Society (£1,000 each); and Sea Ranger Association (£500).

Exclusions

No grants to individuals.

Applications

The trustees meet in May/June and November. Applications should be in writing to the secretary including annual accounts and details of the specific project including running costs and so on. General policy is not to consider any further grant to the same organisation within the next two years.

Common applicant mistakes

'Applying from areas outside the area of benefit stipulated by the trust. Several applications are received from individuals (who we can't help) rather than registered charities. Applicants re-applying too soon when they have been advised of the time scale when a grant has been sent.'

The Elise Pilkington Charitable Trust

Equine animals, aged, infirm and poor

£161,000 (2009/10)

Beneficial area

UK.

Ridgecot, Lewes Road, Horsted Keynes, Haywards Heath, West Sussex RH17 7DY
Tel: 01825 790304
Correspondent: Kenton Lawton, Trust Administrator
Trustees: Caroline Doulton, Chair; Tara Economakis; Revd Rob Merchant; Helen Timpany.
CC Number: 278332

Information available

Accounts were available from the Charity Commission, but without a grants list.

The trust's objects are:
- to prevent cruelty to equine animals, to relieve suffering and distress amongst such equine animals and to care for and protect such equines in need of care and protection
- to provide social services for the relief of the aged, infirm and poor.

The trust supports small specific projects of a capital nature and occasionally larger charities, but over a period of three years. Grants are not usually given towards running costs.

In 2009/10 the trust's assets stood at £2.8 million. It had an income of £89,000 and made 22 grants totalling £161,000, broken down as follows:

To prevent cruelty to equine animals	10	£95,000
To provide help for aged, infirm or poor	12	£66,000

A list of beneficiaries was not available.

Applications

In writing to the correspondent.

Common applicant mistakes

'Applying for grants that do not fit with our objects.'

The Cecil Pilkington Charitable Trust

Conservation, medical research, general

£137,000 (2008/09)

Beneficial area

UK, particularly Sunningwell in Oxfordshire and St Helens.

Duncan Sheard Glass, Castle Chambers, 43 Castle Street, Liverpool L2 9TL
Correspondent: The Administrator
Trustees: A P Pilkington; R F Carter Jonas; M R Feeny.
CC Number: 249997

Information available

Accounts were available from the Charity Commission.

This trust supports conservation and medical research causes across the UK, supporting both national and local organisations. It also has general charitable purposes in Sunningwell in Oxfordshire and St Helens.

In 2008/09 the trust's assets stood at £7.6 million. It had an income of £198,000 and made grants to 35 organisations totalling £137,000.

Beneficiaries included: Psychiatry Research Trust (£50,000); Peninsular Medical School Foundation (£20,000); St Leonard's Church Restoration and SANE (£5,000 each); Wildfowl and Wetlands Trust (£2,000); and Sunningwell School of Art (£1,000).

Exclusions

No grants to individuals or non-registered charities.

Applications

The trust does not respond to unsolicited appeals.

The Sir Harry Pilkington Trust

General charitable purposes

£187,000 (2009/10)

Beneficial area

UK, with a preference for Merseyside.

Liverpool Charity And Voluntary Services, 151 Dale Street, Liverpool L2 2AH
Tel: 0151 227 5177
Website: www.merseytrusts.org.uk
Correspondent: The Trustees
Trustee: Liverpool Charity and Voluntary Services.
CC Number: 206740

Information available

Accounts were available from the Charity Commission.

In 2009/10 the trust had assets of £4.7 million and an income of £169,000. Grants were made totalling £187,000.

Beneficiaries included: Liverpool Charity and Voluntary Services (£40,000); The Basement Night Drop-in Centre (£4,000); Albion Youth Club, Barnstondale Centre and Disability and Deaf Arts (£3,000 each); Dovecot Multi Activity Centre (£2,800); Healthy Energy Advice Team, Hetherlow Community Centre Association, Merseyside Caribbean Council and Pre School Equipment and Resource Centre (£2,000 each); and Woodlands Residents Association and Writing On the Wall (£1,000 each).

Applications

In writing to the correspondent. The trust welcomes an initial phone call to discuss the proposal.

Common applicant mistakes

'Not speaking to us before applying.'

The Austin and Hope Pilkington Trust

Categories of funding repeated in a three-year rotation (see the entry for further information)

£210,000 (2009)

Beneficial area

Unrestricted, but see exclusions field.

PO Box 124, Stroud, Gloucestershire GL6 7YN
Email: admin@austin-hope-pilkington.org.uk
Website: www.austin-hope-pilkington.org.uk
Correspondent: Karen Frank, Administrator
Trustees: Jennifer Jones; Deborah Nelson; Penny Shankar.
CC Number: 255274

Information available

Full accounts were available from the Charity Commission website; the trust has a useful website.

The trustees welcome applications for projects within the following areas for the next three years. These categories are then repeated in a three-year rotation.

- 2011: music and the arts; overseas (the last year grants will be made to overseas projects)
- 2012: community; medical
- 2013: children & youth
- 2014: music and the arts; elderly.

Registered charities only. National projects are preferred to those with a local remit. Grants are usually between £1,000 and £3,000. The majority of grants made were for £1,000, the trustees deciding to make a large number of small grants in order to make the trust's resources as effective as possible given the exceptional demand on the charity. Exceptionally, grants of up to £10,000 are made, but these are usually for medical research projects. Grants are usually awarded for one year only.

In 2009 the trust had assets of £8.9 million and an income of £217,000. Grants were made totalling £210,000. The priorities for the charity in 2009 were community and disability.

Community beneficiaries included: The Connection at St Martin in the Fields (£5,000); Resources for Autism, Enterprise Education Trust (£3,000 each); Get Hooked on Fishing, Blind in Business, ASGMA, Crime Diversion Scheme, Women in Prison, Hope Centre Ballymena and Normandy Community Therapy Garden (£1,000 each).

Disability beneficiaries included: Action Space, Parentline Plus, Tourettes Action (£3,000 each); YWCA, Vassall Centre trust, Spadework, Multiple Sclerosis Trust and Disability Alliance (£1,000 each).

Exclusions

Grants only to registered charities. No grants to individuals, including individuals embarking on a trip overseas with an umbrella organisation. Overseas projects are no longer supported. National organisations are more likely to be supported than purely local organisations. Charities working in the following areas are not supported: religion (including repair of Church fabric); animals (welfare and conservation); scouts, guides, cubs, brownies; village halls; individual hospices (national organisations can apply); capital appeals; schools; and minibuses.

Applications

Applicants are strongly advised to visit the trust's website as projects supported and eligibility criteria change from year to year. Grants are made twice a year, with deadlines for applications being 1 June and 1 November.

Applications should be made in writing to the correspondent – do not use signed for or courier. To apply for a grant, please submit *only* the following:

- A letter summarising the application, including acknowledgement of any previous grants awarded from the trust.
- A maximum of two sides of A4 (including photographs) summarising the project.
- A detailed budget for the project.
- A maximum of two sides of A4 (including photographs) summarising the charity's general activities.
- The most recent accounts and annual report.

The trust asks the following:

Please do not send CDs, DVDs, or any other additional information. If we require further details, we will contact the charity directly. Charities are therefore advised to send in applications with sufficient time before the June or November deadlines to allow for such enquiries.

With the increased level of applications, the trust has stated that all successful applicants will in future be listed on their website on the 'recent awards' after each trustee meeting. All applicants will still be contacted by letter in due course. Early applications are strongly encouraged.

The Col W W Pilkington Will Trusts – The General Charity Fund

Medical, arts, social welfare, international charities, drugs misuse, environment

£46,000 (2009/10)

Beneficial area

Mainly UK, with a preference for Merseyside.

PO Box 8162, London W2 1GF
Correspondent: The Clerk
Trustees: Arnold Pilkington; Hon. Mrs Jennifer Jones; Neil Pilkington Jones.
CC Number: 234710

Information available

Accounts were on file at the Charity Commission.

The trust gives grants to registered charities only, with a preference for the Merseyside area.

In 2009/10 the trust had assets of £1.5 million and an income of £56,000. Grants were made to organisations totalling £46,000, which were broken down as follows:

Medical	7
Environment	6
Arts	4
International	4
Welfare	2
Drugs	2

Beneficiaries included: Halle Concerts Society, the New Works, Narconon, No Panic, Mary Seacole House, Buglife, Wildlife Trust for Lancs, Manchester and North Merseyside and Minority Rights Group International (£1,500 each).

Exclusions

No support for non-registered charities, building projects, animal charities or individuals.

Applications

In writing to the correspondent.

Miss A M Pilkington's Charitable Trust

General

Around £120,000 (2009/10)

Beneficial area

UK, with a preference for Scotland.

Carters Chartered Accountants, Pentland House, Saltire Centre, Glenrothes, Fife KY6 2AH
Correspondent: The Clerk
SC Number: SC000282

Information available

Despite making a written request for the accounts of this trust, they were not provided. The following entry is based, therefore, on information filed with the Office of the Scottish Charity Regulator.

The trust supports a wide variety of causes in the UK, with few causes excluded (see exclusions). In practice there is a preference for Scotland – probably half the grants are given in Scotland. There is a preference for giving recurring grants, which normally range from £500 to £1,500.

In 2009/10 the trust had an income of £136,000.

Exclusions

Grants are not given to overseas projects or political appeals.

Applications

The trustees state that, regrettably, they are unable to make grants to new applicants since they already have 'more than enough causes to support'.

The DLA Piper Charitable Trust

General

£50,000 (2009/10)

Beneficial area

UK.

Fountain Precinct, Balm Green, Sheffield S1 1RZ

Tel: 0114 267 5594
Email: godfrey.smallman@wrigleys.co.uk
Correspondent: G J Smallman, Secretary
Trustees: N G Knowles; P Rooney.
CC Number: 327280

Information available

Accounts were received at the Charity Commission, but were not available to view.

In 2009/10 this trust had an income of £500 and a total expenditure of £53,000. In the previous year £132,000 was given in grants to 96 organisations.

Previous beneficiaries included: the Cutty Sark Trust (£10,000); Solicitors' Benevolent Association (£8,500); Christie's Hospital, Green Belt Movement International and the Prince's Trust (£5,000 each); and Yorkshire Air Ambulance and South Yorkshire Community Foundation Flood Disaster Relief Fund. A one-off donation of £51,000 was awarded to the University of Michigan Law School to fund the employment of a new professorial chair.

Other donations of less than £1,000 each totalled £17,000.

Exclusions

No grants to individuals.

Applications

In writing to the correspondent, for consideration every three months.

The Platinum Trust

Disability

£559,000 (2009/10)

Beneficial area

UK.

Sedley Ricchard Laurence Voulters, 89 New Bond Street, London W1S 1DA
Tel: 020 7079 8814
Correspondent: The Secretary
Trustees: Georgios K Panayiotou; Stephen Marks; C D Organ.
CC Number: 328570

Information available

Accounts were available from the Charity Commission.

This trust gives grants in the UK for the relief of children with special needs and adults with mental or physical disabilities 'requiring special attention'. The trust was established by Georgios Panayiotou, AKA the singer George Michael.

In 2009/10 the trust had an income of £687,000 and assets stood at £282,000. Grants to 16 organisations totalled £559,000.

Beneficiaries included: Goss Michael Foundation – restricted funds (£353,000); Disability, Pregnancy and Parenthood International (£45,000); Centre for Studies on Inclusive Education (£30,000); Alliance for Inclusive Education (£20,000); Parents for Inclusion (£20,000); Independent Panel for Special Education Advice (£15,000); Disabled Parents Network (£10,000); DEMAND (£5,000); and Clear Vision (£300).

All the trustees are also trustees of Platinum Overseas Trust (Charity Commission no. 1004176) and Stephen Marks is also a trustee of The Mill Charitable Trust (Charity Commission no. 1128056).

Exclusions

No grants for services run by statutory or public bodies, or from mental-health organisations. No grants for: medical research/treatment or equipment; mobility aids/wheelchairs; community transport/disabled transport schemes; holidays/exchanges/holiday playschemes; special-needs playgroups; toy and leisure libraries; special Olympic and Paralympics groups; sports and recreation clubs for people with disabilities; residential care/sheltered housing/respite care; carers; conservation schemes/city farms/horticultural therapy; sheltered or supported employment/community business/social firms; purchase/construction/repair of buildings; and conductive education/other special educational programmes.

Applications

The trust does not accept unsolicited applications; all future grants will be allocated by the trustees to groups they have already made links with.

G S Plaut Charitable Trust Limited

Sickness, disability, Jewish, elderly, general

£47,000 (2009/10)

Beneficial area

Predominantly UK.

39 Bay Road, Wormit, Newport-on-Tay, Fife DD6 8LW
Correspondent: Dr R A Speirs, Secretary
Trustees: Mrs A D Wrapson; Miss T A Warburg; Mr W E Murfett; Mrs B A Sprinz; Miss R E Liebeschuetz.
CC Number: 261469

Information available

Accounts were available from the Charity Commission.

This trust appears to make grants across the whole spectrum of the voluntary sector, however it may have some preference for charities in those fields listed above.

In 2009/10 the trust's assets totalled £1.2 million, it had an income of £49,000 and grants totalled £47,000.

Beneficiaries included: Dogs for the Disabled, Magen David Adom UK and Children In Touch – 1978 (£3,000 each); Médecins Sans Frontières (£2,500); Toybox Charity, Tear Fund, Carers UK and Anglo Jewish Association (£2,000 each); Ex-Services Mental Welfare Society – Combat Stress (£1,500); and Sight Savers International, the Sobriety Project and British Retinitis Pigmentosa Society (£1,000 each).

Exclusions

No grants to individuals or for repeat applications.

Applications

In writing to the correspondent. Applications are reviewed twice a year. An sae should be enclosed. Applications will not be acknowledged.

The George and Esme Pollitzer Charitable Settlement

Jewish, general

£79,500 (2009/10)

Beneficial area

UK.

Saffery Champness, Beaufort House, 2 Beaufort Road, Clifton, Bristol B58 2AE
Tel: 01179 151617
Correspondent: Miss L E Parrock
Trustees: J Barnes; Catherine Alexander Charles; R F C Pollitzer.
CC Number: 212631

Information available

Accounts were available from the Charity Commission.

This trust has general charitable purposes with no exclusions. Most funds are given to Jewish causes.

In 2009/10 the settlement's assets stood at £2.8 million. It had an income of £95,000 and made grants to 49 organisations totalling £79,500. A large proportion of grants were for £1,000 and £1,500 each.

Beneficiaries included: Jewish Museum (£10,000); Norwood Children and Families First and The Royal College of Surgeons (£2,000 each); Alexandra Rose Day, Anthony Nolan Trust, The Big Issue, Cove Park, Deafblind UK, Fields in Trust, Foundation for Conductive Education, Sense, Swinfen Charitable Trust, The Weiner Library and Who Cares Trust (£1,500 each); and Jewish Council for Racial Equality and Target Ovarian Cancer (£1,000 each).

Applications

In writing to the correspondent.

The J S F Pollitzer Charitable Settlement

General

£44,000 (2009/10)

Beneficial area

UK and overseas.

Mary Street House, Mary Street, Taunton, Somerset TA1 3NW
Tel: 01823 286096
Correspondent: Trust Accountant
Trustees: R F C Pollitzer, Chair; Mrs E Pettit; Mrs S C O'Farrell.
CC Number: 210680

Information available

Accounts were available from the Charity Commission.

The trust supports a range of UK and local charities. In 2009/10 the trust had assets of £672,000 and an income of £48,000. Grants were made to 44 organisations totalling £44,000; all grants were for amounts of £1,000 each. Grants were broken down into the following categories:

Health	£11,000
Children and youth	£7,000
Cultural	£7,000
Social and community welfare	£7,000
Disabled	£4,000
Conservation/environment	£3,000
Education, science and technology	£3,000
Hospices	£2,000

Beneficiaries included: Aidis Trust, Cruse Bereavement Care, Dyson Perrins Museum Trust, Education Uganda, Florence Nightingale Hospice Charity, Girls' Venture Corps Air Cadets, the Herpetological Conservation Trust, Highland Budokan Judo Club, Little Ouse Headwaters Project, MDF the Bipolar Association, the Memorial Arts Charity and the Sequal Trust.

Exclusions

No grants to individuals or students, i.e. those without charitable status.

Applications

In writing to the correspondent. Grants are distributed twice a year, usually around April/May and November/December.

Edith and Ferdinand Porjes Charitable Trust

Jewish, general

£57,000 (2009/10)

Beneficial area

UK and overseas.

Adelaide House, London Bridge, London EC4R 9HA
Tel: 020 7760 1000
Correspondent: M D Paisner, Trustee
Trustees: M D Paisner;
A S Rosenfelder; H Stanton.
CC Number: 274012

Information available

Accounts were on available from the Charity Commission website.

Although the trust has general charitable purposes, the trust is inclined to support applications from the Jewish community in the UK and overseas. The trustees have set aside a fund, referred to as the 'British Friends of the Art Museums of Israel Endowment fund' with the specific aim of supporting the British Friends of the Art Museums of Israel.

In 2009/10 the trust had assets of £1.4 million and an income of £48,000 with grants to six organisations totalling £57,000.

Beneficiaries included: the Jewish Museum (£25,000); Jewish Book Council (£20,000); Yesodey Hatorah Grammar School (£7,500); British Friends of the Art Museums of Israel (£4,000); and British Friends of OHEL Sarah (£2,500).

Applications

In writing to the correspondent.

The Porter Foundation

Jewish charities, environment, arts, general

£551,000 (2009/10)

Beneficial area

Israel and the UK.

Blick Rothenburg, Trust Department, 12 York Gate, Regent's Park, London NW1 4QS
Tel: 020 7544 8863
Email: theporterfoundation@ btinternet.com
Correspondent: Paul Williams, Executive Director
Trustees: David Brecher; Albert Castle; Dame Shirley Porter; Steven Porter; Sir Walter Bodmer; John Porter; Linda Streit.
CC Number: 261194

Information available

Accounts were available from the Charity Commission.

Summary

The foundation supports 'projects in the fields of education, the environment, culture and health and welfare, which encourage excellence, efficiency and innovation and enhance the quality of people's lives'.

During recent years it has cut back on the number of beneficiaries supported and is making fewer, larger grants, mainly to the connected Porter School of Environmental Studies at Tel Aviv University, or the university itself, and to other causes in Israel. This has led to a temporary reduction in UK-based activity. A limited number of community awards continue to be given, though usually to organisations already known to the foundation.

General

The foundation was set up in 1970 by Sir Leslie Porter and Dame Shirley Porter, a former leader of Westminster City Council.

In 2009/10 the foundation had assets of £46 million and an income of £804,000. Over £120,000 was spent on governance. During the year the trust made uncommitted charitable donations totalling £241,000 and paid £259,000 in respect of binding charitable commitments. There was one new commitment of £101,000 to the Tel Aviv Foundation.

Beneficiaries of uncommitted grants included: Friends of Daniel for Rowing Association (£63,000); New

Israel Fund (£42,000); Tel Aviv University Trust (£40,000); Friends of the Israeli Opera (£20,000); Oxford Centre of Hebrew and Jewish Studies (£9,500); Beit Issie Shapiro (£2,000); and Whitechapel Gallery (£1,000).

Exclusions

The foundation makes grants only to registered charitable organisations or to organisations with charitable objects that are exempt from the requirement for charitable registration.

Grants will not be made to:
- general appeals such as direct mail circulars
- charities which redistribute funds to other charities
- third-party organisations raising money on behalf of other charities
- cover general running costs.

No grants are made to individuals.

Applications

An initial letter summarising your application, together with basic costings and background details on your organisation, such as the annual report and accounts, should be sent to the director. Speculative approaches containing expensive publicity material are not encouraged.

If your proposal falls within the foundation's current funding criteria you may be contacted for further information, including perhaps a visit from the foundation staff. There is no need to fill out an application form.

Applications fulfilling the criteria will be considered by the trustees, who meet three times a year, usually in March, July and November. You will hear shortly after the meeting whether your application has been successful. Unfortunately, it is not possible to acknowledge all unsolicited applications (unless a stamped, addressed envelope is enclosed). If you do not hear from the foundation, you can assume that your application has been unsuccessful. Due to limits on funds available, some excellent projects may have to be refused a grant. In such a case the trustees may invite the applicant to re-apply in a future financial year, without giving a commitment to fund.

The Portrack Charitable Trust

General

£69,500 (2009/10)

Beneficial area

Some preference for Scotland.

Butterfield Bank, 99 Gresham Street, London EC2V 7NG
Tel: 020 7776 6700
Correspondent: The Trustees
Trustees: Charles Jencks; Keith Galloway; John Jencks.
CC Number: 266120

Information available

Accounts were available from the Charity Commission.

In 2009/10 the trust had assets of £3.2 million and an income of £70,000. Grants were made totalling £69,500. The majority of the 32 grants made were for £1,000.

Beneficiaries included: Maggie's Cancer Caring Centres (£30,000); Yale University Press (£10,000); Medical Aid for Palestinians (£2,000); Carers UK, Listening Books, National Museums Scotland and Princess Royal Trust for Carers (£1,000 each); and St Andrew's Youth Club and University of Glasgow (£500 each).

Charles Alexander Jencks is also a trustee of the Keswick Foundation Limited (Charity Commission no. 278449); and Keith Galloway is also a trustee of Rockliffe Charitable Trust (Charity Commission no. 274117).

Exclusions

Grants are not given to individuals.

Applications

In writing to the correspondent.

The J E Posnansky Charitable Trust

Jewish charities, health, social welfare and humanitarian

£139,000 (2009/10)

Beneficial area

UK and overseas.

Sobell Rhodes, Monument House, 215 Marsh Road, Pinner, London WA5 5NE
Tel: 020 7431 0909
Fax: 020 7435 1516
Correspondent: Mr N S Posnansky, Trustee
Trustees: Mrs G Raffles; A Posnansky; P A Mishcon; Mrs E J Feather; N S Posnansky.
CC Number: 210416

Information available

Accounts were available from the Charity Commission.

The trust was created in 1958 for general charitable purposes in the UK and elsewhere and grant giving now concentrates on the areas of Jewish, health, education, social welfare and humanitarian causes. The trust incorporates the A V Posnansky Charitable Trust.

In 2009/10 the trust had assets of £3.8 million and an income of £80,000. Grants totalled £139,000.

Beneficiaries included: Magen David Adom UK (£20,000); Friends of Alyn (£15,000); Jewish Care (£7,500); Norwood (£5,000); Terence Higgins Trust (£2,000); Tay Sachs Screening Programme (£1,000); and the Sue Ryder Foundation (£500).

Exclusions

No grants to individuals.

Applications

Unsolicited applications will not be considered.

The David and Elaine Potter Foundation

Human rights, education, research and the arts

£3.2 million (2009)

Beneficial area

UK and overseas with particular emphasis on the developing world.

10 Park Crescent, London W1B 1PQ
Tel: 0207 291 3993
Fax: 020 7291 3991
Email: info@potterfoundation.com
Website: www.potterfoundation.com/
Correspondent: Mrs Angela Seay, Director
Trustees: Michael S Polonsky; Michael Langley; Dr David Potter; Elaine Potter; Samuel Potter.
CC Number: 1078217

Information available

Latest accounts were available from the Charity Commission. The foundation also has a helpful and informative website.

Established in 1999, the foundation has general charitable purposes but focuses on supporting education, human rights, the arts and the general strengthening of civil society. The following description of the settlor's motivations are given on the foundation's website:

> The David and Elaine Potter Foundation is motivated to use philanthropy to encourage the values and beliefs of the founders within society in its largest definition. The Potters believe in 'the constructs of the rational mind – the great edifice of human thought – science, philosophy, the social sciences, the arts and ethics'. The underpinnings of their views are intellectual and moral without being oriented towards religions or nationalism. They believe passionately in the power of reason and in the significance and importance of all individuals in society. By extension, their principles embrace tolerance and an intolerance to intolerance.

Areas of interest

The foundation makes grants under the following categories:

Civil Society

A strong civil society holds governments accountable, enhances democratic institutions and the quality of life of its citizens, helping to strengthen and sustain economic, civil and legal rights.

One of our most important aims as a foundation is to help to create societies – both locally and worldwide – that are driven by equality and fairness. The means by which we and others can foster civil society are varied. We support projects that give people opportunities to take part in and to shape society; which enable the most disadvantaged people to play a full role in developing a fair civil society; and which foster dialogue across national and cultural boundaries. We do this by investing in a diverse array of projects: supporting education with an emphasis on commitment to civil society at the University of Cape Town; by funding the Centre for Investigative Journalism in its training of investigative journalists and other independent journalism efforts; by funding Global Witness in its efforts to highlight corruption and misuse of natural resources and many others.

Human Rights

Global society cannot be fair or equal while human rights are abused. We provide grants to organisations that defend human rights, protect individuals and campaign for change.

Because of the nature of human rights work, many of the organisations we support are international, though we also support smaller, local projects. We may fund specific projects within a large organisation. For example we have supported Amnesty International's annual Greetings Card Campaign for a number of years – and recently made a large general grant to underpin the whole range of the organisation's work.

Education

At the root of a strong civil society is an educated populace with access to good quality information. Without education, people struggle to participate in decision-making and change: the Foundation therefore supports projects which promote education for all people and particularly ones that give opportunities to those who would otherwise be excluded.

Whilst in the past the Foundation made occasional grants to individuals, today we focus our support on organisations and institutions. These bodies offer educational opportunities which will enable students to develop their skills and abilities. We hope that these students will become leaders and opinion formers and will make real contributions towards a fairer civil society.

A prime example of this ethos is our grants scheme at the University of Cape Town. Each year we offer a number of scholarships to high achieving students to enable them to pursue their studies – a requirement of the grant is that they share their research within the university and use it to contribute to wider society.

Research

A fair and strong civil society makes rational decisions and plans based on sound, well-researched information. Our grants enable academic institutions to carry out high quality research that will underpin these rational choices and suggest new, fairer ways of organising society.

A number of our educational grants will also produce significant research. For example, the new Centre of Governance and Human Rights at the University of Cambridge will certainly produce exciting new work, bringing together as it does researchers and practitioners across a range of disciplines.

Arts

The Potters feel strongly that the performing arts contribute to civil society and to quality of life in general, enhancing individual understanding and promoting independent thought. The Foundation supports a range of London-based organisations and one in New York City. The foundation tends to provide small grants for its funding in the arts; it is not a primary area of focus.

Guidelines

The following information on funding guidelines is taken from the foundation's website:

The foundation's funding is divided into five categories: Education, Civil society, Research, Human rights and Arts. The trustees are interested in lasting social change, and in forming long-term partnerships with the organisations the foundation supports.

The David and Elaine Potter Foundation will consider: general or core funding; specific programme grants; small lead gifts for innovative, new or enhanced programmes; challenge gifts to encourage the participation of other donors; and one-time and short-term gifts to sustain a programme until its long-term funding is realised.

The foundation prefers to use its funding to leverage other donor participation. Requests for endowment, capital campaigns, construction, equipment purchases and debt reduction should not be submitted.

Support can only be given to organisations or groups that are charitable within the UK meaning of that term. This includes UK registered charities and exempt charities such as

hospitals, educational establishments, museums, and housing corporations. Applications from individuals or for individual research or study cannot be considered and the trustees do not generally support humanitarian aid or animal welfare charities.

The foundation strongly prefers to fund strategically; for capacity building, to 'grow' a specific charity or area of interest, or to leverage additional support for an organisation.

Charities are asked not to re-apply within twelve months of an appeal to the foundation, whether they have received a grant or not. Grants are normally made by means of a single payment unless it is a multi-year grant.

The trustees meet on a regular basis to review submissions. The foundation has a rolling programme and deals with the letters of enquiry and applications in order of receipt. It normally takes between two and three months for each stage of the process, but things can proceed more quickly depending on the timing of the trustees' meetings. The trustees will provide multi-year or forward funding grants in some cases.

Due to the volume of material received and the foundation's small staff, the paperwork for unsuccessful letters of enquiry is not retained and it is therefore not possible to comment on individual cases.

The trustees are happy for the foundation to be acknowledged along with other donors.

Grantmaking

In 2009 the foundation marked its tenth anniversary; over this period the foundation has awarded over £11.4 million in grant funding to over 100 charitable organisations, schools and universities, in areas ranging from education, research and human rights, to the arts. During the year, it had assets of £22.6 million and an income of £1.6 million. Grants totalled £3.2 million, which included commitments from the previous year. An exceptional grant of £2 million to be paid over five years was approved to support a new initiative, the Bureau of Investigative Journalism.

Grants were made in six main categories as follows:

Civil society	£2.2 million
Education	£557,000
Human rights	£206,000
Research	£150,000
Arts	£79,000

Beneficiaries included: Bureau of Investigative Journalism (£2 million); CIDA – UK Foundation, Independent Diplomat and the Royal Society

(£150,000 each); Business Bridge Initiative (£90,000); Reprieve (£60,000); Room to Read (£31,000); Performa (£25,000); UCL Development Fund (£10,000); Royal Court Theatre (£5,000); and Global Dialogue – ARIADNE (£2,500).

Exclusions

No grants to individuals, animal welfare charities or humanitarian aid. Requests for endowment, capital campaigns, construction, equipment purchases and debt reduction will not be considered.

Applications

The following details on how to apply to the foundation are taken from its website:

The grant application process is divided into two stages: a letter of enquiry and an application.

An applicant is invited to submit a full proposal only if their letter of enquiry has been accepted.

There are no deadlines for letters of enquiry, as the foundation reviews these requests regularly. The members of the board of trustees request that correspondence be submitted to the foundation office in place of personal or written contact with individual board members.

Stage 1 – Letter of Enquiry

In order to initiate a proposal to the David and Elaine Potter Foundation, please submit a one to two-page letter of enquiry. Your letter should include the following information:

- contact name
- contact telephone numbers/fax number
- contact email
- organisation background and brief description of activities
- total income of the organisation in the last complete financial year
- brief project synopsis, time frame, and anticipated outcome
- grant amount requested and total project cost
- charity status, charity registration number if applicable.

Once the foundation director has reviewed your letter, we will contact you via email to acknowledge receipt. The contact information listed on your letter of enquiry is where all correspondence will be sent. If you do not receive email notification within two weeks, please contact us. Following up on a letter of enquiry is the organisation's responsibility.

Stage 2 – Application

Should the foundation approve your letter of enquiry, you may then complete and submit a formal application. Your formal application must include all information originally provided in the letter of enquiry and expand on details appropriately and as suggested by the foundation trustees.

In assessing applications, the trustees consider the following information:

- whether the aims of the organisation meet the foundation priorities
- a copy of the most recent report and audited accounts
- a full description of the project requiring funding, with details of who will benefit
- a complete budget for the project, with amount requested from the foundation
- a description of how the project/ programme will be evaluated and outcomes measured.

What happens next

The foundation director screens letters of enquiry and applications to establish whether sufficient information has been submitted. Additional details are sometimes requested before any further action is taken. At any point, a visit might also be arranged in order to gain greater insight into an organisation. All letters of enquiry and applications are considered on an individual basis by the trustees. Applicants are notified of the outcome of each stage by letter.

Evaluation

The foundation requires evaluation information about the expenditure of grants and/or programme outcomes every six months after grant monies are received and until the funds have been expended. A final report on the grant will be required within three months of completion of the project/programme. If relevant to the grant evaluation process or to consider future funding, a site visit may be arranged at this time.

Prairie Trust

International development, climate change, conflict prevention

£254,000 (2009/10)

Beneficial area

Worldwide.

83 Belsize Park Gardens, London NW3 4NJ
Email: info@frederickmulder.com
Correspondent: The Administrator
Trustees: Dr Frederick Mulder; Hannah Mulder.

CC Number: 296019

Information available

Accounts were available from the Charity Commission.

The trust does not consider unsolicited applications and instead develops its own programme to support a small number of organisations working on issues of third world development, climate change and conflict prevention, particularly to support policy and advocacy work in these areas. The trustees are also interested in supporting innovative and entrepreneurial approaches to traditional problems.

Many grants are now made through the Funding Network, to projects which have presented at both the London and non-London events, and the trust also helps to support the Network's operating costs. The trust states that this trend is likely to continue and possibly increase in future years.

In 2009/10 the trust had an income of £24,000 and made grants totalling £254,000. Investments stood at £449,000 and the trust transferred a further £631,000 into its CAF Gold account during the year.

Beneficiaries included: Not Stupid (£69,000 in 4 grants); the Funding Network (£60,000 in 16 grants across a number of groups); P8 (£30,000); Landmatters (£14,000); Institute of Fundraising (£3,100); Women in Need (£2,500); British Museum and Olivia Hodson Cancer Fund (£1,000 each); Royal Opera House Foundation (£320); and Ashmolean Museum (£100).

Exclusions

No grants to individuals or for expeditions.

Applications

The trust states: 'As we are a proactive trust with limited funds and administrative help, we are unable to consider unsolicited applications.'

The W L Pratt Charitable Trust

General

£59,000 (2009/10)

Beneficial area

UK, particularly York, and overseas.

Grays, Duncombe Place, York
YO1 7DY
Tel: 01904 634771
Email: christophergoodway@
grayssolicitors.co.uk
Correspondent: C C Goodway,
Trustee
Trustees: J L C Pratt; C M Tetley;
C C Goodway.
CC Number: 256907

Information available

Accounts were available from the
Charity Commission.

The trust divides its grant-giving
between overseas charities, local
charities in the York area and UK
national charities. UK and overseas
grants are restricted to well-known
registered charities.

Support is given:

- In the UK: to support religious and
  social objectives with a priority for
  York and district, including health
  and community services.
- Overseas: to help the developing
  world by assisting in food
  production and relief of famine
  and disease.

In 2009/10 the trust's assets stood at
£1.6 million. It had an income of
£47,000 and made grants totalling
£59,000, broken down into the
following categories:

Local charities	20	£24,000
One-off donations	19	£14,000
UK National charities	15	£11,000
Overseas	7	£10,000

Beneficiaries included: York Diocesan
Board of Finance and York Minister
Development Campaign (£5,000
each); Christian Aid, Sightsavers
International and Wilberforce Trust
(£2,000); Oxfam and Save the
Children (£1,000 each); and Action
Research, Age Concern, Camphill
Village Trust (Croft Community),
Live Music Now, Mercy Ships,
NSPCC, Shelter and Yorkshire Young
Musicians (£500 each).

Exclusions

No grants to individuals. No grants
for buildings or for upkeep and
preservation of places of worship.

Applications

In writing to the correspondent.
Applications will not be
acknowledged unless an sae is
supplied. Telephone applications are
not accepted.

Premierquote Ltd

Jewish, general

£560,000 (2009/10)

Beneficial area

Worldwide.

18 Green Walk, London NW4 2AJ
Tel: 0207 247 8376
Correspondent: D Last, Trustee
Trustees: D Last; Mrs L Last; H Last;
M Weisenfeld.
CC Number: 801957

Information available

Accounts were on file at the Charity
Commission, but without a list of
grants.

The trust was established in 1985 for
the benefit of Jewish organisations,
the relief of poverty and general
purposes. In 2009/10 the trust had
assets of £7 million and an income of
£897,000. Grants to organisations
totalled £560,000.

A full list of beneficiaries for the year
was not included with the accounts,
however, previous beneficiaries have
included: Achisomoch, Belz Yeshiva
Trust, Beth Jacob Grammar School
for Girls Ltd, British Friends of
Shuvu, Friends of Ohel Moshe,
Friends of Senet Wiznitz, Friends of
the United Institutions of Arad, Kehal
Chasidel Bobov, Meadowgold
Limited, Menorah Primary School,
North West London Communal
Mikvah and Torah Vedaas Primary
School.

Applications

In writing to the correspondent.

Premishlaner Charitable Trust

Jewish

£119,000 (2009/10)

Beneficial area

UK and worldwide.

186 Lordship Road, London N16 5ES
Tel: 020 8802 4449
Correspondent: C M Margulies,
Trustee
Trustees: C Freudenberger;
C M Margulies.
CC Number: 1046945

Information available

Accounts were available from the
Charity Commission.

This trust was founded in 1995; its
principal objects are:

- to advance orthodox Jewish
  education
- to advance the religion of the
  Jewish faith in accordance with the
  Orthodox practice
- the relief of poverty.

In 2009/10 the trust's assets stood at
£422,000 and it had an income of
£126,000. It awarded grants totalling
£119,000.

Beneficiaries included: Chen
Vochessed Vrachamim (£19,000);
Tchabe Kollel (£18,000); Marcaz
Hayahalom (£12,000); Beis Rochel
(£10,000); Yeshiva and Cong
Machizikei (£7,000); and CMZ
(£5,000).

Other donations under £5,000 each
totalled £47,000.

Applications

In writing to the correspondent.

The Primrose Trust

General

£75,000 (2009/10)

Beneficial area

UK.

5 Callaghan Square, Cardiff CF10 5BT
Tel: 02920 264394

Correspondent: Steven Allan
Trustees: M G Clark; Susan Boyes-Korkis.
CC Number: 800049

Information available

Accounts were available from the Charity Commission.

The trust was established in 1986 with general charitable purposes. In 2009/10 the trust had assets of £3.5 million and an income of £121,000. Grants were made to eight organisations totalling £75,000.

Grant recipients were: Badger Trust (£20,000); Animal Health Trust (£15,000); Langford Trust and Sea Shepherd (£10,000 each); and Barn Owl Trust, Community of the Holy Fire Loving Caring Members, Scottish Badgers and Vale Wildlife Hospital (£5,000 each).

Exclusions

Grants are given to registered charities only.

Applications

In writing to the correspondent, including a copy of the most recent accounts. The trust does not wish to receive telephone calls.

Princess Anne's Charities

Children, medical, welfare, general

£107,000 (2009/10)

Beneficial area

UK.

Buckingham Palace, London SW1A 1AA
Correspondent: Capt. N Wright
Trustees: Hon. M T Bridges; Vice Admiral T J H Laurence; B Hammond.
CC Number: 277814

Information available

Accounts were available from the Charity Commission, but without a list of grants.

This trust has general charitable purposes, with a preference for

registered charities in which the Princess Royal has a particular interest. In 2009/10 the trust had assets of £4.9 million and an income of £133,000. Grants were made to 30 organisations totalling £107,000, broken down as follows:

Social welfare	12	£41,000
Children and youth	3	£25,000
Medical	9	£24,000
Armed forces	4	£10,000
Environment and wildlife	2	£7,500
General	–	–

Previous beneficiaries have included: Butler Trust, the Canal Museum Trust, Cranfield Trust, Dogs Trust, Dorothy House Foundation, Durrell Wildlife Conservation Trust, the Evelina Children's Hospital Appeal, Farms for City Children, Farrer and Co Charitable Trust, Fire Services National Benevolent Fund, the Home Farm Trust, Intensive Care Society, International League for the Protection of Horses, King Edward VIII Hospital-Sister Agnes, National Autistic Society, Minchinhampton Centre for the Elderly, Mission to Seafarers, Princess Royal Trust for Carers, REDR, RYA Sailability, Save the Children Fund, Scottish Field Studies Association, Scottish Motor Neurone Disease Association, SENSE, Spinal Injuries Association, Strathcarron Hospice, Transaid, London Bombing Relief Charitable Fund, Victim Support, VSO and Women's Royal Navy Benevolent Trust.

Exclusions

No grants to individuals.

Applications

The trust states:

> The trustees are not anxious to receive unsolicited general applications as these are unlikely to be successful and only increase the cost of administration of the charity. The trustees generally make awards only to those charities of which the Princess is Patron. Other appeals are considered on a case by case basis, but only very few are successful.

The Priory Foundation

Health and social welfare, especially children

£741,000 (2007)

Beneficial area

UK.

c/o Cavendish House, 18 Cavendish Square, London W1G 0PJ
Correspondent: The Trustees
Trustees: N W Wray; L E Wray; T W Bunyard; D Poutney.
CC Number: 295919

Information available

Last accounts available at the Charity Commission website were for 2007.

The trust was established in 1987 to make donations to charities and appeals that directly benefit children.

In 2007 it had assets of £1.9 million and an income of £143,000. Grants totalled £741,000.

There were 46 grants listed in the accounts of £1,000 or more. Beneficiaries included: Saracens Foundation (£34,000); Infer Trust and Ovarian Cancer Action (£30,000 each); London Borough of Barnet (£29,000); Wellbeing (£25,000); Arundel Castle Cricket Foundation (£24,000); Watford Palace Theatre (£21,000); Get-A-Head Appeal (£19,000); Barnet CAB (£6,500); Barnet Primary Care NHS Trust (£3,400); Children for Peace (£2,500); Disability Aid Fund (£1,000); Tim Parry Jonathan Ball Foundation for Peace and Dame Vera Lynn Trust (£2,500 each); and Mill Hill School (£1,000).

Applications

In writing to the correspondent.

Prison Service Charity Fund

General

£111,000 (2010)

Beneficial area
UK.

The Lodge, 8 Derby Road, Garstang, Preston PR3 1EU
Tel: 01995 604997
Email: bob@pscf.co.uk
Website: www. prisonservicecharityfund.co.uk
Correspondent: The Trustees
Trustees: A N Joseph, Chair; P Ashes; J Goldsworthy; P McFall; C F Smith; K Wingfield MBE; J White MBE.
CC Number: 801678

Information available
Full accounts were available from the Charity Commission website.

In 2010 the fund's assets stood at £643,000. It had an income of £182,000 and made 188 grants totalling £111,000, the majority of which were for less than £1,000 each.

Grant beneficiaries included: Motor Neurone Association and British Disabled (£2,000) Velindre Hospital Cancer Centre (£1,600); Legacy Rainbow House, Cancer Research UK, Villa Real Special School (£1,000 each); Anthony Nolan Appeal (£800); Rainbow Children's Hospice (£700); Robbie Jones Appeal (£630); Macmillan Cancer Support, Help for Heroes and Scope (£500 each); M.I.N.D (£350) and Rowan Park Special School (£150).

Applications
The trust does not accept outside applications – the applicant must be a member of staff.

The Puebla Charitable Trust

Community development work, relief of poverty

£371,000 (2009/10)

Beneficial area
Worldwide.

Ensors, Cardinal House, 46 St Nicholas Street, Ipswich IP1 1TT
Tel: 01473 220 022
Correspondent: The Clerk
Trustees: J Phipps; M A Strutt.
CC Number: 290055

Information available
Accounts were available from the Charity Commission.

The trust has stated that: 'At present, the council limits its support to charities which assist the poorest sections of the population and community development work – either of these may be in urban or rural areas, both in the UK and overseas.'

Grants are normally in the region of £5,000 to £20,000, with support given over a number of years where possible. Most of the trust's income is therefore already committed, and the trust rarely supports new organisations.

In 2009/10 the trust's assets stood at £215 million and an income of £102,000. Grants were made to nine organisations totalling £371,000.

Beneficiaries were : Child Poverty Action Group, Family Action Group, Shelter and South West London Law Centres (£60,000 each); Action on Disability and Development and Mines Advisory Group (£45,000 each); SOS Sahel and Donald Woods Trust (£20,000 each); and Chikupira (£1,000).

Exclusions
No grants for capital projects, religious institutions, research or institutions for people who are disabled. Individuals are not supported and no scholarships are given.

Applications
In writing to the correspondent. The trustees meet in July. The trust is unable to acknowledge applications.

The Richard and Christine Purchas Charitable Trust

Medical research, medical education and patient care

£9,000 (2009/10)

Beneficial area
UK.

46 Hyde Park Gardens Mews, London W2 2NX
Tel: 0207 580 2448
Correspondent: Daniel Auerbach, Trustee
Trustees: Daniel Auerbach; Mrs Pauline Auerbach; Dr Douglas Rossdale; Robert Auerbach.
CC Number: 1083126

Information available
Basic information taken from the Charity Commission website.

Registered with the Charity Commission in October 2000, in 2009/10 this trust had an income and total expenditure of almost £9,000.

Previously the trust has part-funded the post of Consultant Speech Therapist at the Charing Cross Hospital in association with Macmillan Cancer Relief.

Applications
In writing to the correspondent.

The Pyne Charitable Trust

Christian, health

£135,000 (2010)

Beneficial area
UK and overseas, particularly Malawi, Moldova, Slovakia and Ukraine.

26 Tredegar Square, London E3 5AG
Tel: 0208 980 4853
Correspondent: Pauline Brennan, Secretary

Trustees: Michael Brennan; Pauline Brennan; Mike Mitchell.
CC Number: 1105357

Information available

Accounts were on file at the Charity Commission.

In 2010 the trust had an income of £154,000 mostly from voluntary income. Grants to organisations totalled £135,000. Assets stood at £35,000.

Grant beneficiaries included: Good Shepherd Mission (£60,000); Affordable Christian Housing Association (£21,000); Disasters Emergency Appeal (Haiti) (£20,000); Great Ormond Street Children's Hospital (£15,000); NSPCC (£10,000); Teen Challenge London (£7,000); and Crossroads Christian Housing Association (£1,000).

Applications

Ongoing support appears to be given to projects selected by the trustees.

The Queen Anne's Gate Foundation

Educational, medical and rehabilitative charities and those that work with underprivileged areas of society

£809,000 (2009/10)

Beneficial area

UK and overseas.

WillcoxLewis LLP, The Old Coach House, Bergh Apton, Norwich, Norfolk NR15 1DD
Correspondent: The Trustees
Trustees: N T Allan; J M E Boyer; G Lewis.
CC Number: 1108903

Information available

Accounts were available from the Charity Commission. The foundation's 2009/10 annual report states:

The foundation seeks to support projects and charities within the following broad criteria. It seeks to make a contribution that is meaningful in the context of the project/charity with which it is working. It tries to focus in particular on projects which might be said to make potentially unproductive lives productive. This tends to mean a bias towards educational, medical and rehabilitative charities and those that work with underprivileged areas of society. There is an attempt to focus a significant proportion of donations on Asia, Malawi and the UK.

In 2009/10 the foundation had an income of £185,000, mostly from voluntary income. Donations to other charities totalled £809,000. The sum of £3.6 million was carried forward at year end.

Beneficiaries included: Merlin (£80,000); St Mungo's (£50,000); English National Opera (£35,000); Policy Exchange and Families for Children (adoption) (each £30,000); World Medical Fund and Udanum Karangal (orphanage) (each £25,000); Blue Sky (£12,000); and Hackney Music Development Trust (£10,000).

Applications

In writing to the correspondent.

Quercus Trust

Arts, general

£131,000 (2009/10)

Beneficial area

UK.

Chantrey Vellacott DFK, Russell Square House, 10–12 Russell Square, London WC1B 5LF
Tel: 020 7509 9000
Correspondent: Chris Jones, Trust Administrator
Trustees: Lady Angela Bernstein; Kate E Bernstein.
CC Number: 1039205

Information available

Full accounts were available from the Charity Commission website.

In February 1999 the trustees declared by deed that distributions would in future be directed principally (but not exclusively) to the arts and any other objects and purposes which seek to further public knowledge, understanding and appreciation of any matters of artistic, aesthetic, scientific or historical interest.

In 2009/10 the trust had assets of £5.2 million and an income of £128,000. Grants were made to 14 organisations totalling £131,000.

The largest grant of £70,000 went to Dance UK.

Other beneficiaries were: Royal National Theatre (£20,000); Royal Opera House, Covent Garden and Kettle's Yard (£10,000 each); Royal Opera House Foundation (£7,500); Artichoke Trust (£5,000); British Friends of the Art Museums of Israel (£2,000); ORH Charitable Fund (£1,500); British Humanist Association, Donmar Warehouse Projects, Gala for Africa, Tate Foundation and Young Vic Theatre Company (£1,000 each); and Hofesh Shechter Company (£500).

Exclusions

No grants to individuals.

Applications

In writing to the correspondent, but please note, the trust has previously stated: 'All of the trust's funds are currently earmarked for existing projects.' In order to keep administrative costs to a minimum, the trust does not reply to any unsuccessful applicants.

R J M Charitable Trust

Jewish

£218,000 (2009/10)

Beneficial area

UK and worldwide.

84 Upper Park Road, Salford M7 4JA
Tel: 0161 720 8787
Email: joshua@broomwell.com
Correspondent: Joshua Rowe, Trustee
Trustees: Joshua Rowe; Michelle Rowe.
CC Number: 288336

Information available

Accounts were available from the Charity Commission.

In 2009/10 the trust had assets of £102,000 and an income of £201,000. Grants were made to 63 organisations totalling £218,000.

Beneficiaries of the largest grants included: UJIA (£100,000); Kings David (£50,000); KD AD Min (£19,000); and CRT (£10,000).

Beneficiaries of smaller grants included: CST and Aish Hatorah (£5,000 each); North Salford Synagogue (£3,300); Broughton Park Primary School (£2,500); Policy Exchange (£2,000); Henry Jackson Society, Central Region Chaplaincy Board and Friends of Bnei Akiva (£1,000 each); Sterecourt (£704); Reshet (£300); Manchester Jewish Museum (£150); Jerusalem Educational Trust (£100); and Yeshiva (£50).

Applications

In writing to the correspondent.

R S Charitable Trust

Jewish, welfare

£280,000 (2009/10)

Beneficial area

UK.

138 Stamford Hill, London N16 6QT
Correspondent: Max Freudenberger, Trustee
Trustees: Harvey Freudenberger; Michelle Freudenberger; Stuart Freudenberger; Max Freudenberger.
CC Number: 1053660

Information available

Accounts were available from the Charity Commission.

Established in 1996, this trust states that it supports Jewish organisations and other bodies working towards the relief of poverty.

In 2009/10 the trust had assets of £1.8 million and an income of £611,000. Grants were made totalling £280,000. A full list of beneficiaries was not included in the annual reports.

Previous beneficiaries have included British Friends of Tshernobil, Forty Ltd, NRST, Society of Friends of the

Torah, Talmud Hochschule, Viznitz, Yeshiva Horomo and Yeshivas Luzern.

Applications

In writing to the correspondent.

The R V W Trust

Music education and appreciation

£330,000 (2010)

Beneficial area

UK.

7–11 Britannia Street, London WC1X 9JS
Email: helen@rvwtrust.org.uk
Website: www.rvwtrust.org.uk
Correspondent: Ms Helen Faulkner, Administrator
Trustees: Hugh Cobbe, Chair; Dr Michael Kennedy; The Lord Armstrong of Ilminster; Andrew Hunter Johnston; Sir John Manduell; Jeremy Dale Roberts; John Axon-Musicians Benevolent Fund.
CC Number: 1066977

Information available

Accounts were available from the Charity Commission.

The trust's current grant-making policies are as follows:
1   To give assistance to British composers who have not yet achieved a national reputation.
2   To give assistance towards the performance and recording of music by neglected or currently unfashionable 20th century British composers, including performances by societies and at festivals which include works by such composers in their programmes.
3   To assist UK organisations that promote public knowledge and appreciation of 20th and 21st century British music.
4   To assist education projects in the field of music.
5   To support post-graduate students of composition taking first masters degrees at British universities and conservatoires.

In 2010 the trust's assets stood at £1.4 million with an income of £386,000. Grants were made totalling £330,000, broken down as follows:

Public performance	68	£136,000
Music festivals	21	£65,800
Public education	26	£119,000
Education grants	12	£30,000

Grant beneficiaries included: Vaughan Williams Memorial Library/ English Folk Dance & Song Society (£25,000); Park Lane Group (£15,000); Huddersfield Contemporary Music Festival (£12,000); Royal Philharmonic Society Composition Prize (£7,500); Scottish Opera, NMC, New London Orchestra and English Touring Opera (£5,000 each) and Artisan Trio, Sound and Buxton Festival (£2,500 each).

Exclusions

No grants for local authority or other government-funded bodies, nor degree courses, except first Masters' degrees in musical composition. No support for dance or drama courses. No grants for workshops without public performance, private vocal or instrumental tuition or the purchase or repair of musical instruments. No grants for concerts that do not include music by 20th and 21st century composers or for musicals, rock, pop, ethnic, jazz or dance music. No grants for the construction or restoration of buildings. The trust is not able to make grants towards the music of Ralph Vaughan Williams.

Applications

All potential applicants should contact the trust for further details of current grant-making policy and details of how to apply by emailing the secretary. The trust holds three main grant-making meetings a year. Closing dates for applications are 2 January, 1 May and 1 September. Applicants are notified of the results approximately 8 weeks after these dates.

Common applicant mistakes

'Failing simple eligibility criteria.'

The Monica Rabagliati Charitable Trust

Children, humanitarian, medical, general

£52,000 (2009/10)

Beneficial area

UK.

S G Hambros Bank Limited, Norfolk House, 31 St James's Square, London W1Y 4JR
Tel: 0207 597 3060
Website: www.rabagliati.org.uk
Correspondent: Shirley Baines, Administrator
Trustees: S G Hambros Trust Company Limited; R L McLean
CC Number: 1086368

Information available

Accounts were available from the Charity Commission.

This trust was registered with the Charity Commission in April 2001. It makes grants in support of organisations that focus on the alleviation of child suffering and deprivation. The trust also supports humanitarian and medical causes and has stated: 'The trustees have decided to prioritise small/medium sized organisations where possible.'

In 2009/10 the trust had assets of over £1.8 million and an income of £44,000. Grants to 17 organisations were made totalling £52,000

Beneficiaries included: Rwanda Aid and St Joseph Priestly Scholarships (£10,000 each); The Africa Foundation and U Turn (£5,000 each); International Childcare Trust (£3,000); Hereford Cathedral (£2,500); Dream Makers, Down Syndrome International Swimming Organisation and Everychild (£2,000 each); FORWARD (£1,000); and The Warfield Churches for the Bethany Project (£500).

Applications

The trustees report for 2009/10 states: 'The charity does not solicit applications but considers all relevant applications and the trustees give any such applications fair consideration.'

The Radcliffe Trust

Music, crafts, conservation

£334,000 (2009/10)

Beneficial area

UK.

6 Trull Farm Buildings, Tetbury, Gloucestershire GL8 8SQ
Tel: 01285 841900
Email: radcliffe@thetrustpartnership.com
Website: www.theradcliffetrust.org
Correspondent: Belinda Hunt, Correspondent
Trustees: Felix Warnock, Chair; Sir Henry Aubrey-Fletcher; Lord Balfour of Burleigh; Christopher Butcher; Mary Ann Sieghart.
CC Number: 209212

Information available

Accounts were available from the Charity Commission.

The Radcliffe Trust was established in 1714 as a charitable trust under the will of Dr. John Radcliffe, the most eminent physician of his day. The will was provided for a permanent endowment, and the income is used exclusively for charitable purposes.

By his will, Dr. Radcliffe directed his Trustees to spend £40,000 on building a library, and today the Radcliffe Camera is one of Oxford's architectural glories. The trustees subsequently built two other important Oxford landmarks, the Radcliffe Observatory and the Radcliffe Infirmary, precursor of the modern John Radcliffe Hospital. In 1970 the agricultural holdings which Dr. Radcliffe had bought in 1713 were acquired to become the new town of Milton Keynes, leaving the trustees with a substantial endowment and increased income.

Today the trust has a policy of making grants principally in two sectors: Music and Heritage & Crafts. The following information on these two programmes is taken from the trust's website:

Music

The Radcliffe Trust supports classical music performance and training especially chamber music, composition and music education. Particular interests within music education are music for children and adults with special needs, youth orchestras and projects at secondary and higher levels, including academic research.

Craft

The Radcliffe Trust supports the development of the skills, knowledge and experience that underpin the UK's traditional cultural heritage and crafts sectors. This includes support for craft and conservation training, for practical projects and for strategic projects which demonstrate clear benefits to individuals and to the sector. However, the Trust remains committed to flexible, open and inclusive grant-giving and will consider other projects, should they fall broadly within its remit. The Radcliffe Trust wishes to promote standards of excellence through all its support.

Applications are considered under two headings:
▪ Heritage
▪ Crafts.

In 2009/10 it had assets of £13.7 million, and an income of £406,000. Grants were made totalling £334,000, broken down as follows:

Heritage and Crafts	38	£209,000
Music	32	£122,000
Miscellaneous	2	£2,000

The Allegri String Quartet (£22,000); Monastery of St Francis & Gorton Trust and National Library of Scotland (£15,000 each); Edward Barnsley Education Trust (£12,500 University of Oxford Bodleian Library (£12,000); Scottish Lime Centre (£10,000); The Bronte Society (£9,000); Clerkenwell Green Association (£8,000); Weald and Downland Open Air Museum and Church Buildings Council (£7,500 each); University of Nottingham (£6,000); English National Opera, Guideposts Trust, Halle Concerts Society, Kettles Yard and Music in Country Churches (£5,000 each); Lake District Summer Music and Leicestershire Chorale (£2,000 each); Dante Quartet (£1,000); and St Bartholomew's Hospital (£600).

For full details of the trust's guidelines please visit its website.

Exclusions

No grants to individual applicants. No retrospective grants are made, nor for deficit funding, core costs, general appeals or endowment funds. No new building appeals.

Applications

The trustees meet twice yearly to oversee the charity's activities and to make decisions on grants. The Trust works with specialist advisers in each of its main sectors of activity: Mrs Sally Carter, Music Adviser and Ms Carole Milner, Heritage & Crafts Adviser. There is also a Music Panel and a Heritage & Crafts Committee which each meet twice a year to consider applications. The day-to-day running of the Trust's financial and administrative affairs and processing of grant applications is undertaken by The Trust Partnership.

How to apply

Please note that it is advisable to submit an application well in advance of the deadline.

- **Music deadline:** January 31st for the June Trustee meeting; August 31st for the December Trustee meeting.
- **Heritage & Crafts deadline:** February 28th for the June Trustee meeting; August 31st for the December Trustee meeting.

All applications must include:

- a cover letter, which should include official address, telephone number, email address and charity registration number. The letter should be headed with the project title and the applicant should make clear his/her position in the charity. Please note that this letter should NOT include information on the project itself as this should be within the grant request.
- no more than three pages outlining the proposal and the specific request to the Trust. This should be structured as follows:
  - the project title
  - a summary of the request in no more than 40 words
  - the timing of the project
  - the project background and description

- a budget including a financial breakdown and total cost of the project as well as other income secured or requested and from what sources
- the amount requested either as a one-off or recurrent grant
- an indication of past grants from the Radcliffe Trust (year, amount and purpose)

- other relevant supporting information, although applicants should be aware that this may not be circulated to Trustees.

The cover letter and grant request should be emailed to the Administrator as Word or Excel documents and a hard copy also sent by post.

The Bishop Radford Trust

Church of England

£319,000 (2009/10)

Beneficial area

UK.

Devonshire House, 1 Devonshire Street, London W1W 5DR
Correspondent: The Secretary
Trustees: Stephen Green; Janian Green; Suzannah O'Brien; Ruth Dare.
CC Number: 1113562

Information available

Accounts were available from the Charity Commission.

The trust was set up in 2006 to help 'promote the work of the Christian church in a manner consistent with the doctrines and principles of the Church of England'. During 2009/10 the trust held assets of £4.3 million, received income of £812,000, mostly from donations, and made grants for church related projects totalling £319,000.

Beneficiaries included: Anglican Investment Agency Trust (£130,000); Diocese of Liverpool (£45,000); International Needs (£40,000); Save the Children (£33,000); Diocese of London (£20,000); and Cambourne Parish (£5,000).

Applications

In writing to the correspondent.

The Rainford Trust

Social welfare, general

£141,000 (2009/10)

Beneficial area

Worldwide, with a preference for areas in which Pilkington plc have works and offices, especially St Helens and Merseyside.

c/o Pilkington plc, Prescot Road, St Helens, Merseyside WA10 3TT
Tel: 01744 20574
Email: rainfordtrust@btconnect.com
Correspondent: W H Simm, Secretary
Trustees: Dr F Graham; Mrs A J Moseley; H Pilkington; Lady Pilkington; D C Pilkington; S D Pilkington; Mrs I Ratiu; Mrs L F Walker.
CC Number: 266157

Information available

Accounts were available from the Charity Commission.

The trust's accounts stated that its objectives are to: 'apply money for charitable purposes and to charitable institutions within the St Helens MBC area, and other places in the UK or overseas where Pilkington has employees. This does not prejudice the trustees' discretion to help charities that operate outside those areas.'

Further to this the trust's charitable purposes are to support:

- the relief of poverty, the aged, the sick, helpless and disabled, and the unemployed.
- the advancement of education including the arts, and other purposes with wide benefit for the community such as environmental and conservation projects.

In 2009/10 the trust had assets of £6.7 million and an income of £147,000, generated from investments. Grants were made totalling £141,000 and were broken down as following:

Education	20	£60,000
Welfare	48	£42,000
Humanities	6	£25,000
Medical	11	£13,000
Environmental	2	£1,500

Beneficiaries included: The Citadel Arts Centre and Hope Academy (£20,000 each); Clonter Opera (£16,000); WASOT UK (£5,000); Hand in Hand (£2,500); National M E Centre (£2,000); The Arkwright Scholarship Trust and International Spinal Research Trust (£1,000 each); and Raynauds and Scleroderma Association (£500).

Exclusions

Funding for the arts is restricted to St Helens only. Applications from individuals for grants for educational purposes will be considered only from applicants who are normally resident in St Helens.

Applications

On a form available from the correspondent. Applications should be accompanied by a copy of the latest accounts and cost data on projects for which funding is sought. Applicants may apply at any time. Only successful applications will be acknowledged.

Common applicant mistakes

'Not being concise enough and providing too much irrelevant information. Failing to provide up to date annual reports and accounts.'

The Peggy Ramsay Foundation

Writers and writing for the stage

£191,000

Beneficial area

British Isles.

Harbottle and Lewis Solicitors, Hanover House, 14 Hanover Square, London W1S 1HP
Tel: 020 7667 5000
Fax: 020 7667 5100
Email: laurence.harbottle@harbottle.com

Website: www.peggyramsayfoundation.org
Correspondent: G Laurence Harbottle, Trustee
Trustees: G Laurence Harbottle; Simon P H Callow; Michael Codron; Sir David Hare; John Tydeman; Harriet Walter; Tamara C Harvey; Mr Neil Adleman; Mr Rupert J Rhymes.
CC Number: 1015427

Information available

Accounts were obtained from the Charity Commission website. The trust also has a useful website.

This trust was established in 1992, in accordance with the will of the late Peggy Ramsay. The foundation's website gives the following background information:

> Peggy Ramsay was one of the best-known play agents in the United Kingdom during the second half of the twentieth century. When she died in 1991 her estate was left for charitable purposes to help writers and writing for the stage.

The objects of the trust are:

- the advancement of education by the encouragement of the art of writing
- the relief of poverty among those practising the arts, together with their dependants and relatives, with special reference to writers
- Any charitable purpose which may, in the opinion of the trustees, achieve, assist in, or contribute to, the achievement of these objectives.

Grants are made to:

- writers who have some writing experience who need time to write and cannot otherwise afford to do so
- companies which might not otherwise be able to find, develop or use new work
- Projects which may facilitate new writing for the stage.

The main priority of the trust is to support semi-professional writers who fulfil the trust's application criteria. The trust also supports organisations and projects, which they review annually. Please visit the trust's website for further information.

In 2010 the trust had assets of £5 million and an income of

£229,000. Grants were made totalling £191,000, of which £182,000 was distributed to 94 individuals.

Organisational beneficiaries included: Clean Break Theatre (£5000); Definitely Theatre (£2,500); Society of Authors (£1,500).

Exclusions

No grants are made for productions or writing not for the theatre. Adaptations and plays intended primarily for younger audiences are accepted only in special circumstances which imply wider originality. Commissioning costs are often considered as part of production costs. Course fees are not considered. Aspiring writers without some production record are not usually considered.

Applications

Applications should be made in writing, including:

- a short letter explaining the need, the amount hoped for and the way in which any grant would be spent
- a full CV not limited to writing
- separate sheet answers to these questions:
  1. when and where was the first professional production of a play of yours
  2. who produced the play which qualifies you for a grant
  3. when and where was your qualifying play produced, what was its run and approximate playing time and has it been revived
  4. for that production were the director and actors all professionals engaged with Equity contracts
  5. did the audience pay to attend

Trustees meet quarterly, but applications are considered between meetings. Allow six to eight weeks for a definitive answer. Urgent appeals can be considered at other times. All appeals are usually acknowledged.

Common applicant mistakes

'The fact that they are not qualified because they had not previously had a play professionally produced for an adult audience.'

The Joseph and Lena Randall Charitable Trust

General

£96,000 (2009/10)

Beneficial area
Worldwide.

Europa Residence, Place des Moulins, Monte-Carlo MC98 000
Tel: 00377 9350 0382
Correspondent: David Anthony Randall, Correspondent
Trustee: Rofrano Trustee Services Ltd.
CC Number: 255035

Information available
Accounts were available from the Charity Commission, but without a list of grants.

It is the policy of this trust to provide regular support to a selection of charities providing medical, educational and cultural facilities.

In 2009/10 the trust's assets totalled £1.9 million, it had an income of £103,000 and grants totalled £96,000.

Previous beneficiaries have included: Cancer Research UK, Community Security Trust, Diabetes UK, Downe House 21st Century Appeal, Holocaust Educational Trust, Jewish Care, Jewish Deaf Association, LPO, LSE Foundation, Motor Neurone Disease Association, ROH Foundation and Transplant Trust.

Exclusions
No grants to individuals.

Applications
The trust has stated that funds are fully committed and that it was 'unable to respond to the many worthy appeals'.

Common applicant mistakes
'Appeals not personally signed. Unfocused, prolix, unclear appeals from those that are too categorical.'

Ranworth Trust

General

£515,000 (2009/10)

Beneficial area
UK and developing countries, with a preference for East Norfolk.

The Old House, Ranworth, Norwich NR13 6HS
Website: www.ranworthtrust.org.uk
Correspondent: Hon. Jacquetta Cator, Trustee
Trustees: Hon. Jacquetta Cator; Charles Cator; Mark Cator.
CC Number: 292633

Information available
Accounts were obtained from the Charity Commission website. The trust has a very basic website.

This trust supports local registered charities in East Norfolk which are involved in care and education in the community and international charities with long-term commitment in providing technological initiative and support.

In 2009/10 the trust's assets stood at £4 million. It had an income of £168,000 and made grants to 25 organisations totalling £515,000.

The largest grant of £350,000 was given to Norfolk Community Foundation to establish The Ranworth Grassroots Fund. The aim of the fund is to support a wide range of charitable, voluntary and community activities across Norfolk.

Other beneficiaries included: Practical Action and Water Aid (£20,000 each); Cancer Research UK (£15,000); Sightsavers, Médecins Sans Frontières and BREAK (£10,000 each); Reach Foundation and Hope and Homes for Children (£5,000 each); Fairhaven CE VA Primary School – South Walsham (£3,500); Samaritans – Norfolk Branch (£2,000); and Mango Tree and Canine Partners for Independence (£1,000 each).

Exclusions
No grants to non-registered charities.

Applications
The trust's website states that it will not be considering any new applications until 2012.

The Fanny Rapaport Charitable Settlement

Jewish, general

Around £20,000

Beneficial area
North west England.

Kuit Steinart Levy Solicitors, 3 St Mary's Parsonage, Manchester M3 2RD
Correspondent: J S Fidler, Trustee
Trustees: J S Fidler; N Marks.
CC Number: 229406

Information available
Accounts had been received at the Charity Commission but were not available to view.

The trust supports mainly, but not exclusively, Jewish charities and health and welfare organisations, with a preference for the north west of England.

In 2009/10 the charity had both an income and expenditure of £22,000. Further information was not available.

Previous beneficiaries included Brookvale, Christie Hospital NHS Trust, Community Security Trust, Delamere Forest School, the Heathlands Village, King David Schools, Manchester Jewish Federation, South Manchester Synagogue, United Jewish Israel Appeal and World Jewish Relief.

Exclusions
No grants to individuals.

Applications
Trustees hold meetings twice a year in March/April and September/October with cheques for donations issued shortly thereafter. If the applicant does not receive a cheque by the end of April or October, the application

will have been unsuccessful. No applications are acknowledged.

The Ratcliff Foundation

General

£170,000 (2009/10)

Beneficial area

UK, with a preference for local charities in the Midlands, North Wales and Gloucestershire.

Woodlands, Earls Common road, Stock Green, Redditch B96 6TB
Tel: 01386 792116
Email: chris.gupwell@btinternet.com
Correspondent: Christopher J Gupwell, Secretary and Trustee
Trustees: David M Ratcliff, Chair; Edward H Ratcliff; Carolyn M Ratcliff; Gillian Mary Thorpe; James M G Fea; Christopher J Gupwell.
CC Number: 222441

Information available

Accounts were available from the Charity Commission.

The foundation was established in 1961, by Martin Rawlinson Ratcliff. Grants are made to any organisation that has charitable status for tax purposes.

In 2009/10 it had assets of £3.2 million and an income of £193,000. There were 76 grants made totalling £170,000, of which 54 were for £2,000 or more each.

Beneficiaries included: Avoncroft Museum of Historic Buildings and Multiple Births Foundation (£5,000 each); Harbury Village Hall (£4,000); Cottage and Rural Enterprises Ltd and White Ladies Aston PCC (£3,000 each); Focus Birmingham, Full House Furniture and Recycling Service Ltd and Gloucestershire Wildlife Trust (£2,000 each); and Colwyn Choral Society (£1,000).

There were 22 grants of less than £2,000 each that totalled £10,000.

Exclusions

No grants to individuals.

Applications

In writing to the correspondent.

Common applicant mistakes

'Applications by individuals. Grants to individuals are not permitted by the trust deed.'

The E L Rathbone Charitable Trust

Social work charities

£76,000 (2009/10)

Beneficial area

UK, with a strong preference for Merseyside.

Rathbone Investment Management Ltd, Port of Liverpool Building, Pier Head, Liverpool L3 1NW
Tel: 0151 236 6666
Correspondent: The Secretary
Trustees: J B Rathbone; Mrs S K Rathbone; Mrs V P Rathbone; R S Rathbone.
CC Number: 233240

Information available

Accounts were on file at the Charity Commission.

The trust has a special interest in social work charities. There is a strong preference for Merseyside with local beneficiaries receiving the major funding.

In 2009/10 the trust had assets of £1.9 million, which generated an income of £71,000. Grants were made to 47 organisation totalling £76,000.

Beneficiaries included: Sheila Kay Fund (£5,000); St Aidan's Catholic Primary and YKIDS (£3,000 each); Wirral Community Narrow Boat Trust (£2,000); Liverpool Cathedral Girls' Choir and Sanctuary Family Support (£1,500 each); Fairbridge in Merseyside and Friends of the Elderly (£1,000 each); and Hope Centre (£500).

Exclusions

No grants to individuals seeking support for second degrees.

Applications

In writing to the correspondent.

The Eleanor Rathbone Charitable Trust

Merseyside, women, 'unpopular causes'

£216,000 (2009/10)

Beneficial area

UK, with the major allocation for Merseyside; also international projects (Africa, the Indian Sub Continent, plus exceptionally Iraq and Palestine).

546 Warrington Road, Rainhill, Merseyside L35 4LZ
Email: eleanor.rathbone.trust@ tinyworld.co.uk
Correspondent: Mrs Liese Astbury, Administrator
Trustees: William Rathbone; Jenny Rathbone; Andrew Rathbone; Lady Morgan; Mark Rathbone.
CC Number: 233241

Information available

Full accounts were available from the Charity Commission.

The trust concentrates its support largely on the following:

- charities and charitable projects focused on Merseyside.
- charities benefiting women and unpopular and neglected causes but avoiding those with a sectarian interest.
- charities with which any of the trustees have a particular knowledge or association or in which it is thought Eleanor Rathbone or her father William Rathbone VI would have had a special interest.
- charities providing holidays for disadvantaged people from Merseyside.

International Grants

The trust also makes international grants which are governed by the following criteria:

- The trust will only consider projects from Africa, the Indian Sub Continent, plus exceptionally Iraq and Palestine.
- Applications will be considered only from small or medium sized charities.
- Projects must be sponsored and monitored by a UK based charity. In addition, projects must meet one or more of the following criteria: (i) they will benefit women or orphan children; (ii) they will demonstrate local involvement in scoping and delivery, except where skills required are not currently available e.g. eye surgeons in remote rural areas (iii) they will aim to repair the damage in countries recently ravaged by international or civil war; (iv) they will deliver clean water.

In 2009/10 the trust's assets stood at £7.4 million. It had an income of £267,000 and made grants totalling £216,000, which are broken down as follows:

Merseyside	60	£86,000
International	46	£52,000
National/Regional	34	£70,000
Holidays	10	£8,000

Most donations are on a one-off basis, although requests for commitments over two or more years are considered. Grants are made in the range £100 to £3,000 and exceptionally higher.

Beneficiaries included: Haven Project (£19,000); Queen's Nursing Institute (£15,000); Wirral Churches Arc Project (£5,000); Social Partnership; NMP Anti-racist trust (£3,000 each); St Gregory's Youth; Community Initiative; Somali Women's Group (£2,000 each); After Adoptio; Zero Centre (£1,500 each); Wells For India; Volunteer Reading Help; Barnstondale Centre (£1,000 each); Sunseed Tanzania Trust (£900); LCVS (£500); and Mary Seacole House (£300).

Exclusions

Grants are not made in support of: any activity which relieves a statutory authority of its obligations; individuals, unless (and only exceptionally) it is made through a charity and it also fulfils at least one of the other positive objects

mentioned above; overseas organisations without a sponsoring charity based in the UK.

The trust does not generally favour grants for running costs, but prefers to support specific projects, services or to contribute to specific developments.

Applications

There is no application form. The trust asks for a brief proposal for funding including costings, accompanied by the latest available accounts and any relevant supporting material. It is useful to know who else is supporting the project.

To keep administration costs to a minimum, receipt of applications is not usually acknowledged. Applicants requiring acknowledgement should enclose an sae.

Trustees currently meet three times a year on varying dates (contact the Administrator for information on the latest deadlines).

The Rayden Charitable Trust

Jewish

£45,000 (2009/10)

Beneficial area

UK.

c/o Beavis Morgan LLP, 82 St John Street, London EC1M 4JN
Tel: 020 7417 0417
Correspondent: The Trustees
Trustees: Shirley Rayden; Clive Rayden; Paul Rayden.
CC Number: 294446

Information available

Accounts were available from the Charity Commission.

In 2009/10 the trust had an income from Gift Aid of £46,000 and made grants totalling £45,000. Assets stood at £12,000.

Most grants are for under £500. Beneficiaries of these larger grants included: NWJDS (£7,000); Or Chadash (£6,500); Yesodey Hatorah (£3,000); Holocaust Education and Jewish Care (£2,500); and Central

London Mikveh and CTN Jewish Life (£1,000 each).

Applications

In writing to the correspondent.

The Roger Raymond Charitable Trust

Older people, education, medical

£209,000 (2009/10)

Beneficial area

UK (and very occasionally large, well-known overseas organisations).

Suttondene, 17 South Border, Purley, Surrey CR8 3LL
Tel: 020 8660 9133
Email: russell@pullen.cix.co.uk
Correspondent: R W Pullen, Trustee
Trustees: R W Pullen; M G Raymond.
CC Number: 262217

Information available

Accounts were available from the Charity Commission. The trust's 2009/10 annual report states:

> The Roger Raymond Charitable Trust owns 100% of the issued share capital of Shaw White Estates Limited whose principle business is that of property investment. Any profits attributable to the subsidiary undertaking are covenanted up to The Roger Raymond Charitable Trust.

In 2009/10 the trust had assets of £11.6 million and an income of £252,000. Grants totalled £209,000.

The principal beneficiary during the year, as in previous years, was Bloxham School, which received a donation of £184,000.

Other beneficiaries of grants over £2,000 and listed in the accounts were: Alzheimer's Society (£3,000); and DEC Haiti and Garvald West Linton (£2,000 each). Grants totalling £18,000 were also made but not listed in the accounts.

Exclusions

Grants are rarely given to individuals.

Applications

The trust stated that applications are considered throughout the year, although funds are not always available.

The Rayne Trust

Jewish organisations, older and young people and people disadvantaged by poverty or socially isolation

£102,000 (2009/10)

Beneficial area

Israel and UK.

Carlton House, 33 Robert Adam Street, London W1U 3HR
Correspondent: Tim Joss, Director
Trustees: Lady Jane Rayne; the Hon. Robert A Rayne.
CC Number: 207392

Information available

Accounts were available from the Charity Commission.

The Rayne Trust was established by Lord Rayne to support organisations in which its trustees (Lady Rayne and the Hon. Robert A Rayne) have a close personal interest.

The trust's mandate, as determined by the trustees, is to understand and engage with the needs of UK and Israeli society. The trust is involved in social bridge building, and looks for four main outcomes:

- Enlarging sympathies – increasing tolerance and understanding between communities and people of different backgrounds.
- Reduced exclusion – helping to bring people in from the margins of society.
- Reduced conflict in society – helping to heal divisions in society.
- New productive relationships – bringing unconnected people and organisations together to benefit society.

The trust's work is measured, as is that of its partnerships and social investments, by the degree to which each contributes to the four bridge building outcomes and:

- can have wider than just local application or is of national importance
- helps the most vulnerable or disadvantaged
- provides direct benefits to people and communities
- tackles neglected causes
- levers other funds and encourages the involvement of other organisations
- strives to achieve excellence.

In 2009/10 it had assets of £15.9 million and an income of £275,000. Grants were given to 66 organisations and totalled £102,000.

In the UK 3 grants of £10,000 or more were payable totalling £65,000. There was one grant relating to an Israel based charity of £42,000. Other grants of less than £10,000 totalled £8,000. Grants cancelled during the year totalled £13,000.

Beneficiaries included: Language as a Cultural Bridge and Mirkam/Nasij (£42,000); The Jewish Joint Distribution Committee (£40,000); UK Task Force on Arab Citizens of Israel (£15,000); and North London Hospice (£10,000).

Exclusions

No grants to individuals or non-registered charities.

Applications

If you are considering applying to the trust you should first discuss your proposal with the Grants Manager at The Rayne Foundation (tel. 020 7487 9630).

The John Rayner Charitable Trust

General

£33,000 (2009/10)

Beneficial area

England, with a preference for Merseyside and Wiltshire.

Manor Farmhouse, Church Street, Great Bedwyn, Marlborough, Wiltshire SN8 3PE
Correspondent: Mrs J Wilkinson, Trustee
Trustees: Mrs J Wilkinson; Dr J M H Rayner; Louise McNeilage.
CC Number: 802363

Information available

Accounts were available from the Charity Commission.

This trust has general charitable purposes in the UK, with a preference for Merseyside and Wiltshire. Support is given to smaller organisations.

In 2009/10 the trust had assets of £791,000 and an income of £29,000. 11 grants were made totalling £33,000.

Grants were distributed in the following categories and amounts:

Medical	£10,000
Arts	£7,000
Disability	£6,000
Children	£5,000
General	£5,000

Beneficiaries were: Age UK, Marie Curie Cancer Care and Music in Hospitals (£4,000 each); ACIR Bowel Cancer Appeal, Blackheath Halls, Countryside Foundation for Education, Jubilee Sailing Trust, Theodora Children's Trust and Whizz-Kids (£3,000 each); Swindon Sea Cadet Unit (£2,000); and Gt Bedwyn School Association (£1,000).

Exclusions

No grants to individuals or non-registered charities.

Applications

In writing to the correspondent by 31 January each year. Trustees meet to allocate donations in February/March. Only successful applicants will be contacted. There are no application forms or guidelines.

Common applicant mistakes

'Individuals applying; applications made by email.'

Eva Reckitt Trust Fund

Welfare, relief-in-need, extension and development of education, victims of war

Around £50,000

Beneficial area
UK and overseas.

1 Somerford Road, Cirencester, Gloucestershire GL7 1TP
Email: davidbirch50@googlemail.com
Correspondent: David Birch, Trustee
Trustees: Anna Bunney; Chris Whittaker; David Birch; Diana Holliday.
CC Number: 210563

Information available
Accounts had been submitted to the Charity Commission, but were not available to view.

Registered in October 1962, in 2009 the trust had an income of £22,000 and a total expenditure of £52,000.

Previous beneficiaries included: Children of the Andes, Christian Engineers in Development, Computer Aid International, Crisis, Medical Foundation for the Care of Victims of Torture, One World Action, Orbis, Prisoners of Conscience Appeal Fund, Send a Cow, St John of Jerusalem Eye Hospital, St Mungo's, Stephen Lawrence Charitable Trust, Traidcraft, Water and Sanitation for the Urban Poor and World Development Movement.

Applications
In writing to the correspondent.

The Red Rose Charitable Trust

General with particular reference to educational expenses for students and ill health

£22,000 (2009/10)

Beneficial area
UK with a preference for Lancashire and Merseyside.

c/o Rathbones, Port of Liverpool Building, Pier Head, Liverpool L3 1NW
Correspondent: J N L Packer, Trustee
Trustees: James N L Packer; Jane L Fagan; Julian B Rathbone.
CC Number: 1038358

Information available
Accounts were available from the Charity Commission.

This trust was established in 1994. It has a preference for supporting charities working with older people and people who have physical or mental disabilities and providing education expenses of students whose parents or guardians cannot afford the same. Grants are also made to individuals within these categories.

In 2009/10 the trust had assets of almost £900,000 and an income of £34,000. Grants were made to 18 organisations totalling £22,000. All grants bar one were for £1,000.

Beneficiaries included: Liverpool Cathedral Centenary Fund (£5,000); and Brainwave, Clatterbridge Cancer Research Trust, Help the Aged, Make a Wish Foundation, Mango Tree, Sense and Sue Ryder Care (£1,000 each).

Applications
In writing to the correspondent.

The C A Redfern Charitable Foundation

General
£179,000 (2009/10)

Beneficial area
UK.

PricewaterhouseCoopers, 9 Greyfriars Road, Reading, Berkshire RG1 1JG
Correspondent: The Trustees
Trustees: Sir Robert Clark; William Maclaren; David Redfern; Terence Thornton; Simon Ward.
CC Number: 299918

Information available
Accounts were on file at the Charity Commission.

This foundation supports a wide range of organisations with some preference for those concerned with health and welfare. In 2009/10 the foundation had assets of £4.2 million, which generated an income of £157,000. Grants were made to 53 organisations totalling £179,000.

The largest grants went to: South Bucks Riding for the Disabled (£35,000); Saints and Sinners (£30,000); and White Ensign (£10,000).

Other beneficiaries included: Live Music Now, Reed School Foundation Appeal and Special Yoga Centre (£5,000 each); the Royal College of Surgeons (£2,500); Whitefield Development Trust (£1,000); and Motor Neurone Disease Association and Thames Valley Hospice (£500 each); and The Camphill Family and the Pasque Charity (£250 each).

Exclusions
No grants for building works or individuals.

Applications
The foundation does not accept unsolicited applications.

The Max Reinhardt Charitable Trust

Deafness, fine arts promotion

£32,000 (2009/10)

Beneficial area
UK.

Flat 2, 43 Onslow Square, London SW7 3LR
Correspondent: The Secretary to the Trustees
Trustees: Joan Reinhardt; Veronica Reinhardt; Magdalen Wade.
CC Number: 264741

Information available
Accounts were available from the Charity Commission.

The trust supports organisations benefiting people who are deaf and fine arts promotion. In 2009/10 the trust had assets of £732,000 and an income of £39,000. Grants were made to 26 charities totalling £32,000.

Beneficiaries include: Paintings in Hospitals (£20,000); The Art Room (£6,000); Auditory Verbal UK and Modern Art Museum, Oxford (£1,000 each); Deafblind UK (£250); and Dogs Trust, Friends of the Earth, National Trust, Thrive, West London Homeless, Young and Free and Zane (£100 each).

Exclusions
No grants to individuals.

Applications
In writing to the correspondent.

REMEDI

Medical research

£107,000 (2009/10)

Beneficial area
UK.

Elysium House, 126–128 New Kings Road, London SW6 4LZ
Tel: 020 7384 2929
Email: research@remedi.org.uk
Website: www.remedi.org.uk
Correspondent: Rosie Wait, Director
Trustees: James Moseley; Brian Winterflood; Dr Anthony K Clarke; Jerry Hansford; Prof Nick Bosanquet; Dr Adrian H M Heagerty; Michael Hines; Colin Maynard; Karin Russell; Dr Anthony B Ward.
CC Number: 1063359

Information available
Accounts were available from the Charity Commission.

Remedi provides funds for medical research projects in the UK, which it hopes will result in new rehabilitation procedures, improved medical equipment, services and facilities that dramatically improve the quality of life for babies, children and adults and make the journey from illness or disability back to a normal life a reality.

The trust receives most of its income from companies and other trusts, which is then given towards researchers carrying out innovative and original work who find it difficult to find funding from larger organisations. Grants are generally for one year, although funding for the second year is considered sympathetically and for a third year exceptionally. There is a preference for awarding a few sizeable grants rather than many smaller grants.

The medical research supported by the trust in rehabilitation and disability projects, often complete the 'incubator' or pilot study stage and this enables researchers to then seek funding from large organisations such as the Medical Research Council, who will then fund a much larger project to complete the studies which enable new advances in care for these diseases.

In 2009/10 the trust's assets stood at £213,000. It had an income of £130,000 and made grants totalling £107,000.

Previous beneficiaries include: Dr Brona McDowell et al – Musgrave Park Hospital, Belfast; Professor Lalit Kalra – Kings College London; and, Professor Nadina Lincoln – University of Nottingham.

Applications
Firstly, applicants should email a short summary of their project (two pages of A4), including a breakdown of costs, proposed start date and length of the research programme. If the project is considered of interest to the trustees they will request that a full application form be completed. Full applications are peer reviewed and, if successful, passed on to the trustees for a final decision at their biannual meetings (usually in June and December).

For full guidelines please visit the trust's website.

Common applicant mistakes
'They do not give enough detail about the benefit of the research nor the timeplan and project plan to support the application and validate the costs.'

The Rest Harrow Trust

Jewish, general

£45,000 (2009/10)

Beneficial area
UK.

c/o Portrait, Solicitors, 1 Chancery Lane, London WC2A 1LF
Tel: 020 7092 6990
Correspondent: Miss Judith S Portrait
Trustees: Mrs J B Bloch; Miss J S Portrait; H O N and V Trustee Limited; Dominic B Flynn.
CC Number: 238042

Information available
Accounts were available from the Charity Commission.

This trust was established in 1964, its main objectives are to distribute grants from its income for education, housing and to assist the deprived and the elderly.

In 2009/10 the trust had an income of £58,000 and made grants totalling £45,000. Its assets stood at £857,000. There were 216 grants made totalling £45,000, of which the vast majority were under £500 each.

The largest grants were those made to: Nightingale House, Pinhas Rutenberg Educational Trust and Weizmann UK (£2,000 each); and British Friends of the Hebrew University, Jewish Care and World Jewish Relief (£1,000 each).

Smaller grants included those made to: Magen David Adorn UK (£700); Canon Collins Trust, Council of Christians & Jews and Friends of Israel Educational Foundation (£500 each); Sightsavers International, Spiro Ark, St Christopher's Hospice, Barnardo's, Bath Institute of Medical Engineering (BIME), Blond Mclndoe Research Foundation, Book Aid International, Books Abroad, Bowel Disease Research Foundation, Brain Research Trust (£200 each); and Build Africa, Catch 22, Central & Cecil Housing Trust, Charity Search, ChildHope, Children's Adventure Farm Trust, Church Army and Church Housing Trust(£100 each).

Exclusions

No grants to non-registered charities or to individuals.

Applications

In writing to the correspondent. Applications are considered quarterly. Only submissions from eligible bodies are acknowledged.

The Rhododendron Trust

Overseas aid and development, social welfare and culture

£50,000 (2009/10)

Beneficial area

UK and overseas.

Cedar House, Sandbrook Business Park, Sandbrook Way, Rochdale OL11 1LQ
Correspondent: P E Healey, Trustee
Trustees: Peter Edward Healey; Dr Ralph Walker; Mrs Sarah Ray; Mrs Sarah Oliver.
CC Number: 267192

Information available

Accounts were available from the Charity Commission.

It is the current policy of the trustees to divide donations as follows: (i) 50% to charities whose work is primarily overseas; (ii) 40% for UK social welfare charities; and (iii) 10% for UK cultural activities.

In 2009/10 the trust had assets of £1.4 million and an income of £104,000. Grants of £500 or £1,000 are made generally to charities which have been supported in the past although a few new beneficiaries are included each year. In 2009/10 the trust made 85 grants totalling £50,000.

Grant recipients included: Cambodia Trust, Children in Crisis, Fauna and Flora International and Friends of Hlekweni (£1,000 each) and Beyond the Streets, Book Aid International, Brandon Centre, Contact the Elderly, Corrymeela, Crisis, Working with Massai, World Wildlife Fund and Zero Centre (£500 each).

Exclusions

The trust does not support medical research, individual projects, or local community projects in the UK.

Applications

In writing to the correspondent at any time. The majority of donations are made in March. Applications are not acknowledged.

Common applicant mistakes

'Individuals apply (we are only allowed to support trusts and do not like to support organisations such as Raleigh Trust in respect of an individual. Also we do not support medical research and these charities occasionally apply.'

Daisie Rich Trust

General

£49,000 to organisations (2009/10)

Beneficial area

UK, with a preference for the Isle of Wight.

The Hawthorns, School Lane, Arreton, Newport, Isle of Wight PO30 3AD
Tel: 07866 449 855
Email: daisierich@yahoo.co.uk
Correspondent: Mrs L Mitchell, Administrator
Trustees: Adrian H Medley, Chair; Ann C Medley; Maurice J Flux; David J Longford.
CC Number: 236706

Information available

Accounts were on file at the Charity Commission.

The trust makes grants to former employees, or their spouses, of Upward and Rich Limited. Further grants are made mainly to Isle of Wight institutions, charities and individuals.

In 2009/10 the trust had assets of £3.2 million and an income of £102,000. Grants totalled £82,000 and were distributed as follows:

Organisations	£49,000
Ex-employees of Upward and Rich Ltd	£32,000
Other individuals	£586

The largest grant again went to the Earl Mountbatten Hospice (£10,000).

Other beneficiaries included: Shanklin Voluntary Youth and Community Centre (£6,000); Isle of Wight RCC 'Helping Hands', Hampshire and Isle of Wight Air Ambulance and SSAFA Isle of Wight (£3,000 each); Isle of Wight Citizens Advice Bureau (£2,000); St Vincent's Care Home (£1,200); Macmillan Cancer Relief, Marie Curie Nurses and Parkinson's Disease Society (£1,000 each); Friends of Brading Roman Villa (£800); Fishbourne Sailability Club, Girls' Brigade 3rd Ryde Company and Challenge and Adventure (£500 each); and Isle of Wight Hospital Broadcasting Association (£250).

Applications

In writing to the correspondent. The trustees hold regular meetings to decide on grant applications and are assisted by information gathered by the administrator.

C B Richard Ellis Charitable Trust

General

£18,000 (2009/10)

Beneficial area

Unrestricted.

St Martin's Court, 10 Paternoster Row, London EC4M 7HP
Tel: 020 7182 3452
Correspondent: A C Naftis, Secretary to the Trustees
Trustees: Kevin Bramley; Matthew D Black; Michael J Prentice; Nick R Martel; Lena Patel; Nicholas E Compton.
CC Number: 299026

Information available

Accounts were available from the Charity Commission.

The aim of the trust is primarily to respond to clients of C B Richard Ellis Ltd requests for support and to provide sponsorship to staff who are personally involved in fundraising activities. The trust will also consider applications from any other party with whom C B Richard Ellis has a significant relationship.

In 2009/10 the trust had assets of £70,000 and an income of £76,000. Grants were made totalling £18,000, down significantly from £66,000 in 2008/09. Unfortunately, no explanation was given for the fall.

Donations were made to 89 organisations across a wide range of areas including health, welfare and overseas development. Beneficiaries included: Breast Cancer Care (£1,100); Richard House Children's Hospice (£930); British Heart Foundation (£720); Macmillan Cancer Support (£627); Help for Heroes (£525); Shelter (£290); Yorkhill Children's Foundation (£200); Scottish Community Foundation, Suffolk Historic Churches Trust, Land Aid and National Woodland Trust (£150 each); UNICEF (£100); Oxfam (£75); Veterans Aid (£50); and Rainbow Trust (£20).

Exclusions

Recognised charitable causes only. No grants to third parties, such as fundraising organisations or publication companies producing charity awareness materials.

Applications

In writing to the correspondent.

The trust stated that in recent years they have received as many as two hundred unsolicited requests for support that do not meet with the above donations criteria. Given the size of the trust, a response to such requests is not always possible.

The Violet M Richards Charity

Older people, ill health, medical research and education

£54,000 (2009/10)

Beneficial area

UK, with a preference for East Sussex, particularly Crowborough.

c/o Wedlake Bell, 52 Bedford Row, London WC1R 4LR
Tel: 020 7395 3155
Fax: 020 7395 3100
Email: chicks@wedlakebell.com
Correspondent: Charles Hicks, Secretary
Trustees: Mrs E H Hill; G R Andersen; C A Hicks; Mrs M Burt; Dr J Clements.
CC Number: 273928

Information available

Accounts were available from the Charity Commission.

The trust's objects are the relief of age and ill health, through the advancement of medical research (particularly into geriatric problems), medical education, homes and other facilities for older people and those who are sick. Applications from East Sussex, particularly the Crowborough area are favoured by the trustees. The trustees are happy to commit themselves to funding a research project over a number of years, including 'seed corn' projects.

In 2009/10 the trust had assets of £1.9 million and an income of £63,000. The only beneficiary organisation in this financial year was: Brain Research Trust (£54,000).

Exclusions

No support for individuals.

Applications

In writing to the correspondent, however the trust states in its accounts that the trustees 'prefer to be proactive with charities of their own choice, rather than reactive to external applications.' The trustees generally meet to consider grants twice a year in the spring and the autumn. There is no set format for applying and only successful applications are acknowledged. Due to the change of grant policy to focus on a smaller number of projects, external applications are unlikely to be successful and are therefore discouraged.

Common applicant mistakes

'Individuals who we do not help continue to apply despite publicity to the contrary. Applicants in fields where we are not interested also apply.'

The Clive Richards Charity

Churches, schools, arts, disability and poverty

£208,000 (2009/10)

Beneficial area

UK, with a preference for Herefordshire.

Lower Hope, Ullingswick, Herefordshire HR1 3JF
Tel: 01432 820557
Fax: 01432 820772
Correspondent: Peter Henry, Trustee
Trustees: Peter Henry; Clive Richards; Sylvia Richards.
CC Number: 327155

Information available

Accounts were available from the Charity Commission.

The trust gives predominantly to schools, churches and organisations which support disability and the arts. Help is also available to individuals, particularly those who suffer from disabilities.

In 2009/10 the trust had assets of £51,000 and an income of £311,000, which mostly came from donations. Grants were made to organisations totalling £208,000.

Beneficiaries included: the Hydosense Charitable Organisation – Hydosense Appeal (£123,000); Belmont Abbey General Fund (£22,000); the Mary Rose Appeal (£10,000); Welsh National Opera (£5,000); Royal National College for the Blind (£3,000); St Joseph's Church – Bromyard (£2,500); and Bishop Vesey's Grammar School (£1,000).

Applications
In writing to the correspondent. The trustees meet monthly to consider applications. Please note, the trust has previously stated that due to its resources being almost fully committed it is extremely selective in accepting any requests for funding.

Common applicant mistakes
'Applicants assume that the charity makes payments replacing benefits that the applicant might otherwise have obtained. Donations are made mainly to applicants in the local Herefordshire area.'

The Ripple Effect Foundation

General, particularly disadvantaged young people, the environment and overseas development
£200,000 (2009/10)

Beneficial area
UK, with a preference for the South West of England.

Marlborough Investment Consultants Ltd, Wessex House, Oxford Road, Newbury, Berkshire RG14 1PA
Tel: 01635 814 470

Correspondent: Caroline D Marks, Trustee
Trustees: Caroline D Marks, Chair; I R Marks; I S Wesley.
CC Number: 802327

Information available
Information taken from the Charity Commission website.

The accounts of this charity state:

> The objectives of the trustees are to support a range of charitable causes over a few years that meet their funding criteria. They proactively seek out projects that meet their criteria and do not respond to unsolicited applications.

In 2009/10 the trust had an income of £24,000 and a total expenditure of £204,000.

Previous beneficiaries included: the Devon Community Foundation to help identify and fund community initiatives which support vulnerable young people; the Network for Social Change which passed on to other organisations largely for environmental work, both in the UK and overseas; the Smart Justice campaign; and Homestart UK to assist 10 families in being able to access the West Devon Family Group.

Exclusions
No grants are made to individuals.

Applications
The trust states that it does not respond to unsolicited applications.

Common applicant mistakes
'That they apply unsolicited. We do not accept, respond to or acknowledge unsolicited applications.'

The Sir John Ritblat Family Foundation

Jewish, general
£270,000 (2009/10)

Beneficial area
UK.

Baker Tilly, 1st Floor, 46 Clarendon Road, Watford WD17 1JJ
Tel: 01923 816400
Correspondent: The Clerk

Trustees: Sir John Ritblat; N S J Ritblat; C B Wagman; J W J Ritblat.
CC Number: 262463

Information available
Full accounts were available from the Charity Commission website.

In 2009/10 the trust had assets of £715,000 and an income of £56,000. Grants were made to 25 organisations totalling £270,000.

Beneficiaries included: Weizman UK (£60,000); Eton College (£50,000); The Wallace Collection (£45,000); London Business School (£13,000); The Royal Opera House Foundation (£9,000); Tate Foundation (£6,000); International Students House (£5,000); Tzedek (£500); and Venice in Peril (£200).

The trust makes grants primarily to long-established organisations. Please note, the trust was previously known as The John Ritblat Charitable Trust No. 1.

Exclusions
No grants to individuals.

Applications
The trust has previously stated that its funds are fully committed.

The River Farm Foundation

General, older people, young people, animal welfare and the environment
£10,000 (2009/10)

Beneficial area
UK.

The Old Coach House, Bergh Apton, Norwich NR15 1DD
Tel: 01508 480100
Email: info@willcoxlewis.co.uk
Correspondent: M D Willcox, Trustee
Trustees: Mark Haworth; Nigel Jeremy Langstaff; Michael David Willcox.
CC Number: 1113109

Information available

Accounts were available from the Charity Commission.

The foundation was set up in February 2006. The trustees to date have made small grants for the benefit of the elderly, young people, animals and the environment.

In 2009/10 the foundation had assets of £32 million and an income of £28.6 million. Only one grant was made in this financial year, it went to Busoga Trust (£10,000), while governance costs were almost £63,000.

The trustees annual report for 2009/10 states:

> One of the trustees, Michael Willcox is a Principal Member of WillcoxLewis LLP, a firm of solicitors which raises invoices to the Foundation for legal and administrative services rendered. Michael Willcox is also a beneficiary of the trust which owns 100% of the shares in OCH Services Limited, an accountancy firm which raises invoices to the Foundation for services rendered. Payment of these invoices is authorised by the other trustees. No trustees expenses have been reimbursed during the year.

> Due to the receipt of the £28.6 million received by the trustees during the year, we would expect grant-making to increase significantly from now on.

Applications

The trustees decide on the grants to be made after careful review of the applications received. This strategy will continue to be implemented for as long as the number of applications remains relatively small. As the activities of the foundation expand in the future, it is envisaged that a more refined administrative process of assessment will be put in place.

The River Trust

Christian

£106,000 (2009/10)

Beneficial area

UK, with a preference for Sussex.

c/o Kleinwort Benson Trustees Ltd, PO Box 57005, 30 Gresham Street, London EC2V 7PG
Tel: 020 3207 7337
Fax: 020 3207 7665
Correspondent: The Trustees

Trustee: Kleinwort Benson Trustees Ltd.
CC Number: 275843

Information available

Accounts were available from the Charity Commission.

Gillian Warren formed the trust in 1977 with an endowment mainly of shares in the merchant bank Kleinwort Benson. It is one of the many Kleinwort trusts. The River Trust is one of the smaller of the family trusts. It supports Evangelical Christian causes.

In 2009/10 the trust had assets of £639,000 and an income of £157,000. Grants were made totalling £106,000. These were divided into the following categories:

Religious education	20	£42,000
Advancement of the Christian faith	10	£37,000
Religious welfare work	12	£14,000
Church funds	4	£10,000
Missionary work	3	£3,000
Miscellaneous	1	£500

Grant recipients included: Youth with a Mission (£20,500); Barcombe PCC (£8,000); The Genesis Arts Trust (£5,000); Care for the Family (£4,000); Society of Mary and Martha (£3,000); and African Enterprise and Release International (£1,000 each).

Exclusions

Only appeals for Christian causes will be considered. No grants to individuals. The trust does not support 'repairs of the fabric of the church' nor does it give grants for capital expenditure.

Applications

In writing to the correspondent. It is unusual for unsolicited appeals to be successful. Only successful applicants are notified of the trustees' decision. Some charities are supported for more than one year, although no commitment is usually given to the recipients.

Riverside Charitable Trust Limited

Health, welfare, older people, education, general

£148,000 to organisations and individuals (2009/10)

Beneficial area

Mainly Rossendale, Lancashire.

E Sutton and Sons Ltd, PO Box 2, Bacup OL13 0DT
Tel: 01706 874 961
Correspondent: Brian Terry, Trustee
Trustees: Leslie Clegg; Annie Higginson; Barry John Lynch; Frederick Drew; Gilbert Maden; Harry Francis; Ian Barrie Dearing; Jacqueline Davidson; Brian Terry; Angela O'Gorman; Mark Butterworth.
CC Number: 264015

Information available

Accounts were obtained from the Charity Commission website.

The trust's objects are to support the following: poor, sick and older people; education; healthcare; the relief of poverty of people employed or formerly employed in the shoe trade; and other charitable purposes. There is a preference for activities in the Rossendale area of Lancashire.

In 2009/10 the trust held assets of £2.1 million and an income of £60,000. The trustees made 182 grants totalling £148,000. Grants were broken down into the following categories:

Relief for sickness, infirmity and for the elderly	23	£42,000
General charitable public benefit	74	£60,000
Relief of poverty	60	£44,000
Death grants	20	£2,300

Exclusions

No grants for political causes.

Applications

In writing to the correspondent.

The Daniel Rivlin Charitable Trust

Jewish, general

Around £8,000 (2009/10)

Beneficial area

UK.

Manor House, Northgate Lane, Linton, Wetherby, West Yorkshire LS22 4HN
Tel: 01937 589645
Correspondent: D R Rivlin, Trustee
Trustees: D R Rivlin; N S Butler; M Miller.
CC Number: 328341

Information available

Basic information available from the Charity Commission website.

In 2009/10 the trust had no income and a total expenditure of £8,000.

We do not know why the charity had no income in this financial year, we do know that it remains on the Central Register of Charities and so has not as yet been dissolved. There was no information available regarding beneficiary organisations but previously they included: Donisthorpe Hall; Friends of Israel; Hay on Wye Festival of Literature; Makor Charitable Trust; Make a Dream; Pocklington and Market Weighton Rotary Club; UJIA; Yad Vashem.

Applications

The trust states that funds are fully committed and does not welcome unsolicited applications.

Rix-Thompson-Rothenberg Foundation

Learning disabilities

£118,000 (2010).

Beneficial area

UK.

RTR Administrative Office, White Top Research Unit, Springfield House, 15/16 Springfield, Dundee DD1 4JE
Tel: 01382 384654
Email: P-RTR@dundee.ac.uk
Correspondent: The Administrator
Trustees: Lord Rix; Walter Rothenberg; Loretto Lambe; Fred Heddell; Barrie Davis; Jonathan Rix; Brian Baldock; Suzanne J. Marriott.
CC Number: 285368

Information available

Accounts were on file on the Charity Commission. The 2010 board of governors report and accounts provides the following information:

> The Foundation is dedicated to supporting projects connected with the care, education, training, development and leisure activities of people with learning disabilities.

> It makes grants to a variety of organisations which aim to benefit people with learning disabilities and their carers. A special emphasis is given to grants that will enhance opportunity and lifestyle.

> The foundation maintains a close relationship with the Baily Thomas Charitable Fund which gives it substantial donations towards the annual grant-making activity.

Set up in 1982, in 2010 the foundation had assets of £1.3 million and an income of £127,000, including £75,000 from donations. Grants totalled £118,000.

Grant beneficiaries include: Llandovery Theatre (£6,000); Magpie Dance (£5,000); FAIR, Birmingham Royal Ballet and Avon North Mencap Ltd. (£4,000 each); Crossroads and SMILE (£3,000 each) and Sunflower Music Hall Ltd. (£1,200);

Exclusions

Applications for specific learning difficulties are not supported.

Applications

In the first instance contact should be made through the RTR Administration office, at least two months prior to the next relevant meeting. Once successfully through the application process, submissions are considered by the board of governors at their twice yearly meetings held in June and December and a decision made. No unsolicited applications are considered. The foundation does not support specific learning difficulties initiatives/ projects.

Common applicant mistakes

'Sending applications which do not fit our criteria – we support projects involving people with learning disabilities, not specific learning difficulties.'

Thomas Roberts Trust

Medical, disability, relief in need

45000 (2009/10)

Beneficial area

UK.

5–6 The Square, Winchester, Hampshire SO23 9WE
Tel: 01962 843 211
Fax: 01962 843 223
Email: trtust@thomasroberts.co.uk
Correspondent: James Roberts, Trustee
Trustees: R E Gammage; J Roberts; G Hemmings.
CC Number: 1067235

Information available

Accounts were received at the Charity Commission but unable to view.

Established in November 1997, this trust mainly makes grants to medical (particularly cancer support and research), disability and welfare organisations. Applications from employees and former employees of the Thomas Roberts Group of companies are also considered.

In 2009/10 the trust had an income of £24,000 and expenditure of £45,000.

Past beneficiaries included: Cancer Research UK ; Macmillan Cancer Relief; Marie Curie Cancer Care ; Age Concern; Winchester Churches Nightshelter; Diabetes UK; Riding for the Disabled ; Parkinson's Disease Society and Breast Cancer Campaign.

Information about grant amounts was not available.

Applications

In writing to the correspondent. Applicants are required to provide a summary of their proposals to the trustees, explaining how the funds would be used and what would be achieved.

Edwin George Robinson Charitable Trust

Medical research

Around £35,000 (2009/10)

Beneficial area
UK.

71 Manor Road South, Esher, Surrey KT10 0QB
Tel: 020 8398 6845
Correspondent: E C Robinson, Trustee
Trustees: E C Robinson; Mrs S C Robinson.
CC Number: 1068763

Information available
Accounts were received by the Charity Commission but were not available to view.

The trust supports organisations which provide care for people with disabilities and older people, particularly in the area of medical research. Grants tend to be made for specific research projects and are not usually made to fund general operating costs.

In 2009/10 the trust had an income of £8,100 and a total expenditure of £36,000. No further information was available.

Previous beneficiaries include: Marie Curie Cancer Care; Diabetes UK; Bath Institute of Medical Engineering; Deafness Research; Brainwave; Action for Medical Research; Ness Foundation; Cure Parkinson's; Holly Lodge Centre and Salvation Army.

Exclusions
No grants to individuals or for general running costs for small local organisations.

Applications
In writing to the correspondent.

Robyn Charitable Trust

General charitable purposes, particularly the support of young people

Around £30,000 (2009/10)

Beneficial area
UK and overseas.

c/o Harris and Trotter, 65 New Cavendish Street, London W1G 7LS
Tel: 020 7467 6300
Correspondent: The Trustees
Trustees: Malcolm Webber; Mark Knopfler; Ronnie Harris.
CC Number: 327745

Information available
Basic information was available from the Charity Commission website.

This trust was established in 1988 to advance education and relieve need amongst children in any part of the world.

In 2009/10 the trust had an unusually low income of £709 and a total expenditure of £35,000. No further information was available.

Previous beneficiaries have included: One to One Children's Fund, The Purcell School, Variety Club, The Honeypot Charity, Malawi Against Aids and Teenage Cancer Trust.

Exclusions
No grants to individuals.

Applications
In writing to the correspondent.

The Rock Foundation

Christian ministries and charities

£176,000 (2009/10)

Beneficial area
Worldwide.

Park Green Cottage, Barhatch Road, Cranleigh, Surrey GU6 7DJ
Tel: 01483 274556
Correspondent: The Trustees
Trustees: Richard Borgonon; Andrew Green; Kevin Locock; Jane Borgonon; Colin Spreckley; Peter Butler.
CC Number: 294775

Information available
Accounts were available from the Charity Commission.

Formed in 1986, this charity seeks to support charitable undertakings which are built upon a clear biblical basis and which, in most instances, receive little or no publicity. It is not the intention of the foundation to give widespread support, but rather to specifically research and invest time and money in the work of a few selected Christian ministries. As well as supporting such ministries, grants are also made to registered charities.

In 2009/10 the foundation had an income of £790,000 and made grants totalling £176,000.

There were 16 grants of £5,000 or more listed in the accounts. Beneficiaries included: Proclamation Trust (£17,000); Carter (£14,000); Bible College of Victoria (£10,000); Relite Africa Trust (£6,000); and Soweto Church (£1,000).

The sum of £71,000 was distributed to 18 individuals.

Applications
The trust has previously stated:

> The trust identifies its beneficiaries through its own networks, choosing to support organisations it has a working relationship with. This allows the trust to verify that the organisation is doing excellent work in a sensible manner in a way which cannot be conveyed from a written application. As such, all appeals from charities the foundation do not find through their own research are simply thrown in the bin. If an sae is included in an application, it will merely end up in the foundation's waste-paper bin rather than a post box.

The Rock Solid Trust

Christian causes

£18,000 (2007/08)

Beneficial area

Worldwide.

8 Cupar Road, London SW11 4JW
Correspondent: J D W Pocock, Trustee
Trustees: J D W Pocock; T P Wicks; T G Bretell.
CC Number: 1077669

Information available

Accounts were received at the Charity Commission but not available to view online. Information taken from the Commission's website.

This trust supports:

- Christian charitable institutions and the advancement of Christian religion
- the maintenance, restoration and repair of the fabric of any Christian church
- the education and training of individuals
- relief in need.

In 2009/10 it had an income of £13,000 and a total expenditure of almost £18,000.

Previous beneficiaries have included: Christchurch Clifton and Sherborne School Foundation (£20,000 each); Bristol University (£5,000); Chain of Hope and London School of Theology (£500 each); and RNLI (£100).

Applications

In writing to the correspondent.

The Rofeh Trust

General, religious activities

£57,000 (2009/10)

Beneficial area

UK.

44 Southway, London NW11 6SA
Tel: 020 8458 7382

Correspondent: The Trustees
Trustees: Martin Dunitz; Ruth Dunitz; Vivian Wineman; Henry Eder.
CC Number: 1077682

Information available

An annual report was available from the Charity Commission but there were no accounts to view.

In 2009/10 the trust had an income of £50,000 and a total expenditure of £57,000. There was no further financial information given in the annual report filed with the Charity Commission.

Applications

In writing to the correspondent.

Richard Rogers Charitable Settlement

General

£127,000 (2007/08)

Beneficial area

UK.

Lee Associates, 5 Southampton Place, London WC1A 2DA
Tel: 020 7025 4600
Correspondent: K A Hawkins
Trustees: Lord R G Rogers; Lady R Rogers.
CC Number: 283252

Information available

The latest accounts available from the Charity Commission website were for 2007/8.

The latest accounts available were from 2007/8. The trust had assets of £992,000 and an income of £80,000. Grants were made to 40 organisations totalling £127,000.

The largest grants went to: National Communities Research Centre (£50,000); the Constant Gardener Trust and the National Community Resource Ltd (£13,000 each); Serpentine Gallery (£11,000); Refuge (£10,000); Tree House (£6,400); and Crisis (£1,000).

Smaller grants of less than £1,000 each went to: Trafford Hall (£900);

British Heart Foundation (£500); Scientists for Global Responsibility (£330); Walk the Walk Worldwide (£300); and The RSA (£95).

Applications

In writing to the correspondent.

Rokach Family Charitable Trust

Jewish, general

£185,000 (2008/09)

Beneficial area

UK.

20 Middleton Road, London NW11 7NS
Tel: 020 8455 6359
Correspondent: Norman Rokach, Trustee
Trustees: N Rokach; Mrs H Rokach; Mrs E Hoffman; Mrs M Feingold; Mrs A Gefilhaus; Mrs N Brenig.
CC Number: 284007

Information available

Accounts for 2009/10 overdue. Information taken from 2008/09 accounts.

This trust supports Jewish and general causes in the UK. Accounts for this trust are consistently very overdue when submitted to the Commission and we have used the accounts for the year 2008/09 as the latest available. Investment management costs were £286,000 and governance costs were £8,000. Assets stood at £2 million and the trust had an income of £434,000. The total awarded in grants was £185,000.

Beneficiaries were: Cosmon Belz Limited (£110,000); Moreshet Hatorah Ltd (£26,000); Belz Israel (£23,000); Friends of Wiznitz (£5,000); L & N Brenig Family Trust (£4,000); Society of Friends of the Torah (£3,000); and Lolev (£2,000).

Applications

In writing to the correspondent.

The Helen Roll Charitable Trust

General

£122,000 (2009/10)

Beneficial area

UK.

30 St Giles, Oxford OX1 3LE
Tel: 01865 559 900
Correspondent: F R Williamson, Trustee
Trustees: Christine Chapman; Christine Reid; Patrick J R Stopford; Paul Strang; Frank R Williamson; Jennifer C Williamson; Peter R Williamson; Stephen G Williamson.
CC Number: 299108

Information available

Accounts were available from the Charity Commission. The trust's 2009/10 annual report states:

> One of the trustees' aims is to support work for which charities find it difficult or impossible to obtain funds from other sources. Some projects are supported on a start-up basis, others involve funding over a longer term.

The charities supported are mainly those whose work is already known to the trustees and who report on both their needs and achievements. Each year a handful of new causes are supported. However the trust has previously stated that 'the chances of success for a new application are about 100–1'.

In 2009/10 the trust had assets of £1.5 million and an income of £50,000. Grants were made to 36 organisations totalling £122,000.

Grants included those made to: Home Farm Trust (£12,000); Trinity College of Music (£6,000); Alzheimer's Research Trust (£5,000); Dartington International Summer School (£4,000); Friends of Animal League (£3,000); Oxfordshire Association for the Blind, Oxfordshire Family Mediation and Perthes Association (£2,000 each); Compassionate Friends (£1,500); and Barn Owl Trust (£1,000).

Exclusions

No support for individuals or non-registered charities.

Applications

In writing to the correspondent during the first fortnight in February. Applications should be kept short, ideally on one sheet of A4. Further material will then be requested from those who are short-listed. The trustees normally make their distributions in March.

Common applicant mistakes

'Some applications are not within the application window. Personal applications from individuals, which do not qualify, are also received.'

The Sir James Roll Charitable Trust

General

£145,000 (2009/10)

Beneficial area

UK.

5 New Road Avenue, Chatham, Kent ME4 6AR
Tel: 01634 830 111
Correspondent: N T Wharton, Trustee
Trustees: N T Wharton; B W Elvy; J M Liddiard.
CC Number: 1064963

Information available

Accounts were available from the Charity Commission.

The trust's main objects are the:

- promotion of mutual tolerance, commonality and cordiality in major world religions
- promotion of improved access to computer technology in community based projects other than political parties or local government
- funding of projects aimed at early identification of specific learning disorders
- other charitable projects as the trustees see fit.

In 2009/10 the trust had assets totalling £3.9 million and an income of £191,000. Grants were made to 146 beneficiaries totalling £145,000. Grants ranged from £700 to £10,000.

Beneficiaries included: DEC Haiti Earthquake Appeal (£10,000); CRISIS and DEC Indonesia Philippines & Vietnam (£5,000 each); Action Medical Research, Africa Equipment for Schools, Appropriate Technology Asia, Bowel Disease Research Foundation, Crime Diversion Scheme, Jessie May Trust, Link Community Development, Manna Society, Tall Ships Youth Trust Treehouse Trust and Whizz-Kidz (£1,250 each); and Crossroads Association, Konnect 9 Worldwide, Respite Association, Strongbones Children's Foundation and Young Minds (£700 each).

Applications

In writing to the correspondent. The trustees usually meet around four times a year to assess grant applications.

Rosa – the UK fund for women and girls

Women's organisations and projects supporting women

£96,000 (2009/10)

Beneficial area

UK.

c/o Women's Resource Centre, Ground Floor East, 33–41 Dallington Street, London EC1V 0BB
Tel: 020 7324 3044
Email: info@rosauk.org
Website: www.rosauk.org
Correspondent: Anya Stern
Trustees: Mrs Marilyn List; Ms Maggie Baxter; Ms Gillian Egan; Ms Lindsay Driscoll; Ms Natalie Szeszkowski; Ms Aisha Gill; Ms Tania Bronstein; Ms Ruth Pearson.
CC Number: 1124856

Information available

Information was available on the Rosa website and at the Charity Commission.

> Rosa is a charitable fund set up to support initiatives that benefit women and girls in the UK. Because, while many women and girls here do enjoy

freedom of choice and the opportunity for success in their lives, that's simply not true for all. Our vision is of equality and justice for all women and girls in the UK. Women aren't short of ideas to help create positive change in their lives, but they are often short of the money needed to turn those ideas into reality. That's why Rosa was launched in 2008 – to help raise more money for women's projects and organisations. We do this in three key ways: We champion funding for women and girls – we can help inform, influence and advise other funders to promote greater investment in organisations working with women and girls. We raise funds and invest in change – Rosa raises money from individuals, companies, foundations and statutory donors so we can make grants to initiatives and groups that tackle specific issues around women's safety, economic justice, health and wellbeing, and representation in society. We act as a connector and advocate – by promoting awareness of women's organisations and the issues they tackle, showing how donations will help create lasting change, and bringing donors closer to the causes they support.

How we make a difference

Through Rosa you can support projects working with women and girls on these issues:

- Safety
- Economic Justice
- Health and wellbeing
- Leadership and representation

The Rosa website provides some information about the grants the charity has made to date and lists its current priorities as its Girls and Young Women Fund and its Challenge Fund. In 2012 the charity plans to support organisations working with young women in two specific areas: violence, and issues of self-esteem and aspiration. As the fund's website notes:

> We plan to establish a young women's fund to support creative approaches that will unearth the roots of the issue and encourage individuals to find solutions for themselves and their communities.

In 2009/10 the organisation had assets of £47,000 and an income of £131,000. Grants were made totalling £96,000.

Beneficiaries included: Funding initiative against Female Genital Mutilation (£29,000); Lankelly Chase Foundation (£25,000); Body Image (£24,500); Sheila McKennie Foundation's Women Creating Change award (£15,000).

Applications

The fund encourages organisations running projects or initiatives which match the current strategic priorities of the fund to contact them to discuss how the fund may be able to help. Potential applicants may contact the trust via email, phone or by visiting the office. The fund changes its priorities regularly so applicants are encouraged to visit the website regularly.

Exclusions

The charity does not make grants to individuals.

Alexandra Rose Charities

Supporting charities helping people in need

£103,000 (2010)

Beneficial area

England and Wales.

5 Mead Lane, Farnham, Surrey
GU9 7DY
Tel: 01252 726171
Fax: 01252 727559
Email: enquiries@alexandrarose.org.uk
Website: www.alexandrarosecharities.org.uk
Correspondent: The National Director
Trustees: Andrew Mitchell MP; Lady Kathleen Grade; Iain Matthewson; Angela Anderson; Sonja Miller; Lady Marianna Falconer of Thoroton; Roger Lomax; Mike Morris; Lord Anthony St John of Bletso; Dominic Tayler; Sophia Tayler; Alan Kirby; Elizabeth Keir; Michael Mackenzie.
CC Number: 211535

Information available

Accounts were available from the Charity Commission.

Since its establishment in 1912 by Queen Alexandra to sell pink roses on one day of the year to help the needy of London, Alexandra Rose Charities has moved with the times and now helps small charities and community organisations raise money throughout the year on a national basis. These charities look after the needs of children, people with disabilities, vulnerable adults, at risk people of all ages, ex-service personnel, the lonely, the elderly and the bereaved.

Charities taking part in Rose Days keep 90% of the money collected, though organisations getting involved for the first time are required to pay a £50 registration fee. The charity also runs an annual Rose Raffle which allows small charities to sell raffle tickets on behalf of the Alexandra Rose Charities and keep 80% of the sales income.

A special appeal fund is available to organisations which have been involved in Rose Day collections and/or the Rose Raffle. Please note the following details taken from the charities' website:

> Each year Alexandra Rose Charities raises funds from events and corporate donors to supplement our Special Appeal Fund. Any charity may apply to us for a grant as long as they have taken part in either an annual collection or sold raffle tickets from our Rose Raffle. In each case applicants must have generated at least £100 from the activity. Any qualifying organisation may apply to us for a project grant of up to £1,000 or for those with an income of less than £100,000 they can request a core cost grant of up to £500 if they do not have a specific project in mind.

In 2010 the charities had assets of £628,000 and an income of £281,000. Grants totalling £119,000 were approved.

Beneficiaries included: Manor Farm Boys Club (£3,200); Royal Naval Association Cardiff (£2,500); St Vincent de Paul Society (£1,700); It's Fun to Dance (£1,600) RNA – Dorchester (£1,300); and Blue Badge Network (£1,100).

Applications

Only charities participating in Rose Days or the Rose Raffle are eligible to apply. Please see the website for further information on how to get involved.

The Cecil Rosen Foundation

Welfare, especially older people, infirm, people who are mentally or physically disabled

£218,000 (2009/10)

Beneficial area
UK.

22 Lisson Grove, London NW1 6TT
Correspondent: M J Ozin, Trustee
Trustees: M J Ozin; J A Hart; P H Silverman.
CC Number: 247425

Information available
Accounts were available from the Charity Commission, but without a list of grants and only a limited review of activities.

Established in 1966, the charity's main object is the assistance and relief of the poor, especially older people, the infirm or people who are disabled.

The correspondent has previously stated that almost all the trust's funds are (and will always continue to be) allocated between five projects. The surplus is then distributed in small donations between an unchanging list of around 200 organisations. 'Rarely are any organisations added to or taken off the list.'

In 2009/10 the foundation had assets of £5.7 million and an income of £410,000. Grants totalled £218,000, of which one grant was recorded. This was £75,000 given to the Jewish Blind and Physically Handicapped Society (of which one of the trustees is the director).

Exclusions
No grants to individuals.

Applications
The correspondent has previously stated that 'no new applications can be considered'. Unsuccessful applications are not acknowledged.

The Rothermere Foundation

Education, general

£206,000 (2009/10)

Beneficial area
UK.

Beech Court, Canterbury Road, Challock, Ashford, Kent TN25 4DJ
Tel: 01233 740 641
Correspondent: V P W Harmsworth, Secretary
Trustees: Rt Hon. Viscount Rothermere; Viscountess Rothermere; V P W Harmsworth; J G Hemingway; Hon. Esme Countess of Cromer.
CC Number: 314125

Information available
Information was on file at the Charity Commission.

This trust was set up for the establishment and maintenance of Rothermere Scholarships to be awarded to graduates of the Memorial University of Newfoundland to enable them to undertake further periods of study in the UK; and general charitable causes. In 2005 the trustees made the decision to designate £200,000 each year for the following seven years to form a fund to make grants to the Rothermere fellows and to support other such long term scholarships.

In 2009/10 the foundation had assets of £27.3 million and an income of £730,000. Grants totalled £206,000, broken down in the following categories:

Medical research
Beneficiaries included: King Edward VII Hospital (£30,000); Paula D'Auria Cancer Centre (£10,000) and Baby Bio Bank- wellbeing of women (£5,000).

Educational/children's charities
Beneficiaries included: Harmsworth Professorship (£61,000); St Peter's College, Oxford (£50,000) and National Literacy Trust (£5,000).

Religious organisations
Beneficiaries included: Sacred Heart Parish Tisbury, Wardour Chapel

Trust (£2,500 each) and Daylesford Church (£300).

Other charitable donations
Beneficiaries included: Bomber Command Memorial (£10,000); Great Dixter Charitable Trust (£5,000); Caza Alianza Charity (£2,000) and Salisbury & South Wilts Museum (£1,000).

Three fellowship grants were awarded totalling £57,000.

Applications
In writing to the correspondent.

The Rowing Foundation

Water sports

£28,000 (2010)

Beneficial area
UK.

6 Lower Mall, Hammersmith, London W6 9DJ
Tel: 020 8878 3723
Fax: 020 8878 6298
Email: p.churcher@sky.com
Website: www.ara-rowing. org/rowing-foundation
Correspondent: Pauline Churcher, Secretary
Trustees: John Buchan; Simon Goodey; Philip J Phillips; Iain Reid; Roger S Smith; John Chick; Christopher Sprague.
CC Number: 281688

Information available
Accounts were available from the Charity Commission.

The Rowing Foundation was set up in 1981 to generate and administer funds for the aid and support of young people (those under 18 or 23 if still in full-time education) and people who have disabilities, of all ages, through their participation in water sports, particularly rowing. Its income is mainly dependent on donations from the rowing fraternity.

Grants are made in the range of £500 and £2,000 to support youth and adaptive rowing and particularly to pump-prime projects. The foundation is anxious to help organisations and clubs whose requirements may be too small or who may be otherwise ineligible for an approach to the Big Lottery Fund or other similar sources of funds. It has also helped to get rowing started in areas where it did not exist or was struggling. Grants are not restricted to boats/sculls and have also been made for buoyancy aids, splash suits, canoes and 'taster' rowing courses.

In 2010 the foundation had an income of £23,000 and a total expenditure of over £28,000.

Previous beneficiaries have included: Headway, which received £4,800. Other beneficiaries during the year included London Youth (£3,000); Cranmore School RC (£2,000); University of Derby and Oarsport – Sculls (£1,200 each); and Back Up Trust (£900).

Exclusions

The foundation does not give grants to individuals, only to clubs and organisations, and for a specific purpose, not as a contribution to general funds.

Applications

Applications should be made on a form, available to download from the Amateur Rowing Association website.

Common applicant mistakes

'Ignoring the fact that the foundation only makes grants to rowing clubs, i.e. not sailing or swimming clubs. Applying on behalf of organisations which have nothing to do with water sports at all.'

The Rowland Family Foundation

Relief-in-need, education, religion, community

£379,000 (2009/10)

Beneficial area

UK and overseas.

Harcus Sinclair, 3 Lincoln's Inn Fields, London WC2A 3AA

Tel: 020 7242 9700
Email: lucy.gibson@harcus-sinclair.co.uk
Correspondent: Lucy Gibson
Trustees: Mrs A M Rowland; N G Rowland.
CC Number: 1111177

Information available

Accounts were available from the Charity Commission.

The foundation was registered with the Charity Commission in 2005. Its principal objectives are the relief of poverty, the advancement of education, the advancement of religion or other purposes beneficial for the community.

In 2009/10 the foundation had assets of £5.2 million and an income of £621,000. Grants totalled £379,000.

Beneficiaries during the year were: Hope and Homes for Children (£195,000); Chailey Heritage School (£142,000); Child Welfare Scheme (£40,000 each); and Royal Marsden Hospital (£2,000).

Applications

In writing to the correspondent.

The Rowlands Trust

General, but mainly medical research, social welfare, music and the arts and the environment

£482,000 (2010)

Beneficial area

West and South Midlands including Hereford and Worcester, Gloucester, Shropshire and Birmingham.

c/o Mills and Reeve, 78–84 Colmore Row, Birmingham B3 2AB
Tel: 0121 456 8341
Fax: 0121 200 3028
Email: nicola.fenn@mills-reeve.com
Correspondent: Ms N Fenn, Clerk to the Trustees
Trustees: A C S Hordern, Chair; Mrs F J Burman; Mrs A M I Harris; G Barber; T Jessop.

CC Number: 1062148

Information available

Accounts were available from the Charity Commission.

The trust primarily has an interest in supporting projects in the West Midlands, the South Midlands including Hereford and Worcester, Gloucester, Shropshire and Birmingham. Grants are given in the following areas:

- research, education and training in the broadest sense with special regard to medical and scientific research
- the sick, poor, disabled and elderly
- music and the Arts
- the environment.

In 2010 the trust had assets of £5.3 million and an income of almost £170,000. Grants paid in the year totalled £482,000.

Research, education and training	46	£287,000
Sick, poor, the elderly and those with disabilities	42	£97,000
Music and the arts	24	£95,000
Environment	4	£4,000

The largest grants went to: CTC Kinghurst Academy (£15,000); Baverstock School (£13,000); Longmynd Adventure Camp and New College, Worcester (£10,000); Carpet Museum Trust, Creation Skatepark and Walsall Hospice (£5,000 each); Cerebral Palsy Midlands (£3,000); Pentabus Arts Ltd – Ludlow, Warwickshire & Northamptonshire Air Ambulance (£2,000 each); and Birmingham Hippodrome Theatre Development Trust, Birmingham Symphonic Winds, Camp XL – Whitbourne, Warley Woods Community Trust Ltd and Wellington Cottage Care Trust (£1,000 each); and Worcestershire Wildlife Trust (£750).

Exclusions

No support for individuals or to animal charities. No support is given for revenue funding.

Applications

Applications forms are available from the correspondent and are the preferred means by which to apply. Completed forms should be returned with a copy of the most recent accounts. The trustees meet to consider grants four times a year.

Royal Artillery Charitable Fund

Service charities

£202,000 to organisations (2010)

Beneficial area

UK and overseas.

Artillery House, Artillery Centre, Larkhill, Wiltshire SP4 8QT
Tel: 01980 845698
Email: AC-RHQRA-RACF-WelfareClk2@mod.uk
Website: www.theraa.co.uk/
Correspondent: The Welfare Secretary
Trustees: Maj. Gen. J Milne; Brig. A Gordon; Col. G Gilchrist; Col. A Jolley; Col. C Fletcher-Wood; Maj. ATG Richards; Maj. AJ Dines; Brig. D E Radcliffe; Brig. R Haldenby; Brig. W J F Bramble; Col. M J Thornhill; Col. B W Jenkins; Col. IA Vere Nicoll.
CC Number: 210202

Information available

Accounts were on file at the Charity Commission.

The fund promotes the efficiency and welfare of all ranks of the Royal Artillery and gives relief and assistance to any past or present members, living or deceased, their dependants and families who are in need of such assistance by way of poverty, illness or disability.

In 2010 the trust had assets of £14 million and an income of £937,000. Grants were made totalling £978,000, of which £202,000 was given to organisations and the remaining £776,000 was distributed to individuals.

Grants to organisations included: Army Benevolent Fund (£55,000); Regiment and Batteries (£51,500); Royal Artillery Institution (£35,000); Gunner Magazine (£20,000); King Edward VII Hospital (£2,800); and Erskine Homes (£1,000).

Applications

In writing to the correspondent.

Royal Masonic Trust for Girls and Boys

Children, young people

£219,000 to non-Masonic charities (2010)

Beneficial area

UK.

Freemasons' Hall, 60 Great Queen Street, London WC2B 5AZ
Tel: 020 7405 2644
Fax: 020 7831 4094
Email: info@rmtgb.org
Website: www.rmtgb.org
Correspondent: Leslie Hutchinson, Chief Executive
Trustee: Council members appointed by a resolution of a General Court.
CC Number: 285836

Information available

Accounts were available from the Charity Commission.

This trust was established in 1982 and is largely focused on making grants to individual children of Freemasons who are in need. Grants are also made to UK non-Masonic organisations working with children and young people and to support bursaries at cathedrals and collegiate chapels.

In 2010 the trust had assets of £125 million and an income of £5.2 million. Grants made to non-Masonic charities totalled £219,000. Other grants totalled £4.9 million, and a further £512,000 went to individuals through the TalentAid programme.

The non masonic grants were divided between the Choral Bursaries (£180,000) and 'other non masonic charities'.

Applications

In writing to the correspondent.

Please note: the trust states on its website that, 'at present, the Trust's resources are sufficient only to support its primary beneficiaries and its existing projects. It is not able to consider applications for new non-Masonic grants at this time'.

Any change to this policy will be noted on the trust's website.

The RRAF Charitable Trust

General, medical research, children who are disadvantaged, religious organisations, aid for the developing world and support for the elderly

£43,000 (2009/10)

Beneficial area

UK and the developing world.

Rathbone Trust Company Limited, 159 New Bond Street, London W1S 2UD
Tel: 020 7399 0807
Correspondent: The Administrator
Trustees: Rathbone Trust Company Limited; Claire Tufnell; Emilie Astley-Arlington; Joanne Mcarthy; Rosemary Mcarthy; Elizabeth Astley-Arlington.
CC Number: 1103662

Information available

Accounts were available from the Charity Commission.

This trust was established in 2004. In 2009/10 it had assets of £628,000 and an income of £25,000. Grants were made to seven organisations totalling £43,000.

Beneficiaries during the year were: Refugee Support Network (£14,000); Dove Association and Kids Company (£7,000 each); Reaching Orphans for Care (£5,800); Hamlin Fistula (£5,000); Blues in Schools (£3,000); and Living Links (£1,500).

Applications

In writing to the correspondent. Only successful applicants are notified of the trustees' decision.

William Arthur Rudd Memorial Trust

General in the UK, and selected Spanish charities

£50,500 (2009)

Beneficial area

In practice UK and Spain.

12 South Square, Gray's Inn, London WC1R 5HH
Tel: 020 7405 8932
Email: mail@mmandm.co.uk
Correspondent: A A Sarkis, Trustee
Trustees: A A Sarkis; D H Smyth; R G Maples.
CC Number: 326495

Information available

Accounts were on file at the Charity Commission, without a narrative report or a list of beneficiaries.

In 2009 the trust had assets of £864,000, an income of £56,000 and made grants totalling £50,500.

The trust's accounts state that donations were made to registered charities in the UK and to selected Spanish charities; however, no grants list was provided.

Applications

The trust's 2009/10 annual report states:

> As the objects of the Charity are not linked to any specific areas of charitable activity, the Trustees receive a large number of applications for donations. They review the applications received and any wishes expressed by the Settlor at their annual meeting and make their awards.

The Russell Trust

General charitable purposes

£252,000 (2008/9)

Beneficial area

UK, especially Scotland.

Markinch, Glenrothes, Fife KY7 6PB

Tel: 01592 753311
Email: russelltrust@trg.co.uk
Correspondent: Iona Russell, Administrator and Trustee
Trustees: Fred Bowden; Mrs Cecilia Croal; Graeme Crombie; David Erdal; Don Munro; Ms Iona Russell; Alan Scott; C A G Parr.
SC Number: SC004424

Information available

Accounts for 2008/09 supplied by the Russell Trust.

This family trust was established in 1947 in memory of Capt. J P O Russell who was killed in Italy during the Second World War. The trustees prefer to make grants to pump-prime new projects, rather than giving on an ongoing basis. Grants of up to £10,000 can be distributed; however, generally the amounts given are for between £250 and £2,000. Three or four larger grants of up to £20,000 may be awarded annually.

In 2008/09 the trust had assets of £9.4 million and an income of £262,000. Grants were made totalling £252,000. No grants list was available, but donations were broken down as follows:

- Youth work – £55,000
- Health and welfare – £47,000
- Education – £36,000
- Local – £26,000
- St Andrew's University – £25,500
- Music and the Arts – £23,000
- Church – £18,000
- Preservation/Conservation – £12,000
- Archaeology – £9,500

Exclusions

Only registered charities or organisations with charitable status are supported.

Applications

On a form available from the correspondent. A statement of accounts must be supplied. Trustees meet quarterly, although decisions on the allocation of grants are made more regularly.

Ryklow Charitable Trust 1992

Education, health, environment and welfare

£108,000 to organisations (2009/10)

Beneficial area

UK and overseas, with a preference for the East Midlands.

c/o Robinsons Solicitors, 10–11 St James Court, Friar Gate, Derby DE1 1BT
Tel: 01332 254 157
Fax: 01332 254 142
Email: ryklow@robinsons-solicitors.co.uk
Website: ryklowcharitabletrust.org
Correspondent: Stephen Marshall
Trustees: Andrew Williamson; Ernest J S Cannings; Philip W Hanson; Sheila Taylor.
CC Number: 1010122

Information available

Accounts were available online at the Charity Commission; the trust has a useful website.

The trust (also known as A B Williamson Charitable Trust) was established by Mr A B Williamson, a midlands industrialist, to provide financial assistance to small or individual charitable projects, students, and people in need, throughout the world.

Funding is given for the following activities:

- projects in the developing world, especially those which are intended to be self sustaining or concerned with education
- help for vulnerable families, minorities and the prevention of abuse or exploitation of children and young persons
- conservation of natural species, landscape and resources.

Annual grants usually range between £500 and £3,000 and are generally given to small charities or start up charities.

In 2009/10 the trust had assets of £1.9 million and an unusually low income of £69,000 (£514,000 in 2008/09) largely due to the lack of voluntary donations. Grants were made to 50 organisations totalling £108,000 and were distributed as follows:

Medical research	2	£5,000
Projects in the developing world	23	£46,000
Help for vulnerable families, minorities and children	18	£39,000
Conservation of natural species, landscape and resources	6	£12,000
The benefit of the local community in Belper, Derbyshire	1	£5,000

A full grants list was unavailable but the trust did note the two largest beneficiaries in its accounts. They were: Safe and Sound (£6,300) and Field Row Unitarian Chapel Belper (£5,000).

One grant of £4,000 was made to an individual.

Exclusions

Only organisations which are UK registered, have a UK sponsor, or are affiliated to a UK registered charity will be considered.

Applications

On a form available from the correspondent or to download from the trust's website. Applications should be brief and include an audited financial report (or at least a statement of finances).

Forms should be submitted between 1 September and 31 December. The trustees usually make a decision once a year in March, with grants being awarded by the end of the month. Only in cases of real emergency will applications be considered at other times.

Only successful applicants will be notified.

The Jeremy and John Sacher Charitable Trust

General, including arts, culture and heritage, medical and disability, community and welfare, education, science and technology, children and youth, and religion

£97,000 (2009/10)

Beneficial area

UK and Israel.

Acre House, 11–15 William Road, London NW1 3ER
Tel: 020 7388 7000
Correspondent: The Trustees, c/o H W Fisher & Company
Trustees: Simon John Sacher; Jeremy Michael Sacher; Hon. Mrs Rosalind E C Sacher; Mrs Elisabeth J Sacher.
CC Number: 206321

Information available

Accounts were available from the Charity Commission

This trust has general charitable purposes, with some interest in Jewish/Israeli organisations. In 2009/10 the trust had assets of £4.4 million and an income of £124,000. Grants were made to 41 organisations totalling £97,000 and were broken down into the following categories:

Arts, culture, heritage	11	£30,000
Community and welfare	6	£26,000
Education, science and technology	2	£20,000
Medical and disability	7	£12,000
Wildlife	1	£7,000
Children and youth	5	£1,300
Environment	3	£600
General	1	£500
Religion	1	£100

Beneficiaries included: Community Security Trust and Kings College London (£20,000 each); The National Gallery (£11,000); Royal Opera House Foundation (£6,800); New Israel Fund (£4,000); Beaminster Festival (£2,000); Army Benevolent Fund (£1,000); and Dorset Children's Hospice (£150).

Applications

In writing to the correspondent at any time.

The Michael Harry Sacher Trust

General, with a preference for arts, education, animal welfare, Jewish, health and social welfare

£76,000 (2009/10)

Beneficial area

UK and overseas.

c/o H W Fisher and Co, Acre House, 11–15 William Road, London NW1 3ER
Tel: 020 7388 7000
Correspondent: The Trustees
Trustees: Nicola Shelley Sacher; Michael Harry Sacher.
CC Number: 288973

Information available

Accounts were on file at the Charity Commission.

The trust was established in 1984 and makes donations to registered charities which support a wide range of causes. Grants are only made to charities known personally to the trustees and generally range from £250 to £30,000.

In 2009/10 the trust had assets of almost £2.2 million and an income of £64,000. Grants were made to 20 organisations totalling £76,000 and were broken down into the following categories:

Culture and arts	6	£36,500
Community care	4	£12,600
Overseas aid	3	£11,000
Health	3	£6,000
General	1	£3,400
Animals	1	£3,300
Children and youth	1	£2,000
Religion	1	£750

Beneficiaries included: British Friends of the Art Museums of Israel (£18,500); National Gallery Trust (£10,000); Jewish Care and Nightingale House (£5,000 each); Jeremy and John Sacher Charitable

Trust (£3,400); Whale and Dolphin Conservation Society (£3,300); The Mariinsky Theatre Trust (£375); and Venice in Peril (£250).

Exclusions

No grants to individuals or organisations which are not registered charities.

Applications

In writing to the correspondent.

The Sackler Trust (Formerly Dr Mortimer and Theresa Sackler Foundation)

Arts and culture, science, medical

£203,000 (2010)

Beneficial area

UK.

9th Floor, New Zealand House, 80 Haymarket, London SW1Y 4TQ
Tel: 020 7930 4944
Correspondent: Christopher B Mitchell, Trustee
Trustees: Theresa Sackler; Christopher Mitchell; Raymond Smith; Marissa Sackler; Peter Stormonth Darling; Sophie Sackler Dalrypmle; Michael Sackler; Marianne Mitchell.
CC Number: 1132097

Information available

Accounts were on file at the Charity Commission but were unable to view.

The foundation was set up in 1988 to support the advancement of the public in the UK and elsewhere in the fields of art, science and medical research generally.

In 2009 the trust underwent restructuring meaning that the original trust's (Dr Mortimer and Theresa Sackler Foundation) assets were transferred to the new trust (The Sackler Trust). The previous trust still exists but its income and expenditure are insignificant (£8,000 and £4,000 respectively).

In 2010 the trust had an income of £26.3 million (due to assets being transferred), assets of £26.1 million and made grants totalling £203,000.

Beneficiaries included: Turquoise Mountain Trust (£150,000); Glyndebourne Arts Trust (£25,000); Southbank Centre (£10,000).

The trust also made miscellaneous donations of under £10,000 totalling £18,000.

Applications

In writing to the correspondent.

The Ruzin Sadagora Trust

Jewish

£260,000 (2009/10)

Beneficial area

UK and Israel.

Israel Moshe Friedman, 269 Golders Green Road, London NW11 9JJ
Tel: 0208 806 9514
Correspondent: Rabbi I M Friedman, Trustee
Trustees: Rabbi I M Friedman; Mrs S Friedman.
CC Number: 285475

Information available

Accounts were on file at the Charity Commission without a list of grants.

The charity funds the cost, upkeep and activities of The Ruzin Sadagora Synagogue in London. The charity also funds and supports the parent and other associated and affiliated Sadagora institutions and other religious Jewish causes and charities.

In 2009/10 the trust had assets of £500,000, an income of £250,000 and made grants totalling £260,000. The trust's accounts were without a list of grants.

Previous grants beneficiaries include: Beth Israel Ruzin Sadagora (£196,000); Friends of Ruzin Sadagora (£180,000); Beth Kaknesset Ohr Yisroel (£91,600); Mosdos Sadigur (£40,000); Yeshivas Torah Temimah (£9,000); Chevras Moaz Lodol (£6,500); Pardes House (£2,000).

Applications

In writing to the correspondent.

The Jean Sainsbury Animal Welfare Trust

Animal welfare

£315,000 (2010)

Beneficial area

UK registered charities.

PO Box 469, London W14 8PJ
Tel: 0207 602 7948
Website: jeansainsburyanimalwelfare.org.uk/
Correspondent: Madeleine Orchard, Administrator
Trustees: Colin Russell; Gillian Tarlington; James Keliher; Mark Spurdens; Adele Sparrow; Valerie Pike; Michelle Francine Allen.
CC Number: 326358

Information available

Accounts were available from the Charity Commission.

The trust was established in 1982 with the objective of benefiting and protecting animals from suffering. The policy of the trustees is to support smaller charities concerned with the following areas:
- benefiting or protecting animals
- relieving animals from suffering
- conserving wild life
- encouraging the understanding of animals.

Grants are given towards general running costs, veterinary fees, neutering campaigns and major items such as vehicles, veterinary equipment, kennels and cattery units. Capital building projects will be considered under certain circumstances. Charities must be registered in the UK, though their work can take place overseas. However, at least 90% of the trust's donated income must be given to those who operate in the UK.

In 2010 a major donation was made to the Royal Veterinary College of £1 million, in memory of Jean Sainsbury, for the refurbishment of the college's first opinion clinic at its base in Camden Town, London. In recognition of the donation, the hospital will be re-launched in 2011 as the Beaumont Sainsbury Animal Hospital.

Donations were made to smaller UK registered animal welfare charities. These charities rescue and rehome domestic animals and rehabilitate wildlife and some exotic species. Most donations were given towards running costs, vet fees, kennels and catteries. Conditional pledges were made towards building and refurbishment projects. A number of UK registered charities working overseas were also helped, mainly with neutering and veterinary projects including mobile clinics.

In 2010 the trust had assets of £12.5 million Grants were made to 87 organisations totalling £315,000.

Beneficiaries included: Folly Wildlife Rescue (£35,000); North Clwyd Animal Rescue (£12,500); Doris Banham Sanctuary, RSPCA Norfolk West and Retired Greyhound Trust (£10,000 each); Boxer Welfare Scotland, Exotic Pet Refuge, Oldies Club and Twinkle Trust Animal Aid (£5,000 each); Cat and Rabbit Rescue and Labrador Welfare (£2,000 each); Friends of the Strays of Greece and Safe Haven for Donkeys in the Holy Land (£1,000 each) and Compassion in World Farming (£300).

Exclusions

No grants are given to charities which:

- are mainly engaged with the preservation of specific species of wild animals
- have available reserves equal to more than one year's running costs (unless it can be demonstrated that reserves are being held for a designated project)
- are offering sanctuary to animals, with no effort to re-home, foster or rehabilitate
- do not have a realistic policy for animals that cannot be given a reasonable quality of life
- are involved with assistance animals e.g. Hearing Dogs for the Deaf, Riding for the Disabled etc

- spend more than a reasonable proportion of their income on administration or cannot justify their costs per animal helped
- are registered outside the UK.

No support is given to veterinary schools (unless the money can be seen to be directly benefiting the type of animals the trust would want to support). No individuals are supported.

Applications

On a form available from the correspondent or to download from the trust's website. Applicants should complete and return seven copies of the form, their latest set of audited accounts and any other information which may be relevant to the application. Please note: the trust requests that you do not send originals as these cannot be returned.

There are three trustees' meetings every year, usually in March, July and November and applications should be submitted by 1 February, 1 June and 1 October respectively. Further application information and policy guidelines are available by visiting the trust's website.

Saint Luke's College Foundation

Research or studies in theology

£137,000 to organisations and individuals (2009/10)

Beneficial area

UK and overseas, with some preference for Exeter and Truro.

15 St Maryhaye, Tavistock, Devon PL19 8LR
Tel: 01822 613143
Email: director@st-lukes-foundation. org.uk
Website: www.st-lukes-foundation. org.uk
Correspondent: Dr David Benzie, Director
Trustees: Prof Mark Overton; The Bishop Of Exeter; Prof Grace Davie; Very Reverend Cyril Jonathan

Meyrick; Dr Barbara Wintersgill; Dr Michael Wykes; Alyson Sheldrake; David Cain; Alice Hutchings; Dick Powell; The Rev Dr David Rake.
CC Number: 306606

Information available

Accounts were available from the Charity Commission.

This foundation encourages original work and imaginative new projects in theology. It supports St Luke's Chapel and funds the post of St Luke's Chaplain at Exeter University. It also supports the subject of Theology at Exeter and regional initiatives in ministerial formation.

Other awards are made in two main areas:

- *Corporate awards* are made to departments of Theology and RE in universities, colleges and other agencies operating at university level, to enhance their capacity to provide theological and religious education. The awards are usually small and short-term and, consequently, priority is given to pump-priming initiatives and other such situations where, if the initiative proves itself, it may enable the grant-holder to demonstrate success to bodies which engage in longer-term funding.
- *Personal awards* are made to support individuals who are studying Theology or RE; or who are undertaking research leading to a Masters' degree or PhD in these fields.

In 2009/10 the foundation had assets of £3.7 million and an income of £175,000. Grants were made totalling £137,000 which was broken down as follows:

Chapel and chaplaincy	£44,000
University of Exeter – Department of Theology	£31,000
Personal and corporate grants	£62,000

Exclusions

Funding is not available for building work or to provide bursaries for institutions to administer. Schools are not supported directly (although support is given to teachers who are taking eligible studies). Grants are not normally made for periods in excess of three years.

Applications

From 1st January each year, applicants can request an application pack from the correspondent. Applications are considered once a year and should be received by 1st May for grants starting in September.

Saint Sarkis Charity Trust

Armenian churches and welfare, offenders

£204,000 (2009/10)

Beneficial area

UK and overseas.

50 Hoxton Square, London N1 6PB
Tel: 020 7012 1408
Email: info@saintsarkis.org.uk
Website: www.saintsarkis.org.uk
Correspondent: Louisa Hooper, Secretary to the Trustees
Trustees: Martin Sarkis Essayan; Boghos Parsegh (Paul) Gulbenkian; Rita Vartoukian; Robert Brian Todd.
CC Number: 215352

Information available

Accounts were available from the Charity Commission.

The Saint Sarkis Charity Trust funds the following organisations:

- the Armenian Church of Saint Sarkis in London
- the Gulbenkian Library at the Armenian Patriarchate in Jerusalem
- registered charities concerned with the Armenian community in the UK and/or overseas
- UK-registered charities developing innovative projects to support prisoners in the UK and so reduce the rates of re-offending; in particular, the trust is interested in helping people with short-term sentences to cope on their release from prison, women offenders and the families of offenders.

In 2009/10 the trust had an income of £266,000 and made grants totalling £204,000. Its assets stood at £7.4 million. Grants were divided into two categories:

Armenian projects (£193,000)
The largest grants were made to: Armenian Church of Saint Sarkis (£71,000); Armenian Patriarchate (£29,000); and Oxfam (£25,000).

Other grants included those to: Friends of Armenia (£15,000); Terre et Culture (£12,000); Tate Gallery (£10,000); London Armenian Poor Relief (£8,500); Anahid Association (£3,000); and University of London (£1,600).

Other projects (£11,000)
Beneficiaries were: Relate (£5,800); and Worldwide Volunteering (£5,000).

Exclusions

The trust does not give grants to:
- individual applicants
- organisations that are not registered charities
- registered charities outside the UK, unless the project benefits the Armenian community in the UK and/or overseas.

The trust does not fund:
- general appeals
- core costs or salaries (as opposed to project costs)
- projects concerning substance abuse
- medical research.

Applications

In writing to the correspondent. There is no standard application form so applicants should write a covering letter including the following:
- an explanation of the exact purpose of the grant
- how much is needed, with details of how the budget has been arrived at
- details of any other sources of income (firm commitments and those still being explored)
- the charity registration number
- the latest annual report and audited accounts
- any plans for monitoring and evaluating the work.

Common applicant mistakes

'Not reading the eligibility criteria on our website.'

The Saintbury Trust

General

150,000 (2010)

Beneficial area

West Midlands and Warwickshire (which the trust considers to be post code areas B, CV, DY, WS and WV), Worcestershire, Herefordshire and Gloucestershire (post code areas WR, HR and GL).

P O Box 464, Abinger Hammer, Dorking, Surrey RH4 9AF
Tel: 01306 730119
Correspondent: Mrs J P Lewis, Trustee
Trustees: Victoria K Houghton; Anne R Thomas; Jane P Lewis; Amanda E Atkinson-Willes; Harry O Forrester.
CC Number: 326790

Information available

Accounts were on file at the Charity Commission but unavailable to view.

The trust gives grants for general charitable purposes, although the trust deed states that no grants can be given to animal charities. Grants are made to registered charities in Gloucestershire, West Midlands and Worcestershire. Areas of work include addiction, arts and leisure, care of the dying, childhood and youth, community work, disability, education, environment, health, heritage, homelessness, old age, other special needs and prisons.

In 2010 the trust had an income of £142,000 and a total expenditure of £153,000. No further information for 2010 was available however based upon previous years the total grants was approximately £150,000.

Previous beneficiaries included: Birmingham Children's Hospitals Charities (£20,000); Trinity Winchester (£10,000); Nelson Trust; UCE Birmingham Conservatoire; Pimlico Opera (£5,000 each); Myton Hamlet Hospice Trust (£4,000); Tettenhall Wood School Fund; Good Gardeners' Foundation; Kings Norton PCC Restoration; St Basil's (£2,000 each); Adoption Support; Blind Art;

Age Concern Malvern; Hop Skip and Jump – Cotswold (£1,000 each).

Exclusions
No grants to animal charities, individuals (including individuals seeking sponsorship for challenges in support of charities), 'cold-calling' national charities or local branches of national charities. The trust only gives grants to charities outside of its beneficial area if the charity is personally known to one or more of the trustees.

Applications
In writing to the correspondent. Applications are considered twice a year, usually in April and November.

Common applicant mistakes
'Not within our defined geographical area; national charities trying to be local.'

The Saints and Sinners Trust

General but in practice mainly welfare and medical
£95,000 (2009/10)

Beneficial area
Mostly UK.

Lewis Golden and Co., 40 Queen Anne Street, London W1G 9EL
Tel: 020 7580 7313
Correspondent: N W Benson, Trustee
Trustees: N W Benson; Sir Donald Gosling; David Edwards; I A N Irvine.
CC Number: 200536

Information available
Accounts were available from the Charity Commission.

This trust supports welfare and medical causes through the proceeds of its fundraising efforts. In 2009/10 the trust had assets of £265,000 and an income of £88,000. Grants were made to 40 organisations totalling £95,000.

Beneficiaries included: Nordoff Robins Music Therapy, Royal Shakespeare Company and White

Ensign Association Limited (£5,000 each); National Talking Newspapers and White Lodge Centre (£3,000 each); Oxford Children's Hospital Appeal and Police Rehabilitation Trust (£2,000 each); and Sandy Gall's Afghanistan Appeal, Sightsavers International and Society for Welfare of Horses and Ponies (£1,000 each).

Exclusions
No grants to individuals or non-registered charities.

Applications
Applications are not considered unless nominated by members of the club.

The Salamander Charitable Trust

Christian, general charitable purposes
£73,000 (2009/10)

Beneficial area
Worldwide.

Threave, 2 Brudenell Avenue, Canford Cliffs, Poole, Dorset BH13 7NW
Tel: 01202 706661
Correspondent: Sheila M Douglas, Trustee
Trustees: Sheila M Douglas; Alison Hardwick; Phillip Douglas.
CC Number: 273657

Information available
Accounts were available from the Charity Commission.

Founded in 1977, the principal objects of the trust are:
- the relief and assistance of poor and needy persons of all classes, irrespective of colour, race or creed
- the advancement of education and religion
- the relief of sickness and other exclusively charitable purposes beneficial to the community.

In 2009/10 the trust had assets of £1.4 million and an income of £64,000. Grants were made to 96 organisations totalling £73,000, ranging from £250 to £2,000. A list of beneficiaries was not available.

Previous beneficiaries have included: SAT-7 Trust, All Nations Christian College, All Saints in Branksome Park, Birmingham Christian College, Christian Aid, Churches Commission on Overseas Students, FEBA Radio, International Christian College, London Bible College, Middle East Media, Moorland College, St James PCC in Poole, SAMS, Trinity College and Wycliffe Bible Translators.

Exclusions
No grants to individuals. Only registered charities are supported.

Applications
The trust's income is fully allocated each year, mainly to regular beneficiaries. The trustees do not wish to receive any further new requests.

Salters' Charitable Foundation

General, with project grants focused specifically on the environment, citizenship and community development and health
£126,000 (2009/10)

Beneficial area
Greater London and the UK.

The Salters' Company, Salters' Hall, 4 Fore Street, London EC2Y 5DE
Tel: 020 7588 5216
Fax: 020 7638 3679
Email: charities@salters.co.uk
Website: www.salters.co.uk
Correspondent: Vicky Chant, Charities Development Manager
Trustee: The Salters' Company.
CC Number: 328258

Information available
Accounts were available from the Charity Commission.

The foundation makes donations for a range of charitable purposes including: children and young people, health, homelessness, the developing world, the environment and members of the armed forces. Priority is given to funding small nationwide charities and organisations connected with the City of London, where the trust's contribution would make a 'real difference'. As a livery company, the trust pays particular attention to charities a liveryman is involved with. Many beneficiaries have received grants over a number of years.

The trust has two main grantmaking programmes:

- **Project grants:** three year grants of up to £20,000 are available. The foundation is currently prioritising the environment, citizenship and community development, and health as areas of focus for its project grant support.
- **General support:** a limited amount of small donations (up to £3,000) are available as general grants outside of the project grant programme. Applicants must have the support of a member of the Salters' Company to be eligible.

In 2009/10 the trust had assets of £314,000, up from £1,900 in 2008/09, largely due to the transfer of assets (£277,000) from the Salters' Company Charity for Relief in Need (charity number: 244092) following its amalgamation with the Salters' Charitable Foundation in June 2010. The trust had an income of £154,000 and grants were made to 62 organisations totalling £126,000 and were broken down as follows:

Medical	14	£31,000
City of London	10	£25,000
Environment/developing countries	6	£20,000
Children, schools and youth	7	£17,000
Homelessness	3	£8,000
Armed forces	5	£7,400
Other	8	£11,000
Masters' discretionary fund	6	£5,000
Subscriptions	3	£795

Beneficiaries included: United Nations Environment Programme – World Conservation Monitoring Centre (£9,000); Guildhall School Trust (£7,500); Arkwright Schools Scholarship (£5,400); Drapers' Charitable Fund – Olympics (£4,000); Home Farm Trust, Providence Row and Federation of London Youth Clubs (£3,000 each); City of London Migraine Clinic, London Sea Cadet Corps – District 5 NE, Diabetes UK,

City University London and Blind in Business (£2,000 each); Royal Naval Benevolent Trust (£1,500); Ulysses Trust (£1,000); Banana Tree Project (£500); and Royal British Legion – City of London Poppy Appeal (£150).

Exclusions

Please see the foundation's guidelines for information on restrictions.

Applications

Applicants must follow the relevant Guidelines ('Project Grant' or 'General Support') depending on the type of grant they are requesting:

- *Project grant* applicants need to fill in an application form, available from the foundation's website when the programme is open. The last deadline passed in January 2011.
- *General support* applicants need to submit a covering letter, supporting document and annual report and accounts.

Applications can be made via email or post. All supported organisations are regularly reviewed and visited by the Charities Development Manager, members of the Charity Committee and other interested parties within the company.

The Andrew Salvesen Charitable Trust

General

Around £70,000 (2009/10)

Beneficial area

UK, with a preference for Scotland.

c/o Meston Reid and Co., 12 Carden Place, Aberdeen AB10 1UR
Tel: 01224 625554
Email: info@mestonreid.com
Correspondent: The Trustees
Trustees: A C Salvesen; Ms K Turner; V Lall.
SC Number: SC008000

Information available

The following entry is based on information filed with the Office of the Scottish Charity Regulator.

The trust gives grants for general charitable purposes; in particular it will support the arts, education/training, medical sciences and welfare of people who are young, elderly or ill.

In 2009/10 the trust had an income of £78,000 and made grants totalling around £70,000.

Previous beneficiaries have included: Bield Housing Trust, William Higgins Marathon Account, Multiple Sclerosis Society in Scotland, Royal Zoological Society of Scotland, Sail Training Association, Scottish Down's Syndrome Association and Sick Kids Appeal.

Exclusions

No grants to individuals.

Applications

The trustees only support organisations known to them through their personal contacts. The trust has previously stated that all applications sent to them are 'thrown in the bin'.

The Sammermar Trust

General

£232,000 (2009)

Beneficial area

UK and overseas.

Swire House, 59 Buckingham Gate, London SW1E 6AJ
Tel: 020 7834 7717
Correspondent: Mrs Yvonne Barnes
Trustees: Lady Judith Swire; M Dunne; M B Swire; M V Allfrey.
CC Number: 800493

Information available

Accounts for 2009 were available from the Charity Commission website.

The trust, formerly known as the Adrian Swire Charitable Trust, was established in 1988 with general charitable purposes.

The latest accounts available were for 2008/9 when the trust made grants totalling £232,000. They had an income of £265,000 and assets of £10.9 million.

Beneficiaries included: Head and Neck Cancer Research Trust £30,000); West Dean College; Maggie's (Oxford) (£15,000 each); The Mango Tree (£12,000); Family Friends (£10,000); Acre Housing ; Chipping Norton Theatre; Internally Displaced Persons, Sri Lanka; Oxford Philomusica (£5,000 each); and Wycombe Air Centre and Cheltenham Festivals (£2,000 each).

The trust also gave £8,700 in grants less than £1,000.

Applications

In writing to the correspondent. The trust states that: 'although the trustees make some grants with no formal applications, they normally require organisations to submit a request saying how the funds could be used and what would be achieved'. The trustees usually meet monthly.

The Hon. M J Samuel Charitable Trust

General, Jewish

£105,000 (2009/10)

Beneficial area

UK and overseas.

35 Connaught Square, London W2 2HL
Correspondent: The Secretary
Trustees: Hon. Michael Samuel; Hon. Mrs Julia A Samuel; Viscount Bearsted.
CC Number: 327013

Information available

Accounts were available from the Charity Commission.

The trust supports a wide range of causes, many of them Jewish, environmental or concerned with mental health.

In 2009/10 the trust had assets of almost £3.4 million, which generated an income of £90,000. There were 30 grants made totalling £105,000.

Beneficiaries of grants of £1,000 or more included: Oxfam (£32,000); Full Fact (£31,000); Child Bereavement Trust (£10,000); Chicken Shed

Theatre Company (£2,500); ChildLine/Dyslexia Action, Hazara Charitable Trust and Oxford Radcliffe Children's Hospital (£2,000 each); Community Security Trust (£1,500); James Wentworth-Stanley Memorial Fund and National Hospital Development Foundation (£1,000 each).

In addition 13 (2009:15) other donations were made to institutions of less than £1,000 each totalling just over £5,000.

Exclusions

No grants to individuals.

Applications

In writing to the correspondent.

Basil Samuel Charitable Trust

General charitable purposes

£261,000 (2009/10)

Beneficial area

Worldwide, in practice, mainly UK.

Smith & Williamson, 25 Moorgate, London EC2R 6AY
Tel: 020 7131 4376
Correspondent: Mrs Coral Samuel, Trustee
Trustees: Coral Samuel; Richard M Peskin.
CC Number: 206579

Information available

Accounts were available from the Charity Commission.

The trust was established in 1959 for such charitable purposes as the trustees decide, either in the UK or elsewhere. The trust describes its activities as making grants to medical, socially supportive, educational and cultural charities plus a number of donations to other charities.

In 2009/10 it had assets of £10.2 million and an income of £371,500. Grants were made to 28 organisations totalling £261,000. Most grants were for £5,000, and were categorised as follows:

Medical	£115,000
Cultural	£85,000
Socially supportive	£45,000
Educational	£16,000

Beneficiaries included: Macmillan Cancer Support (£60,000); Royal National Theatre (£20,000); Prince's Trust and the Victoria and Albert Museum (£10,000 each); Attingham Trust, London's Air Ambulance, Museum of London, NSPCC and the Cystic Fibrosis Trust (£5,000 each); Hammerson Home Charitable Trust (£2,000); and St John of Jerusalem Eye Hospital Group (£1,000).

Exclusions

Grants are given to registered charities only.

Applications

In writing to the correspondent. The trustees meet on a formal basis annually and more frequently on an informal basis to discuss proposals for individual donations.

Coral Samuel Charitable Trust

General, with a preference for educational, cultural and socially supportive charities

£101,000 (2009/10)

Beneficial area

UK.

c/o Smith and Williamson, 25 Moorgate, London EC2R 6AY
Tel: 020 7131 4376
Correspondent: Coral Samuel, Trustee
Trustees: Coral Samuel; Peter Fineman.
CC Number: 239677

Information available

Accounts were on file at the Charity Commission.

This trust was established in 1962 and makes grants to educational, cultural and socially supportive charities, plus a number of other charities.

In 2009/10 the trust had assets totalling £5.3 million and an income of £191,000. Grants were made to 28 organisations totalling £101,000.

Beneficiaries included: Royal National Theatre and Sir John Soane's Museum (£10,000 each); Glyndebourne Arts Trust (£6,000); Burlington Magazine Foundation, SAVE and Royal Geographic Society (£5,000 each); Child Bereavement Charity (£3,000); Winston's Wish (£2,600); Commonwealth Jewish Trust (£2,000); RVC Animal Care Trust (£1,500); Maccabi GB and the Art Fund (£1,000 each); Personal Support Trust (£500); and JMI (£350).

Exclusions

Grants are only made to registered charities.

Applications

In writing to the correspondent.

The Peter Samuel Charitable Trust

Health, welfare, conservation, Jewish care

£90,000 (2009/10)

Beneficial area

UK, with some preference for local organisations in South Berkshire, Highlands of Scotland and East Somerset.

The Estate Office, Farley Hall, Castle Road, Farley Hill, Berkshire RG7 1UL
Tel: 0118 973 0047
Fax: 0118 973 0385
Email: emma@farleyfarms.co.uk
Correspondent: Miss Emma Chapman, Trust Administrator
Trustees: Hon. Viscount Bearsted; Hon. Michael Samuel.
CC Number: 269065

Information available

Full accounts were available from the Charity Commission website.

The trust was established in 1975 and supports medical sciences, Jewish concerns, heritage, forestry/land restoration and the quality of life in local areas (south central Berkshire, east Somerset and the Highlands of Scotland).

In 2009/10 the trust had assets of nearly £3.6 million, which produced an income of £110,000. Grants were made to 35 organisations totalling £90,000.

The largest grants went to DEC Haiti Earthquake Appeal and Peter Samuel Royal Free Charitable Trust (£10,000 each).

Other grants made included those to: Campaign for the University of Oxford, Anna Freud Centre and Game and Wildlife Conservation Trust (£5,000 each); Jewish Care and Norwood Ravenswood (£2,500 each); Berkshire Community Foundation and the RNID (£1,000 each); Anne Frank and You, Isle of Man and Woodland Trust (£500 each); and SANE (£250).

The Hon Michael Samuel is also a trustee of: Col. Wilfred Horatio Micholls Deceased Charitable Trust Fund (Charity Commission no. 267472); The Hon. A G Samuel Charitable Trust (Charity Commission no. 1090481); The M J Samuel Charitable Trust (Charity Commission no. 327013); and The Peter Samuel Royal Free Fund (Charity Commission no. 200049).

Exclusions

No grants to purely local charities outside Berkshire or to individuals.

Applications

In writing to the correspondent. Trustees meet twice-yearly.

The Camilla Samuel Fund

Medical research

Around £4,500 (2009/10)

Beneficial area

UK.

40 Berkeley Square, London W1J 5AL
Tel: 0207 581 9099
Correspondent: The Secretary to the Trustees

Trustees: Sir Ronald Grierson; Hon. Mrs Waley-Cohen; Dr Hon. J P H Hunt.
CC Number: 235424

Information available

Basic information was obtained from the Charity Commission website.

The fund supports medical research projects in a discipline agreed by the trustees at their annual meetings.

In 2009/10 the fund had an income of £16,000 and a total expenditure of £4,500. Further information was not available. Previous beneficiaries have included Imperial Cancer Research Fund and EORTC.

Exclusions

Individuals, general appeals.

Applications

The trustees will request written applications following the recommendation of a suitable project by the medical trustees. However, please note as all the money available, together with the fund's future income, has been earmarked for four years for an important research project, the fund will not be in a position to consider any applications for grants during this period.

The Sandhu Charitable Foundation

General

£77,000 (2009/10)

Beneficial area

Worldwide.

C/o The Stanton Group, 3rd Floor, Saunders House, 52–53 The Mall, Ealing SW1X 7LY
Tel: 020 3159 5071
Email: enquiries@santoncapital.com
Correspondent: The Trustees
Trustees: B S Sandhu, Chair; S Carey.
CC Number: 1114236

Information available

Accounts were available from the Charity Commission.

The foundation was established in 2006 as a focus for the philanthropic activities of Bim and Pardeep Sandhu and their family.

In 2009/10 it had an income of £1.4 million. Assets stood at £3.2 million at year end. The trustees made 17 grants totalling £77,000.

Beneficiaries included: Magic Bus UK (£12,000); Dec Haiti Appeal and Young Enterprise South East of England (£10,000 each); Jubilee Boy Hill School (£9,000); Latymer Foundation (£4,000); and Joint Educational Trust (£3,000).

Applications

'The charity is to support individual charities or charitable causes, mainly on a single donation basis, which they themselves identify.'

The Sants Charitable Trust

General

£91,000 (2009/10)

Beneficial area

UK.

17 Bradmore Road, Oxford OX2 6QP
Tel: 01865 310813
Correspondent: The Trustees
Trustees: Alexander Sants; Mrs Caroline Sants; Hector W H Sants; John H Ovens.
CC Number: 1078555

Information available

Accounts were available from the Charity Commission.

Registered with the Charity Commission in December 1999, the trust has general charitable purposes.

In 2009/10 the trust had assets of £1 million and an income of £85,000. Grants were made to 15 organisations during the year totalling £91,000.

Beneficiaries of £1,000 or more included: St Paul's Theological Centre (£25,000); Radley Foundation (£22,000); Footsteps Foundation (£10,000); Ashmolean Museum and Garsington Opera (£5,000 each); and Trinity College (£300).

Applications

In writing to the correspondent.

Jimmy Savile Charitable Trust

General

£35,000 (2008/9)

Beneficial area

UK.

22 Lake View Court, Leeds LS8 2TX
Correspondent: The Trustees
Trustees: James Collier; Luke Lucas; Dr Roger Bodley.
CC Number: 326970

Information available

The latest accounts available at the Charity Commission were for 2008/9.

The trust was established by the late Sir Jimmy Savile and other trustees in 1984. It provides funds for the relief of poverty, sickness and other charitable purposes which are beneficial to the community, including the provision of recreational and other facilities for people with disabilities. Grants are made to charitable organisations and individuals.

In 2008/9 the charity had assets of £3.7 million and an income of £159,000. Grants in the year totalled £35,000.

Grants of £1,000 or more went to: A.A.I. Scientific Cultural Services (£15,000); John Augar – Cardiac Research Software (£5,000); Apostleship of the Sea and Inst. of Cancer Research (£1,000 each); The C Group (Royal Marines) (£2,000).

Grants of less than £1,000 included: Music in Hospitals (£430); Leeds Teaching Hospitals (£750); Cleft Plate Charity (£350); S.E.N.S.E (£500); Guide Dogs (£250).

Applications

The trust does not respond to unsolicited applications.

The Scarfe Charitable Trust

Churches, arts, music, environment

£44,000 (2009/10)

Beneficial area

UK, with an emphasis on Suffolk.

Salix House, Falkenham, Ipswich, Suffolk IP10 0QY
Tel: 01394 448 339
Fax: 01394 448 339
Email: ericmaule@hotmail.com
Correspondent: Eric Maule, Trustee
Trustees: Sean McTernan; E Maule; John McCarthy.
CC Number: 275535

Information available

Accounts were available from the Charity Commission.

The trust was established in 1978 by W S N Scarfe and supports mainly art and musical projects and the restoration of churches in Suffolk.

In 2009/10 the trust had an income of £51,000 and made grants totalling £44,000. Its assets stood at £1.2 million. 12 grants were made to churches in Suffolk and 46 grants to organisations.

Beneficiaries included: Aldeburgh Music (£10,000); Aldeburgh Young Musicians (£2,500); Disability Advice Service, High Tide, Liveability, St Andrews, Hasketon and St Augustine's , Ashen (£1,000 each); Trinity College of Music (£850.00); Marie Curie Cancer Care (£750); St Helen's, Ipswich, St Mary's, Bacton, St Mary's, Cratfield and St Peters, Westleton (£500 each); RNID (£350); and Ipswich Chamber Music (£100).

Applications

In writing to the correspondent by post or email. The trustees meet quarterly to consider applications.

The Schapira Charitable Trust

Jewish, health, education

£552,000 (2010)

Beneficial area
UK.

2 Dancastle Court, 14 Arcadia Avenue, Finchley, London N3 2JU
Tel: 020 8371 0381
Email: londonoffice@istrad.com
Correspondent: The Trustees
Trustees: Issac Y Schapira; Michael Neuberger; Suzanne L Schapira.
CC Number: 328435

Information available
Accounts were available from the Charity Commission.

This trust was established in 1989 and has a policy of supporting Jewish organisations relating to religion, health or education.

In 2010 the trust had an income of £202,000 and held assets of £6.4 million. Grants were made totalling £552,000.

The two most significant beneficiaries were: Emuno Educational Centre Ltd (£143,000) and Friends of Tashbar Chazon Ish (£134,000).

Other beneficiaries included: The New Rachmistrivke Synagogue (£38,000); Friends of Mir (£16,000); British Friends of Ramoth Jerusalem (£9,000); Chevras Machzikel Mesifta (£8,000); Yesamach Levav (£3,500); and BCDT Limited (£4,000).

8 grants of £1,000 or less were also made including: Before Trust (£1,000) and Torah (5759) Limited (£720).

Applications
In writing to the correspondent.

The Annie Schiff Charitable Trust

Orthodox Jewish education

£101,000 (2009/10)

Beneficial area
UK, overseas.

8 Highfield Gardens, London NW11 9HB
Tel: 020 8458 9266
Correspondent: Joseph Pearlman, Trustee
Trustees: Joseph Pearlman; Ruth Pearlman.
CC Number: 265401

Information available
Full accounts were available from the Charity Commission website.

The trust's objectives are:
- relief of poverty, particularly amongst the Jewish community
- advancement of education, particularly the study and instruction of Jewish religious literature
- advancement of religion, particularly Judaism.

In 2009/10 the trust had assets of £234,000 and an income of £74,000. Grants were made to 13 organisations totalling £101,000.

Grant recipients included: Chevras Mo'oz Ladol (£22,000); Gevruth Ari Torah Academy Trust (£16,000); Yesamech Levav Trust and Friends of Beis Yisrael Trust (£10,000 each); United Torah Association (£8,000); Yeshivo Horomo Talmudical College (£6,500); Beth David Institute (£6,000); WST Charity Limited (£5,000); Friends of Yeshivat Meor Hatalmud (£3,000); Yesodey Hatorah Schools (£2,000); and Society of Friends of the Torah (£1,800).

Exclusions
No support for individuals and non-recognised institutions.

Applications
In writing to the correspondent. Grants are generally made only to registered charities.

The Schmidt-Bodner Charitable Trust

Jewish, general

£68,000 (2009/10)

Beneficial area
UK and overseas.

5 Fitzhardinge Street, London W1H 6ED
Tel: 020 7486 3111
Correspondent: Harvey Rosenblatt, Trustee and Correspondent
Trustees: Harvey Rosenblatt; Daniel Dover; Martin Paisner.
CC Number: 283014

Information available
Full accounts were available from the Charity Commission website.

This trust mainly supports Jewish organisations though it has also given a few small grants to medical and welfare charities. In 2009/10 the trust had assets of £2 million and an income of £1 million. Grants were made to 12 organisations totalling £68,000.

The largest grants went to: Lubavitch Foundation (£20,000); Jewish Care (£12,500); and United Synagogue (£11,000).

Smaller grants of £10,000 or less went to: British Friends of Or Chadash (£5,000); Yesodey Hatorah School (£3,000); SEED and Simon Marks Junior Primary School Trust (£2,000 each); and British Friends of Ohel Sarah (£250).

Applications
In writing to the correspondent.

The R H Scholes Charitable Trust

General, including children and young people who have disabilities or are disadvantaged, hospices, preservation and churches

£34,000 (2009/10)

Beneficial area
England.

Danehurst Corner, Danehurst Crescent, Horsham, West Sussex RH13 5HS
Tel: 01403 263482
Email: roger@rogpat.plus.com
Correspondent: R H C Pattison, Trustee
Trustees: R H C Pattison; Mrs A J Pattison.
CC Number: 267023

Information available
Accounts were available from the Charity Commission.

This trust currently only supports organisations in which the trustees have a special interest, knowledge of, or association with. Both recurrent and one-off grants are made depending upon the needs of the beneficiary. Core costs, project and research grants are made. Funding for more than three years will be considered.

In 2009/10 the trust had assets of £554,000 and an income of £155,000. Grants totalling £34,000 were made to 86 charities during the year. Grants of £1,200 were made to The Church of England Pensions Board, The Friends of Lancing Chapel and National Churches Trust. All other grants were between £100 and £1,010.

Exclusions
Grants only to registered charities. No grants to individuals, animal charities, expeditions or scholarships. The trust tries not to make grants to more than one charity operating in a particular field, and does not make grants to charities outside England.

Applications
Due to a lack of funds the trust is not currently accepting unsolicited applications from organisations it is not already supporting.

The Schreiber Charitable Trust

Jewish with a preference for education, social welfare and medical

£155,000 (2009/10)

Beneficial area
UK.

PO Box 35547, The Exchange, 4 Brent Cross Gardens, London NW4 3WH
Tel: 020 8457 6500
Email: graham@schreibers.com
Correspondent: G S Morris, Trustee
Trustees: Graham S Morris; David A Schreiber; Sara Schreiber.
CC Number: 264735

Information available
Accounts were available from the Charity Commission.

In 2009/10 the trust had assets of £3.8 million and an income of £178,000. Grants totalling £146,000 were made for education and £9,000 for social welfare.

Beneficiaries included: Friends of Rabbinical College Kol Tora, Jerusalem Foundation, SOFT, Gateshead Talmudical College, Dalaid Limited and Aish Hatorah UK Limited.

Applications
The trust states that the trustees 'regularly appraise new opportunities for direct charitable expenditure and actively seek suitable causes to reduce the unrestricted fund to the appropriate level'.

Schroder Charity Trust

General

£165,000 (2009/10)

Beneficial area
Worldwide, in practice mainly UK.

81 Rivington Street, London EC2A 3AY
Correspondent: Sally Yates, Secretary
Trustees: Claire Fitzalan Howard; Charmaine Mallinckrodt; Bruno Schroder; T B Schroder; Leonie Fane; Frederick Schroder.
CC Number: 214050

Information available
Accounts were available from the Charity Commission.

This trust was established in 1944 and supports a wide range of charitable causes in the areas of health and welfare, community, education, international relief and development, young people, arts, culture and heritage, the environment and rural issues. Preference is given to UK registered charities with a proven track record and those in which the trust has a special interest.

In 2009/10 the trust had assets of £6.9 million and an income of £173,000. 89 grants were made totalling £165,000.

Beneficiaries included: Tavistock Trust for Aphasia (£11,000); Catholic Trust for England and Wales – Mallinckrodt Foundation (£10,000); Atlantic Education Project (£5,000); Cirencester Parish Church (£4,500); Water Aid (£3,000); Tax Help for Older People and Africa Now (£2,500 each); Game Conservancy Trust, Queen Victoria School – Dunblane, Tree Aid and Moorfields Eye Hospital Trust (£2,000 each); Skillshare International and Amber Foundation (£1,500 each); Leukaemia Research Fund (£1,200); National Society for Epilepsy and Borealis Theatre (£1,000 each); Silversmiths and Jewellers Charity (£500); and Winston Churchill Foundation of the United States (£210).

Exclusions

No grants to individuals.

Applications

In writing to the correspondent. Applicants should briefly state their case and enclose a copy of their latest accounts or annual review. Requests will be acknowledged in writing. The trust does not have the capacity to correspond with organisations on the progress of their application. Therefore, if you have not heard from the trust after six months, you can assume that the application has not been successful.

The Scotshill Trust

General, particularly health, arts, conservation, education, social needs, animal welfare and conservation

£1 million (2009/10)

Beneficial area

UK and overseas.

Trustee Management Limited, 19 Cookridge Street, Leeds LS2 3AG
Tel: 0113 243 6466
Correspondent: The Trust Manager
Trustees: Amanda Claire Burton; Paul Howard Burton; Deborah Maureen Hazan; Jeremy John Burton.
CC Number: 1113071

Information available

Accounts were available from the Charity Commission.

Donations are made at the discretion of the trustees and grants are normally made for the following objects:

▶ the advancement of education of all members of the public in the arts, but in particular those that are disadvantaged by reason of poverty, disability, ill health, youth or age and those attending performing arts colleges;

▶ to educate the public in matters pertaining to animal welfare in general and the prevention of cruelty and suffering among animals;

▶ the advancement of education and relief of poverty for those who are disadvantaged by reason of youth, age, ill health, disability, financial hardship or other disadvantage;

▶ to promote for the benefit of the public the conservation, protection and improvement of the physical and natural environment;

▶ the advancement of health for the saving of lives;

▶ such other charitable purposes for the benefit of the community.

In 2009/10 the trust had assets of £6 million and an income of £150,000. Grants to organisations totalled £1 million. There were 166 grants made during the year.

Third World and human rights	41	£446,000
Social welfare	44	£318,000
Health	22	£121,000
Education and arts	20	£65,000
Disability	23	£76,000
Conservation	11	£29,000
Animal welfare	5	£3,500

There was no list of beneficiary organisations but the following have previously been awarded grants from the trust:

Oxfam (£50,000); UJIA (£30,000); Samaritans (£25,000); Crisis (£20,000); Amarderm Research Trust, Amnesty International, Big Issue, Richmond Fellowship and Salvation Army (£10,000 each); Canine Partners, Demand, SNAP and SoundAbout (£5,000 each); Nightstop (£2,500); Amber Trust (£1,500); the Horse Trust, Redwings Horse and Prisoners Abroad (£1,000 each); and Happy Wonderers (£250).

Exclusions

No grants to individuals.

Applications

Appeals should be in writing only to the trust managers. Unsuccessful appeals will not necessarily be acknowledged.

Scott (Eredine) Charitable Trust

Service and ex-service charities, medical, welfare

£189,000 (2010)

Beneficial area

Not defined.

Harcus Sinclair, 3 Lincoln's Inn Fields, London WC2A 3AA
Tel: 020 7242 9700
Correspondent: Keith Bruce-Smith, Trustee
Trustees: M B Scott; Keith Bruce-Smith; A J Scott.
CC Number: 1002267

Information available

Accounts were available from the Charity Commission.

Set up in 1999, in 2010 the trust held assets of £204,000, had an income of £186,000 and made 62 grants totalling £189,000.

Beneficiaries included: Charitable Fund (£35,000); Scots Guards Charitable Funds (£10,000); Household Division Sailing Association (£7,000); Scottish Veterans Residences (£5,000); King Edward VII Hospital for Officers, National Star Centre, St Dunstan's and The Erskine Hospital (£4,000 each); Taste for Adventure Centre (£3,000); Starlight Children's Foundation, World Vision and ZANE (£2,000 each); The Asker Appeal and The Fire Fighters Charity (£1,000 each); and The League of Remembrance (£500).

Applications

In writing to the correspondent.

Sir Samuel Scott of Yews Trust

Medical research

£245,000 (2009/10)

Beneficial area

UK.

c/o Currey and Co, 21 Buckingham Gate, London SW1E 6LS

Tel: 020 7802 2700

Correspondent: The Secretary

Trustees: Lady Phoebe Scott; Hermione Stanford; Edward Perks.

CC Number: 220878

Information available

Accounts were available from the Charity Commission.

In 2009/10 the trust had assets of £5.6 million and an income of £108,000. There were 38 grants made to organisations totalling £245,000.

By far the largest grant of £103,000 went to the Gray Institute at the University of Oxford.

Other beneficiaries included: Royal College of Surgeons, Alzheimer's Research Trust and Bath Institute of Medical Engineering (£10,000 each); Bristol Eye Hospital – National Eye Research Centre, International Spinal Research, Wellbeing of Women and Joint Action (£5,000 each); Meningitis UK (£4,000); Brain Research Trust (£3,000); Deafness Research UK and Ovarian Cancer Action (£2,000 each); and Marfan Trust and University of London – School of Pharmacy (£1,000 each).

Exclusions

No grants for: core funding; purely clinical work; individuals (although research by an individual may be funded if sponsored by a registered charity through which the application is made); research leading to higher degrees (unless the departmental head concerned certifies that the work is of real scientific importance); medical students' elective periods; or expeditions (unless involving an element of genuine medical research).

THE SCOULOUDI FOUNDATION

	Historical awards	Regular donations	Special donations	Total
Humanities	£63,000	£14,000	£1,000	£78,000
Medicine, health and hospices		£26,000		£26,000
People with disabilities		£22,500		£22,500
Famine relief and overseas aid		£14,000	£5,000	£19,000
Children and youth		£11,000	£5,000	£16,000
Environment		£7,500	£5,000	£12,500
Social welfare		£12,500		£12,500
Aged		£9,000		£9,000
Welfare of armed forces/sailors		£9,000		£9,000

Applications

In writing to the correspondent. Trustees hold their half-yearly meetings in April and October and applications have to be submitted two months before. There are no special forms, but applicants should give the following information: the nature and purpose of the research project or programme; the names, qualifications and present posts of the scientists involved; reference to any published results of their previous research; details of present funding; and if possible, the budget for the next 12 months or other convenient period.

All applications are acknowledged and both successful and unsuccessful applicants are notified after each meeting of the trustees. No telephone calls.

The Scouloudi Foundation

General charitable purposes

£204,000 (2009/10)

Beneficial area

UK charities working domestically or overseas.

c/o Haysmacintyre, (The Scouloudi Foundation), Fairfax House, 15 Fulwood Place, London WC1V 6AY

Tel: 020 7969 5500

Fax: 020 7969 5600

Correspondent: The Administrators

Trustees: Sarah Stowell; David Marnham; James Sewell.

CC Number: 205685

Information available

Full accounts were available from the Charity Commission website.

The foundation has three types of grants:

- Historical grants are made each year to the Institute of Historical Research at University of London for fellowships, research and publications, to reflect the interests of the settlor, Irene Scouloudi, who was a historian
- Regular grants, generally of £1,300 each, are made to organisations on a five-year cycle
- Special grants are one-off grants in connection with capital projects.

In 2009/10 the foundation had assets of £5.2 million and an income of £233,000. Grants were made totalling £204,000, broken down as shown in the table above.

By far the largest donation was a historical grant made to the University of London – Institute of Historical Research (£68,000).

Other grants included those made to: British Red Cross Disaster Fund, Friends of Kew and Richard's House Children's Hospice (£5,000 each); Brain Research Trust, British Records Association, British & International Sailors Society, CORDA the Heart Charity, Macmillan Cancer Support, Marie Curie Cancer Care, Mental Health Foundation, National Society for Epilepsy, Samaritans and Voluntary Service Bureau (£1,250 each); and British Library (£1,000).

Exclusions

Donations are not made to individuals, and are not normally made for welfare activities of a purely local nature. The trustees do not make loans or enter into deeds of covenant.

365

Applications

Only Historical grants are open to application. Copies of the regulations and application forms for 'Historical Awards' can be obtained from: The Secretary, The Scouloudi Foundation Historical Awards Committee, c/o Institute of Historical Research, University of London, Senate House, Malet Street, London WC1E 7HU.

Seamen's Hospital Society

Seafarers

£361,000 to organisations (2010)

Beneficial area

UK.

29 King William Walk, Greenwich, London SE10 9HX
Tel: 020 8858 3696
Fax: 020 8293 9630
Email: admin@seahospital.org.uk
Website: www.seahospital.org.uk
Correspondent: Peter Coulson, General Secretary
Trustees: Capt. D Glass; J C Jenkinson; P McEwan; R Chichester; A R Nairne; Capt. A J Speed; Capt. C Stewart; J Newton; Dr C Mendes da Costa; Mark Carden; Anthony Lydekker; Commander Frank Leonard; Max Gladwyn; Graham Lane.
CC Number: 231724

Information available

Accounts were available from the Charity Commission.

This trust makes grants to medical, care and welfare organisations working with seafarers and to individual seafarers and their dependants. In 2010 the society had assets of £8 million and an income of £494,000. £361,000 was distributed to organisations helping seafarers, with a further £108,500 going to individuals.

The largest grant went to the Seafarers' Benefits Advice Line (£250,000) which the society operates to help provide free confidential advice and information on welfare benefits, housing, consumer problems, legal matters, credit and debt, matrimonial and tax.

Other beneficiaries included: MCFG Development Programme (£40,000); Nautilus Welfare Fund – Mariners' Park (£30,000); Merchant Seamen's War Memorial Society (£17,500); Royal Alfred Seafarers' Society (£10,000); Royal National Mission to Deep Sea Fishermen (£7,500); Scottish Nautical Welfare Society (£3,000); Queen Victoria Seamen's Rest (£2,500); and Annual National Service for Seafarers (£100).

Applications

On a form available from the correspondent. Grants are awarded in November of each year.

The Searchlight Electric Charitable Trust

General

£71,000 (2009/10)

Beneficial area

UK, with a preference for Manchester.

Searchlight Electric Ltd, 900 Oldham Road, Manchester M40 2BS
Tel: 0161 203 3300
Email: heh@slightdemon.co.uk
Correspondent: H E Hamburger, Trustee
Trustees: D M Hamburger, Chair; H E Hamburger; M E Hamburger.
CC Number: 801644

Information available

Basic information was available from the Charity Commission website.

This trust has general charitable purposes, although most grants are given to Jewish organisations. A large number of grants are made in the Manchester area.

In 2009/10 the trust had an unusually low income of £14,000. Total expenditure for that year was £71,000.

Previous beneficiaries include: UJIA (£45,000); CST (£6,000); Bnei a Kivah Sefer Torah (£5,000); Guide Dogs for the Blind (£4,000); Young Israel Synagogue (£2,600); the Federation (£2,000); and Langdon College (£1,500).

Smaller grants of £1,000 or less have included those made to: Heathlands, Lubavitch Manchester and Manchester Eruv Committee (£1,000 each); Reshet and the Purim Fund (£750 each); and Sense, Nightingales and Chabad Vilna (£500 each).

Exclusions

No grants for individuals.

Applications

In writing to the correspondent, but please note that in the past the trustees have stated that it is their policy to only support charities already on their existing list of beneficiaries or those already known to them.

The Searle Charitable Trust

Youth development with a nautical basis

£88,000 (2009/10)

Beneficial area

UK.

30 Watling Street, St Albans AL1 2QB
Correspondent: Sarah Sharkey
Trustees: Andrew D Searle; Victoria C Searle.
CC Number: 288541

Information available

Full accounts were available from the Charity Commission website.

This trust was established in 1982 by Joan Wynne Searle. Following the death of the settlor in 1995 the trust was split into two. One half is administered by the son of the settlor (Searle Charitable Trust) and the other half by her daughter (Searle Memorial Trust).

The Searle Charitable Trust only supports projects/organisations for youth development within a nautical framework.

In 2009/10 the trust had assets of £3.6 million and an income of £81,000. Only one grant was made this financial year, it went to RONA Trust, also a major beneficiary in previous years.

Exclusions

No grants for individuals or for appeals not related to sailing.

Applications

In writing to the correspondent.

The Helene Sebba Charitable Trust

Medical, disability and Jewish

£109,000 (2009/10)

Beneficial area

UK, Canada and Israel.

PO Box 326, Bedford MK40 3XU
Tel: 01234 266657
Correspondent: David L Hull
Trustees: Mrs N C Klein; Mrs
I C Sebba; L Sebba.
CC Number: 277245

Information available

Full accounts were available from the Charity Commission.

The trust supports disability, medical and Jewish organisations and in the past has made grants to causes in the UK, Canada and Israel. In 2009/10 the trust had assets of £2.4 million and an income of £52,000. Grants totalled £109,000 and were divided between two categories: 'Welfare, health including medical research' and 'other'.

Grants included those made to: Friends of Israel Sports Centre for the Disabled (£32,000); SAS Success after Stoke (£7,000); Ferring Country Centre (£5,000); the Prostrate Cancer Charity (£4,000); Friends of Morris Fienmann Homes (£3,000); Foundation Training Company (£2,000); North London Hospice (£1,000); National Jewish Chaplaincy (£500).

Applications

In writing to the correspondent.

The Seedfield Trust

Christian, relief of poverty

£80,000 (2010)

Beneficial area

Worldwide.

3 Woodland Vale, Lakeside, Ulverston, Cumbria LA12 8DR
Tel: 015395 30359
Correspondent: The Trustees
Trustees: Paul Vipond; Keith Buckler; David Ryan; Janet Buckler; Valerie James.
CC Number: 283463

Information available

Accounts were available from the Charity Commission.

The trust's main objects are the furthering of Christian work and the relief of poverty. The trust rarely makes grants towards core funding or for activities that may require funding over a number of years, preferring to make one-off grants for projects which are also receiving support from other sources.

In 2010 the trust had assets of £2.4 million and an income of £105,000. Grants to 33 organisations totalled £80,000.

Beneficiaries included: Overseas Missionary Fellowship (£10,000); European Christian Mission (International) – (£6,000); Mullers (£5,000); Gideons International (£3,000); Capernwary Hall, Choices, Islington and Operation Mobilisation (£2,000 each); Leprosy Mission, Manchester Mission and MECO UK/Ireland (£1,000 each); and Acorn Christian Healing Foundation (£500).

Exclusions

No grants to individuals.

Applications

In writing to the correspondent, for consideration by the trustees who meet twice each year. Please enclose an sae for acknowledgement.

Common applicant mistakes

'Applicants asking for unrealistic amounts; not including an sae.'

Leslie Sell Charitable Trust

Scout and guide groups

£86,000 (2009/10)

Beneficial area

UK, with some preference for the Bedfordshire, Hertfordshire and Buckinghamshire area.

Ashbrittle House, 2a Lower Dagnall Street, St Albans, Hertfordshire AL3 4PA
Tel: 01727 843 603
Fax: 01727 843 663
Email: admin@iplltd.co.uk
Website: www.lesliesellct.org.uk
Correspondent: Sharon Long, Secretary
Trustees: Mary Wiltshire; Adrian Sell; John Byrnes.
CC Number: 258699

Information available

Accounts were on file at the Charity Commission, without a list of grants.

Established in 1969 by the late Leslie Baden Sell, the trust mainly supports scout and guide groups. Most grants are made towards small projects such as building repair works, transport or equipment. Grants are also available to individuals and groups making trips in the UK and overseas.

In 2011 the trust set up the Peter Sell Annual Award, in memory of Peter Sell, a trustee and later chair of the Leslie Sell Charitable Trust who died in 2007. The award will give up to £5,000 to a project aimed at widening engagement and involvement in scouting and guiding.

In 2009/10 the trust had assets totalling £2.9 million and an income of £118,000. Grants were made totalling £86,000.

Applications

In writing to the correspondent. Applications should include clear details of the project or purpose for which funds are required, together with an estimate of total costs and details of any funds raised by the group or individual for the project. The trust states that: 'Applications are usually treated sympathetically provided they are connected to the Scouting or Guide movement'.

Applications to the Peter Sell Annual Award usually have to be submitted by the end of September. Please see the website for full guidelines and accurate future deadlines.

Common applicant mistakes
'Insufficient information about why they are applying for a grant; they forget to include details of where to send the grant to.'

Sellata Ltd

Jewish, welfare
£103,000 (2009/10)

Beneficial area
UK.

29 Fontayne Road, London N16 7EA
Correspondent: Eliezer Benedikt, Trustee
Trustees: Eliezer Benedikt; Nechy Benedikt; Pinchas Benedikt; Joseph Stern.
CC Number: 285429

Information available
Accounts were on file at the Charity Commission, but without a list of grants.

The trust says it supports the advancement of religion and the relief of poverty. In 2009/10 the trust had assets of £311,000 and an income of £220,000. Grants were made totalling £103,000. A list of beneficiaries was not available.

Applications
In writing to the correspondent.

SEM Charitable Trust

General, with a preference for educational special needs and Jewish organisations
£120,000 (2009/10)

Beneficial area
Mainly South Africa, Israel and UK.

Reeves and Co LLP, 37 St Margaret's Street, Canterbury, Kent CT1 2TU
Tel: 01227 768231
Email: info@semtrust.org.uk
Website: www.semcharitabletrust.org
Correspondent: The Trustees
Trustees: Sarah Radomir; Michael Radomir.
CC Number: 265831

Information available
Accounts were available from the Charity Commission.

The trust operates in two main ways:
- supporting and operating educational and training initiatives in South Africa
- making ad hoc grants to organisations in the UK and Israel, particularly those supporting educational special needs.

In 2009/10 the trust had assets of £1.1 million and an income of £89,000. Grants were made to 34 organisations totalling £120,000. A significant amount (£84,000) was also spent on support costs.

By far the largest grant went to Natal Society for Arts (£81,000).

Other beneficiaries included: Jewish Aid Community (£4,500); Tiverton MKT (£3,000); Lotem (£2,500); Care Ltd and Nicky Alliance Day Centre (£2,000 each); SOS Children's Villages, Friends of the Elderly, Disabled on Line Ltd and the Valley Trust (£1,000 each); and Skillforce, CP Sport and Trustees of Snowden (£500 each).

Exclusions
No grants to individuals.

Applications
In writing to the correspondent.

The Ayrton Senna Foundation

Children's health and education
nil (2010)

Beneficial area
Worldwide, with a preference for Brazil.

8th Floor, 6 New Street Square, London EC4A 3AQ
Tel: 020 7842 2000
Correspondent: Christopher Bliss, Trustee
Trustees: Viviane Lalli; Milton Guerado Theodoro da Silva; Neyde Joanna Senna da Silva; Leonardo Senna da Silva; Christopher Bliss; Stephen Howard Ravenscroft.
CC Number: 1041759

Information available
Accounts were available from the Charity Commission.

The trust was established in 1994 by the father of the late Ayrton Senna, in memory of his son, the racing driver. The trust was given the whole issued share capital of Ayrton Senna Foundation Ltd, a company set up to license the continued use of the Senna trademark and copyrights. The trust supports the relief of poverty and the advancement of education, religion and health, particularly the provision of education, healthcare and medical support for children.

In 2010 the foundation had assets of £492,000, with an income of £45,000. In 2010 the trust did not make any donations (£2.8 million in 2009). In 2009 a significant amount of the trust's expenditure (£290,000) was spent on 'governance costs, including foreign exchange movements'. There was one grant made to Instituto Ayrton Senna totalling £2.8 million, a substantial increase from the previous year (£146,000).

Exclusions

No grants to individuals.

Applications

In writing to the correspondent.

The Seven Fifty Trust

Christian causes

£22,000 (2009/10)

Beneficial area

UK and worldwide.

All Saints Vicarage, Church Road, Crowborough, East Sussex TN6 1ED
Tel: 01892 667384
Correspondent: Revd Andrew C J Cornes, Trustee
Trustees: Rev Andrew C J Cornes; Katherine E Cornes; Peter N Collier; Rev Susan M Collier.
CC Number: 298886

Information available

Full accounts were available from the Charity Commission website.

This trust is for the advancement of the Christian religion in the UK and throughout the world. In 2009/10 it had assets of £1.9 million and an income of £65,000. Grants were made totalling £22,000.

The largest grant again went to All Saints Church – Crowborough (£21,000). There were only two other beneficiary organisations: Compassion (£700); and Universities and Colleges Christian Fellowship (£100).

Exclusions

No support for unsolicited requests.

Applications

Unsolicited applications will not be considered.

Common applicant mistakes

'Applying despite unsolicited applications being ineligible.'

SFIA Educational Trust Limited

Education

£280,000 (2009/10)

Beneficial area

UK.

Tectonic Place, Holyport Road, Maidenhead, Berkshire SL6 2YE
Tel: 01628 502040
Fax: 01628 502049
Email: trust@plans-ltd.co.uk
Website: www.plans-ltd.co.uk/trusts
Correspondent: Anne Feek, Chief Executive
Trustees: Beatrice Roberts; Anthony Hastings; David Prince; John Rees; Hugh Monro.
CC Number: 270272

Information available

Full accounts were available from the Charity Commission website.

The trust is focused on the furtherance of education for children and young people under 18. Grants are only awarded to schools/educational organisations towards bursaries to cover part fees for pupils with the following needs:
- special learning difficulties
- social deprivation
- emotional/behavioural difficulties
- physical disabilities
- gifted in a specialist area
- boarding need

Grants are also given towards educational projects, books, equipment and school trips to promote the advancement of learning. Grants will only be considered for specific projects. Recipients will be asked to complete a declaration confirming that the funds will be used for the nominated purpose.

In 2009/10 the trust had assets of £5.4 million and an income of £298,000. Grants were made to 59 institutions totalling £280,000 and were divided as follows:

Educational organisations	38	£170,000
Schools	21	£111,000

Beneficiaries included: Prince's Trust (£35,000); Emmott Foundation (£30,000); Royal Wolverhampton School and King Edward's School – Witley (£15,000 each); Wildfowl and Wetland Trust (£10,000); Arkwright Scholarships (£9,000); Choir Schools' Association (£8,000); Cardiff County Council and Stubbers Adventure Centre (£5,000 each); National Youth Orchestra (£2,800); Beverley School (£2,000); Musicworks (£1,000); and Rainbow Under 5's Playgroup (£100).

Exclusions

No applications will be considered from individuals or from schools/organisations in respect of pupils/students over the age of 18.

Applications

Application forms are available on the trust's website. All applications should be received by 31 January accompanied by the most recent set of audited accounts. Applications are considered in March/April each year. After the meeting, all applicants will be informed of the outcome as soon as possible.

The Cyril Shack Trust

Jewish, general

£150,000 (2009/10)

Beneficial area

UK.

c/o Lubbock Fine, Chartered Accountants, Russell Bedford House, City Forum, 250 City Road, London EC1V 2QQ
Tel: 020 7490 7766
Correspondent: The Clerk
Trustees: J Shack; C C Shack.
CC Number: 264270

Information available

Accounts were available from the Charity Commission, but without a list of grants.

In 2009/10 the trust's assets totalled £680,000. It had an income of £99,000 and made grants totalling £150,000. Mainly Jewish organisations are supported.

No grants list was available. The most recent list of beneficiaries available from the Charity Commission website was from 1996/97. Jewish organisations supported have included: Finchley Road Synagogue, Nightingale House and St John's Wood Synagogue. UK organisations to benefit have included Breakthrough Breast Cancer, Crisis, Golf Aid, Hampstead Theatre, Hartsbourne Ladies Charity, London Library, Prisoners of Conscience, Samaritans, St John's Hospice and University of the Third Age – London.

Exclusions

No grants for expeditions, travel bursaries, scholarships or to individuals.

Applications

In writing to the correspondent.

The Jean Shanks Foundation

Medical research and education

£307,000 (2009/10)

Beneficial area

UK.

Peppard Cottage, Peppard Common, Henley on Thames, Oxon RG9 5LB
Email: barbara.sears@ukgateway.net
Website: jeanshanksfoundation.
org/index.html
Correspondent: Mrs B Sears
Trustees: Prof. Sir Dillwyn Williams; Dr Julian Axe; Alistair Jones; Eric Rothbarth; Prof. Dame Lesley Rees; Prof. Andrew Carr; Prof. Sir James Underwood; Prof. Sir Nicholas Wright.
CC Number: 293108

Information available

Accounts were available from the Charity Commission.

Registered with the Charity Commission in November 1985 this foundation supports medical research and education, particularly in the area of pathology. Grants are made to fund medical students who wish to have an extra research year at medical school and also to other research

projects the trustees consider worthwhile.

In 2009/10 the foundation had assets amounting to £17.1 million and an income of £1.5 million. Grants were made to 24 institutions totalling £307,000.

Beneficiaries included: Royal College of Pathologists (£53,000); University of Oxford (£24,000); University of Cambridge (£21,000); Academy of Medical Sciences (£20,000); and University of Southampton, University of Leicester, University of Manchester, University of Sheffield, University of Hull, University of Cardiff, University of Liverpool, Keele University, Brighton and Sussex Medical School and Queen's University Belfast (£7,500 each).

Exclusions

No grants for capital items. No grants for research which is already supported by another grant giving body or for projects of the type normally dealt with by bodies such as the MRC or Wellcome Trust.

Applications

In writing to the correspondent. Please note: full grant guidelines are available on the foundation's website.

The Shanley Charitable Trust

Relief of poverty

£230,000 (2009/10)

Beneficial area

Worldwide.

Knowles Benning Solicitors, 32 High Street, Shefford, Bedfordshire SG17 5DG
Tel: 01462 814824
Correspondent: S J Atkins, Trustee
Trustees: C A Shanley; R F Lander; S J Atkins.
CC Number: 1103323

Information available

Accounts were available from the Charity Commission.

The trustees make grants to recognised international charities that operate for the relief of poverty.

In 2009/10 the trust had assets of £2 million, an income of £77,000 and made grants totalled £230,000. Beneficiaries were: Children in Crisis, Red Cross, Save the Children and SOS Children (£40,000 each); DEC Haiti Appeal and Water Aid (£30,000); and DEC Philippine Appeal (£10,000).

Applications

In writing to the correspondent.

The Shanti Charitable Trust

General, Christian, international development

£76,000 (2009/10)

Beneficial area

UK, with preference for West Yorkshire, and developing countries (especially Nepal).

Baker Tilly, The Waterfront, Salts Mill Road, Saltaire, Shipley BD17 7EZ
Tel: 01274 536 400
Correspondent: Timothy Parr, Trustee
Trustees: Barbara Gill; Timothy Parr; Ross Hyett.
CC Number: 1064813

Information available

Accounts were available from the Charity Commission.

This trust is a long term supporter of the International Nepal Fellowship, although other funding is given. The trust states that most of the beneficiaries are those which the trustees already have links with.

In 2009/10 the trust had assets of £161,000 and an income of £37,000. Grants were made to 13 organisations totalling £76,000.

Beneficiaries included: Missionaries of Charity (£30,000); International Nepal Fellowship (£10,500); Protac/Theotac, Nepal (£8,000); The Joshua Project and Western Nepal Disability Trust (£5,000 each); EWI-UK (£1,000); and Christian Links in Keighley Schools and CMS (£500 each).

Exclusions

No grants to gap year students, or political or animal welfare causes.

Applications

In writing to the correspondent. Please note, most beneficiaries are those the trustees already have contact with.

The Linley Shaw Foundation

Conservation

£95000 (2009/10)

Beneficial area

UK.

Natwest Trust Services, 5th Floor, Trinity Quay 2, Avon Street, Bristol BS2 0PT
Tel: 0117 940 3283
Fax: 0117 940 3275
Correspondent: The Trust Section
Trustee: National Westminster Trust Services.
CC Number: 1034051

Information available

Brief accounts available at the Charity Commission website.

The foundation supports charities working to conserve, preserve and restore the natural beauty of the UK countryside for the public benefit.

Generally the trustees prefer to support a specific project, rather than give money for general use. In his will, Linley Shaw placed particular emphasis on those charities which organise voluntary workers to achieve the objects of the foundation. This may be taken into account when considering applications. Grants can be given towards any aspect of a project. Previous examples include the cost of tools, management surveys and assistance with the cost of land purchase.

In 2009/10 the trust had an income of £43,000. Grants were made to 25 charitable organisations totalling £95,000 and ranging in value from £500 to £16,000. Grant beneficiaries included: Plantlife, Kent Wildlife Trust, Devon Wildlife Trust, Essex Wildlife Trust; Gazen Salts Nature Reserve, The Barn Owl Trust, The National Trust Brecon Beacons, Trees for Life, Scottish Sea Bird Centre and Ty-Croeso Centre.

Exclusions

No grants to non-charitable organisations, or to organisations whose aims or objects do not include conservation, preservation or restoration of the natural beauty of the UK countryside, even if the purpose of the grant would be eligible. No grants to individuals.

Applications

Applications must be in writing to the correspondent. All material will be photocopied by the trust so please avoid sending bound copies of reports and so on. Evidence of aims and objectives are needed, usually in the forms of accounts, annual reports or leaflets, which cannot be returned. Applications are considered in February/early March and should be received by December/early January.

The Sheldon Trust

General charitable purposes

£116,000 (2009/10)

Beneficial area

West Midlands.

White Horse Court, 25c North Street, Bishop's Stortford, Hertfordshire CM23 2LD
Tel: 01279 506 421
Email: charities@pwwsolicitors.co.uk
Website: www.pwwsolicitors.co.uk/charitable-applications
Correspondent: The Trust Administrator
Trustees: A Bidnell; Revd R S Bidnell; J K R England; R V Wiglesworth; Mrs R Beatton; Mrs R Gibbins; Paul K England.
CC Number: 242328

Information available

Full accounts were available from the Charity Commission website.

The trust's geographical area of giving is the West Midlands, with particular emphasis on the areas of Birmingham, Coventry, Dudley, Sandwell, Solihull, Wolverhampton and Warwickshire. The main aims continue to be the relief of poverty and distress in society, concentrating grants on community projects as well as those directed to special needs groups, especially in deprived areas. The trustees review their policy and criteria regularly and 'although they have a central policy, flexibility is retained to allow for reaction to changes in the environment and the community alike'.

In 2009/10 the trust had assets of £3.8 million and an income of £180,000. Grants were made to 37 organisations totalling £116,000. The average grant size was £4,000.

Grants were broken down in the accounts as follows:

Holiday projects: Grants totalling £6,000 for holiday projects included those awarded to: Bethany Christian Fellowship, Birmingham Phab Camps, CF Dream Holidays and Farms for City Children.

Grants for special needs groups: Beneficiaries included: Birmingham Centre for Arts Therapies, Birmingham Focus on Blindness, Sound It Out Community Music and The Society of Mary and Martha.

Continuing grants: Four new continuing grants were approved by the trustees: The Birmingham Centre for Arts Therapies, Mercia MS Therapy Centre, Signhealth and St George House Charity.

Community projects: Organisations supported during the year included: Bentley Beginnings, Guy's Gift, Home Start Winson Green, Karis Neighbour Scheme, St Martin's Social Care Project and Warwickshire Clubs for Young People.

Continuing grants: Five new continuing grants were approved by the trustees: Bentley Beginnings, Guy's Gift, Kingsbury Village Pre School, National Youth Theatre of Great Britain and Safeline.

Exclusions

The trust does not consider general appeals from national organisations and does not usually consider appeals in respect of the cost of buildings.

Applications

Application forms are available from the correspondent but the trust prefers applicants to complete and submit their application online. The trustees meet three times a year, in April, August and November. Application forms, including the most recent signed accounts, a project budget and a job description (if applying for a salary) should be received at least six weeks before the date of the next meeting.

Successful organisations will be sent a grant offer and any conditions. Unsuccessful applicants will have to wait two years before re-applying.

Please note: a designated sum is set aside for the holiday grants programme and applications are considered in April each year. Applications should be submitted by the end of February.

Common applicant mistakes

'Not supplying the supporting documentation required for an application.'

P and D Shepherd Charitable Trust

General charitable purposes particularly those involving young people

£97,000 to organisations (2009/10)

Beneficial area

Worldwide, particularly the north of England and Scotland.

5 Cherry Lane, Dringhouses, York YO24 1QH
Correspondent: The Trustees
Trustees: Mrs P Shepherd; Mrs J L Robertson; Patrick M Shepherd; Annabel Robertson; I O Robertson; Mrs C M Shepherd; Michael James Shepherd; J O Shepherd; R O Robertson.
CC Number: 272948

Information available

Full accounts were available from the Charity Commission website.

The trust makes grants through charitable organisations to benefit people in need and society in general. There is a preference for supporting charities in the north of England and Scotland, or those connected with the trustees.

Patrick Shepherd is also a trustee of York Against Cancer (Charity Commission no. 1130835).

In 2009/10 the trust had assets of £497,000 and an income of £179,000. Grants were made to 156 organisations totalling almost £97,000 and grants totalling £500 were made to two individuals.

Beneficiaries of grants of £1,000 or more during this period included: Special Boat Service Association and York Air Museum (£10,000 each); Army Benevolent Fund and York Air Ambulance (£5,000 each); Help for Heroes (£5,000); and Survive (£1,000).

Applications

In writing to the correspondent.

The Archie Sherman Cardiff Foundation

Health, education, training, overseas aid, community and Jewish

£156,000 (2009/10)

Beneficial area

UK, Canada, Australia, New Zealand, Pakistan, Sri Lanka, South Africa, India, Israel, USA and other parts of the British Commonwealth.

Rothschild Trust Corp Ltd, New Court, St Swithins Lane, London EC4P 4DU
Tel: 020 7280 5000
Correspondent: The Trustees
Trustee: Rothschild Trust Corporation Ltd.
CC Number: 272225

Information available

Full accounts were available from the Charity Commission website.

Established in 1976, this foundation supports health and educational charities in the UK and overseas. The foundation is empowered to distribute its income as it sees fit but it tends to pay special regard to the following organisations: Society of Friends of the Jewish Refugees, UJIA, British Organisation for Rehabilitation and Training, JNF Charitable Trust, British Council of the Shaare Zedek Hospital, British Technion Society and Friends of the Hebrew University.

In 2009/10 the foundation had assets of £2.3 million and an income of £108,000. Grants were made totalling £156,000, broken down as follows:

Health	2	£99,000
Community	1	£47,500
Education and training	1	£10,000

Beneficiaries were: Magen David Adom UK (£60,000); United Jewish Israel Appeal (£47,500); Merephdi Foundation (£39,000); and Friends of Bar Ilan University (£10,000).

Exclusions

No grants to individuals.

Applications

In writing to the correspondent.

The Barnett and Sylvia Shine No 2 Charitable Trust

General

£41,000 (2009/10)

Beneficial area

Worldwide.

Berwin Leiton Paisner, Adelaide House, London Bridge, London EC4R 9HA
Tel: 020 7760 1000
Fax: 020 7760 1111
Correspondent: M D Paisner, Trustee
Trustees: M D Paisner; Barbara J Grahame; Prof R Grahame.
CC Number: 281821

Information available

Accounts were available from the Charity Commission.

In 1980, half the assets of the No 1 Charitable Trust (see separate entry) were transferred to the No 2 Charitable Trust. In 1981, the executors of the estate of the late Sylvia Shine transferred several paintings, jewellery and cash to the trusts. The No 2 fund has some preference for organisations working with children and young adults, the elderly and people with disabilities.

In 2009/10 the trust had assets of £1.3 million and an income of £44,000. Grants were made to 17 organisations totalling £41,000.

Beneficiaries included: Médecins Sans Frontières (£10,000); Macmillan Cancer Support (£3,000); Lifeboats, the Samaritans, the Smile Train – UK, St Mungo's and Water Aid (£2,000 each); and Chernobyl Children's Project – UK, One-to-One Children's Fund, the Royal Parks Foundation, and Send a Cow to Africa (£1,000).

Exclusions

No grants to individuals.

Applications

In writing to the correspondent.

The Bassil Shippam and Alsford Trust

Young and older people, health, education, learning disabilities, Christian

£116,000 to organisations (2009/10)

Beneficial area

UK, with a preference for West Sussex.

Thomas Eggar, The Corn Exchange, Baffins Lane, Chichester, West Sussex PO19 1GE
Tel: 01243 786111
Fax: 01243 775640
Correspondent: Simon MacFarlane, Clerk to the Trustees

Trustees: J H S Shippam; C W Doman; S A E MacFarlane; S W Young; Mrs M Hanwell; R Tayler; Mrs S Trayler.
CC Number: 256996

Information available

Full accounts were available from the Charity Commission website.

This trust supports charities active in the fields of care for young and older people, health, education and religion. Many of the organisations supported are in West Sussex. In 2009/10 the trust had assets of £3.6 million and an income of £142,000. Grants were made to 152 organisations totalling £116,000, which were made under the following categories:

Furtherance of education	£62,000
Social welfare	£50,000
Performing arts	£1,800
Medical research	£1,200
Welfare of people in financial need	£350

Beneficiaries included: Donnington House and Fordwater School (£10,000 each); Christian Youth Enterprise Sailing Centre and St Wilfrid's Hospice (£5,000 each); Newell Centre Association (£3,500); Pailant House Gallery, Crime Diversion Scheme and TEAR Fund – Haiti Donation (£1,000 each); Careforce, Cancerwise and Petworth Festival(£500 each); Disability Awareness UK and St John Ambulance – Sussex (£350 each); Miracles, the Chichester Stroke Club and the Meningitis Trust (£250 each); Action Medical Research (£200); and the Honeypot Trust (£100).

An additional £7,000 was given in grants to 20 individuals.

Applications

In writing to the correspondent, including a copy of the latest set of reports, accounts and forecasts. The trustees meet three times a year to consider applications.

Common applicant mistakes

'Applying from the wrong geographical area (i.e. not within the scope of the trust).'

The Shipwrights' Company Charitable Fund

Maritime or waterborne connected charities

£87,000 (2009/10)

Beneficial area

UK, with a preference for the City of London.

Ironmongers' Hall, Shaftesbury Place, Barbican, London EC2Y 8AA
Tel: 020 7606 2376
Fax: 020 7600 8117
Email: clerk@shipwrights.co.uk
Website: www.shipwrights.co.uk
Correspondent: The Clerk
Trustees: The Worshipful Company of Shipwrights; William D Everard; Simon Sherrard; Sir Jock Slater; M Simon Robinson; Graham Clarke.
CC Number: 262043

Information available

Accounts were available from the Charity Commission.

The Shipwrights' Company is a Livery Company of the City of London and draws its members from all the various aspects of marine commerce and industry in the UK. Its charitable interests therefore focus on the maritime, with an emphasis on young people, church work and the City.

Applications from individuals or, for example, schools to join sail training voyages are considered. It supports sailing for people with disabilities, with both the Jubilee Sailing Trust and the Challenger class.

In 2009/10 the trust had assets of £2.5 million and an income of £179,000. Grants to 34 organisations totalled around £87,000 and are categorised as general donations, outdoor activity bursaries and special donations.

Grant recipients included: Tall Ships Youth Trust (£20,000); Marine Society and Sea Cadets (£17,000); George Green's School (two grants totalling £10,500); Jubilee Training Trust and Tower Hamlets – Summer University (£5,000 each); City of London Unit, Sea Cadet Corps, HMS

373

Belfast (£3,000); and Maritime Rescue Institute, Ocean Youth Trust South, Thames Shipwright and the Trinity Sailing Trust (£1,000 each).

Exclusions

Any application without a clear maritime connection.

Applications

In writing to the correspondent. Applications and guidelines are available from the trust's website. Applications are considered in February, June and November.

The trust gave us the following information: 'Send requests by email – letters take time to process. In particular give an email address to reply to, particularly as 5 out of 6 are rejected.'

Common applicant mistakes

'Not reading the specific criteria that we are unable to consider to circular letters which are sent, thus wasting the applicant's postage and assessor's time.'

The Charles Shorto Charitable Trust

General

£936,000 (2010/11)

Beneficial area

UK.

c/o Taylors, Mercury House, 1 Mason Road, Redditch, Worcestershire B97 5DA
Tel: 01527 544 221
Email: tom@taylorssolicitors.com
Correspondent: T J J Baxter
Trustees: Joseph A V Blackham; Brian M Dent.
CC Number: 1069995

Information available

Accounts were available from the Charity Commission.

This trust was established under the will of Edward Herbert Charles Shorto with general charitable purposes. Whilst welcoming applications, the trustees also like to identify causes that they know

Charles Shorto had an interest in. There is a preference for projects benefiting disadvantaged and disabled people and their carers.

In 2010/11 the trust had assets of £2 million and an income of almost £90,000. Grants were made to five organisations totalling £936,000.

The largest grant went to: The Barnard Kenneth Hufton Trust (£740,000). Other beneficiaries were: Sacred Heart & Holy Souls Catholic Church (£97,000); League of Friends of the Budleigh Salterton Hospital (£50,000); Oxford Youth Works (£3,000); Cumnor PCC (£1,700).

According to the trust's 2007/08 accounts: 'The fund is to be distributed finally between 2nd October 2007 and 2nd October 2012.'

Applications

In writing to the correspondent at any time. The trustees meet four times a year.

The Barbara A Shuttleworth Memorial Trust

People with disabilities

£30,000 (2009/10)

Beneficial area

UK, with a preference for West Yorkshire.

Baty Casson Long, Shear's Yard, 21 Wharf Street, The Calls, Leeds LS2 7EQ
Tel: 0113 242 5848
Fax: 0013 247 0342
Email: baty@btinternet.com
Correspondent: John Baty, Chair
Trustees: John Alistair Baty, Chair; Barbara Anne Shuttleworth; John Christopher Joseph Eaton; William Fenton.
CC Number: 1016117

Information available

Information was obtained from the Charity Commission website.

The trust gives grants to organisations that aim to improve the circumstances of people who are disabled, and particularly those

helping children. The trust prefers to make grants for what it calls 'hard' benefits such as equipment, premises or other permanent facilities but it will consider funding 'soft' benefits like holidays, training courses and visits.

In 2009/10 the trust had an income of £22,000 and a total expenditure of £39,000. Grants are likely to have totalled around £30,000, further information was not available.

Previous beneficiaries have included: National Deaf Children's Society (£2,300); Chapel Grange Special School and Children's Liver Disease Foundation (£2,000 each); Aidis Trust (£1,500); United Response – York and Sunny Days Children's Charity (£1,000 each); St James's Hospital for 'Chemo Ducks' (£900); Muscular Dystrophy Group (£600); Symbol Trust (£500); Rutland House School for Parents (£350); and British Diabetic Association (£250).

Applications

In writing to the correspondent.

The Leslie Silver Charitable Trust

Jewish, general

Around £208,000 (2009/10)

Beneficial area

UK, but mostly West Yorkshire.

R S M Tennon Ltd, 2 Wellington Place, Leeds LS1 4AP
Tel: 0113 244 5451
Fax: 0113 242 6308
Correspondent: Ian J Fraser, Trustee
Trustees: Leslie H Silver; Mark S Silver; Ian J Fraser.
CC Number: 1007599

Information available

Accounts received at the Charity Commission but unavailable to view.

This trust principally supports Jewish-based charities and appeal funds launched in the West Yorkshire area. In 2009/10 the trust had an income of £11,000 and a total expenditure of £208,000.

Previous beneficiaries included: Donisthorpe Hall (£55,000); Leeds

Centre for Deaf and Blind People £16,000); and Holocaust Centre and Variety Club Children's Charity £10,000 each); UJIA and Jewish National Fund (£5,000 each); the Zone (£4,000); Children in Crisis and Lord Mayor's Charity Appeal (£2,000 each); Second World War Experience £1,000); and Holocaust Educational Trust (£500).

Exclusions

No grants to individuals or students.

Applications

In writing to the correspondent following a specific format. Please note the trust has previously stated: the recipients of donations are restricted almost exclusively to the concerns in which the trustees take a personal interest and that unsolicited requests from other sources, although considered by the trustees, are rejected almost invariably'.

The Simpson Education and Conservation Trust

Environmental conservation

£43,000 (2009/10)

Beneficial area

UK and overseas, with a preference for the neotropics (South America).

Honeysuckle Cottage, Tidenham Chase, Chepstow, Gwent NP16 7JW
Tel: 01291 689423
Fax: 01291 689803
Correspondent: N Simpson, Chair
Trustees: Nigel Simpson, Chair; Prof. D M Broom; Dr J M Lock; Prof. S Chang; Dr Katherine Simpson.
CC Number: 1069695

Information available

Accounts were available from the Charity Commission.

Established in 1998, the main objectives of this trust are:

- the advancement of education in the UK and overseas, including medical and scientific research

- the conservation and protection of the natural environment and endangered species of plants and animals with special emphasis on the protection of forests and endangered avifauna in the neotropics (South America).

The trust receives its income mainly from Gift Aid donations, which totalled £33,000 in 2009/10. Its priority for this year was again to support the Jocotoco Foundation in Ecuador (£40,000). This charity is dedicated to the conservation of endangered special birds through the acquisition of forest habitat. The chair of this trust, Dr RNF Simpson, an expert in ornithology and conservation, is also on the board of trustees for Jocotoco Conservation Foundation (JFC).

Other grants were awarded to: World Land Trust (£2,000) for a school environmental educational project; and Linnean Society of London (£1,000) for the preparation of Field Guides for the African Violet Conservation Project in Tanzania (sixth year).

Exclusions

No grants to individuals.

Applications

In writing to the correspondent. The day-to-day activities of this trust are carried out by email, telephone and circulation of documents, since the trustees do not all live in the UK.

Common applicant mistakes

This trust was established to make available grants to overseas NGOs with minimum overhead costs in processing the grants. It does not make donations to individual applicants, and usually the trust has in-depth knowledge about the recipient NGO. It specialises in Tropical Americas. Donations within the UK are made by personal Gift Aid process, usually not involving the trust.

Donations to individuals are not possible, but the trust does receive a lot of such applications – say 30 to 50 a year.

The Simpson Foundation

Roman Catholic purposes

£29,000 (2009/10)

Beneficial area

UK.

Pothecary Witham Weld, 70 St George's Square, London SW1V 3RD
Tel: 020 7821 8211
Fax: 020 7630 6484
Correspondent: P J O Herschan, Trustee
Trustees: C E T Bellord; P J M Hawthorne; P J O Herschan.
CC Number: 231030

Information available

Basic information taken from the Charity Commission website.

The trust supports charities favoured by the founder in his lifetime and others with similar objects, mainly Catholic charities. Only registered charities are supported.

In 2009/10 it had an income of £15,000 and a total expenditure of £29,000. No information on grant beneficiaries for this year was available.

Beneficiaries in previous years have included: Venerable Collegio Inglese, St Benedict's Abbey, Sisters of Charity of Jesus and Mary, The Access Partnership, Congregation of the Blessed Sacrament and Providence Row Night Refuge and Home.

Exclusions

No grants to non-registered charities or individuals.

Applications

In writing to the correspondent, at any time. No telephone applications will be considered.

The Huntly and Margery Sinclair Charitable Trust

General

£42,000 (2009/10)

Beneficial area

UK.

c/o Vernor-Miles and Noble Solicitors, 5 Raymond Buildings, Gray's Inn, London WC1R 5DD
Tel: 020 7242 8688
Fax: 020 7242 3192
Email: wilfridvm@vmn.org.uk
Correspondent: Wilfrid Vernor-Miles, Administrator
Trustees: Mrs A M H Gibbs; Mrs M A H Windsor; Mrs J Floyd.
CC Number: 235939

Information available

Full accounts were available from the Charity Commission website.

This trust has general charitable purposes at the discretion of the trustees. However, the trust states that nearly all grants are made to organisations already known to the trustees so unsolicited applications are rarely successful.

In 2009/10 the trust had assets of £1.3 million and an income £48,000. Grants were made to 32 organisations totalling £42,000.

Grants included those made to: King Edward VII Hospital (£5,000); Too Many Women (£3,000); Injured Jockey's Fund (£2,500); Cheltenham Festival (£2,000); St Rose's Special School (£1,000); and Tiger Awareness (£500).

Applications

Unsolicited applications are rarely successful and due to the high number such requests the trust is not able to respond to them or return any printed materials supplied.

Sino-British Fellowship Trust

Education

£334,000 to organisations (2010)

Beneficial area

UK and China.

Flat 23 Bede House, Manor Fields, London SW15 3LT
Tel: 020 8788 6252
Correspondent: Mrs Anne Ely
Trustees: Prof. H Baker; A Ely; P Ely; Prof. Sir Heap; Dr J Langton; L Thompson; Prof. Sir Todd; Lady Pamela Youde.
CC Number: 313669

Information available

Full accounts were available from the Charity Commission website.

The trust makes grants to institutions benefiting individual postgraduate students. It does this through: scholarships to Chinese citizens to enable them to pursue their studies in Britain; grants to British citizens in China to educate/train Chinese citizens in any art, science or profession.

In 2010 the trust had assets of £12.7 million and an income of £397,000. A total of £414,000 was made in grants. Of this total £334,000 was made in grants to organisations in the UK and China, with the remainder awarded as individual scholarships.

Grants to institutions included: Royal Society (£120,000); China Scholarship Council (£26,000); British Academy (£22,000 in two grants); Great Britain China Educational Trust (£20,000); Chinese University of Hong Kong and Open University of Hong Kong (£16,500 each); and School of Oriental and African Studies (£10,000).

Applications

On a form available by writing to the correspondence address.

The Charles Skey Charitable Trust

General

£92,000 (2009/10)

Beneficial area

UK.

Flint House, Park Homer Road, Colehill, Wimborne, Dorset BH21 2SP
Correspondent: J M Leggett, Trustee
Trustees: C H A Skey, Chair; J M Leggett; C B Berkeley; Revd J H A Leggett.
CC Number: 277697

Information available

Accounts were available from the Charity Commission.

The trust's 2009/10 annual report states:

> The trustees support causes on an annual basis, irregularly and on a one-off basis. For those charities receiving annual donations, the amount to be given is reviewed annually. For those receiving periodic donations, the trustees are the judge of when a further grant should be made. For one-off donations, the trustees examine the requests which have been received and have sole authority as to which to support. In general, the trust supports those causes where the grant made is meaningful to the recipient.

In 2009/10 the trust had assets of £3.5 million and an income of £200,000. Grants were made to organisations totalling £92,000, which were distributed as follows:

Education, training, medical, health, sickness and disability	23	£72,000
Environmental conservation and heritage	3	£8,000
Religious activities	3	£8,000
General purposes	2	£4,000

Beneficiaries included: Arnold Foundation – Rugby School, Lloyds Patriotic Fund and Royal Fusiliers Museum Appeal (£10,000 each); Trinity Hospice (£7,500); Roses Charitable Trust (£5,000); Camphill Village Trust (£3,000); the Dagenham Gospel Trust (£2,000); and Heritage of London Trust (£1,000).

Applications

The trust has previously stated that no written or telephoned requests for support will be entertained.

The John Slater Foundation

Medical, animal welfare, general

£169,000 (2009/10)

Beneficial area

UK, with a strong preference for the north west of England especially West Lancashire.

HSBC Trust Services, 10th Floor, Norwich House, Nelson Gate, Commercial Road, Southampton
Tel: 023 8072 2231
Fax: 023 8072 2250
Correspondent: R Thompson, Trust Manager
Trustee: HSBC Trust Co. (UK) Ltd.
CC Number: 231145

Information available

Accounts were obtained from the Charity Commission website.

The foundation gives grants for £1,000 to £5,000 to a range of organisations, particularly those working in the fields of medicine or animal welfare.

In 2009/10 it had assets of £3.9 million and an income of £454,000. Grants were made to 82 organisations totalling £169,000.

Beneficiaries included: The Wellspring – Stockport (£18,000); Macmillan and Trinity Hospice (£10,000 each); Blackpool Ladies Sick Poor Association, Superintendent Gerald Richardson Memorial and Addlington Community Centre (£8,000); St John's Church, Levens (£5,000); RSPCA, RSPB, RNLI (£4,000 each); PDSA, Asthma Relief, Conquest Art (£2,000 each); Blue Cross (£1,000).

Exclusions

No grants to individuals.

Applications

In writing to the correspondent, including accounts. Applications are considered twice a year, in May and November.

Rita and David Slowe Charitable Trust

General

£68,000 (2009/10)

Beneficial area

UK and overseas.

32 Hampstead High Street, London NW3 1JQ
Tel: 020 7435 7800
Correspondent: The Trustees
Trustees: Elizabeth Slowe; Graham Weinberg; Jonathan Slowe.
CC Number: 1048209

Information available

Accounts were available from the Charity Commission.

The trust makes grants to a range of registered charities. In 2009/10 the trust held assets of £660,000 and had an income of £82,000. Grants were made to eight organisations totalling £68,000.

Grants went to: Shelter and Computer Aid International (£13,000 each); David Baum International Foundation (£10,000); Books Abroad, Excellent Development and Wells for India (£7,500 each); and Send a Cow and Big Issue Foundation (£5,000 each).

Exclusions

No grants are made to individuals (including gap year students) or religious bodies.

Applications

In writing to the correspondent.

Common applicant mistakes

'Applicants not having accounts available on their website.'

The SMB Charitable Trust

Christian, general charitable purposes

£212,000 (2009/10)

Beneficial area

UK and overseas.

15 Wilman Rd, Tunbridge Wells, Kent TN4 9AJ
Tel: 01892 537 301
Fax: 01892 618 202
Email: smbcharitabletrust@googlemail.com
Correspondent: Mrs B M O'Driscoll, Trustee
Trustees: E D Anstead; P J Stanford; Barbara O'Driscoll; J A Anstead; Claire Swarbrick.
CC Number: 263814

Information available

Accounts were available from the Charity Commission.

The trust supports charities which meet one of the following criteria:

- support of the Christian faith
- provision of social care in the UK and abroad
- provision of famine or emergency aid
- protection of the environment and wildlife
- support of education or medical research.

Grants are generally of £1,000 each, although this can vary. The trustees make regular grants to a large number of 'core' charities, so while new applications are considered, only a small minority is likely to be successful. The founder's preferences are taken into account when deciding which of the applicants will be supported.

In 2009/10 the trust had assets of £8.2 million and an income of £323,000. Grants were made to 178 organisations totalling £212,000.

Beneficiaries included: Pilgrim Homes (£4,000); British Red Cross and Salvation Army (£3,000 each); Baptist Missionary Society and Mission Aviation Fellowship (£2,500); Marie Curie Foundation and West Ham

Central Mission (£2,000 each); Shaftesbury Society (£1,500); Share Jesus International (£1,000); and Sports Reach (£500).

Exclusions

Grants to individuals are not normally considered, unless the application is made through a registered charity which can receive the cheque.

Applications

In writing to the correspondent, including the aims and principal activities of the applicant, the current financial position and details of any special projects for which funding is sought. Application forms are not used. Trustees normally meet in March, June, September and December and applications should be received before the beginning of the month in which meetings are held. Because of the volume of appeals received, unsuccessful applicants will only receive a reply if they enclose an sae. However, unsuccessful applicants are welcome to reapply.

The N Smith Charitable Settlement

General including social work, medical research, education, environment/animals, arts and overseas aid

£117,000 (2009/10)

Beneficial area

Worldwide.

Linder Myers, Phoenix House, 45 Cross Street, Manchester M2 4JF
Tel: 0161 832 6972
Fax: 0161 834 0718
Correspondent: Anne E Merricks
Trustees: T R Kendal; Miss A E Merricks; J H Williams-Rigby; G Wardle.
CC Number: 276660

Information available

Full accounts were available from the Charity Commission website.

This trust was established in 1978. In 2009/10 the trust had assets of £4.1 million and an income of £140,000. Grants were made totalling £117,000 and were broken down as follows:

Social work	72	£45,000
Overseas aid	28	£22,500
Medical research	13	£17,000
Arts	16	£10,500
Environment/animals	17	£9,500
Education	10	£6,500

Beneficiaries included: Migraine Trust (£2,000); Nepal Leprosy Trust and East Cheshire Hospice (£1,000 each); Animal Health Trust (£650); Action for Kids, Autism West Midlands, Eden Project, Listening Books, Opera North, Royal British Legion and Whoopsadaisy (£500 each).

Exclusions

Grants are only made to registered charities and not to individuals.

Applications

In writing to the correspondent. The trustees meet twice a year.

The Smith Charitable Trust

General charitable purposes

£92,000 (2009/10)

Beneficial area

UK and overseas.

c/o Moon Beever, Solicitors, 24 Bloomsbury Square, London WC1A 2PL
Tel: 020 7637 0661
Correspondent: Paul Shiels, Trustee
Trustees: A G F Fuller; P A Sheils; R I Turner; R J Weetch.
CC Number: 288570

Information available

Accounts were available from the Charity Commission.

The trust supports registered charities, which are usually larger well-known UK organisations. Beneficiaries are chosen by the settlor and he has a set list of charities that are supported twice a year. Other charities are unlikely to receive a grant.

In 2009/10 the trust had assets of £5.3 million and an income of £157,000. Grants were made to 22 organisations totalling £92,000.

Grants included those made to: Sue Ryder Care (£9,000); Research Institute for the Care of the Elderly, Macmillan Cancer Relief and RNLI (£6,000 each); St Nicholas' Hospice and Help the Heroes (£5,000 each); and the Marine Society and Sea Cadets, MIND, SENSE and SCOPE (£3,000 each).

Exclusions

No grants to animal charities or to individuals.

Applications

Unsolicited applications are not considered.

The E H Smith Charitable Trust

General

Around £40,000

Beneficial area

UK, some preference for the Midlands.

Westhaven House, Arleston Way, Shipley, West Midlands B90 4LH
Tel: 0121 706 6100
Correspondent: K H A Smith, Trustee
Trustees: K H A Smith; Mrs B M Hodgskin-Brown; D P Ensell.
CC Number: 328313

Information available

Full accounts were available from the Charity Commission website.

This trust has general charitable purposes and supports a range of local and national organisations. In 2009/10 the trust had an income of £10,000 and a total expenditure of £42,000.

Previous beneficiaries included: Romania Challenge (£4,900); Betel (£2,500); Solihull Hall (£1,500); Cancer Research UK (£900); County Air Ambulance (£700); Smile Train UK (£600); and Crash Christmas Cards, NSPCC and Junior Heybridge Swifts FC (£500 each).

Exclusions

No grants to political parties. Grants are not normally given to individuals.

Applications

In writing to the correspondent at any time.

The Amanda Smith Charitable Trust

General

Around £1,400 (2010)

Beneficial area

UK.

1 Manchester Square, London W1U 3AB
Tel: 02032 192600
Correspondent: Neil Bradley
Trustees: C Smith, Chair; Ms A Smith.
CC Number: 1052975

Information available

Information was obtained from the Charity Commission website.

This trust was established in 1996. The trust's income is derived mainly from the rent of a shopping centre and a housing estate. The trust stated that this is gradually decreasing. The trust makes grants irregularly.

In 2010 the trust had no income and a total expenditure of £1,400. Further information was not available, except that it remains on the Central Register of Charities and so has not been dissolved. Previous beneficiaries have included Cedar School and Nordoff Robbins Music Therapy.

Applications

In writing to the correspondent.

The Martin Smith Foundation

Art, music, sports and education

£204,000 (2005/06)

Beneficial area

UK.

4 Essex Villas, London W8 7BN
Tel: 020 7937 0027
Correspondent: Martin Smith
Trustees: Martin G Smith, Chair; Elise Smith; Jeremy J G Smith; Katherine Wake; Elizabeth F C Buchanan; B Peerless.
CC Number: 1072607

Information available

Accounts were available from the Charity Commission.

This trust mainly gives to projects and organisations connected to art, music, sports and education. In 2009/10 the trust had assets of £95,000 and an income of £78,000. Grants were made to 8 organisations totalling £154,000.

The two largest grants went to: Orchestra of the Age of Enlightenment – Smith Challenge (£62,000); and St Edmund Hall (£50,000).

Other grants of £15,000 or less included those made to: Bath Mozartfest (£15,000); The Beckett Collection (£12,500); Inside World Imagine (£5,000); and London School Symphony Orchestra (£1,000).

Grants totalling £100 were also made to individuals.

Applications

This trust does not consider unsolicited applications.

The Leslie Smith Foundation

Children with illnesses, orphans and schools

£181,000 (2009/10)

Beneficial area

UK with a preference for Wiltshire, Norfolk, Middlesex, London and Dorset.

c/o Willcox & Lewis, The Old Coach House, Sunnyside, Bergh Apton, Norwich NR15 1DD
Tel: 01508 480100
Fax: 01508 480001
Email: info@willcoxlewis.co.uk
Correspondent: The Trustees
Trustees: M D Willcox; H L Young Jones.
CC Number: 250030

Information available

Accounts were obtained from the Charity Commission website.

The foundation, which regularly reviews its grant-making policy, is currently focusing on:

- Children with illnesses, both terminal and non-terminal, in the UK, excluding respite care and research
- Orphans
- Schools, specifically special needs schools based in the UK.

In 2009/10 the trust had an income of £56,000 and made grants totalling £181,000. Its assets stood at almost £2.9 million. Grants were broken down as follows:

Health and allied services	£52,000
Poverty	£43,000
Miscellaneous	£37,000
Children's welfare	£28,000
Ex-service welfare	£10,000
Counselling services	£10,000

Grants included those made to: Comic Relief (£43,000); Shakespeare Globe (£25,000); Gaddum Centre, Joseph Weld Hospice and Royal British Legion (£10,000 each); Shooting Star Children's Hospice and Prisoners Abroad (£5,000 each); The Community Foundation and Step by Step (£2,500 each); and Norfolk Accident Rescue Service (£2,000).

Exclusions

Grants are given to registered charities only. No grants for individuals.

Applications

In writing to the correspondent, including a summary of the project and a copy of the latest accounts. Only successful applications are acknowledged.

The Stanley Smith UK Horticultural Trust

Horticulture

£121,000 (2009/10)

Beneficial area

UK and overseas.

Cory Lodge, PO Box 365, Cambridge CB2 1HR
Tel: 01223 336 299
Fax: 01223 336 278
Correspondent: James Cullen, Director
Trustees: C D Brickell; Lady Renfrew; J B E Simmons; A De Brye; P R Sykes; Dr D A H Rae; E Reed.
CC Number: 261925

Information available

Accounts were available from the Charity Commission.

Established by deed in 1970, the trust's objects are the advancement of horticulture. In particular, the trustees have power to make grants for the following purposes:

- horticultural research
- the creation, development, preservation and maintenance of public gardens
- the promotion of the cultivation and wide distribution of plants of horticultural value/other value to mankind
- the promotion of the cultivation of new plants
- publishing books and work related to horticultural sciences.

In 2009/10 the trust had assets of £3.2 million and an income of £135,000. Grants to 34 organisations and individuals totalled £121,000.

Beneficiaries from the general fund included: The Belmont Trust, Unst, Shetland and WB School (£5,000 each); Bristol University Botanic Garden, GardenAfrica, HM Prison Shepton Mallet and Trees for Cities (£2,500 each); Castle Howard Arboretum Trust and Fokas-Cosmetatos Foundation, Cephalonia, Greece (£2,000 each); and Combe Reading Room, Combe, Oxfordshire,

Jane Austen's House, Chawton, Hampshire, Plant Heritage (NCCPG) and The Garden Museum, Lambeth, London (£1,000 each).

The director continues to provide advice to actual and potential applicants, and to established projects which have already received grants. Any grant provided by the trust bears the condition that the recipient should provide within six months, or some other agreed period, a report on the use of the grant.

Exclusions

Grants are not made for projects in commercial horticulture (crop production) or agriculture, nor are they made to support students taking academic or diploma courses of any kind, although educational institutions are supported.

Applications

In writing to the correspondent. Guidelines for applicants are available from the trust. The director is willing to give advice on how applications should be presented.

Grants are awarded twice a year, in spring and autumn. To be considered in the spring allocation, applications should reach the director before 15 February of each year; for the autumn allocation the equivalent date is 15 August. Potential recipients are advised to get their applications in early.

Common applicant mistakes

'Many applicants seem not to read the trust's guidelines. Applicants often give excessive detail from which it is difficult to pick out what they are actually applying for.'

Philip Smith's Charitable Trust

Welfare, older people, children, environment, armed forces

£97,000 (2009/10)

Beneficial area

UK with a preference for Gloucestershire.

Bircham Dyson Bell, 50 Broadway, London SW1H 0BL
Tel: 020 7783 3685
Fax: 020 7222 3480
Email: helendmonte@bdb-law.co.uk
Correspondent: Helen D'Monte
Trustees: Hon. Philip R Smith; Mary Smith.
CC Number: 1003751

Information available

Accounts were obtained from the Charity Commission website.

The trusts grantmaking policy is outlined in the 2009/10 accounts:

> The trustees have adopted a policy of donating to those charities within the Gloucestershire area and also national charities supporting the environment, the elderly, the armed forces, children and the needy.

In 2009/10 the trust had assets of £1.1 million and an income of £57,000. Grants were made to 41 organisations totalling £97,000.

Grants included those made to: NSPCC (£20,000); Merlin (£13,000 in two grants); Save the Children (£10,000); Chipping Campden Playing Field and Recreation Ground (£7,000 in two grants); Game and Wildlife Conservation Trust (£5,000); St James PCC Chipping Campden (£3,500 in two grants); the Connection at St Martin's (£2,500); Wester Ross Fisheries Trust and Combat Stress (£2,000 each); Farms for City Children (£1,300); British Red Cross and Countryside Foundation for Education (£1,000 each); Independent Age (£750); Family Haven (£500); and Royal Green Jackets (£100).

Applications

In writing to the correspondent. The trustees meet regularly to consider grants. A lack of response can be taken to indicate that the trust does not wish to contribute to an appeal.

Solev Co Ltd

Jewish charities

£435,000 (2009/10)

Beneficial area

UK.

1 Spaniards Park, Columbas Drive, London NW3 7JD
Correspondent: R Tager, Trustee
Trustees: R Tager; S Tager; J Tager; C M Frommer.
CC Number: 254623

Information available

Accounts were available from the Charity Commission, but without a list of grants.

In 2009/10 the charity had assets of £3.7 million and an income of £704,000. Grants were made totalling £435,000. No information on beneficiaries has been included in the accounts in recent years.

In 1996/97 the following two donations were mentioned in the annual report: '£100,000 to the Dina Perelman Trust Ltd, a charitable company of which Mr Perelman and Mr Grosskopf are governors; and £40,000 to Songdale Ltd, a charity of which Mr M Grosskopf is a governor.'

A comprehensive grants list has not been included in the accounts since 1972/73, when £14,000 was given to 52 Jewish charities. Examples then included Society of Friends of the Torah (£3,900), Finchley Road Synagogue (£2,300), NW London Talmudical College (£1,500), Yesodey Hatorah School (£700), and Gateshead Talmudical College (£400).

Applications

In writing to the correspondent.

The Solo Charitable Settlement

Jewish, general

£34,000 (2009/10)

Beneficial area

UK and Israel.

c/o Randall Greene, Parallel House, 32–34 London Road, Guildford, Surrey GU1 2AB
Tel: 01483 230440
Correspondent: The Trustees
Trustees: Peter D Goldstein; Edna A Goldstein; Paul Goldstein; Dean Goldstein; Jamie Goldstein; Tammy Ward.
CC Number: 326444

Information available

Full accounts were obtained from the Charity Commission website.

Peter David Goldstein established the trust in 1983. The main object of the trust is to support Jewish charities, and where possible, to concentrate their efforts on the relief of suffering and poverty, and on education. The majority of grants was given to organisations that focused on Jewish related causes, medical research, the arts and palliative care.

In 2009/10 the trust had assets of £5.3 million and an income of £232,000. Grants were made to 23 organisations totalling £34,000.

Beneficiaries included: Norwood Ravenswood (£10,500); Nightingale House (£6,000); Dulwich College (£5,000); Beth Shalom Holocaust Centre (£2,500); UCLH Fund No 1051 and Yad Vashem UK Foundation (£1,000 each); Future Dreams Trust (£500); Langdon Foundation, British ORT and Cystic Fibrosis Charity (£250 each); One to One Children's Fund and Combat Stress (£200 each); and British WIZO, Royal Marsden Charity and One Family UK (£100 each).

Applications

In writing to the correspondent.

David Solomons Charitable Trust

Learning difficulties

£78,000 (2009/10)

Beneficial area

UK.

Jasmine Cottage, 11 Lower Road, Breachwood Green, Hitchin, Hertfordshire SG4 8NS
Tel: 01438 833254
Email: g.crosby@waitrose.com
Correspondent: Graeme Crosby, Administrator
Trustees: J L Drewitt; J J Rutter; Dr R E B Solomons; M T Chamberlayne; Dr L B Cooke; D J Huntingford.
CC Number: 297275

Information available

Accounts were available from the Charity Commission.

This trust supports research into, or the treatment and care of, people with learning difficulties, with a preference for smaller or localised charities. Most grants range from £1,000 to £2,000, although larger and smaller amounts are given. Administrative expenses and large building projects are not usually funded, although grants can be made towards furnishing or equipping rooms.

In 2009/10 the trust had assets of £2.2 million, an income of £87,000 and made grants to 82 organisations totalling £78,000.

The largest grant was made to Down's Syndrome Association (£8,000).

Other grants included: Autism Bedfordshire and Special Yoga Centre (£3,000 each); Sarum Orchestra (£2,300); Martha Trust (£2,000); Support for Living, Art and Power, Into Work, National Trust for Scotland and Bishopswood School Association (£1,000 each); Pathway Workshop (£750); SEN, Stallcombe House, Adventure Farm Trust and Musical Keys (£500 each); and Swiss Cottage School (£375).

Exclusions

No grants to individuals.

Applications

The trustees conduct their own research into potential applicants.

Common applicant mistakes

'They do not appreciate that the trust only gives grants to charitable organisations that support those suffering from learning difficulties as opposed to mental illness.'

Songdale Ltd

Jewish, education

£260,000 (2009/10)

Beneficial area

UK and Israel.

6 Spring Hill, London E5 9BE
Tel: 020 8806 5010
Correspondent: Yechiel Grosskopf, Trustee
Trustees: Yechiel Grosskopf; Myer Grosskopf; Malka Gitel Grosskopf.
CC Number: 286075

Information available

Accounts were available from the Charity Commission, but without a list of grants.

In 2009/10 the trust had assets of £2.4 million and an income of £237,000. Grants were made totalling £260,000. A list of grant beneficiaries was not provided in the latest accounts.

Previous beneficiaries include: Cosmon Belz Ltd, Kollel Belz, BFOT, Ezras Yisroel, Forty Limited, Darkei Ovois, Germach Veholachto, Keren Nedunnia Lchasanim, Belz Nursery and Bais Chinuch.

Applications

In writing to the correspondent.

The E C Sosnow Charitable Trust

Mainly education and arts

£51,000 (2009/10)

Beneficial area

UK and overseas.

PO Box 13398, London SW3 6ZL
Correspondent: The Trustees
Trustees: E R Fattal; Mrs F J M Fattal.
CC Number: 273578

Information available

Full accounts were on file at the Charity Commission.

The trust makes grants mainly to organisations working in education and the arts. Other potential areas of interest mentioned in its annual report are disadvantage, healthcare and emergency relief. In 2009/10 the trust had assets of £1.8 million and an income of £53,000. Grants were made to 26 organisations totalling £51,000.

Grants included those made to: LSE (£5,000); Weizmann UK (£4,000); School Bursary Trust (£3,000); Brent Adolescent Centre (£2,500); Chicken Shed (£2,000); Spanish and Portuguese Congregation (£1,000); and Woodstock Sinclair Trust (£500).

Exclusions

No grants are made to individuals.

Applications

In writing to the correspondent.

The South Square Trust

General

£215,000 (2009/10)

Beneficial area

UK, with a preference for London and the Home Counties.

PO Box 169, Lewes, East Sussex BN7 9FB
Tel: 01825 872264
Website: www.southsquaretrust.org.uk
Correspondent: Mrs Nicola Chrimes, Clerk to the Trustees
Trustees: Andrew Blessley; W P Harriman; C P Grimwade; D B Inglis; R S Baldock.
CC Number: 278960

Information available

Accounts were available from the Charity Commission.

The South Square Trust is governed by a trust deed dated 12 November 1979 and is established for general charitable purposes but in particular, education. The trustees having due regard to the wishes of the original settlor, apply the income to such charities they choose and to such schools, colleges and other institutions selected by them which offer appropriate courses in the Fine and Applied Arts. Grants are also made to individuals in connection with degree level educational courses in the Fine and Applied Arts (especially goldsmithing and silversmithing), to include music, drama and dance.

The trustees have set up Scholarship Awards with a number of colleges, a full list of which can be obtained from the clerk to the trustees.

In 2009/10 the trust had assets of £3.3 million and an income of £174,000. Grants were made totalling £215,000 of which £197,000 went to 69 organisations and £18,000 to individuals. Grants were broken down as follows:

General charitable donations	£48,000
Bursaries and scholarships to schools/colleges	£149,000
Directly aided students and single payment grants	£18,000

Beneficiary organisations included: Byam Shaw School of Art (£26,000); St Paul's School (£23,000); Textile Conservation Foundation (£12,000); Bristol Old Vic Theatre School, Guildford School of Acting and RADA (£10,000 each); Royal College of Music (£10,000); The Cass, London Metropolitan University (£9,000);and Royal Northern College of Music and School of Jewellery, Birmingham (£8,000 each).

Exclusions

No support for building projects, salaries or individuals wishing to start up a business. No grants given to individuals under 18 or those seeking funding for expeditions, travel, courses outside the UK, short courses or courses not connected with fine and applied arts.

Applications

Registered charities
In writing to the correspondent with details about your charity and the reason for requesting funding. Applications are considered three times a year, in November, March and June, and should be submitted at least one month before the next meeting. It is advisable to telephone the correspondent for up-to-date information about the criteria for funding.

Individuals

Standard application forms are available from the correspondent. Forms are sent out between January and April only, to be returned by the end of April for consideration for the following academic year.

The Stephen R and Philippa H Southall Charitable Trust

General

£143,000 (2009/10)

Beneficial area

UK, but mostly Herefordshire.

Porking Barn, Clifford, Hereford HR3 5HE
Tel: 01497 831243
Correspondent: Philippa Southall, Trustee
Trustees: Stephen Readhead Southall; Philippa Helen Southall; Anna Catherine Southall; Candia Helen Compton.
CC Number: 223190

Information available

Accounts were obtained from the Charity Commission website.

This trust has general charitable purposes, with a preference for promoting education and conservation of the natural environment and cultural heritage. A large number of grants are made in Herefordshire. The trust has previously stated that it uses its surplus income for world emergencies and the development of Hereford Waterworks Museum.

In 2009/10 the trust had assets of £2.9 million and an income of £145,000. Grants were made to 23 organisations totalling £143,000.

Beneficiaries listed in the accounts were: The Worgan Trust – Mount Pleasant School Farm (£75,000); Hereford Waterworks Museum Trust (£49,000); Clifford PCC and Tobacco Factory Arts Trust (£5,000 each); and BODS (£2,500).

Applications

The trust makes several repeat donations and has previously stated that: 'no applications can be considered or replied to'.

The W F Southall Trust

Quaker, general

£286,000 (2009/10)

Beneficial area

UK and overseas.

c/o Rutters Solicitors, 2 Bimport, Shaftesbury, Dorset SP7 8AY
Tel: 01747 852377
Fax: 01747 851989
Email: southall@rutterslaw.co.uk
Correspondent: The Secretary
Trustees: Donald Southall, Chair; Joanna Engelkamp; Claire Greaves; Mark Holtom; Daphne Maw; Annette Wallis; Richard Maw; Hannah Engelkamp.
CC Number: 218371

Information available

Accounts were available from the Charity Commission.

This trust prefers to support innovative projects from smaller charities where the grant will make a more significant difference. Areas of work supported are: Society of Friends; peace-making and conflict resolution; alcohol, drug abuse and penal affairs; environmental action; homelessness; community action; and overseas development.

In 2009/10 the trust had assets of £7.4 million and an income of £273,000. Grants were made totalling £286,000 and were broken down as follows:

Overseas development	50	£96,000
Quaker and Society of Friends charities	9	£89,000
Peace and reconciliation	13	£30,000
Community action	17	£35,000
Environmental action	10	£24,000
Alcohol and drug abuse and penal affairs	7	£12,000
Homelessness	1	£1,000

Grant recipients included: Yearly Meeting – Society of Friends (£55,000); Woodbrooke Quaker Study Centre (£10,000); International Voluntary Services (£6,500); Centre for Alternative Technology and St Augustine's Centre (£5,000 each); British Friends of Neve Shalom, Children in Crisis, Mend UK and Peace Direct (£3,000 each); and Refugee Council (£2,000).

Exclusions

No grants to individuals or large national charities.

Applications

In writing to the correspondent (via post or email), requesting an application form. Applications are usually considered in February/March and November. Applications received between meetings are considered at the next meeting.

R H Southern Trust

Education, disability, relief of poverty, environment, conservation

£225,000 to organisations (2009/10)

Beneficial area

Worldwide.

23 Sydenham Road, Cotham, Bristol BS6 5SJ
Tel: 0117 942 5834
Correspondent: The Trustees
Trustees: Marion Wells; Charles Wells; James Bruges; Colkin Trustee Company Limited.
CC Number: 1077509

Information available

Accounts were available from the Charity Commission.

This trust was registered with the Charity Commission in 1999. Grants tend to be made to a small number of organisations, mostly for long-term core funding and special projects. The trust's objects are:

▶ the advancement of education (including medical and scientific research)
▶ the relief of poverty
▶ disability

383

▶ the preservation, conservation and protection of the environment (especially climate change).

The trust favours projects where the work is innovative, connected to other disciplines/bodies and has diverse application.

In 2009/10 the trust had assets of £3.2 million and an income of £128,000. Grants were made to 20 organisations totalling £225,000 and were broken down as follows:

Education	4	£66,000
Poverty	5	£50,000
Disabilities	2	£35,000
Environment	9	£75,000

Beneficiaries included: Feasta (£41,000 in five grants); Soil Association (£26,000 in five grants); Equal Adventure (£20,000); Motivation (£15,000); Accord – Just Change (£11,000); Action Village India, Corporate European Observatory and Friends of the Earth (£10,000 each); EI Rural Links – Tamwed (£8,500); Global Witness and Sustrans (£5,000 each); and Ragmans Lane Farm (£246).

One grant of £15,000 was also made to an individual working on the Soil Fertility Project (charcoal project).

Applications
In writing to the correspondent, though at present the trust's funds are fully committed.

Spar Charitable Fund

General, with a preference for children and young people

£115,000 (2009/10)

Beneficial area
UK.

Mezzanine Floor, Hygeia Building, 66–68 College Road, Harrow, Middlesex HA1 1BE
Tel: 020 8426 3700
Email: philip.marchant@spar.co.uk
Correspondent: Philip Marchant, Director and Company Secretary
Trustee: The National Guild of Spar Ltd.

CC Number: 236252

Information available
Accounts were available from the Charity Commission.

This trust tends to choose one main beneficiary, which receives most of its funds, with smaller grants being made to similar beneficiaries each year.

In 2009/10 it had assets of £799,000 and an income of £91,000. Grants were made totalling £115,000.

The main beneficiary was the NSPCC, which received £91,000. Grants were also made to: Business in the Community (£12,000); Clubs for Young People (£6,000); Caravan – NGBF (£5,000); Scottish Grocers Benevolent Fund (£1,300); and Kenia (£450).

Applications
In writing to the correspondent.

The Spear Charitable Trust

General, with some preference for animal welfare, the environment and health

£123,000 to organisations (2007)

Beneficial area
UK.

Roughground House, Beggarmans Lane, Old Hall Green, Ware, Hertfordshire SG11 1HB
Tel: 01920 823071
Fax: 01920 823071
Correspondent: Hazel E Spear, Secretary
Trustees: P N Harris; F A Spear; H E Spear; N Gooch.
CC Number: 1041568

Information available
Full accounts were available from the Charity Commission website.

Established in 1994 with general charitable purposes, this trust has particular interest in helping employees and former employees of J W Spear and Sons plc and their families and dependants.

In 2010 the assets totalled £4.7 million and generated an income of £124,000. Grants were made to 46 organisations totalling £123,000, while ex-employees received £11,000 in total. Management and administration charges were quite high at £19,000.

Beneficiaries included: Nuremberg Toy Museum and RSPCA – Enfield (£8,000 each); Imagine (Mozambique) (£6,000); Barnet and Chase Farm NHS Trust, Tree Aid and The Woodland Trust (£5,000 each); Lake Malawi Projects and Marine Conservation Society (£2,500 each); Grasslands Trust and No Panic (£2,000 each); and Jewish Care, Mayhew International and Scottish Seabird Sanctuary (£1,000 each).

Exclusions
Appeals from individuals are not considered.

Applications
In writing to the correspondent.

Spears-Stutz Charitable Trust

Relief of poverty, general

Around £90,000 (2009/10)

Beneficial area
Worldwide.

Berkeley Law, 4th Floor, 19 Berkeley Street, London W1J 8ED
Tel: 020 7399 0930
Correspondent: The Trustees
Trustees: Glenn Hurstfield; Jonathan Spears.
CC Number: 225491

Information available
Accounts were available from the Charity Commission but without a list of grants.

This trust was previously known as the Roama Spears Charitable Settlement. It states that it makes grants to organisations towards the relief of poverty worldwide. In practice it appears to support a range of organisations including a number of museums and arts organisations. It as some preference for Jewish causes.

n 2009/10 the trust had assets of 4.2 million and an income of 93,000. Grants totalled £90,000 and were made to various local and national charities, ranging from donations of £250 to £30,000. A list of grants was not provided in the accounts.

Previous beneficiaries include: Cancer Macmillan Fund, Royal Academy Trust, Royal Academy of Arts, Wellbeing, King Edward Hospital, Help the Aged and Westminster Synagogue.

Applications
In writing to the correspondent.

The Worshipful Company of Spectacle Makers' Charity

Visual impairment, City of London, general

£64,000 (2009/10)

Beneficial area
Worldwide, with a preference for the City of London.

Apothecaries Hall, Blackfriars Lane, London EC4V 6EL
Tel: 020 7236 2932
Email: clerk@spectaclemakers.com
Website: www.spectaclemakers.com
Correspondent: John Salmon, Clerk
Trustees: Brian Mitchell; Christine Tomkins; Venerable John Morrison; Liz Shilling; Edward Middleton; James Osborne.
CC Number: 1072172

Information available
Accounts were on file at the Charity Commission.

Registered with the Charity Commission in October 1998, this livery company supports causes related to visual impairment and the City of London, however it has also supported a wide range of other projects worldwide. Grants tend to be made for specific projects, not general

funds, and to national campaigns rather than local causes.

In 2009/10 the charity had assets of £700,000 and an income of £82,500. Grants were made to organisations totalling £64,000.

The charity's website lists a number of beneficiaries, without details of the value of individual grants. These included: Action for Blind People, Blind in Business, Childhood Eye Cancer Trust, Eyeless Trust, St John's Eye Hospital in Jerusalem, Prison Fellowship, Optical Workers' Benevolent Fund, British Council for the Prevention of Blindness, Vision 2020UK, Livings Paintings Trust, Vision Aid Overseas, Macular Disease Society, British Blind Sport and the Talking Newspaper Association.

Exclusions
No grants are made to individuals.

Applications
In writing to the correspondent including details of how the grant will be used and a copy of the latest audited accounts. Please note: the trustees meet in early spring to decide on grants, meaning that applications received between June and March are unlikely to be addressed quickly.

Common applicant mistakes
'Applicants not understanding our core purpose, which is fighting visual impairment.'

The Jessie Spencer Trust

General

£160,000 (2009/10)

Beneficial area
UK, with some preference for Nottinghamshire.

Berryman Shacklock LLP, Park House, Friar Lane, Nottingham NG1 6DN
Tel: 0115 945 3700
Fax: 0115 948 0234
Correspondent: The Trustees
Trustees: Victor W Semmens; Mrs B Mitchell; David Wild.
CC Number: 219289

Information available
Accounts were available from the Charity Commission.

The trust supports a range wide of causes, including welfare, religion and the environment amongst others. Whilst grants are made UK-wide, there is a preference for work in Nottinghamshire.

In 2009/10 the trust had assets of £3.4 million and an income of £128,000. Grants were made totalling £160,000 and were distributed as follows:

Accommodation	£41,000
Medical/disabled	£26,000
Welfare	£25,000
Churches	£12,000
Arts	£7,000
Groups/clubs	£5,000
Education	£5,000
Environment	£2,000
Services	£2,000
Heritage	£1,500
Individuals	£550
Other	£33,000

Beneficiaries included: Nottinghamshire Community Foundation (£30,000); Core – Digestive Disorders Foundation (£5,000); Marie Curie Cancer Care (£3,000); SSAFA (£1,500); Binns Organ Trust, the Jonathan Young Memorial Trust, Not Shut Up and Rutland House School (£1,000 each); Enterprise Education Trust (£750); and ASBAH, the Rehearsal Orchestra, York Foundation for Conservation and Craftsmanship and the Woodland Trust (£500 each).

Exclusions
Grants are rarely made for the repair of parish churches outside Nottinghamshire.

Applications
In writing to the correspondent, including the latest set of audited accounts, at least three weeks before the trustees' meetings in March, June, September and December. Unsuccessful applications will not be notified.

The Moss Spiro Will Charitable Foundation

Jewish welfare

About £14,000 (2009/10)

Beneficial area
UK.

Crowndean House, 26 Bruton Lane, London W1J 6JH
Tel: 020 7491 9817
Fax: 020 7499 6850
Email: trevor@assassin.co.uk
Correspondent: Trevor Spiro, Trustee
Trustees: Trevor David Spiro; Melvin Clifford Kay.
CC Number: 1064249

Information available

Accounts were received but not available to view from the Charity Commission website.

The trust makes grants towards Jewish welfare. In 2009/10 the trust had an income of £45 and a total expenditure of £14,000. Further information was not available.

Previous beneficiaries have included American Friends of Yershivas Birchas Ha Torah, Lubavitch Foundation, J T Tannenbaum Jewish Cultural Centre, Friends of Neve Shalom, Jewish Care and HGS Emunah.

Applications
In writing to the correspondent.

Spring Harvest

The promotion of Christianity

£199,000 (2009/10)

Beneficial area
UK and overseas.

14 Horsted Square, Bellbrook Industrial Estate, Uckfield, East Sussex TN22 1QG
Tel: 01825 769000
Fax: 01825 748899
Email: offerings@springharvest.org
Website: www.springharvest.org

Correspondent: Pete Broadbent, Chair
Trustees: Pete Broadbent, Chair; Krish Kandiah; Ian White; Peter Martin; Wendy Beech-Ward; Russell Rook; Geoff Booker; Ruth Valerio; David Dorricott; Allistair Watson.
CC Number: 1014540

Information available
Accounts were available from the Charity Commission.

Spring Harvest began as a one week event in Wales in 1979. Since then the event has grown into a multi-resort event. In 2009 Spring Harvest merged with ICC Media Group to form the new Memralife Group. Although Spring Harvest retains its own original identity the trust is wholly administered by the Memralife Group (registered charity number: 1126997). The two bodies have a common board of trustees and Spring Harvest grants are distributed by Memralife – details of which are contained in the annual report of the Memralife Group.

The trust's website says:

> Within our stated aim to 'equip the Church for action', we seek to encourage Christians to think about their faith, to be transformed through the renewing of our minds and to engage in the mission of God in the world. Those who speak at Spring Harvest events are understood to be speaking, living and acting within that framework.

The 2009/10 annual report of the Memralife group notes that:

> Funds for grantmaking derived largely from the generosity of guests at the Spring Harvest event in supporting the Offering appeal.

> The trust's policy is to channel funds to other organisations through which a range of Christian work in the UK and worldwide can be supported. Most grants are to other UK registered charities. It may on occasion give support to individuals involved in Christian work or support the work of organisations which are not registered charities.

The focus for funding in 2012 (as stated under the heading 'No ceiling to hope' in the 'Offerings' section of the trust's website), is for projects which:

▶ demonstrate local church involvement
▶ are outside your immediate church and congregational pastoral responsibilities.

Preference will be given to:

▶ partnership projects involving more than one local church
▶ innovative or new initiatives in your community.

Most grants are for up to £5,000 but the trust will consider applications for higher sums. As the focus for grant giving changes annually applicants are encouraged to check the up-to-date criteria on the trust's website.

The trust also notes: 'We warmly endorse short term mission and Bible College training, but are no longer able to financially support individuals to attend or take part in this sort of work.'

Grants in 2009/10
In 2009/10 the Memralife Group had total assets of £2.4 million and an income of £9.3 million, £350,000 of which came directly from donations at the Spring Harvest event. Grants totalling £199,000 were made to 49 organisations. They were broken down as follows:

Open Doors with Brother Andrew	£30,000
XLP	£30,000
FRRME (Foundation for Relief and Reconciliation in the Middle East)	£8,000
Jubilee Action	£8,000
London City Mission	£8,000
Lifecentre	£7,000
The Message Trust	£6,000
Military Ministries International/ ACCTS General	£6,000
Redeeming Our Communities	£6,000
Children Worldwide	£5,200
CLAAS (Centre for Legal Aid, Assistance and Settlement)	£5,000
The Bless Network	£4,000
Scripture Union International	£4,000
Viva	£4,000
A Rocha UK	£3,000
AE Evangelistic Enterprise Ltd	£3,000
Bible Society	£3,000
Five Talents	£3,000
Heart of the Father	£3,000

Grants of under £3,000 totalled £53,000 to 31 other institutions.

The trust also makes sums available to individuals and families in receipt of state benefits to enable people on a low income to attend the Spring Harvest event. In 2010, £21,600 was spent in this way.

Exclusions
Grants are not made for salaries.

Applications
There is one round of funding applications per year, usually at the end of November/early December, for

distribution the following year. An application form is made available on the trust's website in Spring.

Applications can be for any amount up £5,000. If your application requests substantially more the trust will consider, but it is unlikely to be able to offer the total amount needed.

Applications from non-UK organisations can only be considered if you have a UK office or a UK contact that knows you well and is able to comment on your work.

All applications must be submitted on our application form.

We have one funding round per year and look particularly for applications with a Christian bias where there's a link to our annual theme.

We can't commit to on-going funding, so we don't usually support salary costs unless it is clear that the project can be sustained in the long term.

Rosalyn and Nicholas Springer Charitable Trust

Welfare, Jewish, education, general

£120,000 (2009/10)

Beneficial area
UK.

5 Park Village West, London NW1 4AE
Tel: 020 7253 7272
Correspondent: Nicholas Springer, Trustee
Trustees: Rosalyn Springer; Nicholas Springer; Judith Joseph.
CC Number: 1062239

Information available
Accounts were available from the Charity Commission.

This trust supports the relief and assistance of people in need, the advancement of education, religion and other purposes beneficial to the community.

In 2009/10 the trust had assets of £48,000 and an income of £156,000. Grants were made to 72 organisations totalling £120,000 and were distributed as follows:

Medical, health and sickness	20	£36,000
Education and training	11	£29,000
Arts and culture	10	£22,000
Religious activities	4	£7,300
Relief of poverty	11	£16,000
General charitable purposes	16	£10,000

Beneficiaries included: UJIA (£20,000); Royal Opera House Foundation (£15,000); Chai-Lifeline Cancer Care (£10,000); MDA UK (£6,300); World Jewish Relief (£4,200); Belsize Square Synagogue (£3,400); Norwood Ravenswood (£3,000); Holocaust Educational Trust (£2,000); Presidents Club Charitable Trust (£1,300); Cystic Fibrosis Trust (£800); London Arts Museum and Foundation of Nursing Studies (£500 each); Jewish Child's Day (£400); and Derby Toch Children's Camp (£150).

Applications
The trust has previously stated that it only supports organisations it is already in contact with. 99% of unsolicited applications are unsuccessful and because of the volume it receives, the trust is unable to reply to such letters. It would therefore not seem appropriate to apply to this trust.

The Spurrell Charitable Trust

General

£80,000 (2009/10)

Beneficial area
UK, with some preference for Norfolk.

Apartment 7, 99 Warwick Park, Tunbridge Wells, Kent TN2 5FD
Tel: 01892 541565
Correspondent: A T How, Trustee
Trustees: Alan T How; Mrs Inge H Spurrell; Martyn R Spurrell.
CC Number: 267287

Information available
Accounts were available from the Charity Commission.

The trust has previously stated that grants are only distributed to charities known personally to the trustees and that its funds are fully committed.

In 2009/10 the trust had assets of £2.2 million and an income of £61,000. Grants were made totalling £80,000.

Beneficiaries included: Merlin (£10,000; East Anglian Air Ambulance (£7,000); Break (£5,000); Aylesbury High School (£3,000); Alzheimer's Research Trust, Brain & Spine Foundation, Camphill Village Trust and North Norfolk Multiple Sclerosis Society (£1,200 each); Norfolk Deaf Association, Norwich & Central Norfolk MIND, Wireless for the Bedridden and Woodlands Trust (£600 each) and Felbrigg Crusaders, Sheringham & Cromer Choral Society and Sustead Village Hall Fund (£300 each).

In 2009/10 income fell to £61,000. Commitments are likely to be reduced as a result.

Applications
Unsolicited applications are not considered.

Common applicant mistakes
'Applications from individuals, especially students, who are encouraged to write for support instead of working for it, e.g. Operation Wallacea.'

St Gabriel's Trust

Higher and further religious education

£138,000 to organisations (2010)

Beneficial area
Mainly in the UK.

Ladykirk, 32 The Ridgeway, Enfield, Middlesex EN2 8QH
Tel: 020 8363 6474
Correspondent: Peter Duffell, Clerk
Trustees: Dr Priscilla Chadwick, Chair; James Cowen; Revd Janina Ainsworth; John Keast; Jessica Giles; Barbara Lane; Mary Halvorson; Deborah Weston; Bruce Gill; Prof Liam Gearon; Rosemary Walters.
CC Number: 312933

Information available

Accounts were available from the Charity Commission.

The trust is concerned with the advancement of higher and further education in one or more of the following ways:

- promotion of the education and training of people who are, or intend to become, engaged as teachers or otherwise in work connected with religious education;
- promotion of research in, and development of, religious education;
- promotion of religious education by the provision of instruction, classes, lectures, books, libraries and reading rooms;
- granting of financial assistance to institutions of higher or further education established for charitable purposes only;
- provision and conduct of a chapel and chaplaincy providing religious worship, care and instruction.

In 2010 the trust had assets of £6.6 million and an income of £305,000. Grants totalling £259,000 were made comprising £138,000 in 12 corporate awards, £114,000 to St Gabriel's Programme (see below) and £7,000 in total to 9 individuals.

The corporate beneficiaries included: ACCT Virtual RE Centre, RE Council DFE think tank and RE Festival (£20,000 each); All Faiths and None (£12,500); Bible Reading Fellowship (£10,000); Spinnaker Trust (£7,000); and National Society – Bicentenary 2011 (£5,000).

The trustees have committed funds for several corporate projects including:

- an initiative to develop a virtual RE Centre, in conjunction with other trusts;
- the St Gabriel's Programme, an ongoing venture which has been run jointly with The Culham Institute, 'to develop thought and action in support of RE teachers'.

Awards to individuals are given towards course fees and expenses for teachers taking part-time RE courses whilst continuing their teaching jobs. Occasional grants have been given to those undertaking specialist research

that will clearly benefit the religious education world.

Exclusions

Grants are not normally available for: any project for which local authority money is available, or which ought primarily to be funded by the church – theological study, parish or missionary work – unless school RE is involved; and research projects where it will be a long time before any benefit can filter down into RE teaching. No grants are made to schools as such; higher and further education must be involved.

Applications

In writing to the correspondent with an sae. Applicants are asked to describe their religious allegiance and to provide a reference from their minister of religion. Applications need to be received by the beginning of January, April or September as trustees meet in February, May and October.

St James' Trust Settlement

General
£100,000 (2009/10)

Beneficial area
Worldwide, with a preference for the UK and USA.

Epworth House, 25 City Road, London EC1Y 1AR
Tel: 020 7628 5801
Correspondent: The Trustees
Trustees: Jane Wells; Cathy Ingram; Simon Taffler.
CC Number: 280455

Information available
Full accounts were on available from the Charity Commission website.

The trust's main aims are to make grants to charitable organisations that respond to areas of concern which the trustees are involved or interested in. In the UK, the main concerns are health, education and social justice; in the USA the main areas are in education, especially to the children of very disadvantaged families, and in community arts projects. Grants are

made by the trustees through their involvement with the project. Projects are also monitored and evaluated by the trustees.

In 2009/10 the trust had assets of £3.5 million and an income of £91,000. Grants payable in the year were almost £100,000, which went to 10 organisations the UK amounting to £33,000 and 25 in the USA amounting to £67,000.

In the UK grants were made to organisations including: Highbury Vale Blackstock Trust (£12,000); Prisoners Abroad (£10,000); CARIS, and Rainforest Foundation (£5,000 each); and World Children Unite (£2,500).

Exclusions
No grants to individuals.

Applications
The trust states that it 'does not seek unsolicited applications for grants and, without paid staff, are unable to respond to such applications'.

St Michael's and All Saints' Charities

Health, welfare
£100,000 (2010)

Beneficial area
City of Oxford.

St Michael's Church Centre, St Michael at the North Gate, Cornmarket Street, Oxford OX1 3EY
Tel: 01865 240940
Email: robert.hawes@smng.org.uk
Correspondent: Robert J Spencer Hawes
Trustees: P Beavis; The Very Revd. R Wilkes; Prof. P Langford; M Lear; Lord Krebs; The Ven J Hubbard; Ruth Loseby; R Earl; P Dailey; S Shibli.
CC Number: 202750

Information available
Accounts were available from the Charity Commission.

Income of the charity is applied to relieve, either generally or individually, persons resident in the city of Oxford who are in conditions of need, hardship or distress. Grants may be made to institutions or organisations which provide services or facilities for such people.

In 2010 the trust had assets of £1.4 million and an income of £113,000. Grants were made to 26 organisations totalling £100,000.

Beneficiaries included: Abbeyfield and Leys Youth Programme (£10,000 each); Oxford Homeless Pathways (£8,000); Donnington Doorstep Family Centre (£6,000); Oxford Sexual Abuse & Rape Crisis Line (£5,000); Seesaw (£3,000); and Soup Kitchen (£2,000).

Exclusions
Individuals are very rarely supported.

Applications
In writing to the correspondent.

St Monica Trust Community Fund

Older people, disability
£139,000 to organisations (2010)

Beneficial area
Preference for the south west of England, particularly Bristol and the surrounding area.

Cote Lane, Westbury-on-Trym, Bristol BS9 3UN
Tel: 0117 949 4003
Fax: 0117 949 4044
Email: kate.stobie@stmonicatrust.org.uk
Website: www.stmonicatrust.org.uk
Correspondent: Kate Stobie, Community Fund Manager
Trustees: Revd Ian Gobey; Jane Edwards Cork; Trevor Smallwood; John Laycock; Gillian Camm; Charles Hunter; Dr. Pippa Marsh; Ms H E Evans; C A Griffiths; M D Lea; P J Rilett; Dr R Slinn; Lady Wills; A Burnett; R T Wynn-Jones.
CC Number: 202151

Information available
Accounts were available from the Charity Commission.

This St Monica Trust has provided accommodation, care and support for older and disabled people for over 85 years. Another branch of its work, the St Monica Trust Community Fund, gives grants to individuals and organisations to help improve the daily lives of people with a physical or sensory impairment or long-term physical health problem.

Grants of up to £10,000 each are available to organisations. Grants may be awarded for small capital items and/or for running costs. To be considered, organisations must meet all five of the following criteria:
1 Benefit people (over 16 years old) who have a physical or sensory impairment or long-term physical health problem, including those with infirmities due to old age.
2 Benefit people living in Bristol or the surrounding area (North Somerset, Somerset, South Gloucestershire, Gloucestershire, Bath and North East Somerset and Wiltshire).
3 Make a real difference to people's daily lives.
4 Be both properly constituted and a not-for-profit organisation.
5 Fit in with the fund's current theme (see below).

Each year has a different theme – the 2009 grants scheme was open to organisations working with older people living with a long-term physical disability, impairment or physical health problem where substance misuse has been a contributing factor. Please see the fund's website for up-to-date information.

In 2010 the trust gave grants to 14 organisations totalling £139,000. The trust's Community Fund is working alongside agencies in Bristol, as well as all its surrounding counties to support older people with alcohol, drug and prescribed medication addiction. This year the Fund supported 14 applications from organisations that demonstrated their impact on people's daily lives, providing support or counselling or undertaking research or training that directly relates to this issue.

Previous beneficiaries included: Citizen's Advice Bureau (£9,800); St Peter's Hospice, Headway Bristol

and Motor Neurone Disease Association (£7,500 each); IT Help@Home (£5,000); the New Place (£3,900); Bristol and Avon Chinese Women's Group (£2,000); Bath Institute of Medical Engineering (£1,500); and Western Active Stroke Group (£1,000).

The trust accepts applications from organisations that it has previously funded.

Exclusions
No grants to fund buildings, adaptations to buildings or minibus purchases.

Applications
On a form available from the correspondent, or to download from the fund's website. All applicants must submit a form together with additional information that is requested, for example, an annual report.

Applications are considered once a year; please see the fund's website for deadline dates.

All applications will be considered by the Community Fund Committee of the fund. Notification of the outcome will be made in writing.

The fund states:

> We receive many more requests than we have funds available. For example, we [have previously] received 35 applications with requests totalling over £318,000: well above the £110,000 we had available. In practice this means that we do not give grants to organisations which do not fully meet our criteria.

The Late St Patrick White Charitable Trust

General
£47,000 (2009/10)

Beneficial area
UK, with a possible preference for Hampshire.

HSBC Trust Co UK Ltd, Norwich House, Nelson Gate, Commercial Road, Southampton SO15 1GX
Tel: 023 8072 2240

Correspondent: Lee Topp, Trust Manager
Trustee: HSBC Trusts Co. (UK) Ltd.
CC Number: 1056520

Information available

Accounts were available from the Charity Commission.

The objects of the charity are to pay or to apply the income from the trust fund for the benefit of Barnardo's, Guide Dogs for the Blind, The Salvation Army, Age Concern and other charities benefiting people who are blind, cancer research, arthritis and rheumatism research.

In 2009/10 the trust had assets of £1.9 million and an income of £15,000. Grants were made totalling £47,000. Beneficiaries included: Age Concern, Arthritis Care, Barnardo's, Guide Dogs for the Blind Association and The Salvation Army (£5,000 each); Help the Aged (£3,000); and Prostrate Cancer Charity and the Foundation for Prevention of Blindness (£2,000 each).

Applications

In writing to the correspondent. Applications are considered in February, May, August and November.

St Teilo's Trust

Evangelistic work in the Church in Wales

Around £41,000 (2009/10)

Beneficial area

Wales.

Stradey Estate Office, 53 New Road, Llanelli SA15 3DP
Tel: 01554 773059
Email: info@saintteilostrust.org.uk
Website: www.saintteilostrust.org.uk
Correspondent: Rev P Mansel Lewis
Trustees: Revd P C A Mansel Lewis, Chair; Mrs C Mansel Lewis; Revd Canon S R Bell; Revd Dr W A Strange; Revd P A Bement; Revd Bob Capper.
CC Number: 1032405

Information available

Information taken from the Charity Commission website and the trust's website.

The trust supports evangelical work in the Church in Wales. It provides funding towards the cost of evangelical initiatives in parishes, Alpha courses, evangelical events and literature distribution for example. Grants are usually one-off and range from £50 to £1,000.

In 2009/10 the trust had an income of £5,000 and expenditure of £41,000. No grants list was available but examples of grant support are detailed on the trust's website.

Previous beneficiaries include: Llandeilo PC, Gobaith Gymru, St Michael's Aberyswyth, Cilcoed Christian Centre, Parish of Bargoed, Postal Bible School and St David's Diocesan Council.

Applications

In writing to the correspondent. Trustees meet in February, May and September. Applications should be sent by January, April and August. Guidelines are available from the trust.

Common applicant mistakes

'Applications outside the trust's grant making categories; failure to supply a financial breakdown of the cost of the project supported by statement of existing resources.'

The Stanley Foundation Ltd

Older people, medical care and research, education, social welfare

£269,000 (2009/10)

Beneficial area

UK.

Flat 3, 19 Holland Park, London W11 3TD
Tel: 020 7792 3854
Email: nick@meristan.com
Correspondent: N Stanley, Secretary

Trustees: C Shale; Georgina Stanley; N Stanley, Chair; S R Stanley; Elodie Stanley; S H Hall.
CC Number: 206866

Information available

Full accounts were available from the Charity Commission.

The trust has traditionally supported medical care and research, education and social welfare charities. In 2009/10 it had assets of over £3.2 million and an income of £98,000. Grants were made to 53 organisations totalling £269,000.

Beneficiaries included: Royal Opera House (£19,000); Tusk (£15,000); Action Against Addiction, National Gallery and Sculpt the Future (£10,000 each); Churches Conservation Trust, Dyslexia Association and Honeypot (£5,000); Independent Age (£3,000); British Museum (£2,000); and Friends of Chievely Church, Hospice in the Weald, Kathmandu Arts Centre and Tate Patrons (£1,000 each).

Exclusions

No grants to individuals.

Applications

In writing to the correspondent.

The Star Charitable Trust

General

Around £23,000 (2009/10)

Beneficial area

UK.

2nd Floor, 16–18 Hatton Garden, London EC1N 8AT
Tel: 020 7404 2222
Fax: 020 7404 3333
Correspondent: The Trustees
Trustees: D D Fiszman; P I Propper; D A Rosen.
CC Number: 266695

Information available

Basic information was obtained from the Charity Commission website.

Connected to the Star Diamond group of companies, this trust was established in March 1974. In 2009/10

he trust had an income of £22,000
nd a total expenditure of £23,000.
'urther information was not
vailable.

Applications

n writing to the correspondent.

The Peter Stebbings Memorial Charity

General charitable purposes

£351,000 to institutions (2009/10)

Beneficial area

JK and developing countries.

5 Pont Street, London SW1X 0BX
Tel: 020 7591 3333
Correspondent: Andrew Stebbings,
Trustee
Trustees: A J F Stebbings; N F Cosin;
Mrs J A Clifford.
CC Number: 274862

Information available

Accounts were available from the
Charity Commission.

The trust makes grants for a range of
charitable purposes and the objects of
he trust are to fund, in particular,
medical research and education, and
the welfare of those who are poor, old
or sick.

The trustees' annual report for
2009/10 states:

> Following a review of the charity's
> activities and the use of its assets in
> 2006, the trustees agreed that the
> charity should be more strategic in its
> grant making in order to maximise the
> impact of its donations. Changes to the
> assets have increased the charity's
> grant giving capacity very considerably
> and the income is now being applied in
> making more substantial grants to a
> limited number of charities. The
> principal grant has been a grant of
> £150,000 over three years to the Liver
> Group at the Royal Free Hospital. The
> trustees have agreed a grant of
> £250,000 over three years to the Royal
> Marsden Hospital.

In 2009/10 the charity had assets of
£6.7 million and an income of
£210,000. Grants were made to
organisations totalling £351,000.

Beneficiaries included: Liver Group
and The Medical Foundation for
Victims of Torture (£50,000 each);
Bromley by Bow Centre (£42,000);
The Maya Centre (£30,000); Berkeley
Reforestation Trust (£20,000); Bibic
(£10,000); Mercy Ships and Tools for
Self Reliance (£5,000 each); and
Amnesty International (£1,000).

Exclusions

No grants to individuals, non-
registered charities or for salaries.

Applications

It is the trustees' policy to make more
substantial grants to a limited
number of charities. Please note: the
trust has previously stated that it does
not respond to unsolicited
applications and that its funds are
fully committed.

The Steinberg Family Charitable Trust

Jewish, health

£441,000 (2009/10)

Beneficial area

UK, with a preference for Greater
Manchester.

Lime Tree Cottage, Bollingway, Hale,
Altrincham WA15 0NZ
Tel: 0161 903 8851
Email: admin@steinberg-trust.co.uk
Correspondent: Jonathan Steinberg
Trustees: Dominic Burke, Chairman;
Beryl Steinberg; Jonathan Steinberg;
Lynne Attias.
CC Number: 1045231

Information available

Accounts for 2010 were available at
the Charity Commission.

Whilst the objects of the founding
deed are very wide, the trust is
primarily concerned with the support
of charities located in the North West
region or active within the Jewish
Community (whether in the North
West or Israel), particularly those
involved with the provision of social
or health services. There is a
particular emphasis on the needs of

children and young people within
those areas.

During 2009/10 the trust had an
income of £1.4 million, held assets of
£13 million and made grants totalling
£441,000.

The most significant beneficiaries for
this year were: Fed (£27,500) and
Integrated Education Fund (£25,000).

Beneficiaries of £10,000 or less
included: Aish; Centre for Torah
Education Trust; Crimestoppers;
Imperial War Museum North;
Yeshiva Orchos Chaim (£10,000
each); Lubavitch South Manchester;
Holocaust Centre (£7,500 each);
Genesis Appeal (£5,000); Manchester
Junior Girls' School; St John's
Hospice (£2,500 each); and Royal
British Legion (£1,000).

Over the last 5 years this charity has
been on average well over a year late
in submitting their accounts to the
Charity Commission.

Exclusions

Registered charities only.

Applications

In writing to the correspondent,
including evidence of charitable
status, the purpose to which the
funds are to be put, evidence of other
action taken to fund the project
concerned, and the outcome of that
action.

The Sigmund Sternberg Charitable Foundation

Jewish, inter-faith causes, general

£200,000 (2009/10)

Beneficial area

Worldwide.

Star House, 104/108 Grafton Road,
London NW5 4BA
Tel: 020 7431 4200
Correspondent: Sir S Sternberg,
Trustee
Trustees: Sir S Sternberg;
V M Sternberg; Lady Sternberg; Rev

M C Rossi Braybrooke;
M A M Slowe; R Tamir; M D Paisner.
CC Number: 257950

Information available

Full accounts were on file at the Charity Commission.

This trust supports the furtherance of interfaith activities to promote racial and religious harmony, in particular between Christian, Jewish and Muslim faiths, and the education in, and understanding of, their fundamental tenets and beliefs. Most grants are made to Jewish and Israeli charities. The trust makes a small number of large grants, generally of £10,000 to £80,000 each, and a large number of smaller grants.

In 2009/10 the trust had an income of £300,000 and made 145 grants totalling £200,000. Its assets stood at £4.7 million.

Grant beneficiaries included: Three Faiths Forum (£83,000); The Movement for Reform Judaism (£70,000); The Board of Deputies Charitable Foundation (£9,000); Leo Baeck College Centre for Jewish Education (£5,000); World Congress of Faiths (£3,000) and Jewish National Fund (£1,100).

There were a further 104 grants of less than £1,000 each, totalling £13,000.

Exclusions

No grants to individuals.

Applications

In writing to the correspondent.

Stervon Ltd

Jewish

£267,000 (2009)

Beneficial area

UK.

c/o Stervon House, 1 Seaford Road, Salford, Greater Manchester M6 6AS
Tel: 0161 737 5000
Correspondent: A Reich, Secretary
Trustees: A Reich; G Rothbart.
CC Number: 280958

Information available

The latest accounts available at the Charity Commission were for 2009.

The principal objective of the company is the distribution of funds to Jewish, religious, educational and similar charities.

The latest accounts available were for 2009. During the year the trust held assets of £114,000 and received an income of £270,000. The trustees made grants totalling £267,000.

Previous beneficiaries include: Eitz Chaim, Rehabilitation Trust, Chasdei Yoel, Beis Yoel, Friends of Horeinu, Beis Hamedrash Hachadash, Tashbar, Tov V' Chessed, Beth Sorah Schneirer and Asser Bishvil.

Applications

In writing to the correspondent.

Stevenson Family's Charitable Trust

Culture and arts, conservation and heritage, health, education, overseas aid and general charitable purposes

£183,000 (2009/10)

Beneficial area

Worldwide, in practice mainly UK.

Old Waterfield, Winkfield Road, Ascot SL5 7LJ
Correspondent: Sir Hugh Stevenson, Trustee
Trustees: Sir Hugh Stevenson; Lady Catherine Stevenson.
CC Number: 327148

Information available

Accounts were available from the Charity Commission.

This is the family trust of Hugh and Catherine Stevenson. A well known City of London figure, Hugh Stevenson was formerly the chair of one of London's largest investment management companies. The trust is operated personally with no premises or salaried staff of its own and is probably best seen simply as the vehicle for the personal donations of Mr and Mrs Stevenson, rather than as an institution with an independent existence.

The current policy of the trustees is in the main to support charitable causes in the fields of culture and the arts, conservation and heritage, and education, but they can exercise their discretion to make donations for other charitable purposes. In accordance with this policy the main donations made by the trustees during the year were in favour of places of culture and arts.

In 2009/10 the trust had assets of £2.4 million and an income of £161,000. Grants were made to 39 organisations totalling £183,000 and were categorised as follows:

General charitable purposes	15	£84,000
Culture and arts	12	£34,000
Conservation and heritage	4	£29,000
Overseas aid	2	£29,000
Health and medicine	4	£7,300
Education and training	2	£750

Beneficiaries included: Berkshire Community Foundation (£50,000); University of Cape Town Trust (£28,000); National Trust for Scotland (£25,000); St Michael and All Angels – Sunninghill (£15,000); Royal Chapel Appeal and St Mary's PCC (£10,000 each); Sick Children's Trust (£5,000); Charleston Trust (£2,000); British Museum Society (£1,500); Merlin (£1,000); Camphill Village Trust Appeals Fund (£500); Reed's School Foundation Appeal and Cancer Research (£250 each); and Glyndebourne Arts Trust (£150).

Applications

The trust states that: 'No unsolicited applications can be considered as the charity's funds are required to support purposes chosen by the trustees.'

Common applicant mistakes

'Submitting unsolicited applications.'

The Stewards' Charitable Trust

Rowing

£288,000 (2009/10)

Beneficial area

Principally the UK.

Regatta Headquarters, Henley-on-Thames, Oxfordshire RG9 2LY
Tel: 01491 572153
Fax: 01491 575509
Website: www.hrr.co.uk/
Correspondent: Daniel Grist, Secretary
Trustees: M A Sweeney; G V Davidge; C L Baillieu; C Lester; Sir S Redgrave.
CC Number: 299597

Information available

Accounts were available from the Charity Commission.

The Stewards' Charitable Trust was formally established by the governing body of the Henley Regatta in June 1988. The principal objective of the trust was to provide funds to encourage and support young people (still receiving education or undergoing training) to row or scull.

The trust's website provides the following information:

> The trust receives the bulk of its money from substantial annual donations made by Henley Royal Regatta and its trading arm, Henley Royal Regatta Limited, but also benefits from the generosity of other donors, both corporate and individual, including several members of the Stewards' Enclosure.

The trust makes grants to organisations and clubs benefiting boys and girls involved in the sport of rowing. It supports rowing at all levels, from grassroots upwards; beneficiaries should be in full-time education or training. Support is also given to related medical and educational research projects. The trust works closely with the ARA and plans to offer long term support to their various coaching schemes. Grants can be one-off or recurring and are especially made where matched funds are raised elsewhere.

In 2009/10 the trust had assets of £5.6 million and an income of £301,000, including £176,000 in donations received from the Henley Royal Regatta Limited. Grants were made to nine organisations totalling £288,000.

The beneficiaries were: British Rowing Scholarships (£204,000); London Youth Rowing (£37,500); Rowing Foundation (£15,000); Project Oarsome (£12,000); Upper Thames Rowing Club – Junior Development (£10,000); Ball Cup Regatta (£4,500); Junior Inter-Regional Regatta (£3,000); World University Rowing Championships (£1,000); and Regatta for the Disabled (£500).

Exclusions

No grants to individuals or for building or capital costs.

Applications

In writing to the correspondent. Applications are usually first vetted by Amateur Rowing Association.

The Andy Stewart Charitable Foundation

General

£109,000 (2010)

Beneficial area

Worldwide.

The Andy Stewart Charitable Foundation, 18 Curzon Street, London W1J 7TA
Tel: 020 7397 8900
Website: www.cenkos.com
Correspondent: The Trustees
Trustees: Andy Stewart; Mark Stewart; Paul Stewart.
CC Number: 1114802

Information available

Accounts were on file at the Charity Commission.

The foundation was set up in 2006. During 2010 it had assets of £529,000 and an income of £290,000 which included a large donation of £250,000

from Cenkos Holdings. Grants to 28 charities totalled £109,000.

Grant beneficiaries included: Spinal Research (£72,000); Sir Peter O'Sullivan Charitable Trust (£10,000); Spinal Injuries (£6,200); Moorcroft Trust (£4,350); Brompton Foundation (£2,500) and Racing Welfare (£1,100). Further donations for £1,000 or less totalled £7,000.

Applications

In writing to the correspondent.

The Stoller Charitable Trust

Medical, children, general

£252,000 (2009/10)

Beneficial area

UK, with a preference for the Greater Manchester area.

PO Box 164, Middleton, Manchester M24 1XA
Tel: 0161 653 3849
Correspondent: Alison M Ford, Secretary
Trustees: Norman K Stoller, Chair; Roger Gould; Jan Fidler; Sheila M Stoller.
CC Number: 285415

Information available

Accounts were available from the Charity Commission.

The trust supports a wide variety of charitable causes, but with particular emphasis on those that are local (Greater Manchester), medically related or supportive of children. It also endeavours to maintain a balance between regular and occasional donations and between large and smaller grants. Grants can be considered for buildings, capital costs, projects, research costs, recurring costs and start-up costs. As well as one-off grants, funding may also be given for up to three years.

In 2009/10 the trust had assets of £5.8 million and an income of £64,000. Grants were made to 66 organisations totalling £252,000.

Grants included those made to: Bauern Helfen Baeurn (£25,000); Onside North West (£25,000); Broughton House (£20,000); Central Manchester Children's Hospitals and Live Music Now (£10,000 each); Christie Hospital, Greater Manchester Appeal, Imperial War Museum North and National Memorial Arboretum (£5,000 each); Cancer Research UK and Oldham Liaison of Ex-Services Associations (£2,500); Church Housing Trust, Commandery of John of Gaunt and Mines Advisory Group (£1,000 each); Salvation Army Eden Project (£400); and Windermere Air Show (£250).

Exclusions

No grants to individuals.

Applications

In writing to the correspondent. Applications need to be received by February, May, August or November. The trustees usually meet in March, June, September and December.

The M J C Stone Charitable Trust

General

Around £90,000 (2010)

Beneficial area

UK.

Estate Office, Ozleworth Park, Wotton-under-Edge, Gloucestershire GL12 7QA
Tel: 01453 845591
Correspondent: Michael Stone, Trustee
Trustees: Michael Stone; Louisa Stone; Charles Stone; Andrew Stone; Nicola Farquhar.
CC Number: 283920

Information available

Accounts had been received at the Charity Commission but were not available to view.

While the trust has general charitable objects, giving to a range of causes, it stated that its main area of interest is the advancement of education. In 2010 the trust had an income of just £900 and a total expenditure of £93,000. No further information was available. In the past grants have been awarded under five categories which were: education; health and medical; environment and countryside; the relief of poverty and religious purposes.

Previous beneficiaries have included: Westonbirt School (£50,000); Bradfield Foundation and Great North Air Ambulance (£26,000 each); Wotton Under Edge Community Sports Fund (£20,000); Maggie Keswick Jencks Cancer (£10,000); National Trust (£5,000); Zimbabwe Rhodesia Relief and Gloucestershire Society (£1,000 each) and CDTR – Peruvian Appeal, Royal British Legion and Tewkesbury Abbey Appeal Trust (£250 each).

Applications

The trust does not accept unsolicited applications.

Common applicant mistakes

'Disregarding the fact that we do not consider unsolicited applications.'

The Stone-Mallabar Charitable Foundation

Medical, arts, religion, overseas appeals, welfare and education

£37,000 (2008/9)

Beneficial area

UK.

41 Orchard Court, Portman Square, London W1H 6LF
Email: jmls@ymail.com
Correspondent: Jonathan Stone, Trustee
Trustees: Jonathan Stone; Thalia Stone; Robin Paul; Graham Hutton.
CC Number: 1013678

Information available

Accounts were on file at the Charity Commission for 2008/9.

The foundation supports a range of charitable purposes including religion, overseas appeals, welfare and education but tends to have a preference for medical causes and the arts.

The latest accounts available were for 2008/9 when the trust held assets of £521,000, had an income of £39,000 and made grants of £37,000.

The trust gave £5,000 in grants of less than £1,000 and 13 grants of £1,000 or over including: Sheffield Institute Foundation for Motor Neurone Disease £8,000; Bolshoi Ballet School Sally Oakley Smith- Motor Neurone Disease Event (£4,000); Alzheimer's Concern Ealing (£3,000); The Hard Man Trust £2,500; Thalidomide at 50 (£2,500); West London Mission; Christian Concern Crewe; Dermatrust; Cini UK; Pearson Holiday Fund (£1,000 each).

Exclusions

No grants to individuals.

Applications

In writing to the correspondent.

The Samuel Storey Family Charitable Trust

General

£93,000 (2009/10)

Beneficial area

UK, with a preference for Yorkshire.

21 Buckingham Gate, London SW1E 6LS
Tel: 020 7802 2700
Correspondent: Hon. Sir Richard Storey, Trustee
Trustees: Hon. Sir Richard Storey; Wren Hoskyns Abrahall; Kenelm Storey.
CC Number: 267684

Information available

Accounts were available from the Charity Commission.

This trust has general charitable purposes, supporting a wide range of causes, including the arts, children, gardens and churches. The grants list shows a large number of beneficiaries in Yorkshire. In 2009/10 the trust had assets of £4.6 million and an income f £138,000. Grants were made to 118 organisations totalling £93,000.

The largest grant again went to Hope and Homes for Children (£29,000). Other beneficiaries included: York University (£20,000); Pebbles Project (£2,000); Molly's Fund and RLNI (£1,000 each); Sistema Scotland (£500); World Monument Fund in Britain (£250); Smile Train UK (£200) and Woodland Trust (£65).

Exclusions

The trust does not support non-registered charities or individuals.

Applications

In writing to the correspondent.

Common applicant mistakes

'Taking insufficient trouble in approaching the trust (i.e. in the form of a letter). In order to give appropriately, we only really do so to personalised applications.'

Peter Stormonth Darling Charitable Trust

Heritage, medical research, sport

£93,500 (2010)

Beneficial area

UK.

Moditic Ltd, 12 Charles II Street, London SW1Y 4QU
Correspondent: Peter Stormonth Darling
Trustees: Tom Colville; John Lodwell; Peter Stormonth Darling; Elizabeth Cobb; Arabella Johannes; Christa Taylor.
CC Number: 1049946

Information available

Accounts were available from the Charity Commission.

The trust makes grants towards heritage, education, healthcare and sports facilities. In 2010 it had assets of £2.8 million and an income of £150,000. Grants were made to 17 organisations totalling £93,500.

The largest grants were made to Winchester College Wykeham Campaign (£50,000) and Friends of East Sussex Hospices (£10,000).

Smaller grants included those to: Reed's School (£4,000); Cheltenham Festivals (£2,500); Canine Partners and Chelsea Physic Garden (£2,000 each); and Brittle Bone Society, Courtauld Institute of Art and Sussex Community Foundation (£1,000 each).

Exclusions

No grants to individuals.

Applications

This trust states that it does not respond to unsolicited applications.

Peter Storrs Trust

Education

£86,000 (2009/10)

Beneficial area

UK.

c/o Smithfield Accountants, 117 Charterhouse Street, London EC1M 6AA
Tel: 020 7253 3757
Fax: 020 7253 3761
Correspondent: The Trustees
Trustees: Geoffrey Adams; Arthur Curtis; Julie Easton.
CC Number: 313804

Information available

Accounts were available from the Charity Commission.

The trust makes grants to registered charities working for the advancement of education in the UK.

In 2009/10 the trust had assets of £2.3 million and an income of £102,000. Grants were made to 37 organisations totalling £86,000.

Beneficiaries included: Peter House (£5,400); RNIB and Eggington Memorial Trust (£5,000 each); Skillforce and British Schools Exploring Society – Next Generation Initiative (£3,000 each); Barnardo's, British Bible Society, African Medical, World Wildlife Fund, Dorothy Kerin Trust, British Aid to Refugees, Royal

Academy of Arts, Voluntary Services Overseas, Oxford Mission and Bath Church Houses (£2,000 each); and Zebra Trust (£1,500).

Applications

In writing to the correspondent. Applications are considered every three to six months. Please note the trust receives far more applications than it is able to support, many of which do not meet the criteria outlined above. This results in a heavy waste of time and expense for both applicants and the trust itself.

Common applicant mistakes

'We cannot entertain applications from individuals. Our principle constraint is availability of funds (from annual income). As we have a number of recipients to whom we make annual awards our unallocated income is generally small.'

The Strawberry Charitable Trust

Jewish, youth

£113,000 (2009/10)

Beneficial area

Not defined but with a preference for Manchester.

4 Westfields, Hale, Altrincham WA15 0LL
Tel: 0161 980 8484
Email: anthonysula@hotmail.com
Correspondent: Anthony Leon, Trustee
Trustees: Emma Myers; Laura Avigdori; Anthony Leon.
CC Number: 1090173

Information available

Accounts were available from the Charity Commission.

Set up in January 2000, this trust supports the relief of poverty and hardship amongst Jewish persons and the advancement of the Jewish religion.

In 2009/10 the trust had assets of £483,000 and an income of £44,000. Grants were made totalling £113,000. There were 16 grants made during the year.

Beneficiaries included: United Jewish Israel Appeal (£35,000); Community Security Trust (£15,000); The Fed (£10,000); Lubavitch South Manchester (£8,000); King David School (£6,000); World Jewish Relief (£5,000); Belz and St John's Wood Synagogue (£3,000); Action on Addiction and Mew Children's Hospital (£2,000 each); and Tickets for Troops (£1,000).

Smaller grants of less than £1,000 were not listed separately, but totalled £14,000.

Applications

In writing to the correspondent.

The W O Street Charitable Foundation

Education, people with disabilities, young people, health, social welfare

£314,000 (2010)

Beneficial area

UK, with a preference for the North West of England, primarily Lancashire and Jersey.

c/o Barclays Bank Trust Company Ltd, PO Box 15, Osborne Court, Gadbrook Park, Northwich CW9 7UR
Tel: 01606 313 417
Correspondent: The Trust Officer
Trustees: Barclays Bank Trust Co. Ltd;
CC Number: 267127

Information available

Accounts were available from the Charity Commission.

In considering grants the trustees pay close regard to the wishes of the late Mr. Street who had particular interests in education, support for people with financial difficulties (particularly the elderly, people who are blind or who have other disabilities), health and social welfare generally. Special support is given to the North West of England and Jersey.

In 2010 the trust had an income of £382,000 and assets of over £16 million. Grants were made totalling £314,000. In line with the grant making policies of the foundation, £40,000 (a proportion of the available income annually, not exceeding 10%) was paid by grant to the W O Street Jersey Charitable Trust. £52,000 was also given in educational bursaries. In addition the foundation supports the Combined Trusts Scholarship Trust (a separate registered charity – numbered 295402).

Beneficiaries included: W O Street Jersey Charitable Trust (£40,000); Emmott Foundation (£30,000); The museum of Science and Industry in Manchester (£10,000); Nightstop in Stockport and Trafford (£8,000); SignHealth (£6,600); Bury Parish Church (£5,000); Harmony Youth Project (£4,000); Caring Today (£3,500 each); Stick n Step (£2,500); The Sailors Families Society (£1,400); Scottish Spina Bifida Association (£327).

Exclusions

No grants towards:
- medical research
- animal welfare
- overseas projects or charities.

Applications directly from individuals are not considered.

Applications

In writing to the correspondent. Applications are usually considered on a quarterly basis, at the end of January, April, July and October.

The A B Strom and R Strom Charitable Trust

Jewish, general

£45,000 (2009/10)

Beneficial area

UK.

c/o 11 Gloucester Gardens, London NW11 9AB
Tel: 020 8455 5949
Email: m@michaelpasha.worldonline.co.uk

Correspondent: Regina Strom, Trustee
Trustees: Regina Strom; Debbie Weissbraun.
CC Number: 268916

Information available

Accounts were available from the Charity Commission, but without a list of grants.

The objects of the charity are stated as follows:
- the advancement of education according to the tenets of the Orthodox Jewish faith
- the relief of poverty and sickness.

However, according to our correspondence with the trust: 'the trust only supports a set list of charities working with elderly people, schools/colleges, hospitals and Christian causes. It does not have any money available for any charities not already on the list'.

In 2009/10 the trust had assets of £619,000 with an income of £60,000. Grants totalled £45,000. No further information was available.

Previously, grants in excess of £1,000 each were made to Yeshivas Hanegev (£10,000), JRRC (£10,000 in two grants) and Redcroft and Russian Immigrants (£5,000 each).

Applications

Please note that the same organisations are supported each year, therefore the trust does not want to receive any applications for funding.

Sueberry Ltd

Jewish, welfare

£172,000 (2009/10)

Beneficial area

UK and overseas.

18 Clifton Gardens, London N15 6AP
Correspondent: D S Davis, Trustee
Trustees: D S Davis, Chair; C Davis; Mrs H Davis; J Davis; Mrs M Davis; A D Davis; S M Davis; Y Davis.
CC Number: 256566

Information available

Accounts were available from the Charity Commission, but without a list of grants.

The trust makes grants to Jewish organisations and to other UK welfare, educational and medical organisations benefiting children and young adults, at risk groups, people who are disadvantaged by poverty, or socially isolated people.

In 2009/10 the trust had assets of £51,000 and an income of £123,000. Grants were made totalling £172,000. A list of beneficiaries was not available. In previous years the trust has supported educational, religious and other charitable organisations.

Applications

In writing to the correspondent.

The Alan Sugar Foundation

Jewish charities, general

£283,000 (2009/10)

Beneficial area

UK.

Sterling House, Langston Road, Loughton, Essex IG10 3TS
Tel: 020 3225 5560
Email: colin@amsprop.com
Correspondent: Colin Sandy, Trustee
Trustees: Lord Alan Sugar; Colin Sandy; Simon Sugar; Daniel Sugar; Louise Baron.
CC Number: 294880

Information available

Accounts were available from the Charity Commission.

This trust was established by the well-known creator of The Apprentice and ex-chair of Tottenham Hotspur FC. It gives a small number of substantial grants each year to registered charities that are of current and ongoing interest to the trustees.

In 2009/10 the trust had assets of £1.1 million and an income of £927,000. Grants were made totalling £283,000.

Beneficiaries were: Jewish Care (£200,000); Sport Relief (£50,000); MacMillan Cancer (£25,000); Children in Need (£3,000); Prostate Cancer Charitable Fund and Cancer Research UK (£2,000 each); and St Michael's Hospice (£500).

Exclusions

No grants for individuals or to non-registered charities.

Applications

This trust states that it does not respond to unsolicited applications. All projects are initiated by the trustees.

The Adrienne and Leslie Sussman Charitable Trust

Jewish, general

£57,000 (2009/10)

Beneficial area

UK, in practice Greater London, particularly Barnet.

25 Tillingbourne Gardens, London N3 3JJ
Correspondent: Adrienne Sussman, Trustee
Trustees: Adrienne Sussman; Leslie Sussman; Martin Paisner.
CC Number: 274955

Information available

Accounts were available from the Charity Commission, but without a list of grants.

The trust supports a variety of Jewish, medical and social welfare organisations, including many in the Greater London area. In 2009/10 the trust had assets of £1.8 million and an income of £65,000. Grants were made totalling £57,000.

A list of beneficiaries was not available, however previous beneficiaries have included; BF Shvut Ami, Chai – Lifeline and B'nai B'rith Hillel Fund, Child Resettlement, Children and Youth Aliyah, Finchley Synagogue, Jewish Care, Nightingale House, Norwood Ravenswood and Sidney Sussex CLL.

Exclusions

No grants to branches of UK charities outside Barnet, non-registered charities and individuals.

Applications

In writing to the correspondent.

The Sutasoma Trust

Education, general

£100,000 (2009/10)

Beneficial area

UK and overseas.

PO Box 157, Haverhill, Suffolk CB9 1AH
Tel: 07768 245384
Email: sutasoma.trust@btinternet.com
Correspondent: Jane M Lichtenstein, Trustee
Trustees: Dr Angela R Hobart; Marcel A Burgauer; Jane M Lichtenstein; Prof. Bruce Kapferer; Dr Sally Wolfe; Dr Piers Vitebsky.
CC Number: 803301

Information available

Accounts were available from the Charity Commission.

The trust's objects are: 'to advance education and humanitarian activities by providing bursaries and support to institutions in the field of social sciences, humanities and humanitarian activities'. General grants may also be made. The trustees have indicated in the past that they prefer that annual donations should be made available to organisations on a recurring basis for the mid to long term.

In 2009/10 the trust had assets of £2.5 million and an income of £101,000. Grants were made totalling £100,000. The largest grants went to Lucy Cavendish College Fellowship (£19,500) and University of Bergen (£12,000).

Other grants included those made to: Amrita Performing Arts (£8,000); LACP Zambia (£7,000); Emslie Horniman Fund and School of Oriental and African Studies (£5,000 each); Merlin Medical Relief (£3,000);

Corporation of Haverford and Practical Action (£2,000 each); Lewa Wildlife Conservation (£1,000); and Anti-Slavery International (£500).

Applications

In writing to the correspondent.

The Suva Foundation Limited

General

£138,000 (2009/10)

Beneficial area

Unrestricted with a preference for Henley-on-Thames.

The Old Rectory, 17 Thameside, Henley-on-Thames RG9 1BH
Tel: 01491 848876
Correspondent: Philip Kent
Trustees: A Nicoll; P Nicoll.
CC Number: 1077057

Information available

Accounts were available from the Charity Commission.

Set up in 1999, the following was taken from the foundation's 2007/08 annual report:

> The charity's principal activity during the year was the support of charities through the payments of donations. The objects of the charity are to promote any charitable purpose or support any charity selected by the directors. It is expressly contemplated that The Langley Academy may be a beneficiary of the charity.

In 2009/10 the foundation had assets of almost £9.5 million and an income of £297,000. Grants totalled £138,000 of which £92,000 went to the Langley Academy.

Other beneficiaries included: Great Ormond Street Hospital (£27,000); Chiltern Centre for Disabled Children, Lambrook School Trust and Natural History Museum (£5,000 each); CLIC Sargent (£2,500); ORH Charitable Funds (£1,000); Remenham PCC and The Royal Marsden Cancer Charity (£500 each); and Friends of Henley Festival Society (£250).

Applications

This trust does not accept unsolicited applications.

Swan Mountain Trust

Mental health, penal affairs

Around £30,000 (2009/10)

Beneficial area

UK.

7 Mount Vernon, London NW3 6QS
Tel: 020 7794 2486
Correspondent: Janet Hargreaves, Trustee
Trustees: Dodie Carter; Janet Hargreaves; Peter Kilgarriff; Calton Younger.
CC Number: 275594

Information available

Limited information was available from the Charity Commission website.

This trust supports organisations which are actively involved in the fields of mental health and penal affairs. Provision is also made to help prisoners with educational needs. Grants are made to meet specific needs and rarely exceed £1,500.

The trust has previously stated in its advice to applicants:

> We are a very small grantmaking trust; as such we like to ensure that our limited resources are used as effectively as possible. We do not consider contributing to a large appeal but would rather consider a piece of equipment or an activity for which we can consider meeting the total cost, somewhere around £500. Alternatively, we will consider meeting the final amount of a larger appeal when most of the rest has been found.

In 2009/10 the trust had an income of £27,000 and a total expenditure of £37,000. No further information was available.

Previous beneficiaries include: AVID – Association of Visitors to Immigrant Detainees, Sheffield MIND, Prison Advice and Care Trust – London, HMP Morton Hall, Community Action Halfway Home, Foundation for the Arts and Mental

Health, Lifecraft – Cambridge, Corner House Resource Centre and Wigan and Leigh CVS – Freebirds Mental Health Group.

Exclusions

No grants for annual holidays, debt repayment, large appeals or for causes outside the trust's two main areas of work.

Applications

In writing to the correspondent, enclosing an up-to-date report on fundraising, and a copy of the most recent annual report and accounts (or any financial information available). The trustees meet in early February, June and October each year, but can occasionally reach decisions quickly in an emergency. Applications should be made at least four weeks before the trustees' next meeting. The trust tries to be as responsive as it can be to appropriate applicants.

Common applicant mistakes

'They don't know our criteria; don't reply to a request for more information; and don't wait two years before submitting a further application.'

The John Swire (1989) Charitable Trust

General

£477,000 (2009)

Beneficial area

UK.

Swire House, 59 Buckingham Gate, London SW1E 6AJ
Tel: 020 7834 7717
Correspondent: Michael Todhunter, Charities Administrator
Trustees: Sir John Swire; J S Swire; B N Swire; M C Robinson; Lady M C Swire.
CC Number: 802142

Information available

Full accounts were on file at the Charity Commission.

Established in 1989 by Sir John Swire of John Swire and Sons Ltd, merchants and ship owners, the trust supports a wide range of organisations including some in the area of arts, welfare, education, medicine and research.

In 2009 the trust had assets of £16.4 million and an income of £5.4 million. Grants were made totalling £477,000. The largest grants included those to: St John of Jerusalem Eye Hospital (£102,000); New Marlow Theatre Development Trust (£75,000); Breast Cancer Hope Charity (£30,000); British Cardiovascular Society (£25,000); Krishna Gurung (£23,000); St Anthony's College (£13,000); and Carers First (£10,000).

Other grants included those to: Action for ME (£7,500); Canterbury Festival (£6,000); Crimestoppers, Faversham Society, St Mary the Virgin – Great Parndon (£5,000 each); St Clare Hospice (£3,000); Ataxia-Telangiectasia Society, Changing Faces (£2,500 each); Caldecott Foundation, Kent Scouts (£2,000 each); Age Concern and Citizens Advice Bureau in Swale (£1,000 each).

Grants of less than £1,000 amounted to a total of £39,000.

Applications
In writing to the correspondent.

The Swire Charitable Trust

General
£490,000 (2009)

Beneficial area
Worldwide.

The Swire Charitable Trust, Swire House, 59 Buckingham Gate, London SW1E 6AJ
Tel: 020 7834 7717
Trustees: Sir J Swire; Sir Adrian Swire; B N Swire; J S Swire; M Swire; J W J Hughes-Hallett.
CC Number: 270726

Information available
Full accounts were on file at the Charity Commission.

In 2009 the trust had an income of £526,000 – almost entirely from donations received from John Swire & Sons Limited. Assets stood at £57,000 and grants totalled £490,000.

Grants of £1,000 or more were listed in the accounts. Beneficiaries of the five largest grants were: Help for Heroes, Marine Society & Sea Cadets (£25,000 each); Air League Educational Trust (£23,500); Breast Cancer Haven (£20,000) and Royal Air Force Benevolent Fund (£15,000).

Other beneficiaries included: Internally Displaced Persons in Sri Lanka (£11,000); Autism Speaks, Brydges Centre, Rethink, Royal National College for the Blind (£10,000 each); The Japan Society (£7,500); Child Bereavement Charity, Commonwealth War Graves Commission (£5,000 each); Cleft Lip and Palate Association (£3,000); Helping Uganda Schools, Heritage of London Trust (£2,500 each); and Living Paintings (£1,500).

Grants of less than £1,000 each totalled £4,000.

Applications
In writing to the correspondent. Applications are considered throughout the year.

The Hugh and Ruby Sykes Charitable Trust

General, medical, education, employment
£136,000 (2009/10)

Beneficial area
Principally South Yorkshire, also Derbyshire.

The Coach House, Brookfield Manor, Hathersage, Hope Valley, Derbyshire S32 1BR
Tel: 01433 651190
Email: info@brookfieldmanor.com
Correspondent: Brian Evans, Administrator
Trustees: Sir Hugh Sykes; Lady Ruby Sykes.
CC Number: 327648

Information available
Accounts were available at the Charity Commission, but without a list of grants.

This trust was set up in 1987 for general charitable purposes by Sir Hugh Sykes and his wife Lady Sykes. It supports local charities in South Yorkshire and Derbyshire, some major UK charities and a few medical charities.

In 2009/10 the trust had assets of £1.9 million and an income of £88,000. Grants were made totalling £136,000. A list of beneficiaries was not included in the accounts.

Exclusions
No grants are made to individuals. Most grants are made to organisations which have a connection to one of the trustees.

Applications
Applications can only be accepted from registered charities and should be in writing to the correspondent. In order to save administration costs, replies are not sent to unsuccessful applicants. If the trustees are able to consider a request for support, they aim to express interest within one month.

The Sylvanus Charitable Trust

Animal welfare, Roman Catholic
£27,000 (2010)

Beneficial area
Europe and North America.

Hunters, 9 New Square, London WC2A 3QN
Tel: 020 7412 0050
Correspondent: John C Vernor Miles, Trustee
Trustees: John C Vernor Miles; Alexander D Gemmill; Wilfred E Vernor Miles; Gloria Taviner.
CC Number: 259520

Information available
Accounts were available from the Charity Commission.

399

This trust was established in 1968 by the Countess of Kinnoull, who spent the last 40 years of her life in California, and supports animal welfare, the prevention of animal cruelty and the teachings and practices of the Roman Catholic Church pre Second Vatican Council. Organisations in North America and Europe are supported, with the trust splitting its finances into two sections, namely, the sterling section (Europe) and the Dollar section (North America) to avoid currency troubles.

As the dollar section focuses solely on US giving (and information on it was unavailable), only the sterling section is described here.

In 2010 it had assets of £2 million and an income of £68,000. Grants were made to 11 organisations totalling £27,000.

The beneficiaries included: Society of St Pius X (£5,000); FRAME (£3,000); Durrell Wildlife Conservation Trust and Fauna & Flora International (£2,000 each); and Animal Health Trust and Help in Suffering (£1,000 each).

Exclusions
No grants for expeditions, scholarships or individuals.

Applications
The trustees usually make grants to charities known personally to them but occasionally make grants in response to unsolicited appeals. When considering applications for funding the trustees take into account how many years' reserves are held by an applicant and the proportionate costs of administration and fund-raising. They also consider the degree to which the trustees have been informed of progress made since previous grants. The trustees do not give grants to individuals. Apply in writing to the correspondent. The trustees meet once a year.

T & S Trust Fund

Orthodox Jewish

£110,000 (2008/09)

Beneficial area
Greater London, Gateshead, Manchester City.

96 Whitehall Road, Gateshead, Tyne And Wear NE8 4ET
Tel: 0191 482 5050
Correspondent: A Sandler, Trustee
Trustees: A T Sandler; Mrs S Sandler; E Salomon.
CC Number: 1095939

Information available
The most recent accounts available from the Charity Commission were those for 2008/09.

According to these accounts:

> The objects of the charity are the advancement of education according to the tenets of the Orthodox Jewish Faith, the advancement of the Orthodox Jewish Religion and the relief of poverty amongst the elderly or persons in need, hardship and distress in the Jewish Community.

In 2008/09 the trust had assets of £523,000 and an income of£125,000. Grants were made to fifteen organisations and totalled £110,000.

The beneficiaries were: Orphan children fund (£59,000); Centre for Advanced Rabbinics (£8,000); New Hall Charitable Trust (£7,000); Rozac Charitable Trust (£6,000); Etz Chaim School (£4,500); Yeshaya Adler Memorial Fund (£2,000) and Tashbar (£1,000)

In addition to the above there were 'relief of poverty grants' (£4,000).

Applications
In writing to the correspondent.

The Tabeel Trust

Evangelical Christian

£63,000 (2009/10)

Beneficial area
Worldwide with a preference for Clacton (Essex).

3 Oak Park, West Byfleet, Surrey KT14 6AG
Tel: 01932 343808
Correspondent: Barbara Carter, Trustee
Trustees: Douglas K Brown; Pauline M Brown; Barbara J Carter; Dr Mary

P Clark; Jean A Richardson; James Davey; Sarah Taylor; Nigel Davey.
CC Number: 266645

Information available
Basic information taken from the Charity Commission website.

This trust primarily supports Evangelical Christian activities and projects which are either based in Clacton or are personally known to one or more of the trustees. In 2009/10 it had an income of £21,000 and a total expenditure of nearly £64,000.

Previous beneficiaries included: St George's Crypt – Leeds (£30,000); Essex County Evangelists' – Accommodation Trust (£10,000); ZACS (£6,000); Radio Worldwide (£5,000); Barnabas Fund (£4,000); Viz a Viz (£3,000); Tabernacle Baptist Church – Penarth (£2,000); Christian Institute (£1,000); and Upesi and Salvation Army – Clacton (£500 each).

Applications
Only charities with which a trustee already has contact should apply. Grants are considered at trustees' meetings in May and November.

Tadlus Limited

Orthodox Jewish

£0 (2009/10)

Beneficial area
UK and Israel.

6 Spring Hill, London E5 9BE
Correspondent: Jacob Grosskopf, Trustee
Trustees: Jacob Grosskopf; Myer Grosskopf; Chaim Grosskopf.
CC Number: 1109982

Information available
Accounts were available from the Charity Commission.

Set up in 2005, this trust supports the advancement of religion in accordance with the orthodox Jewish faith. Grants are made to promote and maintain institutions, organisations and individuals involved in religious education and worship, and for the relief of individuals in need.

In 2009/10 the trust had an income of £45,000. At year end it had a deficit of £1 million in its reserves. This was due to ongoing problems with both of the trust's investment properties, which have led to their devaluation. The trustees state that they are, 'actively monitoring the situation and seeking negotiations with their bankers and creditors'. No grants were made during the year. No details on when the issues might be resolved were given in the accounts.

Applications

In writing to the correspondent.

The Gay and Keith Talbot Trust

Overseas aid, health, famine relief

Around £40,000 (2009/10)

Beneficial area

Worldwide.

Fold Howe, Kentmere, Kendal, Cumbria LA8 9JW
Correspondent: Keith Talbot, Chair
Trustees: Keith Talbot, Chair; Gay Talbot.
CC Number: 1102192

Information available

Information was available from the Charity Commission.

Established in 2004, this trust mainly supports charities working in developing countries. In 2009/10 the trust had an income of £1,600 and a total expenditure of £44,000.

Previous beneficiaries included: CAFOD – Sudan, Cystic Fibrosis Trust, Door of Hope, Medical Missionaries of Mary – Uganda and Nigeria, Our Lady of Windermere and St Herbert, Rwanda Group Trust, SVP – Sudan, Impact Foundation – Bangladesh and Uganda Childbirth Injury Fund.

Applications

In writing to the correspondent.

Common applicant mistakes

'We are very specific about the type of project for which we give grants. Most refusals are because they are not relevant to our cause.'

The Talbot Village Trust

General

£884,000 (2010)

Beneficial area

The boroughs of Bournemouth, Christchurch and Poole; the districts of east Dorset and Purbeck.

Dickinson Manser, 5 Parkstone Road, Poole, Dorset BH15 2NL
Tel: 01202 673071
Email: garycox@dickinsonmanser.co.uk
Correspondent: Gary S Cox, Clerk
Trustees: Christopher Lees, Chair; James Fleming; Sir George Meyrick; Sir Thomas Salt; Russell Rowe; Earl of Shaftesbury.
CC Number: 249349

Information available

Accounts were available from the Charity Commission.

Support is given to other charitable bodies, churches, schools and the like for projects which support youth, the elderly and the disadvantaged in the boroughs of Bournemouth, Christchurch and Poole and the districts of East Dorset and Purbeck.

In addition, the trust also gives extensive support to charities in the form of loans. The charity owns and manages land and property at Talbot Village, Bournemouth, including almshouses which it maintains through an associated trust. There is a strong property focus to much of the trust's work.

As part of the trust's rolling five year plan it aims to make grants and loans averaging £800,000 per annum, in addition to its regular support of St Mark's Church, St Mark's School, the University Chaplaincy and others. The majority of grants are made for capital costs such as, equipment, refurbishment and building extensions.

In 2010 the trust held assets of £36.1 million, had an income of £1.8 million and made grants totalling £884,000, in line with the five year grant expenditure plan.

Grants authorised and paid during the year included those to: Cherry Tree Nursery (£75,000); The Beacon Church (£50,000); Deancry Youth Worker Project (£47,000); Diverse Abilities (£40,000); Colehill & Wimborne Youth & Community Centre (£30,000); Carter Community School (£25,000); Alderholt Chapel; Life Education Wessex; Wessex Autistic Society (£20,000 each); The Variety Club Children's Charity (£12,000); Motability; 1st Woodcutts Scout Group (£10,000 each); The Salvation Army (£9,000); and Broadstone United Reform Church (£4,000).

Exclusions

No grants for individuals.

Applications

In writing to the correspondent.

Talteg Ltd

Jewish, welfare

£245,000 (2010)

Beneficial area

UK, with a preference for Scotland.

90 Mitchell Street, Glasgow G1 3NQ
Tel: 0141 221 3353
Correspondent: Fred Berkley, Trustee
Trustees: Fred Berkley; Adam Berkley; Delia Lynn Berkley; Maxwell Berkley.
CC Number: 283253

Information available

Accounts were available from the Charity Commission but without a grants list.

In 2010 the trust had assets totalling £3.6 million and an income of £371,000. Grants were made during the year totalling £245,000. A list of grants has not been available since 1993.

Previous beneficiaries include: British Friends of Laniado Hospital, Centre for Jewish Studies, Society of Friends of the Torah, Glasgow Jewish

Community Trust, National Trust for Scotland, Ayrshire Hospice, Earl Haig Fund – Scotland and RSSPCC.

Applications

In writing to the correspondent.

The Lady Tangye Charitable Trust

Catholic, overseas aid, general

Around £33,000 (2009/10)

Beneficial area

UK and worldwide, with some preference for the Midlands.

55 Warwick Crest, Arthur Road, Birmingham B15 2LH
Correspondent: Colin Ferguson Smith, Trustee
Trustees: Gitta Clarisse Gilzean Tangye; Colin Ferguson Smith; Michael Plaut.
CC Number: 1044220

Information available

Accounts were available from the Charity Commission.

This trust has general charitable purposes, with a preference for work in the Midlands and the developing world. Christian and environmental causes are well represented in grants awarded.

In 2009/10 it had an income of £27,000 and an expenditure of £33,000.

Previous beneficiaries have included: West Midland Urban Wildlife Trust (£3,000); Spana, ChildLine – Midlands and Aid to the Church in Need (£2,000 each); Amnesty International, Priest Training Fund and Crew Trust (£1,500 each); St Saviour's Church, Walsall and District Samaritans, Life and European Children's Trust (£1,000 each); and Charity Ignite – Big Ideal (£500).

Applications

In writing to the correspondent.

The David Tannen Charitable Trust

Jewish

£134,000 (2009/10)

Beneficial area

UK.

c/o Sutherland House, 70–78 West Hendon Broadway, London NW9 7BT
Tel: 020 8202 1066
Correspondent: Jonathon Miller
Trustees: Jonathon Miller; Alan Rose; David Tannen.
CC Number: 280392

Information available

Accounts were on file at the Charity Commission, without a list of grants.

The trust makes grants for the advancement of the Jewish religion.

In 2009/10 it had assets of £23.6 million and an income of £2.3 million. Grants were made totalling £134,000. A list of grant beneficiaries was not included in the trust's accounts.

Previous beneficiaries included: Cosmon Beiz Academy, Gevurath Ari Trust, Telz Academy Trust, Friends of Ohr Elchonon, Beis Ahron Trust, Wlodowa Charity, Chai Cancer Care, Kollel Skver Trust, Centre for Torah Trust, Gateshead Talmudical College, Jewish Women's Aid Trust, Torah 5759 Ltd and YTAF.

Applications

In writing to the correspondent.

The Tanner Trust

General

£396,000 (2009/10)

Beneficial area

UK, with a slight preference for the South of England, and overseas.

c/o Blake Lapthorn Tarlo Lyons, Harbour Court, Compass Road, Portsmouth PO6 4ST
Tel: 02392 221 122

Fax: 02392 221 123
Correspondent: Celine Lecomte, Trust Administrator
Trustees: Alice P Williams; Lucie Nottingham.
CC Number: 1021175

Information available

Accounts were available from the Charity Commission.

This trust has general charitable purposes, supporting organisations worldwide. The grants list shows no cause or geographical regions favoured or missing, although there appear to be many organisations concerned with youth, welfare and relief work.

In 2009/10 the trust had assets of £7.4 million, an income of £629,000 and made about 150 grants totalling £396,000.

Beneficiaries included: National Trust (£6,500); CRCC and Great Dixter Charitable Trust (£6,000 each); Berkshire Community Foundation, Falmouth and Penryn Sea Cadets Group and Helford River Children's Sailing Trust (£5,000 each); JOLT (£4,000); Industrial Trust and Mercy Ships (£3,000 each); Mango Tree and PlantHeritage (£2,000 each); and Oxford Deaf and Hard of Hearing Centre (£300).

Exclusions

No grants to individuals.

Applications

The trust states that unsolicited applications are, without exception, not considered. Support is only given to charities personally known to the trustees.

The Lili Tapper Charitable Foundation

Jewish

£77,000 (2009/10)

Beneficial area

UK.

Yew Tree Cottage, Artists Lane, Nether Alderley, Macclesfield SK10 4UA

Correspondent: Michael Webber, Trustee

Trustees: Michael Webber; Dr Jonathan Webber.

CC Number: 268523

Information available

Accounts were available from the Charity Commission, but without a grants list.

The trust primarily supports organisations benefiting Jewish people.

In 2009/10 it had assets of £3.1 million, which generated an income of £115,000. Grants were made to 25 organisations totalling £77,000. No details of grant beneficiaries were available.

Previous beneficiaries include: UJIA, CST, Manchester Jewish Foundation, Teenage Cancer Trust, Keshet Eilon, Israel Educational Foundation, Chicken Shed Theatre Company and Jewish Representation Council.

Exclusions

No grants to individuals.

Applications

The trust states that it does not respond to any unsolicited applications.

The Taurus Foundation

General

£77,000 (2009/10)

Beneficial area

UK.

Forsters LLP, 31 Hill Street, London W1J 5LS

Tel: 020 7863 8333

Email: carole.cook@forsters.co.uk

Correspondent: Carole Cook

Trustees: Denis Felsenstein; Michael Jacobs; Alan Fenton; Anthony Forwood; Priscilla Fenton.

CC Number: 1128441

Information available

Basic information was available from the Charity Commission.

The foundation was established in 2009 for general charitable purposes.

In 2009/10 the foundation had assets of £699,000 and an income of £770,500, mainly from donations. Grants were made to 12 organisations totalling £77,000.

The beneficiaries were: Norwood Ravenswood, Jewish Care, Rainbow Trust, Clic Sargent and Chance UK (£10,000 each); Camp Simcha, Child Welfare Scheme, Momentum, Aspire and Just for Kids Law (£5,000 each); and Almeida Theatre and Donmar Warehouse Projects (£1,000 each).

Applications

The foundation states: 'The foundation does not consider unsolicited applications and does not have the resources to respond to any unsolicited applications.'

The Tay Charitable Trust

General

Around £180,000 (2009/10)

Beneficial area

UK, with a preference for Scotland, particularly Dundee.

6 Douglas Terrace, Broughty Ferry, Dundee DD5 1EA

Correspondent: Mrs E A Mussen, Trustee

Trustees: Mrs E A Mussen; Mrs Z C Martin; G C Bonar.

SC Number: SC001004

Information available

Basic information taken from the Office of the Scottish Charities Regulator website.

This trust has general charitable purposes and supports a wide range of causes. Grants of up to £5,000 are generally made to UK-wide charities or organisations benefitting Scotland or Dundee, although local groups elsewhere can also be supported.

In 2009/10 the trust had an income of £188,000.

Previous beneficiaries of grants of £1,000 or more included: Dundee Heritage Trust and RNLI (£5,000 each); Boarders Forest Trust,

DermaTrust, Edinburgh World Heritage Trust, Maritime Volunteer Service and University of St Andrews – Low Scholarship (£3,000 each); Bowel Cancer UK, High Blood Pressure Foundation, John Muir Trust and National Trust for Scotland (£2,000 each); Princess Royal Trust for Carers (£1,500); and Army Benevolent Fund, Changing Faces, Dundee Symphony Orchestra, Guide Dogs for the Blind, Lincoln Cathedral, Samaritans, Scottish Countryside Alliance Trust, Skillforce Development and Tayside Council on Alcohol (£1,000 each).

Exclusions

Grants are only given to charities recognised by the Inland Revenue. No grants to individuals.

Applications

No standard form; applications in writing to the correspondent, including a financial statement. An sae is appreciated.

Common applicant mistakes

'Not stating whether they are a registered charity; not giving any financial details.'

C B and H H Taylor 1984 Trust

Quaker, general

£255,000 (2009/10)

Beneficial area

West Midlands, Ireland and overseas.

14 Chamberlain Road, Worcester WR2 4PR

Correspondent: Clare Norton, Trustee

Trustees: James Taylor; Constance Penny; Elizabeth Birmingham; Clare Norton; John Taylor; Thomas Penny; Robert Birmingham; Simon Taylor.

CC Number: 291363

Information available

Accounts were on file at the Charity Commission.

The trust's geographical areas of benefit are:

▶ organisations serving Birmingham and the West Midlands

- organisations outside the West Midlands where the trust has well-established links
- organisations in Ireland
- UK-based charities working overseas.

The general areas of benefit are:
- the Religious Society of Friends (Quakers) and other religious denominations
- healthcare projects
- social welfare: community groups; children and young people; older people; disadvantaged people; people with disabilities; homeless people; housing initiatives; counselling and mediation agencies
- education: adult literacy schemes; employment training; youth work
- penal affairs: work with offenders and ex-offenders; police projects
- the environment and conservation work
- the arts: museums and art galleries; music and drama
- Ireland: cross-community health and social welfare projects
- UK charities working overseas on long-term development projects.

About 60% of grants are for the work and concerns of the Religious Society of Friends (Quakers). The trust favours specific applications. It does not usually award grants on an annual basis for revenue costs. Applications are encouraged from minority groups and women-led initiatives. Grants, which are made only to or through registered charities, mostly range from £500 to £5,000.

In 2009/10 the trust had assets of £9 million and an income of £335,000. Grants to 131 organisations totalled £255,000.

The largest grant went to Britain Yearly Meeting (£30,000).

Other beneficiaries included: Central England Quakers (£9,500); Friends of Swanivar (£7,000); Cape Town Quaker Peace Centre (£6,000); Oxfam, UNICEF, Christian Aid and Merlin (£5,000 each); Birmingham Settlement (£4,000); Salvation Army (£3,500); Action Aid (£3,000); Ironbridge Gorge Museum (£2,000); Bournville Parish Church, Birmingham Boys'/Girls' Union, Concern Africa, Dalit Solidarity Network and Shelter (£1,000 each);

Cornwall Quakers (£850); Kanga Project and Home from Hospital (£500 each); and Birmingham Botanical Gardens (£250).

Exclusions

The trust does not fund: individuals (whether for research, expeditions, educational purposes and so on); local projects or groups outside the West Midlands; or projects concerned with travel or adventure.

Applications

There is no formal application form. Applicants should write to the correspondent giving the charity's registration number, a brief description of the charity's activities, and details of the specific project for which the grant is being sought. Applicants should also include a budget of the proposed work, together with a copy of the charity's most recent accounts. Trustees will also wish to know what funds have already been raised for the project and how the shortfall will be met.

The trust states that it receives more applications than it can support. Therefore, even if work falls within its policy it may not be able to help, particularly if the project is outside the West Midlands.

Trustees meet twice each year, in May and November. Applications will be acknowledged if an sae is provided.

The Cyril Taylor Charitable Trust

Education

£124,000 (2009/10)

Beneficial area

Generally in Greater London.

Penningtons, Abacus House, 33 Gutter Lane, London EC2V 8AR
Tel: 020 7457 3000
Fax: 020 7457 3240
Email: chris.lintott@penningtons.co.uk
Correspondent: Christopher Lintott, Trustee
Trustees: Sir Cyril Taylor, Chair; Clifford D Joseph; Robert W Maas; Peter A Tchereprine; Stephen Rasch;

Christopher Lintott; Lady June Taylor; Michael Berry; William Gertz; Marcie Schneider.
CC Number: 1040179

Information available

Accounts were available from the Charity Commission.

This trust makes grants to organisations benefiting students in particular those studying at Richmond College and the American International University in London.

In 2009/10 the trust had assets of £249,000 and an income of £211,000. Grants were made to 11 organisations totalling £124,000.

Beneficiaries included: Richmond Foundation (£100,000); Institute of Economic Affairs (£6,000); the British Friends of Harvard Business School (£3,000); and Trinity Hall, Cambridge (£1,000).

Applications

In writing to the correspondent.

The Connie and Albert Taylor Charitable Trust

Medical research, hospices, education and recreation, preservation

£450,000 (2010)

Beneficial area

West Midlands.

The Farmhouse, Darwin Park, Abnalls Lane, Lichfield, Staffordshire WS13 8BJ
Email: applications@taylortrust.co.uk
Website: www.taylortrust.co.uk
Correspondent: Harry Grundy, Trustee
Trustees: Alan Foster; Harry Grundy; Richard D Long.
CC Number: 1074785

Information available

Accounts were available from the Charity Commission.

The trust was established by the will of Constance Iris Taylor in 1998 for he benefit of the West Midlands with he following objects:

- research into the cure and causes of cancer, blindness and heart disease
- provision and maintenance of nursing homes for older people or people who are unable to look after themselves
- provision of maintenance of hospices for people with terminal illnesses
- facilities for the education and recreation of children and young people
- the preservation, protection and improvements of any amenity or land of beauty, scientific or of horticultural interest and any building of historical, architectural or artistic or scientific interest

n 2010 the trust had assets of almost 5 million and an income of 285,000. Grants were made totalling 450,000, broken down as follows:

Care/hospice	£250,000
Education of children and young people	£135,000
Medical research	£45,000
Other donations	£13,000

Grant beneficiaries included: National tar College – Cheltenham £100,000); Birmingham Children's Hospital (£70,000); Compton Hospice – Wolverhampton (£60,000); t Vincent's and St George's Association (£50,000); Wellbeing of Women (£25,000); South taffordshire Medical Foundation £20,000); Katherine House Hospice £13,000) and National Blind Children (£2,000).

Applications

n writing to the correspondent, the rustees prefer to receive applications ia email. The trust may visit applicants/beneficiaries.

Rosanna Taylor's 1987 Charity Trust

General

£40,000 (2009/10)

Beneficial area

UK and overseas, with a preference for Oxfordshire and West Sussex.

The Cowdray Trust Ltd, Pollen House, 10–12 Cork Street, London W1S 3LW
Tel: 020 7439 9061
Email: charity@mfs.co.uk
Correspondent: Laura Gosling, Trust Administrator
Trustee: The Cowdray Trust Limited.
CC Number: 297210

Information available

Accounts were available from the Charity Commission.

The trust has general charitable purposes, including support for medical, cancer, child development and environmental charities.

In 2009/10 it had assets of £1.1 million, an income of £30,000 and made grants to four organisations totalling £40,000.

Beneficiaries were: Charities Aid Foundation (£24,000); Pearson Taylor Trust (£10,000); Disaster Emergencies Committee – Haiti Appeal (£5,000); and Resonance FM (£500).

Exclusions

No grants to individuals or non-registered charities.

Applications

In writing to the correspondent. Acknowledgements are not sent to unsuccessful applicants.

Tegham Limited

Orthodox Jewish faith, welfare

£231,000 (2009/10)

Beneficial area

UK.

22 Park Way, London NW11 0EX
Email: admin@geraldkreditor.co.uk
Correspondent: Sylvia Fluss, Trustee
Trustees: Sylvia Fluss; Nizza Fluss.
CC Number: 283066

Information available

Accounts were available from the Charity Commission, but without a list of grants.

This trust supports the promotion of the Jewish Orthodox faith and the relief of poverty.

In 2009/10 the trust had assets of £1.5 million, an income of £236,000 and made grants totalling £231,000. Unfortunately no grants list was available for this period.

Applications

The trust has stated that it has enough causes to support and does not welcome other applications.

Thackray Medical Research Trust

Research of medical procedures/products, medical supply trade

£163,000 (2009/10)

Beneficial area

Worldwide.

c/o Thackray Museum, Beckett Street, Leeds LS9 7LN
Email: w.k.mathie@leeds.ac.uk
Website: www.tmrt.co.uk
Correspondent: The Chair of the Trustees
Trustees: William Kendall Mathie; Matthew Wrigley; Martin Schweiger; Christin Thackray; John Campbell.
CC Number: 702896

Information available

Accounts were obtained from the Charity Commission. The trust has a clear and concise website.

The following details on the trust's objects have been taken from its website:

Objects
The trust has three main purposes.
- To support the Thackray Museum (Object 1)
- To support charitable international medical supply organisations (Objects 2 and 3)
- To support research into and publication of, the history of medical procedures and products. (Objects 4 to 7).

Objects and Notes on the Objects
Object 1
To support a museum in or near Leeds which has its objective bringing a greater awareness to the general public

of advances in medical treatment, science, research and development with particular reference to the medical supply trade, with special regards to links with northern Great Britain and in particular Leeds and generally to educate the public in matters relating to the medical, technical and social aspects of medical products and procedures.

Note: This object relates to the establishment of the museum and only the Thackray Museum may apply for funding under this heading.

Object 2
To support charitable international medical supply organisations, and in particular the Joint Missions Hospital Equipping Board (ECHO), for exceptional expenditure in the course of their charitable work in under-developed/Third World Countries.

Note: Grants are provided for charitable organisations which specialise in supplying medical equipment to or within the third world. Support is unlikely to be for actual funding of equipment purchases but instead may be for 'pump-priming', start-up or organisational expenses where alternative funding is not available. Preference will be given where the charity is involved in value-for-money projects, e.g. the supply of used rather than new equipment.

Object 3
To relieve and prevent disease and sickness in under-developed or third-world countries by supporting for the public benefit appropriate research and manufacture of medical products calculated to achieve that aim.

Object 4
To promote research for the public benefit in the evaluation of medical procedures and products.

Object 5
To commission, fund and publish the results of research into the effect of health service investment decisions and product-related medical regulations on the supply of health services and the British health service in particular.

Object 6
To provide grants for research into, and publication of, the history of medical products and supplies.

Object 7
To provide grants for lectureships and prize money for essay competitions on the subjects of medical supplies, value-for-money evaluation of medical products and medical product history.

In 2009/10 the trust had assets of £5.6 million and an income of £172,000. Grants awarded totalled £163,000, of which £154,000 went to the Thackray Museum.

The remaining £8,900 was distributed to the Paul Thackray Heritage Foundation (£5,000); BMA (£2,500); and the Liverpool School of Tropical Medicine (£1,400).

Applications

Application forms and guidance notes are available from the trust's website. Applications are usually considered in October and April but may be considered at other times. The closing date for applications is the last day of July and January respectively.

The Thames Wharf Charity

General charitable purposes

£531,000 (2009/10)

Beneficial area

UK.

HW Lee Associates, New Derwent House, 69/73 Theobalds Road, London WC1X 8TA
Tel: 020 7025 4600
Correspondent: Kenneth Hawkins
Trustees: Avtar Lotay; Patrick Burgess; Graham Stirk.
CC Number: 1000796

Information available

Accounts were available from the Charity Commission.

In 2009/10 the charity had an income of £820,000 and made grants to over 160 organisations totalling £531,000. Assets totalled £2.5 million.

Beneficiaries included: Alzheimer's Society (£37,000); Cancer Research UK (£19,000); Ellenor Hospice Care (£13,000); Architectural Association, British Museum Friends and Schumacher College (£12,000); National Society for the Prevention of Cruelty to Children (£11,000); Friends of Vineyard School (£10,000); Age UK Age Concern (£6,000); British Heart Foundation and Practical Action (£5,000); Open City Architecture (£3,500); Nottingham Regional Society for Adults and Children with Autism (£2,000); Prisoners of Conscience Appeal Fund

(£1,000); and West Suffolk Special Care Baby Unit (£275).

Exclusions

No grants for the purchase of property, motor vehicles or holidays.

Applications

In writing to the correspondent.

The Thistle Trust

Arts

£31,000 (2009/10)

Beneficial area

UK.

Kleinwort Benson, 30 Gresham Street, London EC2V 7PG
Correspondent: Ran Amin
Trustees: Madeleine, Lady Kleinwort; Catherine Trevelyan; Neil Morris; Donald McGilvray; Nicholas Kerr-Sheppard.
CC Number: 1091327

Information available

Accounts were available from the Charity Commission.

This trust was established in 2002, and during the following year it received a £1 million endowment from the settlor. Its main objects are to promote study and research in the arts and to further public knowledge and education of art.

In 2009/10 the trust had assets of £1.1 million and an income of £33,000. Grants totalling £31,000 were made to 23 organisations. A further £17,000 was spent on investment advice and governance.

Beneficiaries included: Graeae Theatre, National Youth Theatre, Orchestra Europa Limited, Place and Royal School of Needlework (£2,000 each); Birmingham Royal Ballet, Bishopsgate Institute, City of Birmingham Symphony Orchestra and Corn Exchange Newbury (£1,000 each); Shakespeare Schools Festival (£900); and Dance Umbrella Ltd (£500).

Exclusions

No grants to individuals.

Applications

In writing to the correspondent including most recent report and financial accounts. The trustees meet at least once a year with only successful applicants notified of the trustees' decision.

The Loke Wan Tho Memorial Foundation

Environment and conservation, medical causes, overseas aid

£15,000 (2009/10)

Beneficial area

Worldwide.

RBC Trust Company (International) Ltd, La Motte Chambers, St Helier, Jersey, Channel Islands JE1 1BJ
Tel: 01534 602000
Correspondent: The Secretary
Trustees: Lady Y P McNeice; Mrs P S Tonkyn; A P Tonkyn.
CC Number: 264273

Information available

Accounts were available from the Charity Commission.

The trust supports environment/ conservation organisations, medical causes and overseas aid organisations. In 2009/10 it had assets of £5.4 million and an income of £114,000. Grants totalled £15,000.

Only two organisations received grants during the year: Durrell Wildlife Conservation (£9,400); and University of Adelaide (£5,500).

Applications

In writing to the correspondent.

The Maurice and Vivien Thompson Charitable Trust

General

£107,000 (2009/10)

Beneficial area

UK.

2 The Orchard, London W4 1JX
Tel: 020 8995 1547
Correspondent: M N B Thompson, Trustee
Trustees: M N B Thompson; Mrs V Thomson; P Rhodes.
CC Number: 1085041

Information available

Accounts were available from the Charity Commission.

In 2009/10 the trust had assets of £1.2 million and an income of £48,500. Unusually only one substantial grant was made and this was almost £107,000 to Leicestershire First. A further £250 was awarded to other organisations not listed in the accounts.

Previous beneficiaries were: Beacon Fellowship Charitable Trust (£15,000); Martin Johnson Development Scholarship (£7,500); Pelican Cancer Foundation (£3,000); Leicester and Rutland Crimebeat (£1,800); Shackleton Foundation and Sight for Africa (£1,000 each); RIED (£200); and Bridge2Aid (£100).

Applications

In writing to the correspondent.

The Sue Thomson Foundation

Christ's Hospital School, education

£108,000 (2009/10)

Beneficial area

UK, Sussex, London or Surrey.

3 Danehurst Street, London SW6 6SA
Tel: 07508 038632
Email: stfsusannah@aol.com
Correspondent: Susannah Holliman, Administrator
Trustees: Susan M Mitchell, Chair; Timothy J Binnington; Charles L Corman; Kathleen Duncan.
CC Number: 298808

Information available

Accounts were available from the Charity Commission.

The foundation exists to support children in need in the UK, mainly by helping Christ's Hospital and the school in Horsham which caters specifically for children in need. Other areas of support include educational and self-help organisations and projects. The foundation's policies were reviewed in July 2009 and minor changes implemented. Grants are awarded for education and welfare in one of three categories: Regular, Special, and Christ's Hospital Student Schemes, within annual budgetary limits in all cases.

The foundation also explores, from time to time, new areas for possible future development that may lie outside its existing priority areas.

The trustees' report for 2009/10 states:

> In the year under review we made seven repeat education or welfare grants, awarded in prior years. The foundation's policy was to make no new regular or special grants in 2009/10 in view of the anticipated reduction in endowment income. Nevertheless, the trustees made two exceptional awards to the Disasters Emergency Committee relating to the earthquake in Indonesia and the tsunami in Haiti.

> The main objective for 2010/11 is to meet our existing grant making commitments and resume making new small grants, whilst at the same time adhering to a break-even budget on a cash basis.

In 2009/10 the trust had assets of £2.4 million and an income of £154,000. Grants paid totalled £108,000, divided between education (£76,000) and welfare (£32,000). The total includes £7,000 paid to individual students.

The majority of the funds went to Christ's Hospital, which received £86,000. The foundation nominates one new entrant each year from a needy background to the school, subject to the child meeting Christ's Hospital's own admissions criteria academically, socially and in terms of need. The foundation commits to contributing to the child's costs at a level agreed with Christ's Hospital for as long as each of them remains in the school.

Other beneficiaries included: The Leonard Sainer Legal Education Foundation and the Sussex Snowdrop – Chichester (£3,000 each); Book Trade Benevolent Society and The Bridewell Foundation (£2,000 each); the National Literacy Trust – London (£1,400); and The Publishing Training Centre and the Stationers' Foundation (£500 each).

Exclusions

No grants to large, national charities (except Christ's Hospital) or individuals, except as part of a specific scheme. No research projects, charities concerned with animals, birds, the environment, gardens or historic buildings.

Applications

In writing to the correspondent, or preliminary telephone enquiry. Unsolicited applications are not acknowledged, unless accompanied by an sae or an email address. Grant-making policies are published in the annual report and accounts, available from the Charity Commission website, and in relevant charity sector publications when the trustees are able to do so free of charge. This statement of policies is provided to anyone on request.

The trustees' report for 2009/10 states: 'The foundation's resources are almost wholly committed to its existing projects at the present time and the trustees are therefore able to support only a very small number of unsolicited appeals in 2010/11.'

Common applicant mistakes

'Applying not having read our criteria or made a preliminary phone call.'

The Thornton Foundation

General charitable purposes

£154,000 (2009/10)

Beneficial area

UK.

Stephenson Harwood, 1 St Paul's Churchyard, London EC4M 8SH
Tel: 020 7329 4422
Correspondent: A H Isaacs
Trustees: R C Thornton, Chair; A H Isaacs; H D C Thornton; Mrs S J Thornton.
CC Number: 326383

Information available

Accounts were available from the Charity Commission.

The object of the foundation is to make grants to charities selected by the trustees. The principal guideline of the trust is to use the funds to further charitable causes where their money will, as far as possible, act as 'high powered money', in other words be of significant use to the cause. Only causes that are known personally to the trustees and/or that they are able to investigate thoroughly are supported. The trust states it is proactive rather than reactive in seeking applicants.

In 2009/10 the trust had assets of almost £4.6 million and an income of £58,000. Grants totalling £154,000 were made to 26 organisations, some of which were supported in the previous year.

Beneficiaries included: St Dunstan-in-the-West (£50,000); Institute of Cancer Research (£17,000); The Cirdan Sailing Trust and National Gallery (£10,000 each); The Healing Foundation (£7,500); Museum of London and Helen House (£6,000 each); Action for Blind People, Books Abroad, Keble College – Oxford and Wessex Children's Hospice (£5,000 each); the Tait Memorial Trust (£3,000); BREAK and Prisoners of Conscience (£2,000 each); the Handel Society (£1,000) and British Heart Foundation and Cancer Research UK (£500 each).

Applications

The trust strongly emphasises that it does not accept unsolicited applications, and, as it states above, only organisations that are known to one of the trustees will be considered for support. Any unsolicited applications will not receive a reply.

The Thornton Trust

Evangelical Christianity education, relief of sickness and poverty

£152,000 (2009/10)

Beneficial area

UK and overseas.

Hunters Cottage, Hunters Yard, Debden Road, Saffron Walden, Essex CB11 4AA
Tel: 01799 526712
Correspondent: D H Thornton, Trustee
Trustees: D H Thornton; Mrs B Y Thornton; J D Thornton.
CC Number: 205357

Information available

Accounts were available from the Charity Commission.

This trust was created in 1962 for 'the promotion and furthering of education and the Evangelical Christian faith, and assisting in the relief of sickness, suffering and poverty'.

In 2009/10 it had assets of £970,000 and an income of £67,000. Grants were made to over 60 organisations totalling £152,000.

Beneficiaries included: Africa Inland Mission (£20,000); St Andrew's Church, Hertford (£15,000); Bible Society and Saffron Walden Baptist Church (£11,000 each); London City Mission (£10,000); Redcliffe Missionary College (£6,000); Mission Aviation Fellowship (£4,000); Young Life Hyt (£3,000); Urban Saints (£2,000); Practical Action (£1,000); and National Prayer Breakfast (£100).

Applications

The trust states: 'Our funds are fully committed and we regret that we are unable to respond to the many unsolicited calls for assistance we are now receiving.'

The Three Oaks Trust

Welfare

£189,000 (2009/10)

Beneficial area

UK and overseas, with a preference for West Sussex.

P O Box 893, Horsham, West Sussex RH12 9JD
Email: contact@thethreeoakstrust.co.uk
Website: www.thethreeoakstrust.co.uk
Correspondent: The Trustees
Trustees: Dianne Margaret Ward; Polly Elizabeth Hobbs; Carol Vivian Foreman; Carol Johnson; Pam Wilkinson; Dr P Kane; Sarah A Kane; Giles Duncan Wilkinson; Three Oaks Family Trust Co Ltd.
CC Number: 297079

Information available

Comprehensive accounts were available from the Charity Commission website.

Grants are made to organisations that promote the welfare of individuals and families. Grants are also made to individuals via statutory authorities or voluntary agencies. The trust regularly supports the same welfare organisations in the UK and overseas each year.

In 2009/10 the trust had assets of £5.9 million and a total income of £208,000. Donations made this year totalled £243,000. Of this, £91,000 was donated to UK registered charities and organisations that promote the welfare of individuals and families. As in previous years, a large number of small donations was made more directly for the benefit of individuals via statutory authorities and voluntary agencies. This year 340 such donations were made with a net value, taking account of refunds, of some £57,000.

Donations to charities and organisations whose focus of work is overseas, including donations in kind, were made to a value of £98,000.

Beneficiaries included: Crawley Open House and Dalesdown and Raynauds

Association (£15,000 each); Family Foundation Trust (Dalesdown) and Sussex Probation (£10,000 each); MIND – Brighton and Hove and The Connection at St Martin-in-the-Fields (£5,000 each); and Dermatrust (£3,000).

Exclusions

No direct applications from individuals. Applications from students for gap year activities are not a priority and will not be funded.

Applications

The following guidelines are taken from the 2009/10 annual accounts:

> Grants are made to organisations that promote the welfare of individuals and families. In general, the trustees intend to continue supporting the organisations that they have supported in the past. Periodically and generally annually the trustees review the list of registered charities and institutions to which grants have been given and consider additions and deletions from the list. To save on administration, the trustees do not respond to requests unless they are considering making a donation. Requests from organisations for donations in excess of £2,000 are considered by the trustees on a quarterly basis in meetings usually held in January, April, July and September.

For the full guidelines, please visit the trust's website.

The Thriplow Charitable Trust

Higher and further education and research

£79,000 (2009/10)

Beneficial area

Preference for British institutions.

PO Box 225, Royston SG8 1BG
Correspondent: The Trustees
Trustees: Sir Peter Swinnerton-Dyer, Chair; Dr Harriet Crawford; Prof. Christopher Bayly; Sir David Wallace; Dame Jean Thomas.
CC Number: 1025531

Information available

Accounts were available from the Charity Commission, but without a list of grants.

The charity was established by a trust deed in 1983. Its main aims are the furtherance of higher and further education and research, with preference given to British institutions.

Projects that have generally been supported in the past include contributions to research study funds, research fellowships, academic training schemes, computer facilities and building projects. Specific projects are preferred rather than contributions to general running costs. The trust prefers to support smaller projects where grants can 'make a difference'.

In 2009/10 it had assets of £3.2 million and an income of £453,000. Grants totalled £79,000.

Previous beneficiaries have included Cambridge University Library, Centre of South Asian Studies, Computer Aid International, Fight for Sight, Fitzwilliam Museum, Foundation for Prevention of Blindness, Foundation of Research Students, Hearing Research Trust, Inspire Foundation, Loughborough University, Marie Curie Cancer Care, Royal Botanic Gardens, Royal College of Music, Transplant Trust and University of Reading.

Exclusions

Grants can only be made to charitable bodies or component parts of charitable bodies. In no circumstances can grants be made to individuals.

Applications

There is no application form. A letter of application should specify the purpose for which funds are sought and the costings of the project. It should be indicated whether other applications for funds are pending and, if the funds are to be channelled to an individual or a small group, what degree of supervision over the quality of the work would be exercised by the institution. Trustee meetings are held twice a year – in spring and in autumn.

Common applicant mistakes

'Asking for too much and not being specific about how much they will be spending on each of their applications

– the trust favours properly costed applications.'

The Tinsley Foundation

Human rights, poverty and homelessness and health education in underdeveloped countries

£120,000 (2009/10)

Beneficial area

UK and overseas.

14 St Mary's Street, Stamford, Lincolnshire PE9 2DF
Tel: 01780 762056
Fax: 01780 767594
Email: hctinsley@aol.com
Correspondent: Henry C Tinsley, Trustee
Trustees: H C Tinsley; R C Tinsley; T A Jones.
CC Number: 1076537

Information available

Accounts were available from the Charity Commission.

The foundation was founded by Henry Tinsley in 1999 and will support:

- charities which promote human rights and democratisation and/or which educate against racism, discrimination and oppression
- charities which promote self-help in fighting poverty and homelessness;
- charities which provide reproductive health education in underdeveloped countries, but specifically excluding charities whose policy is against abortion or birth control.

In 2009/10 the foundation had assets of £2.6 million, an income of £152,000 and made 22 grants totalling £120,000.

Beneficiaries included: Human Rights Watch Charitable Trust (£25,000); Article 1 Charitable Trust and Network for Africa (£15,000 each); Medact and Peace Brigades International (£10,000 each); One

World Action (£5,000); Global Dialogue and The Big Issue Foundation (£2,500 each); and Africa Now, Computer Aid International, English National Opera, Gatwick Detainees Welfare Group, Medical Foundation, Release International, St Mungo's and The Cambodia Trust (£1,000 each).

Applications

The trustees have recently stated that: 'while the charity welcomes applications from eligible potential grantees, the trustees seek out organisations that will effectively fulfil our objectives'.

The Tisbury Telegraph Trust

Christian, overseas aid, general

£217,000 (2009/10)

Beneficial area

UK and overseas.

35 Kitto Road, Telegraph Hill, London SE14 5TW
Tel: 020 7732 6550
Correspondent: Mrs E Orr, Trustee
Trustees: Alison Davidson; John Davidson; Eleanor Orr; Roger Orr; Sonia Phippard.
CC Number: 328595

Information available

Accounts were available from the Charity Commission.

In 2009/10 it had assets of £128,000 and an income of £192,000, mostly from donations. Grants were made totalling £217,000. The trust made grants to 64 charities. These included Anglican parishes and dioceses, charities formed for the advancement of the Christian religion or the relief of poverty both in the UK and overseas, and charities working to conserve the natural world and retain its value for the benefit of this and future generations.

Beneficiaries included: World Vision (£77,000); Friends of Kiwoko Hospital (£20,000); All Saints Church (£15,500); St Mary's Building Fund (£15,000); Practical Action (£10,500);

Helen and Douglas House and Romania Care (£10,000 each); Crisis (£2,000 each); and Habitat for Humanity and Salvation Army (£1,000 each).

Exclusions

No applications from individuals for expeditions or courses can be considered.

Applications

In writing to the correspondent. However, it is extremely rare that unsolicited applications are successful and the trust does not respond to applicants unless an sae is included. No telephone applications please.

Common applicant mistakes

'Not sending an sae which means they hear nothing.'

TJH Foundation

Social welfare, medical, racing welfare

£22,000 (2009/10)

Beneficial area

England and Wales with some preference for organisations based in the North West of England.

Gleadhill House, Dawbers Lane, Euxton, Chorley, Lancashire PR7 6EA
Correspondent: J C Kay, Trustee
Trustees: T J Hemmings, Chair; Mrs P A Clare; J C Kay; Ms K Revitt.
CC Number: 1077311

Information available

Income and expenditure details are on file at the Charity Commission.

The TJH Foundation was established in 1999. In 2009/10 it had assets of £309,000 and an income of £25,500. Grants totalled £22,000.

Beneficiaries included: Kevin Gray Memorial Charity (£15,000); The Princess Royal Trust for Carers (£4,000); Marie Curie Cancer Care and R.N.L.I (£500 each); Well Being for Women (£250); Racing Welfare (£50)

Applications

In writing to the correspondent.

Tomchei Torah Charitable Trust

Jewish

£247,500 (2009/10)

Beneficial area

UK.

66 Cranbourne Gardens, London NW11 0HP
Tel: 0208 458 5706
Correspondent: I J Kohn
Trustees: I J Kohn; S M Kohn; A Frei.
CC Number: 802125

Information available

Accounts were received at the Charity Commission but unable to view.

This trust supports Jewish educational institutions. Grants usually average about £5,000.

In 2009/10 the trust had an income of £7,000 mainly from donations. Grants totalled £247,500 and were made to mainly Jewish organisations.

Previous beneficiaries included: Friends of Mir; MST College; Friends of Sanz Institutions; United Talmudical Associates; Ezer North West; Menorah Grammar School; Friends of Torah Ohr; Ruzin Sadagora Trust; Achisomoch Aid Co and Chesed Charity Trust.

Applications

In writing to the correspondent at any time.

The Torah Temimah Trust

Orthodox Jewish

£53,000 (2009/10)

Beneficial area

UK.

16 Reizel Close, Stamford Hill, London N16 5GY
Tel: 020 8800 3021
Correspondent: Mrs E Bernath, Trustee
Trustees: Mrs E Bernath; M Bernath; A Grunfeld.

CC Number: 802390

Information available

Accounts were available from the Charity Commission, but without a list of grants.

This trust was set up in 1980 to advance/promote Orthodox Jewish religious education and religion. In 2009/10 it had an income mainly from donations of £61,000 and grants totalled £53,000. The trust has remaining funds of £115,000.

Applications

In writing to the correspondent.

Toras Chesed (London) Trust

Jewish, education

£215,000 (2009/10)

Beneficial area

Worldwide.

14 Lampard Grove, London N16 6UZ
Tel: 0208 806 9589
Email: ari@toraschesed.co.uk
Correspondent: A Langberg, Trustee
Trustees: A Stenn; S Stern; A Langberg.
CC Number: 1110653

Information available

Accounts were on file at the Charity Commission, without a list of grants.

Set up in 2005, the objects of the charity are:

- the advancement of Orthodox Jewish religious education
- the relief of poverty and infirmity among persons of the Jewish faith
- to provide a safe and user friendly environment to share mutual problems and experiences
- to encourage active parental participation in their children's education.
- the advancement of the Orthodox Jewish faith

The charity achieves its objectives by making grants to qualifying institutions and individuals.

In 2009/10 the trust had an income of £217,000 and made grants totalling

£215,000. There were negative assets of £4,000.

In their annual report the trustees stated that the charity was making various grant applications in order to eliminate the deficit.

Applications

The trust states: 'Applications for grants are considered by the trustees and reviewed in depth for final approval.'

The Tory Family Foundation

Education, Christian, medical

£84,000 (2009/10)

Beneficial area

Worldwide, but principally Folkestone.

The Estate Office, Etchinghill Golf Club, Folkestone, Kent CT18 8FA
Tel: 01303 862280
Correspondent: Paul N Tory, Trustee
Trustees: P N Tory; J N Tory; S A Tory.
CC Number: 326584

Information available

Accounts were available from the Charity Commission, but without a list of grants.

The foundation's 2009/10 annual report stated:

> The charity was formed to provide financial assistance to a wide range of charitable needs. It is currently supporting a wide range of causes both from a national perspective and an international perspective. These causes include educational, religious, social and medical subjects and the donees themselves are often registered charities. The trustees continue to pursue the policy of donations and grants in line with the financial position of the charity.

The charity does not normally aim to fund the whole of any given project, and applicants are expected to demonstrate a degree of existing and regular support.

In 2009/10 the foundation had assets of almost £3.2 million, an income of £83,000 and made grants totalling over £84,000. These were broken down as follows:

Overseas	£22,000
Local	£17,500
Health	£16,000
Education	£16,000
Churches	£3,500
Elderly	£1,500
Other	£7,000

Previous beneficiaries have included: Ashford YMCA, Bletchley Park, Canterbury Cathedral, Concern Worldwide, Deal Festival, Disability Law Service, Folk Rainbow Club, Foresight, Friends of Birzett, Gurkha Welfare, Kent Cancer Trust, Royal British Legion, Uppingham Foundation and Youth Action Wiltshire.

Exclusions

Priority is given to applications from Kent. No grants are given for further education.

Applications

In writing to the correspondent. Applications are considered throughout the year. To keep costs down, unsuccessful applicants will not be notified.

The Toy Trust

Children

£266,000 (2010)

Beneficial area

UK.

c/o British Toy and Hobby Association, 80 Camberwell Road, London SE5 0EG

Tel: 0207 701 7271
Email: admin@btha.co.uk
Website: www.btha.co.uk/
Correspondent: Roland Earl
Trustees: The British Toy and Hobby Association Ltd; N Austin; Clive Jones; Christine Nicholls; Frank Martin.
CC Number: 1001634

Information available

Accounts were available from the Charity Commission.

This trust was registered in 1991 to centralise the giving of the British Toy and Hobby Association. Prior to this, the association raised money from the toy industry, which it pledged to one charity on an annual basis. It was felt that the fundraising activities of the association were probably more than matched by its individual members, and that the charitable giving of the toy industry to children's charities was going unnoticed by the public. The trust still receives the majority of its income from fundraising activities, donating the proceeds to children's charities and charitable projects benefiting children.

In 2010 the trust had an income of £193,000, mostly in donations received and grants were made totalling over £266,000. Assets stood at £104,000.

Beneficiaries included: Great Ormond Street Hospital (£45,000); Samaritans Purse International (£35,000); Christian Resource Ministries and World in Need (£10,000 each); Action for Kids, Alton Castle Children's Retreat and Book Aid International (£5,000 each); and Concern Worldwide and Pathway Project (£4,000 each).

Applications

In writing to the correspondent.

Common applicant mistakes

'Applicants not reading our applicant rules and guidelines and not including a copy of their most recent accounts to support their application.'

Annie Tranmer Charitable Trust

General, young people

£89,000 to organisations (2009/10)

Beneficial area

UK, particularly Suffolk and adjacent counties.

51 Bennett Road, Ipswich IP1 5HX
Correspondent: Mrs M R Kirby, Clerk to the Trustees
Trustees: J F F Miller; Mrs V A Lewis; N J Bonham-Carter.
CC Number: 1044231

Information available

Accounts were obtained from the Charity Commission website.

The objectives of the trust are to:

- make grants in the county of Suffolk and adjacent counties
- make grants to national charities according to the wishes of Mrs Tranmer during her lifetime
- advance education and historical research relating to the national monument known as the Sutton Hoo burial site and Sutton Hoo estate
- protect and preserve the Sutton Hoo burial site
- to further the education of children and young people in Suffolk
- make grants for general charitable purposes.

In 2009/10 the trust had assets of £3.3 million and an income of £107,000. Grants were made totalling £105,000 of which £89,000 was donated to 62 organisations and £16,000 to individuals.

Beneficiaries included: East Anglian Air Ambulance (£10,000); Cancer Research UK and Mid Essex Hospital Services NHS Trust – Burns Unit (£5,000 each); Independent Age and Motor Neurone Disease (£3,000 each); Salvation Army, Age Concern – Suffolk and Headstart 4 Babies (£2,000 each); Liveability, Leveltwo Youth Project, Suffolk Punch Trust and the British Association for Adoption and Fostering (£1,000 each); Listening Books (£600); Ipswich Furniture Project, Optua and the Nancy Oldfield Trust (£500 each); and Jubilee Opera (£200).

Applications

This trust does not accept unsolicited applications.

The Treeside Trust

General

£115,000 (2009/10)

Beneficial area

UK, but mainly local in Oldham.

4 The Park, Grasscroft, Oldham OL4 4ES
Tel: 01457 876422
Correspondent: J R Beresford

Trustees: Mrs C C Gould; R B Gould; J R W Gould; Mrs D M Ives; R J Ives.
CC Number: 1061586

Information available

Accounts were available from the Charity Commission, but without a list of grants.

The trust supports mainly small local charities, and a few UK-wide charities which are supported on a regular basis. The majority of grants are made as a result of half-yearly reviews. In the main, the trustees' policy is to make a limited number of substantial grants each year, rather than a larger number of smaller ones, in order to make significant contributions to some of the causes supported.

In 2009/10 the trust had assets of £1.3 million and an income of £136,000. Grants totalling £115,000 were made during the year, none of which exceeded £15,000. A list of grants for this year was not available.

Applications

The trust has stated that they 'do not welcome unsolicited applications'.

The Tresillian Trust

Overseas aid, welfare

£59,000 (2009/10)

Beneficial area

Worldwide.

Old Coach House, Sunnyside, Bergh Apton, Norwich NR15 1DD
Tel: 01508 480100
Email: info@willcoxlewis.co.uk
Correspondent: M D Willcox, Trustee
Trustees: G E S Robinson; P W Bate; M D Willcox.
CC Number: 1105826

Information available

Accounts were available from the Charity Commission.

The trust is a general purpose charity and the trustees focus on particular areas of benefit from time to time. The strategy of the trustees for 2009/10 and the foreseeable future is to concentrate on donations to charities which fulfil one or more of the following criteria:

- in the UK, community based projects supporting the elderly and young people;
- in Africa, Asia and South America, projects supporting the education and health of women and children; and
- worldwide projects dealing with conflict and disaster areas and the environment.

In 2009/10 this trust had an income of £508,000 and made grants to 15 organisations totalling £59,000. The sum of £2.5 million was carried forward at year end.

Beneficiaries included: Habitat for Humanity (£10,000); Playpumps International (£9,000); Indraprasthra Medic (£6,000); Alive and Kicking UK, Book Aid International, Child Welfare Scheme, Contact the Elderly, Frishta Children's Village – India and Tools for Self Reliance (£1,000 each); and St John of Jerusalem Eye Hospital, TB Alert and Tree Africa (£500 each).

Applications

In writing to the correspondent. The trust states that it 'is very selective in the grant making process and applications are reviewed by the trustees personally.'

Truedene Co. Ltd

Jewish

£960,000 (2009/10)

Beneficial area

UK and overseas.

c/o Cohen Arnold and Co., 1075 Finchley Road, London NW11 0PU
Correspondent: The Trustees
Trustees: Sarah Klein, Chair; Samuel Berger; Solomon Laufer; Sije Berger; Zelda Sternlicht.
CC Number: 248268

Information available

Accounts were on file at the Charity Commission without a list of grant beneficiaries.

In 2009/10 this trust had assets of almost £4.1 million and an income of £1.3 million. Grants were made totalling £960,000.

Previous beneficiaries have included: Beis Ruchel D'Satmar Girls' School Ltd, British Friends of Tchernobyl, Congregation Paile Yoetz, Cosmon Belz Limited, Friends of Mir, Kolel Shomrei Hachomoth, Mesifta Talmudical College, Mosdos Ramou, Orthodox Council of Jerusalem, Tevini Limited, United Talmudical Associates Limited, VMCT and Yeshivo Horomo Talmudical College.

Applications

In writing to the correspondent.

The Truemark Trust

General

£289,000 (2009/10)

Beneficial area

UK.

PO Box 2, Liss, Hampshire GU33 6YP
Tel: 01730 894120
Correspondent: The Trustees
Trustees: Sir T Lucas; S Neil; Mrs W Collett; D Hawkins; Mrs J Hayward; Kate Hussey.
CC Number: 265855

Information available

Accounts were on file at the Charity Commission.

The trust's purpose is to make grants to other charitable bodies for the relief of all kinds of social distress and disadvantage.

Donations are to mostly made to small local charities dealing with all kinds of disadvantage, with preferences to neighbourhood based community projects and for innovatory work with less popular groups.

Grants are usually one-off for a specific project or part of a project. Core funding and/or salaries are rarely considered. The average size of grants is £1,000.

In 2009/10 it had assets of nearly £11 million and an income of £439,000. Grants totalled £289,000.

There were 126 grants made in the year. Beneficiaries included: White Eagle Publishing Trust (£13,000); Quiet Mind Centre (£10,000); Bradford Family Support Network and Ellen Tinkham School – PTFA (£5,000 each); Lighthouse and MS Therapy Centre (£4,000 each); 1st Clanfield Scout Group and At Risk Teenagers (£3,000 each); Avon Riding Centre (£2,500); Disabled on Line and Longcause Community Special School (£2,000 each); Adoption Support and Evergreens (£1,500 each); and Latin American Disabled People's Project, Life Education Centre, Special Toys Educational Postal Service and Wand Mental Health (£1,000 each).

Exclusions

Grants are made to registered charities only. Applications from individuals, including students, are ineligible. No grants are made in response to general appeals from large national charities. Grants are seldom available for churches or church buildings or for scientific or medical research projects.

Applications

In writing to the correspondent, including the most recent set of accounts, clear details of the need the project is designed to meet and an outline budget. Trustees meet four times a year. Only successful applicants receive a reply.

Truemart Limited

General, Judaism, welfare

£92,000 (2009/10)

Beneficial area

UK-wide and overseas, with a preference for Greater London.

34 The Ridgeway, London NW11 8QS
Tel: 0208 455 4456
Correspondent: Mrs S Heitner, Secretary
Trustees: I Heitner; B Hoffman.
CC Number: 1090586

Information available

Accounts were on file at the Charity Commission, without a list of grants.

The trust was set up to promote:

- the advancement of religion in accordance with the Orthodox Jewish faith
- the relief of poverty
- general charitable purposes.

In 2009/10 the trust held assets of £82,000 and had an income from donations of £191,000. Grants totalled £92,000. A list of beneficiaries was not included with the accounts.

Applications

In writing to the correspondent.

Trumros Limited

Jewish

£384,000 (2009)

Beneficial area

UK.

282 Finchley Road, London NW3 7AD
Tel: 0207 431 3282
Email: r.hofbauer@btconnect.com
Correspondent: H Hofbauer, Trustee
Trustees: R S Hofbauer; H Hofbauer.
CC Number: 285533

Information available

Full accounts were on file at the Charity Commission.

In 2009 the trust had assets of £7.3 million and a total income of £880,000. A total of £384,000 was given in about 131 grants.

Beneficiaries included: Before Trust (£51,000); Beis Yosef Zvi (£36,000); Chevras Mo'oz Ladol (£29,000); Hamayon (£25,000); Yaldei Yisroel (£20,000); Kupas Tsedoko Vochessed £13,500; Achisomoch Aid Co (£13,000); London Academy of Jewish Studies (£11,000); Jewish Learning Exchange (£10,000).

Applications

In writing to the correspondent, but note that the trust states it is already inundated with applications.

Tudor Rose Ltd

Jewish

£268,000 (2009/10)

Beneficial area

UK.

c/o Martin and Heller, 5 North End Road, London NW11 7RJ
Correspondent: Samuel Taub, Secretary
Trustees: M Lehrfield; S Taub; S L Taub.
CC Number: 800576

Information available

Accounts were on file at the Charity Commission without a list of grant beneficiaries.

This trust works for the promotion of the Orthodox Jewish faith and the relief of poverty.

In 2009/10 it had assets of £3.1 million. Total income was £435,000, mainly from property income. Grants were made totalling £268,000.

Past beneficiaries have included: Lolev Charitable Trust; Woodlands Charity; KTV; Bell Synagogue; Hatzola; Lubavitch Centre; and TCT.

Applications

In writing to the correspondent.

The Tufton Charitable Trust

Christian

£363,000 (2010)

Beneficial area

UK.

Tufton Place, Ewhurst Place, Northiam, East Sussex TN31 6HL
Correspondent: The Trustees
Trustees: Sir Christopher Wates; Lady Wates; J R F Lulham; Wates Charitable Trustees Ltd.
CC Number: 801479

Information available

Accounts were available from the Charity Commission.

This trust supports Christian organisations, by providing grants as well as allowing them to use premises leased by the trust for retreats.

In 2010 the trust had an income of £449,000 and grants totalled £363,000. Assets stood at £589,000.

There were over 15 grants listed in the accounts. Beneficiaries included: Emmaus UK (£75,000); Glyndebourne (£30,000); Caritas Foundation of Western Kansas (£29,000); the Arts Educational School (£27,000); Soul Survivor (£10,000); St John Ambulance (£7,000); and Institute of Economic Affairs, Catholic Evangelisation Services and The Turner Contemporary (£5,000 each).

Exclusions

No grants for repair or maintenance of buildings.

Applications

In writing to the correspondent, including an sae.

The R D Turner Charitable Trust

General

£162,500 (2009/10)

Beneficial area

UK, with a preference for the Worcestershire area.

3 Poplar Piece, Inkberrow, Worcester WR7 4JD
Tel: 01386 792014
Email: timpatrickson@hotmail.co.uk
Correspondent: Timothy J Patrickson, Administrator
Trustees: J M Del Mar, Chair; D P Pearson; S L Preedy; P J Millward; J M G Fea.
CC Number: 263556

Information available

Accounts were available from the Charity Commission.

This trust has general charitable purposes and the trustees have resolved that the following objectives be adopted:

- To support by means of grants and loans other registered charities, particularly in the Worcestershire area.
- To maintain and enhance the amenities of the villages of Arley and Upper Arley.
- Such other general charitable purposes in connection with the villages of Arley and Upper Arley as the trustees shall in their absolute discretion determine/ decide.

In 2009/10 it had assets of £27 million and an income of £975,000. The upkeep of the Arley Estate was maintained at £584,500, with grants to 42 organisations totalling £162,500. Grants were broken down as follows:

The elderly	£29,000
Environment and heritage	£25,500
People with disabilities and health	£24,000
Work in the community	£23,000
Hospices	£20,000
The Arts	£19,500
Children and young people	£16,500
Medical research	£5,000

There was no list of grant recipients with the accounts but previous beneficiaries have included: St Richard's Hospice (£15,000); Worcestershire and Dudley Historic Churches Trust (£12,000); British Red Cross Hereford and Worcester (£10,000); ARCOS, Cobalt Appeal Fund and Motor Neurone Disease Association (£5,000 each); County Air Ambulance Trust and Relate Worcestershire (£3,000); Sunfield Children's Homes (£2,000); Listening Books (£1,000); and Talking Newspapers of the UK (£500).

Exclusions

No grants to non-registered charities or to individuals.

Applications

The trust does not have a grant application form. Applicant Charities are requested to send a letter of no more than two pages describing their appeal, together with a copy of their latest accounts, to the Trust Administrator at the Grants Office.

The Florence Turner Trust

General

£182,000 (2009/10)

Beneficial area

UK, but with a strong preference for Leicestershire.

c/o Harvey Ingram Owston, 20 New Walk, Leicester LE1 6TX
Correspondent: The Trustees
Trustees: Roger Bowder; Allan A Veasey; Caroline A Macpherson.
CC Number: 502721

Information available

Accounts were available from the Charity Commission.

This trust has general charitable purposes, giving most of its support in Leicestershire. Grants are made to organisations and individuals. Smaller projects are favoured where (in the words of the trust's annual reports) donations will make a 'quantifiable difference to the recipients rather than favouring large national charities whose income is measured in millions rather than thousands.' Grants are made for the benefit of individuals through a referring agency such as social services, NHS trusts or similar responsible bodies.

In 2009/10 it had assets of £5.2 million and an income of £176,000. Grants totalled £182,000.

There were 191 grants made in the year, of which 41 were listed in the accounts. Beneficiaries included: Leicester Charity Link (£12,000); Leicester Grammar School – Bursary (£10,000); Age Concern Leicester, Leicester and Leicestershire Historic Churches Preservation Trust and VISTA (£2,400 each); LOROS (£2,000); New Parks Club for Young People (£1,500); and Four Twelve Ministries and Help for Heroes (£1,000 each).

A further 150 grants below £1,000 each totalled £76,000.

Exclusions

The trust does not support individuals for educational purposes.

Applications

In writing to the correspondent. Trustees meet every eight or nine weeks.

The TUUT Charitable Trust

General, particularly trade-union-favoured causes

Around £65,000 (2009/10)

Beneficial area

Worldwide.

Congress House, Great Russell Street, London WC1B 3LQ
Tel: 020 7637 7116
Fax: 020 7637 7087
Email: info@tufm.co.uk
Website: www.tufm.co.uk
Correspondent: Ann Smith, Secretary
Trustees: Lord Christopher; A Tuffin; M Walsh; M Bradley; B Barber; Lord Brookman; E Sweeney.
CC Number: 258665

Information available

The following information was taken from the trust's website:

> The TUUT Charitable Trust was set up by the trade union movement in 1969 for the sole purpose of owning TU Fund Managers Limited. The intention was – and still is – that profits distributed by the company should go to good causes rather than individual shareholders.
>
> It is a requirement of the trust deed that all the trustees must be trades unionists, the intention being to ensure that causes benefiting should broadly be those that would be supported by the movement. Trade unions – and indeed individuals – are free to nominate favoured causes, all of which are reviewed by the trustees before any payment is made.

The trust considers requests from small to medium sized non-religious charitable organisations based in the UK.

In 2009/10 the trust had an income of £11,000 and a total expenditure of around £65,000.

Previous beneficiaries have included: NACRO (£40,000); Alma Hospital and PFA Centenary Fund (£5,000 each); Macmillan Cancer Relief (£3,000); Evelina Children's Hospital Appeal (£2,300); CCA, Concern Worldwide and Scrap Poverty in Africa (£2,000 each); UK Sports Association and Woking Hospice (£1,000 each); and World Development Movement Trust, Hope and Homes for Children, Cruse Bereavement Care and the Respite Association (£500 each).

Exclusions

No grants to individuals or to charities based overseas.

Applications

The trust has stated in its annual report:

> To apply for a grant, charitable organisations should apply for a Form of Request and submit this, duly completed. The Trustees meet three times a year to consider requests received.

Common applicant mistakes

'Simply asking for a sum of money without any details of what it is to be spent on. Our trustees prefer to fund projects or specific items.'

TVML Foundation

General

£77,000 (2010)

Beneficial area

UK and overseas, with a preference for Brazil, Israel and the USA.

Spinnaker Capital Limited,
6 Grosvenor Street, London W1K 4DJ
Tel: 020 7903 2900
Fax: 020 7903 2999
Email: marcos.lederman@ spinnakercapital.com
Correspondent: Marcos Lederman, Trustee
Trustees: Marcos Lederman; Vivian Lederman; Marcelo Steuer.
CC Number: 1135495

Information available

Accounts were available from the Charity Commission.

(The Vivian and Marcos Lederman) Foundation was established in 2010 for general charitable purposes. The settlor of the foundation is Marcos Lederman, founding partner of the hedge fund Spinnaker Capital Limited.

In 2010 the foundation received an income from Spinnaker Capital Limited of £1.6 million and made grants to organisations and individuals totalling £77,000.

There were no details of beneficiaries listed in the accounts, although the trust states that grants were to support 'educational and lifehood initiatives in Brazil and Israel'.

Applications

In writing to the correspondent.

Ulting Overseas Trust

Theological training

£114,000 (2009/10)

Beneficial area

The developing world (mostly, but not exclusively, Asia, Africa and South and Central America).

Pothecary Witham Weld,
70 St George's Square, London SW1V 3RD
Correspondent: T B Warren, Trustee
Trustees: A J Bale, Chair; Mrs M Brinkley; D Ford; J C Heyward; J Kapolyo; Dr J B A Kessler; R Pearce; K-S Tan; T B Warren.
CC Number: 294397

Information available

Accounts were on file at the Charity Commission.

The trust exists solely to provide bursaries, normally via grants to Christian theological training institutions or organisations with a training focus, for those in the developing world who wish to train for the Christian ministry, or for those who wish to improve their ministry skills. It gives priority to the training of students in their home countries or continents.

In 2009/10 it had assets of £3.5 million and an income of £108,000. There were 33 grants made in the year totalling £114,000.

Beneficiaries included: IFES (£16,500); Scripture Union international (£15,000); Langham

Trust (£13,500); Oxford Centre for Mission Studies (£7,000); Pan African Christian College (£5,500); Asian Theological Seminary (£5,000); Cornerstone Christian College (£2,000); and Arab World Ministries (£1000).

Exclusions

No grants are given for capital projects such as buildings or library stock, nor for training in subjects other than Biblical, theological and missionary studies. Grants are only made to institutions to pass on to their students; direct grants to individuals cannot be made.

Applications

The funds of the trust are already committed. Unsolicited applications cannot be supported.

The Ulverscroft Foundation

People who are blind or partially sighted, ophthalmic research

£58,000 (2009/10)

Beneficial area

Worldwide.

1 The Green, Bradgate Road, Anstey, Leicester LE7 7FU
Tel: 0116 236 1595
Fax: 0116 236 1594
Email: foundation@ulverscroft.co.uk
Website: www.foundation.ulverscroft.com/
Correspondent: Joyce Sumner, Secretary
Trustees: A W Leach, Chair; P H F Carr; Pat Beech; D Owen; R Crooks.
CC Number: 264873

Information available

Accounts were available from the Charity Commission.

Ulverscroft Large Print Books Limited, was formed in 1964. The company republished existing books in large type to sell to libraries and donate the profits to sight-related charitable causes. In 1972 The Ulverscroft Foundation was created.

The foundation supports projects which will have a positive effect on the quality of life of visually impaired people (blind and partially sighted). Funding is channelled via recognised organisations which help the visually impaired, for example, libraries, hospitals, clinics, schools and colleges, and social and welfare organisations.

In 2009/10 the foundation had a total income of £12.7 million, including £12.4 million from trading income. Out of a total expenditure of £11.9 million, grants totalled £58,000.

Beneficiaries included: Calibre and Sight Savers International (£5,000 each); J S Smith French Eye Diseases (£4,000); Birmingham Talking Newspaper, Blind in Business and Sense International (£2,000 each); and Intercare, Listening Books, John Fawcett Foundation, St John of Jerusalem and York Blind & Partially Sighted Society (£1,000 each).

Exclusions

Applications from individuals are not encouraged. Generally, assistance towards salaries and general running costs are not given.

Applications

In writing to the correspondent including the latest annual report and accounts, there is no application form. Proposals should be as detailed as possible, including: details of the current service provided to the visually impaired (if any) and how the proposed project will be integrated or enhanced; an estimate (if possible) of how many visually impaired people use/will use the service; the amount of funding obtained to date (if any); and the names of any other organisations to whom funding applications have been made.

Trustees meet quarterly to consider appeals in January, April, July and October each year; deadlines for appeals are the last day of the previous month.

Due to the large number of appeals received, the foundation will not consider fresh appeals until a period of 12 to 18 months has elapsed since the last application. The success of any appeal is dependent on the level of funding available at the time of consideration.

Common applicant mistakes

'Not looking at our guidelines for applying for funding.'

The Union of Orthodox Hebrew Congregation

Jewish

£453,000 (2009)

Beneficial area

UK.

Landau Morley, Lanmor House, 370–386 High Road, Wembley HA9 6AX
Tel: 020 8903 5122
Correspondent: The Administrator
Trustees: B S F Freshwater; C Konig; Rabbi A Pinter.
CC Number: 249892

Information available

Accounts were available from the Charity Commission, but without a grants list.

The operational charity works to protect and to further in every way the interests of traditional Judaism in Great Britain and to establish and support such institutions as will serve this object.

In 2009 it had assets of £1.5 million and an income of £1.4 million. Out of a total charitable expenditure of £1.4 million, grants to organisations totalled £437,000, with £16,000 donated to individuals.

Previous beneficiaries have included: Addas Yisoroel Mikva Foundation, Achieve Trust, Atereth Shau, Beis Malka, Beis Shmuel, Belz Nursery, Bnos Yerushaim, Chesed Charity Trust, London Board of Schechita, Mutual Trust, Maoz Ladol, North West London Mikvah, Needy Families and Poor Families Pesach, Society of Friends of the Torah, Talmud Centre Trust and VMCT.

Applications

In writing to the correspondent.

The David Uri Memorial Trust

Jewish, general

£89,000 (2009/10)

Beneficial area

Worldwide.

Suite 511, 19–21 Crawford Street, London W1H 1PJ
Correspondent: The Trustees
Trustees: Mrs S Blackman; Mrs B Roden; B Blackman.
CC Number: 327810

Information available

Accounts were available from the Charity Commission, but without a grants list.

In 2009/10 the trust's assets totalled £2.9 million and it had an income of £285,000, mainly from property investment revenue. It made grants to organisations totalling £89,000.

Previous beneficiaries have included: National Jewish Chaplaincy Board, Age Concern, Crisis at Christmas, Jefferies Research Wing Trust, NSPCC and Yakar Education Foundation.

Exclusions

No grants to individuals.

Applications

In writing to the correspondent.

Vale of Glamorgan – Welsh Church Fund

General

£33,000 (2009/10)

Beneficial area

Vale of Glamorgan and City of Cardiff council areas.

The Vale of Glamorgan Council, Civic Offices, Holton Rd, Barry CF63 4RU
Tel: 01446 709250
Email: adwilliams@valeofglamorgan.gov.uk
Correspondent: A D Williams, Director of Finance, ICT and Property
Trustee: Vale of Glamorgan County Borough Council.
CC Number: 506628

Information available

Accounts were on file at the Charity Commission

The Fund makes grants in the following areas:
- education
- relief in sickness
- relief in need
- libraries, museums, art galleries
- social and recreational
- protection of historical buildings
- medical and social research treatment
- probation
- older people
- the blind
- places of worship and burial grounds
- emergencies or disasters
- other charitable purposes

In 2009/10 it had assets of £3.7 million and an income of £48,000. Grants were made totalling £32,500.

Grants are given on a one-off basis. Whilst no maximum/minimum grant levels are stipulated, awards are usually in the region of £1,500.

Beneficiaries included: Holy Trinity Presbytarian Church, Barry (£10,000); The United Reform Church, Barry (£10,000); Bethel Baptist Church, Barry (£8,500); Elfred Avenue United Church, Penarth (£500)

Exclusions

No grants to individuals.

Applications

For organisations based in the Vale of Glamorgan, further information can be obtained from the correspondent. For organisations based in Cardiff, please contact R Anthony at Cardiff County Council (tel. 029 20 872395).

The Albert Van Den Bergh Charitable Trust

Medical research, disability, community, general

£90,000 (2009/10)

Beneficial area

UK and overseas.

Trevornick Farmhouse, Holywell Bay, Newquay, Cornwall TR8 5PW
Correspondent: Jane Hartley, Trustee
Trustees: Jane Hartley; Nicola Glover; Bruce Hopkins.
CC Number: 296885

Information available

Accounts were available from the Charity Commission, but without a list of grants.

The trust was established in 1987. The majority of the organisations who receive donations are in the UK and concerned with health research and care for patients with cancer, multiple sclerosis, Parkinson's disease and other diseases and disabilities. Institutions which care for the elderly and children's charities are also supported.

In 2009/10 the trust had assets of £3.1 million and an income of £104,000. Grants to 79 organisations totalled £90,000 and were broken down as follows:

Medical research, care and support	£37,000
Help in the community	£8,500
Overseas	£8,500
Disability	£8,000
Hospices	£6,000
Older people	£5,800
Cultural	£5,000
Outward bound	£3,500
Conservation	£3,000
Disadvantaged	£2,000
Homelessness	£1,000
Services	£500
Other	£2,000

Previous beneficiaries have included: BLISS, Bishop of Guildford's Charity, British Heart Foundation, Counsel and Care for the Elderly, Leukaemia Research Trust, Multiple Sclerosis Society, Parentline Surrey, National Osteoporosis Society, RNID, Riding for the Disabled – Cranleigh Age Concern, SSAFA, St John Ambulance

...nd United Charities Fund – Liberal ...ewish Synagogue.

Applications

...n writing to the correspondent, ...ncluding accounts and budgets.

The Van Neste Foundation

Welfare, Christian, developing world

£215,000 (2009/10)

Beneficial area

UK (especially the Bristol area) and overseas.

...5 Alexandra Road, Clifton, Bristol ...S8 2DD
Tel: 01179 735167
Correspondent: Fergus Lyons, Secretary
Trustees: M T M Appleby, Chair; ... J F Lyons; G J Walker; J F Lyons; ... M Appleby; Michael Lyons; Tom Appleby.
CC Number: 201951

Information available

Accounts were available from the Charity Commission.

The trustees currently give priority to the following:

- developing world
- people who are disabled or elderly
- advancement of religion and respect for the sanctity and dignity of life
- community projects.

These objectives are reviewed by the trustees from time to time but applications falling outside them are unlikely to be considered.

In 2009/10 the trust had assets of £6.4 million and an income of £227,000. Grants were made totalling £215,000.

Donations were broken down as follows:

Community and Christian family life	14	£73,000
People with disabilities and the elderly	11	£46,000
Respect for dignity and the sanctity of life	3	£45,000
'Developing world'	7	£41,500

Beneficiaries included: Life (£30,000); CCS Adoption (£20,000); CAFOD in Bolivia (£15,000); Moquegua Project Peru and Windmill Hill City Farm (£10,000 each); Royal West of England Academy (£6,000); African Initiatives, Home Start, Prisoners Abroad and Rainbow Development Africa (£5,000 each); St Peter's Church Henleaze – Bristol (£1,000); Dolphin Society (£250).

Exclusions

No grants to individuals or to large, well-known charities. Applications are only considered from registered charities.

Applications

Applications should be in the form of a concise letter setting out the clear objectives to be obtained, which must be charitable. Information must be supplied concerning agreed funding from other sources together with a timetable for achieving the objectives of the appeal and a copy of the latest accounts. The foundation does not normally make grants on a continuing basis. To keep overheads to a minimum, only successful applications are acknowledged. Appeals are considered by the trustees at their meetings in January, June and October.

Mrs Maud Van Norden's Charitable Foundation

General

£40,000 (2010)

Beneficial area

UK.

BM Box 2367, London WC1N 3XX
Correspondent: The Trustees
Trustees: Ena Dukler; John Gordon; Elizabeth Humphryes; Neil Wingerath.
CC Number: 210844

Information available

Accounts were available from the Charity Commission.

Established in 1962, in 2010 the trust had assets of £1 million and an income of £39,000. There were 27 grants agreed totalling £40,000.

All but four of grants agreed for the year were for £1,500 each. Beneficiaries included: Princess Royal Trust for Carers (£3,000); Royal Hospital for Neuro-disability (£2,500); Changing Faces, Church Urban Fund, Home Warmth for the Aged, Humane Slaughter Association, National Rheumatoid Arthritis Society, Police Community Clubs of Great Britain, and Vitalise (£1,500 each); Ellen Macarthur Cancer Trust (£500).

Exclusions

No grants to individuals, expeditions or scholarships. The trustees make donations to registered UK charities only.

Applications

All appeals should be by letter containing the following:

- aims and objectives of the charity
- nature of the appeal
- total target, if for a specific project
- contributions received against target
- registered charity number
- any other factors.

Letters should be accompanied by a copy of the applicant's latest reports and accounts.

The Vandervell Foundation

General

£391,000 (2010)

Beneficial area

UK.

Hampstead Town Hall Centre, 213 Haverstock Hill, London NW3 4QP
Tel: 2074357546
Correspondent: Valerie Kaye, Administrator
Trustee: Directors of the Vandervell Foundation Ltd
CC Number: 255651

Information available

Full accounts were on file at the Charity Commission.

This trust has general charitable purposes, supporting both individuals and organisations. A wide range of causes has been supported, including schools, educational establishments, hospices and other health organisations, with the trust stating there are no real preferences or exclusions. Grants generally range from £1,000 to £20,000.

In 2010 the trust had assets of over £6.5 million, an income of £258,000 and gave a total of £391,000 in grants. Of this, £387,000 was given in 92 grants to organisations and £4,000 was given in 3 grants to individuals.

Advancement of education	18	170,500
Medical research	20	48,500
Performing arts	15	64,000
Environmental regeneration	4	9,500
Social Welfare	35	94,500

Beneficiaries included: Big Issue (£30,000); Prisoners Educational Trust (£20,000); Oxford Medical School (£18,000); PMS Foundation; QMUL; King's College London School of Medicine (£15,000 each); Lucy Cavendish College; Weekend Arts College(£10,000 each); London Air Ambulance; and Royal National Theatre (£5,000 each).

Applications

In writing to the correspondent. Grants are reviewed by the board of the trustees which meets every two months.

Common applicant mistakes

'We fund very few individuals and never help those who have a shortfall in funding due to entirely foreseen circumstances.'

Roger Vere Foundation

General

£244,000 (2009/10)

Beneficial area

UK and worldwide, with a special interest in High Wycombe.

19 Berwick Road, Marlow, Buckinghamshire SL7 3AR

Correspondent: Peter Allen, Trustee
Trustees: Rosemary Vere, Chair; Marion Lyon; Peter Allen.
CC Number: 1077559

Information available

Accounts were available from the Charity Commission, but without a list of grants.

This trust was established in September 1999 and it supports, worldwide:

- the relief of financial hardship in and around, but not restricted to, High Wycombe
- advancement of education
- advancement of religion
- advancement of scientific and medical research
- conservation and protection of the natural environment and endangered plants and animals
- relief of natural and civil disasters
- general charitable purposes.

In 2009/10 the trust had assets of £3.5 million and an income of £145,000. Grants were made totalling £244,000.

Previous beneficiaries include: Cord Blood Charity, the Leprosy Mission, Claire House Children's Hospice, Angels International, Signalong Group, Changing Faces, Women's Aid, St John Water Wing, UK Youth and Jubilee Plus.

Applications

In writing to the correspondent. The trustees meet regularly to consider requests.

The Nigel Vinson Charitable Trust

Economic/community development and employment, general

£105,000 (2009/10)

Beneficial area

UK, with a preference for north east England.

Hoare Trustees, 37 Fleet Street, London EC4P 4DQ
Tel: 020 7353 4522
Correspondent: The Trustees

Trustees: Hon. Rowena A Cowan; Rt Hon. Lord Vinson of Roddam Dene; Thomas O C Harris; Hon. Miss Bettina C Witheridge; Hon. Antonia C Bennett; Miss E Passey.
CC Number: 265077

Information available

Full accounts were available from the Charity Commission website.

This trust was established in 1972. It supports economic/community development and employment as well as making grants to other causes.

In 2009/10 the trust had assets of £4.2 million and an income of £104,000. Grants were made totalling £105,000.

There were 12 grants of £1,000 or more listed in the accounts. Beneficiaries included: Institute for Policy Research (£28,000); Civitas (£17,000); Institute of Economic Affairs (£12,000); Hampden Trust (£10,000); Politics and Economics Research Trust (£5,000); Christian Institute (£4,000); Songbird Survival (£2,000); and Elizabeth Finn Care (£1,500).

Applications

In writing to the correspondent. The trustees meet periodically to consider applications for grants of £1,000 and above. All grants below £1,000 are decided by The Rt. Hon. Nigel Lord Vinson on behalf of the trustees.

Vision Charity

Children who are blind, partially sighted or dyslexic

£116,000 (2009/10)

Beneficial area

UK and overseas.

PO Box 553, Chatham ME4 9AN
Website: www.visioncharity.co.uk
Correspondent: The Trustees
Trustees: Herbert Brenninkmeijer, Chair; Bill Bohanna; Larry Davis; David Pacy.
CC Number: 1075630

Information available

Accounts were on file at the Charity Commission.

The objects of the charity are to combine the fundraising efforts of companies and individuals who use or benefit from, or work in, the visual communications industry for the benefit of children who are blind, partially sighted or dyslexic.

The following information is taken from the charity's website:

> The monies raised are used expressly to purchase equipment, goods or specialist services. The Vision Charity will make cash donations only in very exceptional circumstances, as approved by its Board of Trustees.

> Vision is keen to emphasize its increasing international focus, both it terms of its fundraising activities and in directing its donations.

In 2009/10 it had assets of £378,000 and an income of £644,000, most of which came from donations received and various fundraising events organised by the charity.

Grants were made totalling £116,000.

There were 14 grants of £1,000 or more listed in the accounts. Beneficiaries included: Dyslexia Action (£25,000); London Society for the Blind – Dorton House School (£17,000); Blind in Business (£10,000); Autism Independent UK (£8,500); Royal Blind Society (£7,500); Moorfields Eye Hospital (£5,000).

Applications

A brief summary of the request should be sent to the correspondent. If the request is of interest to the trustees, further details will be requested. If the request has not been acknowledged within three months of submission, the applicant should assume that it has not been successful. The charity is interested to receive such applications but regrets that it is not able to acknowledge every unsuccessful submission.

Vivdale Ltd

Jewish

£109,000 (2009/10)

Beneficial area

UK.

17 Cheyne Walk, London NW4 3QH
Correspondent: D H Marks, Trustee
Trustees: D H Marks; L Marks; F Z Sinclair.
CC Number: 268505

Information available

Accounts were available at the Charity Commission, without a list of grants.

In 2009/10 the trust's assets totalled £2.4 million, it had an income of £93,500 and made grants totalling £109,000.

Previous beneficiaries have included: Achisomach Aid Company Ltd, Beis Soroh Schneirer, Beis Yaakov Town, Beis Yisroel Tel Aviv, Comet Charities Ltd, Friends of Harim Bnei Brak, Jewish Teachers Training College Gateshead, Mosdos Bnei Brak, Torah Vechesed Ashdod and Woodstock Sinclair Trust.

Applications

In writing to the correspondent.

The Viznitz Foundation

Jewish

£0 (2009/10)

Beneficial area

UK and abroad.

23 Overlea Road, London E5 9BG
Tel: 020 8557 9557
Correspondent: H Feldman, Trustee
Trustees: H Feldman; E Kahan.
CC Number: 326581

Information available

Accounts were available from the Charity Commission.

The objects of the charity are to pay and apply and appropriate the whole of the trust fund to those purposes both in the UK and abroad recognised as charitable by English Law and in accordance with the trust deed and the wishes of the Grand Rabbi of Viznitz.

In 2009/10 the foundation had assets of £1.9 million and an income of £218,000. No grants were made in this particular financial year. In 2008/09 grants were made totalling £146,000.

Applications

In writing to the correspondent.

The Scurrah Wainwright Charity

Social reform

£97,000 (2009/10)

Beneficial area

Preference for Yorkshire, South Africa and Zimbabwe.

16 Blenheim Street, Hebden Bridge, West Yorkshire HX7 8BU
Email: admin@wainwrighttrusts.org.uk
Website: www.wainwrighttrusts.org.uk
Correspondent: Kerry McQuade, Administrator
Trustees: M S Wainwright, Chair; R R Bhaskar; H P I Scott; H A Wainwright; J M Wainwright; P Wainwright; T M Wainwright.
CC Number: 1002755

Information available

Accounts were available from the Charity Commission.

The following extract is adapted from the charity's website:

> The Wainwright family runs two trusts, one charitable [The Scurrah Wainwright Charity], one non-charitable [The Andrew Wainwright Reform Trust Ltd], which prioritises grants for political and pressure group work that a registered charity could not support. The AWRT has a wide-ranging remit, striving for a just and democratic society, redressing political and social injustices.

> The trusts are based on the family's traditions of liberal values and support for the socially disempowered. The trustees are all family members, based in West Yorkshire.

> ▶ The charity funds projects in England, primarily in Yorkshire and the North of England, as well as Zimbabwe and Southern Africa. It

- rarely funds work in any other part of the world.
- It looks for innovative work in the field of social reform, with a preference for 'root-cause' rather than palliative projects.
- It favours causes that are outside the mainstream, and unlikely to be funded by other charities.
- It will contribute to core costs.

Typically, grants are between £1,000 and £5,000, but in cases of exceptional merit larger grants may be awarded.

In 2009/10 the trust had assets of £1.7 million, an income of £57,000 and made 40 grants totalling £97,000.

Beneficiaries included: Oxfam (£24,000); Fawcett Society (£10,000); CHAS Bradford (£5,000); Circle of Support and Accountability (£5,000); Food Aware (£3,000); Bar Human Rights (£2,500); Beatrix Campbell, Spinwatch, Stamp Out Poverty, Riders for Health and Forum for Discussion of Israel and Palestine (£2,000 each); and Essential Needs, Salvation Army, Million Women Rise and Robin Hood Project (£1,000 each).

Exclusions

No support is given to:
- individuals
- animal welfare
- buildings
- medical research or support for individual medical conditions
- substitution for Government funding (e.g. in education and health)
- charities that send unsolicited general appeal letters.

Applications

Follow these preliminary steps:
- check that the amount of money you need falls within the charity's limits
- check deadlines: the trustees meet three times a year – in March, July and November – and applications must be submitted by 1 February, 1 June or 1 October respectively.

Write a succinct but complete application that should include:
- an opening section that gives the name and postal address of your organisation, details of a named contact for the application and where you heard about the charity;
- background information about you and/or your organisation;
- the nature of the project you wish to pursue and what it seeks to achieve;
- your plans for practical implementation of the work and a budget;
- your most recent accounts and details of any additional sources of funding already secured or to be sought;
- whether you will accept a contribution to the amount requested.
- If the above information (excluding your accounts) takes up more than two sides of A4, please include a summary of that information on no more than two sides of A4, using a font no smaller than 12-point.

Applicants may contact the administrator, preferably by email, for any clarification.

If you have not heard from the administrator by the end of the month in which the trustees' meeting was held you must assume your application was not successful.

Common applicant mistakes

'Seeking funding in a part of the world that SWC doesn't cover; sending round-robin circular type appeals that the trustees won't consider.'

Wakeham Trust

Community development, education, community service by young people

£61,000 (2009/10)

Beneficial area

UK.

Wakeham Lodge, Rogate, Petersfield, Hampshire GU31 5EJ
Tel: 01730 821748
Email: wakehamtrust@mac.com
Website: www.wakehamtrust.org
Correspondent: The Trustees

Trustees: Harold Carter; Barnaby Newbolt; Tess Silkstone.
CC Number: 267495

Information available

Accounts were on file at the Charity Commission. Full and detailed guidelines can be found at the trust's website from which the following extract is taken:

> We provide grants to help people rebuild their communities. We are particularly interested in neighbourhood projects, community arts projects, projects involving community service by young people, or projects set up by those who are socially excluded.

> We also support innovative projects to promote excellence in teaching (at any level, from primary schools to universities), though we never support individuals.

> We aim to refresh the parts that other funding sources can't reach, especially new ideas and unpopular causes. Because we don't appeal to the public for funds, we can take risks.

> Because we are mostly run by volunteers, we can afford to make very small grants, without our funds being eaten up by administration costs.

> We favour small projects – often, but not always, start-ups. We try to break the vicious circle whereby you have to be established to get funding from major charities, but you have to get funding to get established. Grants are normally given where an initial £75 to £750 can make a real difference to getting the project up and running.

In 2009/10 the trust's assets totalled £1.5 million and it had an income of £29,500. Grants were made totalling £61,000.

Beneficiaries included: Archdiocese of Pondicherry (£5,000); ATD Fourth World (£1,000); Bridport Arts (£500); Bath Youth for Christ (£200); Chichester Family Church (£150).

Exclusions

No grants to individuals or large, well-established charities, or towards buildings and transport.

Applications

By letter or by filling in the online form. The trust prefers online applications. Full guidelines are available on the trust's website.

Common applicant mistakes

'Common mistakes vary. Sometimes too much/too many words and nformation, other times, it's not nough.'

The Thomas Wall Trust

Education, welfare

£27,000 to organisations (2009/10)

Beneficial area
UK.

Skinners' Hall, 8 Dowgate Hill, London EC4R 2SP
Tel: 020 7213 0564
Email: information@thomaswalltrust. org.uk
Website: www.thomaswalltrust.org.uk
Correspondent: Ms Sue Ellis, Charities Officer
Trustees: Dr G M Copland, Chair; Mrs M A Barrie; P Bellamy; C R Broomfield; Miss A S Kennedy; Miss A-M Martin; Mrs A Mullins; Revd Dr R Waller.
CC Number: 206121

Information available
Accounts were available from the Charity Commission.

This trust makes grants to both individuals and charitable organisations. The applying organisation, movement or institution has to be a registered charity with objects in a broad sense educational and/or concerned with social service.

Note on grants to individuals:

The trustees consider applications from UK nationals only who are in financial need and who wish to undertake educational courses at any level and duration, especially courses which are vocational or are concerned with social service in a broad sense and which will lead to paid employment.

In 2009/10 the trust had assets of £2.6 million and an income of £112,000. Grants to organisations totalled £27,000 and to individuals over £40,000.

Beneficiaries included: Careers 'N' Kids (£2,000); Behind Closed Doors (£1,500); Just Different (£1,200); and Adventure Unlimited, Caboodle Theatre, Hackney Quest, Just 42, One in a Million and West London

Churches Homeless Concern (£1,000 each).

Exclusions
Grants are not made: towards the erection, upkeep or renovation of buildings; to hospitals, almshouses or similar institutions; for objects which are purely medical; for projects outside of the UK.

Applications
There is no application form for charitable organisations to use except that all applicants must complete a cover sheet which can be downloaded from the trust's website. A copy of the latest available set of accounts for their charity should be included along with an sae, which will be used to acknowledge receipt of application.

The trustees meet twice a year, in July and November. Applications for the July meeting must be received by mid-May and for the November meeting by end of September.

Common applicant mistakes
'Organisations not applying on headed paper or providing accounts as requested.'

Wallace and Gromit's Children's Foundation

Improving the quality of life for sick children

£125,500 (2009/10)

Beneficial area
UK.

PO Box 2186, Bristol BS99 7NT
Email: info@wrongtrousersday.org
Website: www. wallaceandgromitfoundation.org
Correspondent: The Company Secretary
Trustees: I Hannah, Chair; S Cooper; P Lord; J Moule; N Park; D Sproxton.
CC Number: 1096483

Information available
Accounts were on file at the Charity Commission.

Wallace & Gromit's Children's Foundation is a national charity raising funds to improve the quality of life for children in hospitals and hospices throughout the UK.

The foundation states: 'We are the ONLY national charity raising funds for LOCAL children's hospitals and hospices to improve the quality of life for sick children across the UK.'

The foundation provides funding to support the following projects:

- Arts, music play and entertainment programmes to stimulate young minds and divert attention away from illness.
- Providing welcoming and accessible environments and surroundings, designed specifically for children in a fun and engaging way.
- Funding Education and Information Programmes to educate young people and recognising the importance of self help and health related issues.
- Helping to fund the acquisition of medical facilities, which can help to improve diagnosis and treatment of a wide range of conditions and illnesses in children.
- Sustaining family relationships helping to keep families together during emotionally difficult times.
- Helping to meet the cost of care in a children's hospice where children and their families are cared for during good days, difficult days and last days.
- Supporting children with physical and emotional difficulties empowering and increasing confidence.

Wallace and Gromit's Wrong Trousers Day is the foundation's primary fundraising event which encourages the general public to wear the wrong trousers for the day and donate funds raised to the foundation. In 2009/10 it had an income of £199,000 and made grants to 16 organisations totalling £125,500; £93,500 of which went to Children's Hospitals and £32,000 went to Children's Hospices.

Beneficiaries included: Birmingham Children's Hospital (£10,000); SICK kids friends foundation (£8,000); Alder Hey IMAGINE Appeal (£5,000); CHASE Hospice care for children (£4,000)

Exclusions

The foundation will not fund:

- charities not supporting children's healthcare
- organisations that do not have charitable status
- animal, religious or international charities
- organisations that do not work within a hospital or hospice environment
- organisations that provide excursions, holidays or away days
- no grants will be made to individuals.

The foundation does not give retrospective funding, grants to individuals or grants to replace statutory funding.

Applications

Grants are distributed on an annual basis. Application forms and guidelines are posted on the foundation's website from October and the closing date for applications is usually in December. All awards are made by the end of March.

The F J Wallis Charitable Settlement

General

£37,000 (2009/10)

Beneficial area

UK, with some interest in Hampshire and Surrey.

c/o Bridge House, 11 Creek Road, Hampton Court, East Molesey, Surrey KT8 9BE
Correspondent: F H Hughes, Trustee
Trustees: F H Hughes; A J Hills; Revd J J A Archer.
CC Number: 279273

Information available

Accounts were available from the Charity Commission.

Registered in 1979, the settlement has a criteria-based approach to grantmaking. The trustees usually rotate the areas of charitable activity that will receive grants, alternating between disability, children's charities and medical research/health and sickness in one year and animal charities, community charities and hospices in the next.

In 2009/10 the settlement had assets of £1.2 million and an income of £45,000. Grants to organisations totalled £37,000. The majority of grants given were for £1,000 each.

Beneficiaries included: the PSP Association (£2,000); Abbeyfield, Carroll Centre, Conquest Art, Fields in Trust, QUIT, Slough Furniture Project, Target Ovarian Cancer and WWT London Wetland Centre (£1,000 each); Hampshire and Isle of Wight Wildlife Trust and St Luke's Church – Stoke Hammond (£500 each); and St Clare Hospice (£250).

Exclusions

No grants to individuals or to local charities except those in Surrey or in Hampshire. The same organisation is not supported twice within a 24-month period.

Applications

In writing to the correspondent. No telephone calls. Applications are not acknowledged and unsuccessful applicants will only be contacted if an sae is provided. Trustees meet in March and September and applications need to be received the month prior to the trustees' meeting.

The Ward Blenkinsop Trust

Medicine, social welfare, arts, education, general

£157,000 (2009/10)

Beneficial area

UK, with a special interest in Merseyside and surrounding counties.

PO Box 28840, London SW13 0WZ
Tel: 020 8878 9975

Correspondent: Charlotte Blenkinsop, Trustee
Trustees: A M Blenkinsop; Ms S J Blenkinsop; Ms C A Blenkinsop; Mrs F A Stormer; Mrs H E Millin.
CC Number: 265449

Information available

Brief accounts were available from the Charity Commission website, without a list of grants.

The trust is established for general charitable purposes and currently supports charities in the Merseyside area and charities of a medical nature. We understand all requests for funds are considered.

In 2009/10 the trust had assets of £2.1 million and an income of £194,000. Grants totalled £157,000.

Previous beneficiaries have included Action on Addiction, BID, Chase Children's Hospice, Clatterbridge Cancer Research, Clod Ensemble, Comic Relief, Depaul Trust, Fairley House, Give Youth a Break, Halton Autistic Family Support Group, Hope HIV, Infertility Network, George Martin Music Foundation, Royal Academy of Dance, St Joseph's Family Centre, Strongbones Children's Charitable Trust, Walk the Walk, Winchester Visitors Group and Wirral Holistic Care Services.

Exclusions

No grants to individuals.

Applications

In writing to the correspondent.

The Barbara Ward Children's Foundation

Children

£507,000 (2010)

Beneficial area

England and Wales.

Copyhold, Lock Lane, Partridge Green, Horsham RH13 8EF
Website: www.bwcf.org.uk
Correspondent: Christopher Banks, Trustee

Trustees: Barbara Irene Ward, Chair; D C Bailey; J C Banks; A M Gardner; C R Parker; B M Walters.
CC Number: 1089783

Information available

Accounts were available from the Charity Commission.

This foundation makes grants to organisations working with children who are seriously or terminally ill, disadvantaged or otherwise. Grants made can range from one-off grants to project-related grants that run for two or three years.

In 2010 it had assets of £8.5 million and an income of £493,000. Grants to 56 organisations totalled £507,000.

The largest grants were made to: the Rainbow Centre and MERU (£35,000 each); BIBIC (£29,000); Reedham Trust (£29,000); National Blind Children's Society and New College Worcester (£25,000 each); and WellChild (£22,000).

Other beneficiaries included: The Rainbow Centre (£19,000); The Bobath Centre, The Food Chain and Hop, Skip and Jump – South West (£12,000 each); Changing Faces and Disability Challengers (£10,000 each); Army Cadet Force Association, Arts for All, Asian Students Christian Trust, CHICKS, Child Care Action Trust, Dandelion Trust, Hopscotch, Over the Wall, Peter Pan Nursery, Suffolk School for Parents and Huntington's Disease Association (£5,000 each); Let Us Play and STEPS (£4,000 each); Pearson's Holiday Fund (£3,000); and the Elizabeth Svendsen Trust for Children and Donkeys (£2,000).

Applications

In writing to the correspondent including latest set of audited financial statements. The trustees usually meet quarterly.

G R Waters Charitable Trust 2000

General

£375,000 to organisations (2009/10)

Beneficial area

UK, also North and Central America.

Finers Stephens Innocent, 179–185 Great Portland Street, London W1W 5LS
Tel: 0207 323 4000
Correspondent: Michael Lewis
Trustees: M Fenwick; C Organ.
CC Number: 1091525

Information available

Accounts were on file at the Charity Commission.

This trust was registered with the Charity Commission in 2002, replacing Roger Waters 1989 Charitable Trust (Charity Commission number 328574), which transferred its assets to the new trust (the 2000 in the title refers to when the declaration of trust was made.) Like the former trust, it receives a share of the band, Pink Floyd's, royalties as part of its annual income. It has general charitable purposes throughout the UK, as well as North and Central America.

In 2009/10 the trust had assets of £1.1 million, an income of £94,000 and made grants totalling £383,000.

Beneficiaries included: Fundacion Un Techo Para Chile (£132,000); Cinema Jenin Association – Palestine (£126,000); Nordoff Robbins Music Therapy, Mandeville School (£50,000 each); Cystic Fibrosis Dream Holidays, Dream Connection (£5,000 each); Royal British Legion and Help for Heroes (£3,000); Rainbow for Conductive Education (£2,000); and Amnesty International (£1,000).

Grants totalling £8,000 were also made to 2 individuals.

Applications

In writing to the correspondent.

Blyth Watson Charitable Trust

UK-based humanitarian organisations, hospices

£96,000 (2009/10)

Beneficial area

UK.

50 Broadway, Westminster, London SW1H 0BL
Tel: 020 7227 7000
Correspondent: The Trustees
Trustees: Nicholas Brown; Ian McCulloch.
CC Number: 1071390

Information available

Accounts were on file at the Charity Commission.

The trust dedicates its grant-giving policy in the area of humanitarian causes based in the UK. A number of hospices are supported each year.

In 2009/10 the trust had assets of £2.6 million and an income of £84,000. Grants, including support costs, totalled £96,000.

Beneficiaries included: Connection at St Martin's, Society for the Relief of Distress, Royal Academy of Music and Journey of a Lifetime.

Applications

In writing to the correspondent. Trustees usually meet twice during the year in June and December.

Common applicant mistakes

'Applicants not matching our criteria.'

Weatherley Charitable Trust

General

£131,000

Beneficial area

Unrestricted.

Northampton Science Park Ltd, Newton House, Kings Park Road Moulton Park, Northampton NN3 6LG
Correspondent: Christine Weatherley, Trustee
Trustees: Christine Weatherley; Richard Weatherley; Steven Chambers.
CC Number: 1079267

Information available

Accounts were on file at the Charity Commission, without a list of grants.

This trust was established in 1999 for general charitable purposes. In 2009/10 it had no income. Grants were made totalling £75,000. A list of grants was not included with the accounts.

Applications

This trust does not accept unsolicited applications.

The Weavers' Company Benevolent Fund

Helping disadvantaged young people, offenders and ex-offenders

£258,000 (2010)

Beneficial area

UK.

The Worshipful Company of Weavers', Saddlers' House, Gutter Lane, London EC2V 6BR

Tel: 020 7606 1155

Fax: 020 7606 1119

Email: clerk@weaversco.co.uk

Website: www.weavers.org.uk/

Correspondent: John Snowdon, Clerk

Trustee: The Worshipful Company of Weavers.

CC Number: 266189

Information available

Accounts were available from the Charity Commission. The trust also has a useful website.

This benevolent fund was set up in 1973 with funds provided by the Worshipful Company of Weavers, the oldest of the City of London Livery Companies. Its priorities as outlined on its website are:

1. Helping disadvantaged young people

The object of the fund is to support projects working with disadvantaged young people to ensure that they are given every possible chance to meet their full potential and to participate fully in society. We normally define young people as being aged from 5 to 30 years.

2. Offenders and ex-offenders, particularly those under 30 years of age

Many offenders and ex-offenders suffer from a variety of difficult and complex problems and they are amongst the most vulnerable members of society. We will fund work that addresses the social and economic problems faced by this group and their families, and provide them with support, life skills training and a way back into education, training and/or employment, so that they may reintegrate and make a positive contribution to society.

We are especially interested in helping smaller organisations which offer direct services. They must be registered charities or in the process of applying for registration. Our grants are relatively modest, usually with an upper limit of £15,000 per annum, and to make sure grants of this size have an impact, we will not fund large organisations.

Applicants must show that they have investigated other sources of funding and made plans for the future, which should include replacement funding if appropriate.

What will we fund?

Size of organisation

To be eligible for funding, local organisations such as those working in a village, estate or small town should normally have an income of less than about £100,000. Those working across the UK should normally have an income of not more than about £250,000.

Funding limit

Grants are usually up to £15,000 per annum but smaller applications are also welcomed.

Duration

Grants may be awarded for up to three years.

Pump-priming

The trust particularly welcome applications for pump-priming grants from small community-based organisations where a grant would form a major element of the funding. It prefers to support projects where our grant will be used for an identified purpose.

Core costs

Applications for core funding will be considered, such as general administration and training that enable an organisation to develop and maintain expertise.

Innovative or pioneering work

We like to encourage new ideas and to fund projects that could inspire similar work in other areas of the country.

Continuation funding

The trust appreciates the importance of providing ongoing funding for successful projects, which have proved their worth.

Salaries

Normally funded for up to three years but payment of the second and third year grants are subject to satisfactory progress reports.

Emergency or deficit funding

In exceptional circumstances, the trust may provide emergency or deficit funding for an established organisation Applicants most likely to be granted emergency funding are charities which the company knows or has previously supported.

In 2010 the trust had assets of £7.9 million, an income of £362,000 and made grants totalling £258,000.

Beneficiaries included: Cowpen Quay Association and Worldwide Volunteering (£15,000 each); Upper Room and Urban Hope (£13,000 each); Footprints and The Prison Reform Trust (£10,000 each); Youth Empowerment Crime Diversion Scheme (£8,000); Leys Youth Programme and The Premises Music Education (£5,000 each); CMO Productions and Guildhall School of Music and Drama (£3,000 each); The Evelina's Children's Hospital (£2,000); Cana Ethiopia and St Paul's Cathedral (£500 each); and City of London Festival and Movement of Peasant Workers, Guatemala (£250 each).

Exclusions

The website lists the following exclusions.

What will we not fund?

- **General appeals:** We will not support sponsorship, marketing or other fundraising activities.
- **Endowment funds:** We will not support endowment funds, nor bursaries or long-term capital projects.
- **Grant-giving charities.**
- **Retrospective funding:** We will not make grants for work that has been completed or will be completed while the application is being considered.
- **Replacement funding:** We will not provide grants for work that should be covered by statutory funding.
- **Building projects:** We will not fund building work but may help with the cost of equipment or furnishings.
- **Disability Discrimination Act:** We will not fund capital projects to provide access in compliance with the DDA.
- **Personal appeals:** We will not make grants to individuals. Applicants must be registered charities, in the process of registering, or qualified as charitable.

- **Umbrella bodies or large, established organisations:** We will not normally support projects in which the charity is collaborating or working in partnership with umbrella bodies or large, established organisations.
- **Overseas:** We will not support organisations outside the UK, nor overseas expeditions or travel.

Work that we cannot normally support includes:

- Work with children under 5 years of age.
- Universities or colleges.
- Medical charities or those involved in medical care.
- Organisations of and for disabled people.
- Environmental projects.
- Work in promotion of religious or political causes.

Applications

Detailed guidelines are available from the Weaver's Company website, from where forms can also be downloaded.

The grants committee meets in February, June and October of each year, it may take up to four months for applications to be processed.

Common applicant mistakes

They do not read or comply with criteria, clearly stated and available.'

Webb Memorial Trust

Education, politics, social policy

£202,500 (2008/09)

Beneficial area

UK and Eastern Europe.

Mount Royal, Allendale Road, Hexham, Northumberland NE46 2NJ
Website: www.webbmemorialtrust.org.uk/
Correspondent: Mike Parker, The Hon. Secretary
Trustees: Richard Rawes, Chair; Mike Parker; Robert Lloyd-Davies; Dianne Hayter; Mike Gapes; Barry Knight.
CC Number: 313760

Information available

Information was provided by the trust.

The Webb Memorial Trust is a registered charity; it was established in 1947 as a memorial to the socialist pioneer Beatrice Webb.

The trust is set up with the aims of the advancement of education and learning with respect to the history and problem of government and social policy (including socialism, trade unionism and co-operation) in Great Britain and elsewhere by:

1 research
2 lectures, scholarships and educational grants
3 such other educational means as the trustees may from time to time approve.

Since 1987 the trust has provided £70,000 a year to fund a variety of projects in the UK and Eastern Europe.

In 2008/9 the trust had an income of £71,500, assets of £1,643,000 and gave grants totalling £202,500.

Beneficiaries were Ruskin College (£126,000) and the Fabian Society (£76,500).

Half of the trust's grant expenditure goes towards funding students from Eastern Europe attending Ruskin College – Oxford to study courses relevant to the trust's objects. The remainder goes on projects either within the UK or overseas in Europe.

Exclusions

No grants in support of any political party.

Applications

See the trust's website for details of availability.

Common applicant mistakes

'Applicants don't read our website. Too many individual students apply.'

The David Webster Charitable Trust

Ecological and broadly environmental projects

£190,000 (2009/10)

Beneficial area

UK.

Marshalls, Marshalls Lane, High Cross, Ware, Hertfordshire SG11 1AJ
Tel: 01920 462001
Correspondent: N Thompson
Trustees: T W D Webster; N Thompson.
CC Number: 1055111

Information available

Accounts were on file at the Charity Commission.

Set up in 1995, in 2009–10 the trust had assets of £3.2 million, an income of £183,000 and made 12 grants totalling £190,000.

Beneficiaries included: Bird Life International (£100,000); Wells Cathedral (£25,000); Herts & Middlesex Wildlife Trust, Rosslyn Chapel, Isabel Hospice, The Tank Museum, Royal Navy Submarine Museum (£10,000 each); National Trust, Beds & Cambs Wildlife Trust (£5,000 each); Bat Conservation Trust, Norfolk Wherry Trust (£2,000); and High Cross PCC (£1,000).

Applications

In writing to the correspondent.

The Weinberg Foundation

General

Around £85,000 (2009/10)

Beneficial area

UK and overseas.

Munslows, 2nd Floor, Manfield House, 1 Southampton Street, London WC2R 0LR
Tel: 020 7845 7500
Correspondent: Nathan Steinberg
Trustees: Sir Mark Weinberg; Joy Whitehouse.
CC Number: 273308

Information available

Information was available the Charity Commission.

Established in 1971 for general charitable purposes, this is the foundation of the financier Sir Mark Weinberg.

In 2009/10 the foundation had an income of £2,100 and a total expenditure of £93,000. Grants were made totalling around £85,000.

Previous beneficiaries included: Natan Foundation; Friends of EORTC; Amnesty International; Community Security Trust; Ability Net; Philharmonia Orchestra; Royal Shakespeare Theatre; St James's Palace Foundation; University of Cambridge; UJIA Campaign; South Bank Foundation; and the Elton John AIDS Foundation.

Applications

In writing to the correspondent.

The Weinstein Foundation

Jewish, medical, welfare

£68,000 (2009/10)

Beneficial area

Worldwide.

32 Fairholme Gardens, Finchley, London N3 3EB
Tel: 020 8346 1257
Correspondent: M L Weinstein, Trustee
Trustees: Stella Weinstein; Michael Weinstein; Philip Weinstein; Lennne Newman.
CC Number: 277779

Information available

Accounts were available from the Charity Commission.

This trust mostly supports Jewish organisations, although it does have general charitable purposes and supports a wide range of other causes, notably medical-related charities.

In 2009/10 the foundation had assets of £1.5 million, an income of 45,000 and made grants totalling £68,000.

Previous grants include: Chevras Evas Nitzrochim Trust; Friends of Mir; SOFT UK; Chesed Charitable Trust; and Youth Aliyah.

Exclusions

No grants to individuals.

Applications

In writing to the correspondent.

The Weinstock Fund

General

Around £255,000 (2009/10)

Beneficial area

Unrestricted, but with some local interest in the Wiltshire and Newbury area.

PO Box 17734, London SW18 3ZQ
Correspondent: Miss Jacqueline Elstone, Trust Administrator
Trustees: Susan G Lacroix; Michael Lester; Laura H Weinstock.
CC Number: 222376

Information available

Accounts were available from the Charity Commission.

The trustees support a wide range of charitable causes, particularly in the field of welfare, children, education, medicine and arts. Only UK registered charities are considered.

In 2009/10 the fund had assets of £9.8 million and an income of £417,000. Grants were made totalling around £255,000.

Beneficiaries included: St George's Hospital (£25,000); St Peter's College Oxford (£20,000); Canterbury Cathedral (£10,000); Newbury Spring Festival (£6,000); and the Philharmonia Orchestra, Ashmolean Museum and Cambridge University (£5,000 each).

Exclusions

No grants to individuals or unregistered organisations.

Applications

In writing to the correspondent. There are no printed details or applications forms. Previous information we have received stated: 'Where nationwide charities are concerned, the trustees prefer to make donations centrally.' Donations can only be made to registered charities, and details of the registration number are required before any payment can be made.

The James Weir Foundation

Welfare, education, general

£203,000 (2010)

Beneficial area

UK, with a preference for Ayrshire and Glasgow.

Mercer & Hole Trustees Ltd, Gloucester House, 72 London Road, St Albans, Herts AL1 1NS
Tel: 01727 869141
Correspondent: The Secretary
Trustees: Simon Bonham; William Ducas; Elizabeth Bonham.
CC Number: 251764

Information available

Accounts were available from the Charity Commission.

The foundation has general charitable purposes, giving priority to schools and educational institutions; Scottish organisations, especially local charities in Ayrshire and Glasgow; and charities with which either James Weir or the trustees are particularly associated. These preferences, however, do not appear to be at the expense of other causes, UK-wide charities or local organisations outside of Scotland. The following six charities are listed in the trust deed as potential beneficiaries:

▸ The Royal Society
▸ The British Association for Advancement of Science
▸ The RAF Benevolent Fund
▸ The Royal College of Surgeons
▸ The Royal College of Physicians
▸ The University of Strathclyde.

In 2010 the trust had an income of £190,000 and made 71 grants totalling £203,000. Assets stood at £6.8 million.

Beneficiaries included those organisations listed above which each received £5,000, except the University of Strathclyde which received (£9,500).

Other beneficiaries included: Aberlour, Age Concern Scotland, Brainwave, Breast Cancer Campaign, Hopscotch, Jubilee Sailing Trust, Lee Smith Foundation and Youth Action

Wiltshire (£3,000 each); ABF The Soldiers' Charity and Epilepsy Scotland (£2,000 each); and Bi Polar Scotland, Borderline and New Dimensions (£1,000 each).

Exclusions

Grants are given to recognised charities only. No grants to individuals.

Applications

In writing to the correspondent. Distributions are made twice-yearly in June and November when the trustees meet. Applications should be received by May or October.

The Barbara Welby Trust

General

£28,000 (2009/10)

Beneficial area

UK, with a preference for Lincolnshire.

Hunters, 9 New Square, Lincoln's Inn, London WC2A 3QN
Correspondent: The Trustees
Trustees: N J Barker; C W H Welby; C N Robertson.
CC Number: 252973

Information available

Accounts were on file at the Charity Commission

The trust states that it considers supporting a range of charities, but has a preference for those of which the founder had special knowledge and for charities which have objects with which she was especially associated.

In 2009/10 the trust had assets of £963,000 and an income of £33,000. Grants were made totalling £28,000.

Beneficiaries included: Launde Abbey (£5,000); Lincolnshire Agricultural Society (£2,500); Be Your Best Foundation, The Connection at St Martin's, St Wulfram's Church and St Luke's Hospital for the Clergy (£1,000 each); and Elizabeth Finn Care, Grantham & District Phab, Strut in the Community and The Kings School New Trust (£500 each).

Exclusions

Applications for individual assistance are not normally considered unless made through an established charitable organisation.

Applications

In writing at any time to the above address, although the trustees usually meet to consider grants in March and October.

The Wessex Youth Trust

Youth, general

£147,000 (2009/10)

Beneficial area

Worldwide.

Chelwood, Rectory Road, East Carleton, Norwich NR14 8HT
Tel: 01508 571230
Correspondent: Jenny Cannon
Trustees: Mark Foster-Brown; Malcolm Cockren; Denise Poulton; Robert Clinton; Kate Cavelle; Richard Parry
CC Number: 1076003

Information available

Accounts were on file at the Charity Commission.

The trust states that:

> The charity's primary aim is to assist other registered charities and charitable causes and in particular those with which Their Royal Highnesses have personal connection or interests. The charity is particularly, although not exclusively, interested in supporting projects which provide opportunities to help, support and advance young people.

Most grants are one-off, although substantial grants may be made for up to five years.

In 2009/10 the trust had an income of £281,000 mainly from donations. Assets stood at £508,000. Grants to 28 organisations totalled £147,000.

Beneficiaries have included: Blind in Business, the Brainwave Centre, Cardboard Citizens, Caring for Life, Children's Adventure Farm Trust, Classworks Theatre, the Country Trust, Demelza Hospice Care for Children, East Reading Explorer

Scouts, East Anglia Children's Hospice, Happy Days Children's Charity, Kidscape, Project Scotland, Tolerance International UK and National Autistic Society.

The accounts stated: 'The Charities Commission has been supplied with details of amounts given to each charity together with an explanation of the reasons for the non-disclosure of individual amounts in the financial statements.'

Non-disclosure of grants information should only be made where the information being made public may be potentially harmful to the trust or its recipients; failing to disclose information without providing an explanation in the public sphere may prompt unjustified speculation about the nature of grants made.

Exclusions

No grants are made to:
- non-registered charities or causes
- individuals, including to people who are undertaking fundraising activities on behalf of a charity
- organisations whose main objects are to fund or support other causes
- organisations whose accounts disclose substantial financial resources and that have well-established and ample fundraising capabilities
- fund research that can be supported by government funding or that is popular among trusts.

Applications

In writing to the correspondent in the first instance. A response will be made within two weeks in the form of an application form and guidelines to eligible applicants or a letter of rejection if more appropriate. Completed forms, which are not acknowledged upon receipt, need to be submitted by 1 May or 1 November, for consideration by the end of the month. Clarity of presentation and provision of financial details are among the qualities which impress the trustees. Successful applicants will receive a letter stating that the acceptance of the funding is conditional on an update being received before the next meeting. The trust's criteria state other correspondence cannot be entered into, and organisations cannot reveal the size of any grants they receive.

West London Synagogue Charitable Fund

Jewish, general

£30,000 (2010)

Beneficial area
UK.

33 Seymour Place, London W1H 5AU
Correspondent: The Fund Coordinator
Trustees: Simon Raperport; Jane Cutter; Michael Cutter; Francine Epstein; Vivien Feather; Jacqui Green; Ruth Jacobs; Hermy Jankel; Monica Jankel; Phyllis Levy; Elaine Parry; Jean Regen; Vivien Rose and four ex-officio trustees.
CC Number: 209778

Information available
Accounts were available from the Charity Commission.

The trust has stated that it makes grants to both Jewish and non-Jewish organisations. It prefers to be involved with charities which synagogue members are involved with or helped by. In 2010 it had an income of £31,000, mostly from charity events and made around 40 grants totalling £30,000.

Beneficiaries included: Admiral Nurses and the Psoriasis Association (£4,000 each); Rabbi Freeman's Discretionary Fund (£1,000); Down's Syndrome Association and Save A Child's Heart (£500 each); Bet Shalom, Bobath Centre and Respite Carers (£300 each).

Exclusions
No grants to individuals.

Applications
In writing to the correspondent.

The Westcroft Trust

International understanding, overseas aid, Quaker, Shropshire

£92,500 (2009/10)

Beneficial area
Unrestricted, but with a special interest in Shropshire.

32 Hampton Road, Oswestry, Shropshire SY11 1SJ
Correspondent: Mary Cadbury, Managing Trustee
Trustees: Mary C Cadbury; Richard G Cadbury; James E Cadbury; Erica R Cadbury.
CC Number: 212931

Information available
Accounts were on file at the Charity Commission.

Currently the trustees have five main areas of interest:
- international understanding, including conflict resolution and the material needs of the developing world
- religious causes, particularly social outreach, usually of the Society of Friends (Quakers) but also for those originating in Shropshire
- development of the voluntary sector in Shropshire
- needs of people with disabilities, primarily in Shropshire
- development of community groups and reconciliation between different cultures in Northern Ireland.

Medical education is only helped by support for expeditions overseas that include pre-clinical students. Medical aid, education and relief work in developing countries is mainly supported through UK-registered organisations. International disasters may be helped in response to public appeals.

The trust favours charities with low administrative overheads and that pursue clear policies of equal opportunity in meeting need. Grants may be one-off or recurrent;

recurrent grants are rarely made for endowment or capital projects.

In 2009/10 the trust had assets of £2.2 million, which generated an income of £94,000. Grants were made totalling £92,000, broken down as follows:

Overseas Aid	£35,000
Social services/Health/Education	£28,000
Religious Society of Friends	£29,000
Shropshire organisations	£12,000

Beneficiaries included: Oxfam (£2,500); Liverpool School of Tropical Medicine (£900); Save the Children Fund (£850); Action Village India (£750); Macmillan Shropshire (£500); Telford Christian Council (£450) and Shropshire Playbus (£250).

Exclusions
Grants are given to charities only. No grants to individuals or for medical electives, sport, the arts (unless specifically for people with disabilities in Shropshire) or armed forces charities. Requests for sponsorship are not supported. Annual grants are withheld if recent accounts are not available or do not satisfy the trustees as to continuing need.

Applications
In writing to the correspondent. There is no application form or set format but applications should be restricted to a maximum of three sheets of paper, stating purpose, overall financial needs and resources together with previous years' accounts if appropriate. Printed letters signed by 'the great and good' and glossy literature do not impress the trustees, who prefer lower-cost applications. Applications are dealt with about every two months. No acknowledgement will be given. Replies to relevant but unsuccessful applicants will be sent only if an sae is enclosed. As some annual grants are made by Bank Telepay, details of bank name, branch, sort code, and account name and number should be sent in order to save time and correspondence.

Common applicant mistakes
'It might appear that applicants have not paid any regard to the published aims and objectives of the trust.'

The Barbara Whatmore Charitable Trust

Arts and music, relief of poverty

£49,000 (2009/10)

Beneficial area

UK.

Spring House, Priors Way, Aldeburgh, Suffolk IP15 5EW
Tel: 01728 452885
Correspondent: Mrs P M Cooke-Yarborough, Chair
Trustees: Patricia Cooke-Yarborough, Chair; David Eldridge; Denis Borrow; Gillian Lewis; Luke Gardiner; Sally Carter; Stephen Bate.
CC Number: 283336

Information available

Accounts were on file at the Charity Commission.

This trust was registered with the Charity Commission in October 1981. In 2009/10 it had assets of £1.3 million. It had an income of £44,000 and made 30 grants to organisations totalling £49,000.

Beneficiaries included: National Youth Orchestra (£6,000); Campaign for Drawing (£3,500); Theatre 503 (£3,000); Royal School of Needlework and the Wallace Collection (£2,000); Wonderful Beast Theatre Company (£1,000); Cambridge University Library (£500); and New Lanark Conservation (£250).

Applications

In writing to the correspondent.

The Whitaker Charitable Trust

Music, environment, countryside conservation

£185,000 (2009/10)

Beneficial area

UK, but mostly East Midlands and Scotland.

c/o Currey and Co., 21 Buckingham Gate, London SW1E 6LS
Tel: 0207 802 2700
Correspondent: The Trustees
Trustees: E R H Perks; D W J Price; Lady Elizabeth Whitaker.
CC Number: 234491

Information available

Accounts were on file at the Charity Commission.

The trust has general charitable objects, although with stated preferences in the following fields:

- local charities in Nottinghamshire and the east Midlands
- music
- agriculture and silviculture
- countryside conservation
- Scottish charities.

In 2009/10 the trust had assets of £7.3 million, it generated an income of £206,000. Grants to 73 organisations totalled £185,000.

A substantial grant of £42,000 was made to Atlantic College. Other beneficiaries include: Leith School of Art £13,000; Nottingham University, Bristol University, Phoenix Foundation, Game and Wildlife Conservation Trust Scotland and Teaching Trees – £10,000 each; Live Music now £6,000; Heritage Trust of Lincolnshire £3,750; Bassetlaw Hospice £3,000

Exclusions

Support is given to registered charities only. No grants are given to individuals or for the repair or maintenance of individual churches.

Applications

In writing to the correspondent. Applications should include clear details of the need the intended project is designed to meet plus a copy of the latest accounts available and an outline budget. If an acknowledgement of the application, or notification in the event of the application not being accepted is required, an sae should be enclosed. Trustees meet on a regular basis.

The Simon Whitbread Charitable Trust

Education, family welfare, medicine, preservation

Around £139,000 (2009/10)

Beneficial area

UK, with a preference for Bedfordshire.

Hunters, 9 New Square, Lincoln's Inn, London WC2A 3QN
Correspondent: E C A Martineau
Trustees: Sir Samuel Charles Whitbread; E C A Martineau; Mrs E A Bennett.
CC Number: 200412

Information available

Accounts were available from the Charity Commission.

The trust supports general causes in Bedfordshire, and education, family welfare, medicine, medical research and preservation UK-wide.

In 2009/10 the trust had assets of £63,000, an income of £121,000 and a total charitable expenditure of £139,000.

Previous beneficiaries have included All Saints Church, Army Benevolent Fund, Arthritis Care, Bedfordshire Historical Records Society, Bedfordshire Music Trust, Chillingham Wild Cattle, Countryside Foundation for Education, Gravenhurst Parish Council, Mencap, National Association of Widows, St Luke's Hospital for the Clergy, Spurgeons Child Care, Royal Green Jackets, Retirement Education Centre Bedfordshire, RSPB, St Mungo's and SCOPE.

Exclusions

Generally no support for local projects outside Bedfordshire.

Applications

In writing to the correspondent. Acknowledgements are not given. Please do not telephone.

Common applicant mistakes

'Many applicants quite evidently have done no research and are using a scattergun approach. Some use first class postage – which is noted.'

The Colonel W H Whitbread Charitable Trust

Education, preservation of places of historic interest and natural beauty

£102,500 (2010)

Beneficial area

UK, with an interest in Gloucestershire.

Fir Tree Cottage, World's End, Sinton Green, Worcestershire WR2 6NN
Tel: 07812 454321
Email: whwhitbread.trust@googlemail.com
Correspondent: Susan M Smith
Trustees: H F Whitbread; J R Barkes; R T Foley.
CC Number: 210496

Information available

Accounts were available from the Charity Commission.

The trustees have resolved to support charitable organisations and general areas of charitable activity which were, or in the opinion of the trustees would have been, of interest to the trust's founder, the late Colonel William Henry Whitbread, which, according to its 2008/09 trustees' report, comprise the following:

1　The promotion of education and in particular: (a) the provision of financial assistance towards the maintenance and development of Aldenham School, and (b) the creation of Colonel W H Whitbread scholarships or bursaries or prizes to be awarded to pupils at Aldenham School.
2　Charitable organisations within Gloucestershire.
3　The preservation, protection and improvement for the public benefit of places of historic interest and natural beauty.

The trustees will only in exceptional circumstances consider grant applications for purposes which fall outside those described above. Within this framework the trustees will distribute a minimum of £500 per distribution.

The trustees make charitable distributions on an arbitrary basis, having reviewed all applications and considered other charities that they wish to benefit.

In 2010 the trust had assets of £7.3 million and an income of £102,000. Grants made to organisations totalled £102,500.

Previous beneficiaries have included: 1st Queen's Dragon Guards Regimental Trust, Abbey School Tewkesbury, Army Benevolent Fund, CLIC Sargent, DEC Tsunami Earthquake Appeal, Friends of Alderman Knights School, Gloucestershire Historic Churches Trust, Great Ormond Street Hospital Children's Charity, Household Cavalry Museum Appeal, Hunt Servants' Fund, Queen Mary's Clothing Guild, Royal Hospital Chelsea and St Richard's Hospice.

Applications

A brief summary (no more than one side of A4) in writing (by email if possible) to the correspondent. It is not necessary to send any accompanying paperwork at this stage. Should the trustees wish to consider any application further, then an application form will be sent.

The Melanie White Foundation Limited

General – see below

£242,000 (2009/10)

Beneficial area

Unrestricted.

Boodle Hatfield Secretarial Limited, 89 New Bond Street, London W1 S 1 DA
Correspondent: The Trustees
Trustees: Mrs. M White; A White.
CC Number: 1077150

Information available

Accounts were available from the Charity Commission.

Set up in 1999, the following was taken from the foundation's 2009/10 annual report:

> The charity's principal activity during the year was the support of charities through the payments of donations. The objects of the charity are to promote any charitable purpose or support any charity selected by the directors. It is expressly contemplated that CLIC Sargent may be a beneficiary of the application of some or all funds or other benefits by the charity.

The major beneficiary is usually The Arbib Foundation (charity registration number 296358), of which, Sir Martyn Arbib, the father of Mrs. Melanie White, is a trustee, but this has changed for the year 2009/10.

In 2009/10 the foundation had assets of £10 million and an income of £313,000. Grants payable amounted to £242,000. A major grant of £235,000 was given to CLIC Sargent. Other beneficiaries were: A Team Foundation (£2,500); Multiple Sclerosis Society (£2,000); The Guards Museum (£1,000); Alzheimer's Research Trust, Help for Heroes and Paul Laurie Foundation (£500 each); and Shooting Stars Children's Hospice (£250).

Applications

This trust does not accept unsolicited applications.

The Whitecourt Charitable Trust

Christian, general

£50,000 (2009/10)

Beneficial area

UK and overseas, with a preference for South Yorkshire.

48 Canterbury Avenue, Fulwood, Sheffield S10 3RU
Tel: 0114 230 5555
Correspondent: Mrs G W Lee, Trustee
Trustees: P W Lee; G W Lee; M P W Lee.
CC Number: 1000012

Information available

Accounts were on file at the Charity Commission.

Most of the grants given by the trust are recurrent and to Christian causes in the UK and overseas. Other grants are given to a few Christian and welfare causes in Sheffield.

In 2009/10 there were 139 grants made totalling £50,000, of which Christ Church Fulwood received £9,750.

Other beneficiaries included: Monkton Combe School Bursary Fund (£3,000); Oaks Building Appeal (£2,500); Christian Aid (£2,000); Church Missionary Society and South Yorkshire Community Foundation (£1,100 each); and St John's College, Nottingham and Whirlow Grange (£1,000 each).

Exclusions

No support for animal or conservation organisations or for campaigning on social issues.

Applications

In writing to the correspondent, at any time. However, the trust states very little money is available for unsolicited applications, due to advance commitments.

A H and B C Whiteley Charitable Trust

Art, environment, general

£30,000 (2009/10)

Beneficial area

England, Scotland and Wales, with a special interest in Nottinghamshire.

Marchants Solicitors, Regent Chambers, Regent Street, Mansfield, Nottinghamshire NG18 1SW
Tel: 01623 655111
Correspondent: E G Aspley, Trustee
Trustees: E G Aspley; K E B Clayton.
CC Number: 1002220

Information available

Accounts were available from the Charity Commission.

The trust was established in 1990 and derives most of its income from investments. The trust deed requires the trustees to make donations to registered charities in England, Scotland and Wales but with particular emphasis on charities based in Nottinghamshire.

In 2009/10 the trust had assets of £1.3 million and an income of £40,000. Grants were made to four organisations totalling £30,000.

Beneficiaries were: National Trust and Collier Charity (£10,000 each); and Cats Protection League and Mansfield Choral Society (£5,000 each).

The trusts management and administration costs totalled £11,000.

Applications

The trust does not seek applications.

The Norman Whiteley Trust

Evangelical Christianity, welfare, education

£85,000 (2009/10)

Beneficial area

Worldwide, although in practice mainly Cumbria.

High Barugh, Gaisgill, Penrith, Cumbria CA10 3UD
Correspondent: The Trustees
Trustees: Miss P Whiteley; P Whiteley; D Dickson; J Ratcliff.
CC Number: 226445

Information available

Accounts were available from the Charity Commission.

This trust supports the furtherance of the Gospel, the relief of poverty and education. Grants can be made worldwide, but in practice are usually restricted to Cumbria and the surrounding areas.

In 2009/10 the trust had assets of £2.6 million and an income of £147,000. Grants were made to 36 organisations totalling £85,000.

Beneficiaries included: Kinder Und Jugendwerk (£9,000); South Lakes Youth for Christ and Kisi Kids – Kinder Machen (£6,000 each);

Greenstones Christian Trust and Osterreichische Evangelische Allianz (£5,000 each); New Life Church (£4,000); Let TL Children Come and Scripture Union (£2,700); Richard Foster and Step by Step (£1,000 each); and Harbour Light Church and The Olive Branch (£500 each).

Exclusions

Whilst certain overseas organisations are supported, applications from outside of Cumbria are not accepted.

Applications

In writing to the correspondent. Trustees meet to consider applications twice a year.

The Whitley Animal Protection Trust

Protection and conservation of animals and their environments

£367,000 (2009)

Beneficial area

UK and overseas, with a preference for Scotland.

Padmore House, Hall Court, Hall Park Way, Telford TF3 4LX
Tel: 01952 641651
Correspondent: M T Gwynne, Secretary
Trustees: E Whitley, Chair; Mrs P A Whitley; E J Whitley; J Whitley.
CC Number: 236746

Information available

Full accounts were on file at the Charity Commission.

This trust supports the prevention of cruelty to animals and the promotion of their conservation and environment. Grants are made throughout the UK and the rest of the world, with about 20% of funds given in Scotland.

In 2009 the trust had assets of £8 million and an income of £371,000. Grants to 16 organisations totalled £367,000.

Beneficiaries included: Whitley Fund for Nature (£192,700); Fauna and Flora International Northern White Rhino (£50,000); Fauna and Flora International and River and Fisheries Trust, Scotland (£20,000 each); and Edinburgh Zoo (£5,000).

Exclusions

No grants to non-registered charities.

Applications

The trust has previously stated that: 'The trust honours existing commitments and initiates new ones through its own contacts rather than responding to unsolicited applications.'

The Lionel Wigram Memorial Trust

General

£54,000 (2009/10)

Beneficial area

UK, with a preference for Greater London.

Highfield House, 4 Woodfall Street, London SW3 4DJ
Tel: 020 7730 6820
Correspondent: Tracy Pernice, PA to A F Wigram
Trustees: A F Wigram; Mrs S A Wigram.
CC Number: 800533

Information available

Accounts were available from the Charity Commission.

The trustees have particular regard to projects which will commemorate the life of Major Lionel Wigram who was killed in action in Italy in 1944. The trust makes grants to a wide range of organisations, especially in the illness and disabilities sector.

In 2009/10 the trust's assets totalled £685,000 and it had an income of £69,000. Grants totalled £54,000. The 49 donations (to 44 organisations) made in the year were broken down as follows:

Coping with illness and disability	22	£40,750
Community projects/helping the disadvantaged	20	£8,000
Performing arts	3	£3,500
Historical/restoration	2	£1,000
Conservation	1	£500
Research and prevention of Illness	1	£50

Beneficiaries included: U Can Do IT (£32,000 in four grants); Newbury Spring Festival Society Limited (£3,500 in three grants); Dressability, Eyeless Trust, Marine Conservation Society, The Respite Association, Access to Art, The Manna Society, The Passage and War Memorials Trust (£500 each); Child Bereavement Charity and Royal Hospital Chelsea (£100 each); and Jo's Trust (£50).

Applications

In writing to the correspondent.

The Richard Wilcox Welfare Charity

Health, medical research, welfare of patients, hospitals, animal welfare

£669,000 (2009/10)

Beneficial area

UK.

Herschel House, 58 Herschel Street, Slough SL1 1PG
Tel: 01753 551111
Correspondent: Richard Oury, Administrator
Trustees: John Ingram; Nick Sargent; Roger Danks.
CC Number: 1082586

Information available

Accounts were available from the Charity Commission.

Registered with the Charity Commission in September 2000, the objects of the trust are to:

- Prevent cruelty and to relieve the suffering and distress of animals of any species who are in need of care, attention and protection.
- Relieve sickness and protect and preserve good health.
- Promote the research and advancement of the causes and treatment of diseases.
- Relieve patients receiving treatment in hospital or on their discharge.
- Provide, maintain and improve hospitals and other institutions providing medical treatment.
- Assist or promote any charitable organisation or charitable purpose.

The following statement is taken from the trustees 2009/10 annual report:

Grants were given to a number of organisations including those operating the following charitable functions:

- Hospices
- Air Ambulance Rescue Services
- Wildlife Hospital
- Relief for those suffering from Aids in Africa
- Medical Research
- Parental guidance and training

The trustees have decided to close the charity and plan to wind up the affairs during the next 12 months.

In 2009/10 the charity had assets of almost £1.5 million and an income of £165,000. Grants totalled £669,000.

Beneficiaries were: Harlington Hospice (£500,000); Tiggywinkles (£100,000); Chiltern Air Ambulance and Nyumbarni (£60,000); Fairbridge (£25,000); Vision Aid Overseas and Friends & Family (£10,000 each) and Motor Neurone Disease Association (£4,000). The accounts listed 'DNA (accrual reversal) – £100,000)'.

Applications

In writing to the correspondent. The trustees meet quarterly to assess grant applications.

The Felicity Wilde Charitable Trust

Children, medical research

£138,000 (2009/10)

Beneficial area

UK.

Barclays Bank Trust Company Ltd, Estates and Trusts, Osborne Court, Gadbrook Park, Northwich, Cheshire CW9 7UE
Correspondent: Sarah Buckley, Trust Officer

Trustee: Barclays Bank Trust Co Ltd.
CC Number: 264404

Information available

Accounts were available from the Charity Commission.

The trust supports children's charities and medical research, with particular emphasis on research into the causes or cures of asthma. In 2009/10 it had assets of £1.6 million and an income of £71,000. Grants were made to 77 organisations totalling £138,000.

Grants included those made to: Asthma UK (£30,000); James Hopkins Trust and Joint Action (£5,000 each); Kidney Research UK and West Scotland Deaf Children's Society (£3,000 each); Happy Days Children's Charity and Medic Alert (£2,000 each); Kidscan, Shared Care Network (£1,000 each); and Christian Lewis Trust (£500).

Exclusions

No grants to individuals or non-registered charities.

Applications

In writing to the correspondent at any time. Applications are usually considered quarterly.

The Wilkinson Charitable Foundation

Scientific research

£38,000 (2009/10)

Beneficial area

UK.

c/o Lawrence Graham LLP, 4 More London Riverside, London SE1 2AU
Correspondent: B D S Lock, Trustee
Trustees: B D S Lock; G C Hurstfield.
CC Number: 276214

Information available

Full accounts were on file at the Charity Commission.

The trust was set up for the advancement of scientific knowledge and education at Imperial College – University of London. Grants are only given to academic institutions.

The trustees have continued their policy of supporting research and initiatives commenced in the founder's lifetime and encouraging work in similar fields to those he was interested in.

In 2009/10 the foundation had assets of £1.4 million and an income of £33,000. Grants to eight organisations totalled £38,000.

Beneficiaries included: Wolfson College – Oxford (£31,000); University College – London and Lady Margaret Hall Development Fund – Oxford (£2,500 each); British Heart Foundation and Alzheimer's Society (£500 each).

Exclusions

No grants to individuals.

Applications

In writing to the correspondent.

Common applicant mistakes

'They ignore the parameters set out in DSC publications and do not tailor their application.'

The Williams Charitable Trust

Education, medicine, theatre, general

£60,000 (2009/10)

Beneficial area

UK.

85 Capital Wharf, 50 Wapping High Street, London E1W 1LY
Correspondent: Stuart Williams, Trustee
Trustees: S K M Williams; H A Williams; J Riddick; A M Williams; M T M Williams.
CC Number: 1086668

Information available

Accounts were on file at the Charity Commission.

The objects of the trust are to support education and training, the advancement of medicine and general charitable purposes.

In 2009/10 the trust had assets of £2.5 million, an income of £42,000 and made 12 grants totalling £60,000.

Beneficiaries included: Donmar Warehouse (£25,000); Young Disciples (£10,000); Wilton Music Hall Trust (£5,000); Myelomia UK and Help for Heroes (£2000 each)

Applications

In writing to the correspondent.

The Williams Family Charitable Trust

Jewish

£33,500 (2010)

Beneficial area

Worldwide.

192 Gilbert Road, Cambridge CB4 3PB
Tel: 01223 570417
Email: bl10@cam.ac.uk
Correspondent: Barry Landy, Trustee
Trustees: Shimon Benison; Arnon Levy; Barry Landy.
CC Number: 255452

Information available

Information was on file at the Charity Commission, without a list of grants.

In 2010 this trust had an income of £41,000 and made grants totalling £33,500. Cash funds at year end were £13,400. No further information regarding grant giving was available for this year.

Previous beneficiaries have included But Chabad, Friends of Mifalhtorah for Shiloh, Holon Association for Absorption of Immigrants, Ingun Yedidut, Israel Concern Society, Karen Denny Pincus, Mogdal Un, Yedidut Maabeh Eliahu and Yesodrey Hetorah Schools.

Applications

In writing to the correspondent.

Dame Violet Wills Charitable Trust

Evangelical Christianity

£62,000 (2010)

Beneficial area

UK and overseas, but there may be a preference for Bristol.

3 Cedar Way, Portishead, Bristol BS20 6TT
Correspondent: Julian Marsh, Treasurer
Trustees: Julian Marsh; Margaret Lewis; Revd Dr Ernest Lucas; Revd Alexander Cooper; Revd Ray Lockhart; Derek Cleave; John Dean; Rosalind Peskett; Stuart Burton; Janet Persson; Rachel Daws; David Caporn; Mrs E Street.
CC Number: 219485

Information available

Accounts were obtained from the Charity Commission website.

The trust continues to operate within the original terms of reference, supporting evangelical Christian activities both within the UK and overseas. It is not the practice of the trustees to guarantee long-term support to any work, however worthy. The trust does not commonly supply funds to non-registered charities.

In 2010 the trust had assets of £1.6 million and an income of £72,000. Grants were made to 83 organisations totalling £62,000.

Beneficiaries included: WC and SWET – Evangelists Fund (£12,000); Bath Youth for Christ – Hope in our Schools and Echoes of Service – Bristol Missionaries (£2,000 each); Bristol International Student Centre (£1,200); Living Waters Radio Ministry (£500); and Langham Partnership – Hippo Project (£375).

Exclusions

No grants to individuals.

Applications

In writing to the correspondent. Trustees meet in March and in September.

Sumner Wilson Charitable Trust

General

£46,000 (2009/10)

Beneficial area

UK.

Munslows Accountants, Mansfield House, 2nd Floor, 1 Southampton Street, London WC2R 0LR
Tel: 020 7845 7500
Email: mail@munslows.co.uk
Correspondent: N A Steinberg, Trust Administrator
Trustees: Lord Joel G Joffe; Amanda W S Christie; Michael S Wilson.
CC Number: 1018852

Information available

Accounts were available from the Charity Commission.

This trust has general charitable purposes, with no preferences or exclusions. In 2009/10 it had assets of £2.5 million, an income of £34,000 and made grants totalling £46,000.

There were 19 grants of £1,000 or more listed in the accounts. Beneficiaries included: St James's Place Foundation (£19,000); Prostate Cancer Charitable Trust (£2,800); Full Circle Fund (£2,500); Friends of Young Carers – Swindon (£2,000); St Edwards School (£1,100); and Relate, Ride High, Lewisham Theatre, Breakthrough Cancer, AMREF and Rushmoor Healthy Living (£1,000 each).

Applications

In writing to the correspondent, or to the trustees.

The Benjamin Winegarten Charitable Trust

Jewish

£87,000 to organisations (2009/10)

Beneficial area

UK.

25 St Andrew's Grove, Stoke Newington, London N16 5NF
Correspondent: B A Winegarten, Trustee
Trustees: B A Winegarten; E Winegarten.
CC Number: 271442

Information available

Accounts were available from the Charity Commission, but without a list of grants.

This trust makes grants for the advancement of the Jewish religion and religious education. In 2009/10 it had assets of £768,000 and an income of £131,000, including £100,000 from donations and grants. Grants were made to 20 organisations totalling £87,000, with a further £5,000 going to 6 individuals.

Previous beneficiaries have included Hechal Hatovah Institute, the Jewish Educational Trust, the Mechinah School, Merkaz Lechinuch Torani Zichron Ya'akov, Ohr Someach Friends, Or Akiva Community Centre, Yeshivo Hovomo Talmudical College and ZSVT.

Applications

In writing to the correspondent.

The Francis Winham Foundation

Welfare of older people

£216,000 (2009/10)

Beneficial area

England.

41 Langton Street, London SW10 0JL
Tel: 020 7795 1261
Email: francinetrust@btopenworld.com
Correspondent: Mrs J Winham, Trustee
Trustees: Francine Winham; Josephine Winham; Elsa Peters.
CC Number: 278092

Information available

Accounts were available from the Charity Commission.

Grants are given to both national organisations (including their local branches) and local charities. Many organisations are regular recipients, although not necessarily on an annual basis.

In 2009/10 the trust had assets of £2.4 million, which generated an income of £81,000. There were 57 grants made totalling £216,000 (previously £1.5 million; which can be equated to a significant drop in investment income during the year).

Beneficiaries included: Pasque Charity – Keech Hospice Care (£50,000); SAFA (£22,000 in 70 donations); Help the Hospices (£15,000); Home Warmth for the Aged (£10,000); and Independence at Home (£5,000).

Applications

In writing to the correspondent. The trust regrets it cannot send replies to applications outside its specific field of help for older people. Applications should be made through registered charities or social services departments only.

Anona Winn Charitable Trust

Health, welfare, general

£105,000 (2009)

Beneficial area

UK.

New Inn Cottage, Croft Lane, Winstone, Cirencester GL7 7LN
Correspondent: The Trustees
Trustee: Trefoil Trustees Ltd.
CC Number: 1044101

Information available

Accounts were available from the Charity Commission.

Registered with the Charity Commission in February 1995, the trustees maintain a list of charitable organisations which it supports; this list is reviewed periodically. The trust will generally only support charities which are related to medicine, young people, people with disabilities, the arts and the armed forces.

In 2009 the trust had assets of £865,000 and an income of £37,000.

Grants to 17 organisations totalled £105,000.

Beneficiaries included: Charities Aid Foundation (£40,000); St Wilfrid's Hospice and Sussex Snowdrop Trust (£6,000 each); Ovarian Cancer Action and Help for Heroes (£5,000 each); Smile Train and Motor Neurone Disease Association (£4,000 each); Foundation for the Study of Infant Deaths (£3,000); Stonepillow and Beat (£2,000 each); and Racing Welfare (£1,000).

Exclusions

No applications are considered from individuals.

Applications

Applications will only be considered if received in writing and accompanied by the organisation's latest report and full accounts. The trustees usually meet in February and July to decide on distributions.

The Witzenfeld Foundation

General

£100,000 (2009/10)

Beneficial area

UK and Israel.

9 Chadwick Road, Westcliff on Sea, Essex SS0 8LS
Correspondent: Alan Witzenfeld, Trustee
Trustees: Alan Witzenfeld; Lyetta Witzenfeld; Emma Witzenfeld; Mark Witzenfeld.
CC Number: 1115034

Information available

Accounts are on file at the Charity Commission, without a list of donations.

Set up in 2006, in 2009/10 the foundation had an income of £86,000 and made grants totalling £100,000. Assets totalled £5,000.

The foundation's annual reports state:

> The foundation endeavours to distribute all the income it receives. During the year the foundation made donations to a variety of charities in both the UK and Israel.

Applications

In writing to the correspondent.

The Michael and Anna Wix Charitable Trust

Older people, disability, education, medicine and health, poverty, welfare, Jewish

£65,000 (2009/10)

Beneficial area

UK.

Portrait Solicitors, 1 Chancery Lane, London WC2A 1LF
Tel: 020 7092 6985
Correspondent: Sarah Hovil, Correspondent
Trustees: Mrs J B Bloch; D B Flynn; Miss Judith Portrait.
CC Number: 207863

Information available

Full accounts were available from the Charity Commission website.

In 2009/10 the trust had assets of £1.7 million and an income of £72,000. Grant Management and administration costs were £18,000. The accounts state that Miss J S Portrait and Mr D B Flynn are partners of Portrait Solicitors to whom fees of £11,272 (2009 -£10,612) including VAT were paid for legal services. Grants were made to 227 organisations totalling £65,000.

Beneficiaries included: British Friends of the Hebrew University, British Technion Society, Nightingale and Weizmann UK (£5,000 each); Jewish Care, Norwood and Pinhas Rutenberg Educational Trust (£2,000 each); World Jewish Relief (£1,000); Age Concern/Help the Aged, Alzheimer's Research Trust, Association of Jewish Refugees, British Friends of Neve Shalom, British Friends of Rambam Medical Centre, British ORT, Council of Christians and Jews, Friends of Alyn, Langdon Foundation, Shaare Zedek UK, UJIA and Wiener Library (£500 each). The remaining grants were for £200 or less and beneficiaries included: Action for Children, Action for Kids, Action for ME, Action for Russia's Children, British Liver Trust, British Lung Foundation, British Red Cross Society, Canine Partners, Care International UK, Magen David Adorn UK, Manchester Jewish Community Care, Medical Engineering Resource Unit, Meningitis Research Foundation, Target Ovarian Cancer, Target Tuberculosis, Vitalise, WellChild, Who Cares? Trust, WIZO UK and Youth Aliyah.

Exclusions

Applications from individuals are not considered. Grants are to national bodies rather than local branches or local groups.

Applications

In writing to the trustees. Applications are considered half-yearly. Only applications from registered charities are acknowledged. Frequent applications by a single charity are not appreciated.

Women's World Day of Prayer

Promotion of the Christian faith through education and literature and audio-visual material

£228,000 (2010)

Beneficial area

UK and worldwide.

Commercial Road, Tunbridge Wells, Kent TN1 2RR
Tel: 01892 541 411
Fax: 01892 541745
Email: office@wwdp-natcomm.org
Website: www.wwdp-natcomm.org
Correspondent: Mrs Mary Judd, Administrator
Trustees: Mrs J Hackett; Mrs Emma Wilcock; Mrs M M Barton.
CC Number: 233242

Information available

Accounts were available from the Charity Commission.

The trust makes grants to charitable Christian educational projects and Christian organisations publishing literature and audio-visual material designed to advance the Christian faith. Its full name is: National Committee of the Women's World Day of Prayer for England, Wales and Northern Ireland.

The main object of the trust is to unite Christians in prayer, focused in particular on a day of prayer in March each year. The trust's income is mainly from donations collected at this event. After the trust's expenses, including the costs of running the day of prayer, the income can be used for grantmaking.

In 2010 the trust had assets of £364,000 and an income of £538,000. Grants were made totalling £228,000.

Beneficiaries included: United Society of Christian Literature, Feed the Minds, Bible Society (£18,000 each); World in Need, Christian Aid, Wycliffe UK Ltd (£10,000 each); Bible Reading Fellowship, International Bible Reading Association (£7,500 each); Royal National Institution for the Blind (£4,000 each).

Exclusions

No grants to individuals.

Applications

In writing to the correspondent, before the end of June. Grants are made in November.

Common applicant mistakes

'Applicants which are not Christian charities apply.'

The Woodcock Charitable Trust

General, children

£129,000 (2010/11)

Beneficial area

UK.

Harcus Sinclair, 3 Lincoln's Inn Fields, London WC2A 3AA
Tel: 0207 242 9700
Correspondent: Lucy Gibson
Trustees: M N Woodcock; S M Woodcock.

CC Number: 1110896

Information available

Accounts were available from the Charity Commission.

Set up in 2005, in 2010/11 the trust had assets of £82,000 and an income of £128,000, mostly from donations and made grants totalling £129,000.

Grants included those to: Egmont Trust (£90,000); RNIB (£11,000); George Adamson Wildlife Preservation Trust and Kids Company (£5,000 each); Walden Spoon (£4,500); Surrey Air Ambulance and Tusk Trust (£1,000 each); and Action on Addiction (£750).

Applications

In writing to the correspondent.

Woodlands Green Ltd

Jewish

£230,000 (2009/10)

Beneficial area

Worldwide.

19 Green Walk, London NW4 2AL
Correspondent: J A Ost, Secretary
Trustees: A Ost; E Ost; D J A Ost; J A Ost; A Hepner.
CC Number: 277299

Information available

Accounts were on file at the Charity Commission, without a list of grants.

The trust's objectives are the advancement of the Orthodox Jewish faith and the relief of poverty. It mostly gives large grants to major educational projects being carried out by orthodox Jewish charities.

In 2009/10 the trust had assets of £1.3 million and both an income and expenditure of £230,000. During the year, the trust gave grants to over 40 organisations. No further information was available.

Previous beneficiaries have included Achisomoch Aid Co, Beis Soro Schneirer, Friends of Beis Yisroel Trust, Friends of Mir, Friends of Seret Wiznitz, Friends of Toldos Avrohom itzchok, JET, Kahal Imrei Chaim, Dizer Dalim Trust, NWLCM, TYY Square and UTA.

Exclusions

No grants to individuals, or for expeditions or scholarships.

Applications

In writing to the correspondent.

Woodroffe Benton Foundation

General

£217,000 (2009/10)

Beneficial area

UK.

6 Fernleigh Court, Harrow, London HA2 6NA
Tel: 020 8421 4120
Email: alan.king3@which.net
Correspondent: Alan King, Secretary
Trustees: J J Hope, Chair; P M Miles; C G Russell; Mrs Rita Drew; P Foster.
CC Number: 1075272

Information available

Accounts were available from the Charity Commission.

This trust makes grants towards:
- people in need, primary care of people who are sick or elderly or those affected by the results of a local or national disaster
- promotion of education
- conservation and improvement of the environment.

Most grants are for less than £2,000 – the trust does not normally make more than one grant to the same charity in a 12 month period.

In 2009/10 it had assets of £6.1 million and an income of £205,000. Grants totalled £217,000.

Beneficiaries included: Queen Elizabeth's Grammar School (£26,000); ; Community Links (£13,000); Ifield Park Care Home (£12,500); Furniture Re-use Network, Friendship Works, Young People's Trust for the Environment and Prisoners' Families and Friends (£5,000 each).

Exclusions

Grants are not made outside the UK and are only made to registered charities. No grants to individuals. Branches of UK charities should not apply, as grants, if made, would go to the charity's headquarters.

Applications

On a form available from the correspondent. Full guidance notes on completing the form and procedures for processing applications are sent with the form. Trustees meet quarterly.

The Woodward Charitable Trust

General

£240,000 (2009/10)

Beneficial area

Unrestricted.

Allington House, 1st Floor, 150 Victoria Street, London SW1E 5AE
Tel: 020 7410 0330
Fax: 020 7410 0332
Email: contact@woodward charitabletrust.org.uk
Website: www.woodward charitabletrust.org.uk
Correspondent: Karin Hooper, Administrator
Trustees: Camilla Woodward; Rt Hon. Shaun A Woodward; Judith Portrait.
CC Number: 299963

Information available

Annual report and accounts were available from the Charity Commission. The trust also has a clear and simple website.

This is one of the Sainsbury Family Charitable Trusts which share a joint administration but it operates quite differently to most others in this group in that it gives a large number of small grants in response to open application. It is the trust of Camilla Woodward (née Sainsbury) and her husband Shaun Woodward MP, Northern Ireland Secretary.

Guidelines

The following guidance is offered by the trust on its website:

The trustees favour small-scale, locally based initiatives. Funding is primarily for one-off projects, but the trustees are willing to consider funding for start-up or running costs (including core costs and salaries).

Please be clear when applying who the target users are and what your projected outcomes are. If this is a continuation of existing work what are your outcomes to date? If your project is on-going, how will it be sustainable? What are your plans for future/ongoing funding? If your request is for a one-off project, what will be its legacy? How many people will benefit from the grant? Trustees are interested in helping smaller organisations which offer direct services. Any participation by past or current users of the service should be mentioned and is encouraged.

Applications will only be considered if they fall within the following areas:

1 Children and young people who are isolated, at risk of exclusion or involved in anti-social behaviour.
2 Minority groups including refugees, gypsies and travellers. Projects that promote integration and community cohesion will be favoured.
3 Prisoners and ex-offenders. Projects that help the rehabilitation and resettlement of prisoners and/or ex-offenders are supported as well as requests to help prisoners families.
4 Disability projects which can include rehabilitation and training for people who are either physically disabled or learning disabled, as well as help to improve employment prospects.
5 Homelessness, especially affecting young people and women, and covering facilities such as women's refuges.
6 Arts outreach work by local groups for the benefit of disadvantaged people.
7 Environmental projects, especially with a strong educational element.

Exclusions

Trustees review grant applications twice a year, usually in January and July. Please consult the diary page for up-to-date deadlines for receipt of applications.

Types of grants

- Small grants, £100–£5,000 (around 100 grants made per year). Charities should note that only 19 grants for £3,000 or more were made in 2010/11).
- Large grants, over £5,000 (around 6 grant are made per year). Large grants are mainly give to charities already known to the Trustees.

Please note that applications for large grants will automatically be rejected unless they are discussed with the administrator prior to submission.

- Children's summer playscheme grants £500–£1,000 (about 35 grants made per year). Applications for these are made separately and considered in May each year. The charities annual income should be under £100,000.

Grantmaking in 2009/10

In 2009/10 the trust had assets of £9.9 million and an income of £318,000. Grants were paid during the year totalling £240,000, and were categorised as follows:

Community and social welfare	42	£144.000
Disability and health	17	£39,000
Summer schemes	31	£29,000
Education	4	£14,600
Arts	2	£6,000
Environment	2	£7,000
Total	**98**	**£240,000**

The following are examples of grants that were made during the year, including a description of the trust's interests in each category taken from the accounts.

Community and social welfare

Grants funded in this category cover projects which range from: employment skills training; services for victims of domestic violence; English lessons for refugees and asylum seekers and computer classes and life skills for ex-offenders.

Beneficiaries included: Unlock-National Association of Reformed Offenders (£15,000); International Children's Trust (£10,000); Friends, Families and Travellers (£7,700); First Step Drop-in Centre (£5,000); Friends First (£4,000); Changing Tunes (£3,000); Behind Closed Doors (£2,500); East Cleveland Youth Housing Trust (£1,200) and Get Hooked on Fishing Midlands (£1,000).

Disability and health

This year disability and health grants were awarded to young adults for help with learning difficulties, horticultural skills, equipment, court hire and transport for BME disabled basketball players, amongst other things.

Beneficiaries included: Soundabout (£5,000); U Can Do It (£4,800); Oxford Parent-Infant Project (£3,000); Reach Inclusive Arts

(£2,500) and Anglo-Egyptian Society (£1,000).

Summer schemes

The trustees' 2010 annual report states:

> Every year the trustees make small grants for summer playschemes during the long summer holidays for children between the ages of 5–16 who come from disadvantaged backgrounds. Only charities whose annual income is £100,000 or less can apply. The playschemes funded are inclusive and encourage integration both by accepting those of differing abilities as well as different social and racial backgrounds. Funds have also been made to train past users to come back as volunteers.

Beneficiaries included: Derby Kids Camp; Hart Voluntary Action; Hollow Lane Club; Rainbow Film Society (£1,000 each).

Education

The report outlines this area as follows:

> The education grants have varied from funding education offers to museums to family literacy projects in the community and upgrading equipments in museums for public use

Beneficiaries were: Story Museum (£5,000); Reading Quest (£3,000) and The Sainsbury Archive (£1,000).

Arts

It goes on to detail arts projects as follows:

> Arts projects which the trustees favour have a variety of purposes. Through art, music or performing arts, projects funded help to combat social isolation and change the behaviour of those 'at risk' providing an arena in which to address social problems and help disadvantaged young people achieve their potential.

Beneficiaries were: National Opera Studio (£5,000); Theatre Modo and Young Musicians Symphony Orchestra (£3,000).

And finally, the report states:

Environment
The trustees have supported schemes to help volunteers recycle goods that might have gone to landfill sites and redistribute them to people suffering from poverty. Other grants have funded programmes in schools to inspire and empower young people to look after their environment for the future as well as encouraging sustainable energy projects.

Beneficiaries were: The Ashden Awards (£5,000) and Wester Hailes Youth Agency (£2,000).

Exclusions

Trustees will not normally fund:

- charities whose annual turnover exceeds £250,000
- construction projects such as playgrounds, village halls, and disabled accesses
- general school appeals including out of hours provision
- hospices
- medical research
- parish facilities
- playgroups and pre-school groups
- requests for vehicles.

Trustees will definitely not support

- individuals in any capacity
- educational fees.

Applications

On simple application forms available from the trust, or via its website. Potential applicants are invited to telephone the administrator in advance to discuss the advisability of making an application.

Main grants are allocated following trustees' meetings in January and July each year, with the exception of summer schemes, which are considered at the beginning of May each year. All application forms are assessed on arrival and if additional information is required you will be contacted further. Applicants must make sure the trust receives a project budget and audited accounts.

The trust's website has a useful diary of trustees' meetings and of the cut-off dates for applications.

The A and R Woolf Charitable Trust

General

£28,000 (2009/10)

Beneficial area

Worldwide; UK, mainly in Hertfordshire.

c/o Griffiths Preston Accountants, Aldbury House, Dower Mews,

08 High Street, Berkhamsted,
Hertfordshire HP4 2BL
Tel: 01442 870277
Correspondent: The Trustees
Trustees: Andrew Rose; Dr Gillian
Edmonds; Stephen Rose; Joyce Rose.
CC Number: 273079

Information available

Accounts were available from the
Charity Commission.

The trust supports a range of causes,
including animal welfare and
conservation causes, Jewish
organisations, children and health
and welfare charities. Both UK and
overseas charities (through a British-
based office) receive support, together
with local charities. Most of the
grants are recurrent.

In 2009/10 the trust had assets of
£2.6 million and an income of
£50,000. Grants totalled £28,000. A
detailed grants list was not provided
but the trust did make the following
comments on one of its major
beneficiaries:

> Amongst the donations for the year
> was a donation of £10,000 to UNICEF.
> It is intended to continue our policy of
> making donations to UNICEF in
> subsequent years as the trustees are
> impressed with the work of that
> organisation in health and education
> provision internationally, particularly in
> Africa and Afghanistan for women and
> children.

Previous beneficiaries include: Central
British Fund for World Jewish Relief,
the Peace Hospice, University of
Hertfordshire Charitable Trust,
Northwood Pinner Liberal
Synagogue, RSPCA, WWF UK, the
Multiple Sclerosis Society, Jewish
Child's Day, Wellbeing for Women,
National Schizophrenia Fellowship,
International Primate Protection
League UK, the Hertfordshire and
Middlesex Wildlife Trust and
Senahasa Trust.

Exclusions

No grants to individuals or non-
registered charities unless schools,
hospices and so on.

Applications

Support is only given to projects/
organisations/causes personally known
to the trustees. The trust does not
respond to unsolicited applications.

The Fred and Della Worms Charitable Trust

Jewish, social welfare, health, education, arts, youth

£78,000 (2009/10).

Beneficial area

UK.

35 King David Gardens, 27 King
David Street, Jerusalem, 94101, Israel
Tel: 00 972 2 6246 993
Email: fredsimonworms@gmail.com
Correspondent: The Trustees
Trustees: Mrs D Worms;
M D Paisner; F S Worms;
A D Harverd.
CC Number: 200036

Information available

Accounts were available from the
Charity Commission.

In 2009/10 the trust had assets of
£1.9 million and an income of
£81,000. Grants were made totalling
£78,000 and were categorised as
follows:

Social and healthcare	£54,000
Education	£17,000
Youth	£5,000
Arts	£1,000
Religion	£800

Grant beneficiaries included: British
Friends of Jerusalem Foundation
(£50,000); UJIA (£10,000); Maccabi
GB (£5,000); JNF Charitable Trust
and Highgate Synagogue (£1,000);

Exclusions

No grants to individuals.

Applications

The trust has previously stated that
its funds were fully committed.

The Diana Edgson Wright Charitable Trust

Animal conservation, social welfare, general

£54,000 (2009)

Beneficial area

UK with some preference for Kent.

c/o 2 Stade Street, Hythe, Kent
CT21 6BD
Correspondent: R H V Moorhead,
Trustee
Trustees: R H V Moorhead; P Edgson
Wright; H C D Moorhead.
CC Number: 327737

Information available

Full accounts were available from the
Charity Commission.

The trust has general charitable
purposes; the policy is to support a
small number of charities. In 2009 the
trust had assets of £1.3 million, which
generated an income of £46,000.
Grants were made to 51 organisations
totalling £54,000.

Grants included those made to:
Barbourne Church of England School
(£5,000); Gurkha Welfare Trust
(£3,000); Chernobyl Children's
Lifeline (£2,000); Smeeth Parish Club
(£1,500); Caledott Foundation, the
Donkey Sanctuary and Kent Air
Ambulance (£1,000 each); Camphill
Family, Folkestone Rainbow Trust,
Kent Minds and Mouth and Foot
Painting Artists (£500 each).

Applications

In writing to the correspondent.

The Matthews Wrightson Charity Trust

General, smaller charities

£72,000 to organisations and
individuals (2010)

Beneficial area

UK and some overseas.

The Old School House, Church Lane, Easton, Hampshire S021 1 EH
Tel: 0845 2412574
Correspondent: Jon Mills, Secretary and Administrator
Trustees: Priscilla W Wrightson; Robert Partridge; Guy D G Wrightson; Isabelle S White; Maria de Broe Ferguson.
CC Number: 262109

Information available

Accounts were on file at the Charity Commission.

The trustees favour smaller charities or projects e.g. those seeking to raise under £25,000 and usually exclude large national charities and those with turnover in excess of £250,000.

In 2010 it had assets of £1.4 million and an income of £64,000. There were 133 grants made totalling £72,000, including grants to individuals. Donations were broken down as follows:

Youth	26	£12,000
Third world	9	£7,000
Disabled	31	£15,500
Individuals	8	£3,000
Christian	7	£4,000
Rehabilitation	3	£4,000
Arts	20	£15,000
Poor and homeless	9	£4,000
Medical	7	£2,700
Elderly	2	£1,000
Miscellaneous	7	£3,000

The trustees gave to a wide range of charities. Help Tibet, Karuna Home, Nisthma Rural Health Centre and Pimlico Opera each received £1,200. Most other donations, with a few exceptions, were for £500.

Awards totalling £10,000 were made to support students at the Royal College of Art who find their grants and other income inadequate (hardship grants), and awards totalling £5,000 were made to students to further ideas for UK industrial production (starting your own business awards).

In addition to donations to charitable bodies and students at the RCA, the MWCT also gives to trainee doctors for medical elective expenses and to individual students taking 'gaps' abroad for personal development. In particular, a close relationship exists with the Daneford Trust, and several of its clients received grants from the trust. In both categories preference is given to those undertaking charitable projects when abroad or visiting third-world countries in need. By spreading its donations, the MWCT avoids becoming too significant a funder of any charity.

Previous beneficiaries of larger grants included: Tools for Self-Reliance (£2,400); and the Butler Trust, Childhood First, the Daneford Trust, DEMAND, Live Music Now! New Bridge and Practical Action (£1,200 each). Most other donations, with a few exceptions, were for £400 or £500 each.

Exclusions

The trust states: 'The trustees would not normally support the maintenance of the fabric of churches, schools and village halls, and do not make donations to animal charities.'

Applications

In writing to the correspondent including a set of accounts. Applications received are considered by the trustees on a monthly basis. Applicants who wish to be advised of the outcome of their application must include an sae. Successful applicants are advised of the trustees' decision at the earliest opportunity.

Wychdale Ltd

Jewish

£430,000 (2009/10)

Beneficial area

UK and abroad.

89 Darenth Road, London N16 6EB
Correspondent: The Secretary
Trustees: C D Schlaff; J Schlaff; Mrs Z Schlaff.
CC Number: 267447

Information available

Accounts were on file at the Charity Commission.

The objects of this charity are the advancement of the Orthodox Jewish religion and the relief of poverty in the UK and abroad. The charity stated in its 2009/10 accounts that it 'invites applications from religious and educational institutions as well as organisations providing services for the relief of poverty both in the UK and abroad'.

In 2009/10 the trust had assets of £1.5 million and an income of £218,000. Grants were made totalling £430,000 and were broken down into the following categories:

General charitable purposes	£47,000
Advancement of religion	£103,000
Religious education	£79,000
Relief of poverty	£194,000

Beneficiaries included: Dajtrain Ltd (£28,000); United Ttalmudical Associates (£24,000); the Society of Friends of the Torah (£18,000); Chevras Mo'oz Ladol (£16,000); and Tomchei Sharei Zion (£10,000).

Exclusions

Non-Jewish organisations are not supported.

Applications

In writing to the correspondent.

Wychville Ltd

Jewish, education, general

About **£600,000** (2009/10)

Beneficial area

UK.

44 Leweston Place, London N16 6RH
Correspondent: Mrs S Englander, Secretary
Trustees: B Englander, Chair; S Englander; E Englander; B R Englander.
CC Number: 267584

Information available

Accounts were on file at the Charity Commission, but without a list of grants.

This trust supports educational, Jewish and other charitable organisations.

In 2009/10 the trust had assets of £105,000 and an income of £622,000, mostly from donations. No further information was available.

Applications

In writing to the correspondent.

The Wyseliot Charitable Trust

Medical, welfare, arts

£98,000 (2009/10)

Beneficial area

UK.

7 Chelsea Square, London SW3 6LF
Correspondent: J H Rose, Trustee
Trustees: Jonathan Rose; Emma Rose; Adam Raphael.
CC Number: 257219

Information available

Accounts were on file at the Charity Commission.

This trust gives grants in the following areas: medical, especially cancer research and care; welfare; and arts, including music, visual arts and literature.

In 2009/10 the trust had assets of £1.57 million, which generated an income of £96,000. Grants were made to 25 organisations totalling £98,000.

Beneficiaries included: Alzheimer's Trust, Cystic Fibrosis Trust, Royal Marsden Cancer Fund, MIND, Royal College of Music, Trinity Hospice, Cancer Relief Macmillan Fund and St Mungo's Trust (£5,000 each); Notting Hill Foundation (£4,000); and Runnymede Trust (£2,000).

Exclusions

Local charities are not supported. No support for individuals; grants are only made to registered charities.

Applications

In writing to the correspondent; however, note that the trust states that the same charities are supported each year, with perhaps one or two changes. It is unlikely new charities sending circular appeals will be supported and large UK charities are generally not supported.

Yankov Charitable Trust

Jewish

£120,000 (2009/10)

Beneficial area

Worldwide.

40 Wellington Avenue, London N15 6AS
Tel: 2030143974
Correspondent: The Trustees
Trustees: J Schonberg; Mrs B S Schonberg.
CC Number: 1106703

Information available

Accounts were on file at the Charity Commission without a list of grant beneficiaries.

The trust was established in 2004 for the advancement of the Jewish religion and culture among the Jewish community throughout the world.

In 2009/10 the trust had assets of £116,000 and an income of £250,000 including £200,000 from donations received. Grants totalled £120,000. No further grant information was available.

Previous grant beneficiaries include: European Yarchei Kalloh (£53,000); Keren Machzikei Torah (£23,000); Kollel Tiferes Chaim (£21,000); Agudas Israel Housing Association (£12,000); Ponovez Hachnosos Kalloh (£7,600); Freiman Appeal (£7,200); Beth Jacob Grammar School (£4,000); British Friends of Tiferes Chaim (£3,000); Yeshiva Tzemach Yisroel (£2,000); British Friends of Rinat Ahsron (£1,500); and Yeshivat Givat Shaul (£1,000).

Applications

In writing to the correspondent.

The Yapp Charitable Trust

Social welfare

£293,000 (2009/10)

Beneficial area

England and Wales.

8 Leyburn Close, Ouston, Chester le Street DH2 1TD
Tel: 0191 4922118
Email: info@yappcharitabletrust.org.uk
Website: www.yappcharitabletrust.org.uk
Correspondent: Joanne Anderson, Administrator
Trustees: David Aeron-Thomas; Revd Timothy C Brooke; Annette Figueiredo; Ron Lis; Stephanie Willats.
CC Number: 1076803

Information available

Accounts were on file at the Charity Commission. The trust has a clear and helpful website.

The Yapp Charitable Trust was formed in 1999 from the Yapp Welfare Trust (two-thirds share) and Yapp Education and Research Trust (one-third share). However, rather than combining the criteria for the two trusts, the trustees decided to focus on small charities, usually local rather than UK wide charities. The trust now accepts applications only from small charities and organisations with a turnover of less than £60,000 in the year of application. The objects are restricted to registered charities in England or Wales.

The trust's website has a link to its *Printed Guidelines* which gives the following information and advice:

Eligibility Criteria

We only offer grants for core funding to registered charities with a total annual expenditure of less than £40,000 who are undertaking work that focuses on one of our priority groups:

- Elderly people
- Children and young people aged 5–25
- People with disabilities or mental health problems
- Moral welfare–people trying to overcome life-limiting problems of a social, rather than medical, origin (such as addiction, relationship difficulties, abuse, offending)
- Education and learning (with a particular interest in people who are educationally disadvantaged, whether adults or children)

We only make grants for core funding. We define core funding as the costs associated with regular activities or services that have been ongoing for at least a year. We can not fund new projects, extra services or additional delivery costs. This includes creating a paid post for work that is currently undertaken on a voluntary basis or rent for premises that are currently cost free.

We can only offer grants to registered charities that have been formally established for a minimum of 3 years.

Newly registered charities may apply but the organisation must have appointed a management committee and adopted a governing document at least 3 years ago.

To ensure that our grants offer some realistic help we will not contribute towards organisational budgets with a shortfall in excess of £10,000 in the first year.

Grant Making Policy

We will fund running costs for up to three years. Grants are normally for a maximum of £3,000 per year. Most of our grants are for more than one year because we like to fund ongoing needs. We prefer to make a grant when other funding is coming to an end. We prioritise:

- Work that is unattractive to the general public or unpopular with other funders
- Services that help to improve the lives of marginalised, disadvantaged or isolated people
- Applicants that can demonstrate an effective use of volunteers
- Charities that seek to be preventive and aim to change opinion and behaviour through raising awareness of issues, education and campaigning
- Applicants that can demonstrate (where feasible) an element of self sustainability by charging subscriptions/fees to service users

Applications that don't address at least two of the above are unlikely to receive a grant.

In 2009/10 the trust had assets of £5.4 million and an income of £207,000. Grants totalled £293,000.

Beneficiaries included: Working together (£9,000); Disability Advice Service (East Suffolk) (£7,500); Hillingdon Asian Women Group (£6,000); Community Transport Helpline (£4,500); Carrs Lane Counselling Centre (£4,000) and Four Seasons Activity Group (£3,000)

Exclusions

The *Printed Guidelines* give the following exclusions:

- Charities with a total annual expenditure of more than £40,000
- Charities that are not registered with the Charity Commission in England & Wales. You must have your own charity number or be excepted from registration. Industrial Provident Societies and Community Interest Companies are not eligible to apply
- Work that is based in Scotland or Northern Ireland
- Charities with unrestricted reserves that equate to more than 12 months expenditure

- Branches of National Charities. You must have your own charity number, not a shared national registration
- New organisations – you must have been operating as a fully constituted organisation for at least 3 years, even though you may have registered as a charity more recently
- New work that has not been occurring for at least a year
- New paid posts – even if the work is now being done by volunteers
- Additional activities, expansion or development plans
- Special events, trips or outings
- Capital expenditure – including equipment, buildings, renovations, furnishings, minibuses
- Work with under 5s
- Childcare
- Holidays and holiday centres
- Core funding of charities that benefit the wider community such as general advice services and community centres unless a significant element of their work focuses on one of our priority groups
- Bereavement support
- Debt advice
- Community safety initiatives
- Charities raising money to give to another organisation, such as schools, hospitals or other voluntary groups
- Individuals – including charities raising funds to purchase equipment for or make grants to individuals

Applications

The application form is available to download on the trust's website. The *Printed Guidelines* give the following information on the trust's new applications policy:

In August 2011 we revised our criteria and funding priorities following a review of our grant making policy and updated our guidelines and application form at the same time. Please read these updated guidelines carefully as they outline some important changes to what we can fund. We stopped considering requests for funding made on the old application form from 30th September 2011.

One of the biggest changes is that we can now only offer grants to registered charities with an annual expenditure of less than £40,000.

Common applicant mistakes

'Applying with expenditure over £60,000 per annum; not a registered charity; individuals applying.'

The Yardley Great Trust

General

£55,000 (2010)

Beneficial area

The ancient parish of Yardley now part of the County of West Midlands. This includes the wards of Yardley, Acocks Green, Fox Hollies, Billesley, Hall Green and parts of the wards of Hodge Hill, Shard End, Sheldon, Small Heath, Sparkhill, Moseley, Stechford, Sparkbrook and Brandwood. (A map is available on request.).

Old Brookside, Yardley Fields Road, Stechford, Birmingham B33 8QL
Tel: 0121 784 7889
Fax: 0121 785 1386
Email: enquiries@ygtrust.org.uk
Website: www.yardley-great-trust.org.uk
Correspondent: Mrs K L Grice, Clerk to the Trustees
Trustees: Mrs I Aylin, Chair; Revd A Bullock; Mrs J Hayes; Mrs J Holt; Cllr Mrs B Jackson; C James; Revd J Ray; Revd J Richards; K Rollins; Revd J Self; Revd D Senior; M Cox; W Sands; A Veitch; R Jones.
CC Number: 216082

Information available

Accounts were available from the Charity Commission.

This charity is probably the earliest recorded Birmingham charity, originating when John de Yeardley made over all his lands to the poor in 1335. In 1531, other local charities were grouped together under the title the Yardley Great Trust. The trust still owns the freehold land, on which it has built five sheltered housing complexes and a care home and has a piece of land covering about eight acres in Sparkhill which is used for allotments.

The trust's priority is maintaining its own properties mentioned above. After this it makes grants to help the fight against poverty in South East Birmingham, supporting organisations as well as providing basic household essentials such as cookers and beds directly to individuals. In line with the trust's second broad aim of providing high quality care and housing for older people the trust also owns a nursing home, which is operated by another charity.

In 2010 the trust had assets of £6.3 million and an income of £1.6 million. Grants to organisations totalled £30,000.

Christmas monies were distributed totalling £2,400. A further £24,000 was disbursed in grants of less than £500 to individuals.

Grants to organisations included: Birmingham and Solihull Women's Aid (£7,500); St Richard's Community Centre (£5,000); Greswold House £2,000); St Michaels Meals on Wheels & Day Centre, Ninestiles School/Westmidlands Police (1,500 each); Stay (£1,000); and Church of Ascension (£600).

Applications
On a form available from the correspondent. Applications from individuals should be via a third party. Applications are considered on the second Thursday of each month.

Common applicant mistakes
Not supplying enough information about why they need us to provide funding, or whether they have already exhausted all other avenues.'

The Dennis Alan Yardy Charitable Trust

General
£28,000 (2009/10)

Beneficial area
Overseas and UK with a preference for the East Midlands.

PO Box 5039, Spratton, Northampton NN6 8YH
Correspondent: The Secretary
Trustees: Dennis Alan Yardy, Chair; Mrs Christine Anne Yardy; Jeffrey Creek; Mrs Joanne Stoney.
CC Number: 1039719

Information available
Accounts were available from the Charity Commission, but without a grants list.

This trust was established in 1993. It supports major UK and international charities and those within the East Midlands area. In 2009/10 the trust had assets of £512,000, an income of £24,000 and made grants totalling £28,000.

Exclusions
No grants to individuals or non-registered charities.

Applications
In writing to the correspondent.

The York Children's Trust

Young people under the age of 25
£76,000 (2010)

Beneficial area
Within 20 miles of York City.

29 Whinney Lane, Harrogate, North Yorkshire HG2 9LS
Tel: 01423 524765
Email: yorkchildrenstrust@hotmail.co.uk
Correspondent: Margaret Brien, Secretary
Trustees: Colin Stroud; Mark Sessions; Lenore J Hill; Keith Hayton; Peter Watson; William Miers; Lynn Wagstaff; Alan D Ward; Anne Kelly; Percy Roberts; Rosalind F Fitter; Julie A Simpson; Dawn M Moores; Kathy Pickard; Kitty Lamb.
CC Number: 222279

Information available
Accounts were on file at the Charity Commission

The trust's objects are the relief of needy children and needy young persons under 25 years of age, including the advancement of the education of such children and young persons living within a 20 mile radius of York.

In 2010 the trust had assets of £2.1 million and an income of

£79,000. Grants totalled £76,000, of which £36,000 was made to organisations and £40,000 to individuals.

Beneficiaries included: City of York Council (£8,000); CFS York (£5,000); Calvert Carpets (£4,000); Heworth Green Nursery (£3,000); York City Knights Foundation, Child Development Centre (£2,000 each); Home Start York (£1,500); Market Weighton Scout & Guide HQ, LIPA and Peter Pan Nursery (£1,000 each).

Exclusions
The trust will not normally give grants for private education fees. Exceptions may be made where unforeseen circumstances, such as the death of a parent, would prevent a child completing the last year of a critical stage of education such as A-levels.

Applications
In writing to the correspondent.

The John Young Charitable Settlement

General
£47,000 (2009/10)

Beneficial area
UK and overseas.

c/o Lee Associates, 5 Southampton Place, London WC1A 2DA
Tel: 020 7025 4600
Correspondent: Ken Hawkins
Trustees: J M Young; D P H Burgess.
CC Number: 283254

Information available
Basic details taken from the Charity Commission website.

In 2009/10 the trust had no income and an expenditure of £47,000. Accounts were not required by the Charity Commission because of the low (nil) income figure.

Previous beneficiaries included: Caius House (£13,000); the Boulase Smart, Médecins du Monde, Pancreatic Cancer Research Fund, RSBP and St Barnabas Hospice Trust (£5,000 each); Chichester Harbour Trust (£2,000); and Action Aid (£250).

Applications

In writing to the correspondent.

The William Allen Young Charitable Trust

General, health, social welfare

£470,000 (2009/10)

Beneficial area

UK, with a preference for South London, occasionally overseas.

Young & Co.'s Brewery PLC, Riverside House, 26 Osiers Road, London SW18 1NH
Tel: 0208 875 7000
Correspondent: Torquil Sligo-Young
Trustees: T C Young; J G A Young; T F B Young.
CC Number: 283102

Information available

Accounts were available from the Charity Commission.

The trust supports humanitarian causes, with a large number of health organisations supported each year. Grants are made to local and national organisations throughout the UK, although there appears to be a preference for South London.

In 2009/10 the trust had assets of £16.8 million with an income of £420,000 and made 281 grants totalling £470,000.

Beneficiaries included: Anti Slavery International, the British Consular Age Concern Partnership Project and Gonville and Caius College, Cambridge (£20,000 each); British Benevolent Fund of Madrid and the Cardinal Hume Centre (£10,000 each); Somerset Otter Group (£8,000); Wimbledon Cricket Club (£5,000).

Applications

The trust has stressed that all funds are committed and consequently unsolicited applications will not be supported.

Zephyr Charitable Trust

Community, environment, social welfare

£48,000 (2009/10)

Beneficial area

UK and worldwide.

Luminary Finance LLP, PO Box 135, Longfield, Kent DA3 8WF
Correspondent: The Trust Administrator
Trustees: Elizabeth Breeze; Marigo Harries; David Baldock; Donald I Watson.
CC Number: 1003234

Information available

Accounts were on file at the Charity Commission.

The trust's grants are particularly targeted towards three areas:
- enabling lower income communities to be self-sustaining
- the protection and improvement of the environment
- providing relief and support for those in need, particularly from medical conditions or social or financial disadvantage.

In 2009/10 the trust had assets of £1.3 million and an income of £45,000. There were 21 grants made totalling £48,000 which were listed in the accounts as 21 'subscriptions'.

Beneficiaries during the year included: Friends of the Earth Trust; Medical Foundation for the Victims of Torture (£2,500 each); Organic Research Centre – Elm Farm; Hearing Research Trust (Deafness Research UK), UNICEF and Womankind (£2,000 each); Margaret Pyke Trust and MERLIN (Medical Emergency Relief International) (£1,500 each).

Exclusions

No grants to individuals, expeditions or scholarships.

Applications

In writing to the correspondent. The trustees usually meet to consider grants in July each year. Unsolicited

applications are unlikely to be successful, since the trust makes annual donations to a list of beneficiaries. However, the trust stated that unsolicited applications are considered on a quarterly basis by the trustees and very occasional support is given. Telephone applications are not accepted.

The Marjorie and Arnold Ziff Charitable Foundation

General, education, Jewish, arts, youth, older people, medicine

£1.5 million (2009/10)

Beneficial area

UK, with a preference for Yorkshire, especially Leeds and Harrogate.

Town Centre House, The Merrion Centre, Leeds LS2 8LY
Tel: 0113 222 1234
Correspondent: Ann McGookin, Secretary
Trustees: Dr Marjorie E Ziff; Michael A Ziff; Edward M Ziff; Mrs Ann L Manning.
CC Number: 249368

Information available

Full accounts were available from the Charity Commission website.

This trust likes to support causes that will provide good value for the grant made by benefiting a large number of people, as well as encouraging others to make contributions to the work. This includes a wide variety of schemes that involve the community at many levels, including education, public places, the arts and helping people who are disadvantaged. Capital costs and building work are particularly favoured by the trustees, as they feel projects such as these are not given the support they deserve from statutory sources.

In 2009/10 the trust had assets of £4.9 million and an income of £625,000. There were 127 grants made totalling £1.5 million.

The beneficiaries of the largest grants were: the University of Leeds (£1.25 million); United Jewish Israel Appeal (£67,000); Leeds Jewish Welfare Board (£34,000); Leeds International Pianoforte Competition and Maccabi GB (£13,000 each); and the Chief Rabbinate Charitable Trust and Wellington College (£10,000 each).

Other beneficiaries included: Lifeline for the Old and Western Marble Arch Synagogue (£6,000 each); Aish Hatorah UK Limited, Donisthorpe Hall and Leeds Lubavitch (£5,000 each); Community Security Trust (£3,000); Keren Roi and YABC – Club for Young People (£2,000 each); United Synagogue and Yorkshire Chaplaincy Board (£1,000 each); Marie Curie Cancer Care, The Place2Be (£500 each); Friends of Roundhay Park (£200); and Havens Christian Hospice and The Anne Frank Trust (£50 each).

Exclusions
No grants to individuals.

Applications
In writing to the correspondent. Replies will only be given to a request accompanied by an sae. Please note that funds available from the trust are limited and requests not previously supported are unlikely to be successful. Initial telephone calls are welcome but please note the foregoing comments.

Subject index

The following subject index begins with a list of categories used. The categories are very wide-ranging to keep the index as simple as possible. DSC's subscription website (www.trustfunding.org.uk)has a much more detailed search facility on the categories. There may be considerable overlap between the categories – for example, children and education, or older people and social welfare.

The list of categories is followed by the index itself. Before using the index, please note the following:

How the index was compiled

1) The index aims to reflect the most recent grant-making practice. It is therefore based on our interpretation of what each trust has actually given to, rather than what its policy statement says or its charitable objects allow it to do in principle. For example, where a trust states that it has general charitable purposes, but its grants list shows a strong preference for welfare, we index it under welfare.

2) We have tried to ensure that each trust has given significantly in the areas where it is indexed (usually at least £15,000). Thus small, apparently untypical grants have been ignored for index purposes.

3) The index has been complied from the latest information available to us.

Limitations

1) Policies may change; some more frequently than others.

2) Sometimes there will be a geographical restriction on a trust's grantgiving which is not shown in this index, or the trust may not give for the specific purposes you require under that heading. It is important to read each entry carefully.

You will need to check:

(a) The trust gives in your geographical area of operation.

(b) The trust gives for the specific purposes you require.

(c) There is no other reason to prevent you making an application to this trust.

3) It is worth noting that one or two of the categories list almost half the trusts included in this guide.

Under no circumstances should the index be used as a simple mailing list. Remember: each trust is different. Often the policies or interests of a particular trust do not fit easily into the given categories. Each entry must be read individually before you send off an application. Indiscriminate applications are usually unsuccessful. They waste time and money and greatly annoy trusts.

The categories are as follows:

Arts, culture, sport and recreation *page 449*

A very wide category including performing, written and visual arts, crafts, theatres, museums and galleries, heritage, architecture and archaeology, sports.

Children and young people *page 450*

Mainly for welfare and welfare-related activities.

Development, housing and employment *page 452*

This includes specific industries such as leather making or textiles.

Disability *page 452*

Disadvantaged people *page 453*

This includes people who are:

- Socially excluded
- socially and economically disadvantaged
- unemployed
- homeless
- offenders
- educationally disadvantaged
- victims of social/natural occurrences, including refugees and asylum seekers.

Education and training *page 454*

Environment and animals *page 456*

This includes:

- agriculture and fishing
- conservation
- animal care
- environment and education
- transport
- sustainable environment.

General charitable purposes *page 457*

This is a very broad category, and includes trusts that often have numerous specific strands to their programmes a well as those that will consider any application (subject to other eligibility criteria).

Arts, culture, sport and recreation

Children and young people

The Ayrton Senna Foundation
SFIA Educational Trust Limited
The P and D Shepherd Charitable Trust
The Bassil Shippam and Alsford Trust
The Shipwrights' Company Charitable Fund
The Barbara A Shuttleworth Memorial Trust
The Leslie Silver Charitable Trust
The Leslie Smith Foundation
Philip Smith's Charitable Trust
The E C Sosnow Charitable Trust
Spar Charitable Fund
The Steinberg Family Charitable Trust
The Stoller Charitable Trust
The Strawberry Charitable Trust
The W O Street Charitable Foundation
Sueberry Ltd
The Connie and Albert Taylor Charitable Trust
The Sue Thomson Foundation
The Toy Trust
Annie Tranmer Charitable Trust
The Tresillian Trust
The Albert Van Den Bergh Charitable Trust
The Viznitz Foundation
Wallace and Gromit's Children's Foundation
The Barbara Ward Children's Foundation
The Wessex Youth Trust
The Felicity Wilde Charitable Trust
Anona Winn Charitable Trust
The Woodcock Charitable Trust
The Woodward Charitable Trust
The A and R Woolf Charitable Trust
The Fred and Della Worms Charitable Trust
The Yapp Charitable Trust
The York Children's Trust
The Marjorie and Arnold Ziff Charitable Foundation

Development, housing and employment

The Ajahma Charitable Trust
The Ashley Family Foundation
The Oliver Borthwick Memorial Trust
R S Brownless Charitable Trust
Henry T and Lucy B Cadbury Charitable Trust
The Cooks Charity

The Helen and Geoffrey De Freitas Charitable Trust
The Dyers' Company Charitable Trust
The Edith Maud Ellis 1985 Charitable Trust
The Emmandjay Charitable Trust
The Football Association National Sports Centre Trust
The Oliver Ford Charitable Trust
Sydney E Franklin Deceased's New Second Charity
Jacqueline and Michael Gee Charitable Trust
Grand Charitable Trust of the Order of Women Freemasons
The Harbour Foundation
The Haymills Charitable Trust
The Horne Trust
The Hyde Charitable Trust – Youth Plus
The Irish Youth Foundation (UK) Ltd
The Johnson Foundation
Jusaca Charitable Trust
The Peter Kershaw Trust
LandAid Charitable Trust
Liberum Foundation
The Lotus Foundation
The Charlotte Marshall Charitable Trust
Matliwala Family Charitable Trust
The Merchants' House of Glasgow
The Millfield House Foundation
Monmouthshire County Council Welsh Church Act Fund
The Kitty and Daniel Nabarro Charitable Trust
The Nadezhda Charitable Trust
The Noon Foundation
The Norda Trust
The Norton Foundation
Prairie Trust
The Puebla Charitable Trust
Ranworth Trust
The Searle Charitable Trust
The Shanti Charitable Trust
The Sheldon Trust
The Hugh and Ruby Sykes Charitable Trust
The Nigel Vinson Charitable Trust
The Scurrah Wainwright Charity
Wakeham Trust

Disability

The Acacia Charitable Trust
The Company of Actuaries' Charitable Trust Fund
The Adamson Trust
The Green and Lilian F M Ainsworth and Family Benevolent Fund

The Ajahma Charitable Trust
The Alchemy Foundation
Alexandra Rose Charities
The Appletree Trust
The Astor Foundation
The BACTA Charitable Trust
The Baker Charitable Trust
Barchester Healthcare Foundation
The Bintaub Charitable Trust
Blatchington Court Trust
The Boshier-Hinton Foundation
The Bothwell Charitable Trust
The Harry Bottom Charitable Trust
P G and N J Boulton Trust
John Bristow and Thomas Mason Trust
The British Council for Prevention of Blindness
R S Brownless Charitable Trust
The Joseph and Annie Cattle Trust
The Pamela Champion Foundation
Chrysalis Trust
CLA Charitable Trust
The Cleopatra Trust
Harold and Daphne Cooper Charitable Trust
The Cotton Trust
Disability Aid Fund
The Dorus Trust
The Dumbreck Charity
The Sir John Eastwood Foundation
Gilbert Edgar Trust
The Vernon N Ely Charitable Trust
The Emerton-Christie Charity
The Emmandjay Charitable Trust
The Epigoni Trust
Samuel William Farmer Trust
The Fawcett Charitable Trust
Dixie Rose Findlay Charitable Trust
The Rose Flatau Charitable Trust
The Ian Fleming Charitable Trust
Florence's Charitable Trust
The Follett Trust
The Forbes Charitable Foundation
Ford Britain Trust
The Oliver Ford Charitable Trust
The Jill Franklin Trust
The Joseph Strong Frazer Trust
The Frognal Trust
The Fuserna Foundation
The G D Charitable Trust
The Robert Gavron Charitable Trust
Generations Charitable Trust
The B and P Glasser Charitable Trust
The Sydney and Phyllis Goldberg Memorial Charitable Trust
The Good Neighbours Trust
Grand Charitable Trust of the Order of Women Freemasons
The Constance Green Foundation
The Philip Green Memorial Trust
The Harebell Centenary Fund

The Alfred And Peggy Harvey
Charitable Trust
Hasluck Charitable Trust
The Hawthorne Charitable Trust
The Dorothy Hay-Bolton
Charitable Trust
May Hearnshaw's Charity
The Charles Littlewood Hill Trust
R G Hills Charitable Trust
The Sir Julian Hodge Charitable
Trust
The Cuthbert Horn Trust
The Horne Trust
The Hospital Saturday Fund
The Clifford Howarth Charity Trust
The Humanitarian Trust
The Iliffe Family Charitable Trust
The Ruth and Lionel Jacobson
Trust No. 2
The Lillie Johnson Charitable Trust
The Judith Trust
The Anton Jurgens Charitable Trust
The Ian Karten Charitable Trust
The Kohn Foundation
The David Laing Foundation
The Lambert Charitable Trust
Mrs F B Laurence Charitable Trust
The Edgar E Lawley Foundation
The Raymond and Blanche Lawson
Charitable Trust
The Leach Fourteenth Trust
The John Spedan Lewis Foundation
The Sir Edward Lewis Foundation
Lifeline 4 Kids
The William and Katherine
Longman Trust
The Loseley and Guildway
Charitable Trust
Paul Lunn-Rockliffe Charitable
Trust
Lord and Lady Lurgan Trust
The E M MacAndrew Trust
Macdonald-Buchanan Charitable
Trust
Ian Mactaggart Trust
The Marchday Charitable Fund
The Marsh Christian Trust
The Charlotte Marshall Charitable
Trust
The Jim Marshall Charitable Trust
The Violet Mauray Charitable Trust
The Robert McAlpine Foundation
The McKenna Charitable Trust
D D McPhail Charitable Settlement
Brian Mercer Charitable Trust
The Merchant Taylors' Company
Charities Fund
The Merchants' House of Glasgow
Mickleham Charitable Trust
Gerald Micklem Charitable Trust
The Miller Foundation
The Peter Minet Trust

Minge's Gift and the Pooled Trusts
The Mitchell Charitable Trust
The Mountbatten Memorial Trust
Murphy-Neumann Charity
Company Limited
The Kitty and Daniel Nabarro
Charitable Trust
Newby Trust Limited
The Norton Foundation
The Odin Charitable Trust
Old Possum's Practical Trust
The O'Sullivan Family Charitable
Trust
The Constance Paterson Charitable
Trust
The Susanna Peake Charitable
Trust
The Persula Foundation
The Austin and Hope Pilkington
Trust
The Platinum Trust
G S Plaut Charitable Trust Limited
The Red Rose Charitable Trust
The Max Reinhardt Charitable
Trust
The Clive Richards Charity
The River Farm Foundation
Rix-Thompson-Rothenberg
Foundation
Thomas Roberts Trust
The Cecil Rosen Foundation
The Rowlands Trust
The Scotshill Trust
The Helene Sebba Charitable Trust
SEM Charitable Trust
SFIA Educational Trust Limited
The Charles Shorto Charitable
Trust
The Barbara A Shuttleworth
Memorial Trust
David Solomons Charitable Trust
R H Southern Trust
The Worshipful Company of
Spectacle Makers' Charity
St Monica Trust Community Fund
The W O Street Charitable
Foundation
The Ulverscroft Foundation
The Albert Van Den Bergh
Charitable Trust
The Van Neste Foundation
Vision Charity
The Viznitz Foundation
The Westcroft Trust
The Lionel Wigram Memorial Trust
Anona Winn Charitable Trust
The Michael and Anna Wix
Charitable Trust
The Woodward Charitable Trust
The Yapp Charitable Trust
The York Children's Trust

Disadvantaged people

The A B Charitable Trust
The Company of Actuaries'
Charitable Trust Fund
The Green and Lilian F M
Ainsworth and Family Benevolent
Fund
The Ajahma Charitable Trust
The Alchemy Foundation
The Pat Allsop Charitable Trust
The Appletree Trust
The BACTA Charitable Trust
The Bintaub Charitable Trust
The Oliver Borthwick Memorial
Trust
P G and N J Boulton Trust
John Bristow and Thomas Mason
Trust
R S Brownless Charitable Trust
Buckingham Trust
Consolidated Charity of Burton
upon Trent
The C Charitable Trust
Henry T and Lucy B Cadbury
Charitable Trust
The Calpe Trust
Chrysalis Trust
CLA Charitable Trust
The Cleopatra Trust
The Coltstaple Trust
The Cotton Trust
The Violet and Milo Cripps
Charitable Trust
The Dorus Trust
Double 'O' Charity Ltd
The Doughty Charity Trust
Dromintee Trust
Gilbert Edgar Trust
The Ellinson Foundation Ltd
The Edith Maud Ellis 1985
Charitable Trust
The Emmandjay Charitable Trust
The Epigoni Trust
The Ericson Trust
The Doris Field Charitable Trust
The Rose Flatau Charitable Trust
The Follett Trust
The Anna Rosa Forster Charitable
Trust
Sydney E Franklin Deceased's New
Second Charity
The Jill Franklin Trust
Maurice Fry Charitable Trust
The G D Charitable Trust
The Angela Gallagher Memorial
Fund
The Robert Gavron Charitable
Trust
Jacqueline and Michael Gee
Charitable Trust
Generations Charitable Trust

Education and Training

Ranworth Trust
The Roger Raymond Charitable Trust
The Eva Reckitt Trust Fund
The Red Rose Charitable Trust
The Clive Richards Charity
The Violet M Richards Charity
Riverside Charitable Trust Limited
Rix-Thompson-Rothenberg Foundation
The Sir James Roll Charitable Trust
The Rothermere Foundation
The Rowland Family Foundation
The Rowlands Trust
Royal Masonic Trust for Girls and Boys
Ryklow Charitable Trust 1992
The Michael Harry Sacher Trust
Saint Luke's College Foundation
The Saintbury Trust
The Andrew Salvesen Charitable Trust
Basil Samuel Charitable Trust
Coral Samuel Charitable Trust
Schroder Charity Trust
The Scott Bader Commonwealth Ltd
SEM Charitable Trust
The Ayrton Senna Foundation
SFIA Educational Trust Limited
The Jean Shanks Foundation
The Archie Sherman Cardiff Foundation
The Bassil Shippam and Alsford Trust
Sino-British Fellowship Trust
The Leslie Smith Foundation
The Martin Smith Foundation
The E C Sosnow Charitable Trust
The South Square Trust
The Stephen R and Philippa H Southall Charitable Trust
R H Southern Trust
Rosalyn and Nicholas Springer Charitable Trust
St Gabriel's Trust
The Stanley Foundation Ltd
Stevenson Family's Charitable Trust
The Stone-Mallabar Charitable Foundation
Peter Storrs Trust
The W O Street Charitable Foundation
Sueberry Ltd
The Sutasoma Trust
The Hugh and Ruby Sykes Charitable Trust
The Connie and Albert Taylor Charitable Trust
The Cyril Taylor Charitable Trust
The Thomas Wall Trust
The Thornton Trust
The Thriplow Charitable Trust
The Tory Family Foundation
TVML Foundation

Vale of Glamorgan – Welsh Church Fund
Roger Vere Foundation
Wakeham Trust
The Ward Blenkinsop Trust
Webb Memorial Trust
The James Weir Foundation
The Whitaker Charitable Trust
The Colonel W H Whitbread Charitable Trust
The Simon Whitbread Charitable Trust
The Williams Charitable Trust
The Michael and Anna Wix Charitable Trust
Woodroffe Benton Foundation
The Fred and Della Worms Charitable Trust
The Yapp Charitable Trust
The York Children's Trust
The Marjorie and Arnold Ziff Charitable Foundation

Environment and animals

The Alborada Trust
The Animal Defence Trust
A J H Ashby Will Trust
The Astor Foundation
The Astor of Hever Trust
Harry Bacon Foundation
The Balney Charitable Trust
Lord Barnby's Foundation
The Blair Foundation
The Bothwell Charitable Trust
Briggs Animal Welfare Trust
C J Cadbury Charitable Trust
The Christopher Cadbury Charitable Trust
The G W Cadbury Charitable Trust
The Edward and Dorothy Cadbury Trust
The Carron Charitable Settlement
The Leslie Mary Carter Charitable Trust
The Wilfrid and Constance Cave Foundation
The Cemlyn-Jones Trust
CLA Charitable Trust
J A Clark Charitable Trust
The Cleopatra Trust
The Robert Clutterbuck Charitable Trust
The John Coates Charitable Trust
The Marjorie Coote Animal Charity Trust
The Craignish Trust
The Ronald Cruickshank's Foundation
The Dennis Curry Charitable Trust
The Helen and Geoffrey De Freitas Charitable Trust

William Dean Countryside and Educational Trust
The Delves Charitable Trust
Dischma Charitable Trust
The Dorus Trust
The Dumbreck Charity
The Houghton Dunn Charitable Trust
The Dunn Family Charitable Trust
EAGA Partnership Charitable Trust
Audrey Earle Charitable Trust
The Edinburgh Trust, No. 2 Account
The Elmgrant Trust
The Ericson Trust
The Alan Evans Memorial Trust
The Beryl Evetts and Robert Luff Animal Welfare Trust
Samuel William Farmer Trust
The Flow Foundation
Ford Britain Trust
The Oliver Ford Charitable Trust
The Anna Rosa Forster Charitable Trust
Sydney E Franklin Deceased's New Second Charity
The Gordon Fraser Charitable Trust
Maurice Fry Charitable Trust
The G D Charitable Trust
The Galanthus Trust
Generations Charitable Trust
The GNC Trust
The Gough Charitable Trust
The Barry Green Memorial Fund
The Gunter Charitable Trust
The Hamamelis Trust
The Harebell Centenary Fund
The Edith Lilian Harrison 2000 Foundation
The G D Herbert Charitable Trust
The Joanna Herbert-Stepney Charitable Settlement
The Holly Hill Charitable Trust
The J G Hogg Charitable Trust
The Homestead Charitable Trust
The Cuthbert Horn Trust
The Reta Lila Howard Foundation
The Geoffrey C Hughes Charitable Trust
The Michael and Shirley Hunt Charitable Trust
The Idlewild Trust
The John Jarrold Trust
Rees Jeffreys Road Fund
The Kennel Club Charitable Trust
The Kreitman Foundation
John Laing Charitable Trust
The Christopher Laing Foundation
The Martin Laing Foundation
Lancashire Environmental Fund
The Langley Charitable Trust
Mrs F B Laurence Charitable Trust
The Leach Fourteenth Trust
The John Spedan Lewis Foundation
The Limbourne Trust

Limoges Charitable Trust
Llysdinam Charitable Trust
The William and Katherine
 Longman Trust
The Lotus Foundation
The Lyons Charitable Trust
The Mahavir Trust
Marchig Animal Welfare Trust
Michael Marks Charitable Trust
Marmot Charitable Trust
The Marsh Christian Trust
The Metropolitan Drinking
 Fountain and Cattle Trough
 Association
T and J Meyer Family Foundation
 Limited
Millennium Stadium Charitable
 Trust
The Miller Foundation
The Millichope Foundation
The Millward Charitable Trust
The Peter Minet Trust
The Minos Trust
The D C Moncrieff Charitable
 Trust
The Montague Thompson Coon
 Charitable Trust
The Morel Charitable Trust
The Kitty and Daniel Nabarro
 Charitable Trust
The Sir Peter O'Sullevan Charitable
 Trust
The Oakdale Trust
Old Possum's Practical Trust
The John Oldacre Foundation
Onaway Trust
The Owen Family Trust
Panton Trust
The Frank Parkinson Agricultural
 Trust
The Persula Foundation
The Petplan Charitable Trust
The Cecil Pilkington Charitable
 Trust
The Elise Pilkington Charitable
 Trust
The Col W W Pilkington Will
 Trusts The General Charity Fund
The Porter Foundation
Prairie Trust
Princess Anne's Charities
The Rhododendron Trust
The Ripple Effect Foundation
The River Farm Foundation
The Rowlands Trust
Ryklow Charitable Trust 1992
The Michael Harry Sacher Trust
The Jean Sainsbury Animal Welfare
 Trust
The Saintbury Trust
The Saints and Sinners Trust
Salters' Charitable Foundation
The Hon. M J Samuel Charitable
 Trust
The Peter Samuel Charitable Trust

The Scarfe Charitable Trust
Schroder Charity Trust
The Scotshill Trust
The Scott Bader Commonwealth
 Ltd
The Scouloudi Foundation
The Linley Shaw Foundation
The Shipwrights' Company
 Charitable Fund
The Simpson Education and
 Conservation Trust
The John Slater Foundation
The SMB Charitable Trust
The N Smith Charitable Settlement
The Stanley Smith UK
 Horticultural Trust
Philip Smith's Charitable Trust
The South Square Trust
The Stephen R and Philippa H
 Southall Charitable Trust
The W F Southall Trust
R H Southern Trust
Stevenson Family's Charitable Trust
The Sylvanus Charitable Trust
The Connie and Albert Taylor
 Charitable Trust
The Loke Wan Tho Memorial
 Foundation
Roger Vere Foundation
The David Webster Charitable
 Trust
The Whitaker Charitable Trust
The Colonel W H Whitbread
 Charitable Trust
The Simon Whitbread Charitable
 Trust
A H and B C Whiteley Charitable
 Trust
The Whitley Animal Protection
 Trust
The Richard Wilcox Welfare
 Charity
Woodroffe Benton Foundation
The Woodward Charitable Trust
The A and R Woolf Charitable
 Trust
The Diana Edgson Wright
 Charitable Trust
Zephyr Charitable Trust

General charitable purposes

The Acacia Charitable Trust
The Adnams Charity
The Green and Lilian F M
 Ainsworth and Family Benevolent
 Fund
The Sylvia Aitken Charitable Trust
The Albion Trust
D G Albright Charitable Trust

AM Charitable Trust
The Amalur Foundation Limited
Sir John and Lady Amory's
 Charitable Trust
The Ampelos Trust
Andor Charitable Trust
The Henry Angest Foundation
The Annandale Charitable Trust
The Anson Charitable Trust
The John Apthorp Charitable Trust
The John M Archer Charitable
 Trust
The Ardwick Trust
The Argentarius Foundation
The Armourers' and Brasiers'
 Gauntlet Trust
The Ashworth Charitable Trust
The Ian Askew Charitable Trust
The Astor Foundation
The Avenue Charitable Trust
The BACTA Charitable Trust
The Bagri Foundation
The Andrew Balint Charitable Trust
The George Balint Charitable Trust
The Paul Balint Charitable Trust
Balmain Charitable Trust
Peter Barker-Mill Memorial Charity
Lord Barnby's Foundation
The Barnsbury Charitable Trust
The Misses Barrie Charitable Trust
The Bartlett Taylor Charitable Trust
The Paul Bassham Charitable Trust
The Batchworth Trust
The Bay Tree Charitable Trust
The Beaverbrook Foundation
The Becker Family Charitable Trust
The Peter Beckwith Charitable
 Trust
The David and Ruth Behrend Fund
Bellasis Trust
The Benham Charitable Settlement
Michael and Leslie Bennett
 Charitable Trust
The Ruth Berkowitz Charitable
 Trust
The Billmeir Charitable Trust
Birthday House Trust
The Michael Bishop Foundation
The Bertie Black Foundation
The Blair Foundation
The Sir Victor Blank Charitable
 Settlement
The Neville and Elaine Blond
 Charitable Trust
The John and Celia Bonham
 Christie Charitable Trust
The Charlotte Bonham-Carter
 Charitable Trust
The Linda and Gordon Bonnyman
 Charitable Trust
The William Brake Charitable Trust
The Bransford Trust
The Brendish Family Foundation
The Roger Brooke Charitable Trust
Bill Brown's Charitable Settlement

West London Synagogue Charitable Fund
The Melanie White Foundation Limited
The Whitecourt Charitable Trust
A H and B C Whiteley Charitable Trust
The Lionel Wigram Memorial Trust
The Williams Charitable Trust
Sumner Wilson Charitable Trust
The Witzenfeld Foundation
The Woodcock Charitable Trust
The Woodward Charitable Trust
The A and R Woolf Charitable Trust
The Diana Edgson Wright Charitable Trust
The Matthews Wrightson Charity Trust
Wychville Ltd
The Yardley Great Trust
The Dennis Alan Yardy Charitable Trust
The John Young Charitable Settlement
The William Allen Young Charitable Trust
The Marjorie and Arnold Ziff Charitable Foundation

Illness

The A B Charitable Trust
The Appletree Trust
The BACTA Charitable Trust
The Baker Charitable Trust
The Ruth Berkowitz Charitable Trust
The Bintaub Charitable Trust
The Tony Bramall Charitable Trust
John Bristow and Thomas Mason Trust
R S Brownless Charitable Trust
Buckingham Trust
P H G Cadbury Charitable Trust
Child Growth Foundation
The Cleopatra Trust
Criffel Charitable Trust
The Violet and Milo Cripps Charitable Trust
The Dorus Trust
Dromintee Trust
The Sir John Eastwood Foundation
Gilbert Edgar Trust
The Emmandjay Charitable Trust
The Epigoni Trust
Samuel William Farmer Trust
Dixie Rose Findlay Charitable Trust
Bud Flanagan Leukaemia Fund
The Rose Flatau Charitable Trust
Florence's Charitable Trust
The Follett Trust
The Forte Charitable Trust

The Jill Franklin Trust
The Fuserna Foundation
Generations Charitable Trust
The B and P Glasser Charitable Trust
The Constance Green Foundation
Grimmitt Trust
The Harris Family Charitable Trust
The Edith Lilian Harrison 2000 Foundation
May Hearnshaw's Charity
The Christina Mary Hendrie Trust for Scottish and Canadian Charities
R G Hills Charitable Trust
The Clifford Howarth Charity Trust
The Humanitarian Trust
The Iliffe Family Charitable Trust
The Ruth and Lionel Jacobson Trust No. 2
The Judith Trust
The Anton Jurgens Charitable Trust
The Ian Karten Charitable Trust
The Caron Keating Foundation
The Kohn Foundation
The R J Larg Family Charitable Trust
The Kathleen Laurence Trust
The Leigh Trust
The Linden Charitable Trust
The Loftus Charitable Trust
Ian Mactaggart Trust
The Marchday Charitable Fund
The Marsh Christian Trust
The Charlotte Marshall Charitable Trust
Brian Mercer Charitable Trust
The Merchants' House of Glasgow
Mercury Phoenix Trust
Gerald Micklem Charitable Trust
The Miller Foundation
The Montague Thompson Coon Charitable Trust
The Peter Morrison Charitable Foundation
The Owen Family Trust
The Panacea Society
The Park Charitable Trust
The Constance Paterson Charitable Trust
G S Plaut Charitable Trust Limited
Riverside Charitable Trust Limited
Thomas Roberts Trust
The Rowlands Trust
The Andrew Salvesen Charitable Trust
The Hon. M J Samuel Charitable Trust
Swan Mountain Trust
The Connie and Albert Taylor Charitable Trust
The Thornton Trust
The Weinstein Foundation
The Lionel Wigram Memorial Trust
The Woodward Charitable Trust

Medicine and health

The Company of Actuaries' Charitable Trust Fund
The Adamson Trust
The Adint Charitable Trust
The Green and Lilian F M Ainsworth and Family Benevolent Fund
The Sylvia Aitken Charitable Trust
The Ajahma Charitable Trust
The Alchemy Foundation
The Pat Allsop Charitable Trust
Andor Charitable Trust
The Armourers' and Brasiers' Gauntlet Trust
The Artemis Charitable Trust
The Astor Foundation
The Astor of Hever Trust
Harry Bacon Foundation
The Baker Charitable Trust
The Barbers' Company General Charities
The Barbour Foundation
The Barcapel Foundation
Barchester Healthcare Foundation
The Misses Barrie Charitable Trust
The Batchworth Trust
The John Beckwith Charitable Trust
The Peter Beckwith Charitable Trust
The Ruth Berkowitz Charitable Trust
The Bestway Foundation
The Billmeir Charitable Trust
The Bintaub Charitable Trust
The Birmingham Hospital Saturday Fund Medical Charity and Welfare Trust
Sir Alec Black's Charity
The Boltons Trust
The Booth Charities
The Boshier-Hinton Foundation
The Bothwell Charitable Trust
The Harry Bottom Charitable Trust
P G and N J Boulton Trust
Sir Clive Bourne Family Trust
The Bowerman Charitable Trust
The Tony Bramall Charitable Trust
The Breast Cancer Research Trust
The Brendish Family Foundation
The British Council for Prevention of Blindness
The British Dietetic Association General and Education Trust Fund
The David Brooke Charity
Bill Brown's Charitable Settlement
R S Brownless Charitable Trust
Buckland Charitable Trust
The Burden Trust
The Burry Charitable Trust

Older people

Religion – Christianity

Religion – Inter-faith activities

Religion – Islam

Religion – Judaism

Religion – Religious understanding

Philanthropy and the voluntary sector

Rights, law and conflict

Science and technology

Social sciences, policy and research

Social welfare

Geographical index

The following geographical index aims to highlight when a trust gives preference for, or has a special interest in, a particular area: county, region, city, town or London borough. Please note the following:

) Before using this index please read the following information, as well as the introduction to the subject index on page 448. We must emphasise that this index:

(a) should not be used as a simple mailing list, and

(b) is not a substitute for detailed research.

When you have used this index to identify relevant trusts, please read each entry carefully before making an application. Simply because a trust gives grants in your geographical area does not mean that it gives to your type of work.

) Most trusts in this list are not restricted to one area; usually the geographical index indicates that the trust gives some priority for the area(s).

) Trusts which give throughout England or the UK have been excluded from this index, unless they have a particular interest in one or more locality.

) Each section is ordered alphabetically according to the name of the trust. The categories for the overseas and UK indices are as follows:

England

We have divided England into the following nine categories:

North East *page 472*

North West *page 472*

Yorkshire and the Humber *page 472*

East Midlands *page 472*

West Midlands *page 472*

Eastern England *page 472*

South East *page 472*

South West *page 472*

Greater London *page 472*

Some trusts may be found in more than one category due to them providing grants in more than one area e.g. those with a preference for northern England.

Wales *page 473*

Scotland *page 473*

Northern Ireland *page 473*

Republic of Ireland *page 473*

Europe *page 473*

Overseas categories

Developing world page 473

This includes trusts which support missionary organisations when they are also interested in social and economic development.

Individual continents page 474

The Middle East has been listed separately. Please note that most of the trusts listed are primarily for the benefit of Jewish people and the advancement of the Jewish religion.

England

North East

The Barbour Foundation
Chrysalis Trust
The Catherine Cookson Charitable Trust
The Dickon Trust
The Ellinson Foundation Ltd
The GNC Trust
The Millfield House Foundation
T and S Trust Fund

North West

The Booth Charities
The Harold and Alice Bridges Charity
The Ellerdale Trust
The Eventhall Family Charitable Trust
The Fairway Trust
Famos Foundation Trust
The GNC Trust
The Johnson Foundation
The Johnson Group Cleaners Charity
The J E Joseph Charitable Fund
The Peter Kershaw Trust
The Ann and David Marks Foundation
Matliwala Family Charitable Trust
The Mushroom Fund
The Fanny Rapaport Charitable Settlement
T and S Trust Fund
The Norman Whiteley Trust

Yorkshire and the Humber

The Joseph and Annie Cattle Trust
The Marjorie Coote Animal Charity Trust
The A M Fenton Trust
The GNC Trust
The Constance Green Foundation
The Mayfield Valley Arts Trust
W W Spooner Charitable Trust
The Scurrah Wainwright Charity
The York Children's Trust

East Midlands

The Jack and Ada Beattie Foundation
The Michael Bishop Foundation
Ford Britain Trust
The GNC Trust
The Joanna Herbert-Stepney Charitable Settlement
The Hesed Trust

West Midlands

The Jack and Ada Beattie Foundation
The Michael Bishop Foundation
The Bransford Trust
Consolidated Charity of Burton upon Trent
The Dumbreck Charity
The John Feeney Charitable Trust
The GNC Trust
Grimmitt Trust
Alan Edward Higgs Charity
John Martin's Charity
The Bernard Piggott Trust
The Sheldon Trust
C B and H H Taylor 1984 Trust
The Connie and Albert Taylor Charitable Trust
The Yardley Great Trust

Eastern England

The Adnams Charity
The Bedfordshire and Hertfordshire Historic Churches Trust
The Chapman Charitable Trust
The Ebenezer Trust
Educational Foundation of Alderman John Norman
The Essex Youth Trust
Farthing Trust
Ford Britain Trust
The GNC Trust
The John Jarrold Trust
The D C Moncrieff Charitable Trust
The Music Sales Charitable Trust
The Norwich Town Close Estate Charity
The A and R Woolf Charitable Trust

South East

John Bristow and Thomas Mason Trust
The Chapman Charitable Trust
The John and Freda Coleman Charitable Trust
The Dugdale Charitable Trust
The Gilbert and Eileen Edgar Foundation
Ford Britain Trust
The Friends of Kent Churches
T F C Frost Charitable Trust
The GNC Trust
The Walter Guinness Charitable Trust
William Harding's Charity
The Dorothy Hay-Bolton Charitable Trust
R G Hills Charitable Trust
Stuart Hine Trust
The Iliffe Family Charitable Trust

The Ingram Trust
The James Trust
The JMK Charitable Trust
The Emmanuel Kaye Foundation
The Leach Fourteenth Trust
The Leonard Trust
The Jim Marshall Charitable Trust
Gerald Micklem Charitable Trust
The Moss Charitable Trust
The Earl of Northampton's Charity
The David Pickford Charitable Foundation
The Rothermere Foundation
The Sants Charitable Trust
St Michael's and All Saints' Charities

South West

The Chipping Sodbury Town Lands Charity
The Joyce Fletcher Charitable Trust
The Fulmer Charitable Trust
The GNC Trust
The Walter Guinness Charitable Trust
The Heathcoat Trust
The Michael and Ilse Katz Foundation
The Leach Fourteenth Trust
The Moss Charitable Trust
The Norman Family Charitable Trust
The Rock Solid Trust
Saint Luke's College Foundation
St Monica Trust Community Fund
The Talbot Village Trust

Greater London

The Avenue Charitable Trust
Barleycorn Trust
The Jack and Ada Beattie Foundation
The Bintaub Charitable Trust
The Sir Victor Blank Charitable Settlement
The British Council for Prevention of Blindness
The Chapman Charitable Trust
Coutts Charitable Trust
Dischma Charitable Trust
The Edinburgh Trust, No. 2 Account
Elshore Ltd
The Vernon N Ely Charitable Trust
Sir John Evelyn's Charity
Finnart House School Trust
Ford Britain Trust
Friends of Wiznitz Limited
The B and P Glasser Charitable Trust
The Grahame Charitable Foundation Limited

Africa

Americas and the West Indies

Asia

Middle East

Alphabetical index